HENRY ADAMS

HENRY ADAMS

HISTORY OF THE
UNITED STATES OF AMERICA
DURING THE ADMINISTRATIONS OF
JAMES MADISON

THE LIBRARY OF AMERICA

The paper used in this publication meets the
minimum requirements of the American National Standard
for Information Sciences—Permanence of Paper for
Printed Library Materials, ANSI Z39.48-1984.

Distributed to the trade in the United States
and Canada by the Viking Press.

Published outside North America by the Press Syndicate
of the University of Cambridge,
The Pitt Building, Trumpington Street, Cambridge CB2 IRP, England
ISBN 0 521 32484 X

Library of Congress Catalog Card Number: 85-23098
For cataloging information, see end of *Notes* section.
ISBN 0-940450-35-6

92-93-3493

Second Printing

Manufactured in the United States of America

EARL N. HARBERT
WROTE THE NOTES AND SELECTED
THE TEXTS FOR THIS VOLUME

Grateful acknowledgement is made to the National Endowment for the Humanities and the Ford Foundation for their generous financial support of this series.

Contents

Each section has its own table of contents.

The First Administration of James Madison   1

The Second Administration of James Madison 615

Index 1347

Chronology. 1419

Note on the Texts 1426

Notes 1434

HISTORY OF
THE UNITED STATES
OF AMERICA

DURING THE FIRST ADMINISTRATION OF

JAMES MADISON

1809–1813

Contents

VOLUME ONE

I. Subsidence of Faction 7

II. Alienation from France 20

III. Canning's Concessions 33

IV. Erskine's Arrangement 49

V. Disavowal of Erskine 64

VI. Francis James Jackson 79

VII. Napoleon's Triumph 96

VIII. Executive Weakness 110

IX. Legislative Impotence 125

X. Incapacity of Government 141

XI. The Decree of Rambouillet 156

XII. Cadore's Letter of August 5 171

XIII. The Marquess Wellesley 185

XIV. Government by Proclamation 203

XV. The Floridas and the Bank 221

XVI. Contract with France 235

XVII. Dismissal of Robert Smith 249

XVIII. Napoleon's Delays 264

XIX. Russia and Sweden 280

VOLUME TWO

I. Pinkney's Inamicable Leave 297

II. The "Little Belt" 313

III. Madison Triumphant 327

IV. Harrison and Tecumthe 342

V. Tippecanoe 359

VI. Meeting of the Twelfth Congress 374

VII. War Debates 387

VIII. War Legislation 401

IX. Madison as Minerva 416

X. Hesitations 432

XI. War 446

XII. Joel Barlow 463

XIII. Repeal of the Orders in Council 478

XIV. Invasion of Canada 492

XV. Hull's Surrender 510

XVI. The Niagara Campaign 528

XVII. Naval Battles 550

XVIII. Discord 566

XIX. Executive Embarrassments 582

XX. War Legislation 598

MAPS AND PLANS

Indiana Territory 344

Seat of War about Lake Erie 498

Detroit River 512

Straits of Niagara from Lake Erie
   to Lake Ontario 530

Chapter I

THE "NATIONAL INTELLIGENCER," which called public attention only to such points of interest as the Government wished to accent, noticed that President Madison was "dressed in a full suit of cloth of American manufacture" when he appeared at noon, March 4, 1809, under escort of the "troops of cavalry of the city and Georgetown," amid a crowd of ten thousand people, to take the oath of office at the Capitol. The suit of American clothes told more of Madison's tendencies than was to be learned from the language of the Inaugural Address, which he delivered in a tone of voice so low as not to be heard by the large audience gathered in the new and imposing Representatives' Hall.[1] Indeed, the Address suggested a doubt whether the new President wished to be understood. The conventionality of his thought nowhere betrayed itself more plainly than in this speech on the greatest occasion of Madison's life, when he was required to explain the means by which he should retrieve the failures of Jefferson.

"It is a precious reflection," said Madison to his anxious audience, "that the transition from this prosperous condition of our country to the scene which has for some time been distressing us, is not chargeable on any unwarrantable views, nor as I trust on any voluntary errors, in the public councils. Indulging no passions which trespass on the rights or the repose of other nations, it has been the true glory of the United States to cultivate peace by observing justice, and to entitle themselves to the respect of the nations at war by fulfilling their neutral obligations with the most scrupulous impartiality. If there be candor in the world, the truth of these assertions will not be questioned; posterity at least will do justice to them."

Since none of Madison's enemies, either abroad or at home, intended to show him candor, his only hope was in

[1] Diary of J. Q. Adams, March 4, 1809; i. 544.

posterity; yet the judgment of posterity depended chiefly on the course which the new President might take to remedy the misfortunes of his predecessor. The nation expected from him some impulse toward the end he had in mind; foreign nations were also waiting to learn whether they should have to reckon with a new force in politics; but Madison seemed to show his contentment with the policy hitherto pursued, rather than his wish to change it.

"This unexceptionable course," he continued, "could not avail against the injustice and violence of the belligerent Powers. In their rage against each other, or impelled by more direct motives, principles of retaliation have been introduced equally contrary to universal reason and acknowledged law. How long their arbitrary edicts will be continued, in spite of the demonstrations that not even a pretext for them has been given by the United States, and of the fair and liberal attempt to induce a revocation of them, cannot be anticipated. Assuring myself that under every vicissitude the determined spirit and united councils of the nation will be safeguards to its honor and essential interests, I repair to the post assigned me, with no other discouragement than what springs from my own inadequacy to its high duties."

Neither the actual world nor posterity could find much in these expressions on which to approve or condemn the policy of Madison, for no policy could be deduced from them. The same iteration of commonplaces marked the list of general principles which filled the next paragraph of the Address. Balancing every suggestion of energy by a corresponding limitation of scope, Madison showed only a wish to remain within the limits defined by his predecessor. "To cherish peace and friendly intercourse with all nations having corresponding dispositions" seemed to imply possible recourse to war with other nations; but "to prefer in all cases amicable discussion and reasonable accommodation of differences to a decision of them by an appeal to arms" seemed to exclude the use of force. "To promote by authorized means improvements friendly to agriculture, to manufactures, and to external as well as internal commerce" was a phrase so cautiously framed that no one could attack it. "To support the Constitution, which is the cement of the Union, as well in its limitations as in its authorities," seemed a duty so guarded as to need no further antithesis; yet Madison did not omit the usual obligation "to respect the rights and authorities reserved to the States and to the people, as equally incorporated with, and essential to, the success of the general system." No one could object to the phrases with which the Address defined Executive duties; but no one could point out a syllable implying that Madison would bend his energies with sterner purpose to maintain the nation's rights.

At the close of the speech Chief-Justice Marshall administered the oath; the new President then passed the militia in review, and in the evening Madison and Jefferson attended an inauguration ball, where "the crowd was excessive, the heat oppressive, and the entertainment bad."[1] With this complaint, so familiar on the occasion, the day ended, and President Madison's troubles began.

About March 1, Wilson Cary Nicholas had called on the President elect to warn him that he must look for serious opposition to the expected appointment of Gallatin as Secretary of State. Nicholas had the best reason to know that Giles, Samuel Smith, and Leib were bent on defeating Gallatin.

"I believed from what I heard he would be rejected," wrote Nicholas two years afterward;[2] "and that at all events, if he was not, his confirmation would be by a bare majority. During my public service but one event had ever occurred that gave me as much uneasiness: I mean the degradation of the country at that very moment by the abandonment of [the embargo]."

The two events were in fact somewhat alike in character. That Gallatin should become Secretary of State seemed a point of little consequence, even though it were the only remaining chance for honorable peace; but that another secretary should be forced on the President by a faction in the Senate, for the selfish objects of men like Samuel Smith and Giles, foreboded revolution in the form of government.

[1] Diary of J. Q. Adams, i. 544.
[2] W. C. Nicholas to ——. Nicholas MSS.

Nicholas saw chiefly the danger which threatened his friends; but the remoter peril to Executive independence promised worse evils than could be caused even by the overthrow of the party in power at a moment of foreign aggression.

The effort of Giles and Smith to control Madison had no excuse. Gallatin's foreign birth, the only objection urged against him, warranted doubt, not indeed of his fitness, but of difficulty in obliging European powers to deal with a native of Geneva, who was in their eyes either a subject of their own or an enemy at war; but neither Napoleon nor King George in the year 1809 showed so much regard to American feelings that the United States needed to affect delicacy in respect to theirs; and Gallatin's foreign birth became a signal advantage if it should force England to accept the fact, even though she refused to admit the law, of American naturalization. Gallatin's fitness was undisputed, and the last men who could question it were Giles and Samuel Smith, who had been his friends for twenty years, had trusted their greatest party interests in his hands, had helped to put the Treasury under his control, and were at the moment keeping him at its head when they might remove him to the less responsible post of minister for foreign affairs. Any question of Gallatin's patriotism suggested ideas even more delicate than those raised by doubts of his fitness. A party which had once trusted Burr and which still trusted Wilkinson, not to mention Giles himself, had little right to discuss Gallatin's patriotism, or the honesty of foreign-born citizens. Even the mild-spoken Wilson Cary Nicholas almost lost his temper at this point. "I honestly believe," he wrote in 1811, "if all our *native* citizens had as well discharged their duty to their country, that we should by our energy have extorted from both England and France a respect for our rights, and that before this day we should have extricated ourselves from all our embarrassments instead of having increased them." The men who doubted Gallatin's patriotism were for the most part themselves habitually factious, or actually dallying with ideas of treason.

Had any competent native American been pressed for the Department of State, the Senate might still have had some pretext for excluding Gallatin; but no such candidate could be

suggested. Giles was alone in thinking himself the proper secretary; Samuel Smith probably stood in the same position;
Monroe still sulked in opposition and discredit; Armstrong,
never quite trusted, was in Paris; William Pinkney and J. Q.
Adams were converts too recent for such lofty promotion;
G. W. Campbell and W. H. Crawford had neither experience
nor natural fitness for the post. The appointment of Gallatin
not only seemed to be, but actually was, necessary to Madison's Administration.

No argument affected the resistance of Giles and Samuel
Smith, and during the early days of March Madison could see
no means of avoiding a party schism. From that evil, at such
a stage, he shrank. While the subject still stood unsettled,
some unknown person suggested a new idea. If Robert Smith
could be put in the Treasury, his brother Samuel would vote
to confirm Gallatin as Secretary of State. The character of
such a transaction needed no epithet; but Madison went to
Robert Smith and offered him the Treasury.[1] He knew Smith
to be incompetent, but he thought that with Gallatin's aid
even an incompetent person might manage the finances; and
perhaps his astuteness went so far as to foresee what was to
happen,—that he should deal with the Smiths on some better
occasion in a more summary manner. Madison's resemblance
to a cardinal was not wholly imaginary.[2]

While Robert Smith went to inquire into the details of
Treasury business before accepting the offered post, the President consulted with Gallatin, who rejected the scheme at
once. He could not, he said, undertake the charge of both
departments; the President would do better to appoint Robert Smith Secretary of State, and leave the Treasury as it was.
Madison seized this outlet of escape. He returned to Robert
Smith with the offer of the State Department, which Smith
accepted. In making this arrangement Madison knew that he
must himself supply Smith's deficiencies; but stronger wills
than that of Madison had yielded to party discontent, and he
gained much if he gained only time.

The true victim of the bargain was Gallatin, who might
wisely have chosen the moment for retiring from the Cabinet;

[1] Robert Smith's Address to the People, June 7, 1811.
[2] First Administration of Jefferson, p. 128.

but after declining an arrangement in his favor, he could not fairly desert the President, who had offered to sacrifice much for him, and he was too proud to avow a personal slight as the motive of his public action. Weakened already by the unexpected decline of his influence in the Senate, his usefulness was sure to be still further lessened by the charge of clinging to office; but after weighing the arguments for retirement he decided to remain,[1] although he could not, even if he would, forget that the quarrel which had been forced upon him must be met as vigorously as it was made.

The War and Navy Departments remained to be filled. Dearborn, who had continued in the War Department chiefly to oblige President Jefferson, retired in the month of February to become Collector of the port of Boston. As his successor, Madison selected William Eustis, of Boston, who had served in Congress during Jefferson's first Administration. Eustis was about fifty-six years old; in the Revolutionary War he had filled the post of hospital surgeon, and since the peace he had practised his profession in Boston. Little could be said of the appointment, except that no other candidate was suggested who seemed better qualified for the place.[2]

To succeed Robert Smith at the Navy Department, Madison selected Paul Hamilton, of South Carolina. Nothing was known of Hamilton, except that he had been governor of his State some ten years before. No one seemed aware why he had attracted the President's attention, or what qualities fitted him for the charge of naval affairs; but he appeared in due time at Washington,—a South Carolinian gentleman, little known in society or even to his colleagues in the government, and little felt as an active force in the struggle of parties and opinions.

From the outset Madison's Cabinet was the least satisfactory that any President had known. More than once the Federalist cabinets had been convulsed by disagreements, but the Administration of Madison had hardly strength to support two sides of a dispute. Gallatin alone gave it character, but was himself in a sort of disgrace. The Secretary of State, the Secretary of War, and the Secretary of the Navy, over-

[1] Gallatin to Jefferson, Nov. 8, 1809; Adams's Gallatin, p. 408.
[2] Madison to Henry Lee, February, 1827; Works, iii. 562, 564.

shadowed in the Cabinet by Gallatin, stood in a position of inevitable hostility to his influence, although they represented neither ideas nor constituents. While Gallatin exacted economy, the army and navy required expenditures, and the two secretaries necessarily looked to Robert Smith as their friend. Toward Robert Smith Gallatin could feel only antipathy, which was certainly shared by Madison. "We had all been astonished at his appointment," said Joel Barlow two years afterward;[1] "we all learned the history of that miserable intrigue by which it was effected." Looking upon Robert Smith's position as the result of a "miserable intrigue," Gallatin could make no secret of his contempt. The social relations between them, which had once been intimate, wholly ceased.

To embroil matters further, the defalcation of a navy agent at Leghorn revealed business relations between the Navy Department and Senator Samuel Smith's mercantile firm which scandalized Gallatin and drew from him a sharp criticism. He told Samuel Smith that the transactions of the firm of Smith and Buchanan were the most extraordinary that had fallen within his knowledge since he had been in the Treasury, and had left very unfavorable impressions on his mind.[2] Smith was then struggling for a re-election to the Senate, and felt the hand of Gallatin as a chief obstacle in his way. The feud became almost mortal under these reciprocal injuries; but Samuel Smith gained all his objects, and for the time held Gallatin and Madison at his mercy. Had he been able to separate them, his influence would have had no bounds, except his want of ability.

Yet Madison was always a dangerous enemy, gifted with a quality of persistence singularly sure in its results. An example of this persistence occurred at the moment of yielding to the Smiths' intrigues, when, perhaps partly in the hope of profiting by his sacrifice, he approached the Senate once more on the subject of the mission to Russia. February 27, the nomination of William Short to St. Petersburg had been unanimously rejected. March 6, with the nominations of Robert Smith and William Eustis to the Cabinet, Madison sent the

[1] National Intelligencer, July, 1811.
[2] Gallatin to Samuel Smith, June 26, 1809; Adams's Gallatin, p. 402.

names of J. Q. Adams as minister at St. Petersburg, and of Thomas Sumter as minister to Brazil. He asked the Senate to establish two new missions at once. March 7 the Senate confirmed all the other nominations, but by a vote of seventeen to fifteen, adhered to the opinion that a mission to Russia was inexpedient. Both Giles and Samuel Smith supported the Government; but the two senators from Pennsylvania, the two from Kentucky, together with Anderson of Tennessee and William H. Crawford, persisted in aiding the Federalists to defeat the President's wish. Yet the majority was so small as to prove that Madison would carry his point in the end. Senators who rejected the services of Gallatin and John Quincy Adams in order to employ those of Robert Smith, Dr. Eustis, and Governor Hamilton could not but suffer discredit. Faction which had no capacity of its own, and which showed only dislike of ability in others, could never rule a government in times of danger or distress.

After thus embarrassing the President in organizing his service the Senate rose, leaving Madison in peace until May 22, when the Eleventh Congress was to meet in special session. The outlook was more discouraging than at the beginning of any previous Administration. President Jefferson had strained his authority to breaking, and the sudden reaction threw society as well as government into disorder. The factiousness at Washington reflected only in a mild form the worse factiousness elsewhere. The Legislature of Massachusetts, having issued its Address to the People, adjourned; and a few days afterward the people, by an election which called out more than ninety thousand votes, dismissed their Republican governor, and by a majority of two or three thousand chose Christopher Gore in his place. The new Legislature was more decidedly Federalist than the old one. New Hampshire effected the same revolution. Rhode Island followed. In New York the Federalists carried the Legislature, as they did also in Maryland.

Even in Pennsylvania, although nothing shook the fixed political character of the State, the epidemic of faction broke out. While the legislatures of Massachusetts and Connecticut declared Acts of Congress unconstitutional, and refused aid to execute them, the legislature of Pennsylvania authorized

Governor Snyder to resist by armed force a mandate of the Supreme Court; and when the United States marshal attempted to serve process on the person of certain respondents at the suit of Gideon Olmstead, he found himself stopped by State militia acting under orders.

In a country where popular temper had easier means of concentrating its violence, government might have been paralyzed by these proofs of low esteem; but America had not by far reached such a stage, and dark as the prospect was both within and without, Madison could safely disregard dangers on which most rulers had habitually to count. His difficulties were only an inheritance from the old Administration, and began to disappear as quickly as they had risen. At a word from the President the State of Pennsylvania recovered its natural common-sense, and with some little sacrifice of dignity gave way. The popular successes won by the Federalists were hardly more serious than the momentary folly of Pennsylvania. As yet, the Union stood in no danger. The Federalists gained many votes; but these were the votes of moderate men who would desert their new companions on the first sign of a treasonable act, and their presence tended to make the party cautious rather than rash. John Henry, the secret agent of Sir James Craig, reported with truth to the governor-general that the Federalist leaders at Boston found disunion a very delicate topic, and that "an unpopular war . . . can alone produce a sudden separation of any section of this country from the common head."[1] In public, the most violent Federalists curbed their tongues whenever the Union was discussed, and instead of threatening to dissolve it, contented themselves by charging the blame on the Southern States in case it should fall to pieces. Success sobered them; the repeal of the embargo seemed so great a triumph that they were almost tempted into good humor.

On the people of New England other motives more directly selfish began to have effect. The chief sources of their wealth were shipping and manufactures. The embargo destroyed the value of the shipping after it had been diminished by the belligerent edicts; the repeal of the embargo restored

---

[1] Henry to Craig, March 13, 1809; State Papers, iii. 550.

the value. The Federalist newspapers tried to prove that this was not the case, and that the Non-intercourse Act, which prohibited commerce with England, France, or their dependencies, was as ruinous as embargo itself; but the shipping soon showed that Gottenburg, Riga, Lisbon, and the Spanish ports in America were markets almost as convenient as London or Havre for the sale of American produce. The Yankee ship-owner received freights to Europe by circuitous routes, on the accumulations of two years in grain, cotton, tobacco, and timber, of the whole United States, besides the freights of an extended coast-trade. Massachusetts owned more than a third of the American registered tonnage, and the returns for 1809 and 1810 proved that her profits were great. The registered tonnage of Massachusetts employed in foreign trade was 213,000 tons in 1800, and rose to 310,000 tons in 1807 before the embargo; in 1809 it rose again to 324,000; in 1810 it made another leap to 352,000 tons. The coasting trade employed in 1807 about 90,000 tons of Massachusetts shipping which was much increased by the embargo, and again reduced by its repeal; but in 1809 and 1810 this enrolled shipping still stood far above the prosperous level of 1807, and averaged 110,000 tons for the two years.[1]

Such rapid and general improvement in shipping proved that New England had better employment than political factiousness to occupy the thoughts of her citizens; but large as the profits on freights might be, they hardly equalled the profits on manufactures. In truth, the manufactories of New England were created by the embargo, which obliged the whole nation to consume their products or to go without. The first American cotton mills, begun as early as 1787, met with so little success that when the embargo was imposed in 1807, only fifteen mills with about eight thousand spindles were in operation, producing some three hundred thousand pounds of yarn a year. These eight thousand spindles, representing a capital of half a million dollars, were chiefly in or near Rhode Island.

The embargo and non-importation Acts went into effect in the last days of 1807. Within less than two years the number

[1] State Papers, Commerce and Navigation, pp. 897, 898.

of spindles was increased, or arrangements were made for increasing it, from eight thousand to eighty thousand.[1] Nearly four million dollars of capital were invested in mills, and four thousand persons were in their employ, or expected soon to be employed in them. The cotton cost about twenty cents a pound; the yarn sold on an average at about $1.12½ a pound. Besides these mills, which were worked mostly by water but partly by horse-power, the domestic manufacture of cotton and linen supplied a much larger part of the market. Two thirds of the clothing and house-linen used in the United States outside of the cities was made in farm-houses, and nearly every farmer in New England sold some portion of the stock woven every year by the women of his household. Much of this coarse but strong flaxen material, sold at about fifteen or twenty cents a yard by the spinner, was sent to the Southern States.[2]

While the cotton and linen industries of the North became profitable, the manufactures of wool lagged little behind. William Whittemore, who owned the patent for a machine which manufactured wool and cotton cards, reported from Cambridge in Massachusetts, Nov. 24, 1809, that only the want of card-wire prevented him from using all his machines to the full extent of their power.[3] "Since the obstructions to our foreign trade, the manufactures of our country have increased astonishingly," he wrote. "The demand for wool and cotton cards the present season has been twice as great as it has been any year preceding." Scarcity of good wool checked the growth of this industry, and the demand soon roused a mania among farmers for improving the breed of sheep. Between one hundred and three hundred per cent of profit attended all these industries, and little or no capital was required.

All the Northern and Eastern States shared in the advantages of this production, for which Virginia with the Western and Southern States paid; but in the whole Union New England fared best. Already the development of small industries had taken place, which, by making a varied aggregate, became the foundation and the security of Yankee wealth. Massachu-

[1] Gallatin's Report, April 17, 1810; State Papers, Finance, ii. 427.
[2] Gallatin's Report, April 17, 1810; State Papers, Finance, ii. 435.
[3] Gallatin's Report, April 17, 1810; State Papers, Finance, ii. 436.

setts taxed her neighbors on many small articles of daily use. She employed in the single manufacture of hats four thousand persons,—more than were yet engaged in the cotton mills. More than a million and a half of hats were annually made, and three fourths of these were sold beyond the State; between three and four million dollars a year flowed into Massachusetts in exchange for hats alone.[1] At Lynn, in Massachusetts, were made one hundred thousand pairs of women's shoes every year. The town of Roxbury made eight hundred thousand pounds of soap. Massachusetts supplied the country with cut-iron nails to the value of twelve hundred thousand dollars a year. Connecticut supplied the whole country with tin-ware.

New industries sprang up rapidly on a soil and in a climate where the struggle of life was more severe than elsewhere in the Union, and where already capital existed in quantities that made production easy. One industry stimulated another. Women had much to do with the work, and their quickness and patience of details added largely to the income of New England at the cost of less active communities. Their hands wove most of the cotton and woollen cloths sent in large quantities to the West and South; but they were inventors as well as workmen. In 1801, when English straw-bonnets were in fashion, a girl of Wrentham, not far from Boston, found that she could make for herself a straw-hat as good as the imported one. In a few months every girl in the county of Norfolk made her own straw-bonnet; and soon the South and West paid two hundred thousand dollars a year to the county of Norfolk for straw hats and bonnets.[2]

At no time could such industries have been established without the stimulus of a handsome profit; but when Virginia compelled Massachusetts and the Northern States to accept a monopoly of the American market, the Yankee manufacturer must have expected to get, and actually got, great profits for his cottons and woollens, his hats, shoes, soap, and nails. As though this were not more than enough, Virginia gave the Northern shipowners the whole freight on Southern produce, two thirds of which in one form or another went into the

[1] Gallatin's Report, April 17, 1810; State Papers, Finance, ii. 428.
[2] Gallatin's Report, April 17, 1810; State Papers, Finance, ii. 439.

hands of New England shipbuilders, shippers, and merchants. Slowly the specie capital of the Union drifted towards the Banks of Boston and New Haven, until, as the story will show, the steady drain of specie eastward bankrupted the other States and the national government. Never, before or since, was the country so racked to create and support monopolies as in 1808, 1809, and 1810, under Southern rule, and under the system of the President who began his career by declaring that if he could prevent the government from wasting the labors of the people under the pretence of protecting them, they must become happy.[1] The navy and army of the United States were employed, and were paid millions of dollars, during these years in order to shut out foreign competition, and compel New England at the cannon's mouth to accept these enormous bribes.

The Yankee, however ill-tempered he might be, was shrewd enough to see where his profit lay. The Federalist leaders and newspapers grumbled without intermission that their life-blood was drained to support a negro-slave aristocracy, "baser than its own slaves," as their phrase went; but they took the profits thrust upon them; and what they could not clutch was taken by New York and Pennsylvania, while Virginia slowly sank into ruin. Virginia paid the price to gratify her passion for political power; and at the time, she paid it knowingly and willingly. John Randolph protested almost alone. American manufactures owed more to Jefferson and Virginians, who disliked them, than to Northern statesmen, who merely encouraged them after they were established.

These movements and tendencies were rather felt than understood amid the uproar of personal and local interests; but the repeal of the embargo had the effect intended by the Virginians,—it paralyzed Pickering and the party of forcible resistance. New England quickly turned from revolutionary thoughts while she engaged in money-making; and as though the tide of fortune had at last set in Madison's favor, a stroke of his diplomacy raised the tottering Administration to a sudden height of popularity such as Jefferson himself had never reached.

[1] History of First Administration of Jefferson, p. 152.

Chapter II

WHEN NAPOLEON, Aug. 3, 1808, heard at Bordeaux that the Spaniards had captured Dupont's army at Baylen and Rosily's ships at Cadiz, and had thrown eighty thousand French troops back upon the Pyrenees, his anger was great; but his perplexity was much greater. In a character so interesting as that of Napoleon, the moments of perplexity were best worth study; and in his career no single moment occurred when he had more reason to call upon his genius for a resource than when he faced at Bordeaux the failure of his greatest scheme. From St. Petersburg to Gibraltar every shopkeeper knew that England had escaped, and all believed that no combination either of force or fraud could again be made with reasonable hope of driving her commerce from its channels. On this belief every merchant, as well as every government in the world, was actually shaping calculations. Napoleon also must shape his calculations on theirs, since he had failed to force theirs into the path of his own. The escape of England made useless the machinery he had created for her ruin. Spain, Russia, and Austria had little value for his immediate object, except as their control was necessary for the subjection of England; and the military occupation of Spain beyond the Ebro became worse than a blunder from the moment when Cadiz and Lisbon, Cuba and Mexico, Brazil and Peru threw themselves into England's arms.[1]

More than once this history has shown that Napoleon never hesitated to throw aside a plan which had miscarried. If he did not in the autumn of 1808 throw aside his Spanish schemes, the reason could only be that he saw no other resource, and that in his belief his power would suffer too much from the shock of admitting failure. He showed unusual signs of vacillation, and of a desire to escape the position into which his miscalculations had led him. Instead of going at once to Spain and restoring order to his armies, he left his brother helpless at Vittoria while he passed three months in negotiations looking toward peace with England. In September he went to Germany, where he met the Czar of Russia at

[1] Correspondance de Napoléon, xxxii. 265, 272, 359–370.

Erfurt, and induced Alexander, or consented to his inducement, to join in an autograph letter to the King of England,
marked by the usual Napoleonic character, and offering the
principle of *uti possidetis* as the preliminary to a general peace.
England regarded this advance as deceptive, and George Canning was never more successful than in the gesture of self-
restrained contempt with which he tossed back the letter that
Napoleon and Alexander had presumed to address to a constitutional King of England; but even Canning could hardly
suppose that Napoleon would invite an insult without a motive. From whatever side Napoleon approached the situation
he could invent no line of conduct which did not imply the
triumph of England. Study the problem as he might, he could
not escape from the political and military disadvantages he
incurred from the Spanish uprising. Without the consent of
England he could neither free his civil government from the
system of commercial restriction, nor free his military
strength from partial paralysis in Spain; and England refused
to help him, or even to hear reason from Alexander.

Thenceforward a want of distinct purpose showed itself in
Napoleon's acts. Unable either to enforce or to abandon his
Continental system, he began to use it for momentary objects,—sometimes to weaken England, sometimes to obtain
money, or as the pretext for conquests. Unable to hold the
Peninsula or to withdraw from it, he seemed at one time resolved on conquest, at another disposed toward retreat. In the
autumn of 1808 both paths ran together, for his credit required him to conquer before he could honorably establish
any dynasty on the throne; and during the months of September and October he marched new French armies across the
Pyrenees and massed an irresistible force behind the Ebro. A
year before, he had thought one hundred thousand men
enough to occupy all Spain and Portugal; but in October,
1808, he held not less than two hundred and fifty thousand
men beyond the Pyrenees, ready to move at the moment of
his arrival.

October 25, after his return from Germany, the Emperor
pronounced a speech at the opening of his legislative chambers; and the embarrassment of his true position was evident
under the words in which he covered it.

"Russia and Denmark," he said, "have united with me against England. The United States have preferred to renounce commerce and the sea rather than recognize their slavery. A part of my army marches against those that England has formed or disembarked in Spain. It is a special benefit of that Providence which has constantly protected our arms, that passion has so blinded English councils as to make them renounce the protection of the sea and at last present their armies on the Continent. I depart in a few days to place myself at the head of my army, and with God's aid to crown the King of Spain in Madrid, and plant my eagles on the forts of Lisbon."

He left Paris October 29, and ten days later, November 9, began the campaign which still attracts the admiration of military critics, but which did not result in planting his eagles on the forts of Lisbon. "To my great astonishment," he afterward said,[1] "I had to fight the battles of Tudela, Espinosa, Burgos, and Somo Sierra, to gain Madrid, which, in spite of my victories, refused me admission during two days." After disposing in rapid succession of all the Spanish armies, he occupied Madrid December 4, and found himself at the end of his campaign. The conquest of Lisbon and Cadiz required more time, and led to less military result than suited his objects. At that moment he learned that an English army under Sir John Moore had ventured to march from Portugal into the north of Spain, and had already advanced so far toward Burgos as to make their capture possible. The destruction of an English army, however small, offered Napoleon the triumph he wanted. Rapidly collecting his forces, he hurried across the Guadarrama Mountains to cut off Moore's retreat; but for once he was out-generalled. Sir John Moore not only saved his own army, but also led the French a long and exhausting chase to the extreme northwestern shore of Spain, where the British fleet carried Moore's army out of their reach.

Napoleon would not have been the genius he was had he wasted his energies in following Moore to Corunna, or in trying to plant his eagles on the forts of Lisbon or Cadiz. A

[1] Correspondance de Napoléon, xxxii. 366.

year earlier, Lisbon and Cadiz had been central points of his scheme; but in December, 1808, they were worth to him little more than any other seaports without fleets or colonies. For Spain and Portugal Napoleon showed that he had no further use. The moment he saw that Moore had escaped, which became clear when the Emperor reached Astorga, Jan. 2, 1809, throwing upon Soult the task of marching one hundred and fifty miles to Corunna after Moore and the British army, Napoleon stopped short, turned about, and with rapidity unusual even for him, quitted Spain forever. "The affairs of Spain are finished," he wrote January 16;[1] although Joseph had the best reason to know and much cause to tell how his brother left nothing finished in Spain. "The circumstances of Europe oblige me to go for three weeks to Paris," he wrote to Joseph early in the morning of January 15; "if nothing prevents, I shall be back again before the end of February."[2] With characteristic mixture of harshness and tenderness toward his elder brother, he wrote at noon the same day another account, equally deceptive, of his motives and intentions:—

"You must say everywhere, and make the army believe, that I shall return in three or four weeks. In fact, my mere presence at Paris will make Austria shrink back to her nullity; and then, before the end of October, I will be back here. I shall be in Paris in five days. I shall go at full speed, day and night, as far as Bordeaux. Meanwhile everything will go on quieting itself in Spain."[3]

Giving out that the conduct of Austria required his presence at Paris, he succeeded in imposing this fiction upon Europe by the empire of his will. Europe accepted the fable, which became history; but although the Emperor soon disposed of Austria, and although Spain was a more difficult problem than Austria ever was, Napoleon never kept his word to Joseph, and never again ventured within sight of the mistakes he could no longer correct.

Meanwhile Armstrong, disgusted with the disappointments and annoyances of his residence at Paris, had become anxious

[1] Napoleon to Jerome, 16 Janvier, 1809; Correspondance, xviii. 237.
[2] Correspondance, xviii. 225.
[3] Correspondance, xviii. 227.

to escape without further loss of credit. His letters to Madison, published by Congress, returned to terrify his French acquaintance, and to close his sources of information. He could see no hope of further usefulness. As early as Oct. 25, 1808, when the Emperor was addressing his legislative chambers before setting out for Spain, Armstrong wrote to Madison that no good could come from keeping an American minister at Paris.[1] Yet in the enforced idleness of the month when Napoleon was in Spain, Armstrong found one ally whose aid was well worth seeking. After the Czar Alexander accepted, at Tilsit, the ascendency of Napoleon, he appointed as his minister of foreign relations the Count Nicholas Roumanzoff. The Czar was still a young man in his thirty-first year, while Roumanzoff, fifty-four years old, had the full powers of maturity. Together they shaped a Russian policy, in the traditional direction of Russian interests, founded upon jealousy of British maritime tyranny. Lord Howick's and Spencer Perceval's Orders in Council served to sharpen Russian as well as American antipathies, and brought the two distant nations into a sympathy which was certainly not deep, but which England had reason to fear. In the autumn of 1808 Count Roumanzoff came to Paris to arrange with Champagny the details of their joint diplomacy; and at the same time, in the month of November, William Short arrived in Paris secretly accredited as minister plenipotentiary at St. Petersburg, but waiting confirmation by the Senate before going to his post. When Armstrong told Roumanzoff that an American minister would soon be on his way to St. Petersburg, the count was highly pleased, and promised at once to send a full minister to replace André Daschkoff, the chargé at Washington. "Ever since I came into office," he said to Armstrong,[2] "I have been desirous of producing this effect; for in dissolving our commercial connections with Great Britain it became necessary to seek some other power in whom we might find a substitute; and on looking round I could see none but the United States who were at all competent to this object." So far as concerned England, the alliance promised great advantages; but Armstrong's chief anxiety affected

[1] Armstrong to Madison, Oct. 25, 1808; MSS. State Department Archives.
[2] Armstrong to Madison, Nov. 24, 1808; MSS. State Department Archives.

France, and when he attempted to enlist Roumanzoff in resistance to Napoleon's robberies, he found no encouragement. Roumanzoff had already tried his influence with Napoleon on behalf of the Danes, who wanted compensation for their plundered commerce. "Give them a civil answer," replied Napoleon,[1] "but of course one never pays for this sort of thing,— *On ne paye jamais ces choses-là, n'est-ce pas?*" From Roumanzoff's refusal, Armstrong inferred that no change need be hoped in Napoleon's conduct.

"On the contrary," he wrote to Madison, the day when Napoleon abandoned the pursuit of Sir John Moore,[2] "their anti-neutral system is more rigidly observed; the embargo on ships of the United States found here before the imperial decrees were issued is continued; every ship of ours coming into a port of France or of her allies is immediately seized and sequestered; cargoes regularly admitted to entry by the custom-houses are withheld from their owners; ships most obviously exceptions to the operation of the Decrees have been recently condemned; and—what in my view of the subject does not admit of aggravation— the burning of the ship 'Brutus' on the high seas, so far from being disavowed, is substantially justified."

Had this been all, perhaps President Madison and Congress might have waited with courtesy, if not with hope, for Napoleon's pleasure; but grievances equally serious ran back to the year 1803, and not one of them had been redressed by France.

"It is now three years since one of her admirals, on the principle of self-preservation, burnt four of our ships at sea, and the Emperor immediately acknowledged the debt and repeatedly promised to discharge it; but not a shilling has yet been paid, nor is it probable that a shilling ever will be paid. Besides this breach of justice in the first instance and of promise in the last, we have to complain that bills of exchange drawn to the order of citizens of the United States by the public functionaries of France, to the amount

[1] Gallatin's Writings, ii. 490.
[2] Armstrong to Madison, Jan. 2, 1809; MSS. State Department Archives.

of many millions of dollars, and for articles of the first necessity, and drawn many years ago, are not only not paid,
but are officially denounced as not payable."

Armstrong's temper, bad in the winter, became worse in
the spring, until his letters to the Department of State seemed
to leave no remedy but war for the grievances he described.
The angry tone of his despatches was not counteracted by fair
words in the instructions sent by Champagny to Turreau,
which were calculated to irritate President Madison beyond
patience.

"You cannot too much call attention to the grievances of
the Americans against England in order to make them
more sensibly felt," wrote Champagny to Turreau, after the
Emperor went to Spain.[1] "The Americans would like
France to grant them commercial privileges which no nation at present enjoys. . . . But . . . hitherto it has not
seemed proper, in the execution of general measures, to introduce exceptions which would have really destroyed their
effect. If the rules adopted against English commerce had
not been made common, that commerce would continue
through every opening left to it; England would preserve
the same resources as before for supporting the war. A system of exception for one people would turn the rule into
an injustice toward all others; all would have right to complain of a privilege granted to the Federal government
which themselves would not enjoy."

Unanswerable as this reasoning was from the Napoleonic
standpoint, it was open to the objection of placing Madison
among the belligerents at war with England, and of obliging
him not only to accept the rules imposed by Napoleon on the
allies of France, but also to admit the corresponding right of
British retaliation, even to the point of war. Until President
Madison made up his mind to war with England, he could
hardly be induced by Napoleon's diplomacy to overlook his
causes of war with France.

Had Napoleon acted according to rules of ordinary civilization, he would at least have softened the harshness of his

[1] Champagny to Turreau, Dec. 10, 1808; Archives des Aff. Étr. MSS.

commercial policy toward America by opening to the American President some vista of compensation elsewhere. Florida seemed peculiarly suited for this object, and no one so well as Napoleon knew the anxiety of the late Administration to obtain that territory, which, for any legitimate purpose, was useless and worthless to France. In December, 1808, Napoleon could have retained little or no hope of controlling the Spanish colonies by force; yet he ordered the American government to leave them alone, as he ordered it to adopt the French system of commercial restraint. "I venture to presume," continued Champagny to Turreau, "that if his Majesty has no reason to complain of the disposition shown by the United States toward him, he will show himself more and more inclined to treat them favorably. What will most influence his course will be the conduct pursued by the United States toward the Spanish colonies, and the care that shall be taken to do nothing in regard to them which can contravene the rights of the mother-country."

Thus from Turreau's attitude as well as from Armstrong's letters, the government at Washington was advised that neither favor nor justice need be expected from Napoleon. This impression, strengthened by all the private advices which arrived from France during the winter of 1808–1809, even though partly balanced by the bulletins of the Emperor's splendid Spanish campaign, had much to do with the refusal of Congress to declare a double war, which, however general in terms, must in effect be waged against England alone. Anger with France affected Republicans almost as strongly as fear of Napoleon excited Federalists. When the final struggle took place in Congress over the embargo, no small share of the weakness shown by the Administration and its followers was due to their consciousness that the repeal of the embargo would relieve them from appearing to obey an imperial mandate.

Turreau understood the repeal in no other light, and was extremely irritated to see the decline of his influence. Men who had given him pledge upon pledge that the embargo should be withdrawn only when war against England should be declared, could plead no better excuse for failing to keep their promise than that Napoleon had forfeited his claim to their support. March 19, two weeks after Congress rose, Turreau wrote from Baltimore to Champagny,[1] —

"You will have judged from my last despatches that the Embargo Law would be repealed. It has been so, in fact, despite my efforts to maintain it, and notwithstanding the promise of quite a large number of influential Representatives, especially among the senators, who had guaranteed to me its continuance till the next Congress, and who have voted against their political conscience. I had informed your Excellency of the disunion projects shown by some of the Northern States. Their avowed opposition to the continuance of the embargo, and their threats to resist its execution, terrified Congress to such a degree that the dominant party became divided, and the feebleness (faiblesse) of Mr. Jefferson sanctioned the last and the most shameful act of his Administration. . . . I say it with regret,—and perhaps I have said it too late,—I am convinced there is nothing to hope from these people."

Erskine, whose persistent efforts to conciliate had also something to do with the action of Congress, made Turreau's anger the subject of a despatch, doubtless hoping it might guide Canning's thoughts toward the wisdom of conciliation.[2] "The French minister it seems is so much offended at the Non-intercourse Law which has been lately passed, and is so little pleased with the general disposition, as he conceives it, of the new Administration of the United States toward France, that he has quitted this city, having previously given up his house and removed all his furniture, without calling either upon the new President or any of the members of the Administration, as was his uniform custom in former years, and as is always done by foreign ministers." Robert Smith informed Erskine that the Government would consider it to be their duty, which he was sure they would feel no disposition to shrink from, to recommend to the new Congress to enter upon immediate measures of hostility against France in the event of Great Britain giving way as to her Orders so far

[1] Turreau to Champagny, 19 March, 1809; Archives des Aff. Étr., MSS.
[2] Erskine to Canning, March 17, 1809; MSS. British Archives.

as to afford an opportunity to the United States to assert their rights against France.

During the month of March, Turreau watched the workings of the Non-intercourse Act, but found little encouragement. "Generally the ventures have not been so numerous as was to be expected from the well-known avidity of American merchants, and the privations they have suffered from the embargo."[1] Most of the outgoing vessels had cleared for the West Indies or the Azores, "but the French government may rest assured that among a hundred ships leaving the ports of the Union for the high seas, ninety of them will have the real object of satisfying the wants and demands of England." Such a commerce was in his opinion fair prey. England had gained the upper-hand in America; English superiority could no longer be contested; and to France remained only the desperate chances of the political gambler.

"To-day not only is the separation of New England openly talked about, but the people of those five States wish for this separation, pronounce it, openly prepare it, will carry it out under British protection, and probably will meet with no resistance on the part of the other States. Yet this project, which is known and avowed; the last proceedings of Congress, which are blamed; the progress of the Federalists; the alarms of commerce; the feebleness of the highest authorities (*des premiers pouvoirs*), and the doubts regarding the capacity and the party views of the new President,—cause a ferment of public opinion; and perhaps the moment has come for forming a party in favor of France in the Central and Southern States, whenever those of the North, having given themselves a separate government under the support of Great Britain, may threaten the independence of the rest."[2]

Turreau's speculations might show no great sagacity, but they opened a glimpse into his mind, and they were the chief information possessed by Napoleon to form his estimate of American character. Nothing could more irritate the Emperor than these laments from his minister at Washington over the

[1] Turreau to Champagny, 15 April, 1809; Archives des Aff Étr. MSS.
[2] Turreau to Champagny, 20 April, 1809; Archives des Aff. Étr. MSS.

victory of English interests in the United States. The effect of
such reports on Napoleon was likely to be the more decided
because Turreau saw everything in darker colors than the facts
warranted. Deceived and defeated in the case of the embargo,
he imagined himself also in danger on the other main point
of his diplomacy,—the Spanish colonies. The old Spanish
agents, consular and diplomatic, mostly patriots, were still officially recognized or privately received at Washington. Rumor said that troops were collecting at New Orleans to
support a movement of independence in Florida; that General
Wilkinson, on his way to take command in Louisiana, had
stopped at Havana and Pensacola; that President Jefferson, on
the eve of quitting the Presidency, had been heard to say,
"We must have the Floridas and Cuba." Anonymous letters,
believed by Turreau to be written by one of the clerks in the
State Department, warned him against the intrigues of the
Federal government in the Spanish colonies. So much was he
troubled by these alarms, that April 15 he addressed an unofficial note on the subject to Robert Smith.[1]

The President, having no wish to quarrel with the French
minister, and probably aware of his irritation, asked Gallatin,
on his way northwards, to call on Turreau at Baltimore and
make to him such soothing explanations as the case seemed
to require. The interview took place during the last week of
April, and Turreau's report threw another ray of light into the
recesses of Jefferson's councils.[2]

   " 'I am specially charged,' said Gallatin, 'to assure you
   that whatever proceedings of General Wilkinson may seem
   to warrant your suspicions must not be attributed to the
   Executive, but solely to the vanity, the indiscretion, and the
   ordinary inconsistencies of that General, whom you know
   perhaps as well as we. . . . We are and we wish to be
   strangers to all that passes in the Floridas, in Mexico, and
   also in Cuba. You would be mistaken if you supposed that
   Mr. Madison wishes the possession of the Floridas. That
   was Mr. Jefferson's hobby (*marotte*),—it has never been

[1] Turreau to Champagny, 22 April, 1809; Archives des Aff. Étr., MSS.
[2] Turreau to Champagny, 1 June, 1809; Archives des Aff. Étr., MSS. Cf.
Madison to Jefferson, May 1, 1809; Writings, ii. 440.

the wish of his Cabinet; and Mr. Madison values to-day the possession of the Floridas only so far as they may be thought indispensable to prevent every kind of misunderstanding with Spain, and to secure an outlet for the produce of our Southern States. We have had no part in the meetings which have taken place in the Floridas, and we could not know that General Wilkinson has been ill received there.' (This is true.) 'As for the possession of Cuba, this was also a new idea of Mr. Jefferson which has not been approved by the Executive council; and I am authorized to protest to you that even if Cuba were offered us as a gift, we would not accept it. We are also opposed to every step which would tend, under the pretext of commerce, to involve us in the politics of France and Spain, and we shall see to it that any persons undertaking such enterprises are properly dealt with. I flatter myself therefore that you will believe the Cabinet to be firmly resolved carefully to avoid every disturbance of the good understanding between the United States and France.' "

Gallatin was a persistent enemy of the Florida intrigue, and doubtless believed that Madison held opinions like his own; but Madison's opinions on this subject, as on some others, were elusive,—perhaps no clearer to himself than to readers of his writings; and Gallatin had yet to learn that the instinct which coveted Florida could not be controlled by a decision of the Cabinet. Yet he said only what he seemed authorized to say; and his reference to the *marotte* of President Jefferson was significant. For the moment the weakness seemed cured. Gallatin gave Turreau to understand that President Madison would not intrigue in Florida or Cuba, and to that extent he was doubtless expressly authorized by the President. Perhaps only on his own authority he went a step further, by hinting that Napoleon need no longer dangle Florida before Madison's eyes.

A rupture with France seemed certain. Turreau expected it and hoped only to delay it. In his eyes the Emperor had suffered an indignity that could not be overlooked, although he asked that retaliation should be delayed till autumn. "However dissatisfied the French government may be by the last measures adopted by Congress, I believe it would be well to await the result of the next session two months hence before taking a severer course against the Americans. This opinion, which I express only with doubt, is yet warranted by advices which I have received within a few days, and which have been given me by men who know the Executive intentions, and who at least till now have not deceived me." Turreau believed that when the Emperor learned what the late Congress had done, he would strike the United States with the thunderbolt of his power. Doubtless the same impression was general. Even after Napoleon's character has been the favorite study of biographers and historians for nearly a hundred years, the shrewdest criticism might fail in the effort to conjecture what shape the Emperor's resentment took. This story has shown many of his processes from the time when he met the resistance of the Haytian negroes in 1803 to the time when he met the uprising of the Spanish patriots in 1809; but even with the advantage of his own writings as a guide, neither friend nor enemy could test theories of his character better than by attempting to divine the conduct he was to pursue toward the United States after their defiance of his wishes in the repeal of the embargo.

As though to remove the last doubt of rupture with Napoleon, the President startled the country by suddenly announcing a settlement of his disputes with England. April 7 Erskine received new instructions from London, and during the next two weeks he was closeted with the President and the Cabinet. April 21 the "National Intelligencer" announced the result of their labors.

Chapter III

IN CANNING's note to Pinkney of Sept. 23, 1808,—the same paper which expressed his Majesty's regret for the embargo "as a measure of inconvenient restriction upon the American people,"—a paragraph easily overlooked had been inserted to provide for future chances of fortune:—

"It is not improbable, indeed, that some alterations may be made in the Orders of Council as they are at present framed,—alterations calculated, not to abate their spirit or impair their principle, but to adapt them more exactly to the different state of things which has fortunately grown up in Europe, and to combine all practicable relief to neutrals with a more severe pressure upon the enemy. But of alterations to be made with this view only it would be uncandid to take any advantage in the present discussion, however it might be hoped that in their practical effect they might prove beneficial to America, provided the operation of the embargo were not to prevent her from reaping that benefit."

This intended change in the orders depended on the political change which converted Spain from an enemy into an ally. Spencer Perceval did not care to press the cause of British commerce so far as to tax American wheat and salt-fish on their way to Spain and Portugal, where he must himself provide money to pay for them after they were bought by the army commissaries. Accordingly, in December, 1808, a new Order in Council appeared, doing away with the export duties lately imposed by Parliament on foreign articles passing through England. Thenceforward American wheat might be shipped at Liverpool for the Spanish peninsula without paying ten shillings a quarter to the British Treasury,[1] if only the embargo did not prevent American wheat from entering Liverpool at all.

In a short note, dated December 24, Canning enclosed to Pinkney a copy of the new order; and while taking care to

[1] Act of Geo. III. 1808; Cap. xxvi. American State Papers, iii. 274.

explain that this measure conceded nothing in principle, he offered it as a step toward removing the most offensive, if not the most oppressive, restraint imposed on American commerce by the Orders of 1807: —

> "As I have more than once understood from you that the part of the Orders in Council which this order goes to mitigate is that which was felt most sorely by the United States, I have great pleasure in being authorized to communicate it to you."

Pinkney was in no humor to bear more of what he considered Canning's bad taste, and he could have but one opinion of the measure which Canning announced. "This order is a shadow," he wrote to Madison,[1] "and if meant to conciliate us, ridiculous." His reply to Canning verged for the first time on abruptness, as though the moment were near when he meant to speak another language.

> "It is perfectly true," began Pinkney's acknowledgment of Dec. 28, 1808,[2] "as the concluding paragraph of your letter supposes me to believe, that the United States have viewed with great sensibility the pretension of this Government (which, as a pretension, the present order reasserts without much if at all modifying its practical effect) to levy imposts upon their commerce, outward and inward, which the Orders in Council of the last year were to constrain to pass through British ports. But it is equally true that my Government has constantly protested against the entire system with which that pretension was connected, and has in consequence required the repeal, not the modification, of the British Orders in Council."

This reception roused the temper of Canning, who could not understand, if Pinkney honestly wished harmony, why he should repel what might be taken as a kindness; yet the same reasons which induced him to make the advance impelled him to bear with the American minister's roughness. The moment was ill adapted for more quarrels. Napoleon had occupied Madrid three weeks before, and was driving Sir John Moore's

[1] Pinkney to Madison, Dec. 25, 1808; Wheaton's Pinkney.
[2] Pinkney to Canning, Dec. 28, 1808; State Papers, iii. 240.

army in headlong flight back to England; the dreams of mid-summer had vanished; the overthrow of France was no nearer than before the Spanish uprising; the United States were seriously discussing war, and however loudly a few interested Englishmen might at times talk, the people of England never wanted war with the United States. Canning found himself obliged to suppress his irritation, and so far from checking the spirit of concession to America, was drawn into new and more decided advances. Spencer Perceval felt the same impulse, and of his own accord proposed other steps to his colleague, after Pinkney's letter of December 28 had been read and considered by the Cabinet. With the impression of that letter fresh in the minds of both, Canning wrote to Perceval on the last day of the year:[1] —

"We have given quite proof enough of our determination to maintain our principle to enable us to relax, if in other respects advisable, without danger of being suspected of giving way. The paragraph in my letter to Pinkney, of September 23, prepares the world for any relaxations that we may think fit to make, provided they are coupled with increased severity against France; and though this last consideration is something impaired by my last communication to Pinkney, yet the manner in which he has received that communication (with respect to which reception I partake of the fury which you describe as having been kindled in Hammond) leaves us quite at liberty to take any new steps without explanation, and exempts us from any hazard of seeing them too well received."

The year 1809 began with this new spirit of accommodation in British councils. The causes which produced it were notorious. From the moment Europe closed her ports, in the autumn of 1807, articles commonly supplied from the Continent rose to speculative prices, and after the American embargo the same effect followed with American produce. Flax, linseed, tallow, timber, Spanish wool, silk, hemp, American cotton doubled or trebled in price in the English markets during the years 1807 and 1808.[2] Colonial produce declined in the same

[1]Canning to Perceval, Dec. 31, 1808; Perceval MSS.
[2]Tooke's History of Prices, i. 274–279.

proportion. Quantities of sugar and coffee overfilled the ware-houses of London, while the same articles could not be bought at Amsterdam and Antwerp at prices three, four, and five times those asked on the Royal Exchange. Under the Orders in Council, the whole produce of the West Indies, shut from Europe by Napoleon and from the United States by the embargo, was brought to England, until mere plethora stopped accumulation.

Debarred from their natural outlets, English merchandise and manufactures were forced into every other market which seemed to offer a hope of sale or barter. When Portugal fell into Napoleon's hands, and the royal family took refuge in Brazil under British protection, English merchants glutted Brazil with their goods, until the beach at Rio Janeiro was covered with property, which perished for want of buyers and warehouses. The Spanish trade, thrown open soon afterward, resulted in similar losses. In the effort to relieve the plethora at home, England gorged the few small channels of commerce that remained in her control.

These efforts coincided with a drain of specie on government account to support the Spanish patriots. The British armies sent to Spain required large sums in coin for their supplies, and the Spaniards required every kind of assistance. The process of paying money on every hand and receiving nothing but worthless produce could not long continue without turning the exchanges against London; yet a sudden call for specie threatened to shake the foundations of society. Never was credit so rotten. Speculation was rampant, and inflation accompanied it. None of the familiar signs of financial disaster were absent. Visionary joint-stock enterprises flourished. Discounts at long date, or without regard to proper security, could be obtained with ease from the private banks and bankers who were competing for business; and although the Bank of England followed its usual course, neither contracting nor expanding its loans and issues, suddenly, at the close of 1808, gold coin rose at a leap from a nominal rate of 103 to the alarming premium of 113. The exchanges had turned, and the inevitable crash was near.

The political outlook took the same sombre tone as the finances. The failure of the Spaniards and the evacuation of

Spain by the British army after the loss of Sir John Moore at Corunna, January 16, destroyed confidence in all political hopes. Lord Castlereagh, as war-secretary, was most exposed to attack. Instead of defending him, Canning set the example of weakening his influence. Aware that the Administration had not the capacity to hold its own, Canning undertook to reform it. As early as October, 1808, he talked freely of Castlereagh's incompetence, and made no secret of his opinion that the Secretary for War must go out.[1] Whether his judgment of Castlereagh's abilities were right or wrong was a matter for English history to decide; but Americans might at least wonder that the Convention of Cintra and the campaign of Sir John Moore were not held to be achievements as respectable as the American diplomacy of Canning or the commercial experiments of Spencer Perceval. Canning himself agreed that Perceval was little, if at all, superior to Castlereagh, and he saw hope for England chiefly in his own elevation to the post of the Duke of Portland.

Although no one fully understood all that had been done by the Portland ministry, enough was known to render their fall certain; and Canning saw himself sinking with the rest. He made active efforts to secure his own safety and to rise above the misfortunes which threatened to overwhelm his colleagues. Among other annoyances, he felt the recoil of his American policy. The tone taken by Pinkney coincided with the warlike threats reported by Erskine, and with the language of Campbell's Report to the House of Representatives. Erskine's despatch of November 26, in which Campbell's Report was enclosed, and his alarming despatches of December 3 and 4 were received by Canning about the middle of January,[2] at a time when the Ministry was sustained only by royal favor. The language and the threats of these advices were such as Canning could not with dignity overlook or with safety resent; but he overlooked them. January 18, at a diplomatic dinner given by him on the Queen's birthday, he took Pinkney aside to tell him that the Ministry

[1] Brougham to Grey, Nov. 25, 1809, Brougham's Memoirs, i. 417; Temple's Courts and Cabinets, iv. 276, 283; Canning to the Duke of Portland, March 24, 1809; Walpole's Spencer Perceval, i. 347, 350.

[2] Canning to Erskine, Jan. 23, 1809; Cobbett's Debates, xvii, cxix.

were willing to consider the Resolutions proposed in Campbell's Report as putting an end to the difficulties which prevented a satisfactory arrangement.[1] Pinkney, surprised by Canning's "more than usual kindness and respect," suggested deferring the subject to a better occasion; and Canning readily acquiesced, appointing January 22 as the day for an interview.

The next morning, January 19, Parliament met, and American affairs were instantly made the subject of attack on ministers. In the Lords, Grenville declared that "the insulting and sophistical answer" returned by Canning to the American offer, persuaded him "that the intention of the King's government is to drive things to extremity with America." Lord Hawkesbury the Home Secretary, who had succeeded his father as Earl of Liverpool, replied in the old tone that ministers felt no disposition to irritate America, but that national dignity and importance were not to be sacrificed "at the very moment when America seemed so blind to her own interest, and betrayed so decided a partiality in favor of France."[2] In the Commons, Whitbread and the other leaders of opposition echoed the attack, but Canning did not echo the reply.

"The same infatuation," said Whitbread,[3] "seems now to prevail that existed in the time of the late American war. There were the same taunts, the same sarcasms, and the same assertions that America cannot do without us." Only a few weeks earlier or later, Canning would have met such criticisms in his loftiest tone, and with more reason than in 1807 or in 1808. In his desk were Erskine's latest despatches, announcing impending war in every accent of defiance and in many varieties of italics and capital letters; fresh in his memory was his own official pledge that "no step which could even mistakenly be construed into concession should be taken" while a doubt existed whether America had wholly abandoned her attempt at commercial restriction. Yet instead of maintaining England's authority at the moment when for the first time it was threatened by the United States, Canning

[1] Pinkney to Madison, Jan. 23, 1809; Wheaton's Pinkney, p. 420.
[2] Cobbett's Debates, xii. 25.
[3] Cobbett's Debates, p. 69.

became apologetic and yielding. Repeating the commonplaces of the newspapers that America had sided with France, and even going so far as to assert, what he best knew to be an error, that the Orders in Council had not been the cause of the embargo, and "it was now a notorious fact that no such ground had been laid for the embargo;" after declaring the exclusion of British war-vessels from American harbors to have been the chief obstacle to the compromise offered by America,—treading, with what seemed a very uncertain foot, among these slippery and ill-balanced stepping-stones, he reached the point where he meant to rest. The "Chesapeake" Proclamation, which excluded British war-ships from American harbors, being his chief grievance, any settlement which removed that grievance would be so far satisfactory; and for this reason the measures proposed in Campbell's Report, though clothed in hostile language, might, if made known to the British government in amicable terms, have led to the acceptance of the compromise proposed, since they excluded French as well as English ships of war from American ports.

Canning next turned to Pinkney to ascertain how much concession would be safe. The interview took place January 22; but Pinkney's powers had been withdrawn, and he neither could nor would furnish Canning with any assurance on which a concession could be offered with the certainty either that it would be accepted, or that it would be refused. Canning seemed particularly anxious to know how the embargo could be effectually enforced against commerce with France, after being removed in regard to England.[1] He "presumed that the government of the United States would not complain if the naval force of this country should assist in preventing such a commerce."[2] Pinkney felt many doubts of Canning's good faith,[3] and had every reason for avoiding committal of himself or of his Government. According to his own account, he declined to enter into the discussion of details, and confined himself to general encouragement of Canning's good disposition.[4]

[1] Pinkney to Madison, Jan. 23, 1809; Wheaton's Pinkney, p. 423.
[2] Brief Account, etc., Jan. 23, 1809; State Papers, iii. 299.
[3] Pinkney to Madison, Jan. 23, 1809; Wheaton's Pinkney, p. 424.
[4] Pinkney to R. Smith, June 6, 1809; State Papers, iii. 303.

After experimenting upon Pinkney, much as he had sounded Parliament, Canning lost not an hour in composing the new instructions to Erskine. Four in number, all bearing the same date of January 23, they dealt successively with each of the disputed points; but in order to understand the embroilment they caused, readers must carry in mind, even at some effort of memory, precisely what Canning ordered Erskine to do, and precisely what Erskine did.

The first instruction dealt with the "Chesapeake" affair, and the Proclamation occasioned by it. Accepting Gallatin's idea that the Proclamation being merged in the general non-intercourse would cease to exist as a special and separate provision of law, Canning instructed Erskine that if French ships of war should be excluded from American ports, and if the Proclamation should be tacitly withdrawn, he need no longer insist upon the formal recall. Further, Gallatin had suggested that Congress was about to exclude foreign seamen by law from national ships; and Canning admitted also this evasion of his demand that the United States should engage not to countenance desertions. Finally, he withdrew the demand for disavowals which had wrecked Rose's mission.

Evidently the British government wished to settle the "Chesapeake" affair. Had Canning in like manner swept away his old conditions precedent to withdrawal of the Orders in Council, his good faith would have been above suspicion; but he approached that subject in a different spirit, and imposed one condition after another while he adopted the unusual course of putting each new condition into the mouth of some American official. He drew from Erskine's despatches the inference that Madison, Smith, and Gallatin were willing to recognize in express terms the validity of the British "Rule of 1756."[1] For this misunderstanding Erskine was to blame,[2] but Canning was alone responsible for the next remark, that "Mr. Pinkney has recently, but for the first time, expressed to me his opinion that there will be no indisposition on the part of his Government to the enforcement, by the naval power of Great Britain," of the Act of Congress declaring non-intercourse with France. On the strength of these supposed

[1] Canning to Erskine, Jan. 23, 1809; American State Papers, iii. 300.
[2] Second Administration of Jefferson, pp. 1194–1195.

expressions of William Pinkney, Madison, Smith, and Gallatin, none of which was official or in writing, Canning concluded: —

> "I flatter myself that there will be no difficulty in obtaining a distinct and official recognition of these conditions from the American government. For this purpose you are at liberty to communicate this despatch *in extenso* to the American government."

The chief interest of these instructions lay in the question whether Canning meant in good faith to offer on any conditions a withdrawal of the Orders in Council. The course of his own acts and of Perceval's measures, suggested that he did not intend to offer any terms which the United States could accept. His remark to Perceval three weeks before, that they were quite at liberty to take new steps without "any hazard of seeing them too well received," pointed in the same direction. Yet motives were enigmas too obscure for search, and the motives of Canning in this instance were more perplexing than usual. If he was serious in hoping an agreement, how could he insist on requiring official recognition of the right of Great Britain to enforce the municipal laws of the United States when he afterward admitted that such a claim "could not well find its way into a stipulation; that he had nevertheless believed it proper to propose the condition to the United States; that he should have been satisfied with the rejection of it; and that the consequence would have been that they should have intercepted the commerce to which it referred, if any such commerce should be attempted"?[1] In the instructions to Erskine he imposed the condition as essential to the agreement, — the same condition which he thought "could not well find its way into a stipulation," and which "he should have been satisfied" to see rejected.

For two years Canning had lost no opportunity of charging the American government with subservience to Napoleon; even in these instructions he alleged Jefferson's "manifest partiality" to France as a reason why England could entertain no propositions coming from him. He had in his hands

[1] Pinkney to R. Smith, June 23, 1809; State Papers, iii. 303.

Madison's emphatic threats of war; how then could he conceive of obtaining from Madison an express recognition of the British Rule of 1756, which Madison had most deeply pledged himself to resist?

On the other hand, Canning showed forbearance and a wish for peace, by leaving Erskine minister at Washington as well as by passing unnoticed Madison's threats of war; and he betrayed a singular incapacity to understand the bearing of his own demands when he directed Erskine to communicate his instructions *in extenso* to the American government. Had he intelligently acted in bad faith, he would not have given the President, whose attachment to France he suspected, the advantage of seeing these instructions, which required that America should become a subject State of England.

Perhaps a partial clew to these seeming contradictions might be found in the peculiar traits of Canning's character. He belonged to a class of men denied the faculty of realizing the sensibilities of others. At the moment when he took this tone of authority toward America, he gave mortal offence to his own colleague Lord Castlereagh, by assuming a like attitude toward him. He could not understand, and he could never train himself to regard, the rule that such an attitude between States as between gentlemen was not admitted among equals.

Whatever was the reason of Canning's conduct, its effect was that of creating the impression of bad faith by offering terms intended to be refused. The effect of bad faith was the more certain because the instructions closed by giving Erskine some latitude, not as to the conditions which were to be distinctly and officially recognized, but as to the form in which the recognition might be required: —

> "Upon the receipt here of an official note containing an engagement for the adoption of the three conditions above specified, his Majesty will be prepared on the faith of such engagement,—either immediately, if the repeal shall have been immediate in America or on any day specified by the American government for that repeal,—reciprocally to recall the Orders in Council."

The form of the required engagement was left to Erskine's

discretion; and in case Erskine failed, Canning would be still at liberty to claim, as he afterward did, that his conditions were not so rigorously meant as Erskine should have supposed them to be.

Meanwhile the Government of England was falling to pieces. Day by day the situation became more alarming. For months after these despatches were sent, the Commons passed their time in taking testimony and listening to speeches intended to prove or disprove that the Duke of York, commander-in-chief of the army, was in the habit of selling officers' commissions through the agency of his mistress, a certain Mrs. Clarke; and although the Duke protested his innocence, the scandal drove him from his office. The old King, blind and infirm, was quite unfit to bear the shame of his son's disgrace; while the Prince of Wales stood no better than the Duke of York either in his father's esteem or in public opinion. The Ministry was rent by faction; Perceval, Castlereagh, and Canning were at cross purposes, while the Whigs were so weak that they rather feared than hoped their rivals' fall. Whatever might be the factiousness of Congress or the weakness of government at Washington, the confusion in Parliament was worse, and threatened worse dangers.

"All power and influence of Perceval in the House is quite gone by," wrote a Whig member, February 16.[1] "He speaks without authority and without attention paid to him; and Canning has made two or three such rash declarations that he is little attended to. You may judge the situation of the House, when I tell you we were last night nearly three quarters of an hour debating about the evidence of a drunken footman by Perceval suggesting modes of ascertaining how to convict him of his drunkenness,— Charles Long [one of the Administration], near whom I was sitting telling me at the time what a lamentable proof it was of the want of some man of sense and judgment to lead the House. There is no government in the House of Commons,—you may be assured the thing does not exist; and whether they can ever recover their tone of power

[1] W. H. Fremantle to the Marquis of Buckingham, Feb. 16, 1809; Courts and Cabinets of George III., iv. 318.

remains to be proved. At present Mr. Croker, Mr. D. Brown, and Mr. Beresford are the leaders. . . . The Cintra Convention, or the general campaign, or the American question, are minor considerations, and indeed do not enter into the consideration of any one."

The House of Lords maintained more appearance of dignity; and there, February 17, four-and-twenty hours after Colonel Fremantle wrote this letter, Lord Grenville began a debate on American affairs. As a test of Tory sincerity in view of what Erskine was soon to do at Washington, the debate— as well as all else that was said of American affairs during the session—deserved more than ordinary notice, if only in justice to the British ministry, whose language was to receive a commentary they did not expect.[1]

The most significant speech came from Lord Sidmouth. The conservatism of this peer stood above reproach, and compared closely with that of Spencer Perceval. Rather than abandon the "established principle" of the Rule of 1756, he far preferred an American war. He proved his stubborn Tory consistency too clearly, both before and after 1809, to warrant a suspicion of leanings toward liberal or American sympathies; but his speech of February 17 supporting Grenville, and charging ministers with bad faith, was long and earnest. He called attention to the scandal that while the Government professed in the speech from the Throne a persuasion "that in the result the enemy will be convinced of the impolicy of persevering in a system which retorts upon himself, in so much greater proportion, those evils which he endeavors to inflict," yet instead of retorting those evils, Perceval licensed the export and import both with France and Holland of the very articles which those countries wished to sell and buy, while Canning at the same moment rejected the American offers of trade because he thought it "important in the highest degree that the disappointment of the hopes of the enemy should not have been purchased by any concession."

Ministers might disregard Grenville's furious denunciation of the orders as an act of the most egregious folly and the most unexampled ignorance that ever disgraced the councils

---

[1] Cobbett's Debates, xii. 771–803.

of a State; they might even close their ears to Sidmouth's charge that the folly and ignorance of the orders were surpassed by their dishonesty,—but not even Spencer Perceval could deny or forget that while a year before, Feb. 15, 1808, forty-eight peers voted against him, on Feb. 17, 1809, seventy lords, in person or by proxy, supported Grenville. While the opposition gained twenty-two votes, the government gained only nine.

The impression of weakness in the ministry was increased by the energy with which the authors of the orders stood at bay in their defence. When Whitbread in the House of Commons renewed the attack, and the House, March 6, entered on the debate, James Stephen came forward as the champion of his own cause. Stephen's speech,[1] published afterward as a pamphlet, was intended to be an official as well as a final answer to attacks against the orders, and was conclusive in regard to the scope and motives of Perceval's scheme. Neither Canning nor Liverpool spoke with personal knowledge to be compared with that of Stephen. Canning in particular had nothing to do with the orders except as a subject of diplomatic evasion. Stephen, Perceval, and George Rose were the parents of commercial restriction, and knew best their own objects. With frankness creditable to him, but contrasting with the double-toned language of Perceval and Canning, Stephen always placed in the foreground the commercial objects he wanted and expected to attain. His speech of March 6, 1809, once more asserted, in language as positive as possible, that the orders had no other purpose than to stop the American trade with France because it threatened to supplant British trade. The doctrine of retaliation, or the object of retorting evils on France, had nothing to do with Stephen's scheme. His words were clear, for like a true enthusiast he was wholly intent on the idea in which he thought safety depended.

Canning also planted himself on advanced ground. The question, he said, was between England and France; not between England and America. On the principles of international law he had no defence to offer for the Orders in Council as between England and America. "He was willing

---

[1] Cobbett's Debates, xiii. App. no. 2, xxxi.

to admit that it was not upon the poor pretence of the existing law of nations, but upon the extension of that law (an extension just and necessary), that his Majesty's ministers were to rely, in the present instance, for justification." This extension rested on the excuse that France had first discarded the law of nations; and America, in attempting to give to Great Britain the priority in wrong, had incurred this censure,—"that she had brought a false charge, and persisted in it." In his opinion, the American offer to withdraw the embargo in favor of England and to enforce it against France, "was illusory; he might add, in the language of Mr. Madison, 'it was insulting.'" Those who accused ministers of a disinclination to adopt pacific measures respecting America had lost sight of the facts. "We had rather gone too far than done too little. We twice offered to negotiate; yet the Non-importation Act was not revoked."

If this was Canning's true state of mind, his instructions to Erskine less than a month before, offering to abandon the Orders in Council, seemed to admit no defence. Still less could be explained how President Madison, after reading these speeches, should have expected from Canning the approval of any possible arrangement. Yet the irritation of Canning's tone showed him to be ill at ease,—he felt the ground slipping under his feet. The public had become weary of him and his colleagues. The commercial system they had invented seemed to create the evils it was made to counteract. The press began to complain. As early as January 13 the "Times" showed signs of deserting the orders, which it declared to be no "acts of retaliation," but "measures of counteraction," complicated by transit duties doubtful either in expediency or justice. "If America will withdraw her Embargo and Non-importation Acts as far as they relate to England, provided we rescind the Orders in Council, we cannot consider this as a disgraceful concession on our part." After the debate of March 6, the "Times" renewed its complaints. Every day increased the difficulties of ministers, until mere change became relief.

At length, April 26, the reality of the weakness of Perceval and Canning became clear. On that day a new Order in

Council[1] appeared, which roused great interest because it seemed to abandon the whole ground taken in the Orders of November, 1807, and to return within the admitted principles of international law. The machinery of the old orders was apparently discarded; the machinery of blockade was restored in its place. The Order of April 26, 1809, declared that the old orders were revoked and annulled except so far as their objects were to be attained by a general blockade of all ports and places under the government of France. The blockade thus declared was to extend northward as far as Ems, and was to include on the south the ports of northern Italy. Of course the new blockade was not even claimed to be effective. No squadrons were to enforce its provisions by their actual presence before the blockaded ports. In that respect the Order of April 26, 1809, was as illegal as that of Nov. 11, 1807; but the new arrangement opened to neutral commerce all ports not actually ports of France, even though the British flag should be excluded from them,—retaliating upon France only the injury which the French decrees attempted to inflict on England.

Pinkney was greatly pleased, and wrote to Madison in excellent spirits[2] that the change gave all the immediate benefits which could have arisen from the arrangement proposed by him in the previous August, except the right to demand from France the recall of her edicts. "Our triumph is already considered as a signal one by everybody. The pretexts with which ministers would conceal their motives for a relinquishment of all which they prized in their system are seen through, and it is universally viewed as a concession to America. Our honor is now safe; and by management we may probably gain everything we have in view." Canning said to Pinkney: "If these alterations did not do all that was expected, they at least narrowed extremely the field of discussion, and gave great facilities and encouragement to reviving cordiality."[3] Government took pains to impress the idea that it had done much, and wished to do more for conciliation; yet the doubt remained

---

[1] Order in Council of April 26, 1809; State Papers, iii. 241.
[2] Pinkney to Madison, May 3, 1809; Wheaton's Pinkney, p. 428.
[3] Pinkney to R. Smith, May 1, 1809. MSS. State Dep. Archives.

whether Government was acting in good faith. Pinkney over-
estimated its concessions. If the British navy was to blockade
Holland, France, and northern Italy only in order that British
commerce might be forced, through the blockade and license
system, into the place of neutral commerce, the new system
was only the old one in disguise. Under a blockade, in good
faith, licenses seemed to have no place. In that case, the Order
in Council of April 26 might lead to a real settlement; but
how was it possible that Perceval, George Rose, and James
Stephen should have given up what they believed to be the
only hope for England's safety?

If one frank and straightforward man could be found
among the ministerial ranks, James Stephen had a right to
that distinction, and to his language one might hope to look
with confidence for the truth; yet Stephen seemed for once
not to understand himself. In publishing his speech of March
6, he added an appendix on the new order, and closed his
remarks by a prayer that seemed meant to open the way for
the full admission of American offers: —

> "It is not strange that a measure so indulgent [as the new
> Order] should be generally approved by the American mer-
> chants and agents resident in England. The most eminent
> of the gentlemen of that description who opposed the Or-
> ders of November have openly professed their satisfaction
> at this important change. May the same sentiment prevail
> on notice of it beyond the Atlantic! Or, what would be still
> better, may an amicable arrangement there have already ter-
> minated all the differences between us and our American
> brethren on terms that will involve a complete revocation
> of our retaliatory orders, and impose on America herself,
> by her own consent, the duty of vindicating effectually the
> rights of neutrality against the aggressions of France!"

Chapter IV

EARLY IN FEBRUARY, when Congress refused to support Madison's war-policy,—the mere shadow of which brought Perceval and Canning almost to their senses,—Canning's instructions were despatched from the Foreign Office. April 7, more than a month after the Tenth Congress had expired, amidst political conditions altogether different from those imagined by Canning, the instructions reached Washington; and Erskine found himself required to carry them into effect.

A cautious diplomatist would have declined to act upon them. Under pretext of the change which had altered the situation he would have asked for new instructions, while pointing out the mischievous nature of the old. The instructions were evidently impossible to execute; the situation was less critical than ever before, and Great Britain was master of the field.

On the other hand, the instructions offered some appearance of an advance toward friendship. They proved Canning's ignorance, but not his bad faith; and if Canning in good faith wanted a settlement, Erskine saw every reason for gratifying him. The arrogance of Canning's demands did not necessarily exclude further concession. The great governments of Europe from time immemorial had used a tone of authority insufferable to weaker Powers, and not agreeable to one another; yet their tone did not always imply the wish to quarrel, and England herself seldom resented manners as unpleasant as her own. Used to the rough exchange of blows, and hardened by centuries of toil and fighting, England was not sensitive when her interests were at stake. Her surliness was a trick rather than a design. Her diplomatic agents expected to enjoy reasonable liberty in softening the harshness and in supplying the ignorance of their chiefs of the Foreign Office; and if such latitude was ever allowed to a diplomatist, Erskine had the best right to use it in the case of instructions the motives of which he could not comprehend.

Finally, Erskine was the son of Lord Erskine, and owed his appointment to Charles James Fox. He was half Republican by education, half American by marriage; and probably, like all British liberals, he felt in secret an entire want of confidence in Canning and a positive antipathy to the Tory commercial system.

Going at once to Secretary Robert Smith, Erskine began on the "Chesapeake" affair, and quickly disposed of it. The President abandoned the American demand for a court-martial on Admiral Berkeley, finding that it would not be entertained.[1] Erskine then wrote a letter offering the stipulated redress for the "Chesapeake" outrage, and Madison wrote a letter accepting it, which Robert Smith signed, and dated April 17.

Two points in Madison's "Chesapeake" letter attracted notice. Erskine began his official note[2] by alluding to the Non-intercourse Act of March 1, as having placed Great Britain on an equal footing with the other belligerents, and warranting acknowledgment on that account. The idea was far-fetched, and Madison's reply was ambiguous:—

> "As it appears at the same time, that in making this offer his Britannic Majesty derives a motive from the equality now existing in the relations of the United States with the two belligerent Powers, the President owes it to the occasion and to himself to let it be understood that this equality is a result incident to a state of things growing out of distinct considerations."

If Madison knew precisely what "distinct considerations" had led Congress and the country to that state of things to which the Non-intercourse Act was incident, he knew more than was known to Congress; but even though he owed this statement to himself, so important an official note might have expressed his ideas more exactly. "A result incident to a state of things growing out of distinct considerations" was something unusual, and to say the least wanting in clearness, but seemed not intended to gratify Canning.

The second point challenged sharper criticism.

> "With this explanation, as requisite as it is frank,"

[1] Erskine to Canning, April 18, 1809; Cobbett's Debates, xvii. Appendix, cxlvii.

[2] Erskine to R. Smith, April 17, 1809; State Papers, iii. 295.

Smith's note continued, "I am authorized to inform you that the President accepts the note delivered by you in the name and by the order of his Britannic Majesty, and will consider the same with the engagement therein, when ful-filled, as a satisfaction for the insult and injury of which he has complained. But I have it in express charge from the President to state that while he forbears to insist on the further punishment of the offending officer, he is not the less sensible of the justice and utility of such an example, nor the less persuaded that it would best comport with what is due from his Britannic Majesty to his own honor."

According to Robert Smith's subsequent account, the last sentence was added by Madison in opposition to his secre-tary's wishes.[1] One of Madison's peculiarities showed itself in these words, which endangered the success of all his efforts. If he wished a reconciliation, they were worse than useless; but if he wished a quarrel, he chose the right means. The President of the United States was charged with the duty of asserting in its full extent what was due to his own honor as representative of the Union; but he was not required, either by the laws of his country or by the custom of nations, to define the conduct which in his opinion best comported with what was due from his Britannic Majesty to the honor of En-gland. That Erskine should have consented to receive such a note was matter for wonder, knowing as he did that Kings of England had never smiled on servants who allowed their sov-ereign's honor to be questioned; and the public surprise was not lessened by his excuse.

"It appeared to me," he said,[2] "that if any indecorum could justly be attributed to the expressions in the official notes of this Government, the censure due would fall upon them; and that the public opinion would condemn their bad taste or want of propriety in coldly and ungraciously giving up what they considered as a right, but which they were not in a condition to enforce."

Under the impression that no "intention whatever existed

[1] Robert Smith's Address to the People, 1811.
[2] Erskine to Canning, Aug. 3, 1809; Cobbett's Debates, xvii. clvi.

in the mind of the President of the United States to convey a disrespectful meaning toward his Majesty by these expressions," Erskine accepted them in silence, and Madison himself never understood that he had given cause of offence.

Having thus disposed of the "Chesapeake" grievance, Erskine took up the Orders in Council.[1] His instructions were emphatic, and he was in effect ordered to communicate these instructions *in extenso* to the President, for in such cases permission was equivalent to order. He disobeyed; in official sense he did not communicate his instructions at all. "I considered that it would be in vain," he afterward said. This was his first exercise of discretion; and his second was more serious. After reading Canning's repeated and positive orders to require from the American government "a distinct and official recognition" of three conditions, he decided to treat these orders as irrelevant. He knew that the President had no Constitutional power to bind Congress, even if Madison himself would patiently bear a single reading of three such impossible requirements, and that under these circumstances the negotiation had better never begin than end abruptly in anger. Erskine would have done better not to begin it; but he thought otherwise. Under more favorable circumstances, Monroe and Pinkney had made the same experiment in 1806.

Canning offered to withdraw the Orders in Council, on three conditions precedent:—

(1) That all interdicts on commerce should be revoked by the United States so far as they affected England, while they were still to be enforced against France. When Erskine submitted this condition to Robert Smith, he was assured that the President would comply with it, and that Congress would certainly assert the national rights against France, but that the President had no power to pledge the government by a formal act. Erskine decided to consider Canning's condition fulfilled if the President, under the eleventh section of the Non-intercourse Act, should issue a proclamation renewing trade with Great Britain, while retaining the prohibition against France. This settlement had the disadvantage of

[1] Erskine to Canning, April 30, 1809; Aug. 7, 1809. Erskine to Robert Smith, Aug. 14, 1809. Cobbett's Debates, xvii. cli. clxx. State Papers, iii. 305.

giving no guarantee to England, while it left open the trade with Holland, which was certainly a dependency of France.

(2) Canning further required that the United States should formally renounce the pretension to a colonial trade in war which was not permitted in time of peace. To this condition, which Erskine seems to have stated as applying only to the direct carrying-trade to Europe, Robert Smith replied that it could not be recognized except in a formal treaty; but that it was practically unimportant, because this commerce, as well as every other with France or her dependencies, was prohibited by Act of Congress. Erskine accepted this reasoning, and left the abstract right untouched.

(3) Canning lastly demanded that the United States should recognize the right of Great Britain to capture such American vessels as should be found attempting to trade with any of the Powers acting under the French Decrees. To this suggestion Secretary Smith replied that the President could not so far degrade the national authority as to authorize Great Britain to execute American laws; but that the point seemed to him immaterial, since no citizen could present to the United States government a claim founded on a violation of its own laws. Erskine once more acquiesced, although the trade with Holland was not a violation of law, and would probably give rise to the very claims which Canning meant to preclude.

Having thus disposed of the three conditions which were to be distinctly and officially recognized, Erskine exchanged notes with Robert Smith, bearing date April 18 and 19, 1809, chiefly admirable for their brevity, since they touched no principle. In his note of April 18, Erskine said that the favorable change produced by anticipation of the Non-intercourse Act had encouraged his Government to send out a new envoy with full powers; and that meanwhile his Majesty would recall his Orders in Council if the President would issue a Proclamation renewing intercourse with Great Britain. Secretary Smith replied on the same day that the President would not fail in doing so. April 19, Erskine in a few lines announced himself "authorized to declare that his Majesty's Orders in Council of January and November, 1807, will have been withdrawn as respects the United States on the 10th of June next." Secretary Smith answered that the President would immediately issue his Proclamation. Two days afterward the four notes and the Proclamation itself were published in the "National Intelligencer."

The United States heard with delight that friendship with England had been restored. Amid an outburst of joy commerce resumed its old paths, and without waiting for June 10 hurried ships and merchandise to British ports. No complaints were heard; not a voice was raised about impressments; no regret was expressed that war with France must follow reconciliation with England; no one found fault with Madison for following in 1809 the policy which had raised almost a revolution against President Washington only fourteen years before. Yet Madison strained the law, besides showing headlong haste, in acting upon Erskine's promises without waiting for their ratification, and without even asking to see the British negotiator's special powers or instructions. The haste was no accident or oversight. When Turreau remonstrated with Gallatin against such precipitate conduct contrary to diplomatic usage, Gallatin answered,—

"The offers could not be refused."

"But you have only promises," urged Turreau; "and already twelve hundred vessels, twelve thousand sailors, and two hundred million [francs] of property have left your ports. May not the English take all this to serve as a guarantee for other conditions which their interest might care to impose?"

"We would like it!" replied the Secretary of the Treasury. "Perhaps our people may need such a lesson to cure them of British influence and the mania of British commerce."[1]

Impatient at the conduct of Congress and the people, Madison was glad to create a new situation, and preferred even hostilities to the Orders in Council. Erskine's conduct was unusual, yet Great Britain had shown no such regard for Madison's feelings that Madison should hesitate before the eccentricities of British diplomacy. Perplexed to account for Canning's sudden change, the President and his friends quieted their uneasiness by attributing their triumph to their

[1] Turreau to Champagny, 1 June, 1809; Archives des Aff. Étr. MSS.

own statesmanship. The Republican newspapers, the "National Intelligencer" at their head, announced that England had been conquered by the embargo, and taunted not only the Federalists but also the Northern Republicans with the triumph. While nothing could be more positive than the language thus encouraged by the Government, the error was partly redeemed by the tenderness with which it was used to soothe the wounded feelings of Jefferson.

> "The bright day of judgment and retribution has at length arrived," said the "National Intelligencer" of April 26, "when a virtuous nation will not withhold the tribute of its warmest thanks from an Administration whose sole ambition has ever been to advance the happiness of its constituents, even at the sacrifice of its present popularity. Thanks to the sage who now so gloriously reposes in the shades of Monticello, and to those who shared his confidence! . . . It may be boldly alleged that the revocation of the British Orders is attributable to the embargo."

President Madison wrote to Jefferson somewhat more cautiously:[1] "The British Cabinet must have changed its course under a full conviction that an adjustment with this country had become essential." Accepting quietly a turn of fortune that would have bewildered the most astute diplomatist, Madison made ready to meet the special session of Congress.

The Eleventh Congress differed little in character from its predecessor, but that little difference was not to its advantage. G. W. Campbell of Tennessee, David R. Williams of South Carolina, Joseph Clay of Pennsylvania, Joseph Story of Massachusetts, and Wilson Cary Nicholas of Virginia disappeared from the House, and no one of equal influence stepped into their places. The mediocrity of the Tenth Congress continued to mark the character of the Eleventh. John W. Eppes became chairman of the Committee of Ways and Means. Varnum was again chosen Speaker, while Vice-President George Clinton still presided over the deliberations of thirty-four men whose abilities were certainly not greater than those of any previous Senate.

---

[1] Madison to Jefferson, April 24, 1809; Madison's Writings, ii. 439.

May 23 President Madison's first Annual Message was read. No objection could be made to its brief recital of the steps which led to the arrangement with Erskine; but the next paragraph not only provoked attack, it threatened the country also with commercial wars to the end of time:—

> "Whilst I take pleasure in doing justice to the councils of his Britannic Majesty which, no longer adhering to the policy which made an abandonment by France of her Decrees a prerequisite to the revocation of the British Orders, have substituted the amicable course which has issued thus happily, I cannot do less than refer to the proposal heretofore made on the part of the United States, embracing a like restoration of the suspended commerce, as a proof of the spirit of accommodation which has at no time been intermitted, and to the result which now calls for our congratulations as corroborating the principles by which the public councils have been guided during a period of the most trying embarrassments."

When Madison spoke of the "principles by which the public councils have been guided," he meant to place at their head the principles of embargo and non-intercourse,—a result of Erskine's arrangement hardly more agreeable to commercial America than to despotic England; but however England might resent what Canning would certainly think an offence, Americans were in no humor for fault-finding, and they received Madison's allusions with little protest. The remainder of the Message contained nothing that called for dispute.

The Federalist minority—strong in numbers, flushed by victory over Jefferson, and full of contempt for the abilities of their opponents—found themselves suddenly deprived by Erskine and Madison of every grievance to stand upon. For once, no one charged that Madison's act was dictated from the Tuileries. The Federalist newspapers, like their Republican rivals, advanced the idea that their success was the natural result of their own statesmanship. Their efforts against the embargo had opened the path for Canning's good-will to show itself, and the removal of Jefferson's sinister influence accounted for the brilliancy of Madison's success. The attempt to approve Erskine's arrangement without approving Jefferson's system, required ingenuity as great as was shown in the similar attempt of Madison to weigh down Erskine's arrangement by coupling it with the embargo. These party tactics would hardly deserve notice had not John Randolph, in drawing a sharp line between Jefferson and Madison, enlivened the monotony of debate by comments not without interest.

"Without the slightest disposition to create unpleasant sensations," said he, "to go back upon the footsteps of the last four years, I do unequivocally say that I believe the country will never see such another Administration as the last. It had my hearty approbation for one half of its career; as for my opinion of the remainder of it, it has been no secret. The lean kine of Pharaoh devoured the fat kine; the last four years, with the embargo in their train, ate up the rich harvest of the first four; and if we had not had some Joseph to have stepped in and changed the state of things, what would have been now the condition of the country? I repeat it,—never has there been any Administration which went out of office and left the country in a state so deplorable and calamitous as the last."

Not satisfied with criticising Jefferson, Randolph committed himself to the opinion that Canning had been influenced by the same antipathy, and had been withheld from earlier concessions only by Jefferson's conduct:—

"Mr. Canning obtained as good a bargain from us as he could have expected to obtain; and those gentlemen who speak of his having heretofore had it in his power to have done the same, did not take into calculation the material difference between the situation in which we now stand and the situation in which we before stood."

In the virulence of temper with which Randolph blackened the Administration of Jefferson, he could not help committing himself to unqualified support of Madison; and even Barent Gardenier, whose temper was at least as indiscreet as Randolph's, seemed to revel in the pleasure of depressing the departed President in order to elevate the actual Executive, whose eight years of coming power were more dangerous to the opposition than the eight years of Jefferson had ever been.

"I am pretty well satisfied," said Barent Gardenier,[1] "that when the secret history of the two last years is divulged, it will be found that while the former President was endeavoring to fan the flames of war, the Secretary of State . . . was smoothing the way for the happy discharge of his Presidential duties when he should come to the chair. I think it did him honor. . . . It is for the promptitude and frankness with which the President met the late overture that I thank him most cordially for my country. I approve it most heartily. . . . And it is now in proof before us, as I have said and contended, that nothing was wanting but a proper spirit of conciliation, and fair and honorable dealing on the part of this country, to bring to a happy issue all the fictitious differences between this country and Great Britain."

Political indiscretion could go no further. The rule that in public life one could never safely speak well of an opponent, was illustrated by the mistake of the Federalists in praising Madison merely to gratify their antipathy to Jefferson. Had they been silent, or had they shown suspicion, they would have been safe; but all admitted that French influence and hostility to England had vanished with Jefferson; all were positive that England had gained what she had sought, and that Canning had every reason to be satisfied. For the moment Madison was the most popular President that ever had met Congress. At no session since 1789 had such harmony prevailed as during the five weeks of this political paradise, although not one element had changed its character or position, and the harmony, like the discord, was a play of imagination. Congress passed its bills with unanimity altogether new. That which restored relations of commerce with England passed without discussion, except on the point whether French ships of war should be admitted to American ports. Somewhat to the alarm of the Eastern men, Congress decided not to exclude French national vessels,—a decision which threw some doubt on Madison's wish to push matters to a

[1] Annals of Congress, 1809–1810, p. 210.

head with Napoleon. Yet care was taken to avoid offence to
Great Britain. Little was said and nothing was done about
impressments. An attempt to increase the protective duties
was defeated. Not a voice was raised on behalf of France; not
a fear of Napoleon's revenge found tongue.

Although no one ventured to avow suspicion that Canning
would refuse to ratify Erskine's act, news continued to arrive
from England which seemed hard to reconcile with any immediate thought, in the British ministry, of giving up their
restrictive system. June 10, the day when amid universal delight the new arrangement went into effect, the public pleasure was not a little disturbed by the arrival of news that on
April 26 the British government had issued a very important
Order in Council, revoking the order of Nov. 11, 1807, and
establishing in its place a general blockade of Holland,
France, and Italy. This step, though evidently a considerable
concession,—which would have produced its intended effect
in checking hostile feeling if Erskine had not intervened,—
roused anxiety because of its remote resemblance to Erskine's
arrangement, which it seemed to adopt by means that the
United States could not admit as legal or consistent with the
terms of Erskine's letters.

"The new Orders," wrote Madison to Jefferson,[1] . . .
"present a curious feature in the conduct of the British
Cabinet. It is explained by some at the expense of its sincerity. It is more probably ascribed, I think, to an awkwardness in getting out of an awkward situation, and to
the policy of withholding as long as possible from France
the motive of its example to have advances on her part toward adjustment with us. The crooked proceeding seems
to be operating as a check to the extravagance of credit
given to Great Britain for the late arrangement with us, and
so far may be salutary."

Such reasoning was soon felt to be insufficient. The more
the new order was studied, the less its motive was understood. How could Canning in January have authorized Erskine to withdraw the orders of 1807 without reserve, when

[1] Madison to Jefferson, June 12, 1809; Madison's Writings, ii. 443.

in April, without waiting to hear from Erskine, he himself
withdrew those orders only to impose another that had every
mark of permanence? How could Erskine, April 18, have been
authorized to throw open the ports of Holland, when his
Government, April 26, was engaged in imposing a new blockade upon them? So rapidly did the uneasiness of Congress
increase that Erskine was obliged to interpose. June 15 he
wrote an official note to the Secretary of State, which the
President sent the same day to Congress.[1]

"I have the honor," said Erskine, "to enclose a copy of
an Order of his Majesty in Council issued on the 26th of
April last. In consequence of official communications sent
to me from his Majesty's government since the adoption of
that measure, I am enabled to assure you that it has no
connection whatever with the overtures which I have been
authorized to make to the government of the United
States; and that I am persuaded that the terms of the agreement so happily concluded by the recent negotiation will
be strictly fulfilled on the part of his Majesty."

The expressions of this letter, if carefully read, still left
cause for doubt; and Madison saw it, although he clung to
what he thought he had gained. June 20 he wrote again to
Jefferson:[2] —

"The 'Gazette' of yesterday contains the mode pursued
for reanimating confidence in the pledge of the British government given by Mr. Erskine in his arrangement with this
government. The puzzle created by the Order of April
struck every one. Erskine assures us that his Government
was under such impressions as to the views of this, that not
the slightest expectation existed of our fairly meeting its
overtures, and that the last order was considered as a sea-
sonable mitigation of the tendency of a failure of the experiment. This explanation seems as extraordinary as the
alternative it shows. The fresh declarations of Mr. Erskine
seem to have quieted the distrust which was becoming very
strong, but has not destroyed the effect of the ill grace

[1] Message of June 15, 1809; State Papers, iii. 297.
[2] Madison to Jefferson, June 20, 1809; Madison's Writings, ii. 443.

stamped on the British retreat, and of the commercial rigor evinced by the new and insidious duties stated in the newspapers. It may be expected, I think, that the British government will fulfil what its minister has stipulated; and that if it means to be trickish, it will frustrate the proposed negotiation, and then say their orders were not permanently repealed but only withdrawn in the mean time."

Madison had chosen to precipitate a decision, with a view to profiting in either case, whether England consented or refused to have her hands thus forced. Indeed, if he had not himself been old in the ways of diplomacy, Turreau was on the spot to warn him, and lost no chance of lecturing the Administration on the folly of trusting Erskine's word.

Meanwhile Turreau so far lost his temper as to address to Secretary Smith a long letter complaining of the persistently unfriendly attitude of the United States government toward France. So strong was the language of the letter that Turreau was obliged to withdraw it.[1] Robert Smith attempted to pacify him by assurances that the new Administration would respect the Spanish possessions more strictly than the old one had done.

"The Secretary of State did not deny that there might have been some attempt in that direction," reported Turreau, June 14,[2] "but at the same time, while himself alluding to the affair of Miranda, he attributed these events to causes independent of the actual Administration and anterior to its existence, and especially to the weakness and the indiscretions of Mr. Jefferson; that he [Smith] was then in the Cabinet, and knew better than any one how much the want of vigor (*mollesse*), the uncertainty, and absence of plan in the Executive head had contributed to the false steps of the Federal government."

The new Administration meant to show vigor. Every act and expression implied that its path was to be direct to its ends. The President and Congress waited with composure for the outcome of Erskine's strange conduct.

[1]Turreau to Smith, June 14, 1809. John Graham to the editors of the Federal Republican, Aug. 31, 1813. Niles, v. 37–40.

[2]Turreau to Champagny, 14 June, 1809; Archives des Aff. Étr. MSS.

No new measure was suggested, after June 10, to provide for the chance that Erskine's arrangement might fail, and that the Order in Council of April 26, 1809, might prove to be a permanent system. Congress seemed disposed to indulge the merchants to the utmost in their eagerness for trade. The nearest approach to suspicion was shown in the House by appropriating $750,000 for fortifications. Randolph, Macon, Eppes, and Richard M. Johnson tried to reduce the amount to $150,000. The larger appropriation was understood to mean an intention of preparing for attack, and eighty-four members sustained the policy against a minority of forty-seven; but notwithstanding this vote and the anxiety caused by the new Order in Council, Congress decided to stop enlistments for the army; and by an Act approved June 28 the President was authorized, "in the event of a favorable change in our foreign relations," to reduce the naval force, although the words of the Act implied doubt whether the favorable change would take place.

Nothing could be happier for Madison than this situation, where all parties were held in check not only by his success but by his danger. So completely was discipline restored, that June 27 he ventured to send the name of J. Q. Adams a second time to the Senate as minister to Russia; and nineteen Republicans confirmed the nomination, while but one adhered to the opinion that the mission was unnecessary. The power of England over America was never more strikingly shown than by the sudden calm which fell on the country, in full prospect of war with France, at a word from a British minister. As Canning frowned or smiled, faction rose to frenzy or lay down to slumber throughout the United States. No sooner did the news of Erskine's arrangement reach Quebec May 1, than Sir James Craig recalled his secret agent, John Henry, from Boston, where he still lingered. "I am cruelly out of spirits," wrote Secretary Ryland to Henry,[1] "at the idea of Old England truckling to such a debased and accursed government as that of the United States;" but since this was the case, Henry's services could no longer be useful. He returned to Montreal early in June.

[1] Ryland to Henry, May 1, 1809; State Papers, iii. 552.

June 28 Congress adjourned, leaving the Executive, for the first time in many years, almost without care, until the fourth Monday in November.

Chapter V

ERSKINE'S DESPATCHES were received by Canning May 22, and the "Morning Post" of the next day printed the news with approval: "Upon this pleasing event we sincerely congratulate the public." The "Times" of May 24 accepted the arrangement: "We shall not urge anything against the concessions." May 25, with "considerable pain though but little surprise," the same newspaper announced that Erskine was disavowed by the Government.

Canning's abrupt rejection of Erskine's arrangement without explanation must have seemed even to himself a high-handed course, at variance with some of his late professions, certain to injure or even to destroy British influence in America, and likely to end in war. To the settlement as a practical measure no objection could be alleged. No charge of bad faith could be supported. No shadow of law or reason could be devised for enforcing against America rights derived from retaliation upon France, when America enforced stronger measures of retaliation upon France than those imposed by the Orders in Council. Neither the Non-importation Act of 1806, nor the "Chesapeake" proclamation of 1807, nor the embargo, nor the Non-intercourse Act of March, 1809, could be used to justify the rejection of an arrangement which evaded or removed every British grievance. Even the subject of impressments had been suppressed by the American government. Madison flung himself into Canning's arms, and to fling him back was an effort of sheer violence.

Perhaps the effort gave to Canning's conduct an air that he would not naturally have cared to betray; for his manner was that of a man irritated by finding himself obliged to be brutal. In the want of a reason for rejecting the American arrangement, he was reduced to rejecting it without giving a reason. The process of disciplining Erskine was simple, for Erskine had disregarded instructions to an extent that no government could afford to overlook; but President Madison was not in the employ of the British king, and had a right to such consideration at least as one gentleman commonly owes to another.

Canning addressed himself first to the simpler task. May 22, a few hours after receiving the despatches from Washington, he wrote a despatch to Erskine in regard to the "Chesapeake" arrangement.[1] He reminded Erskine that his instructions had required the formal exclusion of French war-vessels and the formal withdrawal of the "Chesapeake" proclamation before any arrangement should be concluded. Not only had these conditions been neglected, but two other less serious errors had been made.

Variations from the rigor of instruction might be ground for reproving Erskine, but could hardly excuse a disavowal of the compact; yet the compact was disavowed. An impression was general that the Ministry were disposed to ratify it, but were withheld by the paragraph in Robert Smith's letter defining what was due from his Britannic Majesty to his own honor. Milder Foreign Secretaries than George Canning would have found themselves obliged to take notice of such a reflection, and Canning appeared at his best when his adversaries gave him an excuse for the lofty tone he liked to assume.

"It remains for me," he continued, "to notice the expressions, so full of disrespect to his Majesty, with which that note concludes; and I am to signify to you the displeasure which his Majesty feels that any minister of his Majesty should have shown himself so far insensible of what is due to the dignity of his sovereign as to have consented to receive and transmit a note in which such expressions were contained."

Canning was hardly the proper person to criticise Robert Smith's disrespectful expressions, which, whatever their intention, failed to be nearly as offensive as many of his own; but this was a matter between himself and Erskine. Even after granting the propriety of his comment, diplomatic usage seemed to require that some demand of explanation or apology from the American government should precede the rejection of an engagement otherwise satisfactory; but no such step was in this case taken through Erskine. His settlement

[1] Canning to Erskine, May 22, 1809; Cobbett's Debates, xvii. App. cxxvii.

of the "Chesapeake" outrage was repudiated without more words, and the next day Canning repudiated the rest of the arrangement.

Nothing could be easier than to show that Erskine had violated his instructions more plainly in regard to the Orders in Council than in regard to the "Chesapeake" affair. Of the three conditions imposed by Canning, not one had been fulfilled. The first required the repeal of all Non-intercourse Acts against England, "leaving them in force with respect to France;" but Erskine had doubly failed to secure it:[1] —

"As the matter at present stands before the world in your official correspondence with Mr. Smith, the American government would be at liberty to-morrow to repeal the Non-intercourse Act altogether, without infringing the agreement which you have thought proper to enter into on behalf of his Majesty; and if such a clause was thought necessary to this condition at the time when my instructions were written, it was obviously become much more so when the Non-intercourse Act was passed for a limited time. You must also have been aware at the time of making the agreement that the American government had in fact formally exempted Holland, a Power which has unquestionably 'adopted and acted under the Decrees of France,' from the operation of the Non-intercourse Act,—an exemption in direct contravention of the condition prescribed to you, and which of itself ought to have prevented you from coming to any agreement whatever."

Here, again, sufficient reasons were given for punishing Erskine; but these reasons were not equally good for repudiating the compact with the United States. No American vessels could enter a Dutch port so long as the British blockade lasted; therefore the exemption of Holland from the non-intercourse affected England only by giving to her navy another chance for booty, and to the Americans one more empty claim. Canning himself explained to Pinkney[2] "that the exemption of Holland from the effect of our embargo and non-intercourse would not have been much objected to by the

[1]Canning to Erskine, May 23, 1809; MSS. British Archives.
[2]Pinkney to Robert Smith, June 23, 1809; State Papers, iii. 303.

British government" if the President had been willing to pledge himself to enforce the non-intercourse against France; but for aught that appeared to the contrary, "the embargo and non-intercourse laws might be suffered without any breach of faith to expire, or might even be repealed immediately, notwithstanding the perseverance of France in her Berlin and other edicts; and that Mr. Erskine had in truth secured nothing more, as the consideration of the recall of the Orders in Council, than the renewal of American intercourse with Great Britain."

Thus Canning justified the repudiation of Erskine's arrangement by the single reason that the United States government could not be trusted long enough to prove its good faith. The explanation was difficult to express in courteous or diplomatic forms; but perhaps its most striking quality, next to its want of courtesy, was its evident want of candor. Had the American government evaded its obligation, the British government held the power of redress in its own hands. Clearly the true explanation was to be sought elsewhere, in some object which Canning could not put in diplomatic words, but which lay in the nature of Perceval's system. Even during the three days while the decision was supposed to be in doubt, alarmed merchants threw themselves in crowds on the Board of Trade, protesting that if American vessels with their cheaper sugar, cotton, and coffee were allowed to enter Amsterdam and Antwerp, British trade was at an end.[1] The mere expectation of their arrival would create such a fall in prices as to make worthless the accumulated mass of such merchandise with which the warehouses were filled, not only in London, but also in the little island of Heligoland at the mouth of the Elbe, where a system of licensed and unlicensed smuggling had been established under the patronage of the Board of Trade. Deputations of these merchants waited on Earl Bathurst to represent the danger of allowing even those American ships to enter Holland which might have already sailed from the United States on the faith of Erskine's arrangement. Somewhat unexpectedly ministers refused to gratify this prayer. An Order in Council of May 24, while

---

[1] The Courier, May 26, 1809.

announcing the Royal repudiation of Erskine's arrangement, declared that American vessels which should have cleared for Holland between April 19 and July 20 would not be molested in their voyage.

The chief objection to Erskine's arrangement, apart from its effect on British merchants, consisted in the danger that by its means America might compel France to withdraw her decrees affecting neutrals. The chance that Erskine's arrangement might involve America in war with Napoleon was not worth the equal chance of its producing in the end an amicable arrangement with Napoleon which would sacrifice the last defence of British commerce and manufactures. Had the British government given way, Napoleon, to whom the most solemn pledges cost nothing, would certainly persuade President Madison to lean once more toward France. The habit of balancing the belligerents—the first rule of American diplomacy—required the incessant see-saw of interest. So many unsettled questions remained open that British ministers could not flatter themselves with winning permanent American favor by partial concession.

To Canning's despatch repudiating the commercial arrangement, Erskine made a reply showing more keenness and skill than was to be found in Canning's criticism.

"It appears from the general tenor of your despatches," wrote Erskine[1] on receiving these letters of May 22 and 23, "that his Majesty's government were not willing to trust to assurances from the American government, but that official pledges were to have been required which could not be given for want of power, some of them also being of a nature which would prevent a formal recognition. Had I believed that his Majesty's government were determined to insist upon these conditions being complied with in one particular manner only, I should have adhered implicitly to my instructions; but as I collected from them that his Majesty was desirous of accomplishing his retaliatory system by such means as were most compatible with a good understanding with friendly and neutral Powers, I felt confident

[1] Erskine to Canning, Aug. 7, 1809; Cobbett's Debates, xvii. App. clx.– clxiii.

that his Majesty would approve of the arrangement I had concluded as one likely to lead to a cordial and complete understanding and co-operation on the part of the United States, which co-operation never could be obtained by previous stipulations either from the government of the United States, who have no power to accede to them, or from Congress, which would never acknowledge them as recognitions to guide their conduct."

This reply, respectful in form, placed Secretary Canning in the dilemma between the guilt of ignorance or that of bad faith; but the rejoinder of a dismissed diplomatist weighed little except in history, and long before it was made public Erskine and his arrangement had ceased to interest the world. Canning disposed of both forever by a third despatch, dated May 30, enclosing to Erskine an Order in Council disavowing his arrangement and ordering him back to England.

When the official disavowal appeared in the newspapers of May 25, Canning had an interview with Pinkney.[1] At great length and with much detail he read the instructions he had given to Erskine, and commented on the points in which Erskine had violated them. He complained of unfriendly expressions in the American notes; but he did not say why the arrangement failed to satisfy all the legitimate objects of England, nor did he suggest any improvement or change which would make the arrangement, as it existed, agreeable to him. On the other hand, he announced that though Erskine would have to be recalled, his successor was already appointed and would sail for America within a few days.

If Canning showed, by his indulgence to American vessels and his haste to send out a new minister, the wish to avoid a rupture with the United States, his selection of an agent for that purpose was so singular as to suggest that he relied on terror rather than on conciliation. In case Erskine had obeyed his instructions, which ordered him merely to prepare the way for negotiation, Canning had fixed upon George Henry Rose as the negotiator.[2] Considering the impression left in America by Rose on his previous mission, his appointment

---

[1] Pinkney to R. Smith, May 28, 1809; MSS. State Department Archives.
[2] Pinkney to Madison, Dec. 10, 1809; Wheaton's Pinkney, p. 434.

seemed almost the worst that could have been made; but bad as the effect of such a selection would have been, one man, and perhaps only one, in England was certain to make a worse; and him Canning chose. The new minister was Francis James Jackson. Whatever good qualities Jackson possessed were overshadowed by the reputation he had made for himself at Copenhagen. His name was a threat of violence; his temper and manners were notorious; and nothing but his rank in the service marked him as suitable for the post. Pinkney, whose self-control and tact in these difficult circumstances could hardly be too much admired, listened in silence to Canning's announcement, and rather than risk making the situation worse, reported that Jackson was, he believed, "a worthy man, and although completely attached to all those British principles and doctrines which sometimes give us trouble will, *I should hope*, give satisfaction." The English press was not so forbearing. The "Morning Chronicle" of May 29 said that the appointment had excited general surprise, owing to "the character of the individual;" and Pinkney himself, in a later despatch, warned his Government that "it is rather a prevailing notion here that this gentleman's conduct will not and cannot be what we all wish, and that a better choice might have been made."[1]

Jackson himself sought the position, knowing its difficulties. May 23, the day of his appointment, he wrote privately to his brother in Spain: "I am about to enter upon a most delicate—I *hope* not desperate—enterprise."[2] At a later time, embittered by want of support from home, he complained that Canning had sent him on an errand which he knew to be impossible to perform.[3] So well understood between Canning and Jackson was the nature of the service, that Jackson asked and received as a condition of his acceptance the promise that his employment should last not less than twelve months.[4] The delicate enterprise of which he spoke could

[1] Pinkney to R. Smith, June 23, 1809; MSS. State Department Archives.

[2] Bath Archives; Diaries and Letters of Sir George Jackson, ii. 447.

[3] Bath Archives; Diaries and Letters of Sir George Jackson, Second Series, i. 109.

[4] Bath Archives; Diaries and Letters of Sir George Jackson, Second Series, i. 24, 46.

have been nothing more than that of preventing a rupture between England and America; but until he studied his instructions, he could hardly have known in its full extent how desperate this undertaking would be.

Canning made no haste. Nearly two months elapsed before Jackson sailed. After correcting Erskine's mistake and replacing the United States in their position under the Orders in Council of April 26, Canning, June 13, made a statement to the House of Commons. Declining to touch questions of general policy for the reason that negotiations were pending, he contented himself with satisfying the House that Erskine had acted contrary to instructions and deserved recall. James Stephen showed more clearly the spirit of Government by avowing the opinion "that America in all her proceedings had no wish to promote an impartial course with respect to France and this country." The Whigs knew little or nothing of the true facts; Erskine's conduct could not be defended; no one cared to point out that Canning left to America no dignified course but war, and public interest was once more concentrated with painful anxiety on the continent of Europe. America dropped from sight, and Canning's last and worst acts toward the United States escaped notice or knowledge.

The session of Parliament ended June 21, a week before the special session of Congress came to an end; and while England waited impatiently for news from Vienna, where Napoleon was making ready for the battle of Wagram, Canning drew up the instructions to Jackson,—the last of the series of papers by which, through the peculiar qualities of his style even more than by the violence of his acts, he embittered to a point that seemed altogether contrary to their nature a whole nation of Americans against the nation that gave them birth. If the famous phrase of Canning was ever in any sense true,—that he called a new world into existence to redress the balance of the old,—it was most nearly true in the sense that his instructions and letters forced the United States into a nationality of character which the war of the Revolution itself had failed to give them.

The instructions to Jackson[1]—five in number—were dated

---

[1] Canning to F. J. Jackson, Nos. 1–5, July 1, 1809; MSS. British Archives, America, vol. xcv.

July 1, and require careful attention if the train of events which brought the United States to the level of war with England is to be understood.

The first instruction began by complaint of Erskine's conduct, passing quickly to a charge of bad faith against the American government, founded on "the publicity so unwarrantably given" to Erskine's arrangement:—

> "The premature publication of the correspondence by the American government so effectually precluded any middle course of explanation and accommodation that it is hardly possible to suppose that it must not have been resorted to in a great measure with that view.

> "The American government cannot have believed that such an arrangement as Mr. Erskine consented to accept was conformable to his instructions. If Mr. Erskine availed himself of the liberty allowed to him of communicating those instructions on the affair of the Orders in Council, they must have known that it was not so; but even without such communication they cannot by possibility have believed that without any new motive, and without any apparent change in the dispositions of the enemy, the British government could have been disposed at once and unconditionally to give up the system on which they have been acting, and which they had so recently refused to relinquish, even in return for considerations which though far from being satisfactory were yet infinitely more so than anything which can be supposed to have been gained by Mr. Erskine's arrangement."

Canning attributed this conduct to a hope held by President Madison that the British government would feel itself compelled, however reluctantly, to sanction an agreement which it had not authorized. In this case the American government had only itself to blame for the consequences:—

> "So far, therefore, from the American government having any reason to complain of the non-ratification of Mr. Erskine's unauthorized agreement, his Majesty has on his part just ground of complaint for that share of the inconvenience from the publication which may have fallen upon

his Majesty's subjects, so far as their interests may have been involved in the renewed speculations of their American correspondents; and his Majesty cannot but think any complaint, if any should be made on this occasion in America, the more unreasonable, as the government of the United States is that government which perhaps of all others has most freely exercised the right of withholding its ratification from even the authorized acts of its own diplomatic agents."

In this spirit Jackson was to meet any "preliminary discussion" which might arise before he could proceed to negotiation. Canning did not touch on the probability that if Jackson met preliminary discussion in such a spirit as this, he would run something more than a risk of never reaching negotiation at all; or if Canning considered this point, he treated it orally. The other written instructions given to Jackson dealt at once with negotiation.

The "Chesapeake" affair came first in order, and was quickly dismissed. Jackson was to require from the President a written acknowledgment that the interdict on British ships was annulled before any settlement could be made. The Orders in Council came next, and were the subject of a long instruction, full of interest and marked by many of Canning's peculiarities. Once more he explained that Erskine had inverted the relation of things by appearing to recall the orders as an inducement to the renewal of trade,—"as if in any arrangement, whether commercial or political, his Majesty could condescend to barter objects of national policy and dignity for permission to trade with another country. The character even more than the stipulations of such a compact must under any circumstances have put out of question the possibility of his Majesty's consenting to confirm it." He related the history of the orders, which he called "defensive retaliation," and explained why Erskine's arrangement failed to effect the object of that system:—

"In the arrangement agreed to by Mr. Erskine the incidental consequence is mistaken for the object of the negotiation. His Majesty is made by his minister to concede the whole point in dispute by the total and unconditional recall of the Orders in Council; and nothing is done by the United States in return except to permit their citizens to renew their commercial intercourse with Great Britain. Whereas, before his Majesty's consent to withdraw or even to modify the Orders in Council was declared, the United States should have taken upon themselves to execute in substance the objects of the Orders in Council by effectually prohibiting all trade between their citizens and France, or the Powers acting under her decrees, and by engaging for the continuance of that prohibition so long as those decrees should continue unrepealed."

As in the "Chesapeake" affair, so in regard to the orders,— Canning's objection to Erskine's arrangement was stated as one of form. That the "Chesapeake" proclamation was no longer in force; that Congress had effectually prohibited trade with France; and that the President had engaged as far as he could to continue that prohibition till the French Decrees were repealed,—these were matters of notoriety. England took the ground that the United States were liable to the operation of the British retaliatory orders against France, even though Congress should have declared war upon France, unless the declaration of war was regularly made known to the British minister at Washington, and unless "the United States should have taken upon themselves," by treaty with England, to continue the war till France repealed her decrees.

Canning was happy in the phrase he employed in Parliament, March 6, to justify the course of ministers toward America. "Extension of the law of nations" described well the Orders in Council themselves; but the instruction to Jackson was remarkable as a prodigious extension of the extended orders. The last legal plea was abandoned by these instructions, and the subject would have been the clearer for that abandonment were it not that owing to the rapidity of events the new extravagance was never known; with Canning himself the subject slipped from public view, and only the mystery remained of Canning's objects and expectations.

Another man would have temporized, and would have offered some suggestion toward breaking the force of such a blow at a friendly people. Not only did Canning make no new suggestion, but he even withdrew that which he had made in February. He told Jackson to propose nothing whatever:—

> "You are to inform the American Secretary of State that in the event of the government of the United States being desirous now to adopt this proposal, you are authorized to renew the negotiation and to conclude it on the terms of my instructions to Mr. Erskine; but that you are not instructed to press upon the acceptance of the American government an arrangement which they have so recently declined, especially as the arrangement itself is become less important, and the terms of it less applicable to the state of things now existing."

The remainder of this despatch was devoted to proving that the late order of April 26 had so modified that of November, 1807, as to remove the most serious American objections; and although the blockade was more restrictive than the old orders as concerned French and Dutch colonies, yet the recent surrender of Martinique had reduced the practical hardship of this restriction so considerably that it was fairly offset by the opening of the Baltic. America had the less inducement to a further arrangement which could little increase the extent of her commerce, while England was indifferent provided she obtained her indispensable objects:—

> "I am therefore not to direct you to propose to the American government any formal agreement to be substituted for that which his Majesty has been under the necessity of disavowing. You are, however, at liberty to receive for reference home any proposal which the American government may tender to you; but it is only in the case of that proposal comprehending all the three conditions which Mr. Erskine was instructed to require."

The fourth instruction prescribed the forms in which such an arrangement, if made, must be framed. The fifth dealt with another branch of the subject,—the Rule of 1756. Canning declined to accept a mere understanding in regard to this rule. Great Britain would insist on her right to prohibit neutral trade with enemies' colonies, "of which she has permitted the exercise only by indulgence; . . . but the indulgence which was granted for peculiar and temporary reasons being now withdrawn, the question is merely whether the rule from which such an indulgence was a deviation shall be established by the admission of America or enforced as heretofore by the naval power of Great Britain." As a matter of courtesy the British government had no objection to allowing the United States to sanction by treaty the British right, so that legal condemnations should be made under the authority of the treaty instead of an Order in Council; "but either authority is sufficient. No offence is taken at the refusal of the United States to make this matter subject of compact. The result is that it must be the subject of an Order in Council."

The result was that it became the subject of a much higher tribunal than his Majesty's Council, and that the British people, and Canning himself, took great offence at the refusal of the United States to make it a subject of one-sided compact; but with this concluding touch Canning's official irony toward America ended, and he laid down his pen. About the middle of June, Jackson with three well-defined *casus belli* in his portfolio, and another—that of impressments—awaiting his arrival, set sail for America on the errand which he strangely hoped might not be desperate. With his departure Canning's control of American relations ceased. At the moment when he challenged for the last time an instant declaration of war from a people who had no warmer wish than to be permitted to remain his friends, the career of the Administration to which he belonged came to an end in scandalous disaster.

Hardly had the Duke of York stopped one source of libel, by resigning May 16 his office of commander-in-chief, when fresh troubles from many directions assailed ministers. As early as April 4, Canning had satisfied the Duke of Portland that he must dismiss Castlereagh for incompetence, and every Cabinet minister except Castlereagh himself was acquainted with this decision; but contrary to Canning's wishes no action was taken, and the conduct of the war was left at a critical moment in the hands of a man whose removal for incompetence had been decreed by his own colleagues. The summer campaign was then fought. April 9 Austria had begun another war with Napoleon. At Essling, May 21, she nearly won a great victory; at Wagram, July 6, she lost a battle, and soon afterward entered on negotiations which ended, October 20, in the treaty of Vienna. While this great campaign went on, Sir Arthur Wellesley drove Soult out of Portugal much as Napoleon had driven Sir John Moore out of Spain; and then marching up the valley of the Tagus scared Joseph a second time from Madrid, and fought, July 28, the desperate battle of Talavera. In any case the result of the Austrian war would have obliged him to retreat; but the concentration of the French forces in his front quickly drove the British army back toward Lisbon, and ended all hope of immediate success in the Peninsula. A third great effort against Napoleon was directed from London toward the Scheldt and Meuse. The Cabinet, June 14, decided that Castlereagh should attempt this experiment; for raids of the kind had charms for a naval power, and although success could affect the war but little, it might assist smuggling and destroy a naval depot of Napoleon. Castlereagh sent to the Scheldt forty thousand soldiers who were grievously wanted on the Tagus. July 28, while Wellington fought the battle of Talavera, Lord Chatham's expedition started from the Downs, and reaching the mouth of the Scheldt occupied itself until August 15 with the capture of Flushing. In gaining this success the army was worn out; nearly half its number were suffering from typhoid, and September 2 the Cabinet unanimously voted to recall the expedition.

Talavera and Flushing closed Castlereagh's career in the War Office, as Jackson's mission closed that of Canning in American diplomacy. Defeat abroad, ruin at home, disgrace and disaster everywhere were the results of two years of Tory administration. August 11 the Duke of Portland was struck by paralysis; and deprived of its chief, the Cabinet went to pieces. September 7 Castlereagh was gently forced to resign. Canning, refusing to serve under Perceval or under any one whom Perceval suggested, tendered his own resignation. In the course of the complicated negotiations that followed, Perceval showed to Castlereagh letters in which for a year past Canning had pressed Castlereagh's removal from office. Then at last Castlereagh discovered, as he conceived, that Canning was not a gentleman or a man of honor, and having called him out, September 21, in a duel on Putney Heath shot him through the thigh.

Such an outcome was a natural result of such an Administration; but as concerned the United States Canning had already done all the harm possible, and more than three generations could wholly repair.

Chapter VI

THE NEWS OF Erskine's disavowal reached America so slowly that merchants enjoyed three months of unrestricted trade, and shipped to England or elsewhere the accumulations of nearly two years' produce. From April 21 till July 21 this process of depletion continued without an anxiety; and when July 21 news arrived that the arrangement had been repudiated, merchants still had time to hurry their last cargoes to sea before the government could again interpose.

The first effect of Canning's disavowal seemed bewilderment. No one in the United States, whether enemy or friend of England, could for a time understand why Canning had taken so perplexing a course. Very few of England's friends could believe that her conduct rested on the motives she avowed; they sought for some noble, or at least some respectable, object behind her acts. For several months the Federalist newspapers were at a loss for words, and groped in the dark for an English hand to help them; while the Republican press broke into anger, which expressed the common popular feeling. "The late conduct of the British ministry," said the "National Intelligencer" of July 26, "has capped the climax of atrocity toward this country." Every hope of reconciliation or even of peace with England seemed almost extinguished; yet the country was still far from a rupture. Not until popular feeling could express itself in a new election would the national will be felt; and the next election was still more than a year away, while the Congress to be then chosen would meet only in December, 1811. Until then war was improbable, perhaps impossible, except by the act of England.

When the news arrived, President Madison was at his Virginia plantation. During his absence Gallatin was in charge of matters at Washington, and on the instant wrote that he thought the President should return. In a letter of July 27, three days after the news reached Washington, Gallatin gave his own view of the situation:[1] —

"I will not waste time in conjectures respecting the true

[1] Gallatin to Montgomery, July 27, 1809; Adams's Gallatin, p. 395.

79

cause of the conduct of the British government, nor can we, until we are better informed, lay any permanent plan of conduct for ourselves. I will only observe that we are not so well prepared for resistance as we were one year ago. Then all or almost all our mercantile wealth was safe at home, our resources entire, and our finances sufficient to carry us through during the first year of the contest. Our property is now all afloat; England relieved by our relaxations might stand two years of privations with ease. We have wasted our resources without any national utility; and our treasury being exhausted, we must begin our plan of resistance with considerable and therefore unpopular loans."

The immediate crisis called first for attention. Gallatin held that the Non-intercourse Act necessarily revived from the moment the supposed fact on which alone its suspension rested was shown not to have taken place. The remoter problem of Jackson's mission seemed to the secretary simpler than the question of law:[1] —

"If we are too weak or too prudent to resist England in the direct and proper manner, I hope at least that we shall not make a single voluntary concession inconsistent with our rights and interest. If Mr. Jackson has any compromise to offer which would not be burdened with such, I shall be very agreeably disappointed. But judging by what is said to have been the substance of Mr. Erskine's instructions, what can we expect but dishonorable and inadmissible proposals? He is probably sent out like Mr. Rose to amuse and to divide; and we shall, I trust, by coming at once to the point, bring his negotiation to an immediate close."

The President heard the news with as much perplexity as anger, and even tried to persuade himself that Canning would be less severe than he threatened. Madison still clung to hope when he first replied to Gallatin's summons:[2] —

"The conduct of the British government in protesting the arrangement of its minister surprises one in spite of all

[1] Gallatin to Montgomery, July 27, 1809; Adams's Gallatin, p. 395.
[2] Madison to Gallatin, July 28, 1809; Gallatin's Works, i. 454.

their examples of folly. If it be not their plan, now that they have filled their magazines with our supplies and ascertained our want of firmness in withholding them, to adopt openly a system of monopoly and piracy, it may be hoped that they will not persist in the scandalous course in which they have set out. Supposing Erskine to have misunderstood or overstrained his instructions, can the difference between our trading directly and indirectly with Holland account for the violent remedy applied to the case? Is it not more probable that they have yielded to the clamors of the London smugglers in sugar and coffee, whose numbers and impudence are displayed in the scandalous and successful demand from their government that it should strangle the lawful trade of a friendly nation lest it should interfere with their avowed purpose of carrying on a smuggling trade with their enemies? Such an outrage on all decency was never before heard of even on the shores of Africa."

Madison exaggerated. The outrage on decency committed by the British government in May, 1809, was on the whole not so great as that of Sir William Scott's decision in the case of the "Essex" in July, 1805; or that of the blockade of New York and the killing of Pierce in April, 1806; or that of Lord Howick's Order in Council of January, 1807, when the signatures to Monroe's treaty were hardly dry; or that of Spencer Perceval's Orders in November, 1807, and the speeches made in their defence; or the mission of George Henry Rose in the winter of 1807–1808; or Erskine's letter of February 23, or Canning's letters of September 23, 1808,—for all these left the United States in a worse position than that created by the disavowal of Erskine. Indeed, except for the disgrace of submitting to acts of illegal force, the United States stood in a comparatively easy attitude after the orders of April 26, 1809, so long as Napoleon himself enforced within his empire a more rigid exclusion of neutral commerce than any that could be effected by a British blockade.

"Still, I cannot but hope," continued Madison, "on the supposition that there be no predetermined hostility against our commerce and navigation, that things may take

another turn under the influence of the obvious and striking considerations which advise it."

The hope vanished when Erskine's instructions became
known, and was succeeded by consternation when the public
read the reports made by Erskine and Canning of the language used by Madison, Gallatin, and Pinkney. For the first
time in this contest, Englishmen and Americans could no
longer understand each other's meaning. Erskine had so confused every detail with his own ideas, and Canning's course
on one side the Atlantic seemed so little to accord with his
tactics on the other, that neither party could longer believe in
the other's good faith. Americans were convinced that Canning had offered terms which he intended them to refuse.
Englishmen were sure that Madison had precipitated a settlement which he knew could not be carried out. Madison credited Canning with fraud as freely as Canning charged
Madison with connivance.

> "I find myself under the mortifying necessity of setting
> out to-morrow morning for Washington," wrote Madison
> to Jefferson, August 3.[1] "The intricate state of our affairs
> with England produced by the mixture of fraud and folly
> in her late conduct, and the important questions to be de-
> cided as to the legal effect of the failure of the arrangement
> of April on our commercial relations with her are thought
> by the heads of departments to require that I should join
> them. . . . You will see by the instructions to Erskine, as
> published by Canning, that the latter was as much deter-
> mined that there should be no adjustment as the former
> was that there should be one."

The President remained three days in Washington in order
to sign, August 9, a Proclamation reviving the Non-intercourse Act against Great Britain. On the same day the Secretary of the Treasury enclosed this Proclamation to the
Collectors of Customs in a circular, with instructions not to
enforce the penalties of the law against vessels entering American ports on the faith of Erskine's arrangement. This done,
Madison returned to Montpelier, August 10, leaving Erskine

[1] Madison to Jefferson, Aug. 3, 1809; Madison's Works, ii. 449.

to exchange apologetic but very unsatisfactory explanations with Robert Smith and Gallatin.

The Proclamation of August 9 was sharply criticised, and with reason; for Congress had given the President no express authority to revive the Non-intercourse Act, and he had clearly exceeded his powers, if not in the Proclamation which revived the Act, then certainly in the original Proclamation of April 19, which set it aside. Even this stretch of authority hardly equalled Gallatin's assumption of the power to admit what vessels he pleased without regard to the Non-intercourse Act. Yet right or wrong the President had no choice but to use all the powers he needed. Evidently his original mistake in opening intercourse was a greater stretch of authority than any subsequent act could be, except that of leaving it open after the mistake was admitted. Sullenly and awkwardly the Government restored some degree of order to its system, and then President and Cabinet scattered once more, leaving the village of Washington to the solitude of August and September.

A month passed without further change, until September 5 Jackson landed at Annapolis, whence he reached Washington September 8. He came with his wife—a fashionable Prussian baroness with a toilette—and young children, for whose health a Washington September was ill suited; he came too with a carriage and liveries, coachmen and servants, and the outfit of a long residence, as though neither he nor Canning doubted his welcome.

Francis James Jackson had many good qualities, and was on the whole the only English minister of his time so severely treated by the American government as to warrant almost a feeling of sympathy. He was probably suffering from some organic disease which made his temper irritable, while his instructions were such as to leave him no room to show his best capacities in his profession. In ordinary times a man of his experience, intelligence, and marked character might have succeeded in winning at Washington a name for ability and straightforwardness; but he was ill fitted for the special task he had undertaken, and had no clear idea of the dangers to which he was exposed. Gallatin expressed the feeling of the Administration when he advised coming at once to the point with Jackson, and bringing his negotiation to an immediate close. Madison could not have wished to repeat his experience with Rose, or to allow a British minister to reside at Washington for the sole purpose of dividing American counsels and intriguing with Senator Pickering. Had Jackson been quick in his perceptions, he would have seen early that nothing but mortification could be in store for him; but he had the dogged courage and self-confidence of his time, and undertook to deal single-handed with a government and people he did not trouble himself to understand.

The President was not in Washington when the British minister drove into that "famous city," as he called it, which "resembles more nearly Hampstead Heath than any other place I ever saw."[1] Robert Smith apologized for the incivility of leaving him without the usual public recognition, and explained that the risk of fever and the fatigue of four days' journey made the President extremely unwilling to return before October 1, the day fixed for Jackson's reception. Indirectly Smith suggested that Jackson might visit the President at Montpelier, or even begin negotiation before being officially received; but the minister replied that he would cheerfully wait. Gallatin wrote to the President, September 11,—

> "I do not think that there is any necessity to hurry yourself beyond your convenience in returning here. It will be as well the 10th as the 1st of October, for I am sure, although I have not seen Mr. Jackson and can judge only from what has passed between him and Mr. Smith, that he has nothing to say of importance, or pleasant."[2]

Madison replied, proposing to set out for Washington about the 29th, but agreeing with Gallatin that in view of "Jackson's apparent patience and reserve," his disclosures "would not be either operative or agreeable."[3]

Whether Jackson showed patience or activity, he could not avoid giving offence; and perhaps he did wisely to gain all the time he could, even if he gained nothing else. Unlike some of his predecessors, he understood how to make the best of his

[1] Bath Archives; Second Series, i. 9.
[2] Gallatin to Madison, Sept. 11, 1809; Works i. 461.
[3] Gallatin's Works, i. 462.

situation. He found amusement for a month of idleness, even though the month was September and the place was Washington. He took the house which Merry and Erskine had occupied,—a house that stood amid fields looking over Rock Creek to Georgetown:

> "Erskine had let it go to such a state of ruin and dirt that it will be several weeks before we can attempt to move into it. A Scotchman with an American wife who would be a fine lady, are not the best people to succeed on such an occasion.
>
> "It is but justice to say that I have met with nothing but the utmost civility, and with none of those hardships and difficulties of which the Merrys so bitterly complained. The travelling is not worse than much that I have met with before in my life, and the accommodations are better than many I have thought supportable. The expense is about the same as in England, and must be considered most exorbitant when the inferiority of their arrangements to ours and the greater cheapness of provisions are taken into account."[1]

As the season advanced, Jackson began to enjoy his autumn picnic on the heath of Washington. He had an eye for the details which gave interest to travel. "I put up a covey of partridge," he wrote October 7, "about three hundred yards from the House of Congress, yclept the Capitol." He had the merit of being first to discover what few men of his time had the taste to feel,—that Washington was beautiful:—

> "I have procured two very good saddle-horses, and Elizabeth and I have been riding in all directions round this place whenever the weather has been cool enough. The country has a beautifully picturesque appearance, and I have nowhere seen finer scenery than is composed by the Potomac and the woods and hills about it; yet it has a wild and desolate air from being so scantily and rudely cultivated, and from the want of population. . . . So you see we are not fallen into a wilderness,—so far from it that I

[1] F. J. Jackson to Mrs. Jackson, Oct. 7, 1809; Bath Archives, Second Series, i. 17.

am surprised no one should before have mentioned the great beauty of the neighborhood. The natives trouble themselves but little about it; their thoughts are chiefly of tobacco, flour, shingles, and the news of the day. The Merrys, I suppose, never got a mile out of Washington, except on their way to Philadelphia."

Part of Jackson's leisure was employed in reading Erskine's correspondence, although he would have done better had he neglected this customary duty, and had he brought to his diplomacy no more prejudices than such as belonged to his nature and training. His disgust with Erskine only added to his antipathy for Erskine's objects, methods, and friends.

"My visitors," he wrote, "are a different set from Erskine's, I perceive; many of them he says he never saw. Per contra, many of the Democrats who were his intimates never come to me, and I am well pleased and somewhat flattered by the distinction. . . . Erskine is really a greater fool than I could have thought it possible to be, and it is charity to give him *that* name. . . . Now that I have gone through all his correspondence, more than ever am I at a loss to comprehend how he could have been allowed to remain here for the last two years. . . . To be obliged to wade through such a mass of folly and stupidity, and to observe how our country has been made, through Erskine's means, the instrument of these people's cunning, is not the least part of my annoyance. Between them our cause is vilified indeed. The tone which Erskine had accustomed them to use with him, and to use without any notice whatever being taken of it, is another great difficulty I have had to overcome. Every third word was a declaration of war."

The month passed only too soon for Jackson's comfort, and October 1, punctual to his word, the President arrived. The next day Erskine had his farewell audience, and October 3 Jackson was officially received. Merry's experience had not been without advantage to both sides; and Jackson, who seemed to feel more contempt for his own predecessors— Merry and Erskine—than for his American antagonists, accepted everything in good part.

"Madison, the President, is a plain and rather mean-looking little man, of great simplicity of manners, and an inveterate enemy to form and ceremony; so much so that I was officially informed that my introduction to him was to be considered as nothing more than the reception of one gentleman by another, and that no particular dress was to be worn on the occasion,—all which I was very willing to acquiesce in. Accordingly I went in an afternoon frock, and found the President in similar attire. Smith, the Secretary of State, who had walked from his office to join me, had on a pair of dusty boots, and his round hat in his hand. When he had introduced us he retired, and the President then asked me to take a chair. While we were talking, a negro servant brought in some glasses of punch and a seed-cake. The former, as I had been in conference the whole morning, served very agreeably to wet, or whet, my whistle, and still more strongly to contrast this audience with others I had had with most of the sovereigns of Europe."

Perhaps this passing allusion to previous acquaintance with "most of the sovereigns of Europe" threw a light, somewhat too searching, into the recesses of Jackson's character. The weakness was pardonable, and not specially unsuited to success in his career, but showed itself in private as a form of self-deception which promised ill for his coming struggle. Madison's civility quite misled him.

"I do not know," he wrote October 24, "that I had ever more civility and attention shown me than at a dinner at the President's yesterday, where I was treated with a distinction not lately accorded to a British minister in this country. A foolish question of precedence, which ever since Merry's time has been unsettled, and has occasioned some heart-burnings among the ladies, was also decided then by the President departing from his customary indifference to ceremony and etiquette, and taking Elizabeth in to dinner, while I conducted Mrs. Madison."

Evidently this deference pleased the British minister, who saw nothing behind it but a social triumph for himself and his wife; yet he had already been forced to protest against the ceremonial forms with which Madison studiously surrounded him, and had he read Shakspeare rather than Erskine's writings, he might have learned from Julius Cæsar the general diplomatic law that "when love begins to sicken and decay, it useth ever an enforced ceremony." A man of tact would have seen that from the moment Madison became formal he was dangerous. The dinner of October 23 at the White House came at a moment when Jackson had been so carefully handled and so effectually disarmed as to stand at Madison's mercy; and although he was allowed to please himself by taking Mrs. Madison to dinner, the "mean-looking little man" at the head of the table, was engaged only in thinking by what stroke the British minister's official life should be most quickly and quietly ended.

Jackson's interviews with Robert Smith began immediately after the President's arrival in Washington. The first conversation was reported by the British minister to his Government in language so lifelike, but showing such astonishment on both sides at the attitude of each, as to give it place among the most natural sketches in American diplomatic history. After some fencing on the subject of Erskine's responsibility, Jackson passed to the subject of his own instructions, and remarked that he was ordered to wait for propositions from the President.

"Here the American minister," reported Jackson,[1] "exhibited signs of the utmost surprise and disappointment. He seemed to be so little prepared for this close of my conversation that he was some time before he could recollect himself sufficiently to give me any answer at all. Expecting to meet suggestions of a totally different nature, and finding that what he had ready to say to them did not suit the occasion, he seemed to require some time and reflection to new arrange his thoughts. Accordingly a considerable pause in our conversation took place, which at length he broke in upon by saying: 'Then, sir, you have no proposal to make to us,—no explanation to give? How shall we be able to get rid of the Non-intercourse Act?' "

Robert Smith was a wearisome burden to Madison, and his

[1] Jackson to Canning, Oct. 17, 1809; MSS. British Archives.

incompetence made no agreeable object of study; but his apparent bewilderment at Jackson's audacity was almost as instructive as the sincere astonishment of the Englishman at the effect of his own words. The game of cross-purposes could not be more naturally played. Robert Smith had been requested by Madison to ascertain precisely what Jackson's instructions were; and both at the first and at a second interview he pressed this point, always trying to discover what Jackson had to offer, while the Englishman always declined to offer anything whatever. Two conversations satisfied the President that Jackson's hands were fast tied, and that he could open no door of escape. Then Madison gently set the Secretary of State aside, and, as openly as the office of Chief Magistrate permitted, undertook to deal with the British minister.

October 9 the Secretary of State sent to the British Legation a formal letter, written, like all Robert Smith's important papers, by the President.[1] After recapitulating the negative results reached in the two interviews, Jackson was asked whether he had been rightly understood; and the letter ended by saying, that, "to avoid the misconceptions incident to oral proceeding, I have also the honor to intimate that it is thought expedient that our further discussions on the present occasion be in the written form."[2]

Jackson saw a challenge in this change of attitude, and undertook to meet it by vigorous resistance. He had no mind to be thrown on the defensive; as he wrote to Canning, he wished to teach the American government not to presume on his patience.

"On connecting all these circumstances," he reported,[3] — "the manner in which Mr. Smith had conducted our conferences; the abruptness, especially, with which he had put an end to them; and the style in which he announces to me, without leaving any choice or alternative, but as the absolute decision of his Government, 'that it is thought expedient that our future discussions on the present occasion'

[1] Madison's Works, ii. 499.
[2] Secretary of State to Mr. Jackson, Oct. 9, 1809; State Papers, iii. 308.
[3] Jackson to Canning, Oct. 18, 1809; MSS. British Archives.

(*i. e.*, the only occasion of doing away existing differences) 'should be in the written form,'—it occurred to me to be necessary to put the matter on such a footing as to preclude, *in limine*, the idea that every species of indirect obloquy was to be patiently submitted to by his Majesty's minister in this country."

In this temper Jackson wrote a long letter, dated October 11, for the purpose, as he reported to Canning,[1] of checking "that spirit which can never lead to conciliation, by which America thinks herself entitled to make her will and her view of things the criterion by which they are to be generally approved or condemned." Beginning with the assertion that "there does not exist in the annals of diplomacy a precedent" for stopping verbal communication within so few days after the delivery of credentials, he rehearsed the story of Erskine's arrangement, and justified his refusal of apology or explanation. In doing so, he allowed himself to insinuate what Canning expressly asserted in his instructions, that Robert Smith had connived at Erskine's misconduct:—

> "It was not known when I left England whether Mr. Erskine had, according to the liberty allowed him, communicated to you *in extenso* his original instructions. It now appears that he did not. But . . . I find . . . that he has submitted to your consideration the three conditions specified in those instructions as the groundwork of an arrangement. . . . Mr. Erskine reports, *verbatim et seriatim*, your observations upon each of the three conditions, and the reasons which induced you to think that others might be substituted in lieu of them. It may have been concluded between you that these latter were an equivalent for the original conditions; but the very act of substitution evidently shows that those original conditions were in fact very explicitly communicated to you, and by you, of course, laid before the President for his consideration."

After justifying the disavowal of Erskine on the admitted ground that he had disobeyed instructions, Jackson came to the point of his own powers. "His Majesty has authorized

[1] Jackson to Canning, Oct. 18, 1809; MSS. British Archives.

me," he said, "notwithstanding the ungracious manner in which his former offer of satisfaction for the affair of the 'Chesapeake' was received, to renew that which Mr. Erskine was instructed to make." As for the Orders in Council, these had been so far modified by the blockade of April 26 as to make any formal agreement on that subject seem unnecessary, and he reserved his proposals until he should hear those of the President.

Two days after this letter was despatched, Robert Smith sent a civil message that there had been no intention to stop personal intercourse; "he should be most happy to see me whenever I would call upon him; we might converse upon indifferent subjects; but that his memory was so incorrect that it was on his account necessary that in making his reports to the President he should have some written document to assist him."[1] With this excuse for the secretary's sudden withdrawal from the field the British minister contented himself until October 19, when he received an official letter, signed as usual by Robert Smith, but written with ability such as that good-natured but illiterate Secretary of State never imagined himself to possess.

The American note of October 19, far too long to quote or even to abridge, was perhaps the best and keenest paper Madison ever wrote. His faults of style and vagueness of thought almost wholly disappeared in the heat of controversy; his defence was cool, his attack keen, as though his sixty years weighed lightly the day when he first got his young antagonist at his mercy. He dealt Jackson a fatal blow at the outset, by reminding him that in July, 1808, only the previous year, Canning had put an end to oral communication after two interviews with Pinkney on the subjects under negotiation. He then made three points, well stated and easily remembered: (1) That when a government refuses to fulfil a pledge, it owes a formal and frank disclosure of its reasons. (2) That, in the actual situation, Mr. Erskine's successor was the proper channel for that disclosure. (3) That since Mr. Jackson disclaimed authority to make either explanations or proposals, the President could do no more than express his willingness

---

[1] Jackson to Canning, Oct. 18, 1809; MSS. British Archives.

to favor any honorable mode of settling the matters in dispute.

In enlarging on the subjects touched by Jackson's letter, the President made more than one remark of the kind that most exasperated the British minister. Since no settlement of the dispute was possible or even desired by Jackson, such flashes of Madison's temper were neither harmful nor inappropriate, yet they were certainly on the verge of insult. He told Jackson plainly that Great Britain, by retaining her so-called retaliation after admitting that it no longer retaliated, was guilty of deception: —

> "You cannot but be sensible that a perseverance under such circumstances in a system which cannot longer be explained by its avowed object would force an explanation by some object not avowed. What object might be considered as best explaining it is an inquiry into which I do not permit myself to enter, further than to remark that in relation to the United States it must be an illegitimate object."

On the other hand, Madison seemed not to resent, as warmly as he might have done, the intimation that he had induced Erskine to violate instructions. The President either affected not to see, or failed fully to grasp at first, the serious scope of this charge:

> "The stress you have laid on what you have been pleased to state as the substitution of the terms finally agreed on for the terms first proposed, has excited no small degree of surprise. Certain it is that your predecessor did present for my consideration the three conditions which now appear on the printed document; that he was disposed to urge them more than the nature of two of them (both palpably inadmissible, and one more than merely inadmissible) could permit; and that on finding his first proposals unsuccessful, the more reasonable terms . . . were adopted. And what, sir, is there in this to countenance the conclusion you have drawn in favor of the right of his Britannic Majesty to disavow the proceeding? Is anything more common in public negotiations than to begin with a higher demand, and that failing, to descend to a lower?"

Contenting himself with the remark that he had for the first time learned, from Jackson's note, the restrictions on Erskine's authority, the President passed to other points as though unaware that his good faith was in question.

The letter of October 19 forced Jackson one step backward, and drove him nearly to the wall. Obliged to choose between the avowal that he had no proposal to make, or the assertion that he had both explanations and proposals, he yielded, somewhat surlily, to the weakness of offering explanations, such as they were, and of inviting proposals eventually to be embodied in a convention. In a note dated October 23 he answered the American note of October 19.[1] If Madison had doubted his own advantage, his doubts must have vanished in reading Jackson's second note, which shuffled and evaded the issues in a manner peculiar to disconcerted men; but the most convincing proof of Jackson's weakness appeared in the want of judgment he showed in exposing himself to attack at the moment when he was seeking safety. He committed the blunder of repeating the charge that Madison was responsible for Erskine's violation of instructions: —

"These instructions . . . were at the time, in substance, made known to you. . . . So far from the terms which he was actually induced to accept having been contemplated in that instruction, he himself states that they were substituted by you in lieu of those originally proposed."

Jackson's folly in thus tempting his fate was the more flagrant because his private letters proved that he knew something of his true position. "Madison is now as obstinate as a mule," he wrote October 26.[2] "Until he gets [the absolute surrender of the Orders in Council] he will not even accept any satisfaction for the affair of the 'Chesapeake,' which has been now for the third time offered to him in vain;" and he added: "There is already a great and growing fermentation in the United States, which shows itself in a manner highly prejudicial to the amity and good understanding which doubtless our ministers wish to see established between the two countries."

[1] Jackson to the Secretary of State, Oct. 23, 1809; State Papers, iii. 315.
[2] Bath Archives, Second Series, i. 28.

A few days after writing this evidence of his own uneasiness, the British minister received from the Department of State a third note, dated November 1, which left no doubt that the President meant to push his antagonist to extremes. After accepting the explanations at last made in regard to the Orders in Council, and pointing out that they did not apply to the case of the "Chesapeake," Madison requested Jackson to show his full powers, as an "indispensable preliminary to further negotiation." The letter was short, and ended with a stern warning: —

> "I abstain, sir, from making any particular animadversions on several irrelevant and improper allusions in your letter, not at all comporting with the professed disposition to adjust, in an amicable manner, the differences unhappily subsisting between the two countries; but it would be improper to conclude the few observations to which I purposely limit myself, without adverting to your repetition of a language implying a knowledge on the part of this Government that the instructions of your predecessor did not authorize the arrangement formed by him. After the explicit and peremptory asseveration that this Government had no such knowledge, and that with such a knowledge no such arrangement would have been entered into, the view which you have again presented of the subject makes it my duty to apprise you that such insinuations are inadmissible in the intercourse of a foreign minister with a Government that understands what it owes to itself."

This letter placed Jackson in a position which he could not defend, and from which he thought, perhaps with reason, that he could not without disgrace retreat. The insinuations he had made were but a cautious expression of the views he was expressly ordered to take. November 4 he replied, with more ability than he had hitherto shown, to the letter of November 1; but he gave himself, for a mere point of temper, into Madison's hands.

> "I am concerned, sir, to be obliged, a second time, to appeal to those principles of public law, under the sanction and protection of which I was sent to this country. . . .

You will find that in my correspondence with you I have carefully avoided drawing conclusions that did not necessarily follow from the premises advanced by me, and least of all should I think of uttering an insinuation where I was unable to substantiate a fact. To facts, such as I have become acquainted with them, I have scrupulously adhered; and in so doing I must continue, whenever the good faith of his Majesty's government is called in question, to vindicate its honor and dignity in the manner that appears to me best calculated for that purpose."

When Jackson was sent to Copenhagen with a message whose general tenor resembled that which he brought to the United States, he was fortunate enough to be accompanied by twenty ships of the line, forty frigates, and thirty thousand regular troops. Even with this support, if court gossip could be believed, King George expressed to him surprise that he had escaped being kicked downstairs. At Washington he had no other force on his side than such as his footman or his groom could render, and the destiny that King George predicted for him could not, by any diplomatic weapons, be longer escaped. November 8, Secretary Smith sent to the Legation one more note, which closed Jackson's diplomatic career: —

"SIR,— . . . Finding that in your reply of the 4th instant you have used a language which cannot be understood but as reiterating and even aggravating the same gross insinuation, it only remains, in order to preclude opportunities which are thus abused, to inform you that no further communications will be received from you. . . ."

Chapter VII

THE EFFECT OF American conciliation upon Canning was immediate and simple; but the effect of American defiance upon Napoleon will be understood only by those who forget the fatigue of details in their interest for Napoleon's character. The Emperor's steps in 1809 are not easily followed. He was overburdened with labor; his motives and policy shifted as circumstances changed; and among second-rate interests he lost more habitually than ever the thread of his own labyrinth.

Travelling day and night from Spain in January, 1809, with the same haste and with something of the same motive as when four years afterward he posted back to Paris from his Russian disaster, Napoleon appeared unexpectedly at his capital January 24. The moment was one of crisis, but a crisis of his own making. He had suffered a political check in Spain, which he had but partially disguised by a useless campaign. The same spirit of universal dominion which grasped at Spain and required the conquest of England, roused resistance elsewhere almost as desperate as that of the Spaniards and English. Even the American Congress repealed its embargo and poured its commerce through so-called neutral ports into the lap of England, while at the same moment Austria, driven to desperation, prepared to fight for a fourth time. Napoleon had strong reasons for choosing that moment to force Austria wholly into his system. Germany stood at his control. Russia alone could have made the result doubtful; but the Czar was wholly French. "M. Romanzoff," wrote Armstrong to the State Department,[1] " with the fatalism of the Turk, shakes his head at Austria, and asks what has hitherto been got by opposition; calls to mind the fate of Prussia, and closes by a pious admonition not to resist the will of God."

Toward Austria the Emperor directed all his attention, and rapidly drove her government into an attitude of resistance the most spirited and the most desperate taken by any people of Europe except Spain. Although Austria never wearied

[1] Armstrong to R. Smith, Feb. 16, 1809; MSS. State Department Archives.

of fighting Napoleon, and rarely fought without credit, her effort to face, in 1809, a Power controlling the military resources of France, Italy, and Germany, with the moral support of Russia behind them, had an heroic quality higher than was shown at any time by any other government in Europe. April 9 the Austrian army crossed the Inn, and began the war. April 13 Napoleon left Paris for the Danube, and during the next three months his hands were full. Austria fought with an energy which put Germany and Russia to shame.

Such a moment was ill suited for inviting negotiation on American affairs; but Armstrong received instructions a few days after Napoleon left Paris, and with these instructions came a copy of the Non-intercourse Act of March 1, which, while apparently forbidding intercourse with England and France, notified Napoleon that the United States would no longer obey his wishes, or keep their industries from seeking a British market through indirect channels. Armstrong communicated this Act to the French government in the terms of his instructions:[1] —

"The undersigned is instructed to add that any interpretation of the Imperial Decrees of Nov. 21, 1806, and Dec. 17, 1807, which shall have the effect of leaving unimpaired the maritime rights of the Union, will be instantaneously followed by a revocation of the present Act [as regards France] and a re-establishment of the ordinary commercial intercourse between the two countries."

May 17 Champagny, then at Munich, having received Armstrong's letter of April 29, notified the Minister of Marine,[2] —

"The news of this measure having received an official character by the communication made to me by the United States minister on the part of his Government, I think it my duty to transmit to your Excellency a copy of the law which he has addressed to me."

Armstrong informed Secretary Robert Smith[3] that nothing

[1] Armstrong to Champagny, April 29, 1809; State Papers, iii. 324.
[2] Champagny to Decrès, 17 May, 1809; Archives des Aff. Étr. MSS.
[3] Armstrong to R. Smith, April 27, 1809; MSS. State Department Archives.

need be expected from this step, unless it were perhaps his own summary expulsion from France as a result of offence given either by the Non-intercourse Act or by the language of Armstrong's despatches surreptitiously published. Bitterly as Armstrong detested Napoleon, he understood but little the mind and methods of that unusual character. Never in his career had the Emperor been busier than when Armstrong wrote this note to Champagny, but it caught his attention at once. He had fought one battle after another, and in five days had captured forty thousand men and a hundred pieces of cannon; he had entered Vienna May 10, and had taken his quarters at Schönbrunn, the favorite palace of the Austrian emperor. There he was in a position of no little difficulty, in spite of his military successes, when his courier brought him despatches from Paris containing news that the United States, March 1, had repealed the embargo, and that the British government, April 26, had withdrawn the Orders in Council of November, 1807, and had substituted a mere blockade of Holland, France, and Italy. The effect of these two events was greatly increased by their coming together.

At first Napoleon seemed to feel no occasion for altering his course. After reading Armstrong's letter, he dictated May 18 a reply which was to serve as the legal argument to justify his refusal of concessions. His decrees were founded on eternal principles, and could not be revoked:—

> "The seas belong to all nations. Every vessel sailing under the flag of any nation whatever, recognized and avowed by it, ought to be on the ocean as if it were in its own ports. The flag flying from the mast of a merchantman ought to be respected as though it were on the top of a village steeple. . . . To insult a merchant-vessel carrying the flag of any Power is to make an incursion into a village or a colony belonging to that Power. His Majesty declares that he considers the vessels of all nations as floating colonies belonging to the said nations. In result of this principle, the sovereignty and independence of one nation are a property of its neighbors."[1]

The conclusion that the sovereignty and independence of

[1] Correspondance, xix. 21.

every nation were the property of France, and that a floating
colony denationalized by the visit of a foreign officer became
the property of Napoleon, involved results too extreme for
general acceptance. Arbitrary as the Emperor was, he could
act only through agents, and could not broach such doctrines
without meeting remonstrance. His dissertation on the principles of the *jus gentium* was sent May 18 to Champagny.
Four days afterward, May 22, Napoleon fought the battle of
Essling, in which he lost fifteen or twenty thousand men and
suffered a serious repulse. Even this absorbing labor, and the
critical situation that followed, did not long interrupt his attention to American business. May 26, Champagny made to
the Emperor a report[1] on American affairs, taking ground
altogether different from that chosen by Napoleon. After narrating the story of the various orders, decrees, blockades, embargoes, and non-intercourse measures, Champagny discussed
them in their practical effect on the interests and industries of
France: —

> "The fact cannot be disguised; the interruption of neu-
> tral commerce which has done much harm to England has
> been also a cause of loss to France. The staple products of
> our territory have ceased to be sold. Those that were for-
> merly exported are lost, or are stored away, leaving impov-
> erished both the owner who produced them and the dealer
> who put them on the market. One of our chief sources of
> prosperity is dried up. Our interest therefore leads us to-
> ward America, whose commerce would still furnish an am-
> ple outlet for several of our products, and would bring us
> either materials of prime necessity for our manufactures, or
> produce the use of which has become almost a necessity,
> and which we would rather not owe to our enemies."

For these reasons Champagny urged the Emperor not to
persist in punishing America, but to charge M. d'Hauterive,
the acting Minister of Foreign Relations at Paris, with the
duty of discussing with General Armstrong the details of an
arrangement. Champagny supported his advice by urging
that England had made advances to America, had revoked

[1] Champagny to Napoleon, May 26, 1809; Archives des Aff. Étr. MSS.

her orders of November, 1807, and seemed about to turn the French Decrees against France. "It will always be in your Majesty's power to evade this result. A great step to this end will be taken when Mr. Armstrong is made aware that your Majesty is disposed to interpret your commercial decrees favorably for the Americans, provided measures be taken that no tribute shall be paid to England, and that their efficacy shall be assured. Such will be the object of M. d'Hauterive's mission."

Napoleon, impressed by Champagny's reasoning, fortified by the news that Erskine had settled the commercial disputes between England and America, sent to Champagny the draft of a new decree,[1] which declared that inasmuch as the United States by their firm resistance to the arbitrary measures of England had obtained the revocation of the British Orders of November, 1807, and were no longer obliged to pay imposts to the British government, therefore the Milan Decree of Dec. 17, 1807, should be withdrawn, and neutral commerce should be replaced where it stood under the Berlin Decree of Nov. 21, 1806.

This curious paper was sent June 10 to Paris for a report from the Treasury as to its probable effects. June 13 Champagny sent instructions to Hauterive[2] directing him to begin negotiation with Armstrong. Far from overlooking either the intention or the effect of the Non-intercourse Act, Champagny complained that it was unfair to France and "almost an act of violence;" but he did not resent it. "The Emperor is not checked by this consideration; he feels neither prejudice nor resentment against the Americans, but he remains firm in his projects of resisting British pretensions. The measures taken by England will chiefly decide his measures." Champagny explained that the Emperor hesitated to issue the new decree already forwarded for the inspection of the customs authorities, not because any change had taken place in the reasons given for its policy, but because the arrangement of Erskine was said to be disavowed.

"What has prevented the Emperor till now from coming

[1] Napoleon to Champagny, June 10, 1809; Correspondance, xix. 95.
[2] Champagny to Hauterive, June 13, 1809; Archives des Aff. Étr. MSS.

to a decision in this respect is the news contained in the English journals of an arrangement between England and America, and announced by a Proclamation of the President of the United States, April 19, 1806. If from this act should result the certainty that the English renounce their principle of blockade, then the Emperor would revoke the whole of his measures relative to neutral commerce. But the 'Gazette de France' of June 5, for I have no other authority, pretends that the British ministry refuse to sanction the arrangement concluded in America; and the result of all this is an extreme uncertainty, which prevents a decision as to the course proper to be taken."

This was the situation of the American dispute June 13, 1809, at Vienna, at the moment Canning's disavowal of Erskine became certain. Thus far Napoleon's mind had passed through two changes,—the first, in consequence of the British Order in Council of April 26, which led him to decide on withdrawing the Milan Decree; the second, in consequence of Erskine's arrangement, which led him to promise America everything she asked. The news of Canning's refusal to carry out the arrangement stopped Napoleon short in his career of concession; he left the American affair untouched until after the battle of Wagram, July 6, which was followed by the submission of Austria, July 12. The battle of Wagram placed him in a position to defy resistance. Immediately afterward he sent orders to Paris to stop Hauterive's negotiation. About the middle of July Hauterive told the American minister "that a change had taken place in the views of the Emperor; and in particular that a decree prepared by his orders as a substitute for those of November, 1806, and December, 1807, and which would have been a very material step toward accommodation, had been laid aside."[1]

In the heat and fury of the battle of Wagram this order must have been given, for it was known at Paris only one week afterward, and Armstrong reported the message, July 24, as a notice that unless America resisted the British doctrines of search and blockade she need expect no relaxation on the part of Napoleon; while this notice was supported by

[1] Armstrong to R. Smith, July 22, 1809; MSS. State Department Archives.

a menace that until the Emperor knew the President's decision he would take no step to make matters worse than they already were.[1]

If Armstrong put trust in this last promise or menace, he showed once more his want of sympathy with the Emperor's character. Quick to yield before an evident disaster, Napoleon was equally quick to exhaust the fruits of an evident victory; and the advantage he had obtained over the United States was as decided, if not as extensive, as that which he had gained over Austria. In one way or another America must pay for rebellion, and she could be made to pay only by the usual process of seizing her commerce.

June 7, while the Emperor was still hesitating or leaning to concession, Decrès, his Minister of Marine, wrote to him that an American schooner with a cargo of colonial produce had arrived at San Sebastian May 20, and that more such vessels must be expected to arrive, since the Non-intercourse Act had opened the trade to Spanish ports. What should be done with them? The French Decrees denationalized every vessel which went to England, or wished to go there, or had been visited by an English cruiser, or had violated the laws of the United States, or had incurred suspicion of fraud; but the schooner in question was under no suspicion of fraud,—she had not been to England, nor had she ever thought of going there; she had not been stopped by any cruiser; she was in a Spanish port, nominally outside of French jurisdiction, and she was authorized in going there by the law of the United States. Here was an unforeseen case, and Decrès properly referred it to the Emperor.[2]

Decrès' letter reached Vienna about June 13, the day when Champagny described the Emperor as vexed by an extreme uncertainty on American affairs. The subject was referred to the Minister of Finance. No decision seems to have been reached until August. Then Maret, the Secretary of State in personal attendance on the Emperor, created Duc de Bassano a few days later, enclosed to Champagny, August 4, the draft

[1] Armstrong to R. Smith, July 24, 1809; MSS. State Department Archives.

[2] Rapport a l'Empereur par le Ministre de la Marine, 7 Juin, 1809. Archives des Aff. Étr. MSS.

of a new decree,[1] which was never published, but furnished the clew to most of the intricate movements of Napoleon for the following year: —

"Napoleon, etc.,—considering that the American Congress by its Act of March 1, 1809, has forbidden the entrance of its ports to all French vessels under penalty of confiscation of ships and cargo,—on the report of our Minister of Finance have decreed and decree what follows: —

"Art. 1. The American schooner loaded with colonial produce and entered at San Sebastian the 20th May, 1809, will be seized and confiscated.

"Art. 2. The merchandise composing the cargo of the vessel will be conveyed to Bayonne, there to be sold, and the produce of the sale paid into the *caisse de l'amortissement* (sinking-fund).

"Art. 3. Every American ship which shall enter the ports of France, Spain, or Italy will be equally seized and confiscated, as long as the same measure shall continue to be executed in regard to French vessels in the harbors of the United States."

Probably the ministers united in objecting to a general confiscation founded on the phrase of a penalty which the customs laws of every country necessarily contained. Whatever the reason, this draft rested in the files of the office over which Champagny presided, and the Emperor seemed to forget it; but its advantages from his standpoint were too great to be lost, and its principle was thenceforward his guide.

Not even Armstrong, suspicious as he was of Napoleon's intentions, penetrated the projected policy; yet Armstrong was by no means an ordinary minister, and his information was usually good. At the moment when he received what he supposed to be the promise that Napoleon would not make matters worse until he heard what the President had to say,

[1] Décret Impérial; Archives des Aff. Étr. MSS. vol. lxii. (États Unis), pièce 166.

Armstrong warned his Government that this assurance was intended as a menace rather than as a pledge:[1] —

"What will satisfy him on even these points, particularly the former, is not distinctly explained. Our creed on this subject is one thing; that of the British government another; and the French doctrine of visit, a third. When we speak of illegal search, we mean that which claims the right of impressment also; but according to the imperial decrees and their commentators, the offence is equally great whatever may be the object of the visit,—whether it be to demand half your crew, or to ascertain only the port from which you sailed, the nature of your cargo, or the character of your flag. This is pushing things to a point whither we cannot follow them, and which, if I do not mistake, is selected because it is a point of that description."

Before the month of August, Napoleon reverted more energetically than ever to his old practice and policy. Within Armstrong's reach remained only one influence strong enough to offer a momentary resistance to imperial orders, and thither he turned. The kingdom of Holland was still nominally independent, and its trade an object of interest. While England shaped her policy to favor the licensed or smuggling trade with Dutch ports, the United States risked their relations with England and France by treating Holland as an independent neutral. Yet the nominal independence of Holland was due only to the accident that had made Louis its king, as it had made his brother Joseph king of Spain,—not wholly with a view to please them, but also to secure obedience to Napoleon's orders and energy to his system. No one would willingly deprive any member of Napoleon's family of virtues which the world allowed them; yet none but a Bonaparte thoroughly understood a Bonaparte, and Napoleon's opinion of his brothers, as their opinions of him, stand highest in authority. Napoleon was often generous and sometimes forbearing with his brothers, and left them no small freedom to seek popularity at his expense; but they were nothing except as they represented him, and their ideas of independence

[1] Armstrong to R. Smith, July 24, 1809; MSS. State Department Archives.

or of philanthropy showed entire misunderstanding of their situation. Of all Napoleon's brothers, Louis was the one with whom he was most reasonably offended. Lucien at least did not wait to be made a king before he rebelled; but Louis accepted the throne, and then intrigued persistently against the Emperor's orders. From the moment he went to Holland he assumed to be an independent monarch, devoted to winning popularity. He would not execute the Berlin Decree until Napoleon threatened to march an army upon him; he connived at its evasion; he issued licenses and admitted cargoes as he pleased; and he did this with such systematic disregard of remonstrance that Napoleon became at last angry.

July 17, some days after the battle of Wagram, the Emperor wrote from Vienna to Louis,[1] —

"You complain of a newspaper article; it is France that has a right to complain of the bad spirit which reigns with you. . . . It may not be your fault, but it is none the less true that Holland is an English province."

At the same time he ordered Champagny to notify the Dutch government officially that if it did not of its own accord place itself on the same footing with France, it would be in danger of war.[2]

While this correspondence was still going on, Armstrong imagined that he might obtain some advantage by visiting Holland. He amused himself during the idle August by a journey to Amsterdam, where he obtained, August 19, a private interview with King Louis. Three days before, Flushing had capitulated to the English expedition which was supposed to be threatening Antwerp. At Vienna Napoleon was negotiating for peace, and between the obstinacy of Austria and the British attacks on Madrid and Antwerp he found himself ill at ease. President Madison had just issued his Proclamation of August 9 reviving the Non-intercourse Act, which kept open the American trade with Holland. Everywhere the situation was confused, irritable, and hard to understand. A general system of cross-purposes seemed to govern the political movements of the world.

[1] Correspondance, xix. 261.
[2] Ibid.

King Louis told Armstrong that he was quarrelling seriously with the Emperor on account of the American trade,
but was bent on protecting it at all hazards. This declaration
to a foreign minister accredited not to himself but to his
brother, showed Louis attempting with the aid of foreign
nations a systematic opposition to Napoleon's will. He denounced his brother's system as "the triumph of immorality
over justice. . . . The system is bad,—so bad that it cannot
last; but in the mean time we are the sufferers." Even the
British expedition to Walcheren troubled Louis chiefly because it forced him under his brother's despotism. "It is an
erring policy, and will have no solid or lasting effect but that
of drawing upon us a French army which will extinguish all
that is left of ancient Holland. Can it be wisdom in England
to see this country a province of France?"

With such comfort as Armstrong could draw from the
knowledge that Napoleon's brothers were as hostile as President Madison to the imperial system, he returned to Paris,
September 6, to wait the further development of the Emper-
or's plans. He found on his arrival two notes from Champagny at Vienna. One of these despatches expressed a civil
hope, hardly felt by the Emperor,[1] that Armstrong would not
for the present carry out his project of returning to America.
The other, dated August 22, was nothing less than a revised
and permanent form of the Emperor's essay on the *jus gentium*, which Champagny since May 18 had kept in his portfolio.[2]

In Champagny's hands Napoleon's views lost freshness
without gaining legality. The "village steeple" disappeared,
but with some modification the "floating colony" remained,
and the principle of free seas was carried to its extreme
results:—

> "A merchant-vessel sailing with all the necessary papers
> (*avec les expéditions*) from its government is a floating col-
> ony. To do violence to such a vessel by visits, by searches,
> and by other acts of an arbitrary authority is to violate the
> territory of a colony; this is to infringe on the indepen-

[1] Napoleon to Champagny, 21 August, 1809; Correspondance, xix. 375.
[2] Correspondance de Napoléon, xix. 374; State Papers, iii. 325.

dence of its government. . . . The right, or rather the pretension, of blockading by a proclamation rivers and coasts, is as monstrous (*révoltante*) as it is absurd. A right cannot be derived from the will or the caprice of one of the interested parties, but ought to be derived from the nature of things themselves. A place is not truly blockaded until it is invested by land and sea."

Every one could understand that to assert such principles was an impossibility for neutrals, and was so meant by Napoleon. He had no thought of making demands which England could accept. The destruction of her naval power was his favorite object after the year 1805. The battle of Wagram confirmed him in his plan, and Louis' opposition counted for even less than Armstrong's diplomacy in checking the energy of his will. As he ordered Louis, so he ordered Madison, to obey; and thanks to the obstinacy of Spencer Perceval, both had no choice but to assist his scheme. As an answer to the American offer expressed in the Non-intercourse Act, Champagny's despatch of August 22 was final; but to preclude a doubt, it closed by saying that the ports of Holland, of the Elbe and the Weser, of Italy and of Spain, would not be allowed to enjoy privileges of which French ports were deprived, and that whenever England should revoke her blockades and Orders in Council, France would revoke her retaliatory decrees.

Without suicide, England could hardly accept the principles required by this note; nor had she reason to suppose that her acceptance would satisfy Napoleon's demands. As though to encourage her in obstinacy, the note was printed in the "Moniteur" of October 6, by the Emperor's order, before it could have reached America. This unusual step served no purpose except to give public notice that France would support England in restricting American rights; it strengthened the hands of Spencer Perceval and took away the last chance of American diplomacy, if a chance still existed. Yet neither this stroke nor the severity foreshadowed by the secret Decree of Vienna was the only punishment inflicted by Napoleon on the United States for the Non-intercourse Act and Erskine's arrangement.

The principle of the Vienna Decree required confiscation of American commerce in retaliation for penalties imposed on French ships that should knowingly violate the Non-intercourse Act. Although this rule and the Bayonne Decree seemed to cover all ordinary objects of confiscation, the Emperor adopted the supplementary rule that American merchandise was English property in disguise. In the month of November a cotton-spinner near Paris, the head of a very large establishment, petitioned for leave to import about six hundred bales of American cotton. His petition was returned to him with the indorsement: "Rejected, as the cotton belongs to American commerce." The severity of the refusal surprised every one the more because the alternative was to use Portuguese—that is to say English—cotton, or to encourage the consumption of fabrics made wholly in England, of English materials.[1] Having decided to seize all American merchandise that should arrive in France on private account, and having taken into his own hands the business of selling this property as well as of admitting other merchandise by license, Napoleon protected what became henceforward his personal interests, by shutting the door to competition.[2] Armstrong caught glimpses of this stratagem even before it had taken its finished shape.

"I am privately informed," wrote Armstrong December 10, "that General Loison has left Paris charged to take hold of all British property, or property suspected of being such in the ports of Bilbao, San Sebastian, Pasages, etc. The latter part of the rule is no doubt expressly intended to reach American property. With the General goes a mercantile man who will be known in the market as his friend and protégé, and who of course will be the exclusive purchaser of the merchandise which shall be seized and sold as British. This is a specimen at once of the violence and corruption which enter into the present system; and of a piece with this is the whole business of licenses, to which, I am sorry to add, our countrymen lend themselves with great facility."

[1] Armstrong to R. Smith, Nov. 18, 1809; MSS. State Department Archives.
[2] Mémoires de Mollien, iii. 133–135.

Under such conditions commerce between the United States and France seemed impossible. One prohibition crowded upon another. First came the Berlin Decree of Nov. 21, 1806, which turned away or confiscated every American vessel voluntarily entering a British port after that date. Second, followed the Milan Decree of Nov. 11, 1807, which denationalized and converted into English property every American ship visited by a British cruiser or sent into a British port, or which had paid any tax to the British government. Third, the Bayonne Decree of April 5, 1808, sequestered all American vessels arriving in France subsequent to the embargo, as being presumably British property. Fourth, the American Non-intercourse Act of March 1, 1809, prohibited all commerce with France or her dependencies. Fifth, the British Orders in Council of April 26, 1809, established a blockade of the whole coast of France. Sixth, the secret Decree of Vienna, of August, 1809, enforced in principle, sequestered every American vessel arriving within the Emperor's military control, in reprisal for the Non-intercourse Act which threatened French ships with confiscation. Yet with all this, and greatly to General Armstrong's displeasure, American ships in considerable numbers entered the ports of France, and, what was still more incomprehensible, were even allowed to leave them.

Chapter VIII

UNDER THESE CIRCUMSTANCES President Madison was to meet Congress; but bad as his situation was in foreign affairs, his real troubles lay not abroad but at home. France never counted with him as more than an instrument to act on England. Erskine and Canning, by their united efforts, had so mismanaged English affairs that Madison derived from their mismanagement all the strength he possessed. The mission of Jackson to Washington retrieved a situation that offered no other advantage.

Jackson lost no occasion to give the President popularity. Comprehending at last that his high tone had only helped his opponent to carry out a predetermined course, Jackson lost self-confidence without gaining tact. At first he sustained himself by faith in Canning; but within a short time he heard with alarm the news from England that Canning was no longer in office or in credit. For a few days after the rupture he had a right to hope that the quarrel would not be pressed to a scandal; but November 13, the "National Intelligencer" published an official statement which embarrassed Jackson to the last point of endurance.

> "I came prepared to treat with a regular government," he wrote to his brother,[1] "and have had to do with a mob, and mob leaders. That I did not show an equal facility with Erskine to be duped by them has been my great crime."

That Jackson should be angry was natural, and if he was abusive, he received an ample equivalent in abuse; but his merits as a diplomatist were supposed to be his courage and his truth, and these he could not afford to compromise. He had neither said nor done more than stood in his express orders. Canning's instructions charged Madison with fraud:

> "The American government cannot have believed that such an arrangement as Mr. Erskine consented to accept was conformable to his instructions. . . . They cannot by possibility have believed that without any new motive, and

[1] Bath Archives, Second Series, i. 44.

without any apparent change in the dispositions of the enemy, the British government could have been disposed at once and unconditionally to give up the system on which they had been acting."

This ground Jackson had been ordered to take in any "preliminary discussion" which might "in all probability" arise before he could enter on the details of his negotiation. In obedience to these instructions, and well within their limits, Jackson had gone as near as he dared to telling the President that he alone was to blame for the disavowal of Erskine, because Erskine's instructions " were at the time in substance made known" to him. In subsequently affirming that he made no insinuation which he could not substantiate, Jackson still kept to what he believed the truth; and he reiterated in private what he insinuated officially, that Erskine had been "duped" by the American government. November 16 he wrote officially to the Foreign Office that without the slightest doubt the President had full and entire knowledge of Erskine's instruction No. 2.[1] These views were consistent and not unreasonable, but no man could suppose them to be complimentary to President Madison; yet November 13 Jackson caused his secretary, Oakeley, to send in his name an official note to the Secretary of State, complaining of the rupture and rehearsing the charges, with the conclusion that "in stating these facts, and in adhering to them, as his duty imperiously enjoined him to do, Mr. Jackson could not imagine that offence would be taken at it by the American government, as most certainly none could be intended on his part."[2] He then addressed the same counter-statement as a circular to the various British consuls in the United States, and caused it to be printed in the newspapers,[3] —thus making an appeal to the people against their own Government, not unlike the more famous appeal which the French Minister Genet made in 1793 against President Washington.

In extremely bad temper Jackson quitted the capital. His wife wrote to her friends in joy at the prospect of shortening

[1] Jackson to Bathurst, Nov. 16, 1809; MSS. British Archives.
[2] Mr. Oakeley to the Secretary of State, Nov. 13, 1809; State Papers, iii. 319.
[3] National Intelligencer, Nov. 22, 1809.

her stay in a country which could offer her only the tribute
of ignorant admiration; but even she showed a degree of
bitterness in her pleasure, and her comments on American
society had more value than many official documents
in explaining the attitude of England toward the United
States: —

> "Francis, being accustomed to treat with the civilized
> courts and governments of Europe, and not with savage
> Democrats, half of them sold to France, has not succeeded
> in his negotiation."[1]

At Washington she had seen few ladies besides Mrs. Madison, "une bonne, grosse femme, de la classe bourgeoise, . . .
sans distinction," and also, to do her justice, "sans préten-
sions;" who did the British minister's wife the honor to copy
her toilettes. Immediately after the rupture Mrs. Jackson went
to Baltimore, where she was received with enthusiasm by society; but Baltimore satisfied her little better than Washington: "Between ourselves their cuisine is detestable; coarse
table-linen, no claret, champagne and madeira indifferent."
Only as the relative refinement of New York and Boston was
reached, with the flattery lavished upon the British minister
by the Federalist society of the commercial cities, did Mrs.
Jackson and her husband in some degree recover their composure and their sense of admitted superiority.

Incredible as the folly of a political party was apt to be, the
folly of the Federalists in taking up Jackson's quarrel passed
the limits of understanding. After waiting to receive their
tone from England, the Federalist newspapers turned on their
own path and raised the cry that Madison had deceived Erskine, and had knowingly entered into an arrangement which
England could not carry out. The same newspapers which in
April agreed with John Randolph that Canning had obtained
through Erskine all he had ever asked or had a right to expect,
averred in October that Erskine surrendered everything and
got nothing in return. No political majority, still less a minority, could survive a somersault so violent as this; and the
Federalists found that all their late recruits, and many friends

[1] Bath Archives, i. 56.

hitherto stanch, deserted them in the autumn elections. Throughout the country the Administration was encouraged by great changes in the popular vote, even before the rupture with Jackson. With confidence, Madison might expect the more important spring elections to sweep opposition from his path. Although a whole year, and in some cases eighteen months, must pass before a new Congress could be chosen, the people were already near the war point.

Vermont chose a Republican governor and a legislature Republican in both branches. In Rhode Island, Connecticut, and New Jersey the Administration recovered more than the ground lost by the embargo. In Maryland the feud between Samuel Smith and his opponents was ended by a Republican majority so large that nothing could prevent Smith's return to the Senate, although every one knew that he would carry on a system of personal opposition, if he dared, and that a moderate Federalist would be less dangerous to the Administration. In the general return of deserters to the ranks, the party would not be too strict in its punishments; and the President set the example by clemency to the worst offender, except John Randolph, of all the trusted lieutenants in the party service. He held out a hand to Monroe.

Madison's reasons for winning Monroe were strong. The more he had to do with Robert Smith, the more intolerable became the incubus of Smith's incompetence. He had been obliged to take the negotiations with Erskine and Jackson wholly on his own shoulders. The papers drafted by Smith were, as Madison declared,[1] brought from the Department of State in a condition "almost always so crude and inadequate that I was, in the more important cases, generally obliged to write them anew myself, under the disadvantage sometimes of retaining through delicacy some mixture of his draft." Smith had not even the virtue of dulness. He could not be silent, but talked openly, and criticised freely the measures of Government, especially those of commercial restriction.

Complicated with this incessant annoyance was Gallatin's feud. The combination of the Smiths with Giles, Leib, and Duane's "Aurora" against Gallatin had its counterpart in the

[1] Works, ii. 499.

Clintonian faction which made Madison its target; and whenever these two forces acted together, they made, with the Federalists, a majority of the Senate. Gallatin saw the necessity of breaking down this combination of intrigue which had already done incalculable harm by forcing Robert Smith into the State Department. He foresaw the effects of its influence in weakening the Treasury in order to expel himself. On a visit to Monticello in August he spoke plainly to Jefferson and Madison, and pointed out the probability that he should be forced to resign. Jefferson reflected six weeks on this communication, and then wrote entreating him to stand firm.[1] November 8, the day of the rupture with Jackson, Gallatin answered Jefferson's appeal in a long and outspoken letter evidently meant for communication to Madison: —

"It has seemed to me from various circumstances that those who thought they had injured were disposed to destroy, and that they were sufficiently skilful and formidable to effect their object. As I may not, however, perhaps, see their actions with an unprejudiced eye, nothing but irresistible evidence both of the intention and success will make me yield to that consideration. . . . I do not ask that in the present situation of our foreign relations the debt be reduced, but only that it shall not be increased so long as we are not at war. I do not pretend to step out of my own sphere and to control the internal management of other departments; but it seems to me that as Secretary of the Treasury I may ask, that, while peace continues, the aggregate of the expenditure of those departments be kept within bounds such as will preserve the equilibrium between the national revenue and expenditure without recurrence to loans. I cannot consent to act the part of a mere financier, to become a contriver of taxes, a dealer of loans, a seeker of resources for the purpose of supporting useless baubles, of increasing the number of idle and dissipated members of the community, of fattening contractors, pursers, and agents, and of introducing in all its ramifications that system of patronage, corruption, and rottenness which you so justly execrate."

[1] Jefferson to Gallatin, Oct. 11, 1809; Works, v. 477.

From this avowal Madison's difficulties could be understood and his course foreseen. Very slow to move, he was certain at last to quarrel with the senatorial faction that annoyed him. He could not but protect Gallatin, and dismiss Smith. At the end of the vista, however far the distance, stood the inevitable figure of Monroe. Scarcely another man in public life could fill precisely the gap, and none except Armstrong could give strength to the President by joining him. Perhaps Littleton Tazewell, another distinguished Virginian of the same school, would have answered the President's purpose as well as Monroe; but probably Tazewell would have declined to accept a seat in the Cabinet of a President whose election he had opposed.[1] Madison decided to take the first step. He had reason to think that Monroe repented his course, at least to the extent of wishing reconciliation. He authorized Jefferson to act as mediator; and the Ex-President, who spared no effort for harmony, hastened to tell Monroe that the government of Louisiana was still at his disposal.[2] Monroe declined the office as being beneath his previous positions, but said that he would have accepted the first place in Madison's Cabinet, and was sincere in his desire for the success of the Administration; he even pledged his support, and intimated that he had lost favor with John Randolph owing to his exertions for Madison. When Jefferson reported the result of this interview, the President replied:[3] "The state of Colonel Monroe's mind is very nearly what I had supposed; his willingness to have taken a seat in the Cabinet is what I had not supposed." Considering the state of Monroe's mind in 1808, Madison might be excused for failing to see that Monroe would accept the State Department in February, 1809. Indeed, the suddenness of the change would have startled Monroe's best friends; and even in December, 1809, he would have fared ill had his remarks to Jefferson been brought to John Randolph's ears.

Monroe's adhesion having been thus attested, Madison made no immediate use of the recruit, but held him in reserve until events should make action necessary. Perhaps this delay

[1] Grigsby's Tazewell, p. 87.

[2] Jefferson to Madison, Nov. 30, 1809; Works, v. 481. Cf. Monroe to Colonel Taylor, Feb. 25, 1810; Monroe MSS. State Department Archives.

[3] Madison to Jefferson, Dec. 11, 1809; Works, ii. 460.

was one of Madison's constitutional mistakes, and possibly a prompt removal of Robert Smith might have saved some of the worst disasters that befell the Government; but in truth Madison's embarrassments rose from causes that only time could cure, and were inherent in American society itself. A less competent administrative system seldom drifted, by reason of its incompetence, into war with a superior enemy. No department of the government was fit for its necessary work.

Of the State Department, its chief, and its long series of mortifying disasters, enough has been said. In November, 1809, it stood helpless in the face of intolerable insults from all the European belligerents. Neither the diplomatic nor the consular system was better than a makeshift, and precisely where the Government felt most need of ministers,—at Copenhagen, Stockholm, Berlin, and St. Petersburg,—it had no diplomatic and but few consular agents, even these often of foreign allegiance.

The Treasury, hitherto the only successful Executive department, showed signs of impending collapse, not to be avoided without sacrifices and efforts which no one was willing to make. The accounts for the year ending September 30 showed that while the receipts had amounted to $9,300,000, the actual expenses had exceeded $10,600,000. The deficit of $1,300,000, as well as reimbursements of debt to the amount of $6,730,000, had been made good from the balance in the Treasury. The new fiscal year began with a balance of only $5,000,000; so that without a considerable curtailment of expenses, a loan or increased taxation, or both, could not be avoided. Increased taxation was the terror of parties. Curtailment of expense could be effected only on the principle that as the government did nothing well, it might as well do nothing. Any intelligent expenditure, no matter how large or how small, would have returned a thousand-fold interest to the country, whatever had been the financial cost; but the waste of money on gunboats and useless cruisers, or upon an army so badly organized and commanded as to be a hindrance in war, was an expense that might perhaps be curtailed, though only by admitting political incapacity.

Naturally Gallatin threatened to resign. Even by submitting to the Smiths, Duanes, Gileses, and Leibs, and allowing them to cut off the sources or waste the supplies of public revenue until the government became an habitual beggar, he could promise himself no advantage. Never had the chance of finding an end to the public embarrassments seemed so remote. The position in which the government stood could not be maintained, but could be abandoned only by creating still greater difficulties. Intended merely as a makeshift, the Non-intercourse Act of March 1, 1809, had already proved more mischievous to America than to the countries it purported to punish. While the three great commercial nations—France, England, and the United States—were forcing trade into strange channels or trying to dam its course, trade took care of itself in defiance of war and prohibitions. As one coast after another was closed or opened to commerce, countries whose names could hardly be found on the map—Papenburg, Kniphausen, Tönningen—became famous as neutrals, and their flags covered the sea, because England and France found them convenient for purposes of illegitimate trade. The United States had also their Papenburg. Amelia Island and the St. Mary's River, which divided Florida from Georgia, half Spanish and half American waters, became the scene of a trade that New York envied. While the shore was strewn with American cotton and other produce waiting shipment in foreign vessels, scores of British ships were discharging merchandise to be smuggled into the United States, or were taking on board heavy freights of cotton or naval stores on American account. To the United States this manner of trading caused twofold loss. Not only were the goods charged with a double voyage and all the costly incidents of a smuggling business, and not only did the American shipowner lose the freight on this American merchandise, both outward and inward, but the United States government collected no duties on the British goods smuggled from Amelia Island, Bermuda, and Halifax. The Non-intercourse Act prohibited French and British merchandise; but in disregard of the prohibition such goods were freely sold in every shop. Erskine's arrangement, short as it was, brought in a fresh and large supply; custom-house oaths were cheap; custom-house officials did not inquire closely whether cloth was made in England, France, Holland, or Germany, or whether rum, sugar, and coffee came from

St. Kitt's or St. Bart's. Some sorts of English goods, such as low-priced woollens, were necessities; and the most patriotic citizen could hardly pay so much respect to the laws of his country as to dispense with their use by his family, whatever he did on his own account. Finally, a law which in the eyes of a community was not respectable was not respected. The community had no other defence against bad legislation; and in a democracy the spirit of personal freedom deserved cultivation to the full as much as that of respect for bad law. The Non-intercourse Act was not only a bad law,—the result of admitted legislative imbecility,—but it had few or no defenders even among those who obeyed it.

Ingenuity could hardly have invented a system less advantageous for the government and people who maintained it. The government lost its revenue, the shipping lost much of its freight, the people paid double prices on imports and received half-prices for their produce; industry was checked, speculation and fraud were stimulated, while certain portions of the country were grievously wronged. Especially in the Southern States all articles produced for exchange were depressed to the lowest possible value, while all articles imported for consumption were raised to extravagant rates. Elisha Potter, a Congressman from Rhode Island, complained with reason that the system made the rich more rich and the poor more poor.[1] In a crowded or in a highly organized society such a system would probably have created a revolution; but America had not yet reached such a stage of growth or decay, and the worst effect of her legislation was to impoverish the government which adopted and the class of planters who chiefly sustained it.

Gallatin best knew how much the Non-intercourse Act or any other system of commercial restriction weakened the Treasury. He knew that neither the President nor Congress offered the germ of a better plan. He faced an indefinite future of weakness and waste, with a prospect of war at the end; but this was not the worst. His enemies who were disposed to destroy, were skilful enough to invent the means of destruction. They might deprive him of the United States

[1] Annals of Congress, 1809–1810, p. 1263.

Bank, his only efficient ally; they might reject every plan, and let the Treasury slowly sink into ruin; they might force the country into a war for no other object than to gratify their personal jealousies. Gallatin believed them capable of all this, and Madison seemed to share the belief. The Treasury which had till that time sustained the Republican party through all its troubles, stood on the verge of disaster.

From the military and naval departments nothing had ever been expected; but their condition was worse than their own chiefs understood. The machinery of both broke down as Madison took control. The navy consisted of a few cruisers and a large force of gunboats. Neither were of immediate use; but a considerable proportion of both were in active service, if service could be called active which chiefly consisted in lying in harbor or fitting for harbor defence when no enemy was expected. No sooner had Paul Hamilton succeeded Robert Smith at the navy department than the new secretary became aware that his predecessor had wasted a very large sum of money.[1] Hamilton made no concealment of his opinion that gunboats were expensive beyond relation to their value.[2] He intimated that the life of gunboats hardly exceeded one year, and that their value depended on the correct answer to the inquiry whether war was a defensive or aggressive operation. This hint that gunboats could do no harm to their enemies seemed to gain force from the suggestion that they had yet to prove their uses for their friends; but if Jefferson's gunboat system should prove to be a failure, nothing would be left of the navy except a few frigates and sloops which could hardly keep the sea in the event of war with England. The navy was a sink of money.

The army was something worse. At least the navy contained as good officers and seamen as the world could show, and no cruisers of their class were likely to be more efficient than the frigates commanded by Rodgers, Bainbridge, and Decatur, provided they could escape a more numerous enemy; but the army was worthless throughout, and its deficiency in equipment was a trifling evil compared with the

[1] *Infra*, chap. x.

[2] Secretary Hamilton to Joseph Anderson, June 6, 1809; State Papers, Naval Affairs, p. 194.

effects of political influence on its organization. The first attempt to raise the army to efficiency ended in scandalous failure within a few months. Among a thousand obstacles to any satisfactory reform in the military service, the most conspicuous if not the most fatal was General Wilkinson, whom President Jefferson could not and would not sacrifice, but whose character and temper divided the army into two hostile camps. Wade Hampton, the next general officer in rank, regarded Wilkinson with extreme contempt, and most of the younger officers who were not partisans of Jefferson shared Hampton's prejudice; but July 4, 1808, a military court of inquiry formally acquitted Wilkinson of being a Spanish pensioner. President Jefferson had already saved him from court-martial on account of his relations with Burr, and Secretary Dearborn restored him to command over an army whose interests required an officer of other qualities.

When Madison and Gallatin in December, 1808, looked to a declaration of war, their first anxiety concerned New Orleans and West Florida. December 2, 1808, Secretary Dearborn gave Wilkinson, then at Washington, orders to direct the new levies of troops toward New Orleans, and to be ready to take command there in person as soon as practicable. In pursuance of these orders, two thousand raw soldiers were directed upon New Orleans from different quarters, and in the midst of war preparations, Jan. 24, 1809, Wilkinson himself embarked from Baltimore.[1] Stopping at Annapolis, Norfolk, and Charleston, he passed six weeks on the Atlantic coast. After the overthrow of the war policy and the close of the session he sailed March 12 from Charleston, and in his mysterious way stopped at Havana and then at Pensacola, "under a special mission from the Executive of the United States." April 19 he re-entered New Orleans, the scene of his exploits three years before; and he returned as a victor, triumphant over Daniel Clark and the Burr conspirators, as well as over Governor Claiborne, Wade Hampton, and all ill-wishers in the subordinate ranks of the army, of whom Captain Winfield Scott was one.

Wilkinson found at New Orleans, in his own words,[2] —

[1] Wilkinson's Memoirs, ii. 344.
[2] Wilkinson's Memoirs, ii. 346.

"A body of two thousand undisciplined recruits, men and officers with a few exceptions sunk in indolence and dissipation; without subordination, discipline, or police, and nearly one third of them sick; . . . without land or water transport for a single company; medical assistance for two thousand men dependent on two surgeons and two mates, one of the former confined to his bed; a majority of the corps without paymasters; the men deserting by squads; the military agent representing the quartermaster's department without a cent in his chest, his bills protested, and he on the eve of shutting up his office; a great deficiency of camp equipage; not a haversack in store; the medicine and hospital stores scarcely sufficient for a private practitioner."

The General decided that, first of all, the troops must be removed from the city and sent into camp; but rains made encampment impossible until the river should fall, and May 12 nothing had been done excepting to notify the Secretary of War that in the course of the following week the General meant to select an encampment which would be so placed as to meet an attack from every hostile quarter.[1] His decision was made known to the Secretary of War in a letter dated May 29:—

"With the general voice of American and Creole in favor of it, I have selected a piece of ground on the left bank of the Mississippi, below this city about four leagues, which I find perfectly dry at this moment, although the surface of the river, restrained by its dykes, is in general three feet above the level of the country. You will put your finger on the spot, at the head of the English turn, just where the road to the settlements on the Terre aux Boeufs leaves the river."[2]

June 10 the main body of troops moved down the river to the new camp. More than five hundred sick were transported with the rest, suffering chiefly from chronic diarrhœa, bilious or intermittent fevers, and scurvy.

[1] Wilkinson's Memoirs, ii. 351.
[2] Wilkinson's Memoirs, ii. 358.

Secretary Eustis, who in March succeeded Dearborn at the War Department, being an army-surgeon by profession, noticed, before Wilkinson's arrival at New Orleans, the excessive proportion of troops on the sick-list. Quickly taking alarm, he wrote April 30 directing Wilkinson to disregard Dearborn's previous instructions, and after leaving a garrison of old troops at New Orleans, to transport the rest up the river to the high ground in the rear of Fort Adams, or Natchez. The orders were peremptory and pressing.[1]

This letter, dated April 30, should have gone, and was believed to have gone, by the post which left Washington May 6, and reached New Orleans May 25; another post followed a week later, and still another arrived June 8, two days before the troops moved to Terre aux Boeufs. According to Wilkinson the letter did not arrive by any of these mails, but came only by the fourth post, which reached New Orleans June 14, after he and his troops were fixed in camp. The cost of a bad character was felt at such moments. No one believed Wilkinson; his reputation for falsehood warranted suspicion that he had suppressed the orders in the belief that he knew best what the troops required. Such insubordination was no new thing on his part. Instead of expressing regret, he wrote to Eustis that even had he received the orders of April 30 in time, he should still "have not sought the position you recommended," because the labor of ascending the river would have diseased nine tenths of the men, the expense would have exceeded twelve thousand dollars, and the position of Fort Adams was ill-suited for the protection of New Orleans.[2]

On the troops the first effect of their encampment was good; but after the middle of June rains began, generally several showers on the same day, and the camp was deep in mud. The number of sick made proper sanitary care impossible. The police officer's report of July 12[3] gave a revolting picture of the sanitary conditions: "The whole camp abounds with filth and nastiness of almost every kind." The sick-list rose to six hundred and sixty in a force of sixteen hundred and eighty-nine non-commissioned officers and men; in August it

[1] State Papers, Military Affairs, i. 269.
[2] Ibid.
[3] Wilkinson's Memoirs, ii. Appendix cvii.

rose to nine hundred and sixty-three in a total force of fifteen hundred and seventy-four. The camp was a fever hospital, the suffering beyond experience. Food, medicine, shelter, clothing, and care were all wanting either to the sick or to the well:[1] —

> "The sick and the well lived in the same tents; they generally subsisted on the same provisions, were equally exposed to the constant and incessant torrents of rain, to the scorching heat of the sun, and during the night to the attacks of numberless mosquitoes. They manifested the pains and sufferings they experienced by shrieks and groans which during the silence of the night were distinctly to be heard from one end of the line to the other. It is my candid belief the mosquitoes produced more mischief than any other cause. In the night the air was filled with them, and not a man was provided with anything like a bar or net. Thus situated, the sufferings of the unfortunate sick can perhaps better be imagined than described."

Before the army had been a month in camp, the officers petitioned the General for removal. He could not but refuse. He had no means of escape, and to do him justice, he bore with courage the consequences of his own mistake. He did whatever occurred to him to protect his men. Secretary Eustis took the matter less calmly. No sooner did the secretary learn, through Wilkinson's letters written in May, that he seriously meant to encamp the troops at Terre aux Boeufs, than official orders, admitting no discretion, were despatched as early as June 22 from the Department, directing that the whole force should be instantly embarked for Natchez and Fort Adams.

The letter arrived July 19. Wilkinson dared not again disobey, although he might be right in thinking that the risks of removal were greater than those of remaining. Every resource of the army and navy was put at Wilkinson's command, and every man at Terre aux Boeufs was eager to escape; yet week after week passed without movement. The orders which arrived July 19 were not made public till the end of August, and only September 14 was the camp evacuated. The effective

[1] Deposition of John Darrington, Captain Third Infantry; State Papers, Military Affairs, i. 282.

force was then about six hundred men in charge of nine hundred invalids. The strength of all had been reduced, until they were unequal to the fatigues of travel. Only one hundred and twenty-seven men died at Terre aux Boeufs between June 10 and September 14; but two hundred and fifty died on their way up the river, before October 31, and altogether seven hundred and sixty-four, out of two thousand soldiers sent to New Orleans, died within their first year of service. The total loss by death and desertion was nine hundred and thirty-one.

Wilkinson himself was attacked by fever in passing New Orleans, September 19, and on proceeding to Natchez soon received a summons to Washington to answer for his conduct. Brigadier-General Wade Hampton succeeded him in command of what troops were still alive at New Orleans. The misfortune was compensated only by the advantage of affording one more chance to relieve the army and the government of a general who brought nothing but disaster.

With the four departments of Executive government in this state of helplessness, President Madison met Congress, the least efficient body of all.

Chapter IX

THE PRESIDENT's Annual Message, read November 29 before Congress, threw no light on the situation. If Madison's fame as a statesman rested on what he wrote as President, he would be thought not only among the weakest of Executives, but also among the dullest of men, whose liveliest sally of feeling exhausted itself in an epithet, and whose keenest sympathy centred in the tobacco crop; but no statesman suffered more than Madison from the constraints of official dress. The Message of 1809 hinted that England had no right to disavow her minister's engagement, and that Jackson's instructions as well as his conduct betrayed a settled intent to prevent an understanding; but these complaints led to no corrective measures. The President professed himself still willing to listen with ready attention to communications from the British government through any new channel, and he seemed to fall back on Jefferson's "painful alternatives" of the year before, rather than on any settled plan of his own: —

"In the state which has been presented of our affairs with the parties to a disastrous and protracted war, carried on in a mode equally injurious and unjust to the United States as a neutral nation, the wisdom of the national Legislature will be again summoned to the important decision on the alternatives before them. That these will be met in a spirit worthy of the councils of a nation conscious both of its rectitude and of its rights, and careful as well of its honor as of its peace, I have an entire confidence. And that the result will be stamped by a unanimity becoming the occasion, and be supported by every portion of our citizens with a patriotism enlightened and invigorated by experience, ought as little to be doubted."

Such political formulas, conventional as a Chinese compliment, probably had value, since they were current in every government known to man; but that President Madison felt entire confidence in the spirit of the Eleventh Congress could not be wholly believed. John Randolph best described

Madison's paper in a letter to Judge Nicholson, a few days afterward:[1]

"I have glanced over the President's Message, and to say the truth it is more to my taste than Jefferson's productions on the same occasions. There is some cant to be sure; but politicians, priests, and even judges, saving your honor's presence, must cant, 'more or less.'"

Probably the colorless character of the Message was intended to disarm criticism, and to prevent Randolph and the Federalists from rousing again the passions of 1808; but sooner or later some policy must be adopted, and although the Message suggested no opinion as to the proper course, it warned Congress that the crisis was at hand: "The insecurity of our commerce and the consequent diminution of the public revenue will probably produce a deficiency in the receipts of the ensuing year." The moment when a Republican administration should begin to borrow money for ordinary expenses in time of peace would mark a revolution in the public mind.

Upon Gallatin, as usual, the brunt of unpopular responsibility fell. His annual Report, sent to the House December 8, announced that a loan, probably of four million dollars, would be required for the service of 1810; that the Non-intercourse Law, as it stood, was "inefficient and altogether inapplicable to existing circumstances;" and finally that "either the system of restriction, partially abandoned, must be reinstated in all its parts, and with all the provisions necessary for its strict and complete execution, or all the restrictions, so far at least as they affect the commerce and navigation of citizens of the United States, ought to be removed." This subject, said Gallatin, required immediate attention; but in regard to the wider question of war or peace he contented himself with a reference to his two preceding reports.

Congress showed more than usual unwillingness to face its difficulties. The episodes of Erskine and Jackson supplied excuse for long and purposeless debates. In the Senate, December 5, Giles reported from a special committee the draft of a Resolution denouncing Jackson's conduct as indecorous,

[1] Randolph to Nicholson, Dec. 4, 1809; Nicholson MSS.

insolent, affronting, insidious, false, outrageous, and premeditated,—epithets which seemed to make superfluous the approval of Madison's course or the pledge of support with
which the Resolution ended. Giles reviewed the conduct of
Jackson and Canning, entreating the Senate to banish irritation and to restore harmony and mutual good-will, "the most
fervent prayer of one who in the present delicate, interesting
crisis of the nation feels a devotion for his country beyond
everything else on this side of heaven."[1] The experience of
many years warranted Giles's hearers in suspecting that when
he professed a wish for harmony, the hope of harmony must
be desperate, for his genius lay in quite another direction; and
when he laid aside partisanship, his party had reason to look
for some motive still narrower. His course quickly proved the
sense in which he understood these phrases.

January 3, 1810, the President recommended by message the
enlistment for a short period of a volunteer force of twenty
thousand men, and a reorganization of the militia; adding
that it would rest with Congress also "to determine how far
further provision may be expedient for putting into actual service, if necessary, any part of the naval armament not now
employed." No one knew what this language meant. Crawford of Georgia, with his usual bluntness, said:[2] "This Message, in point of obscurity, comes nearer my ideas of a
Delphic oracle than any state paper which has come under
my inspection. It is so cautiously expressed that every man
puts what construction on it he pleases." Giles pleased to put
upon it a warlike construction. January 10 he reported a bill
for fitting out the frigates; January 13 he supported this bill in
a speech which surprised Federalists and Republicans alike, if
they could be still surprised at the varieties of Giles's political
philosophy.

"The visionary theory of energy," said he, " was the fatal
error of the Federal party, and that error deprived it of the
power of the nation. The government being thus placed in
the hands of the Republicans, while heated by the zeal of
opposition to the Federal doctrines and flushed with their

[1] Annals of Congress, 1809–1810, p. 509.
[2] Annals of Congress, 1809–1810, p. 544.

recent triumph, it was natural for them, with the best intentions, to run into the opposite extreme; to go too far in
the relaxations of the powers of the government, and to
indulge themselves in the delightful visions of extending
the range of individual liberty. . . . It was natural that in
the vibration of the political pendulum, it should go from
one extreme to another; and that this has been too much
the case with the Republican administration, he regretted
to say, he feared would be demonstrated by a very superficial review of the events of the last two or three years."

Energy was a fatal mistake in the Federalists; relaxation was
an equally fatal mistake in the Republicans,—and the remedy
was a show of energy where energy did not exist. Giles won
no confidence by thus trimming between party principles; but
when Samuel Smith argued for Giles's bill on grounds of
economy, friends of the Administration felt little doubt of the
motives that guided both senators. Had they declared for
war, or for peace; had they proposed to build more frigates
or ships-of-the-line, or to lay up those in active service,—had
they committed themselves to a decided policy of any kind,
their motives would have offered some explanation consistent
with a public interest; but they proposed merely to fit out the
frigates while giving them nothing to do, and the Republican
party, as a whole, drew the inference that they wished to
waste the public money, either for the personal motive of
driving Madison and Gallatin from office, or for the public
advantage of aiding the Federalists to weaken the Treasury
and paralyze the nation.

Crawford replied to Giles with some asperity; but although
Crawford was known to represent the Treasury, so completely
had the Senate fallen under the control of the various cabals
represented by Vice-President Clinton, Giles, Smith, and Michael Leib of Pennsylvania, with their Federalist associates,
that Crawford found himself almost alone. Twenty-five senators supported the bill; only six voted against it.

Giles impressed the least agreeable qualities of his peculiar
character on this Senate,—a body of men easily impressed by
such traits. By a vote of twenty-four to four, they passed the
Resolution in which Giles showed energy in throwing epi-

thets at the British government, as they passed the bill for employing frigates to pretend energy that was not in their intentions. No episode in the national history was less encouraging than the conduct of Congress in regard to Giles's Resolution. From December 18 to January 4, the House wasted its time and strength in proving the helplessness of Executive, Congress, parties, and people in the grasp of Europe. With painful iteration every Republican proved that the nation had been insulted by the British minister; while every Federalist protested his inability to discern the insult, and his conviction that no insult was intended. Except as preliminary to measures of force, Giles's Resolution showed neither dignity nor object; yet the Republicans embarrassed themselves with denials of the Federalist charge that such language toward a foreign government must have a warlike motive, while the Federalists insisted that their interests required peace.

If the Resolution[1] was correct in affirming as it did that the United States had suffered "outrageous and premeditated insults" from Jackson, Congress could not improve the situation by affirming the insult without showing even the wish to resent it by means that would prevent its repetition; but the majority saw the matter in another light, and when the Federalists resorted to technical delays, the Republicans after a session of nineteen hours passed the Resolution by a vote of seventy-two to forty-one. Macon, Stanford, and the old Republicans voted with the Federalists in the minority, while Randolph was ill and absent throughout the debate.

The Resolution marked the highest energy reached by the Eleventh Congress. Giles's bill for fitting out the frigates was allowed to slumber in committee; and a bill for taking forty thousand volunteers for one year into government service never came to a vote in the Senate. Congress was influenced by news from England to lay aside measures mischievous except as a prelude to hostilities. The change of Administration in London opened the way to new negotiations, and every fresh negotiation consumed a fresh year.

No course would have pleased Congress so much as to do

[1] Resolution approved Jan. 12, 1810; Annals of Congress, 1809–1810, p. 2590.

nothing at all; but this wish could not be fully gratified. The Non-intercourse Act of March 1, 1809, was to expire by limitation with the actual session. As early as December 1 the House referred the matter to a committee with Macon for its head. Macon probably went to the Treasury for instructions. A plan drawn by Gallatin, and accepted without opposition by the Cabinet, was reported December 19 to the House in the form of a bill which had less the character of a Non-intercourse than of a Navigation Act; for while it closed American ports to every British or French vessel public and private, it admitted British and French merchandise when imported directly from their place of origin in vessels wholly American. The measure was as mild a protest as human skill could devise if compared with the outrages it retaliated, but it had the merit of striking at the British shipping interest which was chiefly to blame for the conduct of the British government. Under the provisions of the bill, American shipping would gain a monopoly of American trade. Not a British vessel of any kind could enter an American port.

Macon's bill came before the House Jan. 8, 1810, for discussion, which lasted three weeks. The opposition objected to the new policy for the double reason that it was too strong and too weak. St. Loe Livermore, a Massachusetts Federalist, began by treating the measure as so extreme that England and France would resent it by shutting their ports to all American ships; while Sawyer of North Carolina denounced it as evaporating the national spirit in mere commercial regulations, when no measure short of war would meet the evil. According as commerce or passion weighed with the reasoners, the bill was too violent or disgracefully feeble. Throughout the winter, these contradictory arguments were pressed in alternation by speaker after speaker. Macon reflected only the views of Madison and Gallatin when he replied that if England and France should retaliate by excluding American shipping from their ports, they would do what America wanted; for they must then enforce the non-intercourse which the United States had found impossible to enforce without their aid. He agreed with the war-members that the bill showed none too much energy, but he argued that the nation was less prepared for war than in 1808 and 1809; while as for Jackson's quarrels, he declined to admit that they changed the affair one iota.

Although the two extremes still stood so far apart that their arguments bore no relation to each other, the violence of temper which marked the embargo dispute, and which was to mark any step toward actual measures of force, did not appear at this session. Indeed, the Federalists themselves were not unanimous; some of the most extreme, like Barent Gardenier and Philip Barton Key, supported Macon's plan, while some of the extremists on the other side, like Troup of Georgia, voted against it. January 29, by a vote of seventy-three to fifty-two, the House passed the bill. The Senate soon afterward took it up; and then, as was to be expected, the factions broke loose. February 21, at the motion of Senator Samuel Smith, by a vote of sixteen to eleven the Senate struck everything from the bill except the enacting clause and the exclusion of belligerent war-vessels from United States' harbors.

An Administration measure could not without rousing angry feelings be so abruptly mutilated by a knot of Administration senators. Samuel Smith's motives, given in his own words, were entitled to proper attention; but President Madison's opinion on the subject, whether correct or mistaken, had even more effect on what was to follow. Madison believed that the rejection of the bill was an intrigue of the Smiths for selfish or personal objects. He recorded the language which he felt himself obliged to use on the subject, twelve months afterward, to Robert Smith's face:[1] —

"For examples in which he had counteracted what he had not himself disapproved in the Cabinet, I referred to the bills called Macon's bills, and the Non-intercourse Bill, on the consultation on which he appeared to concur in their expediency; that he well knew the former, in its outline at least, had originated in the difficulty of finding measures that would prevent what Congress had solemnly protested against,—to wit, a complete submission to the belligerent edicts; that the measure was considered as better than nothing, which seemed to be the alternative, and as part only of whatever else might in the progress of the

[1] Madison's Works, ii. 498.

business be found attainable; and that he neither objected to what was done in the Cabinet (the time and place for the purpose), nor offered anything in the place of it, yet it was well understood that his conversations and conduct out of doors had been entirely of a counteracting nature; that it was generally believed that he was in an unfriendly disposition personally and officially; and that although in conversations with different individuals he might not hold the same unfavorable language, yet with those of a certain temper it was no secret that he was very free in the use of it, and had gone so far as to avow a disapprobation of the whole policy of commercial restrictions from the embargo throughout."

Robert Smith, doubtless believing that all his actions had been above question or reproach, protested warmly against these charges of unfriendliness and intrigue; but Madison, with a feminine faculty for pressing a sensitive point, insinuated that in his opinion both the Smiths were little better than they should be. "With respect to his motives for dissatisfaction I acknowledged that I had been, for the reasons given by him, much puzzled to divine any natural ones without looking deeper into human nature than I was willing to do." The meaning of the innuendo was explained by Joel Barlow the following year in the "National Intelligencer," where he acted as Madison's mouthpiece in defending the Administration from Robert Smith's attacks. One of Smith's complaints rested upon Macon's bill. Barlow asked, "What gives Mr. Smith a right at this day to proclaim himself in opposition to that bill? Was it ever laid before the Cabinet and opinions taken? Did he there oppose it? Did he not rather approve it, and give his vote for every article? Did he ever utter a syllable against it till his more acute brother discovered the commercial bearing that it would have upon the house [of Smith and Buchanan], and concluded that their interest required its rejection?"

Perhaps this explanation, however offensive to the Smiths, injured them less than the other suspicion which had as much vogue as the first,—that their conduct toward Macon's bill was a part of their feud against Gallatin, and proved their determination to oppose everything he suggested. At the moment when Samuel Smith revolted against Macon's measure, Washington was filled with tales of quarrels in the Cabinet. In truth, these reports were greatly exaggerated. Robert Smith had not the capacity to develop or to pursue a difficult line of argument even without opposition. Against Gallatin he could not, and as Madison testified did not, open his mouth, nor did Gallatin or Madison ever complain except of Smith's silence in the Cabinet; but he talked freely in society, and every one heard of battles supposed to be raging. Walter Jones, one of the most respectable Virginia members, wrote to Jefferson, February 19, imploring him to intervene:[1] —

"Before you quitted this place you knew that causes of dissension subsisted in the Executive departments. So ominous an event has not failed to be an object of my continued and anxious attention, and I am now fully persuaded that these unfriendly feelings are fast approaching to a degree of animosity that must end in open rupture, with its very injurious consequences to the Republican cause. . . . This break of harmony in the Executive departments, added to the extreme points of difference in opinion among the majority in Congress in relation to the great questions of peace and war, renders the apathy and inaction of the Republicans here extremely mortifying. I never knew them more disconnected in sentiment and system, as probably may have been made manifest to you by the desultory and inconclusive work of nearly three months. . . . You will recollect that at the close of the last Congress the appearance of umbrage was confined to Mr. Gallatin and Mr. R. Smith; indeed, excepting themselves there were no other secretaries effectively in office. It is now supposed, and I believe with truth, that the former stands alone against the more or less unfriendly dispositions of all the rest. Their *main abettors* of last spring have abated nothing of their strong and indecent zeal."

Upon feelings so irritable and at a moment when schism was imminent, as Walter Jones described, the action of

[1] Walter Jones to Jefferson, Feb. 19, 1810; Jefferson MSS.

Samuel Smith and Michael Leib with six or eight more Republican senators, in emasculating Macon's bill, left small chance of reconciliation. Giles, having declared himself in favor of energy, did not vote at all. The debate being for the most part not reported, the arguments of the dissenting senators have been lost. One speaker alone broke the monotony of the discussion by an address that marked the beginning of an epoch.

Henry Clay had been barely two weeks a senator, when, February 22, he rose to move that the bill as amended by Samuel Smith be recommitted; and this motion he supported by a war speech of no great length, but full of Western patriotism.

> "The conquest of Canada is in your power," he said. "I trust I shall not be deemed presumptuous when I state that I verily believe that the militia of Kentucky are alone competent to place Montreal and Upper Canada at your feet. . . . The withered arm and wrinkled brow of the illustrious founders of our freedom are melancholy indications that they will shortly be removed from us. Their deeds of glory and renown will then be felt only through the cold medium of the historic page; we shall want the presence and living example of a new race of heroes to supply their places, and to animate us to preserve inviolate what they achieved. . . . I call upon the members of this House to maintain its character for vigor. I beseech them not to forfeit the esteem of the country. Will you set the base example to the other House of an ignominious surrender of our rights after they have been reproached for imbecility and you extolled for your energy! But, sir, if we could be so forgetful of ourselves, I trust we shall spare you [Vice-President George Clinton] the disgrace of signing, with those hands so instrumental in the Revolution, a bill abandoning some of the most precious rights which it then secured."

Other members both of the House and of the Senate had made war speeches, and in Clay's harangue no idea could be called original; yet apart from the energy and courage which showed a new and needed habit of command, these sentences of Clay's maiden speech marked the appearance of a school which was for fifty years to express the national ideals of statesmanship, drawing elevation of character from confidence in itself, and from devotion to ideas of nationality and union, which redeemed every mistake committed in their names. In Clay's speech almost for the first time the two rhetorical marks of his generation made their appearance, and during the next half century the Union and the Fathers were rarely omitted from any popular harangue. The ideas became in the end fetiches and phrases; but they were at least more easily understood than the fetiches and phrases of Jeffersonian re-publicanism which preceded them. Federalists used the name of Washington in the same rhetorical manner, but they used it for party purposes to rebuke Washington's successors. The Union and the Fathers belonged to no party, and might be used with equal advantage by orators of every section. Clay enjoyed almost alone for years the advantage of winning popularity by this simple means; but in 1810, at least along the Atlantic coast, such appeals had little popular success. Least of all had they weight in the Senate, which listened unmoved to Clay's oratory, and replied to it immediately on the same day by passing the "ignominious surrender" of national rights by a vote of twenty-six to seven. Giles did not vote. Samuel Smith, Leib, and even Crawford were in the majority.

Macon's bill came back to the House as a law for the exclusion of British and French war-vessels from American harbors. The House resented the treatment, and after another long debate, March 5, refused to concur in the Senate's amendments. By a vote of sixty-seven to forty-seven the bill was sent back to the Senate in its original form. A long wrangle ensued; a committee of conference failed to agree, and March 16 the Senate was obliged to decide whether it would yield to the House, or allow the bill to fail.

On that question Samuel Smith made a speech,[1] which he afterward printed, and which demanded attention because it forced President Madison into a course that exposed him to severe and perhaps deserved criticism. The Senate was equally balanced. Samuel Smith's voice and vote decided the result. His reasons were such as no one could misunderstand.

[1] Annals of Congress, 1809–1810, p. 602.

"I found in it," said he, criticising Macon's bill, "or believed I did, that which would be ruinous to the commerce of the United States, and therefore felt myself bound by the duty I owe to my constituents to remove the veil and leave the measure open to public view. . . . Is there no danger, Mr. President, to be apprehended from the Emperor if the bill should pass with this provision [that any British or French ship hereafter arriving in an American harbor should with its cargo be seized and condemned]? His character for decision is well known. Might we not fear that he would retort our own measure upon us by causing all the property of our merchants now under sequestration (amounting to at least three millions of dollars) to be condemned? . . . But what will England do should this law pass? Will the King and Council retaliate our measure? I confess, Mr. President, that I think they will. . . . What will be the consequence? Ruin to your merchants and destruction to the party which now governs this country. . . . But I have been told that if England should retaliate, her retaliation would operate as a complete nonintercourse between the two countries, and in a way that would be effectual; and that as I had always approved those measures, this view of the subject must meet my approbation,—that it would precisely create that which I have said was a powerful measure against Great Britain: to wit, an embargo. I never will agree, Mr. President, in this side-way to carry into execution a great national measure."

The speech excited surprise that Samuel Smith, a man accounted shrewd, should suppose such arguments to be decent, much less convincing. From Federalists, who conscientiously wished submission to British policy, Smith's reasoning would have seemed natural; but Smith protested against submission, and favored arming merchant-ships and providing them with convoy,—a measure useless except to bring on war in a "side-way." Congress preferred to choose its own time for fighting, and declined listening to Smith's advice, although the Senate sustained him in rejecting Macon's bill. On this occasion Giles appeared, and voted with the Administration; but sixteen senators followed Smith, while only fifteen could be found to act in concert with the House and the Executive.

After the Senate had thus put an end to Macon's bill, the House after much hesitation, March 31, put an end to Smith's bill. After five months of discussion Congress found itself, April 1, where it had been in the previous November.

Rather than resume friendly relations with both belligerents without even expressing a wish for the recovery of national self-respect, the House made one more effort. April 7 Macon reported a new bill, which was naturally nicknamed Macon's bill No. 2. This measure also seems to have had the assent of the Cabinet, but Macon himself neither framed nor favored it. "I am at a loss to guess what we shall do on the subject of foreign relations," he wrote to his friend Judge Nicholson, three days later.[1] "The bill in the enclosed paper, called Macon's No. 2, is not really Macon's, though he reports it as chairman. It is in truth Taylor's. This I only mention to you, because when it comes to be debated I shall not act the part of a father, but of a step-father." The Taylor who took this responsibility was a member from South Carolina, whose career offered no other great distinction than the measure which produced a war with England.

Macon's bill No. 2 was the last of the annual legislative measures taken by Congress to counteract by commercial interest the encroachments of France and Great Britain. The first was the Partial Non-intercourse Act of April, 1806; the second was the Embargo Act with its supplements, dating from Dec. 22, 1807; the third was the Total Non-intercourse Act of March 1, 1809; and the fourth was Macon's bill No. 2. Each year produced a new experiment; but the difference could be easily remembered, for after the climax of the embargo each successive annual enactment showed weakening faith in the policy, until Macon's bill No. 2 marked the last stage toward the admitted failure of commercial restrictions as a substitute for war. Abandoning the pretence of direct resistance to France and England, this measure repealed the Non-intercourse Act of March 1, 1809, leaving commercial relations with all the world as free as ever before, but autho-

[1] Nicholson MSS.

rizing the President "in case either Great Britain or France shall, before the 3d day of March next, so revoke or modify her edicts as that they shall cease to violate the neutral commerce of the United States," to prohibit intercourse with the nation which had not revoked its edicts.

The objections to the bill were overpowering, for its effect was equivalent to alliance with England. Had the United States taken active part in the war against France, they could have done Napoleon no greater injury than by the passage of this Act, which invited Great Britain to control American commerce for her military purposes. On the other hand the bill conferred on the President a discretion dangerous, unconstitutional, and unnecessary,—a power once before conferred by the Non-intercourse Act of March 1, 1809, and then resulting in the mistakes of Erskine's arrangement, which seemed warning enough against repeating the same risk.

These objections were well understood and forcibly pointed out, while the arguments in support of the bill were melancholy in their admissions. The records of Congress could hardly parallel the disregard of dignity with which Taylor defended his bill in a tone that could have been endured only by an assembly lost to the habits of self-respect. His denunciation of war expressed party doctrine, and he harmed no one by repeating the time-worn moral drawn from Greece and Rome, the Persian millions, Philip of Macedon, Syracuse and Carthage,—as though the fate of warlike nations proved that they should have submitted to foreign outrage, or as though the world could show either arts or liberty except such as had sprung from the cradle of war; but feeling perhaps that classical authority proved too little or too much, he told the House frankly why those members who like himself opposed war found themselves unable to maintain the pledge of resistance they had given in imposing the embargo:—

"But concerning the breaking down of the embargo! Let the truth come out! Neither this plea nor the other miserable one of the fear of insurrections, and what not, will do. . . . The embargo repealed itself. The wants created by it to foreigners, and the accidental failure of crops in England had reduced the thing in one article to plain calculation. The vote of this House to repeal the law gave from four to five dollars rise on each barrel of flour. This was the weight that pulled us down."

The admission could not inspire enthusiasm or raise the moral standard of Congress; but the House accepted it, and amended the bill only by adding fifty per cent to the existing duties on all products of Great Britain and France. The amendment was also a business speculation, for it was intended to protect and encourage American manufactures; but it did not come directly from the manufacturers. Richard M. Johnson of Kentucky moved the amendment. "Kentucky, Pennsylvania, New Jersey, and the New England Republicans," wrote Macon,[1] "are full of manufacturing. To these may be added some of the Virginia Republicans. This plan is said to be a Cabinet project; if so, it satisfies me that the Cabinet is hard pushed for a plan."

April 19 the bill passed the House by a vote of sixty-one to forty. The Senate referred it to a select committee with Samuel Smith at its head,—a committee made for Smith to control. As before, he reported the measure with its only effective provision—the additional duty—struck out, and with the addition of a convoy-clause. The Senate, by nineteen votes to eight, sustained Smith; nor did one New England senator, Federalist or Republican, vote for the protection offered by Kentucky and Virginia. The bill went to a third reading by a vote of twenty-one to seven, and April 28, having passed the Senate as Smith reported it without a division, was sent back to the House for concurrence.

Irritated though the House was by the Senate's hostility to every measure which had support from the Treasury or was calculated to give it support, the members were for the most part anxious only to see the session ended. Nó one cared greatly for Macon's bill No. 2 in any shape. The House refused to accept the Senate's amendments, and found itself May 1 within a few hours of adjournment, and within the same time of seeing the Non-intercourse Act expire, without having made provision for the commercial relations that were to follow. Perhaps Congress might have shown wisdom by

[1] Macon to Nicholson, April 21, 1810; Nicholson MSS.

doing nothing; but the instinct to do something was strong, and party feeling mixed with the sense of responsibility. At five o'clock in the afternoon committees of conference were appointed, and at the evening session, Samuel Smith having abandoned his convoy-clause, the House gave up its extra duties and the bill came to its passage. All the Federalists voted against it with Macon, Randolph, and Matthew Lyon,—a minority of twenty-seven. Sixty-four Republicans recorded themselves in its favor, and made the bill a law.

Chapter X

RANDOLPH, WHO had been ill at home during the winter of 1809–1810, appeared in public affairs only after the debates were mostly ended. March 22 he moved a Resolution that the military and naval establishments ought to be reduced. He wished to bring Madison's administration back to the point where Jefferson's administration eight years before had begun; and in truth the country could choose only between the practices of 1801 and those of 1798. Randolph, who shunned no assumption of fact which suited his object, asked the House whether any one "seriously thought of war, or believed it a relation in which we could be placed": —

> "With respect to war we have—thank God!—in the Atlantic a fosse wide and deep enough to keep off any immediate danger to our territory. The belligerents of Europe know as well as we feel that war is out of the question. No, sir! if our preparation was for battle, the State physicians have mistaken the state of the patient. We have been embargoed and non-intercoursed almost into a consumption, and this is not the time for battle."

Randolph easily proved the need of retrenchment. His statements were not to be denied. President Washington, with a gross income of fifty-eight million dollars in eight years, spent eleven millions and a quarter on the army and navy. John Adams in four years spent eighteen millions, and was supposed to have been driven from office for extravagance. President Jefferson in his first four years cut down these expenses to eight million, six hundred thousand dollars; in his second term he raised them again to sixteen millions, or nearly to the point reached by John Adams at a time of actual hostilities with France,—although President Jefferson relied not on armaments, but on peaceable coercion, which cost very large sums besides. At last the country had reached a point where, after refusing either to fight its enemies or resent its injuries, it had begun to run in debt for armaments it would not use. This waste needed to be stopped.

Three fourths of the Republican party and all the Federalists were of the same mind with Randolph,—that an army led by Wilkinson and a navy of gunboats, when the country refused to fight under any provocation, were not worth maintaining; and when Eppes of Virginia, April 14, brought forward the budget for the coming year, he started by assuming that the military and naval expenditure might be reduced three million dollars, which would still leave a deficiency of two millions and a half, and would require an increase of customs-duties. If three millions and a half could be saved, members wanted to know why the whole military and naval expenditure, which had required only six millions in 1809, might not be cut off.

Macon, who supported Randolph with the ardor of 1798, urged nothing less than this sweeping reform.

"If the army were disbanded and the navy sold," he argued,[1] "we should not perhaps want half a million,—not a million and a half, on the outside. That might be obtained by loans payable at short date. . . . You must get clear of the navy-yards; if you do not put them down, unquestionably they will put you down. How is it with the army? Has it been employed to more advantage? Its situation is too melancholy to be spoken of; and if anything could disgust the people of the territory we acquired some years since, it must be the management of that army, for however much they hear of our good government, after such a specimen they must have a despicable opinion of it indeed. . . . I will not raise a tax of a cent to support the present plan. I have no hesitation in saying that I shall feel bound to vote down the additional force of six thousand men whenever the subject shall come before us. I voted for it; but found that then, as now, we talk a great deal about war, and do nothing."

Not a member supported Eppes's motion for increased taxes. Democrats and Federalists, one after another, rose to oppose an increase, and to favor disbanding the additional army.

"I shall certainly vote to reduce the army of the United

[1] Annals of Congress, 1809–1810, p. 1828.

States," said Burwell of Virginia;[1] "and if the House should decide that it will not employ the navy of the United States in the protection of commerce, I shall certainly vote also to reduce the naval establishment. I am perfectly convinced that the circumstances under which I voted for the increase of the army and navy have passed away; and as our revenue has diminished, I shall vote for a reduction of our expenses. . . . So far from considering the country in a deplorable situation, as my colleague (Mr. Randolph) has represented it, I think that in many points of view we have every reason to congratulate ourselves. It is a singular phenomenon to see any nation enjoying peace at this time. This exemption from the general lot claims the gratitude of every man in the country. So far as I am concerned in the affairs of the nation, I have but a single object in view,—namely, to preserve peace; and my votes are predicated on that ground."

The war men voted with the peace men for reasons given by Troup of Georgia:[2] —

"I am as well convinced of the fact as that I am now addressing you, that the people will not consent to pay an additional tax for the support of armies and navies raised to oppose the injurious acts of the belligerents against our rights, after we have abandoned those rights and dishonorably withdrawn from the contest."

After much contradictory talk of this kind, Nelson of Maryland told the House that they were behaving like schoolboys.

"It is a perfect child's game," said he.[3] "At one session we pass a law for raising an army, and go to expense; in another year, instead of raising money to pay the expense by the means in our power, we are to disband the army we have been at so much pains to raise. We shall well deserve the name of children instead of men if we pursue a policy of this kind."

The warning had no perceptible weight with the House,

[1] Annals of Congress, 1809–1810, pp. 1855–1857.
[2] Annals of Congress, 1809–1810, p. 1862.
[3] Annals of Congress, 1809–1810, p. 1864.

where the peace party were in a majority and the war party were in a passion, not with the foreign enemy, but with their neighbors and friends. Richard M. Johnson almost avowed that he should vote for reducing army and navy in order to punish the men who had made them useless: —

"To our humiliation and everlasting degradation we have refused to use the means in our power to induce foreign nations to do us justice. . . . The annals of human nature have not given to the world the sad example of a nation so powerful, so free, so intelligent, so jealous of their rights and at the same time so grossly insulted, so materially injured, under such extraordinary forbearance. . . . We are afraid to trust ourselves, and we pretend that we are afraid to trust the people. My hopes have rested and always will rest upon the people; they constitute my last hope. We may disgrace ourselves, but the people will rise in the majesty of their strength, and the world will be interested in the spectacle."

With the advocates of war in a temper so unmanageable, and the advocates of peace in a majority so decisive, the House showed unanimity by passing in committee, without a dissenting voice, a Resolution that the military and naval establishments ought to be reduced. April 16 this vote was reached in committee; and the next day, by a vote of sixty to thirty-one, the Resolution was formally adopted by the House. Of the minority, two thirds were Northern men and all were Republicans.

In obedience to the order, Randolph promptly reported a bill for reducing the navy.[1] All the gunboats, all but three of the frigates, and all other armed vessels—three only excepted—were to be sold, their officers and crews discharged; the navy-yards, except at Boston, New York, and Norfolk, to be disused, and the marine corps reduced to two companies. A few days later, April 24, Smilie of Pennsylvania reported a bill for a similar reduction of the military establishment to three regiments. These measures seemed to carry out the express will and orders of the House; but no sooner did the

[1] Annals of Congress, 1809–1810, p. 1933.

House go into committee than the members astonished themselves by striking out each section in succession. Gunboats,
frigates, navy-yards, and marines, each managed in turn to
obtain a majority against reduction.

Then Randolph rose,—not in wrath, for he spoke with unusual calm, but with a force which warranted the sway he so
often exercised over men whose minds were habitually in
doubt. He had ever believed, he said, that the people of the
United States were destined to become a great naval power,
but if anything could prevent this result it would be the premature attempts of the last two Administrations to force it. A
naval power necessarily grew out of tonnage and seamen,
but both tonnage and seamen had been systematically discouraged:—

> "It has always been understood, according to my view of
> the subject, that one of the principal uses of a navy was to
> protect commerce; but our political rule for some time past
> has been that of inverse proportion, and we have discov-
> ered that commerce is the natural protector of a navy."

The inconsistency of Jefferson's principles and practice was
a target which could be hit by the most inexperienced marks-
man, but Randolph struck it with something more solid than
an epigram when he discussed its expense.

> "Against the administration of Mr. Adams," he said, "I,
> in common with many others, did and do yet entertain a
> sentiment of hostility, and have repeatedly cried out against
> it for extravagance and for profusion and for waste—wan-
> ton waste—of the public resources. I find, however, upon
> consideration,—whether from the nature of men, or from
> the nature of things, or from whatever other cause,—that
> that Administration, grossly extravagant as I did then and
> still do believe it to have been, if tried by the criterion of
> the succeeding one, was a pattern of retrenchment and
> economy."

In order to prove this charge he attacked Robert Smith's
administration of the navy, asserting that while in 1800 each
seaman cost about four hundred and seventy-two dollars a
year, in 1808 each seaman cost nearly nine hundred dollars a

year; and that the same excess existed in regard to officers, marines, clothing, and provisions:—

"Yes, sir! we have economized until we absolutely have reduced the annual cost of a seaman from $472—as it was under the very wasteful expenditure of Mr. Adams's administration—down to the moderate sum of $887. We have economized until a paltry fleet consisting of vessels built to our hand, to say nothing of those that have been sold, and the warlike stores of which have been retained and preserved,—which fleet was built, equipped, and every cannon and implement of war purchased under the old Administration,—has cost us twelve million dollars, when it cost the preceding Administration but nine millions."

Only one member replied on behalf of the Government to these criticisms. Burwell Bassett of the naval committee ventured somewhat timidly to defend, not so much Robert Smith as Secretary Hamilton, who, he said, had reduced expenses at the navy-yard about one third. Most of the frigates had been so thoroughly repaired as to be more valuable than when first built. In the navy-yard itself everything was in good condition and well conducted. Bassett's testimony hardly met Randolph's charges, but the House sustained him on every point; and Boyd of New Jersey so far forgot the respect due to a former vote, in which the House had resolved by a majority of two to one that the army and navy ought to be reduced, as to say that never since the government was formed had so preposterous a proposition been offered. The end of the session arrived before the discussion ceased.

The same inability to act, even where no apparent obstacle existed, was shown in regard to the United States Bank, whose charter, granted for twenty years by the First Congress in February, 1791, was to expire March 4, 1811. In the days of Federalist sway the Republicans had bitterly opposed the Bank and denied the constitutional power of Congress to grant the charter; but during the eight years of Jefferson's rule the Bank had continued without a question to do the financial work of government, and no other agency existed or could be readily created capable of taking the place of this machine, which, unlike any other in the government, worked excellently well.

If its existence was to be continued, public interest required that the Act should be passed at this session, since the actual charter was to expire in ten months. If a new charter was to be refused, public interest required even more urgently that ample warning of so radical a change should be given, that the Treasury might not be suddenly crippled or general bankruptcy be risked without notice.

No complaint of any kind was at that time made against the Bank; no charge was brought against it of interference in politics, of corrupt influence, or of mismanagement. Gallatin was known to favor it; the President was not hostile, nor was any influence in the government opposed; the Federalists who had created were bound to support it; and except for the principles of some Southern Republicans who regarded functions of government as germs of despotism, every political faction in the country seemed consenting to the charter. January 29 the subject was referred to a special committee. The committee reported a Resolution, and in due course John Taylor of South Carolina brought in a bill, the result of negotiations between the Treasury and the Bank, granting a new charter on condition that the Bank should increase its capital two-and-a-half million dollars, half of which should be paid outright to the government; that, further, the Bank should bind itself to lend the government at three months' notice any amount not exceeding in the whole five million dollars at a rate not exceeding six per cent; that on all government deposits above the sum of three millions, which should remain for one year, the Bank should pay interest at the rate of three per cent; and that the government should have the right at any time to increase the capital stock, and subscribe and own the new stock to a fixed amount. These terms were especially valuable at the moment, because they assisted the Treasury to meet an actual deficit, and provided, as far as human foresight went, for financial dangers that might rise from further foreign troubles. No serious opposition showed itself. April 21 the House, by a majority of seventy-five to thirty-five, voted to accept the price fixed for the charter; but the session closed without further action.

When Congress adjourned, May 2, 1810, the result attained during five months passed in continuous labor amounted to little more than the constitutional necessities of government,—the appropriation bills; a loan for five million dollars; an Act for taking a census of persons; an Act appropriating sixty thousand dollars toward making the Cumberland Road; an appropriation of five thousand dollars for experiments on Fulton's torpedoes; in regard to foreign affairs, Giles's Resolution blaming the conduct of the British minister, and Macon's or Taylor's Act, which condoned that conduct. The old Non-intercourse Act of March 1, 1809, expired by limitation with the expiring Congress May 1, 1810.

"We adjourned last night," wrote Randolph to Nicholson the next day,[1] "a little after twelve, having terminated a session of more than five months by authorizing a loan of as many millions, and—all is told. The incapacity of Government has long ceased to be a laughing matter. The Cabinet is all to pieces, and the two Houses have tumbled about their own ears."

With all Randolph's faults, he had more of the qualities, training, and insight of a statesman than were to be found elsewhere among the representatives in the Eleventh Congress; and although himself largely the cause of the chaos he described, he felt its disgraces and dangers. Society in general troubled itself little about them. The commercial class, pleased to be freed from restraints, and the agricultural class, consoled by the fair prices of their produce, thought as little as possible about their failure in government; what was called good society for the most part drew a bitter pleasure from it. Yet beneath the general physical contentment almost equally general moral disgust existed and made itself felt. President Madison, who was in the best position to gauge popular opinion, began to suspect the hardly perceptible movement of a coming tide. After the adjournment he wrote to William Pinkney at London:[2] —

"Among the inducements to the experiment of an un-

[1] Nicholson MSS.
[2] Madison to Pinkney, May 23, 1810; Works, ii. 474.

restricted commerce now made were two which contributed essentially to the majority of votes in its favor,—first, a general hope, favored by daily accounts from England, that an adjustment of differences there, and thence in France, would render the measure safe and proper; second, a willingness in not a few to teach the advocates for an open trade the folly as well as degradation of their policy. . . . It will not be wonderful, therefore, if the passive spirit which marked the late session of Congress should at the next meeting be roused to the opposite point, more especially as the tone of the nation has never been so low as that of its representatives."

Madison still held to his favorite doctrine, and meant no more by his warning than that the Eleventh Congress might be expected to reimpose measures of commercial restriction:—

"The experiment [of free commerce] about to be made will probably open too late the eyes of the people to the expediency and efficacy of the means [the embargo] which they have suffered to be taken out of the hands of the Government and to be incapacitated for future use."[1]

This condolence with Jefferson over the fate of their experiment showed the direction toward which Madison's eyes were still turned; but, though a firm believer in his own theory of peaceable coercion, he was ready and had always been ready to accept and carry out any stronger scheme that Congress might prefer. He had no definite plan of his own; he clung to the idea that England and France could be brought by patience to respect neutral claims of right; but he felt that the actual submission made by Congress was apparent rather than real, and might be followed within a year by renewed resistance.

Meanwhile nothing could be more dangerous to the Americans than the loss of self-respect. The habit of denouncing themselves as cowards and of hearing themselves denounced as a race that cared only for money tended to produce the qualities imputed. Americans of 1810 were persuaded that they

[1] Madison to Jefferson, April 23, 1810; Works, ii. 472.

could not meet Englishmen or Frenchmen on equal terms, man against man, or stand in battle against the veterans of Napoleon or Nelson. The sense of national and personal inferiority sank astonishingly deep. Reasonable enough as regarded the immense superiority of Europe in organization, it passed bounds when it condemned everything American as contemptible, or when the Federalist gentry refused to admit the Democrats of Pennsylvania or the Republicans of Virginia or the Government at Washington into the circle of civilized life. Social self-abasement never went so far as in its efforts to prove to Francis James Jackson, the British minister, that he was right in treating the national government with contempt. Englishman as Jackson was, and ready to assume without question every claim of superiority that might be made for his country or his class, he was surprised at the force of American allegiance to himself. As he travelled northward, after his dismissal from Washington, his private letters gave a strange idea of the chaos in American society. He wrote from Philadelphia, —

"The tide has turned completely in our favor. At Washington they are in a state of the most animated confusion, the Cabinet divided, and the Democratic party going various ways. . . . Their foreign politics embarrass them even more than home ones. One moment they want another embargo; the next, to take off the restrictions; then, to arm their merchantmen; and next, to declare war. In short, they do not know what to be at. . . . Notwithstanding all that has passed,—which would fill volumes to relate in full,— and the Government being at open war with me, 'the respectability' has been both here and at Baltimore so anxious to show that they did not share the sentiments of the Democrats that we have had throngs of visitors and innumerable invitations that we could not accept, though we have dined at home but twice during the month we have been here. To prevent this, the savages have threatened in one of their papers to tar and feather every man who should ask me to his house."[1]

Pleased with his social success at Baltimore and Phila-

[1] Bath Archives, Second Series, i. 78.

delphia, Jackson found New York and New England fairly delightful. His vogue in Baltimore and Philadelphia meant little
more than curiosity to see his wife and her toilettes; but as he
approached New England he became a personage in politics,
and received attentions such as he could hardly have expected
even from those European courts whose civility lingered in
his mind. February 25 he wrote from New York:[1] —

> "As we get farther north and east, the said Yankees im-
> prove very much. New York is a fine town, unlike any other
> in America, and resembling more the best of our country
> towns, with the additional advantage of the finest water
> that can be imagined. There is as much life and bustle as at
> Liverpool or any other of our great commercial towns; and
> like them New York has inhabitants who have made and
> are making rapid and brilliant fortunes by their enterprise
> and industry. . . . We have met with unbounded civility
> and good-will, and may be said to live here in triumph. We
> are now engaged to dinner every day but two, till the end
> of the first week in March. . . . The governor of Massa-
> chusetts has written to me to invite me to Boston, where,
> he says, he and many others will be happy to receive me.
> That State, which is one of the most populous and enlight-
> ened of the States of the Union, and, as you know, is the
> birthplace of American independence, has done more to-
> ward justifying me to the world than it was possible from
> the nature of things that I or any other person could do in
> the present stage of the business. The legislature, which is
> not a mob like many that have passed resolutions, has
> agreed to a report of a joint committee, and passed resolu-
> tions in conformity with it, exculpating me altogether, and
> in the most direct manner censuring the conduct of the
> President and of the general government."

Boston newspapers of Feb. 9, 1810, contained the report
and resolutions in which the Massachusetts legislature, by a
vote of two hundred and fifty-four to one hundred and forty-
five, declared that "they can perceive no just or adequate
cause" for breaking relations with the British minister, F. J.

[1] Bath Archives, Second Series, i. 82.

Jackson; and this challenge to their own Government, backed by Governor Gore's invitation of Jackson to Boston, was intended to carry political weight, even to the extent of forcing Madison to renew political relations, as he had been forced to resume commercial relations, with England. Had public opinion taken the intended course, Jackson's visit to Boston would have marked a demonstration of popular feeling against the national government; nor were the Federalists in any way parties consenting to the defeat of the scheme. The measures adopted by the Massachusetts legislature in February came before the people at the State election early in April, only six weeks after the General Court and Governor Gore had condemned Madison. More than ninety thousand votes were cast, and the Republican party, by a majority of about two thousand, not only turned Governor Gore out of office, but also chose a General Court with a Republican majority of twenty. At the same time similar changes of public opinion restored New Hampshire to Republican control, and strengthened the Republicans in New York and the Middle States. Not a doubt could exist that the country sustained Madison, and that Jackson was not only an object of decided unpopularity in America, but was far from being favored in England. The advantage to be derived from his visit to Boston was no longer evident, and after Governor Gore ceased to hold office, the good taste of acting on an invitation thus practically withdrawn seemed doubtful; but Jackson was not daunted by doubts.

Holding the promise of his Government that his mission should last at least a year, Jackson beguiled the interval by such amusements as offered themselves. In May he retired to a country-house on the North River, about eight miles above New York, where he caught a glimpse of an American invention which, as he had the good sense to suspect, was more important than all the diplomatic quarrels in which he had ever engaged:—

"One of the curiosities that we daily see pass under our windows is the steamboat,—a passage-vessel with accommodation for near a hundred persons. It is moved by a steam-engine turning a wheel on either side of it, which acts like the main wheel of a mill, and propels the vessel against wind and tide at the rate of four miles an hour. As soon as it comes in sight there is a general rush of our household to watch and wonder till it disappears. They don't at all know what to make of the unnatural monster that goes steadily careering on, with the wind directly in its teeth as often as not. I doubt that I should be obeyed were I to desire any one of them to take a passage in her."[1]

After thus entertaining himself on the Hudson, the British minister made his triumphal trip to Boston early in June, where he found a gratifying welcome from society if not from the governor and legislature: —

"At Boston, 'the headquarters of good principles,' we were feasted most famously, and I made there many interesting acquaintances. After living nine days in clover at about eighteen of the principal houses, — having never less than two engagements per day, — they gave me on the 10th a public dinner, at which near three hundred persons were present, and where we had toasts and cheering and singing in the best style of Bishopsgate Street or Merchant Taylor's Hall. A party of gentlemen met me at the last stage on entering Boston, and accompanied me to the first on my departure. At another public dinner I was invited to on the 4th of June (the Ancient and Honorable Artillery election dinner), and at which the governor, who is a Democrat, was present, the clergy, the magistrates, the heads of the University of Cambridge, and the military came to the top of the room in their respective bodies to be introduced to and to compliment me. There is at Washington in consequence much ' wailing and gnashing of teeth.' "

At the public dinner given to Jackson June 11, after the guest of the evening had retired, Senator Pickering gave a toast which became a party cry: "The world's last hope, — Britain's fast-anchored isle!"[2]

From the moment the State officials withdrew from the reception, little importance attached to the private acts of a

[1] Bath Archives, Second Series, i. 118.
[2] Upham's Life of Pickering, iv. 172.

society which might easily look with interest at the rare appearance of a British minister in Boston; but the political and social feeling was the same as though Governor Gore were still in power, and created natural disgust among Republicans, who believed that their Federalist opponents aimed at a dissolution of the Union and at a retreat within the protection of Great Britain. If such ideas existed, they showed themselves to Jackson in no recorded form. His visit to Boston was a social amusement; and he regarded it, like the conduct of Congress, as a triumph to himself only because it increased the mortifications of President Madison, which counterbalanced in some degree his own want of energetic support from Canning's successor at the Foreign Office.

The history of Jackson and his mission did not quite end with his departure from Boston in June, 1810, under escort of a mounted procession of Boston Federalists. He thence went to Niagara,—a difficult journey; and descending to Montreal and Quebec, returned to Albany, where he had the unusual experience of seeing himself burned in effigy.

During all these wanderings he was a victim to the constant annoyance of being able to quarrel neither with President Madison nor with his new official chief, who showed a wish to quarrel as little as possible. Jackson was as willing to find fault with one Government as with the other.

"I look forward with full confidence," he wrote to his brother,[1] "for a full approbation of what I have done. Ministers cannot disapprove of though they may be sorry for it; and if they are sorry, it must be for the trouble it occasions them, for as I have told them there is no loss of any adjustment of difficulties, that being impracticable with this country upon the principles of my instructions. I hope they are adopting the line that I recommended to them,—that of procrastinating any decision whatever; but they might as well have told me so for my own guidance and information, instead of leaving me a prey to all the lies and misrepresentations which the Democrats have found it necessary to propagate on the subject for election purposes. It would be an absolute disgrace to the country, and would produce

[1] Bath Archives, Second Series, i. 109.

an impression never to be got over here,—the ill effects of which in all future transactions we should not fail to be made sensible of,—if another minister were to be sent out without some sort of satisfaction being taken or received for the treatment I have experienced. They ought to insist on my being reinstated."

The British government held a different opinion; and accordingly, at the expiration of his stipulated twelve months, Sept. 16, 1810, Jackson set sail for Europe, leaving J. P. Morier in charge of the British legation at Washington.

Chapter XI

IF THE NON-INTERCOURSE ACT of March 1, 1809, irritated Napoleon, Macon's Act of May 1, 1810, might be expected to work in a manner still more active.

The story has shown that Napoleon, toward the end of the year 1809, felt many difficulties in giving new shape to his American policy after it had been ruined by the Non-intercourse Act. His fixed idea required the seizure of every American ship in Europe beyond the borders of France, as he had for years seized American ships in his own ports. In part this wish sprang from the Continental system, and was excused to some extent by the plea that American commerce could be carried on only under British protection; in part the seizure of American ships was a punishment for defying the Emperor's orders; and in part it was due to his necessities of finance.

December 19, 1809, Napoleon wrote a brief order to Berthier, ordering the seizure of all American vessels in the Spanish ports within his control;[1] vessels and cargoes, he said, were to be considered good prize. Having taken this measure, he called a council of ministers for the next day, and ordered Maret to bring there "everything relating to the judgments of the prize-court; to the merchandise sequestered in the ports, which is spoiling. If you have not all the information, ask the Minister of Finance."[2]

The meaning of this preparation was to be sought in the Cabinet itself, and in the Emperor's surroundings. Peace with Austria left many vexations in Napoleon's path. Perhaps the unhappy situation of his brother Joseph at Madrid troubled him less than the difficulty of reconciling the Empress Josephine to a divorce, or the mortifications of negotiating for a wife among Russian, German, and Austrian princesses; but annoyances like these, though serious for ordinary men, could not be compared with the constant trouble created by the Continental system of commercial restrictions and the want of money it caused. Threatened with financial difficulties, and

[1] Napoleon to the Prince of Neuchatel, Dec. 19, 1809; Correspondance, xx. 78.

[2] Napoleon to Maret, Dec. 19, 1809; Correspondance, xx. 77.

obliged to study economies as well as to press contributions of war, the Emperor found himself met by something resembling opposition among his own ministers. As was his habit, he yielded at first to the advice he disliked, and promised to do something for French industry. In November he appointed a new Minister of the Interior, Montalivet, and lectured him on the slowness of his bureaus in acting for the good of commerce.[1] From such a mouth such a lesson startled the hearer, and Montalivet threw himself with zeal into the prescribed work. To Fouché the Emperor read another lecture compared with which the discourse to Montalivet was commonplace. Fouché, a pronounced opponent of Napoleon's commercial restrictions, during the Emperor's absence in Austria distributed too freely his licenses for foreign trade: "I recognize always the same course in your acts," Napoleon wrote him. "You have not enough legality in your head."[2]

While thus teaching one minister to cherish commerce, and another to respect legality, the Emperor listened to Champagny, who lost no chance of advising the encouragement of neutral trade; and these three ministers—Champagny, Fouché, and Montalivet—found a strong ally in the Minister of the Treasury, Mollien, who has left the recorded opinion that the Imperial system of commercial restriction was "the most disastrous and the most false of fiscal inventions."[3] The bias of Decrès, the Minister of Marine, may be inferred from a story told by Marshal Marmont,[4] who, coming to Paris at the close of 1809, called on his old friend and talked with the enthusiasm of a successful soldier about the Emperor. "Well, Marmont," replied Decrès, "you are pleased at being made a marshal; you see everything in bright colors. Do you want me to tell you the truth and to unveil the future? The Emperor is mad—absolutely mad! He will upset us all, and everything will end in a terrible disaster." Taken in connection with King Louis' attitude in Holland, the Cabinet opposition of December, 1809, amounted to rebellion against Napoleon's authority.

[1] Note pour le Comte de Montalivet, 16 Nov. 1809; Correspondance, xx. 35.
[2] Napoleon to Fouché, Sept. 29, 1809; Correspondance, xix. 535.
[3] Mémoires, iii. 134.
[4] Mémoires de Marmont, iii. 336.

At the Cabinet council of December 20 Montalivet made a written report on the subject of American cotton, which threw so much blame on the Imperial policy as to call a written contradiction from Napoleon. "An American vessel," the Emperor replied the next day,[1] "coming from Louisiana to France will be well received here, no act of the government forbidding the admission of American ships into French ports." The Americans, he explained, had prohibited commerce with France while permitting it with Holland, Spain, and Naples; and in consequence "his Majesty has used his right of influence over his neighbors because he was unwilling that they should be treated differently from France, and he has sequestered the ships destined for their ports;" but no such provision had been made against American ships entering French ports.

Naturally piqued at an Imperial assertion that he had shown ignorance of facts that deeply concerned his department, Montalivet sent to the Treasury for information, with which, a few days afterward, he routed the Emperor from the field. Unable to answer him, Napoleon referred his report to Gaudin, Minister of Finance, with a curious marginal note, which showed—what his ministers evidently believed—that the Emperor understood neither the workings of his own system nor the laws of the United States:—

"Referred to the Minister of Finance to make me a report on this question: (1) How is it conceivable that American ships come from America in spite of the embargo? (2) How distinguish between ships coming from America and those coming from London?"

Armstrong obtained immediate and accurate knowledge of this struggle in council. Only a week after the Emperor wrote his note on the margin of Montalivet's report, Armstrong sent home a despatch on the subject:[2]—

"The veil which for some weeks past has covered the proceedings of the Cabinet with regard to neutral com-

[1] Note pour le Ministre de l'Intérieur, 21 Dec. 1809; Correspondance, xx. 81.

[2] Armstrong to R. Smith, Jan. 6, 1810; MSS. State Department Archives.

merce is now so far withdrawn as to enable us to see with sufficient distinctness both the actors and the acting. The Ministers of Police and of the Interior (Fouché and Montalivet) have come out openly and vigorously against the present anti-commercial system, and have denounced it as 'one originating in error and productive only of evil, and particularly calculated to impoverish France and enrich her enemy.' While they have held this language in the Cabinet they have held one of nearly the same tenor out of it, and have added (we may suppose on sufficient authority) the most solemn assurances that the Emperor 'never meant to do more than to prevent the commerce of the United States from becoming *tributary* to Great Britain; that a new decision would soon be taken by him on this subject, and that from this the happiest results were to be expected.' "

As though to prevent President Madison from showing undue elation at this announcement for the fiftieth time that the happiest results were to be expected from the future, Armstrong wrote another letter, four days afterward,[1] on the new confiscations and their cause. Frenchmen he said would reason thus: "There is a deficit of fifty millions in the receipts of last year. This must be supplied. Why not then put our hands into the pockets of your citizens once more, since, as you continue to be embroiled with Great Britain, we may do it with impunity." Armstrong was angry, and could not analyze to the bottom the Emperor's methods or motives. Thiers, in later years having the advantage of studying Napoleon's papers, understood better the nature of his genius. "To admit false neutrals in order to confiscate them afterward, greatly pleased his astute (*rusé*) mind," wrote the French historian and statesman,[2] "little scrupulous in the choice of means, especially in regard to shameless smugglers who violated at once the laws of their own country and those of the country that consented to admit them." This description could not properly be applied to Americans, since they violated neither their own law nor that of France by coming to Amsterdam,

---

[1] Armstrong to R. Smith, Jan. 10, 1810; MSS. State Department Archives. Cf. Thiers' Empire, xii. 45.

[2] Thiers, xii. 48, 49.

San Sebastian, and Naples; but Thiers explained that the Emperor considered all Americans as smugglers, and that he wrote to the Prussian government: "Let the American ships enter your ports! Seize them afterward. You shall deliver the cargoes to me, and I will take them in part payment of the Prussian war-debt."[1]

Meanwhile the confiscation of American ships helped in no way the objects promised by Napoleon to Montalivet and Fouché. At a loss to invent a theory on which neutrals could be at the same time plundered and encouraged, the Emperor referred the subject to Champagny, January 10, in an interesting letter.[2] He called for a complete history of his relations with the United States since the treaty of Morfontaine. He ordered the recall of Turreau, in whom he said he had little confidence, and who should be replaced by a more adroit agent: —

"Have several conferences, if necessary, with the American minister as well as with the Secretary of Legation who has just come from London; in short, let me know your opinion on the measures proper to be taken to get out of the position we are in (*pour sortir de la position où nous nous trouvons*).

"All the measures I have taken, as I have said several times, are only measures of reprisal. . . . It was only to the new extension given to the right of blockade that I opposed the Decree of Berlin; and even the Decree of Berlin ought to be considered as a Continental, not as a maritime blockade, for it has been carried out in that form. I regard it, in some sort, only as a protest, and a violence opposed to a violence. . . . Down to this point there was little harm. Neutrals still entered our ports; but the British Orders in Council necessitated my Milan Decree, and from that time there were no neutrals. . . . I am now assured that the English have given way; that they no longer levy taxes on ships. Let me know if there is an authentic act which announces it, and if there is none, let me know if the fact is true; for once I shall be assured that a tax on

[1] Thiers, xii. 50.
[2] Napoleon to Champagny, Jan. 10, 1810; Correspondance, xx. 109.

navigation will not be established by England, I shall be able to give way on many points."

All Napoleon's ministers must have known that these assertions of his commercial policy were invented for a momentary purpose. He had himself often declared, and caused them to declare, that his Continental system, established by the Berlin Decree and enforced before the Orders in Council were issued, had a broad military purpose quite independent of retaliation,—that it was aimed at the destruction of England's commerce and resources. As for his profession of ignorance that England had abandoned her transit duties on neutral merchandise, every minister was equally well aware that only six months before, the Emperor had discussed with them the measures to be taken in consequence of that abandonment; had sent them the draft of a new decree founded upon it, and had finally decided to do nothing only because England had again quarrelled with America over Erskine's arrangement. The pretexts alleged by Napoleon were such as his ministers could not have believed; but they were satisfied to obtain on any grounds the concessions they desired, and Champagny—or as he was thenceforward called, the Duc de Cadore—sent to Armstrong for the information the Emperor professed to want.

January 18, M. Petry, at the order of Cadore, called on the American minister, and requested from him a written memorandum expressing the demands of his Government. Armstrong drew up a short minute of the provisions to be made the material of a treaty.[1] The first Article required the restoration of sequestered property; the next stipulated that any ship which had paid tribute to a foreign Power should be liable to confiscation, but that with this exception commerce should be free. Cadore sent this paper to the Emperor, and within a few hours received a characteristic reply.

"You must see the American minister," wrote Napoleon.[2] "It is quite too ridiculous (*par trop ridicule*) that he should write things that no one can comprehend. I prefer him to write in English, but fully and in a manner that we

[1] Armstrong to R. Smith, Jan. 28, 1810; Document G. MSS. State Department Archives.
[2] Napoleon to Champagny, Jan. 19, 1810; Correspondance, xx. 132.

can understand. [It is absurd] that in affairs so important he should content himself with writing letters of four lines. . . . Send by special courier a cipher despatch to America to let it be understood that that government is not represented here; that its minister does not know French; is a morose man with whom one cannot treat; that all obstacles would be raised if they had here an envoy to be talked with. Write in detail on this point."

Petry returned to Armstrong with the condemned paper, and received another, somewhat more elaborate, but hardly more agreeable to the Emperor. January 25, Cadore himself sent for the American minister, and discussed the subject. The Emperor, he said, would not commit himself to the admission of colonial produce; he wished to restrict American commerce to articles the growth or manufacture of the two countries; he would not permit his neighbors to carry on a commerce with America which he denied to himself; but the "only condition required for the revocation by his Majesty of the Decree of Berlin will be a previous revocation by the British government of her blockade of France, or part of France (such as the coast from the Elbe to Brest, etc.), of a date anterior to that of the aforesaid decree; and if the British government would then recall the Orders in Council which had occasioned the Decree of Milan, that decree should also be annulled." This pledge purported to come directly from the Emperor, and at Armstrong's request was repeated in the Emperor's exact words.[1]

Neither the Minister of the Interior, the Minister of the Treasury, nor the Emperor in these discussions alluded to the proposed Decree of Vienna, the draft of which was sent to Paris in August, confiscating all American ships in reprisal for the seizures of French ships threatened by the Non-intercourse Act. Although that decree was the point which the Emperor meant to reach, not until January 25—when Champagny, after dismissing Armstrong, reported the interview to Napoleon, bringing with him at the Emperor's request the text of the Non-intercourse Act—did the Emperor at last revert to the ideas of the Vienna Decree. The long hesitation

[1] Note pour le Général Armstrong, 25 Jan., 1810. Correspondance, xx. 141.

proved how little satisfactory the plea of retaliation was; but no other excuse could be devised for a measure which Napoleon insisted upon carrying out, and which Champagny had no choice but to execute. The Emperor dictated the draft of a note,[1] in which the principles of confiscation were to be laid down: —

"If American ships have been sequestered in France, France only imitates the example given her by the American government; and the undersigned recalls to Mr. Armstrong the Act of Congress of March 1, 1809, which orders in certain cases the sequestration and confiscation of French ships, excludes them from American ports, and interdicts France to the Americans. It is in reprisal of this last provision that the American ships have been seized in Spain and Naples. The league against England, which has the cause of neutrals for its object, embraces now all the Continental peoples, and permits none of them to enjoy commercial advantages of which France is deprived. France will permit it in no place where her influence extends; but she is ready to grant every favor to the ships of a neutral Power which shall not have subjected themselves to a tribute, and shall recognize only the laws of their own country, not those of a foreign government. . . . If the Minister of the United States has the power to conclude a convention proper to attain the object indicated, the undersigned is ordered to give all his care to it, and to occupy himself upon it without interruption."

Perhaps this was the only occasion in Napoleon's life when he stood between a nation willing to be robbed and a consciousness that to rob it was a blunder. The draft of his note showed his embarrassment. Remarkable in many ways, it required special notice in two points. The proposed Vienna Decree confiscated American ships because French ships were forbidden under threat of confiscation to enter American ports. The note of January 25 suggested a variation from this idea. American ships were to be confiscated everywhere except in France, because they were forbidden to enter France.

[1] Projet de Note, Jan. 25, 1810; Correspondance, xx. 141.

As they were also confiscated in France because they were
forbidden to leave America, the Emperor had nothing more
to demand. His reasoning was as convincing as a million bayonets could make it; but perhaps it was less Napoleonic than
the avowal that for six months the Emperor had been engaged in inveigling American property into neutral ports in
order that he might seize it.

Apparently Cadore still raised obstacles to the Emperor's
will. For some three weeks he held this note back, and when
at last, February 14, he sent it to Armstrong, he made changes
which were not all improvements in the Emperor's text. Indeed, Napoleon might reasonably have found as much fault
with Champagny as he found with some of his generals, for
failing to carry out the orders he dictated: —

> "His Majesty could place no reliance on the proceedings
> of the United States, who, having no ground of complaint
> against France, comprised her in their acts of exclusion, and
> since the month of May have forbidden the entrance of
> their ports to French vessels, under the penalty of confis-
> cation. As soon as his Majesty was informed of this mea-
> sure, he considered himself bound to order reprisals on
> American vessels, not only in his territory, but likewise in
> the countries which are under his influence. In the ports of
> Holland, of Spain, of Italy, and of Naples, American vessels
> have been seized because the Americans have seized French
> vessels."

After such long discussions and so many experiments, Napoleon had become reckless of appearances when he allowed
his foreign secretary to send this note of Feb. 14, 1810, in
which every line was a misstatement, and every misstatement,
as far as concerned America, was evident in its purpose; while
apart from these faults, the note erred in trying to cover too
much ground of complaint against the United States. Napoleon had, in the projected Decree of Vienna, ordered retaliation everywhere for the confiscation threatened by the Non-
intercourse Act. Made to feel the impossibility of this course,
he changed his ground, continuing to confiscate American
ships in France under the old Bayonne Decree, and ordering
the sequestration of American ships throughout the rest of

Europe on the plea that other countries must not enjoy a commerce interdicted to France. Cadore's note abandoned this ground again, in order to return to the doctrine of the projected Vienna Decree; and in the effort to give it a color of reason, he asserted that the Americans had seized French vessels.

Such a letter was a declaration of war six months after beginning hostilities; and it made no offer of peace except on condition that the United States should pledge themselves to resist every British blockade which was not real in the sense defined by Napoleon. Armstrong wrote to his Government, in language as strong as he could use, that nothing was to be expected from a policy that had no other foundation than force or fraud. His angry remonstrances had embroiled him with the Emperor, and he was on the point of quitting France. Under such circumstances he did not insist on breaking off further conversations with Petry, but February 25 he positively assured Petry that neither would the President and Senate ratify, nor would he himself as negotiator accept, a treaty in any form which did not provide reparation for the past as well as security for the future;[1] and March 10 he replied to the Duc de Cadore in what the Emperor would have called a morose tone, denying every assertion made in Cadore's note,—reminding Cadore that the Emperor had received knowledge of the Non-intercourse Act at the time of its passage without a sign of protest or complaint; and, finally, renewing his old, long-standing grievances against "the daily and practical outrages on the part of France."[2]

When the Emperor received Armstrong's letter, which was excessively strong, and ended in a suggestion that Napoleon was trying to cover theft by falsehood, he showed no sign of anger, but became almost apologetic, and wrote to Cadore,[3]—

"Make a sketch of a reply to the American minister. It will be easy for you to make him understand that I am master to do here what America does there; that when

---

[1] Armstrong to R. Smith, Feb. 25, 1810; MSS. State Department Archives.
[2] Armstrong to Cadore, March 10, 1810; State Papers, iii. 381.
[3] Napoleon to Cadore, March 20, 1810; Correspondance, xx. 273.

America embargoes French ships entering her ports, I have the right to reciprocate. You will explain to him how that law came to our knowledge only a short time ago, and only when I had knowledge of it did I immediately prescribe the same measure; that a few days before, I was busying myself with provisions for raising the actual prohibitions on American merchandise, when the course of commerce (*la voie du commerce*) made known to me that our honor was involved, and that no compromise was possible; that I conceive America as entitled to prevent her ships from coming to England and France; that I approved this last measure, though there was much to be said about it; but that I cannot recognize that she should arrogate the right of seizing French ships in her ports without putting herself in the case of incurring reciprocity."

One must answer as one can the question why Cadore, who had in his hands Armstrong's letter of April 29, 1809,[1] officially communicating the Non-intercourse Act, should not have suggested to Napoleon that some limit to his failings of memory ought to be observed. Napoleon's memory was sometimes overtasked by the mass of details he undertook to carry in his mind, but a striking incident always impressed itself there. Mme. de Rémusat[2] told how Grétry, who as member of the Institute regularly attended the Imperial audiences, was almost as regularly asked by Napoleon, "Who are you?" Tired at last of this rough question, Grétry replied by an answer equally blunt: "Sire, toujours Grétry;" and thenceforward the Emperor never failed to remember him. The United States in a similar tone recalled their affairs to the Emperor's memory by the Non-intercourse Act; but had this "toujours Grétry" not been enough, Napoleon's financial needs also made him peculiarly alive to every event that could relieve them, and his correspondence proved that the Non-intercourse Act as early as May, 1809, impressed him deeply. Yet in March, 1810, he not only convinced himself that this Act had just come to his knowledge, producing in him an outburst of national dignity, but he also convinced his

[1] State Papers, iii. 324. See *supra*, p. 97.
[2] Mémoires, ii. 77.

Minister of Foreign Relations, who knew the contrary, that these impressions were true, and made him witness them by his signature.

Acting without delay on the theory of sudden passion, the Emperor signed, three days afterward, March 23, a decree known as the Decree of Rambouillet, in which the result of these long hesitations was at last condensed.[1] This document was a paraphrase of the projected Decree of Vienna of Aug. 4, 1809; and it showed the tenacity with which Napoleon, while seeming to yield to opposition, never failed to return to a purpose and effect its object. In order to carry out the Decree of Vienna in that of Rambouillet he was forced into a *coup d'état*. He had not only to expel his brother Louis from Holland, and annex Holland to France, but also to drive his ablest minister, Fouché, from the Cabinet.

Of the steps by which he accomplished his objects, something can be seen in his letters; of his motives, no doubt ever existed. Armstrong described them in strong language; but his language was that of a party interested. Thiers recounted them as a panegyric, and his language was even clearer than Armstrong's. He made nothing of the Emperor's pretence that his seizures were in reprisal for the Non-intercourse Act. "This was an official reason (*une raison d'apparat*)," said Thiers.[2] "He was in search of a specious pretext for seizing in Holland, in France, in Italy, the mass of American ships which smuggled for the English, and which were within his reach. He had actually sequestered a considerable number; and in their rich cargoes were to be found the means of furnishing his Treasury with resources nearly equal to those procured for him by the contributions of war imposed on the vanquished."

The system of treating the United States as an enemy conquered in war rested on a foundation of truth; and as usual with conquered countries it met with most resistance, not from them but from by-standers. The Emperor of Russia, the kings of Prussia, Sweden, and Denmark, the Hanse Towns, and King Louis of Holland were the chief obstacles to the success of the scheme to which they were required to be

[1] State Papers, iii. 384.
[2] Empire, xii. 45.

parties. King Louis of Holland refused to seize the American ships at Amsterdam, and forced his brother to the conclusion that if nothing else could be done, Holland must be annexed to France.

For many reasons the annexation of Holland met with little favor in the Emperor's family and among his Council. Chief among its opponents was Fouché, who sacrificed himself in his efforts to prevent it. Driven to the conviction that nothing but peace with England could put an end to the Emperor's experiments on the welfare of France, Fouché resolved that peace should be made, and invented a scheme for bringing it about. As Minister of Police he controlled secret means of intrigue, and probably he acted without concert with his colleagues; but the motives which guided him were common to almost all Napoleon's Cabinet. The only difference between ministers was, that while Cadore, Montalivet, Mollien, and Decrès stopped their opposition when it became dangerous, Fouché undertook to act.

Something of this came to Armstrong's ears. As early as January 10[1] he reported a remark which he could not understand. " 'Do not believe,' said a minister to me the other day, 'that peace between us and England is impossible. If we offer to her the commerce of the world, can she resist it?' " Unknown to Armstrong, Napoleon had already made an advance to England. For this purpose he employed Labouchere, the chief banker of Holland, whose association with the Barings of London fitted him to act as an intermediary. The message sent by the Emperor through Labouchere could hardly be called an offer of terms; it amounted only to a threat that unless England made peace Holland should be annexed to France, and every avenue of illicit commerce in northern Europe should be stopped. In itself this message could hardly serve as ground for a treaty; but Fouché, without the Emperor's knowledge, sent to London at the same time, about January 18, a secret agent named Fagan, to suggest that if Great Britain would abandon Spain, France would join in creating from the Spanish-American colonies a

---

[1] Armstrong to R. Smith, Jan. 10, 1810; MSS. State Department Archives.

monarchy for Ferdinand VII., and from Louisiana, at the expense of the United States, a kingdom for the French Bourbons.[1]

This last idea bore on its face the marks of its origin. Fouché had listened to Aaron Burr, who after years of effort reached Paris, and presented to the government a memoir showing that with ten thousand regular troops, and a combined attack from Canada and Louisiana, the destruction of the United States was certain.[2] The scheme for placing the Spanish Bourbons on a Spanish-American throne probably came from the same Ouvrard whom Napoleon imprisoned at Vincennes, and whom Fouché took into favor.

Labouchere and Fagan went to England, and early in February had interviews with the British ministers, who quickly dismissed them. The only impression made on the British government by the double mission was one of perplexity at the object of an errand which appeared too absurd for discussion. The two agents returned to the Continent, and reported the result of their journey. Meanwhile Napoleon ordered Marshal Oudinot to march his army-corps into Holland, a step which brought King Louis to immediate submission. "I promise you," wrote Louis, "to follow faithfully all the engagements you shall impose upon me. I give you my word of honor to follow them faithfully and loyally from the moment I shall have undertaken them."[3] While Cadore was still negotiating with Armstrong for an arrangement with America, he was also employed in framing a treaty with Louis, which exacted the seizure of all American ships and merchandise in Dutch ports.[4] Louis came to Paris, and March 16 signed the treaty which by a secret stipulation provided for the seizure of American property.[5]

Matters stood thus April 1, 1810, when the ceremonies of the Imperial marriage interrupted for the moment further

[1] Thiers, xii. 126.
[2] Armstrong to R. Smith, July 18, 1810; MSS. State Department Archives. Cf. Correspondance de Napoleon, xx. 450, 451, *note*.
[3] Thiers, xii. 117.
[4] Napoleon to Champagny, Feb. 22, 1810; Correspondance, xx. 235.
[5] Thiers, xii. 117.

action. Napoleon had carried his point in regard to the punishment of America; but the difficulties he had already met were trifling compared with the difficulties to come.

Chapter XII

NAPOLEON SET OUT, April 27, with his new Empress on a wedding journey to Holland. In the course of his journey an accident revealed to him the secret correspondence which Fouché had conducted through Fagan with the British government. Nothing criminal was alleged, nor was it evident that the Minister of Police had acted contrary to the Emperor's admitted wishes; but since the fall of Talleyrand, Fouché alone had considered himself so necessary to the Imperial service as to affect independence, and the opportunity to discipline him could not be lost. June 3 he was disgraced, and exiled to Italy. General Savary, Duc de Rovigo, succeeded him as Minister of Police.

The fate of King Louis was almost equally swift. When he returned to Holland after promising entire submission and signing the treaty of March 16, he could not endure the disgrace of carrying his pledges into effect. He tried to evade the surrender of the American ships, and to resist the military occupation of his kingdom. He showed public sympathy with the Emperor's opponents, and with riotous popular proceedings at Amsterdam. Once more the Emperor was obliged to treat him as an enemy. June 24 the French troops were ordered to occupy Amsterdam, and July 3 Louis, abdicating his throne, took refuge in Germany. July 8 Napoleon signed a Decree annexing Holland to France.[1]

The United States at the same time received their punishment for opposing the Imperial will. The Decree of Rambouillet, though signed March 23, was published only May 14, when the sequestrations previously made in Holland, Spain, Italy, and France became in a manner legalized. The value of the seizures in Holland and Spain was estimated by the Emperor in arranging his budget for the current year as follows:[2] American cargoes previously seized at Antwerp, two million dollars; cargoes surrendered by Holland, two million four hundred thousand dollars; seizures in Spain, one million six hundred thousand dollars.

[1] Napoleon to Decrès, 8 July, 1810. Correspondance, xx. 450.
[2] Note, July 5, 1810; Correspondance, xx. 444.

In this estimate of six million dollars the seizures in France, Denmark, Hamburg, Italy, and Naples were not included. The American consul at Paris reported to Armstrong that between April 1809 and April 1810 fifty-one American ships had been seized in the ports of France, forty-four in the ports of Spain, twenty-eight in those of Naples, and eleven in those of Holland.[1] Assuming an average value of thirty thousand dollars, these one hundred and thirty-four American ships represented values exceeding four millions. Adding to Napoleon's estimate of six millions the Consul's reported seizure of seventy-nine ships in France and Naples, a sum of nearly $8,400,000 was attained. In this estimate the seizures at Hamburg, in Denmark, and in the Baltic were not included. On the whole the loss occasioned to Americans could not be estimated at less than ten millions, even after allowing for English property disguised as American. The exports from the United States during the six months after the embargo amounted to fifty-two million dollars,[2] exclusive of the ships; and as England offered a less profitable market than the Continent, one fifth of this commerce might easily have fallen into Napoleon's hands. Twenty years afterward the government of France paid five million dollars as indemnity for a portion of the seizures, from which Napoleon by his own account received not less than seven millions.

Profitable as this sweeping confiscation was, and thoroughly as Napoleon overbore opposition in his family and Cabinet, such measures in no way promised to retrieve the disaster his system suffered from the defection of America. While England protected American ships in their attempts to counteract his system in Spain, Holland, and in the Baltic, the Emperor regarded American trade as identical with British, and confiscated it accordingly; but by doing so he exhausted his means of punishment, and since he could not march armies to New York and Baltimore as he marched them to Amsterdam and Hamburg, he could only return on his steps and effect by diplomacy what he could not effect by force. The Act of March 1, 1809, was a thorn in his side; but the news

[1] Rapport à l'Empereur, 25 Août, 1810; Archives des Aff. Étrs. MSS.
[2] Gallatin to the Speaker, Feb. 7, 1810; State Papers, Commerce and Navigation, i. 812.

which arrived toward the end of June, 1810, that Congress had repealed even that slight obstacle to trade with England made some corrective action inevitable. The Act of May 1, 1810, struck a blow at the Emperor such as no Power in Europe dared aim, for it threw open to British trade a market in the United States which would alone compensate England for the loss of her trade with France and Holland. Macon's Act made the Milan Decree useless.

Napoleon no sooner learned that Congress had renewed intercourse with England and France, than he wrote an interesting note[1] to Montalivet dated June 25, the day after he ordered his army to seize Amsterdam.

"The Americans," he said, "have raised the embargo on their ships so that all American ships can leave America to come to France; but those which should come here would be sequestered, because all would either have been visited by English ships or would have touched in England. It is therefore probable that no American ship will come into our ports without being assured of what France means to do in regard to them."

France could evidently do one of three things,—either avowedly maintain her decrees, or expressly revoke them, or seem to revoke them while in fact maintaining them. The process by which Napoleon made his choice was characteristic.

"We may do two things," he continued,—"either declare that the Decrees of Berlin and Milan are repealed, and replace commerce where it formerly was; or announce that the Decrees will be repealed September 1, if on that date the English have repealed the Orders in Council. Or the English will withdraw their Orders in Council, and then we shall have to ascertain whether the situation that follows will be advantageous to us."

Assuming that the decrees and orders were withdrawn, and American ships admitted as neutrals, the Emperor explained how he should still enforce his system as before:—

[1] Notes pour le Ministre de l'Intérieur, 25 Juin, 1810; Correspondance, XX. 431.

"This situation will have no influence on the customs legislation, which will always regulate arbitrarily duties and prohibitions. The Americans will be able to bring sugar and coffee into our ports,—the privateers will not stop them because the flag covers the goods; but when they come into a port of France or a country under the influence of France, they will find the customs legislation, by which we shall be able to say that we do not want the sugar and coffee brought by the Americans because they are English merchandise; that we do not want tobacco, etc.; that we do not want such or such goods, which we can as we please class among prohibited goods. Thus it is evident that we should commit ourselves to nothing."

Again and again, orally and in writing, in the presence of the whole Council and in private to each minister, the Emperor had asserted positively and even angrily that "all the measures I have taken, as I have said several times, are only measures of reprisal;" yet after assuming that his reprisals had succeeded, and that England had withdrawn her orders as France should have withdrawn her decrees, he told Montalivet, as though it were a matter of course, that he should carry out the same system by different means. This method of fighting for the rights of neutrals differed but little, and not to advantage, from the British method of fighting against them.

The Emperor put his new plan in shape. He proposed to recognize neutral rights by issuing licenses under the name of permits for a score of American vessels, and for the introduction of Georgia cotton, the article for which Montalivet made his long struggle. This measure was to be so organized that the shipments could take place only in a single designated port of America, only with certificates of origin delivered by a single French consul also to be designated; that the ship could enter only at one or two designated ports of France; that independently of the certificates of origin a cipher-letter should be written to the Minister of Foreign Relations by the consul who should have given them; finally, that the ships should be required to take in return wines, cognac, silks, and other French goods for the value of the cargo.

Deep was Armstrong's disgust when an Imperial Decree[1] appeared, dated July 15, authorizing licenses for thirty American ships to sail from Charleston or New York under the rigorous conditions detailed by this note; but the thirty licenses were merely a beginning. Once having grasped the idea that something must be done for French industry, the Emperor pressed it with his usual energy and with the usual results. During the months of June and July, while annexing Holland to his empire, he worked laboriously on his new commercial system. He created a special Council of Commerce, held meetings as often as twice a week, and issued decrees and orders by dozens. The difficulty of understanding his new method was great, owing to a duplication of orders not unusual with him; the meaning of a public decree was affected by some secret decree or order not made public, and as never failed to happen with his civil affairs, the whole mass became confused.

Apparently the new system[2] rested on a decree of July 25, 1810, which forbade any ship whatever to leave a French port for a foreign port without a license; and this license, in the Emperor's eyes, gave the character of a French ship to the licensed vessel,—"that is to say, in two words, that I will have no neutral vessel; and in fact there is none really neutral,— they are all vessels which violate the blockade and pay ransom to the English." In other words the Emperor's scheme was founded on his Berlin and Milan Decrees, and left them intact except within the operation of the licenses. "For these [licensed] ships," he said,[3] "the Decrees of Berlin and Milan are null and void; . . . my licenses are a tacit privilege of exemption from my decrees, on condition of conforming to the rules prescribed by the said licenses." The licenses themselves were classified in thirty different series,[4]—for the ocean, the Mediterranean, England, etc.,—and prescribed the cargoes to be carried both on the inward and outward voyages.[5] They made no distinction between neutrals and enemies; the license

---

[1] State Papers, iii. 400.
[2] Napoleon to Prince Lebrun, Aug. 20, 1810; Correspondance, xxi. 53.
[3] Napoleon to Eugene Napoleon, Sept. 19, 1810; Correspondance, xxi. 134.
[4] Napoleon to Montalivet, Aug. 10, 1810; Correspondance, xxi. 29.
[5] Napoleon to Montalivet, Aug. 11, 1810; Correspondance, xxi. 35.

that authorized a voyage from London was the same, except for its series, as that which covered a cargo of cotton from Charleston; and such distinction as appeared, was limited to imposing on the neutral additional trouble to prove that his goods were not English. In theory the import of such British merchandise as would relieve England's distress was forbidden, and the export of French merchandise was encouraged, not only in order to assist French industry, but also in order to drain England of specie. Especially the sugar, coffee, and cotton of the colonies were prohibited; but when captured by privateers or confiscated on land, colonial produce was first admitted to the custom-house at a duty of fifty per cent, and then sold for the benefit of the Imperial treasury.

This system and tariff Napoleon imposed on all the countries subject to his power, including Switzerland, Naples, Hamburg, and the Hanse Towns; while he exerted all his influence to force the same policy on Prussia and Russia. As far as concerned the only neutral, the United States, the system classified American ships either as English when unlicensed, or as French when licensed; it imposed Imperial functions inconsistent with local law on the French consuls in America, and violated both international and municipal law only to produce another form of the Berlin and Milan Decrees, in some respects more offensive than the original.

The character and actions of Napoleon were so overpowering that history naturally follows their course rather than the acts of the undecided and unenergetic governments which he drove before him; and for this reason the replies made by Secretary Robert Smith to the flashes of Imperial temper or policy have not hitherto been noticed. In truth, Secretary Smith made no attempt to rival Napoleon in originality or in vigor of ideas or expression. Neither his genius nor that of Madison shone bright in the lurid glare of the Emperor's planet. When Champagny's letter of Aug. 22, 1809, reached Washington with its novel views about floating colonies, rights of search, identity of blockade with siege, and warning of confiscations in Holland, Spain, and Italy, President Madison, replying through Robert Smith, Dec. 1, 1809, contented himself with silence in regard to the threats, and with a mild dissent from the Emperor's exposition of the *jus gentium*.

"However founded the definition of M. Champagny may be in reason and general utility, and consequently however desirable to be made the established law on the subject of blockades, a different practice has too long prevailed among all nations, France as well as others, and is too strongly authenticated by the writers of admitted authority, to be combated by the United States."

A touch of Madison's humor brightened the monotony of these commonplaces, but was not granted the freedom which the subject might have allowed. The President felt no wish to dwell on what was unreasonable or violent in Napoleon's conduct. He passed lightly over the floating colony, ignored the threatened seizure of American commerce, and fastened on the closing paragraph of Champagny's note, which promised that if England would revoke her blockades, the decrees of France should fall of themselves. This proposition, defined by Champagny and commented by Armstrong, required that England should admit the whole doctrine of floating colonies and siege-blockades. Madison knew it to be impracticable and deceptive; but he was not bound to go beyond the letter of the pledge, and although he declined to admit Napoleon among those " writers of admitted authority" whose law prevailed among nations, he instructed Armstrong to act without delay in the sense of Champagny's suggestion.

"You will of course," wrote Secretary Smith to Armstrong, Dec. 1, 1809, "understand it to be wished that you should ascertain the meaning of the French government as to the condition on which it has been proposed to revoke the Berlin Decree. On the principle which seems to be assumed by M. Champagny, nothing more ought to be required than a recall by Great Britain of her proclamation or illegal blockades which are of a date prior to that of the Berlin Decree, or a formal declaration that they are not now in force."[1]

January 25, 1810, Armstrong asked Cadore the question thus dictated, and received for answer that the Emperor required only the revocation of the British blockades as a condition of

[1] Robert Smith to Armstrong, Dec. 1, 1810; State Papers, iii. 326.

recalling the Decree of Berlin,—a reply which Armstrong communicated the same day to Minister Pinkney at London. No further instructions from Washington seem to have reached the United States Legation at Paris until news arrived that on May 1 the Non-intercourse Act had been repealed. No official information of the repeal was received by Armstrong, but an American who brought despatches from Pinkney in London brought also a printed copy of the Act of May 1, 1810. In the want of official advices, probably July 9, Armstrong communicated the Act of May 1 to the Duc de Cadore in the unofficial form of a newspaper. Cadore replied that being so entirely unofficial, it could not be made the groundwork of any government proceeding;[1] but he took it to the Emperor, and Armstrong waited for some striking exhibition of displeasure.

From that moment Armstrong's relations with Cadore became mysterious. Something unrecorded passed between them, for, July 19 Napoleon ordered Cadore to write to the French ambassador at St. Petersburg a message for the American minister at that Court:[2] —

"Charge the Duc de Vicence to tell Mr. Adams that we have here an American minister who says nothing; that we need an active man whom one can comprehend, and by whose means we could come to an understanding with the Americans."[3]

For three weeks Napoleon made no decision on the subject of the American Act; then, after settling the annexation of Holland, he wrote to Cadore July 31:[4] —

"After having much reflected on the affairs of America, I have thought that to repeal my Decrees of Berlin and Milan would have no effect; that it would be better for you to make a note to Mr. Armstrong by which you should let him know that you have put under my eyes the details contained in the American newspaper; that I should have liked

[1] Armstrong to Robert Smith, July 10, 1810; MSS. State Department Archives.
[2] Napoleon to Champagny, 19 July, 1810; Correspondance, xx. 505.
[3] Napoleon to Champagny, 13 July, 1810; Correspondance, xx. 554.
[4] Correspondance, xxi. 1.

to have a more official communication, but that time passes, and that,—since he assures me we may regard this as official,—he can consider that my Decrees of Berlin and Milan will have no effect, dating from November 1; and that he is to consider them as withdrawn in consequence of such Act of the American Congress, on condition that (*à condition que*) if the British Council does not withdraw its Orders of 1807, the United States Congress shall fulfil the engagement it has taken to re-establish its prohibitions on British commerce. This appears to me more suitable than a decree which would cause a shock (*qui ferait secousse*) and would not fulfil my object. This method appears to me more conformable to my dignity and to the seriousness of the affair."

The Emperor himself, August 2, dictated the letter,—the most important he ever sent to the United States government. During the next three days he made numerous changes in the draft; but at last it was signed and sent to the American Legation.[1] Upon that paper, long famous as Cadore's letter of Aug. 5, 1810, turned the course of subsequent events; but apart from its practical consequences the student of history, whether interested in the character of Napoleon or of Madison, or in the legal aspects of war and peace, or in the practice of governments and the capacity of different peoples for self-government, could find few examples or illustrations better suited to his purpose than the letter itself, the policy it revealed, and the manner in which it was received by the United States and Great Britain.

Cadore began by saying that he had communicated to the Emperor the newspaper containing the Act of Congress of May 1. The Emperor could have wished that all the acts of the United States government which concerned France had always been officially made known to him:—

"In general, he has only had indirect knowledge of them after a long interval of time. From this delay serious inconveniences have resulted which would not have existed had these acts been promptly and officially communicated.

[1] Cadore to General Armstrong, Aug. 5, 1810; State Papers, iii. 386.

"The Emperor applauded the general embargo laid by the United States on all their vessels, because that measure, if it has been prejudicial to France, had in it at least nothing offensive to her honor. It has caused her to lose her colonies of Martinique, Guadeloupe, and Cayenne; the Emperor has not complained of it. He has made this sacrifice to the principle which has determined the Americans to lay the embargo. . . . The Act of March 1 [1809] raised the embargo and substituted for it a measure the most injurious to the interests of France. This Act, of which the Emperor knew nothing until very lately, interdicted to American vessels the commerce of France at the time it authorized that to Spain, Naples, and Holland,—that is to say, to the countries under French influence,—and denounced confiscation against all French vessels which should enter the ports of America. Reprisal was a right, and commanded by the dignity of France,—a circumstance on which it was impossible to make a compromise (*de transiger*). The sequestration of all the American vessels in France has been the necessary consequence of the measure taken by Congress."

This preamble, interesting for the novelty of its assertions both of fact and law, led to the conclusion that the Act of May 1, 1810, was a retreat from the Act of March 1, 1809, and warranted France in accepting the offer extended by both laws to the nation which should first "cease to violate the neutral commerce of the United States."

"In this new state of things," concluded Cadore, "I am authorized to declare to you, sir, that the Decrees of Berlin and Milan are revoked, and that after November 1 they will cease to have effect,—it being understood (*bien entendu*) that in consequence of this declaration the English are to revoke their Orders in Council, and renounce the new principles of blockade which they have wished to establish; or that the United States, conformably to the Act you have just communicated, cause their rights to be respected by the English."

No phraseology could have more embarrassed President

Madison, while, as Napoleon had remarked to Montalivet a few days before, "it is evident that we commit ourselves to nothing."[1] So closely was the Imperial promise imitated from that given by Erskine that the President could hardly reject it, although no American merchant would have risked so much as a cargo of salt-fish on a pledge of such a kind from such a man. As though to warn the Americans, Napoleon added personal assurances that gave to the whole proceeding an unpleasant air of burlesque: —

> "It is with the most particular satisfaction, sir, that I make known to you this determination of the Emperor. His Majesty loves the Americans. Their prosperity and their commerce are within the scope of his policy. The independence of America is one of the principal titles of glory to France. Since that epoch the Emperor is pleased in aggrandizing the United States; and under all circumstances that which can contribute to the independence, to the prosperity, and to the liberty of the Americans the Emperor will consider as conformable with the interests of his Empire."

One might doubt whether Napoleon or Canning were the more deficient in good taste; but Americans whose nerves were irritated to fury by the irony of Canning, found these expressions of Napoleon's love rather absurd than insulting. So little had the mere fact of violence to do with the temper of politics, compared with the sentiments which surrounded it, that Napoleon could seize without notice ten million dollars' worth of American property, imprisoning the American crews of two or three hundred vessels in his dungeons, while at the same instant he told the Americans that he loved them, that their commerce was within the scope of his policy, and as a climax avowed a scheme to mislead the United States government, hardly troubling himself to use forms likely to conceal his object; yet the vast majority of Americans never greatly resented acts which seemed to them like the exploits of an Italian brigand on the stage. Beyond doubt, Napoleon regarded his professions of love and interest not as irony or

[1] Notes, etc., June 25, 1810; Correspondance, xx. 431.

extravagance, but as adapted to deceive. A few weeks earlier he sent a message to the Czar of Russia, who asked him to disavow the intention of restoring the kingdom of Poland. "If I should ever sign," replied Napoleon,[1] "a declaration that the kingdom of Poland shall never be restored, it would be for the reason that I intended to restore it,—a trap I should set for Russia;" and in signing a declaration to the President that his decrees were repealed, he set a trap for the United States, which he baited with professions of love that to a more refined taste would have seemed fatal to his object.

This mixture of feline qualities,—energy, astuteness, secrecy, and rapidity,—combined with ignorance of other natures than his own, was shown in the act with which he concluded his arrangements of Aug. 5, 1810. About a fortnight before, by a secret decree dated July 22, 1810,[2] he had ordered the proceeds of the American cargoes seized at Antwerp and in Dutch and Spanish ports, valued by him at six million dollars, to be turned into the Treasury as a part of his customs revenue devoted to the service of 1809–10. In French ports he held still some fifty ships in sequestration. Cadore's letter of August 5 mentioned these ships as sequestered,—a phrase implying that they would be held subject to future negotiation and decision, liable to be returned to their owners; yet on the same day Napoleon signed another secret decree[3] which condemned without hearing or judgment all the ships and cargoes declared to be still in sequestration by the letter that could hardly have yet been sent from Cadore's office. Every vessel which had arrived in French ports between May 20, 1809, and May 1, 1810, suffered confiscation by this decree, which further ordered that the American crews should be released from the dungeons where they were held as prisoners of war, and that from August 5 to November 1, 1810, American ships should be allowed to enter French ports, but should not discharge their cargoes without a license.

The Decree of August 5 was never made public. Armstrong indeed employed the last hours of his stay in Paris in asking whether the French government meant to admit further ne-

---

[1] Napoleon to Caulaincourt, July 1, 1810; Correspondance, xx. 158.
[2] Gallatin's Writings, ii. 211.
[3] Gallatin's Writings, ii. 198.

gotiation about these seizures,[1] and Cadore replied that the law of reprisals was final;[2] but when Albert Gallatin, as minister at Paris some ten years afterward, happened to obtain a copy of the document, he expressed his anger at its secrecy in language such as he used in regard to no other transaction of his public life. "No one can suppose," he wrote,[3] "that if it had been communicated or published at the same time, the United States would with respect to the promised revocation of the Berlin and Milan Decrees have taken that ground which ultimately led to the war with Great Britain. It is indeed unnecessary to comment on such a glaring act of combined injustice, bad faith, and meanness as the enacting and concealment of that decree exhibits." These epithets would not have disturbed Napoleon. Politics were to him a campaign, and if his opponents had not the sense to divine his movements and motives, the disgrace and disaster were none of his.

More mysterious than the conduct of Napoleon was that of Armstrong. Contenting himself with whatever the Emperor ordered, he refrained in his despatches from saying more than was necessary for the record. He protected himself from Napoleon's personal attack by sending to the Duc de Cadore an undated letter,[4] referring to the archives of Cadore's department for proof that every public measure of the United States had been promptly and officially communicated to the French government; but he wrote home no report of any conference with Cadore, he expressed no opinion as to the faith of the Emperor's promise, made no further protest against the actual reprisals, and required no indemnity for past spoliations. In fact, no action was asked from him; but he lent himself readily to the silence that was needed. Cadore reported[5] to the Emperor that Armstrong "before his departure wishes to open (*engager*) none of those difficult questions which he foresees must rise between the two

---

[1] Armstrong to Cadore, Sept. 7, 1810; State Papers, iii. 388.
[2] Cadore to Armstrong, Sept. 12, 1810; State Papers, iii. 388.
[3] Gallatin to J. Q. Adams, Sept. 15, 1821; Gallatin's Writings, ii. 196.
[4] State Papers, iii. 387.
[5] Rapport à l'Empereur, Août, 1810; Archives des Aff. Étr. MSS. vol. lxiv. pièce 81.

governments, in order to arrive in America without having seen the fading of the glory he attaches to having obtained the Note of August 5." Too happy in the good fortune that threw an apparent triumph into his hands at the moment when he was ending his diplomatic career in disgust, he felt anxious only to escape before another turn of the wheel should destroy his success. He remained in Paris more than a month after receiving Cadore's letter of August 5, but reserved for a personal interview whatever information he had to give the President; and his letters, like his despatches, expressed no inconvenient opinions. Sept. 12, 1810, his long and extremely interesting mission ended, and he quitted Paris on his homeward journey, leaving the Legation in charge of Jonathan Russell of Rhode Island. Armstrong's last official act was to write from Bordeaux a letter to Pinkney at London, declaring that the conditions imposed by Napoleon on the repeal of his decrees were "not *precedent*, as has been supposed, but *subsequent*."[1]

[1] Armstrong to Pinkney, Sept. 29, 1810; State Papers, iii. 386.

Chapter XIII

WHILE NAPOLEON labored to reconstruct his system mutilated by American legislation, the Government of Great Britain sank lower and lower toward disappearance, while the star of Spencer Perceval shone alone with dull lustre on the British horizon. When the Portland ministry went to pieces in September, 1809, Perceval became of necessity master of the empire. Canning had quarrelled with him, and refused office except as prime minister. Castlereagh had been so lately disgraced that he could bring only weakness to the Government if he rejoined it. Both Castlereagh and Sidmouth refused to serve with Canning on any terms. The Whigs, represented by Lord Grenville and Lord Grey, were excluded by the King's prejudices, by their own pledges to the Irish Catholics, and by the great preponderance of Tory opinion in the country. The Duke of Portland was dying; King George himself was on the verge of insanity, and every one supposed that the Prince of Wales, if he became regent, would at once appoint a ministry from among his Whig friends. This stalemate, where every piece on the chessboard stood in the way of its neighbor, and none could move while the King and Spencer Perceval remained, seemed likely to end in the destruction of the British empire. An economist wiser and better educated than Napoleon might easily have inferred, as he did, that with time England must succumb.

Perceval and his remaining friends—Liverpool, Bathurst, Eldon—looked about them for allies. They would not, indeed they could not, surrender the government to others, for no one offered to take it. In the House of Lords they were strong, but in the Commons they had no speaker except Perceval, while the opposition was strengthened by Canning, and Castlereagh could not be safely reckoned as more than neutral. They sought for allies both old and young in the Commons, but their search was almost fruitless. They could find only young Viscount Palmerston, about five-and-twenty years of age, who took the subordinate place of Secretary at War.

Nothing remained but to carry on the government by the Peers, with Perceval as its only important representative in the

Commons. The Lord Hawkesbury of 1802, who had become Lord Liverpool at his father's death, and was actually head of the Home Office, succeeded Castlereagh as head of the War Department. Spencer Perceval took the Duke of Portland's place as first Lord of the Treasury, retaining his old functions as Chancellor of the Exchequer. These changes brought no new strength into the Cabinet; but Canning's place at the Foreign Office remained to be filled, and common consent fixed upon one person as alone competent to bring with him to the position a weight of character that could overbalance the losses the Cabinet had suffered.

This person, hitherto unmentioned, was Richard Colley Wesley, or Wellesley, born in Ireland in 1760, eldest son of the first Earl of Mornington, whose younger son Arthur was born in 1769. Another brother, Henry, born in 1773, rose to high rank in diplomacy under the later title of Lord Cowley. In 1809 these three brothers were all actively employed in the public service; but the foremost of the three was the eldest, the Marquess Wellesley, whose reputation still overshadowed that of Arthur, then just called to the peerage Sept. 4, 1809, as Viscount Wellington of Talavera, in reward of his recent battle with Marshal Victor.

An Irish family neither wealthy nor very distinguished, the Wellesleys owed their success to their abilities. The second Lord Mornington, Marquess Wellesley, sprang into fame as a favorite of William Pitt, who showed his power by pushing young men like Richard Wesley and George Canning into positions of immense responsibility. Perhaps the favor shown to the former may in part have had its source in some resemblance of character which caused Pitt to feel a reflection of himself, for Mornington was a scholar and an orator. His Latin verses were an ornament of Eton scholarship; his oratory was classic like his verses; and his manners suited the scholarship of his poetry and the Latinity of his orations. Lord Mountmorris, one of his antagonists in the Irish Parliament of 1783, ridiculed his rhetoric: "If formidable spectres portending the downfall of the Constitution were to appear in this House, I admit that the noble Lord is frightened with becoming dignity. The ancient Roscius or the modern Garrick could not stand with a better grace at the appearance of

a spectre." The orator whose air of dignity Lord Mountmorris thought so studied was then twenty-three years old, and
apparently never changed his manner. In the British Parliament, thirteen years afterward, Sheridan described him as
presenting the same figure that Mountmorris laughed at.
"Exactly two years ago," said Sheridan in 1796, "I remember
to have seen the noble Lord with the same sonorous voice,
the same placid countenance, in the same attitude, leaning
gracefully upon the table, and giving an account from shreds
and patches of Brissot that the French republic would last but
a few months longer." The aristocratic affectations, if they
were affectations, of Lord Mornington were conspicuous; but
no man could safely laugh at one of the Wellesleys. In 1797
Mr. Pitt suddenly sent this ornament of the peerage to India
as governor-general, and the world learned that since the time
of Clive no surer or bolder hand had guided the empire of
England in the East.

When he took charge of the Indian government, French
influence contested his own at more than one court of the
powerful native princes, while his resources were neither great
nor easily concentrated. During the eight years of his sway he
extirpated French influence; crushed the power of Tippoo
Sultaun; conquered the empire of Mysore, which had again
and again won victories over English armies within sight of
Madras; broke up the Mahratta confederacy; and doubled the
British territory in India, besides introducing or planning
many important civil reforms. He shocked the Court of Directors by arbitrary rule, extravagance in finance, and favoritism toward his younger brothers; but success was the decisive
answer to hostile criticism, and even fanatics could hardly affirm that a governor-general, though he might have every virtue, was fit for his place if he refused the services of Arthur
Wellesley when they might be had for the asking.

When Lord Wellesley, created an Irish marquess and English baron, returned to England in 1806, he came home with
the greatest name in the empire next to that of Pitt.[1] He was
asked to join the Portland Administration, but declined. Canning was said to have taken offence at his refusal;[2] but at last

[1] Memoirs of R. Plumer Ward, i. 424.
[2] Buckingham Memoirs, iv. 390.

in disgust with Perceval, Canning connected himself more closely than ever with the Marquess, doubtless in the hope of forcing Castlereagh out in order to bring Wellesley in.[1] At Canning's request in April, 1809, the Marquess was appointed to the important and difficult post of Ambassador Extraordinary to the Supreme Junta of Spain, then at Seville; while at the same time his brother Arthur was made general-in-chief in the Peninsula. Lord Wellesley went to Spain with the understanding that he was soon to return and enter the Cabinet.[2] In October he learned that Canning had broken up the Cabinet, and that while Canning himself on one side expected the Wellesleys' support, Perceval on the other was begging for it, and the Whigs were waiting with open arms to welcome their alliance. Canning's duel took place Sept. 21, 1809. October 5 Spencer Perceval wrote to Wellesley at Seville, asking him to accept the Foreign Office; while at the same time Canning informed the King that Lord Wellesley would retire from office with himself.

In such a situation the most astute politician could not trust his own judgment. No one could say whether Wellesley's strength would invigorate the Government, or whether Perceval's weakness would exhaust Wellesley as it had exhausted Canning. Canning and Wellesley held the same estimate of Perceval. Canning had succeeded only in ruining himself by struggling to rid the Government of that incubus, as he regarded it, and Wellesley had no better right to expect success. On the other hand, if the Marquess should join the Government he might assist his brother Arthur, who needed support at home. Probably this idea turned the scale; at all events Wellesley accepted Perceval's offer, and gave his Administration a chance of life.

Wellesley could have had no hope of effecting any considerable object except by carrying out Canning's scheme, which required that Spencer Perceval should be forced from power before the Government could be placed on a strong foundation. His first experiences showed him the difficulties in his way.

December 6, 1809, the Marquess was sworn as Secretary of

[1] Wellington to Wellesley, Oct. 5, 1809; Supplementary Despatches, vi. 386.
[2] Buckingham Memoirs, iv. 392.

State. A few days afterward he appointed his brother Henry to the post he had himself vacated, of Envoy to the Spanish Junta at Seville. The favoritism was unfortunate, but Wellesley troubled himself little about odium; his single thought was to support his "brother Arthur," while England was far from showing equal zeal in Arthur's support. In spite of the success at Talavera, Lord Wellington had been obliged to retreat into Portugal; the Spanish army led by inferior generals ventured to march on Madrid, and November 19 was annihilated by the French at Ocaña, some fifty miles south of that city, leaving the whole south and east of Spain unprotected. The French were certain to reoccupy Seville if not to attack Cadiz. Affairs in the Peninsula were at least as unpromising as they had ever been, and Englishmen might be excused for doubting the policy of wasting British resources in fretting one extremity of Napoleon's enormous bulk.

While the Wellesley interest concentrated on the Peninsula, the Foreign Office was interested in wider fields. The new secretary was expected to devise some system of trade with the Spanish-American colonies which should meet approval from the Junta, jealous with good reason of any foreign interference with Mexico and Peru; but above all he was required to take in hand the quarrel with the United States, and if possible to retrieve the mistakes of Canning. He had been only a few weeks in office when news arrived that President Madison refused to hold further relations with F. J. Jackson, the British minister, and that Madison and Jackson were only agreed in each requiring the punishment of the other. Pinkney soon appeared at the Foreign office with a request for Jackson's recall.

Lord Wellesley was in character to the full as arbitrary as George Canning. Seven years of imperial power in India had trained him in habits of autocratic authority; but he was a man of breeding, courteous, dignified, and considerate of others' dignity. In India he had shown what Canning thought himself to possess,—the hand of iron in the velvet glove. Without a tinge of Canning's besetting vice, the passion to be clever, Wellesley never fell into the fault of putting sarcasms or epigrams into his state papers. So little offensive was he in manner, that although he brought about a war between

England and the United States no American held him as an enemy, or retained so much ill-feeling toward him as to make even his name familiar to American ears. In truth his subordinate position in the Government prevented the exercise of his powers, and left him no opportunity to develop the force of that character which had crushed Tippoo Sultaun and tamed the Mahrattas. His colleagues allowed him to show only the weaknesses of a strong nature, which may have been increased to vices by the exhaustion of eight years' severe labor in an Indian climate. What he might have done had he taken Perceval's place no one can say; what he did or failed to do is more easily told.

When Pinkney came to explain the President's action and wishes in regard to Jackson, Wellesley, in a manner that seemed to the American minister both frank and friendly, showed only the wish to conciliate. In a short time Pinkney became so intimate with the new Foreign Secretary as to excite comment. Nothing could be more encouraging than his reports to the President of the change in disposition which had come over the Foreign Office. Jan. 2, 1810, Pinkney, in a long note, explained to Wellesley the President's reasons for breaking off relations with Jackson.[1] His tone was conciliatory, professing only the wish for friendly accommodation; and Wellesley on his side not only received the note without objection, but encouraged the hope that the President's wishes would be gratified. Pinkney reported that in conversation Lord Wellesley had promised at once to send out a new envoy of diplomatic rank; to lose no time in settling the "Chesapeake" affair; and afterward to take up the commercial questions which had made the substance of Monroe's treaty three years before. The cordiality of these promises satisfied Pinkney that they were not meant to deceive. If any one was deceived, the victim was not Pinkney but Wellesley himself, who overrated his own power and underrated the inert resistance of Spencer Perceval and the army of selfish interests at his back. Even Jackson's affair was not easily managed. Jackson could not be disavowed, for he had done nothing more than his orders required him to do; nor could a new minister

<hr />

[1] Pinkney to Wellesley, Jan. 2, 1810; State Papers, iii. 352.

be appointed until the year elapsed which Canning promised for the term of Jackson's mission. Between Canning on one side and Perceval on the other, Wellesley found himself unable to act, and resorted to delays.

Not until March 14 did Pinkney receive the promised reply[1] to his note of January 2; and this reply was not all that Wellesley had given him to expect. Compared with Canning's notes, Wellesley's letter might be called affectionate; but it was less definite than Pinkney would have liked. His Majesty, said Wellesley, regretted that the President should have interrupted communications before his Majesty could manifest his invariable disposition to maintain the relations of amity with the United States. Mr. Jackson had most positively assured his Government that it was not his purpose to give offence by anything he said or did; in such cases the usual course would have been to convey a formal complaint, which would have prevented the inconvenience of a suspension of relations. Yet his Majesty, always disposed to pay the utmost attention to the wishes and sentiments of States in amity with him, had directed the return of Mr. Jackson, though without marking his conduct with any expression of displeasure, inasmuch as Mr. Jackson's "integrity, zeal, and ability have long been distinguished in his Majesty's service," and he seemed to have committed no intentional offence on the present occasion. Jackson was ordered to deliver his charge into the hands of a properly qualified person, while his Majesty " would receive, with sentiments of undiminished amity and good-will, any communication which the Government of the United States may deem beneficial to the mutual interests of both countries."

This was but Canning once more, without the sarcasm. With his grand air of sultan and viceroy, Wellesley ignored the existence of complaints, and professed himself "ready to receive, with sentiments of undiminished amity and good-will, any communication which the Government of the United States may deem beneficial;" but when his course led, two years afterward, to the only communication which could logically result,—a declaration of war,—Wellesley declared in

[1] State Papers, iii. 355.

Parliament[1] "that a more unjust attack was never made upon the peace of any nation than that of the American government upon England;" and that "the American government had been long infected with a deadly hatred toward this country, and (if he might be allowed an unusual application of a word) with a deadly affection toward France." He blamed only his own colleagues, who "ought in fact to have expected and been fully prepared for war with America."

That the American government and people were infected with a deadly hatred toward England, if not already true, was becoming true with a rapidity which warranted Wellesley in taking it for fact, if he could do nothing to prevent it; but he should at least have explained the reasons why his colleagues, who in his opinion showed culpable neglect, failed to expect war or to prepare for it. In truth his colleagues had as little reason to expect war with America as he had to charge the American government with "deadly affection" toward France. They would do nothing to conciliate the United States because they had what seemed the best ground for thinking that the United States were already conciliated, and that the difficulties between America and France were such as to prevent America from quarrelling with England. Wellesley's note was written March 14; Louis of Holland, March 16, signed the treaty obliging him to seize the American ships in his ports; Napoleon signed, March 23, the Rambouillet Decree. In every country within French control Napoleon was waging avowed war against the United States in retaliation for the Nonintercourse Act; while in America, March 31, Congress abandoned the idea of even a Navigation Act against England, and May 1 restored relations with her, without asking an equivalent or expressing unfriendly feeling. Under such circumstances, ministers more intelligent than Spencer Perceval were warranted in thinking that the part of wisdom was to leave American affairs alone.

The point was all-important in the story of the war. Governments rarely succeed in forethought, and their favorite rule is to do nothing where nothing need be done. Had the British government expected war, even Spencer Perceval would

[1] Cobbett's Debates, Nov. 30, 1812; xxiv. 33, 34.

have bestirred himself to prevent it; but ministers neither expected nor had reason to expect hostilities. On the contrary, the only bright spot in Perceval's horizon was the United States, where his influence seemed paramount. The triumph of Perceval's policy there gave him strength at home to disregard Wellesley's attempts at domination. An intelligent bystander, through whom Lord Wellesley kept up relations with the Whigs, wrote, May 1, to the Marquess of Buckingham a letter,[1] which threw light on the ideas then influencing Wellesley: —

"The only hope Perceval can naturally have is in the turn which peace, or rather accommodation, with America may give the public mind; as also the successes in Spain against France which may be looked for. The former, in my opinion, as well from the devotion of Pinkney to Lord Wellesley as the late rapacious act of Bonaparte, may be looked on as certain."

This letter, showing the certainty felt by all parties in American friendship, happened to be written on the day when the President signed the Act restoring commercial relations. After all that had occurred,—seizures, blockades, impressments, and Orders in Council; the "Chesapeake" affair, Rose's mission, Canning's letters, Erskine's arrangement, and Jackson's dismissal,—the British government counted its American policy as its chief success, and had the strongest reasons for doing so. American legislation was controlled by British influence, and Napoleon reasonably thought that neither robbery nor magnanimity would affect the result.

The Marquess of Buckingham's friend gave him exact information, as the news a few weeks later, of the Act of May 1, proved; but evidence much more convincing of the confidence felt by ministers in the attitude of America was given by George Canning, who claimed the credit for having brought about that settlement which gave a new lease of life to the Perceval Administration. June 15, a week before Parliament rose, Canning spoke.[2]

[1] Buckingham Memoirs, iv. 438.
[2] Cobbett's Debates, xvii. 742.

"The recent proceedings of Congress," he said, "have effected so much of what it was the anxious wish of the Government of which I was a member to attain, that I trust all our difficulties with America may be speedily adjusted. In truth I had never much doubt upon my mind that America, if left to her own policy and to the effect of those discussions which would take place in her own legislatures, general and provincial, would at no distant period arrive at that point at which, by the late Act of Congress, she appears to have arrived. No man is more anxious than I am for an amicable accommodation with that Power; but I trust at the same time that the change in the policy of the United States has not been effected by any improper concessions on our part,—a circumstance which I can fully disclaim during the period that I remained in office. I should rather hope that it has been the consequence of a determined adherence to that system which has been so often declaimed against in this House, but which has proved as clearly beneficial to the commercial interests as it has been consistent with the political dignity of this nation."

While it was possibly true, or soon became true, that the United States were, as Wellesley afterward alleged, infected by a deadly hostility to England, neither Wellesley nor Canning, nor any other English statesman in the year 1810, suspected the strength of that passion, or dreamed of shaping a policy to meet the hatred which ought to have been constantly in their minds. Wellesley's personal wishes were not easy to fathom, but they probably leaned, under Pinkney's influence, toward conciliation. His actual measures showed a want of decision, or a degree of feebleness, unsuspected in his character.

Quite early in Wellesley's career as Foreign Secretary, an opportunity occurred to test his energies. January 25, 1810,[1] Armstrong sent to Pinkney a copy of Napoleon's offer to withdraw the Decree of Berlin, if England would withdraw her previous blockade of the coast from Elbe to Brest. Nothing could be easier for England. The blockade of May 16, 1806, had been invented by Charles James Fox at the begin-

---

[1] Armstrong to Pinkney, Jan. 25, 1810; State Papers, iii. 350.

ning of his short Administration as an act of friendship toward the United States, in order to evade the application of
Sir William Scott's legal principles; it was strictly enforced
only between Ostend and the Seine, a short strip of coast
within the narrow seas completely under British control, and
in part visible from British shores, while the subsequent Orders in Council had substituted a series of other measures in
place of this temporary device, until at last the blockade of
Holland and the Empire, from the river Ems to Trieste,—in
which, April 26, 1809, the restrictive system of England was
merged,—seemed to sweep away all trace of the narrower
restraint. No one but Sir William Scott could say with certainty, as matter of law, whether Fox's blockade was or was
not in force; but for years past England had established a
depot at Helgoland in the mouth of the Elbe, for no other
purpose than to violate its own blockade by smuggling merchandise into Germany, Denmark, and Holland. From every
point of view the continued existence of Fox's blockade
seemed impossible to suppose.

February 15 Pinkney wrote to Wellesley, asking whether
that or any other blockade of France previous to January,
1807, was understood to be in force.[1] March 2 Wellesley replied that the restrictions imposed in May, 1806, " were afterward comprehended in the Order of Council of Jan. 7, 1807,
which order is still in force."[2] This reply encouraged Pinkney
to infer that Fox's blockade had merged in Howick's Order
in Council. March 7 he wrote again to the Marquess,[3] —

"I infer . . . that the blockade . . . is not itself in force,
and that the restrictions which it established rest altogether,
so far as such restrictions exist at this time, upon an Order
or Orders in Council issued since the first day of January,
1807."

To this easy question, which seemed hardly worth answer-
ing in the negative, Wellesley replied, March 26,[4]

"The blockade notified by Great Britain in May, 1806,

[1] Pinkney to Wellesley, Feb. 15, 1810; State Papers, iii. 350.
[2] Wellesley to Pinkney, March 2, 1810; State Papers, iii. 350.
[3] Pinkney to Wellesley, March 7, 1810; State Papers, iii. 350.
[4] Wellesley to Pinkney, March 26, 1810; State Papers, iii. 356.

has never been formally withdrawn. It cannot, therefore, be accurately stated that the restrictions which it established rest altogether on the Order of Council of Jan. 7, 1807; they are comprehended under the more extensive restrictions of that Order."

This explanation, however satisfactory it might be to the admiralty lawyer who may have framed it, conveyed no clear idea to the diplomatic mind. The question whether the blockade of 1806 was or was not still in force remained obscure. Pinkney thought it not in force, and wrote to Armstrong,[1] —

"Certainly the inference is that the blockade of 1806 is virtually at an end, being merged and comprehended in an Order in Council issued after the date of the Edict of Berlin. I am, however, about to try to obtain a formal revocation of that blockade, and of that of Venice [July 27, 1806], or at least a precise declaration that they are not in force."

His hopes were not strong, but he returned patiently to his task, and April 30 wrote a third letter to Lord Wellesley,[2] in which he recited Napoleon's promise in full, and begged Wellesley to say " whether there exists any objection on the part of his Majesty's government to a revocation, or to a declaration that they are no longer in force, of the blockades in question, especially that of May, 1806."

Already Pinkney had waited nearly three months for a plain answer to a question which ought certainly to have received a satisfactory reply within a week. He was destined to wait longer; indeed, the United States waited two years for their answer before they declared war. The reason for this incomprehensible behavior, at a moment when America was thought to be friendly, cannot be fully explained; but evidence published in his brother's papers seems to show that Marquess Wellesley favored giving up not only Fox's blockade, but also the principle of commercial restrictions represented both in the Orders of November, 1807, and in the blockade of April, 1809. "He only agreed with his colleagues in the legality and propriety of the orders when first enacted.

[1] Pinkney to Armstrong, April 6, 1810; State Papers, iii. 355.
[2] Pinkney to Wellesley, April 30, 1810; State Papers, iii. 357.

He contended that they had ceased to be applicable to the state of affairs; that they had become inexpedient with regard to England, and would certainly produce a war with America."[1] That he insisted on this opinion in the Cabinet, or forced an issue with his colleagues on the point, is not to be supposed; but without doubt the treatment his opinions and authority received in the Cabinet was the cause of his strange conduct toward the American minister.

Pinkney's last letter about Fox's blockade was dated April 30. As early as April 25 every well-informed man in London knew that Wellesley was on bad terms with his colleagues. The Marquess of Buckingham's correspondent had the news from Wellesley's own mouth:[2] —

"Lord Wellesley complains that he has no weight whatever in Council; that there is nothing doing there which marks energy or activity; that the affairs of the country are quite at a standstill, and are likely to remain so; and that so little is his private interest in any of the departments, that since his accession to office he has not been able to make an exciseman. . . . Add to all this that he hates, despises, and is out of friendship or even intimacy with every one of his colleagues at this moment."[3]

Two years afterward the Marquess repeated the same story in public:[4] —

"Lord Wellesley," he declared, speaking in the third person, "had repeatedly, with great reluctance, yielded his opinions to the Cabinet on many other important points [besides the war in the Peninsula]. He was sincerely convinced by experience that in every such instance he had submitted to opinions more incorrect than his own, and had sacrificed to the object of accommodation and temporary harmony more than he could justify in point of strict public duty. In fact he was convinced by experience that the Cabinet neither possessed ability nor knowledge to devise a

[1] Memorandum; Supplementary Despatches, vii. 264.
[2] Cf. Lewis's Administrations, 323, *note.*
[3] Buckingham Memoirs, iv. 435.
[4] Statement, etc.; Cobbett's Debates, xxiii. 367, *note.*

good plan, nor temper and discernment to adopt what he now thought necessary, unless Mr. Perceval should concur with Lord Wellesley. To Mr. Perceval's judgment or attainments Lord Wellesley, under the same experience, could not pay any deference without injury to the public service."

Probably Wellesley did not conceal in Council the opinion of his colleagues which he freely expressed in society. In every way they annoyed him. A scholar, who prided himself on his classical studies and refined tastes, he found these colleagues altering his state papers and criticising his style. "He had thought he was among a Cabinet of statesmen," he said; "he found them a set of critics." His own criticisms occasionally touched matters more delicate than style. Once at a Cabinet meeting Lord Westmoreland, the Privy Seal, put his feet on the table while Wellesley was talking. The Foreign Secretary stopped short. "I will go on with my remarks," he said, " when the noble Lord resumes a more seemly attitude."

Americans could hardly be blamed for holding a low opinion of this Administration, when most intelligent Englishmen held the same. If Whigs or Liberals like Grenville, Brougham, and Sydney Smith were prejudiced critics, this charge could hardly be brought against Canning; but if Canning's opinion were set aside, the Wellesleys at least being identified with his administration had every reason to wish Perceval success. How the Marquess hated and despised Perceval; how he struggled to get rid of him, and strained every nerve to bring Canning, Castlereagh, Sidmouth, Grey, or Grenville into the Government as a counter-balancing influence, can be read in the biographies of all these men, and of many less famous. London echoed with the Marquess's deep disgust; every man of fair parts in England sympathized with it, unless his personal interests or feelings bound him to blind devotion. The yoke hung heavy on Whigs and Tories alike. Even Lord Sidmouth rebelled against the commercial system to which Perceval clung more desperately than to his offices or power. "Of that destructive system," wrote Sidmouth in the summer of 1810,[1] "all are weary, 'praeter atrocem animum Catonis.' "

Even Henry Wellesley, at Seville and Cadiz, felt the same

[1] Pellew's Sidmouth, ii. 507.

heavy hand deadening the effect of every effort, and longed
to do at Cadiz what Erskine had done at Washington. March
4, 1810,[1] Perceval wrote to Lord Wellesley begging him to
instruct his brother Henry to obtain from the Spanish Junta
exclusive or at least special privileges in the trade of the Spanish colonies, such as would admit British consuls to the chief
places of South America, and "give us a decided benefit and
preference in the trade." Of course this preference was to be
granted at the expense of the United States, the solitary rival
of England in those waters, but "as nearly hostile to Spain as
she can be without actually declaring war against her." Soon
afterward the "Espagnol," a Spanish periodical published in
England, applauded revolutionary movements in Caracas and
Buenos Ayres, while it asserted the impossibility of preventing the spread of the spirit of independence in the Spanish-
American colonies.

"You can have no idea," wrote Henry Wellesley from
Cadiz, August 31, to his brother Arthur,[2] "of the ferment
occasioned here by this article, which is attributed to the
Government,—as it is supposed, and I believe justly, that
the 'Espagnol' is patronized by the Government, and contains its sentiments with regard to the occurrences in Spain
and the measures necessary in the present crisis of her affairs. . . . It is wonderful that they cannot be satisfied in
England with a commercial arrangement which would be
attended with immense advantages to ourselves, and would
likewise be greatly beneficial to Spain. I apprehend this to
be the true spirit of all commercial treaties; and why are we
to take advantage of the weakness of Spain to endeavor to
impose terms upon her which would be ruinous and disgraceful? I have it in my power to conclude to-morrow a
commercial treaty which, without breaking in upon the
Spanish colonial laws, would pour millions into the pockets
of our merchants, and be equally advantageous to the resources; but this will not do, and we must either have the
trade direct with the colonies, or nothing. However, I have

[1] Walpole's Perceval, ii. 114.
[2] Wellington's Supplementary Despatches, vi. 583.

received my answer, and the Government will not hear of opening the trade."

The coincidence of opinion about Spencer Perceval extended everywhere, except among the Church of England clergy, the country squires, the shipping interests, the Royal household at Windsor, and the Federalists of Boston and Connecticut. As though to make him an object of execration, the long-threatened storm burst on the trade and private credit of Great Britain. For some eighteen months gold stood at a premium of about fifteen per cent; the exchanges remained steadily unfavorable, while credit was strained to the utmost, until in July, 1810, half the traders in England, and private banks by the score, were forced to suspend payment. Never before, and probably never since, has England known such a fall in prices and destruction of credit.[1]

This was the impending situation when Parliament adjourned, June 21, with no bright spot on its horizon but the supposed friendship of America. Meanwhile Pinkney wearied Wellesley for an answer to the question whether Fox's blockade was in force. June 10, June 23, and finally August 6, he renewed his formal request. "No importunity had before been spared which it became me to use."[2] He was met by the same torpor at every other point. Wellesley promised to name a new minister to Washington, but decided upon none. He invited overtures in regard to the "Chesapeake" affair, but failed to act on them. Rumor said that he neglected business, came rarely to Cabinet meetings, shut himself in his own house, saw only a few friends, and abandoned the attempt to enforce his views. He resolved to retire from the Cabinet, in despair of doing good, and waited only for the month before the next meeting of Parliament, which he conceived to be the most proper time for declaring his intention.[3]

In the midst of this chaos, such as England had rarely seen, fell Cadore's announcement of August 5 that the Imperial Decrees were withdrawn, *bien entendu* that before November 1 England should have abandoned her blockades, or America

[1] Tooke's History of Prices.
[2] Pinkney to Robert Smith, Aug. 14, 1810; State Papers, iii. 363.
[3] Memorandum; Supplementary Despatches of Lord Wellington, vii. 266.

should have enforced her rights. Pinkney hastened to lay this information before Lord Wellesley, August 25, and received the usual friendly promises, which had ceased to gratify him. "I am truly disgusted with this," he wrote home, August 29,[1] "and would, if I followed my own inclination, speedily put an end to it." Two days afterward he received from Wellesley a civil note,[2] saying that whenever the repeal of the French Decrees should actually have taken effect, and the commerce of neutral nations should have been restored to the condition in which it previously stood, the system of counteraction adopted by England should be abandoned. This reply, being merely another form of silence, irritated Pinkney still more, while his instructions pressed him to act. He waited until September 21, when he addressed to Wellesley a keen remonstrance. "If I had been so fortunate," he began,[3] "as to obtain for my hitherto unanswered inquiry the notice which I had flattered myself it might receive, and to which I certainly thought it was recommended by the plainest considerations of policy and justice, it would not perhaps have been necessary for me to trouble your Lordship with this letter;" and in this tone he went on to protest against the "unwarrantable prohibitions of intercourse rather than regular blockades," which had helped in nearly obliterating "every trace of the public law of the world": —

"Your Lordship has informed me in a recent note that it is 'his Majesty's earnest desire to see the commerce of the world restored to that freedom which is necessary for its prosperity;' and I cannot suppose that this freedom is understood to be consistent with vast constructive blockades which may be so expanded at pleasure as, without the aid of any new device, to oppress and annihilate every trade but that which England thinks fit to license. It is not, I am sure, to *such* freedom that your Lordship can be thought to allude."

The Marquess of Buckingham's well-advised correspondent

[1] State Papers, iii. 366.
[2] Wellesley to Pinkney, Aug. 31, 1810; State Papers, iii. 366.
[3] Pinkney to Wellesley, Sept. 21, 1810; State Papers, iii. 368.

some weeks afterward[1] remarked that "Pinkney, who was at first all sweetness and complaisance, has recently exhibited in his communications with Lord Wellesley an ample measure of republican insolence." Sweetness and insolence were equally thrown away. Pinkney's letter of September 21, like most of his other letters, remained unanswered; and before November 1, when Napoleon's term for England's action expired, a new turn of affairs made answer impossible. The old King was allowed to visit the death-bed of his favorite daughter the Princess Amelia; he excited himself over her wishes and fare-wells, and October 25 his mind, long failing, gave way for the last time. His insanity could not be disguised, and the Government fell at once into confusion.

[1] Buckingham Memoirs, iv. 482.

Chapter XIV

THE SUMMER OF 1810 was quiet and hopeful in America. For the first time since December, 1807, trade was free. Although little immigration occurred, the census showed an increase in population of nearly thirty-seven per cent in ten years,—from 5,300,000 to 7,240,000, of which less than one hundred thousand was due to the purchase of Louisiana. Virginia and Massachusetts still fairly held their own, and New York strode in advance of Pennsylvania, while the West gained little relative weight. Ohio had not yet a quarter of a million people, Indiana only twenty-four thousand, and Illinois but twelve thousand, while Michigan contained less than five thousand. The third census showed no decided change in the balance of power from any point of view bounded by the usual horizon of human life. Perhaps the growth of New York city and Philadelphia pointed to a movement among the American people which might prove more revolutionary than any mere agricultural movement westward. Each of these cities contained a population of ninety-six thousand, while Baltimore rose to forty-six thousand, and Boston to thirty-two thousand. The tendency toward city life, if not yet unduly great, was worth noticing, especially because it was confined to the seaboard States of the North.

The reason of this tendency could in part be seen in the Treasury reports on American shipping, which reached in 1810 a registered tonnage of 1,424,000,—a point not again passed until 1826. The registered foreign tonnage sprang to 984,000,—a point not again reached in nearly forty years. New vessels were built to the amount of one hundred and twenty-seven thousand tons in the year 1810.[1] The value of all the merchandise exported in the year ending Sept. 30, 1810, amounted to nearly sixty-seven million dollars, and of this sum about forty-two millions represented articles of domestic production.[2] Except in the year before the embargo this

[1] Statement, etc., Dec. 16, 1811; State Papers, Commerce and Navigation, i. 876.
[2] Gallatin to the Speaker, Feb. 6, 1811; State Papers, Commerce and Navigation, i. 866.

export of domestic produce had never been much exceeded.[1]
The imports, as measured by the revenue, were on the same
scale. The net customs-revenue which reached $16,500,000 in
1807, after falling in 1808 and 1809 to about $7,000,000, rose
again to $12,750,000 in 1810.[2] The profits of the export and
import business fell chiefly to Boston, New York, Philadelphia, and Baltimore, where the shipping belonged; and these
cities could not fail to attract labor as well as capital beyond
the degree that a conservative republican of the Revolutionary
time would have thought safe.

More than half of these commercial exchanges were with
England or her dependencies. Great Britain and her American
colonies, Portugal and Spain in her military protection, and
British India consumed at least one half of the exports; while
of the net revenue collected on imports, Gallatin estimated six
and a half millions as derived from articles imported from
Great Britain and the British dependencies, all other sources
supplying hardly six millions.[3] The nature of these imports
could be only roughly given. In general, sugar, molasses, coffee, wines, silk, and tea were not British; but manufactures of
cotton, linen, leather, paper, glass, earthen-ware, iron, and
other metals came chiefly from Great Britain. To the United
States this British trade brought most of the articles necessary
to daily comfort in every part of the domestic economy. The
relief of recovering a full and cheap supply exceeded the satisfaction of handsome profits on the renewed trade. Experience of the hourly annoyance, expense, and physical exposure
caused by deprivation of what society considered necessities
rendered any return to the restrictive system in the highest
degree unwise, especially after the eastern people acquired
conviction that the system had proved a failure.

Thus the summer passed with much of the old contentment
that marked the first Administration of Jefferson. Having lost
sight of national dignity, the commercial class was contented
under the protection of England; and American ships in the
Baltic, in Portugal, and in the West Indies never hesitated to

[1] Statement, etc., Dec. 16, 1811; State Papers, Commerce and Navigation,
i. 929.
[2] Statement, etc., Feb. 28, 1812; State Papers, Finance, ii. 542–552.
[3] Report on the Finances, Nov. 25, 1811; State Papers, Finance, ii. 495.

ask and were rarely refused the assistance of the British navy. From time to time a few impressments were reported; but impressment had never been the chief subject of complaint, and after the withdrawal of the frigates blockading New York, little was heard of British violence. On the other hand, Napoleon's outrages roused great clamor in commercial society, and his needless harshness to every victim, from the Pope to the American sailors whom he shut up as prisoners of war, went far to palliate British offences in the eyes of American merchants.

News of Napoleon's seizures at San Sebastian arrived before the adjournment of Congress May 1; and as fresh outrages were reported from every quarter by every new arrival, and as Cadore's letters became public, even Madison broke into reproaches. May 25 he wrote to Jefferson:[1] "The late confiscations by Bonaparte comprise robbery, theft, and breach of trust, and exceed in turpitude any of his enormities not wasting human blood." These words seemed to show intense feeling, but Madison's temper indulged in outbursts of irritability without effect on his action; in reality, his mind was bent beyond chance of change on the old idea of his Revolutionary education,—that the United States must not regard France, but must resist Great Britain by commercial restrictions. "This scene on the Continent," he continued to Jefferson, "and the effect of English monopoly on the value of our produce are breaking the charm attached to what is called free-trade, foolishly by some and wickedly by others." He reverted to his life-long theory of commercial regulations.

A few days afterward Madison wrote to Armstrong fresh instructions founded on the Act of May 1, which was to be the new diplomatic guide. These instructions,[2] dated June 5, were of course signed by the Secretary of State, Robert Smith, who afterward claimed credit for them; but their style, both of thought and expression, belonged to Madison. Even the unfailing note of his mind—irritability without passion— was not wanting. He would wait, he said, for further advices before making the proper comments on Cadore's letter of February 14 and on its doctrine of reprisals. "I cannot, how-

[1] Madison's Works, ii. 477.
[2] State Papers, iii. 384.

ever, forbear informing you that a high indignation is felt by the President, as well as by the public, at this act of violence on our property, and at the outrage both in the language and in the matter of the letter of the Duc de Cadore." Turning from this subject, the despatch requested that Napoleon would make use of the suggestion contained in the Act of May 1, 1810. "If there be sincerity in the language held at different times by the French government, and especially in the late overture, to proceed to amicable and just arrangements in case of our refusal to submit to the British Orders in Council, no pretext can be found for longer declining to put an end to the decrees of which the United States have so justly complained." One condition alone was imposed on Armstrong preliminary to the acceptance of French action under the law of May 1, but this condition was essential:

> "If, however, the arrangement contemplated by the law should be acceptable to the French government, you will understand it to be the purpose of the President not to proceed in giving it effect in case the late seizure of the property of the citizens of the United States has been followed by an absolute confiscation, and restoration be finally refused. The only ground short of a preliminary restoration of the property on which the contemplated arrangement can be made will be an understanding that the confiscation is reversible, and that it will become immediately the subject of discussion with a reasonable prospect of justice to our injured citizens."

The condition thus prescribed seemed both reasonable and mild in view of the recent and continuous nature of the offence; but Madison could not, even if he would, allow his own or public attention to be permanently diverted from England. As early as June 22 he had begun to reconstruct in his own mind the machinery of his restrictive system. "On the first publication of the despatches by the 'John Adams,'" he wrote to Jefferson,[1] "so strong a feeling was produced by Armstrong's picture of the French robbery that the attitude in which England was placed by the correspondence between

[1] Madison's Works, ii. 480.

Pinkney and Wellesley was overlooked. The public attention is beginning to fix itself on the proof it affords that the original sin against neutrals lies with Great Britain; and that while she acknowledges it, she persists in it."

The theory of original sin led to many conclusions hard to reconcile; but, as regarded Napoleon, Madison's idea seemed both sensible and dignified,—that England's original fault in no way justified the recent acts of France, which were equivalent to war on the United States, not as one among neutrals, but as a particular enemy. Fresh instructions to Armstrong, dated July 5,[1] reiterated the complaints, offers, and conditions of the despatch sent one month before. Especially the condition precedent to action under the law of May 1 was repeated with emphasis:—

"As has been heretofore stated to you, a satisfactory provision for restoring the property lately surprised and seized, by the order or at the instance of the French government, must be combined with a repeal of the French edicts with a view to a non-intercourse with Great Britain, such a provision being an indispensable evidence of the just purpose of France toward the United States. And you will moreover be careful, in arranging such a provision for that particular case of spoliations, not to weaken the ground on which a redress of others may be justly pursued."

The instructions of June 5 and July 5 went their way; but although Armstrong duly received them, and wrote to Cadore a letter evidently founded on the despatch of June 5, he made no express allusion to his instructions in writing either to the French government or to his own. Although he remained in Paris till September 12, and on that day received from Cadore an explicit avowal that the sequestered property would not be restored, but that "the principles of reprisal must be the law," he made no protest.

Equally obscure was the conduct of Madison. Cadore's letter of August 5 announcing that the French Decrees were withdrawn, on the understanding that the United States should by November 1 enforce their rights against England,

[1] State Papers, iii. 385.

reached Washington September 25, but not in official form. Nothing is known of the impression it produced on the Cabinet; nothing remains of any discussions that ensued. If Gallatin was consulted, he left no trace of his opinion. Hamilton and Eustis had little weight in deciding foreign questions. Robert Smith within a year afterward publicly attacked the President for the course pursued, and gave the impression that it was taken on Madison's sole judgment. The President's only authority to act at all without consulting Congress depended on the words of the law of May 1: "In case either Great Britain or France shall, before the third day of March next, so revoke or modify her edicts as that they shall cease to violate the neutral commerce of the United States, which fact the President of the United States shall proclaim by proclamation," the non-intercourse of March 1, 1809, should at the end of three months revive against the nation which had not revoked its edicts. Under this authority, President Madison was required by Cadore's letter to proclaim that France had revoked or modified her edicts so that they ceased to violate the neutral commerce of the United States.

Madison was doubtless a man of veracity; but how was it possible that any man of veracity could proclaim that France had revoked or modified her edicts so that they ceased to violate the neutral commerce of the United States when he had every reason to think that at least the Bayonne Decree, barely six months old, would not be revoked, and when within a few weeks he had officially declared that the revocation of the Bayonne Decree was "an indispensable evidence of the just purpose of France" preliminary to a non-intercourse with England? If the President in June and July thought that provision indispensable to the true intent of the law which he aided in framing, he would assume something more than royal dispensing power by setting the indispensable provision aside in November.

This objection was light in comparison with others. The law required the President to proclaim a fact,—that France had revoked or modified her decrees so that they ceased to violate the commerce of America. Of this fact Cadore's letter was the only proof; but evidently Cadore's letter pledged the Emperor to nothing. "I am authorized to declare to you,"

wrote Cadore, "that the Decrees of Berlin and Milan are revoked, and that after November 1 they will cease to have effect, on the understanding that in consequence of this
declaration . . . the United States, conformably to the Act
you have just communicated, shall cause their rights to be
respected by the English." Napoleon not only reserved to
himself the right of judging whether the measures to be taken
by the United States should "cause their rights to be respected," but in doing so he reversed the process prescribed
by the Act, and required the President to enforce his rights
before the Emperor should withdraw his decrees.

From the standpoint of morality, perhaps the most serious
objection of all was the danger of sacrificing national and personal self-respect by affecting to regard as honest a promise
evidently framed to deceive, and made by a man whom Madison habitually characterized in terms that implied, to speak
mildly, entire want of confidence. If America would consent
to assert her rights against England in no way more straightforward than this, she might perhaps recover her neutral profits, but hardly her national self-respect.

A few months afterward, when Robert Smith gave to the
world the amusing but not wholly new spectacle of a Secretary of State attacking his own President for measures signed
by his own name, Joel Barlow wrote for the "National Intelligencer" a defence of the President's course, in which he
gave reasons supplied by Madison himself for holding that
Cadore's letter satisfied the conditions of Macon's Act.

To the first objection, founded on the Rambouillet and
Bayonne Decrees, Barlow replied that the American government had habitually distinguished between maritime edicts violating neutral rights and municipal edicts attacking private
property. "We could not in strictness arraign such municipal
spoliations under the head of violations of our *neutral* rights,
nor of consequence regard them as contemplated by the Acts
of Congress defining the acts whose revocation would satisfy
the conditions of that Act." This reasoning, though not quite
convincing, might have had weight but for two objections.
First, the President himself, in June and July, had declared
these municipal spoliations to be contemplated by Macon's
Act as "an indispensable evidence of the just purpose of

France;"[1] and, second, the President in November notified Armstrong, that,[2] "in issuing the proclamation, it has been presumed that the requisition contained in that letter [of July 5] on the subject of the sequestered property will have been satisfied." Barlow's idea of a municipal spoliation, independent of the *jus gentium*, was an afterthought intended to hide a miscalculation.

One other argument was advanced by Barlow. Erskine's arrangement having been accepted without question of previous British spoliations, not only did impartiality require the same treatment for France, but a different rule "would have led to the embarrassment of obliging the Executive, in case the British government should be desirous of opening a free trade with the United States by repealing its orders, to make it a prerequisite that Great Britain also should indemnify for her respective spoliations."

Such a prerequisite would have been proper, and ought to have been imposed; but Barlow's argument was again answered by the President himself, who actually insisted on the demand against France, and assumed the demand to be satisfied. If this was partiality to England, the President was guilty of it. Probably at the time he saw reasons for thinking otherwise. The secrecy, the continuance, the pretext of the French seizures, their municipal and vindictive character and direct Imperial agency seemed to set them apart from those of England, which, although equally illegal, were always in the form of lawful trial and condemnation.

The same argument of impartiality served to justify immediate action on Cadore's offer as on Erskine's, without waiting for its execution. That one admitted mistake excused its own repetition in a worse form was a plea not usually advanced by servants, either public or private; but in truth Erskine's pledge was distinct and unconditional, while Cadore's depended on the Emperor's satisfaction with a preliminary act. Had Erskine made his arrangement conditional on Canning's approval of the President's measures, Madison would certainly have waited for that approval before acting under the law; and after the disastrous results of precipitancy in

[1] Cf. Speech of Mr. Eppes, Feb. 2, 1811; Annals of Congress, 1810–1811, 866.
[2] Robert Smith to Armstrong, Nov. 2, 1810; State Papers, iii. 389.

1809, when no one questioned Erskine's good faith, wisdom called for more caution rather than less in acting, in 1810, on an offer or a pledge from a man in whom no one felt any confidence at all.

In truth, Madison's course in both cases was due not to logic, but to impatience. As Barlow admitted: "We know it had been the aim of our government for two or three years to divide the belligerents by inducing one or the other of them to revoke its edicts, so that the example would lead to a revocation by the other, or our contest be limited to a single one." Madison gave the same reason in a letter of October 19 to Jefferson:[1] "We hope from the step the advantage at least of having but one contest on our hands at a time." He was mistaken, and no one expressed himself afterward in language more bitter than he used against Napoleon for conduct that deceived only those who lent themselves to deception.

October 31, Robert Smith sent for Turreau and gave him notice of the decision reached by the President and Cabinet:[2] —

> "The Executive," said Robert Smith, "is determined not to suffer England longer to trammel the commerce of the United States, and he hopes to be sustained by Congress. If, then, England does not renounce her system of paper-blockades and the other vexations resulting from it, no arrangement with that Power is to be expected; and consequently you will see, in two days, the President's proclamation appear, founded on the provisions of the law requiring the non-intercourse to be enforced against either nation which should fail to revoke its edicts after the other belligerent had done so. . . . Although we have received nothing directly from Mr. Armstrong on this subject, which is doubtless very extraordinary, we consider as sufficient for the Government's purposes the communication he made to Mr. Pinkney, which the latter has transmitted to us."

The next day Robert Smith made some further interesting

[1] Works, ii. 484.
[2] Turreau to Champagny, 1 November, 1810 (No. 1); Archives des Aff. Étr. MSS.

remarks.[1] "The Executive thinks," he said, "that the measures he shall take in case England continues to restrict our communications with Europe will lead necessarily to war," because of the terms of the non-intercourse. "We have with us a majority of Congress, which has much to retrieve, and has been accused of weakness by all parties."

On leaving Smith, Turreau went to see Gallatin, " whose opinion in the Cabinet is rarely favorable to us."

"Mr. Gallatin (by the way long since on bad terms with Mr. Smith) told me that he believed in war; that England could not suffer the execution of measures so prejudicial to her, and especially in the actual circumstances could not renounce the prerogatives of her maritime supremacy and of her commercial ascendency."

Both Smith and Gallatin evidently expected that war was to result, not from the further action of the United States, but from the resentment and retaliation of England. They regarded the non-intercourse as a measure of compulsion which would require England either to resent it or to yield.

Having decided to accept Cadore's letter as proof that an actual repeal of the French Decrees, within the meaning of the Act of Congress, had taken place November 1, the President issued, November 2, his proclamation declaring that "it has been officially made known to this Government that the said edicts of France have been so revoked as that they ceased, on the said first day of the present month, to violate the neutral commerce of the United States;" and simultaneously Gallatin issued a circular to the collectors of customs, announcing that commercial intercourse with Great Britain would cease Feb. 2, 1811.

By this means Madison succeeded in reverting to his methods of peaceful coercion. As concerned England, he could be blamed only on the ground that his methods were admittedly inadequate, as Gallatin, only a year before, had officially complained. Toward England the United States had stood for five years in a position which warranted them in adopting any measure of reprisal. The people of America alone had a right

[1] Turreau to Champagny, 2 November, 1810 (No. 6); Archives des Aff. Étr. MSS.

to object that when Madison began his attack on England by proclaiming the French Decrees to be revoked, he made himself a party to Napoleon's fraud, and could scarcely blame the Federalists for replying that neither in honor nor in patriotism were they bound to abet him in such a scheme.

The Proclamation of Nov. 2, 1810, was not the only measure of the autumn which exposed the President to something more severe than criticism. At the moment when he challenged a contest with England on the assertion that Napoleon had withdrawn his decrees, Madison resumed his encroachments on Spain in a form equally open to objection.

The chaos that reigned at Madrid and Cadiz could not fail to make itself felt throughout the Spanish empire. Under British influence, Buenos Ayres in 1810 separated from the Supreme Junta, and drove out the viceroy whom the Junta had appointed. In April of the same year Caracas followed the example, and entered into a treaty with England, granting commercial preferences equally annoying to the Spaniards and to the United States. Miranda reappeared at the head of a revolution which quickly spread through Venezuela and New Grenada. A civil war broke out in Mexico. Even Cuba became uneasy. The bulky fabric of Spanish authority was shaken, and no one doubted that it must soon fall in pieces forever.

England and the United States, like two vultures, hovered over the expiring empire, snatching at the morsels they most coveted, while the unfortunate Spaniards, to whom the rich prey belonged, flung themselves, without leadership or resources, on the ranks of Napoleon's armies. England pursued her game over the whole of Spanish America, if not by government authority, more effectively by private intrigue; while the United States for the moment confined their activity to a single object, not wholly without excuse.

As long as Baton Rouge and Mobile remained Spanish, New Orleans was insecure. This evident danger prompted Madison, when Secretary of State, to make a series of efforts, all more or less unfortunate, to gain possession of West Florida; and perhaps nothing but Napoleon's positive threat of war prevented the seizure of Baton Rouge during Jefferson's time. After that crisis, the subject dropped from diplomatic discussion; but as years passed, and Spanish power waned, American influence steadily spread in the province. Numerous Americans settled in or near the district of West Feliciana, within sight of Fort Adams, across the American border. As their number increased, the Spanish flag at Baton Rouge became less and less agreeable to them; but they waited until Buenos Ayres and Caracas gave notice that Spain could be safely defied.

In the middle of July, 1810, the citizens of West Feliciana appointed four delegates to a general convention, and sent invitations to the neighboring districts inviting them to cooperate in re-establishing a settled government. The convention was held July 25, and consisted of sixteen delegates from four districts, who organized themselves as a legislature, and with the aid or consent of the Spanish governor began to remodel the government. After some weeks of activity they quarrelled with the governor, charged him with perfidy, and suddenly assembling all the armed men they could raise, assaulted Baton Rouge. The Spanish fort, at best incapable of defence, was in charge of young Louis Grandpré, with a few invalid or worthless soldiers. The young man thought himself bound in honor to maintain a trust committed to him; he rejected the summons to surrender, and when the Americans swarmed over the ruinous bastions they found Louis Grandpré almost alone defending his flag. He was killed.

After capturing Baton Rouge, the Americans held a convention, which declared itself representative of the people of West Florida, and September 26 issued a proclamation, which claimed place among the curious products of that extraordinary time. "It is known to the world," began this new declaration of independence,[1] " with how much fidelity the good people of this territory have professed and maintained allegiance to their legitimate sovereign while any hope remained of receiving from him protection for their property and lives." The convention had acted in concert with the Spanish governor "for the express purpose of preserving this territory, and showing our attachment to the government which had heretofore protected us;" but the governor had endeavored to

[1] State Papers, iii. 396.

pervert those concerted measures into an engine of destruction; and therefore, "appealing to the Supreme Ruler of the world for the rectitude of our intentions, we do solemnly publish and declare the several districts composing the territory of West Florida to be a free and independent State."

A few days afterward the convention, through its president, wrote to the Secretary of State, Robert Smith, urging the annexation of the new territory to the United States, but claiming all the public lands in the province for "the people of this Commonwealth, who have wrested the government and country from Spain at the risk of their lives and fortunes."[1] These words accorded ill with their appeal to the Supreme Ruler of the world for the rectitude of their intentions, and their protest of "our inviolable fidelity to our king and parent country while so much as a shadow of legitimate authority remained to be exercised over us." Yet neither with nor without their elaborate machinery of legitimate revolution could Madison have anything to do with them. Innumerable obstacles stood in his way. They declared the independence of territory which he had long since appropriated to the United States. This course alone withheld Madison from recognizing the new State; but other difficulties forbade any action at all. The Constitution gave the President no power to use the army or navy of the United States beyond the national limits, without the authority of Congress; and although extreme emergency might have excused the President in taking such action, no emergency existed in October, 1810, since Congress would meet within six weeks, and neither Spain, France, nor England could interfere in the interval. The President's only legal course was to wait for Congress to take what measures seemed good.

Madison saw all this, but though aware of his want of authority, felt the strongest impulse to act without it. He described his dilemma to Jefferson in a letter written before he received the request for annexation, then on its way from Baton Rouge:[2] —

"The crisis in West Florida, as you will see, has come

[1] State Papers, iii. 395.
[2] Madison to Jefferson, Oct. 19, 1810; Works, ii. 484.

home to our feelings and interests. It presents at the same time serious questions as to the authority of the Executive, and the adequacy of the existing laws of the United States for territorial administration. And the near approach of Congress might subject any intermediate interposition of the Executive to the charge of being premature and disrespectful, if not of being illegal. Still, there is great weight in the considerations that the country to the Perdido, being our own, may be fairly taken possession of, if it can be done without violence; above all, if there be danger of its passing into the hands of a third and dangerous party."

Casuistry might carry the United States government far. The military occupation of West Florida was an act of war against Spain. "From present appearances," continued Madison, "our occupancy of West Florida would be resented by Spain, by England, and by France, and bring on, not a triangular, but quadrangular contest." Napoleon himself never committed a more arbitrary act than that of marching an army, without notice, into a neighbor's territory, on the plea that he claimed it as his own. None of Madison's predecessors ventured on such liberties with the law; none of his successors dared imitate them, except under the pretext that war already existed by the act of the adverse government.

Madison was regarded by his contemporaries as a precise, well-balanced, even a timid man, argumentative to satiety, never carried away by bursts of passion, fretful rather than vehement, pertinacious rather than resolute,—a character that seemed incapable of surprising the world by reckless ambition or lawless acts; yet this circumspect citizen, always treated by his associates with a shade of contempt as a closet politician, paid surprisingly little regard to rules of consistency or caution. His Virginia Resolutions of 1798, his instructions in the Louisiana purchase, his assumption of Livingston's claim to West Florida, his treatment of Yrujo, his embargo policy, his acceptance of Erskine's arrangement, his acceptance of Cadore's arrangement, and his occupation of West Florida were all examples of the same trait; and an abundance of others were to come. He ignored caution in pursuit of an object which seemed to him proper in itself;

nor could he understand why this quiet and patriotic conduct should rouse tempests of passion in his opponents,
whose violence, by contrast, increased the apparent placidity
of his own persistence.

Forestalling the action of Congress which was to meet
within five weeks, President Madison issued, Oct. 27, 1810, a
proclamation announcing that Governor Claiborne would
take possession of West Florida to the river Perdido, in the
name and behalf of the United States. This proclamation, one
of the most remarkable documents in the archives of the
United States government, began by reasserting the familiar
claim to West Florida as included in the Louisiana purchase: —

> "And whereas the acquiescence of the United States in
> the temporary continuance of the said territory under the
> Spanish authority was not the result of any distrust of their
> title, as has been particularly evinced by the general tenor
> of their laws and by the distinction made in the application
> of those laws between that territory and foreign countries,
> but was occasioned by their conciliatory views, and by a
> confidence in the justice of their cause, and in the success
> of candid discussion and amicable negotiation with a just
> and friendly Power; . . . considering, moreover, that un-
> der these peculiar and imperative circumstances a forbear-
> ance on the part of the United States to occupy the
> territory in question, and thereby guard against the confu-
> sions and contingencies which threaten it, might be con-
> strued into a dereliction of their title or an insensibility to
> the importance of the stake; considering that in the hands
> of the United States it will not cease to be a subject of fair
> and friendly negotiation and adjustment; considering finally
> that the Acts of Congress, though contemplating a present
> possession by a foreign authority, have contemplated also
> an eventual possession of the said territory by the United
> States, and are accordingly so framed as in that case to ex-
> tend in their operation to the same," —

Considering all these reasons, substantially the same self-
interest by which France justified her decrees, and England
her impressments, the President ordered Governor Claiborne,

with the aid of the United States army, to occupy the country and to govern it as a part of his own Orleans territory.[1] By a letter of the same date the Secretary of State informed Claiborne, that, "if contrary to expectation, the occupation of this [revolutionized] territory should be opposed by force, the commanding officer of the regular troops on the Mississippi will have orders from the Secretary of War to afford you, upon your application, the requisite aid. . . . Should however any particular place, however small, remain in possession of a Spanish force, you will not proceed to employ force against it, but you will make immediate report thereof to this Department."[2] Having by these few strokes of his pen authorized the seizure of territory belonging to "a just and friendly Power," and having legislated for a foreign people without consulting their wishes, the President sent to the revolutionary convention at Baton Rouge a sharp message through Governor Holmes of the Mississippi territory, to the effect that their independence was an impertinence, and their designs on the public lands were something worse.[3]

A few days after taking these measures, Robert Smith explained their causes to Turreau in the same conversation in which he announced the decision to accept Cadore's letter as the foundation of non-intercourse with England. The wish to preclude British occupation of Florida was the motive alleged by Smith for the intended occupation by the United States.[4]

"As for the Floridas, I swear, General, on my honor as a gentleman," said Robert Smith to Turreau, October 31, "not only that we are strangers to everything that has happened, but even that the Americans who have appeared there either as agents or leaders are enemies of the Executive, and act in this sense against the Federal government as well as against Spain. . . . Moreover these men and some others have been led into these measures by the hope of obtaining from a new government considerable conces-

[1] Proclamation, etc., Oct. 27, 1810; State Papers, iii. 397.

[2] Secretary of State to Governor Claiborne, Oct. 27, 1810; State Papers, iii. 396.

[3] Secretary of State to Governor Holmes, Nov. 15, 1810; State Papers, iii. 398.

[4] Turreau to Champagny, 1 Nov. 1810 (No. 2); Archives des Aff. Étr. MSS.

sions of lands. In any case you will soon learn the measures we have taken to prevent the English from being received at Baton Rouge as they have been at Pensacola, which would render them absolute masters of our outlets by the Mobile and Mississippi. We hope that your Government will not take it ill that we should defend the part of Florida in dispute between Spain and us; and whether our pretensions are well-founded or not, your interest, like ours, requires us to oppose the enterprises of England in that country."

Claiborne took possession of the revolutionized districts December 7, and the Spanish governor at Mobile was not sorry to see the insurgents so promptly repressed and deprived of their expected profits. Yet Claiborne did not advance to the Perdido; he went no farther than the Pearl River, and began friendly negotiations with Governor Folch at Mobile for delivery of the country still held by the Spaniards between the Pearl and the Perdido. Governor Folch had none but diplomatic weapons to use in his defence, but he used these to save that portion of the province for some years to Spain.

The four districts west of the Pearl River were organized by Claiborne as a part of the territory of Orleans, in which shape, the President's proclamation had said, "it will not cease to be a subject of fair and friendly negotiation and adjustment" with Spain. Within a few weeks the President announced to Congress in his Annual Message that "the legality and necessity of the course pursued" required from the Legislature "whatever provisions may be due to the essential rights and equitable interests of the people thus brought into the bosom of the American family." The difficulty of reconciling two such assertions perplexed many persons who in the interests of law and of society wished to understand how a people already brought into the bosom of the American family could remain a subject of fair negotiation with a foreign Power. The point became further complicated by the admission of Louisiana as a State into the Union, with the four districts which were "to be a subject of fair and friendly negotiation."

The first result of these tortuous proceedings was to call a protest from Morier, the British chargé at Washington, who wrote to the Secretary of State, December 15, a letter[1] containing one paragraph worth noting: —

"Would it not have been worthy of the generosity of a free nation like this, bearing, as it doubtless does, a respect for the rights of a gallant people at this moment engaged in a noble struggle for its liberty, — would it not have been an act on the part of this country dictated by the sacred ties of good neighborhood and friendship which exist between it and Spain, to have simply offered its assistance to crush the common enemy of both, rather than to have made such interference the pretext for wresting a province from a friendly Power, and that at the time of her adversity?"

Spain had little reason to draw distinctions between friends, allies, and enemies. She could hardly stop to remember that the United States were filching a petty sand-heap in a remote corner of the world, at a time when England was "wresting" not one but all the splendid American provinces from their parent country, and when France was kneeling on the victim's breast and aiming stab after stab at her heart.

[1] Morier to Robert Smith, Dec. 15, 1810; State Papers, iii. 399.

Chapter XV

THE ELECTIONS for the Twelfth Congress, as far as they took place in 1810, showed a change in public opinion, and not only reduced the Federalists to their old rank of a faction rather than a party, but also weakened the conservative Republicans of Jefferson's school; while the losses of both strengthened a new party, which called itself Republican, but favored energy in government. Henry Clay and William Lowndes, John C. Calhoun and Felix Grundy, Langdon Cheves and Peter B. Porter, whatever they might at times say, cared little for Jeffersonian or Madisonian dogmas. The election which decided the character of the Twelfth Congress, by choosing men of this character to lead it, decided also the popular judgment on the Eleventh Congress, which had as yet run only half its course. Rarely in American history has any particular Congress been held in high popular esteem, but seldom if ever was a Congress overwhelmed by contempt so deep and general as that which withered the Eleventh in the midst of its career. Not only did Republicans and Federalists think alike for once, but even among the members themselves no one of weight had a good word to say of the body to which he belonged.

Quick to feel a popular rebuke, Congressmen submitted to punishment, and obeyed the orders they would rather have resisted; but their work in such a temper was sure to be done without good-will or good faith, for a body which had lost its own respect could hardly respect its successor. The American system of prolonging the existence of one Legislature after electing another, never worked worse in practice than when it allowed this rump Congress of 1809, the mere scourings of the embargo, to assume the task of preparing for the War of 1812, to which it was altogether opposed and in which it could not believe. No Congress had been confronted by greater perplexities. President Madison submitted to it a number of Executive acts more than doubtful in legality, which must all be approved; and these measures, when approved, led to a policy of war with England and Spain, which required great increase of Executive strength, careful reorganization of the Executive machinery, especially great care of the national credit and of its chief financial agents,—political duties of extreme difficulty and delicacy.

President Madison's Annual Message, December 5, called attention to such business as he wished to present. Naturally, the revocation of the French Decrees took the first place. The President assumed that the revocation was complete, and that his proclamation was issued in regular course, "as prescribed by law," the President having no discretion; but he admitted disappointment that the sequestered property had not been restored. "It was particularly anticipated that, as a further evidence of just disposition toward them, restoration would have been immediately made of the property of our citizens, seized under a misapplication of the principle of reprisals, combined with a misconstruction of a law of the United States. This expectation has not been fulfilled." England had not yet relinquished her illegitimate blockades, and she avowed that the blockade of May, 1806, was comprehended in the subsequent Orders in Council; the withdrawal of that blockade had therefore been required by the President as one of the conditions of renewing intercourse with Great Britain. The state of the Spanish monarchy had produced a change in West Florida, a district " which though of right appertaining to the United States had remained in the possession of Spain, awaiting the result of negotiations for its actual delivery to them." The Spanish authority being subverted, the President did not delay taking possession; "the legality and necessity of the course pursued assure me of the favorable light in which it will present itself to the Legislature."

If this sketch of foreign affairs lacked perfect candor, the view of domestic concerns gave matter for other doubts. "With the Indian tribes," said the Message, "the peace and friendship of the United States are found to be so eligible that the general disposition to preserve both continues to gain strength." The story of Tippecanoe and Tecumthe soon threw new light on this assertion. To Indian friendship domestic prosperity succeeded, and the Message praised the economy and policy of manufactures. "How far it may be expedient to guard the infancy of this improvement in the distribution of labor by regulations of the commercial tariff, is a subject

which cannot fail to suggest itself to your patriotic reflections." A navigation law was also required to place American
shipping on a level of competition with foreign vessels. A national university " would contribute not less to strengthen the
foundations than to adorn the structure of our free and happy
system of government." Further means for repressing the
slave-trade were required. Fortifications, arms, and organization of the militia were to be provided. The Military School
at West Point needed enlargement.

Congress found more satisfaction in Gallatin's Annual Report, sent to Congress a week afterward, than they could
draw from Madison's Message, for Gallatin told them that he
had succeeded in bringing the current expenses within the
annual income; and only in case they should decide to prohibit the importation of British goods after Feb. 2, 1811,
should he need further legislation both to make good the revenue and to enforce the prohibition.

Congress lost no time. West Florida called first for attention; and Senator Giles, December 18, reported a bill extending the territory of Orleans to the river Perdido, in
accordance with the President's measures. In the debate
which followed, Federalist senators attacked the President for
exceeding the law and violating the Constitution. Their argument was founded on the facts already told, and required
nothing more to support it; but the defence had greater interest, for no one could foretell with certainty by what expedient senators would cover an Executive act which, like the
purchase of Louisiana itself, had best be accepted in silence as
plainly beyond the Constitution. Henry Clay acted as the
President's champion, and explained on his behalf that the
Act of Oct. 31, 1803, authorizing the President to occupy the
ceded territory of Louisiana, was still in force, although regular possession to the Iberville had been taken, Dec. 20, 1803,
in pursuance of that Act, without further demand on the part
of the United States, and although the Act of March 20, 1804,
providing for the temporary government of the territory, declared that "the Act passed the 31st day of October . . . shall
continue in force until the 1st day of October, 1804." In face
of this double difficulty,—the exhaustion of the power and
its express limitation,—Clay asserted that the power had not

been exhausted, and that the limitation, though apparently general, was intended only for the provisional government established by another portion of the Act of 1803. He produced in his support the Act of Feb. 24, 1804, empowering the President to erect West Florida into a collection district whenever he deemed it expedient. "These laws," continued Clay, "furnish a legislative construction of the treaty correspondent with that given by the Executive, and they vest in this branch of the government indisputably a power to take possession of the country whenever it might be proper in his discretion."

Congress approved this opinion, which was in truth neither weaker nor stronger than the arguments by which the Louisiana purchase itself had been sustained. Fate willed that every measure connected with that territory should be imbued with the same spirit of force or fraud which tainted its title. The Southern States needed the Floridas, and cared little what law might be cited to warrant seizing them; yet a Virginia Republican should have been startled at learning that after October, 1803, every President, past or to come, had the right to march the army or send the navy of the United States at any time to occupy not only West Florida, but also Texas and Oregon, as far as the North Pole itself, since they claimed it all, except the Russian possessions, as a part of the Louisiana purchase, with more reason than they claimed West Florida.

As usual, the most pungent critic of Republican doctrines was Senator Pickering, who if he could not convince, could always annoy the majority. He replied to Clay, and in the course of his speech read Talleyrand's letter of Dec. 21, 1804, which put an end to Monroe's attempt to include West Florida in the Louisiana purchase. Nothing could be more apt; but nothing could be more annoying to the Administration, for Talleyrand's letter was still secret. Confidentially communicated with other papers to Congress by Jefferson, Dec. 6, 1805, the injunction of secrecy had never been removed, and the publication tended to throw contempt on Madison not only for his past but particularly for his present dalliance with Napoleon. Pickering could charge, with more than usual appearance of probability, that West Florida was to be Madison's reward for accepting the plainly deceptive pledge of Cadore's letter of August 5. The Senate, with some doubts, resented Pickering's conduct to a moderate extent. Samuel Smith moved it to be "a palpable violation of the rules;" and with the omission of "palpable," the resolution was adopted. The deference to Executive authority which allowed so important a paper to be suppressed for five years showed more political sagacity than was proved in censuring Pickering by a party vote, which he would regard as a compliment, because he read a document that the Administration should have been ashamed not to publish and resent.

The interlude helped only to embarrass the true question,—what should be done with West Florida. President Madison's doctrine, embodied in Giles's bill, carried out the Livingston-Monroe theory that West Florida belonged to Louisiana. In theory, this arrangement might answer the purpose for which it was invented; but in fact West Florida did not belong to Louisiana, either as a Spanish or as an American province, and could not be treated as though it did. If Mobile Bay and the Gulf coast as far as the Perdido belonged to Louisiana, the territory afterward divided into the States of Alabama and Mississippi had no outlet to the gulf. Georgia would never consent to such treatment, merely to support President Madison in alleging that West Florida was occupied by him as a part of the Orleans territory. Senator Giles's bill was silently dropped.

The Senate reached this point December 31, but meanwhile the House reached the same stand-still from another side. December 17 the Speaker appointed a committee, with Macon at its head, to report on the admission of Orleans territory as a State. The admission of the State of Louisiana into the Union was for many reasons a serious moment in American history; but one of its lesser incidents was the doubt which so much perplexed the Senate, whether Louisiana included West Florida. If this was the case, then by the third article of the treaty of purchase the inhabitants of Mobile and the district between Mobile and Baton Rouge, without division, should be "incorporated in the Union of the United States, and admitted as soon as possible" to the Union as part of the territory of Orleans. This was the opinion of Macon and his committee, as it had been that of Giles and his committee, and of the President and his Cabinet. December 27 Macon reported a bill admitting Louisiana, with West Florida to the Perdido, as a State; but no sooner did the debates begin, than the Georgians for the first time showed delicacy in regard to the rights of Spain. Troup could not consent to include in any State this territory "yet in dispute and subject to negotiation." Bibb held the same misgivings: "The President by his proclamation, although he had required its occupation, had declared that the right should be subject to negotiation; now, if it became a State, would not all right of negotiation be taken from the President?" To prevent this danger, Bibb moved that West Florida, from the Iberville to the Perdido, should be annexed to the Mississippi Territory or made a separate government.

On the other hand, Rhea of Tennessee held that no other course was open to Congress than to admit the Orleans territory in its full extent as ceded by France, according to the President's assertion. The treaty was peremptory, and Congress was bound by it to annex no part of the Orleans purchase to a pre-existing territory. West Florida belonged to Louisiana, and could not lawfully be given to Mississippi.

The House tried as usual to defer or compromise its difficulty. January 9, Macon's bill was so amended as to withdraw West Florida from its operation; but when on the following day two members in succession asked the House to provide a government for West Florida, the House referred the motions back to the committee, and there the matter rested. No man knew whether West Florida belonged to Louisiana or not. If the President was right, Mobile and all the Gulf shore to a point within ten miles of Pensacola, although still held by the Spaniards, made part of the State of Louisiana, and even an Act of Congress could not affect it; while if this was not the case, the President in ordering the seizure of West Florida had violated the Constitution and made war on Spain.

Hardly had the House admitted its helplessness in the face of this difficulty, when it was obliged to meet the larger issue involved in the Louisiana affair; for Jan. 14, 1811, Josiah Quincy, with extreme deliberation, uttered and committed to writing a sentence which remained long famous:—

"If this bill passes, it is my deliberate opinion that it is virtually a dissolution of this Union; that it will free the

States from their moral obligation; and, as it will be the right of all, so it will be the duty of some, definitely to prepare for a separation,—amicably if they can, violently if they must."

The Speaker decided this language to be disorderly; but the House, by a vote of fifty-six to fifty-three, reversed the ruling, and Quincy went on arguing, as Jefferson had argued eight years before, that the introduction of new States, outside the original Union, was no part of the compact, and must end in overwhelming the original partners.

Quincy's protest wanted only one quality to give it force. He spoke in the name of no party to the original compact. His own State of Massachusetts assented to the admission of Louisiana, and neither the governor nor the legislature countenanced the doctrine of Quincy and Pickering. If the partners themselves made no protest, the act had all the legality it needed, in the absence of appeal to higher authority; but it consummated a change in the nature of the United States government, and its results, however slow, could not fail to create what was in effect a new Constitution.

The House, without further delay, passed the bill by a vote of seventy-seven to thirty-six. After some amendment by the Senate, and dispute between the Houses, the bill was sent to the President, and Feb. 20, 1811, received his signature. The Act fixed the Iberville and the Sabine for the eastern and western boundaries of the new State. Meanwhile West Florida remained, till further legislation, a part of Orleans Territory for all purposes except those of admission into the Union; and, according to the view implied by the action of Executive and Legislature, the President retained power to order the military occupation of Texas under the Act of Oct. 31, 1803, subject to government afterward, like West Florida, by the proconsular authority of the Executive.

As though the Florida affair needed still further complication, the President, January 3, sent to Congress a secret message asking authority to seize East Florida:—

"I recommend . . . the expediency of authorizing the Executive to take temporary possession of any part or parts of the said territory, in pursuance of arrangements which may be desired by the Spanish authorities. . . . The wisdom of Congress will at the same time determine how far it may be expedient to provide for the event of a subversion of the Spanish authorities within the territory in question, and an apprehended occupancy thereof by any other foreign Power."

In secret session Congress debated and passed an Act, approved Jan. 15, 1811, authorizing the President to take possession of East Florida, in case the local authority should consent or a foreign Power should attempt to occupy it. The President immediately appointed two commissioners to carry the law into effect. The orders he gave them, the meaning they put on these orders, the action they took, and the President's further measures were to form another remarkable episode in the complicated history of Florida.

Congress next turned to the charter of the United States Bank; but if it succumbed before West Florida, it was helpless in dealing with finance. Long hesitation had ended by creating difficulties. Local interests hostile to the Bank sprang into existence. In many States private banks were applying for charters, and preparing to issue notes in the hope of seizing their share of the profits of the United States Bank. The influence of these new corporations was great. They induced one State legislature after another to instruct their senators on the subject. That Massachusetts, Pennsylvania, and Maryland should wish to appropriate the profits of the National Bank was not surprising, but that Virginia and Kentucky should make themselves instruments of the capitalist States showed little knowledge of their true interests. As the crisis came near, the struggle became hotter, until it rivalled the embargo excitement, and every hour of delay increased the vehemence of opposition to the charter.

The Bank was vulnerable on more than one side. Largely owned in England, it roused jealousy as a foreign influence. Congress could hardly blame this ownership, since Congress itself, in 1802, aided President Jefferson in selling to the Barings, at a premium of forty-five per cent, the two thousand two hundred and twenty Bank shares still belonging to the government. The operation brought to the Treasury not only a profit of four hundred thousand dollars in premiums, but also about thirteen hundred thousand dollars of British capital to be used for American purposes. Fully two thirds of the Bank stock, amounting to ten million dollars, were owned in England; all the five thousand shares originally subscribed by the United States government had been sold to England; and as the Bank was a mere creature of the United States government, these seven millions of British capital were equivalent to a score of British frigates or regiments lent to the United States to use against England in war. By returning them, the United States seriously weakened themselves and strengthened their enemy.

Unfortunately this interest was national. Local interests felt that Englishmen received profits which should belong to Americans; and capitalists in general were not inclined to lower their profits by inviting foreign capital into the country unless they shared its returns. The second misfortune of the Bank was that of being a Federalist creation, chiefly used for the benefit of Federalists, who owned most of the active capital in the country. The third objection went deeper. The Bank was the last vestige of strong government created by the Federalists,—a possible engine of despotism; and no one could deny that if decentralization was wise, the Bank should be suppressed. Finally, the Bank was a bulwark to Gallatin; its destruction would weaken Madison and drive Gallatin from office.

Doubtless the objections to the Bank were so strong as some day to become fatal. In a society and government so little developed as those of America, a National Bank was out of keeping with other institutions. Even in England and France these banks exercised more influence over the Treasury than was proper; and in America, if once the Bank should unite in political sympathy with the Government, it might do no little harm. The necessity for such an institution was merely one of the moment, but in the period of national history between 1790 and 1860, the year 1811 was perhaps the only moment when destruction of the Bank threatened national ruin. A financial cataclysm had prostrated credit from St. Petersburg to New Orleans. Prices were nominal. England owed America large sums of money, but instead of discharging the debt, she was trying to escape payment and withdraw specie. Already the supply of specie in the United States was insufficient to sustain the bank-note circulation. In New York city the State banks were supposed to hold not more than half a million dollars, and in Pennsylvania not much more than a million; while the Bank of the United States had lost three and a half millions in eleven months, and had but five and a half millions left.[1]

Meanwhile the State banks not only expanded their issues, but also rapidly increased in number. Suppression of the National Bank could not fail to stimulate this movement. "The banks established by the State legislatures will scramble for the privilege of filling the chasm to be made by the destruction of the Bank of the United States. Already are they preparing for the patriotic endeavor. Our State legislatures are to be importuned to become bank jobbers and joint undertakers and copartners in the enterprise."[2] Nothing could prevent expansion of credit, drain of specie, bankruptcy and confusion of the currency; and this was to be done at the time the country entered into a war with the only Power whose influence could shake the Union to its foundation.

Madison stood aloof, and left on Gallatin the burden of the struggle; but Gallatin's energies and influence could do little with the Eleventh Congress. He was strongest in the House; but there the debate, after many speeches, ended, January 24, by a vote of sixty-five to sixty-four in favor of indefinite postponement, and by common consent all parties waited for the Senate to decide. The omen was not happy for the Treasury.

Gallatin had at last found a capable senator to support him. The political fortunes of William Henry Crawford, which ended only at the threshold of the White House, drew no small part of their growth from his courageous defence of the Treasury during these chaotic years. Crawford showed the faults of a strong nature,—he was overbearing, high-tempered, and his ambition did not spurn what his enemies called intrigue; but he possessed the courage of Henry Clay, with

[1] Speech of Mr. Tallmadge of Connecticut, Jan. 23, 1811; Annals of Congress, 1810–1811, p. 784.
[2] Speech of Jonathan Fisk of New York, Jan. 17, 1811; Annals of Congress, 1810–1811, p. 612.

more than Clay's intelligence, though far less than his charm.
Crawford was never weak, rarely oratorical; and if he was ever
emotional he reserved his emotion for other places than the
Senate. "One man at last appeared who filled my expectations," wrote Gallatin many years afterward to an old and
intimate friend.[1] "This was Mr. Crawford, who united to a
powerful mind a most correct judgment and an inflexible integrity,—which last quality, not sufficiently tempered by indulgence and civility, has prevented his acquiring general
popularity." February 5 he introduced into the Senate a bill
continuing the old Bank charter for twenty years on certain
conditions; and February 11 he supported the bill in a speech
remarkable for the severity of its truths. He began by challenging the Constitution itself:—

> "Upon the most thorough examination [of the Consti-
> tution] I am induced to believe that many of the various
> constructions given to it are the result of a belief that it is
> absolutely perfect. It has become so extremely fashionable
> to eulogize this Constitution, whether the object of the eu-
> logist is the extension or contraction of the powers of the
> government, that whenever its eulogium is pronounced I
> feel an involuntary apprehension of mischief."

Upon the party theory that Congress could exercise no implied power, and therefore could not charter a corporation,
Crawford fell energetically, until he came in contact with the
instructions of State legislatures, which he swept out of his
path with actual contempt:—

> "What is the inducement with these great States to put
> down the Bank of the United States? Their avarice com-
> bined with their love of domination! . . . The great com-
> mercial States are to monopolize the benefits which are to
> arise from the deposits of your public money. The suppres-
> sion of this Bank will benefit none of the interior or smaller
> States in which there is little or no revenue collected. As
> the whole benefit is to be engrossed by three or four of the
> great Atlantic States, so the whole of the power which the

[1] Adams's Gallatin, p. 598.

dissolution of this Bank will take from the national government will be exclusively monopolized by the same States."

Under Gallatin's teaching, Crawford bade fair to make himself, what the South so greatly needed, a statesman who understood its interests; but he was far in advance of his people.
The society from which he sprang was more correctly represented by Giles, who answered him in the manner for which
the Virginia senator had acquired unpleasant notoriety. February 14 John Randolph, who with all his faults was not so
factious as to join in the scheme of the State banks, wrote to
his friend Nicholson:[1] "Giles made this morning the most unintelligible speech on the Bank of the United States that I ever
heard." Never had Giles taken more trouble to be judicial,
candid, and temperate; no one could have admitted with
more impartiality the force of his opponent's arguments; but
his instincts, stronger than his logic, compelled him to vote
against the Bank. The conclusion was as certain as the process
was vague.

Henry Clay, who followed on the same side, ironically
complimented the Virginia senator, who had "certainly demonstrated to the satisfaction of all who heard him both that it
was constitutional and unconstitutional, highly proper and
improper, to prolong the charter of the Bank;" but Clay's
irony was as unfortunate as Giles's logic. The sarcasm thrown
at Giles recoiled on Clay himself, for he passed the rest of his
life in contradicting and repenting the speech he made at this
moment, in which he took ground against the power of Congress to create corporations. "The power to charter companies is not specified in the grant, and, I contend, is of a nature
not transferable by mere implication. It is one of the most
exalted attributes of sovereignty." The legislation of twenty
years which enforced the opposite opinion he swept aside in
his peculiar manner. "This doctrine of precedents, applied to
the legislature, appears to me to be fraught with the most
mischievous consequences." With more than his ordinary self-
confidence, he affirmed that the Treasury could be as well
conducted without as with the Bank; and he closed with a
burst of rhetoric hardly to be paralleled in his oratory, by

[1] Adams's Gallatin, p. 430.

holding the Bank responsible for not preventing Great Britain from attacking the "Chesapeake," impressing American seamen, and issuing the Orders in Council.

Clay's excuse for extravagances like these was neither his youth nor his ignorance of affairs nor his obedience to instructions, nor yet a certain want of tact which made him through life the victim of needless mistakes, but was rather the simple repentance with which, within five years, he threw himself on the mercy of the public, admitting that had he foreseen the effect of his course he would have acted in a very different way.[1] Even for Giles some apology might be made, for no one could deny that consistency required him to vote as he did, and he could appeal to the record in his defence. The worst offender was not Giles or Clay, but Samuel Smith.

When Crawford flung so freely his charges of avarice and ambition about the Senate chamber, he had Samuel Smith directly in his eye; for Smith's action was avowedly controlled by his interests, and since his speech on Macon's bill his attitude toward public measures was better understood than before. No one could conceive Smith to be influenced by conscientious scruples about implied powers, but many persons besides Madison and Gallatin believed him to be selfish and grasping. Baltimore favored State banks, and Smith lent his reputation as a business man to the service of local politics and interests, except so far as in doing this he aimed at the overthrow of Gallatin. He gave what amounted to a pledge of his character as a merchant to the assertion that the State banks were better, safer, and more efficient agencies for the Treasury than the Bank of the United States could possibly be. In making the speech which advanced these doctrines, he threw out an express challenge to Gallatin. "The secretary is considered by his friends a very great man in fiscal operations; in commercial matters I may be permitted to have opinions of my own." As a commercial authority he asserted that government had much greater control over the State banks than over the United States Bank; that more confidence could be put in the security of the State banks than in that of the National Bank; that they could more easily effect the necessary

---

[1] Address to Constituents; Annals of Congress, 1815—1816, p. 1193.

exchanges; that they were as prudently conducted; that the National Bank did not act as a check upon them, but they acted as a check upon it; that the ordinary and extraordinary business of the Treasury could be as effectually and securely done by the State banks; and that the liquidation of the United States Bank would "be remembered nine days and not much longer." When five years afterward the fallacy of these opinions became too notorious for question, Smith did not, like Clay, throw himself on the justice of his country or admit his errors, but he voted to re-establish the Bank in a far more extensive form, and took the ground that it was the only means of repairing mistakes which he had been a principal agent in making.

The other speeches made in this debate, although quite equal in ability to these, carried less political weight, for they implied less factiousness. One remained, which excited no small curiosity and some amusement.

When the Senate, February 20, divided on the motion to strike out the enacting clause, seventeen senators voted for the Bank and seventeen voted against it. Nine Northern senators voted in its favor, including seven of the ten from New England, and nine on the opposite side. Eight Southern senators voted one way, and eight the other. Of the twenty-seven Republican senators, seventeen voted against the Bank, and ten in its favor; while the three senators who were supposed to be in personal opposition to the President—Giles, Samuel Smith, and Michael Leib—all voted in opposition. The force of personal feeling was credited with still another vote; for when the result was announced, the Vice-President, George Clinton, whose attitude was notorious, made a short address to the effect that "the power to create corporations is not expressly granted; it is a high attribute of sovereignty, and in its nature not accessorial or derivative by implication, but primary and independent." On this ground he threw his casting vote against the bill.

So perished the first Bank of the United States; and with its destruction the Federalist crisis, so long threatened, began at last to throw its shadow over the government.

Chapter XVI

WHILE CONGRESS recoiled from the problem of West Florida, and by a single voice decreed that the United States Bank should cease to exist, nothing had yet been decided in regard to England and France.

This delay was not due to negligence. From the first day of the session anxiety had been great; but decision, which even in indifferent matters was difficult for the Eleventh Congress, became impossible in so complicated a subject as that of foreign relations. The President's proclamation named Feb. 2, 1811, as the day when intercourse with England was to cease. Congress had been six weeks in session, and had barely a fortnight to spare, when at last the subject was brought before the House, January 15, by John W. Eppes of Virginia, chairman of the committees of Ways and Means and Foreign Relations, who reported a bill for regulating commercial intercourse with Great Britain. As a third or fourth commercial experiment,—a companion to the partial Non-intercourse Act of April, 1806; the embargo of December, 1807; and the total Non-intercourse Act of March, 1809,—the new bill promised more discontent in America than it was ever likely to create in England. The measure was not a non-intercourse, but a non-importation, severe and searching, in some ways almost as violent as the embargo; and was to be passed by a Congress elected expressly for the purpose of repealing the embargo.

The proposed bill lay on the Speaker's table. February approached, and still Congress did nothing; yet this delay substituted in place of the Constitution a system of government by proclamation. In two instances involving not only foreign war, but also more than half the foreign trade and several principles of fundamental law, the country depended in February, 1810, on two Executive proclamations, which rested on two assertions of fact that no one believed to be true. In spite of Madison and his proclamations, West Florida was not a part of Louisiana; Napoleon had not withdrawn his decrees,—and Congress was unwilling to support either assertion.

Unless the Berlin and Milan Decrees were repealed Nov. 1, 1810, as Cadore's letter was held to promise, neither President nor Congress could reasonably take the ground that Cadore's letter, of itself, revived the non-intercourse against England. The United States had the right to make war on England with or without notice, either for her past spoliations, her actual blockades, her Orders in Council other than blockades, her Rule of 1756, her impressments, or her attack on the "Chesapeake," not yet redressed,—possibly also for other reasons less notorious; but the right to make war did not carry with it the right to require that the world should declare to be true an assertion which the world knew to be false. Unless England were a shrew to be tamed, President Madison could hardly insist on her admitting the sun to be the moon; and so well was Congress aware of this difficulty that it waited in silence for two months, until, February 2, the President's proclamation went into effect; while the longer Congress waited, the greater became its doubts.

Only one proof could be admitted as sufficient evidence that the French Decrees were repealed. The Emperor had violated American rights by decree, and until he restored them by decree no municipal order of his subordinates could replace the United States in the position they claimed. For this reason the President and Congress waited anxiously for news from Paris to November 1, when the decree of appeal should have issued. The news came, but included no decree. The President then assumed that at least the Decrees of Berlin and Milan would not be enforced in France after November 1; but letters from Bordeaux, dated Dec. 14, 1810, brought news that two American vessels which entered that port about December 1 had been sequestered. No other American vessels were known to have arrived in French ports except with French licenses.

This intelligence was a disaster. The President communicated it to Congress in a brief message[1] January 31; and so serious was its effect that on February 2, when the non-intercourse revived by proclamation, Eppes rose in the House and moved to recommit his bill on the ground that the

[1] State Papers, iii. 390.

behavior of France gave no excuse for action against England. "The non-intercourse went into operation to-day," he said. "It had been considered by the Committee of Foreign Relations that in the present state of our affairs it would be better to provide for the relief of our own citizens and suspend the passage of the law for enforcing the non-intercourse until the doubts hanging over our foreign relations were dissipated."

The opposition would have done well to let Eppes struggle with his difficulties as he best could without interference; but Randolph, who liked to press an advantage, professing a wish to relieve the President "from the dilemma in which he must now stand," moved the repeal of the Non-intercourse Act of March 1, 1809,—a step which if taken would have repealed also the President's proclamation. The motion brought on a premature debate. Out-reasoned, out-manœuvred, and driven to the wall, the Republicans could only become dogged and defiant. They took the ground that retreat was impossible. Eppes avowed that he considered the national faith pledged to France; and although he would not enforce the non-intercourse against England until he had certain knowledge that the French Decrees were withdrawn, he must have unequivocal evidence that France had "violated the faith pledged to this nation" before he would vote to repeal the law. Apologetic throughout, he admitted that indemnity for the French seizures had always been considered an essential part of any arrangement with Napoleon, yet held that the national faith was pledged to that arrangement, although an essential part of the Emperor's obligation was omitted. Every speaker on the Republican side, with the exception of Dr. Samuel L. Mitchill of New York, asserted with increasing vehemence that the Act of May 1, 1810, created a contract with France, made perfect by Cadore's letter of August 5. This legal view of Napoleonic statesmanship had much force with the Republican lawyers of the Eleventh Congress, although its necessary consequence followed its announcement; for since law, whatever lawyers might sometimes seem to assert, was not politics,—differing especially in the point that law had a sanction of force, while international politics had none,— and since Napoleon could in no way be controlled by any sanction, and still less be trusted, the so-called contract, while binding on America, in no way bound France.

Even Langdon Cheves, the new member from South Carolina, maintained that the United States could no longer break their compact with the Emperor. "Was it not better," he asked, "that the nation should preserve all it had left,—its good faith? Its property and honor had been sacrificed, and all that was left was its good faith." Cheves admitted that his doctrine of "good faith" had an ulterior motive, which was to force a conflict with England. "He had never been satisifed with the wisdom or propriety of the law of May last in any other view than one. He believed it would make the country act a part worthy of its character; it would precipitate us on a particular enemy,—and this, he believed, the country required." He went so far as to assert "that the decrees were removed, and that if the violation of our rights continued to-morrow, yet the decrees were so revoked on the 1st of November last as that they did cease to violate our commerce. If our rights are now violated, it is a violation independent of the decrees, by the mere will of an arbitrary and powerful government." Rhea of Tennessee went further still. "If any compact," said he, "can be of greater dignity than a treaty, the law of May 1, made by the constituted authorities of the United States, and agreed to and acted on by the constituted authorities of France, forms that compact."

When one nation is agreed in the policy of fighting another any pretext will answer, and Government need not even be greatly concerned to give any reason at all; but in the condition of America in 1810, grave dangers might result from setting aside the four or five just issues of war with England in order to insist on an issue that revolted common-sense. If ingenuity had been provoked to suggest the course which would rouse most repugnance in the minds of the largest possible number of Americans, no device better suited for its purpose than the theory of Eppes, Cheves, and Rhea could have been proposed; and if they wished to exasperate the conscience of New England in especial to fanatical violence, they came nearest their end by insisting on an involuntary, one-sided compact, intended to force Massachusetts and Connecticut to do the will of the man whom a majority of the people in New England seriously regarded as anti-Christ. Even on the floor of the House no Republican could stand a moment before John Randolph without better protection than this compact with France, which France herself did not recognize.

"This is the 2d of February," said Randolph. "The time has arrived, the hour now is, when gentlemen by their own arguments, if their arguments be just, are bound to fulfil the contract, which I do not undertake to expound, but which they say has been made—certainly in a manner very novel to our Constitution—between the House of Representatives on the one hand and Bonaparte on the other,—a bargain which, like the bargains of old with the Devil, there is no shaking off. It is a bargain which credulity and imbecility enter into with cunning and power. . . . I call upon gentlemen to make good their promise to his Majesty the Emperor of the French and King of Italy; to redeem their pledge; to cut off in fact nearly the whole of our existing trade in return for the liberty of trading by license from the three favored ports which it has pleased his Imperial Majesty to privilege. No man believes—I beg pardon, sir; I was going to say, but I will not, that no man believes one syllable of this breach of faith on our part. I have too much confidence in the honor of gentlemen not to be convinced that they have persuaded themselves to this effect, although it is incomprehensible to me. Bound, sir, to whom? To Bonaparte? Bound to Shylock? Bound to render up not only the pound of flesh, but every jot of blood in the Constitution? Does he come forward with his pockets swelled with American treasure; do his minions, fattened upon our soil, whether obtained by public rapine or private extortion, do they come forward, calling upon us to make sacrifices of our best interest on the shrine of their resentments, in the name, too, of good faith?"

The majority showed its usual weakness in debate, but rejected Randolph's motion by a vote of sixty-seven to forty-five; and after rejecting it, knew not what to do. Eppes reported a new bill to suspend for a time the operation of the non-intercourse, and a new debate began. February 9 Eppes rejoiced the House by opening a fresh hope of some decided policy. A new French minister was soon to arrive in place of Turreau, and further legislation must wait his arrival.

"He has left France," said Eppes, "at a time to bring us certain information on this question. I have no wish to enter on this interesting question with a bandage round my eyes. Whether France has complied with her engagements, whether France has failed in her engagements, cannot be a subject of ingenious speculation many days longer."

Further proceedings were suspended until Congress should learn what Napoleon's agent would say.[1]

The new minister arrived almost immediately. Unlike Turreau, Serurier was a diplomate by profession. He had last served as French minister at the Hague, where, by no fault of his own, he drove King Louis of Holland from his throne. February 16 he was presented to the President, and the next day had a long interview with Robert Smith, who learned that he brought no instructions or information of any kind on the one subject that engrossed diplomatic attention. The scene with Francis James Jackson was repeated with the French minister. Again and again Smith pressed his inquiries, which Serurier politely declined to answer except by resenting any suggestion that the Emperor would fail to keep his word.[2]

After this interview, on the same day, the President apparently held a Cabinet meeting, and probably also consulted certain party leaders in Congress; but no record of such conferences has been preserved, nor is anything known of the arguments that ended in the most hazardous decision yet risked. If disagreement took place,—if Gallatin, Eppes, Robert Smith, or Crawford remonstrated against the course pursued, not a whisper of their arguments was heard beyond the Cabinet. Serurier himself is the only authority for inferring that some conference was probably held; but he knew so little, that in giving to his Government an account of his first day in Washington he closed the despatch by reporting in a few lines the decision, of which he could have hardly suspected the importance. His interview with Robert Smith took

[1] Robert Smith's Address to the People, June 7, 1811.
[2] Serurier to Maret, Feb. 17, 1811; Archives des. Aff. Étr. MSS.

place on the morning of February 17; the afternoon was probably passed by the President and Cabinet in conference; in the evening Mrs. Madison held a reception, where Serurier was received with general cordiality: —

"In coming away, Mr. Smith—probably intending to say something agreeable, and something that I might regard as the effect of our first conversations—assured me that he was authorized to give me the pledge that if (*pour peu que*) England should show the least new resistance to the withdrawal of her orders, the Government had decided to increase the stringency of the non-intercourse, and to give that measure all the effect it ought to have."

The decision to enforce and re-enforce the non-intercourse against England implied that the President considered Napoleon's Decrees to be withdrawn. February 17, at latest, the decision was made. February 19 the President sent to Congress a Message containing two French documents.[1] The first was a letter, dated December 25, from the Duc de Massa, Minister of Justice, to the President of the Council of Prizes, which recited the words of Cadore's letter and the measures taken by the American government in consequence, and ordered that all captured American vessels should thenceforward not be judged according to the principles of the Decrees of Berlin and Milan, which "shall remain suspended;" but such captured vessels should be sequestrated, "the rights of the proprietors being reserved to them until the 2d of February next, the period at which the United States, having fulfilled the engagement to cause their rights to be respected, the said captures shall be declared null by the Council." The second letter, of the same date, was written by Gaudin, Duc de Gaete, Minister of Finance, to the Director-General of the Customs, directing him thenceforward not to enforce the Berlin and Milan Decrees against American vessels.

On these letters, not on any communications from Serurier, the President rested his decision that the Decrees of Berlin and Milan were so revoked as no longer to violate the neutral commerce of the United States. Obviously they failed to

[1] State Papers, iii. 393.

prove more than that the decrees were partially suspended. According to these orders the decrees were not under any circumstances to be revoked, but their operation upon American commerce in France was to cease in case the Emperor should be satisfied that America had previously enforced against England the principles of the decrees. This was the converse of the American demand, and was in effect the attitude of England. The same packet which brought Jonathan Russell's despatch containing the two letters of the French ministers brought also the "Moniteur" of December 15, which contained the Duc de Cadore's official Report on Foreign Relations,—a paper understood to express the Emperor's own language, and to be decisive as to the meaning of his foreign policy:—

> "Sire, as long as England shall persist in her Orders in Council, your Majesty will persist in your decrees; will oppose the blockade of the Continent to the blockade of the coast, and the confiscation of British merchandise on the Continent to the pillage on the seas. My duty obliges me to say to your Majesty, You cannot henceforward hope to recall your enemies to more moderate ideas except by perseverance in this system."

These documents, combined with a knowledge of the license system, showed the true scope and meaning of Cadore's pledge so clearly as to leave no possibility of doubt. If America chose to accept these limitations of her neutral rights, she was at liberty to do so; but she could hardly require England to admit that the Berlin and Milan Decrees were in any sense revoked because American ships were thenceforward to be admitted to France subject to the system of those decrees. Napoleon concealed neither his policy nor his motives, and as these did not warrant the assertion that France had ceased to violate the neutral rights of America, President Madison was obliged to assume that the Emperor meant to do more. A month after his decision was made, he wrote to Jefferson a letter of speculation as to the reasons that prevented the Emperor from taking the action assumed to belong to his plans:[1]—

[1] Madison to Jefferson, March 18, 1811; Works, ii. 490.

"It is, as you remark, difficult to understand the meaning of Bonaparte toward us. There is little doubt that his want of money and his ignorance of commerce have had a material influence. He has also distrusted the stability and efficacy of our pledge to renew the non-intercourse against Great Britain, and has wished to execute his in a manner that would keep pace only with the execution of ours, and at the same time leave no interval for the operation of the British Orders without a counter-operation in either his or our measures. In all this his folly is obvious."

Such language was not only inconsistent with the doctrine that the French Decrees stood repealed in such a manner as no longer to violate American commerce, but it also showed that Madison deceived himself as to Napoleon's character and his policy. Of all theories on which to found political action, the least reasonable was that of assuming Napoleon to be foolish; yet his "obvious folly" was Madison's explanation of an ingenious and successful device to enforce the Continental system.

Having adopted a policy, Madison could not but carry it to its practical results. Robert Smith came to him February 20 with the draft of a note addressed to Serurier, asking for information—as to the withdrawal of the decrees,—a course similar to that adopted with Jackson. "I was, to my astonishment, told by him that it would not be expedient to send to Mr. Serurier any such note. His deportment during this interview evinced a high degree of disquietude, which occasionally betrayed him into fretful expressions."[1]

Smith did not understand the uselessness of asking Serurier for information he could not give, after deciding to act on such information as though it had been given. Although every one knew privately that Serurier would say nothing on the subject, the President could not afford to give the silence official emphasis; and he probably regarded Smith's attempt to do so as a part of his general effort to discredit the whole system of commercial restrictions. The proposed letter to Serurier could be of no use except to embarrass Congress in legislating against England. Already the first steps for this

[1] Address to the People of the United States, by Robert Smith, 1811.

purpose had been arranged, and the next day, February 21, Eppes moved in the House to amend his bill by substituting two new sections, which revived the non-intercourse of March, 1809, against England in respect to all vessels which left a British port after Feb. 2, 1811, and forbade the courts to entertain the question whether the French edicts were or were not revoked.

Nothing short of a revolution in the form of government could force such a bill through Congress at so late an hour; but the Republican party having decided on the measure, did not shrink from employing the means.

February 23 the House went into committee and took up Eppes's new bill. That it was unsatisfactory could not be denied. Robert Wright of Maryland—a new member, of the war party—moved to amend by requiring from England an arrangement about impressments as an additional condition of restoring intercourse, and had the Government intended to make war its ultimate object it would have adopted Wright's motion; but the House had no such object. Impressment was not one of the grievances which of late had been urged against England; indeed, the subject had somewhat fallen out of sight, and so little did the House care to insist upon it, that only twenty-one votes supported Wright's motion. On the other hand, the conduct of France was hotly discussed, but only by Federalists. The Republicans sat silent.

After one day's debate the bill was reported, and February 26 the true struggle began. The House sat eighteen hours, while the minority consumed time by long speeches and dilatory motions. During the last four hours no quorum was present, and the Speaker decided that in the absence of a quorum no compulsory process could be issued. When the House reassembled at half-past ten on the morning of February 27, long speeches were resumed. The evening session began at six o'clock, when on both sides patience was exhausted. Randolph made two successive motions to postpone. Eppes declared that Randolph's motive was to delay and defeat the bill; Randolph retorted by the lie direct, and for a time the House fell into confusion, while Eppes wrote a challenge on the spot, and sent it by Richard M. Johnson to Randolph, who left the House to instruct his second.

Until half-past two o'clock in the morning of February 28 time was consumed in these tactics,—about eighty members being present, and the majority keeping silence. At that hour Barent Gardenier was on the floor making another diffuse harangue, when Thomas Gholson of Virginia called for the previous question on the last motion before the House. According to the rules, Speaker Varnum stated the motion: "Shall the main question be now put?" It was decided in the affirmative. Gardenier immediately attempted to speak on the main question, when Gholson called him to order. Then followed the *coup d'état*.

"The Speaker decided that according to the late practice of the House it was in order to debate the main question after the previous question had been taken. He said that this practice had been established by the House by a decision two years ago, in opposition to an opinion which he himself had always entertained and had then declared. His decision on that occasion was reversed, and he felt himself bound by that expression of the House."

Gholson appealed. The Speaker decided that the appeal was debatable, but his decision was reversed by a vote of sixty-six to thirteen. The House then, without a division, reversed his first ruling, and ordered that thenceforth, after the motion for the previous question should have been decided in the affirmative, the main question should not be debated.

By this means and by persistent silence the majority put an end to debate. When Randolph returned to the hall and heard what had been done, he burst into reproaches that the House had disgraced itself; but his outcry, which like his language to Eppes was attributed to drink, received no answer except cries to order. Further resistance was not carried to extremes; perhaps the dilatory tactics of later times were hardly applicable to so small a body as the House of 1811, or needed time for development; at all events the bill was forced to its passage, and at about five o'clock on the morning of February 28 the House passed it by a vote of sixty-four to twelve. March 2 it passed the Senate, and was approved by the President. Of all the Republicans, Macon alone in the House and Bradley of Vermont in the Senate voted against it. Matthew

Lyon, who also opposed it, left the House in disgust without voting.

The rule of the previous question thus adopted has been the subject of much criticism, and doubtless tended among other causes to affect the character of the House until in some respects it became rather a court of registration than a deliberative body. With few exceptions in history, this result has proved inevitable in large assemblies whose cumbrous inefficiency has obstructed public needs or interests; and perhaps the House of Representatives in 1811 was not to blame for seeking to correct vices inherent in its character. Such great and permanent changes implied a sufficient cause behind them, even though they led to worse evils. The previous question was a rude expedient for removing wanton obstruction, and might have been the source of benefit rather than of injury to the public service had the House succeeded in giving its new character systematic improvement; but in American history the previous question became an interesting study, because it marked deterioration. Of all the defences provided by the Constitution for special or feeble interests, the right of debate was supposed to be the most valuable; and nowhere was this right so necessary as in Congress. Not even in the courts of justice was deliberation more essential than in the House of Representatives. The Republicans came into office in 1801 to protect special and feeble interests, and had no other reason for existence than as the enemies of centralized power; yet circumstances drove them to impose silence on the voice of a minority that wanted only to prevent an improper act, and they did so by methods substantially the same as those used by Cromwell or Napoleon. In neither case was the minority consulted or its protest regarded. The difference was rather in the character of the actors. The great usurpers of history had in one sense a sufficient motive, for they needed the power they seized, and meant to use it. The Republican majority in the Eleventh Congress neither needed power nor meant to use it. Their object was not to strengthen government, or to prepare for war, or even to suppress popular liberties for their own pleasure, but merely to carry out an Executive scheme which required no haste, and was to be followed by no strong measures. As far as human intelligence could be called blind, the intelligence which guided the House was the blind instinct of power.

The same instinct was shown in the behavior of Congress toward other matters of legislation. Under Executive pressure, the Acts authorizing or approving the seizure of East and West Florida, the admission of Louisiana as a State, and the revival of non-intercourse against England were passed; and this series of measures seemed to a large minority a domestic revolution preliminary to foreign war. Naturally the Federalists and independent Republicans looked for the measures to be taken in order to meet or to escape the dangers thus invited. The Federalists had no small share of English respect for whatever was fixed, and they needed only to be satisfied that the Union was strong in order to yield whatever obedience it required; but they wondered how Madison with his weak Cabinet and Eppes with his still less intelligent majority meant to create and handle the weapons that were to drive Old England from the ocean and to hold New England on the land. They could not believe that a government would fling itself headlong out of the window in order to oblige the people to save it from breaking its neck.

So far from grasping at weapons, Congress and the Executive seemed bent only on throwing away the weapons they held. The Bank perished almost with the same breath that revived the non-intercourse against England. By abolishing the Bank, Congress threw away a large sum of money which Gallatin hoped to employ for his current demand and for possible war. By forbidding the importation of English merchandise, Congress further struck off one half the annual revenue. Gallatin foresaw the danger to the Treasury long before it was realized, and January 28 wrote a letter to Eppes advising a general increase of duties on such importations as might be permitted by law. February 6 Eppes reported from the Ways and Means Committee a bill to this effect; but the House failed to act upon it. Congress would consent to no new taxation; and as the Treasury could not be allowed to fail in its engagements, the House authorized a loan of five million dollars.

Such financial expedients looked toward any result except a policy of vigor, and the rest of the winter's legislation bore out the belief that no vigor was in the mind of Government. The Tenth Congress had increased the military establishment, until in 1808 the appropriations exceeded $4,700,000. The Eleventh Congress reduced them in 1809–1810 to about $3,100,000; in 1811 Congress appropriated barely $3,000,000. The naval appropriations in 1809 reached nearly $3,000,000; in 1810 they were reduced to about $1,600,000; in 1811 Congress appropriated $1,870,000. Even in a time of profound peace, when no thought of war disturbed the world, such armaments would have been hardly sufficient for purposes of police on the coasts and in the territories.

A short debate took place at the last moment of the session, on a bill authorizing the President to accept a corps of fifty thousand volunteers. The measure had been reported by Crawford of Georgia in the Senate, from a committee appointed to consider the occupation of West Florida. March 1 the Senate passed the bill without a division, for it implied neither a new principle nor any necessary expense; while the President, without such authority, would find himself helpless to deal with any trouble that might arise from the affairs of Florida. When the bill reached the House, John Dawson of Virginia urged its adoption; "it was incumbent on them," he said, "to do something to provide for defence." Matthew Lyon said he had frequently voted for such bills when there was no prospect of war; "and now, when we were going to war [with Spain], and giving the provocation ourselves, he was of opinion it ought to be passed." The House, without a division, indefinitely postponed the bill; and thus refusing to do more business of any kind, toward midnight of Sunday, March 3, the Eleventh Congress expired, leaving behind it, in the minds of many serious citizens, the repute of having brought Government to the last stage of imbecility before dissolution.

Chapter XVII

THE GOVERNMENT of the United States reached, March 4, 1811, the lowest point of its long decline. President Madison had remained so passive before domestic faction, while so active in foreign affairs, that the functions of government promised to end in confusion. Besides the greater failures of the last session, more than one personal slight had been inflicted on the President. He obtained the confirmation of Joel Barlow as Armstrong's successor at Paris, by a vote of twenty-one to eleven in the Senate; but when he nominated Alexander Wolcott of Connecticut to succeed Justice Cushing on the Supreme Bench, he met a sharp rebuff. The selection was far from brilliant, but New England offered no great choice among Republicans suited to the bench. Sullivan was dead; Levi Lincoln declined the office; Barnabas Bidwell, detected in a petty defalcation, had absconded to Canada; Joseph Story, still a young man, only thirty-one years of age, was obnoxious to many Republicans on account of his hostility to the embargo, and particularly to Jefferson, who took personal interest in this appointment.[1] The President could think of no one who brought stronger recommendations than Wolcott, and accordingly sent his name to the Senate. A few days afterward John Randolph wrote to his friend Nicholson,[2] —

"The Senate have rejected the nomination of Alexander Wolcott to the bench of the Supreme Court, twenty-four to nine. The President is said to have felt great mortification at this result. The truth seems to be that he is President *de jure* only. Who exercises the office *de facto* I know not, but it seems agreed on all hands that 'there is something behind the throne greater than the throne itself.'"

February 21 the President nominated J. Q. Adams, then absent as minister at St. Petersburg, to the same place, and the Senate unanimously confirmed the appointment. The rejection of Wolcott had no meaning further than showing the

[1] Jefferson to Madison, Sept. 27, 1810; Works, v. 548.
[2] Adams's Gallatin, p. 430.

opinion held by the Republican party of their President's judgment.

"Our Cabinet presents a novel spectacle in the world;" continued Randolph. "Divided against itself, and the most deadly animosity raging between its principal members, — what can come of it but confusion, mischief, and ruin? Macon is quite out of heart."

Gallatin was also out of heart. The conduct of Duane and his "Aurora" put additional venom into the wounds made by the session. Commonly some foundation of truth or probability lay beneath political attacks; some show of evidence or some responsible voucher was alleged if not produced, and the charges against public men, to be accepted, were shaped to suit the known character and habits of the victims; but this was not the case with Duane's assertions of Gallatin's wealth, speculations, embezzlements, and secret intrigues. Duane assumed the truth of his own inventions, and although few persons might be so credulous as to believe him, many were so far influenced as to draw aside and leave Gallatin and the Smiths to fight out their battles as they liked. This withdrawal of active support chiefly weakened the Administration. President Madison had no hold over his friends so long as he refused to declare whom he regarded as friends. He lost not only the Smiths, but also Gallatin, by standing aloof.

"Things as they are cannot go on much longer," wrote Randolph, February 17. "The Administration are now in fact aground at the pitch of high tide, and a spring tide too. Nothing then remains but to lighten the ship, which a dead calm has hitherto kept from going to pieces. If the cabal succeed in their present projects, and I see nothing but promptitude and decision that can prevent it, the nation is undone."

This judgment was so far true that none but persons hostile to all central government could look toward the future without alarm; for if the system continued in the future to lose energy as in the ten years past, the time was not far distant when the country must revert to the old Confederation, or to ties equally weak. Such a result was the outcome of Randolph's principles, and he should have welcomed it; but Randolph was a creature of emotions; with feminine faults he had feminine instincts and insight, which made him often shrink from results of his own acts. At this crisis he showed more political judgment than could be expected from wiser men. Though a Republican of the narrowest Virginia creed, he would take part with none of the factions that racked the government. He opposed vehemently not only the legislative assertion that the French Decrees were withdrawn, but also the legislative violence that overthrew the constitution of the House by means of the previous question. If Randolph was wrong on either of these points, he was at least wrong in company with history itself. He favored his old policy of peace, economy, and a decentralized government, and lost his temper with his colleague Eppes, to the verge of a duel; but for this course he was little to be blamed, since the policy was that of his party, and the contest was not of his making. He gave to Gallatin all the support he had to give. Though more deeply committed than any regular party man to the Constitutional doctrines of narrow construction, he voted with the friends of the Bank. "Randolph's opinion on the bill to renew the charter of the United States Bank is, I believe, unknown to every person except himself," wrote Macon, February 20,[1] —although Macon, himself opposed to the Bank, was Randolph's intimate friend. Disgusted with the factiousness of others, Randolph became almost statesmanlike, and for a brief moment showed how valuable he might have been had his balance equalled his intelligence.

Randolph had long since ceased to hold direct relations with Gallatin, but neither then nor ever afterward did he doubt that Gallatin was the only capable character in the Government, and that he must be supported. "The cabal," whose influence excited disgust in his mind as it did in that of Macon, ought to be put down, and Randolph said plainly to Gallatin's friends that the President must be compelled to do it.[2] This dreaded cabal drew life only from the President himself; in any other sense it was a creature of the imagination. So little did Randolph and Macon know about it that they

[1] Macon to Nicholson, Feb. 20, 1811; Nicholson MSS.
[2] Adams's Gallatin, p. 431.

called its members "the invisibles," and puzzled themselves to account for the influence it appeared to exert. In truth, the cabal had no strength that warranted the alarm it roused. Samuel Smith's abilities have shown themselves in the story. Few men of the time stand more definitely imaged than he in speeches, letters, intrigues, and ambitions, for the exactest measurement; but measured in whatever way he pleased, he was rather mischievous than alarming. His brother Robert, whom he had made Secretary of State, was a mere instrument. Giles possessed more ability, but could never become the leader of a party, or win the confidence of the public. Vice-President Clinton and his friends were an independent faction, ready to coalesce with the Smiths and Giles for any personal objects; but they had little more capacity than the Marylanders. Michael Leib and Duane of the "Aurora" were more useful as intriguers, because they had less to lose; but they were also more dangerous to their friends. Seven or eight Federalist senators also could be depended upon as allies for all ordinary purposes of faction. Yet in such a combination no solidarity existed; no common head, no plan, no object held its members together. The persons engaged in this petty and vexatious war on the Administration could not invent a scheme of common action, or provide a capable leader, or act in unison on any two measures. As Randolph justly said:[1]

> "I am satisfied that Mr. Gallatin, by a timely resistance to their schemes, might have defeated them and rendered the whole cabal as impotent as Nature would seem to have intended them to be; for in point of ability (capacity for intrigue excepted), they are utterly contemptible and insignificant."

Randolph had ruined himself by impetuosity; his only idea of resistance implied violence. Gallatin never used the knife except when every other means had been tried; but when he did so, his act was proof that no other outlet could be opened by the clearest head and the most patient temper of his time. For two years he had waited, while the problem he placed before Madison and Jefferson in 1809 became more perplexed

[1] Adams's Gallatin, p. 432.

and less soluble with every month; but when the Eleventh Congress expired, he reached the same conclusion with Randolph, that promptitude and decision could alone save Madison. Acting on this belief, he wrote a letter of resignation.[1]

"It appears to me," he told the President, "that not only capacity and talents in the Administration, but also a perfect heartfelt cordiality among its members, are essentially necessary to command the public confidence, and to produce the requisite union of views and action between the several branches of government. In at least one of these points your present Administration is defective; and the effects, already sensibly felt, become every day more extensive and fatal. New subdivisions and personal factions, equally hostile to yourself and the general welfare, daily acquire additional strength. Measures of vital importance have been and are defeated; every operation, even of the most simple and ordinary nature, is prevented or impeded; the embarrassments of government, great as from foreign causes they already are, are unnecessarily increased; public confidence in the public councils and in the Executive is impaired,— and every day seems to increase every one of these evils. Such a state of things cannot last; a radical and speedy remedy has become absolutely necessary."

Gallatin's resignation obliged the President to act. How long he might still have waited had Gallatin taken no step, only those can say who best understand the peculiarities of his temper; but in any case he could hardly have much longer postponed a crisis. Not only were his ablest supporters, like Crawford, as impatient as Randolph of the situation, but his own personal grievances were becoming intolerable. He could acquiesce with patience while Gallatin and the Treasury were sacrificed; but he could not bear to be crossed in his foreign policy, or to be opposed on his sensitive point,—the system of commercial restrictions. Gallatin probably liked the nonintercourse as little as it was liked by the Smiths; but he did not, as a Cabinet minister, intrigue against the President's policy, while Robert and Samuel Smith did little else.

[1] Adams's Gallatin, p. 434.

When Gallatin, probably March 5, sent, or brought, his resignation to the White House, Madison declined to accept it, and at once authorized Gallatin to sound James Monroe on the offer of the State Department. Gallatin sent for Richard Brent, Giles's colleague in the Senate, who wrote to Monroe March 7. Brent's letter, followed by others, opened another act in the political drama, for it made Monroe Secretary of State and President of the United States, and prolonged the Virginia dynasty for eight years; but in order to reach this result, Monroe himself had to thread more than one dark and dangerous passage, which would have wrecked the fortunes of any man not born to carry a charmed political life.

Monroe's return to the paths of promotion had been steady and even rapid. In 1808 he was the rival candidate for the Presidency, on the ground that he leaned toward reconciliation with England, while Madison leaned toward France. Without wholly abandoning this attitude, Monroe was invited to become the Republican governor of Virginia; and when attacked for his want of sympathy with Madison, he made explanations, both public and private, which so much irritated his old friend John Randolph as to draw from him a letter, Jan. 14, 1811,[1] telling Monroe of reports industriously circulated, "that in order to promote your election to the chief magistracy of this Commonwealth, you have descended to unbecoming compliances with the members of the Assembly, not excepting your bitterest personal enemies; that you have volunteered explanations to them of the differences heretofore subsisting between yourself and the Administration which amount to a dereliction of the ground which you took after your return from England, and even of your warmest personal friends." The charge was never answered to Randolph's satisfaction.[2] Monroe could not publicly avow that he had made a succession of mistakes, partly under Randolph's influence, which he wished to correct and forget; but on this tacit understanding he was elected governor of Virginia, and for the rest of his life became to John Randolph an object of little esteem considering the confidence and admiration he had so long inspired.

[1] Adams's Randolph, p. 243.
[2] Monroe to Randolph, Feb. 13, 1811; Monroe MSS.

More than most men, Randolph could claim the merits of his own defects. If he was morbidly proud and sensitive, he was at least quick to understand when he had lost a friend. Of him Monroe rid himself without trouble; but Monroe labored under the misfortune that his other oldest and best friends were of the same political stamp. Chief among these, the Mentor of Virginia politics, was John Taylor of Caroline,—a man whose high character, consistent opinions, and considerable abilities made him a valuable ally. Another was Littleton Walker Tazewell. To them, after the rupture with Randolph, Monroe wrote, excusing his course in becoming the Republican candidate for governor, and reasserting in sufficiently strong terms his want of confidence in President Madison:[1] —

> "I fear, if the system of policy which has been so long persevered in, after so many proofs of its dangerous tendency, is still adhered to, that a crisis will arise the dangers of which will require all the virtue, firmness, and talents of our country to avert. And that it will be persevered in seems too probable while the present men remain in power. . . . And if the blame of improvident and injudicious measures is ever to attach to them among the people, it must be by leaving to the authors of those measures the entire responsibility belonging to them."

Within six weeks after this letter had been written, Monroe was asked to join the men in power, and to share the blame of those "improvident and injudicious measures," the responsibility for which ought, as he conceived, to be left entirely to their authors. He wrote at once to Colonel Taylor for advice; and the reply threw much light on the personal and public motives supposed to guide the new Secretary of State. Colonel Taylor advised Monroe to accept the President's invitation, for several reasons.[2] Assuming that Monroe was to succeed Madison as the next Republican candidate for the Presidency, he took for granted that Monroe was to follow

---

[1] Monroe to Tazewell, Feb. 6, 1811; Monroe MSS.

[2] Colonel Taylor to Monroe, March 24, 1811; Monroe MSS. State Department Archives.

the lines of his old opinions, and to correct Madison's leanings toward France.

"Our foreign relations," continued Taylor, "seem to be drawing to a crisis, and you ought to be in the public eye when it happens, for your own sake, independently of the services you can render your country. It is probable that this crisis will occur on a full discovery that France will not do our commerce any substantial good without an equivalent which would amount to its destruction. So soon as this discovery is made, the Government, in all its departments, will alter its policy, and your occupancy of a conspicuous station will shed upon you the glory of its having come round to your opinion."

Colonel Taylor gave no thought to the opposite possibility that Monroe might come round to the opinion of the Government; yet his argument seemed to place Monroe in a position where, if he could not convert Madison, he would have no choice but to let Madison convert him.

"This offer to you is an indication of a disposition in Mr. Madison to relieve himself of the burden [of certain persons and measures]; and if you suffer yourself to lose the benefit of this disposition, another will gain it to your inestimable injury. Suppose this other should be a competitor for the Presidency, will it not be a decisive advantage over you? General Armstrong is probably taking measures for this object. . . . One consideration of great weight is that the public think you an honest man. If this opinion is true, the acceptance seems to be a duty toward relieving it from the suspicion that there are too many avaricious or ambitious intriguers of apparent influence in the government. I suppose the President and Gallatin (whom I know) to be wholly guided by what they think to be the public good; and should you happen to concur with them, it will abate much of the jealousy (though I hope it will never be smothered) with which Executive designs are viewed; and to moderate it, under the perilous situation of the country, is in my view desirable."

The country reached a perilous pass when John Taylor of

Caroline made plans to strengthen the Executive; but he could not have calculated on Monroe's readiness to follow this course so far as it ended in leading him. Taylor's advice threw Monroe into the full current of Executive influence. Alliance with Madison and Gallatin, rupture with France, antagonism to the Smiths and Clintons, jealousy of Armstrong, and defiance of Duane were sound policy, and united honesty with self-interest; but their success depended on elements that Taylor could not measure.

That Monroe shared these views, that they were in fact the common stock of his personal party, might be seen not only in his previous letters, but even more in his reply to Senator Brent,[1] written March 18.

"You intimate," said Monroe to Brent, "that the situation of the country is such as to leave me no alternative. I am aware that our public affairs are far from being in a tranquil and secure state. I may add that there is much reason to fear that a crisis is approaching of a very dangerous tendency,—one which menaces the overthrow of the whole Republican party. Is the Administration impressed with this sentiment, and prepared to act on it? Are things in such a state as to allow the Administration to take the whole subject into consideration, and to provide for the safety of the country and of free government by such measures as circumstances may require, and a comprehensive view of them suggest? Or are we pledged by what is already done to remain spectators of the interior movement, in the expectation of some change abroad as the ground on which we are to act? I have no doubt, from my knowledge of the President and Mr. Gallatin,—with the former of whom I have been long and intimately connected in friendship, and for both of whom, in great and leading points of character, I have the highest consideration and respect,—that if I came into the Government the utmost cordiality would subsist between us, and that any opinions which I might entertain and express respecting our public affairs would receive, so far as circumstances would permit, all the attention to which they might be entitled; but if our course is

[1] Adams's Gallatin, p. 435; Gallatin's Writings, i. 497.

fixed, and the destiny of our country dependent on arrangements already made, I do not perceive how it would be possible for me to render any service at this time in the general government."

If the President's proclamation of Nov. 2, 1810, and the Act of Congress passed March 2, 1811, three weeks before Monroe wrote this letter, had not fixed the course and destiny of the country, instructions to Pinkney and Jonathan Russell—on which those two agents had already acted, and which would be the first papers to be read by Monroe as Secretary of State—seemed certainly to fix beyond recall the course about which Monroe inquired. Even a man more liberal than Madison in professions might have hesitated to say that the future secretary was free to break with France, or to enter on other arrangements with England than those already imposed. Monroe's letter implied disapproval of the course hitherto taken, and a wish, if possible, to change it. Madison was well acquainted not only with Monroe's opinions on foreign affairs, but also with those of Monroe's friends, who held that the course taken by the President ought to be reversed; and with this knowledge of all the circumstances Madison replied[1] to Monroe's inquiry:—

"With the mutual knowledge of our respective views of the foreign as well as domestic interests of our country, I see no serious obstacle on either side to an association of our labors in promoting them. In the general policy of avoiding war by a strict and fair neutrality toward the belligerents, and of settling amicably our differences with both,—or with either, as leading to a settlement with the other,—or, that failing, as putting us on better ground against him, there is and has been an entire concurrence among the most enlightened who have shared in the public councils since the year 1800. . . . In favor of a cordial accommodation with Great Britain there has certainly never ceased to be a prevailing disposition in the Executive councils since I became connected with them. In the terms of accommodation with that as with other Powers, differences

[1] Madison to Monroe, March 26, 1811; Monroe MSS. State Department Archives.

of opinion must be looked for, even among those most agreed on the same general views. These differences, however, lie fairly within the compass of free consultation and mutual concession as subordinate to the unity belonging to the Executive department. I will add that I perceive not any commitments, even in the case of the abortive adjustment with that Power, that could necessarily embarrass deliberations on a renewal of negotiations."

From these letters, the attitude of Monroe in entering Madison's Cabinet may be understood. Committed to the doctrine that Madison had leaned toward France, and that this bias should be corrected, Monroe and his personal party looked on Madison's offer of the State Department as the pledge of a change in policy which should have a rupture with France for its immediate object, and the Presidency for its ultimate reward. Madison, on his side, understanding this scheme saw no objection to it, and was unconscious of having committed the government to any position that could necessarily embarrass Monroe. Monroe's acceptance of this situation was as natural as his refusal would have been surprising, for no man who wanted office, and who saw the Presidency in his grasp, could be required to show rigorous consistency. Madison's attitude was somewhat different; and his assurance, in March, 1811, that he saw no commitment which could necessarily embarrass Monroe in renewing negotiations with England, showed not only that Madison, notwithstanding Robert Smith's assertions to Turreau, still counted on no war with England, but felt no suspicion that his measures within little more than a twelvemonth would lead him to a recommendation of war. The policy of commercial restrictions still satisfied his mind.

Madison was not alone in this ignorance. Monroe himself, still less conscious than Madison of a war spirit, expected to reach the Presidency by conciliating England. Even Robert Smith, to the surprise of the world, posed as the victim of his hostility to France, and hoped to become the centre of a combination of Smiths, Clintons, Federalists, and Duane Pennsylvanians, who charged that Madison was less friendly to England than he might have been. The President suffered

much annoyance from the Smiths because he could not disprove their assertions or demonstrate his good-will for Great
Britain.

As soon as Madison learned through Senator Brent that
Monroe made no serious difficulty in accepting the State Department, he sent for Robert Smith. A faithful account of the
conversations that followed would add vivacity to the story,
for Madison seemed at times to enjoy commenting not only
on the acts of his opponents, but also on their motives; while
Robert Smith, being easily disconcerted and slow in defence
or attack, offered a tempting mark for arrows of temper. The
first interview took place March 23,[1] and Madison made a
long memorandum of what passed.

> "I proceeded to state to him," recorded Madison,[2] "that
> it had long been felt and had at length become notorious
> that the administration of the Executive department la-
> bored under a want of the harmony and unity which were
> equally necessary to its energy and its success; that I did
> not refer to the evil as infecting our Cabinet consultations,
> where there had always been an apparent cordiality and
> even a sufficient concurrence of opinion, but as showing
> itself in language and conduct out of doors, counteracting
> what had been understood within to be the course of the
> Administration and the interest of the public; that truth
> obliged me to add that this practice, as brought to my
> view, was exclusively chargeable on him; and that he had
> not only counteracted what had been the result of consul-
> tations apparently approved by himself, but had included
> myself in representations calculated to diminish confidence
> in the administration committed to me."

Robert Smith protested, in his somewhat incoherent way,
against the truth of this charge; and the President, roused by
resistance, spoke with more preciseness, instancing Smith's
conduct in regard to Macon's bills in 1810, as evidence of the
secretary's bad faith.

> "With respect to his motives for dissatisfaction, I ac-

[1] Serurier to Champagny, March 26, 1811; Archives des Aff. Étr. MSS.
[2] Madison's Works, ii. 494.

knowledged that I had been, for the reasons given by him, much puzzled to divine any natural ones, without looking deeper into human nature than I was willing to do; . . . that whatever talents he might possess, he did not, as he must have found by experience, possess those adapted to his station; . . . that the business of the Department had not been conducted in the systematic and punctual manner that was necessary, particularly in the foreign correspondence, and that I had become daily more dissatisfied with it."

The man must have been easy-tempered who could listen to these comments on conduct, motives, and abilities without sign of offence; but Robert Smith showed no immediate resentment, for when the President closed by offering to send him to St. Petersburg to succeed J. Q. Adams, who was to take Justice Cushing's place on the Supreme Bench, Smith showed no unwillingness, although he avowed his preference for the other vacancy on the bench soon to be caused by Justice Chase's death, or for the English mission left vacant by Pinkney's return. Madison declined to encourage these ambitions, and Smith retired to consider the offer of St. Petersburg. For several days the President supposed the arrangement to be accepted; but meanwhile Robert Smith consulted his friends, who held other views on the subject of his dignity and deserts. When he next saw the President he declined the mission, declaring that acceptance would be only indirect removal from office, the result of "a most shameful intrigue." After trying in vain the characteristic task of convincing him that he altogether exaggerated his own consequence, Madison accepted his resignation and left him to carry out his threat of appealing to the country. "He took his leave with a cold formality," concluded Madison, "and I did not see him afterward."

For ten years Robert Smith had been one of the most powerful influences in politics, trusted with the highest responsibilities and duties, seeming more than any other single Cabinet officer to affect the course of public affairs; when at a breath from the President his official life was snuffed out, his reputation for ability vanished, and the Republican party, which had so long flattered him, suddenly learned to belittle his name. Under the shadow of monarchical or absolute governments such tales of artificial greatness were common, and their moral was worn thin by ages of repetition; but in the democratic United States, and from the bosom of Jefferson's political family, this experience of Robert Smith was a singular symptom.

Never again did this genial gentleman sun himself in the rays of Executive power, or recover the smallest share of influence. He returned to Baltimore, where he lived thirty years longer without distinguishing himself; but about three months after his retirement from office, in the month of June, 1811, he published an Address to the People, charging President Madison with offences more or less grave, and surprising every one by representing himself as having persistently but vainly opposed Madison's fixed purpose of making a virtual alliance with France. The evidence of the late Secretary of State, who might reasonably be thought the best informed and most competent judge, confirmed the Federalist and British theory that Madison was under secret pledges to Napoleon. So gravely did it compromise Madison that he caused Joel Barlow to write a semi-official reply in the "National Intelligencer;" and although Barlow wrote in a bad temper, Madison himself wrote privately in a worse.

> "You will have noticed in the 'National Intelligencer,'" he told Jefferson July 8,[1] "that the wicked publication of Mr. Smith is not to escape with impunity. It is impossible, however, that the whole turpitude of his conduct can be understood without disclosures to be made by myself alone, and of course, as he knows, not to be made at all. Without these his infamy is daily fastening upon him, leaving no other consolation than the malignant hope of revenging his own ingratitude and guilt on others."

Robert Smith hardly deserved such invective. If the taunts of Madison, Barlow, and the Republican press and party at his incompetence were well-founded, the party had only itself to blame for putting such a man in so high a position. If

[1] Madison's Works, ii. 513.

triumphant in nothing else, Smith overthrew both Madison and Barlow by the retort with which he met their sneers, and retaliated the charge of incompetence.

"This advocate," replied Smith (in the "Baltimore American") to Barlow (in the Washington "Intelligencer"), "would have us believe that many persons both in and out of Congress thought that Mr. Smith from want of talents and integrity was quite unfit for the Department of State, and that his appointment was the effect of an intrigue. Were there any truth in this remark, it could not fail to convince every person of the utter unfitness of Mr. Madison himself for *his* office. It in plain English says that from the officious persuasion of a few intriguers he had appointed to the most important and the highest station in the government a person without talents and without integrity; and this person not a stranger, respecting whom he might have been misled, but one who had been his colleagues in office during the long term of eight years, and of whose fitness he of course had better means of judging than any other person or persons whatever; nay, more,—to this same person, without talents or integrity, was offered by Mr. Madison not only the mission to Russia, but the important office of the Treasury Department."

Chapter XVIII

APRIL 1, 1811, Monroe took charge of the State Department. The first person to claim his attention was the French Emperor, and Monroe had reasons for knowing that diplomatists of reputed sagacity found use for uninterrupted attention when they undertook to deal with Napoleon.

Monroe stood in a situation of extreme difficulty, hampered not only by the pledges of his own government, but still more by the difficulty of dealing at all with the government of France. When Armstrong quitted Paris in September, 1810, being obliged to fix upon some American competent to take charge of the legation at Paris, he chose Jonathan Russell. The selection was the best he could make. Jonathan Russell possessed advantages over ordinary ministers coming directly from America. A native of Rhode Island, educated at Brown University, after leaving college he followed the business of a merchant, and in November, 1809, sailed from Boston in a ship of his own, which arrived at Tönning in Denmark only to be at once sequestered under Napoleon's Decrees. He passed several months in efforts to recover the property, and acquired experience in the process. About forty years old, and more or less acquainted with the people, politics, and languages of Europe, he was better fitted than any secretary of legation then abroad for the burden that Armstrong had found intolerable; yet the oldest and ablest diplomatist America ever sent to Europe might have despaired of effecting any good result with such means as were at the disposal of this temporary agent, who had not even the support of a direct commission from the President.

Russell felt the embarrassment of the position he was called to fill. Armstrong departed September 12, bearing Cadore's promise that the decrees should cease to operate November 1, and saying as little as possible of a condition precedent. The 1st of November came, and Russell asked the Duc de Cadore whether the revocation had taken place; but a month passed without his receiving an answer. December 4, 1810, Russell wrote to the Secretary of State,[1] —

---

[1] Russell to Robert Smith, Dec. 4, 1810; MSS. State Department Archives.

"No one here except the Emperor knows if the Berlin and Milan Decrees be absolutely revoked or not; and no one dares inquire of him concerning them. The general opinion of those with whom I have conversed on the subject is that they are revoked. There are indeed among those who entertain this opinion several counsellors of State; but this is of little importance, as the construction which the Emperor may choose to adopt will alone prevail."

At about the same time Russell wrote to Pinkney at London a letter[1] expressing the opinion that, as the decrees had not been executed for one entire month against any vessel arriving in France, this fact created a presumption that the decrees were repealed. He could not be blamed for an opinion so cautious, yet he was mistaken in committing himself even to that extent, for he learned a few days afterward that two American vessels had been seized at Bordeaux, and he found himself obliged to write the Duc de Cadore a strong remonstrance on the ground that as this was the first case that had occurred since November 1 to which the decrees could have applied, the seizures created a presumption that the decrees were not repealed.[2] Russell's instructions from America, including the President's proclamation of November 2, arrived three days later, December 13, requiring him to assume the revocation of the decrees; but only two days after receiving them, he read in the "Moniteur" of December 15 Cadore's official report to the Emperor declaring that the decrees would never be revoked as long as England maintained her blockades; and again, December 17, he found in the same newspaper the Count de Semonville's official address before the Senate, declaring that the Decrees of Berlin and Milan should be the "palladium of the seas."

Yet Russell's position was not quite so desperate as it seemed. Certainly the decrees were not revoked; but he had a fair hope of obtaining some formal act warranting him in claiming their revocation. Although Napoleon's motives often seemed mysterious except to men familiar with his mind, yet one may venture to guess, since guess one must, that he had

[1] Russell to Pinkney, Dec. 1, 1810; State Papers, iii. 390.
[2] Russell to Cadore, Dec. 10, 1810; State Papers, iii. 391.

looked for little success from the manœuvre of announcing the revocation of his decrees as concerned the United States. Perhaps he dictated Cadore's letter of August 5 rather in order to prevent America from declaring war against himself than in the faith that a trick, that to his eye would have been transparent, could effect what all his efforts for ten years past had failed to bring about,—a war between the United States and Great Britain. The Emperor showed certainly almost as lively surprise as pleasure, when December 12 he received the President's proclamation of November 2, reviving the non-intercourse against England. His pleasure was the greater when he learned that President Madison had adopted his suggestion not only in this instance, but also in requiring of England the withdrawal of Fox's blockade of 1806 as a *sine qua non* of any future renewal of commerce. Delighted with his success, not only did the Emperor take no offence at the President's almost simultaneous proclamation for the seizure of West Florida, but rather his first impulse was to lose not a moment in fixing Madison in his new attitude. He wrote a hurried letter[1] on the instant to Cadore, ordering him if possible to send fresh instructions to Serurier, who was already on his way to succeed Turreau as French minister at Washington:—

"Send me the draft of a despatch for M. Serurier, if he is still at Bayonne. . . . You will show in this letter the satisfaction I have felt in reading the last letters from America. You will give the assurance that if the American government is decided to maintain the independence of its flag, it will find every kind of aid and privileges in this country. Your letter will of course be in cipher. In it you will make known that I am in no way opposed to the Floridas becoming an American possession; that I desire, in general, whatever can favor the independence of Spanish America. You will make the same communication to the American *chargé d'affaires*, who will write in cipher to his Government that I am favorable to the cause of American independence; and that as we do not found our commerce on exclusive pretensions, I shall see with pleasure the independence of a great nation, provided it be not under the influence of England."

[1] Napoleon to Champagny, Dec. 13, 1810; Correspondance, xxi. 316.

This hasty note still throws out flashes of the fire that consumed the world. Silent as to the single question that America wanted him to answer, the Emperor not only resumed his old habit of dangling the Floridas before the President's eyes, but as though he were glad to escape from every Spanish tie, he pressed on Madison the whole of Spanish America. Once more one is reduced to guess at the motive of this astonishing change. No one knew better than Napoleon that the independence of Spanish America could benefit England alone; that England had fought, intrigued, and traded for centuries to bring this result about, and that the United States were altogether unable to contest English influence at any point in Central and South America. He knew, too, that the permanent interests of France could only be injured by betraying again the Spanish empire, and that nothing could exceed the extravagance of intriguing for the revolt of Mexico and Peru while his armies were exhausting themselves in the effort to make his own brother King of Spain. Such sudden inconsistencies were no new thing in Napoleon's career. The story of the Floridas repeated the story of Louisiana. As in 1803 Napoleon, disgusted with his failure at St. Domingo, threw Louisiana to Jefferson, so in 1810, disgusted with his failure at Madrid, he threw Spanish America in a mass to Madison. What was more serious still, as in 1803 Germany could foresee that she must pay on the Rhine for the losses of France at St. Domingo and New Orleans, so in 1810 the Czar Alexander already could divine that the compensation which Napoleon would require for Mexico and Peru would lie somewhere in the neighborhood of Poland. Thus much at least had been gained for the United States and England. Napoleon took no more interest in the roads to Lisbon and Cadiz, and studied only those that led to Wilna, Moscow, and St. Petersburg.

Read in this sense, Napoleon's instructions to Cadore and Serurier told most interesting news; but on the point likely to prove a matter of life and death to Madison, the Emperor spoke so evasively as to show that he meant to yield nothing he could retain. He ordered Cadore to talk with Jonathan Russell about commercial matters: —

"Have a conference with this *chargé d'affaires* in order to understand thoroughly what the American government wants. You will tell him that I have subjected ships coming from America to certain formalities; that these formalities consist of a letter in cipher, joined with licenses, which prove that the ship comes from America and has been loaded there, but that I cannot admit American ships coming from London, since this would upset my system; that there is no way of knowing the fact [of their American character], and that there are shipowners who for mercantile objects foil the measures of the American government; in short, that I have made a step; that I will wait till February 2 to see what America will do, and that in the mean time I will conduct myself according to circumstances, but so as to do no harm to ships really coming from America; that the question is difficult, but that he should give the positive assurance to his Government of my wish to favor it in everything; that he knows, moreover, that several ships coming from America since the last measures were known have obtained permission to discharge their cargoes in France; finally, that we cannot consider as American the ships conveyed to the Baltic, which have double papers, etc. It would be well if you could engage this *chargé* to answer you by a note, and to agree that he disowns the American ships which navigate the Baltic. This would be sent to Russia, and would be useful. In general, employ all possible means of convincing this *chargé d'affaires*, who I suppose speaks French, of the particularly favorable disposition I feel toward the Americans; that the real embarrassment is to recognize true Americans from those who serve the English; and that I consider the step taken by the American government as a first step taken toward a good result."

When Napoleon used many words and became apologetic, he was least interesting, because his motives became most evident. In regard to America, he wished to elude an inconvenient inquiry whether the Berlin and Milan Decrees were or were not revoked. Consequently he did not mention those decrees, although credulity itself could not have reconciled his pledge to wait until February 2, with his official assertion of

August 5 that the decrees would be withdrawn on November 1. Such a course was fatal to Madison, for it forced him to appear as accepting the Berlin and Milan Decrees after so long protesting against them. So justly anxious was the President to protect himself from this risk, that in sending to Russell the Non-intercourse Proclamation of November 2 he warned the *chargé* against the doctrine of a condition precedent involved in Cadore's "bien entendu." The Emperor was to understand that the United States acted on the ground that "bien entendu" did not mean "condition precedent."[1] "It is to be remarked, moreover, that in issuing the Proclamation, it has been presumed that the requisition . . . on the subject of the sequestered property will have been satisfied."

December 13, at the moment when Napoleon was writing his instructions to Cadore, Jonathan Russell was reading the instructions of President Madison. No diplomatist could have found common ground on which to reconcile the two documents. Madison's knowledge of the Napoleonic idiom was certainly incomplete. Whatever "bien entendu" meant in the dictionaries, it meant in Napoleon's mouth the words "on condition,"—and something more. In further assuming that the sequestered property had been restored, President Madison might with equal propriety have assumed that it had never been seized. Russell did what he could to satisfy Madison's wishes, but he could not hope to succeed.

Bound by these instructions to communicate the President's proclamation in language far from according with Napoleon's ideas, Russell wrote to Cadore, December 17, a note,[2] in which he not only repeated the President's assumptions in regard to the revocation of the decrees, but also ventured beyond the scope of his instructions: he demanded an explanation of the language used by Cadore himself in his report to the Emperor, and by Semonville in the Senate. As though such a demand under such circumstances were not indiscreet enough, Russell strengthened the formal and perfunctory protests of the President by adding an assurance of his own that the United States, after cutting off their own intercourse with England, would not consent to "any

[1] Smith to Armstrong, Nov. 2, 1810; State Papers, iii. 389.
[2] Russell to Cadore, Dec. 17, 1810; MSS. State Department Archives.

commercial intercourse whatever, under licenses or otherwise, between France and her enemy."

Russell's note of December 17 was never answered by the French government, and, as was equally natural, it was never published by the President or made known to Congress. Fortunately for Russell, the Emperor was in good humor, and Cadore was in haste to convey his master's wishes to the American *chargé d'affaires*. December 22 Russell was summoned to the minister, and a very interesting interview took place. Cadore gently complained of the tone in which Russell's note had been written, but put into his hands, as its result and answer, the two letters written by the ministers of Justice and Finance,—which allowed American vessels to enter French ports, subject only to provisional sequestration, until February 2, at which time all vessels sequestered since November 1 would be restored. "When I had read these letters," reported Russell,[1] "I returned them to the Duke of Cadore, and expressed to him my regret that the general release of American vessels detained under the Berlin and Milan Decrees should be deferred until the 2d of February, as this delay might throw some doubt on the revocation of those decrees." Cadore replied that the time thus taken was intended to afford an opportunity for forming some general rule by which the character of the property could be decided. Russell then complained that by assigning the second day of February,—the very day on which the non-intercourse with England would be revived,—this event was made to appear as a condition precedent to the abrogation of the French edicts; and thereby the order in which the measures of the two governments ought to stand was reversed. In reply Cadore repeated the general assurances of the friendly disposition of the Emperor, and that he was determined to favor the trade of the United States so far as it did not cover or promote the commerce of England. He said the Berlin and Milan Decrees, "inasmuch as they related to the United States," were at an end; that the Emperor was pleased with what the United States had already done, but that he could not "throw himself into their arms" until they had accomplished their undertaking.

[1] Russell to Robert Smith, Dec. 29, 1810; MSS. State Department Archives.

Nothing could be more gentle than this manner of saying that the revocation of November 1 was and was not founded on a condition precedent; that the decrees themselves were and were not revoked; but when Russell still pressed for a categorical answer, Cadore declared at last, " with some vivacity, that the Emperor was determined to persevere in his system against England; that he had overturned the world in adopting this system, and that he would overturn it again to give it effect." On the third point Cadore was equally unyielding. Not a word could Russell wring from him in regard to the confiscated property of American merchants. "His omission to notice the last is more to be lamented, as I have reason to believe that this conversation was meant to form the only answer I am to receive to the communications which I have addressed to him."

The conduct of Cadore warranted Russell's conclusion that "upon the whole this interview was not calculated to increase my confidence in the revocation of the decrees." Although President Madison reached a different conclusion, and on the strength of this conference caused Congress to adopt the Non-Intercourse Act of March 2, Russell's opinion could not be disputed. At the end of another week Cadore sent word that one of the American vessels, the "Grace Ann Greene," arrived at Marseilles since November 1, had been released; and Russell wrote to Pinkney that this release might be considered conclusive evidence of the revocation.[1] A month afterward he wrote to the Secretary of State on the same subject in a different tone,[2] saying that the United States had not yet much cause to be satisfied; that no vessel arrived since November 1 had been permitted to discharge her cargo, and that tedious delays were constantly interposed. As for the property confiscated before November 1, Russell avowed himself afraid to make the reclamation ordered by the President: "I ascertained indirectly that a convention to this effect would not be entered into at this moment; and I thought it indiscreet to expose the United States, with all the right on their side, to a refusal." No

---

[1] Russell to Pinkney, Dec. 30, 1810; State Papers, iii. 417.
[2] Russell to Robert Smith, Jan. 28, 1811; MSS. State Department Archives.

action of the United States, he feared, could redeem the unfortunate property.[1]

Failure on these points was accompanied by a promise of success on others. The President had remonstrated against the Emperor's scheme of issuing licenses through the French consuls to vessels in ports of the United States; and Russell wrote to Cadore, Jan. 12, 1811, that such consular superintendence was inadmissible, and would not be permitted.[2] January 18 Cadore returned an answer, evidently taken from the Emperor's lips:[3]

"I have read with much attention your note of January 12, relative to the licenses intended to favor the commerce of the Americans in France. This system had been conceived before the revocation of the Decrees of Berlin and Milan had been resolved on. Now circumstances are changed by the resolution taken by the United States to cause their flag and their independence to be respected. That which has been done before this last epoch can no longer serve as a rule under actual circumstances."

Although this letter said that the Berlin and Milan Decrees were repealed,—not on Nov. 1, 1810, but at some indeterminate time afterward, in consequence of the President's proclamation of November 2,—yet it officially declared that whatever the date might be, on January 18, when Cadore wrote, the revocation was complete. Russell sent the letter to the President, and the President sent it nearly ten months afterward to Congress as proof that the decrees were revoked. He could not send, for he could not know, another letter written by Cadore to Serurier three weeks later, which instructed him to the contrary:[4] —

"I send you the copy of a letter addressed by me to Mr. Russell, January 18, on the permits that had been at first delivered to American ships. I cannot assure you that the permits are no longer to be issued, although this letter gives it to be understood in an explicit manner. Continue

[1] Russell to Robert Smith, Feb. 13, 1811; MSS. State Department Archives.
[2] State Papers, iii. 501.
[3] Ibid.
[4] Champagny to Serurier, Feb. 9, 1811; Archives des Aff. Étr. MSS.

to conduct yourself with the reserve heretofore recommended to you, and compromise yourself by no step and by no official promise. Circumstances are such that no engagement can be taken in advance. It is at the date of February 2 that the United States were to execute their act of non-intercourse against England; but before being officially informed in France of what they have done at that time, we cannot take here measures so decisive in favor of the Americans as after news to February 2 shall have arrived from America. This motive will serve to explain to you whatever uncertainty may appear in the conduct of France toward the United States."

From these official instructions the facts were easy to understand. The decrees had not been revoked on Aug. 5 or Nov. 1, 1810; they were not revoked Jan. 18, 1811; they were not to be revoked on February 2; but the Emperor would decide in the spring, when news should arrive from America, whether he would make permanent exceptions in favor of American commerce. In principle, the decrees were not to be revoked at all.

For four years President Madison had strenuously protested that France and England must withdraw their decrees as a condition precedent to friendly relations with America. For four years Napoleon had insisted that America should submit to his decrees as a condition precedent to friendly relations with France. February 2, 1811, he carried his point. The decisive day passed without action on his part. Six weeks followed, but March 15 Russell still wrote to the Secretary of State as doubtfully as he wrote in the previous December:[1] "The temper here varies in relation to us with every rumor of the proceedings of our government. One day we are told that the Emperor has learned that the Non-intercourse Law will be severely executed,—that he is in good humor, and that everything will go well; the next day it is stated that he has heard something which has displeased him, and that the American property lately arrived in this country is in the utmost jeopardy. Every general plan here is evidently suspended

[1] Russell to Robert Smith, March 15, 1811; MSS. State Department Archives.

until the course we may elect to pursue be definite and certain."

Russell made no further attempt to maintain the fact of revocation. Indeed, if the decrees were revoked, American rights were more lawlessly violated than before. As ship after ship arrived from the United States, he saw each taken, under one pretext or another, into the Emperor's keeping:—

> "To countenance delay, no doubt, a new order was issued to the custom-houses on the 18th ult., that no vessels not having licenses, coming from foreign countries, be admitted without the special authority of the Emperor. This indeed makes the detention indefinite, as when once a case is before the Emperor it can no longer be inquired after, much less pressed, and it is impossible to say when it may attract the Imperial attention. It is my belief that our property will be kept within the control of this government until it is officially known here that the Non-intercourse Act against England went into operation with undiminished rigor on the 2d of February."

Under such circumstances, the idea that the United States were bound by a contract with France—the principle on which Congress legislated in the month of February—had no meaning to Jonathan Russell at Paris, where as late as April 1 not a step had yet been taken toward making the contract complete. "I trust," wrote Russell, March 15, "that I shall not be understood in anything which I have written in this letter to urge any obligation on the United States to execute *at all* the Non-intercourse Law; this obligation is certainly weakened, if not destroyed, by the conduct of the Government here."

Russell never misunderstood the situation or misled his Government. Although Napoleon's habit of deception was the theme of every historian and moralist, the more remarkable trait was his frequent effort to avoid or postpone an evidently necessary falsehood, and, above all, his incapacity to adhere to any consistent untruth. Napoleon was easily understood by men of his own stamp; but he was not wholly misunderstood by men like Armstrong and Russell. He did not choose to revoke the decrees, and he made no secret of his reasons even to the American government.

In the spring of 1811 the Emperor was surrounded by difficulties caused by his interference with trade. The financial storm which overspread England in 1810 extended to France in the following winter, and not only swept away credit and capital throughout the empire, but also embarrassed Napoleon's finances and roused fresh resistance to his experiments on commerce. The resistance irritated him, and he showed his anger repeatedly in public. At the Tuileries, March 17, he addressed some deputies of the Hanseatic League in a tone which still betrayed an effort at self-control:[1] —

"The Decrees of Berlin and Milan are the fundamental laws of my empire. They cease to have effect only for nations that defend their sovereignty and maintain the religion of their flag. England is in a state of blockade for nations that submit to the decrees of 1806, because the flags so subjected to English laws are denationalized; they are English. Nations on the contrary that are sensible of their dignity, and that find resources enough in their courage and strength for disregarding the blockades by notice, commonly called paper blockades, and enter the ports of my empire, other than those really blockaded, — following the recognized usage and the stipulations of the Treaty of Utrecht, — may communicate with England; for them England is not blockaded. The Decrees of Berlin and Milan, founded on the nature of things, will form the constant public law of my empire during the whole time that England shall maintain her Orders in Council of 1806 and 1807, and shall violate the stipulations of the Treaty of Utrecht in that matter."

The sudden appearance of the Treaty of Utrecht had an effect of comedy; but the speech itself merely reasserted the rules of 1806 and 1807, which time had not made more acceptable to neutrals. Again and again, by every means in his power and with every accent of truth, Napoleon asserted that his decrees were not and never should be revoked, nor

[1] Correspondance, xxi. 284.

should they be even suspended except for the nations that conformed to them. Though America had rejected this law in 1807, she might still if she chose accept it in 1811; but certainly she could not charge Napoleon with deception or concealment of his meaning. A week after the address to the Hanseatic deputies, on Sunday, March 24, he made another and a more emphatic speech. The principal bankers and merchants of Paris came to the Tuileries to offer their congratulations on the birth of a son. Napoleon harangued them for more than half an hour in the tone he sometimes affected, of a subaltern of dragoons,—rude, broken, and almost incoherent, but nervous and terrifying:—

"When I issued my Decrees of Berlin and Milan, England laughed; you made fun of me; yet I know my business. I had maturely weighed my situation with England; but people pretended that I did not know what I was about,—that I was ill-advised. Yet see where England stands to-day! . . . Within ten years I shall subject England. I want only a maritime force. Is not the French empire brilliant enough for me? I have taken Holland, Hamburg, etc., only to make my flag respected. I consider the flag of a nation as a part of herself; she must be able to carry it everywhere, or she is not free. That nation which does not make her flag respected is not a nation in my eyes. The Americans—we are going to see what they will do. No Power in Europe shall trade with England. Six months sooner or later I shall catch up with it (*je l'attendrai*),—my sword is long enough for that. I made peace at Tilsit only because Russia undertook to make war on England. I was then victorious. I might have gone to Wilna; nothing could stop me but this engagement of Russia. . . . At present I am only moderately desirous of peace with England. I have the means of making a navy; I have all the products of the Rhine; I have timber, dock-yards, etc.; I have already said that I have sailors. The English stop everything on the ocean; I will stop everything I find of theirs on the Continent. Their Miladies, their Milords,—we shall be quit! (*Leurs Miladies, leurs Milords—nous serons à deux de jeu!*)"

This hurried talk, which was rather a conversation than a

speech, lasted until the Emperor's voice began to fail him. He flung defiance in the face of every nation in the Christian world, and announced in no veiled terms the coming fate of Russia. His loquacity astounded his hearers, and within a few days several reports of what he said, differing in details, but agreeing in the main, were handed privately about Paris, and were on their way to St. Petersburg, London, and New York.[1] One account varied in regard to the words used about America: —

"The Decrees of Berlin and Milan are the fundamental laws of my empire," began the second report. "As for neutral navigation, I regard the flag as an extension of territory; the Power which lets it be violated cannot be considered neutral. The lot of American commerce will be soon decided. I will favor it if the United States conform to those decrees; in the contrary case, their ships will be excluded from the ports of my empire."

Russell sent to Monroe these private accounts, adding a few details to show more exactly the Emperor's meaning. Writing April 4, he said that no American vessel had been allowed an entry since February 4 unless carrying a license; that a secret order had then been given to the custom-house to make no reports on American cases; that the Council of Prizes had suspended its decisions; and that, notwithstanding Cadore's promise, licenses were still issued. "If the license system," concluded Russell, "were concerned, as the Duke of Cadore suggests, to favor American commerce during the existence only of the Berlin and Milan Decrees, it is probably necessary to infer from the excuse of that system the continuance of those decrees."

Left without powers or instructions, Russell could thenceforward do nothing. Remonstrance was worse than useless. "A representation of this kind," he wrote, "however mildly it might portray the unfriendly and faithless conduct of this Government, might have hastened a crisis which it does not become me to urge."

At length, April 25, despatches arrived from America en-

[1] Russell to Robert Smith, April 4, 1811; MSS. State Department Archives. Cf. Thiers's Empire, xiii. 27–33.

closing the Non-intercourse Act of March 2 and the secret Act for taking possession of Florida. The President's accompanying instructions[1] ordered Russell to explain that the different dates fixed by the Proclamation and by the Act for enforcing the non-intercourse against England were owing to the different senses in which Cadore's letter had been construed in France and America,—the President having assumed that the decrees would have been extinct Nov. 1, 1810, while the French government, "as appears from its official acts, admits only a suspension with a view to a subsequent cessation." These instructions, as well as Russell's despatches for the most part, were never communicated to Congress.

April 17, a week before these documents arrived, Napoleon made a sudden change in his Cabinet, by dismissing Cadore and appointing Hugues Maret, Duc de Bassano, as his Minister of Foreign Affairs. No one knew the cause of Cadore's fall. He was mild, modest, and not given to display. He "lacked conversation," Napoleon complained. Probably his true offence consisted in leaning toward Russia and in dislike for the commercial system, while Maret owed promotion to opposite tendencies. Maret's abilities were undoubted; his political morality was no worse than that of his master, and perhaps no better than that of Cadore or of Talleyrand whom he hated.[2] He could hardly be more obedient than Cadore; and as far as America was concerned, he could do no more mischief.

When Russell repaired to the Foreign Office, April 28, he was received by the new minister, who availed himself of his inexperience to ask many questions and to answer none. Russell had a long interview with no results; but this delay mattered little, for the Emperor needed no information. No sooner had he received the Non-intercourse Act of March 2 than he ordered his ministers to make a report on the situation of American commerce.[3] The order was due not so much to a wish of hearing what his ministers had to say as of telling them what they were to report:—

"The United States have not declared war on England,

[1] Robert Smith to Russell, March 5, 1811; MSS. State Department Archives.
[2] Maret, Duc de Bassano; Par Ernouf., 285–299.
[3] Note dictée en Conseil, 29 avril, 1811; Correspondance, xxii. 122.

but they have recognized the Decrees of Berlin and Milan, since they have authorized their citizens to trade with France, and have forbidden them every relation with England. In strict public right, the Emperor ought to exact that the United States should declare war against England; but after all it is in some sort to make war when they consent that the Decree of Berlin should be applied to ships which shall have communicated with England. On this hypothesis, one would say: 'The Decrees of Berlin and Milan are withdrawn as regards the United States; but as every ship which has touched in England, or is bound thither, is a vagrant that the laws punish and confiscate, it may be confiscated in France.' If this reasoning could be established, nothing would remain but to take precautions for admitting none but American products on American ships."

This view of the contract to which American faith was bound, though quite the opposite of Madison's, was liberal compared with its alternative: —

"Finally, if it should be impossible to trace out a good theory in this system, the best would be to gain time, leaving the principles of the matter a little obscure until we see the United States take sides; for it appears that that Government cannot remain long in its actual situation toward England, with whom it has also political discussions concerning the affairs of Spanish America."

The Emperor's will was law. The Council set itself accordingly to the task of "leaving the principles of the matter a little obscure" until the United States should declare war against England; while the Emperor, not without reason, assumed that America had recognized the legality of his decrees.

Chapter XIX

THE EMPEROR'S decision was made known to the American government by a letter[1] from Bassano to Russell, dated May 4, 1811, almost as curt as a declaration of war: —

> "I hasten to announce to you that his Majesty the Emperor has ordered his Minister of Finance to authorize the admission of the American cargoes which had been provisionally placed in deposit on their arrival in France. I have the honor to send you a list of the vessels to which these cargoes belong; they will have to export their value in national merchandise, of which two thirds will be in silks. I have not lost a moment in communicating to you a measure perfectly in accord with the sentiments of union and of friendship which exist between the two Powers."

This was all. No imperial decree of repeal was issued or suggested. President Madison cared little for the released ships; he cared only for the principle involved in the continued existence of the decrees, and Bassano's letter announced by silence, as distinctly as it could have said in words, that the principle of the decrees was not abandoned. Such were Napoleon's orders; and in executing them Bassano did not, like Cadore or Talleyrand, allow himself the license of softening their bluntness. Russell knew the letter to be fatal to any claim that the French decrees were withdrawn, but he could do nothing else than send it to London as offering, perhaps, evidence of the "actual relations growing out of the revocation of the Berlin and Milan Decrees."[2] He wrote to Bassano a letter asking the release of the American vessels captured and brought into French ports as prizes since November 1, but he obtained no answer.[3] A month afterward he wrote again, remonstrating against the excessive tariff duties and the requirement that American vessels should take two thirds of their return cargoes in French silks; but this letter received as little notice as the other. Russell had the mortification of

---

[1] Duke of Bassano to Mr. Russell, May 4, 1811; State Papers, iii. 505.
[2] Russell to J. S. Smith, May 10, 1811; State Papers, iii. 502.
[3] Russell to Bassano, May 11, 1811; State Papers, iii. 506.

knowing, almost as well as Bassano himself, the motives that guided the Emperor; and July 13 he recited them to the President in language as strong as propriety allowed:[1] —

"The temper here toward us is professedly friendly, but unfortunately it is not well proved to be so in practice. It is my conviction, as I before wrote you, that the great object of the actual policy is to entangle us in a war with England. They abstain therefore from doing anything which would furnish clear and unequivocal testimony of the revocation of their decrees, lest it should induce the extinction of the British orders and thereby appease our irritation against their enemy. Hence, of all the captured vessels since November 1, the three which were liberated are precisely those which had not violated the decrees. On the other hand, they take care, by not executing these decrees against us, to divert our resentment from themselves. I have very frankly told the Duke of Bassano that we are not sufficiently dull to be deceived by this kind of management. He indeed pretends that they are influenced by no such motive; and whenever I speak to him on the subject, he reiterates the professions of friendship, and promises to endeavor to obtain the release of the remainder of our vessels captured since November 1. I fear, however, that he will not succeed."

Even in case of war with England, Russell warned the President to look for no better treatment from Napoleon, who might then consider America as "chained to the imperial car, and obliged to follow whithersoever it leads." He pointed out that concessions had never produced any return from the Emperor except new exactions and new pretensions. If war with England became inevitable, care must be taken to guard against the danger that France should profit by it. French trade was not worth pursuing. The tariff on imports, reinforced by the restrictions on exports, created a practical nonintercourse.

Napoleon's writings furnish evidence that the Emperor's chief object was not so much to entangle America in war with

[1] Russell to Monroe, July 13, 1811; MSS. State Department Archives.

England as to maintain the decrees which he literally overturned the world to enforce. When he suspended their enforcement against American ships in his own ports, he did so
only because his new customs' regulations had been invented
to attain by other means the object of the decrees. When he
affirmed and reaffirmed that these decrees were the fundamental law of his empire, he told a truth which neither England nor America believed, but to which he clung with
energy that cost him his empire.

Russell made no more efforts, but waited impatiently for
the arrival of Joel Barlow, while Napoleon bethought himself
only of his favorite means for quieting Madison's anger. August 23 the Emperor ordered[1] Bassano to give his minister at
Washington instructions calculated to sharpen the cupidity of
the United States. Serurier was to be active in effecting the
independence of Spanish America, was to concert measures
for that purpose with the President, promise arms and supplies, employ the American government and American agents
for his objects, and in all respects give careful attention to
what passed in the colonies; yet in regard to Florida, the only
Spanish colony in which Madison took personal interest,
Napoleon hinted other views to Bassano in a message[2] too
curious for omission.

"You spoke to me this morning," he wrote August 28,
"of instructions received by the American *chargé* on the affair of Florida. You might insinuate the following idea,—
that in consideration of some millions of piastres, Spain in
her present condition of penury would cede the Floridas.
Insinuate this, while adding that though I do not take it ill
that America should seize the Floridas, I can in no way
interfere, since these countries do not belong to me."

With this touch of character, the great Emperor turned
from American affairs to devote all his energies to matters
about the Baltic. Yet so deeply were American interests
founded in the affairs of Europe that even in the Baltic they
were the rock on which Napoleon's destiny split; for the
quarrels which in the summer of 1811 became violent between

[1] Napoleon to Maret, Aug. 23, 1811; Correspondance, xxii. 432.
[2] Napoleon to Maret, Aug. 28, 1811; Correspondance, xxii. 448.

France and the two independent Baltic Powers—Russia and Sweden—were chiefly due to those omnipresent American ships, which throve under pillage and challenged confiscation. Madison's wisdom in sending a minister to St. Petersburg was proved more quickly than he could have expected. Between March 1 and Nov. 1, 1811, at one of the most critical moments in the world's history, President Madison had no other full minister accredited in Europe than his envoy to Russia; but whatever mortifications he suffered from Napoleon, were more than repaid by means of this Russian mission.

The new minister to Russia, J. Q. Adams, sailed from Boston August 5, 1809, and on arriving at Christiansand in Norway, September 20, he found upward of thirty masters of American vessels whose ships had been seized by Danish privateers between April and August, and were suffering trial and condemnation in Danish prize courts. He reported that the entire number of American ships detained in Norway and Denmark was more than fifty, and their value little less than five million dollars.[1] The Danes, ground in the dust by England and France, had taken to piracy as their support; and the Danish prize-courts, under the pressure of Davout, the French general commanding at Hamburg, condemned their captures without law or reason. Adams made what remonstrance he could to the Danish government, and passed on to Cronstadt, where he arrived Oct. 21, 1809. He found a condition of affairs in Russia that seemed hopeless for the success of his mission. The alliance between Russia and France had reached its closest point. Russia had aided Napoleon to subdue Austria; Napoleon had aided Russia to secure Finland. At his first interview with the Russian Foreign Minister, Adams received official information of these events; and when he called attention to the conduct of the Danish privateers, Count Roumanzoff, while expressing strong disapprobation of their proceedings, added that a more liberal system was a dream.[2]

The Foreign Minister of Russia, Count Roumanzoff, officially known as Chancellor of the Empire, and its most

[1] J. Q. Adams to R. Smith, Oct. 4, 1809; MSS. State Department Archives.
[2] J. Q. Adams to R. Smith, Oct. 26, 1809; MSS. State Department Archives.

powerful subject, favored the French alliance. From him Adams could expect little assistance in any case, and nothing but opposition wherever French interests were involved. Friendly and even affectionate to America as far as America was a rival of England, Roumanzoff could do nothing for American interests where they clashed with those of France; and Adams soon found that at St. Petersburg he was regarded by France as an agent of England. He became conscious that French influence was unceasingly at work to counteract his efforts in behalf of American interests.

Adams's surprise was the greater when, with the discovery of this immense obstacle, he discovered also an equally covert influence at work in his favor, and felt that the protection was stronger than the enmity. By a good fortune almost equal to that which brought Monroe to Paris on April 12, 1803, Adams was officially received at St. Petersburg on October 25, 1809, only two days before the Czar first revolted against Napoleon's authority.[1] Of this revolt, in the mysterious atmosphere of the Russian court, Adams could know nothing. At the outset, obliged to ask the Czar's interference on behalf of the plundered American merchants in Denmark, he could regard himself only as performing an official duty without hope of more than a civil answer. This was in fact the first result of the request; for when, Dec. 26, 1809, he opened the subject to Roumanzoff, the chancellor gave him no encouragement. The Danes, he said, had been forced by France to do what they were doing. France viewed all these American ships as British; and "as this was a measure emanating from the personal disposition of the Emperor of France, he was apprehensive there existed no influence in the world of sufficient efficacy to shake his determination."[2] Adams resigned himself to this friendly refusal of a request made without instructions, and implying the personal interference of the Czar with the most sensitive part of Napoleon's system.

Three days afterward, December 29, Adams saw Roumanzoff again, who told him, with undisguised astonishment,

---

[1] Tatistcheff, Alexandre Iᵉʳ et Napoléon, p. 512. Vandal, Napoléon et Alexandre Iᵉʳ, II., 167 ff.

[2] Diary of J. Q. Adams, Dec. 26, 1809, ii. 83, 87. Adams to R. Smith, Jan. 7, 1810; MSS. State Department Archives.

that he had reported to the Czar the American minister's request for interference in Denmark and his own refusal; and that the Czar had thought differently, and had "ordered him immediately to represent to the Danish government his wish that the examination might be expedited, and the American property restored as soon as possible; which order he had already executed."[1]

If Adams had consciously intrigued for a rupture between France and Russia, he could have invented no means so effective as to cause the Czar's interference with Napoleon's control of Denmark; but Adams's favor was far from ending there. The winter of 1809–1810 passed without serious incident, but when spring came and the Baltic opened, the struggle between France and the United States at St. Petersburg began in earnest. Adams found himself a person of much consequence. The French ambassador, Caulaincourt, possessed every advantage that Napoleon and Nature could give him. Handsome, winning, and in all ways personally agreeable to the Czar, master of an establishment more splendid in its display than had been before known even at the splendid court of St. Petersburg, he enjoyed the privilege, always attached to ambassadors, of transacting business directly with the Czar; while the American minister, of a lower diplomatic grade, far too poor to enter upon the most modest social rivalry, labored under the diplomatic inferiority of having to transact business only through the worse than neutral medium of Roumanzoff. Caulaincourt made his demands and urged his arguments in the secrecy that surrounded the personal relation of the two Emperors, while Adams could not even learn, except indirectly after much time, what Caulaincourt was doing or what arguments he used.

Already in April, 1810, Adams reported[2] to his Government that the commercial dispute threatened a rupture between France and Russia. On one hand, Napoleon's measures would prove ineffectual if Russia admitted neutral vessels, carrying as they would cargoes more or less to the advantage of England; on the other, Russia must become avowedly bankrupt if denied exports and restricted to imports of French luxuries,

[1] Diary, ii. 88.
[2] Adams to R. Smith, April 19, 1810; MSS. State Department Archives.

such as silks and champagnes, to be paid in specie. Russia, at war with Turkey and compelled to maintain an immense army with a depreciated currency, must have foreign trade or perish.

Napoleon wanted nothing better than to cripple Russia as well as England, and was not disposed to relax his system for the benefit of Russian military strength. During the summer of 1810 he redoubled his vigilance on the Baltic. Large numbers of vessels, either neutral or pretending to be neutral, entered the Baltic under the protection of the British fleet. Napoleon sent orders that no such vessels should be admitted. June 15 Denmark issued an ordinance prohibiting its ports to all American vessels of every description, and August 3 another to the same effect for the Duchy of Holstein. July 19 a similar ordinance was published by Prussia, and July 29 Mecklenburg followed the example. The same demand came from Caulaincourt to the Czar, and the French ambassador pressed it without intermission and without disguising the dangers which it involved to the peace of Europe. Alexander's reply never varied.

"I want to run no more risks," he told Caulaincourt.[1] "To draw nearer England I must separate from France and risk a new war with her, which I regard as the most dangerous of all wars. And for what object? To serve England; to support her maritime theories which are not mine? It would be madness on my part! . . . I will remain faithful to this policy. I will remain at war with England. I will keep my ports closed to her,—to the extent, however, which I have made known, and from which I cannot depart. In fact I cannot, as I have already told you, prohibit all commerce to my subjects, or forbid them to deal with the Americans. . . . We must keep to these terms, for I declare to you, were war at our doors, in regard to commercial matters I cannot go further."

Thus the American trade became the apparent point of irritation between Alexander and Napoleon. The Russians were amused by Cadore's letter to Armstrong of August 5, saying

[1] Thiers's Empire, xiii. 56.

that the decrees were revoked, and that Napoleon loved the Americans; for they knew what Napoleon had done and was trying to do on the Baltic. The Czar was embarrassed and harassed by the struggle; for the American ships, finding themselves safe in Russian ports, flocked to Archangel and Riga, clamoring for special permission to dispose of their cargoes and to depart before navigation closed, while Napoleon insisted on their seizure, and left no means untried of effecting it. He took even the extravagant step of publicly repudiating the very licenses he was then engaged in forcing American ships to carry. July 10, 1810, the "Moniteur" published an official notice that the certificates of French consuls in the United States carried by American vessels in the Baltic were false, "and that the possessors of them must be considered as forgers," inasmuch as the French consuls in America had some time before ceased to deliver any such certificates; and not satisfied with this ministerial act, Napoleon wrote with his own hand to the Czar that no true American trade existed, and that not a single American ship, even though guaranteed by his own licenses, could be received as neutral.

In the heat of this controversy Adams was obliged to ask, as a favor to the United States, that special orders might be given on behalf of the American vessels at Archangel. As before, Roumanzoff refused; and once more the Czar directed that the special orders should be given.[1] This repeated success of the American minister in overriding the established rules of the government, backed by the whole personal influence of Napoleon, made Roumanzoff uneasy. Friendly and even confidential with Adams, he did not disguise his anxiety; and while he warned the American minister that Cadore's letter of August 5 had made no real change in Napoleon's methods or objects, he added that the Americans had only one support, and this was the Czar himself, but that as yet the Czar's friendship was unshaken. "Our attachment to the United States is obstinate,—more obstinate than you are aware of."[2]

Adams then saw the full bearing of the struggle in which

[1] Diary, ii. 143–160. Adams to R. Smith, Sept. 5, 1810; MSS. State Department Archives.

[2] Diary, Oct. 9, 1810, ii. 180–181. Adams to R. Smith, Oct. 12, 1810; MSS. State Department Archives.

he was engaged; his sources of information were extended, his social relations were more intimate, and he watched with keen interest the effect of his remonstrances and efforts. He had every reason to be anxious, for Napoleon used diplomatic weapons as energetically as he used his army corps. Only ten days after Roumanzoff made his significant remark about the Czar's obstinacy, Napoleon sent orders to Prussia, under threat of military occupation, to stop all British and colonial merchandise; and the following week, October 23, he wrote with his own hand to the Czar a letter of the gravest import:[1] —

"Six hundred English merchant-vessels which were wandering in the Baltic have been refused admission into Mecklenburg and Prussia, and have turned toward your Majesty's States. . . . All this merchandise is on English account. It depends on your Majesty to obtain peace [with England] or to continue the war. Peace is and must be your desire. Your Majesty is certain to obtain it by confiscating these six hundred ships or their cargoes. Whatever papers they may have, under whatever names they may be masked,—French, German, Spanish, Danish, Russian, Swedish,—your Majesty may be sure that they are English."

If Napoleon aimed at crippling Russia by forcing her into the alternative of bankruptcy for want of commerce or invasion as the penalty of trade, he followed a clear and skilful plan. Alexander answered his appeal by pleading that Russia could not seize neutral property, and would not harm England even by doing so.[2] November 4, two days after President Madison proclaimed the revocation of the French Decrees, Napoleon rejoined:[3] —

"As for the principle advanced,—that though wishing war on England we do not wish to wage it on neutrals,— this principle arises from an error. The English want no neutrals and suffer none; they allow the Americans to

[1] Correspondance, xxi. 233, 234.
[2] Alexander to Napoleon. Tatistcheff, pp. 542, 548, 549. Vandal, 509.
[3] Napoleon to Champagny, Nov. 4, 1810; Correspondance, xxi. 252.

navigate, so far as they carry English merchandise and sail on English account; all the certificates of French consuls and all other papers with which they are furnished are false papers. In short, there is to-day no neutral, because the English want none, and stop every vessel not freighted on their account. Not a single vessel has entered the ports of Russia with so-called American papers which has not come really from England."[1]

Armstrong, quitting Paris Sept. 10, 1810, wrote to Madison in his last despatch a few significant words on the subject,[2] suggesting that Napoleon's true motive in reviving the energy of his restrictions on commerce was, among others, the assistance it lent to his views and influence on the Baltic. No other explanation was reasonable. Napoleon intended to force Russia into a dilemma, and he succeeded. The Czar, pressed beyond endurance, at last turned upon Napoleon with an act of defiance that startled and delighted Russia. December 1 Roumanzoff communicated to Caulaincourt the Czar's refusal to seize, confiscate, or shut his ports against colonial produce.[3] At about the same time the merchants of St. Petersburg framed a memorial to the Imperial council, asking for a general prohibition of French luxuries as the only means of preventing the drain of specie and the further depreciation of the paper currency. On this memorial a hot debate occurred in the Imperial council. Roumanzoff opposed the measure as tending to a quarrel with France; and when overruled, he insisted on entering his formal protest on the journal.[4] The Czar acquiesced in the majority's decision, and December 19 the Imperial ukase appeared, admitting American produce on terms remarkably liberal, but striking a violent blow at the industries of France.

Napoleon replied by recalling Caulaincourt and by sending a new ambassador, Count Lauriston, to St. Petersburg, carrying with his credentials an autograph letter to the Czar.[5]

---

[1] Cadore to Kourakine, 2 Dec., 1810; Correspondance, xxi. 297.
[2] Armstrong to Smith, Sept. 10, 1810; MSS. State Department Archives.
[3] Adams to Robert Smith, Dec. 17, 1810; MSS. State Department Archives.
[4] Adams to Robert Smith, Jan. 27, 1811; MSS. State Department Archives.
[5] Napoleon to Alexander, Feb. 28, 1811; Correspondance, xxi. 424.

"Your Majesty's last ukase," said this letter, "in substance, but particularly in form, is directed specially against
France. In other times, before taking such a measure
against my commerce, your Majesty would have let me
know it, and perhaps I might have suggested means which,
while accomplishing your chief object, might still have prevented it from appearing a change of system in the eyes of
France. All Europe has so regarded it; and already, in the
opinion of England and of Europe, our alliance exists no
longer. If it were as entire in your Majesty's heart as in
mine, this general impression would be none the less a
great evil. . . . For myself, I am always the same; but I am
struck by the evidence of these facts, and by the thought
that your Majesty is wholly disposed, as soon as circumstances permit it, to make an arrangement with England,
which is the same thing as to kindle a war between the two
empires."

Adams's diplomatic victory was Napoleonic in its magnitude and completeness. Even Caulaincourt, whom he
overthrew, good-naturedly congratulated him after he had
succeeded, against Caulaincourt's utmost efforts, in saving all
the American ships. "It seems you are great favorites here;
you have found powerful protection," said the defeated ambassador.[1] The American minister felt but one drawback,—
he could not wholly believe that his victory was sure. Anxious
by temperament, with little confidence in his own good fortune,—fighting his battles with energy, but rather with that
of despair than of hope,—the younger Adams never allowed
himself to enjoy the full relish of a triumph before it staled,
while he never failed to taste with its fullest flavor, as though
it were a precious wine, every drop in the bitter cup of his
defeats. In this, the most brilliant success of his diplomatic
career, he could not be blamed for doubting whether such
fortune could last. That the Czar of Russia should persist in
braving almost sure destruction in order to defend American
rights which America herself proclaimed to be unassailed,
passed the bounds of fiction.

Yet of all the facts with which Monroe, April 1, 1811, had to

[1] Diary, Feb. 15, 1811, ii. 226.

deal, this was the most important,—that Russia expected to fight France in order to protect neutral commerce. Already, Dec. 27, 1810, Adams notified his Government that Russia had determined to resist to the last, and that France had shown a spirit of hostility that proved an intention to make war. A few weeks later he wrote that military movements on both sides had begun on such a scale that the rumor of war was universal.[1] Napoleon's harangue of March 24, 1811, to the Paris Chamber of Commerce was accepted in Russia as the announcement of a coming declaration, and the Russians waited uneasily for the blow to be struck which the Czar would not himself strike.

They waited, but Napoleon did not move. Hampered by the Spanish war and by the immense scale on which a campaign in Russia must be organized, he consumed time in diplomatic remonstrances which he knew to be useless. April 1, 1811, a week after his tirade to the Paris merchants, he dictated another lecture to the Czar, through Count Lauriston:[2] "Doubtless the smugglers will try every means of forming connections with the Continent; but that connection I will cut, if necessary, with the sword. Until now I have been indulgent; but this year I am determined to use rigor toward those who are concerned in contraband." A great convoy, he said, was at that moment collecting in English ports for the Baltic; but the goods thus introduced would be everywhere seized, "even in Russia, whatever might be said to the contrary, because the Emperor Alexander has declared his wish to remain at war with the English as the only means of maintaining the peace of the Continent." A few days afterward, April 5, Cadore was ordered to write again:[3] "It is probable that the least appearance of a peace with England will be the signal of war unless unforeseen circumstances lead the Emperor to prefer to gain time." Alexander wished the moral advantage of appearing to be attacked, and he allowed Napoleon to gain time in these pretended remonstrances. Roumanzoff replied to them as seriously as though they were seriously meant. Once he quoted the American minister as

[1] Adams to Robert Smith, Feb. 12, 1811; MSS. State Department Archives.
[2] Napoleon to Champagny, April 1, 1811; Correspondance, xxii. 3.
[3] Napoleon to Champagny, April 5, 1811; Correspondance, xxii. 28.

authority for the genuine character of the admitted vessels. Napoleon treated the appeal with contempt:[1] "Let him know that there are no American ships; that all pretended American ships are English, or freighted on English account; that the English stop American vessels and do not let them navigate; that if the American minister sustains the contrary, he does not know what he is talking about."

The American minister no longer needed to sustain the contrary; he had passed that stage, and had to struggle only with the completeness of his success. Although a large British squadron kept the Baltic open to commerce, few British merchantmen visited those waters in 1811. Their timidity was due to the violence with which Napoleon had seized and destroyed British property in 1810 wherever he found it, without respecting his own licenses. In consequence of British abstention, American vessels swarmed in Russian ports. In July, 1811, Adams wrote that two hundred American ships had already arrived,[2] and that Russia was glutted with colonial goods until the cargoes were unsalable at any price, while the great demand for return cargoes of Russian produce had raised the cost of such articles to extravagance. America enjoyed a monopoly of the Baltic trade; and Adams's chief difficulty, like that of Napoleon, was only to resist the universal venality which made of the American flag a cover for British smuggling. Adams seemed unable to ask a favor which the Czar did not seem eager to grant; for in truth the result of admitting American ships pleased the friendly Czar and his people, who obtained their sugar and coffee at half cost, and sold their hemp and naval stores at double prices.

The Russians knew well the price they were to pay in the end, but in the mean time Napoleon became more and more pacific. If war was to come in 1811, every one supposed it would be announced in the French Emperor's usual address to his legislative body, which opened its session June 16. The Address was brought in hot haste by special courier to St. Petersburg; but to the surprise of every one it contained no allusion to Russia. As usual, Napoleon pointed in the direc-

[1] Napoleon to Maret, July 15, 1811; Correspondance, xxii. 327.
[2] Adams to Monroe, July 22, 1811; MSS. State Department Archives.

tion he meant not to take, and instead of denouncing Russia, he prophesied disaster to the victorious English in Spain:—

> "When England shall be exhausted; when she shall have felt at last the evils that she has for twenty years poured with so much cruelty over the Continent; when half of her families shall be covered by the funeral veil,—then a thunder-stroke will end the peninsula troubles and the destinies of her armies, and will avenge Europe and Asia by closing this second Punic war."

This Olympian prophecy meant only that Napoleon, for military reasons, preferred not to invade Russia until 1812. As the question of neutral trade was but one of the pretexts on which he forced Russia into war, and as it had served its purpose, he laid it aside. He closed the chapter August 25 by directing his ambassador, Lauriston, to cease further remonstrance.[1] One hundred and fifty ships, he said, under false American colors had arrived in Russia; the projects of Russia were unmasked; she wanted to renew her commerce with England; she no longer preserved appearances, but favored in every way the English trade; further remonstrance would be ridiculous and diplomatic notes useless.

War for the spring of 1812 was certain. So much harm, at least, the Americans helped to inflict on Napoleon in return for the millions he cost them; but even this was not their whole revenge.

The example of Russia found imitation in Sweden, where Napoleon was most vulnerable. Owing to a series of chances, Bernadotte, who had happened to attract the attention of the Swedes, was made Prince of Sweden in October, 1810, and immediately assumed the government of the kingdom. Bernadotte as an old republican, like Lucien Bonaparte, never forgave Napoleon for betraying his party, and would long since have been exiled like Moreau had he not been the brother-in-law of Joseph and a reasonably submissive member of the Imperial family. Napoleon treated him as he treated Louis, Lucien, Joseph, Jerome, Eugene, and Joachim Murat, —loading them with dignities, but exacting blind obedience;

[1] Napoleon to Maret, Aug. 25, 1811; Correspondance, xxii. 441.

and instantly on the new king's accession, the French minister informed him that he must within five days declare war on England. Bernadotte obeyed. Napoleon next required the confiscation of English merchandise and the total stoppage of relations between Sweden and England.[1] As in the case of Holland and the Baltic Powers, this demand included all American ships and cargoes, which amounted to one half of the property to be seized. Bernadotte either could not or would not drag his new subjects into such misery as Denmark and Holland were suffering; and within five months after his accession, he already found himself threatened with war. "Tell the Swedish minister," said Napoleon to Cadore,[2] "that if any ship loaded with colonial produce—be it American or Danish or Swedish or Spanish or Russian—is admitted into the ports of Swedish Pomerania, my troops and my customs officers shall immediately enter the province." Swedish Pomerania was the old province still held by Sweden on the south shore of the Baltic, next to Mecklenburg; and Stralsund, its capital, was a nest of smugglers who defied the Emperor's decrees.

In March, 1811, Davout, who commanded at Hamburg, received orders[3] to prepare for seizing Stralsund at the least contravention of the commercial laws. Bernadotte's steps were evidently taken to accord with those of the Czar Alexander; and at last Napoleon found himself in face of a Swedish as well as a Russian, Spanish, and English war. In the case of Russia, American commerce was but one though a chief cause of rupture;[4] but in the case of Sweden it seemed to be the only cause. In August, Napoleon notified the Czar of his intentions against Stralsund; in November, he gave the last warning to Sweden,—and in both cases he founded his complaints on the toleration shown to American commerce. Nov. 3, 1811, he wrote to Bassano: "If the Swedish Government does not renounce the system of escorting by its armed ships the vessels which English commerce covers with the American flag, you will order the *chargé d'affaires* to quit Stockholm with all the legation." He returned again and again to the

---

[1] Napoleon to Alquier, Dec. 22, 1810; Correspondance, xxi. 328.

[2] Napoleon to Champagny, March 25, 1811; Correspondance, xxi. 510.

[3] Correspondance, xxi. 506.

[4] Tatistcheff, Alexandre 1ᵉʳ et Napoléon, p. 578.

grievance: "If Sweden does not desist from this right of escorting American ships which are violating the Decrees of Berlin and Milan, and maintains the pretension to attack my privateers with her ships-of-war, the *chargé d'affaires* will quit Stockholm. I want to preserve peace with Sweden,—this wish is palpable,—but I prefer war to such a state of peace."[1]

Once more the accent of truth sounded in these words of Napoleon. He could not want war with Sweden, but he made it because he could not otherwise enforce his Berlin and Milan Decrees against American commerce. Although a part of that commerce was fraudulent, Napoleon, in charging fraud, wished to condemn not so much the fraudulent as the genuine. In order to enforce his Berlin and Milan Decrees against American commerce, he was, as Cadore had threatened, about to overturn the world.

This was the situation when Joel Barlow, the new American minister to France, arrived at Paris Sept. 19, 1811, bringing instructions dated July 26, the essence of which was contained in a few lines.[2]

"It is understood," said the President, "that the blockade of the British Isles is revoked. The revocation having been officially declared, and no vessel trading to them having been condemned or taken on the high seas that we know of, it is fair to conclude that the measure is relinquished. It appears, too, that no American vessel has been condemned in France for having been visited at sea by an English ship, or for having been searched or carried into England, or subjected to impositions there. On the sea, therefore, France is understood to have changed her system."

Of all the caprices of politics, this was the most improbable,—that at the moment when the Czar of Russia and the King of Sweden were about to risk their thrones and to face the certain death and ruin of vast numbers of their people in order to protect American ships from the Berlin and Milan Decrees, the new minister of the United States appeared in Paris authorized to declare that the President considered those decrees to be revoked and their system no longer in force!

[1] Napoleon to Maret, Nov. 3, 1811; Correspondance, xxii. 552.
[2] Monroe to Barlow, July 26, 1811; State Papers, iii. 510.

Chapter I

RARELY HAD A great nation approached nearer than England to ruin without showing consciousness of danger. Napoleon's boast to his Chamber of Commerce, that within ten years he would subject his rival, was not ill-founded. The conquest of Russia, which Napoleon meant to make certain, combined with a war between the United States and Great Britain, coming immediately upon the destruction of private credit and enterprise in 1810, could hardly fail to shake the British empire to its foundation; and perhaps the worst sign of danger was the absence of popular alarm. The intelligence of all England with feelings equally strong, whether mute or vociferous, was united in contempt for the stolid incompetence of the Tory faction beyond anything known in England since the Stuarts; but both Houses of Parliament, as well as the Crown, were conscious of needing no better representatives than Perceval and Eldon, and convulsions that shook the world never stirred the composure of these men. The capital and credit on which England's power rested were swept away; the poorer classes were thrown out of employment; the price of wheat,[1] which averaged in 1807 seventy-eight shillings per quarter of eight bushels, in 1808 eighty-five shillings, and in 1809 one hundred and six shillings, in 1810 rose to one hundred and twelve shillings, or about three dollars and a half a bushel, and remained at or above this rate until the autumn of 1813; while abroad, the Spanish peninsula was subdued by Napoleon, whose armies occupied every part of Spain and Portugal except Cadiz and Lisbon. Sweden, the last neutral in Europe, elected a French general of Bonaparte's family as king, and immediately afterward declared war on England; and the United States closed their ports to British commerce, and menaced a declaration of war. The exports of Great Britain fell off one third in the year 1811. The sources of England's strength showed exhaustion.

Neither these arguments nor even the supreme argument

[1] Tooke's Prices, ii. 389, 390.

of war shook the steadfast mind of Spencer Perceval. Responsibilities that might have driven him to insanity took the form of religious duties; and with the support of religious or patriotic formulas statesmen could sleep in peace amidst the wreck of nations. After the insanity of King George was admitted, at the beginning of November, 1810, Spencer Perceval became for a time the King of England, but a king without title. The Prince of Wales, the future regent, was obliged to wait for an Act of Parliament authorizing him to assume power. The Prince of Wales had all his life detested the Tory influence that surrounded the throne, and had associated with Whigs and liberals, like Sheridan and Fox. Perceval expected to retire; the prince could not yet take control, and this deadlock put a stop to serious government. Nothing but business of routine could be undertaken.

If the United States could wait till spring, their friends were likely to be once more in power, or the Tory influence would be so far shaken that the danger of war might pass. For this possible revolution both Madison and Pinkney twelve months before would have waited with confidence and pleasure; but repeated disappointments had convinced them that their patience was useless. Pinkney had asked and received instructions to require a decision or to quit England. When November arrived, the day on which Napoleon's Decrees stood revoked according to the Duc de Cadore, Pinkney acted in London on his own responsibility, as Madison acted at Washington, and sent to Lord Wellesley a note, dated November 3, asking for an immediate repeal of the British Orders in Council, on the ground that Napoleon's revocation had taken effect. "That it has taken effect cannot be doubted," he said;[1] but he offered no evidence to support his assertion. He also assumed that England was bound to withdraw Fox's blockade of the French coast from Brest to the Elbe, as well as Spencer Perceval's subsequent measures which were called into existence by Napoleon's Continental system, and were to cease with it. Both these demands were made without instructions founded on the knowledge of Cadore's letter.

At that moment Lord Wellesley was full of hope that at last

[1] State Papers, iii. 373.

he should remove Spencer Perceval from his path. Every one supposed, and had good ground for believing, that the Prince of Wales would at once form a new Government, with Wellesley and the Whigs for its support. At such a crisis Wellesley could not expect or indeed wish to effect a partial and sudden change of foreign policy. He waited a month before taking official notice of Pinkney's letter, and when he replied,[1] December 4, said only that "after the most accurate inquiry" he had been unable to obtain any authentic intelligence of the French repeal, and begged the American minister to furnish whatever information he possessed on the subject.

The American minister possessed no information on the subject, but he received, December 11, news of the President's proclamation founded on the French repeal, and was the more decided to insist on his ground. Finding that conversations produced no effect, Pinkney took his pen once more,— and then began another of the diplomatic duels which had occurred so often in the course of the last six years; but for the first time the American champion with weak arguments and indifferent temper used the kind of logic likely to produce conviction in the end.

Pinkney maintained that the French Decrees were revoked and that Fox's blockade was illegal. Neither position was beyond attack. The American doctrine of blockade was by no means clear. The British government never attempted to defend its sweeping Orders of 1807 and 1809 on the ground of legality; these were admittedly illegal, and a proper *casus belli* if America chose to make war on their account. England claimed only that the United States were bound to make war on France for the Berlin Decree of Nov. 21, 1806, before making war on England for her retaliatory Orders of 1807. In order to evade this difficulty, France declared that her Decree of November, 1806, was retaliatory on Fox's blockade of May, 1806. America began by maintaining that as far as concerned neutral commerce both belligerents used retaliation for illegitimate objects, and that the United States might rightfully declare war against either or both. The position was easily understood, and had the advantage of being historically true;

[1] State Papers, iii. 376.

but the United States stood on less certain ground when they were drawn into discussion of the legal theory involved in Fox's blockade.

England held[1] that Fox's blockade of May, 1806, covering the French coast from the Elbe to Brest, was a lawful blockade, supported by a particular naval force detached for that special purpose and sufficient for its object, until the blockade itself was merged in the avowedly extra-legal paper-blockades of 1809; and that if the paper-blockades were withdrawn, Great Britain had the right to re-establish Fox's blockade with an efficient naval force to execute it.

President Madison held a different opinion. He insisted,[2] and ordered Pinkney to insist, that a particular port must be invested by a particular naval force; and that Great Britain ought not to contend that her naval force was adequate to blockade a coast a thousand miles long. On this ground the President, July 5, 1810,[3] instructed Pinkney to require the annulment of Fox's blockade as "palpably at variance with the law of nations." In order to prove the impartiality of this demand, the President promised to insist that the repeal required from France as its counterpart should "embrace every part of the French Decrees which violate the neutral rights guaranteed to us by the law of nations."

No worse ground could have been found for Pinkney to stand upon. He was obliged to begin by asserting, what every public man in Europe knew to be untrue, that "every part of the French Decrees which violated the neutral rights" of America had been repealed by Cadore's letter of August 5. His next contention, that coasts could not be blockaded, was at least open to dispute when the coast was that of the British Channel. Pinkney's arguments became necessarily technical, and although technical reasoning might be easily understood in a Court of Admiralty, the attempt to treat politics as a branch of the profession of the law had the disadvantage of refining issues to a point which no large society could comprehend. When Wellesley, Dec. 4, 1810, asked for evidence

[1] Instructions of Wellesley to Foster, April 10, 1811; Papers presented to Parliament, February, 1813.
[2] Robert Smith to Pinkney, July 2, 1810; State Papers, iii. 360.
[3] Smith to Pinkney, July 5, 1810; State Papers, iii. 362.

that Napoleon's Decrees were repealed, Pinkney replied, in a long note dated December 10,[1] that Cadore's letter of August 5 stated two disjunctive conditions of repeal,—the first depending on Great Britain, the last on the United States; that although Great Britain had not satisfied the first condition, the United States would undoubtedly satisfy the last; therefore the French Decrees stood repealed. This proposition, not even easy to understand, was supported by a long argument showing that Cadore could not without absurdity have meant anything else. As for further proof, not only had Pinkney none to offer, but he gravely offered his want of evidence as evidence:—

> "On such an occasion it is no paradox to say that the want of evidence is itself evidence. That certain decrees are not in force is proved by the absence of such facts as would appear if they were in force. Every motive which can be conjectured to have led to the repeal of the edicts invites to the full execution of that repeal, and no motive can be imagined for a different course. These considerations are alone conclusive."

The argument might have escaped ridicule had not Jonathan Russell been engaged at the same moment[2] in remonstrating with the Duc de Cadore because the "New Orleans Packet" had been seized at Bordeaux under the Berlin and Milan Decrees; and had not the "Moniteur," within a week, published Cadore's official Report, declaring that the decrees would never be repealed as long as England maintained her blockades; and had not the Comte de Semonville, within another week, announced in the French Senate that the decrees were the palladium of the seas.

Wellesley answered Pinkney, December 29, in a note[3] comparatively short, and more courteous than any important State paper that had come from the British government since Fox's death.

> "If nothing more had been required from Great Britain

[1] Pinkney to Wellesley, Dec. 10, 1810; State Papers, iii. 376.
[2] Russell to Cadore, Dec. 10, 1810; State Papers, iii. 391.
[3] Wellesley to Pinkney, Dec. 29, 1810; State Papers, iii. 408.

than the repeal of our Orders in Council," he said, "I should not have hesitated to declare the perfect readiness of this Government to fulfil that condition. On these terms the Government has always been sincerely disposed to repeal the Orders in Council. It appears, however, not only by the letter of the French minister, but by your explanation, that the repeal of the Orders in Council will not satisfy either the French or the American government. The British government is further required by the letter of the French minister to renounce those principles of blockade which the French government alleges to be new. . . . On the part of the American government, I understand you to require that Great Britain shall revoke her Order of Blockade of May, 1806."

Wellesley declined to entertain this demand. He appealed to the justice of America not to force an issue on such ground, and he protested that the Government retained an anxious solicitude to revoke the Orders in Council as soon as the Berlin and Milan Decrees should be effectually repealed, without conditions injurious to the maritime rights of Great Britain.

To this declaration Pinkney replied, Jan. 14, 1811, in a letter[1] defending his own position and attacking the good faith of the British government. He began by defending the temper of his late remonstrances: —

"It would not have been very surprising nor very culpable, perhaps, if I had wholly forgotten to address myself to a spirit of conciliation which had met the most equitable claims with steady and unceasing repulsion; which had yielded nothing that could be denied, and had answered complaints of injury by multiplying their causes. With this forgetfulness, however, I am not chargeable; for against all the discouragements suggested by the past, I have acted still upon a presumption that the disposition to conciliate, so often professed, would finally be proved by some better evidence than a perseverance in oppressive novelties, as obviously incompatible with such a disposition in those who

[1] Pinkney to Wellesley, Jan. 14, 1811; State Papers, iii. 409.

enforce them as in those whose patience they continue to exercise."

America, continued Pinkney, was not a party, either openly or covertly, to the French requisition. "What I have to request of your Lordship is that you will take our views and principles from our own mouths." The rejoinder was not so convincing as it would have been had Pinkney wholly discarded French views; but on the point of Fox's blockade, the American and the French demand was the same. Pinkney was obliged to show that the two identical conditions rested on different grounds. At some length he laid down the law as the United States understood it.

"It is by no means clear," he began, "that it may not be fairly contended, on principle and early usage, that a maritime blockade is incomplete with regard to States at peace unless the place which it would affect is invested by land as well as by sea. The United States, however, have called for the recognition of no such rule. They appear to have contented themselves with urging in substance that ports not actually blockaded by a present, adequate, stationary force employed by the Power which attacks them shall not be considered as shut to neutral trade in articles not contraband of war; . . . that a vessel cleared or bound to a blockaded port shall not be considered as violating in any manner the blockade unless on her approach to such port she shall have been previously warned not to enter it; . . . that whole coasts and countries shall not be declared (for they can never be more than *declared*) to be in a state of blockade; . . . and lastly, that every blockade shall be impartial in its operation."

On these definitions of law, and not to satisfy Napoleon's requirement, the President insisted on the abandonment of Fox's blockade.

The withdrawal of the Orders in Council, on the other hand, was required on the ground that England had pledged her faith to withdraw them whenever France revoked her decrees. France had revoked her decrees, and England could not honorably refuse to withdraw the orders.

"As to the Orders in Council which professed to be a reluctant departure from all ordinary rules, and to be justified only as a system of retaliation for a pre-existing measure of France, their foundation, such as it was, is gone the moment that measure is no longer in operation. But the Berlin Decree is repealed, and even the Milan Decree, the successor of your Orders in Council, is repealed also. Why is it, then, that your orders have outlived those edicts?"

In both instances the American position lost character by connection with Napoleon's acts. Pinkney repudiated such a connection in the first case, and his argument would have been stronger could he have repudiated it in the second. Unable or unwilling to do this, he had no resource but to lose his temper, which he did with proper self-control. The correctness of his reasoning or of his facts became less important from the moment he showed himself in earnest; for then the controversy entered a new phase.

In making an issue of war, President Madison needed to exercise extreme caution not to shock the sentiment of New England, but he needed to observe no such delicacy in regard to the feelings of the British Tories. In respect to the British government, the nature of the issue mattered little, provided an issue were made; and Pinkney might reasonably think that the more paradoxical his arguments the more impression they would produce. Centuries of study at Oxford and Edinburgh, and generations devoted to the logic or rhetoric of Aristotle, Cicero, and Quintilian, had left the most educated classes of Great Britain still in the stage of culture where reasoning, in order to convince, must cease to be reasonable. As Pinkney became positive and arrogant, Wellesley became conciliatory and almost yielding. The American note of January 14, written in a tone that had not hitherto been taken in London, was coupled with a notice that brought the two governments in presence of the long-threatened rupture. Pinkney informed Lord Wellesley that as the British government, after a lapse of many months, had taken no steps to carry out the assurance of sending a new minister to Washington, the United States government could not retain a minister at London. Therewith Pinkney requested an audience of leave.

Although Wellesley had never avowed a political motive for his systematic delays, no one could doubt that he intentionally postponed not only concession on the Orders in Council, but also a settlement of the "Chesapeake" affair and the appointment of a new minister at Washington, because his colleagues, as he hinted[1] to Pinkney, were persuaded "that the British interest in America would be completely destroyed by sending thither at this time a minister plenipotentiary," and of course by any other frank advance. The influence of F. J. Jackson with the Government was perhaps strong enough to check action that would have amounted to a censure on his own conduct; and although the American elections showed that Jackson had for the time so much reduced British influence in America as to make some change of policy necessary if it were to be revived, Jackson, in daily intercourse with the Foreign Office and with ministers, was exerting every effort to maintain his credit. Nothing less than Pinkney's request for an audience of leave was likely to end these ministerial hesitations.

For the moment, as Pinkney knew, his request could not be granted, because the King was insane and could give audience to no one. Since Nov. 1, 1810, Parliament had done no other business than such as related to the regency; yet on Jan. 14, 1811, when Pinkney's two notes were written, the Regency Bill had not been brought before the Commons. Introduced on the following day, Parliament showed extraordinary energy by making it law in little more than a fortnight; yet the Prince Regent, who took the oaths February 6, still required time to settle his government.

Everything depended on the Prince Regent's action. Had he followed the expected course,—had he dismissed Spencer Perceval, and put himself in the hands of Wellesley, Grenville, Grey, and Holland,—the danger of an American war might possibly have vanished. The Orders in Council might have been withdrawn, the "Chesapeake" affair might have been settled, a friendly minister would have been sent to Washington, and the war party in the Twelfth Congress would have been thrown into a minority. After much manœuvring, the Prince

---

[1] Pinkney to Madison, Dec. 17, 1810; Wheaton's Pinkney, p. 452.

of Wales at last avowed his decision. February 4 he wrote to Spencer Perceval, announcing the wish, wholly in deference to the King's feelings, that the late ministers should remain in charge of the government. The Whigs were once more prostrated by this desertion, and the Marquess Wellesley abandoned his last hope of saving the government from Perceval's control.

The effect of the Prince Regent's course was instantly felt. His letter to Perceval was written February 4; he assumed the royal office February 6; and February 11 Wellesley was able to answer[1] Pinkney's note on blockades.

> "France requires," said he, "that Great Britain shall not only repeal the Orders in Council, but renounce those principles of blockade which are alleged in the same letter to be new,—an allegation which must be understood to refer to the introductory part of the Berlin Decree. If Great Britain shall not submit to those terms, it is plainly intimated in the same letter that France requires America to enforce them. To these conditions his Royal Highness, on behalf of his Majesty, cannot accede. No principles of blockade have been promulgated or acted upon by Great Britain previously to the Berlin Decree which are not strictly conformable to the rights of civilized war and to the approved usages and laws of nations. . . . I am commanded to inform you that his Royal Highness cannot consent to blend the question which has arisen upon the Orders in Council with any discussion of the general principles of blockade."

In a note of two lines, Pinkney replied[2] that he had no inducement to trouble his Lordship further on the subject. The same day he received a notice that the Prince Regent would hold his first diplomatic levee February 19; but instead of accepting the invitation, Pinkney wrote with the same brevity to ask at what time the Prince Regent would do him the honor to give his audience of leave.[3]

This abrupt course brought the Government partially to reason. Within forty-eight hours Wellesley wrote to Pinkney

[1] Wellesley to Pinkney, Feb. 11, 1811; State Papers, iii. 412.
[2] Pinkney to Wellesley, Feb. 13, 1811; State Papers, iii. 412.
[3] Pinkney to Wellesley, Feb. 13, 1811; State Papers, iv. 413.

a private letter[1] of apology for the delay in appointing a minister to Washington, and of regret that this delay should have been misunderstood; he announced that Augustus J. Foster, late British minister in Sweden, would be immediately gazetted as minister to the United States; and his letter closed by a remark which came as near deprecation as Pinkney's temper would allow: "You will, of course, exercise your own judgment, under these circumstances, respecting the propriety of requiring an audience of leave on the grounds which you have stated." With this private letter, Lord Wellesley sent an official notice that the Prince Regent would receive Mr. Pinkney February 19, by his desire, for an audience of leave.

The responsibility thus thrown upon Pinkney was more serious than had ever before, or has ever since, fallen to the share of a minister of the United States in England. The policy of withdrawing the United States minister from London might be doubted, not so much because it was violent, as because it was likely to embarrass the President more than it embarrassed England. If the President was indeed bent on war, and wished to hasten its declaration, the recall of his minister in London might be proper; but if he still expected to negotiate, London was the spot where he needed to keep his strongest diplomatist, and, if possible, more than one. Yet the worst possible mistake was to recede once more,—to repeat the comedy of American errors, and to let the British government assume that its policy was still safe.

Pinkney hesitated, and consulted his instructions.[2] These were dated Nov. 15, 1810, and ordered Pinkney, in case no successor to F. J. Jackson should then have been appointed, to take leave of absence, entrusting the legation to a *chargé d'affaires*; but this positive order was practically revoked in the concluding sentence: "Considering the season at which this instruction may have its effect, and the possibility of a satisfactory change in the posture of our relations with Great Britain, the time of your return to the United States is left to your discretion and convenience."

These instructions did not warrant Pinkney in demanding

[1] Wellesley to Pinkney, Feb. 15, 1811; State Papers, iii. 413.
[2] Smith to Pinkney, Nov. 15, 1810; State Papers, iii. 375.

leave of absence on any other ground than that of failure to appoint a minister at Washington. They did not warrant him in returning to America at all if he saw the possibility of such an appointment. Pinkney was obliged to put a free construction on the President's language. Abandoning the ground that his departure was a necessary result of the absence of a British minister at Washington, he asked Lord Wellesley, in an official note, dated February 17, what Mr. Foster was to do when he arrived there?[1] "I presume that for the restoration of harmony between the two countries, the Orders in Council will be relinquished without delay; that the blockade of 1806 will be annulled; that the case of the 'Chesapeake' will be arranged in the manner heretofore intended; and in general that all such just and reasonable acts will be done as are necessary to make us friends." So important a letter was probably never written by any other American diplomatist without instructions from his Government,—for it was in effect an ultimatum, preliminary to the rupture of relations and ultimate war; yet even in this final list of American demands made by the American minister in withdrawing from London, impressment was not expressly mentioned.

Wellesley replied in a private letter[2] dated February 23, with the formal avowal that "it would be neither candid toward you, nor just toward this Government, to countenance any interpretation which might favor a supposition that it was intended by this Government to relinquish any of the principles which I have so often endeavored to explain to you." Nothing in Wellesley's letter showed a desire to irritate, and his refusals left less sting than was left by Canning's concessions; but the issue was fairly joined, and America was at liberty to act upon it as she pleased.

In order to leave no doubt of his meaning, Pinkney instantly[3] claimed his audience of leave for February 28, declining, in the mean time, to attend the diplomatic levee which by postponement took place only February 26. His conduct was noticed and understood, as he meant it should be; and as his audience still remains the only occasion when

[1] Pinkney to Wellesley, Feb. 17, 1811; State Papers, iii. 414.

[2] Wellesley to Pinkney, Feb. 23, 1811; State Papers, iii. 415.

[3] Pinkney to Wellesley, Feb. 23, 1811; State Papers, iii. 415.

an American minister at London has broken relations in a hostile manner, with resulting war, it has an interest peculiar to itself. Several accounts were preserved of what passed at the interview. Pinkney's official report recorded the words used by him:[1] —

> "I stated to the Prince Regent the grounds upon which it had become my duty to take my leave and to commit the business of the legation to a *chargé d'affaires*; and I concluded by expressing my regret that my humble efforts in the execution of the instructions of my Government to set to rights the embarrassed and disjointed relations of the two countries had wholly failed; and that I saw no reason to expect that the great work of their reconciliation was likely to be accomplished through any other agency."

According to Pinkney, and according to the official report of Lord Wellesley,[2] the Prince Regent replied in terms of the utmost amity toward the United States. Another account of the interview gave the impression that the Prince Regent had not shown himself so gracious toward the departing minister as the official reports implied. Francis James Jackson, who dogged Pinkney's footsteps with the personal malevolence he had almost a right to feel, and who haunted the Court and Foreign Office in the hope of obtaining—what he never received—some public mark of approval, wrote to Timothy Pickering a long letter on Pinkney's departure:[3] —

> "It has occasioned much surprise here that exactly at the moment of Pinkney's demand being complied with he should nevertheless take what he calls an inamicable leave. . . . It was not expected that he would depart so far from his usual urbanity as to decline the invitation that was sent him in common with the rest of the foreign ministers to attend the Regent's levee. It was not probable after this that the audience of leave which he claimed should answer his expectation. It was very short. Mr. Pinkney was told that the Regent was desirous of cultivating a good under-

[1] Pinkney to Robert Smith, March 1, 1811; State Papers, iii. 415.
[2] Wellesley to Foster, April 29, 1811; Papers, etc., 1813, p. 294.
[3] F. J. Jackson to Pickering, April 24, 1811; New England Federalism, p. 382.

standing with the United States; that he had given a proof of it in the appointment of a minister as soon as his acceptance of the Regency enabled him to appoint one; that the Orders in Council would have been repealed, but that his Royal Highness never could or would surrender the maritime rights of his country. Mr. Pinkney then made some profession of his personal sentiments, to which he was answered: 'Sir, I cannot look into men's minds; I can only judge of men's motives by their conduct.' And then the audience ended."

So closed Pinkney's residence in London. He had passed there nearly five years of such violent national hostility as no other American minister ever faced during an equal length of time, or defied at last with equal sternness; but his extraordinary abilities and character made him greatly respected and admired while he stayed, and silenced remonstrance when he left. For many years afterward, his successors were mortified by comparisons between his table-oratory and theirs. As a writer he was not less distinguished. Canning's impenetrable self-confidence met in him powers that did not yield, even in self-confidence, to his own; and Lord Wellesley's oriental dignity was not a little ruffled by Pinkney's handling. As occasion required, he was patient under irritation that seemed intolerable, as aggressive as Canning himself, or as stately and urbane as Wellesley; and even when he lost his temper, he did so in cold blood, because he saw no other way to break through the obstacles put in his path. America never sent an abler representative to the Court of London.

Pinkney sailed from England a few weeks afterward, leaving in charge of the legation John Spear Smith, a son of Senator Samuel Smith, who had been for a time attached to the Legation at St. Petersburg; had thence travelled to Vienna and Paris, where he received Pinkney's summons to London,—the most difficult and important diplomatic post in the world. Simultaneously, Lord Wellesley hurried Foster to the United States. The new British minister was personally acceptable. By birth a son of the actual Duchess of Devonshire by her first husband, he had the advantage of social and political backing, while he was already familiar with America, where he had served as Secretary of Legation. Just dismissed from Sweden by Bernadotte's election and the declaration of war against England which followed it, Foster would hardly have sought or taken the mission to Washington had not Europe been closed to English diplomacy. Even F. J. Jackson, who spoke kindly of few people, gave a pleasant account of his successor.[1] "Foster is a very gentlemanlike young man, quite equal to do nothing at his post, which is now the best possible policy to follow;" but in the same breath, "that most clumsy and ill-conditioned minister," as Pinkney described Jackson,[2] added that the police office was the proper place to train officials for service at Washington. "One of the best magistrates as minister, and a good sharp thief-taker for secretary, would put us in all respects much upon a level with their Yankeeships." The phrase implied that Jackson felt his own career at Washington to have been mortifying, and that he had not been on a level with his opponents. Possibly the sense of mortification hurried the decline which ended in his death, three years afterward, in the midst of the war he did so much to cause.

Wellesley's instructions to Foster were dated April 10,[3] and marked another slight step toward concession. Once more he discussed the Orders in Council, but on the ground taken by Pinkney could come to no other conclusion than that the President was mistaken in thinking the French Decrees repealed, and extravagant in requiring the blockade of 1806 to be repealed in consequence; yet as long as any hope remained of prevailing with the President to correct his error, American ships, captured while acting in pursuance of it, should not be condemned. Even under the challenge expressly proclaimed by the non-importation, the British government anxiously desired to avoid a positive rupture. As for the "Chesapeake" affair, Foster was ordered to settle it to suit the American government, guarding only against the admission of insulting expressions. He was to remonstrate and protest against the seizure of the Floridas,[4] but was not to commit his Govern-

---

[1] Bath Archives, Second Series, i. 219.
[2] Pinkney to Madison, Aug. 13, 1810; Wheaton's Pinkney, p. 444.
[3] Papers relating to America, C, presented to Parliament, February, 1813.
[4] Instruction No. 3; MSS. British Archives.

ment further. Finally, a secret instruction[1] notified Foster that in case America should persist in her non-importation, England would retaliate,—probably by increasing her import duties, and excluding American commerce from the East Indies.

These instructions conformed with the general attitude of English society. Though sobered by the disasters that attended Tory government, England had not yet passed beyond the stage when annoyances created only the wish to ignore them. No one would admit serious danger from America. In Parliament, Pinkney's abrupt and hostile departure was barely mentioned, and ministers denied it importance. The "London Times," of March 1, complained that no one could be induced to feel an interest in the American question. "There is certainly great apathy in the public mind generally upon the questions now at issue between us and our quondam colonies, which it is difficult to arouse, and perhaps useless to attempt." Here and there the old wish for a war with the United States was still felt;[2] but the public asked only to hear no more on American subjects. Even the "Times" refused, April 13, to continue discussion on matters "upon which the feelings of the great bulk of the nation are peculiarly blunt." Wellesley's course and Foster's instructions reflected only the lassitude and torpor of the day; but within eighteen months Wellesley, in open Parliament, criticised what he charged as the policy, not of himself, but of his colleagues, in language which implied that the public apathy was assumed rather than real. "The disposition of the American government was quite evident," he said, Nov. 30, 1812;[3] "and therefore common policy should have urged ministers to prepare fully for the event; and they should have made adequate exertion either to pacify, to intimidate, or to punish America." Knowing this, they sent out Foster, powerless either for defence or attack, to waste his time at Washington, where for ten years his predecessors had found the grave of their ambitions.

[1] Instruction No. 8; MSS. British Archives.
[2] Bath Archives, Second Series, i. 221.
[3] Cobbett's Debates, xxiv. 34.

Chapter II

THE DIPLOMATIC insolvency inherited from Merry, Rose, Erskine, and Jackson became more complete with every year that passed; and even while Foster was on the ocean, a new incident occurred, which if it did not prove a catastrophe to be inevitable, showed at least how small was his chance of averting it.

On the renewal of trade between America and France, the British navy renewed its blockade of New York. If nothing more had happened, the recurrence of this vexation would alone have gone far to destroy the hopes of diplomacy; but this was not all.

The "Melampus" reappeared, having for a companion the "Guerriere," commanded by Captain Dacres, and supposed to be one of the best British frigates of her class. Early in May, when Foster sailed from England, these cruisers, lying off Sandy Hook, began to capture American vessels bound for France, and to impress American sailors at will. No sooner did these complaints reach Washington than Secretary Hamilton, May 6,[1] ordered Commodore John Rodgers, whose flag-ship, the 44-gun frigate "President," was lying at Annapolis, to sail at once to protect American commerce from unlawful interference by British and French cruisers. Rodgers sailed from Annapolis May 10, and May 14 passed the capes. The scene of the "Chesapeake's" unredressed outrage lay some fifteen or twenty miles to the southward, and the officers and crew of the "President" had reason to think themselves expected to lose no fair opportunity of taking into their own hands the redress which the British government denied. For the past year Rodgers had carried orders "to vindicate the injured honor of our navy and revive the drooping spirits of the nation; . . . to maintain and support at any risk and cost the honor" of his flag; and these orders were founded chiefly on "the inhuman and dastardly attack on our frigate 'Chesapeake,'—an outrage which prostrated the flag of our country,

---

[1] Secretary Hamilton to Commodore Rodgers, May 6, 1811; MSS. Navy Department Archives.

and has imposed on the American people cause of ceaseless mourning."[1]

Rodgers was bound for New York, but on the morning of May 16 was still about thirty miles from Cape Charles and eighteen miles from the coast, when toward noon he saw a ship to the eastward standing toward him under a press of canvas. As the vessel came near, he could make her out from the shape of her upper sails to be a man-of-war; he knew of no man-of-war except the "Guerriere" on the coast; the new-comer appeared from the quarter where that frigate would be looked for, and Rodgers reasoned that in all probability she was the "Guerriere." He decided to approach her, with the object of ascertaining whether a man named Diggio, said to have been impressed a few days before by Captain Dacres from an American brig, was on board. The spirit of this inquiry was new.

Until quarter before two o'clock in the afternoon the ships stood toward each other. The stranger showed no colors, but made signals, until finding them unanswered, she changed her course and stood to the southward. Rodgers then made sail in chase, his colors and pennant flying. At half-past three, the stranger's hull began to be visible from the "President's" deck, but as the wind failed the American frigate gained less rapidly. In latitude 37° the sun, May 16, sets at seven o'clock, and dusk comes quickly on. At quarter-past seven the unknown ship again changed her course, and lay to, presenting her broadside to the "President," and showing colors, which in the gathering twilight were not clearly seen. The ship had the look of a frigate.

At quarter before eight, Rodgers ordered his acting commandant to bring the "President" to windward of the supposed frigate within speaking distance,—a manœuvre which naturally caused the stranger uneasiness, so that she wore three times to prevent the "President" from getting under her stern. At half-past eight, according to the American account,—at quarter-past eight, according to the British story,—the "President" rounded to, within pistol-shot. On both ships every gun in the broadside was run out and trained

[1] Secretary Hamilton to Commodore Rodgers, June 9, 1810; MSS. Navy Department Archives.

on the opposite vessel, and out of every port a dozen eyes were strained to catch sight, through the dusk, of what passed in the stranger.

By the dim light Rodgers saw the supposed "Guerriere," her maintopsail to the mast, waiting with apparent confidence the next act of the audacious American frigate which had chased a British man-of-war all day, and had at last run up close to windward,—a manœuvre which British frigates were disposed to resent. To this point the reports showed no great disagreement; but in regard to what followed, one story was told by Rodgers and all his ship's company, while a wholly different story was told by the British captain and his officers.

Rodgers reported that while rounding to, he hailed the unknown vessel through his trumpet, calling out: "What ship is that?" The question, "What ship is that?" was immediately echoed back. Rodgers had time to tell his acting captain that the "President" was forging too fast ahead, before he hailed again: "What ship is that, I say?" Instantly a flash was seen from the dark where the stranger's hull lay, and a double report told that the ball had struck the "President," lodging in the mainmast. Taken by surprise, Rodgers turned to his commandant of marines and asked, "What the devil was that?" but before he gave an order his third lieutenant, Alexander James Dallas, who was watching at the first port forward of the gangway and saw the flash, leaped to one of the guns in his division and discharged it. The "Chesapeake's" disaster had done away with the old-fashioned logger-heads and matches; the "President's" guns were fitted with locks, and were discharged in an instant. Immediately afterward three guns were fired by the enemy, and the report of muskets was heard. Then Rodgers gave the order to fire, and the "President" opened with a whole broadside, followed by another. In about five minutes the enemy seemed to be silenced, and Rodgers gave the order to cease firing; but some three minutes afterward the stranger opened again, and the "President" resumed fire until she desisted. From the "President's" deck enough could be seen of the enemy's behavior to prove that whoever she might be, she was not the "Guerriere;" and Rodgers then made the remark that either she had received some unfortunate shot at the outset, or she was a vessel of force very inferior to what he had taken her for,—although she was still supposed to be nothing less than a 36-gun frigate. Disabled she certainly was, for she lay ungovernable, with her bow directly under the "President's" broadside.

Rodgers hailed once more, and understood the stranger to answer that she was a British ship-of-war in great distress. At nine o'clock at night the "President" began to repair damages, and beat about within reach, on different tacks, with lights displayed, until daybreak, when she ran down to the British vessel, and sent a boat on board. Then at last Rodgers learned, certainly to his great disappointment, that he had been fighting a single-decked vessel of less than half his force. His mistake was not so surprising as it seemed. The British cruiser might easily at a distance, or in the dark, be taken for a frigate. Her great length; her poop, top-gallants, forecastle; her deep bulwarks; the manner of stowing her hammocks; and room on each side to mount three more guns than she actually carried,—were decisive to any one who could not see that she carried but one tier of guns.[1]

Captain Bingham of the "Little Belt," a British corvette, rated at twenty guns, gave a very different account of the affair. He had been ordered from Bermuda to carry despatches to the "Guerriere;" had run north toward New York without finding her; and on his return southward, at eleven o'clock on the morning of May 16, had seen a strange sail, to which he gave chase. At two o'clock in the afternoon, concluding that she was an American frigate, he abandoned the chase, and resumed his course. The rest of his story is to be told in his own words:[2] —

> "Hoisted the colors, and made all sail south, . . . the stranger edging away, but not making any more sail. At 3.30 he made sail in chase. . . . At 6.30, finding he gained so considerably on us as not to be able to elude him during the night, being within gunshot, and clearly discerning the stars in his broad pennant, I imagined the most prudent

[1] Rodgers's Report of May 23, 1811; State Papers, Foreign Affairs, iii. 497.
[2] Niles's Register, i. 34.

method was to bring to, and hoist the colors, that no mistake might arise, and that he might see what we were. The ship was therefore brought to, her colors hoisted, her guns double-shotted, and every preparation made in case of a surprise. By his manner of steering down, he evidently wished to lay his ship in a position for raking, which I frustrated by wearing three times. At about 8.15 he came within hail. I hailed and asked what ship it was. He again repeated my words and fired a broadside, which I instantly returned. The action then became general, and continued so for three quarters of an hour, when he ceased firing, and appeared to be on fire about the main hatchway. He then filled, . . . hailed, and asked what ship this was. He fired no more guns, but stood from us, giving no reason for his most extraordinary conduct."

Bingham's report was afterward supported by the evidence of his two lieutenants, his boatswain, purser, and surgeon, at the official inquiry made May 29, at Halifax.[1] Rodgers's report was sustained by the searching inquiry made by the American government to ascertain the truth of Bingham's assertions.[2] The American investigation was naturally much more thorough in consequence of Bingham's charges, so that not only every officer, but also every seaman of the "President's" company gave evidence under oath. All agreed in swearing to the facts as they have been related in the American story.

About a month after the action, two sailors claiming to be deserters from the "President" arrived at Halifax and made affidavits,[3] which gave a third account quite different from the other two. One of these men, an Englishman, swore that he had been stationed in the second division, on the gun-deck of the "President;" that a gun in that division went off, as he thought, by accident, four or five men leaning on it; that he had turned to acquaint Lieutenant Belden, who commanded that division, of the fact, but before he could do this, though the lieutenant was only three guns from him, the whole

[1] American State Papers, Foreign Affairs, iii. 473.
[2] State Papers, iii. 477.
[3] London Times, Dec. 7, 1811; Palladium, Feb. 18, 1812.

broadside of the "President" was discharged. This story was the least probable of the three. The evidence of a deserter, under every motive to ingratiate himself with his future officers, would be suspicious, even if he were proved to have been in the "President's" crew, which was not the case; but it became valueless when the rolls showed no Lieutenant Belden on board the "President," but that the second division on the gun-deck was commanded by Lieut. A. J. Dallas,—and Lieutenant Dallas swore that he himself fired the first gun from the "President," without orders, in answer to the "Little Belt's" discharge. The evidence of every other officer and man at the guns supported his assertion.

When the contradictory reports of Rodgers and Bingham were published, a controversy arose between the newspapers which sympathized with the different captains. Rodgers was vehemently attacked by the English and Federalist press; Bingham was as hotly scouted by the American newspapers friendly to Madison. The dispute was never settled. Perhaps this was the only instance where the honor of the services was so deeply involved on both sides as to make the controversy important; for if Rodgers, all his officers, and his whole crew behaved as Bingham alleged, and perjured themselves afterward to conceal it, they were not the men they were supposed to be; and if Bingham swore falsely, he went far to establish the worst American charges against the character of the British navy.

For this reason some little effort to form an opinion on the subject deserves to be made, even at the risk of diffuseness. The elaborate investigation by the United States government settled the weight of testimony in favor of Rodgers. Other evidence raised doubts of the accuracy of Bingham's report.

This report was dated May 21, five days after the battle, in "lat. 36° 53′ N.; long. 71° 49′ W. Cape Charles bearing W. 48 miles,"—which, according to the senior lieutenant's evidence, May 29, was about the spot of the action, from fifty to fifty-four miles east of Cape Charles. Yet a glance at the map showed that these bearings marked a point more than two hundred miles east of Cape Charles. This carelessness could not be set to the account of a misprint.

The date proved only inaccuracy; other parts of Bingham's

report showed a willingness to confuse the facts. He claimed to have hoisted his colors at two o'clock in the afternoon, after making out the American commodore's pennant and resuming a southerly course. Rodgers averred that the "Little Belt" obstinately refused to show colors till darkness concealed them; and Bingham's report itself admitted that at 6.30 he decided to hoist his colors, "that no mistake might arise." During the five hours' chase his colors were not flying. His assertion, too, that at 6.30 the American frigate was within gunshot, and that the "Little Belt" was brought to because she could not escape, agreed ill with his next admission, that the "President" consumed nearly two hours in getting within hailing distance.

The most evident error was at the close of the British story. Bingham declared that the general action lasted three quarters of an hour, and that then the enemy ceased firing; appeared to be on fire about the main hatchway, and "stood from us," firing no more guns. The two lieutenants, boatswain, and purser of the "Little Belt" swore that the action lasted "about an hour;" the surgeon said "about forty-five minutes." Every American officer declared under oath that the entire action, including the cessation of firing for three minutes, did not exceed a quarter of an hour, or eighteen minutes at most. On this point the American story was certainly correct. Indeed, two years later, after the "Constitution" had silenced the "Guerriere" in thirty-five minutes, and the "United States" had, in a rough sea and at comparatively long range, left the "Macedonian" a wreck in less than two hours of action, no officer in the British service would have sacrificed his reputation for veracity by suggesting that a British corvette of eighteen guns could have lain nearly an hour within pistol-shot, in calm weather, under the hot fire of an American "line-of-battle ship in disguise." The idea of forcing her to "stand from us" would have seemed then mere gasconade. Some fifteen months afterward, the British sloop-of-war "Alert," of twenty guns, imitated the "Little Belt" by attacking Commodore Porter's 32-gun frigate "Essex," and in eight minutes struck her colors in a sinking condition. If the "President" had been no heavier than the "Essex," she should still have silenced the "Little Belt" in a quarter of an hour.

The "Little Belt" escaped destruction, but she suffered severely. Bingham reported: "I was obliged to desist from firing, as, the ship falling off, no gun would bear, and had no after-sail to help her to; all the rigging and sails cut to pieces; not a brace nor a bowline left. . . . I have to lament the loss of thirty-two men killed and wounded, among whom is the master. His Majesty's ship is much damaged in masts, rigging, and hull; . . . many shot through between wind and water, and many shots still remain inside, and upper works all shot away; starboard pump also." He did not know his good fortune. Two years afterward he would have been well content to escape from the "President" on any terms, even though the "Little Belt" had been twice the size she was. The "President's" loss consisted of one boy wounded, and some slight damage to the rigging.

Bingham's report was accepted by the British government and navy with blind confidence, and caused no small part of the miscalculation which ended in disasters to British pride. "No one act of the little navy of the United States," said the British historian five years afterward, "had been at all calculated to gain the respect of the British. First was seen the 'Chesapeake' allowing herself to be beaten with impunity by a British ship only nominally superior to her. Then the huge frigate 'President' attacks and fights for nearly three quarters of an hour the British sloop 'Little Belt.' "[1] So self-confident was the British navy that Bingham was believed to have fought the "President" with credit and success; while, on the American side, Rodgers and his ship's company believed that the British captain deliberately delayed the meeting until dark, with the view of taking advantage of the night to punish what he thought the insolence of the chase.

Whatever opinion might be formed as to the conduct of the two captains, the vehemence of feeling on each side was only to be compared with the "Chesapeake" affair; but in this instance the grievance belonged to the British navy, and Dacres and the "Guerriere" felt the full passion and duty of revenge. The news met Foster on his arrival at Norfolk, a few weeks afterward, and took away his only hope of a cordial

[1] James. Naval Occurrences, p. 97.

reception. His instructions intended him to conciliate good-will by settling the "Chesapeake" outrage, while they obliged him to take a tone of refusal or remonstrance on every other subject; but he found, on arriving, that the Americans cared nothing for reparation of the "Chesapeake" outrage, since Commodore Rodgers had set off against it an outrage of his own, and had killed four men for every one killed by Captain Humphries. Instead of giving redress, Foster found himself obliged to claim it.

July 2 Foster was formally received by the President; and the same day, as though he had no other hope but to take the offensive, he began his official correspondence by a letter on the seizure of West Florida, closing with a formal notice that if the United States persevered in their course, his orders required him to present the solemn protest of his Government "against an attempt so contrary to every principle of public justice, faith, and national honor."

The language was strong; but unfortunately for Foster's influence, the world at the moment showed so little regard for justice, faith, or honor, that the United States had no reason to be singular in Quixotism; and although in logic the *tu quoque* was an argument hardly deserving notice, in politics it was only less decisive than cannon. The policy of Foster's remonstrance was doubtful in another respect. In proportion as men exposed themselves to reprimands, they resented the reprimand itself. Madison and Monroe had each his sensitive point. Madison resented the suggestion that Napoleon's decrees were still in force, regarding the matter as involving his veracity. Monroe equally resented the assertion that West Florida belonged to Spain, for his character as a man of sense, if not of truth, was involved in the assertion that he had himself bought West Florida in his Louisiana purchase. Yet the mildness of his reply to Foster's severe protest proved his earnest wish to conciliate England. In a note[1] of July 8 he justified the seizure of West Florida by the arguments already used, and offered what he called a "frank and candid explanation" to satisfy the British government. In private he talked with more freedom, and—if Foster could be believed—

---

[1] Monroe to Foster, July 8, 1811; State Papers, iii. 543.

showed himself in a character more lively if not more moral than any the American people would have recognized as his. July 5 Foster wrote to Wellesley:[1] —

"It was with real pain, my Lord, that I was forced to listen to arguments of the most profligate nature, such as that other nations were not so scrupulous; that the United States showed sufficient forbearance in not assisting the insurgents of South America and looking to their own interests in the present situation of that country."

Foster was obliged to ignore the meaning of this pointed retort; while his inquiries how far the American government meant to carry its seizures of Spanish territory drew from Monroe no answer but a laugh. The Secretary of State seemed a transformed man. Not only did he show no dread of interference from England in Florida, but he took an equally indifferent air on every other matter except one. He said not a word about impressments; he betrayed no wish to trouble himself about the "Chesapeake" affair; he made no haste in apologizing for the attack on the "Little Belt;" but the Orders in Council—these, and nothing else—formed the issue on which a change of policy was to depend.

Precisely on the Orders in Council Foster could offer no hope of concession or compromise. So far from withdrawing the orders, he was instructed to require that the United States should withdraw the Non-intercourse Act, under threat of retaliation; and he carried out his instructions to the letter. After protesting, July 2, against the seizure of West Florida, he wrote, July 3, a long protest against the non-importation.[2] His demand savored of Canning's and Jackson's diplomacy; but his arguments in its support were better calculated for effect, and his cry for justice claimed no little sympathy among men who shared in the opinion of Europe that France was the true object of attack, and that Napoleon's overthrow, not the overthrow of England, was the necessary condition of restoring public order. Foster's protest against including Fox's blockade among the admittedly illegal Orders in Council, brought the argument to a delicate issue of law and fact.

[1] Foster to Wellesley, July 5, 1811; MSS. British Archives.
[2] Foster to Monroe, July 3, 1811; State Papers, iii. 435.

"In point of date," he said, "the blockade of May, 1806, preceded the Berlin Decree; but it was a just and legal blockade, according to the established law of nations, because it was intended to be maintained, and was actually maintained, by an adequate force appointed to guard the whole coast described in the notification, and consequently to enforce the blockade."

In effect this argument conceded Madison's principle; for the further difference between blockading a coast and blockading by name the several ports on a coast, was hardly worth a war; and the question whether an estuary, like the British Channel, the Baltic Sea, or Chesapeake Bay, could be best blockaded by a cruising or by a stationary squadron, or by both, called rather for naval than for legal opinion. Foster repudiated the principle of paper-blockades; and after showing that Fox's blockade was defended only as far as it was meant to be legal, he made the further concession of admitting that since it had been merged in the Orders in Council, it existed only as a part of the orders; so that if the orders were repealed, England must either make Fox's blockade effective, or abandon it. By this expedient, the issue was narrowed to the Orders in Council retaliatory on Bonaparte's decrees, and intended to last only as long as those decrees lasted. Foster appealed to Napoleon's public and official language to prove that those decrees were still in force, and therefore that the United States government could not, without making itself a party to Napoleon's acts and principles, demand a withdrawal of the British Orders. If the orders were not to be withdrawn because they were illegal, they ought not to be withdrawn on the false excuse that Napoleon had withdrawn his decrees. Against such a demand England might reasonably protest:—

"Great Britain has a right to complain that . . . not only has America suffered her trade to be moulded into the means of annoyance to Great Britain under the provisions of the French Decrees, but construing those decrees as extinct, upon a deceitful declaration of the French Cabinet, she has enforced her Non-importation Act against England. Under these circumstances I am instructed by my Government to urge to that of the United States the injustice of thus enforcing that Act against his Majesty's dominions; and I cannot but hope that a spirit of justice will induce the United States government to reconsider the line of conduct they have pursued, and at least to re-establish their former state of strict neutrality."

President Madison had put himself, little by little, in a position where he had reason to fear the popular effect of such appeals; but awkward as Madison's position was, that of Monroe was many degrees worse. He had accepted office in April as the representative of Republicans who believed that Napoleon's decrees were not repealed, and the objects of his ambition seemed to depend on reversing Madison's course. In July he found himself in painful straits. Obliged to maintain that Napoleon's decrees were repealed, he was reduced to sacrifice his own official agent in the effort. Foster reported, as a matter of surprise to himself, remarks of Monroe still more surprising to history.

"I have urged," reported Foster, July 7,[1] "with every argument I could think of, the injustice of the Non-importation Act which was passed in the last session of Congress, while there were doubts entertained even here as to the repeal of the Berlin and Milan Decrees; but to my surprise I find it now maintained that there existed no doubt on the subject at the time of passing the Act, and Mr. Russell is censured by his Government for publicly averring that the ship 'New Orleans Packet' was seized under their operation,—not that it is denied, however, that she was seized under them by our construction. Mr. Monroe, indeed, though he qualified his blame of Mr. Russell by praising his zeal, yet allowed to me that much of their present embarrassment was owing to his statement."

"It would be fatiguing to your Lordship," continued Foster, "were I to describe the various shadows of argument to which the American minister had recourse in order to prove his statement of the decrees having been repealed in as far as America had a right to expect."

[1] Foster to Wellesley, July 7, 1811; MSS. British Archives.

These shadows of argument, however elaborately described, could be reduced to the compass of a few lines; for they all resulted in a doctrine which became thenceforward a dogma. Napoleon's decrees, so viewed, had two characters,— an international, and a municipal. The international character alone could give the right of international retaliation; and the Emperor, since November 1, had ceased to enforce his edicts in this character. The municipal character, whether enforced or not, in no way concerned England.

Such was, indeed, Napoleon's object in substituting customs regulations for the rules of his decrees in his own ports. After that change, he applied the decrees themselves to every other part of Europe, but made an apparent exception for American commerce with France, which was forced to conform to his objects by municipal licenses and prohibitory duties. Monroe took the ground that since November 2 the decrees stood repealed, and the "New Orleans Packet" had been seized under a "municipal operation" with which England had nothing to do. The argument, though perhaps casuistic, seemed to offer a sufficient excuse for England, in case she should wish to abandon her own system as she saw danger approaching; but it brought Monroe, who used it profusely, into daily mortification, and caused the President, who invented and believed it, a world of annoyance,—for Napoleon, as Monroe had personal reason to remember, never failed to sacrifice his allies, and was certain to fail in supporting a theory so infirm as this.

For the moment, Monroe made no written reply to Foster's letter of July 3; he was tormented by the crisis of his career, and Foster ceased to be important from the moment he could do nothing toward a repeal of the orders. With the usual misfortune of British diplomatists, Foster became aggressive as he lost ground, and pushed the secretary vigorously into Napoleon's arms. July 14 Foster wrote again, in a threatening tone, that measures of retaliation for the Act of March 2 were already before his Government, and if America persisted in her injurious course of conduct, the most unfriendly situation would result. While this threat was all that England offered for Monroe's friendship, news arrived on the same day that Napoleon, May 4, had opened his ports to

American commerce. Not till then did Monroe give way, and turn his back upon England and his old political friends. The course taken by Foster left no apparent choice; and for that reason chiefly Monroe, probably with many misgivings, abandoned the theory of foreign affairs which had for five years led him into so many mortifications at home and abroad.

July 23 Monroe sent his answer[1] to the British minister's argument. In substance this note, though long, contained nothing new; but in effect it was an ultimatum which left England to choose between concession and war. As an ultimatum, it was weakened by the speciousness of its long argument to prove that the French Decrees were repealed. The weakness of the ground required double boldness of assertion, and Monroe accepted the whole task. He showed further willingness to accept an issue on any point England might select. Foster's remonstrance in regard to the "Little Belt" called from Monroe a tart reference to the affair of the "Chesapeake," and a refusal to order an inquiry, as a matter of right, into the conduct of Commodore Rodgers. He showed equally little disposition to press for a settlement of the "Chesapeake" affair. Foster had been barely two weeks at Washington when he summed up the result of his efforts in a few words,[2] which told the situation, as Monroe then understood it, a year before war was declared:—

> "On the whole, their view in this business [of the 'Little Belt'] is to settle this, with every other difference, in the most amicable manner, provided his Majesty's Orders in Council are revoked; otherwise, to make use of it, together with all other topics of irritation, for the purpose of fomenting a spirit of hatred toward England, and thereby strengthening their party. Your Lordship cannot expect to hear of any change till Congress meet."

[1] Monroe to Foster, July 23, 1811; State Papers, iii. 439.
[2] Foster to Wellesley, July 18, 1811; MSS. British Archives.

Chapter III

$\mathbf{B}$EFORE THE FAMILIAR figure of Robert Smith quite fades from the story of his time, the mystery which he succeeded in throwing around his true sympathies needs explanation. When dismissed from the Cabinet in March, he was supposed to be a friend of France and of the President's French policy. In June he appeared before the public as an opponent of Madison and of French influence. Perhaps in reality he neither supported nor opposed either policy; but he deserves such credit as friendly hands gave him at the moment of his disgrace, and on no one had he made a happier impression than on Serurier, the new French minister. After six weeks' experience, Serurier, who looked upon Gallatin as little better than an enemy, regarded Robert Smith as a friend. March 5, while Gallatin was writing his resignation, Serurier wrote a despatch to Cadore giving his estimates of the two Cabinet officers:[1] —

"Mr. Gallatin, perhaps the most capable man in the Republic, under an exterior rigidly Republican hides his ambitious designs, his feelings of superiority, which torment him without his being able to satisfy them. People maintain that all his system as a financier is English,—a thing simple enough; and that, on another side, he thinks himself obliged to expiate the sin of being a stranger and born on our frontiers, by separating himself from us in his political principles. I am told also that he has seen with annoyance the occupation by France of Geneva, his country,— whither he expected to withdraw himself with his riches, if his ambition should be crossed here by events. I have as yet no cause for complaint in regard to him, but this is the way he is talked about by the Frenchmen here, and by the party most nearly in sympathy with us (*le parti qui se rapproche le plus de nous*)."

The fable of Gallatin's *richesses* revealed the source of Serurier's information. The party most nearly in sympathy with France was the "Aurora" faction, which spread stories of

[1] Serurier to Champagny, No. 5, March 5, 1811. Archives des Aff. Étr. MSS.

Gallatin's peculations and treated him with vindictive enmity, but regarded Robert Smith as a friend. Serurier's description of Gallatin's character contrasted darkly with his portrait of Robert Smith: —

"Mr. Smith shows certainly a character equally decided, but more open. His system seems more Continental; at least he wishes me to think so. With perhaps less breadth of mind, he has more elevation. I know that he nourishes a secret admiration of the Emperor, which he very wisely hides. I dined with him three days ago; it was my first dinner. On leaving the table he sent for a bust and an engraving of his Majesty, and on this subject said to me things full of politeness. In the conversation which followed, he became more expansive: 'The nation' (it is he who is speaking) 'is bold and enterprising at sea; and if war should break out with England, supposing this rupture to be accompanied by a full reconciliation with France, the commerce between Europe and America might become more active than ever. The Americans possess a sort of vessels called schooners, the swiftest sailers in the world, and for that reason beyond insult and capture; while their sailors are full of confidence in the advantage given them by this sort of vessel in time of war.' He affirmed to me that the great majority of the nation, if satisfied on the side of France, will be much inclined to war with her rival; but that the mild, prudent, and perhaps too timid administration of Mr. Jefferson heretofore, and now that of Mr. Madison, had thus far repressed the national enthusiasm; but he was convinced that under the administration, for example, of the Vice-President General Clinton, or of any other statesman of his character, war would have already broken out."

This was not the only occasion when Robert Smith showed himself to the French minister as restive under restraint.

"I asked him," reported Serurier at another time,[1] " what the Government expected to do if the English resented its pretension to the independence of its flag? 'War,' he replied

[1] Serurier to Champagny, Feb. 17, 1811; Archives des Aff. Étr. MSS.

with perfect frankness, 'is the inevitable result of our position toward the English if they refuse to recognize our
rights.' Mr. Smith then admitted to me that his Government certainly had the best founded hope that the establishment of the regency in England would bring about a
change of ministry and probably of system, and that the
Orders in Council would be repealed; that in this case, neutral rights being re-established, the motive for all this discussion would cease. But he repeated to me that in the
contrary case war would, in his eyes, be inevitable, and that
the Americans, in deciding on this course, had perfectly
foreseen where it would lead them, without being, on that
account, deterred from a decision dictated by their honor
or their interest."

These remarks were made February 17, the day when the
President decided to accept Napoleon's conditions; and they
helped to convince Serurier that Robert Smith was more
"continental," or Napoleonic, than Gallatin. For this reason,
when he heard that Gallatin had prevailed, and Smith was to
take the Russian Mission, he wrote to his Government with
regret:[1] —

"The Secretary of State has taken his resolution like a
man of courage. Instead of sulking and going to intrigue
in his province, he has preferred to remain attached to the
government of his country, and to go for some time to
enjoy the air of our Europe, whither his tastes lead him,
and to reserve himself for more favorable circumstances.
His frank and open character makes him generally regretted. I think he must have had a share at the time in the fit
of energy which his Government has shown. His language
was measured; but very certainly his system drew him
much nearer to France than to England."

Perhaps Serurier was misled by Robert Smith's habit of taking tone from the person nearest him; but as the French minister learned more of Monroe, his regrets for Smith became
acute. "I regard as an evil," he wrote, April 5,[2] "the removal

[1] Serurier to Champagny, March 26, 1811; Archives des Aff. Étr. MSS.
[2] Serurier to Champagny, April 5, 1811; Archives des Aff. Étr. MSS.

of a man whose elevated views,—noble in foreign policy at least,—and whose decided character, might have given to affairs a direction which must be at least counteracted by his absence, and especially by the way in which his place is filled."

Monroe took charge of the State Department April 1, and within a few days Serurier became unpleasantly conscious of the change. He still met with civility, but he felt new hesitation. Joel Barlow had been appointed minister to France, and should have started instantly for his post. Yet Barlow lingered at Washington; and when Serurier asked the reason of the delay, Monroe merely said he was waiting for the arrival of the frigate "Essex" with despatches from France and England to the middle of April. The expected despatches did not arrive until July; and in the interval Serurier passed a season of discomfort. The new Secretary of State, unlike his predecessor, showed no admiration for Napoleon. Toward the end of June, the French consuls in the United States made known that they were still authorized and required by the Emperor to issue permits or certificates to American vessels destined for France. Monroe sent at once for Serurier, and admonished him in language that seemed to the French minister altogether out of place:[1] —

"Mr. Monroe's countenance was absolutely distorted (*tout-à-fait décomposée*). I could not conceive how an object, apparently so unimportant, could affect him so keenly. He continued thus: 'You are witness, sir, to the candor of our motives, to the loyalty of our principles, to our immovable fidelity to our engagements. In spite of party clamor and the extreme difficulty of the circumstances, we persevere in our system; but your Government abandons us to the attacks of its enemies and ours, by not fulfilling on its side the conditions set forth in the President's proclamation. We are daily accused of a culpable partiality for France. These cries were at first feeble, and we flattered ourselves every day to be able to silence them by announcing the Emperor's arrangements in conformity with ours; but they become louder by our silence. The Administration finds itself

[1] Serurier to Maret, June 30, 1811; Archives des Aff. Étr. MSS.

in the most extreme embarrassment (*dans le plus extrême embarras*); it knows neither what to expect from you, nor what to say to its constituents. Ah, sir!' cried Mr. Monroe, 'if your sovereign had deigned to imitate the promptness (*empressement*) which our President showed in publishing his proclamation; if he had re-opened, with the necessary precautions, concerted with us, his ports and his vessels,— all the commerce of America was won for France. A thousand ships would have sailed at all risks to your ports, where they would have sought the products of your manufactures which are so much liked in this country. The English would have certainly opposed such a useful exchange between the two peoples; our honor and interest would have united to resist them; and the result, for which you are doubtless more desirous than you admit, could not have failed to happen at last.' "

Serurier tried in vain to soothe the secretary; Monroe was not to be appeased. Oratory so impassioned was not meant for mere show; and as causes of grievance multiplied, the secretary gathered one after another, evidently to be used for a rupture with France. Each stage toward his end he marked by the regular shade of increasing displeasure that he had himself, as a victim, so often watched. Enjoying the pleasure of doing to others what Cevallos and Harrowby, Talleyrand and Canning had done to him, Monroe, familiar with the accents of the most famous school in European diplomacy, ran no risk of throwing away a single tone.

When the secretary told Serurier that Joel Barlow's departure depended on the news to be brought by the "Essex," he did not add that he was himself waiting for the arrival of Foster, the new British minister; but as it happened, Foster reached Washington July 1, at the same instant with the despatches brought by the "Essex." The crisis of Serurier's diplomatic fortune came with the arrival of Foster, and during the next two weeks the French minister passed through many uncomfortable scenes. He knew too little of American affairs to foresee that not himself, but Monroe, must in the end be the victim. As soon as the "Essex" was announced, bringing William Pinkney from London and Jonathan Russell's des-

patches from Paris,—including his report of Napoleon's tirade to the Paris merchants, but no sign that his decrees were
repealed,—Serurier called at the Department to learn what
Monroe had to say. "I found him icy; he told me that, contrary to all the hopes of the Government, the 'Essex' had
brought nothing decisive, and asked if I was more fortunate."[1] Serurier had despatches, but as the story has shown[2]
they were emphatic in forbidding him to pledge himself in
regard to the Emperor's course. Obliged to evade Monroe's
inquiry, he could only suggest hopes of more decisive news
by the next arrival, and then turned the subject to Napoleon's
zeal in revolutionizing Spanish America:—

> "I was heard with politeness, but coldly. Then I talked
> of the abrupt and improper tone of Mr. Russell's corre-
> spondence. I said that it did not offend, because Mr. Rus-
> sell was not of enough consequence to give offence; but
> that it was considered altogether indecorous. I made him
> aware, on this occasion, of the necessity that the Republic
> should have a minister at Paris. Mr. Monroe answered that
> the Government had already made that remark; he repeated
> to me that he had intended, long before, to send away Mr.
> Barlow, but that the daily expectation of despatches from
> France had made him always delay. Here he stopped him-
> self, and returned for the tenth time upon the difficult po-
> sition of the Government; upon the universal outcry of
> commerce, which would become a kind of revolt in the
> North if the Government could offer nothing to counteract
> it. He recalled to me the effect produced by the announce-
> ment of new licenses issued at Boston and Baltimore, and
> the equally annoying effect of a pamphlet by the ex-Secre-
> tary of State, Mr. Smith, which revealed to the public the
> declaration made by me on my arrival, that the old confis-
> cations made by way of reprisals, could not be matter of
> discussion,—'information,' said he, ' which had at the time
> profoundly afflicted the Administration, and which it had
> counted on publishing only at the moment when it could
> simultaneously announce a better outlook, and the absolute

[1] Serurier to Maret, July 5, 1811; Archives des Aff. Étr. MSS.
[2] See pp. 272–73.

restoration of commercial relations.' He ended, at last, this conference by telling me that he had not yet finished reading all his papers; that the Government was that moment deliberating on its course, and that in a few days we would have a new conference."

Serurier felt his danger, and expected to be sacrificed. Society turned against him. Even Duane became abusive of France.

"Already, within a few days, I notice a change in the manners of every one about me. The general attention of which I was the object during the first five months has been suddenly followed by a general reserve; people are civil, but under a thousand pretexts they avoid being seen in conversation with me. The journals hitherto most favorable to France begin to say that since we will not keep our engagements, a rupture must take place."

Thinking that he had nothing to lose, the French minister took a high tone, and July 3, through a private channel, conveyed to the President a warning that the course threatened might lead too far.

"The person in question having answered that I might depend on the Government's fidelity to its engagements, I replied that I would believe it all if the new American minister should be despatched to Paris, and that I would believe nothing if this departure were again postponed."

Everything depended on Foster, who had been received by the President July 2, the day before Serurier's message was sent. Apparently, the first impression made by Foster's letters and conversation was decisive, for Monroe told the French minister at the public dinner of July 4, that Barlow was to start at once on his mission.

"This news," reported Serurier, "caused me great pleasure. This success, though doubtless inconsiderable, made all my ambition for the moment; it delays for several months the crisis that the English party was trying to force, in the hope of making it decisive against us; it neutralizes the effect of the arrival of the British minister, whose want of influence down to this point it reveals; it withdraws the initiative from the President and restores to his Majesty the decision of our great affairs."

No sooner had this decision been made, than Monroe seemed to repent it. The conduct of France had been of late more outrageous than that of England; and Monroe, who found his worst expectations fulfilled, could not easily resign himself to accepting a yoke against which he had for five years protested. The departure of Barlow, ordered July 4, was countermanded July 5; and this proof of Monroe's discontent led to a striking interview, July 9, in which the Secretary of State became more impassioned than ever.[1] Serurier began by asking what he was to think of the Government's conduct. Monroe replied by recalling what had happened since the appointment of Barlow as minister to France, a fortnight after Serurier's arrival. Then the Proclamation of November 2 had been supposed sufficient to satisfy the Emperor; the Non-intercourse Act followed,—yet the President was still waiting for the assurance that the French Decrees were repealed, without which knowledge Barlow's instructions could not be written.

"So we reached the day when the 'Essex' arrived," continued Monroe. "Not an officer of the government, not a citizen in the Republic, but was convinced that this frigate brought the most satisfactory and the most decisive news. Yet to our great astonishment—even to our confusion—she has brought nothing. In spite of a deception so afflicting, the President had still decided to make a last attempt, and this was to send off Mr. Barlow. I had the honor to announce it to you; but on the news of our frigate's arrival without satisfactory information from France, a general cry of discontent rose all over the Republic, and public opinion pronounced itself so strongly against Mr. Barlow's departure that the Government can to-day no longer give the order without raising from all parts of the Union the cry of treason. I am myself a daily witness of the general effervescence that this silence of your Government excites. I cannot

[1] Serurier to Maret, July 10, 1811; Archives des Aff. Étr. MSS.

walk from my house to this office without being accosted
by twenty citizens, who say to me: 'What, sir! shall you
send off a minister to France, when the Imperial government shows itself unwilling to carry out its engagements;
when it treats our citizens with so much injustice, and you
yourself with so much contempt? No! the honor of the Republic will not permit you to send your ambassador under
such circumstances, and you will be responsible for it to
the country.' "

Monroe's objection seemed reasonable. The sending a new
minister to France was in no way necessary for making an
issue with England. Indeed, if only a simple issue with England had been wanted, the permanent presence of British
frigates off Sandy Hook, capturing American vessels and impressing American seamen, was sufficient. No further protest
against it needed to be made, seeing that it had been the subject of innumerable protests. If President Madison wanted an
issue that should oblige Great Britain to declare war, or to
take measures equivalent to war, he could obtain it in a moment by ordering Rodgers and Decatur to drive the British
frigates away and rescue their victims. For such a purpose he
needed no minister in France, and had no occasion to make
himself a party to fraud. Monroe's language implied that he
would have preferred some such issue.

" 'Believe me,' said Mr. Monroe in finishing, and as we
were about to separate, 'the American government will not
be inconsequent; but its patience is exhausted, and as regards foreign Powers it is determined to make itself respected. People in Europe suppose us to be merchants,
occupied exclusively with pepper and ginger. They are
much deceived, and I hope we shall prove it. The immense
majority of citizens do not belong to this class, and are, as
much as your Europeans, controlled by principles of honor
and dignity. I never knew what trade was. The President is
as much of a stranger to it as I; and we accord to commerce
only the protection that we owe it, as every government
owes it to an interesting class of its citizens.' "

Commerce would have listened with more amusement than

conviction to Monroe's ideas on the "principles of honor and dignity" which led a government of Virginia and Pennsylvania farmers to accord protection in the form of embargoes and non-intercourses to commerce which it distrusted and despised; but Monroe meant only that France, as well as England, must reckon on a new national spirit in Virginia,—a spirit which they had themselves roused, and for whose bad qualities they had only themselves to blame.

Yet Monroe found himself in an attitude not flattering to his pride. All his life a representative of the Virginia school,— more conservative than Jefferson, and only to be compared with John Randolph, and John Taylor of Caroline,—he had come to the State Department to enforce his own principles and overrule the President; but he found himself helpless in the President's hands. That the contest was in reality between Monroe's will and Madison's became clear to Serurier; and that Monroe's pliable nature must succumb to Madison's pertinacity, backed as it was by authority, could not be doubtful. Six months seemed to Virginians a short time for Monroe's submission, but in truth Monroe had submitted long before; his rebellion itself had been due to William Pinkney and John Randolph rather than to impulses of his own; he regretted it almost as soon as it was made, and he suffered little in allowing Madison to control the course of events. Yet he would certainly have preferred another result, and his interview with Serurier, July 9, recorded the policy he had meant to impose, while preparing for its abandonment.

The secretary waited only for a pretext to accept Madison's dogma that the French Decrees were withdrawn, although his conversations with Serurier proved his conviction to the contrary. A few days later, a vessel arrived from England bringing unofficial news from France, to May 24, that the Emperor had released the American vessels kept in sequestration since November 1, and had admitted their cargoes for sale. Without the form of further struggle, Monroe followed the footsteps of his predecessor.

"The Secretary of State sent for me three days ago to his office," wrote Serurier, July 20.[1] "After having congratu-

[1] Serurier to Maret, July 20, 1811; Archives des Aff. Étr. MSS.

lated me on this decision [of the Emperor], he told me that he had no doubt of its producing on the public the same excellent impression it had made on the Government; but he added that as it was not official, the President would like to have me write a letter as confirmative as possible, in the absence of instructions, both of these events and of his Majesty's good intentions; and that if I could write him this letter, Mr. Barlow should immediately depart."

The only instructions possessed by Serurier on the subject of the decrees warned him against doing what Monroe asked; but the temptation to win a success was strong, and he wrote a cautious letter,[1] dated July 19, saying that he had no official knowledge on the subject, but that "it is with reason, sir, that you reject the idea of a doubt on the fidelity of France in fulfilling her engagements; for to justify such a doubt one must have some contradictory facts to cite,—one must show that judgments have been rendered in France on the principle of maintaining the Decrees of Berlin and Milan, or that a series of American ships coming from England to America, or from America to England, have been captured by our privateers in virtue of the blockade of the British Isles. Nothing of the sort has become known to any of us, and, on the contrary," all advices showed that the decrees in France and on the ocean had ceased to affect American commerce.

Probably this letter disappointed the President, for it was never published, nor was any allusion made to it in the correspondence that followed. Without even such cover, Monroe ordered Barlow to depart, and made the decision public. Serurier, puzzled though delighted by his success, groped in the dark to discover how the Government had reached its decision. Foster's attitude failed to enlighten him; and he could see no explanation, except that the result was a personal victory of Madison over Monroe and the Cabinet.

"The joy is general among the authorities," he wrote July 20,[2] "except among some friends of Mr. Foster; but more than any one else, Mr. Madison seems enchanted to see himself confirmed (*raffermi*) in a system which is wholly

[1] Serurier to Monroe, July 19, 1811; MSS. State Department Archives.
[2] Serurier to Maret, July 20, 1811; Archives des Aff. Étr. MSS.

his own, but which he began to see no means of maintaining. I do him the justice to say that if he had a movement of hesitation on the point of Mr. Barlow's departure, it was more the effect of public clamor than of his own sentiments,—a movement of spite (*dépit*) and discouragement, rather than of inclination toward England, which he frankly detests, as does his friend Mr. Jefferson,—and that he has not been for a moment unfaithful to his engagements with us. I have never seen him more triumphant. The Secretaries of State, of the Treasury, and of War are doubtful, perhaps, and conduct themselves more according to events; but happily the President, superior to them in enlightenment as in position, governs entirely by himself, and there is no reason to fear his being crossed by them."

Serurier knew Madison and Jefferson only as a Frenchman might, and his ideas of their feelings toward England were such as a Frenchman could understand. In truth, Madison did not want a distinct issue of peace or war with England. Had he wished for such an issue, he would have made it. Disbelieving in war, as war approached, he clung to the last chances of peaceful coercion. The fiction that Napoleon's decrees were repealed enabled him to enforce his peaceful coercive measures to avoid war. Not because he wanted war, but because he wanted peace, Madison insisted that the decrees were withdrawn. As he carried each point, he stood more and more alone; he was misunderstood by his enemies and overborne by his friends; he failed in his policy of peace, and knew himself unfit to administer a policy of war. Yet he held to his principle, that commercial restrictions were the true safeguards of an American system.

A man of keen intelligence, Madison knew, quite as well as Monroe, Serurier, or Foster, that the French Decrees were not repealed. His alleged reason for despatching Barlow was unsatisfactory to himself as to Monroe, and doubly worthless because unofficial. Even while he insisted on his measures, he made no secret of his discontent. When official despatches arrived a few days later, Serurier was puzzled at finding Madison well aware that the Emperor had not withdrawn and did not mean to withdraw his decrees. July 23 Serurier communicated[1] to Monroe the substance of the despatches from France. The next day he called at the Department and at the White House to watch the effect of his letter, which announced the admission of American merchandise into French ports.

"Mr. Monroe showed himself less satisfied than I had hoped, either because the President had so directed, in order to reserve the right of raising new pretensions, or because, already advised by Mr. Russell, he had been at the same time informed that the prizes made since November by our privateers were not restored; and these restrictions had been represented in an unfavorable light by the *chargé d'affaires*. He confined himself to telling me that certainly there were things agreeable to the American government in the Emperor's arrangements, but that there were others wholly contrary to expectation, and that before his departure he would send me a list of the complaints left unsatisfied. . . . As the President is to start to-morrow for his estate in Virginia, I called this morning to bid him goodby. I had on this occasion with Mr. Madison an interview which put the last stroke to my suspicions. When I told him that I was glad to see him a last time under auspices so happy as the news I had officially given him the evening before, he answered me that he had learned with pleasure, though without surprise, the release of the sequestered ships and the Emperor's decision to admit American products; but that one thing pained him profoundly. This was that the American ships captured since last November, under pretext of the Berlin and Milan Decrees, had not been released with those which voluntarily entered French ports; and he pretended that this failure to execute the chief of our engagements destroyed the effect of all the rest."[2]

The opinion scarcely admitted dispute. Reversing Madison's theory, Napoleon had relieved American vessels from the "municipal operation" of his decrees in France, while he enforced that international operation on the high seas which alone Madison declared himself bound by the law of nations

[1] Serurier to Monroe, July 23, 1811; State Papers, iii. 508.
[2] Serurier to Maret, July 24, 1811; Archives des Aff. Étr. MSS.

to resist. The blockade thus enforced by Napoleon against England was more extravagant than any blockade England had ever declared. Of his acts in Denmark and on the Baltic Madison took no notice at all, though these, more than the detention of American prizes in France, "destroyed the effect of all the rest." If, then, the decrees were still enforced on the ocean,—as Madison insisted they were,—they could not have been repealed; and Madison, by submitting to their enforcement on the ocean, not only recognized their legality, but also required England to make the same submission, under penalty of a declaration of war from the United States. This dilemma threatened to overthrow Madison's Administration, or even to break up the Union. Serurier saw its dangers, and did his utmost to influence Napoleon toward concessions:

> "The revocation of the Decrees of Milan and Berlin has become a personal affair with Mr. Madison. He announced it by proclamation, and has constantly maintained it since. The English party never stops worrying him on this point, and saying that he has been made a tool of France,—that the decrees have not been repealed. He fears the effect of this suspension, and foresees that it will cause great discussions in the next Congress, and that it alone may compromise the Administration, triumphant on all other points."

Under such circumstances, Monroe needed more than common powers in order to play his part. Talleyrand himself would have found his impassive countenance tried by assuring Foster in the morning that the decrees were repealed, and rating Serurier in the afternoon because they were in force. Such conversations, extended over a length of time, might in the end raise doubts of a statesman's veracity; yet this was what Monroe undertook. On the day when Serurier communicated the news that disturbed the President, Monroe sent to the British minister the note maintaining broadly that France had revoked her decrees. Three days later, after the President had told Serurier that "the failure to execute the chief of our engagements destroyed the effect of all the rest," Monroe gave to Barlow his instructions founded on the revocation of the decrees. Doubtless this double-dealing exasperated all the actors concerned in it. Madison and Monroe at heart were more angry with France than with England, if indeed degrees in anger could be felt where the outrages of both parties were incessant and intolerable. Yet Barlow took his instructions and set sail for France; a proclamation appeared in the "National Intelligencer" calling Congress together for November 1; and the President and his Secretary of State left Washington for their summer vacation in Virginia, having accepted, once for all, the conditions imposed by Napoleon.

For some years afterward Monroe said no more about old Republican principles; but twelve months later he wrote to Colonel Taylor a letter[1] which began with a candid confession:—

"I have been afraid to write to you for some time past, because I knew that you expected better things from me than I have been able to perform. You thought that I might contribute to promote a compromise with Great Britain, and thereby prevent a war between that country and the United States; that we might also get rid of our restrictive system. I own to you that I had some hope, though less than some of my friends entertained, that I might aid in promoting that desirable result. This hope has been disappointed."

[1] Monroe to Taylor, June 13, 1812; Monroe MSS.

Chapter IV

ALTHOUGH NO ONE doubted that the year 1812 was to witness a new convulsion of society, if signs of panic occurred they were less marked in crowded countries where vast interests were at stake, than in remote regions which might have been thought as safe from Napoleon's wars as from those of Genghis Khan. As in the year 1754 a petty fight between two French and English scouting parties on the banks of the Youghiogheny River, far in the American wilderness, began a war that changed the balance of the world, so in 1811 an encounter in the Indian country, on the banks of the Wabash, began a fresh convulsion which ended only with the fall of Napoleon. The battle of Tippecanoe was a premature outbreak of the great wars of 1812.

Governor William Henry Harrison, of the Indiana Territory, often said he could tell by the conduct of his Indians, as by a thermometer, the chances of war and peace for the United States as estimated in the Cabinet at London. The remark was curious, but not surprising. Uneasiness would naturally be greatest where least control and most irritation existed. Such a region was the Northwestern Territory. Even the spot where violence would break out might be predicted as somewhere on the water-line of the Maumee and the Wabash, between Detroit at one extremity and Vincennes at the other. If a guess had been ventured that the most probable point would be found on that line, about half way between Lake Erie and the Ohio River, the map would have shown that Tippecanoe Creek, where it flowed into the Wabash, corresponded with the rough suggestion.

The Indiana Territory was created in 1800; and the former delegate of the whole Northwestern Territory, William Henry Harrison, was then appointed governor of the new division. Until the year 1809, Illinois formed part of the Indiana Territory; but its single settlement at Kaskaskia was remote. The Indiana settlement consisted mainly of two tracts,—one on the Ohio, opposite Louisville in Kentucky, at the falls, consisting of about one hundred and fifty thousand acres, called Clark's Grant; the other, at Vincennes on the Wabash, where the French had held a post, without a definite grant of lands, under an old Indian treaty, and where the Americans took whatever rights the French enjoyed. One hundred miles of wilderness separated these two tracts. In 1800, their population numbered about twenty-five hundred persons; in 1810, nearly twenty-five thousand.

Northward and westward, from the bounds of these districts the Indian country stretched to the Lakes and the Mississippi, unbroken except by military posts at Fort Wayne and Fort Dearborn, or Chicago, and a considerable settlement of white people in the neighborhood of the fortress at Detroit. Some five thousand Indian warriors held this vast region, and were abundantly able to expel every white man from Indiana if their organization had been as strong as their numbers. The whites were equally eager to expel the Indians, and showed the wish openly.

Governor Harrison was the highest authority on matters connected with the northwestern Indians. During eight years of Harrison's government Jefferson guided the Indian policy; and as long as Jefferson insisted on the philanthropic principles which were his pride, Harrison, whose genius lay in ready adaptation, took his tone from the President, and wrote in a different spirit from that which he would have taken had he represented an aggressive chief. His account of Indian affairs offered an illustration of the law accepted by all historians in theory, but adopted by none in practice; which former ages called "fate," and metaphysicians called "necessity," but which modern science has refined into the "survival of the fittest." No acid ever worked more mechanically on a vegetable fibre than the white man acted on the Indian. As the line of American settlements approached, the nearest Indian tribes withered away.

Harrison reported conscientiously the incurable evils which attended the contact of the two hostile forms of society. The first, but not the most serious, was that the white man, though not allowed to settle beyond the Indian border, could not be prevented from trespassing far and wide on Indian territory in search of game. The practice of hunting on Indian lands, in violation of law and existing treaties, had grown into a monstrous abuse. The Kentucky settlers crossed the Ohio

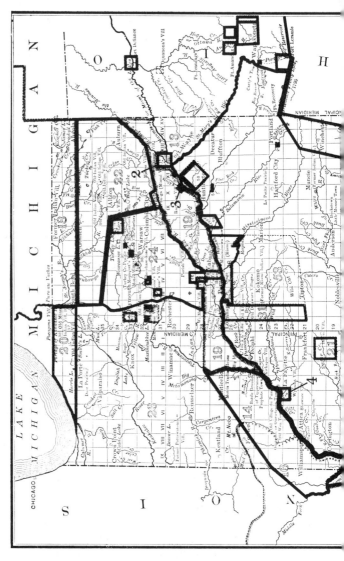

CESSIONS OF INDIAN TERRITORY IN INDIANA, 1795–1810.

1. *Tract ceded by Treaty of Greenville, August 3rd, 1795; 2. Tract about Fort Wayne, ceded by the same Treaty; 3. Two miles square on the Miami portage, ceded by the same Treaty; 4. Six miles square at Old Wea Town on the Wabash, ceded by the same Treaty; 5. Clark's Grant on the Ohio, reserved by the same*

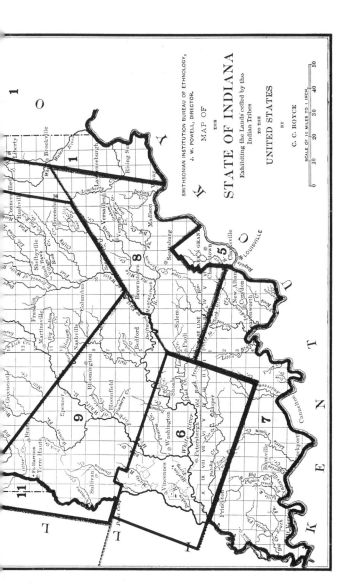

Treaty; 6. *Vincennes tract, reserved by the same Treaty;* 7. *Tract ceded by Treaties of August 18th and 27th, 1804;* 8. *Tract ceded by Treaty of August 21st, 1805;* 9, 10, 11. *Tracts ceded by Treaty of September 30th, 1809;* 12. *Tract ceded by Treaty of December 9th, 1809.*

River every autumn to kill deer, bear, and buffalo for their skins, which they had no more right to take than they had to cross the Alleghanies, and shoot or trap the cows and sheep in the farm-yards of Bucks County. Many parts of the Northwestern Territory which as late as 1795 abounded in game, ten years afterward contained not game enough to support the small Indian parties passing through them, and had become worthless for Indian purposes except as a barrier to further encroachment.[1]

The tribes that owned these lands were forced either to remove elsewhere, or to sell their old hunting-grounds to the government for supplies or for an annuity. The tribes that sold, remaining near the settlements to enjoy their annuity, were more to be pitied than those that removed, which were destined to destruction by war. Harrison reported that contact with white settlements never failed to ruin them. "I can tell at once," he wrote in 1801,[2] "upon looking at an Indian whom I may chance to meet, whether he belongs to a neighboring or to a more distant tribe. The latter is generally well-clothed, healthy, and vigorous; the former half-naked, filthy, and enfeebled by intoxication, and many of them without arms excepting a knife, which they carry for the most villanous purposes." Harrison estimated the number of Indian warriors then in the whole valley of the Wabash as not exceeding six hundred; the sale of whiskey was unlawful, yet they were supposed to consume six thousand gallons of whiskey a year, and their drunkenness so often ended in murder that among three of the tribes scarcely a chief survived.

"I have had much difficulty," wrote Harrison in the same letter from Vincennes, " with the small tribes in this immediate neighborhood; namely the Piankeshaws, the Weas, and the Eel River Miamis. These three tribes form a body of the most depraved wretches on earth. They are daily in this town in considerable numbers, and are frequently intoxicated to the number of thirty or forty at once, when they commit the greatest disorders, drawing their knives and stabbing every one they meet with; breaking open the

---

[1] Dawson's Harrison, p. 8.
[2] Dawson's Harrison, p. 11.

houses of the citizens, killing their cattle and hogs, and breaking down their fences. But in all their frolics they generally suffer the most themselves. They kill each other without mercy. Some years ago as many as four were found dead in a morning; and although those murders were actually committed in the streets of the town, yet no attempt to punish them has ever been made."

The Piankeshaws were reduced to twenty-five or thirty warriors; the Weas and Eel River Indians were mere remnants. The more powerful tribes at a distance saw with growing alarm the steady destruction of the border warriors; and the intelligent Indians everywhere forbade the introduction of whiskey, and tried to create a central authority to control the degraded tribes.

A third evil was much noticed by Harrison. By treaty, if an Indian killed a white man the tribe was bound to surrender the murderer for trial by American law; while if a white man killed an Indian, the murderer was also to be tried by a white jury. The Indians surrendered their murderers, and white juries at Vincennes hung them without scruple; but no jury in the territory ever convicted a white man of murdering an Indian. Harrison complained to the President of the wanton and atrocious murders committed by white men on Indians, and the impossibility of punishing them in a society where witnesses would not appear, criminals broke jail, and juries refused to convict. Throughout the territory the people avowed the opinion that a white man ought not in justice to suffer for killing an Indian;[1] and many of them, like the uncle of Abraham Lincoln,[2] thought it a virtuous act to shoot an Indian at sight. Harrison could combat this code of popular law only by proclamations offering rewards for the arrest of murderers, who were never punished when arrested. In 1801 the Delawares alone complained of six unatoned murders committed on their tribe since the Treaty of Greenville, and every year increased the score.

"All these injuries," reported Harrison in 1801, "the Indians have hitherto borne with astonishing patience; but

[1] Dawson's Harrison, pp. 7, 31, 32.
[2] Life of Lincoln, by Hay and Nicolay, chap. i.

though they discover no disposition to make war on the United States at present, I am confident that most of the tribes would eagerly seize any favorable opportunity for that purpose; and should the United States be at war with any of the European nations who are known to the Indians, there would probably be a combination of more than nine tenths of the Northern tribes against us, unless some means are used to conciliate them."

So warmly were the French remembered by the Indians, that if Napoleon had carried out his Louisiana scheme of 1802 he could have counted on the active support of nearly every Indian tribe on the Mississippi and the Lakes; from Pensacola to Detroit his orders would have been obeyed. Toward England the Indians felt no such sentimental attachment; but interest took the place of sentiment. Their natural line of trade was with the Lakes, and their relations with the British trading-post at Malden, opposite Detroit, became more and more close with every new quarrel between Washington and London.

President Jefferson earnestly urged the Indians to become industrious cultivators of the soil; but even for that reform one condition was indispensable. The Indians must be protected from contact with the whites; and during the change in their mode of life, they must not be drugged, murdered, or defrauded. Trespasses on Indian land and purchases of tribal territory must for a time cease, until the Indian tribes should all be induced to adopt a new system. Even then the reform would be difficult, for Indian warriors thought death less irksome than daily labor; and men who did not fear death were not easily driven to toil.

There President Jefferson's philanthropy stopped. His greed for land equalled that of any settler on the border, and his humanity to the Indian suffered the suspicion of having among its motives the purpose of gaining the Indian lands for the whites. Jefferson's policy in practice offered a reward for Indian extinction, since he not only claimed the territory of every extinct tribe on the doctrine of paramount sovereignty, but deliberately ordered[1] his Indian agents to tempt

[1] Jefferson to Harrison, Feb. 27, 1803; Works, iv. 471.

the tribal chiefs into debt in order to oblige them to sell the tribal lands, which did not belong to them, but to their tribes: —

> "To promote this disposition to exchange lands which they have to spare and we want, for necessaries which we have to spare and they want, we shall push our trading-houses, and be glad to see the good and influential individuals among them in debt; because we observe that when these debts get beyond what the individuals can pay, they become willing to lop them off by a cession of lands."

No one would have felt more astonishment than Jefferson had some friend told him that this policy, which he believed to be virtuous, was a conspiracy to induce trustees to betray their trusts; and that in morals it was as improper as though it were not virtuously intended. Shocked as he would have been at such a method of obtaining the neighboring estate of any Virginia family, he not only suggested but vigorously carried out the system toward the Indians.

In 1804 and 1805, Governor Harrison made treaties with the Miamis, Eel Rivers, Weas, Piankeshaws, and Delawares, — chiefly the tribes he called "a body of the most depraved wretches upon earth," — by which he obtained the strip of country, fifty miles wide, between the Ohio and the White rivers, thus carrying the boundary back toward the Wabash. The treaty excited deep feeling among the better Indians throughout the territory, who held long debates on their means of preventing its execution.

Among the settlers in Indiana, an internal dispute mingled with the dangers of Indian relations. For this misfortune Harrison himself was partially to blame. A Virginian by birth, naturally inclined toward Southern influences, he shared the feelings of the Kentucky and Virginia slave-owners who wanted the right of bringing their slaves with them into the Territory, contrary to the Ordinance of 1787. The men who stood nearest the governor were earnest and active in the effort to repeal or evade the prohibition of slavery, and they received from Harrison all the support he could give them. With his approval, successive appeals were made to Congress. Perhaps the weightiest act of John Randolph's career as leader of the Republican majority in the House was to report, March 2, 1803, that the extension of slavery into Indiana was "highly dangerous and inexpedient," and that the people of Indiana "would at no distant day find ample remuneration for a temporary privation of labor and immigration" in the beneficence of a free society. Cæsar Rodney, of Delaware, in March, 1804, made a report to a contrary effect, recommending a suspension for ten years of the anti-slavery clause in the Ordinance; but the House did not act upon it.

The advocates of a slave system, with Harrison's co-operation, then decided that the Territory should pass into the second grade, which under the Ordinance of 1787 could be done when the population should number five thousand male whites of full age. The change was effected in the winter of 1804–1805, by means open to grave objection.[1] Thenceforward Harrison shared his power with a Legislative Council and a House of Representatives; while the legislature chose a territorial delegate to Congress. The first territorial legislature, in 1805, which was wholly under Harrison's influence, passed an Act, subsequently revised and approved Sept. 17, 1807, permitting owners of slaves to bring them into the Territory and keep them there for a number of days, during which time the slave might be emancipated on condition of binding himself to service for a term of years to which the law set no limit.[2]

The overpowering influence and energy of the governor and his Southern friends gave them during these years undisputed control. Yet the anti-slavery sentiment was so strong as to make the governor uncomfortable, and almost to endanger his personal safety; until at last, in 1808, the issue was fairly brought before the people in the elections. Both in that and in the following year the opponents of slavery outvoted and defeated the governor's party. Feelings became exceedingly bitter, and the Territory was distracted by feuds which had no small influence on matters of administration, and on the Indian troubles most of all. Between the difficulties of introducing negroes and expelling Indians, Harrison found that his

[1] Dunn's Indiana (American Commonwealths), p. 324.
[2] Dillon's History of Indiana, App. G. p. 617.

popularity had been lessened, if not lost.[1] He could not fail to see that a military exploit was perhaps his only hope of recovering it; and for such an exploit he had excuses enough.

The treaties of 1804–1805, which threatened the Indians with immediate loss of their hunting-grounds in the Wabash valley, caused a fermentation peculiarly alarming because altogether new. Early in 1806 Harrison learned that a Shawanee Indian, claiming to be a prophet, had gathered a number of warriors about him at Greenville, in Ohio, and was preaching doctrines that threatened trouble. Harrison attributed the mischief to the Prophet; but he learned in time that the Prophet's brother Tecumseh—or more properly Tecumthe— gave the movement its chief strength.

Indians and whites soon recognized Tecumthe as a phenomenon. His father was a Shawanee warrior, in no way distinguished; his mother, a Creek or Cherokee Indian, captured and adopted by the Shawanee,—and of these parents three children at one birth were born about the year 1780, a few miles from Springfield, Ohio. The third brother lived and died obscure; Tecumthe and the Prophet became famous, although they were not chiefs of their tribe, and had no authority of office or birth. Such of the chiefs as were in the pay or under the power of the United States government were jealous of their influence, and had every reason for wishing to suppress the leaders of a movement avowedly designed to overthrow the system of tribal independence. From the first, Tecumthe aimed at limiting the authority of the tribes and their chiefs in order to build up an Indian confederacy, embracing not the chiefs but the warriors of all the tribes, who should act as an Indian Congress and assume joint ownership of Indian lands.

This scheme was hostile to the plans though not to the professions of President Jefferson. Its object was to prevent the piecemeal sale of Indian lands by petty tribal chiefs, under pressure of government agents. No one could honestly deny that the object was lawful and even regular; for in the Treaty of Greenville in 1795, which was the only decisive authority or precedent, the United States had admitted and acted on the

---

[1] Dunn's Indiana, p. 397.

principle for which Tecumthe contended,—of accepting its cessions of land, not from single tribes, but from the whole body of northwestern Indians, without entering on the subject of local ownership.[1] Governor Harrison and President Jefferson were of course aware of the precedent, and decided to disregard it[2] in order to act on the rule better suited to their purposes; but their decision was in no way binding on Tecumthe or the tribes who were parties to the treaty of Greenville.

During the year 1807 Tecumthe's influence was increased by the "Chesapeake" excitement, which caused the Governor-general of Canada to intrigue among the Indians for aid in case of war. Probably their increase of influence led the Prophet and his brother, in May or June, 1808, to establish themselves on Tippecanoe Creek, the central point of Indian strategy and politics. Vincennes lay one hundred and fifty miles below, barely four-and-twenty hours down the stream of the Wabash; Fort Dearborn, or Chicago, was a hundred miles to the northwest; Fort Wayne the same distance to the northeast; and excepting a short portage, the Tippecanoe Indians could paddle their canoes to Malden and Detroit in one direction, or to any part of the waters of the Ohio and Mississippi in the other. At the mouth of Tippecanoe Creek the reformers laid out a village that realized Jefferson's wish, for the Indians there drank no whiskey, and avowed themselves to be tillers of the soil. Their professions seemed honest. In August, 1808, the Prophet came to Vincennes and passed two weeks with Governor Harrison, who was surprised to find that no temptation could overcome the temperance of the Prophet's followers. The speech then made in the public talk with the governor remains the only record of the Prophet's words, and of the character he wished to pretend, if not to adopt.

> "I told all the redskins," he said to Harrison, "that the way they were in was not good, and that they ought to abandon it; that we ought to consider ourselves as one

---

[1] Treaty of Greenville; State Papers, Indian Affairs, p. 562.
[2] Harrison to the Secretary of War, March 22, 1814; Drake's Tecumseh, p. 161.

man, but we ought to live agreeable to our several customs,—the red people after their mode, and the white people after theirs; particularly that they should not drink whiskey; that it was not made for them, but the white people, who alone know how to use it; and that it is the cause of all the mischiefs which the Indians suffer. . . . Determine to listen to nothing that is bad; do not take up the tomahawk, should it be offered by the British or by the Long-knives; do not meddle with anything that does not belong to you, but mind your own business, and cultivate the ground, that your women and your children may have enough to live on. I now inform you that it is our intention to live in peace with our father and his children forever."

Whatever want of confidence Harrison felt in these professions of peace, he recorded his great surprise at finding the temperance to be real; and every one who visited the settlement at Tippecanoe bore witness to the tillage, which seemed to guarantee a peaceful intent; for if war had been in Tecumthe's mind, he would not have placed town, crops, and stock within easy reach of destruction.

Nothing could be more embarrassing to Jefferson than to see the Indians follow his advice; for however well-disposed he might be, he could not want the Indians to become civilized, educated, or competent to protect themselves,—yet he was powerless to protect them. The Prophet asked that the sale of liquor should be stopped; but the President could no more prevent white settlers from selling liquor to the Indians than he could prevent the Wabash from flowing. The tribes asked that white men who murdered Indians should be punished; but the President could no more execute such malefactors than he could execute the smugglers who defied his embargo. The Indians had rights recognized by law, by treaty, and by custom, on which their existence depended; but these rights required force to maintain them, and on the Wabash President Jefferson had less police power than the Prophet himself controlled.

Wide separation could alone protect the Indians from the whites, and Tecumthe's scheme depended for its only chance of success on holding the white settlements at a distance. The

Prophet said nothing to Harrison on that point, but his silence covered no secret. So notorious was the Indian hostility to land-cessions, that when Governor Hull of Michigan Territory, in November, 1807, negotiated another such cession at Detroit,[1] the Indian agent at Fort Wayne not only doubted its policy, but insinuated that it might have been dictated by the British in order to irritate the Indians; and he reported that the Northern Indians talked of punishing with death the chiefs who signed it.[2]

Aware of the danger, Harrison decided to challenge it. The people of his Territory wanted the lands of the Wabash, even at the risk of war. The settlement at Tippecanoe was supposed to contain no more than eighty or a hundred warriors, with four or five times that number within a radius of fifty miles. No immediate outbreak was to be feared; and Harrison, "conceiving that a favorable opportunity then offered"[3] for carrying the boundary from the White River to the Wabash, asked authority to make a new purchase. Secretary Eustis, July 15, 1809, wrote him a cautious letter,[4] giving the required permission, but insisting that, "to prevent any future dissatisfaction, the chiefs of all the nations who had or pretended right to these lands" were to be present as consenting parties to the treaty. On this authority Harrison once more summoned together "the most depraved wretches upon earth,"—Miamis, Eel Rivers, Delawares, Pottawatomies, and Kickapoos,—and obtained from them, Sept. 30, 1809, several enormous cessions of territory which cut into the heart of the Indian country for nearly a hundred miles up both banks of the Wabash valley. These transfers included about three million acres.

Harrison knew that this transaction would carry despair to the heart of every Indian in his Territory. The Wabash valley alone still contained game. Deprived of their last resource, these Indians must fall back to perish in the country of the Chippewas and Sioux, their enemies.[5] Already impoverished

---

[1] Treaty of Nov. 7, 1807; State Papers, Indian Affairs, p. 747.

[2] Dawson's Harrison, p. 106.

[3] Dawson, p. 129.

[4] Eustis to Harrison, July 15, 1809. Indian Affairs, p. 761.

[5] Harrison to the Secretary of War, March 22, 1814; Drake's Tecumseh, p. 162.

by the decrees of Napoleon, the Orders in Council, and the embargo, which combined to render their peltry valueless, so that they could scarcely buy the powder and shot to kill their game,[1] the Indians had thenceforward no choice but to depend on British assistance. Harrison's treaty immediately strengthened the influence of Tecumthe and the Prophet. The Wyandots, or Hurons, regarded by all the Indian tribes in the Territory as first in dignity and influence, joined Tecumthe's league, and united in a declaration that the late cessions were void, and would not be recognized by the tribes. The winter of 1809–1810 passed quietly; but toward May, 1810, alarming reports reached Vincennes of gatherings at the Prophet's town, and of violence to be expected. When the salt, which was part of the usual annuity, reached Tippecanoe, Tecumthe refused to accept it, and drove the boatmen away. He charged the American government with deceiving the Indians; and he insisted, as the foundation of future peace, that the cessions of 1809 should be annulled, and no future cession should be good unless made by all the tribes.

Harrison knew that his treaties of 1809 opened an aggressive policy, which must naturally end in an Indian war. Some of the best citizens in the Territory thought that the blame for the consequences ought not to rest on the Indians.[2] Since the election of Madison to the Presidency in November, 1808, war with England had been so imminent, and its effect on the Indians so marked, that Harrison could not help seeing the opportunity of a military career, and he had given much study to military matters.[3] His plans, if they accorded with his acts, included an Indian war, in which he should take the initiative. His treaties of 1809 left him no choice, for after making such a war inevitable, his only safety lay in crushing the Indians before the British could openly aid them. Unfortunately, neither Madison nor Eustis understood his purpose, or would have liked it. They approved his land-purchases, which no

[1] Dawson, p. 142.
[2] Harrison to Eustis, July 4, 1810; Dawson, p. 149. Harrison to Governor Scott, Dec. 13, 1811; Dawson, p. 244. Badollet's Letters to Gallatin; Gallatin MSS. Dillon's Indiana, p. 455.
[3] Harrison to Governor Scott of Kentucky, March 10, 1809; Dawson, p. 119.

Administration and no citizen would have dared reject; but they were very unwilling to be drawn into an Indian war, however natural might be such a consequence of the purchases.

So it happened that as early as the summer of 1810 war was imminent in the Wabash and Maumee valleys, and perhaps only British influence delayed it. British interests imperatively required that Tecumthe's confederacy should be made strong, and should not be wrecked prematurely in an unequal war. From Malden, opposite Detroit, the British traders loaded the American Indians with gifts and weapons; urged Tecumthe to widen his confederacy, to unite all the tribes, but not to begin war till he received the signal from Canada. All this was duly reported at Washington.[1] On the other hand, Harrison sent for Tecumthe; and August 12, 1810, the Indian chief came for a conference to Vincennes. Indians and whites, in considerable numbers, armed and alert, fearing treachery on both sides, witnessed the interview.

Tecumthe took, as his right, the position he felt himself to occupy as the most powerful American then living,—who, a warrior himself, with five thousand warriors behind him, held in one hand an alliance with Great Britain, in the other an alliance with the Indians of the southwest. Representatives of the Wyandots, Kickapoos, Pottawatomies, Ottawas, and Winnebagoes announced the adhesion of their tribes to the Shawanee Confederacy and the election of Tecumthe as their chief. In this character he avowed to Harrison, in the broadest and boldest language, the scope of his policy:[2] —

"Brother, since the peace was made in 1795 you have killed some of the Shawanee, Winnebagoes, Delawares, and Miamis, and you have taken our land from us; and I do not see how we can remain at peace with you if you continue to do so. . . . You try to force the red people to do some injury; it is you that are pushing them on to do mischief. You endeavor to make distinctions; you wish to prevent the Indians from doing as we wish them,—from uniting and considering their land as the common property of the

[1] State Papers, Indian Affairs, p. 799.
[2] War Department Archives, MSS.

whole. You take tribes aside and advise them not to come into this measure. . . . The reason, I tell you, is this: You want, by your distinctions of Indian tribes, in allotting to each a particular tract of land, to make them to war with each other. You never see an Indian come and endeavor to make the white people do so. You are continually driving the red people; and at last you will drive them into the great lake, where they cannot either stand or work.

"Since my residence at Tippecanoe we have endeavored to level all distinctions, to destroy village chiefs by whom all mischief is done: it is they who sell our lands to the Americans. Our object is to let all our affairs be transacted by warriors. This land that was sold, and the goods that were given for it, was only done by a few. The treaty was afterward brought here, and the Weas were induced to give their consent because of their small numbers. . . . In future we are prepared to punish those chiefs who may come forward to propose to sell their land. If you continue to purchase of them, it will produce war among the different tribes, and at last I do not know what will be the consequence to the white people."

Earnestly denying the intention of making war, Tecumthe still declared that any attempt on Harrison's part to enter into possession of the land lately ceded would be resisted by force. In the vehemence of discussion he used language in regard to the United States which caused great excitement, and broke up the meeting for that day; but he lost no time in correcting the mistake. After the conference closed, he had a private interview with Harrison, and repeated his official ultimatum. He should only with great reluctance make war on the United States, against whom he had no other complaint than their land-purchases; he was extremely anxious to be their friend, and if the governor would prevail upon the President to give up the lands lately purchased, and agree never to make another treaty without the consent of all the tribes, Tecumthe pledged himself to be a faithful ally to the United States, and to assist them in all their wars with the English; otherwise he would be obliged to enter into an English alliance.

Harrison told him that no such condition had the least

chance of finding favor with the Government. "Well," re-joined Tecumthe, as though he had expected the answer, "as the great chief is to decide the matter, I hope the Great Spirit will put sense enough into his head to induce him to direct you to give up this land. It is true, he is so far off he will not be injured by the war; he may sit still in his town and drink his wine, while you and I will have to fight it out."

Therewith Tecumthe and Harrison parted, each to carry on his preparations for the conflict. The Secretary of War wrote to Harrison in November instructing him to defer the military occupation of the new purchase on the Wabash, but giving no orders as to the policy intended to be taken by the Government. Wanting peace, he threw on Harrison the responsibility for war.[1]

"It has indeed occurred to me," wrote the secretary, "that the surest means of securing good behavior from this conspicuous personage [Tecumthe] and his brother, would be to make them prisoners; but at this time more particularly, it is desirable that peace with all the Indian tribes should be preserved; and I am instructed by the President to express to your Excellency his expectation and confidence that in all your arrangements this may be considered (as I am confident it ever has been) a primary object with you."

[1] Dawson, pp. 173, 174.

Chapter V

NOTWITHSTANDING the hostile spirit on both sides, the winter of 1810–1811 passed without serious disturbance on the Wabash, and the summer of 1811 arrived before Harrison thought proper to take the next step. Then, June 24, he sent to Tecumthe and the Prophet a letter, or speech, intended to force an issue.

"Brothers," he wrote,[1] "this is the third year that all the white people in this country have been alarmed at your proceedings. You threaten us with war; you invite all the tribes to the north and west of us to join against us. Brothers, your warriors who have lately been here deny this, but I have received the information from every direction. The tribes on the Mississippi have sent me word that you intended to murder me, and then to commence a war upon our people. I have also received the speech that you sent to the Pottawatomies and others to join you for that purpose; but if I had no other evidence of your hostility to us, your seizing the salt which I lately sent up the Wabash is sufficient."

Except the seizure of five barrels of salt intended for other Indians, in June, 1811, no overt act yet showed the intention to begin a war, and certainly no such immediate intention existed; but two white men were at that moment murdered in the Illinois Territory, a drunken Indian was murdered at Vincennes, and these acts of violence, together with the general sense of insecurity, caused the government officials to write from all quarters to the War Department that Tecumthe must be suppressed. Tecumthe himself seemed disposed to avoid cause for attack. July 4 he sent word that he would come to Vincennes; and to Harrison's alarm he appeared there, July 27, with two or three hundred warriors for an interview with the governor. The act proved courage, if not rashness. Harrison's instructions hinted advice to seize the two Indian leaders, if it could be done without producing a war, and Harrison had ample time to prepare his measures.

[1] Dawson's Harrison, p. 179.

Tecumthe came and remained two days at Vincennes, explaining, with childlike candor, his plans and wishes. As soon as the council was over, he said, he should visit the Southern tribes to unite them with those of the North in a peaceful confederacy; and he hoped no attempt would be made to settle the disputed territory till his return in the spring. A great number of Indians were to come in the autumn to live at Tippecanoe; they must use the disputed region for hunting-ground. He wished everything to remain in its present situation till his return; he would then go and see the President and settle everything with him. The affairs of all the tribes in that quarter were in his own hands, and he would despatch messengers in every direction to prevent the Indians from doing further mischief.

Tecumthe seemed to think that his wish would prevent Harrison from further aggression for the time. A few days afterward he passed down the Wabash, with some twenty warriors, on his diplomatic errand to the Creeks; but before he was fairly out of sight, July 31, a number of citizens met at Vincennes, and adopted resolutions demanding that the settlement at Tippecanoe should be broken up. Immediate action, before Tecumthe should return, was urged by Harrison's party, and by many frightened settlers. Harrison's personal wish could not be doubted.

The Secretary of War had already ordered the Fourth Regiment of U. S. Infantry, under Colonel Boyd, with a company of riflemen,—making in the whole a force of five hundred regular troops,—to descend the Ohio from Pittsburg as rapidly as possible, and place themselves under Harrison's orders; but Eustis added instructions not easily followed or understood. July 17 he wrote to Harrison,[1] —

> "In case circumstances shall occur which may render it necessary or expedient to attack the Prophet and his followers, the force should be such as to insure the most complete success. This force will consist of the militia and regular troops. . . . If the Prophet should commence or seriously threaten hostilities, he ought to be attacked."

Under these instructions, Harrison was warranted in doing

[1] Dawson, p. 190.

what he pleased. Not even Tecumthe denied the seriousness
of his hostile threats, and Harrison had every reason to begin
the war at once, if war must be; but although Eustis spoke
his own mind clearly, he failed to reckon upon the President,
and this neglect was the cause of another letter to Harrison,
written three days later:[1] —

> "Since my letter of the 17th instant, I have been particu-
> larly instructed by the President to communicate to your
> Excellency his earnest desire that peace may, if possible, be
> preserved with the Indians, and that to this end every
> proper means may be adopted. . . . Circumstances con-
> spire at this particular juncture to render it peculiarly desir-
> able that hostilities of any kind or to any degree, not
> indispensably required, should be avoided. The force under
> Colonel Boyd has been ordered to descend the Ohio, . . .
> and although the force is at the disposal of your Excellency,
> I am instructed to inform you that the President indulges
> the hope and expectation that your exertions and measures
> with the Indians will be such as may render their march to
> the Indian Territory unnecessary, and that they may remain
> liable to another disposition."

Without paying attention to the President's wishes emphatically expressed in these orders of July 20, Harrison
passed the next month in raising forces for an expedition to
satisfy the wishes of the Western people. No doubt was felt
on the Ohio that Harrison meant to attack the Indians at
Tippecanoe; and so serious a campaign was expected that
Kentucky became eager to share it. Among other Kentuckians, Joseph H. Daveiss, Aaron Burr's persecutor, wrote,[2] August 24, to Harrison, offering himself as a volunteer: "Under
all the privacy of a letter," said he, "I make free to tell you
that I have imagined there were two men in the West who
had military talents; and you, sir, were the first of the two.
It is thus an opportunity of service much valued by me."
Daveiss doubted only whether the army was to attack at once,
or to provoke attack.

Harrison   accepted   Daveiss's   services,   and   gave   him

[1] Dawson, p. 191.
[2] Dawson, p. 200.

command of the dragoons, a mounted force of about one hundred and thirty men from Indiana and Kentucky. The Fourth U. S. Infantry, three hundred strong according to Colonel Boyd who commanded it,[1] arrived in the Territory at the beginning of September. As rapidly as possible Harrison collected his forces, and sent them up the river to a point in the new purchase about sixty-five miles above Vincennes. The exact force was afterward much disputed.[2] Harrison reported his effectives as a few more than nine hundred men. Some sixty Kentucky volunteers were of the number.

The last instructions from the Department, dated August 29,[3] made no change in the tenor of the President's orders. When Harrison joined his army, October 6, at the camp above Vincennes, he wrote to Eustis,[4] —

"I sincerely wish that my instructions were such as to authorize me to march up immediately to the Prophet's town. The troops which I command are a fine body of men, and the proportion of regulars, irregulars, infantry, and dragoons such as I could wish it. I have no reason to doubt the issue of a contest with the savages, and I am much deceived if the greater part of both officers and men are not desirous of coming in contact with them."

In doubt what to do next, Harrison waited while his army built a small wooden fort, to which he gave his own name, and which was intended to establish formal possession of the new purchase. While the army was engaged in this work, one of the sentinels was fired at and wounded in the night of October 10 by some person or persons unseen and unknown. Harrison regarded this as a beginning of hostilities by the Prophet, and decided to act as though war was declared. October 12 he received from Secretary Eustis a letter dated September 18, never published though often referred to,[5] which is not found in the records of the government. Harrison replied the next day:[6] —

[1] Boyd to Eustis, Dec. 10, 1811; MSS. War Department Records.
[2] Marshall's Kentucky, ii. 509.
[3] Dawson, p. 195. Cf. McAffee, p. 18.
[4] Harrison to Eustis, Oct. 6, 1811; MSS. War Department Archives.
[5] Dawson, p. 253.
[6] Harrison to Eustis, Oct. 13, 1811; MSS. War Department Archives.

"Your letter of the 18th ult. I had the honor to receive yesterday. My views have hitherto been limited to the erection of the fort which we are now building, and to a march, by way of feint, in the direction of the Prophet's town, as high, perhaps, as the Vermilion River. But the powers given me in your last letter, and circumstances which have occurred here at the very moment on which it was received, call for measures of a more energetic kind."

With this despatch Harrison enclosed a return of the soldiers present under his command. "You will observe," he said, "that our effectives are but little over nine hundred." The rank-and-file consisted of seven hundred and forty-two men fit for duty. Harrison thought this force too small, and sent back to Vincennes for four companies of mounted riflemen. Two of the four companies joined him,[1] but their strength was not reported. These returns showed that the army, with the two additional companies, numbered at least one thousand effectives. One of the officers of the Fourth U. S. Infantry, writing November 21, said that the force was a little upward of eleven hundred men.[2]

While the Americans were determined not to return without a battle, the Indians had been strictly ordered by Tecumthe to keep the peace, and showed the intention to avoid Harrison's attack. As early as September 25, the Prophet sent a number of Indians to Vincennes to protest his peaceful intentions, and to promise that Harrison's demands should be complied with.[3] Harrison returned no answer and sent no demands. October 28 he broke up his camp at Fort Harrison, and the army began its march up the river. The governor remained one day longer at the fort, and from there, October 29, sent some friendly Indians to the Prophet with a message requiring that the Winnebagoes, Pottawatomies, and Kickapoos, at Tippecanoe, should return to their tribes; that all stolen horses should be given up, and that murderers should be surrendered. He intended at a later time to add a demand

---

[1] Harrison to Eustis, Nov. 2, 1811; MSS. War Department Archives.
[2] Letter in New England Palladium, Dec. 24, 1811.
[3] Dawson, p. 196.

for hostages,[1] in case the Prophet should accede to these preliminary terms.

Harrison did not inform the friendly Indians where they
would find him, or where they were to bring their answer.[2]
Crossing to the west bank of the Wabash to avoid the woods,
the troops marched over a level prairie to the mouth of the
Vermilion River, where they erected a blockhouse to protect
their boats. The Vermilion River was the extreme boundary
of the recent land-cession; and to cross it, under such circumstances, was war. Harrison looked for resistance; but not an
Indian was seen, and November 3 the army resumed its
march, keeping in the open country, until on the evening of
November 5 it arrived, still unmolested, within eleven miles
of the Prophet's town. From the Vermilion River to Tippecanoe was fifty miles.

The next morning, November 6, the army advanced toward
the town, and as the column approached, Indians were frequently seen in front and on the flanks. Interpreters tried to
parley with them, but they returned no answer except insulting or threatening gestures. Two miles from the town the
army unexpectedly entered a difficult country, thick with
wood and cut by deep ravines, where Harrison was greatly
alarmed, seeing himself at the mercy of an attack; but no attack was made. When clear of the woods, within a mile and
a half of the town, he halted his troops and declared his intention to encamp. Daveiss and all the other officers urged
him to attack the town at once; but he replied that his instructions would not justify his attacking the Indians unless
they refused his demands, and he still hoped to hear something in the course of the evening from the friendly Indians
sent from Fort Harrison. Daveiss remonstrated, and every officer in the army supported him. Harrison then pleaded the
danger of further advance. "The experience of the last two
days," he said,[3] "ought to convince every officer that no reliance ought to be placed upon the guides as to the topography
of the country; that, relying on their information, the troops

[1] Dawson, p. 196.
[2] Speech of Captain Charley, July 10, 1814; State Papers, Indian Affairs, i.
830.
[3] Dawson, p. 206.

had been led into a situation so unfavorable that but for the celerity with which they changed their position a few Indians might have destroyed them; he was therefore determined not to advance to the town until he had previously reconnoitred."

The candor of this admission did not prove the military advantages of the halt; and neither of Harrison's reasons was strengthened by a third, which he gave a month afterward in a letter to the Governor of Kentucky. "The success of an attack upon the town by day," he said,[1] " was very problematical. I expected that they would have met me the next day to hear my terms; but I did not believe that they would accede to them, and it was my determination to attack and burn the town the following night." Daveiss and the other officers, looking at the matter only as soldiers, became more urgent, until Harrison at last yielded, and resolving no longer to hesitate in treating the Indians as enemies,[2] ordered an advance, with the determination to attack. "I yielded to what appeared the general wish," he said in his official report,[3] "and directed the troops to advance." They advanced about four hundred yards, when three Indians sent by the Prophet came to meet them, bringing a pacific message, and urging that hostilities should if possible be avoided. Harrison's conscience, already heavy-ladened, again gave way at this entreaty.[4] "I answered that I had no intention of attacking them until I discovered that they would not comply with the demands that I had made; that I would go on and encamp at the Wabash, and in the morning would have an interview with the Prophet and his chiefs, and explain to them the determination of the President; that in the mean time no hostilities should be committed."

Had Harrison's vacillation been due to consciousness of strength, his officers would have had no just reason for remonstrance; but he estimated his force at about eight hundred effective men, and the Indians at more than six hundred.[5] He knew that no victory over the Northern Indians

---

[1] Harrison to Governor Scott, Dec. 13, 1811; Dawson, p. 244.
[2] McAffee, p. 25. Dawson, p. 206.
[3] Harrison to Eustis, Nov. 18, 1811; State Papers, Indian Affairs, p. 776.
[4] Harrison to Eustis, Nov. 18, 1811; State Papers, Indian Affairs, p. 776.
[5] Dawson, p. 216.

had ever been won where the numbers were anything like equal.[1] Before him was an unknown wilderness; behind him was a line of retreat, one hundred and fifty miles long, and he had supplies for very few days. He could not trust the Indians; and certainly they could not trust him, for he meant in any case to surprise their town the next night. Delay was dangerous only to the whites,—advantageous only to the Indians. Daveiss felt so strongly the governor's hesitation that he made no secret of his discontent, and said openly not only that the army ought to attack,[2] but also that it would be attacked before morning, or would march home with nothing accomplished.[3] Indeed, if Harrison had not come there to destroy the town, he had no sufficient military reason for being there at all.

Having decided to wait, Harrison had next to choose a camping-ground. The army marched on, looking for some spot on the river where wood as well as water could be obtained, until they came within one hundred and fifty yards of the town, when the Indians, becoming alarmed, called on them to stop. Harrison halted his men and asked the Indians to show him a place suitable for his purpose, which they did;[4] and the troops filed off in front of the town, at right angles to the Wabash, till they reached a creek less than a mile to the northwest. Next to the town was a marshy prairie; beyond the marsh the ground rose about ten feet to a level covered with oaks; and then about a hundred yards farther it suddenly dropped to the creek behind, where the banks were thick with willow and brushwood. No spot in the neighborhood was better suited for a camp than this saddle-back between the marsh and the brook, but Harrison saw that it offered serious disadvantages. "I found the ground destined for the encampment," he reported, "not altogether such as I could wish it. It was, indeed, admirably calculated for regular troops that were opposed to regulars, but it afforded great facility to the approach of the savages."

There Harrison camped. The troops were stationed in a

[1] Dawson, pp. 216, 250.
[2] Dawson, p. 211.
[3] McAffee, p. 28.
[4] Harrison to Eustis, Nov. 18, 1811; State Papers, Indian Affairs, p. 776.

sort of triangle, following the shape of the high land,[1] —the base toward the northeast, the blunt apex toward the southwest; but at no part of the line was any attempt made to intrench, or palisade, or in any way to cover the troops. Harrison afterward explained that he had barely axes enough to procure firewood. The want of axes had been discovered at Fort Harrison, and hardly excused the neglect to intrench at Tippecanoe, for it had not prevented building the fort. The army pitched its tents and lighted its fires for the night, with no other protection than a single line of sentries, although the creek in the rear gave cover to an attack within a few yards of the camp.

The night was dark, with light rain at intervals; the troops slept on their arms, and their rest was disturbed by no sound. Many accounts have been given of what passed in the Prophet's town,[2] but none of them deserve attention. During the night neither Harrison nor his sentinels heard or saw anything that roused their suspicions. Harrison, in a brief report of the next day,[3] said that the first alarm was given at half-past four o'clock in the morning. His full report of November 18 corrected the time to a few minutes before four. Still another account, on the day after the battle, named five o'clock as the moment.[4] Harrison himself was about to leave his tent, before calling the men to parade, when a sentinel at the farthest angle of the camp above the creek fired a shot. In an instant the Indian yell was raised, and before the soldiers at that end of the camp could leave their tents, the Indians had pierced the line, and were shooting the men by the light of the camp-fires. Within a few moments, firing began along the whole line, until the camp, except for a space next the creek, was encircled by it. Fortunately for Harrison, the attacking party at the broken angle had not strength to follow up its advantage, and the American line was soon reformed in the rear. Harrison rode to the point, and at the northeast angle met Daveiss and his dismounted dragoons. Daveiss reported

---

[1] See Plan of Camp. Lossing, p. 205.

[2] Lossing, p. 203.

[3] Harrison to Eustis, Nov. 8, 1811; National Intelligencer, Nov. 30, 1811. Niles, i. 255.

[4] William Taylor to ——, Nov. 8, 1811; National Intelligencer, Dec. 7, 1811.

that the Indians, under cover of the trees, were annoying the troops severely, and asked leave to dislodge them. The order was given; and Daveiss, followed by only a few men, rushed forward among the trees, where he soon fell, mortally wounded. The troops, after forming, held their position without further disaster till daybreak, when they advanced and drove the Indians into the swamp. With this success the battle ended, having lasted two hours.

For the moment the army was saved, but only at great cost. Daveiss, who held an anomalous position almost as prominent as that of Harrison himself, died in the afternoon. Captain Baen, acting major of the Fourth Regiment, two lieutenants, and an ensign of the same regiment, were killed or wounded; two lieutenant-colonels, four captains, and several lieutenants of the Indiana militia were on the same list, and the general's aid-de-camp was killed. One hundred and fifty-four privates were returned among the casualties, fifty-two of whom were killed or mortally wounded. The total loss was one hundred and eighty-eight, of whom sixty-one were killed or mortally wounded.[1] The bodies of thirty-eight Indians were found on the field.

If the army had cause for anxiety before the battle, it had double reason for alarm when it realized its position on November 7. If Harrison's own account was correct, he had with him only eight hundred men. Sixty-one had been killed or mortally wounded, and he had near a hundred and fifty wounded to carry with him in his retreat. His effective force was diminished more than one fourth, according to his biographer;[2] his camp contained very little flour and no meat, for the few beeves brought with the army were either driven away by the Indians or stampeded by the noise of the battle; and his only base of supplies was at Vincennes, one hundred and seventy miles away. The Indians could return in greater numbers, but his own force must steadily grow weaker. Harrison was naturally a cautious man; he felt strongly the dangers that surrounded him, and his army felt them not less.[3]

The number of Indian warriors engaged in the night attack

[1] General Return; State Papers, Indian Affairs, i. 779.
[2] Dawson, p. 233.
[3] Dawson, p. 233. Lossing, p. 206, *note*.

was estimated by Harrison at six hundred.[1] The law of exaggeration, almost invariable in battle, warrants belief that not more than four hundred Indians were concerned in the attack. The Prophet's Indians were few. Tecumthe afterward spoke of the attack as an "unfortunate transaction that took place between the white people and a few of our young men at our village,"[2] — as though it was an affair in which the young warriors had engaged against the will of the older chiefs. Tecumthe commonly told the truth, even with indiscretion; and nothing in the American account contradicted his version of the affair at Tippecanoe. Harrison's ablest military manœuvre had been the availing himself of Tecumthe's over-confidence in quitting the country at so critical a moment.

Although Harrison did not venture to send out a scout for twenty-four hours, but remained in camp waiting attack, no further sign of hostilities was given. "Night," said one of the army,[3] "found every man mounting guard, without food, fire, or light, and in a drizzling rain. The Indian dogs, during the dark hours, produced frequent alarms by prowling in search of carrion about the sentinels." On the morning of November 8, the dragoons and mounted riflemen approached the town and found it deserted. Apparently the Indians had fled in haste, leaving everything, even a few new English guns and powder. The army took what supplies were needed, and set fire to the village. Meanwhile every preparation had been made for rapid retreat. The wagons could scarcely carry all the wounded, and Harrison abandoned the camp furniture and private baggage. "We managed, however, to bring off the public property," he reported. At noon of November 9 the train started, and by night-fall had passed the dangerous woods and broken country where a few enemies could have stopped it. No Indians appeared; the march was undisturbed; and after leaving a company of the U. S. Fourth Regiment at Fort Harrison, the rest of the force arrived, November 18, at Vincennes.

The battle of Tippecanoe at once became a point of pride

[1] Report of Nov. 18, 1811; Niles, i. 304.
[2] Dawson, p. 267.
[3] Lossing, p. 206, *note*.

throughout the Western country, and Harrison received the official applause and thanks of Kentucky, Indiana, and Illinois; but Harrison's account of his victory was not received without criticism, and the battle was fought again in the press and in private. The Fourth Regiment more than hinted that had it not been for their steadiness the whole party would have been massacred. At Vincennes, Harrison was severely attacked. In Kentucky criticism was open, for the family and friends of Joseph Daveiss were old Federalists, who had no interest in the military triumphs of a Republican official. Humphrey Marshall, Daveiss's brother-in-law, published a sharp review of Harrison's report, and hinted plainly that Daveiss had fallen a victim to the General's blunders. With characteristic vigor of language, Marshall called Harrison "a little, selfish, intriguing busybody," and charged him with having made the war without just cause, for personal objects.[1] These attacks caused the Western Republicans to sustain with the more ardor their faith in Harrison's military genius, and their enthusiasm for the victory of Tippecanoe; but President Madison and Secretary Eustis guarded themselves with some care from expressing an opinion on the subject.

Whatever his critics might say, Harrison gained his object, and established himself in the West as the necessary leader of any future campaign. That result, as far as it was good, seemed to be the only advantage gained at Tippecanoe. Harrison believed that the battle had broken the Prophet's influence, and saved the frontier from further alarm; he thought that in the event of a British war, the Indians would remain neutral having "witnessed the inefficacy of British assistance;"[2] he expected the tribes to seek peace as a consequence of what he considered the severest defeat they had ever received since their acquaintance with the white people;[3] and the expectation was general that they would deliver the Prophet and Tecumthe into the hands of the American government. For a time these impressions seemed reasonable. The Prophet lost influence, and the peace was not further dis-

[1] Marshall's Kentucky, ii. 507, 521.
[2] Harrison to J. M. Scott, Dec. 2, 1811. Niles, i. 311.
[3] Harrison to Eustis, Dec. 4, 1811; State Papers, Indian Affairs, p. 779.

turbed; but presently the Western people learned that the Prophet had returned to Tippecanoe, and that all things had resumed their old aspect, except that no one could foresee when the Indians would choose to retaliate for Harrison's invasion.

Toward January, Tecumthe returned from the South, and sent word that he was ready to go to Washington. March 1, 1812, a deputation of some eighty Indians visited Vincennes, and told Harrison that the whole winter had been passed in sending messages to the different villages to consult on their future course, and that all agreed to ask for peace. They blamed the Prophet for the affair at Tippecanoe, and asked leave to visit Washington to obtain peace from the President. Harrison gladly assented, for a delegation of Indians sent to Washington was a guaranty of peace during the time of their absence. He expected them to appear at Fort Wayne in April, ready for the journey.

The Indian hesitation was probably due to doubt whether war would take place between the United States and England. The whole influence of the British agents was exerted to unite the Indians and to arm them, but to prevent a premature outbreak. The British Indian agent at Amherstburg sent Tecumthe a message blaming the attack on Harrison. Tecumthe replied:[1] —

"You tell us to retreat or turn to one side should the Big Knives come against us. Had I been at home in the late unfortunate affair I should have done so; but those I left at home were (I cannot call them men) a poor set of people, and their scuffle with the Big Knives I compared to a struggle between little children who only scratch each other's faces. The Kickapoos, Winnebagoes have since been at Post Vincennes and settled the matter amicably."

The situation was well understood. "If we have a British war, we shall have an Indian war," wrote the commandant from Fort Wayne.[2] "From the best information I can get, I have every reason to believe we shall have an Indian war this spring, whether we have a British war or not." Harrison must

[1] MSS. Canadian Archives. C. 676, p. 147.
[2] J. Rhea to Eustis, March 14, 1812; State Papers, Indian Affairs, p. 806.

himself have felt that the campaign to Tippecanoe could only add to his dangers unless it was followed up. After April 1, 1812, illusions vanished; for Indian hostilities began all along the border. April 6 two settlers were murdered within three miles of Fort Dearborn, at Chicago; several murders were committed near Fort Madison, above St. Louis, on the Mississippi; but the warning which spread wild alarm throughout Indiana was the murder of a whole family early in April within five miles of Vincennes, and April 14 that of a settler within a few miles of the Ohio River. Another murder a few weeks afterward, on the White River, completed the work of terror.

Then a general panic seized the people. The militia dared not turn out; for while they collected at one spot, the Indians might attack their isolated cabins. Even Vincennes was thought to be in danger, and the stream of fugitives passed through it as rapidly as possible on their way southward, until depopulation threatened the Territory.[1] "Most of the citizens in this country," reported Harrison, May 6,[2] "have abandoned their farms, and taken refuge in such temporary forts as they have been able to construct. Nothing can exhibit more distress than those wretched people crowded together in places almost destitute of every necessary accommodation." Misled by the previous peaceful reports, the Government had sent the Fourth Regiment to Detroit; not even a company of militia could be procured nearer than the falls of the Ohio; and Harrison called for help in vain.

Fortunately, Tecumthe was not yet ready for war. Six weeks after the hostilities began he appeared at a grand council, May 16, at Massassinway on the Wabash, between Tippecanoe and Fort Wayne. His speech to the tribes assembled there was more temperate than ever.[3]

"Governor Harrison made war on my people in my absence," he said. "It was the will of God that he should do so. We hope it will please God that the white people may let us live in peace; we will not disturb them, neither have

[1] Dawson, p. 263.
[2] State Papers, Indian Affairs, p. 808.
[3] Dawson, p. 266.

we done it, except when they came to our village with the intention of destroying us. We are happy to state to our brothers present that the unfortunate transaction that took place between the white people and a few of our young men at our village has been settled between us and Governor Harrison; and I will further state, had I been at home there would have been no bloodshed at that time."

He added that the recent murders had been committed by Pottawatomies not under his control, and he offered no excuse for them.

"Should the bad acts of our brothers the Pottawatomies draw on us the ill-will of our white brothers, and they should come again and make an unprovoked attack on us at our village, we will die like men; but we will never strike the first blow. . . . We defy a living creature to say we ever advised any one, directly or indirectly, to make war on our white brothers. It has constantly been our misfortune to have our views misrepresented to our white brethren. This has been done by pretended chiefs of the Pottawatomies and others that have been in the habit of selling land to the white people that did not belong to them."

This was the situation on the Wabash in May and June, 1812. Not only was Tecumthe unwilling to strike the first blow, but he would not even retaliate Harrison's invasion and seizure of the disputed territory. He waited for Congress to act, but every one knew that whenever Congress should declare war against England, war must also be waged with the Indians; and no one could doubt that after provoking the Indian war, Americans ought to be prepared to wage it with effect, and without complaint of its horrors.

Chapter VI

THE WAR FEVER of 1811 swept far and wide over the country, but even at its height seemed somewhat intermittent and imaginary. A passion that needed to be nursed for five years before it acquired strength to break into act, could not seem genuine to men who did not share it. A nation which had submitted to robbery and violence in 1805, in 1807, in 1809, could not readily lash itself into rage in 1811 when it had no new grievance to allege; nor could the public feel earnest in maintaining national honor, for every one admitted that the nation had sacrificed its honor, and must fight to regain it. Yet what honor was to be hoped from a war which required continued submission to one robber as the price of resistance to another? President Madison submitted to Napoleon in order to resist England; the New England Federalists preferred submitting to England in order to resist Napoleon; but not one American expected the United States to uphold their national rights against the world.

Politicians of the old school looked coldly on the war spirit. Nations like individuals, when driven to choose between desperate courses, might at times be compelled to take the chances of destruction, often destroying themselves, or suffering irreparable harm. Yet the opponents of war could argue that Americans were not placed between desperate alternatives. They had persevered hitherto, in spite of their leaders, in the policy of peace; had suffered much injury and acute mortification, but had won Louisiana and West Florida, had given democracy all it asked, and had remained in reasonable harmony with the liberal movement of the world. They were reaping the fruit of their patient and obstinate husbandry; for Russia and Sweden were about to fight their battles without reward. Napoleon offered them favors more or less real, and even England could not long resist the pressure of her interests. Jefferson's policy had wrought all the evil it could cause,—perhaps it had cost the highest price the nation could pay; but after the nation had suffered the evil and paid the price, it had a right to the profit. With more force than in 1798, the old Republicans pleaded that if they should throw aside their principles and plunge into hostilities with England, they would not only sacrifice the results of six years' humiliation, but would throw the United States athwart the liberal movement of Europe, destroy the hopes of pure government at home, and with more eagerness than they had shown for the past ten years in stripping government of its power, must devote themselves to the task of rebuilding a sovereignty as terrible in peace as in war.

The moment for fighting, conservatives argued, had come in 1807, had passed in 1809; and henceforward good policy called only for perseverance in the course that had been so persistently preferred. Not merely old Republicans, but an actual majority of the people probably held these opinions; yet the youthful energy of the nation, which had at last come to its strength under the shelter of Jefferson's peaceful rule, cried out against the cowardice of further submission, and insisted on fighting if only to restore its own self-respect.

The course of Massachusetts had much to do with changing the current of opinion. Hitherto this State had barred the way to a British war. Although the Republican party in Massachusetts several times elected their candidate for governor by majorities more or less decisive, they failed to gain full control of the State legislature before 1811. In 1810 they elected Elbridge Gerry and a majority of the representatives, but they still lacked one vote to give them control of the Senate. In April, 1811, Gerry succeeded once more, defeating Christopher Gore, the Federalist candidate, by a majority of three thousand votes; while the House, which consisted of some six hundred and fifty members, chose a Republican speaker by a majority of thirty-one. For the first time the Republicans controlled also a majority, though only of one vote, in the State Senate. This success, gained in spite of the unpopular Non-importation Act, gave extraordinary confidence to the Government, and left the Federalists powerless. Timothy Pickering lost his seat in the United States Senate, and Speaker Varnum received it. The Republicans hastened to introduce, and to carry through the Massachusetts legislature, measures that threatened to upturn the foundation of Federalist society. Other measures still more radical were expected. Jefferson's hopes of reforming Massachusetts were almost fulfilled; but the success which gave reality to them removed the last obstacle to war with England.

As the autumn advanced, the Republican newspapers broke into a general cry for war. The British minister's refusal to withdraw the Orders in Council, the return of Pinkney from London, the affair of the "Little Belt," the notorious relations between the northwestern Indians and the British traders,— all served to increase the ill-temper of a public trying to lash itself into an act it feared. Even the battle at Tippecanoe, although evidently contrary to British interest, was charged to British influence. As though England had not already given cause for a score of wars, the press invented new grievances, and became as eager to denounce imaginary crimes as to correct flagrant and chronic wrongs.

The matter of impressments then began to receive the attention which had never yet been given it. Hitherto neither Government nor people had thought necessary to make a *casus belli* of impressments. Orders in Council and other measures of Great Britain which affected American property had been treated as matters of vital consequence; but as late as the close of 1811, neither the President, the Secretary of State, nor Congress had yet insisted that the person of an American citizen was as sacred as his property. Impressments occurred daily. No one knew how many native-born Americans had been taken by force from the protection of the American flag; but whether the number was small or great, neither Republican nor Federalist had ventured to say that the country must at all hazards protect them, or that whatever rules of blockade or contraband the belligerents might adopt against property, they must at least keep their hands off the persons of peaceable Americans whether afloat or ashore. President Madison had repeated, until the world laughed in his face, that Napoleon no longer enforced his decrees, and that therefore if England did not withdraw her blockade, war would result; but he had never suggested that America would fight for her sailors. When he and his supporters in earnest took up the grievances of the seamen, they seemed to do so as an afterthought, to make out a cause of war against England, after finding the public unwilling to accept the cause at first suggested. However unjust the suspicion might be, so much truth existed in

this Federalist view of Madison's course as warranted the belief that if England in July, 1811, had yielded to the demand
for commercial freedom, the Government would have become deaf to the outcry of the imprisoned seamen. Only by
slow degrees, and in the doubtful form of a political manœuvre, did this, the worst of all American grievances, take
its proper place at the head of the causes for war.

Winter drew near, finding the public restless, irritable,
more than half afraid of its own boldness, but outspoken at
last. British frigates once more blockaded New York, seizing
ships and impressing men without mercy, while the British
prize-courts, after a moment's hesitation, declared that the
French Decrees were not repealed, and that American vessels
sailing to France were good prize. Under these irritations the
temper of the American press became rapidly worse, until war
was declared to be imminent, and the conquest of Canada
became the favorite topic of newspaper discussion.

Yet the true intentions of the President and his Cabinet
were as uncertain as those of the Twelfth Congress, which
had not yet met. A very large part of the public could not
believe war to be possible, and the Government itself shared
so far in the doubt as to wait for Congress to give the impulse
so often refused. When the President and his Cabinet met in
Washington to prepare for the session of Congress called for
November 4, a month earlier than usual, neither the Cabinet
nor the congressmen felt a certainty of the future; and so little
did the outside world believe in war, that Madison, Monroe,
and Gallatin were supposed to be aiming at a diplomatic
rather than at a military victory. In truth they had no well-
defined plan. The process by which a scattered democracy
decided its own will, in a matter so serious as a great and
perhaps fatal war, was new to the world; bystanders were
surprised and amused at the simplicity with which the people
disputed plans of war and peace, giving many months of
warning and exact information to the enemy, while they
showed no sign of leadership, discipline, or union, or even a
consciousness that such qualities were needed. Men like Josiah Quincy, Rufus King, John Randolph, and even Madison
and Gallatin, seeing that the people themselves, like the machine of government they had invented, were incompetent to

the work of war, waited with varied emotions, but equally believing or fearing that at last a fatal crisis was at hand.

Monroe was far from easy; but he had accepted, as was his wont, the nearest dominating will, and he drifted without an effort, although his old friends had already parted company with him. Though obliged to support the President in holding that Napoleon's decrees were withdrawn so that they had ceased to violate the neutral commerce of the United States, he showed that he did so, not so much because he thought it the truth, as because England gave him no choice. To Serurier, the French minister, Monroe made little concealment of his real wishes; and when Serurier first called at the Department after Monroe's return from Virginia, he heard nothing that greatly pleased him.

"I found the Secretary of State," wrote Serurier, October 23,[1] "nearly in the same state of mind in which I left him at his departure for Virginia. He told me at the outset that although the information received by the President during the last two months had added to his hopes, it had not yet completed his conviction on the decrees; that he could not believe them entirely repealed so long as there remained in our ports a single vessel captured by our privateers since November. . . . He pretended that very recent advices from Naples announced an order sent lately from Paris to sell the American prizes, and this news had been very disagreeable to the Executive, and had thrown it into new uncertainties. . . . He returned again to our customs-tariff, and the indispensability of its reduction."

Serurier exerted himself to infuse what he called proper spirit into the secretary's temper, complaining that England was actually engaged in making war on American commerce with France while enjoying all the advantages of American trade,—

"A very dangerous situation for an alliance, I added, where all the advantage is for your enemies, and all the loss is for your friends. Mr. Monroe agreed to all this; but he pretended that this false position could be viewed only as a

[1] Serurier to Maret, Oct. 23, 1811; Archives des Aff. Étr. MSS.

transition to a more decided state of things; that the present situation was equally burdensome and intolerable to the citizens, and little suited to the dignity of the Government; that it was necessary to wait for despatches from Mr. Barlow. Then he fell back once more on his theme,—that whenever they should be perfectly satisfied on the side of France, and also of the Emperor's friendship, they would certainly adopt very energetic measures toward England. . . . 'We shall not go backward,' said Mr. Monroe to me; 'we shall be inflexible about the repeal of the Orders in Council. But in order to go further, to bring us to great resolutions, the Emperor must aid us; private and public interest must make the same demand. The President does indeed hold the rudder of the Ship of State; he guides, but it is public opinion which makes the vessel move. On France depends the winning of public opinion; and we wish for it, as you can well conceive that in our position we should.'"

Serurier knew no more than this, which was no more than all the world could see. The British minister was not so well informed. After an exchange of notes with Monroe, which left matters where they were, Foster learned from Monroe, October 30, that the Government was waiting for Barlow's despatches, and if these should prove unsatisfactory, some restriction of French commerce would be imposed by way of retaliation on the restrictions imposed by Napoleon.[1] Foster hoped for a turn in affairs favorable to himself, and tried to bring it about, not only by suggesting to Lord Wellesley the wisdom of concessions from England, but also by offering a frank and fair reparation for the "Chesapeake" outrage. He wrote, November 1, to the Secretary of State renewing the formal disavowal of Berkeley's unauthorized act, and offering to restore the men to the vessel from which they had been taken, with compensation to themselves and families. Somewhat coldly Monroe accepted the offer. The two surviving seamen were in due time brought from their prison at Halifax and restored to the deck of the "Chesapeake" in Boston harbor; the redress was made as complete as such tardy justice

[1] Foster to Wellesley, Nov. 5, 1811; MSS. British Archives.

could ever be, but the time had passed when it could atone for the wrong.

Both Foster and Serurier felt that the people were further advanced than the Government in hostility to England, and that this was especially true in the matter of impressments; but no one, even at the White House, knew certainly what to expect from the new Congress assembling at Washington Nov. 4, 1811. That this body differed greatly from any previous Congress was clear, if only because it contained some seventy new members; but another difference, less easily measured, was more serious. The active leaders were young men. Henry Clay of Kentucky, William Lowndes, John Caldwell Calhoun, David R. Williams, Langdon Cheves of South Carolina, Felix Grundy of Tennessee, Peter Buell Porter of New York, Richard Mentor Johnson of Kentucky, had none of them reached his fortieth year; while Madison and his Cabinet belonged to a different generation. None of the new leaders could remember the colonial epoch, or had taken a share in public life except under the Constitution of 1789, or had been old enough to feel and understand the lessons taught by opposition to the Federalist rule. They knew the Federalists only as a faction, more or less given to treasonable talk, controlling some thirty or forty votes in the House, and proclaiming with tedious iteration opinions no one cared to hear. The young war Republicans, as they were called, felt only contempt for such a party; while, as their acts showed, they were filled with no respect for the technicalities of their Executive head, and regarded Gallatin with distrust. Of statesmanship, in the old sense, they took little thought. Bent on war with England, they were willing to face debt and probable bankruptcy on the chance of creating a nation, of conquering Canada, and carrying the American flag to Mobile and Key West.

After ten years devoted to weakening national energies, such freshness of youth and recklessness of fear had wonderful popular charm. The reaction from Jefferson's system threatened to be more violent than its adoption. Experience seemed to show that a period of about twelve years measured the beat of the pendulum. After the Declaration of Independence, twelve years had been needed to create an efficient

Constitution; another twelve years of energy brought a reaction against the government then created; a third period of twelve years was ending in a sweep toward still greater energy; and already a child could calculate the result of a few more such returns.

Had the majority of the House been in a gentler mood, its choice for Speaker should have fallen on Macon, once more a sound party man prepared to support war; but Macon was set aside. Bibb of Georgia, a candidate of the minority, received only thirty-eight voices, while seventy-five were given for Henry Clay. Clay was barely thirty-four years of age, and was a new member of the House; but he was the boldest and most active leader of the war Republicans. He immediately organized the committees for war. That on Foreign Relations, the most immediately important, was put into the hands of Porter, Calhoun, and Grundy. Military affairs were placed in charge of David R. Williams. Langdon Cheves became chairman of the Naval Committee. Ezekiel Bacon and Cheves stood at the head of the Ways and Means.

November 5 the President's Message was read, and its account of the situation seemed to offer hardly the chance of peace. England, it said, had refused the "reasonable step" of repealing its Orders in return for the extinction of the French Decrees; while the new British minister had made "an indispensable condition of the repeal of the British Orders, that commerce should be restored to a footing that would admit the productions and manufactures of Great Britain, when owned by neutrals, into markets shut against them by her enemies,—the United States being given to understand that in the mean time a continuation of their Non-importation Act would lead to measures of retaliation." Instead of repealing the orders, the British government, "at a moment when least to have been expected," put them into more rigorous execution; "indemnity and redress for other wrongs have continued to be withheld; and our coasts and the mouths of our harbors have again witnessed scenes not less derogatory to the dearest of our national rights than vexatious to the regular course of our trade." In some respects Madison's statement of grievances sounded almost needlessly quarrelsome; yet even in this list of causes which were to warrant a declaration of war, the President did not expressly mention impressments, in comparison with which his other grievances sank, in the afterthought, to insignificance.

Of France, also, the President spoke in language far from friendly. Although the decrees were revoked, "no proof is yet given," he said, "of an intention to repair the other wrongs done to the United States, and particularly to restore the great amount of American property seized and condemned under edicts . . . founded in such unjust principles that the reparation ought to have been prompt and ample." In addition to this, the United States had much reason to be dissatisfied with "the rigorous and unexpected restrictions" imposed on their trade with France, which if continued would lead to retaliation. Not a word did the Message contain of friendly or even civil regard for the French government.

Then followed the sentences which could be read only in the sense of an invitation to war: —

"I must now add that the period has arrived which claims from the legislative guardians of the national rights a system of more ample provisions for maintaining them. Notwithstanding the scrupulous justice, the protracted moderation, and the multiplied efforts on the part of the United States to substitute for the accumulating dangers to the peace of the two countries all the mutual advantages of re-established friendship and confidence, we have seen that the British Cabinet perseveres not only in withholding a remedy for other wrongs so long and so loudly calling for it, but in the execution, brought home to the threshold of our territory, of measures which, under existing circumstances, have the character as well as the effect of war on our lawful commerce. With this evidence of hostile inflexibility in trampling on rights which no independent nation can relinquish, Congress will feel the duty of putting the United States into an armor and an attitude demanded by the crisis, and corresponding with the national spirit and expectations."

The report of Secretary Gallatin, sent to the House November 22, bore also a warlike character. For the past year Gallatin told a cheerful story. In spite of the non-importation, the receipts from customs and other revenue exceeded $13,500,000, while the current expenses had not reached $8,000,000. If war should be declared, the secretary asked only for an increase of fifty per cent in the duties, in order to make sure of a fixed revenue of nine million dollars; and should this increase of duty be insufficient for the purpose, the deficiency could be supplied without difficulty by a further increase of duties, by a restoration of the impost on salt, and by "a proper selection of moderate internal taxes." With a revenue of nine million dollars secured, the Treasury could rely on loans to defray extraordinary expenses, and a few years of peace would supply the means of discharging the debt incurred.

If this was different finance from that which Gallatin had taught in other days, and by which he had risen to popularity and power, it was at least as simple as all that Gallatin did; but the simplicity of his methods, which was their chief professional merit, caused also their chief reproach. History showed the financial charlatan to be popular, not so much because he was dishonest as because he gratified an instinct for gambling as deep as the instinct of selfishness; and a common notion of a financier was that of a man whose merit lay in the discovery of new sources of wealth, or in inventing means of borrowing without repayment. Gallatin professed to do neither. He did not recommend the issue of paper money; he saw no secret hoards buried in the unsold public lands; he would listen to no tricks or devices for raising money. If money was needed he would borrow it, and would pay whatever it was worth; but he would not suggest that any device could relieve the public from taxing itself to pay whatever the public chose to spend.

"The ability and will of the United States faithfully to perform their engagements are universally known; and the terms of loans will in no shape whatever be affected by want of confidence in either. They must, however, depend not only upon the state of public credit, and on the ability to lend, but also on the existing demand for capital required for other objects. Whatever this may be, the money wanted by the public must be purchased at its market price.

. . . The most simple and direct is also the cheapest and safest mode."

Gallatin instanced, as an extreme case, the borrowing of forty millions at eight instead of the legal rate of six per cent, which he declared an inconsiderable difference if compared with the effects of other modes of raising money. No one whose judgment deserved respect doubted the correctness of his opinion; but Republican congressmen had for twelve years denounced the Federalist loan of 1798, when five millions had been borrowed at eight per cent, and they hardly dared face their constituents when their own Secretary of the Treasury talked of borrowing forty millions at the same exorbitant rate. Gently as Gallatin hinted at "a proper selection of moderate internal taxes," they remembered that these internal taxes had broken the Federalist party to pieces. They were angry with Gallatin for not providing other means for the war than loans and taxes, and they regarded him as not unwilling to check and chill the military ardor of the nation.

The President's Message, as far as it regarded foreign affairs, was referred in the House, November 11, to a select committee, the chairman of which was Peter B. Porter, with Calhoun and Grundy to support his well-known opinions. Although the nature of their report could hardly be doubted, no one seemed confident that it would be taken seriously. Macon wrote privately, November 21, to his old friend Joseph Nicholson, that he was still ignorant of the leaders' intentions:[1] —

"At this place we are nearly all too wise or too mysterious to form hasty conclusions; it is, however, probable that there are not more than five or six opinions among us, varying from open war to repealing the present restrictive system. I have had but little communication with the knowing ones, and have in some degree guessed at the number of different opinions. I am almost certain that no plan is yet adopted by the leaders in the House."

Within a week Macon found that a plan was made, but it seemed to come wholly from the White House. The Secretary

[1] Macon to Nicholson, Nov. 21, 1811; Nicholson MSS.

of War appeared before the Committee of Foreign Relations and explained what the President wanted;[1] at the same time Secretary Monroe communicated to the French minister the nature of the Executive plan.[2]

"Mr. Monroe added," wrote Serurier, November 28, ". . . that the situation of affairs should leave me no doubt as to his Excellency's [the President's] disposition; that the Government had lost every illusion as to the repeal of the Orders in Council, and was decided in adopting measures of rigor; that we might be assured it would not retreat; that ten thousand regulars were to be raised and placed at the disposition of the Executive, with a great number of volunteers; that the posts would be put in a state of defence, the navy increased, and merchants authorized to arm for the protection of their commerce; that this measure, now that our decrees were withdrawn, could strike at England alone; that the Administration in taking this resolution had perfectly seen where it led; that evidently this situation would not last three months, and would inevitably lead to a decision for which the country was prepared; that the Committee of Foreign Relations in the House of Representatives would report within a few days, and he had no doubt that these measures would pass by a great majority."

A few days later Serurier had conversations with Monroe and Madison on the subject of the Spanish American colonies, whose independence they agreed to assist not only by moral but also by material aid. The French minister closed his despatch by adding that Congress was at the moment listening to the report of the Committee of Foreign Relations. "Mr. Monroe repeated to me that he considered war as pretty nearly decided."

If the British minister knew less exactly what was happening behind the scenes, he still knew enough to alarm him. He reported that the Government was actively organizing its party in Congress; that different sets of members met every evening in caucus, and were instilled with the ideas of the

[1] Annals of Congress, 1811–1812, p. 715.
[2] Serurier to Maret, Nov. 28, 1811; Archives des Aff. Étr. MSS.

Administration;[1] but that while the members of the Government were to all appearance still undecided themselves, it would be rash for other persons to express a decided opinion. A few days after writing in this doubtful sense, Foster was electrified by an outburst of temper from Monroe, who told him that the Government would send no new minister to England, and that it "had reason to believe Great Britain really wished for war with the United States."[2] Monroe added that he felt some difficulty in talking openly about the views of the Government, as some of his disclosures might be regarded as menaces. The President, though less warm than the Secretary, talked not less decidedly:

> "He owned to me that the situation of America was very embarrassing; that anything was better than remaining in such a state; and though he very strongly asserted the impossibility of America receding from the grounds she had taken, . . . said that he would ask no sacrifice of principle in Great Britain, and would have no objection to some conventional arrangement between the two countries if it should be judged necessary in the event of the Orders in Council being withdrawn. This was, however, an indispensable preliminary, for he must consider the French Decrees as revoked so far as Great Britain had a right to expect America should require their revocation."

Although Foster became more nervous from day to day, and showed strong symptoms of a wish that the Orders in Council might be modified or withdrawn, neither he nor the President informed the British government that any other cause of war existed, or that the United States meant to insist on further concessions. In secret, diplomacy flattered itself that war would still be avoided; but it reckoned without taking into account the temper of Congress.

[1] Foster to Wellesley, Nov. 9, 1811; MSS. British Archives.
[2] Foster to Wellesley, Nov. 21, 1811; Papers presented to Parliament in 1813, p. 417.

Chapter VII

T HE LEADERS of the war party next performed in Congress a scene in some respects new in the drama of history.

November 29, Peter B. Porter of New York, from the Committee of Foreign Relations, presented to the House his report, in part.

"Your committee will not incumber your journals," it began, "and waste your patience with a detailed history of all the various matters growing out of our foreign relations. The cold recital of wrongs, of injuries, and aggressions known and felt by every member of this Union could have no other effect than to deaden the national sensibility, and render the public mind callous to injuries with which it is already too familiar."

Admission of weakness in the national sensibility gave the key-note of the report, and of the speeches that supported it. Even the allusion to the repeal of the French Decrees showed fear lest the truth might make the public mind callous to shame: —

"France at length . . . announced the repeal . . . of the Decrees of Berlin and Milan; and it affords a subject of sincere congratulation to be informed, through the official organs of the Government, that those decrees are, so far at least as our rights are concerned, really and practically at an end."

Porter had not studied the correspondence of the Department of State so thoroughly as to learn that Russia and Sweden were in the act of making war to protect American rights from the operation of those decrees which, as he was informed, were "really and practically at an end." His report ignored these difficulties, but added that England affected to deny the practical extinction of the French Decrees. In truth, England not affectedly but positively denied the extinction of those decrees; the United States offered no sufficient evidence to satisfy even themselves; and a declaration of war founded on England's "affected" denial was in a high degree likely to deaden the national sensibility. With more reason and effect, the committee dwelt on the severity with which England enforced her blockades as far as the American coast; and last of all, added, almost in a tone of apology, an allusion to the practice of impressments:—

"Your committee are not, however, of that sect whose worship is at the shrine of a calculating avarice; and while we are laying before you the just complaints of our merchants against the plunder of their ships and cargoes, we cannot refrain from presenting to the justice and humanity of our country the unhappy case of our impressed seamen. Although the groans of these victims of barbarity for the loss of (what should be dearer to Americans than life) their liberty; although the cries of their wives and children, in the privation of protectors and parents, have of late been drowned in the louder clamors at the loss of property,— yet is the practice of forcing our mariners into the British navy, in violation of the rights of our flag, carried on with unabated rigor and severity. If it be our duty to encourage the fair and legitimate commerce of this country by protecting the property of the merchant, then indeed, by as much as life and liberty are more estimable than ships and goods, so much more impressive is the duty to shield the persons of our seamen, whose hard and honest services are employed equally with those of the merchants in advancing under the mantle of its laws the interests of their country."

Truisms like these, matters of course in the oldest despotisms of Europe, and the foundation of even Roman society, sounded altogether new in the mouth of a democratic Legislature, which uttered them as though their force were not universally admitted. The weakness of the report in its premises was not strengthened by vigor in the self-excuses that followed, more apologetic than convincing:—

"If we have not rushed to the field of battle, like the nations who are led by the mad ambition of a single chief or the avarice of a corrupted court, it has not proceeded from a fear of war, but from our love of justice and humanity."

As the sway of Jefferson's philosophy ceased, these formulas, never altogether pleasing, became peculiarly repulsive. Indeed, the only sentence in the committee's report that commanded respect was its concluding appeal to the people to abandon the policy which had proceeded, as it claimed, from their love of justice and humanity: —

"The period has arrived when in the opinion of your committee it is the sacred duty of Congress to call forth the patriotism and resources of the country. By the aid of these, and with the blessing of God, we confidently trust we shall be enabled to procure that redress which has been sought for by justice, by remonstrance, and forbearance in vain."

The report closed with six Resolutions, recommending an increase of ten thousand men to the regular army; a levy of fifty thousand volunteers; the outfit of all the vessels of war not in actual service; and the arming of merchant vessels.

In opening the debate on the report, Porter spoke in language more candid than the report itself. "It was the determination of the committee," he said, "to recommend open and decided war, — a war as vigorous and effective as the resources of the country and the relative situation of ourselves and our enemy would enable us to prosecute." He went so far as to point out the intended military operations, — the destruction of British fisheries, and of British commerce with America and the West Indies, and the conquest of Canada. "By carrying on such a war at the public expense on land, and by individual enterprise at sea, we should be able in a short time to remunerate ourselves ten-fold for all the spoliations she had committed on our commerce."

Such ideas were not unbecoming to Porter, who began life as a Federalist, and had no philosophical theories or recorded principles to explain or defend; but what Porter might advise without a qualm, was much less simple for Republicans from the South; and while his speech had its value for the public as a straightforward declaration, it had little or none for individuals who were conscious that it advised what they had always condemned. The true spokesman of the committee was not Porter, but Felix Grundy of Tennessee.

Grundy, like Henry Clay a Virginian by birth and born the same year, 1777, like Clay began his career in Kentucky, where he rose to be chief-justice of the State before he was thirty years old. In 1807 he removed from Kentucky to Tennessee, and was next elected to the Twelfth Congress expressly to advocate war. As a new member, whose duty, like that of all new members, required him to exchange some controversial hostilities with John Randolph, he could not afford to miss his mark; and when Randolph called upon him by a sneering request to tell what were the constitutional resources of the committee and its talents, Grundy spoke. He apologized for his remarks as embarrassed, and indeed his speech showed less fluency than the subject and occasion seemed to warrant; but though it made no pretence of wit or rhetoric, it went to the heart of the subject, and dealt seriously with the difficulties which Grundy and his party felt.

"What cost me more reflection than anything else," he admitted, "was the new test to which we are to put this government. We are about to ascertain by actual experiment how far our republican institutions are calculated to stand the shock of war; and whether, after foreign danger has disappeared, we can again assume our peaceful attitude without endangering the liberties of the people."

At the outset, Grundy stumbled upon the difficulty which checked every movement of his party. Obliged to reconcile his present action with the attitude taken by his friends in opposition to the Federalist armaments of 1798, he could only charge that the armaments of 1798 were made not for war, but to provide Executive patronage and affect domestic politics, — a charge which, whether true or not, did not meet the objection.

"If your minds are resolved on war," continued the speaker, "you are consistent, you are right, you are still Republican; but if you are not resolved, pause and reflect, for should this Resolution pass and you then become faint-hearted, remember that you have abandoned your old principles and trod in the paths of your predecessors."

Thus, according to Grundy, from the moment a party

intended in earnest to make war against a foreign enemy, armies, loans, patronage, taxes, and every following corruption, with all the perils of European practice, became Republican. Only when armies were to be raised for domestic purposes were they unrepublican. The Administration of 1798 would gladly have accepted this test, had the Republicans then been willing to permit armaments on any terms.

Grundy weakened the argument further by attempting to show that in the present case, unlike that of 1798, sufficient cause for war existed: "It is the right of exporting the productions of our own soil and industry to foreign markets." The statement, considering Grundy's reputation, was not skilfully made. The blockades maintained by England in 1811 were less hostile to American products and industry than were the decrees of Napoleon, or the French Decrees of 1798, which confiscated every American ship laden in whole or in part with goods of English origin, and closed France to every American ship that entered an English port. Grundy still maintained that the decrees of 1798 had not justified the Federalist armaments; he could hardly maintain that the British blockades of 1811 alone gave cause for armaments of the same kind,—yet this he did. "What are we now called on to decide?" he asked. "It is whether we will resist by force the attempt . . . to subject our maritime rights to the arbitrary and capricious rule of her will."

Grundy spoke of impressments as an outrage which called loudly for the interposition of the government, but he did not allege them as in themselves a sufficient cause for war. He laid more weight on the influence of England in turning the minds of the northwestern Indians toward hostilities. "War is not to commence by land or sea; it is already begun," he said, alluding to the battle of Tippecanoe, fought a month before; yet if ever a war was aggressive, it was the war which Harrison had begun for no other object than to win the valley of the Wabash, and England had interfered neither directly nor indirectly to produce the outbreak of these hostilities.

Grundy's next argument was still less convincing. The pledge given to France, he said, made necessary the Nonimportation Law against England; but this act was an intolerable burden to the United States:—

"Ask the Northern man, and he will tell you that any state of things is better than the present. Inquire of the Western people why their crops are not equal to what they were in former years, they will answer that industry has no stimulus left, since their surplus products have no markets. Notwithstanding these objections to the present restrictive system, we are bound to retain it; this, and our plighted faith to the French government have tied the Gordian knot. We cannot untie it. We can cut it with the sword."

Reasoning like this was dear to John Randolph, never so happy as when he had such a slip to expose. In defiance of remonstrance, the President and Congress had insisted upon imposing the non-importation, on the ground that they had entered into a contract with France; and no sooner had they done so, than, in order to free themselves from their contract with France, they insisted upon war with England. On the same reasoning their only means of rendering the contract void was by annexing themselves to the empire of Napoleon. Finally Grundy appealed to an argument wholly new: —

"This war, if carried on successfully, will have its advantages. We shall drive the British from our continent. . . . I am willing to receive the Canadians as adopted brethren. It will have beneficial political effects; it will preserve the equilibrium of the government. When Louisiana shall be fully peopled, the Northern States will lose their power; they will be at the discretion of others; they can be depressed at pleasure, and then this Union might be endangered. I therefore feel anxious not only to add the Floridas to the South, but the Canadas to the North of this empire."

Grundy was the first of Southern statesmen to express publicly the Southern belief that when Louisiana and Florida should be peopled, the Northern States would lose their power and be at the discretion of others, to be depressed at pleasure. Such was the theory of the time, and the political history of the United States seemed to support it; but the Republican party in 1798 would have looked on any of its representatives as insane who had proposed to make war on England in order to give more power to the Northern States.

To this speech John Randolph replied in his usual keen and desultory style; but Randolph's arguments had lost historical interest, for the question was not so much whether war should be made, as upon what new ground the United States should stand. The Federalists, conscious of the change, held their peace. The Republicans, laboring to convince not their opponents but themselves, argued day after day that cause for war existed, as though they doubted their own assertion; but no sooner did they reach delicate ground than they became confused. Many of the speakers avoided argument, and resorted to declamation. The best representative of this class was R. M. Johnson of Kentucky, who, after five years of national submission to both European belligerents, declared that a sixth year would prove fatal: "We must now oppose the further encroachments of Great Britain by war, or formally annul the Declaration of Independence." On this doubtful foundation he imagined visionary conquests. "I should not wish to extend the boundary of the United States by war if Great Britain would leave us to the quiet enjoyment of independence; but considering her deadly and implacable enmity, and her continued hostilities, I shall never die contented until I see her expulsion from North America, and her territories incorporated with the United States." Probably these appeals carried weight with the Western people; but even earnest supporters of war might doubt whether men of sense could be conciliated or persuaded by such oratory, or by descriptions of Harrison's troops at Tippecanoe, "in the silent watches of the night, relieved from the fatigues of valor, and slumbering under the perfidious promises of the savages, who were infuriated and made drunk by British traders," and so massacred unawares.

Among the Republican speakers was J. C. Calhoun, who had lately taken his seat as a member for South Carolina. Of all the new men, Calhoun was the youngest. He had not yet reached his thirtieth birthday, and his experience in life was slight even for his years; but his speech of December 12 much excelled that of Grundy in merit, showing more clearness of statement, and fairly meeting each successive point that had been made by Randolph. Little could be added to what Calhoun said, and no objection could be justly made against it, except that as an expression of principles it had no place in the past history of the Republican party.

"Sir," exclaimed Calhoun, "I know of but one principle to make a nation great, to produce in this country not the form but the real spirit of union; and that is to protect every citizen in the lawful pursuit of his business. . . . Protection and patriotism are reciprocal. This is the road that all great nations have trod."

Of the tenets held by the Virginia school, none had been more often or more earnestly taught than that the United States ought not to be made a great nation by pursuing the road that all great nations had trod. Had Calhoun held such language in 1798, he would have been branded as a monocrat by Jefferson, and would not long have represented a Republican district; but so great was the revolution in 1811 that Calhoun, thinking little of his party and much of the nation, hardly condescended to treat with decent respect the "calculating avarice" which, though he alluded to its authors only in vague words, had been the pride of his party.

"It is only fit for shops and counting-houses," he said, "and ought not to disgrace the seat of sovereignty by its squalid and vile appearance. Whenever it touches sovereign power, the nation is ruined. It is too short-sighted to defend itself. It is an unpromising spirit, always ready to yield a part to save the balance. It is too timid to have in itself the laws of self-preservation. It is never safe but under the shield of honor."

Not without reason did Stanford of North Carolina retort that he very well recollected to have heard precisely the same doctrines in a strain of declamation at least equally handsome, upon the same subject, and from the same State; but the time was in 1799, and the speaker was the Federalist leader of the House,—Robert Goodloe Harper.

Troup of Georgia presently followed with a criticism that seemed more sensible than any yet made. He was ready to vote, but he begged for some discretion in debate. He threatened to call for the previous question if idle verbiage and empty vociferations were to take the place of energetic conduct. "Of what avail is argument, of what avail is eloquence, to convince, to persuade—whom? Ourselves? The people? Sir, if the people are to be reasoned into a war now, it is too soon, much too soon, to begin it; if their representatives here are to be led into it by the flowers of rhetoric, it is too soon, much too soon, to begin it." The House, he said, had chosen to debate in public a subject which should have been discussed with closed doors, to announce that its measures were intended as measures of offensive hostilities, that its army was to attack Canada; and what was all this but a declaration of war, contrary to all warlike custom,—a magnanimous notice to the enemy when, where, and how the blow would fall? Troup protested against this novel strategy, and pointed out the folly of attacking Canada if England were given such liberal notice to reinforce it; but sensible as the warning was, the debate, which was meant to affect public opinion both in America and in England rather than to prepare for hostilities, went on as before. Even Macon insisted on the wisdom of talking, and pledged himself to support war in order to maintain "the right to export our native produce;" while old William Findley, who had sat in almost every Congress since 1790, voted for the Resolutions on the unrepublican principle that the best means to prevent war was to prepare for it. No concealment was affected of conquests to be made in the Canadas. "Ever since the report of the Committee on Foreign Relations came into the House," said Randolph on the last day of the debate, " we have heard but one word,—like the whippoorwill, but one monotonous tone,—Canada, Canada, Canada!"

Stanford of North Carolina made one of the peculiar speeches in which he delighted, but which had ceased to irritate his party, even though he went so far as to aver that the Federalists in 1798 had more cause for war with France than existed in 1811 with England, and though he declared the Sedition Law of 1798 to be no more direct an attack on free discussion than was the "previous question" of 1810. He showed little mercy to Grundy and Calhoun, and he proved to the delight of the Federalists the inconsistency of his party; while Randolph, in another speech, redoubled his bitter comments on the changes of political faith which left no one but

Stanford and himself true to the principles for which they had taken office. They talked to deaf ears. The Republican party no longer cared for principles. Under the beneficent pressure of England, the theories of Virginia were, for the time, laid aside.

The Resolutions proposed by the Committee on Foreign Relations were adopted, December 16, by what was in effect a unanimous vote. Only twenty-two members recorded their names against the increase of the regular army, and only fifteen voted against fitting out the navy. A still stronger proof of political revolution was the vote of ninety-seven to twenty-two in favor of the Resolution which authorized merchant vessels to arm. This measure had the effect of a declaration of war. In former years it had been always rejected as improper, because it created a private war, taking from the Government and giving to private citizens the control over war and peace; but December 19 the House adopted this last and decisive measure, and while many Republicans would not vote at all, and even Lowndes and Macon voted against it, Josiah Quincy, Timothy Pitkin, and most of the extreme Federalists recorded their votes in its favor.

Meanwhile the Senate had acted. In the want of reports, no record remains of what passed in debate before December 17; but the Journal shows that William B. Giles was made chairman of the Committee on Foreign Relations, with Crawford and five other senators as his associates; and that Giles reported December 9 a bill for raising, not ten thousand regular troops, as the President recommended, but ten regiments of infantry, two of artillery, and one of cavalry,—in all twenty-five thousand men for five years, in addition to an existing army nominally ten thousand strong. Each regiment was to number two thousand men, and whether its ranks were filled or not, required a full complement of officers. Rumor reported, and Giles admitted, that his bill was not an Administration measure, but on the contrary annoyed the Administration, which had asked for all the regular force it could raise or organize within a year. The public, though unwilling to side with Giles against the President, could not but admit that the conquest of Canada by ten thousand men was uncertain, even with the assistance of volunteers and militia, while the entire scheme of war would become a subject of ridicule if Congress avowed the intention of vanquishing all the forces of Great Britain with only ten thousand raw troops.

Perhaps a better economy would have covered the ocean with cruisers, and have used the army only for defence; but although in any case the military result would probably have been what it was, the party which undertook to wage a great war by a government not at all equipped for the purpose, without experience and with narrow resources, proved wisdom in proportion as it showed caution. The President evidently held this opinion. Senator Anderson of Tennessee, acting probably on Executive advice, moved to amend the bill with a view of returning to the original plan of ten or twelve thousand additional troops; and on this motion, December 17, Giles made a speech that could not have been more mischievous had he aimed only to destroy public trust in the Government. He avowed the difference between himself and the Secretary of War in regard to the number of troops needed, and he showed only too easily that the force he proposed was not more than competent to the objects of the Government; but not content with proving himself wiser than the President and the Secretary of War, he went out of his way to attack the Secretary of the Treasury with virulence that surprised the Federalists themselves.

The decrepit state of the Treasury, said Giles, was the tenderest part of the discussion; but instead of dealing tenderly with it, he denounced Gallatin, whose financial reputation, he declared, was made to his hand by others, and was founded less on facts than on anticipation. "If reliance can be placed on his splendid financial talents, only give them scope for action, apply them to the national ability and will, let them perform the simple task of pointing out the true *modus operandi*, and what reason have we to despair of the republic? What reason have we to doubt of the abundance of the Treasury supplies? Until now the honorable secretary has had no scope for the demonstration of his splendid financial talents." He went so far as to assert that during the last three years all the measures that had dishonored the nation were, in a great degree, attributable to the unwillingness of Jefferson and Madison to disturb Gallatin's popularity and repose; that the repeal of the salt tax, the failure of the embargo, the refusal to issue letters of marque, were all due to Gallatin's influence; and that it would have been infinitely better to leave the national debt untouched, than to pay it by surrendering the smallest attribute of national sovereignty.

Giles had long been in open opposition to the President, he had intrigued with every other factious spirit to embarrass the Government, and had scandalized his own State by the bitterness of his personal hatreds; but he had not before shown himself ready to sacrifice the nation to his animosities. Every one knew that had he expected to give the Administration the splendid success of a military triumph, he would never have thrust upon it an army competent to the purpose. Every one believed that he hoped to ruin President Madison by the war that was threatened, and wished to hasten the ruin before the next autumn election. Those who had watched Giles closely knew how successfully he had exerted himself to cripple the Treasury,—how he had guided the attacks on its resources; had by his single vote destroyed Gallatin's only efficient instrument, the Bank; had again by his single vote repealed the salt tax against Gallatin's wishes; and how he had himself introduced and supported that repeal of the embargo which broke the influence of Gallatin and went far to ruin Madison's Administration before it was fairly in office. So notorious was his conduct that Senator Anderson of Tennessee and his colleague G. W. Campbell, in replying, went to the verge of the rules in charging Giles with motives of the blackest kind. Campbell pointed out that Giles's army would frustrate its own objects; would be unable to act against Canada as quickly as would be necessary, and would cause needless financial difficulty. "I trust," continued Campbell, "it is not the intention of any one by raising so large a regular force, thereby incurring so great an expenditure beyond what it is believed is necessary, to drain your treasury, embarrass your fiscal concerns, and paralyze the best concerted measures of government. If, however, such are the objects intended, a more effectual mode to accomplish them could not be adopted." Giles's speech offered an example, unparalleled in American history, of what Campbell described as "the malignity of the human mind;" but although his object was evident, only twelve senators supported Madison, while twenty-one voted for Giles's army. As though to prove the true motive of the decision, every Federalist senator voted with Giles, and their votes gave him a majority.

Giles's bill passed the Senate December 19, and was referred at once to the House Committee on Foreign Relations, which amended it by cutting down the number of troops from twenty-five thousand to fifteen thousand men; but when this amendment was proposed to the House, it met, in the words of Peter B. Porter, with a gust of zeal and passion. Henry Clay and the ardent war democrats combined with the Federalists to force the larger army on the President, although more than one sound Democrat invoked past experience and ordinary common-sense to prove that twenty-five thousand men—or even half that number—could not be found in the United States willing to enlist in the regular army and submit for five years to the arbitrary will of officers whom they did not know and with whom they had nothing in common. The House voted to raise Giles's army, but still took the precaution of requiring that the officers of six regiments only should be commissioned, until three fourths of the privates for these six regiments should have been enlisted. Another amendment was proposed giving the President discretion to raise only these six regiments, if he thought circumstances rendered the larger force unnecessary; but Grundy defeated this effort of caution by the argument that too much power had formerly been given to the Executive, and therefore Congress must insist on leaving him no discretion, but obliging him to take twice the army and double the patronage he had asked or could use. More than twenty Federalists supported Grundy, and gave him a majority of sixty-six to fifty-seven. Calhoun came to Grundy's assistance with a more reasonable argument. Delay was becoming dangerous; the New Year had arrived; the public began to doubt whether Congress meant to act; he would vote to prevent delay.

At length, January 6, the bill passed the House by a vote of ninety-four to thirty-four. Six or eight Federalists, including Josiah Quincy, voted with the majority; six or eight Republicans, including Macon, Randolph, and Stanford, voted with the minority. The bill returned to the Senate, where the amendments were immediately and almost unanimously struck out. The House, in no kind temper, was obliged to discuss the subject once more. Even the most zealous advocates of war were staggered at the thought that all the officers of thirteen new regiments in the regular army must be at once appointed, when no one felt confident that the ranks of these regiments could ever be filled. The support given by the Federalists to every extravagant measure increased the uneasiness of Republicans; and John Randolph's ridicule, founded as it was on truth, did not tend to calm it.

"After you have raised these twenty-five thousand men," said Randolph, "if I may reason on an impossibility,—for it has, I think, been demonstrated that these men cannot be raised, it will be an army on paper only,—shall we form a Committee of Public Safety, or shall we depute the power to the Speaker—I should not wish it in safer hands—to carry on the war? Shall we declare that the Executive, not being capable of discerning the public interest, or not having spirit to pursue it, we have appointed a committee to take the President and Cabinet into custody? . . . You have an agent to execute certain business; he asks from you a certain amount for effecting the business on hand; you give him double,—you force it upon him, you compel him to waste it!"

Again the Federalists decided the result. Half of the Federalist members voted with the extreme war Republicans. The House, by sixty-seven votes to sixty, abandoned its amendments; the bill passed, as Giles had framed it, and January 11 received the President's signature.

Chapter VIII

THE ARMY BILL was understood to decide not so much the war as the change in domestic politics. That the party of Jefferson, Madison, Gallatin, and Monroe should establish a standing army of thirty-five thousand troops in time of peace, when no foreign nation threatened attack, and should do this avowedly for purposes of conquest, passed the bounds of inconsistency and proclaimed a revolution. This radical change was no longer disguised. Clay, Calhoun, Grundy, Lowndes, and Cheves made only a bare pretence of respecting the traditions of their party; while Giles, with a quality peculiar to himself, excused his assaults on Madison by doing public penance for his ancient errors in maligning Washington. "Further information and reflection," he said, "and practical experience of more than twenty years, have completely convinced me of the superiority of the talent of this great man as a statesman as well as a soldier, and have also admonished me of my former errors." If in America any politician could be found to whose public character such an admission was fatal, Giles might be regarded as the person; but conduct that ruined Giles's character only raised the reputations of Clay, Lowndes, and Calhoun. These younger men were not responsible for what had been said and done ten or fifteen years before; they had been concerned in no conspiracy to nullify the laws, or to offer armed resistance to the government; they had never rested their characters as statesmen on the chance of success in governing without armaments, and in coercing Napoleon and Pitt by peaceable means; they had no past to defend or excuse, and as yet no philosophical theories to preach,—but they were obliged to remove from their path the system their party had established, and they worked at this task with more energy and with much more success than they showed in conducting foreign war. Even a return to Washington's system would not answer their purpose, for they were obliged to restore the extreme practices of 1798, and to re-enact the laws which had then been denounced and discarded as the essence of monarchy.

Bitterly as all good Republicans regretted to create a standing army, that vote was easy compared with other votes it made necessary. Doubtless an army was an evil, but the effects of the evil were likely to appear chiefly in the form of taxes; and the stanchest war Republicans flinched at taxation. The British minister, who saw so much of these difficulties that he could not believe in the possibility of war, reported to his Government a story which showed how uneasily the Administration balanced itself between the two bodies of its supporters. In December, during the debate on the Army Bill, the Committee of Ways and Means was repeatedly urged to produce a scheme of war-finance, but failed to do so. Foster reported, on what he called good authority, that when the chairman of that committee went to Gallatin for information to meet questions in the House, the secretary declined giving estimates until the Army Bill should be disposed of; and he explained that if he submitted a plan of taxes, the Government would be charged with wanting to damp the ardor of Congress.[1] Every one knew that the ardor of Congress feared nothing so much as damping; but every one who knew Gallatin was persuaded that as long as he remained Secretary of the Treasury, taxes must proportionally increase with debt.

Foster's story was probably true; for although Ezekiel Bacon, chairman of the Ways and Means Committee, wrote as early as Dec. 9, 1811, to the secretary for advice, the secretary delayed his answer until January 10, the day when Congress agreed to pass the Army Bill. The letter was read to the House January 20, and proved, as had been foreseen, a serious discouragement to the war spirit. Yet Gallatin made an underestimate of financial difficulties; for while he assumed the fixed charges at $9,600,000, and estimated the receipts from customs under the existing duties at only $2,500,000 during war, he assumed also the committee's estimate of $10,000,000 as the annual loan that would be required to meet the expense of war. In order to pay the fixed charges of government, the customs revenue must be raised to $6,000,000; and for this purpose he asked Congress not only to double the existing duties, but also to reimpose the old duty on salt. To meet the remaining charge of $3,600,000 and the accruing interest on

[1] Foster to Wellesley, Jan. 16, 1812; MSS. British Archives.

new loans, he asked for internal taxes to the amount of $5,000,000.

Unfortunately Gallatin had carelessly said, in his annual re-port of November, that a revenue of nine millions would, with the aid of loans, answer the purposes of war; while his letter of January 10 required, as was proper, that the interest of each new loan should be added annually to the nine mil-lions. The difference amounted to $600,000 for the first year alone, and in each successive year increased taxation by at least an equal sum. Gallatin himself was in a defiant mood, as he well might be, since he saw Congress in a position where it must either submit or take the responsibility of bankrupting the Treasury; and he did not content himself with demanding unpopular taxes, but read Congress a lecture on its own con-duct that had made these taxes necessary. He recalled his promise of 1808 that "no internal taxes, either direct or indi-rect, were contemplated even in the case of hostilities carried on against the two great belligerent powers;" and he showed that since 1808 Congress had thrown away his actual or expected balance of twenty millions, had refused to accept twenty millions that might have been obtained from the Bank, and had thus made internal taxes necessary, while mak-ing loans more difficult to obtain even on harder terms.

The sting of this reproof came at the end of the secretary's letter, where he named the objects of internal taxation. These were spirits, refined sugar, licenses to retailers, auctions, stamps, and carriages for conveyance of persons. Here was the whole armory of Federalism, that had once already roused rebellion, and after causing the grievances which brought the Republicans into power, appeared again threatening to ruin them as it had ruined their predecessors. Standing army of thirty-five thousand men, loans, protective duties, stamps, tax on distillation,—nothing but a Sedition Law was wanting; and the previous question, as a means of suppressing discus-sion, was not an unfair equivalent for the Sedition Law.

Gallatin's letter caused no little excitement in the House. Congress recoiled, and for more than a month left the subject untouched. The chance that England might still give way, or that something might at the last prevent actual war, made every member anxious to avoid committing himself on matters of taxation. The number of representatives who favored war was supposed not to exceed forty or fifty in a House of one hundred and forty-one,—as many more would vote for war only in case they must; but the war men and the peace men united in private to fall upon Gallatin,—the first, because he had chilled the national spirit by saying that taxes must be laid; the last, because he had not said it earlier, and had not chilled the national spirit once for all.

Laying aside the question of taxes, Congress took up two other subjects of pressing importance. Every one doubted the possibility of raising a regular army, and those persons who knew best the character of the people were convinced that the war must be waged by militia on land, and by privateers on the ocean.

The House began with the militia. December 26 Porter brought in a bill authorizing the President "to accept of any company or companies of volunteers, either of artillery, cavalry, or infantry, who may associate and offer themselves for the service, not exceeding fifty thousand," officered according to the law of the State to which the companies belonged, and liable to service for one year, with the pay of regular troops. Evidently these volunteers were State militia, and were subject to be used only for purposes defined in the Constitution. In 1798 the attempt to raise such a corps had been denounced as unconstitutional, a device to separate a part of the State militia in order to put it under the President's power in a manner expressly forbidden by the Constitution and peculiarly dangerous to the public liberties; and although the device of 1798 was made more evident, as its efficiency was made more certain, by the provision that these corps should be officered by the President, the device of 1812 was not less offensive to men who held that Congress had no power to call out the State militia except "to execute the laws of the Union, suppress insurrections, and repel invasions," of course only within the limits of the United States. The chief service desired from these volunteer corps was the conquest of Canada and the occupation of Florida; but every principle of the Republican party would be outraged by placing the militia at the President's orders, to serve on foreign soil.

Porter, who wanted express legislation to overcome this

difficulty, stated his dilemma to the House; and the debate began quietly on the assumption that these volunteers were not to serve in Canada or Florida without their own consent, when, January 11, Langdon Cheves, with much seriousness and even solemnity of manner and language, informed the House that the Republican party had hitherto taken a wrong view of the subject. The distinguished South Carolinian affirmed doctrines that had never before been heard from Republican lips:—

"The power of declaring and making war is a great sovereign power, whose limits and extent have long been understood and well established. It has its attributes and incidental powers, which are in the same degree less equivocal than those of other powers as it excels those powers in its importance. Do you ask then for the right of Congress to employ the militia in war? It is found among the attributes of the sovereign power which Congress has to make war. Do you ask for the limits to which this employment may extend? They are coextensive with the objects of the war."

The President himself, added Cheves, was understood to hold this opinion, and ought to be left to act under the high responsibility attached to his office. Anxious as the party was to support the President, Cheves's speech met with protest after protest, until Henry Clay came to his support and adopted his argument. On the other hand, the Federalists, although consistency required them to take the same view, and even war Republicans, like Porter and Grundy, rejected the idea of an unlimited war power, and declared that the volunteers must be retained within the national boundaries. The point was left unsettled; January 17 the House passed the bill by a vote of eighty-seven to twenty-three, leaving the decision in the President's hands, or, what was worst of all, in the hands of the volunteers. In the Senate, Giles made an interesting speech against the bill, avoiding the constitutional question, but arguing that the volunteer force would prove inefficient, and that a regular army could alone serve the purposes of war. He had no difficulty in proving the correctness of his view and the fatal folly of short enlistments; but he could not explain how the ranks of the regular army were to be filled, and his objections took no practical form. The bill passed without a division, and February 6 was approved by the President.

In this matter Congress, without absolutely rejecting Cheves's doctrine, evaded a decision; but another subject remained which was not so gently treated. From the first, the Republican party had opposed a navy. The United States owned five or six frigates, but not one ship-of-the-line; New York or Philadelphia might be blockaded, perhaps ransomed, at any time by a single seventy-four with a frigate or two in company. To seafaring men, the idea of fighting England without ships seemed absurd, but the Republican party was pledged by every line of its history not to create a navy. The dilemma was singular. Either the Republican party must recant its deepest convictions, or the war must be fought without ships except privateers, and England must be left with no anxiety but the defence of Canada.

Once more Langdon Cheves took the lead. January 17, after the House voted on the Volunteer Bill, Cheves as chairman of the Naval Committee asked an appropriation to build twelve seventy-fours and twenty frigates at a cost of seven and a half million dollars.

> "I know," he began, "how many and how strong are the prejudices, how numerous and how deeply laid are the errors which I have to encounter in the discussion of this question,—errors and prejudices the more formidable as they come recommended by the virtues and shielded by the estimable motives of those who indulge them. I have been told that this subject is unpopular, and it has been not indistinctly hinted that those who become the zealous advocates of the bill will not advance by their exertions the personal estimation in which they may be held by their political associates."

In few words Cheves avowed that while he preferred to act with the Republican party, he was in truth independent, and he warned his friends that on the subject of a navy they must in the end either conquer their prejudices or quit office.

After this preamble, Cheves struck once more at the foundations of his party. His argument, as a matter of expediency, was convincing; for every American ship-of-war, even when blockaded in port, would oblige the British to employ three ships of equal or greater size to relieve each other in blockading and watching it. The blockading service of the American station was peculiarly severe. England had no port nearer than Halifax for equipments or repairs; in general all her equipments must be made in Europe, and for only three months' service; in winter she must for months at a time abandon the blockade, and leave the coast free. No method could be devised by which, with so small risk and so little waste of money and life, the resources of England could be so rapidly drained as by the construction of heavy war-vessels. Once at sea, an American seventy-four had nothing to fear except a squadron; and even when dismantled in port, she required the attention of a hostile fleet.

The House had submitted with slowly rising ill-temper to each successive demand of the war it would have preferred to avoid; but this last requirement threw it into open revolt. Cheves found himself for a time almost alone. Even Richard M. Johnson, always ardent for war, became mournful with prophecies of the evils that Cheves was about to bring upon the country. "I will refer to Tyre and Sidon, Crete and Rhodes, to Athens and to Carthage." Plunder, piracy, perpetual war, followed the creation of every navy known to history. Armies might be temporary, but navies were permanent, and even more dangerous to freedom. "Navies have been and always will be engines of power, employed in projects of ambition and war."

These were the old and respected Republican doctrines, still dear to a large majority of the party. William Lowndes came to the support of his colleague, and ridiculed Johnson's lessons from ancient history; Henry Clay protested against the unreasonable prejudice which refused naval assistance, and which left New York and the commerce of the Mississippi at the mercy of single British ships; but when the committee of the whole House came to a vote, Cheves found a majority opposed to him on every motion for the building additional ships of any sort whatever. The House continued the debate for several days, but ended, January 27, by refusing to build frigates. The division was close. Fifty-nine members voted for the frigates; sixty-two voted against them. While Cheves, Lowndes, Calhoun, Troup, Porter, and the Federalists voted for the ships, Ezekiel Bacon, Grundy, R. M. Johnson, D. R. Williams, and the friends of the Administration in general voted against them.

By the middle of February, Congress reached a point of disorganization that threatened disaster. The most ardent urged immediate war, while not a practical step had yet been taken toward fighting. Such was the chaos that Peter B. Porter, who had himself reported the Army and Volunteer bills, asked for a committee to raise another provisional army of twenty thousand men, for the reason that the two armies already provided were useless,—the regular force, because it could not be put into the field within the year; the volunteers, because they could not lawfully be used for offensive war. "What force have we given the President?" asked Porter. "We have made a parade in passing laws to raise twenty-five thousand regular troops, and fifty thousand volunteers; but in truth and in fact we have not given him a single man." The House refused to follow Porter's advice; but as usual the war Republicans were obliged to coalesce with the Federalists in order to maintain themselves against these Executive reproaches. What Porter said was mainly true. With the exception of the peace establishment consisting of nominally ten thousand men, and the vessels of war actually afloat, the President had not yet been given means of defending the coasts and frontiers from hostile forces which, in the case of the northwestern Indians, were already actually attacking them.

In the midst of this general discouragement, February 17, Ezekiel Bacon brought in fourteen Resolutions embodying a scheme for raising money. Gallatin's measures were expected to be harsh, but those proposed by Bacon seemed more severe than had been expected. The customs duties were to be doubled; twenty cents a bushel were laid on salt, fifty cents a gallon on the capacity of stills; licenses and stamps in proportion; and a direct tax of three million dollars was to be apportioned among the States. A loan bill for eleven millions at six per cent was easily passed, but all the force of the war feeling could not overcome the antipathy to taxation. The

Resolution for doubling the customs duties met little resistance; but February 28 the House refused, by sixty to fifty-seven, to impose a duty on imported salt, and for the moment this vote threatened to ruin the whole scheme. The House adjourned for reflection; and on the following Monday a member from Virginia moved to reconsider the vote. "It now seems," he said, "that if the article of salt is excluded, the whole system of taxation will be endangered. We are told in conversation, since the vote on the salt tax, that the system which has been presented by the Committee of Ways and Means is a system of compromise and concession, and that it must be taken altogether, the bad with the good; that if we pay the salt tax, the eastern and the western country will suffer peculiarly by an increase of the impost, and by the land tax." In short, he thought it better to take the whole draught even if it were hemlock.

This view of the case did not find easy acceptance. Nelson of Virginia exhorted the majority not under any circumstances to accept the impost on salt; and Wright of Maryland, a man best known for his extravagances, took the occasion to express against Gallatin the anger which the friends of the Smiths, Giles, and Duane had stored. Gallatin, he said, was trying to fix the odium of these taxes on Congress in order to disgust the people and chill the war spirit; he was treading in the muddy footsteps of his official predecessors, in attempting to strap around the necks of the people this odious system of taxation, for which the Federalists had been condemned and dismissed from power. The salt tax would destroy the present as it had destroyed the old Administration; the true course was to lay taxes directly on property. Probably most of the Republican members sympathized in private with the feelings of Wright, but Gallatin had at last gained the advantage of position; the House voted to reconsider, and by a majority of sixty-six to fifty-four accepted the duty of twenty cents on imported salt.

The salt duty distressed the South, and in revenge many Southerners wished to impose a tax of twenty-five cents a gallon on whiskey, which would be felt chiefly in the West; but this was no part of the Treasury scheme. Grundy and R. M. Johnson succeeded in defeating the motion; and after deciding this contest, the House found no difficulty in adopting all the other Resolutions. March 4 the committee was instructed to report by bill; Bacon sent the Resolutions to the Treasury, and the secretary waited for events. Every one admitted that while war was still uncertain, the financial policy undecided, and a Presidential election approaching, only the prospect of immediate bankruptcy would outweigh the dangers of oppressive taxation.

Four months of continuous session had passed, and spring was opening, when the Legislature reached this point. The result of the winter's labor showed that the young vigor of this remarkable Congress had succeeded only in a small part of the work required to give Jefferson's peaceful system a military shape. Although the nominal regular army had been raised from ten thousand to thirty-five thousand men, the Act of Congress which ordered these men to be enlisted could not show where they were to be found; and meanwhile the sudden strain broke down the War Department. Rumor pointed at Secretary Eustis as incompetent, and the chances were great that any secretary, though sufficiently good for peace, would prove unequal to the task of creating an army without men or material to draw from. Whether the secretary was competent or not, his situation exposed him to ridicule. He had hitherto discharged the duties of Secretary of War, of Quartermaster-General, Commissary-General, Indian Commissioner, Commissioner of Pensions, and Commissioner of Public Lands; and although Congress promised to create a quartermaster's department, and had the bill already in hand, the task of organizing this department, as well as all the other new machinery of war, fell on the secretary and eight clerks, not one of whom had been twelve months in office. Any respectable counting-house would have allowed some distribution of authority and power of expansion; but the secretary could neither admit a partner nor had he the right to employ assistance. Adapted by Jefferson, in 1801, to a peace establishment of three or four regiments, the Department required reorganization throughout, or Congress would be likely to find the operations of war brought to a quick end.

Had Congress undertaken to wage war on the ocean, the same difficulty would have been felt in the navy; but this danger was evaded by the refusal to attempt naval operations. At all times the Republicans had avowed their willingness to part with the five frigates, and these were perhaps to be sent to sea with no great hope in the majority for their success; but the Navy Department was required to make no other exertion. Secretary Hamilton, like Secretary Eustis, was supposed to be unequal to his post; but his immediate burden amounted only to fitting out three frigates in addition to those in actual service, and the expenditure of two hundred thousand dollars annually for three years toward the purchase of ship-timber.

To meet the expenses thus incurred for military purposes, in the absence of taxes which, if imposed, could not be made immediately productive, Congress authorized a loan of eleven million dollars at six per cent, redeemable in twelve years.

An army of thirty-five thousand regulars which could not be raised within a year, if at all, and of fifty thousand volunteers who were at liberty to refuse service beyond the frontier, promised no rapid or extensive conquests. A navy of half-a-dozen frigates and a few smaller craft could not be expected to keep the ports open, much less to carry the war across the ocean. Privateers must be the chief means of annoyance, not so much to British pride or power as to British commerce, and this kind of warfare was popular because it cost the government nothing; but even the privateers were at a great disadvantage if the ports were to be closed to their prizes by hostile squadrons. Such means of offence were so evidently insufficient that many sensible persons could not believe in the threatened war; but these were only the most conspicuous weaknesses. Armies required equipment, and the United States depended on Europe, chiefly on England, for their most necessary supplies. The soldier in Canada was likely to need blankets; but no blankets were to be had, and the Nonimportation Act prevented them from coming into the market, whatever price might be offered.

Not only was the machinery of government unsuited to energetic use, but the Government itself was not in earnest. Hardly one third of the members of Congress believed war to be their best policy. Almost another third were Federalists, who wished to overthrow the Administration; the rest were honest and perhaps shrewd men, brought up in the school of Virginia and Pennsylvania politics, who saw more clearly the evils that war must bring than the good it might cause, and who dreaded the reaction upon their constituents. They could not understand the need of carrying into every detail a revolution in their favorite system of government. Clay and Calhoun, Cheves and Lowndes asked them to do in a single session what required half a century or more of time and experience,—to create a new government, and invest it with the attributes of old-world sovereignty under pretext of the war power. The older Republicans had no liking for such statesmanship, and would gladly have set the young Southerners in their right place.

By force of will and intellect the group of war members held their own, and dragged Congress forward in spite of itself; but the movement was slow and the waste of energy exhausting. Perhaps they failed to carry their points more often than they succeeded. Energetic as their efforts were, after four months of struggle they had settled nothing, and found themselves in March no further advanced than in November. War should already have been declared; but Congress was still trying to avoid it.

Federalists had much to do with causing the confusion of Republicans. Their conduct could seldom be explained on rational grounds, but in January, 1812, they seemed to lose reason. Their behavior, contradicting their own principles, embarrassed their friends still more than it confused their enemies. The British minister wrote to his Government constant complaints of the dangerous course his Federalist allies were pursuing.

"The Federal leaders," Foster wrote Dec. 11, 1811,[1] "make no scruple of telling me that they mean to give their votes for war, although they will remain silent in the debates; they add that it will be a short war of six or nine months. To my observations on the strange and dangerous nature of such a policy, they shrug their shoulders, telling me that they see no end to restrictions and non-importation laws but in war; that war will turn out the Administration, and

[1] Foster to Wellesley, Dec. 11, 1811; MSS. British Archives.

then they will have their own way, and make a solid peace with Great Britain."

To this policy Federalist leaders adhered. As the weeks passed, Foster's situation grew more difficult. Disgusted equally by the obstinacy of his Government and by the vacillations of Congress, he found his worst annoyances in the intrigues of his friends. Toward the close of the year he wrote:[1] —

"The situation that I find myself thus unexpectedly placed in is, I must confess, exceedingly embarrassing. I am aware that H. R. H. the Prince Regent wishes to avoid a rupture with this country, and yet I see that the efforts of a party, hitherto the most adverse to a war with Great Britain, are united with those of another, which till now has been supposed the most considerable in point of numbers, for the purpose of bringing it on; while Government, although wishing for delay, are yet so weak and little to be depended on that it is to be feared if the two Houses were to decide on hostilities, they would not have resolution enough to oppose the measure."

January 16, 1812, he wrote again.[2] Somewhat encouraged by the evident difficulties of the war party in Congress, he was then disposed to look less severely at Federalist tactics: —

"The opposition know the embarrassment of the President, and endeavor to take advantage of it by pushing for measures so decisive as to leave him no retreat. It has been told me in confidence more than once by different leaders, that if the Orders in Council are not revoked he must eventually be ruined in the opinion of the nation. Some individuals have even gone so far as to reproach us for not concerting measures with them for that purpose, observing that the French have managed this country by concert with a party; and that unless Great Britain do the same, the French party will always be predominant. I should mention to your Lordship that the Federalists are by no means united. From twelve to sixteen vote for peace measures,

[1] Foster to Wellesley, Dec. 11, 1811; MSS. British Archives.
[2] Foster to Wellesley, Jan. 16, 1812; MSS. British Archives.

while eight only, though of the leaders, vote the contrary way."

February 1, a fortnight after this letter was written, two Federalist leaders, whose names Foster wisely suppressed, called on the British minister to give him their advice as to the best course his Government could take "in order to produce a thorough amalgamation of interests between America and Great Britain." Their conversation, which seems to have been in no way invited by Foster, was reported by him to Lord Wellesley without comment of any kind.[1] Had the two Federalists foreseen the scandal to be caused, six weeks later, by the publication of John Henry's papers, they would hardly have dared approach the British minister at all; and they would at least have been reminded that such advice as they gave him was not only forbidden by law, but bordered closely upon treason.

"The sum of these suggestions was that we should neither revoke our Orders in Council nor modify them in any manner. They said this Government would, if we conceded, look upon our concessions as being the effect of their own measures, and plume themselves thereon; that they only wanted to get out of their present difficulties, and if we made a partial concession they would make use of it to escape fulfilling their pledge to go to war, still however continuing the restrictory system; whereas if we pushed them to the edge of the precipice by an unbending attitude, that then they must be lost, either by the disgrace of having nearly ruined the trade of the United States and yet failed to reduce Great Britain by their system of commercial restrictions, or else by their incapacity to conduct the government during war. These gentlemen declared they were for war rather than for the continuance of the restrictory system, even if the war should last four years. They thought no expense too great which would lead to the termination of the irritating, fretful feelings which had so long existed between the two countries. They animadverted on the peevish nature of the answers given in the affairs of the

[1] Foster to Wellesley, Feb. 2, 1812; MSS. British Archives.

'Chesapeake' and to my note on the Indians, and whenever any spirit of conciliation was shown by Great Britain, and told me it would ever be so until the people felt the weight of taxes; that nothing would bring them to a right sense of their interests but touching their purses; and that if we did go to war for a time, we should be better friends afterward. In short, they seemed to think that Great Britain could by management bring the United States into any connection with her that she pleased."

The President, as his office required, stood midway between the masses of his followers, but never failed to approve the acts and meet the wishes of the war members. Early in March, at a moment when they were greatly embarrassed, he came to their aid by a manœuvre which excited much feeling on all sides, but especially among the Federalists engaged in abetting the war policy. He seemed to have fallen on the track of a conspiracy such as had overthrown the liberties and independence of classic republics, and which left no alternative but war or self-destruction; but the true story proved more modern, if not less amusing, than the conspiracies of Greece and Rome.

Chapter IX

JOHN HENRY, whose reports from Boston to Sir James Craig at Quebec had been received with favor in 1808 and 1809 both in Canada and in London, not satisfied with such reward as he received from the governor-general, went to England and applied, as was said, for not less than thirty-two thousand pounds, or one hundred and sixty thousand dollars, as the price he thought suitable for his services and his silence.[1] Whatever was the sum he demanded, he failed to obtain it, and left England in ill humor on his return to Canada, carrying his papers with him and an official recommendation to the governor-general.

On the same ship was a Frenchman who bore the title of Count Edward de Crillon. His connections, he said, embraced the noblest and highest families of France; among his ancestors was the "brave Crillon," who for centuries had been known to every French child as the Bayard of his time. The Count Edward's father was the Duc de Crillon; by marriage he was closely connected with Bessières, the Maréchal Duc d'Istrie, Napoleon's favorite. Count Edward de Crillon had fallen into disfavor with the Emperor, and for that reason had for a time quitted France, while waiting a restoration to the army. His manners were easy and noble; he wore the decoration of the Legion of Honor, received and showed letters from his family and from the Duc d'Istrie, and talked much of his personal affairs, especially of his estate called St. Martial, "in Lebeur near the Spanish border," and, he took pride in saying, near also to the Château de Crillon, the home of his ancestors. He had met John Henry in London society. When he appeared on the Boston packet, a friendship arose between these two men so hardly treated by fortune. Henry confided his troubles to the count, and Crillon gave himself much concern in the affair, urging Henry to have no more to do with an ungrateful government, but to obtain from the United States the money that England refused. The count offered to act as negotiator, and use his influence with Serurier,

[1] Crillon's evidence; Annals of Congress, 1811–1812, p. 1222.

416

his minister, to approach the Secretary of State. The count even offered to provide for Henry's subsequent welfare by conveying to him the valuable estate at St. Martial in consideration of the money to be obtained for Henry's documents. At St. Martial, under the protection of the Crillons, John Henry would at last find, together with every charm of climate and scenery, the ease of life and the social refinement so dear to him.

Henry entered into a partnership with the Frenchman, and on their arrival at Boston Crillon wrote to Serurier, introducing himself, and narrating the situation of Henry, whose papers, he said, were in his own control.[1] Serurier made no reply; but Crillon came alone to Washington, where he called on the minister, who after hearing his story sent him to Monroe, to whom he offered Henry's papers for a consideration of $125,000. Serurier liked Crillon, and after some months of acquaintance liked him still more:—

"His conduct and language during six weeks' residence here have been constantly sustained; the attention shown him by this Government, the repentance he displayed for having incurred the displeasure of his sovereign, the constant enthusiasm with which he spoke of the Emperor, the name he bore, the letters he showed from his sister and from the Maréchal Duc d'Istrie, the decoration of the Legion he carried, and finally the persecution he suffered from the British minister and the party hostile to France,—all this could not but win my regard for him."[2]

Yet Crillon did not owe to Serurier his introduction into society, or his success in winning the confidence of Madison and Monroe. Indeed, the French minister could not openly recommend a man who admitted himself to be banished from France by the Emperor's displeasure. On the contrary, the favor that Crillon rapidly won at the White House served rather to establish his credit with his legation. The President and Cabinet ministers were civil to the count, who became a frequent guest at the President's table; and the services he

[1] Les Etats Unis il y a quarante ans; Par Caraman. Revue Contemporaine, 31 Août, 1852, p. 26.
[2] Serurier to Maret, May 27, 1812; Archives des Aff. Étr. MSS.

promised to Serurier's great object were so considerable as to make the French minister glad to assist him. No French comedy was suited with a happier situation or with more skilful actors. During several weeks in January and February, 1812, Count Edward de Crillon was the centre of social interest or hostility at the White House, the State Department, and the French and the British Legations.

The negotiation through Serurier was successful. Henry was secretly summoned to Washington, and consented to desist from his demand for $125,000. Secretary Monroe agreed to give him $50,000, and to promise that the papers should not be made public until Henry himself was actually at sea, while Crillon received the money, delivering to Henry the title-deeds to the estate of St. Martial. The money was paid, February 10, out of the contingent fund for foreign intercourse. Henry left Washington the next day to sail from New York for France in a national ship-of-war, but the Count Edward de Crillon remained. March 2 Serurier reported,[1] —

"The Administration has decided to publish Henry's documents. The order has been sent to New York that in case the ship which was to give him passage has not arrived, he is to be embarked on a merchant-vessel; and then all the papers are to be sent to Congress by special message. Much is expected from this exposition. The conduct of M. Crillon since his arrival here has never ceased to be consistent and thoroughly French. It has drawn on him the hatred of the British minister and of all the British party; but he bears up against it with the noblest firmness, and sometimes even with an intrepidity that I am obliged to restrain. He keeps me informed of everything that he thinks of service to the Emperor; and his loyalty of conduct attaches the members of the Administration to him. I have personally every motive to be satisfied with him, and I hope that the service he has just rendered, the sentiments he professes on all occasions, his so enthusiastic admiration for the Emperor, his devotion, his love of his country and his family, will create for him a title to the indulgence of his sovereign and the return of his favor. He will wait for them

[1] Serurier to Maret, March 2, 1811; Archives des Aff. Étr. MSS.

here, and I pray your Excellency to invoke them on my part."

The President waited only for the news that Henry had sailed, before sending to Congress the evidence of British intrigues and of Federalist treason; but as soon as this news arrived, Saturday, March 7, Monroe sent for Serurier:[1] —

"The Secretary of State asked me to come to his office to inform me of the determination. He asked me if I did not agree with him that it was better not to mention me in the Message, as such mention might injure its effect by giving it a French color. I told Mr. Monroe that I should leave the President entirely free to follow the course he thought best in the matter. He might say that the documents had come into my possession, and that I had at once sent them to him as interesting the Republic exclusively; or he might restrict himself to the communication of the papers without detail as to the route they had followed. That I had taken no credit, as he could remember, in regard to the service I had been so fortunate as to render the Administration; and that I had on my own account no need of newspaper notoriety or of public gratitude."

Monday, March 9, the President sent Henry's papers to Congress, with a message which said nothing as to the manner of acquiring them, but charged the British government with employing a secret agent "in fomenting disaffection to the constituted authorities of the nation, and in intrigues with the disaffected for the purpose of bringing about resistance to the laws, and eventually, in concert with a British force, of destroying the Union and forming the eastern part thereof into a political connection with Great Britain." Serurier reported that the Administration had great hopes through this discovery of deciding the result, inflaming the nation, and throwing it enthusiastically into the war: —

"The American people recalls to me the son of Ulysses on the rock of Calypso's isle; uncertain, irresolute, he knows not to which of his passions to yield, when Minerva,

[1] Serurier to Maret, March 2, 1811; Archives des Aff. Étr. MSS.

flinging him into the sea, fixes his fate, leaving him no other choice than to overcome by his courage and strength the terrible elements she gives him for an enemy."

When John Henry's letters were read in Congress, March 9, 1812, the Federalists for a moment felt real alarm, for they knew not what Henry might have reported; but a few minutes of examination showed them that, as far as they were concerned, Henry had taken care to report nothing of consequence. That he came to Boston as a British agent was hitherto unknown to the Federalists themselves, and the papers showed that he never revealed his secret character to them. His letters were hardly more compromising than letters, essays, and leading articles, sermons, orations, and addresses that had been printed again and again in every Federalist paper in Boston and New York. Here and there they contained rows of mysterious asterisks, but no other sign of acquaintance with facts worth concealing. The Federalists naturally suspected, what is evident on comparison of the papers bought by Madison with the originals in the Record Office at London, that Henry intended to sell as little as possible at the highest price he could exact. His revelations told nothing of his first visit to Boston in 1808, nor was one of the letters published which had been written in that year, although his documents incidentally alluded to information then sent; but what was more singular and fatal to his credit, the letters which he sold as his own were not copies but paraphrases of the originals; the mysterious asterisks were introduced merely to excite curiosity; and except the original instructions of Sir James Craig and the recent letter from Lord Liverpool's secretary, showing that in view of an expected war Henry had been employed as a secret agent to obtain political information by the governor-general, and that his reports had been sent to the Colonial Office, nothing in these papers compromised any one except Henry himself. As for the British government, since war was to be waged with it in any case for other reasons, these papers distracted attention from the true issue.

After a night's reflection the Federalists returned to the Capitol convinced that the President had done a foolish act in throwing away fifty thousand dollars for papers that proved the Federalist party to be ignorant of British intrigues that never existed. Fifty thousand dollars was a large sum; and having been spent without authority from Congress, it seemed to the Federalists chiefly their own money which had been unlawfully used by Madison for the purpose of publishing a spiteful libel on themselves. With every sign of passion they took up the President's personal challenge. A committee of investigation was ordered by the House, and found that Henry, with the Government's privity, had already sailed for Europe. Nothing remained but to examine Crillon, who gave evidence tending to prove only such facts as he thought it best that Congress should believe. In the Senate, March 10, Lloyd of Massachusetts moved a Resolution calling on the President for the names of any persons " who have in any way or manner whatever entered into, or most remotely countenanced," the projects of Sir James Craig. Monroe could only reply that, as John Henry had mentioned no names, the Department was not possessed of the information required. The reply made the Federalists only more angry; they were eager for revenge, and fortune did not wholly refuse it. They never learned that Henry's disclosure was the result of French intrigue, but they learned enough to make them suspect and exult over some mortification of the President.

Soon after Count Edward de Crillon gave his evidence to the investigating committee, news arrived that France was about to make war with Russia, and although Crillon had decided to wait in Washington for his recall to the Emperor's favor, he became suddenly earnest to depart. March 22, Serurier wrote:[1] —

> "At the news of a possible rupture with Russia, the blood of M. de Crillon, always so boiling, has become hotter than ever, and he has decided to return to France without waiting an answer from your Excellency; he wants to throw himself at the Emperor's feet, tell him what he has done, invoke pardon for his errors, and go to expiate them in the advance guard of his armies."

April 1 Crillon left Washington bearing despatches from

[1] Serurier to Maret, March 22, 1811; Archives des Aff. Étr. MSS.

Monroe to Barlow, and from Serurier to Bassano. Neither he nor John Henry is known to have ever again visited the United States, and their names would have been forgotten had not stories soon arrived that caused the Federalists great amusement, and made President Madison very uncomfortable. Barlow wrote to the President that Count Edward de Crillon was an impostor; that no such person was known to the Crillon family or to the French service. Private letters confirmed the report, and added that the estate of St. Martial had no existence, and that Crillon's draughts in Henry's favor were drawn on a person who had been five years dead.

"The President, with whom he has often dined," continued Serurier,[1] "and all the secretaries, whose reception, joined with the political considerations known to your Excellency, decided his admittance to my house, are a little ashamed of the eagerness (*empressement*) they showed him, and all the money they gave him. For my own part, Monseigneur, I have little to regret. I have constantly refused to connect myself with his affairs; I sent him to the Secretary of State for his documents; the papers have been published, and have produced an effect injurious to England without my having bought this good fortune by a single *denier* from the Imperial treasury; and I have escaped at the cost of some civilities, preceded by those of the President, the motive of which I declared from the first to be the services which the Administration told me had been rendered it by this traveller."

Serurier continued to declare that he had honestly believed Crillon to be "something like what he represented himself;" but he could not reasonably expect the world to accept these protestations. He had aided this person to obtain fifty thousand dollars from the United States Treasury for papers not his own, and instead of warning the President against an adventurer whose true character he admitted himself to have suspected, the French minister abetted the impostor. Although he afterwards asserted, and possibly believed, that Crillon was an agent of Napoleon's secret police, he was

[1] Serurier to Maret, May 27, 1812; Archives des Aff. Étr. MSS.

equally unwilling to admit that he had himself been either dupe or accomplice.[1]

That the President should be mortified was natural, but still more natural that he should be angry. He could not resent the introduction of a foreign impostor to his confidence, since he was himself chiefly responsible for the social success of the Count Edward de Crillon; but deception was a part of the French system, and Madison felt the Crillon affair sink into insignificance beside the other deceptions practised upon him by the government of France. He was as nearly furious as his temperament allowed, at the manner in which the Emperor treated him. Before Crillon appeared on the scene, Madison used language to Serurier that betrayed his extreme dissatisfaction at being paraded before the public as a dupe or tool of France. At Savannah a riot took place between French privateersmen and American or English sailors; several men on both sides were killed; the privateers were burned; and Serurier complained in language such as Napoleon might be supposed to expect from his minister in regard to a violent outrage on the French flag. At the White House on New Year's day, 1812, the French minister renewed his complaints, and the President lost patience.

"The President," wrote Serurier,[2] "answered me with vivacity, that doubtless such indignities were subject for much regret; but it was not less distressing to learn what was passing every day in the Baltic and on the routes from America to England, where some American ships were burned, while others were captured and taken into European ports under French influence and condemned; that such proceedings were in his eyes hostilities as pronounced as were those of England, against whom the Republic was at that moment taking up arms. . . . Mr. Madison ended by telling me that he wished always to flatter himself that Mr. Barlow would send immediate explanation of these strange measures, and notice that they had ceased; but that for the moment, very certainly, matters could not be in a worse situation."

[1] Caraman. Revue Contemporaine, 31 août, 1852. Count Edward de Crillon, American Historical Review, October, 1895, pp. 51–69.

[2] Serurier to Maret, Jan. 2, 1812; Archives des Aff. Étr. MSS.

Disconcerted by this sharp rebuff from the President, Serurier went to Monroe, who was usually good-humored when Madison was irritable, and irritable when Madison became mild. This process of alternate coaxing and scolding seemed to affect Serurier more than it affected his master. Monroe made no reproaches, but defended the President's position by an argument which the Republican party did not use in public:—

"He urged that the captures of these ships, though perhaps inconsiderable in themselves, had the unfortunate effect of giving arms to the English party, which obstinately maintains that the repeal of the Berlin and Milan Decrees has not taken place; 'that repeal,' he added, 'on which nevertheless the whole actual system of the Administration is founded, and which, if it be not really absolute, would render the war we are undertaking with England very imprudent and without reasonable object.'"

This admission, although made in private, seemed humiliating enough; but as weeks passed, Monroe's complaints became stronger. March 2 Serurier reported him as avowing that he considered Barlow's mission fruitless;[1]—

"After delays that have lasted three months beyond what we feared, we have as yet received only projects of arrangements, but nothing finished that we can publish. . . . You are witness to our embarrassment. Our position is painful. We will treat with England on no other ground than that of withdrawing the Orders in Council, and nothing promises this withdrawal. We are then decided for war. You see us every day making our preparations. If these meet with obstacles, if they suffer some delay, if Congress seems to grow weak and to hesitate, this slackening is due to the fact that we come to no conclusion with France."

Ships were still captured on their way to England. "If your decrees are in fact repealed," asked Monroe, "why this sequestration?" Serurier strove in vain to satisfy Monroe that the decrees, though repealed in principle, might be still enforced

[1] Serurier to Maret, March 2, 1812; Archives des Aff. Étr. MSS.

in fact. He failed to calm the secretary or the President, whose temper became worse as he saw more clearly that he had been overreached by Napoleon, and that his word as President of the United States had been made a means of deceiving Congress and the people.

Had the British government at that moment offered the single concession asked of it, no war could have taken place, unless it were a war with France; but the British government had not yet recovered its reason. Foster came to Washington with instructions to yield nothing, yet to maintain peace; to threaten, but still conciliate. This mixture of policy, half Canning and half Fox, feeble and mischievous as it was, could not be altered by Foster; his instructions were positive. "Nor can we ever deem the repeal of the French hostile decrees to be effectual," wrote Wellesley in April, 1811, "until neutral commerce shall be restored to the condition in which it stood previously to the commencement of the French system of commercial warfare." Wellesley hinted that the Decrees of Berlin and Milan were no longer important; they were in effect superseded by Napoleon's tariff of prohibitions and prohibitive duties; and until this system of war was abandoned, and neutral rights of trade were respected, Great Britain could not withdraw her blockades. In obedience to these instructions, Foster was obliged to tell Monroe in July, and again in October, 1811, that even if the repeal of the decrees were genuine, it would not satisfy the British government. Not the decrees, but their principle, roused British retaliation.

When the President in his Annual Message represented Foster as requiring that the United States should force British produce and manufactures into France, Foster protested, explained, and remonstrated in vain; he found himself reduced to threats of commercial retaliation which no one regarded, and his position became mortifying beyond any in the experience of his unfortunate predecessors. Compelled to witness constant insults to his country, he was still ordered to maintain peace. As early as Dec. 11, 1811, he notified his Government that unless its system were changed, war was likely to follow. The suggestions offered by the Federalist congressmen, February 1, could hardly fail to show the British government that at last it must choose between war and concession.

Feb. 26, 1812, Foster wrote again that war might be declared within a fortnight. March 9 the revelations of John Henry gave the minister another anxiety, and called from him another lame disavowal. Yet throughout these trying months Foster remained on friendly and almost intimate terms with Monroe, whom he described as "a very mild, moderate man."[1]

Matters stood thus till March 21, 1812, when Washington was excited by news that Foster had received recent instructions from his Government, and the crisis of war and peace was at hand. "The anxiety and curiosity of both Houses of Congress," reported Foster, April 1,[2] "to know the real nature of the despatches was so great that some of the members on committees told me they could not get the common routine of business at all attended to. The Department of State was crowded with individuals endeavoring to obtain information from Mr. Monroe, while I was questioned by all those with whom I happened to be acquainted." A report spread through Washington that the Orders in Council were repealed, and that an immediate accommodation of all differences between England and the United States might be expected.

Foster would have been glad to find his new instructions composed in such a sense; but he hardly expected to find them so positive as they were in an opposite spirit. Lord Wellesley's despatch of Jan. 28, 1812,[3] which may be said to have decided the declaration of war, was afterward published, and need not be quoted in detail. He remonstrated against the arming of merchant vessels, and ordered Foster to speak earnestly on the subject "for the purpose of preventing a state of affairs which might probably lead to acts of force." The pretended revocation of the French Decrees, said Lord Wellesley, was in fact a fresh enactment of them, while the measures of America tended to occasion such acts of violence as might "produce the calamity of war between the two countries." This usual formula, by which diplomacy announced an expected rupture, was reinforced by secret instructions

---

[1] Foster to Wellesley, March 12, 1812; MSS. British Archives.
[2] Foster to Wellesley, April 1, 1812; MSS. British Archives.
[3] Papers communicated to Parliament in 1813, p. 314.

warning Foster cautiously to "avoid employing any suggestions of compromise to the American government which
might induce them to doubt the sincerity or firmness of his
Majesty's government in their determination, already announced, of maintaining steadfastly the system of defence
adopted by them until the enemy shall relinquish his unwarrantable mode of attack upon our interests through the violation of neutral rights."

Foster regarded this order as a rebuke, for he had talked
freely, both to his own Government and in Washington, of
the possibility that the Orders in Council might be withdrawn. The warning gave him a manner more formal than
usual when he went, March 21, to assure Monroe that the
Prince Regent would never give way. Monroe listened with
great attention; "then merely said, with however considerable
mildness of tone, that he had hoped his conversations with
me at the early part of the session would have produced a
different result." Foster left him without further discussion,
and announced everywhere in public that, "far from being
awed and alarmed at the threatening attitude and language"
of Congress, his Government would maintain its system unimpaired.[1]

The President looked upon this declaration as final. Already
every preparation had been made to meet it. Only a fortnight
before, the papers of John Henry had been sent to Congress,
and the halls of Congress, as well as the columns of every
Republican newspaper in the country, were filled with denunciations of England's conduct, while the President prepared a
message recommending an embargo for sixty days,—a measure preliminary to the declaration of war,—when March 23,
two days after Foster's interview, news arrived that a French
squadron, under open orders, had begun to burn and sink
American commerce on the ocean. The American brig
"Thames" reached New York March 9, and her captain, Samuel Chew, deposed before a magistrate that February 2, in the
middle of the Atlantic, his brig on the return voyage from
Portugal was seized by a French squadron which had sailed
from Nantes early in January, and which had already seized

[1] Foster to Wellesley, April 1, 1812; MSS. British Archives.

and burned the American ship "Asia" and the brig "Ger-shom." The French commodore declared that he had orders to burn all American vessels sailing to or from an enemy's port. The American newspapers were soon deluged with affi-davits to the same effect from the captains and seamen of ves-sels burned by these French frigates, and the news, arriving in Washington at a moment when the Federalists were most eager to retaliate the insult of the Henry letters, caused ex-treme sensation. In face of these piratical acts no one longer pretended that the French Decrees were repealed. Republi-cans were angrier than Federalists. Madison and Monroe were angriest of all. Serurier was in despair. "I am just from Mr. Monroe's office," he wrote March 23;[1] "I have never yet seen him more agitated, more discomposed. He addressed me abruptly: 'Well, sir, it is then decided that we are to receive nothing but outrages from France! And at what a moment too! At the very instant when we were going to war with her enemies.'" When the French minister tried to check his ve-hemence of reproach, Monroe broke out again:—

"Remember where we were two days ago. You know what warlike measures have been taken for three months past; adopted slowly, they have been progressively followed up. We have made use of Henry's documents as a last means of exciting (*pour achever d'exalter*) the nation and Congress; you have seen by all the use we have made of them whither we were aiming; within a week we were going to propose the embargo, and the declaration of war was the immediate consequence of it. A ship has arrived from London, bringing us despatches to February 5, which contain nothing offering a hope of repeal of the orders; this was all that was needed to carry the declaration of war, which would have passed almost unanimously. It is at such a moment that your frigates come and burn our ships, de-stroy all our work, and put the Administration in the falsest and most terrible position in which a government can find itself placed."

For the hundredth time Monroe repeated the old story that

[1] Serurier to Maret, March 23, 1812; Archives des Aff. Étr. MSS.

the repeal of the French Decrees was the foundation of the whole American system; "that should the Executive now propose the embargo or the declaration of war, the whole Federal party—reinforced by the Clinton party, the Smith party, and the discontented Republicans—would rise in mass and demand why we persist in making war on England for maintaining her Orders in Council when we have proofs so recent and terrible that the French Decrees are not withdrawn." He added that if the question were put at such a moment, he did not doubt that the Government would lose its majority.

Foster also attempted to interfere in this complicated quarrel:—

"I took an occasion to wait on Mr. Monroe," wrote Foster April 1, "to hear what he would say relative to this outrage. He seemed much struck with the enormity of it, and . . . admitted that there were some circumstances in this particular instance of peculiar violence, and calling for the highest expressions of resentment on the part of this government. He told me that M. Serurier in an interview he had with him on the subject stated his disbelief in the fact."

Foster wrote an official note to Monroe, using the recent French outrages as new ground for demanding to see the instrument by which the decrees were said to be repealed.

Serurier himself was little pleased with the Emperor's conduct, and expressed his annoyance frankly to his Government; but he consoled himself with the conviction that President Madison could no longer recede, even if serious in wishing to do so. Congress was equally helpless. Nothing could exceed the anger of congressmen with France. As Macon wrote to Nicholson, March 24,[1] after Captain Chew's deposition had been read in the House, "the Devil himself could not tell which government, England or France, is the most wicked." The cry for a double war with France as well as with England became strong enough to create uneasiness; and although such a triangular war might be a military mistake, no one could explain the reasoning which led to a declaration of war with England, on the grounds selected by Madison, without

[1] Macon to Nicholson, March 24, 1812; Nicholson MSS.

a simultaneous declaration against France. The responsibility Madison had incurred would have broken the courage of any man less pertinacious. With difficulty could the best Republican conceive how the issue with England could have been worse managed.

At this moment, according to a Federalist legend, Madison was believed to hesitate, and Clay and Grundy coerced him into the recommendation of war by threats of opposing his renomination for the Presidency.[1] In reality, some of the moderate Republicans urged him to send a special mission to England as a last chance of peace.[2] Perhaps Clay and Grundy opposed this suggestion with the warmth ascribed to them, but certainly no sign of hesitation could be detected in Madison's conduct between the meeting of Congress in November and the declaration of war in June.[3] Whatever were his private feelings, he acted in constant agreement with the majority of his party, and at most asked only time for some slight armaments. As to the unprepared state of the country, he said that he did not feel himself bound to take more than his share of the responsibility.[4] Even under the exasperation caused by the conduct of France, he waited only for his party to recover composure. March 31 Monroe held a conference with the House Committee of Foreign Relations, and told them that the President thought war should be declared before Congress adjourned, and that he would send an Embargo Message if he could be assured it would be agreeable to the House.[5] On the same day Foster called at the State Department for an answer to the note in which he had just asked for proof that the French Decrees were repealed. Monroe made him a reply of which Foster seemed hardly to appreciate the gravity.[6]

"He told me, a good deal to my disappointment I confess, that the President did not think it would lead to any

[1] Statesman's Manual, ii. 444, *note*.

[2] Adams's Gallatin, pp. 457–459.

[3] Speech of John Smilie, April 1, 1812; Annals of Congress, p. 1592. Monroe to Colonel Taylor, June 13, 1812; Monroe MSS.

[4] Speech of John Randolph, April 1, 1812; Annals of Congress, p. 1593.

[5] Speech of John Randolph, April 1, 1812; Annals of Congress, p. 1593.

[6] Foster to Wellesley, April 1, 1812; MSS. British Archives.

utility to order an answer to be written to either of my last notes; that he could not now entertain the question as to whether the French Decrees were repealed, having already been convinced and declared that they were so. He said that the case of the two American ships which were burned could not be said to come under the Berlin and Milan Decrees, however objectionable the act was to this Government; that the declaration of the French commodore of his having orders to burn all ships bound to or from an enemy's port was given only verbally, and might not have been well understood by the American captain, who did not very well understand French; while the declaration in writing only alluded to ships bound to or from Lisbon and Cadiz."

Nothing could be more humiliating to Monroe than the resort to subterfuge like this; but the President left no outlet of escape. The Committee of Foreign Relations decided in favor of an embargo; and April 1, the day after this interview, Madison sent to Congress a secret Message, which was read with closed doors: —

"Considering it as expedient, under existing circumstances and prospects, that a general embargo be laid on all vessels now in port or hereafter arriving for the period of sixty days, I recommend the immediate passage of a law to that effect."

Chapter X

WHEN NEWS OF this decisive step became public, the British minister hastened to Monroe for explanations.[1] Monroe "deprecated its being considered as a war measure. He even seemed to affect to consider it as an impartial measure toward the two belligerents, and as thereby complying with one of our demands; namely, putting them on an equality. . . . He used an expression which I had some difficulty in comprehending,—that it was the wish of the Government to keep their policy in their own hands." In truth Monroe seemed, to the last, inclined to leave open a door by which the anger of America might, in case of reconciliation with England, be diverted against France. Madison had no such delusion. Foster went to the President, and repeated to him Monroe's remark that the embargo was not a war measure.[2] "Oh, no!" said Madison, "embargo is not war;" but he added that in his opinion the United States would be amply justified in war, whatever might be its expediency, for Great Britain was actually waging war on them, and within a month had captured eighteen ships of the estimated value of fifteen hundred thousand dollars. He said he should be glad still to receive any propositions England might have to make, and that Congress would be in session at the period fixed for terminating the embargo. Neither Madison nor Monroe could properly say more to the British minister, for they could not undertake to forestall the action of Congress; but the rumor that France might be included in the declaration of war as in the embargo, made the French minister uneasy, and he too asked explanation. To him the secretary talked more plainly.[3]

"Mr. Monroe answered me," wrote Serurier April 9, "that the embargo had been adopted in view of stopping the losses of commerce, and of preparing for the imminent war with England; he protested to me his perfect convic-

[1] Foster to Wellesley, April 2, 1812; Papers, 1813, p. 564.
[2] Foster to Wellesley, April 3, 1812; MSS. British Archives.
[3] Serurier to Maret, April 9, 1812; Archives des Aff. Étr. MSS.

tion that war was inevitable if the news expected from France answered to the hopes they had formed. He gave me his word of honor that in the secret deliberations of Congress no measure had been taken against France. He admitted that in fact the affair of the frigates had produced a very deep impresssion on that body; that it had, even in Republican eyes, seemed manifest proof that the Imperial Decrees were not repealed, and that this unfortunate accident had shaken (*ébranlé*) the whole base of the Administration system; that the Executive, by inclination as much as by system, had always wished to believe in this repeal, without which it was impossible to make issue (*engager la querelle*) with England; that its interest in this respect was perfectly in accord with that of France, but that he had found it wholly impossible to justify the inconceivable conduct of the commander of the frigates. . . . Mr. Monroe insisted here on his former declarations, that if the Administration was abandoned by France it would infallibly succumb, or would be obliged to propose war against both Powers, which would be against its interests as much as against its inclination."

The Embargo Message surprised no one. The Committee of Foreign Relations made no secret of its decision. Calhoun warned Josiah Quincy and other representatives of commercial cities; and on the afternoon of March 31 these members sent an express, giving notice to their constituents that the embargo would be proposed on the following day. Every ship-owner on the seaboard and every merchant in the great cities hurried ships and merchandise to sea, showing that they feared war less than they feared embargo, at the moment when Congress, April 1, went into secret session to discuss the measure intended to protect ship-owners and merchants by keeping their property at home. Porter introduced the bill laying an embargo for sixty days;[1] Grundy declared it to be intended as a measure leading directly to war; Henry Clay made a vehement speech approving the measure on that ground. On the other side Randolph declared war to be impossible; the President dared not be guilty of treason so gross

---

[1] Supplemental Journal, April 1, 1812; Annals of Congress, 1811–1812, p. 1588.

and unparalleled as that of plunging an unprepared nation into such a conflict. Randolph even read memoranda of Monroe's remarks to the Committee of Foreign Relations: "The embargo would leave the policy as respected France, and indeed of both countries, in our hands;" and from this he tried to convince the House that the embargo was not honestly intended as a war measure. The debate ran till evening, when by a vote of sixty-six to forty the previous question was ordered. Without listening to the minority the House then hurried the bill through all its stages, and at nine o'clock passed it by a vote of seventy to forty-one.

The majority numbered less than half the members. In 1807 the House imposed the embargo by a vote of eighty-two to forty-four, yet the country failed to support it. The experience of 1807 boded ill for that of 1812. In the Senate the outlook was worse. The motion to extend the embargo from sixty to ninety days was adopted without opposition, changing the character of the bill at a single stroke from a strong war measure into a weak measure of negotiation; but even in this weaker form it received only twenty votes against thirteen in opposition. The President could not depend on a bare majority in the Senate. The New England Democrats shrank from the embargo even more than from war. Giles and Samuel Smith stood in open opposition. The Clintons had become candidates of every discontented faction in the country. Had the vote in the Senate been counted by States, only six would have been thrown for the embargo, and of these only Pennsylvania from the North. In face of such distraction, war with England seemed worse than a gambler's risk.

Madison, watching with that apparent neutrality which irritated both his friends and his enemies, reported to Jefferson the progress of events.[1] He was not pleased with the Senate's treatment of his recommendations, or with "that invariable opposition, open with some and covert with others, which has perplexed and impeded the whole course of our public measures." He explained the motives of senators in extending the embargo from sixty to ninety days. Some wished to make it a peace measure, some to postpone war, some to allow time

[1] Madison to Jefferson, April 24, 1812; Writings, ii. 532.

for the return of their constituents' ships; some intended it as a ruse against the enemy. For his own part he had regarded a short embargo as a rational and provident measure, which would be relished by the greater part of the nation; but he looked upon it as a step to immediate war, and he waited only for the Senate to make the declaration.

The President asked too much. Congress seemed exhausted by the efforts it had made, and the country showed signs of greater exhaustion before having made any efforts at all. The complaints against France, against the non-importation, against the embargo, and against the proposed war were bitter and general. April 6 Massachusetts held the usual State election. Gerry was again the Republican candidate for governor, and the Federalists had little hope of defeating him; but the Republican Administration had proved so unpopular, the famous Gerrymander by which the State had been divided into districts in party interests had so irritated the conservative feeling, that the new embargo and the expected war were hardly needed to throw the State again into opposition. Not even the revelations of John Henry restored the balance. More than one hundred and four thousand votes were cast, and a majority of about twelve hundred appeared on the Federalist side. Caleb Strong became governor once more at a moment when the change paralyzed national authority in New England; and meanwhile throughout the country the enlistments for the new army produced barely one thousand men.

The month of April passed without legislation that could strengthen Government, except an Act, approved April 10, authorizing the President to call out one hundred thousand militia for six months' service. Congress showed so strong a wish to adjourn that the Administration was obliged to exert its whole influence to prevent the House from imitating the Senate, which by a vote of sixteen to fifteen adopted a Resolution for a recess until June 8. Secretary Gallatin ventured to bring no tax bills before Congress; Lowndes and Cheves made a vigorous effort to suspend the Non-importation Act; and a general belief prevailed that the Government wished to admit English goods in order to evade, by increase of customs-revenue, the necessity of taxation.

Serurier, much discomposed by these signs of vacillation, busied himself in the matter, declaring to his friends in Congress that he should look on any suspension of the Non-importation Act as a formal infraction of the compact with France. When he pressed Monroe with remonstrances,[1] Monroe told him, April 22, that the President and Cabinet had positively and unanimously declared to the Committee of Foreign Relations against the suspension, because it would seem to indicate indecision and inconsequence in their foreign policy; that this remonstrance had caused the plan to be given up, but that the Administration might still be obliged to consent to a short adjournment, so great was the wish of members to look after their private affairs. In fact, Congress showed no other wish than to escape, and leave the President to struggle with his difficulties alone.

If the war party hesitated in its allegiance to Madison, its doubts regarded his abilities rather than his zeal. Whatever might be Madison's genius, no one supposed it to be that of administration. His health was delicate; he looked worn and feeble; for many years he had shown none of the energy of youth; he was likely to succumb under the burden of war; and, worst of all, he showed no consciousness of needing support. The party was unanimous in believing Secretary Eustis unequal to his post, but Madison made no sign of removing him. So general was the impression of Eustis's incapacity that when, April 24, the President sent to Congress a message asking for two Assistant Secretaries of War to aid in conducting the Department, the request was commonly regarded as an evasion of the public demand for a new Secretary of War, and as such was unfavorably received. In the House, where the subject was openly discussed, Randolph defended Eustis in the style of which he was master: "I will say this much of the Secretary of War,—that I do verily believe, and I have grounds to believe it to be the opinion of a majority of this House, that he is at least as competent to the exercise of his duties as his colleague who presides over the Marine." The Senate, wishing perhaps to force the President into reconstructing his Cabinet, laid aside the bill

[1] Serurier to Maret, April 24, 1812; Archives des Aff. Étr. MSS.

creating two Assistant Secretaries of War; and with this action, May 6, ended the last chance of efficiency in that Department.

While Eustis ransacked the country for generals, colonels, and the whole staff of officers, as well as the clothing, arms, and blankets for an army of twenty-five thousand men who could not be found, Gallatin labored to provide means for meeting the first year's expenses. Having no longer the Bank to help him, he dealt separately with the State Banks through whose agency private subscriptions were to be received. The subscriptions were to be opened on the first and second days of May. The Republican newspapers, led by the "National Intelligencer,"[1] expressed the hope and the expectation that twice the amount of the loan would be instantly subscribed. Their disappointment was very great. Federalist New England refused to subscribe at all; and as the Federalists controlled most of the capital in the country, the effect of their abstention was alarming. In all New England not one million dollars were obtained. New York and Philadelphia took each about one and a half million. Baltimore and Washington took about as much more. The whole Southern country, from the Potomac to Charleston, subscribed seven hundred thousand dollars. Of the entire loan, amounting to eleven million dollars, a little more than six millions were taken; and considering the terms, the result was not surprising. At a time when the old six-per-cent loans, with ten or twelve years to run, stood barely at par, any new six-per-cent loan to a large amount, with a vast war in prospect, could hardly be taken at the same rate.

The Federalists, delighted with this failure, said, with some show of reason, that if the Southern States wanted the war they ought to supply the means, and had no right to expect that men who thought the war unjust and unnecessary should speculate to make money from it. Gallatin put a good face on his failure, and proposed soon to reopen subscriptions; but the disappointment was real.

"Whatever the result may be," wrote Serurier to his

[1] National Intelligencer, April 23, 1812.

Government,[1] "they had counted on more national energy on the opening of a first loan for a war so just. This cooling of the national pulse, the resistance which the Northern States seem once more willing to offer the Administration, the defection it meets every day in Congress,—all this, joined to its irritation at our measures which make its own system unpopular, adds to its embarrassment and hesitation."

Gallatin made no complaints, but he knew only too well what lay before him. No resource remained except treasury notes bearing interest. Neither Gallatin, nor any other party leader, cared to suggest legal-tender notes, which were supposed to be not only an admission of national bankruptcy at the start, but also forbidden by the spirit of the Constitution; yet the government could hardly fail to experience the same form of bankruptcy in a less convenient shape. After the destruction of the United States Bank, a banking mania seized the public. Everywhere new banks were organized or planned, until the legislature of New York, no longer contented with small corporations controlling capital of one or two hundred thousand dollars, prepared to incorporate the old Bank of the United States under a new form, with a capital of six millions. Governor Tompkins stopped the project by proroguing the legislature; but his message gave the astonishing reason that the legislature was in danger of yielding to bribery.[2] The majority protested against the charge, and denounced it as a breach of privilege; but whether it was well or ill founded, the influence of the banking mania on State legislatures could not fail to be corrupting. The evil, inherent in the origin of the new banks, was aggravated by their management. Competition and want of experience or of supervision, inevitably led to over-issue, inflation of credit, suspension of specie payments, and paper-money of the worst character. Between a debased currency of private corporations and a debased currency of government paper, the former was the most expensive and the least convenient; yet it was the only support on which the Treasury could depend.

[1] Serurier to Maret, May 4, 1812; Archives des Aff. Étr. MSS.
[2] Message of March 27, 1812; Niles, ii. 39.

Early in May a double election took place, which gave more cause of alarm. New York chose a Federalist Assembly, and Massachusetts chose a General Court more strongly Federalist than any one had ventured to expect. In the face of such a revolution in two of the greatest and richest States in the Union, President, Cabinet, and legislators had reason to hesitate; they had even reason to fear that the existence of the Union might hang on their decision. They knew the Executive Department to be incompetent for war; they had before their eyes the spectacle of an incompetent Congress; and they saw the people declaring, as emphatically as their democratic forms of government permitted, their unwillingness to undertake the burden. Even bold men might pause before a situation so desperate.

Thus the month of May passed, full of discouragement. Congress did not adjourn, but the members went home on leave, with the understanding that no further action should be taken until June. At home they found chaos. Under the coercion of embargo, commerce ceased. Men would do little but talk politics, and very few professed themselves satisfied with the condition into which their affairs had been brought. The press cried for war or for peace, according to its fancy; but although each of the old parties could readily prove the other's course to be absurd, unpatriotic, and ruinous, the war men, who were in truth a new party, powerless to restore order by legitimate methods, shut their ears to the outcry, and waited until actual war should enforce a discipline never to be imposed in peace.

The experiment of thrusting the country into war to inflame it, as crude ore might be thrown into a furnace, was avowed by the party leaders, from President Madison downward, and was in truth the only excuse for a course otherwise resembling an attempt at suicide. Many nations have gone to war in pure gayety of heart; but perhaps the United States were first to force themselves into a war they dreaded, in the hope that the war itself might create the spirit they lacked. One of the liveliest and most instructive discussions of the session, May 6, threw light upon the scheme by which the youthful nation was to reverse the process of Medea, and pass through the caldron of war in confidence of gaining the vigor of age. Mr. Bleecker of New York, in offering petitions for the repeal of the embargo, argued that the embargo could not be honestly intended. "Where are your armies; your navy? Have you money? No, sir! Rely upon it, there will be, there can be, no war—active, offensive war—within sixty days." War would be little short of treason; would bring shame, disgrace, defeat; and meanwhile the embargo alienated the people of States which must necessarily bear much of the burden. These arguments were supported by John Randolph.

> "I am myself," he said, "in a situation similar to what would have been that of one of the unfortunate people of Caracas, if preadvised of the danger which overhung his country. I know that we are on the brink of some dreadful scourge, some great desolation, some awful visitation from that Power whom, I am afraid, we have as yet in our national capacity taken no pains to conciliate. . . . Go to war without money, without men, without a navy! Go to war when we have not the courage, while your lips utter war, to lay war taxes! when your whole courage is exhibited in passing Resolutions! The people will not believe it!"

Richard M. Johnson undertook first to meet these criticisms. Johnson possessed courage and abilities, but he had not, more than other Kentuckians of his day, the caution convenient in the face of opponents. He met by threats the opposition he would not answer. "It was a Tory opposition, in the cities and seaports; and an opposition which would not be quite so bold and powerful in a time of war; and he trusted in that Heaven to which the gentleman from Virginia had appealed, that sixty days would not elapse before all the traitorous combinations and opposition to the laws and the acts of the general government would in a great measure cease, or change, and moderate their tone." Calhoun, who followed Johnson, expressed the same idea in less offensive form, and added opinions of his own which showed the mental condition in which the young war leaders exulted: "So far from being unprepared, sir, I believe that in four weeks from the time that a declaration of war is heard on our frontiers the whole of Upper and a part of Lower Canada will be in our possession."

Grundy, following in the debate, used neither threats like Johnson, nor prophecies like Calhoun; but his argument was not more convincing. "It is only while the public mind is held in suspense," he said; "it is only while there is doubt as to what will be the result of our deliberations,—it is only while we linger in this Hall that any manifestations of uneasiness will show themselves. Whenever war is declared, the people will put forth their strength to support their rights." He went so far as to add that when war should be once begun, the distinction between Federalists and Republicans would cease. Finally, Wright of Maryland, whose words fortunately carried little weight, concluded the debate by saying that if signs of treason and civil war should discover themselves in any part of the American empire, he had no doubt the evil would soon be radically cured by hemp and confiscation; and his own exertions should not be spared to employ the remedy.

The President himself had no other plan than to "throw forward the flag of the country, sure that the people would press onward and defend it."[1] The example he had himself given to the people in 1798 tended to cast doubt on the correctness of his judgment,[2] but his candidacy for the Presidency also shook confidence in his good faith. So deep was the conviction of his dislike for the policy he supported as to lead the British minister, May 3, to inform his Government that the jealousies between the younger and older members of Congress threatened an open schism, in which the President was supposed likely to be involved.[3]

"The reason why there has been no nomination made in caucus yet, by the Democratic members, of Mr. Madison as candidate for the Presidency is, as I am assured in confidence, because the war party have suspected him not to have been serious in his late hostile measures, and wish previously to ascertain his real sentiments. I have been endeavoring to put the Federalists upon insinuating that they will support him, if he will agree to give up the advocates for war."

[1] Adams's Gallatin, p. 460, *note*.
[2] Ante, pp. 100, 101–02.
[3] Foster to Castlereagh, May 3, 1812; MSS. British Archives.

This intrigue was stopped by the positive refusal of the eastern Federalists to support Madison on any terms,—they preferred coalition with DeWitt Clinton and the Republican malcontents; but the time had come when some nomination must be made, and when it arrived, all serious thought of an open Republican schism at Washington vanished. The usual Congressional caucus was called May 18, and was attended by eighty-three members and senators, who unanimously renominated Madison. Seventeen senators, just one half the Senate, and sixty-six members, almost one half the House, joined in the nomination; but only three New York members took part, and neither Giles nor Samuel Smith was present,—they had ceased to act with the Republican party. Only a few weeks before, Vice-President Clinton had died in office, and whatever respect the Administration may have felt for his great name and Revolutionary services, the party was relieved at the prospect of placing in the chair of the Senate some man upon whom it could better depend. The caucus named John Langdon of New Hampshire; and when he declined, Elbridge Gerry, the defeated Governor of Massachusetts, was selected as candidate for the Vice-presidency.

So little cordiality was felt for President Madison by his party that only the want of a strong rival reconciled a majority to the choice; but although Clay, Crawford, and Calhoun accepted the necessity, the State of New York flatly rebelled. At Albany, when the news arrived that the Washington caucus had named Madison for the Presidency, the Republican members of the State legislature called for May 29 a caucus of their own. Their whole number was ninety-five; of these, all but four attended, and eighty-seven voted that it was expedient to name a candidate for the Presidency. Ninety members then voted to support DeWitt Clinton against Madison, and Clinton formally accepted the nomination. This unusual unanimity among the New York Republicans raised the movement somewhat above the level of ordinary New York politics, and pointed to a growing jealousy of Virginia, which threatened to end in revival of the old alliance between New York and New England. Even in quiet times this prospect would have been alarming; in face of war, it threatened to be fatal.

During the entire month of May Congress passed, with

only one exception, no Act for war purposes. While the absent members attended to their private affairs, Government waited for the last despatches from abroad. The sloop-of-war "Hornet," after long delay, arrived at New York, May 19, and three days afterward the despatches reached Washington. Once more, but for the last time, the town roused itself to learn what hope of peace they contained.

As far as concerned Great Britain, the news would at any previous time have checked hostile action, for it showed that the British government had taken alarm, and that for the first time a real change of policy was possible; but this news came from unofficial sources, and could not be laid before Congress. Officially, the British government still stoutly maintained that it could not yield. Lord Wellesley had given place to Lord Castlereagh. In a very long despatch,[1] dated April 10, the new Foreign Minister pleaded earnestly that England could not submit herself to the mercy of France. The argument of Lord Castlereagh rested on an official report made by the Duc de Bassano to the Emperor, March 10, in which Napoleon reasserted his rules regarding neutrals in language quite as strong as that of his decrees, and reasserted the validity of those decrees, without exception, in regard to every neutral that did not recognize their provisions. Certainly, no proof could be imagined competent to show the continued existence of the decrees if Bassano's report failed to do so; and Castlereagh, with some reason, relied on this evidence to convince not so much the American government as the American people that a deception had been practised, and that England could not act as America required without submitting to Napoleon's principles as well as to his arms.

Embarrassing as this despatch was to President Madison, it was not all, or the worst; but Serurier himself described the other annoyance in terms as lively as his feelings:[2] —

"The 'Hornet' has at last arrived. On the rumor of this news, the avenues of the State Department were thronged by a crowd of members of both Houses of Congress, as well as by strangers and citizens, impatient to know what

[1] Papers presented to Parliament, 1813, p. 475.
[2] Serurier to Maret, May 27, 1812; Archives des Aff. Étr. MSS.

this long-expected vessel had brought. Soon it was learned that the 'Hornet' had brought nothing favorable, and that Mr. Barlow had as yet concluded nothing with your Excellency. On this news, the furious declamations of the Federalists, of the commercial interests, and of the numerous friends of England were redoubled; the Republicans, deceived in their hopes, joined in the outcry, and for three days nothing was heard but a general cry for war against France and England at once. . . . I met Mr. Monroe at the Speaker's house; he came to me with an air of affliction and discouragement; addressed me with his old reproach that decidedly we abandoned the Administration, and that he did not know henceforward how they could extricate themselves from the difficult position into which their confidence in our friendship had drawn them."

Serurier had no reason for uneasiness on his own account. The President and his party could not go backward in their path; yet no enemy could have devised a worse issue than that on which the President had placed the intended war with England. Every Act of Congress and every official expression of Madison's policy had been founded on the withdrawal of the French Decrees as they affected American commerce. This withdrawal could no longer be maintained, and Madison merely shook confidence in his own good faith by asserting it; yet he could do nothing else. "It is understood," he wrote to Jefferson at this crisis,[1] "that the Berlin and Milan Decrees are not in force against the United States, and no contravention of them can be established against her. On the contrary, positive cases rebut the allegation." Yet he said that "the business has become more than ever puzzling;" he was withheld only by political and military expediency from favoring war with France. He wrote to Joel Barlow,[2] after full knowledge of Napoleon's conduct, that "in the event of a pacification with Great Britain the full tide of indignation with which the public mind here is boiling will be directed against France, if not obviated by a due reparation of her wrongs; war will be called for by the nation almost *unâ voce.*"

[1] Madison to Jefferson, May 25, 1812; Works ii. 535.
[2] Madison to Barlow, Aug. 11, 1812; Works ii. 540.

A position so inconsistent with itself could not be understood by the people. Every one knew that if the decrees were not avowedly enforced in France against the United States, they were relaxed only because Madison had submitted to their previous enforcement, and had, in Napoleon's opinion, recognized their legality. The Republican press, which supported Madison most energetically, made no concealment of its active sympathies with Napoleon, even in Spain. What wonder if large numbers of good citizens who believed Napoleon to be anti-Christ should be disposed to resist, even to the verge of treason, the attempt to use their lives and fortunes in a service they regarded with horror!

Chapter XI

CASTLEREAGH's long note of April 10, communicated by Foster to the American government, contained a paragraph defining the British doctrine of retaliation:—

"What Great Britain always avowed was her readiness to rescind her orders as soon as France rescinded, absolutely and unconditionally, her decrees. She never engaged to repeal those orders as affecting America alone, leaving them in force against other States, upon condition that France would except, singly and especially, America from the operation of her decrees. She could not do so without the grossest injustice to her allies, as well as all other neutral nations; much less could she do so upon the supposition that the special exception in favor of America was to be expressly granted by France, as it has been hitherto tacitly accepted by America, upon conditions utterly subversive of the most important and indisputable maritime rights of the British empire."

Long afterward Madison objected[1] to the common accounts of the war, that they brought too little into view "the more immediate impulse to it" given by this formal notice communicated to him officially by Foster, which left no choice between war and degradation. He regarded this notice as making further discussion impossible. His idea was perhaps too strongly asserted, for Foster offered, under other instructions, a new and important concession,—that England should give up altogether her system of licensing trade with the Continent, and in its place should enforce a rigorous blockade;[2] but Madison and Monroe declined listening to any offer that did not admit in principle the right of the United States to trade with every European country.[3] Thus at the last moment the dispute seemed to narrow itself to the single point of belligerent right to blockade a coast.

Acting at once on the theory that Castlereagh's instructions

[1] Madison to Henry Wheaton, Feb. 26, 1827; Works iii. 553.
[2] Castlereagh to Foster, April 10, 1812; Papers, etc., 1813, p. 511.
[3] Foster to Castlereagh, June 6, 1812; Papers, etc., 1813, p. 577.

of April 10 gave the last formal notice intended by the British government, President Madison prepared a Message recommending an immediate declaration of war. This Message was sent to Congress June 1; the two Houses instantly went into secret session, and the Message was read. No one could dispute the force of Madison's long recital of British outrages. For five years, the task of finding excuses for peace had been more difficult than that of proving a *casus belli*; but some interest still attached to the arrangement and relative weight of the many American complaints.

Madison, inverting the order of complaints previously alleged, began by charging that British cruisers had been "in the continued practice of violating the American flag on the great highway of nations, and of seizing and carrying off persons sailing under it." The charge was amply proved, was not denied, and warranted war; but this was the first time that the Government had alleged impressment as its chief grievance, or had announced, either to England or to America, the intention to fight for redress,—and England might fairly complain that she had received no notice of intended war on such ground. The second complaint alleged that British cruisers also violated the peace of the coasts, and harassed entering and departing commerce. This charge was equally true and equally warranted war, but it was open to the same comment as that made upon the first. The third grievance on which the President had hitherto founded his coercive measures consisted in "pretended blockades, without the presence of an adequate force and sometimes without the practicability of applying one," by means of which American commerce had been plundered on every sea,—a practice which had come to its highest possible development in the fourth grievance, the sweeping system of blockades known as the Orders in Council. These four main heads of complaint covered numbers of irritating consequences, but no other separate charge was alleged, beyond an insinuation that the hostile spirit of the Indians was connected with their neighborhood to Canada.

On the four great grievances thus defined every American could in theory agree; but these admitted wrongs had hitherto been endured as a matter of expediency, rather than resort to war; and the opposition still stood on the ground that had been so obstinately held by Jefferson,—that war, however just, was inexpedient. If union in the war policy was to be hoped, the President must rather prove its expediency than its justice. Even from his own point of view, two doubts of expediency required fresh attention. For the first time, England showed distinct signs of giving way; while on the other hand France showed only the monomania of insisting on her decrees, even to the point of conquering Russia. In the face of two such movements, the expediency of war with England became more than ever doubtful; and if the President wished for harmony, he must remove these doubts. This he did not attempt, further than by alluding to the sense of Castlereagh's late despatch, as yet not in his possession. What was still more remarkable, he said nothing in regard to the contract with France, which since November, 1809, he had made the ground for every measure of compulsion against England. Indeed, not only was the contract ignored, but if any meaning could be placed on his allusions to France, the theory of contract seemed at last to be formally abandoned.

"Having presented this view of the relations of the United States with Great Britain, and of the solemn alternative growing out of them, I proceed to remark that the communications last made to Congress on the subject of our relations with France will have shown that since the revocation of her decrees, as they violated the neutral rights of the United States, her government has authorized illegal captures by its privateers and public ships; and that other outrages have been practised on our vessels and our citizens. It will have been seen, also, that no indemnity had been provided, or satisfactorily pledged, for the extensive spoliations committed under the violent and retrospective orders of the French government against the property of our citizens, seized within the jurisdiction of France. I abstain at this time from recommending to the consideration of Congress definite measures with respect to that nation."

The war of 1812 was chiefly remarkable for the vehemence with which, from beginning to end, it was resisted and thwarted by a very large number of citizens who were commonly considered, and who considered themselves, by no means the least respectable, intelligent, or patriotic part of the nation. That the war was as just and necessary as any war ever waged, seemed so evident to Americans of another generation that only with an effort could modern readers grasp the reasons for the bitter opposition of large and respectable communities which left the government bankrupt, and nearly severed the Union; but if students of national history can bear with patience the labor of retaining in mind the threads of negotiation which President Madison so thoroughly tangled before breaking, they can partially enter into the feelings of citizens who held themselves aloof from Madison's war. In June, 1812, the reasons for declaring war on Great Britain, though strong enough, were weaker than they had been in June, 1808, or in January, 1809. In the interval the British government had laid aside the arrogant and defiant tones of Canning's diplomacy; had greatly modified the Orders in Council; had offered further modifications; and had atoned for the "Chesapeake" outrage. In 1807 England would have welcomed a war with the United States; in 1812 she wanted peace, and yielded much to secure it. In 1808 America was almost unanimous, her government still efficient, well supplied with money, and little likely to suffer from war; in 1812 the people were greatly divided, the government had been weakened, and the Treasury was empty. Even Gallatin, who in 1809 had been most decided for war, was believed in 1812 to wish and to think that it might be avoided. Probably four fifths of the American people held the same opinion. Not merely had the situation in every other respect changed for the worse, but the moral convictions of the country were outraged by the assertion of a contract with Napoleon—in which no one believed—as the reason for forcing religious and peaceful citizens into what they regarded as the service of France.

The war Message of June 1 rather strengthened than removed grounds of opposition. The President alleged but one reason for thinking war expedient at that moment rather than at another; but when in after years he insisted that Castlereagh's instructions were the immediate cause which precluded further negotiation, he admitted his own mistake, and presumed that had Congress known what was then passing in

England the declaration of war would have been suspended and negotiations renewed.[1] Such a succession of mistakes, admitted one after another almost as soon as they were made, might well give to Madison's conduct the air so often attributed to it, of systematic favor to Napoleon and equally systematic hostility to England.

The House went at once into secret session; the Message was referred to the Committee of Foreign Relations; and two days afterward, June 3, Calhoun brought in a report recommending an immediate appeal to arms. As a history of the causes which led to this result, Calhoun's report was admirable, and its clearness of style and statement forced comparisons not flattering to the President's Message; but as an argument for the immediate necessity of war, the report like the Message contented itself with bare assertions. "The United States must support their character and station among the nations of the earth, or submit to the most shameful degradation." Calhoun's arguments were commonly close in logic, and avoided declamation; but in the actual instance neither he nor his followers seemed confident in the strength of their reasoning.

After the House had listened in secret session, June 3, to the reading of this report, Josiah Quincy moved that the debate should be public. The demand seemed reasonable. That preliminary debates should be secret might be proper, but that war with any Power, and most of all with England, should be declared in secret could not be sound policy, while apart from any question of policy the secrecy contradicted the professions of the party in power. Perhaps no single act, in a hundred years of American history, showed less regard for personal and party consistency than the refusal by the Republicans of 1812 to allow society either rights or privileges in regard to the declaration of war upon England. Quite apart from military advantages to be hoped from secrecy, Henry Clay and his friends were weary of debate and afraid of defeat. Only a few days before, May 29, Clay forced Randolph from the floor by tactics which showed that no more discussion was to be allowed. The secret session gave the Speaker

[1] Madison to Wheaton, Feb. 26, 1827; Madison's Works, iii. 553.

absolute power, and annihilated opposition. By seventy-six votes to forty-six, the House rejected Quincy's motion; and a similar motion by Randolph shared the same fate.

This demand being refused, the minority declined further discussion. They said that any act of theirs which admitted the validity of what they held to be a flagrant abuse of power could do no good, and might create a dangerous precedent. Henceforward they contented themselves with voting. On the same day Calhoun presented the bill declaring war against England, and on the second reading the opposition swelled to forty-five votes; while of the Republican majority, numbering about one hundred and five members, only seventy-six could be brought to the test. June 4 the third reading was carried by a vote of seventy-eight to forty-five, and the same day the bill passed by a vote of seventy-nine to forty-nine.

Proverbially wars are popular at their beginning; commonly, in representative governments, they are declared by aid of some part of the opposition. In the case of the War of 1812 the party in power, instead of gaining strength by the declaration, lost about one fourth of its votes, and the opposition actually gained nearly one fifth of the Administration's strength. In the Senate the loss was still greater. There too the President's Message was debated in secret, but the proceedings were very deliberate. A select committee, with Senator Anderson of Tennessee at its head, took charge of the Message, and consumed a week in studying it. June 8 the committee reported the House bill with amendments. June 11 the Senate, by a vote of seventeen to thirteen, returned the bill to the committee for further amendment. June 12 the committee reported the amendments as instructed. The Senate discussed them, was equally divided, and accordingly threw out its own amendments. June 15 the Senate voted the third reading of the House bill by a vote of nineteen to thirteen. June 16, after a strong speech for delay from Senator James A. Bayard, the Senate again adjourned without action; and only June 18, after two weeks of secret discussion, did the bill pass. Nineteen senators voted in its favor; thirteen in opposition. Samuel Smith, Giles, and Leib, the three Republican senators most openly hostile to Madison, voted with the majority. Except Pennsylvania, the entire representation of no

Northern State declared itself for the war; except Kentucky, every State south of the Potomac and the Ohio voted for the declaration. Not only was the war to be a party measure, but it was also sectional; while the Republican majority, formerly so large, was reduced to dependence on the factious support of Smith, Giles, and Leib.

The bill with its amendments was at once returned to the House and passed. Without a moment's delay the President signed it, and the same day, June 18, 1812, the war began.

"The President's proclamation was issued yesterday," wrote Richard Rush, the comptroller, to his father, June 20;[1] . . . "he visited in person—a thing never known before—all the offices of the departments of war and the navy, stimulating everything in a manner worthy of a little commander-in-chief, with his little round hat and huge cockade."

In resorting to old-fashioned methods of violence, Congress had also to decide whether to retain or to throw away its weapons of peaceful coercion. The Non-importation Act stopped importations from England. If war should be considered as taking the place of non-importation, it would have the curious result of restoring trade with England. Opinions were almost as hotly divided on the question of war with, or war without, non-importation as on the question of war and peace itself; while even this detail of policy was distorted by the too familiar interference of Napoleon,—for the non-importation was a part of his system, and its retention implied alliance with him, while the admission of English merchandise would be considered by him almost an act of war. The non-importation was known to press severely on the industries of England, but it threatened to paralyze America. In the absence of taxation, nothing but the admission of British goods into the United States could so increase the receipts of the Treasury as to supply the government with its necessary resources. Thus, two paths lay open. Congress might admit British goods, and by doing so dispense with internal taxes, relieve the commercial States, and offend France; or might

[1] Richard Rush to Benjamin Rush, June 20, 1812; Rush MSS.

shut out British goods, disgust the commercial States, double the burden of the war to America, but distress England and please Napoleon.

War having been declared June 18, on June 19 Langdon Cheves introduced, from the Committee of Ways and Means, a bill partially suspending the Non-importation Act. He supported his motion by a letter from Gallatin, accepting this bill as an alternative to the tax bills. On the same day news arrived of more American vessels burned by French frigates. Chaos seemed beyond control. War with England was about to restore commerce with her; alliance with France was a state of war with her. The war party proposed to depend on peace taxes at the cost of France their ally, in the interests of England their enemy; the peace party called for war taxes to discredit the war; both parties wanted trade with England with whom they were at war; while every one was displeased with the necessity of assisting France, the only ally that America possessed in the world. Serurier went to the Secretary of State to discuss this extraordinary situation, but found Monroe in no happy temper.[1]

"He began by complaining to me of what, for that matter, I knew already,—that a considerable number of new American ships, going to Spain and Portugal and returning, had been very recently burned by our frigates, and that others had been destroyed on the voyage even to England. The Secretary of State on this occasion, and with bitterness, renewed to me his complaints and those of the Government and of Congress, whose discontent he represented as having reached its height. I am, Monseigneur, as weary of hearing these eternal grumblings as of having to trouble you with them; but I think myself obliged to transmit to you whatever is said of an official character. Mr. Monroe averred that for his part, as Secretary of State, since he had never ceased down to this moment to maintain the repeal of our decrees, he found himself suddenly compromised in the face of his friends and of the public, and he must admit he had almost lost the hope of an arrangement with us. Such were, Monseigneur, his expressions; after which he

[1] Serurier to Maret, June 13, 1812; Archives des Aff. Étr. MSS.

retraced to me the system that the Administration had never ceased pursuing with constancy and firmness for eighteen months, and the last act of which had at length been what I had seen, a formal declaration of war against England by the republic,—'at a moment,' he added, 'when it feels ill-assured of France, and is so ill-treated by her.' He finished at last by saying to me, with a sort of political coquetry, that he was among his friends obliged to admit that they had been too weak toward France, and that perhaps they had been too quick in regard to England."

Serurier wrote that the bitterness against France was really such as would have caused a declaration of war against her as well as against England, if the Administration had not stopped the movement in Congress; nothing prevented the double war except the military difficulties in its way. At the moment when, June 23, the French minister was writing in these terms to the Duc de Bassano, the House of Representatives was considering the action he feared. Cheves had proposed to modify the non-importation,—the Federalists moved to repeal it altogether; and although they were defeated that day in committee, when Cheves's bill came before the House no less a champion than Calhoun rose to advocate the reopening of trade.

Whatever Calhoun in those days did, was boldly and well done; but his speech of June 24, 1812, against commercial restrictions, was perhaps the boldest and the best of his early efforts. Neither great courage nor much intelligence was needed to support war, from the moment war became a party measure; but an attack on the system of commercial restriction was a blow at Madison, which belittled Jefferson, and threw something like contempt on the Republican party from its beginning twenty years before, down to the actual moment. How gently Calhoun did this, and yet how firmly he laid his hands on the rein that was to guide his party into an opposite path, could be seen in his short speech.

"The restrictive system, as a mode of resistance," he said, "and a means of obtaining a redress of our wrongs, has never been a favorite one with me. I wish not to censure the motives which dictated it, or to attribute weakness to those who first resorted to it for a restoration of our rights. . . . I object to the restrictive system, and for the following reasons,—because it does not suit the genius of our people, or that of our government, or the geographical character of our country."

With a single gesture, this young statesman of the new school swept away the statesmanship of Jefferson and Madison, and waved aside the strongest convictions of his party; but he did it with such temperate statement, and with so serious a manner, that although he said in effect little less than had been said for years by Federalists and enemies, he seemed rather to lead than to oppose. "We have had a peace like a war: in the name of heaven let us not have the only thing that is worse,—a war like a peace." That his voice should be at once obeyed was not to be expected; but so many Republican members followed Calhoun, Cheves, and Lowndes, that the Federalists came within three votes of carrying their point; and so equally divided was the House that, June 25, when the Federalists returned to the attack and asked for a committee to report a bill repealing the non-importation, the House divided sixty against sixty, and the Speaker's vote alone defeated the motion.

Greatly to the French minister's relief the storm passed over; but the heroic decision of Congress not only to punish England, but to punish itself by deprivation of everything English,—not only to fight Napoleon's battles, but also to fight them under every disadvantage that Napoleon chose to exact,—could not but increase the vehemence of Northern hatred against the war, as it was certain to increase Southern hatred against taxes. Gallatin knew not what to expect. June 26 he wrote to a friend,[1] —

"We have not money enough to last till January 1 next, and General Smith is using every endeavor to run us aground by opposing everything,—treasury notes, double duties, etc. The Senate is so nearly divided, and the division so increased by that on the war question, that we can hardly rely on carrying anything."

[1] Adams's Gallatin, p. 466.

Although Gallatin caused the necessary bills for the war taxes to be reported to the House June 26, he had no idea of passing them, and was not surprised when by a vote of seventy-two to forty-six the House postponed them to the next session, Calhoun and Cheves voting with the Federalists against postponement. This chronic helplessness could not last in face of war without stopping government itself; and Congress, with a bad grace, yielded at last to necessity. Even while Gallatin was complaining, the Senate passed the bill for issuing five millions in treasury notes. June 30 it passed the bill doubling the duties on imports. In rapid succession, such other bills as were most needed by Government were put upon their passage; and July 6 the exhausted Congress adjourned, glad to escape its struggle with the novel problems of war.

In American history few sessions of Congress left a deeper mark than that of 1811–12; but in the midst of the war excitement several Acts of high importance almost escaped public notice. As far-reaching as the declaration of war itself was the Act, approved April 8, 1812, declaring the State of Louisiana to be admitted into the Union. Representatives of the Eastern States once more protested against the admission of new territory without consulting the States themselves; but Congress followed up the act by one more open to question. West Florida had remained hitherto in the condition of its military occupation a year before. Congress had then found the problem too hard to solve on any theory of treaty or popular rights; but in the excitement of the war fever Government acted on the new principle that West Florida, which had been seized because it was a part of Louisiana, should be treated as though it were a conquered territory. An Act of Congress, approved April 14, divided the district in halves at the Pearl River, and annexed the western half—against the expressed wishes of its citizens[1]—to the new State of Louisiana; the eastern portion was incorporated in the Mississippi Territory by an Act approved May 14, 1812.

To the territory of West Florida the United States had no right. Their ownership of the country between the Iberville

---

[1] Petition of inhabitants; Annals of Congress, 1811–1812, p. 2157.

and the Perdido was a usurpation which no other country was bound to regard; indeed, at the moment when Congress subjected the shores of Mobile Bay to the Mississippi Territorial government, Mobile was still garrisoned by a Spanish force and ruled by the Spanish people. The case of West Florida was the more curious, because in after years the United States government, in order to obtain a title good beyond its own borders, accepted the territory as a formal grant from the King of Spain. Ferdinand VII., the grantor and only rightful interpreter of his own grant,[1] inserted an article into the treaty of 1819 which was intended by him to discredit, and did in fact ignore, the usurpations of the United States: "His Catholic Majesty cedes to the United States, in full property and sovereignty, all the territories which belong to him situated to the eastward of the Mississippi, known by the names of East and West Florida."[2] According to the Acts of Congress, no territory known as West Florida belonged to the King of Spain; it had been ceded to the United States as a part of Louisiana. The admission by treaty in 1819 that Ferdinand VII. was still sovereign over any territory known by the name of West Florida, threw discredit on the previous acts of President and Congress, and following the confusion due to the contradictory systems they had pursued, created a chaos which neither proclamations, Acts of Congress, treaties, nor decisions of the courts, numerous and positive as they might be, could reduce to order. History cannot tell by what single title the United States hold West Florida.

East Florida threatened to become a worse annoyance. In January, 1811, as the story has told, the President, under authority of a secret Act of Congress, sent George Matthews and John McKee to take possession, under certain circumstances, of Mobile and Fernandina. Their written instructions were singularly loose.[3] In general they were to take possession of East Florida only in case the Spanish authorities or "the existing local authority" should wish it, or in case of

[1] United States *vs*. Arredondo, 6 Peters, p. 741.
[2] State Papers, Foreign Relations, iv. 617, 623; Diary of J. Q. Adams, Feb. 15, 1819, iv. 254, 255.
[3] Secretary of State to Gen. George Matthews and John McKee, Jan. 26, 1811; State Papers, Foreign Affairs, iii. 571.

actual British interference; but their conduct was to be "reg-ulated by the dictates of their own judgments, on a close view and accurate knowledge of the precise state of things there, and of the real disposition of the Spanish government." Be-sides these written instructions, Matthews professed to be guided by verbal explanations of a stronger character. With the precedent of Baton Rouge before his eyes, Matthews could not but assume that he was sent to St. Mary's for a practical object; and he found there a condition of affairs that seemed to warrant him in acting with energy. St. Mary's River was filled with British vessels engaged in smuggling British merchandise into the United States in defiance of the Non-importation Act; while Amelia Island, on which the town of Fernandina stood, was a smuggling depot, and the Span-ish authority an empty form, useful only for the protection of illicit trade.

Matthews's official reports assumed as a matter of course an intention in his Government to possess itself of East Florida. His letters made no disguise of his own acts or intentions. After six months of inquiry, he wrote to Secretary Monroe, Aug. 3, 1811, a plain account of the measures necessary to be taken:[1] —

"I ascertained that the quiet possession of East Florida could not be obtained by an amicable negotiation with the powers that exist there; . . . that the inhabitants of the province are ripe for revolt. They are, however, incompe-tent to effect a thorough revolution without external aid. If two hundred stand of arms and fifty horsemen's swords were in their possession, I am confident they would com-mence the business, and with a fair prospect of success. These could be put into their hands by consigning them to the commanding officer at this post, subject to my order. I shall use the most discreet management to prevent the United States being committed; and although I cannot vouch for the event, I think there would be but little danger."

In October, Matthews communicated freely his plans and

[1] Matthews to Monroe, Aug. 3, 1811; Secret Acts, Resolutions, and Instruc-tions under which East Florida was invaded in 1812 and 1813. Washington.

wishes to Senator Crawford, and commissioned him to explain them to the Government.[1] The President was fully acquainted with them, and during six months offered no objection, but waited in silence for Matthews to effect the revolution thus prepared.

Matthews carried out his mission by following the West Florida precedent as he understood it. March 16, 1812, some two hundred self-styled insurgents crossed the river, landed on Amelia Island, and summoned the garrison of Fernandina to surrender. At the same time the American gunboats, stationed on the river, took a position to watch the movement. The Spanish commandant sent to inquire whether the American gunboats meant to assist the insurgents, and receiving an answer in the affirmative, he capitulated to the so-called patriots.[2] Independence was declared; an independent flag was raised; and when this formality ended, the patriots summoned General Matthews, who crossed the river with a company of the regular army, and March 19 took possession of Amelia Island, subject to the President's approval.

Matthews supposed his measures to be warranted by his instructions, and thought the Government bound to sustain him; but the Government took an opposite course. April 4 Monroe wrote to Matthews[3] disavowing the seizure of Amelia Island, and referring to the precedent of Baton Rouge as the proper course to have followed. "The United States did not take possession until after the Spanish authority had been subverted by a revolutionary proceeding, and the contingency of the country being thrown into foreign hands had forced itself into view." Matthews failed to see why one "revolutionary proceeding" was not as good as another, or why the fiction of foreign interference might not serve as well at Fernandina as at Baton Rouge. He was excessively indignant, and believed his disavowal to be due to the publication of John Henry's letters, which had made the President suddenly sensitive to the awkwardness of doing openly acts which he imputed as a crime in the governor-general of Canada to

[1] Matthews to Monroe, Oct. 14, 1811; Secret Acts, Resolutions, and Instructions under which East Florida was invaded in 1812 and 1813. Washington.

[2] Niles, ii. 93.

[3] State Papers, Foreign Affairs, iii. 572.

imagine. Senator Crawford afterward wrote to Monroe[1] that this impression was by no means confined to Matthews; indeed, Crawford himself seemed to share it. Yet governments were not bound to make explanations to their instruments; and Matthews was told only that he had mistaken the President's wishes, and that his instructions were meant in good faith to require that the Spaniards should of their own accord ask to surrender their territory to the United States.

April 24 Madison wrote to Jefferson:[2] "In East Florida Matthews has been playing a strange comedy in the face of common-sense as well as of his instructions. His extravagances place us in the most distressing dilemma." The dilemma consisted in the President's wish to maintain possession of Amelia Island, and the difficulty of doing it. In explaining the matter to the French minister, Monroe made no secret of the President's wishes:[3] —

"Mr. Monroe, in communicating the facts to me at one of our last conversations, told me that General Matthews had gone beyond his orders; that he was told to observe only; and in case a third Power, which could be only England, should present itself to occupy the island, he was to prevent it if possible, and in case of necessity repulse the disembarking troops. He added that nevertheless, now that things had reached their present condition, there would be more danger in retreating than in advancing; and so, while disavowing the General's too precipitate conduct, they would maintain the occupation."

This decision required some double dealing. April 10 Monroe wrote[4] to the governor of Georgia, requesting him to take Matthews's place and to restore Amelia Island to the Spanish authorities; but this order was for public use only, and not meant to be carried into effect. May 27 Monroe wrote again,[5] saying: —

"In consequence of the compromitment of the United

[1] Crawford to Monroe, Aug. 6, 1812; Monroe MSS. State Dep. Archives.
[2] Works, ii. 532.
[3] Serurier to Maret, May 4, 1812; Archives des Aff. Étr. MSS.
[4] State Papers, iii. 572.
[5] State Papers, iii. 573.

States to the inhabitants, you have been already instructed not to withdraw the troops unless you find that it may be done consistently with their safety, and to report to the Government the result of your conferences with the Spanish authorities, with your opinion of their views, holding in the mean time the ground occupied."

Governor Mitchell would have been a poor governor and still poorer politician, had he not read such instructions as an order to hold Amelia Island as long as possible. Instead of reestablishing the Spanish authority at Fernandina, he maintained the occupation effected by Matthews.[1] June 19, the day after declaring war against England, the House took up the subject on the motion of Troup of Georgia, and in secret session debated a bill authorizing the President not to withdraw the troops, but to extend his possession over the whole country of East and West Florida, and to establish a government there.[2] June 25, by a vote of seventy to forty-eight, the House passed this bill, which in due time went successfully through all its stages in the Senate until July 3, when the vote was taken on its passage. Only then three Northern Republicans,—Bradley of Vermont, Howell of Rhode Island, and Leib of Pennsylvania,—joining Giles, Samuel Smith, and the Federalists, defeated, by a vote of sixteen to fourteen, this bill which all the President's friends in both Houses supported as an Administration measure, and upon which the President promised to act with decision; but even after its failure the President maintained possession of Fernandina, with no other authority than the secret Act of Congress which had been improperly made by Matthews the ground of usurping possession.

From the pacific theories of 1801 to the military methods of 1812 was a vast stride. When Congress rose, July 6, 1812, the whole national frontier and coast from Prairie du Chien to Eastport, from Eastport to St. Mary's, from St. Mary's to New Orleans,—three thousand miles, incapable of defence,—was open to the attacks of powerful enemies; while

[1] Governor Garzia to Governor Mitchell, Dec. 12, 1812; Niles, iii. 311.
[2] An Act, etc., Annals of Congress; 12th Congress, 1811–1812, Part I. p. 324.

the Government at Washington had taken measures for the military occupation of the vast foreign territories northward of the Lakes and southward to the Gulf of Mexico.

Chapter XII

WHILE THE Twelfth Congress at Washington from November, 1811, until July, 1812, struggled with the declaration which was to spread war westward to the Mississippi
River, Napoleon at Paris prepared the numberless details of
the coming campaign that was to ravage Europe eastward as
far as Moscow; and in this fury for destruction, no part remained for argument or diplomacy. Yet Joel Barlow, full of
hope that he should succeed in solving the problem which
had thus far baffled his Government, reached Paris, Sept. 19,
1811, and began a new experience, ended a year later at Zarnovitch in Poland by a tragedy in keeping with the military
campaign to which Barlow was in a fashion attached.

Joel Barlow felt himself at home in Paris. In 1788, at the age
of thirty-four, he had first come abroad, and during seventeen
exciting years had been rather French than American. In 1792
the National Convention conferred on him the privileges of
French citizenship,—an honor then shared only by Washington and Hamilton among Americans. He felt himself to be
best understood and appreciated by Frenchmen. His return
to France in 1812 was, he said, attended by a reception much
more cordial and friendly than that which he had received in
America, in 1805, on his return to his native country after seventeen years of absence. He settled with delight into his old
society, even into his old house in the Rue Vaugirard, and
relished the pleasure of recovering, with the highest dignity
of office, the atmosphere of refinement which he always
keenly enjoyed. Yet when these associations lost their freshness, and he turned to his diplomatic task, he found that few
lots in life were harder than that of the man who bound himself to the destinies of Napoleon.

On the success of Barlow's mission the fate of President
Madison might depend. As long as France maintained her
attitude of hostility to the United States, war against England
would be regarded by a majority of the Northern people with
distrust and dislike. On that point Madison was justly timid.
The opposition of New England and New York must be quieted, and in order to quiet it Madison must prove France to

be honest in respecting American rights; he must show that the decrees had been really repealed as he had so often and still so obstinately asserted, and that the vast confiscations of American property under the authority of those decrees would receive indemnity. The public had commonly supposed France to be comparatively a slight aggressor; but to the general surprise, when Congress, before the declaration of war against England, called for a return of captures under the belligerent edicts, Monroe's report showed that the seizures by France and by the countries under her influence in pursuance of the decrees were not less numerous than those made by England under the Orders in Council. The precise values were never known. The confiscations ordered by Napoleon in Spain, Naples, Holland, Denmark, Hamburg, and on the Baltic outnumbered those made in his empire; but all these taken together probably exceeded the actual condemnations in British prize-courts. This result, hardly expected by the American government, added to its embarrassment, but was only a part of its grievances against Napoleon. Not only had France since 1807 surpassed England in her outrages on American property, but while England encouraged American commerce with her own possessions, Napoleon systematically prohibited American commerce with his empire. He forbade American vessels to import sugar or other colonial produce except by special license; he imposed a duty of sixty cents a pound on Georgia cotton worth twenty or twenty-five cents; he refused to take tobacco except in small quantities as a part of the government monopoly; and he obliged every American ship to carry for its return cargo two thirds in silks and the other third in wines, liquors, and such other articles of French produce as he might direct. The official returns made to Congress showed that in 1811 the United States exported domestic produce to the amount of $45,294,000, of which France and Italy took only $1,164,275.

Barlow's instructions required him to reform these evils, but they especially insisted upon indemnity for seizures under the decrees. Haste was required; for Congress could not be expected to adopt extreme measures against England until France should have made such concessions as would warrant the American government in drawing a distinction between the two belligerents. Barlow arrived in Paris September 19, only to learn that on the same day the Emperor set out for Antwerp and Amsterdam. The Duc de Bassano received him kindly, assured him of the Emperor's order to begin upon business at once, and listened courteously to the American complaints and demands. Then he too departed for Holland, whence he returned only November 9, when at Washington Congress had been already a week in session.

Nothing showed this delay to be intentional; but Napoleon never allowed delay when he meant to act, and in the present instance he was not inclined to act. Although the Duc de Bassano made no reply to Barlow, he found time at Amsterdam to write instructions to Serurier.[1] In these he declared that all American vessels captured since November, 1810, had been released, except those coming by way of England, which were not yet condemned, but only sequestered.

"The French government would like to know, before making a decision, how England would act toward American ships bound for France. If I return once more on the motives for this delay, it is only for your personal instruction and without making it a subject of an official declaration on your part. On this question you should speak as for yourself; appear ignorant what are the true motives for still detaining some American ships which have had communication with England; restrict yourself to receiving the representations sent you, and to declaring that you will render an account of them; in short, give no explanation that would imply that the Decrees of Berlin and Milan are not entirely revoked."

While the Emperor was thus secretly determined to enforce his decrees, he was equally determined to pay no indemnities. Against sacrifices of money Napoleon always made unconquerable resistance.

In due time Barlow had his audience of reception, and made to the Emperor a speech, not without flattery. He ventured to mention his commercial objects, in the hope of calling out an answer that would suit his purpose. Napoleon's

---

[1] Maret to Serurier, October, 1811; Archives des Aff. Étr. MSS.

reply proved for the hundredth time the danger of risking such experiments:—

> "As to the commerce between the two Powers, I desire to favor it. I am great enough to be just. But on your part you must defend your dignity against my enemies and those of the Continent. Have a flag, and I will do for you all that you can desire."

In reporting the interview to Monroe, Barlow added that the ambiguity of the Emperor's reply made it unfit for publication.[1] Ambiguity was not the quality that a more sensitive man would have ascribed to a rebuff so sharp; but whatever the President may have thought, he took Barlow's advice. The interview was never made known to Congress.

During the month of November Napoleon busied himself in commercial questions only in order to show liberality to England at the expense of America. He extended his system of licenses to the exchange of French wines for sugar in large quantities, and even to the importation of coffee, indigo, tea, wool, dye-woods, and other articles, all to be obtained from England by license.[2] He discovered that his exchanges would benefit France more than England in the proportion of three to one. "It is therefore the perfected system that has produced this result, which had not been expected for several years. Evidently the system thus established is a permanent system, which can be made perpetual."[3] The motive for this discovery might be traced throughout all his economical experiments. He needed money.

Never had Napoleon's ministers a harder task to give his acts a color of consistency. During the months of November and December Barlow held many interviews with Bassano, and made earnest efforts to obtain some written pledge in favor of American interests, but without success. December 19 he wrote that he was almost discouraged by the unexpected and unreasonable delay.[4] Napoleon made no more seizures, and released such American vessels as were held for violation

---

[1] Barlow to Monroe, Nov. 17, 1812; MSS. State Department Archives.
[2] Notes dictées en conseil, 25 nov. 1811; Correspondance, xxiii. 36.
[3] Note sur le Blocus continental, 13 janvier, 1812; Correspondance, xxiii. 167.
[4] Barlow to Monroe, Dec. 19, 1811; State Papers, Foreign Affairs, iii. 515.

of the decrees; but he conceded nothing in principle, and was far from abandoning his fiscal system against the United States. In order to meet Barlow's complaints, Bassano gathered together every token of evidence that the decrees were not in force; but while he was asking the American minister how these facts could be doubted, a French squadron, Jan. 8, 1812, sailed from Nantes with orders to destroy all neutral ships bound to or from an enemy's port. For several months American commerce was ravaged by these ships under the Emperor's order, in pursuance of his decrees. January 19 Napoleon issued another order of the gravest character. His quarrel with Bernadotte the new king of Sweden had reached a rupture, and he carried out his threat of seizing the Swedish provinces south of the Baltic; but his orders to Marshal Davout were almost as hostile to the United States as to Sweden:[1] "As soon as you shall be sure of seizing a great quantity of colonial merchandise in Swedish Pomerania, you will take possession of that province; and you will cause to be seized both at Stralsund and Anklam, in short at all points in Pomerania, whatever colonial merchandise may be found." January 28 he wrote again:[2] "I wait with impatience your report on the colonial merchandise you shall have found in Pomerania." He made no exceptions in favor of American property, for his need of money was greater than ever.

While Bassano amused Joel Barlow with conversations that resulted in nothing, he drew up a report to the Emperor, to be laid before the conservative Senate, dealing wholly with the question of neutrals. Circumstances made the appearance of this report peculiarly mortifying to Barlow. Jonathan Russell, who had been sent to act as American *chargé* at London, wrote to Barlow asking for additional proofs to satisfy Lord Castlereagh that the decrees were repealed. Barlow replied, March 2, by a letter to Russell, recounting seven cases of ships which had been admitted to French ports contrary to the decrees, while in no case had the decrees been enforced.[3] "It is difficult to conceive," he added, "probably impossible to procure, and certainly insulting to require, a mass of evidence

---

[1] Napoleon to Davout, Jan. 19, 1812; Correspondance, xxiii. 182.
[2] Napoleon to Davout, Jan. 19, 1812; Correspondance, p. 194.
[3] Barlow to Russell, March 2, 1812; State Papers, Foreign Affairs, iii. 518.

more positive than this or more conclusive to every unprejudiced mind." Hardly had he written this letter when news
arrived that French frigates were burning American vessels on
the ocean for infringing the decrees. March 12 he wrote to
Bassano a letter of strong protest against these depredations,
and a demand for redress. His letter received no answer. Had
this been all, gross as the outrage was, nothing need have
become public; but on the heels of this scandal came another
more flagrant. March 16 the "Moniteur" published Bassano's
official report to the Emperor, which had the character of an
Imperial message to the conservative Senate. This document
began by defining neutral rights as claimed by France; and
while one of these claims required that the flag should cover
all goods except arms and other munitions of war, another
declared that no blockade was real except of a port "invested,
besieged, in the presumption of being taken;" and until these
principles should be restored to force by England, "the Decrees of Berlin and Milan must be enforced toward Powers
that let their flags be denationalized; the ports of the Continent are not to be opened to denationalized flags or to
English merchandise." Barlow could imagine no way of
reconciling this language with Bassano's assertions that the
decrees were withdrawn, and he enclosed the report to
Monroe in a letter speculating upon the reason of this contradiction:[1] —

"You will notice that the minister in his report says nothing particular of the United States, and nothing more precise than heretofore on the revocation of the decrees. . . .
I am afraid he is forbidden to designate the United States
as out of the gripe of those decrees, because the Emperor
did not like the bill we have seen before Congress for
admitting English goods contracted for before the Non-
importation Law went into operation."

Barlow could not but maintain that the decrees were repealed; yet the British government could hardly be required
to hold the same opinion. Taking Bassano's report as proof
that the United States would no longer maintain the repeal,

[1] Barlow to Monroe, March 16, 1812; MSS. State Department Archives.

the Prince Regent issued, April 21, 1812, a formal declaration, that in case those decrees should at any future time by an authentic act publicly promulgated be expressly and unconditionally repealed, then the Orders in Council should be wholly and absolutely revoked. This step brought matters to a crisis. As soon as the Prince Regent's declaration reached Paris, May 1, 1812, Barlow wrote to the French government a letter declaring that, between Bassano's report and the Prince Regent's declaration, proof that the decrees were repealed had become absolutely necessary for the United States, and he followed up his notes by a conversation in which he pressed on the French minister the danger of further trifling.[1]

Then came the climax of Imperial diplomacy. Neither Talleyrand nor Champagny had shown repugnance to falsehood; whatever end they wished, they used naturally and without hesitation the most convenient means. Yet free as they were from scruples, one might doubt whether Talleyrand or Champagny would have done what Bassano did; for when the American minister impatiently demanded some authentic evidence that the decrees were repealed, Bassano complained that such a demand should be made when the American government possessed the repealing decree itself. Barlow was struck dumb with astonishment when the French minister then passed to him a decree signed by Napoleon at St. Cloud, April 28, 1811, declaring his previous decrees non-existent for American vessels after Nov. 1, 1810.[2]

That the American minister should have lost self-possession in the face of an act so surprising and so unexpected was natural, for Talleyrand himself could hardly have controlled his features on seeing this document, which for an entire year had been sought by the whole world in vain, and which suddenly appeared as a paper so well known as to need only an allusion. In his embarrassment Barlow asked the vacant question whether this decree had been published, as though his surprise could be no greater had the document been printed in the "Moniteur" and the "National Intelligencer," or been sent to Congress with the President's Annual Message. Bassano replied that it had not been published, but had been

[1] Barlow to Bassano, May 1, 1812; State Papers, iii. 602.
[2] Barlow to Monroe, May 12, 1812; State Papers, iii. 603.

communicated at the time to Jonathan Russell and sent to Serurier with orders to communicate it to the Secretary of State. These assertions increased the American minister's embarrassment, for they implied a reflection on the American government which he could not resent without in his turn implying that Napoleon had invented the story so gravely told. Barlow said no more, but asked for a copy of the repealing decree, which was sent to him May 10.

If evidence were necessary to show that no such decree was issued April 28, 1811, Napoleon's correspondence proves that the Emperor did not consider the subject until April 29, and his note to the Council dated that day is proof that no such decree had then been adopted.[1] Yet such a decree might naturally have been afterward ante-dated without objection. Had the Emperor signed it within the year 1811 he might have set what date upon it he liked, and need have made no mystery of the delay. The interest of Bassano's conduct lay not so much in his producing an ante-dated paper as in his averring that the paper was not ante-dated, but had been communicated to the American government at the time. The flagrancy of the falsehood relieved it from the usual reproach of an attempt to deceive; but if it did not embarrass Bassano in the telling, it embarrassed President Madison beyond calculation in admitting.

Still more characteristic than the calmness with which Bassano made these announcements to the American minister at Paris, was the circumstantial gravity with which he repeated them to his own minister at Washington. Writing the same day, May 10, 1812, he enclosed a copy of the decree, explaining his reasons for doing so:[2] —

"I have learned from Mr. Barlow that he is not acquainted with the Decree of April 28, 1811, . . . and I have addressed a copy to him. You yourself, sir, have never acknowledged its reception; you have never mentioned it in any of your despatches; you have never dwelt upon it in any of your interviews with the American Secretary of State. This silence makes me fear that the communication

[1] See *ante*, p. 278.
[2] Maret to Serurier, May 10, 1812; Archives des Aff. Étr. MSS.

made of it to you under date of May 2, 1811, did not reach you, and I think it proper to enclose herewith a new copy."

He explained at some length why he had ignored this decree in his report to the conservative Senate:

"It had become useless to recall in this report a measure in respect to which no one could longer raise a doubt; it would have been even improper to specify the Americans by name; it would have entailed other citations; it would have required too much prominence to be given to the true motives of the Senatus Consultum which was to be proposed. The Emperor had reason to complain of the numerous infractions made by Russia in the Continental system, in spite of her engagement to co-operate with and maintain it. Therefore against Russia were directed the provisions of that report; but although various circumstances rendered war inevitable, it was still necessary to avoid naming her while preparing forces against her."

Bold and often rash a diplomatist as Napoleon was, he still felt that at the moment of going to war with Russia he could not entirely disregard the wishes of the United States. In appearance he gave way, and sacrificed the system so long and so tenaciously defended; but in yielding, he chose means that involved the United States government in common responsibility for his previous acts.

Even had the Emperor's deception stopped there, it would have offered the most interesting example in American experience of one peculiarity of his genius; but this was not all. He seemed to grudge the success which Barlow had wrung from him. One is tempted to think that this victory cost Barlow his life. The decree he had gained was flung at him like a missile. Bassano's letter was dated May 10; the Emperor already, the day before, had left Paris to take command of his Grand Army on the Russian frontier, and as yet the negotiation had not advanced a step. Meanwhile Barlow took a course of his own. Monroe and Madison cared little for a commercial treaty, but insisted upon indemnities. Barlow, finding that indemnity was for the present out of the question, showed great earnestness to make a commercial treaty, and admitted suggestions altogether displeasing to his Government. Thus June arrived, producing no change in the attitude of France other than the new decree, which was as grave an offence to the President's dignity as though it had been couched in terms of the lie direct.

Deceived and deserted, Madison was driven without an ally into a war that required the strongest alliances. Mortified at the figure he had been made to present, he wrote to Barlow that the shameful conduct of the French government would be an everlasting reproach to it, and that if peace were made with England, "the full tide of indignation with which the public mind here is boiling" would be directed against France. His anger was the more bitter because of his personal outrage. The repealing Decree of April, 1811, spared no kind of humiliation, for it proved, even to himself, his error in asserting that Napoleon imposed no condition precedent on the original promise to withdraw his decrees.[1] On that point the Federalists were shown to be right, and Madison could offer no defence against their charge that he had made himself a tool of Napoleon.

When Bassano left Paris to follow Napoleon into Russia he intrusted the negotiation with Barlow to the Duc Dalberg, by birth a German, who was in the Imperial service. While Dalberg listened to Barlow and wrote long reports to Bassano, Napoleon, entering Russia June 23, five days after Congress declared war against Great Britain, advanced to Wilna in Poland, where he remained until July 17, and then with five hundred thousand men plunged into the heart of Russia, leaving Bassano at Wilna with general charge of matters of state. These events made Barlow conscious that his negotiation was hopeless. His communications with Dalberg must be sent from Paris to Wilna, and thence to Napoleon on the road to Moscow, with the certainty of receiving no attention during the active campaign; while even if Napoleon had been able to give them ample attention, he would soon have taken offence at the increasing ill-temper of their tone, and would have been more likely to show anger than to grant favors. Under new instructions from Monroe, which were almost a

[1] Madison to Barlow, Aug. 11, 1812; Works, ii. 540.

reprimand, Barlow said less and less about a commercial treaty, and pressed harder for indemnities. Under instructions from Bassano, dated August 10,[1] Dalberg was obliged to avoid the discussion of indemnities and to talk only about commerce. Barlow insisted upon explanations in regard to seventeen American vessels recently burned at sea under the Decrees of Berlin and Milan; but no explanation could be obtained from Bassano. When the news arrived that Congress had declared war against England, Bassano, August 10, renewed his instructions to Dalberg without essential change:[2] —

"As for the commercial advantages that his Majesty may be disposed to grant the Americans, particularly since the last measures their Government has taken, communicate to the Minister of Commerce the different demands of Mr. Barlow; consult with him to what points and in what proportion these advantages might be granted, and communicate the result of these interviews to me before concluding anything in that respect with Mr. Barlow. You are to encourage his hopes and his confidence in the benevolent views of his Majesty toward the United States; explain, on the score of his Majesty's distance and the importance of his actual occupations, the kind of languor of the negotiation which has been begun, and the failure to decide some of the questions proposed by that minister; and you can point him to the American declaration of war against England as a motive the more for removing from their proposed arrangements with France whatever would tend to complicate them and too long delay their adoption."

These instructions showed no change in the Imperial policy even in consequence of the war declared by the United States against England. The Decrees of Berlin and Milan were no more repealed by the Decree of 1811, so unexpectedly produced by Bassano, than they had been by Champagny's famous letter of August 5, 1810; no order was ever given to any official of the empire that carried the revocation into effect. While Bassano protested to Barlow against implications of

[1] Bassano to Dalberg, 10 August, 1812; Archives des Aff. Étr. MSS.
[2] Bassano to Dalberg, 10 August, 1812; Archives des Aff. Étr. MSS.

the Emperor's good faith, Bassano's colleagues equally protested to Barlow that they had no authority to exempt American ships from the operation of the decrees. Decrès, the Minister of Marine, gave orders to his cruisers to destroy all vessels infringing the decrees, and not even an apology could be wrung from him for the act. If Barlow lost patience at this conduct, the Duc Dalberg, with German simple-mindedness, felt even more acutely the odium of his part, and sent to Bassano remonstrances as strong as those he received from Barlow. August 11, only one day after Bassano wrote from Wilna the instruction just quoted, Dalberg wrote from Paris in language such as had been of late seldom used in the Emperor's service:[1] —

"If we wish to inspire any confidence in the American government, of what use is an isolated proof of revocation if a little while afterward another proof overthrows it, and if Mr. Barlow, by his means of information at the Department of Commerce, at that of the Marine, at the Council of Prizes, learns that they are ignorant of it; that nothing is changed in that legislation, and that it may at any instant be again enforced? Under such circumstances, I pray you, Monsieur le Duc, to consider what is the good of all the fine phrases and fair words that I may use to Mr. Barlow when he is every moment receiving news that our privateers in the Baltic and on the coast permit themselves the most reckless (*les plus fortes*) violations against the property of Americans. In such circumstances the art of diplomacy becomes insufficient, a sorry game (*triste métier*) of which no one is long the dupe."

Dalberg seemed to suspect that Bassano himself knew little of the true situation: —

"Your Excellency is perhaps not informed of the complaints made by Americans to Mr. Barlow. If you believe that, while nothing is settled in regard to American navigation, the Americans enjoy the favor of navigating freely, of being well treated in our ports, and of being exposed to no annoyance, you deceive yourself. What with the Decrees

[1] Dalberg to Bassano, Aug. 11, 1812; Archives des Aff. Étr. MSS.

of Berlin and Milan, whose revocation is not yet known to the authorities; what with our forms of custom-house examinations; what with the multiplied obstacles to all commercial movement,—this is impossible."

Plain as such language was, it could have no effect; for Bassano could do nothing without Napoleon's approval, and Napoleon was already beyond reach. September 7 he fought the battle of Borodino; September 15 he entered Moscow.

During all these months Barlow received by every packet despatches more and more decided from Monroe, letters more and more threatening from Madison. He told Dalberg in substance that these orders left no choice except between indemnities and war. Dalberg reported his language faithfully to Bassano; and Bassano, struggling with the increasing difficulties of his position, invented a new expedient for gaining time. While Napoleon remained at Moscow, unable to advance and unwilling to retreat, Bassano wrote, October 11, from Wilna a letter to Barlow saying that the Emperor, regretting the delay which attended negotiation conducted at so great a distance, had put an end to the Duc Dalberg's authority and requested Barlow to come in person to Wilna. The request itself was an outrage, for its motive could not be mistaken. For an entire year Barlow had seen the French government elude every demand he made, and he could not fail to understand that the journey to Wilna caused indefinite further delay, when a letter of ten lines to Dalberg might remove every obstacle; but however futile the invitation might be, refusal would have excused the French government's inaction. Throughout life Barlow exulted in activity; a famous traveller, no fatigue or exposure checked his restlessness, and although approaching his sixtieth year he feared no journey. He accepted Bassano's invitation, and October 25 wrote that he should set out the following day for Wilna. A week earlier, Napoleon quitted Moscow, and began his retreat to Poland.

Ten days brought Barlow to Berlin, and already Napoleon's army was in full flight and in danger of destruction, although the winter had hardly begun. November 11 Barlow reached Königsberg and plunged into the wastes of Poland. Everywhere on the road he saw the devastation of war, and when he reached Wilna, November 18, he found only confusion. Every one knew that Napoleon was defeated, but no one yet knew the tragedy that had reduced his army of half a million men to a desperate remnant numbering some fifty thousand. While Barlow waited for Napoleon's arrival, Napoleon struggled through one obstacle after another until the fatal passage of the Beresina, November 27, which dissolved his army and caused him to abandon it. December 5, at midnight, he started for Paris, having sent a courier in advance to warn the Duc de Bassano, who lost no time in dismissing his guests from Wilna, where they were no longer safe. Barlow quitted Wilna for Paris the day before Napoleon left his army; but Napoleon soon passed him on the road. The weather was very cold, the thermometer thirteen degrees below zero of Fahrenheit; but Barlow travelled night and day, and after passing through Warsaw, reached a small village called Zarnovitch near Cracow. There he was obliged to stop. Fatigue and exposure caused an acute inflammation of the lungs, which ended his life Dec. 24, 1812. A week earlier Napoleon had reached Paris.

Barlow's death passed almost unnoticed in the general catastrophe of which it was so small a part. Not until March, 1813, was it known in America; and the news had the less effect because circumstances were greatly changed. Madison's earnestness in demanding satisfaction from France expressed not so much his own feelings as fear of his domestic opponents. The triumph of Russia and England strengthened the domestic opposition beyond hope of harmony, and left the President in a desperate strait. No treaty, either with or without indemnities, could longer benefit greatly the Administration, while Napoleon's overthrow threatened to carry down Madison himself in the general ruin. In his own words,[1] —

"Had the French emperor not been broken down, as he was to a degree at variance with all probability and which no human sagacity could anticipate, can it be doubted that Great Britain would have been constrained by her own situation and the demands of her allies to listen to our reasonable terms of reconciliation? The moment chosen for war

[1] Madison to Wheaton, Feb. 26, 1827; Works, iii. 553.

would therefore have been well chosen, if chosen with a reference to the French expedition against Russia; and although not so chosen, the coincidence between the war and the expedition promised at the time to be as favorable as it was fortuitous."

Thus the year 1812 closed American relations with France in disappointment and mortification. Whatever hopes Madison might still cherish, he could not repeat the happy diplomacy of 1778 or of 1803. From France he could gain nothing. He had challenged a danger more serious than he ever imagined; for he stood alone in the world in the face of victorious England.

Chapter XIII

WHILE NAPOLEON thus tried the temper of America, the Government of England slowly and with infinite reluctance yielded to American demands. Not for the first time experience showed that any English minister whose policy rested on jealousy of America must sooner or later come to ruin and disgrace.

After the departure of Pinkney and Foster in May, 1811, diplomatic action was for a time transferred to Washington. The young American *chargé* in London, John Spear Smith, could only transmit news that came officially to his hands. The Marquess Wellesley, still struggling to reorganize the Ministry, found the Prince Regent less and less inclined to assist him, until at last he despaired. American affairs resumed their old position. In June, 1811, Sir William Scott, after some months of hesitation, rendered final decision that the French Decrees were still in force, and that in consequence all American vessels falling within the range of the British Orders in Council were liable to condemnation.[1] In the Cabinet, Wellesley urged his colleagues either to negotiate with America or to show themselves prepared for war; but his colleagues would do neither.[2] Convinced that the United States would not and could not fight, Perceval and Eldon, Bathurst and Liverpool, were indifferent to Wellesley's discomfort. In the autumn of 1811 nothing in the attitude of the British government, except its previous hesitation, held out a hope of change.

Yet many reasons combined to show that concessions were inevitable. The sweeping ruin that overwhelmed British commerce and industry in 1810 sank deep among the laboring classes in 1811. The seasons doubled the distress. The winter had been intense, the summer was unfavorable; wheat rose in the autumn to one hundred and forty-five shillings, or about thirty-six dollars the quarter, and as the winter of 1811 began, disorders broke out in the manufacturing districts. The inland counties reached a state of actual insurrection which no exercise of force seemed to repress. The American non-

[1] State Papers, iii. 421.
[2] The Courier, Sept. 22, 1812; Letter signed "Vetus."

478

importation aggravated the trouble, and worked unceasingly to shake the authority of Spencer Perceval, already one of the most unpopular ministers England had ever seen.

Popular distress alone could hardly have effected a change in Perceval's system; so great a result was not to be produced by means hitherto so little regarded. The moment marked an era in English history, for the new class of laborers, the mill-operatives and other manufacturing workmen, took for the first time an active share in shaping legislation. In their hostility to Perceval's policy they were backed by their employers; but the united efforts of employers and workmen were not yet equal to controlling the Government, even though they were aided by the American non-importation. They worried Perceval, but did not break him down. At the close of 1811 he showed still no signs of yielding; but news then arrived that the American Congress had met, and that the President's Message, the debates in the House, the tone of the press, and the feelings of the American people announced war. This was a new force with which Perceval could not deal.

No man of common-sense could charge England with want of courage, for if ever a nation had fought its way, England had a right to claim whatever credit such a career bestowed; but England lived in war, she knew its exact cost, and at that moment she could not afford it. The most bigoted Tory could see that if Napoleon succeeded in his coming attack on Russia, as he had hitherto succeeded in every war he had undertaken in Europe even when circumstances were less favorable, he would need only the aid of America to ruin beyond redemption the trade and finances of Great Britain. Little as Englishmen believed in the military capacity of the United States, they needed too much the markets and products of America to challenge war.

The gradual decline of the domineering tone which Canning had made fashionable offered a curious study in politics. In 1807 the affair of the "Little Belt" would have caused violent anger; in 1812 it created hardly a flurry. The Tory "Courier" talked wildly, but the "Times" took the matter with calmness; the Ministry showed no offence, and within a few weeks the affair was forgotten. Even after this irritation, the British public seemed pleased rather than angered to learn that Lord Wellesley had yielded complete apology and redress to America for the "Chesapeake" outrage. The commercial class for many months expected energetic retaliation by their government against the American Non-importation Act; but in September this idea was laid aside, and no one complained. Little by little the press took a defensive tone. In the place of threats the newspapers were filled with complaints. America was unfair, unreasonable, unjust; she called on England to admit that the French Decrees were repealed when in fact they were still in force; she threatened war; she hectored and bullied,—but the more dignified course required England to be temperate though firm.

Parliament met Jan. 7, 1812, and the Prince Regent's speech was studiously moderate in its reference to the United States. In the Commons, January 8, Whitbread attacked ministers for their failure to conciliate America; and Spencer Perceval replied in a manner that could hardly have satisfied himself.

"He would allow," he said,[1] "that a war with America would be an evil to Great Britain, but he also knew that such a war would be a greater evil to America. As an evil to America he was anxious to avert it; he looked upon America as accessory to the prosperity and welfare of Great Britain, and would be sorry to see her impoverished, crushed, or destroyed. . . . Sure he was that no one could construe those truly conciliatory dispositions of England into fear; but he was of the opinion that England, conscious of her own dignity, could bear more from America for peace's sake than from any other Power on earth."

This sentiment was the more significant because the latest news showed that England in the immediate future would be obliged to bear a great deal from America. The news became every day more and more alarming, and was reinforced by steadily increasing outcry from Birmingham, Liverpool, Nottingham, Hull, ending in a general agitation organized by active radicals, with Brougham at their head. So rapidly was one attack followed by another, that Perceval and his lieutenants—George Rose and James Stephen—could no longer

[1] Cobbett's Debates, xxi. 61.

carry their points by mere weight of office. The Marquess Wellesley, refusing to serve longer under Perceval, resigned from the Cabinet January 16, and no one felt confident that Perceval could supply his place. During more than a month negotiations continued without result, until, February 22, Lord Castlereagh received the appointment of Foreign Secretary.

During this interval the movement against the Orders in Council gained strength. In the Commons, February 13, another debate occurred when Whitbread, in a strong American speech, moved for the diplomatic correspondence with the United States, and was answered with some temper by Stephen and Perceval. Stephen went so far as to declare,—and whatever he declared he certainly believed,—that "nothing but the utmost aversion to a quarrel with America would have enabled this country to have borne so much. So far from having done anything to provoke a rupture with America, the strongest, most persevering, and almost even humiliating means had been employed to avoid it;"[1] but he would not surrender to her the carrying and coasting trade of Europe even to prevent a war. Perceval spoke more evasively than usual, defending his commercial system as one that had been begun by his Whig predecessors, and throwing the blame for its irregularities on Napoleon's decrees; but although that day he was supposed to be in extreme peril of losing his majority, he closed his speech by declaring that sooner than yield to the repeal of the Orders in Council he would refuse share in any Administration. Alexander Baring answered that in this case war could hardly be avoided, and made an earnest appeal, founded on the distress of the manufacturing towns, in favor of the direct interference of Parliament to overrule the minister. Even William Wilberforce, whose speeches sometimes recalled those of Polonius, and whose hesitations generally marked the decline rather than the rise of a Ministry in power, felt himself constrained to say that "there was not at all times a sufficient attention in this country to the spirit of conciliation toward other countries, and particularly toward America. It would be well if persons in high situations in

[1] Cobbett's Debates, xxi. 773.

government had been more abundant in their civilities to that nation."

Again, five days afterward, Baring attacked Perceval by an embarrassing motion on the subject of licenses. No such scandal as the license system had been known in England since the monopolies of the Tudors and Stuarts. Most of the trade between Great Britain and the Continent was conducted by the Board of Trade on one side and Napoleon on the other, under special licenses issued for the carriage of specified articles. In 1807 the number of such licenses amounted to sixteen hundred; in 1810 they reached eighteen thousand. Owing to practical difficulties and to Napoleon's dislike, American vessels took few licenses. A nondescript class of so-called neutrals under the flags of Pappenberg, Kniphausen, and Varel, carrying double licenses and double sets of papers, served as the agents for this curious commerce which reeked with fraud and perjury. In the case of the "Æolus," Aug. 8, 1810, the Court said: "It is a matter perfectly notorious that we are carrying on the trade of the whole world under simulated and disguised papers. The commerce of the world unavoidably assumes a disguise; these disguises we ourselves are under the necessity of employing, with simulation and dissimulation." Dr. Joseph Phillimore, perhaps the highest authority on civil law in England, in two strong pamphlets[1] declared that ancient rules and practices had been rendered obsolete, so that the Admiralty Courts were no longer occupied with the law of nations, but only with the interpretation of licenses; and while the property of enemies was as invariably restored as formerly it had been condemned, the condemnation of true neutral property had become as much a matter of course as had been its restitution a few years before. No one, even among the sternest supporters of the Orders in Council, ventured to defend the licenses on any other ground than that of their necessity.

Baring's motion called up Perceval again. "The only principle on which Government acted," said he,[2] "was to secure to the natives of England that trade by means of licenses, the profits of which without them would devolve to the hands of

[1] Reflections, etc.; Letter, etc., February, 1812. By Joseph Phillimore.
[2] Cobbett's Debates, xxi. 847.

aliens." This admission, or avowal, seemed to yield the whole ground of complaint which America had taken; neither Perceval nor Rose ventured to defend the licenses as in themselves deserving support; they stood only by the system. Their attitude led to another and more famous debate, which added an interesting chapter to the history of England.

In the Lords, February 28, the Marquess of Lansdowne moved for a committee to consider the subject of the Orders in Council. Like all that Lord Lansdowne did, his speech was temperate and able; but his arguments were the same that have been so often repeated. Lord Bathurst, President of the Board of Trade, replied. Bathurst's argument was singularly free from the faults of Perceval and Rose; and he went to the verge of destroying his own case by avowing that in the clamor raised about the Orders in Council no one could say what those orders were, or what would be the consequences of yielding to American demands. He was sure that France had suffered from the effect of the system, but he was not so certain that England had been also a sufferer, while he maintained that the licenses tended to diminish the spirit of perjury, and that the abandonment of licenses would only place an additional obstacle in the way of trade. "Were they to put restraints on the freedom of British commerce for the simple purpose of giving the trade of Europe to the Americans?" This avowal, like those made by Perceval and Stephen, seemed to concede the justice of American complaints; but perhaps it admitted only the reply made by Lord Holland, who said in plain words that the choice lay between the orders and war, and that he could not suppose the orders to be their Lordships' preference. Lansdowne's motion was rejected by a vote of one hundred and thirty-five to seventy-one.

In the Commons the great debate took place March 3, when Henry Brougham repeated Lansdowne's motion for a committee, after a speech showing as much self-restraint as clearness and force. In reply, George Rose offered a general denial of the facts which Brougham alleged. He denied that the orders injured the British export trade; that the license system injured British shipping or increased perjury; or that the orders caused manufacturing distress. On all these points he arrayed statistics in his support; but toward the close of his speech he made a remark—such as had been made many times by every defender of the system—surrendering in effect the point in diplomatic dispute between England and the United States. "The honorable gentleman," he said,[1] "had not been correct in calling these orders a system of retaliation; they were rather a system of self-defence, a plan to prevent the whole trade of the world from being snatched away from her." He was followed by Alexander Baring, who condemned the policy which built up the shipping of France at the cost of American shipping, and manufactures in Massachusetts at the cost of British manufactures; and after Baring came James Stephen, who repeated his old arguments without essential change. Then toward midnight, after these four long, serious, statistical speeches, such as usually emptied the House, George Canning rose; and so keen was the interest and anxiety of the moment that more than four hundred members crowded in, curious to learn by what ingenuity Canning would defend a threatened vote against those Orders in Council of which he had been so long the champion.[2]

"For these Orders in Council," he said, "so far as he had been connected with their adoption, he was ready to take his full share of responsibility. What orders were truly meant? Why, they were the Orders in Council which, until he had heard the speech of the right honorable gentleman (Mr. Rose), he had always looked upon as retaliatory upon the enemy; which had been so understood in every instance, until the Vice-President of the Board of Trade, in contradiction to every statement which had hitherto been given to the public on the subject,—in contradiction to every document in office respecting these Orders,—in contradiction to every communication which he (Mr. Canning) had made, and every despatch written in his official character explanatory of their nature and spirit,—in contradiction to every speech which had been made in Parliament in defence of them,—had thought proper to represent them not as measures retaliatory upon the enemy, but as

[1] Times report, March 4; National Intelligencer, April 25, 1812. Cf. London Morning Chronicle, March 4, 1812.
[2] Memoirs of R. Plumer Ward, i. 446.

measures of self-defence. Self-defence, but not retaliatory! . . . If they were to be in no larger a sense retaliatory than as self-defensive,—if they were not to retaliate directly against the enemy, but to be defensive against a rival in trade,—if they were not to be belligerent measures, but purely defensive,—then all the arguments by which they had hitherto been supported would fail to apply."

Again and again Canning returned to this slip of the tongue by which Rose had given him pretext for turning against the Administration.

"If at any time it should appear that these orders did not retort his aggression upon the enemy, but operated solely to the injury of the neutrals; if even the British government should appear to have interfered to relieve their pressure upon the enemy,—they would stand upon far different principles than those upon which he had supported them, and would in his opinion be very proper objects for exam-ination and revision. . . . Were he called upon to state his opinion of what he conceived the Orders in Council should be, he could not do it more fully than by saying that they were most perfect as they approached toward a belligerent measure and receded from a commercial one. Let them have for their object the pressure and distress of the enemy, for the purpose of compelling him to listen to terms of accommodation, and not for the narrow policy of wringing temporary concessions from him with which they might go to his own market."

To the amazement of friend and foe Canning next attacked the license system as one of which he had little knowledge, but whose details required investigation. As for America, as he was the last man who would lay the honor of the country at her feet, so would he be among the first to go far in the work of honorable conciliation, and he would not oppose the motion before the House because it might have incidentally the effect of conciliating her. Finally, if the account of Plumer Ward be true, "he concluded the first dull and flat speech I ever heard him make, without the smallest support from the House, and sat down without a cheer and almost without its being known that he had finished."

Plumer Ward was a passionate admirer of Spencer Perceval, and his anger with Canning showed the soreness caused by Canning's sudden change of front. Perceval was obliged to rescue Rose, but in doing so made the case worse rather than better as far as regarded America. Having declared that the orders were strictly retaliatory, he added, in the same breath, that "the object of Government was to protect and to force the trade of this country. . . . The object of the Orders in Council was not to destroy the trade of the Continent, but to force the Continent to trade with us." Had this assertion been made by Madison or Brougham it would have been instantly contradicted; but Perceval's silence was still less creditable than his avowals. No one knew so well as Perceval where to strike with effect at Canning; for not only could he show that from the first Canning was privy to the system of forcing commerce upon France, but he had preserved the letter in which Canning at the outset advised him to keep out of sight the exceptions which gave the measure the air of a commercial rather than a political transaction. Never had a distinguished man exposed himself with less caution than Canning, by declaring that in his opinion the orders required revision from the moment the British government should appear to intervene to relax their pressure upon the enemy; for during two years of his official life he had given steady though silent support to the Board of Trade in its persistent efforts to supply France, by means of licenses in thousands and smuggling without limit, with every product known to commerce. Such conduct challenged the severest retort, but Perceval made none. He would have been superior to the statesmen of his time had he felt the true nature of that sleight-of-hand which he and Canning practised, and which, like the trick of black-legs on the race-course, consisted in shuffling together the two words, "Retaliation—Self-defence! Self-defence—Retaliation!" but he could at least understand the impossibility of exposing Canning without also exposing himself.

The debate ended in a division. One hundred and forty-four members, including Canning and Wilberforce, went into the lobby with Brougham. Only a majority of seventy-two remained to be overcome; and to Brougham's energetic nature such a majority offered an incentive to exertion. Perceval's friends, on the other hand, exulted because this majority of seventy-two stood by him against the combined forces of Wellesley, Canning, the Radicals, and the Whigs.[1] Except for one danger, Perceval and his system were still secure; but the fear that the Americans meant at last to fight gave him no rest,—it dogged his steps, and galled him at every motion. Neither Rose nor James Stephen could prove, by any statistics under the control of the Board of Trade, that their system would benefit British commerce if it produced an American war. Already the north and west of England, the inland counties, the seaports, had risen in insurrection against the orders. Stephen and Rose exhausted themselves and the House to prove that the balance of profit was still in England's favor; but what would become of their balance-sheet if they were obliged to add the cost of an American war to the debtor side of their account?

In the effort to strengthen his Ministry Perceval persuaded Lord Sidmouth to enter the Cabinet, but only on condition that the orders should be left an open question. Sidmouth plainly said that he would rather give up the orders than face an American war.[2] He also asked that the license system should be renounced. Perceval replied that this would be a greater sacrifice than if the licenses had never been granted.[3] Lord Sidmouth was not a great man,—Canning despised his abilities, and the Prince of Wales called him a blockhead;[4] but he was, except Lord Castlereagh, the only ally to be found, and Perceval accepted him on his own terms. The new Cabinet at once took the American question in hand, and Castlereagh then wrote his instructions of April 10 to Foster, making use of Bassano's report to justify England's persistence in the orders; but besides this despatch Castlereagh wrote another of the same date, in which Sidmouth's idea took shape. If the United States would restore intercourse with Great Britain, the British government would issue no more licenses and would resort to rigorous blockades.[5] This great conces-

---

[1] Memoirs of R. Plumer Ward, i. 450.
[2] Memoirs of R. Plumer Ward, i. 441.
[3] Life of Sidmouth, iii. 74.
[4] Memoirs of R. Plumer Ward, i. 478.
[5] Castlereagh to Foster, April 10, 1812; Papers of 1813, No. 4, p. 505.

sion showed how rapidly Perceval lost ground; but this was not yet all. April 21 the Prince Regent issued his formal declaration that whenever the French government should publish an authentic Act expressly and unconditionally repealing the Berlin and Milan Decrees, the Orders in Council, including that of Jan. 7, 1807, should be wholly and absolutely revoked.

Had the United States at that moment been so fortunate as to enjoy the services of Pinkney in London, or of any man whose position and abilities raised him above the confusion of party politics, he might have convinced them that war was unnecessary. The mere threat was sufficient. Sidmouth's entrance into the Cabinet showed the change of current, and once Perceval began to give way, he could not stop. Unfortunately the United States had no longer a minister in England. In July, 1811, the President ordered Jonathan Russell to London to act as *chargé* until a minister should be appointed, which he added would be done as soon as Congress met;[1] but he changed his mind and appointed no minister, while Jonathan Russell, seeing that Perceval commanded a majority and was determined to maintain his system, reported the situation as hopeless.[2]

Brougham, without taking the precaution of giving Russell the daily information he so much needed, devoted all his energies to pressing the popular movement against the Orders in Council. Petition after petition was hurried to Parliament, and almost every petition caused a new debate. George Rose, who possessed an unhappy bluntness, in conversation with a Birmingham committee said that the two countries were like two men with their heads in buckets of water, whose struggle was which of the two could hold out longest before suffocation. The phrase was seized as a catchword, and helped agitation. April 28 Lord Stanley, in the House, renewed the motion for a committee on the petitions against the orders. Perceval had been asked whether he would consent to the committee, and had refused; but on consulting his followers he found such symptoms of disaffection as obliged him to yield rather than face a defeat. George Rose then announced, greatly against his will, that as a matter of respect to the

[1] Monroe to Russell, July 27, 1811; State Papers, iii. 422.
[2] Russell to Monroe, March, 1812; State Papers, iii. 426, 427.

petitioners he would no longer oppose their request; Castle-reagh and Perceval, cautioning the House that nothing need be expected from the investigation, followed Rose; while Stephen, after denouncing as a foul libel the charge that the orders had been invented to extend the commerce of Great Britain, also yielded to the committee "as a negative good, and to prevent misconstruction."

Stimulated by the threatening news from America, Brougham pressed with his utmost energy the victory he had won. The committee immediately began its examination of witnesses, who appeared from every quarter to prove that the Orders in Council and the subsequent non-importation had ruined large branches of British trade, and had lopped away a market that consumed British products to the value of more than ten million pounds sterling a year. Perceval and Stephen did their best to stem the tide, but were slowly overborne, and seemed soon to struggle only for delay.

Then followed a melodramatic change. May 11, as the prime minister entered the House to attend the investigation, persons about the door heard the report of a pistol, and saw Spencer Perceval fall forward shot through the heart. By the hand of a lunatic moved only by imaginary personal motives, this minister, who seemed in no way a tragical figure, became the victim of a tragedy without example in modern English history; but although England had never been in a situation more desperate, the true importance of Spencer Perceval was far from great, and when he vanished in the flash of a pistol from the stage where he seemed to fill the most considerable part, he stood already on the verge of overthrow. His death relieved England of a burden. Brougham would not allow his inquiry to be suspended, and the premier's assassination rather concealed than revealed the defeat his system must have suffered.

During the negotiations which followed, in the midst of difficulties in forming a new Ministry, Castlereagh received from Jonathan Russell Napoleon's clandestine Decree of Repeal. Brougham asked, May 22, what construction was to be put by ministers on this paper. Castlereagh replied that the decree was a trick disgraceful to any civilized government, and contained nothing to satisfy the conditions required by

England. Apart from the subordinate detail that his view of the decree was correct, his remarks meant nothing. The alarm caused by news that Congress had imposed an embargo as the last step before war, the annoyance created by John Henry's revelations and Castlereagh's lame defence, the weight of evidence pressing on Parliament against the Orders in Council, the absence of a strong or permanent Ministry,—these influences, gaining from day to day, forced the conviction that a change of system must take place. June 8 Lord Liverpool announced that he had formed an Administration, and would deal in due course with the Orders in Council. June 16 Brougham made his motion for a repeal of the orders. When he began his speech he did not know what part the new Ministry would take, but while he unfolded his long and luminous argument he noticed that James Stephen failed to appear in the House. This absence could mean only that Stephen had been deserted by ministers; and doubt ceased when Brougham and Baring ended, for then Lord Castlereagh—after Perceval's death the leader of the House—rose and awkwardly announced that the Government, though till within three or four days unable to deliberate on the subject, had decided to suspend immediately the Orders in Council.

Thus ended the long struggle waged for five years by the United States against the most illiberal Government known in England within modern times. Never since the Definitive Treaty of Peace had America won so complete a triumph, for the surrender lacked on England's part no element of defeat. Canning never ceased taunting the new Ministry with their want of courage in yielding without a struggle. The press submitted with bad grace to the necessity of holding its tongue. Every one knew that the danger, already almost a certainty, of an American war chiefly caused the sudden and silent surrender, and that the Ministry like the people shrank from facing the consequences of their own folly. Every one cried that England should not suffer herself to be provoked by the irritating conduct of America; and at a moment when every word and act of the American government announced war in the rudest terms, not a voice was heard in England for accepting the challenge, nor was a musket made ready for defence. The new Ministry thought the war likely to drive them from office, for they were even weaker than when Spencer Perceval led them. The "Times" of June 17 declared that whatever might be the necessity of defending British rights by an American war, yet it would be the most unpopular war ever known, because every one would say that with happier talents it might have been avoided. "Indeed," it added, "every one is so declaring at the present moment; so that we who have ever been the most strenuous advocates of the British cause in this dispute are really overwhelmed by the general clamor." Bitter as the mortification was, the headlong abandonment of the Orders in Council called out reproaches only against the ministers who originally adopted them. "We are most surprised," said the "Times" of June 18, "that such acts could ever have received the sanction of the Ministry when so little was urged in their defence."

Such concessions were commonly the result rather than the prelude of war; they were not unlike those by which Talleyrand succeeded, in 1799, in restoring friendly relations between France and America. Three months earlier they would have answered their purpose; but the English were a slow and stubborn race. Perhaps that they should have repealed the orders at all was more surprising than that they should have waited five years; but although they acted more quickly and decidedly than was their custom, Spencer Perceval lived three months too long. The Orders in Council were abandoned at Westminster June 17; within twenty-four hours at Washington war was declared; and forty-eight hours later Napoleon, about to enter Russia, issued the first bulletin of his Grand Army.

Chapter XIV

FOR CIVIL AFFAIRS Americans were more or less trained; but they had ignored war, and had shown no capacity in their treatment of military matters. Their little army was not well organized or equipped; its civil administration was more imperfect than its military, and its military condition could hardly have been worse. The ten old regiments, with half-filled ranks, were scattered over an enormous country on garrison service, from which they could not be safely withdrawn; they had no experience, and no organization for a campaign, while thirteen new regiments not yet raised were expected to conquer Canada.

If the army in rank and file was insufficient, its commanding officers supplied none of its wants. The senior major-general appointed by President Madison in February, 1812, was Henry Dearborn, who had retired in 1809 from President Jefferson's Cabinet into the Custom-House of Boston. Born in 1751, Dearborn at the time of his nomination as major-general was in his sixty-second year, and had never held a higher grade in the army than that of deputy quartermaster-general in 1781, and colonel of a New Hampshire regiment after active service in the Revolutionary War had ended.

The other major-general appointed at the same time was Thomas Pinckney, of South Carolina, who received command of the Southern Department. Pinckney was a year older than Dearborn; his military service was chiefly confined to the guerilla campaigns of Marion and Sumter, and to staff duty as aide to General Gates in the Southern campaign of 1780; he had been minister in England and Envoy Extraordinary to Spain, where he negotiated the excellent treaty known by his name; he had been also a Federalist member of Congress in the stormy sessions from 1797 to 1801,—but none of these services, distinguished as they were, seemed to explain his appointment as major-general. Macon, whose opinions commonly reflected those of the Southern people, was astonished at the choice.

"The nomination of Thomas Pinckney for major-general," he wrote,[1] "is cause of grief to all men who wish proper men appointed; not that he is a Federal or that he is not a gentleman, but because he is thought not to possess the talents necessary to his station. I imagine his nomination must have been produced through the means of P. Hamilton, who is about as fit for his place as the Indian Prophet would be for Emperor of Europe. I never was more at a loss to account for any proceeding than the nomination of Pinckney to be major-general."

Even the private report that Pinckney had become a Republican did not reconcile Macon, whose belief that the "fighting secretaries" would not do for real war became stronger than ever, although he admitted that some of the military appointments were supposed to be tolerably good.

Of the brigadier-generals the senior was James Wilkinson, born in 1757, and fifty-five years old in 1812. Wilkinson had recently been tried by court-martial on a variety of charges, beginning with that of having been a pensioner of Spain and engaged in treasonable conspiracy; then of being an accomplice of Aaron Burr; and finally, insubordination, neglect of duty, wastefulness, and corruption. The court acquitted him, and February 14 President Madison approved the decision, but added an irritating reprimand. Yet in spite of acquittal Wilkinson stood in the worst possible odor, and returned what he considered his wrongs by bitter and contemptuous hatred for the President and the Secretary of War.

The next brigadier was Wade Hampton, of South Carolina, who entered the service in 1808, and was commissioned as brigadier in 1809. Born in 1754, he was fifty-seven years old, and though understood to be a good officer, he had as yet enjoyed no opportunity of distinguishing himself. Next in order came Joseph Bloomfield of New Jersey, nominated as brigadier-general of the regular army March 27, 1812; on the same day James Winchester, of Tennessee, was named fourth brigadier; and April 8 William Hull, of Massachusetts, was appointed fifth in rank. Bloomfield, a major in the Revolutionary War, had been for the last ten years Governor of New Jersey. Winchester, another old Revolutionary officer, origi-

[1] Macon to Nicholson, March 25, 1812; Nicholson MSS.

nally from Maryland, though mild, generous, and rich, was not the best choice that might have been made from Tennessee. William Hull, civil Governor of Michigan since 1805, was a third of the same class. All were sixty years of age or thereabout, and none belonged to the regular service. Excepting Hull, none seems ever before to have commanded a regiment in face of an enemy.

Of the inferior appointments, almost as numerous as the enlistments, little could be said. Among the officers of the regiment of Light Artillery raised in 1808, after the "Chesapeake" alarm, was a young captain named Winfield Scott, born near Petersburg, Virginia, in 1786, and in the prime of his energies when at the age of twenty-six he saw the chance of distinction before him. In after life Scott described the condition of the service as he found it in 1808.

> "The army of that day," he said,[1] "including its general staff, the three old and the nine new regiments, presented no pleasing aspect. The old officers had very generally sunk into either sloth, ignorance, or habits of intemperate drinking. . . . Many of the appointments were positively bad, and a majority of the remainder indifferent. Party spirit of that day knew no bounds, and of course was blind to policy. Federalists were almost entirely excluded from selection, though great numbers were eager for the field, and in New England and some other States there were but very few educated Republicans; hence the selections from those communities consisted mostly of coarse and ignorant men. In the other States, where there was no lack of educated men in the dominant party, the appointments consisted generally of swaggerers, dependants, decayed gentlemen, and others, 'fit for nothing else,' which always turned out utterly unfit for any military purpose whatever."

This account of the army of 1808 applied equally, said Scott, to the appointments of 1812. Perhaps the country would have fared as well without a regular army, by depending wholly on volunteers, and allowing the States to choose general officers. In such a case Andrew Jackson would have taken

[1] Autobiography, p. 31.

the place of James Winchester, and William Hull would never have received an appointment from Massachusetts.

No one in the government gave much thought to the military dangers created by the war, yet these dangers seemed evident enough to warrant keen anxiety. The sea-shore was nowhere capable of defence; the Lakes were unguarded; the Indians of the Northwestern Territory were already in arms, and known to be waiting only a word from the Canadian governor-general; while the whole country beyond the Wabash and Maumee rivers stood nearly defenceless. At Detroit one hundred and twenty soldiers garrisoned the old British fort; eighty-five men on the Maumee held Fort Wayne; some fifty men guarded the new stockade called Fort Harrison, lately built on the Wabash; and fifty-three men, beyond possibility of rescue, were stationed at Fort Dearborn, or Chicago; finally, eighty-eight men occupied the Island of Michillimackinaw in the straits between Lake Huron and Lake Michigan. These were all the military defences of a vast territory, which once lost would need another war to regain; and these petty garrisons, with the settlers about them, were certain, in the event of an ordinary mischance, to be scalped as well as captured. The situation was little better in the South and Southwest, where the Indians needed only the support of a British army at New Orleans or Mobile to expel every American garrison from the territory.

No serious preparations for war had yet been made when the war began. In January, Congress voted ten new regiments of infantry, two of artillery, and one of light dragoons; the recruiting began in March, and in June the Secretary of War reported to Congress that although no returns had been received from any of the recruiting offices, yet considering the circumstances "the success which has attended this service will be found to have equalled any reasonable expectations."[1] Eustis was in no way responsible for the failure of the service, and had no need to volunteer an opinion as to the reasonable expectations that Congress might entertain. Every one knew that the enlistments fell far below expectation; but not the enlistments alone showed torpor. In February, Congress

---

[1] Eustis to Anderson, June 6, 1812; State Papers, Military Affairs, i. 319.

authorized the President to accept fifty thousand volunteers for one year's service. In June, the number of volunteers who had offered themselves was even smaller than that of regular recruits. In April, Congress authorized the President to call out one hundred thousand State militia. In June, no one knew whether all the States would regard the call, and still less whether the militia would serve beyond the frontier. One week after declaring war, Congress fixed the war establishment at twenty-five regiments of infantry, four of artillery, two of dragoons, and one of riflemen,—making, with the engineers and artificers, an army of thirty-six thousand seven hundred men; yet the actual force under arms did not exceed ten thousand, of whom four thousand were new recruits. Toward no part of the service did the people show a sympathetic spirit before the war was declared; and even where the war was most popular, as in Kentucky and Tennessee, men showed themselves determined to fight in their own way or not at all.

However inexperienced the Government might be, it could not overlook the necessity of providing for one vital point. Detroit claimed early attention, and received it. The dangers surrounding Detroit were evident to any one who searched the map for that remote settlement, within gunshot of British territory and surrounded by hostile Indian tribes. The Governor of Michigan, William Hull, a native of Connecticut, had done good service in the Revolutionary War, but had reached the age of sixty years without a wish to resume his military career. He preferred to remain in his civil post, leaving to some officer of the army the charge of military operations; but he came to Washington in February, 1812, and urged the Government to take timely measures for holding the Indians in check. He advised the President and Cabinet to increase the naval force on Lake Erie, although he already had at Detroit an armed brig ready to launch, which he thought sufficient to control the upper lakes. The subject was discussed; but the delay necessary to create a fleet must have risked, if it did not insure, the loss of the whole Northwestern Territory, and the President necessarily decided to march first a force to Detroit strong enough to secure the frontier, and, if possible, to occupy the whole or part of the neighboring and friendly British territory in Upper Canada. This decision Hull seems to have suggested, for he wrote,[1] March 6, to Secretary Eustis,—

"A part of your army now recruiting may be as well supported and disciplined at Detroit as at any other place. A force adequate to the defence of that vulnerable point would prevent a war with the savages, and probably induce the enemy to abandon the province of Upper Canada without opposition. The naval force on the Lakes would in that event fall into our possession, and we should obtain the command of the waters without the expense of building such a force."

This hazardous plan required energy in the American armies, timely co-operation from Niagara if not from Lake Champlain, and, most of all, assumed both incompetence and treason in the enemy. Assuming that Hull would capture the British vessels on the Lakes, the President made no further provision for a fleet; but, apparently to provide for simultaneous measures against Lower Canada, the Secretary of War sent to Boston for General Dearborn, who was to command operations on Lake Ontario and the St. Lawrence River. Dearborn hastened to Washington in February, where he remained until the last of April. He submitted to the Secretary of War what was called a plan of campaign,[2] recommending that a main army should advance by way of Lake Champlain upon Montreal, while three corps, composed chiefly of militia, should enter Canada from Detroit, Niagara, and Sackett's Harbor. Neither Dearborn, Hull, Eustis, nor Madison settled the details of the plan or fixed the time of the combined movement. They could not readily decide details before Congress acted, and before the ranks of the army were filled.

While these matters were under discussion in March, the President, unable to find an army officer fitted to command the force ordered to Detroit, pressed Governor Hull to reconsider his refusal; and Hull, yielding to the President's wish, was appointed, April 8, 1812, brigadier-general of the United

<hr />

[1] Hull to Eustis, March 6, 1812; Hull's Defence, pp. 29–32.
[2] Defence of Dearborn, by H. A. S. Dearborn, p. 1. Boston, 1824.

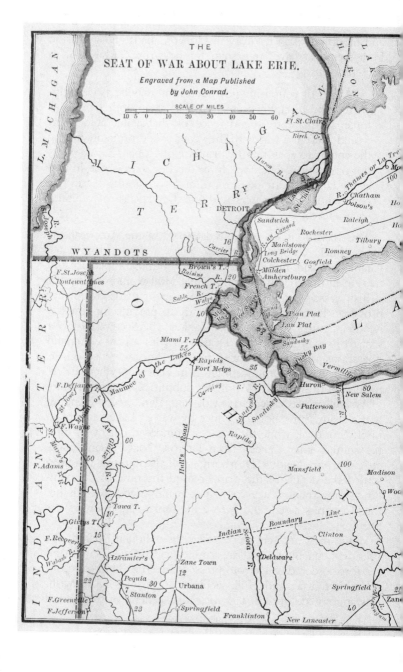

THE

SEAT OF WAR ABOUT LAKE ERIE.

Engraved from a Map Published
by John Conrad.

SCALE OF MILES
10 5 0   10   20   30   40   50   60

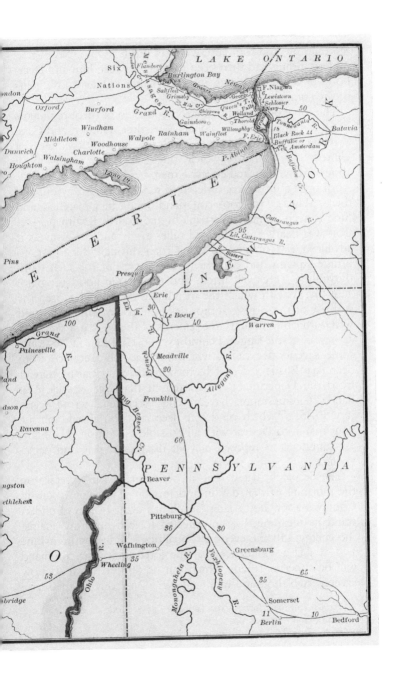

States army, and soon afterward set out for Ohio. No further understanding had then been reached between him and Dearborn, or Secretary Eustis, in regard to the military movements of the coming campaign.

The force destined for Detroit consisted of three regiments of Ohio militia under Colonels McArthur, Findlay, and Cass, a troop of Ohio dragoons, and the Fourth Regiment of United States Infantry which fought at Tippecanoe,—in all about sixteen hundred effective men, besides a few volunteers. April 1 the militia were ordered to rendezvous at Dayton, and there, May 25, Hull took command. June 1 they marched, and June 10 were joined at Urbana by the Fourth Regiment. Detroit was nearly two hundred miles away, and the army as it advanced was obliged to cut a road through the forest, to bridge streams and construct causeways; but for such work the militia were well fitted, and they made good progress. The energy with which the march was conducted excited the surprise of the British authorities in Canada,[1] and contrasted well with other military movements of the year; but vigorous as it was it still lagged behind events. Hull had moved only some seventy-five miles, when, June 26,[2] he received from Secretary Eustis a despatch, forwarded by special messenger from the Department, to warn him that war was close at hand. "Circumstances have recently occurred," wrote Secretary Eustis, "which render it necessary you should pursue your march to Detroit with all possible expedition. The highest confidence is reposed in your discretion, zeal, and perseverance."

The despatch, dated June 18, was sent by the secretary on the morning of that day in anticipation of the vote taken in Congress a few hours later.[3] Hull had every reason to understand its meaning, for he expected to lead his army against the enemy. "In the event of hostilities," he had written June 24,[4] "I feel a confidence that the force under my command will be superior to any which can be opposed to it. It now exceeds two thousand rank and file." On receiving the secre-

[1] Prevost to Brock, July 31, 1812. Tupper's Life of Brock, p. 209.
[2] Hull's Trial; Defence, pp. 21, 22.
[3] Hull's Trial; Evidence of Eustis, Appendix, p. 4.
[4] Defence of Dearborn, p. 9.

tary's pressing orders Hull left his heavy camp-equipage behind, and hurried his troops to the Miami, or Maumee, River
thirty-five miles away. There he arrived June 30, and there, to
save transportation, loading a schooner with his personal baggage, his hospital stores, entrenching tools, and even a trunk
containing his instructions and the muster-rolls of his army,
he despatched it, July 1, up the Lake toward Detroit. He took
for granted that he should receive from his own government
the first notice of war; yet he knew that the steamboat from
New York to Albany and the road from Albany to Buffalo,
which carried news to the British forces at Malden, was also
the regular mode of conveyance for Detroit; and he had every
reason to suspect that as his distance in time from Washington was greater, he might learn of war first from actual hostilities. Hull considered "there was no hazard" in sending his
most valuable papers past Malden;[1] but within four-and-
twenty hours he received a despatch from Secretary Eustis
announcing the declaration of war, and the same day his
schooner was seized by the British in passing Malden to
Detroit.

This first disaster told the story of the campaign. The declaration made at Washington June 18 was published by General Bloomfield at New York June 20, and reached Montreal
by express June 24; the same day it reached the British Fort
George on the Niagara River and was sent forward to Malden, where it arrived June 30. The despatch to Hull reached
Buffalo two days later than the British express, for it went by
ordinary mail; from Cleveland it was forwarded by express,
June 28, by way of Sandusky, to Hull, whom it reached at
last, July 2, at Frenchtown on the river Raisin, forty miles
below Detroit.

The slowness of transportation was made conspicuous by
another incident. John Jacob Astor, being engaged in extensive trade with the Northwestern Indians, for political reasons
had been encouraged by government. Anxious to save the
large amount of property exposed to capture, he not only obtained the earliest intelligence of war, and warned his agents
by expresses, but he also asked and received from the Treasury

[1] Memoirs, p. 36.

orders[1] addressed to the Collectors on the Lakes, directing them to accept and hold such goods as might be brought from Astor's trading-posts. The business of the Treasury as well as that of Astor was better conducted than that of the War Department. Gallatin's letters reached Detroit before Eustis's despatch reached Hull; and this incident gave rise to a charge of misconduct and even of treason against Gallatin himself.[2]

Hull reached Detroit July 5. At that time the town contained about eight hundred inhabitants within gunshot of the British shore. The fort was a square enclosure of about two acres, surrounded by an embankment, a dry ditch, and a double row of pickets. Although capable of standing a siege, it did not command the river; its supplies were insufficient for many weeks; it was two hundred miles distant from support, and its only road of communication ran for sixty miles along the edge of Lake Erie, where a British fleet on one side and a horde of savages on the other could always make it impassable. The widely scattered people of the territory, numbering four or five thousand, promised to become a serious burden in case of siege or investment. Hull knew in advance that in a military sense Detroit was a trap.

July 9, four days after his arrival, Hull received orders from Washington authorizing him to invade Canada:—

> "Should the force under your command be equal to the enterprise, consistent with the safety of your own post, you will take possession of Malden, and extend your conquests as circumstances may justify."

He replied immediately the same day:[1] —

> "I am preparing boats, and shall pass the river in a few days. The British have established a post directly opposite this place. I have confidence in dislodging them, and of being in possession of the opposite bank. . . . The British command the water and the savages. I do not think the

[1] Gallatin's Writings, ii. 503–511.
[2] Armstrong's Notices, i. 48.
[3] Hull's Trial; Hull to Eustis, July 9, 1812, Appendix, p. 9; Clarke's Life of Hull, p. 335.

force here equal to the reduction of Amherstburg (Malden); you therefore must not be too sanguine."

Three days later, July 12, his army crossed the river. Not a gun was fired. The British militia force retired behind the Canard River, twelve miles below, while Hull and his army occupied Sandwich, and were well received by the inhabitants.

Hull had many reasons for wishing to avoid a battle. From the first he looked on the conquest of Canada as a result of his mere appearance. He began by issuing a proclamation[1] intended to win a peaceful conquest.

> "You will be emancipated," said the proclamation to the Canadians, "from tyranny and oppression, and restored to the dignified station of freemen. . . . I have a force which will break down all opposition, and that force is but the vanguard of a much greater. . . . The United States offer you peace, liberty, and security,—your choice lies between these and war, slavery, or destruction. Choose then; but choose wisely." . . .

This proclamation, dated July 12, was spread throughout the province with no small effect, although it contained an apparently unauthorized threat, that "no white man found fighting by the side of an Indian will be taken prisoner; instant death will be his lot." The people of the western province were strongly American, and soon to the number of three hundred and sixty-seven, including deserters from the Malden garrison, sought protection in the American lines.[2] July 19 Hull described the situation in very hopeful terms:[3]—

> "The army is encamped directly opposite to Detroit. The camp is entrenched. I am mounting the 24-pounders and making every preparation for the siege of Malden. The British force, which in numbers was superior to the American, including militia and Indians, is daily diminishing. Fifty or sixty (of the militia) have deserted daily since the American standard was displayed, and taken protection.

[1] Hull's Memoirs, pp. 45, 46. Trial, App. (18).
[2] Hull's Trial; Evidence of Col. Joseph Watson, p. 151.
[3] Hull to Eustis, July 19, 1812; War Department MSS.

They are now reduced to less than one hundred. In a day or two I expect the whole will desert. The Indian force is diminishing in the same proportion. I have now a large council of ten or twelve nations sitting at Brownstown, and I have no doubt but the result will be that they will remain neutral. The brig 'Adams' was launched on the 4th of July. I have removed her to Detroit under cover of the cannon, and shall have her finished and armed as soon as possible. We shall then have the command of the upper lakes."

To these statements Hull added a warning, which carried at least equal weight: —

"If you have not a force at Niagara, the whole force of the province will be directed against this army. . . . It is all important that Niagara should be invested. All our success will depend upon it."

While Hull reached this position, July 19, he had a right to presume that the Secretary of War and Major-General Dearborn were straining every nerve to support him; but in order to understand Hull's situation, readers must know what Dearborn and Eustis were doing. Dearborn's movements, compared day by day with those of Hull, show that after both officers left Washington in April to take command of their forces, Hull reached Cincinnati May 10, while Dearborn reached Albany May 3, and wrote, May 8, to Eustis that he had fixed on a site to be purchased for a military station. "I shall remain here until the erection of buildings is commenced. . . . The recruiting seems going on very well where it has been commenced. There are nearly three hundred recruits in this State."[1] If Dearborn was satisfied with three hundred men as the result of six weeks' recruiting in New York State in immediate prospect of a desperate war, he was likely to take his own duties easily; and in fact, after establishing his headquarters at Albany for a campaign against Montreal, he wrote, May 21, to the Secretary announcing his departure for Boston: "As the quartermaster-general arrived here this day I hope to be relieved from my duties in that line, and shall set out for Pittsfield, Springfield, and Boston;

[1] Dearborn to Eustis, May 8, 1812; War Department MSS.

and shall return here as soon as possible after making the necessary arrangements at those places."

Dearborn reached Boston May 26, the day after Hull took
command at Dayton. May 29 he wrote again to Eustis: "I
have been here three days. . . . There are about three
hundred recruits in and near this town. . . . Shall return to
Albany within a few days." Dearborn found business accumulate on his hands. The task of arranging the coast defences
absorbed his mind. He forgot the passage of time, and while
still struggling with questions of gunboats, garrisons, field-
pieces, and enlistments he was surprised, June 22, by receiving
the declaration of war. Actual war threw still more labor and
anxiety upon him. The State of Massachusetts behaved as ill
as possible. "Nothing but their fears," he wrote,[1] " will prevent their going all lengths." More used to politics than to
war, Dearborn for the time took no thought of military
movements.

Madison and Eustis seemed at first satisfied with this mode
of conducting the campaign. June 24 Eustis ordered Hull to
invade West Canada, and extend his conquests as far as practicable. Not until June 26 did he write to Dearborn,[2] —

"Having made the necessary arrangements for the defence of the sea-coast, it is the wish of the President that
you should repair to Albany and prepare the force to be
collected at that place for actual service. It is understood
that being possessed of a full view of the intentions of Government, and being also acquainted with the disposition of
the force under your command, you will take your own
time and give the necessary orders to the officers on the
sea-coast. It is altogether uncertain at what time General
Hull may deem it expedient to commence offensive operations. The preparations it is presumed will be made to
move in a direction for Niagara, Kingston, and Montreal.
On your arrival at Albany you will be able to form an opinion of the time required to prepare the troops for action."

Such orders as those of June 24 to Hull, and of June 26 to
Dearborn, passed beyond bounds of ordinary incapacity, and

[1] Dearborn to Eustis, June 26, 1812; War Department MSS.
[2] Clarke's Life of Hull, p. 417. Hull's Memoirs, p. 173.

approached the line of culpable neglect. Hull was to move when he liked, and Dearborn was to take his own time at Boston before beginning to organize his army. Yet the letter to Dearborn was less surprising than Dearborn's reply. The major-general in charge of operations against Montreal, Kingston, and Niagara should have been able to warn his civil superior of the risks incurred in allowing Hull to make an unsupported movement from an isolated base such as he knew Detroit to be; but no thought of Hull found place in Dearborn's mind. July 1 he wrote:[1] —

> "There has been nothing yet done in New England that indicates an actual state of war, but every means that can be devised by the Tories is in operation to depress the spirits of the country. Hence the necessity of every exertion on the part of the Government for carrying into effect the necessary measures for defence or offence. We ought to have gunboats in every harbor on the coast. Many places will have no other protection, and all require their aid. I shall have doubts as to the propriety of my leaving this place until I receive your particular directions after you shall have received my letter."

Dearborn complained with reason of the difficulties that surrounded him. Had Congress acted promptly, a large body of volunteers would have been already engaged, general officers would have been appointed and ready for service, whereas no general officer except himself was yet at any post north of New York city. Every day he received from every quarter complaints of want of men, clothing, and supplies; but his remaining at Boston to watch the conduct of the State government was so little likely to overcome these difficulties that at last it made an unfavorable impression on the Secretary, who wrote, July 9, a more decided order from Washington:[2] —

> "The period has arrived when your services are required at Albany, and I am instructed by the President to direct, that, having made arrangements for placing the works on

[1] Dearborn to Eustis, July 1, 1812; War Department MSS.
[2] Eustis to Dearborn, July 9, 1812; War Department MSS.

the sea-coast in the best state of defence your means will permit, . . . you will then order all the recruits not otherwise disposed of to march immediately to Albany, or some station on Lake Champlain, to be organized for the invasion of Canada."

With this official letter Eustis sent a private letter[1] of the same date, explaining the reason for his order: —

"If . . . we divide, distribute, and render inefficient the force authorized by law, we play the game of the enemy within and without. District among the field-officers the sea-board! . . . Go to Albany or the Lake! The troops shall come to you as fast as the season will admit, and the blow must be struck. Congress must not meet without a victory to announce to them."

Dearborn at Boston replied to these orders, July 13,[2] a few hours after Hull's army, six hundred miles away, crossed the Detroit River into Canada and challenged the whole British force on the lakes.

"For some time past I have been in a very unpleasant situation, being at a loss to determine whether or not I ought to leave the sea-coast. As soon as war was declared [June 18] I was desirous of repairing to Albany, but was prevented by your letters of May 20 and June 12, and since that time by the extraordinary management of some of the governors in this quarter. On the receipt of your letter of June 26 I concluded to set out in three or four days for Albany, but the remarks in your letter of the 1st inst. prevented me. But having waited for more explicit directions until I begin to fear that I may be censured for not moving, and having taken such measures as circumstances would permit for the defence of the sea-coast, I have concluded to leave this place for Albany before the end of the present week unless I receive orders to remain."

A general-in-chief unable to decide at the beginning of a campaign in what part of his department his services were

---

[1] Eustis to Dearborn, July 9, 1812; Dearborn MSS.
[2] Dearborn to Eustis, July 13, 1812; War Department MSS.

most needed was sure to be taught the required lesson by the enemy. Even after these warnings Dearborn made no haste. Another week passed before he announced, July 21, his intended departure for Albany the next day, but without an army. "Such is the opposition in this State as to render it doubtful whether much will be done to effect in raising any kind of troops." The two months he passed in Boston were thrown away; the enlistments were so few as to promise nothing, and the governor of Massachusetts barely condescended to acknowledge without obeying his request for militia to defend the coast.

July 26, one week after Hull had written that all his success depended on the movements at Niagara, Dearborn reached Albany and found there some twelve hundred men not yet organized or equipped. He found also a letter, dated July 20, from the Secretary of War, showing that the Government had begun to feel the danger of its position.[1] "I have been in daily expectation of hearing from General Hull, who probably arrived in Detroit on the 8th inst." In fact Hull arrived in Detroit July 5, and crossed into Canada July 12; but when the secretary wrote, July 20, he had not yet heard of either event. "You will make such arrangements with Governor Tompkins," continued Eustis, "as will place the militia detached by him for Niagara and other posts on the lakes under your control; and there should be a communication, and if practicable a co-operation, throughout the whole frontier."

The secretary as early as June 24 authorized Hull to invade Canada West, and his delay in waiting till July 20 before sending similar orders to the general commanding the force at Niagara was surprising; but if Eustis's letter seemed singular, Dearborn's answer passed belief. For the first time General Dearborn then asked a question in regard to his own campaign,—a question so extraordinary that every critic found it an enigma: "Who is to have command of the operations in Upper Canada? I take it for granted that my command does not extent to that distant quarter."[2]

July 26, when Hull had been already a fortnight on British soil, a week after he wrote that his success depended on

[1] Eustis to Dearborn, July 20, 1812; MSS. War Department Records.

[2] Dearborn to Eustis, July 28, 1812. Defence of Dearborn, p. 4.

co-operation from Niagara, the only force at Niagara consisted of a few New York militia, not co-operating with Hull
or under the control of any United States officer, while the
major-general of the Department took it for granted that Niagara was not included in his command. The Government
therefore expected General Hull, with a force which it knew
did not at the outset exceed two thousand effectives, to march
two hundred miles, constructing a road as he went; to garrison Detroit; to guard at least sixty miles of road under the
enemy's guns; to face a force in the field equal to his own,
and another savage force of unknown numbers in his rear; to
sweep the Canadian peninsula of British troops; to capture
the fortress at Malden and the British fleet on Lake Erie,—
and to do all this without the aid of a man or a boat between
Sandusky and Quebec.

Chapter XV

GENERAL HULL, two days after entering Canada, called a council of war, which decided against storming Malden and advised delay. Their reasons were sufficiently strong. After allowing for the sick-list and garrison-duty, the four regiments could hardly supply more than three hundred men each for active service, besides the Michigan militia, on whom no one felt willing to depend. Hull afterward affirmed that he had not a thousand effectives; the highest number given in evidence two years later by Major Jesup was the vague estimate of sixteen or eighteen hundred men. Probably the utmost exertion could not have brought fifteen hundred effectives to the Canadian shore. The British force opposed to them was not to be despised. Colonel St. George commanding at Malden had with him two hundred men of the Forty-first British line, fifty men of the Royal Newfoundland regiment, and thirty men of the Royal Artillery.[1] Besides these two hundred and eighty veteran troops with their officers, he had July 12 about six hundred Canadian militia and two hundred and thirty Indians.[2] The militia deserted rapidly; but after allowing for the desertions, the garrison at Malden, including Indians, numbered nearly nine hundred men. The British had also the advantage of position, and of a fleet whose guns covered and supported their left. They were alarmed and cautious, but though they exaggerated Hull's force they meant to meet him in front of their fortress.[3] Hull's troops would have shown superiority to other American forces engaged in the campaign of 1812 had they won a victory.

The Ohio militia, although their officers acquiesced in the opinion of the council of war, were very unwilling to lose their advantage. If nothing was to be gained by attack, everything was likely to be lost by delay. Detachments scoured the

[1] Richardson, p. 5; Christie, ii. 34; Prevost to Bathurst, Aug. 26, 1812; Brock to Prevost, Aug. 7, 1812; Niles, iii. 265, 266.

[2] Lieutenant-Colonel Raby to Captain Gleg, July 27, 1812. Proctor to Brock, July 26, 1812. MSS. Canadian Archives.

[3] Richardson, p. 9.

country, meeting at first little resistance, one detachment even crossing the Canard River, flanking and driving away the guard at the bridge; but the army was not ready to support the unforeseen success, and the bridge was abandoned. Probably this moment was the last when an assault could have been made with a chance of success. July 19 and 24 strong detachments were driven back with loss, and the outlook became suddenly threatening.

Hull tried to persuade himself that he could take Malden by siege. July 22 he wrote to Eustis that he was pressing the preparation of siege guns:[1] —

> "I find that entirely new carriages must be built for the 24-pounders and mortars. It will require at least two weeks to make the necessary preparations. It is in the power of this army to take Malden by storm, but it would be attended in my opinion with too great a sacrifice under the present circumstances. . . . If Malden was in our possession, I could march this army to Niagara or York (Toronto) in a very short time."

This was Hull's last expression of confidence or hope. Thenceforward every day brought him fatal news. His army lost respect for him in consequence of his failure to attack Malden; the British strengthened the defences of Malden, and August 8 received sixty fresh men of the Forty-first under Colonel Proctor from Niagara;[2] but worse than mutiny or British reinforcement, news from the Northwest of the most disastrous character reached Hull at a moment when his hopes of taking Malden had already faded. August 3 the garrison of Michillimackinaw arrived at Detroit as prisoners-of-war on parole, announcing that Mackinaw had capitulated July 17 to a force of British and savages, and that Hull must prepare to receive the attack of a horde of Indians coming from the Northwest to fall upon Detroit in the rear.

Hull called another council of war August 5, which, notwithstanding this news, decided to attack Malden August 8, when the heavy artillery should be ready; but while they were debating this decision, a party of Indians under Tecumthe

---

[1] Hull to Eustis, July 22, 1812. Hull's Defence, App. No. 2 (10).
[2] Richardson, p. 18.

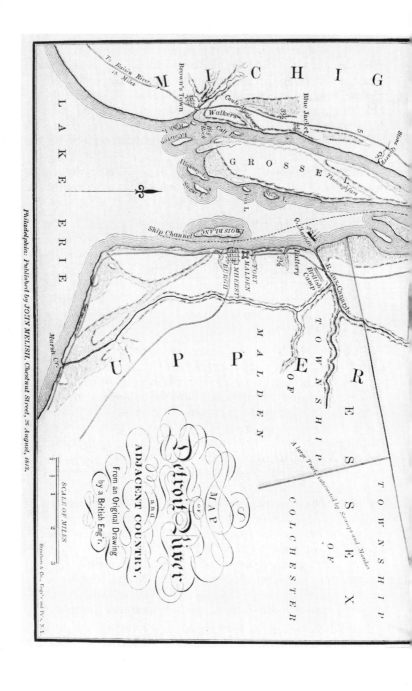

MICHIGA

LAKE ERIE

To Raisin River, 18 Miles

Brown's Town

Coal Mines

Walkers

3½

Blue Jacket

5

Great Turkey Island

GROSSE I.

Thoroughfare

Call I.

Big Rock

Freedom

Hickory I.

Sugar I.

Fish I.

Stony I.

Ship Channel

BOIS BLANC

Q. Charlotte

R. aux Canards

3½

Battery Camp

British Camp

FORT MALDEN

AMHERSTBURGH

UPPER

MALDEN

MARSH Cr.

TOWNSHIP OF ESSEX

A large Tract intersected by Swamps and Marshes

TOWNSHIP OF COLCHESTER

MAP OF
Detroit River
and
ADJACENT COUNTRY,
From an Original Drawing
by a British Eng'r.

SCALE OF MILES
½ ¼ 1 2 3

Philadelphia: Published by JOHN MELISH, Chestnut Street, 26 August, 1813.

Struthers & Co., Eng'r's and Pr's, N.Y.

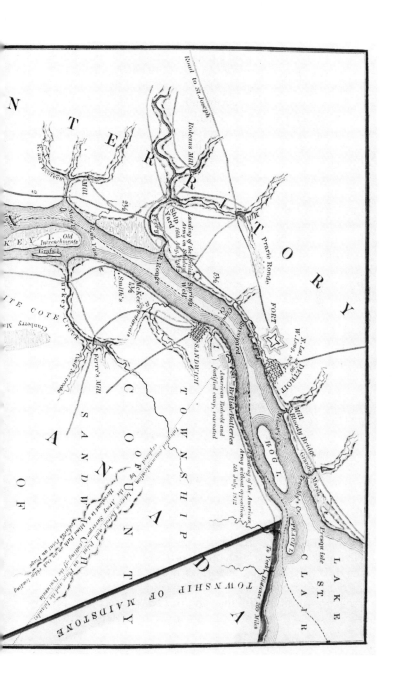

N

TERRITORY

Road to St. Joseph

Roleans Mill

Landing of the British
Army 18th Aug. 1812
Ship
Yard

Prairie Ronde

FORT

Y. Old
Intrenchments
Grafs I.

KEY

R. aux Dindes

Mill

R. aux Pecheurs

Ferry

R. Rouge

Smith's

Dickee's

Turkey Creek

WHITE COTE

Cranberry Ma

Perry's Mill

SANDWICH

American Redoubt and
fortified camp, evacuated

By Batteries

TOWNSHIP

OF SANDWICH

COUNTY

Intended communication opened by
the American Forces

N. Lat.
W. Lon.
DETROIT

Mill
Bloody Bridge
Grands Marais

Grand Marais

Army without opposition,
3th July, 1812

Landing of the American

Scotchyard

Hog's I.

Peche's Cr.

L. O. G. I.

Presque Isle

TOWNSHIP OF MAIDSTONE

To York Distance 205 Miles

LAKE ST. CLAIR

crossing the river routed a detachment of Findlay's Ohio regiment on their way to protect a train of supplies coming from Ohio. The army mail-bags fell into British hands. Hull then realized that his line of communication between Detroit and the Maumee River was in danger, if not closed. On the heels of this disaster he received, August 7, letters from Niagara announcing the passage of British reinforcements up Lake Ontario to Lake Erie and Malden. Thus he was called to meet in his front an intrenched force nearly equal to his own, while at least a thousand Indian warriors were descending on his flank from Lake Huron, and in the rear his line of communication and supply could be restored only by detaching half his army for the purpose.

Hull decided at once to recross the river, and succeeded in effecting this movement on the night of August 8 without interference from the enemy; but his position at Detroit was only one degree better than it had been at Sandwich. He wished to abandon Detroit and retreat behind the Maumee, and August 9 proposed the measure to some of his principal officers. Colonel Cass replied that if this were done every man of the Ohio militia would refuse to obey, and would desert their general;[1] that the army would fall to pieces if ordered to retreat. Hull considered that this report obliged him to remain where he was.

This was the situation at Detroit August 9,—a date prominent in the story; but Hull's true position could be understood only after learning what had been done in Canada since the declaration of war.

The difficulties of Canada were even greater than those of the United States. Upper Canada, extending from Detroit River to the Ottawa within forty miles of Montreal, contained not more than eighty thousand persons. The political capital was York, afterward Toronto, on Lake Ontario. The civil and military command of this vast territory was in the hands of Brigadier-General Isaac Brock, a native of Guernsey, forty-two years old, who had been colonel of the Forty-ninth regiment of the British line, and had served since 1802 in Canada. The appointment of Brock in October, 1811, to the chief

---

[1] Hull's Trial, Cass's testimony. Hull's Memoirs, p. 64.

command at the point of greatest danger was for the British a piece of good fortune, or good judgment, more rare than could have been appreciated at the time, even though Dearborn, Hull, Winchester, Wilkinson, Sir George Prevost himself, and Colonel Proctor were examples of the common standard. Brock was not only a man of unusual powers, but his powers were also in their prime. Neither physical nor mental fatigue such as followed his rivals' exertions paralyzed his plans. No scruples about bloodshed stopped him midway to victory. He stood alone in his superiority as a soldier. Yet his civil difficulties were as great as his military, for he had to deal with a people better disposed toward his enemies than toward himself; and he succeeded in both careers.

Under Brock's direction, during the preceding winter vessels had been armed on Lake Erie, and Malden had been strengthened by every means in his power. These precautions gave him from the outset the command of the lake, which in itself was almost equivalent to the command of Detroit. Of regular troops he had but few. The entire regular force in both Canadas at the outbreak of the war numbered six thousand three hundred and sixty rank and file, or about seven thousand men including officers. More than five thousand of these were stationed in Lower Canada. To protect the St. Lawrence, the Niagara, and the Detroit, Brock had only fourteen hundred and seventy-three rank and file, or including his own regiment,—the Forty-ninth, then at Montreal,—two thousand one hundred and thirty-seven men at the utmost.[1]

When the news of war reached him, not knowing where to expect the first blow, Brock waited, moving between Niagara and Toronto, until Hull's passage of the Detroit River, July 12, marked the point of danger and startled the province almost out of its dependence on England. Sir George Prevost, the governor-general, reported with much mortification the effect of Hull's movement on Upper Canada:

"Immediately upon the invasion of the province," wrote Sir George, August 17,[2] "and upon the issuing of the proc-

[1] Abstracts of General Returns of Troops in Upper and Lower Canada, July 30, 1812. Freer Papers, 1812–1813. MSS. Canadian Archives.

[2] Prevost to Bathurst, Aug. 17, 1812; MSS. British Archives.

lamation by General Hull, which I have the honor of herewith transmitting, it was plainly perceived by General Brock that little reliance could be placed upon the militia, and as little dependence upon the active exertions of any considerable proportion of the population of the country, unless he was vested with full power to repress the disaffected spirit which was daily beginning to show itself, and to restrain and punish the disorders which threatened to dissolve the whole militia force which he had assembled. He therefore called together the provincial legislature on July 27 in the hope that they would adopt prompt and efficient measures for strengthening the hands of the Government at a period of such danger and difficulty. . . . In these reasonable expectations I am sorry to say General Brock has been miserably disappointed; and a lukewarm and temporizing spirit, evidently dictated either by the apprehension or the wish that the enemy might soon be in complete possession of the country, having prevented the Assembly from adopting any of the measures proposed to them, they were prorogued on the 5th instant."

Brock himself wrote to Lord Liverpool a similar account of his trials:—

"The invasion of the western district by General Hull," he wrote August 29,[1] " was productive of very unfavorable sensations among a large portion of the population, and so completely were their minds subdued that the Norfolk militia when ordered to march peremptorily refused. The state of the country required prompt and vigorous measures. The majority of the House of Assembly was likewise seized with the same apprehensions, and may be justly accused of studying more to avoid by their proceedings incurring the indignation of the enemy than the honest fulfilment of their duty. . . . I cannot hide from your Lordship that I considered my situation at that time extremely perilous. Not only among the militia was evinced a disposition to submit tamely, five hundred in the western district having deserted their ranks, but likewise the Indians of the Six Nations,

[1] Brock to Liverpool, Aug. 29, 1812; MSS. British Archives.

who are placed in the heart of the country on the Grand River, positively refused, with the exception of a few individuals, taking up arms. They audaciously announced their intention after the return of some of their chiefs from General Hull to remain neutral, as if they wished to impose upon the Government the belief that it was possible they could sit quietly in the midst of war. This unexpected conduct of the Indians deterred many good men from leaving their families and joining the militia; they became more apprehensive of the internal than of the external enemy, and would willingly have compromised with the one to secure themselves from the other."

Brock's energy counterbalanced every American advantage. Although he had but about fifteen hundred regular troops in his province, and was expected to remain on the defensive, the moment war was declared, June 26, he sent to Amherstburg all the force he could control, and ordered the commandant of the British post at the island of St. Joseph on Lake Huron to seize the American fort at Michillimackinaw. When Hull issued his proclamation of July 12, Brock replied by a proclamation of July 22. To Hull's threat that no quarter should be given to soldiers fighting by the side of Indians, Brock responded by "the certain assurance of retaliation;" and he justified the employment of his Indian allies by arguments which would have been more conclusive had he ventured to reveal his desperate situation. In truth the American complaint that the British employed Indians in war meant nothing to Brock, whose loss of his province by neglect of any resource at his command might properly have been punished by the utmost penalty his Government could inflict.

Brock's proclamation partly restored confidence. When his legislature showed backwardness in supporting him he peremptorily dismissed them, August 5, after they had been only a week in session, and the same day he left York for Burlington Bay and Lake Erie. Before quitting Lake Ontario he could not fail to inquire what was the American force at Niagara and what it was doing. Every one in the neighborhood must have told him that on the American side five or six hundred militiamen, commanded by no general officer, were engaged in patrolling thirty-six miles of river front; that they were undisciplined, ill-clothed, without tents, shoes, pay, or ammunition, and ready to retreat at any sign of attack.[1] Secure at that point, Brock hurried toward Malden. He had ordered reinforcements to collect at Long Point on Lake Erie; and August 8, while Hull was withdrawing his army from Sandwich to Detroit, Brock passed Long Point, taking up three hundred men whom he found there, and coasted night and day to the Detroit River.

Meanwhile, at Washington, Eustis sent letter after letter to Dearborn, pressing for a movement from Niagara. July 26 he repeated the order of July 20.[2] August 1 he wrote, enclosing Hull's despatch of July 19: "You will make a diversion in his favor at Niagara and at Kingston as soon as may be practicable, and by such operations as may be within your control."

Dearborn awoke August 3 to the consciousness of not having done all that man could do. He began arrangements for sending a thousand militia to Niagara, and requested Major-General Stephen Van Rensselaer of the New York State militia to take command there in person. In a letter of August 7 to the Secretary of War, he showed sense both of his mistakes and of their results:[3] —

> "It is said that a detachment [of British troops] has been sent from Niagara by land to Detroit; if so, I should presume before they can march two hundred and fifty miles General Hull will receive notice of their approach, and in season to cut them off before they reach Fort Malden. It is reported that no ordnance or ammunition have reached Niagara this season, and that there is great deficiency of these articles. Not having considered any part of the borders of Upper Canada as within the command intended for me, I have received no reports or returns from that quarter, and did not until since my last arrival at this place give any orders to the commanding officers of the respective posts on that frontier."

[1] Van Rensselaer's Narrative, pp. 9, 10.
[2] Dearborn's Defence of Dearborn, p. 4.
[3] Dearborn's Defence of Dearborn, p. 4.

The consequences of such incapacity showed themselves without an instant's delay. While Dearborn was writing from Albany, August 7, General Brock, as has been told, passed from Lake Ontario to Lake Erie; and the next morning, when Brock reached his detachment at Long Point, Hull evacuated Sandwich and retired to Detroit. Had he fallen back on the Maumee or even to Urbana or Dayton, he would have done only what Wellington had done more than once in circumstances hardly more serious, and what Napoleon was about to do three months afterward in leaving Moscow.

Desperate as Hull's position was, Dearborn succeeded within four-and-twenty hours by an extraordinary chance in almost extricating him, without being conscious that his action more than his neglect affected Hull's prospects. This chance was due to the reluctance of the British government to accept the war. Immediately after the repeal of the Orders in Council the new Ministry of Lord Liverpool ordered their minister, Foster, to conclude an armistice in case hostilities had begun, and requested their governor-general to avoid all extraordinary preparations. These orders given in good faith by the British government were exceeded by Sir George Prevost, who had every reason to wish for peace. Although he could not make an armistice without leaving General Hull in possession of his conquests in Upper Canada, which might be extensive, Prevost sent his adjutant-general, Colonel Baynes, to Albany to ask a cessation of hostilities, and the same day, August 2, wrote to General Brock warning him of the proposed step.[1] Colonel Baynes reached headquarters at Albany August 9, and obtained from Dearborn an agreement that his troops, including those at Niagara, should act only on the defensive until further orders from Washington:—

"I consider the agreement as favorable at this period," wrote Dearborn to Eustis, "for we could not act offensively except at Detroit for some time, and there it will not probably have any effect on General Hull or his movements."[2]

What effect the armistice would have on Hull might be a matter for prolonged and serious doubt, but that it should

[1] Life of Prevost, p. 39; Life of Brock, p. 214.
[2] Dearborn to Eustis, Aug. 9, 1812; Dearborn's Defence, p. 6.

have no effect at all would have occurred to no ordinary commander. Dearborn had been urgently ordered, August 1, to
support Hull by a vigorous offensive at Niagara, yet August
9 he agreed with the British general to act only on the defensive at Niagara. Detroit was not under Dearborn's command,
and therefore was not included in the armistice; but Dearborn
stipulated that the arrangement should include Hull if he
wished it. Orders were sent to Niagara August 9, directing
the commanding officers "to confine their respective operations to defensive measures," and with these orders Dearborn
wrote to Hull proposing a concurrence in the armistice. Had
Brock moved less quickly, or had the British government sent
its instructions a week earlier, the armistice might have saved
Detroit. The chance was narrow, for even an armistice unless
greatly prolonged would only have weakened Hull, especially
as it could not include Indians other than those actually in
British service; but even the slight chance was lost by the delay until August 9 in sending advices to Niagara and Detroit,
for Brock left Long Point August 8, and was already within
four days of Detroit when Dearborn wrote from Albany. The
last possibility of saving Hull was lost by the inefficiency of
American mail-service. The distance from Albany to Buffalo
was about three hundred miles. A letter written at Albany
August 9 should have reached Niagara by express August 13;
Dearborn's letter to Hull arrived there only on the evening of
August 17, and was forwarded by General Van Rensselaer the
next morning.[1] Even through the British lines it could hardly
reach Detroit before August 24.

Slowness such as this in the face of an enemy like Brock,
who knew the value of time, left Hull small chance of escape.
Brock with his little army of three hundred men leaving Long
Point August 8 coasted the shore of the lake, and sailing at
night reached Malden late in the evening of August 13, fully
eight days in advance of the armistice.

Meanwhile Hull was besieged at Detroit. Immediately after
returning there, August 8, he sent nearly half his force—
a picked body of six hundred men, including the Fourth
U. S. Regiment—to restore his communications with Ohio.

---

[1] Van Rensselaer to Dearborn, Aug. 18, 1812; Van Rensselaer's Narrative,
App. p. 25.

Toward afternoon of the next day, when this detachment reached the Indian village of Maguaga fourteen miles south of Detroit, it came upon the British force consisting of about one hundred and fifty regulars of the Forty-first Regiment, with forty or fifty militia and Tecumthe's little band of twenty-five Indians,—about two hundred and fifty men, all told.[1] After a sharp engagement the British force was routed and took to its boats, with a loss of thirteen men or more, while the Indians disappeared in the woods. For some unsatisfactory reason the detachment did not then march to the river Raisin to act as convoy for the supplies, and nothing but honor was acquired by the victory. "It is a painful consideration," reported Hull,[2] "that the blood of seventy-five gallant men could only open the communication as far as the points of their bayonets extended." On receiving a report of the battle Hull at first inclined to order the detachment to the Raisin, but the condition of the weather and the roads changed his mind, and August 10 he recalled the detachment to Detroit.

The next four days were thrown away by the Americans. August 13 the British began to establish a battery on the Canadian side of the river to bombard Detroit. Within the American lines the army was in secret mutiny. Hull's vacillations and evident alarm disorganized his force. The Ohio colonels were ready to remove him from his command, which they offered to Lieutenant-Colonel Miller of the U. S. Fourth Regiment; but Colonel Miller declined this manner of promotion, and Hull retained control. August 12 the three colonels united in a letter to the governor of Ohio, warning him that the existence of the army depended on the immediate despatch of at least two thousand men to keep open the line of communication. "Our supplies must come from our State; this country does not furnish them." A postscript added that even a capitulation was talked of by the commander-in-chief.[3] In truth Hull, who like most commanders-in-chief saw more of the situation than was seen by his subordinates, made no concealment of his feelings. Moody, abstracted, wavering in

[1] Richardson, pp. 16, 24; James's Military Occurrences, i. 65.
[2] Hull to Eustis, Aug. 26, 1812; Niles, iii. 46.
[3] McAffee, pp. 83, 84.

his decisions, and conscious of the low respect in which he was held by his troops, he shut himself up and brooded over his desperate situation.

Desperate the situation seemed to be; yet a good general would still have saved Detroit for some weeks, if not altogether. Hull knew that he must soon be starved into surrender;[1] but though already short of supplies he might by vigorous preparations and by rigid economy have maintained himself a month, and he had always the chance of a successful battle. His effective force, by his own showing, still exceeded a thousand men to defend the fort; his supplies of ammunition were sufficient;[2] and even if surrender were inevitable, after the mortifications he had suffered and those he foresaw, he would naturally have welcomed a chance of dying in battle. Perhaps he might have chosen this end, for he had once been a brave soldier; but the thought of his daughter and the women and children of the settlement left to the mercy of Indians overcame him. He shrank from it with evident horror, exaggerating the numbers and brooding over the "greedy violence" of the bands, "numerous beyond any former example," who were descending from the Northwest.[3] Doubtless his fears were well-founded, but a general-in-chief whose mind was paralyzed by such thoughts could not measure himself with Isaac Brock.

On the evening of August 14 Hull made one more effort. He ordered two of the Ohio colonels, McArthur and Cass, to select the best men from their regiments, and to open if possible a circuitous route of fifty miles through the woods to the river Raisin. The operation was difficult, fatiguing, and dangerous; but the supplies so long detained at the Raisin, thirty-five miles away by the direct road, must be had at any cost, and the two Ohio colonels aware of the necessity promptly undertook the service. Their regiments in May contained nominally about five hundred men each, all told. Two months of severe labor with occasional fighting and much sickness had probably reduced the number of effectives about one half. The report of Colonel Miller of the U. S. Fourth

[1] Hull to Eustis, Aug. 26, 1812; Niles, iii. 55.
[2] Hull's Trial; Evidence of James Dalliby, pp. 80, 81. Life of Brock, p. 289.
[3] Hull to Eustis, Aug. 26, 1812; Niles, iii. 55.

Regiment in regard to the condition of his command showed this proportion of effectives,[1] and the Fourth Regiment was probably in better health than the militia. The two Ohio regiments of McArthur and Cass numbered perhaps six or seven hundred effective men, and from these the two colonels selected three hundred and fifty, probably the best. By nighttime they were already beyond the river Rouge, and the next evening, August 15, were stopped by a swamp less than half way to the river Raisin.

After their departure on the night of August 14 Hull learned that Brock had reached Malden the night before with heavy reinforcements. According to Hull's later story, he immediately sent orders to McArthur and Cass to return to Detroit, giving the reasons for doing so;[2] in fact he did not send till the afternoon of the next day,[3] and the orders reached the detachment four-and-twenty miles distant only at sunset August 15. So it happened that on the early morning of August 16 Hull was guarding the fort and town of Detroit with about two hundred and fifty effective men of the Fourth Regiment, about seven hundred men of the Ohio militia, and such of the Michigan militia and Ohio volunteers as may have been present,—all told, about a thousand effectives. Hull estimated his force as not exceeding eight hundred men;[4] Major Jesup, the acting adjutant-general, reported it as one thousand and sixty, including the Michigan militia.[5] If the sickness and loss of strength at Detroit were in proportion to the waste that soon afterward astonished the generals at Niagara, Hull's estimate was perhaps near the truth.

Meanwhile Brock acted with rapidity and decision. After reaching Malden late at night August 13, he held a council the next day, said to have been attended by a thousand Indian warriors.[6]

"Among the Indians whom I found at Amherstburg," he

[1] Hull's Trial; Evidence of Colonel Miller, p. 111.
[2] Memoir, p. 110.
[3] Hull to Eustis, Aug. 26, 1812; Niles, iii. 55.
[4] Hull to Eustis, Aug. 26, 1812; Niles, iii. 55.
[5] Hull's Trial; Evidence of Major Jesup, p. 96.
[6] Life of Brock, p. 228.

reported to Lord Liverpool,[1] "and who had arrived from distant parts of the country, I found some extraordinary characters. He who attracted most my attention was a Shawnee chief, Tecumset, brother to the Prophet, who for the last two years has carried on contrary to our remonstrances an active warfare against the United States. A more sagacious or more gallant warrior does not, I believe, exist. He was the admiration of every one who conversed with him."

Brock consumed one day in making his arrangements with them, and decided to move his army immediately across the Detroit River and throw it against the fort.

"Some say that nothing could be more desperate than the measure,"[2] he wrote soon afterward; "but I answer that the state of the province admits only of desperate remedies. I got possession of the letters my antagonist addressed to the Secretary of War, and also the sentiments which hundreds of his army uttered to their friends. Confidence in their general was gone, and evident despondency prevailed throughout. I crossed the river contrary to the opinion of Colonel Proctor, etc. It is therefore no wonder that envy should attribute to good fortune what, in justice to my own discernment, I must say proceeded from a cool calculation of the *pours* and *contres*."

Probably Brock received then Sir George Prevost's letter of August 2 warning him of the intended armistice, for Hull repeatedly and earnestly asserted that Brock spoke to him of the armistice August 16; and although twelve days was a short time for an express to pass between Montreal and Malden, yet it might have been accomplished at the speed of about fifty miles a day. If Brock had reason to expect an armistice, the wish to secure for his province the certainty of future safety must have added a motive for hot haste.

At noon August 15 Brock sent a summons of surrender across the river to Hull. "The force at my disposal," he wrote,

---

[1] Despatch of Aug. 29, 1812; MSS. British Archives.
[2] Letter of Sept. 3, 1812; Life, p. 267.

"authorizes me to require of you the surrender of Detroit. It is far from my inclination to join in a war of extermination, but you must be aware that the numerous body of Indians who have attached themselves to my troops will be beyond my control the moment the contest commences." The threat of massacre or Indian captivity struck Hull's most sensitive chord. After some delay he replied, refusing to surrender, and then sent orders recalling McArthur's detachment; but the more he thought of his situation the more certain he became that the last chance of escape had vanished. In a few days or weeks want of provisions would oblige him to capitulate, and the bloodshed that would intervene could serve no possible purpose. Brock's movements increased the general's weakness. As soon as Hull's reply reached the British lines, two British armed vessels—the "Queen Charlotte" of seventeen guns and the "Hunter" of ten guns—moved up the river near Sandwich, while a battery of guns and mortars opened fire from the Canadian shore and continued firing irregularly all night on the town and fort. The fire was returned, but no energetic measures were taken to prepare either for an assault or a siege.

During the night Tecumthe and six hundred Indians crossed the river some two miles below and filled the woods, cutting communication between McArthur's detachment and the fort. A little before daylight of August 16 Brock himself, with three hundred and thirty regulars and four hundred militia, crossed the river carrying with them three 6-pound and two 3-pound guns. He had intended to take up a strong position and force Hull to attack it; but learning from his Indians that McArthur's detachment, reported as five hundred strong, was only a few miles in his rear he resolved on an assault, and moved in close column within three quarters of a mile of the American 24-pound guns. Had Hull prayed that the British might deliver themselves into his hands, his prayers could not have been better answered. Even under trial for his life, he never ventured to express a distinct belief that Brock's assault could have succeeded; and in case of failure the small British force must have retreated at least a mile and a half under the fire of the fort's heavy guns, followed by a force equal to their own, and attacked in flank and rear by McArthur's detachment, which was within hearing of the battle and marching directly toward it.

"Nothing but the boldness of the enterprise could have insured its success," said Richardson, one of Brock's volunteers.[1] "When within a mile and a half of the rising ground commanding the approach to the town we distinctly saw two long, heavy guns, afterward proved to be 24-pounders, planted in the road, and around them the gunners with their fuses burning. At each moment we expected that they would be fired, . . . and fearful in such case must have been the havoc; for moving as we were by the main road, with the river close upon our right flank and a chain of alternate houses and close fences on our left, there was not the slightest possibility of deploying. In this manner and with our eyes riveted on the guns, which became at each moment more visible, we silently advanced until within about three quarters of a mile of the formidable battery, when General Brock, having found at this point a position favorable for the formation of the columns of assault, caused the whole to be wheeled to the left through an open field and orchard leading to a house about three hundred yards off the road, which he selected as his headquarters. In this position we were covered."

All this time Hull was in extreme distress. The cannon-shot from the enemy's batteries across the river were falling in the fort. Uncertain what to do, the General sat on an old tent on the ground with his back against the rampart. "He apparently unconsciously filled his mouth with tobacco, putting in quid after quid more than he generally did; the spittle colored with tobacco-juice ran from his mouth on his neckcloth, beard, cravat, and vest."[2] He seemed preoccupied, his voice trembled, he was greatly agitated, anxious, and fatigued. Knowing that sooner or later the fort must fall, and dreading massacre for the women and children; anxious for the safety of McArthur and Cass, and treated with undisguised contempt by the militia officers,—he hesitated, took no measure to impede

[1] Richardson, p. 30.
[2] Hull's Trial; Evidence of Major Snelling, p. 40.

the enemy's advance, and at last sent a flag across the river to negotiate. A cannon-ball from the enemy's batteries killed four men in the fort; two companies of the Michigan militia deserted,—their behavior threatening to leave the town exposed to the Indians,—and from that moment Hull determined to surrender on the best terms he could get.

As Brock, after placing his troops under cover, ascended the brow of the rising ground to reconnoitre the fort, a white flag advanced from the battery before him, and within an hour the British troops, to their own undisguised astonishment, found themselves in possession of the fortress. The capitulation included McArthur's detachment and the small force covering the supplies at the river Raisin. The army, already mutinous, submitted with what philosophy it could command to the necessity it could not escape.

On the same day at the same hour Fort Dearborn at Chicago was in flames. The Government provided neither for the defence nor for the safe withdrawal of the little garrison, but Hull had sent an order to evacuate the fort if practicable. In the process of evacuation, August 15, the garrison was attacked and massacred by an overwhelming body of Indians. The next morning the fort was burned, and with it the last vestige of American authority on the western lakes disappeared. Thenceforward the line of the Wabash and the Maumee became the military boundary of the United States in the Northwest, and the country felt painful doubt whether even that line could be defended.

Chapter XVI

ALTHOUGH the loss of Detroit caused the greatest loss of territory that ever before or since befell the United States, the public at large understood little of the causes that made it inevitable, and saw in it only an accidental consequence of Hull's cowardice. Against this victim, who had no friend in the world, every voice was raised. He was a coward, an imbecile, but above all unquestionably a traitor, who had, probably for British gold, delivered an army and a province, without military excuse, into the enemy's hands. If any man in the United States was more responsible than Hull for the result of the campaign it was Ex-President Jefferson, whose system had shut military efficiency from the scope of American government; but to Jefferson, Hull and his surrender were not the natural products of a system, but objects of hatred and examples of perfidy that had only one parallel. "The treachery of Hull, like that of Arnold, cannot be a matter of blame to our government," he wrote[1] on learning the story of Lewis Cass and the Ohio militia officers, who told with the usual bitterness of betrayed men what they knew of the causes that had brought their betrayal to pass. "The detestable treason of Hull," as Jefferson persisted in calling it, was the more exasperating to him because, even as late as August 4, he had written with entire confidence to the same correspondent that "the acquisition of Canada this year, as far as the neighborhood of Quebec, will be a mere matter of marching, and will give us experience for the attack of Halifax the next, and the final expulsion of England from the American continent." Perhaps the same expectation explained the conduct of Hull, Madison, Eustis, and Dearborn; yet at the moment when Jefferson wrote thus, Madison was beginning to doubt. August 8, the often-mentioned day when Brock reached Long Point and Hull decided to retreat from Canada, Madison wrote to Gallatin:[2] —

"Should he [Hull] be able to descend upon Niagara and

[1] Jefferson to Duane, Oct. 1, 1812; Works, vi. 79.
[2] Madison to Gallatin, Aug. 8, 1812; Gallatin's Writings, i. 524.

an adequate co-operation be there afforded, our prospect as to Upper Canada may be good enough. But what is to be done with respect to the expedition against Montreal? The enlistments for the regular army fall short of the most moderate calculation; the Volunteer Act is extremely unproductive; and even the militia detachments are either obstructed by the disaffected governors or chilled by the Federal spirit diffused throughout the region most convenient to the theatre. I see nothing better than to draw on this resource as far as the detachments consist of volunteers, who, it may be presumed, will cross the line without raising Constitutional or legal questions."

In contrast with these admissions and their satirical "it may be presumed," the tone of the governor-general, Sir George Prevost, at the same crisis was masterful.[1]

"The Eighth or King's Regiment," he wrote August 17 from Montreal, "has arrived this morning from Quebec to relieve the Forty-ninth Regiment. This fine and effective regiment of the Eighth, together with a chain of troops established in the vicinity of this place consisting of a regular and militia force, the whole amounting to near four thousand five hundred men, effectually serve to keep in check the enemy in this quarter, where alone they are in any strength.

The Canadian outnumbered the American forces at every point of danger on the frontier. A week later Sir George claimed another just credit:[2] —

"The decided superiority I have obtained on the Lakes in consequence of the precautionary measures adopted during the last winter has permitted me to move without interruption, independently of the arrangement [armistice], both troops and supplies of every description toward Amherstburg, while those for General Hull, having several hundred miles of wilderness to pass before they can reach Detroit, are exposed to be harassed and destroyed by the Indians."

[1] Prevost to Bathurst, Aug. 17, 1812; MSS. British Archives.
[2] Prevost to Bathurst, Aug. 24, 1812; MSS. British Archives.

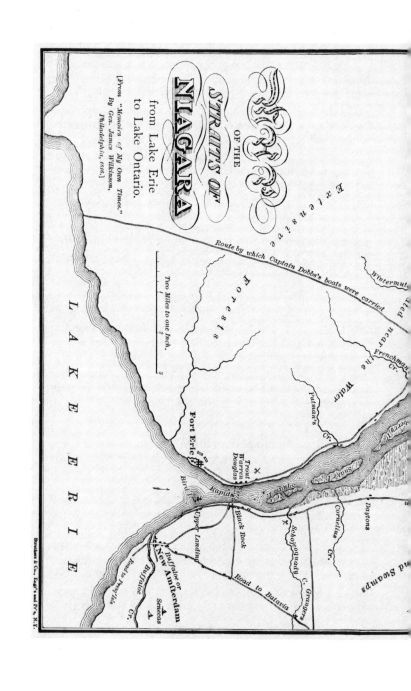

STRAITS OF THE **NIAGARA**

from Lake Erie to Lake Ontario.

[From "Memoirs of My Own Times." By Gen. James Wilkinson, Philadelphia, 1816.]

Two Miles to one Inch.

Route by which Captain Dobbs's boats were carried

L A K E   E R I E

E x t e n s i v e

F o r e s t s

Wintermut

Frenchman Cr.

Water

Putnam's Cr.

Pettisburgh

Fort Erie

Trout

Warren Douglas

Birn

Rapids

Islands

Black Rock

Upper Landing

Cornelius Cr.

Daytons

Schojoquady C.

Grangers

Road to Batavia

Buffaloe or New Amsterdam

Buffaloe Cr.

Seneças

d Swamps

Road to Presq'ile

Strother & Co., Eng'rs and Pr's, N.Y.

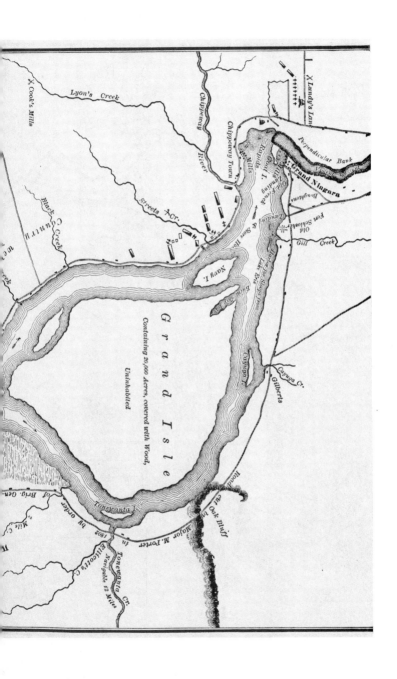

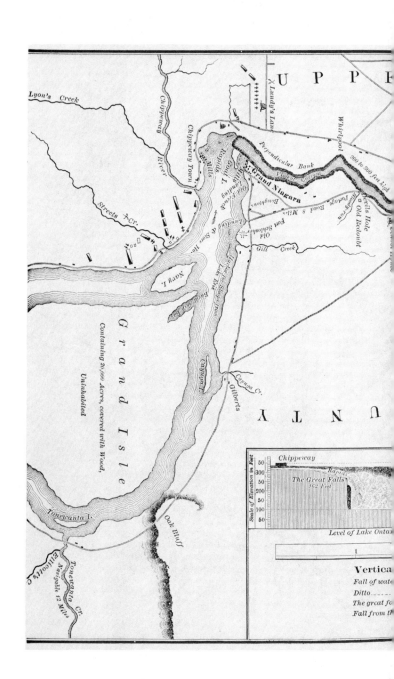

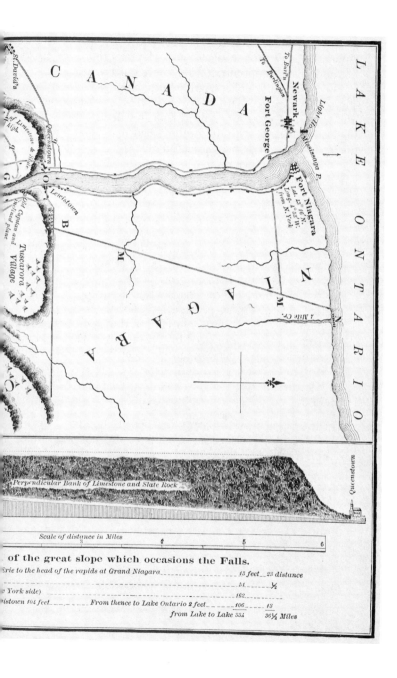

of the great slope which occasions the Falls.

rie to the head of the rapids at Grand Niagara _ _ _ _ _ _ _ _ _ _ _ _ _ _ _ _ *45 feet* _ _ *23 distance*

_ *51* _ _ _ _ _ _ ½

c York side) _ *162* _ _ _ _ _ _ _ _ _ _ _

ristown 104 feet _ _ _ _ _ _ _ _ *From thence to Lake Ontario 2 feet* _ _ _ _ _ *106* _ _ _ _ *13*

from Lake to Lake 334   *36½ Miles*

Not only were the British forces equal or superior to the American at Detroit, Niagara, and Montreal, but they could be more readily concentrated and more quickly supplied.

The storm of public wrath which annihilated Hull and shook Eustis passed harmless over the head of Dearborn. No one knew that Dearborn was at fault, for he had done nothing; and a general who did nothing had that advantage over his rivals whose activity or situation caused them to act. Dearborn threw the whole responsibility on the War Department. August 15 he wrote to President Madison:[1]

"The particular circumstances which have created the most unfortunate embarrassments were my having no orders or directions in relation to Upper Canada (which I had considered as not attached to my command) until my last arrival at this place, and my being detained so long at Boston *by direction*. If I had been directed to take measures for acting offensively on Niagara and Kingston, with authority such as I now possess, for calling out the militia, we might have been prepared to act on those points as early as General Hull commenced his operations at Detroit; but unfortunately no explicit orders had been received by me in relation to Upper Canada until it was too late even to make an effectual diversion in favor of General Hull. All that I could do was done without any delay."

For the moment, such pleas might serve; but after the capture of Detroit, Dearborn's turn came, and nothing could save him from a fate as decided if not as fatal as that of Hull. His armistice indeed would have answered the purpose of protection had the Government understood its true bearing; but Dearborn's letter announcing the armistice reached Washington August 13, and the Secretary of War seeing the dangers and not the advantages of a respite replied, August 15, in language more decided than he had yet used:[2] —

"I am commanded by the President to inform you that there does not appear to him any justifiable cause to vary

[1] Dearborn to Madison, Aug. 15, 1812; Madison MSS. State Department Archives.
[2] Eustis to Dearborn, Aug. 15, 1812; Hull's Memoirs, p. 87.

or desist from the arrangements which are in operation; and I am further commanded to instruct you that from and after the receipt of this letter and allowing a reasonable time in which you will inform Sir George Prevost thereof, you will proceed with the utmost vigor in your operations. How far the plan originally suggested by you of attacking Niagara, Kingston, and Montreal at the same time can be rendered practicable, you can best judge. Presuming that not more than a feint, if that should be deemed expedient, with the troops on Lake Champlain aided by volunteers and militia can be immediately effected against Montreal, and considering the urgency of a diversion in favor of General Hull under the circumstances attending his situation, the President thinks it proper that not a moment should be lost in gaining possession of the British posts at Niagara and Kingston, or at least the former, and proceeding in co-operation with General Hull in securing Upper Canada."

The same day, August 15, the eve of Hull's surrender, Dearborn wrote to the Secretary of War,[1] —

"If the troops are immediately pushed on from the southward, I think we may calculate on being able to possess ourselves of Montreal and Upper Canada before the winter sets in. . . . I am pursuing measures with the view of being able to operate with effect against Niagara and Kingston, at the same time that I move toward Lower Canada. If the Governor of Pennsylvania turns out two thousand good militia from the northwesterly frontier of his State, as I have requested him to do, and the quartermaster-general furnishes the means of transportation and camp-equipage in season, I am persuaded we may act with effect on the several points in the month of October at farthest."

As yet nothing had been done. August 19 General Van Rensselaer reported[2] from Lewiston that between Buffalo and Niagara he commanded less than a thousand militia, without ordnance heavier than 6-pounders and but few of these, without artillerists to serve the few pieces he had, and

[1] Dearborn to Eustis, Aug. 15, 1812; War Department MSS.
[2] Van Rensselaer to Tompkins, Aug. 19, 1812; Narrative, Appendix, p. 27.

the troops in a very indifferent state of discipline. In pursuance of his orders he collected the force within his reach, but August 18 received notice of Dearborn's armistice and immediately afterward of Hull's surrender. August 23 Brock, moving with his usual rapidity, reappeared at Fort George with Hull's army as captives.

Fortunately, not only were the Americans protected by the armistice, but both Prevost and Brock were under orders, and held it good policy, to avoid irritating the Americans by useless incursions. Prevost, about the equal of Madison as a military leader, showed no wish to secure the positions necessary for his safety. Had he at once seized Sackett's Harbor, as Brock seized Detroit, he would have been secure, for Sackett's Harbor was the only spot from which the Americans could contest the control of Lake Ontario. Brock saw the opportunity, and wanted to occupy the harbor, but Prevost did not encourage the idea;[1] and Brock, prevented from making a correct movement, saw no advantage in making an incorrect one. Nothing was to be gained by an offensive movement at Niagara, and Brock at that point labored only to strengthen his defence.

Van Rensselaer, knowing the whole American line to be at Brock's mercy, felt just anxiety. August 31 he wrote to Governor Tompkins,[2] —

> "Alarm pervades the country, and distrust among the troops. They are incessantly pressing for furloughs under every possible pretence. Many are without shoes; all clamorous for pay; many are sick. . . . While we are thus growing weaker our enemy is growing stronger. They hold a very commanding position on the high ground above Queenstown, and they are daily strengthening themselves in it with men and ordnance. Indeed, they are fortifying almost every prominent point from Fort Erie to Fort George. At present we rest upon the armistice, but should hostilities be recommenced I must immediately change my position. I receive no reinforcements of men, no ordnance or munitions of war."

[1] Life of Brock, pp. 293, 294.
[2] Van Rensselaer's Narrative, Appendix, p. 35.

Dearborn replied to this letter September 2, and his alarm was certainly not less than that of Van Rensselaer:[1] —

"From the number of troops which have left Montreal for Upper Canada, I am not without fear that attempts will be speedily made to reduce you and your forces to the mortifying situation of General Hull and his army. If such an attempt of the enemy should be made previous to the arrival of the principal part of the troops destined to Niagara, it will be necessary for you to be prepared for all events, and to be prepared to make good a secure retreat as the last resort."

To the Secretary of War, Dearborn wrote that he hoped there would be nothing worse than retreat.[2] Under such circumstances the armistice became an advantage, for the offensive had already passed into the enemy's hands. Detroit and Lake Erie were lost beyond salvation, but on Lake Ontario supplies and cannon were brought to Niagara by water from Oswego; the vessels at Ogdensburg were moved to Sackett's Harbor and became the nucleus of a fleet; while all the troops, regular and militia, that could be gathered from New England, New York, and Pennsylvania were hurried to the front. September 1 Dearborn wrote to Eustis[3] that he had at Plattsburg, on Lake Champlain, or under marching orders there, five thousand troops, more than half of them regulars, while six thousand, including three regular regiments from the southward, were destined for Niagara.

"When the regular troops you have ordered for Niagara arrive at that post," he wrote to Eustis, September 1, " with the militia and other troops there or on their march, they will be able I presume to cross over into Canada, carry all the works in Niagara, and proceed to the other posts in that province in triumph."

Yet the movement of troops was slow. September 15 Van Rensselaer had only sixteen hundred militia.[4] Not till then

---

[1] Van Rensselaer's Narrative, Appendix, p. 42.
[2] Dearborn to Eustis, Sept. 14, 1812; War Department MSS.
[3] Dearborn to Eustis, Sept. 1, 1812; War Department MSS.
[4] Van Rensselaer to Tompkins, Sept. 15, 1812; Narrative, Appendix, p. 50.

did the reaction from Hull's disaster make itself felt. Commodore Chauncey came to Lake Ontario with unbounded authority to create a fleet, and Lieutenant Elliott of the navy was detached to Lake Erie for the same purpose; ordnance and supplies were hurried to Buffalo, and Dearborn sent two regiments from Albany with two companies of artillery.

"When they arrive," he wrote September 17 to Van Rensselaer,[1] "with the regular troops and militia from the southward and such additional numbers of militia as I reckon on from this State, the aggregate force will I presume amount to upward of six thousand. It is intended to have a force sufficient to enable you to act with effect, though late."

The alarm still continued; and even a week afterward Dearborn wrote as though he expected disaster:[2]

"A strange fatality seems to have pervaded the whole arrangements. Ample reinforcements of troops and supplies of stores are on their way, but I fear their arrival will be too late to enable you to maintain your position. . . . By putting on the best face that your situation admits, the enemy may be induced to delay an attack until you will be able to meet him and carry the war into Canada. At all events we must calculate on possessing Upper Canada before winter sets in."

In Dearborn's letters nothing was said of the precise movement intended, but through them all ran the understanding that as soon as the force at Niagara should amount to six thousand men a forward movement should be made. The conditions supposed to be needed for the advance were more than fulfilled in the early days of October, when some twenty-five hundred militia, with a regiment of Light Artillery without guns, and the Thirteenth U. S. Infantry were in the neighborhood of Lewiston; while a brigade of United States troops, sixteen hundred and fifty strong, commanded by Brigadier-General Alexander Smyth, were on the march to

[1] Dearborn to Van Rensselaer, Sept. 17, 1812; Narrative, Appendix, p. 56.
[2] Dearborn to Van Rensselaer, Sept. 26, 1812; Narrative, Appendix, p. 59.

Buffalo. October 13 Dearborn wrote to Van Rensselaer:[1] "I am confidently sure that you will embrace the first practicable opportunity for effecting a forward movement." This opportunity had then already arrived. Smyth reached Buffalo, September 29, and reported by letter to General Van Rensselaer; but before seeing each other the two generals quarrelled. Smyth held the opinion that the army should cross into Canada above the Falls, and therefore camped his brigade at Buffalo. Van Rensselaer had made his arrangements to cross below the Falls. October 5 Van Rensselaer requested Smyth to fix a day for a council of war, but Smyth paid no attention to the request; and as he was independent of Van Rensselaer, and could not be compelled to obey the orders of a major-general of New York militia, Van Rensselaer decided to act without regard to Smyth's brigade or to his opinions. He knew that the force under his immediate orders below the Falls was sufficient for his purpose.[2]

Van Rensselaer's decision was supported by many different motives,—the lateness of the season, the weather, the sickness and the discontent of the militia threatening actual disbandment, the jealousy of a militia officer toward the regular service, and the additional jealousy of a Federalist toward the Government; for Van Rensselaer was not only a Federalist, but was also a rival candidate against Tompkins for the governorship of New York, and the Republicans were eager to charge him with intentional delay. A brilliant stroke by Lieutenant Elliott at the same moment added to the restlessness of the army. On the night of October 8 Elliott and Captain Towson of the Second Artillery, with fifty sailors and fifty soldiers of Smyth's brigade, cut out two British vessels under the guns of Fort Erie.[3] One of these vessels was the "Adams," captured by Brock at Detroit, the other had belonged to the Northwestern Fur Company, and both were of great value to the British as a reinforcement to their fleet on Lake Erie. The larger was destroyed; the smaller, named the "Caledonia," was saved, and served to increase the little American fleet. Brock felt keenly the loss of these two vessels, which "may reduce us to incalculable distress," he wrote to Prevost, October 11. He watched the progress of Elliott's and Chauncey's naval preparations with more anxiety than he showed in regard to Dearborn's military movements, although he spared no labor in fortifying himself against these.

General Van Rensselaer conceived a plan for a double attack by throwing one body of troops across the river to carry Queenston, while a strong force of regulars should be conveyed in boats by way of the Lake and landed on the Lake shore in the rear of Fort George to take the fort by storm,— a movement afterward successfully made; but owing to Smyth's conduct the double attack was abandoned, and Van Rensselaer decided to try only the simpler movement against Queenston. Brock with less than two thousand men guarded nearly forty miles of front along the Niagara River, holding at Queenston only two companies of the Forty-ninth Regiment with a small body of militia,—in all about three hundred men. Brock was himself at Fort George, some five miles below Queenston, with the greater part of the Forty-first Regiment, which he had brought back from Detroit, and a number of Indians. The rest of his force was at Chippawa and Fort Erie, opposite Buffalo, where the real attack was expected.

Van Rensselaer fixed the night of October 10 for his movement, and marched the troops to the river at the appointed time; but the crossing was prevented by some blunder in regard to boats, and the troops after passing the night exposed to a furious storm returned to camp. After this miscarriage Van Rensselaer would have waited for a council of war, but the tone of his officers and men satisfied him that any sign of hesitation would involve him in suspicion and injure the service.[1] He postponed the movement until the night of October 12, giving the command of the attack to Colonel Solomon Van Rensselaer of the State militia, whose force was to consist of three hundred volunteers and three hundred regular troops under Lieutenant-Colonel Christie of the Thirteenth Regiment.

At three o'clock on the morning of October 13 the first

[1] Van Rensselaer to Secretary Eustis, Oct. 14, 1812; Narrative, Appendix, p. 62.

body of troops embarked. Thirteen boats had been provided. Three of these lost their way, or were forced by the current down stream until obliged to return. Colonel Christie was in one of the boats that failed to land. The command of his men fell to young Captain Wool of the Thirteenth Regiment. The British were on the alert, and although after a volley of musketry they withdrew toward Queenston they quickly returned with reinforcements and began a sharp action, in which Colonel Van Rensselaer was severely wounded and the advance on Queenston was effectually stopped. Daylight appeared, and at a quarter before seven Brock himself galloped up and mounted the hill above the river to watch the contest from an 18-pounder battery on the hill-top.[1] At the same moment Captain Wool with a few men of his regiment climbed up the same heights from the river-side by a path which had been reported to Brock as impassable, and was left unguarded. Reaching the summit, Wool found himself about thirty yards in the rear of the battery from which Brock was watching the contest below. By a rapid flight on foot Brock escaped capture, and set himself immediately to the task of recovering the heights. He had early sent for the Forty-first Regiment under General Sheaffe from Fort George, but without waiting reinforcements he collected a few men—about ninety, it is said—of the Forty-ninth Regiment who could be spared below, and sent them to dislodge Wool. The first British attack was beaten back. The second, in stronger force with the York Volunteers, was led by Brock in person; but while he was still at the foot of the hill, an American bullet struck him in the breast and killed him on the spot.

At ten o'clock in the morning, Captain Wool, though painfully wounded, held the heights with two hundred and fifty men; but the heights had no value except to cover or assist the movement below, where the main column of troops with artillery and intrenching tools should have occupied Queenston, and advanced or fortified itself. When Lieutenant-Colonel Christie, at about seven o'clock, having succeeded in crossing the river, took command of the force on the river bank, he could do nothing for want of men, artillery, and

[1] Life of Brock, p. 330.

intrenching tools.[1] He could not even dislodge the enemy from a stone house whence two light pieces of artillery were greatly annoying the boats. Unable to move without support he recrossed the river, found General Van Rensselaer half a mile beyond, and described to him the situation. Van Rensselaer sent orders to General Smyth to march his brigade to Lewiston " with every possible despatch," and ordered Captain Totten of the Engineers across the river, with intrenching tools, to lay out a fortified camp.

Toward noon General Van Rensselaer himself crossed with Christie to Queenston and climbed the hill, where Lieutenant-Colonel Winfield Scott had appeared as a volunteer and taken the command of Captain Wool's force. Toward three o'clock Lieutenant-Colonel Christie joined the party on the hill. Brigadier-General William Wadsworth of the New York militia was also on the ground, and some few men arrived, until three hundred and fifty regulars and two hundred and fifty militia are said to have been collected on the heights. From their position, at two o'clock, Van Rensselaer and Scott made out the scarlet line of the Forty-first Regiment advancing from Fort George. From Chippawa every British soldier who could be spared hurried to join the Forty-first, while a swarm of Indians swept close on the American line, covering the junction of the British forces and the turning movement of General Sheaffe round the foot of the hill. About one thousand men, chiefly regulars, were concentrating against the six hundred Americans on the heights.[2] General Van Rensselaer, alarmed at the sight, hastened to recross the river to Lewiston for reinforcements.

"By this time," concluded Van Rensselaer in his report of the next day,[3] "I perceived my troops were embarking very slowly. I passed immediately over to accelerate their movements; but to my utter astonishment I found that at the very moment when complete victory was in our hands the ardor of the unengaged troops had entirely subsided. I rode in all directions, urged the men by every consideration to

[1] Christie's Report, Feb. 22, 1813; Armstrong's Notices, i. 207.
[2] Life of Brock, p. 324.
[3] Van Rensselaer to Dearborn, Oct. 14, 1812; Niles, iii. 138.

pass over; but in vain. Lieutenant-Colonel Bloom who had been wounded in the action returned, mounted his horse, and rode through the camp, as did also Judge Peck who happened to be here, exhorting the companies to proceed; but all in vain."

More unfortunate than Hull, Van Rensselaer stood on the American heights and saw his six hundred gallant soldiers opposite slowly enveloped, shot down, and at last crushed by about a thousand men who could not have kept the field a moment against the whole American force. Scott and his six hundred were pushed over the cliff down to the bank of the river. The boatmen had all fled with the boats. Nothing remained but to surrender; and under the Indian fire even surrender was difficult. Scott succeeded only by going himself to the British line through the Indians, who nearly killed him as he went.

In this day's work ninety Americans were reported as killed. The number of wounded can only be estimated. Not less than nine hundred men surrendered, including skulkers and militia-men who never reached the heights. Brigadier-General William Wadsworth of the New York militia, Lieutenant-Colonel Fenwick of the U. S. Light Artillery, Lieutenant-Colonel Winfield Scott of the Second Artillery, and, among officers of less rank, Captain Totten of the Engineers were among the prisoners. Van Rensselaer's campaign did not, like that of Hull, cost a province, but it sacrificed nearly as many effective troops as were surrendered by Hull.

General Van Rensselaer the next day sent his report of the affair to General Dearborn, and added a request to be relieved of his command. Dearborn, who knew little of the circumstances, ordered him to transfer the command to General Smyth, and wrote to Washington a bitter complaint of Van Rensselaer's conduct, which he attributed to jealousy of the regular service.[1]

Hitherto the military movements against Canada had been directed by Eastern men. Alexander Smyth belonged to a different class. Born in Ireland in 1765, his fortunes led him to

---

[1] Dearborn to Eustis, Oct. 21, 1812; War Department MSS. Dearborn to Madison, Oct. 24, 1812; Madison MSS., State Department Archives.

Virginia, where he became a respectable member of the Southwestern bar and served in the State legislature. Appointed in 1808 by President Jefferson colonel of the new rifle regiment, in 1812 he became inspector-general, with the rank of brigadier. By his own request he received command of the brigade ordered to Niagara, and his succession to Van Rensselaer followed of course. Dearborn, knowing little of Smyth, was glad to intrust the army to a regular officer in whom he felt confidence; yet an Irish temperament with a Virginian education promised the possibility of a campaign which if not more disastrous than that led by William Hull of Massachusetts, or by Stephen Van Rensselaer of New York, might be equally eccentric.

October 24 Smyth took command at Buffalo, and three weeks later the public read in the newspapers an address issued by him to the "Men of New York," written in a style hitherto unusual in American warfare.

"For many years," Smyth announced to the Men of New York,[1] "you have seen your country oppressed with numerous wrongs. Your government, although above all others devoted to peace, has been forced to draw the sword, and rely for redress of injuries on the valor of the American people. That valor has been conspicuous. But the nation has been unfortunate in the selection of some of those who have directed it. One army has been disgracefully surrendered and lost. Another has been sacrificed by a precipitate attempt to pass it over at the strongest point of the enemy's lines with most incompetent means. The cause of these miscarriages is apparent. The commanders were popular men, 'destitute alike of theory and experience' in the art of war."

Unmilitary as such remarks were, the address continued in a tone more and more surprising, until at last it became burlesque.

"In a few days the troops under my command will plant the American standard in Canada. They are men accus-

[1] Niles, iii. 203.

tomed to obedience, silence, and steadiness. They will conquer, or they will die.

"Will you stand with your arms folded and look on this interesting struggle? Are you not related to the men who fought at Bennington and Saratoga? Has the race degenerated? Or have you, under the baneful influence of contending factions, forgot your country? Must I turn from you and ask the men of the Six Nations to support the government of the United States? Shall I imitate the officers of the British king, and suffer our ungathered laurels to be tarnished by ruthless deeds? Shame, where is thy blush! No!"

The respectable people of the neighborhood were not wholly discouraged by this call or by a second proclamation, November 17, as little military as the first; or even by an address of Peter B. Porter offering to lead his neighbors into Canada under the command of the "able and experienced officer" who within a few days could and would "occupy all the British fortresses on the Niagara River." A certain number of volunteers offered themselves for the service, although not only the attack but also its details were announced in advance. The British responded by bombarding Black Rock and Fort Niagara; and although their cannon did little harm, they were more effective than the proclamations of the American generals.

November 25 General Smyth issued orders for the invasion, which were also unusual in their character, and prescribed even the gestures and attitudes of the attacking force:[1] "At twenty yards distance the soldiers will be ordered to trail arms, advance with shouts, fire at five paces distance, and charge bayonets. The soldiers will be *silent* above all things." In obedience to these orders, everything was prepared, November 27, for the crossing, and once more orders were issued in an inspiring tone:[2]

"Friends of your country! ye who have 'the will to do, the heart to dare!' the moment ye have wished for has arrived! Think on your country's honors torn! her rights trampled on! her sons enslaved! her infants perishing by the

[1] Lossing, p. 427 *note*.
[2] State Papers, Military Affairs, i. 501.

hatchet! Be strong! be brave! and let the ruffian power of the British king cease on this continent!"

Two detachments were to cross the river from Black Rock before dawn, November 28, to surprise and disable the enemy's batteries and to destroy a bridge five miles below; after this should be done the army was to cross. The British were supposed to have not more than a thousand men within twenty miles to resist the attack of three thousand men from Buffalo. Apparently Smyth's calculations were correct. His two detachments crossed the river at three o'clock on the morning of November 28 and gallantly, though with severe loss, captured and disabled the guns and tore up a part of the bridge without destroying it. At sunrise the army began to embark at the navy yard, but the embarkation continued so slowly that toward afternoon, when all the boats were occupied, only twelve hundred men, with artillery, were on board. "The troops thus embarked," reported Smyth,[1] "moved up the stream to Black Rock without sustaining loss from the enemy's fire. It was now afternoon, and they were ordered to disembark and dine."

This was all. No more volunteers appeared, and no other regulars fit for service remained. Smyth would not cross without three thousand men, and doubtless was right in his caution; but he showed want of courage not so much in this failure to redeem his pledges, as in his subsequent attempt to throw responsibility on subordinates, and on Dearborn who had requested him to consult some of his officers occasionally, and be prepared if possible to cross into Canada with three thousand men at once.[2] Smyth consulted his officers at the moment when consultation was fatal.

"Recollecting your instructions to cross with three thousand men *at once*, and to consult some of my principal officers in 'all important movements,' I called for the field officers of the regulars and twelve-months volunteers embarked."

The council of war decided not to risk the crossing.

[1] Smyth to Dearborn, Dec. 4, 1812; Niles, iii. 282.
[2] Dearborn to Smyth, Oct. 21, 1812; State Papers, Military Affairs, i. 493.

Winder, who was considered the best of Smyth's colonels, had opposed the scheme from the first, and reported the other officers as strongly against it. Smyth was aware of their opinions, and his appeal to them could have no object but to shift responsibility. After receiving their decision, Smyth sent a demand for the surrender of Fort Erie, "to spare the effusion of blood," and then ordered his troops to their quarters. The army obeyed with great discontent, but fifteen hundred men still mustered in the boats, when two days afterward Smyth issued another order to embark. Once more Smyth called a council of war, and once more decided to abandon the invasion. With less than three thousand men in the boats at once, the General would not stir.

Upon this, General Smyth's army dissolved. "A scene of confusion ensued which it is difficult to describe," wrote Peter B. Porter soon afterward,[1] — "about four thousand men without order or restraint discharging their muskets in every direction." They showed a preference for General Smyth's tent as their target, which caused the General to shift his quarters repeatedly. A few days afterward Peter B. Porter published a letter to a Buffalo newspaper, attributing the late disgrace "to the cowardice of General Smyth."[2] The General sent a challenge to his subordinate officer, and exchanged shots with him. Smyth next requested permission to visit his family, which Dearborn hastened to grant; and three months afterward, as General Smyth did not request an inquiry into the causes of his failure, the President without express authority of law dropped his name from the army roll.

When Dearborn received the official report of Smyth's grotesque campaign, he was not so much annoyed by its absurdities as he was shocked to learn that nearly four thousand regular troops sent to Niagara in the course of the campaign could not supply a thousand for crossing the river.[3] Further inquiry explained that sickness had swept away more than half the army. The brigade of regulars at Buffalo, which with the exception of Winder's regiment had never fired a musket, was reduced to less than half its original number, and both officers

[1] Niles, iii. 284.
[2] Niles, iii. 264.
[3] Dearborn to Eustis, December 11, 1812; War Department MSS.

and men were unfit for active duty.[1] Only rest and care could restore the army to efficiency.

The failures of Hull, Van Rensselaer, and Smyth created a scandal so noisy that little was thought of General Dearborn; yet Dearborn still commanded on Lake Champlain the largest force then under arms, including seven regiments of the regular army, with artillery and dragoons. He clung to the idea of an attack on Montreal simultaneous with Smyth's movement at Niagara.[2] November 8, he wrote from Albany to Eustis that he was about to join the army under General Bloomfield at Plattsburg.[3]

"I have been detained several days by a severe rheumatic attack, but I shall, by the aid of Dr. Mann, be able to set off this day toward Lake Champlain, where I trust General Bloomfield will be able to move toward Montreal, and with the addition of three thousand regular troops that place might be carried and held this winter; but I cannot consent to crossing the St. Lawrence with an uncertainty of being able to remain there."

Whatever were Dearborn's motives for undertaking the movement, his official report[4] explained that on arriving at Plattsburg he found General Bloomfield ill, and was himself obliged to take command, November 19, when he marched the army about twenty miles to the Canadian line. At that point the militia declined to go further, and Dearborn as quietly as possible, November 23, marched back to Plattsburg. His campaign lasted four days, and he did not enter Canada.

Whether Dearborn, Smyth, or William Hull would have improved the situation by winning a victory or by losing a battle was a question to be answered by professional soldiers; but the situation at best was bad, and when the report of Smyth's crowning failure reached Dearborn it seemed for a moment to overcome his sorely tried temper. "I had anticipated disappointment and misfortune in the commencement

[1] Major Campbell to General Smyth, Nov. 27, 1812; Military Affairs, i. 500. General Winder to General Smyth, Dec. 2, 1812; Military Affairs, i. 507.
[2] Dearborn to Smyth, Oct. 28 and Nov. 8, 1812; Military Affairs, i. 495, 497.
[3] Dearborn to Eustis, Nov. 8, 1812; War Department MSS.
[4] Dearborn to Eustis, Nov. 24, 1812; War Department MSS.

of the war," he wrote to Eustis,[1] "but I did by no means apprehend such a deficiency of regular troops and such a series of disasters as we have witnessed." He intimated his readiness to accept the responsibility which properly belonged to him, and to surrender his command. "I shall be happy to be released by any gentleman whose talents and popularity will command the confidence of the Government and the country." To the President he wrote at the same time:[2] "It will be equally agreeable to me to employ such moderate talents as I possess in the service of my country, or to be permitted to retire to the shades of private life, and remain a mere but interested spectator of passing events."

[1] Dearborn to Eustis, Dec. 11, 1812; War Department MSS.

[2] Dearborn to Madison, Dec. 13, 1812; Madison MSS., State Department Archives.

Chapter XVII

CULPABLE AS was the helplessness of the War Department in 1812, the public neither understood nor knew how to enforce responsibility for disasters which would have gone far to cost a European war minister his life, as they might have cost his nation its existence. By fortune still kinder, the Navy Department escaped penalty of any sort for faults nearly as serious as those committed by its rival. The navy consisted, besides gunboats, of three heavy frigates rated as carrying forty-four guns; three lighter frigates rated at thirty-eight guns; one of thirty-two, and one of twenty-eight; besides two ships of eighteen guns, two brigs of sixteen, and four brigs of fourteen and twelve,—in all sixteen sea-going vessels, twelve of which were probably equal to any vessels afloat of the same class. The eight frigates were all built by Federalist Congresses before President Jefferson's time; the smaller craft, except one, were built under the influence of the war with Tripoli. The Administration which declared war against England did nothing to increase the force. Few of the ships were in first-rate condition. The officers complained that the practice of laying up the frigates in port hastened their decay, and declared that hardly a frigate in the service was as sound as she should be. For this negligence Congress was alone responsible; but the Department perhaps shared the blame for want of readiness when war was declared.

The only ships actually ready for sea, June 18, were the "President," 44, commanded by Commodore Rodgers, at New York, and the "United States," 44, which had cruised to the southward with the "Congress," 38, and "Argus," 16, under the command of Commodore Decatur. Secretary Hamilton, May 21, sent orders to Decatur to prepare for war, and June 5 wrote more urgently:[1] "Have the ships under your command immediately ready for extensive active service, and proceed with them to New York, where you will join Commodore Rodgers and wait further orders. Prepare for battle, which I hope will add to your fame." To Rodgers he wrote

---

[1] Hamilton to Decatur, June 5, 1812; MSS. Navy Department Records.

on the same day in much the same words:[1] "Be prepared in all respects for extensive service." He asked both officers for their advice how to make the navy most useful. Rodgers's reply, if he made one, was not preserved; but Decatur answered from Norfolk, June 8,[2] —

> "The plan which appears to me to be the best calculated for our little navy . . . would be to send them out with as large a supply of provisions as they can carry, distant from our coast and singly, or not more than two frigates in company, without giving them any specific instructions as to place of cruising, but to rely on the enterprise of the officers."

The Department hesitated to adopt Decatur's advice, and began by an effort to concentrate all its ships at New York,— an attempt in which Secretary Hamilton could not wholly succeed, for the "Constellation" and the "Chesapeake," 38-gun frigates, and the "Adams," 28, were not in condition for sea; the "Essex," 32, was not quite ready, and the "Wasp," 18, was bringing despatches from Europe, while the "Constitution," 44, detained at Annapolis by the difficulty of shipping a new crew, could not sail within three weeks. The secretary ordered Captain Hull, who commanded the "Constitution," to make his way to New York with the utmost speed, and if his crew were in proper condition, to look for the British frigate "Belvidera" on the way. The only ships that could be brought to New York without delay were those of Decatur at Norfolk. To him the secretary, on the declaration of war, sent orders to proceed with all despatch northwards, and "to notice the British flag if it presents itself" on the way. "The 'Belvidera' is said to be on our coast," added the secretary.[3] Before this letter reached Norfolk, Decatur and his squadron sailed from the Chesapeake and were already within sight of Sandy Hook; so that the only orders from the Navy Department which immediately affected the movement of the frigates were those sent to New York for Commodore Rodgers and the

---

[1] Hamilton to Rodgers, June 5, 1812; MSS. Navy Department Records.
[2] Decatur to Hamilton, June 8, 1812; MSS. Navy Department Records.
[3] Hamilton to Decatur, June 18, 1812; MSS. Navy Department Records.

frigate "President," but which included Decatur's squadron when it should arrive.

"For the present," wrote the secretary to Rodgers,[1] "it is desirable that with the force under your command you remain in such position as to enable you most conveniently to receive further more extensive and more particular orders, which will be conveyed to you through New York. But as it is understood that there are one or more British cruisers on the coast in the vicinity of Sandy Hook, you are at your discretion free to strike them, returning immediately after into port. You are free to capture or destroy them."

These orders reached New York June 21. Rodgers in his fine frigate the "President," with the "Hornet," 18, was eager to sail. The hope of capturing the "Belvidera," which had long been an intolerable annoyance to New York commerce, was strong both in the Navy Department and in the navy; but the chance of obtaining prize money from the British West India convoy, just then passing eastward only a few days' sail from the coast, added greatly to the commodore's impatience.[2] Decatur's squadron arrived off Sandy Hook June 19. June 21, within an hour after receiving the secretary's orders of June 18, the whole fleet, including two forty-four and one thirty-eight-gun frigates, with the "Hornet" and the "Argus," stood out to sea.

The secretary might have spared himself the trouble of giving further orders, for many a week passed before Rodgers and Decatur bethought themselves of his injunction to return immediately into port after striking the "Belvidera." They struck the "Belvidera" within forty-eight hours, and lost her; partly on account of the bursting of one of the "President's" main-deck guns, which blew up the forecastle deck, killing or wounding sixteen men, including Commodore Rodgers himself, whose leg was broken; partly, and according to the British account chiefly, on account of stopping to fire at all, when Rodgers should have run alongside, and in that case could not have failed to capture his enemy. Whatever was the

---

[1] Hamilton to Rodgers, June 18, 1812; MSS. Navy Department Records.
[2] Rodgers to Hamilton, Sept. 1, 1812; Official Letters, p. 52.

reason, the "Belvidera" escaped; and Rodgers and Decatur, instead of returning immediately into port as they had been ordered, turned in pursuit of the British West India convoy, and hung doggedly to the chase without catching sight of their game, until after three weeks' pursuit they found themselves within a day's sail of the British Channel and the convoy safe in British waters.

This beginning of the naval war was discouraging. The American ships should not have sailed in a squadron, and only their good luck saved them from disaster. Rodgers and Decatur showed no regard to the wishes of the Government, although had they met with misfortune, the navy would have lost its last hope. Yet if the two commodores had obeyed the secretary's commands their cruise would probably have been in the highest degree disastrous. The Government's true intentions have been a matter of much dispute; but beyond a doubt the President and a majority of his advisers inclined to keep the navy within reach at first,—to use them for the protection of commerce, to drive away the British blockaders; and aware that the British naval force would soon be greatly increased, and that the American navy must be blockaded in port, the Government expected in the end to use the frigates as harbor defences rather than send them to certain destruction.

With these ideas in his mind Secretary Hamilton, in his orders of June 18, told Rodgers and Decatur that "more extensive" orders should be sent to them on their return to New York. A day or two afterward Secretary Gallatin complained to the President that these orders had not been sent.

"I believe the weekly arrivals from foreign ports," said Gallatin,[1] "will for the coming four weeks average from one to one-and-a-half million dollars a week. To protect these and our coasting vessels, while the British have still an inferior force on our coasts, appears to me of primary importance. I think that orders to that effect, ordering them to cruise accordingly, ought to have been sent yesterday, and that at all events not one day longer ought to be lost."

[1] Adams's Gallatin, p. 465.

June 22 the orders were sent according to Gallatin's wish. They directed Rodgers with his part of the squadron to cruise from the Chesapeake eastwardly, and Decatur with his ships to cruise from New York southwardly, so as to cross and support each other and protect with their united force the merchantmen and coasters entering New York harbor, the Delaware, and the Chesapeake. Rodgers and Decatur were then beginning their private cruise across the ocean, and never received these orders until the commerce they were to protect either reached port in safety or fell into British hands.

Probably this miscarriage was fortunate, for not long after Rodgers and Decatur passed the Banks the British Vice-Admiral Sawyer sent from Halifax a squadron to prevent the American navy from doing what Secretary Hamilton had just ordered to be done. July 5 Captain Broke, with his own frigate the "Shannon," 38, the "Belvidera," 36, the "Africa," 64, and "Æolus," 32, put to sea from Halifax and was joined, July 9, off Nantucket by the "Guerriere," 38. Against such a force Rodgers and Decatur, even if together, would have risked total destruction, while a success would have cost more than it was worth. The Americans had nothing to gain and everything to lose by fighting in line-of-battle.

As Broke's squadron swept along the coast it seized whatever it met, and July 16 caught one of President Jefferson's 16-gun brigs, the "Nautilus." The next day it came on a richer prize. The American navy seemed ready to outstrip the army in the race for disaster. The "Constitution," the best frigate in the United States service, sailed into the midst of Broke's five ships. Captain Isaac Hull, in command of the "Constitution," had been detained at Annapolis shipping a new crew, until July 5,[1] — the day when Broke's squadron left Halifax; — then the ship got under way and stood down Chesapeake Bay on her voyage to New York. The wind was ahead and very light. Not till July 10 did the ship anchor off Cape Henry lighthouse,[2] and not till sunrise of July 12 did she stand to the eastward and northward. Light head-winds and a strong current delayed her progress till July 17, when at two o'clock in the afternoon, off Barnegat on the New Jersey coast, the look-

[1] Hull to Secretary Hamilton, July 7, 1812; MSS. Navy Department.
[2] Hull to Secretary Hamilton, July 10, 1812; MSS. Navy Department.

out at the masthead discovered four sails to the northward, and two hours later a fifth sail to the northeast. Hull took them for Rodgers's squadron. The wind was light, and Hull being to windward determined to speak the nearest vessel, the last to come in sight. The afternoon passed without bringing the ships together, and at ten in the evening, finding that the nearest ship could not answer the night signal, Hull decided to lose no time in escaping.

Then followed one of the most exciting and sustained chases recorded in naval history. At daybreak the next morning one British frigate was astern within five or six miles, two more were to leeward, and the rest of the fleet some ten miles astern, all making chase. Hull put out his boats to tow the "Constitution;" Broke summoned the boats of his squadron to tow the "Shannon." Hull then bent all his spare rope to the cables, dropped a small anchor half a mile ahead, in twenty-six fathom water, and warped his ship along. Broke quickly imitated the device, and slowly gained on the chase. The "Guerriere" crept so near Hull's lee-beam as to open fire, but her shot fell short. Fortunately the wind, though slight, favored Hull. All night the British and American crews toiled on, and when morning came the "Belvidera," proving to be the best sailer, got in advance of her consorts, working two kedge-anchors, until at two o'clock in the afternoon she tried in her turn to reach the "Constitution" with her bow guns, but in vain. Hull expected capture, but the "Belvidera" could not approach nearer without bringing her boats under the "Constitution's" stern guns; and the wearied crews toiled on, towing and kedging, the ships barely out of gunshot, till another morning came. The breeze, though still light, then allowed Hull to take in his boats, the "Belvidera" being two and a half miles in his wake, the "Shannon" three and a half miles on his lee, and the three other frigates well to leeward. The wind freshened, and the "Constitution" drew ahead, until toward seven o'clock in the evening of July 19 a heavy rain-squall struck the ship, and by taking skilful advantage of it Hull left the "Belvidera" and "Shannon" far astern; yet until eight o'clock the next morning they were still in sight keeping up the chase.

Perhaps nothing during the war tested American seamanship more thoroughly than these three days of combined skill and endurance in the face of an irresistible enemy. The result showed that Hull and the "Constitution" had nothing to fear in these respects. There remained the question whether the superiority extended to his guns; and such was the contempt of British naval officers for American ships, that with this experience before their eyes they still believed one of their 38-gun frigates to be more than a match for an American forty-four, although the American, besides the heavier armament, had proved his capacity to out-sail and out-manœuvre the Englishman. Both parties became more eager than ever for the test. For once, even the Federalists of New England felt their blood stir; for their own President and their own votes had called these frigates into existence, and a victory won by the "Constitution," which had been built by their hands, was in their eyes a greater victory over their political opponents than over the British. With no half-hearted spirit, the sea-going Bostonians showered well-weighed praises on Hull when his ship entered Boston harbor, July 26, after its narrow escape; and when he sailed again, New England waited with keen interest to learn his fate.

Hull could not expect to keep command of the "Constitution." Bainbridge was much his senior, and had the right to a preference in active service. Bainbridge then held and was ordered to retain command of the "Constellation," fitting out at the Washington Navy Yard; but Secretary Hamilton, July 28, ordered him to take command also of the "Constitution" on her arrival in port. Doubtless Hull expected this change, and probably the expectation induced him to risk a dangerous experiment; for without bringing his ship to the Charlestown Navy Yard, but remaining in the outer harbor, after obtaining such supplies as he needed, August 2, he set sail without orders, and stood to the eastward. Having reached Cape Race without meeting an enemy he turned southward, until on the night of August 18 he spoke a privateer, which told him of a British frigate near at hand. Following the privateersman's directions the "Constitution" the next day, August 19, at two o'clock in the afternoon, latitude 41° 42′, longitude 55° 48′, sighted the "Guerriere."

The meeting was welcome on both sides. Only three days

before, Captain Dacres had entered on the log of a merchant-man a challenge to any American frigate to meet him off Sandy Hook. Not only had the "Guerriere" for a long time been extremely offensive to every sea-faring American, but the mistake which caused the "Little Belt" to suffer so seriously for the misfortune of being taken for the "Guerriere" had caused a corresponding feeling of anger in the officers of the British frigate. The meeting of August 19 had the character of a pre-concerted duel.

The wind was blowing fresh from the northwest, with the sea running high. Dacres backed his main-top-sail and waited. Hull shortened sail and ran down before the wind. For about an hour the two ships wore and wore again, trying to get advantage of position; until at last, a few minutes before six o'clock, they came together side by side, within pistol-shot, the wind almost astern, and running before it they pounded each other with all their strength. As rapidly as the guns could be worked, the "Constitution" poured in broadside after broadside, double-shotted with round and grape,—and, without exaggeration, the echo of these guns startled the world. "In less than thirty minutes from the time we got alongside of the enemy," reported Hull,[1] "she was left without a spar standing, and the hull cut to pieces in such a manner as to make it difficult to keep her above water."

That Dacres should have been defeated was not surprising; that he should have expected to win was an example of British arrogance that explained and excused the war. The length of the "Constitution" was 173 feet; that of the "Guerriere" was 156 feet; the extreme breadth of the "Constitution" was 44 feet; that of the "Guerriere" was 40 feet, or within a few inches in both cases. The "Constitution" carried thirty-two long 24-pounders, the "Guerriere" thirty long 18-pounders and two long 12-pounders; the "Constitution" carried twenty 32-pound carronades, the "Guerriere" sixteen. In every respect, and in proportion of ten to seven, the "Constitution" was the better ship; her crew was more numerous in proportion of ten to six. Dacres knew this very nearly as well as it was known to Hull, yet he sought a duel. What he did not

[1] Hull to Secretary Hamilton, Aug. 28, 1812; MSS. Navy Department.

know was that in a still greater proportion the American officers and crew were better and more intelligent seamen than the British, and that their passionate wish to repay old scores gave them extraordinary energy. So much greater was the moral superiority than the physical, that while the "Guerriere's" force counted as seven against ten, her losses counted as though her force were only two against ten.

Dacres' error cost him dear, for among the "Guerriere's" crew of two hundred and seventy-two, seventy-nine were killed or wounded; and the ship was injured beyond saving before Dacres realized his mistake, although he needed only thirty minutes of close fighting for the purpose. He never fully understood the causes of his defeat, and never excused it by pleading, as he might have done, the great superiority of his enemy.[1]

Hull took his prisoners on board the "Constitution," and after blowing up the "Guerriere" sailed for Boston, where he arrived on the morning of August 30. The Sunday silence of the Puritan city broke into excitement as the news passed through the quiet streets that the "Constitution" was below, in the outer harbor, with Dacres and his crew prisoners on board. No experience of history ever went to the heart of New England more directly than this victory, so peculiarly its own; but the delight was not confined to New England, and extreme though it seemed it was still not extravagant, for however small the affair might appear on the general scale of the world's battles, it raised the United States in one half hour to the rank of a first-class Power in the world.

Hull's victory was not only dramatic in itself, but was also supremely fortunate in the moment it occurred. The "Boston Patriot" of September 2, which announced the capture of the "Guerriere," announced in the next column that Rodgers and Decatur, with their squadron, entered Boston harbor within four-and-twenty hours after Hull's arrival, returning empty-handed after more than two months of futile cruising; while in still another column the same newspaper announced "the melancholy intelligence of the surrender of General Hull and his whole army to the British General Brock." Isaac Hull was

[1] Niles, ii. 333.

nephew to the unhappy General, and perhaps the shattered hulk of the "Guerriere," which the nephew left at the bottom of the Atlantic Ocean, eight hundred miles east of Boston, was worth for the moment the whole province which the uncle had lost, eight hundred miles to the westward; it was at least the only equivalent the people could find, and they made the most of it. With the shock of new life, they awoke to the consciousness that after all the peace teachings of Pennsylvania and Virginia, the sneers of Federalists and foreigners; after the disgrace of the "Chesapeake" and the surrender of Detroit,—Americans could still fight. The public had been taught, and had actually learned, to doubt its own physical courage; and the reaction of delight in satisfying itself that it still possessed the commonest and most brutal of human qualities was the natural result of a system that ignored the possibility of war.

Hull's famous victory taught the pleasures of war to a new generation, which had hitherto been sedulously educated to think only of its cost. The first taste of blood maddens; and hardly had the "Constitution" reached port and told her story than the public became eager for more. The old Jeffersonian jealousy of the navy vanished in the flash of Hull's first broadside. Nothing would satisfy the craving of the popular appetite but more battles, more British frigates, and more daring victories. Even the cautious Madison was dragged by public excitement upon the element he most heartily disliked.

The whole navy, was once more, September 1, safe in port, except only the "Essex," a frigate rated at thirty-two but carrying forty-four guns, commanded by Captain David Porter. She left New York, July 3, with orders,[1] dated June 24, to join Rodgers, or failing this to cruise southwardly as far as St. Augustine. June 11 she met a convoy of seven transports conveying a battalion of the First Regiment, or Royal Scots, from the West Indies to reinforce Prevost and Brock in Canada. Porter cut out one transport. With the aid of another frigate he could have captured the whole, to the great advantage of Dearborn's military movements; but the British

---

[1] Hamilton to Porter, June 24, 1812; MSS. Navy Department Records.

commander managed his convoy so well that the battalion escaped, and enabled Prevost to strengthen the force at Niagara which threatened and defeated Van Rensselaer. August 13 the British 20-gun sloop-of-war "Alert" came in sight, bore down within short pistol-shot, and opened fire on the "Essex." Absurd as the idea seemed, the British captain behaved as though he hoped to capture the American frigate, and not until Porter nearly sunk him with a broadside did the Englishman strike his colors. After taking a number of other prizes, but without further fighting, September 7 Porter brought his ship back to the Delaware River.

The return of the "Essex" to port, September 7, brought all the national vessels once more under the direct control of the Department. Nearly every ship in the service was then at Boston. The three forty-fours—the "Constitution," "United States," and "President"—were all there; two of the thirty-eights—the "Congress" and "Chesapeake"—were there, and the "Constellation" was at Washington. The "Adams," 28, was also at Washington; but the "Hornet," 18, and "Argus," 16, were with Rodgers and Decatur at Boston. The "Syren," 16, was at New Orleans; the "Essex," 32, and the "Wasp," 18, were in the Delaware.

Carried away by Hull's victory, the Government could no longer hesitate to give its naval officers the liberty of action they asked, and which in spite of orders they had shown the intention to take. A new arrangement was made. The vessels were to be divided into three squadrons, each consisting of one forty-four, one light frigate, and one sloop-of-war. Rodgers in the "President" was to command one squadron, Bainbridge in the "Constitution" was to command another, and Decatur in the "United States" was to take the third.[1] Their sailing orders, dated October 2,[2] simply directed the three commodores to proceed to sea: "You are to do your utmost to annoy the enemy, to afford protection to our commerce, pursuing that course which to your best judgment may under all circumstances appear the best calculated to enable you to accomplish these objects as far as may be in your power, re-

[1] Hamilton to Rodgers and Decatur, Sept. 9, 1812; MSS. Navy Department Records.
[2] MSS. Navy Department Records.

turning into port as speedily as circumstances will permit consistently with the great object in view."

Before continuing the story of the frigates, the fate of the little "Wasp" needs to be told. Her career was brief. The "Wasp," a sloop-of-war rated at eighteen guns, was one of President Jefferson's additions to the navy to supply the loss of the "Philadelphia;" she was ship-rigged, and armed with two long 12-pounders and sixteen 32-pound carronades. She carried a crew of one hundred and thirty-seven men, commanded by Captain Jacob Jones, a native of Delaware, lieutenant in the "Philadelphia" when lost in the war with Tripoli. The "Wasp" was attached to Rodgers's squadron, and received orders from the commodore to join him at sea. She sailed from the Delaware October 13, and when about six hundred miles east of Norfolk, October 17, she fell in with the British 18-gun brig "Frolic," convoying fourteen merchantmen to England. The two vessels were equal in force, for the "Frolic's" broadside threw a weight of two hundred and seventy-four pounds, while that of the "Wasp" threw some few pounds less; the "Frolic" measured, by British report,[1] one hundred feet in length, the "Wasp" one hundred and six; their breadth on deck was the same; and although the "Wasp's" crew exceeded that of her enemy, being one hundred and thirty-five men against one hundred and ten, the British vessel had all the men she needed, and suffered little from this inferiority. The action began at half-past eleven in the morning, the two sloops running parallel, about sixty yards apart, in a very heavy sea, which caused both to pitch and roll so that marksmanship had the most decisive share in victory. The muzzles of the guns went under water, and clouds of spray dashed over the crews, while the two vessels ran side by side for the first fifteen minutes. The British fire cut the "Wasp's" rigging, while the American guns played havoc with the "Frolic's" hull and lower masts. The vessels approached each other so closely that the rammers of the guns struck the enemy's side, and at last they fell foul,—the "Wasp" almost squarely across the "Frolic's" bow. In the heavy sea boarding was difficult; but as soon as the "Wasp's" crew could clamber

[1] James, Naval Occurrences, p. 152.

down the "Frolic's" bowsprit, they found on the deck the British captain and lieutenant, both severely wounded, and one brave sailor at the wheel. Not twenty of the British crew were left unhurt, and these had gone below to escape the American musketry. The "Wasp" had only ten men killed and wounded. The battle lasted forty-three minutes.

If the American people had acquired a taste for blood, the battle of the "Wasp" and "Frolic" gratified it, for the British sloop was desperately defended, and the battle, won by the better marksmanship of the Americans, was unusually bloody. Captain Jones lost the full satisfaction of his victory, for a few hours afterward the "Poictiers," a British seventy-four, came upon the two disabled combatants and carried both into Bermuda; but the American people would have been glad to part with their whole navy on such terms, and the fight between the "Wasp" and the "Frolic" roused popular enthusiasm to a point where no honors seemed to satisfy their gratitude to Captain Jones and his crew.

The "Wasp's" brilliant career closed within a week from the day she left the Delaware. A week afterward another of these ship-duels occurred, which made a still deeper impression. Rodgers and Decatur sailed from Boston October 8, with the "President," the "United States," "Congress," and "Argus," leaving the "Constitution," "Chesapeake," and "Hornet" in port. Rodgers in the "President," with the "Congress," cruised far and wide, but could find no enemy to fight, and after making prize of a few merchantmen returned to Boston, December 31. The "Argus" also made some valuable prizes, but was chased by a British squadron, and only by excellent management escaped capture, returning Jan. 3, 1813, to New York. Decatur in the "United States," separating from the squadron October 12, sailed eastward to the neighborhood of the Azores, until, October 25, he sighted a sail to windward. The stranger made chase. The wind was fresh from south-southeast, with a heavy sea. Decatur stood toward his enemy, who presently came about, abreast of the "United States" but beyond gunshot, and both ships being then on the same tack approached each other until the action began at long range. The British ship was the 38-gun frigate "Macedonian" commanded by Captain Carden, and about the same force as the

"Guerriere." At first the "United States" used only her long 24-pounders, of which she carried fifteen on her broadside, while the "Macedonian" worked a broadside of fourteen long 18-pounders. So unequal a contest could not continue. Not only was the American metal heavier, but the American fire was quicker and better directed than that of the Englishman; so that Carden, after a few minutes of this experience, bore down to close. His manœuvre made matters worse. The carronades of the "United States" came into play; the "Macedonian's" mizzen-mast fell, her fore and main top-mast were shot away, and her main-yard; almost all her rigging was cut to pieces, and most of the guns on her engaged side were dismounted. She dropped gradually to leeward, and Decatur, tacking and coming up under his enemy's stern, hailed, and received her surrender.

The British ship had no right to expect a victory, for the disparity of force was even greater than between the "Constitution" and "Guerriere;" but in this case the British court-martial subsequently censured Captain Carden for mistakes. The battle lasted longer than that with the "Guerriere," and Decatur apologized for the extra hour because the sea was high and his enemy had the weather-gauge and kept at a distance; but the apology was not needed. Decatur proved his skill by sparing his ship and crew. His own loss was eleven men killed and wounded; the "Macedonian's" loss was nine times as great. The "United States" suffered little in her hull, and her spars and rigging suffered no greater injury than could be quickly repaired; while the "Macedonian" received a hundred shot in her hull, and aloft nothing remained standing but her fore and main masts and her fore-yard.

Decatur saved the "Macedonian," and brought her back to New London,—the only British frigate ever brought as a prize into an American port. The two ships arrived December 4, and from New London the "Macedonian" was taken to New York and received in formal triumph. Captain Jones of the "Wasp" took command of her in reward for his capture of the "Frolic."

Before the year closed, the "Constitution" had time for another cruise. Hull at his own request received command of the Navy Yard at Charlestown, and also took charge of the naval defences in New York harbor, but did not again serve at sea during the war. The "Constitution" was given to Captain Bainbridge, one of the oldest officers in the service. A native of New Jersey, Bainbridge commanded the "Philadelphia" when lost in the Tripolitan war, and was held for eighteen months a prisoner in Tripoli. In 1812, when he took command of the "Constitution," though a year older than Hull and five years older than Decatur, he had not yet reached his fortieth year, while Rodgers, born in 1771, had but lately passed it. The difference in age between these four naval officers and the four chief generals—Dearborn, Wilkinson, Wade Hampton, and William Hull—was surprising; for the average age of the naval commanders amounted barely to thirty-seven years, while that of the four generals reached fifty-eight. This difference alone accounted for much of the difference in their fortune, and perhaps political influence accounted for the rest.

Bainbridge showed no inferiority to the other officers of the service, and no one grumbled at the retirement of Hull. The "Constitution" sailed from Boston, October 25, with the "Hornet." The "Essex," then in the Delaware, was ordered to join the squadron at certain specified ports in the south Atlantic, and sailed October 28, expecting a very long cruise. December 13 Bainbridge arrived at San Salvador, on the coast of Brazil, where he left the "Hornet" to blockade the "Bonne Citoyenne," a British 18-gun sloop-of-war bound to England with specie. Cruising southward, within sight of the Brazilian coast, in latitude 13° 6′ south, Bainbridge sighted the British frigate "Java," a ship of the same tonnage as the "Guerriere," throwing a slightly heavier broadside and carrying a large crew of four hundred and twenty-six men, if the American account was correct. Bainbridge tacked and made sail off shore, to draw the stranger away from a neutral coast; the British frigate followed him, until at half-past one o'clock in the afternoon Bainbridge shortened sail, tacked again, and stood for his enemy. Soon after two o'clock the action began, the two ships being on the same tack, the "Java" to windward and the better sailer, and both fighting their long-range guns. The British frigate insisted upon keeping at a distance, obliging Bainbridge after half an hour to risk the danger of being raked; and at twenty minutes before three o'clock the "Constitution" closed within pistol-shot.[1] At ten minutes before three the ships were foul, the "Java's" jibboom in the "Constitution's" mizzen rigging; and from that point the battle became slaughter. In fifteen minutes the "Java's" bowsprit, foremast, and main top-mast were cut away, and a few minutes after four o'clock she ceased firing. Her captain, Lambert, was mortally wounded; the first lieutenant was wounded; forty-eight of her officers and crew were dead or dying; one hundred and two were wounded; little more than a hulk filled with wreck and with dead or wounded men floated on the water.

The "Constitution" had but twelve men killed and twenty-two wounded, and repaired damages in an hour. Owing perhaps to the death of Captain Lambert the reports of the battle were more contradictory than usual, but no one disputed that although the "Java" was to windward and outsailed the American frigate, and although her broadside counted as nearly nine against her enemy's ten,—for the "Constitution" on this cruise carried two guns less than in her fight with the "Guerriere,"—yet the "Java" inflicted no more damage than she ought to have done had she been only one fourth the size of the American frigate, although she was defended more desperately than either the "Guerriere" or the "Macedonian."

With this battle the year ended. Bainbridge was obliged to blow up his prize, and after landing and paroling his prisoners at San Salvador sailed for Boston, where he arrived in safety, February 27, 1813. During the six months the war had lasted the little United States navy captured three British frigates, besides the 20-gun "Alert" and the 18-gun "Frolic;" privateers by scores had ravaged British commerce, while the immense British force on the ocean had succeeded only in capturing the little "Nautilus," the 12-gun brig "Vixen," and the "Wasp." The commerce of America had indeed suffered almost total destruction; but the dispute was to be decided not so much by the loss which England could inflict upon America, as by that which America could inflict upon England.

[1] Bainbridge's Journal, Report of Jan. 3, 1813; Niles, iii. 411.

Chapter XVIII

IN SUCH A WAR the people of the United States had only themselves to fear; but their dangers were all the more formidable. Had the war deeply disturbed the conditions of society, or brought general and immediate distress, government and Union might easily have fallen to pieces; but in the midst of military disaster and in plain sight of the Government's incompetence, the general public neither felt nor had reason to fear much change in the routine of life. Commerce had long accustomed itself to embargoes, confiscations, and blockades, and ample supplies of foreign goods continued to arrive. The people made no serious exertions; among a population exceeding seven millions, not ten thousand men entered the military service. The militia, liable to calls to the limit of one hundred thousand, served for the most part only a few weeks in the autumn, went home in whole regiments when they pleased,[1] and in the East refused to go out at all. The scarcity of men was so great that even among the sea-going class, for whose rights the war was waged, only with the utmost difficulty and long delays, in spite of bounties and glory, could sailors be found to man half-a-dozen frigates for a three-months cruise, although the number of privateers was never great.

The nation as a whole saw nothing of actual warfare. While scarcely a city in Europe had escaped capture, and hardly a province of that continent was so remote as not to be familiar with invading armies or to have suffered in proportion to its resources, no American city saw or greatly feared an enemy. The rich farms of New York, New Jersey, Pennsylvania, and Virginia produced their usual harvests, and except on exposed parts of the coast the farmers never feared that their crops might be wasted by manœuvring armies, or their cattle, pigs, and poultry be disturbed by marauders. The country was vast, and quiet reigned throughout the whole United States. Except at the little point of Niagara, occupied by a few hundred scattered farmers, and on the extreme outskirts of Ohio and

[1] Brigadier-General Tannehill to Brigadier-General Smyth, Dec. 7, 1812; State Papers, Military Affairs, i. 507.

Indiana, the occupations and industries of life followed in the main their daily course.

The country refused to take the war seriously. A rich nation with seven million inhabitants should have easily put one hundred thousand men into the field, and should have found no difficulty in supporting them; but no inducement that the Government dared offer prevailed upon the people to risk life and property on a sufficient scale in 1812. The ranks of the army were to be filled in one of two ways,—either by enlistment in the regular service for five years, with pay at five dollars a month, sixteen dollars bounty, and on discharge three months pay and one hundred and sixty acres of land; or by volunteer organizations to the limit of fifty thousand men in all, officered under State laws, to serve for one year, with the pay of regular troops but without bounty, clothed, and in case of cavalry corps mounted, at their own expense. In a society where the day-laborers' wages were nowhere less than nine dollars a month,[1] these inducements were not enough to supply the place of enthusiasm. The patriotic citizen who wished to serve his country without too much sacrifice, chose a third course,—he volunteered under the Act of Congress which authorized the President to call one hundred thousand State militia into service for six months; and upon this State militia Dearborn, Hull, Van Rensselaer, and Smyth were obliged chiefly to depend.

If the war fever burned hotly in any part of the country Kentucky was the spot. There the whole male population was eager to prove its earnestness. When Henry Clay returned to Lexington after the declaration of war, he wrote to Monroe[2] that he was almost alarmed at the ardor his State displayed; about four hundred men had been recruited for the regular army, and although no one had volunteered for twelve months, the quota of six-months militia was more than supplied by volunteers.

"Such is the structure of our society, however," continued Clay, "that I doubt whether many can be engaged for

[1] Remarks of D. R. Williams, Nov. 20, 1812; Annals of Congress, 1812–1813, p. 156.
[2] Clay to Monroe, July 29, 1812; Monroe MSS., State Department Archives.

a longer term than six months. For that term any force whatever which our population can afford may be obtained. Engaged in agricultural pursuits, you are well aware that from about this time, when the crop is either secured in the barn or laid by in the field until the commencement of the spring, there is leisure for any kind of enterprise."

Clay feared only that these six-months militia corps, which had armed and equipped themselves for instant service, might not be called out. His friends were destined not to be disappointed, for early in August pressing letters arrived from Hull's army at Detroit begging reinforcements, and the governor of Kentucky at once summoned two thousand volunteers to rendezvous, August 20, at Newport, opposite Cincinnati. This reinforcement could not reach Detroit before the middle of September, and the difficulties already developed in Hull's path showed that the war could not be finished in a single campaign of six months; but the Kentuckians were not on that account willing to lengthen their term of service even to one year.

The danger revealed by Hull's position threw a double obstacle in the way of public energy, for where it did not check, it promised to mislead enthusiasm, and in either case it shook, if it did not destroy, confidence in the national government. The leaders of the war party saw their fears taking shape. Henry Clay wrote without reserve to Monroe,[1] —

"Should Hull's army be cut off, the effect on the public mind would be, especially in this quarter, in the highest degree injurious. 'Why did he proceed with no inconsiderable a force?' was the general inquiry made of me. I maintained that it was sufficient. Should he meet with a disaster, the predictions of those who pronounced his army incompetent to its object will be fulfilled; and the Secretary of War, in whom already there unfortunately exists no sort of confidence, cannot possibly shield Mr. Madison from the odium which will attend such an event."

Clay was right in thinking that Eustis could not shield

[1] Clay to Monroe, Aug. 12, 1812; Monroe MSS., State Department Archives.

Madison; but from the moment that Eustis could no longer serve that purpose, Clay had no choice but to shield the President himself. When the threatened disaster took place, victims like Eustis, Hull, Van Rensselaer, Smyth, were sacrificed; but the sacrifice merely prepared new material for other and perhaps worse disasters of the same kind. In Kentucky this result was most strongly marked, for in their irritation at the weakness of the national Government the Kentuckians took the war into their own hands, appointed William Henry Harrison to the command of their armies, and attempted to conquer Canada by a campaign that should not be directed from Washington. August 25 Clay described the feelings of his State by a comparison suggesting the greatest military misfortunes known in history:[1]

> "If you will carry your recollections back to the age of the Crusaders and of some of the most distinguished leaders of those expeditions, you will have a picture of the enthusiasm existing in this country for the expedition to Canada and for Harrison as commander."

A week later, September 21, Clay gave another account, even less assuring, of the manner in which the popular energy was exhausting itself: —

> "The capitulation of Detroit has produced no despair; it has, on the contrary, awakened new energies and aroused the whole people of this State. Kentucky has at this moment from eight to ten thousand men in the field; it is not practicable to ascertain the precise number. Except our quota of the hundred thousand militia the residue is chiefly of a miscellaneous character, who have turned out without pay or supplies of any kind, carrying with them their own arms and their own subsistence. Parties are daily passing to the theatre of action; last night seventy lay on my farm; and they go on, from a solitary individual, to companies of ten, fifty, one hundred, etc. The only fear I have is that the savages will, as their custom is, elude them, and upon their return fall upon our frontiers. They have already shocked

[1] Clay to Monroe, Aug. 25, 1812; Monroe MSS., State Department Archives.

us with some of the most horrid murders. Within twenty-four miles of Louisville, on the headwaters of Silver Creek, twenty-two were massacred a few days ago."

The adventures of these volunteers made part of the next campaign. Enthusiastic as Kentucky was, few or none of the eight or ten thousand men under arms offered to serve for twelve months. Excessively expensive, wasteful, insubordinate, and unsteady, no general dared to depend on them. No one could be more conscious of the evils of the system than the Government; but the Government was helpless to invent a remedy.

"Proofs multiply daily," wrote Madison to Monroe, September 21,[1] "of the difficulty of obtaining regulars, and of the fluctuating resource in the militia. High bounties and short enlistments, however objectionable, will alone fill the ranks, and then too in a moderate number."

To dislike of prolonged service even the most ardent Western supporters of the war added distrust of the Executive. The war Republicans of the West and South were hardly less vigorous than the Federalists of Massachusetts and Connecticut in their criticisms of the Government at Washington. John Graham, chief clerk of the State Department, who went to Kentucky in September, wrote to Monroe[2] that "great as is the popularity of the President, it is barely able to resist the torrent of public opinion against the Secretary of War, who, so far as I can judge, is universally considered by the people of this country as incompetent to his present situation." Clay's opinion has already been shown; but the angriest of all the war leaders on hearing of Hull's surrender was Senator Crawford of Georgia.

"Such is my want of confidence in the leaders of our forces," he wrote to Monroe,[3] "and their directors, Eustis

[1] Madison to Monroe, Sept. 21, 1812; Monroe MSS., State Department Archives.

[2] Graham to Monroe, Sept. 27, 1812; Monroe MSS., State Department Archives.

[3] Crawford to Monroe, Sept. 27, 1812; Monroe MSS., State Department Archives.

and Hamilton in the Cabinet, that I am fearful a continuance of the war, unless it should be for several years, will only add to the number of our defeats. The only difficulty I had in declaring war arose from the incompetency of the men to whom the principal management of it was to be confided. A Secretary of War who, instead of forming general and comprehensive arrangements for the organization of his troops and for the successful prosecution of the campaign, consumes his time in reading advertisements of petty retailing merchants to find where he may purchase one hundred shoes or two hundred hats; and a Secretary of the Navy who, in instructing his naval officers, should make the supply of the heads of departments with pineapples and other tropical fruits through the exertions of these officers,—cannot fail to bring disgrace upon themselves, their immediate employers, and the nation. If Mr. Madison finds it impossible to bring his feelings to consent to the dismission of unfaithful or incompetent officers, he must be content with defeat and disgrace in all his efforts during the war. So far as he may suffer from this course he deserves no commiseration, but his accountability to the nation will be great indeed!"

Harsh as these comments were, the Secretary of State found no difficulty in listening to them; indeed, no member of the party was more severe than Monroe. He visited Jefferson, and apparently Jefferson agreed with his criticisms:[1] —

"We conferred on the then state of the Departments of War and Navy, and agreed that whatever might be the merit of the gentlemen in them, which was admitted in certain respects, a change in both was indispensable."

Indeed, Monroe did what no northern Democrat liked to do,—he found fault with Dearborn.

"Our military operations," he told Jefferson, "had been unsuccessful. One army had been surrendered under circumstances which impeached the integrity of the com-

[1] Monroe to Jefferson, June 7, 1813; Jefferson MSS., State Department Archives.

mander; and to the north, in the whole extent of the country, so important and delicately circumstanced as it was, the management had been most wretched. The command at the important post of Niagara had been suffered to fall into State hands, and to be perverted to local and selfish purposes. Van Rensselaer, a weak and incompetent man with high pretensions, took it. It was late in the year before General Dearborn left Boston and repaired to Albany, and had given no impulse to the recruiting business in the Eastern States by passing through them and making appeals to the patriotism of the people; and when he took the command at Albany it was in a manner to discourage all hope of active operations during the favorable season. The commander ought to lead every important movement. If intended to attack Montreal, that being the grand attack, his station was there. If a smaller blow only could be given, the feint against Montreal should have been committed to another, while he commanded in person where real service was to be performed. It was soon seen that nothing would be done against Lower Canada; General Dearborn doubtless saw it on his first arrival at Albany, if he did not anticipate it before he left Boston. Niagara was the object next in importance, and had he taken the command there he might and probably would, by superseding little people and conducting our military operations, have prevented the riotous and contentious scenes exhibited there, saved the country and the Government from the disgraceful defeat of Van Rensselaer, and the more disgraceful and gasconading discomfiture of Smyth. The experience of the campaign had excited a doubt with many, if not with all, whether our military operations would prosper under General Dearborn; . . . he was advanced in years, infirm, and had given no proof of activity or military talent during the year."

The Secretary of State required nothing less than the retirement of the two of his colleagues in the Cabinet, and of the general in chief command of the army. The Secretary of the Treasury, though less censorious than Clay, Crawford, or Monroe, shared their opinions. He spoke of Eustis's incompetence as a matter universally admitted, and wrote to Jefferson that though the three disasters of Hull, Van Rensselaer, and Smyth could not with justice be ascribed to the Secretary of War, "yet his incapacity and the total want of confidence in him were felt through every ramification of the public service."[1] Jefferson abstained from criticising the chief incompetents, but set no bounds to his vindictiveness against the unfortunate generals. "Hull will of course be shot for cowardice and treachery," he wrote to Madison;[2] "and will not Van Rensselaer be broke for incapacity?"

The incapacity of Eustis, Hamilton, Dearborn, Hull, Van Rensselaer, and Smyth pointed directly to the responsible source of appointment,—the President himself; but in face of a general election Republicans could not afford to criticise their President, and only in private could they assail his Cabinet. The Federalists, factious, weak, and unpopular as they were, expressed the secret opinion of the whole country, and could be answered by no facts or arguments except military success, which Madison was admittedly incompetent to win; but perhaps the failure of his Cabinet, of his generals, and of his troops gave the Federalists less advantage than they drew from the failures of diplomacy in which his genius lay. With reasons such as few nations ever waited to collect for an appeal to arms, Madison had been so unfortunate in making the issue that on his own showing no sufficient cause of war seemed to exist. His management was so extraordinary that at the moment when Hull surrendered Detroit, Great Britain was able to pose before the world in the attitude of victim to a conspiracy between Napoleon and the United States to destroy the liberties of Europe. Such inversion of the truth passed ordinary bounds, and so real was Madison's diplomatic mismanagement that it paralyzed one half the energies of the American people.

Largely if not chiefly owing to these mistakes, the New England Federalists were able to convince themselves that Jefferson and Madison were sold to France. From the moment war was declared, the charge became a source of serious danger. Only one more step was needed to throw the clerical

[1] Gallatin to Jefferson, Dec. 18, 1812; Adams's Gallatin, p. 470.
[2] Jefferson to Madison, Nov. 5, 1812; Jefferson's Writings (Ford), ix. 369.

party of New England into open revolution. If the majority meant to close their long career by a catastrophe which should leave the Union a wreck, they had but to try the effects of coercion.

For a time the followers and friends of the Essex Junto had some reason to hope that matters would quickly come to this pass, for the declaration of war caused on both sides an outbreak of temper. In Massachusetts, Governor Strong issued, June 26, a proclamation[1] for a public Fast in consequence of the war just declared "against the nation from which we are descended, and which for many generations has been the bulwark of the religion we profess;" and although such a description of England would in previous times have scandalized the clergy, it was received with general assent. The returning members of Congress who had voted for war met a reception in some cases offensive and insulting, to the point of actual assault. Two of the Massachusetts members, Seaver and Widgery, were publicly insulted and hissed on Change in Boston; while another, Charles Turner, member for the Plymouth district, and Chief-Justice of the Court of Sessions for that county, was seized by a crowd on the evening of August 3, on the main street of Plymouth, and kicked through the town.[2] By energetic use of a social machinery still almost irresistible, the Federalists and the clergy checked or prevented every effort to assist the war, either by money or enlistments. The Supreme Court of Massachusetts, with Chief-Justice Parsons at its head, advised[3] Governor Strong that not to Congress or to the President, but to the governor, belonged the right to decide when the Constitutional exigency existed which should call the State militia into the service of the United States; and Governor Strong decided that neither foreign invasion nor domestic insurrection existed, and that therefore he could not satisfy the President's request for the quota of the United States militia to defend the coast. When, later in the season, the governor called out three companies for the defence of Eastport and Castine, in Maine, the chief-justice privately remonstrated, holding that this act yielded

[1] Niles, ii. 355.
[2] Judge Turner's Affidavit, Boston Patriot, Aug. 19, 1812.
[3] Opinion, etc.; State Papers, Military Affairs, i. 324.

the main point at issue between the State and National government.[1]

General Dearborn's annoyance at the difficulties thrown in the way of enlistments was well-founded. By one favorite device, the creation of fictitious debts, the person enlisting caused himself to be arrested and bailed. The courts held that while the suit was pending the man was the property of his bail, and could not be obliged to resume his military duties.[2] Many such difficulties were created by the activity of individuals; but organized efforts were made with still more effect in counteracting the wishes of government. The Federalist members of Congress issued an Address to their constituents protesting against the action of Congress in suppressing discussion; and this address declared the war to be unnecessary and inexpedient. Immediately after the declaration, the House of Representatives of Massachusetts issued another Address to the People of the State,[3] declaring the war to be a wanton sacrifice of their best interests, and asking their exertions to thwart it.

"To secure a full effect to your object, it will be necessary that you should meet and consult together for the common good in your towns and counties. It is in dark and trying times that this Constitutional privilege becomes invaluable. Express your sentiments without fear, and let the sound of your disapprobation of this war be loud and deep. Let it be distinctly understood that in support of it your conformity to the requisitions of law will be the result of principle and not of choice. If your sons must be torn from you by conscription, consign them to the care of God; but let there be no volunteers except for defensive war."

The people at once acted upon the recommendation to hold town-meetings and county conventions. Among the earliest was a meeting in Essex County, July 21, Timothy Pickering presiding, which adopted a declaration drawn by him, closing with his favorite proposal of a State Convention, to

[1] Sumner's East Boston, p. 738.

[2] Speech of E. Bacon, Nov. 20, 1812; Annals of Congress, 1812–1813, pp. 157, 158.

[3] Address, etc., June 26, 1812; Niles, ii. 417.

which the meeting chose delegates. This step—a revival of the old disunion project of 1804—was received with general favor, and defeated only by the courageous opposition of Samuel Dexter, who, breaking away from his party associates, attacked the scheme so vigorously in Boston town-meeting, August 6 and 7, that though Harrison Gray Otis and other Federalists leaders gave it their public support, and though the motion itself was carried, the plan was abandoned.[1] Thenceforward, while towns and counties continued to adopt addresses, memorials, and resolutions, they avoided committing themselves to expressions or acts for which the time was not ripe. A typical memorial among many that were showered upon the President was adopted by a convention of electors of the county of Rockingham in New Hampshire, August 5, and was the better worth attention because drawn by Daniel Webster, who made there his first appearance as a party leader: —

"We shrink from the separation of the States as an event fraught with incalculable evils; and it is among our strongest objections to the present course of measures that they have in our opinion a very dangerous and alarming bearing on such an event. If a separation of the States ever should take place, it will be on some occasion when one portion of the country undertakes to control, to regulate, and to sacrifice the interest of another; when a small and heated majority in the government, taking counsel of their passions and not of their reason, contemptuously disregarding the interests and perhaps stopping the mouths of a large and respectable minority, shall by hasty, rash, and ruinous measures threaten to destroy essential rights and lay waste the most important interests. It shall be our most fervent supplication to Heaven to avert both the event and the occasion; and the Government may be assured that the tie that binds US to the Union will never be broken *by us*."

The conduct of England strengthened the Federalists. After the repeal of the Orders in Council became known, Monroe, July 27, authorized Jonathan Russell in London to arrange an

[1] Pickering to John Lowell, Nov. 7, 1814; New England Federalism, p. 404. The Palladium, Aug. 7, 1812; The Patriot, Aug. 8, 1812.

armistice, provided the British government would consent to an informal arrangement in regard to impressments and blockades. Hardly had these instructions been sent to England, when from Albany came news that Sir George Prevost had proposed an armistice and General Dearborn had accepted it. This act compelled the President either to stop the war and disorganize his party, or to disapprove Dearborn's armistice without prejudice to the armistice which Russell was to negotiate in London, and also without censure to General Dearborn. To Dearborn the President, as the story has shown, sent immediate orders for the renewal of hostilities; while Monroe, in fresh instructions to Jonathan Russell,[1] explained the disavowal. The explanations given by Monroe were little likely to satisfy Federalists that the Government honestly wished for peace. Monroe alleged that the repeal of the Orders in Council did not satisfy the United States, because the repeal still asserted the principle underlying the orders, which the United States could not admit; but he further maintained that any armistice, made before obtaining redress on the subject of impressments, might be taken as a relinquishment of the claim to redress, and was therefore inadmissible.

However sound in principle these objections were, they seemed to declare perpetual war; for until England should be reduced to the position of Denmark or Prussia, she would not abandon in express terms either the right of impressment or that of blockade. The probable effect of a successful war waged on these grounds would give Canada and the Floridas to the United States as the consequence of aiding Napoleon to destroy European and English liberties. The Federalist clergy had little difficulty in convincing their congregations by such evidence that Madison was bound under secret engagements with Napoleon; and while Madison planted himself in the Napoleonic position of forcing war on a yielding people, the British officials in Canada stood on the defensive, avoided irritation, and encouraged trade and commerce. American merchant-vessels carried British passes; and most of them, to the anger of Napoleon, were freighted with supplies

[1] Monroe to Jonathan Russell, Aug. 21, 1812; State Papers, iii. 587.

for the British army in Portugal and Spain. The attitude of England would have been magnificent in its repose had its dignity not been ruffled by the conduct of Hull, Decatur, and Bainbridge, and by the privateers.

While the New England Federalists, taking the attitude of patriots who strove only to avert impending ruin, made their profit of every new national disaster, and repressed as well as they could the indiscretions of their friends, the war party was not so well disciplined. Democracies in history always suffered from the necessity of uniting with much of the purest and best in human nature a mass of ignorance and brutality lying at the bottom of all societies. Although America was safe for the time from Old World ruin, no political or military error went so far to disgust respectable people with the war and its support, as an uprising of brutality which occurred in Baltimore. Within some twenty years this newest of American cities had gathered nearly fifty thousand inhabitants, among whom were many of the roughest characters in America, fit only for privateersmen or pirates, and familiar with both careers. On the other hand, the State of Maryland like the State of Delaware contained many conservatives, who showed their strength every four years by depriving the Republican candidate for the Presidency of some portion of the State's electoral vote. Under their patronage a newspaper called "The Federal Republican" was published in Baltimore, edited by Jacob Wagner, who had been chief clerk of the State Department under Secretary Pickering, and was retained in that office by Secretary Madison until 1807, when he resigned the place and made use of his knowledge to attack Madison in the press. As an editor, Jacob Wagner belonged to the extreme wing of his party, and scrupled at nothing in the way of an assertion or a slander. His opposition to the war was bitter and unceasing, while the city of Baltimore shared in the feeling common in the South and West, that, after the declaration, opposition to the war amounted to treason and should not be tolerated. June 22, immediately after the declaration, a well-organized mob deliberately took possession of Wagner's printing office and destroyed it, pulling down even the walls, while the citizens looked on and the mayor confined his exercise of authority to deprecations.

Wagner removed to the District of Columbia, and began to publish his paper in Georgetown, where the Government could be made directly responsible in case of further violence; but his associate, A. C. Hanson, and several of the Baltimore Federalists, were not disposed to tolerate the dictation of a mob; and after discussing the matter a month, some of them determined on an attempt as fool-hardy as it was courageous.[1] Monday, July 27, the "Federal Republican" was circulated among its subscribers in Baltimore, purporting to be printed at 45 Charles Street, though really printed at Georgetown; while about twenty persons, under the general direction of Henry Lee,—a Virginian distinguished in the Revolutionary War, and in 1791 governor of his State,—fortified themselves in the house and waited attack. The same evening a mob gathered and broke open the door. The garrison fired, and killed or wounded some of the assailants. The attacking party brought up a cannon, and a serious battle was about to begin, when the mayor with a small squadron of cavalry intervened, and persuaded Hanson and his friends to submit to the civil authority and go to jail to answer for the blood they had shed. General Lee, General Lingan,—also a Revolutionary officer,—Hanson, and the other occupants of the house were marched to the jail through an angry and violent mob. The city was in commotion, the authorities were helpless, the militia when called upon did not appear; and that night the mob, consisting chiefly of low Irish and Germans, entered the jail and took out the prisoners. Some managed to escape in the confusion; the rest were savagely beaten. Eight more or less unconscious victims lay all night and till noon the next day piled on the prison steps, and the crowd, which would not permit their removal, amused itself by cutting and burning the sufferers to ascertain whether they were dead. When at last the rioters permitted them to be removed, General Lingan was in fact dead, General Lee was crippled, and the others were more or less severely injured.

At that moment, and even long after the heat of temper subsided,[2] party feeling tended to favor the rioters rather than the Federalists, who had, as was said, "given aid and comfort

[1] Report of Baltimore City Council; Niles, ii. 376, 377.
[2] Lossing, p. 244.

to the enemy;" but when the political effects of the massacre showed themselves, the war party became aware that a blunder had been committed more serious than any ordinary crime. The Baltimore massacre recalled the excesses of the French Revolution, still fresh in men's minds; and although Democrats in Pennsylvania and Republicans in Virginia might feel themselves too strong for disorder, in the North and East the murder of Lingan shook the foundation of society. Massachusetts and Connecticut looked to their arms. If their political opinions were to be repressed by such means, they had need to be unanimous on their own side. The town of Boston, August 6, declared in strongly worded resolutions[1] that the riot was "the first fruit of the unnatural and dreadful alliance into which we have entered in fact, if not in form," and ordered the magistrates and citizens to be ready at a moment's warning, armed and equipped, to suppress any kind of disorder. Under this excitement, the Federalists at Rockingham, August 5, talked of disunion, and the rabble of Plymouth mobbed Turner on the night of August 3. If the majority alone was to utter opinions, the Republican party north of Pennsylvania might yet be forced to practise the virtue of silence. Not all the political and military disasters of the year harmed the Government and the war more seriously than they were injured by the Baltimore mob.

Under the influence of such passions the Presidential election approached. Except beyond the mountains the war party was everywhere a social minority, and perhaps such strength as Madison retained in the East consisted partly in the popular impression that he was not a favorite with the authors of the war. The true sentiment of the people, if capable of expression, was one of fretful discontent; and the sense of diffused popular restlessness alone explained the obstinacy of De Witt Clinton in refusing to desist from his candidacy, and still more the first prominent appearance of Martin Van Buren as manager of the intrigue for defeating Madison. De Witt Clinton was classed by most persons as a reckless political gambler, but Martin Van Buren when he intrigued commonly preferred to intrigue upon the strongest side. Yet one feeling

[1] The Palladium, Aug. 7, 1812.

was natural to every New York politician, whether a Clinton or a Livingston, Burrite, Federalist, or Republican,—all equally disliked Virginia; and this innate jealousy gave to the career of Martin Van Buren for forty years a bias which perplexed his contemporaries, and stood in singular contradiction to the soft and supple nature he seemed in all else to show.

No canvass for the Presidency was ever less creditable than that of De Witt Clinton in 1812. Seeking war votes for the reason that he favored more vigorous prosecution of the war; asking support from peace Republicans because Madison had plunged the country into war without preparation; bargaining for Federalist votes as the price of bringing about a peace; or coquetting with all parties in the atmosphere of bribery in bank charters,—Clinton strove to make up a majority which had no element of union but himself and money. The Federalists held a conference at New York in September, and in spite of Rufus King, who was said to have denounced Clinton as a dangerous demagogue in almost the words used by Hamilton to denounce Aaron Burr ten years before, after three days debate, largely through the influence of Harrison Gray Otis, the bargain was made which transferred to Clinton the electoral votes of the Federalist States. No one knew what pledges were given by Clinton and his friends; but no man of common-sense who wished to preserve the government and the Union could longer refuse to vote for Madison. Only to that extent could the people be said to have reached any conviction.

Chapter XIX

IN THE MIDST of confusion the election took place. Few moments in the national history were less cheerful. In the Northwest the force organized to recapture Detroit, commanded by General Harrison, was still at Franklinton in the centre of Ohio, unable to advance and preparing to disband. At Niagara, Van Rensselaer had failed, and Smyth was in command. At sea, the "Guerriere" and the "Frolic" had been captured, but Decatur's victory over the "Macedonian" was still unknown. Napoleon, though supposed to be dictating peace at Moscow, was actually in full retreat. Every hope of the war party had already proved mistaken. Canada was not in their hands; no army had been enlisted; the people were less united than ever; taxation and debt could no longer be avoided; and military disgrace had been incurred beyond the predictions of John Randolph and Josiah Quincy. All this took place before the country had seen five hundred enemies except its own Indians on its soil, and when it had no reason to fear immediate attack.

Once more the steadiness of Pennsylvania saved the Administration from its worst perils. The election took place, and the electoral votes of New England, except Vermont, were duly thrown for De Witt Clinton, while under the management of Martin Van Buren the Republicans of the New York legislature chose Clinton electors by Federalist aid. New Jersey and Delaware also voted for Clinton. Maryland gave five of her electoral votes to Clinton, six to Madison, and elected a legislature strongly Federalist. A change of twenty electoral votes would have turned the scale. In 1808, under all the disadvantages of the embargo, Madison received one hundred and twenty-two votes in an Electoral College of one hundred and seventy-five; but in 1812 he obtained only one hundred and twenty-eight votes in an Electoral College of two hundred and seventeen, although the three new votes of Louisiana increased his proportion. In Massachusetts the Federalists surprised even themselves by their immense majority of twenty-four thousand, and the peace party swept the Congressional districts throughout New England and

New York, doubling Federalist strength in the Thirteenth Congress.

If John Taylor of Caroline was to be believed, the support given by Virginia to the Administration was hardly more flattering than the sweeping condemnation of the North and East. The County of Caroline, south of the Rappahannock on the road to Richmond, was distinguished by no peculiarities from the other seaboard counties in the Southern States, and Colonel Taylor himself did not openly oppose the war; but he saw no enthusiasm for it among his neighbors. November 8 he wrote to Monroe,[1] —

"I think I expressed my opinion to you during the last Congress that the people were not for the war in these parts, though they were attached to Mr. Monroe and Mr. Madison. In that opinion I am confirmed by the apathy in choosing electors. Those respectable and popular men, Colonel James Taylor and Dr. Bankhead, could not, I am told, get more than about one hundred and thirty out of about seven hundred free-holders to attend and vote for Mr. Madison. Among these were the most prominent minority-men."

This apathy extended through the three great States of Pennsylvania, Virginia, and North Carolina. Only along the Indian frontier, west of the Alleghany Mountains, could enthusiasm be said to exist, and even there took rather the form of hostilities against the Indians than against the British.

The effect of these embarrassments and difficulties showed itself in wavering and uncertain judgment in the Government, and especially in its diplomacy. The President and the Cabinet hoped and believed, when the news of Hull's surrender arrived, that it would produce an outburst of patriotism. So strong was Monroe's faith in the people that he talked to Serurier, September 1, as though the nation were alive with his own ardor.[2]

"'We want no armistice for the present,' said Mr.

[1] John Taylor to Monroe, Nov. 8, 1812; Monroe MSS. State Department Archives.

[2] Serurier to Maret, Sept. 2, 1812; Archives des Aff. Étr. MSS.

Monroe to me with great energy; 'our resolution is taken. It has been done after long and cool deliberation, and by consent of the whole nation; we shall not easily renounce it. Never, certainly, have we been more determined on war; the disgraceful affront we have lately experienced at Detroit renders its prolongation indispensable until our honor is restored. . . . For myself,' he cried, with indignation altogether military and worthy one of the founders of Independence, 'Secretary of State as I am, if to-morrow a British minister should arrive in Washington to negotiate peace, I would say to him, No; I will not treat with you now! wait till we have given you a better opinion of us! When our honor shall be avenged, when you shall have recrossed the rivers, when our generals shall occupy the best part of your Canada, then I shall be disposed to listen, and to treat of peace.' "

These remarks were made in September. In about six weeks the French minister talked again with the Secretary of State, who assured him, to his astonishment, that peace might be made with England at any moment. Serurier, who took Monroe's pacific temper as seriously as he had taken his warlike expressions, wrote in alarm to his Government,[1] —

"The English want peace with America; they want it at any price; they offer all that America asks, and negotiations are about to open, or rather are continuing, and henceforward openly. Mr. Monroe made me this communication in nearly these terms. . . . 'We did not flatter ourselves on obtaining so quickly such important concessions. Mr. Russell had occasion to see Lord Castlereagh. Discussing with this minister the repeal of the Orders in Council, he asked why the repealing Order treated with such vagueness the renunciation of paper blockades, and whether the Ministry had in fact wholly abandoned them. Lord Castlereagh answered: 'They fall to dust of themselves, and we shall think no more of them.' Mr. Russell having noticed the caution with which the Prince Regent seemed to retain the right to restore at any time the abolished Orders, Lord Castlereagh

[1] Serurier to Maret, Oct. 21, 1812; Archives des Aff. Étr. MSS.

observed that, indeed, something had to be said for the public, but the phrase did no harm.' "

Monroe added that "very certainly the American government would not consent to sign the peace without having obtained from England the renunciation of impressments;" but Serurier had reason for alarm, for Monroe expected an immediate renewal of negotiations. He had received from Admiral Sir John Borlase Warren at Halifax another offer of armistice and negotiation, dated September 30; and soon after the interview with Serurier, Monroe wrote to Admiral Warren a reply, dated October 27,[1] which accepted the armistice on condition that, pending the cessation of hostilities, the practice of impressments should be suspended, while he made the additional offer of negotiating without an armistice if the suspension of impressments should be conceded in principle.

Nothing remained of the refusal to hear England's advances until "our honor shall be restored and our generals shall occupy the best parts of your Canada." The unexpected indifference to the war which made itself so evident in all the Atlantic States paralyzed the government. Even the Federalists of New England, New York, New Jersey, and Maryland spoke to Monroe in tones hardly more emphatic than those used by his oldest Virginia friend, Colonel Taylor, who wrote:[2] "If the President thinks that defeat has raised the spirit of the nation, and goes on with the war on that ground, he will find himself mistaken." The President clearly came to the same conclusion, for he renewed attempts at negotiation a week before Congress met, and a fortnight before the election of November 8.

Thenceforward, Madison risked the charge of continuing the war only to satisfy himself that England could not be forced into an express renunciation of what she called her right of impressment,—a result which the opposition already knew to be certain. The experiment was worth trying, and after the timidity of the American government in past years was well suited to create national character, if it did not

---

[1] Monroe to Admiral Warren, Oct. 27, 1812; State Papers, iii. 596.

[2] John Taylor to Monroe, Nov. 8, 1812; Monroe MSS., State Department Archives.

destroy the nation; but it was not the less hazardous in the face of sectional passions such as existed in New England, or in the hands of a party which held power by virtue of Jefferson's principles. That the British government should expressly renounce its claim to impressment was already an idea hardly worth entertaining; but if the war could not produce that result, it might at least develop a government strong enough to attain the same result at some future time. If a strong government was desired, any foreign war, without regard to its object, might be good policy, if not good morals; and in that sense President Madison's war was the boldest and most successful of all experiments in American statesmanship, though it was also among the most reckless; but only with difficulty could history offer a better example of its processes than when it showed Madison, Gallatin, Macon, Monroe, and Jefferson joining to create a mercenary army and a great national debt, for no other attainable object than that which had guided Alexander Hamilton and the Federalists toward the establishment of a strong government fifteen years before.

Unnatural as Madison's position was, that of Monroe was more surprising. Such were the revolutions of politics that Madison found himself master of the situation, and Monroe was obliged to forego his ancient distrust of Executive power in the effort to prevent his rivals from sharing it. Somewhat to the amusement of the Federalists, who held no high opinion of Monroe's abilities, the Secretary of State was placed before the country in the attitude of Cromwell. He could no longer follow the path of ambition in civil life. If he were to maintain his hold upon the Presidency, he must serve his country in the field where his services were needed, or some bolder man would capture Quebec and the Presidency by a single stroke.

The President himself gave Monroe an early hint to this effect. After the adjournment of Congress, July 6, 1812, and some two months before Hull's surrender was known, Madison suggested[1] to his Secretary of State the idea of leading the advance upon Montreal. Fortunately for Monroe, he could neither out-rank Dearborn, nor serve as a subordinate.

[1] Madison to Monroe, Sept. 5, 1812; Monroe MSS., State Department Archives.

Unable to overcome this objection, Madison laid the subject aside, and soon afterward, toward the end of August, left Washington for Montpelier, where he enjoyed only a few days' rest before the news of Hull's surrender arrived. The idea that he was himself in any degree responsible for Hull's disaster, or for Eustis's or Dearborn's supposed shortcomings, did not distress the President; but he was anxious to restore confidence in the military administration, and Monroe was earnest in the wish to assist him. September 2, immediately after receiving the news, Monroe wrote to the President offering to take a volunteer commission, and to assume command of the fresh force then gathering in Kentucky and Ohio to recapture Detroit. Madison replied September 5,[1] balancing the advantages and objections, but leaning toward the step. The next day he wrote more strongly,[2] urging Monroe to go as a volunteer without rank, if no sufficient commission could be given him. Again, September 10,[3] the President wrote, offering to risk issuing a volunteer commission under a doubt as to the meaning of the Act: "I see no evil in risking your appointment comparable to that which may be obviated by it. The Western country is all in motion and confusion. It would be grievous if so much laudable ardor and effort should not be properly concentrated and directed." Neither the President nor the Secretary was aware that Governor William Henry Harrison had taken steps long in advance for occupying the field on which Monroe's eyes were fixed. Monroe actually made his arrangements, sent off cannon to besiege Detroit, and was himself on the point of starting westward, when letters arrived which showed that Harrison was not only the popular idol of the moment in Kentucky and Ohio, but that he had received from the governor of Kentucky the commission of major-general.[4]

This double set-back from men so inferior as Dearborn and

[1] Madison to Monroe, Sept. 5, 1812; Monroe MSS., State Department Archives.

[2] Madison to Monroe, Sept. 6, 1812; Monroe MSS., State Department Archives.

[3] Madison to Monroe, Sept. 10, 1812; Monroe MSS., State Department Archives.

[4] Monroe to Jefferson, June 7, 1813; Jefferson MSS.

Harrison irritated Monroe, who could not command in the North on account of Dearborn, or in the West without a contest with Harrison and Winchester. Evidently, if he was to take any military position, he must command in chief.

This idea became fixed not only in Monroe's mind, but also in that of the public, particularly among Monroe's personal following. The man who stood closest in his confidence and whose advice weighed most with him in personal matters was his son-in-law, George Hay. September 22 Hay wrote to him from Richmond,[1] —

"It is rumored here that you are to be appointed lieutenant-general. Such an appointment would give, I believe, universal satisfaction. . . . This is indeed a critical moment. Some great effort must be made. Unless something important is done, Mr. Madison may be elected again, but he will not be able to get along. But Mr. Madison ought not to exact any further sacrifices from you. If you go into the army you ought to go with the supreme power in your hand. I would not organize an army for Dearborn or anybody else. Mr. Madison ought not to expect it, and if he did I would flatly and directly reject the proposal. Everybody is looking forward to an event of this kind, and I do not believe that any man calculates that you are to go in a subordinate character. The truth is that Dearborn is laughed at, not by Federalists but by zealous Republicans. I do not give on this subject a reluctant, hesitating opinion. I am clear that if you go into the army (about which I say nothing), you should go as the commander-in-chief."

Monroe also felt no doubt that if he went to the field at all he must go in chief command; but he hesitated. As compared with Madison's major-generals, Monroe was young, being only fifty-four years old; in the Revolutionary War he had risen to the rank of captain, and had seen as much service as made him the military equal of Dearborn or Pinckney, but he felt no such special fitness for carrying out a campaign as for planning and superintending it. Probably he could reconcile the two careers only by some expedient, such as by taking the

[1] Hay to Monroe, Sept. 22, 1812; Monroe MSS.

War Department, and as Secretary of War accompanying the general in command; or by accepting the post of lieutenant-general, and from headquarters advising the Secretary of War as to the conduct of the campaign. The former course seemed to Monroe to imply serious Constitutional difficulties, and he inclined to the latter.

Secretary Eustis waited until Dearborn returned from Lake Champlain to Albany, Smyth failed at Niagara, and Harrison became stationary in Ohio, then, December 3, sent his resignation to the President. Instantly informed of this event, and having reason to suppose that the place would be offered to him, Monroe called his friends to a consultation,[1] the result of which was narrated in a letter written to Jefferson six months afterward:[2] —

> "I stated [to the President] that if it was thought necessary to remove me from my present station in the idea that I had some military experience, and a change in the command of the troops was resolved on, I would prefer it to the Department of War in the persuasion that I might be more useful. In the Department of War a man might form a plan of a campaign and write judicious letters on military operations; but still these were nothing but essays,—everything would depend on the execution. I thought that with the army I should have better control over operations and events, and might even aid, so far as I could give aid at all, the person in the Department of War. I offered to repair instantly to the Northern army, to use my best efforts to form it, to promote the recruiting business in the Eastern States, to conciliate the people to the views of the Government, and unite them so far as it might be possible in the war. The President was of opinion that if I quitted my present station, I ought to take the command of the army. It being necessary to place some one immediately in the Department of War to supply the vacancy made by Mr. Eustis's retreat, the President requested me to take it *pro tempore*, leaving the ultimate decision on the other question open to further consideration. I did so."

[1] Monroe to Crawford, Dec. 3, 1812; Monroe MSS.
[2] Monroe to Jefferson, June 7, 1813; Jefferson MSS.

Monroe, with only the model of Washington before his eyes, felt aggrieved that the Clintons and Armstrongs of the North thought him greedy of power; but the curious destiny which had already more than once made a sport of Monroe's career promised at last to throw the weight of a continent upon his shoulders. Secretary of State, acting Secretary of War, general-in-chief by a double guarantee, and President thereafter, what more could the witches promise on the blasted heath of politics that could tempt ambition? Neither Cromwell nor Napoleon had, at any single moment, laid a broader claim upon the favors of Fortune.

Monroe grasped too much, and the prizes which would have destroyed him slipped through his fingers. The story that he was to be general-in-chief as well as Secretary of War, exaggerated by jealousy, roused a storm of protest. Even the patient Gallatin interposed there, and gave the President to understand that if Monroe were transferred to the army, he should himself claim the vacant Department of State; and Madison admitted the justice of the claim, although the difficulty of filling the Treasury created a new obstacle to the scheme. A greater difficulty arose from sectional jealousies. The loss of New York to the Republican party, due chiefly to dislike of Virginia and to Monroe's previous promotion, was too recent and serious to allow further experiments. The Republican leaders in New York—Governor Tompkins, Judge Spencer, and their connections—felt their hopes depend on checking the open display of Virginia favoritism. Finally, the Federalists made a scandal of the subject. January 5, Josiah Quincy, in a speech which for literary quality was one of the best ever delivered in the House, after giving a keen if not an exact account of the "Cabinet, little less than despotic, composed, to all efficient purposes, of two Virginians and a foreigner, which had for twelve years ruled the nation," rose to a climax by averring that all the new Cabinet projects—the loan of twenty millions, an army of fifty-five thousand regulars, the scheme of mock negotiation—had no other object than to satiate the ambition of a single man:—

"The army for the conquest of Canada will be raised,—

to be commanded by whom? This is the critical question. The answer is in every man's mouth. By a member of the American Cabinet; by one of the three; by one of that trio who at this moment constitute in fact, and who efficiently have always constituted, the whole Cabinet. And the man who is thus intended for the command of the greatest army this New World ever contained,—an army nearly twice as great as was at any time the regular army of our Revolution,—I say the man who is intended for this great trust is the individual who is notoriously the selected candidate for the next Presidency."

In face of these difficulties, Madison could not carry out his scheme. His only object in pushing Monroe forward was to strengthen himself by using what he supposed to be Monroe's popularity; but from the moment it appeared that Monroe, in the War Department or at the head of the Northern army, would be a source of weakness rather than of strength, Madison had no motive to persist; so that Monroe, failing to take a decided step, suddenly found himself—he hardly knew how—in the awkward attitude of a disappointed Cromwell. His rival first withdrew the War Department from his hands. He described to Jefferson[1] the way in which he lost this vantage ground:—

"It was soon found to be improper, at a period of so much danger and urgency, to keep that Department in the hands of a temporary occupant; it ought to be filled by the person who would have to form the plan of the campaign in every quarter, and be responsible for it. It being indispensable to fill it with a prominent character, and the question remaining undecided relative to the command of the army, more persons thinking a change urgent, and the opinion of the President in regard to me being the same, General Armstrong was put in the Department of War. Had it been decided to continue the command of the army under General Dearborn, and the question been with me, 'Would I take the Department of War, the President and

[1] Monroe to Jefferson, June 7, 1813; Jefferson MSS. Cf. Monroe to Madison, Feb. 25, 1813; Monroe, MSS., State Department Archives.

other friends wishing it?' I would not have hesitated a moment in complying; but it never assumed that form."

If Monroe was more jealous of one man than of another,
his antipathies centred upon John Armstrong, the late American minister at Paris. As has been already shown, Monroe
came into the State Department expecting rivalry with Armstrong; but he had no occasion to begin active measures of
hostility. Armstrong's opinions of Madison and Monroe were
known to be the same as those of other New Yorkers; if he
came to the support of the Administration he came not in
order to please the Virginians, but to rescue the government
from what he thought Virginian incompetence or narrow-
ness; and that Armstrong would shut the door of military
glory in the face of the Secretary of State was as certain as
that the Secretary of State would, sooner or later, revenge the
insult by ejecting Armstrong from the Cabinet if he could.

No one denied that Monroe had reason for fearing Armstrong, whose abilities were undoubted and whose scruples
were few. Since his return from Paris, Armstrong had been
known as a discontented Republican, grumbling without reserve at the manner in which public affairs were conducted;
yet this was no more than many other Northern Republicans
had done, and Armstrong behaved better than most. On the
declaration of war he avoided the mistakes of the Clintons,
and acted with Governor Tompkins and Ambrose Spencer in
support of the Administration. July 6, 1812, to the surprise and
anger of the Clinton Republicans, Armstrong accepted the
commission of brigadier-general, and was placed in command
of New York city and its defences. His knowledge of the theory and practice of war was considerable, and his influence as
a politician was likely to be great. In the chronic chaos of
New York politics, Armstrong stood between De Witt Clinton, who wished to win the Presidency by intrigue, and Governor Daniel D. Tompkins, who hoped to become President
by regular party promotion. Ambrose Spencer, who liked neither Clinton nor Tompkins, preferred Armstrong as the candidate of New York. The influence of Spencer in the contest
with De Witt Clinton became for the moment absolute; and
the necessity of securing re-election as governor, in April,

1813, drove Tompkins himself to support Spencer in urging Armstrong's appointment as Secretary of War, although he knew that the appointment of Armstrong to the Cabinet opened to him the door to the Presidency.[1]

In spite of Armstrong's services, abilities, and experience, something in his character always created distrust. He had every advantage of education, social and political connection, ability and self-confidence; he was only fifty-four years old, which was also the age of Monroe; but he suffered from the reputation of indolence and intrigue. So strong was the prejudice against him that he obtained only eighteen votes against fifteen in the Senate on his confirmation; and while the two senators from Virginia did not vote at all, the two from Kentucky voted in the negative. Under such circumstances, nothing but military success of the first order could secure a fair field for Monroe's rival.

The nomination of Armstrong to be Secretary of War was made Jan. 8, 1813, and was accompanied by that of William Jones of Pennsylvania to succeed Paul Hamilton as Secretary of the Navy.

The resignation of Paul Hamilton was supposed to be made at the President's request, for reasons not given to the public. His successor, William Jones, long a prominent Republican, a member of Congress at the beginning of Jefferson's administration, had been offered the Navy Department in 1801, when that Department was offered to almost every leading Republican before falling into the hands of Robert Smith. Jones then declined the task, and soon retired from Congress to follow his private business as a ship-owner in Philadelphia. His appointment in 1812 was probably as good as the party could supply. He was confirmed by the Senate without opposition; but he had little to do with the movement of politics or with matters apart from business.

These changes left no one except Gallatin who belonged to the Cabinet of President Jefferson. Attorney-General Rodney had resigned his position a year before, in natural displeasure because the President nominated Gabriel Duval, the Comptroller of the Treasury, to the vacant seat of Justice Chase on

[1] Hammond, i. 358, 360, 405, 406.

the Supreme Bench, thus passing over the Attorney-General in a manner which could be regarded only as a slight. The President, Dec. 10, 1811, nominated William Pinkney, the late minister at London, to succeed Rodney. The influence and activity of the Attorney-General in the Cabinet were at that time less than they subsequently became; and Pinkney, like Rodney, and like William Wirt afterward, had little responsibility beyond the few cases in which the United States were a party before the Courts.

With this reorganization of the Cabinet Madison's first term of Presidency drew toward a close. Only Congress required his attention, and as some compensation for the cares of war, the cares of Congress diminished. After the general election of Nov. 8, 1812, serious opposition or even faction in Congress became impossible. Madison had no reason to fear anything that could happen in the Legislature, provided he had no difficulties with his Cabinet.

President Madison's Annual Message of Nov. 4, 1812, was an interesting paper. Gliding gently over the disasters of the Northern campaign; dilating on British iniquity in using Indians for allies; commenting on the conduct of Massachusetts and Connecticut with disfavor, because it led to the result that the United States were "not one nation for the purpose most of all requiring it;" praising Rodgers and Hull for the results of their skill and bravery,—the Message next touched upon the diplomatic outlook and the future objects of the war in a paragraph which needed and received much study:—

"Anxious to abridge the evils from which a state of war cannot be exempt, I lost no time, after it was declared, in conveying to the British government the terms on which its progress might be arrested without awaiting the delays of a formal and final pacification; and our *chargé d'affaires* at London was at the same time authorized to agree to an armistice founded upon them. These terms required that the Orders in Council should be repealed as they affected the United States, without a revival of blockades violating acknowledged rules; and that there should be an immediate discharge of American seamen from British ships, and a stop to impressment from American ships, with an understanding that an exclusion of the seamen of each nation from the ships of the other should be stipulated; and that the armistice should be improved into a definite and comprehensive adjustment of depending controversies. Although a repeal of the orders susceptible of explanations meeting the views of this Government had taken place before this pacific advance was communicated to that of Great Britain, the advance [made by us] was declined [by the British government] from an avowed repugnance to a suspension of the practice of impressments during the armistice, and without any intimation that the arrangement proposed with respect to seamen would be accepted. Whether the subsequent communications from this Government, affording an occasion for reconsidering the subject on the part of Great Britain, will be viewed in a more favorable light remains to be known. It would be unwise to relax our measures in any respect on a presumption of such a result."

Not without difficulty could one understand from this statement precisely what prevented the restoration of peace. England had never refused to discharge American seamen on sufficient evidence of wrongful impressment. According to the Message, the President asked only "an immediate discharge of American seamen from British ships, and a stop to impressment from American ships." The demand of this point seemed to imply that England had made or would probably make satisfactory concessions on all others. The Message therefore narrowed the cause of war to the requirement of a formal suspension of impressments from American ships, though not of American citizens on shore, pending negotiations, and to be made permanent by treaty. The demand was proper, and its only fault was to fall short of full satisfaction; but considered in its effect upon the politics of the moment the attitude was new, unsupported by a precedent, unwarranted by any previous decision or declaration of President or Congress, and open to the Federalist charge that Madison sought only an excuse for continuing to stake the national existence on the chance of success in his alliance with Bonaparte. The rest of the Message helped to strengthen the impression that a policy of permanent war was to be fixed upon the country; for it recommended higher pay for recruits and volunteers, an increase in the number of general officers, a reorganization of the general staff of the army, and an increase of the navy. The impression was not weakened by the President's silence in regard to the financial wants of the government, which left to the Secretary of the Treasury the unpleasant duty of announcing that the enormous sum of twenty million dollars must be borrowed for the coming year. Every one knew that such a demand was equivalent to admitting the prospect of immediate bankruptcy.

"I think a loan to that amount to be altogether unattainable," Gallatin told Madison in private.[1] "From banks we can expect little or nothing, as they have already lent nearly to the full extent of their faculties. All that I could obtain this year from individual subscriptions does not exceed three million two hundred thousand dollars."

The President refrained from presenting this demand to Congress, and not until after the election was the financial situation made known; but then Gallatin's report, sent to the House December 5, estimated the military expenses at seventeen millions, the naval at nearly five millions, and the civil at fifteen hundred thousand, besides interest on the public debt to the amount of three million three hundred thousand, and reimbursements of loans, treasury notes, etc., reaching five million two hundred thousand more,—in all, thirty-one million nine hundred and twenty-five thousand dollars. This estimate omitted every expenditure not already authorized by law, such as the proposed increase of army and navy.

To meet these obligations, amounting probably to thirty-three million dollars, Gallatin counted on a revenue of eleven million five hundred thousand dollars from imports, and half a million from the sale of lands,—making twelve millions in all; leaving a sum of at least twenty millions to be borrowed, with an increase of debt to the amount of fifteen millions.

The state of war brought the advantage of compelling the Legislature to act or perish; and although Congress had

[1] Gallatin's Writings, i. 528.

seldom if ever been so unanimously dissatisfied, it was never so docile. For the first time Madison could recommend a measure with some certainty that Congress would listen, and with some confidence that it would act. Faction began to find its limits, and an Executive order had no longer to excuse itself; while Congress, on its side, with shut eyes, broke through the barriers hitherto set to its powers, and roamed almost at will beyond the limits which the Republican party assigned to the Constitution.

Chapter XX

Hardly had Henry Clay seated himself again in the Speaker's chair and appointed the select committee on military affairs, when the process of reorganizing the government on a new and energetic footing began. November 19, David R. Williams, chairman of the military committee, reported a bill raising the soldiers' pay to eight dollars a month, and exempting them from arrest for debt. At any previous moment in national history such a bill would have aroused paroxysms of alarm, but the Republicans of 1812 were obliged to accept it without a protest, and with grave doubts whether it would prove effective; while the Federalists tried only to strike out the clause which allowed minors above eighteen years of age to enlist without the consent of their parents, guardians, or masters. On this subject Josiah Quincy made a vehement speech, which ruffled the temper of David R. Williams. Quincy was defeated in the House; but the Senate by a vote of twenty-six to four saved the rights of parents, guardians, and masters, without reducing the age of enlistments. The bill became law December 12, and was quickly followed by another bill raising the bounty and organizing the recruiting service.

Before this matter was finished, the naval committee reported a bill for increasing the navy; and the two Houses vied with one another in their enthusiasm for this recently unpopular branch of the public service. Here and there an old Republican protested that he could not in conscience violate every fixed idea of his political existence by voting for a large naval establishment; but when the House was asked to appropriate money for four ships-of-the-line and six forty-four-gun frigates, although the Federalists were much divided as to the wisdom of building seventy-fours, and debated the subject at great length with contradictory votes, the House closed the discussion, December 23, by passing the bill as it stood. In the minority of fifty-six were several warm friends of the navy, who thought Congress needlessly extravagant.

"Frigates and seventy-fours," wrote Jefferson,[1] "are a sacri-

[1] Jefferson to Monroe, Jan. 1, 1815; Works, vi. 400.

fice we must make, heavy as it is, to the prejudices of a part of our citizens." No one who saw the quickness of this revolution could doubt that whatever evils war might cause, it was a potent force to sweep nations forward on their destined way of development or decline. Madison, Monroe, Gallatin, as well as Jefferson and the whole Republican party accepted a highly paid mercenary army, a fleet of ships-of-the-line, a great national debt at high interest, and a war of conquest in coincidence with the wars of Napoleon, on ground which fifteen years before had been held by them insufficient to warrant resistance to France.

More serious suggestions were offered by the failure of Congress to act its intended part as the controlling branch of government. The founders of the Constitution had not expected the legislative power whose wishes the President was created to carry out, and which was alone responsible for the policy of government, to prove imbecile; yet every one saw that Congress was sinking, or had already sunk, low in efficiency. Before the declaration of war, this condition of the Legislature was concealed by the factiousness which caused it; but the first meeting of Congress during the war disclosed one of the commonplaces of history,—that no merely legislative body could control a single, concentrated Executive, even though it were in hands as little enterprising as those of President Madison. The declaration of war placed Congress in a new position. Although the sessions were unchanged in character, they became suddenly unimportant compared with Executive acts. Congress no longer counteracted directly the Executive will, or refused what the President required; the wishes expressed in his Annual Message were for the first time carried out like orders. On the other hand the country was excited by a reorganization of the Cabinet, and Congress seemed to feel itself superfluous, while the President decided upon the conflicting claims of politicians to act as channels for dispensing his power.

The exceptions to the newly-established discipline were chiefly found among the war leaders themselves, who had done most to make it necessary. As the demands of the government became greater, they interfered with favorite interests or prejudices. This was particularly the case with the required financial measures. Gallatin made in his annual report no direct recommendations; he contented himself with a brief statement of receipts and estimates; but in a letter to the Committee of Ways and Means, dated November 18, he suggested a resource which might to the extent of a few millions relieve the Treasury from its immediate burden. The resource was accidental. Immediately after the repeal of the British Orders in Council, British merchandise to a great amount was shipped to America in reliance on the Act of Congress of March 2, 1811, which declared that the repeal of the British Orders, at any time, should of itself put an end to the American non-importation. The declaration of war, five days before the British repeal, rendered inoperative the Act of March 2, 1811, so that the importers became liable not only to capture by the public and private armed vessels of both countries, but also to confiscation of their property by the government on its arrival in the United States. Both events occurred. Some vessels were captured at sea, and sent in; but these and all the rest were alike seized on their arrival, and libelled by the government without distinction. The question then arose, what should be done with them.

Under the law of forfeiture, one half was vested in the custom-house officers or informers, the other half in the United States; and the power to remit, in whole or in part, was vested in the Secretary of the Treasury. No one expected the government to exact the full forfeiture, for the importations had been made in good faith, and the property was chiefly American. As though to protect the owners the courts interfered, and in certain districts compelled the collectors to release the cargoes on receiving bonds to their appraised value. The action of the courts obliged the President to make the rule general. All the cargoes were released, the goods passed into the market, and only bonds to the amount of near eighteen million dollars, besides duties to the amount of five millions, remained in charge of the Treasury. The five millions were safe; but the bonds were by no means as good as the gold.

Gallatin expressed to the Committee of Ways and Means the opinion, that in view of the extraordinary profits of the importers, who had no right to any profit at all, substantial justice would be done by remitting that half of the forfeitures which would otherwise fall to the collectors, and by exacting for the public only an equivalent for unexpected war profits. His plan aimed at placing the importers, as nearly as possible, in the condition they had expected, on the withdrawal of the non-importation, when they ordered the importations to be made.[1]

Gallatin's views were explained more fully in the course of the debate. The importers had been aware of their risk, and had not taken it without much hesitation, after consulting Jonathan Russell, then in charge of the legation at London. The Government held non-importation to be more effective than armies or fleets in bringing England to terms, and the non-importation was still in force as a war measure. Gallatin's orders, which admitted these goods for sale, violated the law and the policy of government; but if the goods had been admitted, as was the case, at least they should not be used to diminish the government's receipts from internal taxation. The duties already levied to the amount of five million dollars did not exceed twenty-five per cent on their cost, while the goods themselves commanded war prices, and no other goods of the same kind were allowed to enter the country. The profits could hardly fail to be great, and no small part of these profits, besides the invested capital, was British. Finally, within the wider questions of equity, law, and policy remained the fact that bankruptcy in one form or another stood directly before the Treasury, and that four or five million dollars might be the means of national salvation.

If objections were to be made, one might have supposed that Cheves, Clay, and Calhoun would have resisted Gallatin's idea because it offered too much encouragement to mercantile speculation resting on violation of law; but nothing was more uncertain than the moral sensitiveness of a political body. What seemed to one statesman a right and proper act seemed evident dishonesty to another; nor had the science of ethics made sensible progress toward the invention of practical tests. Statesmen who saw nothing improper in the seizure of West Florida, the attacks on East Florida, or the campaign of

[1]Gallatin to Cheves, Nov. 23, 1812; Annals, 1812–1813, p. 1258.

Tippecanoe; who maintained the doctrine that the admission of Louisiana dissolved the Union, or that Champagny's letters satisfied the demands of government and the Acts of Congress,—war Democrats and Federalists alike, representing the morality and the energy of the country, joined in attacking Gallatin's plan. Langdon Cheves, chairman of the Ways and Means Committee, after reporting from the committee, November 25, a resolution to leave the subject to the Secretary of the Treasury, began a speech, December 4, by declaring that he trembled for the consequences of the measure; it would shake the party to pieces; it would make angels weep.

"I trust in God," cried Cheves, "no man who may be thus consigned by this House to the Secretary of the Treasury to await his decision and to supplicate his clemency, will so far forget what he owes to his own true interests and to his character as a free citizen as to give an equivalent for that sum of money which may be demanded as the government's share of the profits. I would rather see the objects of the war fail,—I would rather see the seamen of the country impressed on the ocean and our commerce swept from its bosom,—than see the long arm of the Treasury indirectly thrust into the pocket of the citizen through the medium of a penal law."

Henry Clay admitted and favored total confiscation, but not the idea of a compromise:—

"The law ought to be enforced or not. He thought a compromise in the case dangerous and undignified; indeed, he felt shocked at the idea of an equivalent. Already are our laws too openly violated or fraudulently eluded. Shall we degrade them still further by carrying them into the market and fixing a price upon their violation? Extend the principle of an equivalent, from cases of prohibition merely, to instances of moral turpitude,—to felony and homicide,—and every gentleman will see its enormity. No, sir! Let us not pollute our hands with this welt-gild!"

Calhoun would not allow that the government could properly act at all:—

"If our merchants are innocent," he said, "they are welcome to their good fortune; if guilty, I scorn to participate in its profits. I will never consent to make our penal code the basis of our Ways and Means, or to establish a partnership between the Treasury and the violators of the Non-importation Law."

William Lowndes fortified his position by an argument showing that "if the plan of confiscation and of a rigid execution of the law were dismissed, no just principles of policy and not even the interests of the Treasury could sanction an exaction which would resolve itself into a tax." Josiah Quincy found himself for once in accord with his chief opponents, and declared that in his opinion highway robbery stood a little higher in point of courage, and was a little less in point of iniquity, than this Treasury attempt to make calumny the basis of plunder. Felix Grundy said: "Gentlemen have assumed a strange, high-minded position in this argument, the force of which, I confess, is beyond my comprehension."

December 11 the House in Committee of the Whole, by a vote of fifty-two to forty-nine, rejected Gallatin's suggestion. December 15 a bill came from the Senate remitting all forfeitures on goods owned by Americans and shipped from England before September 15, when the declaration of war became known there. After a sharp debate this bill passed by a vote of sixty-four to sixty-one,—Calhoun, Cheves, and Lowndes voting with the Federalists and securing its passage. This decision closed one source of revenue for the year.

The course taken by Cheves, Calhoun, and Lowndes was largely due to their dislike of the non-importation system on which the proposed forfeiture rested. They wished to abolish commercial restrictions; they were anxious to avoid internal taxation, and to supply the Treasury with revenue by admitting British goods under heavy duties. So earnest was Cheves in pursuit of this object that he hardly tolerated any other, and made no secret of his hope that the failure to exact these forfeitures and to lay internal taxes would compel Congress to depend upon imports for resources.

"How are the exigencies of the government for the next year to be supplied?" he asked as early as December 4. "Is the deficiency to be derived from [internal] taxes? No! I will tell gentlemen who are opposed to them, for their comfort, that there will be no taxes imposed for the next year. It was said last session that you would have time to lay them for this session, but I then said it was a mistake. You now find this to be the fact. By your indecision then, when the country was convinced they were necessary, you have set the minds of the people against taxes; but were it otherwise, you have not time now to lay them for next year."

Calhoun also laid down emphatic principles on this point, dwelling in strong language on what he held to be the radical error of Virginia statesmanship.

"At the end of the last session," said Calhoun, December 8, "I recommended high duties as a substitute for the Non-importation Act. High duties have no pernicious effects, and are consistent with the genius of the people and the institutions of the country. It is thus we would combine in the highest degree the active resources of the country with the pressure on the manufactures of the enemy. Your army and navy would feel the animating effect. . . . The non-importation as a redress of wrongs is radically defective. You may meet commercial restrictions with commercial restrictions, but you cannot safely confront premeditated insult and injury with commercial restrictions alone. . . . It sinks the nation in its own estimation; it counts for nothing what is ultimately connected with our best hopes,—the Union of these States. Our Union cannot safely stand on the cold calculation of interest alone; it is too weak to withstand political convulsions; we cannot without hazard neglect that which makes man love to be a member of an extensive community,—the love of greatness, the consciousness of strength."

The three South Carolinians—Calhoun, Cheves, and Lowndes—had a financial policy of their own, in which they received some private sympathy, if not much active support, from the Treasury. Gallatin, in his own way, stood in a position almost as solitary as that of John Randolph; but condemned as he was to support the burden of a war which

Congress had insisted upon, with only such financial means as Congress left him, he could feel little sympathy with any financial scheme, for all were more or less clumsy and inefficient. As far as he could see, nothing but peace could save the Treasury. In June, at the time of declaring war, he urged taxation; but the party feared taxation, and preferred to wait the chances of military success. In December these expected successes turned into disasters; the country showed an unforeseen hostility to the war. Taxation might easily be fatal, for the war found little real support except in Kentucky, Tennessee, and the Southern States, precisely where internal taxation would excite deepest resistance. The war leaders would not hear of laying taxes at such a moment, and they had no great difficulty in carrying their point. Gallatin himself could afford to wait. The accidental importations from England after the repeal of the British orders brought five million dollars into the Treasury,—a sum so much greater than had been expected, and so ample for meeting the interest on old and new loans, that Gallatin could not think himself obliged to exhaust his influence and risk that of his party in order to wring taxes from a timid Congress. The secretary's attitude brought upon him a fair and just rebuke from John Randolph, that he had trifled with the dignity of the House.[1] Had Gallatin been inclined to retort, he would have replied that so far as the Treasury knew, the House had no dignity to trifle with; but Gallatin never lost control of his temper or his tongue, and after having been the readiest and boldest adviser of his party he had become a master in the art of silence. He expressed once more his belief in the necessity of taxation;[2] but this done he let Congress go its own gait.

Cheves aspired to abolish the remains of Jeffersonian statesmanship,—non-importations, embargoes, and restrictions,—and to restore the freedom of commerce; and in support of this scheme he obtained from Gallatin a letter dated Feb. 9, 1813,[3] expressing the decided opinion that Congress must not only impose war taxes, both external and internal, but must

[1] Annals of Congress, 1812–1813, p. 800.
[2] Letters of Gallatin, Feb. 3, 1813, and Feb. 9, 1813; Annals of Congress, 1812–1813, p. 1063.
[3] Annals of Congress, 1812–1813, p. 1063.

also repeal the non-importation, if the increased expenditures authorized by law were to be met. February 15 Cheves introduced a bill carrying out the secretary's opinion so far as to suspend the Non-importation Act in part, though continuing it against articles specially enumerated. Two days afterward the House, by a vote of sixty-nine to forty-seven, instructed the Committee of Ways and Means to report tax-bills, although Cheves complained that the instruction was deceptive, and that no system of taxation could possibly be adopted within the fortnight that remained of the session. Apparently Cheves looked on the motion as a manœuvre to save the Non-importation Act; but he could hardly have been prepared to see the Federalist member, Elisha Potter of Rhode Island, rise, February 20, and declare that his constituents had invested a capital of four or five million dollars in manufactures protected by non-importation, and that Cheves's bill, sacrificing as it did the interests of the manufacturing States, ought not to pass.

Such a change of attitude foreshadowed a revolution. New England had her price. The system which Jefferson forced upon her at the cost of the Southern States had begun to work its intended effect. Under the pressure of Virginia legislation, New England was abandoning commerce and creating manufactures. While every Federalist newspaper in the country denounced the restrictive system without ceasing, nearly every Federalist in the House voted with Potter in its favor. By seventy-nine votes to twenty-four, the Committee of the Whole struck out Cheves's proposed relaxation, and converted his bill into a measure for the stricter enforcement of non-importation. Cheves and Lowndes were then obliged to vote against their own bill, so amended, in a minority of forty-five to sixty-seven.

Nothing remained but to depend upon loans and call an extra session to consider the taxes. The loan bill, passed January 26, authorized the President to borrow sixteen million dollars on any terms he could obtain, provided only that the nominal capital might be repaid at the end of twelve years. Attempts to limit the rates of interest and discount were defeated, and the bill passed by a vote of seventy-five to thirty-eight. Another bill immediately followed, authorizing the issue of treasury notes bearing interest at five and two fifths per cent, to be redeemed in one year. Five millions in such notes were to be issued at all events, and five millions more in case the loan should prove less advantageous than the notes. By these means Congress proposed to supply the needed twenty-one million dollars, although no one could say with confidence how much these millions would cost, or whether they could be obtained at any price.

There ended the financial work of the session. The military and naval results were more considerable. Besides the Act increasing the soldiers' pay to eight dollars a month, Congress authorized the President to raise twenty new regiments of infantry for one year's service, with full pay, bounty of sixteen dollars, and invalid pensions of five dollars a month. Six new major-generals and an equal number of brigadiers were authorized February 24; the departments of the commissary and quartermaster-general were placed on a better footing; the general staff was organized with comparative liberality,—until, March 3, 1813, the last day of Madison's first term, the President, who had begun his career of power in an Administration which in effect abolished army and navy, commanded a regular force consisting by law of fifty-eight thousand men,[1] and was surrounded by major-generals and brigadiers by the dozen, instead of the solitary brigadier Wilkinson who had been left to command the frontier garrisons of 1801, while four ships-of-the-line, six forty-fours, and six sloops-of-war were building to reinforce the six frigates and the rest of the navy actually in service; and in addition to all this, an unlimited order had been issued for flotillas on the lakes.

With each new Act, John Randolph showed how his old friends were giving the lie to their old political professions; but by common consent party consistency was admitted to be no longer capable of defence. The party which had taken power in 1801 to carry out the principle that the hopes of society and the rights of the States must not be risked by war for points of pride or profits of commerce, declared with equal energy in 1812 that the country had no choice but to

[1] Organization of the Army. Niles, iv. 145.

sacrifice hopes and rights because England would not expressly abandon a point of pride. Doubtless this momentary position was far beyond the conscious convictions of the party, but it made a precedent; and although political parties were apt to think that precedents could be ignored, history seldom failed to show that they decided the course of law. As far as concerned the old Republican party, the triumph of the national movement was for the time complete.

Yet the government was not so rigid in its logic, even in regard to municipal legislation, as it professed to be. If the dispute about impressment was to be settled, it must be settled by a general consent to abandon the practice. Whether governments consented expressly or tacitly, by a preliminary agreement, by treaty, by legislation, or by simply ceasing to impress, was a matter of little concern provided the practice was stopped. The United States were not obliged to wage war on England or France merely because, under old international law, those governments claimed what they called a right to seize their subjects on the high seas. Indeed, the cause of war would not have been removed by an express surrender of impressment on the high seas, though it had been accompanied by an equally express surrender of the right of search. The difficulty lay deeper and extended further than the American flag had ability to go. Much the larger number of impressments took place on shore or within British waters. Many of the American seamen for whose sake the war continued to be fought were American only in the sense that they carried American papers. They were British-born, in British service, and were impressed in the grog-shops of London or Liverpool. The American government could hardly concede to its seamen the liberty refused to its ships,—of carrying double sets of papers, and appearing as American or British at will; yet if the American protection had legal meaning, it entitled the seaman to complete immunity, no matter where he might be, or might have been in the past, or might intend to be in the future, even though he had never been in the United States in his life. The British officer could not be allowed to disregard the protection, even though such a system would make seamen a privileged class, with double nationality and no allegiance.

Annoyed by this insuperable obstacle to an arrangement, Monroe offered the British government to prohibit by Act of Congress the employment of British seamen in the public or private marine of the United States.[1] The offer was meant as an inducement for England to sacrifice her seamen already naturalized in America, on the chance of recovering those who might not carry American papers; but it bore to England the look of an evasion, and was received by Lord Castlereagh in that sense.[2] The subject had reached this stage when it was brought before Congress by the President's Annual Message, and was referred by the House to the Committee of Foreign Relations. January 29 Felix Grundy made a report from the committee,[3] doubtless written in concert with Monroe and intended to support his position, since it approved what the secretary had done and gave authority to his views. The report asserted with emphasis that impressment alone prevented an armistice. More than once, as though this were the weak point of the government's situation, Grundy returned to the theme that impressment "must be provided for in the negotiation; the omission of it in a treaty of peace would not leave it on its former grounds,—it would in effect be an absolute relinquishment."

The danger of thus committing the government to a *sine qua non* which might need to be abandoned was becoming more evident every day, for already Napoleon was known to have suffered some great disaster in Russia, and his power in Spain was evidently threatened with overthrow. After Napoleon should have been routed in Russia and Spain, and the American armies should have abandoned the hope of conquering Canada, the chance of driving England into an express surrender of impressments would vanish. Wisdom dictated caution; but Monroe's letters and Grundy's report, while committing the government to a *sine qua non* preliminary to negotiation, proposed to escape the inevitable difficulty by an expedient less dignified than the country had a right to expect. Grundy reported a bill to serve as the groundwork for peace.

[1] Monroe to Jonathan Russell, June 26, 1812; State Papers, iii. 585.
[2] Lord Castlereagh to Jonathan Russell, Aug. 29, 1812; State Papers, iii. 589.
[3] Annals of Congress, 1812–1813, p. 932.

This bill began by a prospective, reciprocal prohibition, "from and after the termination of a treaty of peace," to employ on any vessel, public or private, any but actual citizens, "or persons who being resident within the United States at the time of such treaty, and having previously declared agreeably to existing laws their intention to become citizens of the United States, shall be admitted as such within five years thereafter in the manner prescribed by law." With these exceptions, Congress was to dismiss all foreign seamen from the American service, and to forbid forever the sea as a livelihood to persons coming into the country with the intention of acquiring citizenship, after the treaty of peace.

The objections to this measure were evident. It seemed tacitly to admit the right of impressment; it denied to one class of citizens rights in which all others were protected, and its Constitutionality was at least doubtful; it trenched on Executive functions and the treaty-making power; it placed American merchants under great disadvantages, depriving them of seamen, and under many circumstances making it impossible for an American ship to return from a distant port. Yet perhaps its worst practical fault consisted in pressing upon England, as an ultimatum, terms of peace which she had again and again rejected and was certain to reject. Indeed, the only argument of weight advanced in favor of the bill was that its rejection by England would heal the divisions of America. Unfortunately, even this argument seemed to have little foundation.

The bill passed the House by a vote of eighty-nine to thirty-three, and February 12 went to the Senate. There Giles took it in hand, and after sharp opposition it was amended and passed, February 27, by a vote of eighteen to twelve. In its adopted form the Act did not contain the clause that roused most opposition, but reached the same result in a less direct way: —

"From and after the termination of the war," ran the new statute, "it shall not be lawful to employ on board any of the public or private vessels of the United States any person or persons except citizens of the United States, or persons of color, natives of the United States. . . . No person who shall arrive in the United States from and after the time when this Act shall take effect shall be admitted to become a citizen of the United States who shall not for the continued term of five years next preceding his admission as aforesaid have resided within the United States, without being at any time within the said five years out of the territory of the United States."

The subject of impressment was so difficult to understand, even in its simpler facts, that the practical workings of this measure could not be foreseen. No one knew how many naturalized British seamen were in the American service, or how many British seamen not naturalized; and there was no sufficient evidence to serve as the foundation for a probable guess as to the number of impressments from American ships, or how they were distributed among the three classes,—(1) native American citizens; (2) naturalized British seamen; and (3) seamen avowedly British subjects. According to a report made from the Department of State, Feb. 18, 1813,[1] the supposed number of seamen registered in the United States since 1796 amounted to about one hundred and forty thousand. The actual number in any one year was unknown. In 1805 Gallatin estimated them, from the registered tonnage, at fifty thousand.[2]

Foreign seamen served chiefly in the foreign trade; and since the registered tonnage in foreign trade increased from 750,000 tons in 1805 to 984,000 tons in 1810, the number of seamen increased proportionately from 45,000 to 60,000 or thereabout. In 1807 Gallatin estimated the increase at five thousand a year, more than half being British sailors.[3] Probably fifteen thousand seamen, or one fourth of the whole number employed in 1810,[4] were of foreign origin, and might or might not carry American papers. If they did not, the reason could only be that they knew the worthlessness of such papers. Genuine American protections could be bought in any large port for two dollars apiece, while forged protections

[1] Annals of Congress, 1812–1813, p. 93.
[2] Gallatin to Jefferson, November, 1805; Works, i. 267.
[3] Gallatin to Jefferson, April 16, 1807; Works, i. 335.
[4] Dallas to the Committee of Foreign Relations, Jan. 26, 1816. Annals of Congress, 1815–1816, p. 176.

were to be had by the gross.[1] A large proportion of the British seamen in American service carried no evidence of American citizenship.

According to Lord Castlereagh's statement in Parliament, the number of seamen claiming to be Americans in the British service amounted to three thousand five hundred in January, 1811, and to something more than three thousand in February, 1813, at the time he was speaking.[2] Of these, he said, only about one in four, or some eight hundred, could offer proof of any sort, good or bad, of their citizenship; the others had no evidence either of birth or of naturalization in America. If this was true, and the closest American calculation seemed rather to favor Castlereagh's assertion, the new Act of Congress sacrificed much to obtain little; for it authorized the President to expel from American service five or ten thousand seamen, and to forbid future employment or naturalization to all British seamen, if England in return would cease to employ five or six hundred impressed Americans.

The concession was immense, not only in its effect on legitimate American commerce and shipping, but also on the national character. America possessed certainly the right, which England had always exercised, of naturalizing foreign seamen in her service, and still more of employing such seamen without naturalization. In denying herself the practice she made a sacrifice much greater in material cost, and certainly not less in national character, than she ever made by tolerating impressments under protest. The impressments cost her about five hundred seamen a year, of whom only a fraction were citizens; of these such as were natives could in most cases obtain release on giving evidence of their citizenship, while five times the number of native British seamen annually deserted the British service for the American. Thus England was much the greater sufferer from the situation; and America preserved her rights by never for an instant admitting the British doctrine of impressment, and by retaining the ability to enforce at any moment her protest by war. All these advantages were lost by Monroe's new scheme. Under the Act of

[1] Massachusetts Report on Impressed Seamen, 1813, p. 53. Speech of James Emott, Jan. 12, 1813; Annals of Congress, 1812–1813, p. 735.

[2] Cobbett's Debates, Feb. 18, 1813.

1813 America would save her citizens to whatever number they amounted, but she would do so by sacrificing her shipping, by abandoning the practice if not the right of employing and naturalizing British seamen, and by tacitly admitting the right of impressment so far as to surrender the use of undoubted national rights as an equivalent for it.

Numbers of leading Republicans denounced the measure as feeble, mischievous, and unconstitutional. Only as an electioneering argument against the extreme Federalists, and as a means of satisfying discontented Republicans, was it likely to serve any good purpose; but the dangers of discord and the general apathy toward the war had become so evident as to make some concession necessary,—and thus it happened that with general approval the law received the President's signature, and the next day the Twelfth Congress expired. With it expired President Madison's first term of office, leaving the country more than ever distracted, and as little able to negotiate as to conquer.

HISTORY OF
THE UNITED STATES
OF AMERICA

DURING THE SECOND ADMINISTRATION OF

JAMES MADISON

1813–1817

Contents

VOLUME ONE

I. ENGLAND ANGRY 621

II. RUSSIAN MEDIATION 638

III. THE EXTRA SESSION OF 1813 653

IV. THE RIVER RAISIN 669

V. PROCTOR AND PERRY 688

VI. THE BATTLE OF THE THAMES 707

VII. DEARBORN'S CAMPAIGN 718

VIII. WILKINSON'S CAMPAIGN 740

IX. MOBILE AND FORT MIMS 764

X. CAMPAIGNS AMONG THE CREEKS 782

XI. THE BLOCKADE 802

XII. "CHESAPEAKE" AND "ARGUS" 818

XIII. PRIVATEERING 834

XIV. RUSSIA AND ENGLAND 854

XV. THE LAST EMBARGO 871

XVI. MONROE AND ARMSTRONG 889

VOLUME TWO

I. MASSACHUSETTS DECIDES 907

II. CHIPPAWA AND LUNDY'S LANE 923

III. FORT ERIE 952

IV. PLATTSBURG 972

V. BLADENSBURG 993

VI. Baltimore 1016

VII. Sloops-of-war and Privateers. 1033

VIII. Exhaustion 1058

IX. Congress and Currency 1076

X. Congress and Army 1092

XI. The Hartford Convention 1108

XII. New Orleans in Danger 1126

XIII. The Artillery Battle. 1148

XIV. The Battle of New Orleans 1169

VOLUME THREE

I. The Meeting at Ghent 1185

II. The Treaty of Ghent 1200

III. Close of Hostilities 1220

IV. Decline of Massachusetts 1237

V. Peace Legislation 1253

VI. Retirement of Madison 1268

VII. Economical Results 1287

VIII. Religious and Political Thought 1301

IX. Literature and Art 1317

X. American Character. 1331

MAPS AND PLANS

Battle of the Thames 714

East End of Lake Ontario and River St. Lawrence
        from Kingston to French Mills 720

East End of Lake Ontario 734

River St. Lawrence from Williamsburg to Montreal 742

Seat of War among the Creeks 772

Attack on Craney Island 809

Battle of Chippawa 934

Battle of Lundy's Lane, at Sunset 942

Battle of Lundy's Lane, at Ten O'clock 948

Attack and Defence of Fort Erie 955

Naval Battle at Plattsburg 983

Position of British and American Armies at
    Plattsburg 987

Campaign of Washington and Baltimore 994

Battle of Bladensburg 1008

Attack and Defence of Baltimore 1029

Seat of War in Louisiana and West Florida 1124

Attack on Fort Bowyer 1135

Landing of British Army at New Orleans 1144

Attack made by Major General Jackson, Dec. 23, 1814 . 1152

British and American Positions at New Orleans . . 1162

Attack and Defence of the American Lines,
    Jan. 8, 1815 1170

Capture of Fort Bowyer 1182

Chapter I

THE AMERICAN declaration of war against England, July 18, 1812, annoyed those European nations that were gathering their utmost resources for resistance to Napoleon's attack. Russia could not but regard it as an unfriendly act, equally bad for political and commercial interests. Spain and Portugal, whose armies were fed largely if not chiefly on American grain imported by British money under British protection, dreaded to see their supplies cut off. Germany, waiting only for strength to recover her freedom, had to reckon against one more element in Napoleon's vast military resources. England needed to make greater efforts in order to maintain the advantages she had gained in Russia and Spain. Even in America, no one doubted the earnestness of England's wish for peace; and if Madison and Monroe insisted on her acquiescence in their terms, they insisted because they believed that their military position entitled them to expect it. The reconquest of Russia and Spain by Napoleon, an event almost certain to happen, could hardly fail to force from England the concessions, not in themselves unreasonable, which the United States required.

This was, as Madison to the end of his life maintained, "a fair calculation;"[1] but it was exasperating to England, who thought that America ought to be equally interested with Europe in overthrowing the military despotism of Napoleon, and should not conspire with him for gain. At first the new war disconcerted the feeble Ministry that remained in office on the death of Spencer Perceval: they counted on preventing it, and did their utmost to stop it after it was begun. The tone of arrogance which had so long characterized government and press, disappeared for the moment. Obscure newspapers, like the London "Evening Star," still sneered at the idea that Great Britian was to be "driven from the proud pre-eminence which the blood and treasure of her sons have attained for her among the nations, by a piece of striped bunting flying at

[1] Madison to Wheaton, Feb. 26, 1827; Works, iii. 553.

the mastheads of a few fir-built frigates, manned by a handful of bastards and outlaws,"—a phrase which had great success in America,—but such defiances expressed a temper studiously held in restraint previous to the moment when the war was seen to be inevitable.

Castlereagh did not abandon the hope of peace until Jonathan Russell, August 24, reported to him the concessions which the President required antecedent to negotiation,—the stoppage of impressments, dismissal of impressed seamen, indemnity for spoliations, and abandonment of paper blockades. The British secretary intimated that he thought these demands, as conditions precedent to an armistice, somewhat insulting;[1] and in conversation he explained to Russell that such concessions would merely cost the Ministry their places without result. "You are not aware," he said,[2] "of the great sensibility and jealousy of the people of England on this subject; and no administration could expect to remain in power that should consent to renounce the right of impressment or to suspend the practice, without certainty of an arrangement which should obviously be calculated to secure its object." Russell then proposed an informal understanding,—adding of his own accord, without authority from his Government, a proposal, afterward adopted by Congress, that the United States should naturalize no more British seamen. Castlereagh made the obvious reply that an informal understanding offered no more guaranty to England than a formal one; that it had the additional disadvantage of bearing on its face a character of disguise; that in any case the discussion of guaranties must precede the understanding; and that Russell had on this subject neither authority nor instructions.[3]

The correspondence closed September 19, and Russell left England; but not until October 13, after learning that the President had refused to ratify the armistice made by Prevost with Dearborn, did the British government order general reprisals,—and even this order closed with a proviso that nothing therein contained should affect the previous authority

[1] Castlereagh to Russell, Aug. 29, 1812; State Papers, iii. 589.
[2] Russell to Monroe, Sept. 17, 1812; State Papers, iii. 593.
[3] Castlereagh to Russell, Sept. 18, 1812; State Papers, iii. 592.

given to Admiral Sir John Borlase Warren to arrange a cessation of hostilities.

The realization that no escape could be found from an American war was forced on the British public at a moment of much discouragement. Almost simultaneously a series of misfortunes occurred which brought the stoutest and most intelligent Englishmen to the verge of despair. In Spain Wellington, after winning the battle of Salamanca in July, occupied Madrid in August, and obliged Soult to evacuate Andalusia; but his siege of Burgos failed, and as the French generals concentrated their scattered forces, Wellington was obliged to abandon Madrid once more. October 21, he was again in full retreat on Portugal. The apparent failure of his campaign was almost simultaneous with the apparent success of Napoleon's; for the Emperor entered Moscow September 14, and the news of this triumph, probably decisive of Russian submission, reached England about October 3. Three days later arrived intelligence of William Hull's surrender at Detroit; but this success was counterbalanced by simultaneous news of Isaac Hull's startling capture of the "Guerriere," and the certainty of a prolonged war.

In the desponding condition of the British people,—with a deficient harvest, bad weather, wheat at nearly five dollars a bushel, and the American supply likely to be cut off; consols at 57½, gold at thirty per cent premium; a Ministry without credit or authority, and a general consciousness of blunders, incompetence, and corruption,—every new tale of disaster sank the hopes of England and called out wails of despair. In that state of mind the loss of the "Guerriere" assumed portentous dimensions. The "Times" was especially loud in lamenting the capture:—

> "We witnessed the gloom which that event cast over high and honorable minds. . . . Never before in the history of the world did an English frigate strike to an American; and though we cannot say that Captain Dacres, under all circumstances, is punishable for this act, yet we do say there are commanders in the English navy who would a thousand times rather have gone down with their colors flying, than have set their fellow sailors so fatal an example."

No country newspaper in America, railing at Hull's cowardice and treachery, showed less knowledge or judgment than the London "Times," which had written of nothing but war since its name had been known in England. Any American could have assured the English press that British frigates before the "Guerriere" had struck to American; and even in England men had not forgotten the name of the British frigate "Serapis," or that of the American captain Paul Jones. Yet the "Times's" ignorance was less unreasonable than its requirement that Dacres should have gone down with his ship,—a cry of passion the more unjust to Dacres because he fought his ship as long as she could float. Such sensitiveness seemed extravagant in a society which had been hardened by centuries of warfare; yet the "Times" reflected fairly the feelings of Englishmen. George Canning, speaking in open Parliament not long afterward,[1] said that the loss of the "Guerriere" and the "Macedonian" produced a sensation in the country scarcely to be equalled by the most violent convulsions of Nature. "Neither can I agree with those who complain of the shock of consternation throughout Great Britain as having been greater than the occasion required. . . . It cannot be too deeply felt that the sacred spell of the invincibility of the British navy was broken by those unfortunate captures."

Of all spells that could be cast on a nation, that of believing itself invincible was perhaps the one most profitably broken; but the process of recovering its senses was agreeable to no nation, and to England, at that moment of distress, it was as painful as Canning described. The matter was not mended by the "Courier" and "Morning Post," who, taking their tone from the Admiralty, complained of the enormous superiority of the American frigates, and called them "line-of-battle ships in disguise." Certainly the American forty-four was a much heavier ship than the British thirty-eight, but the difference had been as well known in the British navy before these actions as it was afterward; and Captain Dacres himself, the Englishman who best knew the relative force of the ships, told his court of inquiry a different story:[2] "I am so well

[1] Cobbett's Debates, xxiv. 463; Feb. 18, 1813.
[2] James, App. No. 77.

aware that the success of my opponent was owing to fortune, that it is my earnest wish, and would be the happiest period of my life, to be once more opposed to the 'Constitution,' with them [the old crew] under my command, in a frigate of similar force with the 'Guerriere.' " After all had been said, the unpleasant result remained that in future British frigates, like other frigates, could safely fight only their inferiors in force. What applied to the "Guerriere" and "Macedonian" against the "Constitution" and "United States," where the British force was inferior, applied equally to the "Frolic" against the "Wasp," where no inferiority could be shown. The British newspapers thenceforward admitted what America wished to prove, that, ship for ship, British were no more than the equals of Americans.

Society soon learned to take a more sensible view of the subject, but as the first depression passed away a consciousness of personal wrong took its place. The United States were supposed to have stabbed England in the back at the moment when her hands were tied, when her existence was in the most deadly peril and her anxieties were most heavy. England never could forgive treason so base and cowardice so vile. That Madison had been from the first a tool and accomplice of Bonaparte was thenceforward so fixed an idea in British history that time could not shake it. Indeed, so complicated and so historical had the causes of war become that no one even in America could explain or understand them, while Englishmen could see only that America required England as the price of peace to destroy herself by abandoning her naval power, and that England preferred to die fighting rather than to die by her own hand. The American party in England was extinguished; no further protest was heard against the war; and the British people thought moodily of revenge.

This result was unfortunate for both parties, but was doubly unfortunate for America, because her mode of making the issue told in her enemy's favor. The same impressions which silenced in England open sympathy with America, stimulated in America acute sympathy with England. Argument was useless against people in a passion, convinced of their own injuries. Neither Englishmen nor Federalists were open to reasoning. They found their action easy from the moment they classed the United States as an ally of France, like Bavaria or Saxony; and they had no scruples of conscience, for the practical alliance was clear, and the fact proved sufficiently the intent.

This outbreak of feeling took place in the month of October, when the hopes of England were lowest. While Wellington retreated from Madrid and Burgos to Ciudad Rodrigo; while Napoleon was supposed to be still victorious at Moscow, although his retreat began October 19, two days before Wellington abandoned the siege of Burgos; and while, October 18, the "Wasp" captured the "Frolic," and October 25 the "United States" captured the "Macedonian,"—in England public opinion broke into outcry against the temporizing conduct of the government toward America, and demanded vigorous prosecution of the war.

"In any other times than the present," said the "Times" of October 30, "it would appear utterly incredible that men should adopt so drivelling a line of conduct as to think of waging a war of conciliation and forbearance, and that with enemies whom they themselves represent as alike faithless and implacable."

The Government hastened to pacify these complaints. Orders were given to hurry an overwhelming force of ships-of-the-line and frigates to the American coast. Almost immediately England recovered from her dismay; for November 11 news arrived that the Russians were again masters of Moscow, and that Napoleon was retreating. Day after day the posts arrived from Russia, bringing accounts more and more encouraging, until when Parliament met, November 24, the hope that Napoleon might never escape from Russia had become strong.

Thus the new Ministry found themselves able to face opposition with unexpected strength. Madison's calculations, reasonable as they seemed to be, were overthrown, and the glow of English delight over the success of Russia made the burden of the American war seem easy to bear. In Parliament hardly a voice was raised for peace. The Marquess Wellesley in the debate on the King's speech attacked ministers, not because they had brought the country into war with America, but because they had been unprepared for it; "they ought as statesmen to have known that the American government had been long infected with a deadly hatred toward this country, and, if he might be allowed an unusual application of a word, with a deadly affection toward France."[1] America had been suffered to carry on hostilities without danger to herself, and must be convinced of her folly and desperation. Lord Grenville also asserted that the American government was always hostile to England, but that only the conduct of ministers had enabled it to pluck up courage to show its enmity.[2] Canning, in the Commons, attacked still more sharply the forbearance of the Ministry and their silence toward America:

> "It never entered into my mind that the mighty naval power of England would be allowed to sleep while our commerce was swept from the surface of the Atlantic; and that at the end of six months' war it would be proclaimed in a speech from the throne that the time was now at length come when the long-withheld thunder of Britain must be launched against an implacable foe, and the fulness of her power at length drawn out. It never entered into my mind that we should send a fleet to take rest and shelter in our own ports in North America, and that we should then attack the American ports with a flag of truce."[3]

From such criticisms Lord Castlereagh had no difficulty in defending himself. Whitbread alone maintained that injustice had been done to America, and that measures ought to be taken for peace.

This debate took place November 30, two days after the destruction of Napoleon's army in passing the Beresina. From that moment, and during the next eighteen months, England had other matters to occupy her mind than the disagreeable subject of the American war. Napoleon arrived in Paris December 18, and set himself to the task of renewing the army of half a million men which had been lost in Russia, and of strengthening his hold on Germany, where a violent popular emotion threatened to break into open alliance with the

[1] Cobbett's Debates, xxiv. 34; Nov. 30, 1812.
[2] Cobbett's Debates, xxiv. 47, 48; Nov. 30, 1812.
[3] Cobbett's Debates, xxiv. 72; Nov. 30, 1812.

Russian Czar. December 30 the Prussian corps of the Grand Army deserted to the Russians; and soon afterward the French abandoned Poland and the province of old Prussia, and with difficulty, no enemy attacking, held Berlin. The interest of England turned to the negotiations and military movements of the Continent. After January 1, 1813, Englishmen never willingly thought of the American war, or gave attention to terms of peace. They regarded the result in America as dependent on the result in Germany; and they would have ignored the war altogether had not the American frigates and privateers from time to time compelled their attention.

With the prospect of a great trade about to open with the continent of Europe, as the French garrisons were driven out of Germany and Spain, English manufacturers could afford to wait with patience for better times; but although a nation so long accustomed to the chances of war could adapt itself quickly to changes in the course of trade, England felt more than it liked to admit the annoyance of American hostilities on the ocean. During the first few months this annoyance was the greater because it was thought to be the result of official negligence. December 30, a merchant writing to the "Times" declared that "the Americans have taken upward of two hundred sail of British merchantmen and three or four packets from the West Indies. Recent advices from the Windward Islands state that the Admiral is mortified at the depredations of the American privateers, it not being in his power to prevent them, most of the few cruisers under his orders having been out so long from England that their copper is nearly off,—so that the privateers remain unmolested, as they can sail round our ships whenever they think proper; they are in consequence become so daring as even to cut vessels out of harbors, though protected by batteries, and to land and carry off cattle from plantations. The accounts from Jamaica by the mail which arrived on Friday represent that island to be literally blockaded by American privateers."

When the press spoke at all of naval matters, it talked wildly about the American frigates. "Such fearful odds," said the "Morning Post" in regard to the "Macedonian," December 26, " would break the heart and spirit of our sailors, and dissolve that charm, that spell, which has made our navy invincible." "The land-spell of the French is broken, and so is our sea-spell," said the "Times." The American frigates were exaggerated into ships-of-the-line, and were to be treated as such, British frigates keeping out of their way. At first, the British naval officers hesitated to accept this view of a subject which had never before been suggested. Neither Captain Dacres nor his court-martial attributed his defeat to this cause; but before long, nearly all England agreed to rate the American frigates as seventy-fours, and complained that the Americans, with their accustomed duplicity, should have deceived the British navy by representing the "Constitution" and "United States" to be frigates. The "Times" protested in vain against this weakness:—

> "Good God! that a few short months should have so altered the tone of British sentiments! Is it true, or is it not, that our navy was accustomed to hold the Americans in utter contempt? Is it true, or is it not, that the 'Guerriere' sailed up and down the American coast with her name painted in large characters on her sails, in boyish defiance of Commodore Rodgers? Would any captain, however young, have indulged such a foolish piece of vain-boasting if he had not been carried forward by the almost unanimous feeling of his associates?"[1]

To the charge that the British Admiralty had been taken unprepared by the war, the Admiralty replied that its naval force on the American station at the outbreak of hostilities exceeded the American in the proportion of eighty-five to fourteen.

> "We have since sent out more line-of-battle ships and heavier frigates," added the "Times," January 4, 1813. "Surely we must now mean to smother the American navy . . . A very short time before the capture of the 'Guerriere' an American frigate was an object of ridicule to our honest tars. Now the prejudice is actually setting the other way, and great pains seem to be taken by the friends of ministers

[1] The Times, Jan. 2, 1813.

to prepare the public for the surrender of a British seventy-four to an opponent lately so much contemned."

The loss of two or three thirty-eight gun frigates on the ocean was a matter of trifling consequence to the British government, which had a force of four ships-of-the-line and six or eight frigates in Chesapeake Bay alone, and which built every year dozens of ships-of-the-line and frigates to replace those lost or worn out; but although the American privateers wrought more injury to British interests than was caused or could be caused by the American navy, the pride of England cared little about mercantile losses, and cared immensely for its fighting reputation. The theory that the American was a degenerate Englishman,—a theory chiefly due to American teachings,—lay at the bottom of British politics. Even the late British minister at Washington, Foster, a man of average intelligence, thought it manifest good taste and good sense to say of the Americans in his speech of February 18, 1813, in Parliament, that "generally speaking, they were not a people we should be proud to acknowledge as our relations."[1] Decatur and Hull were engaged in a social rather than in a political contest, and were aware that the serious work on their hands had little to do with England's power, but much to do with her manners. The mortification of England at the capture of her frigates was the measure of her previous arrogance.

The process of acquiring knowledge in such light as was furnished by the cannon of Hull, Decatur, and Bainbridge could not be rendered easy or rapid. News of the American victories dropped in at intervals, as though American captains intentionally prolonged the enjoyment of their certain success, in order to keep England in constant ill temper. News of the "Java" arrived about the middle of March, and once more the press broke into a chorus of complaints. The "Times" renewed its outcry; the "Courier" abused the "Times" for its "tone of whining lamentation, of affected sensibility, and puerile grief," but admitted that the behavior of the American frigates seemed extraordinary; while the "Pilot,"

[1] Cobbett's Debates, xxiv. 625; Feb. 13, 1813.

the chief naval authority, lamented in set periods the incomprehensible event: —

"The public will learn, with sentiments which we shall not presume to anticipate, that a third British frigate has struck to an American. This is an occurrence that calls for serious reflection, — this, and the fact stated in our paper of yesterday, that Loyd's list contains notices of upwards of five hundred British vessels captured in seven months by the Americans. Five hundred merchantmen and three frigates! Can these statements be true; and can the English people hear them unmoved? Any one who had predicted such a result of an American war this time last year would have been treated as a madman or a traitor. He would have been told, if his opponents had condescended to argue with him, that long ere seven months had elapsed the American flag would be swept from the seas, the contemptible navy of the United States annihilated, and their maritime arsenals rendered a heap of ruins. Yet down to this moment not a single American frigate has struck her flag. They insult and laugh at our want of enterprise and vigor. They leave their ports when they please, and return to them when it suits their convenience; they traverse the Atlantic; they beset the West India Islands; they advance to the very chops of the Channel; they parade along the coasts of South America; nothing chases, nothing intercepts, nothing engages them but to yield them triumph."

The immediate moral drawn from these complaints was the necessity of punishing the United States; but no one could longer deny that the necessary punishment was likely to prove tedious and costly. February 18 Parliament took up the subject of the American war, and both Houses debated it. In the Lords, Bathurst made a temperate speech devoted to showing that America in claiming immunity from impressments claimed more than England could afford to yield, — "a right hitherto exercised without dispute, and of the most essential importance to our maritime superiority." Lord Lansdowne replied with tact and judgment, rather hinting than saying that the right was becoming too costly for assertion. "Some time ago it was imagined on all hands that in the event of a war with America, the first operation would be the destruction of her navy. What the fact had turned out to be, he was almost ashamed to mention. If any one were asked what had been the success of our navy in this war, he would unfortunately find some difficulty in giving an answer."[1] Lord Liverpool, while defending his administration from the charge of imbecility, tended to strengthen the prevailing impression by the tone of his complaints against America: "Although she might have had wrongs, although she might have had grounds for complaint, although she might have had pressing provocations, yet she ought to have looked to this country as the guardian power to which she was indebted not only for her comforts, not only for her rank in the scale of civilization, but for her very existence."[2] Perhaps these words offered as good an explanation as the Prime Minister could give of the war itself, for apart from the unconscious sarcasm they contained, they implied that England assumed to act as guardian to the United States, and had hitherto denied to the United States the right to act independently.

Both Lord Holland and Lord Erskine gently glanced at this assumption; and Erskine went so far as to intimate that sooner or later England must give way. "It has been said that this war, if the Americans persist in their claims, must be eternal. If so, our prospects are disheartening. America is a growing country,—increasing every day in numbers, in strength, in resources of every kind. In a lengthened contest all the advantages are on her side, and against this country." The warning lost none of its point from Lord Eldon, who, always ready to meet any logical necessity by an equally logical absurdity, granted that "unless America should think proper to alter her tone, he did not see how the national differences could be settled."

Such a debate was little likely to discourage America. Every country must begin war by asserting that it will never give way, and of all countries England, which had waged innumerable wars, knew best when perseverance cost more than concession. Even at that early moment Parliament was evidently perplexed, and would willingly have yielded had it seen

[1] Cobbett's Debates, xxiv. 582.
[2] Cobbett's Debates, xxiv. 586.

means of escape from its naval fetich, impressment. Perhaps the perplexity was more evident in the Commons than in the Lords, for Castlereagh, while defending his own course with elaborate care, visibly stumbled over the right of impressment. Even while claiming that its abandonment would have been "vitally dangerous if not fatal" to England's security, he added that he " would be the last man in the world to underrate the inconvenience which the Americans sustained in consequence of our assertion of the right of search." The embarrassment became still plainer when he narrowed the question to one of statistics, and showed that the whole contest was waged over the forcible retention of some eight hundred seamen among one hundred and forty-five thousand employed in British service. Granting the number were twice as great, he continued, "could the House believe that there was any man so infatuated, or that the British empire was driven to such straits, that for such a paltry consideration as seventeen hundred sailors, his Majesty's government would needlessly irritate the pride of a neutral nation or violate that justice which was due to one country from another?" If Liverpool's argument explained the causes of war, Castlereagh's explained its inevitable result, for since the war must cost England at least ten million pounds a year, could Parliament be so infatuated as to pay ten thousand pounds a year for each American sailor detained in service, when one tenth of the amount, if employed in raising the wages of the British sailor, would bring any required number of seamen back to their ships? The whole British navy in 1812 cost twenty million pounds; the pay-roll amounted to only three million pounds; the common sailor was paid four pounds bounty and eighteen pounds a year, which might have been trebled at half the cost of an American war.

No one rose in the House to press this reasoning. Castlereagh completed his argument, showing, with more temper than logic, that England was wholly in the right and America altogether in the wrong; the American government and people were infatuated; they had an inordinate and insolent spirit of encroachment and unreasonable hostility; had prostituted their character and showed an unexampled degeneracy of feeling. "For America he confessed that he deeply lamented the injury which her character had sustained by the conduct of her government; it was conduct unworthy of any State calling itself civilized and free."

Castlereagh's invective had the merit of being as little serious as his logic, and left as little sting; but what Castlereagh could say without causing more than a smile, never failed to exasperate Americans like drops of vitriol when it came from the lips of George Canning. Canning had not hitherto succeeded better in winning the confidence of England than in curbing the insolence of America; he was still in opposition, while the man whom in 1807 he could hardly condescend to consider a rival was Secretary for Foreign Affairs and leader of the House. Worst of all, Canning could not escape the necessity of supporting him, for Castlereagh's position in regard to America was strong, while Canning's own position was weak and needed constant excuse. In the debate of Feb. 18, 1813, he undertook the difficult task of appearing to attack Castlereagh while defending himself.

Canning's speech began by an argument so characteristic as to win the praise of John Wilson Croker, Secretary to the Admiralty,—a man less than most politicians prone to waste praise on opponents. Whitbread had quoted, in excuse of the American practice of naturalization, two Acts of Parliament,—one the 6th Anne, according to which any foreigner who served two years in any British vessel, military or merchant, without further condition or even oath, or more than the statement of the fact of service, became entitled to every protection of a natural subject of the realm. No words could be more emphatic than those of the statutes. "Such foreign mariner," said the 6th Anne, "shall to all intents and purposes be deemed and taken to be a natural-born subject of his Majesty's kingdom of Great Britain, and have and enjoy all the privileges, powers, rights, and capacities" which a native could enjoy. Again, by the 13th George II. every foreign seaman who in time of war served two years on board an English ship by virtue of the king's proclamation was *ipso facto* naturalized. Other naturalization laws existed, guaranteeing all the privileges of a natural-born subject to foreigners under certain conditions; but the Acts of Anne and George II. were most in point, as they referred to foreign sailors alone; and with these laws on the statute-book Parliament seemed to stand in an unfavorable position for disputing the right of America to adopt a similar system. Canning's argument on the meaning of these statutes was interesting, not only as an example of his own mind, but as the only legal justification of a long war which England fought against America at prodigious expense,—a justification which she maintained for years to be sound.

"My construction of the Acts of Anne was altogether different," said Canning in reply to these quotations. "I understood that by it this country professed to give that only which it is competent to bestow without interfering in any degree with the rights or claims of other Powers; that it imparted to foreigners on certain conditions certain municipal privileges, but leaves untouched and unimpaired their native allegiance. . . . The enactments of this statute are a testimony of national gratitude to brave men of whatever country who may lend their aid in fighting the battles of Great Britain, but not an invitation to them to abandon the cause of their own country when it may want their aid; not an encouragement to them to deny or to undervalue the sacred and indestructible duty which they owe to their own sovereign and to their native soil."

Something peculiarly sacred must have inhered in the statute of Anne which thus conferred naturalization on Dutch or Swedish seamen as "a testimony of national gratitude" for "fighting the battles of Great Britain" for two years in the British merchant service in time of peace, and converted them into citizens enjoying "all the privileges, powers, rights, and capacities" of natural-born subjects of Great Britain, which consisted, according to Canning, only in "certain municipal privileges" in England, subject to the will of a foreign sovereign. Such a definition of the "privileges, powers, rights, and capacities" of a natural-born subject of his Majesty's kingdom of Great Britain seemed new to American lawyers; but it was received with applause by the House, and was further developed by Croker, who laid down the principle, new to the popular view of England's pride, that the naturalized citizen, who was by the law required "to all intents and purposes" to "be deemed and taken to be a natural-born subject," was in fact by the Admiralty "considered as having two countries,— the voluntary service of the one being looked upon as unable to debar the natural allegiance to the other."

The rest of Canning's speech consisted in defence of impressment and of paper blockades, and in panegyric upon European republics at the expense of "the hard features of transatlantic democracy." While assailing the British government because "the arm which should have launched the thunderbolt was occupied in guiding the pen," he expressed his devout wish that the war might not be concluded until England had smothered in victories the disasters to which she was so little habituated. If an harangue of this character served in any degree to guide or aid the councils of England, it served much more effectually the war-party of America, where Canning was held in singular antipathy, and where every admission he made in regard to "the shock of consternation" caused by the American frigates gave pleasure more acute than any pain his sarcastic phrases could thenceforward inflict.

Alexander Baring spoke with his usual good sense, pointing out that Castlereagh's speech proved chiefly the greater interest of England to call for and court negotiation on the subject of impressments. Whitbread challenged public opinion by going to the verge of actual sympathy with America. The debate ended in an unopposed vote for a vigorous prosecution of the war, leaving the subject in truth untouched, except that England had avowed an extreme desire to punish America, and naturally felt an extreme irritation because America showed ability to bear punishment.

The spring came, bringing no new prospects. England refused to make a suggestion on which the governments could discuss terms of peace. She refused even to think upon the problem, but massed a huge armament in Chesapeake Bay and Delaware River to restore her naval invincibility. Yet reflection seemed still to be silently at work, for, March 22, the "Times" interrupted its outcry over the loss of the "Java" by publishing a temperate article on the new Foreign Seamen Bill of Congress,—an article in which the suggestion first appeared that peace might after all be restored by simply omitting in the pacification any mention of impressment. The idea found support nowhere; but while, insufficient as it seemed, the human imagination could hardly conceive of any other expedient, at the same moment the uselessness of trying to obtain peace on any terms was made clear by the interference of the Russian Czar.

Chapter II

NAPOLEON DECLARED war against Russia June 22, four days after the American declaration against England; crossed the Niemen June 24, and August 1 was already at Vitebsk, about three hundred miles south of St. Petersburg, and about equally distant from the frontier and from Moscow. There, in the heart of Russia, he paused to collect his strength for some blow that should lay the Russian empire at his feet; and while he hesitated, the Czar, August 3, returned to his capital to wait. At that moment the chances of war favored Napoleon. Nothing was more likely than his success in destroying the Russian army, and in dictating terms of peace in St. Petersburg.

News of the American declaration of war reached St. Petersburg August 6, and added a new anxiety to the overburdened mind of Alexander. The American minister at that court found himself in a delicate position. His Government declared war against England and became for military purposes an ally of France at the moment when Russia entered into formal alliance with England and went to war with France. If Napoleon caught and crushed the Russian army and marched on St. Petersburg, the American minister would certainly be no favorite with Russians; if Napoleon were beaten, the American minister need expect no consideration, for in that case every influence at the Russian Court was certain to be English, and from England could come no favors.

At the moment when Brock, with his force of a few hundred men attacked Detroit, Napoleon with two hundred thousand men moved upon Smolensk and the Russian army. August 15, he celebrated his fête-day on the banks of the Dnieper; and while Hull was surrendering the fort of Detroit, the Russian army, hardly in better humor than the Ohio militia, were preparing to abandon Smolensk to save themselves from Hull's fate. Napoleon took possession of the town August 18, but failed to destroy the Russian army, and then, turning away from St. Petersburg, pursued his retreating enemy toward Moscow. The battle of Borodino, or Moscowa, followed, September 6, and the French army entered Moscow September 14. There it remained more than a month.

During these weeks of alarm and incessant fighting, the Czar still found time to think of American affairs. The influence of Count Roumanzoff, though lessening every day, still controlled the regular course of foreign relations. September 21 Roumanzoff sent for Adams, and said that the Emperor had been much concerned to find the interests of his subjects defeated and lost by the new war, and it had occurred to him that perhaps an arrangement might be more easily made by an indirect than by a direct negotiation: he wished to know whether an offer of mediation on his part would meet with any difficulty on the part of the United States.[1] Adams replied that his Government could not fail to consider it as a new evidence of the Czar's friendship, but suggested that there was a third party to be consulted,—the British government. Roumanzoff answered that he had already sounded the British minister, who had written to Lord Castlereagh on the subject.

The British minister, lately arrived in Russia, was not a person calculated to aid Roumanzoff. Lord Cathcart, who had been chosen by Castlereagh for the post of ambassador at St. Petersburg, was best known as the commander of the Copenhagen expedition in 1807. Some Americans might perhaps remember that he had served in America during the Revolutionary War. A well-informed writer in the London "Times," who belonged to the Wellesley interest, seemed to doubt Lord Cathcart's qualifications for his new post. "He is only better fitted for it than the horse he rides," was the criticism;[2] but the better he had been fitted for it, the worse he would have suited Roumanzoff's purpose, for his first object could be no other than to overthrow Roumanzoff and thwart his policy. No serious support of Russian mediation could be expected from him. He began his career by seeking access to the Emperor through other channels than the chancellor.[3]

Adams, September 30, advised his Government of the Czar's proposed mediation. October 15, Roumanzoff an-

[1] Diary of J. Q. Adams, Sept. 21, 1812; ii. 401.
[2] VETUS, in the "Times," Oct. 26, 1812.
[3] Diary of J. Q. Adams, Oct. 21, 1812; ii. 414.

nounced that his proposal was ready, and would be sent at once to Washington,—which was actually done, before receiving a reply from London. The step could hardly please the British government; but Roumanzoff seemed almost to take pleasure in disregarding England, and perhaps felt that the course of events must either remove him entirely from the government, or make him independent of British support. He clung to the American mediation as the last remnant of his anti-British policy.

The British government would have preferred to make no answer to the Russian offer of mediation. To English statesmen the idea was absurd that England could allow Russia, more than France or the United States themselves, to mediate on blockade and impressment, or upon points of neutrality in any form; but Castlereagh had every reason to conciliate the Czar, and rather than flatly reject a suggestion from such a source, he replied that he thought the time had not yet come, and that the offer would not be accepted by America.[1] So it happened that the offer of Russian mediation went to America without positive objection from England, finding its way slowly across the Atlantic during the winter months.

With it went the tale of Napoleon's immense disaster. October 23 he began his retreat; November 23 he succeeded in crossing the Beresina and escaping capture; December 5 he abandoned what was still left of his army; and December 19, after travelling secretly and without rest across Europe, he appeared suddenly in Paris, still powerful, but in danger. Nothing could be better calculated to support the Russian mediation in the President's mind. The possibility of remaining without a friend in the world while carrying on a war without hope of success, gave to the Czar's friendship a value altogether new.

Other news crossed the ocean at the same time, but encouraged no hope that England would give way. First in importance, and not to be trifled with, was the British official announcement, dated December 26, 1812, of the blockade of the Chesapeake and Delaware. Americans held that this

[1] Diary of J. Q. Adams, ii. 433. Adams to Monroe, Dec. 11, 1812; State Papers, iii. 626.

blockade was illegal,[1] —a blockade of a coast, not of a port; a paper-blockade, one of the grievances against which the war was waged; but whatever they might choose to call it, they could not successfully disprove its efficiency, or deny that it made Chesapeake Bay, Delaware River, and the Vineyard Sound little better than British waters. Export of American produce from the Chesapeake and Delaware ceased.

The blockade, though serious beyond all other military measures, roused less attention and less protest than another measure of the British government which had the character of a profitable insult. A circular dated November 9, addressed to the governors of West Indian colonies by the British government, authorized them to issue licenses for importation of necessary supplies during the war,—a precaution commonly taken to meet the risk of famine in those regions. The Governor of the Bermudas, in issuing a proclamation January 14, 1813, published the circular, which contained one unusual provision:[2] —

"Whatever importations are proposed to be made, under the order, from the United States of America, should be by your licenses confined to the ports in the Eastern States exclusively, unless you have reason to suppose that the object of the order would not be fulfilled if licenses are not also granted for the importations from the other ports in the United States."

Probably the discrimination was intended, like the exemption from blockade, as a favor to New England, and must have been meant to be more or less secret, since publication was likely to counteract its effect; but in time of war the British government was at liberty to seek supplies where it chose.

Madison thought differently. He sent to Congress, February 24, 1813, a special Message expressing indignation at the conduct of England.

"The policy now proclaimed to the world," he charged, "introduces into her modes of warfare a system equally distinguished by the deformity of its features and the de-

[1] Diary of J. Q. Adams, Feb. 1, 1813; ii. 440.
[2] State Papers, iii. 608.

pravity of its character,—having for its object to dissolve the ties of allegiance and the sentiments of loyalty in the adversary nation, and to seduce and separate its component parts the one from the other. The general tendency of these demoralizing and disorganizing contrivances will be reprobated by the civilized world."

Although many persons shared Madison's view of war as a compulsory process of international law, Federalists and Republicans were at a loss to understand his view of "deformity" and "depravity" in modes of warfare. The whole truth in regard to West and East Florida was not known, but so much was notorious, even in 1811, as to warrant the British minister in protesting "against an attempt so contrary to every principle of public justice, faith, and national honor."[1] What the United States could do in Florida in time of peace, England could surely do in Massachusetts in time of war; but if England's conduct was in reality deformed and depraved, as charged, the celebrated proclamation of William Hull to the Canadians in 1812, inviting them to quit their allegiance and to "choose wisely" the side of the United States, should have been previously disavowed by the United States government. No little ridicule was caused by the contrast between Madison's attitude toward Canada and his denunciation of England's attitude toward Massachusetts.

Taken together, the news from Europe in the last days of winter gave ground for deep reflection. With the overthrow of Napoleon's authority and the close alliance between Great Britain and Russia, the last chance of forcing concessions from England vanished. A long war, with no prospect of success, lay before the United States. New York harbor, the Delaware River, and Chesapeake Bay were already so nearly closed to commerce as to foreshadow complete stoppage; and if Boston was still open, its privileges must soon cease unless Great Britain deliberately intended to regard New England as neutral. All this, though alarming enough, might be met with courage; but against the pronounced disaffection of Massachusetts and Connecticut no defence existed; and whenever those States should pass from stolid inertia into the stage of

[1] Foster to Monroe, July 2, 1811; State Papers, iii. 542.

active resistance to the war, the situation would become hopeless. Under such circumstances England would have a strong motive for refusing peace on any terms.

The shadow of these fears lay over the Inaugural Address which the President pronounced March 4, 1813, after taking for a second time the oath of office at the Capitol. His speech contained only the defence of a war that needed no defence, and complaints against England which were drowned in the tumult of war, the loudest complaint that man could make. Every tone showed that Madison felt doubtful of support, and that in proving the war to be just he betrayed consciousness that it was not energetic. Perhaps the most characteristic sentence in the Address was that in which he congratulated the country " with a proud satisfaction," that in carrying on the war, "no principle of justice or honor, no usage of civilized nations, no precept of courtesy or humanity, have been infringed; the war has been waged on our part with scrupulous regard to all these relations, and in a spirit of liberality which was never surpassed." Madison's phrases were the more remarkable because at about the same time the British government announced its intention of making America feel what war meant. The courtesy and humanity of the war were to be all on the American side; while not a word in the Inaugural Address gave the pledge which could win victories,— the assurance that the President himself had energy and meant to exert it.

Besides the alarming difficulties which rose partly from failure of military calculations at home and abroad, but chiefly from want of national experience in the business of war, other annoyances surrounded the President, and could not fail to make him wish for peace. Armstrong had not been six weeks in the War Department before he set the members of Administration at odds. The factious days of Robert Smith returned, and the President found the task of maintaining discipline as great in the Cabinet as it was in the army. One of the strongest characters called into prominence by the war, who was himself destined to have charge of the War Department, spoke of Armstrong, four months later, in language hinting impatient consciousness of something too complicated to describe. "And Armstrong!—he was the devil from the beginning, is now, and ever will be."[1] Only by studying what Armstrong did, could the causes be understood of the passion which he excited in every man he crossed.

Monroe was the first to resent Armstrong's proceedings. Monroe's character, the opposite of Armstrong's, was transparent; no one could mistake his motives, except by supposing them to be complex; and in his relations with Armstrong his motives were simpler than usual, for Armstrong's views could not be carried into effect without loss of pride to Monroe. Already Monroe had surrendered the War Department to him, with the expectation that if any one was to have general command of the armies in the field, Monroe was to be the man. Down to the time when Armstrong took control, the idea was universal that the next campaign was to be fought by Monroe. Jan. 13, 1813, Serurier wrote to his Government:[2]

"There is much talk of Mr. Monroe for the command of the army, and he has shown a zeal in organizing his Department which tends to confirm me in that belief. . . . Mr. Monroe is not a brilliant man, and no one expects to find a great captain in him; but he served through the War of Independence with much bravery under the orders and by the side of Washington. He is a man of great good sense, of the most austere honor, the purest patriotism, and the most universally admitted integrity. He is loved and respected by all parties, and it is believed that he would soon gain the hearts of all his officers and soldiers. He would be given a staff as good as possible, and with this assistance as well as all his own recognized resources, it is believed that he would be perfectly suited to carry on the campaign about to open against the last continental possession of England in America."

As acting Secretary of War, Monroe had urged Congress to increase the number of major-generals; and after Armstrong took charge of the Department Congress passed the Act of February 24, 1813, authorizing the increase. February 27 the

[1] Adams's Gallatin, p. 488.
[2] Serurier to Bassano, Jan. 13, 1813; Archives des Aff. Étr. MSS.

nominations were sent to the Senate. In a letter to Jefferson, Monroe told the story:[1] —

"On the day that the nomination of these officers was made to the Senate the President sent for me and stated that the Secretary of War had placed me in his list of major-generals, at their head, and wished to know whether I would accept the appointment, intimating that he did not think I ought to do it, nor did he wish me to leave my present station. I asked where I was to serve. He supposed it would be with the Northern army under General Dearborn. I replied that if I left my present office for such a command it would be inferred that I had a passion for military life, which I had not; that in such a station I could be of no service in any view to the general cause or to military operations, even perhaps with the army in which I might serve; that with a view to the public interest the commander ought to receive all the support which the government could give him, and by accepting the station proposed, I might take from General Dearborn without aiding the cause by anything that I might add. I stated, however, that the grade made no difficulty with me, a desire to be useful being my only object; and that if the command was given me even with a lower grade than that suggested, admitting the possibility, I would accept it. The difficulty related to General Dearborn, who could not well be removed to an inactive station."

Monroe said, in effect, that he would have the command in chief or nothing. Armstrong said, in effect, that he meant to be commander-in-chief himself. The new major-generals were James Wilkinson, Wade Hampton, William R. Davy of South Carolina, Morgan Lewis of New York, William Henry Harrison of Indiana Territory, and Aaron Ogden of New Jersey. The command of the Northern army was left to Dearborn, and as the world knew Dearborn's incompetence to conduct a campaign, no one was surprised to learn that Armstrong meant to conduct it as Secretary of War, at the army headquarters in the field, performing the duties of lieutenant-general.

[1] Monroe to Jefferson, June 7, 1813; Jefferson MSS.

No sooner was Monroe satisfied that Armstrong meant to follow this course than he took the unusual step of writing to the President a formal remonstrance against his colleague's supposed plan. The act appointing six major-generals was approved February 24. The same evening Monroe had a conversation on the subject with the President, and the next day, February 25, submitted the substance of his remarks in writing.[1] His argument chiefly regarded the inconvenience and unconstitutionality of separating the War Department from the President and of mixing military with civil functions: —

> "As soon as General Armstrong took charge of the Department at War, I thought I saw his plan; that is, after he had held it a few days. I saw distinctly that he intended to have no grade in the army which should be competent to a general control of military operations; that he meant to keep the whole in his own hands; that each operation should be distinct and separate, with distinct and separate objects, and of course to be directed by himself, not simply in outline but in detail. I anticipated mischief from this, because I knew that the movements could not be directed from this place. I did not then anticipate the remedy which he had in mind."

From that moment began a feud between the two Cabinet ministers. The cause was obvious. Armstrong had found that if a general command were to be created, it must be given to Monroe. Probably he felt no more confidence in Monroe's military abilities than in those of Dearborn; but determined that his hand should not be thus forced, Armstrong decided to retain Dearborn, although his opinion of Dearborn, as shown afterward,[2] made the retention an act of grave responsibility. The decision once taken, he had no choice but to supply Dearborn's wants by his own presence with the army, — a course certain to challenge attack from all Virginia. Had Armstrong been bent on destroying his rival by means which the world could have found no chance to oppose or criticise, he would have removed Dearborn, and would have

[1] Monroe to Madison, Feb. 25, 1813; Monroe MSS. State Department Archives; Gilman's Monroe, p. 108.

[2] Armstrong's Notices of the War, i. 113–116.

sent Monroe to waste his reputation in the task of conquering and holding Canada. The retention of Dearborn was an unfortunate beginning for the new Secretary of War.

The first effect of Armstrong's administration was to turn Monroe into a vindictive enemy; the second was to alienate Gallatin. Of all the old Republican leaders, Gallatin cared least for office and most for consistency. Under any reasonable distribution of party favors, the Presidency should have fallen to him after Madison, not only because he was the fittest man, the oldest, ablest, and most useful member of the Executive government, but also because he represented Pennsylvania; and if any State in the Union had power to select a President, it was she. Madison would have been glad to secure for Gallatin the succession; he had no special love or admiration for Monroe, while his regard for Gallatin was strong and constant; but Pennsylvania cared more for interests than for men, while Virginia cared so much for men that she became prodigal of interests. Pennsylvania allowed Virginia, through the agency of William B. Giles, Samuel Smith, and Michael Leib, to thrust Gallatin aside and to open the path for a third Virginian at the risk of the Union itself. Gallatin, too proud to complain, had no longer an object of ambition; and from the moment ambition ceased abstract ideas of duty alone remained to counteract the disgusts of disappointment.

Gallatin's abstract ideas were those of 1801,—simplicity, economy, and purity. Financiering—the providing of money for wasteful expenditure—was his abhorrence. "I cannot consent to act the part of a mere financier," he wrote to Jefferson in 1809;[1] "to become a contriver of taxes, a dealer of loans, a seeker of resources for the purpose of supporting useless baubles, of increasing the number of idle and dissipated members of the community, of fattening contractors, pursers, and agents, and of introducing in all its ramifications that system of patronage, corruption, and rottenness which you so justly execrate." These words were meant to apply only to a state of peace, but they applied equally well to a state of war from the moment war became useless. In the beginning of Madison's

---

[1] Adams's Gallatin, p. 408.

second term, no man of intelligence denied that the war had failed; that its avowed objects could not be gained; that every month of war increased the danger of disunion, brought national bankruptcy nearer, and fastened habits of extravagance and corruption on the country. From his post at the Treasury, Gallatin could see better than most men the dangers, both financial and political, engendered by the war, while his acquaintance with European affairs showed him the need of rapid diplomacy.

Armstrong represented everything antagonistic to Gallatin; his methods were arbitrary and underhand; his political training was that of the New York school, tempered by personal contact with the court of Napoleon; from him economy could hardly be expected. Yet perhaps the worst feature of his administration was likely to be his use of patronage. The number of Gallatin's personal enemies was small, and the use of patronage in a way that would outrage him seemed difficult; yet within a few weeks Armstrong offended him deeply. March 18, 1813, William Duane, of the "Aurora" newspaper, was appointed to the post of adjutant-general. The appointment was improper, and the motives to which it was sure to be attributed made it more scandalous than the unfitness of the person made it harmful to the service. Gallatin's anger was deep: "Duane's last appointment has disgusted me so far as to make me desirous of not being any longer associated with those who have appointed him."[1]

Into this embroglio of national and personal difficulties Daschkoff, the Russian *chargé* at Washington, suddenly dropped the Czar's offer to mediate a peace. Of its prompt acceptance, under such circumstances, no one could doubt, and on this point the Administration was united. Daschkoff's letter bore date March 8, and Monroe's reply was sent March 11. The letter of reply was a civil and somewhat flattering compliment to Alexander;[2] the mission itself was a matter to be more deliberately arranged.

The next decision regarded the character of the mission. The necessary powers might have been sent, without further form, to Minister Adams at St. Petersburg, but the President

[1] Gallatin to Nicholson, May 5, 1813; Adams's Gallatin, p. 482.
[2] State Papers, iii. 624.

and his advisers thought with reason that the addition of other negotiators to the mission would give more weight and political effect to the measure.[1] They decided to send two new envoys to join Adams; and on the same reasoning to select prominent men. As a guaranty of their wish for peace, they decided that one of these men should be a Federalist, and they chose James A. Bayard of Delaware for the post. For the other, Monroe thought of naming some Western man, to secure the confidence of the Western country, and reconcile it to the result; but a different turn was given to the measure by Gallatin, who asked the appointment for himself. Gallatin's exceptional fitness for the task outweighed all objections. The President consented to appoint him; and Monroe, who had from the first attached himself to Gallatin, acquiesced, although he saw the consequences to the Cabinet and the Treasury.

A question less easy to decide was whether the new mission should be despatched at once, or should wait until England should formally accept the mediation. There again political motives dictated immediate action. If England should accept, much time might be saved if the mission were on the spot; if she did not accept, the peace-party in America would be more effectually silenced. In either case, Russia would be deeply pledged to support her own undertaking.

The President did not intend to lose Gallatin in the Treasury. Abundant precedents warranted the double employment of government officers. In 1794 John Jay, then chief-justice, had been sent to negotiate with England, and the Senate had approved the appointment. In 1799 Oliver Ellsworth, also chief-justice, was sent to negotiate with France, and the Senate had again approved. These were Federalist precedents, supposed to be binding, at least on the Federalist party. If the chief-justice, the head of an independent branch of government, could be sent abroad as an Envoy Extraordinary in Executive employment, no objection could exist to sending an Executive officer on a temporary service of the same kind, unless on the score of expediency. To prevent difficulty on that account, the Secretary of the Navy consented to act as

[1] Monroe to Jefferson, June 7, 1813; Jefferson MSS.

head of the Treasury until Gallatin's return. Gallatin himself inclined to look on his separation from the Treasury as final,[1] but made his arrangements in agreement with the President's views, which looked to his return in the autumn.

Before he could depart he was obliged to complete the necessary financial arrangements for the coming year, on which he was busily engaged at the moment when Daschkoff's letter arrived. First in importance was the loan of sixteen million dollars. March 12, subscription books were opened in all the principal towns, and the public was invited to take the whole amount at seven per cent interest, to be reduced to six per cent at the end of thirteen years. About four million dollars were offered on these terms. Proposals in writing were then invited by a Treasury circular, dated March 18, and after an active negotiation between Gallatin and three or four capitalists of New York and Philadelphia,—John Jacob Astor, Stephen Girard, David Parish,—the remainder of the loan was provided. In all about eighteen millions were offered. Fifteen and a half millions were taken, in the form of six per cent stock, issued at eighty-eight dollars for every hundred-dollar certificate, redeemable after the year 1825. About half a million was taken at par, with an annuity of 1½ per cent for thirteen years, in addition to the six per cent interest.

Calculated as a perpetual annuity, as English borrowers would have viewed it, the rate of this loan was less than seven per cent; but if the nominal capital must or should be repaid after twelve years, the rate was about 7.50 per cent. In the end, the government paid 7.487 per cent, for the use of these sixteen millions for thirteen years. The terms were not excessive when it was considered that New England in effect refused to subscribe. Perhaps the loan could not have been taken at all, had not credit and currency been already expanded to the danger-point, as the allotment showed; for while New England, where most of the specie was held, subscribed less than half a million, and Boston took but seventy-five thousand, Pennsylvania, where banking had become a frenzy, took seven million dollars. New York and Baltimore together contributed only half a million more than was given

[1] Adams's Gallatin. p. 483.

by Philadelphia alone. Ten million dollars were taken by Astor, Girard, and Parish,—three foreign-born Americans, without whose aid the money could not have been obtained on these terms, if at all. Doubtless they were bold operators; but Americans were supposed to be not wanting in the taste for speculation, and the question could not but rise how these men knew the secret of distributing the load which no native American dared carry.

The bargain was completed April 7. At that moment the Treasury was empty, and could not meet the drafts of the other departments; but with sixteen millions in hand, five millions of Treasury notes, and an estimated revenue of something more than nine millions, Gallatin collected about thirty million dollars, and April 17 wrote to the Secretaries of War and Navy,[1] allotting to the one thirteen millions and a quarter, to the other four and a half millions, which could not be exceeded without the consent of Congress. This done, and every question having been settled that could be foreseen,—the tax-bills ready to be laid before Congress, and even the draft for a new bank-charter prepared,—Gallatin bade farewell to the Treasury, and May 9 sailed from the Delaware River, with Bayard, for the Baltic.

Twelve years had passed since Gallatin took charge of the finances, and his retirement was an event hardly less serious than a change of President; for it implied that the political system he had done so much to create and support stood so near the brink of disaster as to call him from the chosen field of his duties into a new career, where, if anywhere, he could save it. As Monroe felt called to the army, so Gallatin turned naturally to diplomacy. He knew that after another year of war the finances must be thrown into disorder like that of the Revolutionary War, beyond the reach of financial skill; and he believed that if any one could smooth the path of negotiation, that person was likely to serve best the needs of the Treasury. Yet he took grave responsibility, of which he was fully aware, in quitting his peculiar post at a moment so serious. Success alone could save him from universal censure; and perhaps nothing in his career better proved the high character he

[1] Gallatin's Writings, i. 535.

bore, and the extraordinary abilities he possessed, than the ease with which he supported responsibility for this almost desperate venture.

The task he had set for himself was hopeless, not so much because of the concessions he was to require, as on account of the change in European affairs which made England indifferent for the moment to any injury the United States could inflict. Monroe's instructions to the new commission, though long, consisted largely in arguments against the legality of impressment as a part of the *jus gentium*; although the legality of European war-measures had long ceased to be worth discussing. As the solution of the dispute, Monroe could offer only the new Foreign Seamen Act, which England had refused from the first to consider, and which was certainly open to objections,—on the American side because it offered too much; on the British side because it offered more than could in practice be performed. To make the utmost possible concession, Monroe proposed that no native-born British subject, thenceforward naturalized in America, should be allowed to serve either in the national or the private vessels of the United States,—a provision which carried one step further the offer to naturalize no British seamen except on condition of leaving the sea, and which went to the verge of conceding the right of impressment. Notwithstanding these concessions, the instructions were still positive on the main point. Without a clear and distinct stipulation against impressments, no treaty was to be signed; negotiations must cease, and the negotiators must return home.[1]

[1] Monroe to the Plenipotentiaries, April 15, 1813; State Papers, iii. 695.

Chapter III

DURING THE WINTER the Republican legislature of New York chose Rufus King, the chief Federalist in the country, to succeed John Smith as United States senator. Some Republicans charged that this election was the price paid by De Witt Clinton for Federalist votes in the Presidential contest; but Clinton's friends declared it to be the price paid by the Administration Republicans for Federalist aid in granting a corrupt bank charter. That the choice was due to a bargain of some kind no one denied, and possibly both stories were true. Rufus King himself stood above suspicion, and had been considered an opponent of the Federalist alliance with Clinton; but he was a powerful recruit to the opposition in the Senate, which numbered thenceforward nine votes, or precisely one fourth of the body. The annoyance to the Administration was the greater because King's Republican colleague, Obadiah German, belonged to the Clintonian opposition, and voted with the Federalists. At the same time Charles Cutts of New Hampshire was succeeded by Jeremiah Mason, a very able and extreme Federalist. Three more senators—Giles, Samuel Smith, and Michael Leib—could be counted as personally hostile to the President. Jesse Franklin of North Carolina was succeeded by David Stone, an independent, opposed to the war. Already the opposition threatened to outweigh the votes on which the President could depend. As though legislation had become a matter of inferior importance, William H. Crawford of Georgia, the only vigorous Republican leader in the Senate, resigned his seat, and followed Gallatin to Europe. He was sent to take the place of Joel Barlow at Paris, and hurried to his post. In this condition of party weakness, the election of Rufus King and Jeremiah Mason to the Senate was a disaster to the Administration; and all the more anxiously the President feared lest the popular election in May should convert New York altogether into a Federalist State, and give Massachusetts the necessary strength to stop the war.

This election, on which the fate of the war was believed to turn, took place as usual, May 1, and began by a Federalist success in the city of New York, followed by another in Kings, Queens, and Westchester counties. These counties before the century ended had a voting population of near half a million, but in 1813 they cast in State elections about eight thousand votes, and gave a majority of eight hundred for the Federalist candidate Stephen Van Rensselaer, the unfortunate general of the Niagara campaign. Throughout the eastern and central counties the election was disputed; three of the four districts into which the State was divided left the result so close—within about three hundred votes—that only the western counties of Cayuga, Seneca, and Genesee turned the scale. Governor Tompkins was re-elected by the moderate majority of three thousand in a total vote of eighty-three thousand; but the Federalists obtained a majority of ten in the Assembly, and gained confidence with their strength. In this election, for the first time, the issue was distinct between those who supported and those who opposed the war. The chief towns, New York, Hudson, and Albany, were strong in opposition; the country districts tended to support.

In Massachusetts the Federalist governor Caleb Strong, who had made himself peculiarly obnoxious by refusing to call out the State's quota of militia, received nearly fifty-seven thousand votes, while Senator Varnum, the Republican candidate, received forty-three thousand. Considering that the population of Massachusetts was about one fourth smaller than that of New York, the vote of one hundred thousand persons in the smaller State, and only eighty-three thousand in the larger, seemed a proof of popular indifference; but in truth the vote of New York was larger than usual, and only one thousand less than at the next election of governor, in 1816. The difference was due to the unequal suffrage, which in New York State elections was restricted to one hundred pound free-holds, while in Massachusetts all citizens worth sixty pounds were entitled to vote.

At the same time John Randolph met with defeat, for the only time in his life. John W. Eppes, one of Jefferson's sons-in-law, took residence within Randolph's district for the purpose of contesting it; and after a struggle succeeded in winning the seat, on the war-issue, by a vote of eleven hundred and twelve to nine hundred and forty-three.[1] This change of membership tended, like the New York election, to show that the people were yielding to the necessity of supporting the war. Yet the process was alarmingly slow. In the second year of hostilities, New Hampshire, Massachusetts, Rhode Island, Connecticut, and New Jersey were Federal in all branches of their State governments; New York, Delaware, and Maryland were partly Republican and partly Federalist; of the eighteen States only ten were wholly Republican, and seven of these were Southern. In the United States Senate the Administration could count upon twenty-two votes, with reasonable certainty; the other fourteen senators were more or less lukewarm or hostile. In the House, one hundred and fourteen members supported the Administration, and sixty-eight opposed it. As far as concerned numbers, the Administration was strong enough in Congress; but the universal want of faith in its capacity to conduct a war of such consequence gave the Federalists an advantage beyond proportion to their numerical strength. The task of opposition was easy, and its force irresistible when the ablest and oldest Republican in office—the Secretary of the Treasury—felt himself helpless in face of the Government's inaptitude for war, and wrote to his closest intimates that no one could "expect much improvement in the manner of making it more efficient. I think that there exists real incapacity in that respect,—an incapacity which must necessarily exhaust our resources within a very short time."[2]

Fortunately for the Government the same slowness of movement which counteracted its undertakings, affected equally its internal enemies in their hostility. The New England extremists wished and expected to act energetically against the war. Chief-Justice Parsons quieted Pickering in the autumn of 1812 by assuring him that the Massachusetts House of Representatives would act at its winter session;[3] yet the legislature met and adjourned without action. The party waited for the spring election of 1813, which was to give them control of New York. Their disappointment at the

[1] Niles, iv. 168.
[2] Gallatin to William Few, May 9, 1813; Gallatin MSS.
[3] Pickering to Lowell, Nov. 7, 1814; New England Federalism, p. 404.

re-election of Governor Tompkins was extreme, and the
temptation to wait until the national government should become bankrupt and disgraced became irresistible. Another
campaign was likely to answer their purpose. While England
grew stronger every day, America grew weaker; the struggle
became more and more unequal, the result more and more
certain; and the hope of peaceably restoring the Federalist
party to power diminished the temptation to adopt measures
of force.

Thus when the Thirteenth Congress met for its extra session, May 24, the Government felt stronger than on March 5,
when the old Congress expired. The elections were safely
passed; the peace negotiations might be considered as begun;
taxation was no longer a matter of taste. The majority liked
taxation as little in 1813 as they had liked it in 1812 or in 1801;
but they could no longer dispute or even discuss it. Gallatin
had gone, leaving the bills for them to pass; and Congress,
which at any other time would have rebelled, had no choice
but to pass them.

Once more Henry Clay was chosen Speaker, and setting
Cheves aside he placed John W. Eppes at the head of the
Ways and Means Committee. The House missed John Randolph, but gained John Forsyth of Georgia, and Daniel Webster,—a new member from New Hampshire, of the same age
as Calhoun and Lowndes, but five years younger than Clay.
Otherwise the members varied little from the usual type, and
showed more than their usual faculty for discussing topics no
longer worth discussion.

President Madison's Message of May 25 challenged no angry comment. Its allusion to the Russian mediation and the
terms of peace had an accent of self-excuse, as though he were
anxious to convince England of her true interests; its allusion
to France contained the usual complaint of delays "so unreasonably spun out;" and its reference to the war and the
finances was rather cheerful than cheering. Daring as
Madison's policy had been, he commonly spoke in tones
hardly to be called bold; and this Message had the disadvantage, which under the circumstances could not be called a
fault, of addressing itself rather to Europe and to enemies,
than to a spirited and united nation. It had also the merit of

directing Congress strictly to necessary business; and Congress acted on the direction.

Nothing less than necessity could at that moment of early summer have induced the members of Congress to remain in session at all. Stout as the majority might be in support of the war, the stoutest were depressed and despondent. They saw themselves disappointed in every hope and calculation on which they had counted a year before. Even their unexpected naval glory was lost for the moment by the victory of Broke's frigate the "Shannon" over the "Chesapeake," June 1, as Congress began its work. Disaster after disaster, disgrace upon disgrace, had come and were every moment multiplying. Suffocated with heat, members were forced to sit day by day in the half-finished Capitol, with a Southern village about them, their nearest neighbor a British fleet. "Defeated and disgraced everywhere," said one of the stanchest war members describing the scene, "Congress was to impose the burden of taxes on a divided people, who had been taught by leaders of the war party to look upon a tax-gatherer as a thief, if not to shoot him as a burglar."[1] According to the same authority, "the country was at the lowest point of depression, where fear is too apt to introduce despair." In this condition of spirits, Gallatin's tax-bills were reported to the House June 10,— measures such as the Republican party had, till very lately, not conceived as within the range of its possible legislation. They included a direct tax of three million dollars; taxes on salt, licenses, spirits, carriages, auctions, sugar refineries; a stamp tax, and a complete machinery for the assessment and collection of these odious and oppressive imposts.

At the same moment, Daniel Webster began his career in Congress by moving Resolutions which caused a long and unprofitable debate on the conduct of France and the character of the French repealing Decree of April 28, 1811,—a debate that could have no other result or object than to mortify and annoy the President, who had been, like so many other rulers, the victim of Napoleon's audacity. Pending this debate, June 13, the President took to his bed with a remittent fever, and for five weeks his recovery was doubtful. Madison was

[1] Ingersoll's History, i. 120.

still confined to his bed, when, July 15, messengers from the lower Potomac brought news that the British fleet, consisting of eight or ten ships-of-the-line and frigates, was in the river, sixty miles below, making its way up the difficult channel to Washington. A reasonable and well-grounded fear took possession of the city. July 21, Serurier wrote to his Government:[1] —

"Every one is making ready to move. I know that they are secretly packing up at the Departments. I have as yet sent nothing away, in order not to show distrust of the Government's power; but I have got ready my most valuable papers, and from the moment the President shall quit his residence, I shall follow where he goes, with my principal portfolios in one of my carriages."

The British ships were approaching the city; the sound of their guns was believed to be heard; and the Government had little means of stopping them. Every man prepared for volunteer duty; other work was suspended. About three thousand militia and volunteers, among whom were all the Cabinet and many members of Congress, were mustered, and marched to Fort Washington, which was occupied by some six hundred regular troops, with the Secretary of War at their head; while the Secretary of the Navy took his post on the 28-gun frigate "Adams" in the river beneath, and the Secretary of State rode down the river shore with a cavalry scouting party to reconnoitre the British ships.[2] July 15 and 16 the House of Representatives ordered a Fast, and went into secret session to consider modes of defence.

Unfortunately the motion for inquiry was made by a Federalist. The majority, determined to make no admissions, referred the subject to the Military Committee, which reported the next day through its chairman, Troup of Georgia, that the preparation was "in every respect adequate to the emergence." When a majority could benefit only its enemies by telling the truth, history showed that honorable men often preferred to tell what was untrue. In this case the British ships made their soundings, and obtained whatever knowledge they sought;

[1] Serurier to Bassano, July 21, 1813; Archives des Aff. Étr. MSS.
[2] National Intelligencer, July 17, 20, 22, 1813.

then left the river to visit other parts of the Bay, but never were so far distant that they might not, with energy and a fair wind, within four-and-twenty hours, have raided the defence-less village. They had but to choose their own time and path. Not a defensible fort or a picket-fence stood within ten miles of Washington, nor could a sufficient garrison be summoned in time for defence. Armstrong, Jones, and Monroe doubtless assured Congress that their means of defence were "in every respect adequate," but Congress took the responsibility on its own shoulders when it accepted their assurance.

Perhaps of all the incompetence shown in the war this ex-ample most exasperated patriotic citizens, because it was shared by every branch of the government. For six months the Administration and its friends had denounced Hull, Van Rensselaer, and Smyth for betraying the government, while the Clintonians and peace Democrats had denounced the President for imbecility; but in regard to the city of Washing-ton the generals were not in question, for no generals were there, while the President was dangerously ill in bed. The Legislature and Cabinet were chiefly responsible for whatever should happen,—the more because their warning was ample, even if under such circumstances warning was needed. If Jef-ferson assumed as a matter of course that William Hull was to be shot and Stephen Van Rensselaer broken for their mis-takes, Republicans might properly ask what punishment should be reserved for Armstrong, Jones, and Monroe of the Cabinet, Troup of Georgia, Sevier of Tennessee, Wright of Maryland, and other members of the Military Committees of the House and Senate for their neglect of the national capital.

The debate on Webster's Resolutions, and the report made in consequence by Monroe, July 12, tended to throw addi-tional discredit on the Government. In no respect did Madi-son's Administration make an appearance less creditable than in its attitude toward Napoleon's Decrees, again and again solemnly asserted by it to have been repealed, in the face of proof that the assertion was unfounded. No Federalist rheto-ric was necessary to make this mortification felt. Madison sel-dom expressed himself with more bitterness of temper than in regard to the Emperor's conduct, and with Monroe the subject drew forth recurrent outbursts of anger and disgust.

His report tacitly admitted everything that the Federalists charged, except that the Administration had a secret engagement with France: it had deceived itself, but it had not wilfully deceived the public.

While the House was busied with these unpleasant subjects, the Senate took up the President's recent nominations. May 29, four names were sent to it for diplomatic appointments,—those of Albert Gallatin, J. Q. Adams, and James A. Bayard, to negotiate treaties of peace and commerce with Great Britain, and a treaty of commerce with Russia; that of Jonathan Russell to be Minister Plenipotentiary to Sweden. Rufus King immediately began opposition by moving three Resolutions of inquiry in regard to the nature of the Russian appointments and the authority under which the Treasury was to be administered in the Secretary's absence. The President replied, June 3, that the duties of the Secretary of the Treasury were discharged by the Secretary of the Navy under the provisions of the Act of 1792. The Senate, by a vote of twenty to fourteen, referred the matter to a committee consisting of Anderson of Tennessee, Rufus King, Brown of Louisiana, and Bledsoe of Kentucky. Anderson, the chairman, wrote to the President and went to see him on behalf of the committee, but received only the answer that the President declined to discuss the matter with them in their official character. The Senate then adopted a Resolution that the functions of Secretary of the Treasury and Envoy Extraordinary were incompatible. The Federalists obtained on this vote the support of Giles, Leib, and Samuel Smith, German of New York, and Gilman of New Hampshire, all of whom were disaffected Republicans; but even with this aid they would have failed without the votes of Anderson, Bledsoe, and the two Louisiana senators, who joined the malcontents.

Madison was then slowly recovering strength, and greatly harassed by anxieties. He would not sacrifice Gallatin to the Senate; he hoped that firmness would carry the point,[1] and at worst he could throw upon senators the charge of factious opposition. This he succeeded in doing. July 16 the Senate

---

[1] Madison to Gallatin, Aug. 2, 1813; Works, ii. 566.

committee, naturally expecting Madison to suggest some arrangement, once more sought and obtained a conference,— "when the President was pleased to observe," said their report,[1] "that he was sorry that the Senate had not taken the same view of the subject which he had done; and that he regretted that the measure had been taken under circumstances which deprived him of the aid or advice of the Senate. After the committee had remained a reasonable time for the President to make any other observations if he thought proper to do so, and observing no disposition manifested by him to enter into further remarks, the committee retired without making any observations on the matter of the Resolutions, or in reply to those made by the President."

Finding itself thus defied, the Senate, without more discussion, rejected Gallatin's nomination by eighteen votes to seventeen, Anderson and the two Louisiana senators still adhering to the hostile interest. Adams and Bayard were then confirmed with little opposition.

After the passage of many years, the propriety of the decision may still be left open to debate. As far as the Federalists were concerned, their votes contradicted their own precedents; and if they conceded, as their precedents required, that the question was not one of law but of expediency, they assumed responsibility in acting as final judges. The incompatibility asserted by them was a matter of dispute. Two successive chief-justices had been sent as envoys abroad. No one could doubt that the Secretary of the Treasury, or any other member of the Executive or Judicial departments, might be appointed to negotiate a treaty in Washington. Temporary absence from Washington had never implied incompatibility. Every one knew that the Secretary of War meant in person to conduct the war on the frontier. No one could question the President's right to appoint acting secretaries. If convenience alone was the point at issue, surely the President knew best the demands of his own Executive departments, and might be trusted with the responsibility which belonged to him. That he should fail to see, as soon as the Senate could discover, an incompatibility that would work only against himself, need

[1] Executive Journal, ii. 388.

not be taken for granted by his own party, whatever might be the case with the opposition.

On the other hand every one might admit that as the country grew, Secretaries of the Treasury were likely to find work in their own Department that would effectually limit their capacity for foreign travel; and if the Senate thought that stage to be already reached, senators were right in insisting upon the appointment of a new secretary in Gallatin's place. Unfortunately for their argument, their power did not extend so far. Gallatin remained Secretary of the Treasury, and continued to negotiate as such, without paying attention to the Senate or its theories.

The Senate further weakened its position in acting on the nomination of Jonathan Russell as Minister to Sweden. The subject was referred, June 2, to a committee consisting of Senator Goldsborough of Maryland, together with Anderson and Rufus King. Jonathan Russell had made himself obnoxious to the peace party by eagerness shown, while he was in charge at London, to bring on the war. The committee not only entered on an investigation of his doings at Paris, but also introduced a Resolution declaring that any mission to Sweden at that time was inexpedient, and by order of the Senate asked a conference with the President. Monroe, angry at this conduct, declared privately that a faction in the Senate, counting on the death not only of President Madison but of Vice-President Gerry, and the election of Giles as President of the Senate, were scheming to usurp the Executive power.[1]

In order to counteract their manœuvre, and also to relieve the President, who was then dangerously ill, Monroe took the ground that the Executive would not confer with a co-ordinate branch of government except through an agent, because his dignity would not allow him to meet a committee except by a committee of his own. Monroe thus expressed this somewhat unrepublican doctrine: "A committee of the Senate ought to confer with a committee of the President through a head of a Department, and not with the Chief Magistrate; for in the latter case a committee of that House is equal to the

[1] Monroe to Jefferson, June 28, 1813; Adams's Gallatin, p. 484.

President."[1] As a necessary conclusion, Monroe's argument seemed to the Senate not beyond dispute; but they answered it, three days afterward, still less logically, by passing Goldsborough's Resolution that it was inexpedient at that time to send a Minister Plenipotentiary to Sweden.

Whatever might have been the case with Gallatin's rejection, no one could doubt that the vote on Russell's appointment was factious. When twenty-two senators, including Jeremiah Mason, Christopher Gore, Samuel Dana, Rufus King, and William B. Giles, declared that a minister resident in Sweden was inexpedient in the summer of 1813, they declared what every other well-informed man knew to be an error. If any American envoy was ever expedient, it was an envoy to Sweden in 1813; for in Sweden at that moment all that was left of American commerce centred after being driven from England, and the political interests of Sweden were greatly involved with those of the United States. The error was the less to be denied, because, only six months afterward, the Senate admitted itself in the wrong, and approved the appointment of Russell.

These votes of the Senate made a deep impression. In time of peace and safety the Senate might show factiousness without necessarily exciting public anger, although at no time was the experiment quite safe; but at a moment like July, 1813, when public opinion tended toward a serious temper, factiousness was out of place, and was the more dangerous because President Madison, though never showing great power as a popular leader, had still a clear perception of the moment when to strike an enemy. He rarely failed to destroy when he struck. The time had come when the Republican party, with one voice, would be obliged to insist that party discipline must be restored; and this result was precipitated by the Senate's conduct in regard to the diplomatic nominations.

An illustration of the dangers into which the spirit of faction at that excited moment led the factious, was furnished by the legislature of Massachusetts, which met, May 26, and after listening to a long speech from Governor Strong arraigning the national government for its injustice to England and

[1] Monroe to Jefferson, June 28, 1813; Adams's Gallatin, p. 484. Cf. Madison to the Senate, July 6, 1813; Executive Journal, ii. 381.

partiality to France, referred the subject to committees which lost no time in reporting. One of these reports, presented June 4 by Josiah Quincy of the State Senate, closed with a Resolution that the Act admitting Louisiana into the Union violated the Constitution, and that the Massachusetts senators in Congress should use their utmost endeavors to obtain its repeal. Another report, by a joint committee, contained a remonstrance addressed to Congress against the war, couched in terms of strong sectional hostility to the Southern States, and marked throughout by a covert argument for disunion. A third report, also by Josiah Quincy, on a naval victory lately won by Captain James Lawrence of the "Hornet," contained a phrase even longer remembered than Quincy's assertion that the Government could not be kicked into a war. The Government had in fact been kicked into the war, but Quincy was not the better pleased. He reported that in order not to give offence to many of the good people of the Commonwealth by appearing to encourage the continuance of an unjust, unnecessary, and iniquitous war, the Massachusetts senate while admiring Lawrence's virtues refrained from approving his acts, —

> "And to the end that all misrepresentations on this subject may be obviated, —
>
> *Resolved*, as the sense of the Senate of Massachusetts, that in a war like the present, waged without justifiable cause, and prosecuted in a manner which indicates that conquest and ambition are its real motives, it is not becoming a moral and religious people to express any approbation of military or naval exploits which are not immediately connected with the defence of our sea-coast and soil."

Such tactics, whether in or out of Congress, were more dangerous to their authors than any blunders of the Administration could ever be to the party in power. If the nation should be successful in the war, it might perhaps in good nature leave unpunished the conduct of its malcontents; but if by their means the nation should be conquered or forced into a humiliating peace, the people would never forget, and never forego revenge. Mere opposition to foreign war rarely injured public men, except while the war-fever lasted. Many distinguished statesmen of Europe and America had been, at one time or another, in opposition to some special war,—as was the case with Talleyrand, Charles James Fox, Lord Grey, Jefferson, and Madison; but opposition became unpardonable when it took a form which could have no apparent object except national ruin. The Federalists who held the ideas expressed by the legislature of Massachusetts could explain or defend their future course only by the conviction that the inevitable and long-expected "crisis" was at hand, which must end either in disunion or in reconstruction of the Union on new ground. As "a moral and religious people," they separated from the common stock, and thenceforward, if the Union lasted, could expect no pardon.

The extravagance of the Massachusetts Federalists was counterbalanced by the same national disasters which caused it. Nothing showed that the war was popular in any of the sea-board States; but the pressure of circumstances, little by little, obliged lukewarm and even hostile communities to support it. Virginia and the Southern States were drawn into relations toward the government which they had never intended to accept. Pennsylvania, Kentucky, and Tennessee submitted to exactions that would at any previous stage of their history have produced a revolution. Perhaps the strongest proof of change in popular prejudices was furnished by the taxes. Tax-bills which were supposed to have already overthrown one great political party,—bills which inflicted the evils so hotly and persistently denounced by Jefferson, Gallatin, and John Randolph in opposition, and which had been long delayed by fear of their popular effect,—were passed by Congress quickly, by decided votes, and with less debate than was given to the discussion whether the President had or had not told all he knew about Bassano's Decree of April 28, 1811. From the time they were approved by the President, in July and August, 1813, to the time of their repeal, neither the President nor his party was troubled by popular discontent on account of the passage of these Acts. They were accepted as a necessary part of the national system, and of a war-policy.

The most curious symptom, and the one which most perplexed the Federalists, was that this popular movement of concentration acted in direct resistance to the movement of events. In every respect as the Federalists looked back at the past twelve years their prophecies had come true. The Republican party, they argued, had proved itself incompetent, and had admitted the failure of its principles; it had been forced to abandon them in practice, to replace the government where the Federalists had put it, and to adopt all the Federalists' methods; and even then the party failed. Equally imbecile in peace and war, the democratic movement had ended in such disgrace and helplessness as few governments had ever outlived, and such as no nation with a near and powerful neighbor could have survived. In 1813 the evidence of downfall had become patent. The government was ruined in credit and character; bankrupt, broken, and powerless, it continued to exist merely because of habit, and must succumb to the first shock. All this the Federalists had long foreseen. Fisher Ames in the press, scores of clergymen in the pulpit, numberless politicians in Congress, had made no other use of their leisure than to point out, step by step, every succeeding stage in the coming decline. The catastrophe was no longer far away, it was actually about them,—they touched and felt it at every moment of their lives. Society held itself together merely because it knew not what else to do.

Under circumstances following each other in necessity so stringent, no Federalist could doubt that society would pursue the predicted course; but it did not. Illogical and perverse, society persisted in extending itself in lines which ran into chaos. The threatened "crisis" had arrived, wanting no characteristic of those so long foretold; but society made no effort to save itself. A vaster ruin and still more terrible retribution lay beyond. The Federalists were greatly and naturally perplexed at discovering the silent under-current which tended to grow in strength precisely as it encountered most resistance from events. They tried to explain the phenomenon in their own way,—the clergy according to religious conceptions, the politicians according to their ideas of popular character. The political theory was the more plausible and less respectable. A. C. Hanson, the extreme Maryland Federalist, mobbed and nearly killed in Baltimore in June, 1812, only to be elected to Congress in November, thought that the national movement of 1813 was due to military glory. Hanson wrote to Pickering on the subject, in the autumn:[1] —

"The war is becoming more popular every day in this State [Maryland]. Our successes, and the weak manner in which it is conducted by the enemy make it so. . . . It would seem that after a while, unless the British can gather the sense and courage to strike some severe blows, the war by its own generative powers will create the means for its support. The vanity of a people cannot bear these brilliant naval victories, and there is no passion to which the rulers of a people can address themselves with greater effect. Even in my district the active opposers of the war are falling off every day, and unless we shortly meet with some reverses, the Administration will shortly find more friends than enemies in this State by a great deal. . . . The impression is becoming universal that the enemy cannot harm us if he would. A few hard blows struck in the right place would be of great service to the country."

A people that could feel its vanity flattered by such glories as the war gave in 1813 must have felt the want of flattery to an unusual degree. The idea was extravagant. Not so much the glories as the disgraces of the war roused public sympathy; not so much the love of victory as the ignominy of defeat, and the grinding necessity of supporting government at any cost of private judgment. At such a moment any success was keenly felt, and covered every failure. The slow conviction that come what would the nation must be preserved, brought one man after another into support of the war, until the Federalists found their feet in a quicksand. The "crisis" produced the opposite effect to that which Burke's philosophy predicted.

Congress finished its work, and August 2 adjourned. Immediately afterward the President went to Montpelier to recover his strength in the air of the Blue Ridge. The session had not been unsatisfactory, for although the Senate refused to impose an embargo, wanted by the President in order to cut off illegitimate trade with England's dependencies, and

[1] Hanson to Pickering, Oct. 16, 1813; Pickering MSS.

although the same body put its negative on the appointments of Gallatin and Jonathan Russell, yet Congress passed the tax-bills, authorized another loan of seven and a half millions, and made the business of trading under a British license a penal offence. The operations of war alone remained to burden the President's mind.

Chapter IV

THE FALL OF Detroit and Chicago in August, 1812, threw the American frontier back to the line of the Wabash and the Maumee, and threatened to throw it still farther back to the Indian boundary itself. The Miami or Maumee River was defended by Fort Wayne; the Wabash had no other defence than the little fort or blockhouse which Harrison built during the Tippecanoe campaign, and named after himself. Fort Harrison stood near the later city of Terre Haute, close to the border of Illinois; Fort Wayne stood within twenty miles of the Ohio border. The width of Indiana lay between the two.

Had Brock been able, after the capture of Detroit, to lead his little army into Ohio, he might have cleared not only the Maumee River, but the whole western end of Lake Erie from American possession. Recalled in haste to defend Niagara, Brock left only two or three companies of troops as garrison at Detroit and Malden. The Indians could do little without the aid of regular forces, but they tried to carry both Fort Wayne and Fort Harrison by stratagem. The attacks were made almost simultaneously a few days after September 1, and not without skill. In the case of Fort Harrison the Indians were nearly successful, not so much in fighting as in burning it. With great difficulty its young captain, Zachary Taylor, of the Seventh Infantry, succeeded in saving his post. Fort Wayne was held by Captain James Rhea of the First Infantry until reinforcements arrived, September 12. Except the usual massacres of scattered families, the Indians accomplished nothing.

Upon the State of Ohio, with its quarter of a million inhabitants, and of Kentucky with four hundred thousand, fell the immediate burden of defending the border between the Ohio and the Lakes. Governor William Henry Harrison of the Indiana Territory leaving Vincennes June 19, the day after the declaration of war, was at Cincinnati when threatening news began to arrive from Detroit. Harrison had military knowledge and instincts. He saw that after the capture of Mackinaw Detroit must fall, and that Hull could save himself only by evacuating it.[1] Harrison's ambition, which had drawn him to Tippecanoe, drew him also to lead the new crusade for the relief or recovery of Detroit. He went to Kentucky at the invitation of Governor Scott, and under the patronage of Scott and Henry Clay he took the direction of military affairs. August 24 news reached Kentucky that Hull was shut in Detroit, and must surrender unless immediately relieved.[2] The Governor of Kentucky at once summoned what was then called a *caucus*, composed of himself, his successor elect Governor Shelby, Henry Clay, Justice Todd of the United States Supreme Court, Major-General Hopkins of the Kentucky militia, various Congressmen, judges, and other citizens,[3] whose whole authority was needed to warrant giving to Harrison, who was not a citizen of Kentucky, the commission of major-general and the command of the expedition to Detroit. By general acclamation, and on the warm assurances of universal popular approval, the measure was taken; and Harrison started at once for Cincinnati and Detroit to organize the campaign. The news of Hull's surrender met him as he left Frankfort.

By this combination of skill and accident, Harrison reached the object of his ambition,—the conduct of war on a scale equal to his faith in his own powers; but the torrent of Western enthusiasm swept him forward faster than his secret judgment approved. Appointed by caucus the general of volunteers, he could keep his position only by keeping his popularity. Without deciding precisely where to march, or what military object to pursue, he talked and acted on the idea that he should recover Detroit by a *coup-de-main*.[4] He knew that the idea was baseless as a practical plan, and futile as a military measure; but nothing less would satisfy the enthusiasm of his Kentucky volunteers, and the national government almost compelled him to pretend what he did not at heart believe possible.

The confusion thus created was troublesome. First, Harrison insisted on commanding the troops marching to relieve

[1] Harrison to Eustis, Aug. 10, 1812; Dawson, p. 273.
[2] Harrison to Eustis, Aug. 28, 1812; Dawson, p. 283.
[3] Harrison to Eustis, Aug. 28, 1812; Dawson, p. 283.
[4] Dawson, p. 296.

Fort Wayne, and obliged the good-natured General Winchester, who outranked him, to yield the point.[1] Then after a forced march with the Kentuckians down the St. Mary's River, having relieved Fort Wayne, Harrison was obliged, September 19, to surrender the command to Winchester, who arrived with orders from the Secretary of War to take general charge of the northwestern army. Harrison then left Fort Wayne for Piqua. Meanwhile the President and Eustis, learning what had been done in Kentucky, September 17, after much debate decided to give to Harrison the commission of brigadier-general, with the command of the northwestern army, to consist of ten thousand men, with unlimited means and no orders except to retake Detroit.[2] Brigadier-General Winchester, who was already at Fort Wayne, was given the option of serving under Harrison, or of joining the army at Niagara.

These new orders reached Harrison September 25 at Piqua. Harrison then resumed command, and two days afterward, September 27, wrote to the secretary, announcing his plan for the autumn campaign. Three columns of troops, from widely distant quarters, were to move to the Maumee Rapids,—the right column, consisting of Virginia and Pennsylvania troops, by way of the Sandusky River; the centre column, of twelve hundred Ohio militia, by Hull's road; the left column, consisting of four Kentucky regiments and the Seventeenth U. S. Infantry, was to descend the Auglaize River to Fort Defiance on the Maumee, and thence to fall down that river to the point of junction with the two other columns.

Compared with Hull's resources, Harrison's were immense; and that he had no serious enemy to fear was evident from his dividing the army into three columns, which marched by lines far beyond supporting distance of each other. At the same time he ordered Major-General Hopkins of the Kentucky militia to march with two thousand men up the Wabash into the Indian country, and to destroy the Indian settlements on the Wabash and Illinois rivers. Had a British force been opposed to the Americans, its general would have had little

[1] Winchester to the "National Intelligencer," Sept. 16, 1816.
[2] Eustis to Harrison, Sept. 17, 1812; Dawson, p. 299. Eustis to Governor Shelby, Sept. 17, 1812. McAffee, p. 117.

difficulty in destroying some one of these four isolated columns, and driving Harrison back to central Ohio; but only bands of Indians, not exceeding five hundred at most, were to be feared before the army should cross the Maumee, and little anxiety existed on account of enemies, unless for the safety of Fort Wayne.

Harrison's anxieties bore a different character. September 23 he wrote to the Secretary of War: "If the fall should be very dry, I will take Detroit before the winter sets in; but if we should have much rain, it will be necessary to wait at the rapids until the Miami of the Lakes is sufficiently frozen to bear the army and its baggage."[1] The promise was rash. However dry the season might be, the task of marching an army with siege-artillery past Malden to Detroit, and of keeping it supplied from a base two hundred miles distant, with the British commanding the Lake, was one which Harrison had too much sense to attempt. Nothing but disaster could have resulted from it, even if Detroit had been taken. In the actual condition of that territory, no army could be maintained beyond the Maumee River without controlling the Lake. Perhaps Harrison was fortunate that constant rains throughout the month of October brought the army to a halt long before it reached the Maumee. Only the left division of five Kentucky regiments succeeded in getting to the river, and camped in the neighborhood of old Fort Defiance, waiting for the other columns to reach the rapids. There the Kentuckians remained, under the command of General Winchester, without food, clothing, or sufficient shelter, in a state of increasing discontent and threatening mutiny, till the year closed.

Within a month after assuming command Harrison found himself helpless either to advance or to retreat, or to remain in any fixed position. The supplies required for ten thousand troops could not be sent forward by any means then known. October 22 the left column, consisting of the Kentucky regiments and some regulars, was at Defiance on the Maumee; the central column of a thousand Ohio troops under General Tupper was on Hull's road, a hundred miles from the Mau-

[1] Dawson, p. 312.

mee, unable to march beyond Urbana, where its supplies were collecting; the right column of Pennsylvanians and Virginians was still farther from the front, slowly approaching the Sandusky River from the southeast, but far out of reach. General Hopkins's expedition up the Wabash ended in failure, his troops becoming a mere mob, and at last disbanding, leaving their general to follow them home. Harrison himself was riding indefatigably through the mud, from one end to the other of his vast concave line,—now at Defiance, making speeches to pacify Winchester's Kentuckians; then at Piqua and Urbana with the Ohioans; soon a hundred miles away at the river Huron, east of Sandusky; next at Wooster, Delaware, or Franklinton, afterward Columbus, in the centre of Ohio, looking for his right wing; but always searching for a passable ridge of dry land, on which his supplies could go forward to the Maumee Rapids. The result of his search was given in a letter of October 22, from Franklinton, to the Secretary of War:—

"I am not able to fix any period for the advance of the troops to Detroit. It is pretty evident that it cannot be done upon proper principles until the frost shall become so severe as to enable us to use the rivers and the margin of the Lake for transportation of the baggage and artillery upon the ice. To get them forward through a swampy wilderness of near two hundred miles, in wagons or on packhorses which are to carry their own provisions, is absolutely impossible."

The obstacle which brought Harrison's autumn campaign to this sudden close was the vast swamp that extended from the Sandusky River on his right to the Auglaize River on his left, and for the moment barred the passage of his necessary supplies as effectually as though it had been the Andes. Hull had crossed it, cutting a road as he went, and no one had then appreciated his effort; but he had marched with a small force in May and June. Harrison tried to transport supplies, heavy guns, military stores, and all the material for an army of ten thousand men on a long campaign, as the autumn rains set in. On the extreme right, with great effort and expense, a considerable quantity of rations was accumulated on the

Sandusky River, to be sent to the Maumee Rapids whenever the frosts should harden the swamps. On the extreme left, desperate efforts were made to carry supplies to Winchester's army at Defiance by way of the Auglaize and St. Mary's rivers. Hull's road was impassable, and for that reason the column of Ohio troops and their supplies were stopped in the neighborhood of Urbana.

Throughout the months of October and November Harrison's army stood still, scattered over the State of Ohio, while wagons and packhorses wallowed in mud toward the Maumee Rapids. None arrived. Sometimes the wagons were abandoned in the mud; sometimes the packhorses broke down; sometimes the rivers were too low for boats; then they froze and stopped water-transport. Universal confusion, want of oversight and organization, added to physical difficulties, gave play to laziness, incapacity, and dishonesty. No bills of lading were used; no accounts were kept with the wagoners; and the teams were valued so high, on coming into service, that the owners were willing to destroy them for the price to be received.[1] The waste of government funds was appalling, for nothing short of a million rations at the Maumee Rapids could serve Harrison's objects, and after two months of effort not a ration had been carried within fifty miles of the spot. In Winchester's camp at Defiance the men were always on half rations, except when they had none at all. During the greater part of December they had no flour, but lived on poor beef and hickory roots. Typhus swept them away by scores; their numbers were reduced to about one thousand. The exact force which Harrison had in the field was matter of conjecture, for he sent no return of any description to the adjutant-general's office.[2] The Government gave him *carte blanche*, and he used it.[3] Chaos and misconduct reigned in every department, while he, floundering through the mud along his line of two hundred miles front, sought in vain for a road.

For the train of errors and disasters in the northwest Secretary Eustis was chiefly responsible, and his resignation, Dec. 3, 1812, left the campaign in this hopeless condition.

[1] McAffee, p. 184.
[2] Armstrong to Harrison, April 4, 1813; Armstrong's Notices, i. 245.
[3] Harrison to Secretary of War, Jan. 4, 1813; Dawson, p. 337.

From Dec. 3, 1812, until Jan. 13, 1813, Monroe acted as Secretary of War; and to him Harrison next wrote from Delaware, December 12, a letter which not only disheartened the Government, but was calculated to create a prejudice against the writer in the mind of any Secretary of War who was not invincibly prejudiced in his favor.[1]

"If there were not some important political reason," said Harrison, "urging the recovery of the Michigan Territory and the capture of Malden as soon as those objects can possibly be effected, and that to accomplish them a few weeks sooner expense was to be disregarded, I should not hesitate to say that if a small proportion of the sums which will be expended in the quartermaster's department in the active prosecution of the campaign during the winter was devoted to obtaining the command of Lake Erie, the wishes of the Government, in their utmost extent, could be accomplished without difficulty in the months of April and May. Malden, Detroit, and Mackinaw would fall in rapid succession. On the contrary, all that I can certainly promise to accomplish during the winter, unless the strait should afford us a passage on the ice, is to recover Detroit. I must further observe that no military man would think of retaining Detroit, Malden being in possession of the enemy, unless his army was at least twice as strong as the disposable force of the enemy. An army advancing to Detroit along a line of operation passing so near the principal force of the enemy as to allow them access to it whenever they think proper, must be covered by another army more considerable than the disposable force of the enemy. I mention this circumstance to show that the attack ought not to be directed against Detroit, but against Malden; and that it depends upon the ice affording a safe passage across the strait, whether I shall be able to proceed in this way or not. Detroit is not tenable. Were I to take it without having it in my power to occupy the opposite shore, I should be under the necessity of hiding the army in the adjacent swamp to preserve it from the effects of the shot and shells which the enemy would throw with impunity from the opposite

[1] Dawson, p. 333. Armstrong's Notices, i. 63, 86.

shore. This result is so obvious to every man who has the least military information, that it appears to me as extraordinary as any other part of General Hull's conduct that he should choose to defend Detroit rather than attack Malden."

Hull could have asked no better apology for his surrender. Harrison did not know that the insubordination and refusal of the Ohio colonels to evacuate Detroit had forced Hull to remain there; but that Detroit was not tenable came at last to the surface as a self-evident truth of the campaign,—which Hull had always seen, and which Harrison himself announced almost as clearly in August as in December, but which he ignored in the interval.

"If it should be asked," he continued, "why these statements were not made sooner,—I answer that although I was always sensible that there were great difficulties to be encountered in the accomplishment of the wishes of the President in relation to the recovery of Detroit and the conquest of the adjacent part of Upper Canada in the manner proposed, I did not make sufficient allowance for the imbecility and inexperience of the public agents and the villany of the contractors. I am still, however, very far from believing that the original plan is impracticable. I believe on the contrary that it can be effected."

The excuse did not satisfy the Cabinet, who thought they saw that Harrison wished to throw upon Government the responsibility for a military failure fatal to himself. Perhaps a simpler motive guided Harrison, who from the first never had known precisely what to do, or had seen any clear path to success. He wrote, January 4, from Franklinton,—

"When I was directed to take the command in the latter end of September, I thought it possible by great exertions to effect the objects of the campaign before the setting in of winter . . . The experience of a few days was sufficient to convince me that the supplies of provisions could not be procured for our autumnal advance; and even if this difficulty was removed, another of equal magnitude existed in the want of artillery. There remained then no alternative but to prepare for a winter campaign."

According to this account he had seen early in October that advance was impossible, yet he wasted millions of money and many of his best troops in attempting it. Winter had come, and he was pledged to a winter campaign as impracticable as the autumn campaign had proved to be. Without the control of the Lake, any army beyond the Maumee must starve or surrender. The government had already paid a vast price in money and men in order to obtain this knowledge; yet Harrison proposed a winter campaign, with full persuasion of its uselessness.

December 20 he sent orders[1] to Winchester to descend the Maumee River from Defiance to the rapids, there to prepare sleds for an expedition against Malden, to be made by a choice detachment when the whole army should concentrate at the rapids. Early in January, the ground being at last frozen, provisions in large quantities were hurried to the Maumee River. Artillery was sent forward. The Pennsylvania and Virginia brigades moved to the Sandusky River, making an effective force of fifteen hundred men at that point. The whole effective force on the frontier amounted to six thousand three hundred infantry.[2] Harrison intended to move his headquarters forward from the Sandusky, and to reach the Maumee Rapids January 20, to which point he supposed General Winchester already in motion from Defiance.[3]

This was the situation January 12; and although Harrison hinted in his reports of January 4 and 8 that his winter campaign would probably fail,[4] he showed the intention of advancing at least as far as the strait opposite Malden, about thirty-five miles beyond the Maumee. This he might venture without much danger; and if he reached that point, supposing the straits to be frozen, the enemy to show little sign of resistance, and the weather to favor, he might attack Malden. Hull had been expected to take Malden with twelve or fourteen hundred men, with an open river behind him, a British fleet on his flank, fifty miles of road to cover, and supplies for only a few days at Detroit; but Harrison with six thousand

[1] Dawson, p. 454.
[2] Harrison to the Secretary of War, Jan. 4, 1813; Dawson, p. 339.
[3] Harrison to the Secretary of War, Jan. 4, 1813; Dawson, p. 339.
[4] Harrison to the Secretary of War, Jan. 4, 1813; Dawson, p. 339.

men, the river frozen and the British fleet frozen in it, a secure base, with a million rations close in his rear, and no Isaac Brock in his front, still spoke with extreme doubt of his prospects, and said that "most of the well-informed men who knew the character of the country"[1] expected a suspension of operations for the winter.

Aware that from a military point of view no land-campaign could, except by accident, effect any result proportionate to its cost, Harrison had placed himself at the head of a popular movement so strong that he would have met the fate of Hull and Alexander Smyth, had he not made at least a demonstration against an enemy whose face he had not yet seen. Forced by his own pledges and the public discontent to enter on an unmilitary campaign, he was anxious to risk as little as possible where he could hardly expect to gain anything; and he would probably have contented himself with his first scheme of a *coup-de-main* against Malden or Detroit, without attempting to hold either place, had not his subordinate, General Winchester, rescued him from an awkward position by a blunder that relieved Harrison of further responsibility.

Brigadier-General Winchester was a planter of Tennessee, sixty-one years old, and formerly an officer in the Revolutionary War. Though outranking Harrison, he had allowed himself to be set aside by what he thought intrigue,[2] and consented to conduct the left wing of the force under Harrison's command. Winchester was not a favorite with his Kentucky militia-men, who had no choice in electing him to their command. Their term of service was to expire in February; they had been imprisoned since September in a wilderness at Defiance,—hungry, cold, sick, and mutinous, able to find no enemy willing to fight them, and disgusted with idleness. No sooner was the ground frozen and the general movement of concentration possible, than Winchester's command by common consent, under Harrison's orders, broke up their camp near Defiance and marched to the rapids, where Hull's road crossed the Maumee. There they arrived January 10, as Harrison expected. They fortified themselves on the north bank,

---

[1] Harrison to the Secretary of War, Jan. 8, 1813; Dawson, p. 339.
[2] Winchester to the "National Intelligencer," Sept. 16, 1817; Major Eves's Statement; Armstrong's Notices, i. 203. Cf. Dawson, p. 443.

and waited for the arrival of Harrison, who intended to join them January 20.

Winchester's force included three regiments of Kentucky militia, numbering nine hundred effectives,[1] and the Seventeenth United States Infantry, numbering three hundred men, also Kentuckians. Altogether he had under his command at the rapids about thirteen hundred men,[2] — a force barely sufficient to hold the exposed position it had taken on the north bank of the river. The three Kentucky militia regiments were soon to go home. The other columns were not yet within supporting distance. If Colonel Proctor, who commanded at Malden, were capable of imitating Brock's enterprise, he would hardly throw away an opportunity, which might never recur, to strike a blow at the Kentuckians, and by defeating them to drive Harrison's army behind the Sandusky River. Every military motive warned Winchester not to divide, detach, or expose his troops without caution. He was himself a detachment, and he had no support nearer than the Sandusky.

While the troops were busily engaged in building a storehouse and throwing up log-works in an injudicious and untenable position,[3] two Frenchmen came into camp, begging protection for the inhabitants of Frenchtown on the river Raisin, thirty miles in front, and within the British lines. Thirty-three families, or about one hundred and fifty persons, were resident at Frenchtown, and the place was held by a few Canadian militia, supposed to consist of two companies, with about as many Indians, — in all, some three hundred men.[4] This force might easily be destroyed, and the loss to the British would be serious. Winchester's troops became eager to dash at them. A council of war decided, January 16, without a voice in remonstrance, that the movement should be made. The most ardent supporter of the adventure was Col. John Allen of the Kentucky Rifle regiment; but no one offered opposition, and Winchester agreed to the council's opinion.[5]

The next morning, Jan. 17, 1813, Col. William Lewis, of the

[1] Winchester's Statement; Armstrong's Notices, i. 197.
[2] McAffee, p. 230.
[3] McAffee, p. 237.
[4] Winchester's Statement; Armstrong's Notices, i. 199.
[5] Winchester to the "National Intelligencer," Dec. 13, 1817.

Fifth Kentucky militia, started for the river Raisin, with four hundred and fifty men.[1] A few hours afterward he was followed by Colonel Allen with one hundred and ten men. No reports told what regiments were taken, or where they were at any moment stationed; but Lewis and Allen probably led twelve companies, drawn from four Kentucky regiments,— the Seventeenth United States Infantry, recruited in Kentucky, commanded by Col. Samuel Wells; the Kentucky Rifles, Col. John Allen; the First Kentucky Infantry; and Colonel Lewis's regiment, the Fifth Kentucky Infantry,—in all, six hundred and sixty men, representing the flower of Kentucky.

They marched on the ice, along the shore of Maumee Bay and Lake Erie, until nightfall, when they camped, and at two o'clock the next afternoon, January 18, reached without meeting resistance the houses on the south bank of the river Raisin. The north bank was occupied, according to British authority,[2] by fifty Canadian militia and two hundred Indians. The British force opened fire with a three-pound howitzer. The action began at three o'clock and lasted till dark, when the enemy after an obstinate resistance was driven about two miles into the woods with inconsiderable loss.[3] The action was sharp, and cost the Americans not less than twelve killed and fifty-five wounded, reducing their effective number to six hundred.

Colonel Lewis had orders to take possession of Frenchtown, and hold it. He reported his success to General Winchester at the rapids, and remained at Frenchtown waiting further orders. Winchester became then aware that the situation was hazardous. Six hundred men were with him in a half-fortified camp on the north bank of the Maumee; six hundred more were thirty miles in advance, at the Raisin River; while fully two thousand—or, according to Harrison's estimate, four thousand[4]—enemies held two fortresses only eighteen miles beyond the Raisin. The Kentuckians at the Maumee, equally aware of their comrades' peril, insisted on

---

[1] Winchester to the "National Intelligencer," Dec. 13, 1817.
[2] James, i. 185; Richardson, p. 74.
[3] Richardson, p. 75.
[4] Winchester's Statement; Armstrong's Notices, i. 198.

going to their aid. Winchester promptly started on the evening of January 19, and arrived at Frenchtown the next morning. Colonel Wells's Seventeenth United States Infantry, two hundred and fifty men, followed, arriving at Frenchtown in the evening.[1]

Winchester, before leaving the Maumee Rapids, sent a despatch to Harrison with a report of the battle of the 18th, which met Harrison on the road hurrying to the Maumee Rapids. The next morning, January 20, Harrison arrived at the camp on the Maumee, and found there about three hundred Kentucky troops,[2] the remainder being all with Winchester at the river Raisin. Probably Harrison, whose own caution was great, felt the peril of Winchester's situation,[3] but he sent his inspector-general, Captain Hart, forward with orders to Winchester "to hold the ground we had got at any rate,"[4] while he wrote to the Secretary of War:—

"Upon my way to this place [Maumee Rapids] last evening, I received the letter from the General [Winchester] of which the enclosed is a copy, informing me of the complete success of the enterprise in the defeat of the enemy and taking the stores they had collected. The detachment under Colonel Lewis remain at the river Raisin, and General Winchester very properly marched yesterday with two hundred and fifty men to reinforce him and take the command. . . . It is absolutely necessary to maintain the position at the river Raisin, and I am assembling the troops as fast as possible for the purpose."[5]

Harrison added that his only fear was lest Winchester should be overpowered. He waited at the Maumee Rapids two days, until at noon, January 22, a messenger arrived with disastrous tidings from the front.

Winchester afterward told the story of his own proceedings

[1] Winchester to the "National Intelligencer," Dec. 17, 1817.
[2] Harrison to the Secretary of War, Jan. 26, 1813; Official Letters, p. 125.
[3] Harrison to Governor Meigs, Jan. 19, 1813; "National Intelligencer," Feb. 11, 1813.
[4] McAffee, p. 210; Armstrong's Notices, i. 200.
[5] Harrison to the Secretary of War, Feb. [Jan.] 20, 1813; MSS. War Department Archives.

with so much candor that his narrative became a necessary part of any explanation of his disaster:—

"Suspecting that Proctor would make an attempt to avenge this stroke, and knowing that our wounded men could not be removed, I hastened to reinforce Colonel Lewis with Wells's regiment, two hundred and fifty men; and set out myself to join him, and arrived on the morning of the 20th. The town, lying on the north side of the river, was picketed on three sides, the longest facing the north, and making the front. Within these pickets Colonel Lewis's corps was found. Not thinking the position eligible, nor the pickets a sufficient defence against artillery, I would have retreated but for the wounded, of whom there were fifty-five; but having no sufficient means for transporting these, and being equally destitute of those necessary for fortifying strongly, I issued an order for putting the place in the best condition for defence that might be practicable, intending to construct some new works as soon as the means for getting out timber might be had. On the evening of the 20th Wells arrived, and was directed to encamp on the right, in an open field, immediately without the picketing. On the 21st a patrol as far as Brownstown [opposite Malden] was sent out, and returned without seeing anything of an enemy. On the same day a man from Malden came in who reported that the enemy were preparing to attack us; but knowing nothing of the kind or extent of the preparation made or making, what he brought was thought to be only conjecture and such as led to a belief that it would be some days before Proctor would be ready to do anything. . . . Neither night-patrol nor night-pickets were ordered by me, from a belief that both were matters of routine and in constant use. . . . Not to discommode the wounded men, . . . I took quarters for myself and suite in a house on the southern bank, directly fronting the troops and only separated from them by the river, then firmly frozen, and but between eighty and a hundred yards wide."

The only educated officer under Harrison's command was Major E. D. Wood of the Engineers, one of the early graduates of West Point, and an officer of high promise. He was not with Winchester's division, but with the right wing on the Sandusky, and arrived at the Maumee Rapids some ten days afterward, where he built Fort Meigs, in February. During the campaign he kept a diary, and his criticisms of Winchester, Lewis, Allen, and their command were quoted with approval by the Kentucky historian,[1] as well as by Harrison's biographer:[2] —

"The troops were permitted to select, each for himself, such quarters on the west side of the river as might please him best, whilst the general . . . took his quarters on the east side,—not the least regard being paid to defence, order, regularity, or system, in the posting of the different corps. . . . With only one third or one fourth of the force destined for that service; destitute of artillery, of engineers, of men who had ever seen or heard the least of an enemy; and with but a very inadequate supply of ammunition,— how he ever could have entertained the most distant hope of success, or what right he had to presume to claim it, is to me one of the strangest things in the world. . . . Winchester was destitute of every means of supporting his corps long at the river Raisin; was in the very jaws of the enemy, and beyond the reach of succor. He who fights with such flimsy pretensions to victory will always be beaten, and eternally ought to be."

Defeat under such conditions was disgraceful enough; but defeat by Colonel Proctor was one of the worst misfortunes that happened to an American general. The Prince Regent took occasion, at the close of the war, to express his official opinion of this officer, then Major-General Proctor, in language of unusual severity.[3] Yet Proctor's first movements at the Raisin River showed no apparent sign of his being "so extremely wanting in professional knowledge, and deficient in those active, energetic qualities which must be required of every officer," as his later career, in the Prince Regent's opinion, proved him to be. He had opposed Brock's bold movement on Detroit; but he did not hesitate to make a somewhat

[1] McAffee, p. 233.
[2] Dawson, p. 364.
[3] Life of Sir George Prevost; App. xxv. p. 74. Christie, ii. 115.

similar movement himself. January 21 he marched with artillery across the river on the ice, to Brownstown opposite Malden, in full view of any American patrol in the neighborhood. His force consisted of six hundred whites, all told,[1] besides either four hundred and fifty, six hundred or eight hundred Indians, under the chief Round Head, Tecumthe being absent collecting reinforcements on the Wabash.[2] This large body of more than a thousand men, without an attempt at concealment, crossed to Brownstown and marched twelve miles, January 21, camping at night within five miles of Frenchtown.[3] If the British historian James was correct, they numbered eleven hundred and eighty men, of whom five hundred and thirty were white, and the rest Indians;[4] but the official return reported the whites, including every person present, at five hundred and ninety-seven men. Two hours before dawn, January 22, they again advanced, and before day-break approached within musket-shot of the picket-fence, and half-formed their line, before an alarm was given.

Had Proctor dashed at once on the defenceless Seventeenth regiment and the fence that covered the militia, he would probably have captured the whole without loss; but he preferred to depend on his three-pound guns, which gave the Kentuckians opportunity to use their rifles. In such fighting the Americans had much the advantage, especially as British regulars were opposite them. Within an hour the Forty-first regiment lost fifteen killed and ninety-eight wounded, and of the entire body of six hundred British troops not less than twenty-four were killed and one hundred and sixty-one wounded.[5] Their three-pound guns were abandoned, so murderous were the Kentucky rifles.[6] Had all the American troops been under cover, the battle would have been theirs; but Wells's Seventeenth regiment was a hundred yards away, on open ground outside the picket-fence on the right, where

[1] Return of the whole of the troops engaged at Frenchtown, Jan. 22, 1813; MSS. Canadian Archives, c. 678, p. 18.
[2] Christie, ii. 69; James, i. 186; Richardson, p. 75.
[3] Proctor's Report of Jan. 25, 1813; James, i. 418.
[4] James, i. 185, 186.
[5] Return, etc.; MSS. Canadian Archives, c. 648, p. 18.
[6] Richardson, p. 76.

it was flanked by the Canadian militia and Indians and driven back toward the river, until Allen's Rifle regiment went out to help it. Gradually forced toward the rear, across the river, this part of the line was at last struck with a panic and fled, carrying with it Winchester himself, Colonel Allen, and Colonel Lewis; while six hundred Indians were in hot pursuit, or already in advance of them.

In the deep snow escape was impossible. Nearly a hundred Kentuckians fell almost side by side, and were scalped. Among these was Colonel Allen. General Winchester and Colonel Lewis were so fortunate as to fall into the hands of the chief Round Head, who first stripped them and then took them to Proctor, who had for the time withdrawn his forces and ceased firing. By Proctor's advice, General Winchester sent an order to the men within the picket-fence to surrender.

By eight o'clock all resistance had ceased except from three hundred and eighty-four Kentuckians who remained within the picket-fence, under the command of Major Madison of the Rifle regiment. Surrounded by a thousand enemies, they had no chance of escape. Their ammunition was nearly exhausted; retreat was impossible; they could choose only between surrender and massacre, and they surrendered.[1] The British officers looked at them with curiosity, as they came within the British line.

"Their appearance," said Major Richardson,[2] "was miserable to the last degree. They had the air of men to whom cleanliness was a virtue unknown, and their squalid bodies were covered by habiliments that had evidently undergone every change of season, and were arrived at the last stage of repair. . . . It was the depth of winter; but scarcely an individual was in possession of a great coat or cloak, and few of them wore garments of wool of any description. They still retained their summer dress, consisting of cotton stuff of various colors shaped into frocks, and descending to the knee. Their trowsers were of the same material. They were covered with slouched hats, worn bare by constant use, beneath which their long hair fell matted and

---

[1] Statement of Madison, March 13, 1813; Niles, iv. 83.
[2] Richardson's War of 1812, p. 79.

uncombed over their cheeks; and these, together with the dirty blankets wrapped round their loins to protect them against the inclemency of the season, and fastened by broad leathern belts, into which were thrust axes and knives of an enormous length, gave them an air of wildness and savageness which in Italy would have caused them to pass for brigands of the Apennines. The only distinction between the garb of the officer and that of the soldier was that the one, in addition to his sword, carried a short rifle instead of a long one, while a dagger, often curiously worked and of some value, supplied the place of the knife."

This description gave a lifelike idea of what Harrison justly thought the best material in the world for soldiery, had it been properly handled. Men who for four months had suffered every hardship, and were still unclothed, unfed, uncared for, and sacrificed to military incompetence, but hardened to cold, fatigue, and danger, had no reason to be ashamed of their misfortunes or of their squalor. Fortunately about five hundred were saved as prisoners, and thirty or forty escaped to the rapids; the rest, four hundred in number, were killed in battle, or massacred afterward.

Had Proctor acted with energy, he might have advanced to the rapids, and there have captured Harrison with his remaining force of nine hundred men, his artillery train and stores. Even with the utmost celerity Harrison could hardly have escaped, if an active pursuit had been made by Indians through the swamp which he had with extreme difficulty crossed two days before,[1] and in the heavy rain which followed the battle;[2] but Proctor had no wish for fighting. So far from thinking of attack, he thought only of escaping it, and hurried back to Malden at noon the same day, leaving the wounded prisoners behind without a guard. Nothing excused such conduct, for Proctor knew the fate to which he was exposing his prisoners. That night the Indians, drunk with whiskey and mad with their grievances and losses, returned to Frenchtown and massacred the wounded. About thirty perished, some apparently burned. Fortunately for the United States the

[1] Dawson, p. 362.
[2] Dawson, p. 356.

glamour of Proctor's victory hid his true character, and he was made a major-general,—the most favorable event of the war for the American armies he was to meet, and one which cost Great Britain even more in pride than in power.

Chapter V

IF PROCTOR was afraid of Harrison, with more military reason Harrison was afraid of Proctor; and while the British
colonel, deserting his wounded prisoners, hurried from the
field of battle, and felt himself in danger until the next day he
was again entrenched at Malden, at the same moment Harrison, burning the post at the Maumee Rapids and destroying
such stores as were collected there, hastened back to the Portage or Carrying River some fifteen miles in the rear. Within
thirty-six hours after the battle, the two enemies were sixty
miles apart. At the Portage River Harrison remained a week,
until he had collected a force of two thousand men. With
these he returned to the rapids February 1, and began to construct a regularly fortified camp on the south bank of the
river. Fort Meigs, as it was called, did credit to the skill of
Major Wood, the engineer officer who constructed it; but
such a fortress seemed rather intended for defence than for
the conquest of Canada.

In fact, Harrison had succeeded only in making the most
considerable failure that had thus far marked the progress of
the war; but while the public was still assuming treason and
cowardice in William Hull, who had been sent with fifteen
hundred men to hold Detroit and conquer Canada, and had
been left unsupported to face destruction,—the same public
admitted the excuses of Harrison, who with ten thousand
men, unlimited means, and active support at Niagara, after
four months of effort, failed even to pass the Maumee River
except with a detachment so badly managed that only thirty-
three men in a thousand escaped. This was the crowning misfortune which wrung from Gallatin the complaint that a "real
incapacity" for war existed in the government itself, and must
inevitably exhaust its resources without good result; but although it drove Gallatin to Europe, it left Harrison on the
Maumee. Harrison would not take on himself the disgrace of
admitting his inability to recapture Detroit, and the President
would not, without his express admission, order him to desist. As Armstrong afterward explained:[1] "The Cabinet, not

[1] Armstrong's Notices, i. 85.

inexpert at deciphering military diplomacy, and peculiarly shy of incurring any responsibility it could avoid, determined, with perhaps less of patriotism than of prudence, to leave the question of continuing the winter campaign exclusively with the General." The General, not inclined to sink into obscurity or to admit failure, set himself to a third campaign as hopeless as either of its predecessors. Ordering all the troops in his rear to join him, making a body of four thousand men, he fixed February 11 as the day for his advance on Malden, not expecting to reduce that place, but merely to raid it.[1] When the day arrived, the roads had again become impassable, the ice was no longer safe; and Harrison, "with much reluctance and mortification,"[2] was reduced to write from the Maumee Rapids to the Secretary of War that the campaign must cease.

Thus the Western movement, likened by Henry Clay to a tenth-century crusade, ended in failure. The Government would have been in a better position had it never sent a man to the Maumee, but merely built a few sloops at Cleveland. The entire result of six months' immense effort was confined to raids into the Indian country; and even these were costly beyond proportion to their results. When the militia of Kentucky and Ohio, which had been mustered in August for six months' service, returned to their homes in February, 1813, not only had they failed to reoccupy a foot of the ground abandoned by Hull, but they left Harrison almost alone at Fort Meigs, trembling lest the enemy should descend on his rear and destroy his supplies, or force him back to protect them.[3] He had accumulated artillery, ammunition, and stores at the Maumee Rapids, in a fortress which itself required a garrison of two thousand men and from which he could neither fall back, as he thought the wiser course,[4] nor remain with safety exposed to an active enemy. He called for more militia from Kentucky and Ohio, but the people no longer felt enthusiasm for war.

"I am sorry to mention," reported Harrison, March 17,[5]

[1] Dawson, p. 370.
[2] McAffee, p. 240.
[3] Dawson, p. 375.
[4] Dawson, p. 373.
[5] Armstrong's Notices, i. 242.

"the dismay and disinclination to the service which appear to prevail in the Western country; numbers must give that confidence which ought to be produced by conscious valor and intrepidity, which never existed in any army in a superior degree than amongst the greater part of the militia who were with me through the winter. The new drafts from this State [Ohio] are entirely of another character, and are not to be depended on."

In short, Harrison, who had in 1812 commanded ten thousand militia, seemed to think double the number necessary for 1813, besides regular troops and a fleet.

President Madison and two successive Secretaries of War had allowed themselves, for fear of displeasing Kentucky, to give Harrison *carte blanche*,[1] which Harrison had used without other limit than that of the entire resources of the West. The time at last came when such management must be stopped, and Secretary Armstrong, naturally impatient under the load of Eustis's and Monroe's failures, quickly decided to stop it. Harrison's letter of February 11, announcing his failure, reached the Department March 1. March 5 the secretary wrote to Harrison ordering him to maintain a threatening attitude, but altering the mode of warfare. Henceforward the army was to be made subordinate,—the navy was to take the lead; and until the middle of May, when the fleet on Lake Erie should be constructed, Harrison was to maintain a strict defensive, and to protect the line of the Maumee with six regular regiments, only three of which had been yet partly raised.

Meanwhile, Harrison had but a few hundred regulars and some Pennsylvania and Virginia militia,—perhaps five hundred men in all,—to hold Fort Meigs, and mere squads of militia to guard eight other posts which had cost the government some millions of dollars. These five hundred troops, whose service was mostly near its end, he left at Fort Meigs, and in the middle of March he set out for Chillicothe and Cincinnati. Greatly annoyed at the summary manner in which Armstrong had put an end to his campaigning, he protested only against the inadequacy of his force for the defence

[1] Dawson, p. 337.

required of it, and insisted on a temporary reinforcement of militia to garrison the fortress that had cost him so much effort to construct at the Maumee Rapids.

Then the value of General Proctor to his enemy became immense. Between January 22, when he attacked Winchester, and the end of April, when he moved on Fort Meigs, Proctor molested in no way the weak and isolated American garrisons. With hundreds of scouts and backwoodsmen at his command, he had not the energy or the knowledge to profit by his opponents' exposed and defenceless condition. He allowed Major Wood to make Fort Meigs capable of standing a siege; he let Harrison, unmolested, pass a month away from his command; he looked on while the Virginia militia marched home, leaving only a handful of sickly men, under a major of artillery, to defend the unfinished fort; he made no attempt to waylay Harrison, who returned with reinforcements by way of the Auglaize River; and not until Harrison had enjoyed all the time necessary to prepare for attack, did Proctor disturb him.

Harrison, expecting an assault, hurried back from Cincinnati to Fort Meigs with some three hundred men, leaving a brigade of Kentucky militia to follow him. April 12 he reached the fort, but not till April 28 did Proctor appear at the mouth of the Maumee, with about five hundred regulars and nearly as many militia,—nine hundred and eighty-three whites, all told, and twelve hundred Indians under Tecumthe and other chiefs.[1] Besides this large force, he brought two twenty-four pound guns with other artillery from Detroit, and two gunboats supported the land-battery. While the guns were placed in position on the north bank of the river, the Indians crossed and surrounded the fort on the south. May 1 the batteries opened, and during four days kept up a heavy fire. Proctor, like Harrison, moved in the wilderness as though he were conducting a campaign on the Rhine; he liked regular modes of warfare, and with a force almost wholly irregular, after allowing Fort Meigs to be built, he besieged it as though he could take it by battering its earthen ramparts. Untaught by his losses at the river Raisin, he gave once more advantage to

[1] Proctor's Report of May 4, 1813; Richardson, p. 94; James, i. 196, 429.

the Kentucky rifle; and with every opportunity of destroying the reinforcement which he knew to be near, he allowed himself to be surprised by it.

The Kentucky brigade of twelve hundred men, under Brigadier-General Green Clay, had descended the Auglaize River in boats, and arrived at Defiance May 3, where they learned that Fort Meigs was invested. So neglectful of his advantages was Proctor that he not only failed to prevent General Clay from advancing, but failed to prevent communication between the besieged fort and the relief-column, so that Harrison was able to arrange a general attack on the investing lines, and came near driving the British force back to Malden with the loss of all its artillery and baggage. At about nine o'clock on the morning of May 5, Clay's brigade descended the rapids, and eight hundred and sixty-six men under Colonel William Dudley,[1] landing on the north side of the river, surprised and took possession of the British batteries, which were entirely unsupported. Had Clay's whole force been on the ground, and had it been vigorously pushed forward, the small British division which held the north bank must have abandoned all its positions; but Dudley's men were under no discipline, and though ready to advance were in no hurry to retreat, even when ordered. Three companies of the British Forty-first, and some of the Canadian militia soon gathered together; and although these could hardly have been half the number of Dudley's force,[2] yet with Tecumthe and a body of Indians they attacked the batteries, drove the Kentuckians out, dispersed them, and either captured or massacred the whole body, under the eyes of Harrison and Fort Meigs.

This affair, though little less fatal to the Americans than that of the river Raisin, was much less dearly bought by the British. Five hundred prisoners fell into Proctor's hands; two or three hundred more of the Kentucky brigade, including "the weak and obstinate but brave"[3] Dudley himself, must have been either killed in battle or massacred after surrender;[4]

[1] Lossing, p. 486, *note*.
[2] Richardson, p. 86; James, i. 198.
[3] Harrison to Armstrong, May 13, 1813; MSS. War Department Archives.
[4] Richardson, pp. 87, 88. Harrison to Armstrong, May 9, 1813; MSS. War Department Archives.

only one hundred and seventy escaped; the boats with the baggage were captured; while the whole British loss on the north side of the river hardly exceeded fifty killed and wounded. A bitter feeling against Proctor was caused by the massacre of some forty American prisoners while under a British guard, and also, as was alleged, under the eyes of General Proctor, who did not interpose, although a soldier of the Forty-first was murdered in trying to protect them. Probably all the prisoners would have been massacred had Tecumthe not ridden up at full speed, tomahawk in hand, and threatened to kill the first Indian who defied his authority.[1]

On the south side Harrison had better fortune, and Colonel John Miller of the Nineteenth U. S. Infantry by a sortie gallantly captured a battery, with some forty prisoners; but neither on the north nor on the south did the fighting of May 5 decide any immediate military result. Besides losing on the north bank half the reinforcement brought by General Green Clay, Harrison had lost in the siege and in the sorties on the south bank nearly three hundred men in killed and wounded.[2] If the numbers loosely reported in the American accounts were correct, the siege cost Harrison one thousand men, or fully half his entire force, including his reinforcements. After the fighting of May 5, he withdrew once more into the fort; the British batteries reopened fire, and the siege went on. No further attempt was made to trouble the enemy in open field. Harrison felt himself too weak for further ventures; yet never had his chance of a great success been so fair.

Proctor's siege of Fort Meigs was already a failure. Not only had the fort proved stronger than he expected, but the weather was bad; his troops were without shelter; dysentery and loss in battle rapidly weakened them; half his militia went home, and, what was fatal to further action, his Indians could not be held together. Within three days after the battle of May 5, the twelve hundred Indians collected by Tecumthe's influence and exertions in the northwest territory dispersed, leaving only Tecumthe himself and a score of other warriors in the British camp.[3] Proctor had no choice

[1] Richardson, p. 88.
[2] Harrison to Armstrong, May 13, 1813; MSS. War Department Archives.
[3] Proctor's Report of May 14, 1813; James, i. 428; Richardson, pp. 93, 94.

but to retire as rapidly as possible, and May 9 embarked his artillery and left his encampment without interference from Harrison, who looked on as a spectator while the movement was effected.

From that time until the middle of July Proctor remained quiet. Harrison moved his headquarters to Upper Sandusky and to Cleveland, and began to prepare for advance under cover of a naval force; but he was not allowed to rest, even though Proctor might have preferred repose. Proctor's position was difficult. Told by Sir George Prevost[1] that he must capture what supplies he needed from the Americans, and must seek them at Erie and Cleveland, since Lower Canada could spare neither food nor transport, he was compelled to look for support to the American magazines. He was issuing ten thousand rations a day to the Indian families at Malden, and his resources were near an end.[2] Leaving Malden with either three hundred and ninety-one regulars, or about five hundred regulars and militia, and by one British account nearly a thousand Indians, by another between three and four thousand,[3] Proctor returned by water to the Maumee Rapids July 20, and tried to draw the garrison of Fort Meigs into an ambush. The attempt failed. General Green Clay, who was in command, had learned caution, and imposed it on his troops. Proctor then found that his Indians were leaving him and returning to Detroit and Amherstburg. To occupy them, Proctor took again to his boats and coasted the Lake shore as far as the Sandusky River, while the Indians who chose to accompany him made their way by land. August 1 the expedition effected a landing at the mouth of the Sandusky, and scattered panic into the heart of Ohio.

In truth, nothing could be more alarming than this movement, which threatened Harrison in all directions,—from Fort Meigs, on the Maumee, to Erie, or Presqu'isle, where Perry's fleet was building. On Sandusky River Harrison had collected his chief magazines. All the supplies for his army were lying at Upper Sandusky, some thirty miles above the British landing-place, and he had only eight hundred raw

[1] Prevost to Proctor, July 11, 1813; Armstrong's Notices, i. 228.
[2] Richardson, p. 111.
[3] James, i. 264, 265; Richardson, p. 104; Christie, p. 117.

recruits to defend their unfortified position.[1] Nothing but an untenable stockade, called Fort Stephenson, on the Sandusky River, where the town of Fremont afterward grew, offered an obstacle to the enemy in ascending; and Tecumthe with two thousand Indians was said to be moving from Fort Meigs by the direct road straight for the magazines, thus flanking Fort Stephenson and every intermediate position on the Sandusky.

In just panic for the safety of his magazines, the only result of a year's campaigning, Harrison's first thought was to evacuate Fort Stephenson in order to protect Upper Sandusky. The flank-attack from two thousand Indians, who never showed themselves, impelled him to retire before Proctor, and to leave the river open. July 29, after a council of war, he sent down a hasty order to young Major Croghan who commanded Fort Stephenson, directing him immediately to burn the fort and retreat up the river or along the Lake shore, as he best could, with the utmost haste.[2] Croghan, a Kentuckian, and an officer of the Seventeenth U. S. regiment, refused to obey. "We have determined to maintain this place, and by Heaven, we will," he wrote back.[3] Harrison sent Colonel Wells, of the same regiment, to relieve him; but Croghan went to headquarters, and by somewhat lame excuses carried his point, and resumed his command the next day. Harrison gave him only conditional orders to abandon the fort,—orders which Croghan clearly could not regard, and which Harrison seemed to feel no confidence in his wishing to follow.[4] In the face of British troops with cannon he was to retreat; but "you must be aware that the attempt to retreat in the face of an Indian force would be vain." Proctor's main force was believed to be Indian.

Neither evacuating nor defending Fort Stephenson, Harrison remained at Seneca, ten miles behind it, watching for Tecumthe and the flank attack, and arranging a plan of battle for his eight hundred men by which he could repel the Indians with dragoons in the open prairie.[5] Croghan remained at

---

[1] Dawson, p. 408.
[2] McAffee, p. 322.
[3] McAffee, p. 323.
[4] Governor Duncan's Report, 1834; Armstrong's Notices, i. 230.
[5] Dawson, p. 408.

Fort Stephenson with one hundred and sixty men, making every preparation to meet an attack. August 1 the woods were already filled with Indians, and retreat was impossible, when the British boats appeared on the river, and Proctor sent to demand surrender of the fort. Immediately on Croghan's refusal, the British howitzers opened fire and continued until it became clear that they were too light to destroy the stockade.

If experience had been of service to Proctor, he should have learned to avoid direct attack on Americans in fortified places; but his position was difficult, and he was as much afraid of Harrison as Harrison was afraid of him. Fearing to leave Croghan's little fort in the rear, and to seek Harrison himself, ten miles above, on the road to Upper Sandusky; fearing delay, which would discontent his Indian allies; fearing to go on to Cleveland or Erie without crippling Harrison; still more afraid to retire to Malden without striking a blow,— Proctor again sacrificed the Forty-first regiment which had suffered at the river Raisin and had been surprised at Fort Meigs. On the afternoon of August 2 the Forty-first regiment and the militia, in three columns of about one hundred and twenty men each,[1] with the utmost gallantry marched to the pickets of Fort Stephenson, and were shot down. After two hours' effort, and losing all its officers, the assaulting column retired, leaving twenty-six dead, forty-one wounded, and about thirty missing, or more than one fifth of their force. The same night the troops re-embarked and returned to Malden.

Proctor's report[2] of this affair was filled with complaints of the Indians, who could not be left idle and who would not fight. At Sandusky, he said, "we could not muster more hundreds of Indians than I might reasonably have expected thousands."

"I could not, therefore, with my very small force remain more than two days, from the probability of being cut off, and of being deserted by the few Indians who had not already done so. . . . On the morning of the 2d inst. the gentlemen of the Indian department who have the direc-

[1] Richardson, p. 105.
[2] Proctor to Prevost, Aug. 9, 1813; MSS. Canadian Archives.

tion of it, declared formally their decided opinion that unless the fort was stormed we should never be able to bring an Indian warrior into the field with us, and that they proposed and were ready to storm one face of the fort if we would attempt another. I have also to observe that in this instance my judgment had not that weight with the troops I hope I might reasonably have expected. . . . The troops, after the artillery had been used for some hours, attacked two faces, and impossibilities being attempted, failed. The fort, from which the severest fire I ever saw was maintained during the attack, was well defended. The troops displayed the greatest bravery, the much greater part of whom reached the fort and made every effort to enter; but the Indians who had proposed the assault, and, had it not been assented to, would have ever stigmatized the British character, scarcely came into fire before they ran out of its reach. A more than adequate sacrifice having been made to Indian opinion, I drew off the brave assailants."

Sir George Prevost seemed to doubt whether Proctor's excuse for the defeat lessened or increased the blame attached to it.[1] The defeat at Sandusky ruined Proctor in the esteem of his men. On the American side, Harrison's conduct roused a storm of indignation. Through the whole day, August 2, he remained at Seneca with eight hundred men, listening to the cannonade at Fort Stephenson till late at night, when he received an express from Croghan to say that the enemy were embarking. The story ran, that as the distant sound of Croghan's guns reached the camp at Seneca, Harrison exclaimed: "The blood be on his own head; I wash my hands of it."[2] Whatever else might be true, his conduct betrayed an extravagant estimate of his enemy's strength. The only British eyewitness who left an account of the expedition reckoned Proctor's force, on its departure from Malden, at about four hundred troops, and "nearly a thousand Indians."[3] The Indians dispersed until those with Proctor at Fort Stephenson probably numbered two or three hundred,[4] the rest having

[1] Life of Prevost, p. 106, *note*.
[2] Governor Duncan's Report, 1834; Armstrong's Notices, i. 230.
[3] Richardson, p. 104.
[4] James, ii. 264.

returned to Detroit and Malden. Harrison reported the British force as five thousand strong, on the authority of General Green Clay.[1]

Whether the British force was large or small, Harrison's arrangements to meet it did not please Secretary Armstrong. "It is worthy of notice," he wrote long afterward,[2] "that of these two commanders, always the terror of each other, one [Proctor] was now actually flying from his supposed pursuer; while the other [Harrison] waited only the arrival of Croghan at Seneca to begin a camp-conflagration and flight to Upper Sandusky."

The well-won honors of the campaign fell to Major George Croghan, with whose name the whole country resounded. Whatever were the faults of the two generals, Major Croghan showed courage and intelligence, not only before and during the attack, but afterward in supporting Harrison against the outcry which for a time threatened to destroy the General's authority. Immediately after the siege of Fort Stephenson every energy of the northwest turned toward a new offensive movement by water against Malden, and in the task of organizing the force required for that purpose, complaints of past failures were stifled. Secretary Armstrong did not forget them, but the moment was not suited for making a change in so important a command. Harrison organized, under Armstrong's orders, a force of seven thousand men to cross the Lake in boats, under cover of a fleet.

The fleet, not the army, was to bear the brunt of reconquering the northwest; and in nothing did Armstrong show his ability so clearly as in the promptness with which, immediately after taking office, he stopped Harrison's campaign on the Maumee, while Perry was set to work at Erie. Feb. 5, 1813, Armstrong entered on his duties. March 5 his arrangements for the new movements were already made. Harrison did not approve them,[3] but he obeyed. The Navy Department had already begun operations on Lake Erie, immediately after Hull's surrender; but though something was accomplished in the winter, great difficulties had still to be overcome when

[1] Dawson, p. 407; McAffee, p. 302.
[2] Armstrong's Notices, i. 166, *note*.
[3] Harrison to Armstrong, March 17, 1813; Notices, i. 242.

February 17 Commander Perry, an energetic young officer on
gunboat service at Newport, received orders from Secretary
Jones to report to Commodore Chauncey on Lake Ontario.
Chauncey ordered him to Presqu'isle, afterward called Erie,
to take charge of the vessels under construction on Lake Erie.
March 27 he reached the spot, a small village in a remote wilderness, where timber and water alone existed for the supply
of the fleets.

When Perry reached Presqu'isle the contractors and carpenters had on the stocks two brigs, a schooner, and three gunboats. These were to be launched in May, and to be ready for
service in June. Besides these vessels building at Erie, a number of other craft, including the prize brig "Caledonia," were
at the Black Rock navy-yard in the Niagara River, unable to
move on account of the British fort opposite Buffalo and the
British fleet on the Lake. Perry's task was to unite the two
squadrons, to man them, and to fight the British fleet, without allowing his enemy to interfere at any stage of these difficult operations.

The British squadron under Commander Finnis, an experienced officer, had entire control of the Lake and its shores.
No regular garrison protected the harbor of Presqu'isle; not
two hundred men could be armed to defend it, nor was any
military support to be had nearer than Buffalo, eighty miles
away. Proctor or Prevost were likely to risk everything in
trying to destroy the shipyard at Erie; for upon that point,
far more than on Detroit, Fort Meigs, Sandusky, or Buffalo,
their existence depended. If Perry were allowed to control the
Lake, the British must not only evacuate Detroit, but also
Malden, must abandon Tecumthe and the military advantages
of three or four thousand Indian auxiliaries, and must fall
back on a difficult defensive at the Niagara River. That they
would make every effort to thwart Perry seemed certain.

Superstition survived in nothing more obstinately than in
faith in luck; neither sailors nor soldiers ever doubted the
value of this inscrutable quality in the conduct of war. The
"Chesapeake" was an unlucky ship to the luckiest commanders, even to the British captain who captured it. The bad luck
of the "Chesapeake" was hardly steadier than the good luck
of Oliver Perry. Whatever he touched seemed to take the

direction he wanted. He began with the advantage of having Proctor for his chief enemy; but Harrison, also a lucky man, had the same advantage and yet suffered constant disasters. Commander Finnis was a good seaman, yet Finnis failed repeatedly, and always by a narrow chance, to injure Perry. Dearborn's incompetence in 1813 was not less than it had been in 1812; but the single success which in two campaigns Dearborn gained on the Niagara obliged the British, May 27, to evacuate Fort Erie opposite Buffalo, and to release Perry's vessels at Black Rock. June 6, at leisure, Perry superintended the removal of the five small craft from the navy-yard at Black Rock; several hundred soldiers, seamen, and oxen warped them up stream into the Lake. Loaded with stores, the little squadron sailed from Buffalo June 13; the wind was ahead; they were five days making eighty miles; but June 19 they arrived at Presqu'isle, and as the last vessel crossed the bar, Finnis and his squadron came in sight. Finnis alone could explain how he, a first-rate seaman, with a strong force and a fair wind, in such narrow seas, could have helped finding Perry's squadron when he knew where it must be.

From June 19 to August 1 Perry's combined fleet lay within the bar at Presqu'isle, while Proctor, with a sufficient fleet and a military force superior to anything on the Lake, was planning expeditions from Malden against every place except the one to which military necessity and the orders of his Government bade him go. August 4, Perry took out the armaments of his two brigs and floated both over the bar into deep water. Had the British fleet been at hand, such a movement would have been impossible or fatal; but the British fleet appeared just as Perry's vessels got into deep water, and when for the first time an attack could not be made with a fair hope of success.

These extraordinary advantages were not gained without labor, energy, courage, and wearing anxieties and disappointments. Of these Perry had his full share, but no more; and his opponents were no better off than himself. By great exertions alone could the British maintain themselves on Lake Ontario, and to this necessity they were forced to sacrifice Lake Erie. Sir George Prevost could spare only a new commander with a few officers and some forty men from the lower Lake to meet the large American reinforcements on the upper. When the commander, R. H. Barclay, arrived at Malden in June, he found as many difficulties there as Perry found at Presqu'isle. Barclay was a captain in the British Royal Navy, thirty-two years old; he had lost an arm in the service, but he was fairly matched as Perry's antagonist, and showed the qualities of an excellent officer.

Perry's squadron, once on the Lake, altogether over-awed the British fleet, and Barclay's only hope lay in completing a vessel called the "Detroit," then on the stocks at Amherst-burg. Rough and unfinished, she was launched, and while Perry blockaded the harbor, Barclay, early in September, got masts and rigging into her, and armed her with guns of every calibre, taken from the ramparts.[1] Even the two American twenty-four pound guns, used by Proctor against Fort Meigs, were put on board the "Detroit." Thus equipped, she had still to be manned; but no seamen were near the Lake. Barclay was forced to make up a crew of soldiers from the hard-worked Forty-first regiment and Canadians unused to service. September 6 the "Detroit" was ready to sail, and Barclay had then no choice but to fight at any risk. "So perfectly destitute of provisions was the port that there was not a day's flour in store, and the crews of the squadron under my command were on half allowance of many things; and when that was done, there was no more."[2]

Early on the morning of September 9 Barclay's fleet weighed and sailed for the enemy, who was then at anchor off the island of Put-in-Bay near the mouth of Sandusky River. The British squadron consisted of six vessels,—the "Detroit," a ship of four hundred and ninety tons, carrying nineteen guns, commanded by Barclay himself; the "Queen Charlotte" of seventeen guns, commanded by Finnis; the "Lady Prevost" of thirteen guns; the "Hunter" of ten; the "Little Belt" carrying three, and the "Chippeway" carrying one gun,—in all, sixty-three guns, and probably about four hundred and fifty men. The American squadron consisted of nine vessels,—the "Lawrence," Perry's own brig, nearly as

[1] Richardson, p. 110; James, Naval Occurrences, p. 285.

[2] Barclay's Report of Sept. 12, 1813; James, Naval Occurrences. Appendix, no. 54.

large as the "Detroit," and carrying twenty guns; the "Niagara," commander Jesse D. Elliott, of the same tonnage, with the same armament; the "Caledonia," a three-gun brig; the schooners "Ariel," "Scorpion," "Somers," "Porcupine," and "Tigress," carrying ten guns; and the sloop "Trippe," with one gun,— in all, fifty-four guns, with a nominal crew of five hundred and thirty-two men, and an effective crew probably not greatly differing from the British. In other respects Perry's superiority was decided, as it was meant to be. The Americans had thirty-nine thirty-two pound carronades; the British had not a gun of that weight, and only fifteen twenty-four pound carronades. The lightest guns on the American fleet were eight long twelve-pounders, while twenty-four of the British guns threw only nine-pound shot, or less. The American broadside threw at close range about nine hundred pounds of metal; the British threw about four hundred and sixty. At long range the Americans threw two hundred and eighty-eight pounds of metal; the British threw one hundred and ninety-five pounds. In tonnage the Americans were superior as eight to seven. In short, the Navy Department had done everything reasonably necessary to insure success; and if the American crews, like the British, were partly made up of landsmen, soldiers or volunteers, the reason was in each case the same. Both governments supplied all the seamen they had.

Between forces so matched, victory ought not to have been in doubt; and if it was so, the fault certainly lay not in Perry. When, at daylight September 10, his look-out discovered the British fleet, Perry got his own squadron under way, and came down with a light wind from the southeast against Barclay's line, striking it obliquely near the head. Perry must have been anxious to fight at close range, where his superiority was as two to one, while at long range his ship could use only two long twelve-pounders against the "Detroit's" six twelves, one eighteen, and two twenty-fours,— an inferiority amounting to helplessness. Both the "Lawrence" and the "Niagara" were armed for close fighting, and were intended for nothing else. At long range their combined broadside, even if all their twelve-pounders were worked on one side, threw but forty-eight pounds of metal; at short range the two brigs were able to throw six hundred and forty pounds at each broadside.

Perry could not have meant to fight at a distance, nor could Commander Elliott have thought it good seamanship. Yet Perry alone acted on this evident scheme; and though his official account showed that he had himself fought at close range, and that he ordered the other commanders to do the same, it gave no sufficient reasons to explain what prevented the whole fleet from acting together, and made the result doubtful. He did not even mention that he himself led the line in the "Lawrence," with two gunboats, the "Ariel" and the "Scorpion," supporting him, the "Caledonia," "Niagara," and three gunboats following. The "Lawrence" came within range of the British line just at noon, the wind being very light, the Lake calm, and Barclay, in the "Detroit," opposite. Perry's report began at that point: —

"At fifteen minutes before twelve the enemy commenced firing; at five minutes before twelve the action commenced on our part. Finding their fire very destructive, owing to their long guns, and its being mostly directed to the 'Lawrence,' I made sail (at quarter-past twelve) and directed the other vessels to follow, for the purpose of closing with the enemy. Every brace and bowline being shot away, she became unmanageable, notwithstanding the great exertions of the sailing-master. In this situation she sustained the action upwards of two hours, within canister-shot distance, until every gun was rendered useless, and a greater part of the crew either killed or wounded. Finding she could no longer annoy the enemy, I left her in charge of Lieutenant Yarnall, who, I was convinced from the bravery already displayed by him, would do what would comport with the honor of the flag. At half-past two, the wind springing up, Captain Elliott was enabled to bring his vessel, the 'Niagara,' gallantly into close action. I immediately went on board of her, when he anticipated my wish by volunteering to bring the schooners, which had been kept astern by the lightness of the wind, into close action. . . . At forty-five minutes past two the signal was made for 'close action.' The 'Niagara' being very little injured, I determined to pass through the enemy's line; bore up, and passed ahead of their two ships and a brig, giving a raking fire to them from the starboard guns, and to a large schooner and sloop, from the larboard side, at half pistol-shot distance. The smaller vessels at this time having got within grape and canister distance, under the direction of Captain Elliott, and keeping up a well-directed fire, the two ships, a brig, and a schooner surrendered, a schooner and sloop making a vain attempt to escape."

From this reticent report, any careful reader could see that for some reason, not so distinctly given as would have been the case if the wind alone were at fault, the action had been very badly fought on the American side. The British official account confirmed the impression given by Perry. Barclay's story was as well told as his action was well fought: —

"At a quarter before twelve I commenced the action by a few long guns; about a quarter-past, the American commodore, also supported by two schooners, . . . came to close action with the 'Detroit.' The other brig [the 'Niagara'] of the enemy, apparently destined to engage the 'Queen Charlotte,' kept so far to windward as to render the 'Queen Charlotte's' twenty-four pounder carronades useless, while she was, with the 'Lady Prevost,' exposed to the heavy and destructive fire of the 'Caledonia' and four other schooners, armed with heavy and long guns. . . . The action continued with great fury until half-past two, when I perceived my opponent [the 'Lawrence'] drop astern, and a boat passing from him to the 'Niagara,' which vessel was at this time perfectly fresh. The American commodore, seeing that as yet the day was against him, . . . made a noble and, alas! too successful an effort to regain it; for he bore up, and supported by his small vessels, passed within pistol-shot and took a raking position on our bow. . . . The weather-gage gave the enemy a prodigious advantage, as it enabled them not only to choose their position, but their distance also, which they [the 'Caledonia,' 'Niagara,' and the gunboats] did in such a manner as to prevent the carronades of the 'Queen Charlotte' and 'Lady Prevost' from having much effect, while their long ones did great execution, particularly against the 'Queen Charlotte.' "

Barclay's report, agreeing with Perry's, made it clear that

while Perry and the head of the American line fought at close quarters, the "Caledonia," "Niagara," and the four gunboats supporting them preferred fighting at long range,—not because they wanted wind, but because the "Caledonia" and gunboats were armed with long thirty-two and twenty-four pounders, while the British vessels opposed to them had only one or two long twelve-pounders. Certainly the advantage in this respect on the side of the American brig and gunboats was enormous; but these tactics threw the "Niagara," which had not the same excuse, out of the battle, leaving her, from twelve o'clock till half-past two, firing only two twelve-pound guns, while her heavy armament was useless, and might as well have been left ashore. Worse than this, the persistence of the "Caledonia," "Niagara," and their gunboats in keeping beyond range of their enemies' carronades nearly lost the battle, by allowing the British to concentrate on the "Lawrence" all their heavy guns, and in the end compelling the "Lawrence" to strike. On all these points no reasonable doubt could exist. The two reports were the only official sources of information on which an opinion as to the merits of the action could properly be founded. No other account, contemporaneous and authoritative, threw light on the subject, except a letter by Lieutenant Yarnall, second in command to Perry on the "Lawrence," written September 15, and published in the Ohio newspapers about September 29,—in which Yarnall said that if Elliott had brought his ship into action when the signal was given, the battle would have ended in much less time, and with less loss to the "Lawrence." This statement agreed with the tenor of the two official reports.

Furious as the battle was, a more furious dispute raged over it when in the year 1834 the friends of Perry and of Elliott wrangled over the action. With their dispute history need not concern itself. The official reports left no reasonable doubt that Perry's plan of battle was correct; that want of wind was not the reason it failed; but that the "Niagara" was badly managed by Elliott, and that the victory, when actually forfeited by this mismanagement, was saved by the personal energy of Perry, who, abandoning his own ship, brought the "Niagara" through the enemy's line, and regained the advantage of her heavy battery. The luck which attended Perry's career on the Lake saved him from injury, when every other officer on the two opposing flagships and four-fifths of his crew were killed or wounded, and enabled him to perform a feat almost without parallel in naval warfare, giving him a well-won immortality by means of the disaster unnecessarily incurred. No process of argument or ingenuity of seamanship could deprive Perry of the fame justly given him by the public, or detract from the splendor of his reputation as the hero of the war. More than any other battle of the time, the victory on Lake Erie was won by the courage and obstinacy of a single man.

Between two opponents such as Perry and Barclay, no one doubted that the ships were fought to their utmost. Of the "Lawrence" not much was left; ship, officers, and crew were shot to pieces. Such carnage was not known on the ocean, for even the cockpit where the sick and wounded lay, being above water, was riddled by shot, and the wounded were wounded again on the surgeon's board. Of one hundred and three effectives on the "Lawrence," twenty-two were killed and sixty-one wounded. The brig herself when she struck was a wreck, unmanageable, her starboard bulwarks beaten in, guns dismounted, and rigging cut to pieces. The British ships were in hardly better condition. The long guns of the gunboats had raked them with destructive effect. Barclay was desperately wounded; Finnis was killed; Barclay's first lieutenant was mortally wounded; not one commander or second in command could keep the deck; the squadron had forty-one men killed and ninety-four wounded, or nearly one man in three; the "Detroit" and "Queen Charlotte" were unmanageable and fell foul; the "Lady Prevost" was crippled, and drifted out of the fight. Perry could console himself with the thought that if his ship had struck her flag, she had at least struck to brave men.

Chapter VI

G ENERAL HARRISON, waiting at Seneca on the Sandusky
River, received, September 12, Perry's famous despatch
of September 10: "We have met the enemy, and they are
ours." The navy having done its work, the army was next to
act.

The force under Harrison's command was ample for the
required purpose, although it contained fewer regular troops
than Armstrong had intended. The seven regular regiments
assigned to Harrison fell short in numbers of the most moderate expectations. Instead of providing seven thousand
rank-and-file, the recruiting service ended in producing
rather more than twenty-five hundred.[1] Divided into two
brigades under Brigadier-Generals McArthur and Lewis
Cass, with a light corps under Lieutenant-Colonel Ball of
the Light Dragoons, they formed only one wing of Harrison's army.

To supply his main force, Harrison had still to depend on
Kentucky; and once more that State made a great effort. Governor Shelby took the field in person, leading three thousand
volunteers,[2] organized in eleven regiments, five brigades, and
two divisions. Besides the militia, who volunteered for this
special purpose, Harrison obtained the services of another
Kentucky corps, which had already proved its efficiency.

One of Armstrong's happiest acts, at the beginning of his
service as War Secretary,[3] was to accept the aid of Richard M.
Johnson in organizing for frontier defence a mounted regiment of a thousand men, armed with muskets or rifles, tom-
ahawks, and knives.[4] Johnson and his regiment took the
field about June 1, and from that time anxiety on account of
Indians ceased. The regiment patrolled the district from Fort
Wayne to the river Raisin, and whether in marching or fighting proved to be the most efficient corps in the Western country. Harrison obtained the assistance of Johnson's regiment

[1] McAffee, p. 334.
[2] Harrison to Meigs, Oct. 11, 1813; Official Letters, p. 239.
[3] Armstrong, i. 171, *note*; McAffee, p. 286.
[4] R. M. Johnson to Armstrong, Dec. 22, 1834; Armstrong, i. 232.

for the movement into Canada, and thereby increased the efficiency of his army beyond the proportion of Johnson's numbers.

While the mounted regiment moved by the road to Detroit, Harrison's main force was embarked in boats September 20, and in the course of a few days some forty-five hundred infantry were safely conveyed by way of Bass Island and Put-in-Bay to Middle Sister Island, about twelve miles from the Canadian shore.[1] Harrison and Perry then selected a landing place, and the whole force was successfully set ashore, September 27, about three miles below Malden.

Although Proctor could not hope to maintain himself at Malden or Detroit without control of the Lake, he had still the means of rendering Harrison's possession insecure. According to the British account, he commanded at Detroit and Malden a force of nine hundred and eighty-six regulars, giving about eight hundred effectives.[2] Not less than thirty-five hundred Indian warriors had flocked to Amherstburg, and although they greatly increased the British general's difficulties by bringing their families with them, they might be formidable opponents to Harrison's advance. Every motive dictated to Proctor the necessity of resisting Harrison's approach. To Tecumthe and his Indians the evacuation of Malden and Detroit without a struggle meant not only the sacrifice of their cause, but also cowardice; and when Proctor announced to them, September 18, that he meant to retreat, Tecumthe rose in the council and protested against the flight, likening Proctor to a fat dog that had carried its tail erect, and now that it was frightened dropped its tail between its legs and ran.[3] He told Proctor to go if he liked, but the Indians would remain.

Proctor insisted upon retiring at least toward the Moravian town, seventy miles on the road to Lake Ontario, and the Indians yielded. The troops immediately began to burn or destroy the public property at Detroit and Malden, or to load on wagons or boats what could not be carried away. September 24, three days before Harrison's army landed, the British evacuated Malden and withdrew to Sandwich, allowing

---

[1] Perry to Secretary Jones, Sept. 24, 1813; Official Letters, p. 215.
[2] James, i. 269.
[3] Richardson, p. 119.

Harrison to establish himself at Malden without a skirmish, and neglecting to destroy the bridge over the Canards River. Harrison was surprised at Proctor's tame retreat.

"Nothing but infatuation," he reported,[1] "could have governed General Proctor's conduct. The day that I landed below Malden he had at his disposal upward of three thousand Indian warriors; his regular force reinforced by the militia of the district would have made his number nearly equal to my aggregate, which on the day of landing did not exceed forty-five hundred . . . His inferior officers say that his conduct has been a series of continued blunders."

This crowning proof of Proctor's incapacity disorganized his force. Tecumthe expressed a general sentiment of the British army in his public denunciation of Proctor's cowardice. One of the inferior British officers afterward declared that Proctor's "marked inefficiency" and "wanton sacrifice" of the troops raised more than a doubt not only of his capacity but even of his personal courage, and led to serious thoughts of taking away his authority.[2] The British at Sandwich went through the same experience that marked the retreat of Hull and his army from the same spot, only the year before.

Harrison on his side made no extreme haste to pursue. His army marched into Malden at four o'clock on the afternoon of September 27,[3] and he wrote to Secretary Armstrong that evening: "I will pursue the enemy to-morrow, although there is no probability of my overtaking him, as he has upwards of a thousand horses, and we have not one in the army."[4] The pursuit was not rapid. Sandwich, opposite Detroit, was only thirteen miles above Malden, but Harrison required two days to reach it, arriving at two o'clock on the afternoon of September 29. From there, September 30, he wrote again to Secretary Armstrong that he was preparing to pursue the enemy on the following day;[5] but he waited for R. M. Johnson's

---

[1] Harrison to Meigs, Oct. 11, 1813; Official Letters, p. 239.
[2] Richardson, pp. 126, 133, 134.
[3] Perry to Secretary Jones, Sept. 27, 1813; Official Letters, p. 220.
[4] Harrison to Armstrong, Sept. 27, 1813; Dawson, p. 421.
[5] Harrison to Armstrong, Oct. 9, 1813; Official Letters, p. 233.

mounted regiment, which arrived at Detroit September 30, and was obliged to consume a day in crossing the river. Then the pursuit began with energy, but on the morning of October 2 Proctor had already a week's advance and should have been safe.

Proctor seemed to imagine that the Americans would not venture to pursue him. Moving, according to his own report,[1] "by easy marches," neither obstructing the road in his rear nor leaving detachments to delay the enemy, he reached Dolson's October 1, and there halted his army, fifty miles from Sandwich, while he went to the Moravian town some twenty-six miles beyond. He then intended to make a stand at Chatham, three miles behind Dolson's.

> "I had assured the Indians," said Proctor's report of October 23, "that we would not desert them, and it was my full determination to have made a stand at the Forks (Chatham), by which our vessels and stores would be protected; but after my arrival at Dover [Dolson's] three miles lower down the river, I was induced to take post there first, where ovens had been constructed, and where there was some shelter for the troops, and had accordingly directed that it should be put into the best possible state of defence that time and circumstances would admit of; indeed it had been my intention to have opposed the enemy nearer the mouth of the river, had not the troops contrary to my intention been moved, during my absence of a few hours for the purpose of acquiring some knowledge of the country in my rear."

The British army, left at Dolson's October 1, without a general or orders,[2] saw the American army arrive in its front, October 3, and retired three miles to Chatham, where the Indians insisted upon fighting; but when, the next morning, October 4, the Americans advanced in order of battle,[3] the Indians after a skirmish changed their minds and retreated. The British were compelled to sacrifice the supplies they had brought by water to Chatham for establishing their new base,

[1] Report of Oct. 23, 1813; MSS. British Archives. Lower Canada, vol. cxxiii.
[2] Richardson, pp. 133, 134.
[3] Harrison's Report, Oct. 9, 1813; Official Letters, p. 234.

and their retreat precipitated on the Moravian town the confusion of flight already resembling rout.

Six miles on their way they met General Proctor returning from the Moravian town, and as much dissatisfied with them as they with him. Pressed closely by the American advance, the British troops made what haste they could over excessively bad roads until eight o'clock in the evening, when they halted within six miles of the Moravian town.[1] The next morning, October 5, the enemy was again reported to be close at hand, and the British force again retreated. About a mile and a half from the Moravian town it was halted. Proctor had then retired as far as he could, and there he must either fight, or abandon women and children, sick and wounded, baggage, stores, and wagons, desert his Indian allies, and fly to Lake Ontario. Probably flight would not have saved his troops. More than a hundred miles of unsettled country lay between them and their next base. The Americans had in their advance the mounted regiment of R. M. Johnson, and could outmarch the most lightly equipped British regulars. Already, according to Proctor's report, the rapidity of the Americans had destroyed the efficiency of the British organization:[2] —

"In the attempt to save provisions we became encumbered with boats not suited to the state of navigation. The Indians and the troops retreated on different sides of the river, and the boats to which sufficient attention had not been given became particularly exposed to the fire of the enemy who were advancing on the side the Indians were retiring, and most unfortunately fell into possession of the enemy, and with them several of the men, provisions, and all the ammunition that had not been issued to the troops and Indians. This disastrous circumstance afforded the enemy the means of crossing and advancing on both sides of the river. Finding the enemy were advancing too near I resolved to meet him, being strong in cavalry, in a wood below the Moravian town, which last was not cleared of Indian women and children, or of those the troops, nor of the sick."

[1] Narrative of Lieutenant Bullock, Dec. 6, 1813; Richardson, p. 137.
[2] Proctor's Report of Oct. 23, 1813; MSS. British Archives.

The whole British force was then on the north bank of the river Thames, retreating eastward by a road near the river bank. Proctor could hardly claim to have exercised choice in the selection of a battleground, unless he preferred placing his little force under every disadvantage. "The troops were formed with their left to the river," his report continued, "with a reserve and a six-pounder on the road, near the river; the Indians on the right." According to the report of officers of the Forty-first regiment, two lines of troops were formed in a thick forest, two hundred yards apart. The first line began where the six-pound field-piece stood, with a range of some fifty yards along the road. A few Canadian Light Dragoons were stationed near the gun. To the left of the road was the river; to the right a forest, free from underbrush that could stop horsemen, but offering cover to an approaching enemy within twenty paces of the British line.[1] In the wood about two hundred men of the British Forty-first took position as well as they could, behind trees, and there as a first line they waited some two hours for their enemy to appear.

The second line, somewhat less numerous, two hundred yards behind the first, and not within sight, was also formed in the wood; and on the road, in rear of the second line, Proctor and his staff stationed themselves. The Indians were collected behind a swamp on the right, touching and covering effectually the British right flank, while the river covered the left.

Such a formation was best fitted for Harrison's purposes, but the mere arrangement gave little idea of Proctor's weakness. The six-pound field-piece, which as he afterward reported "certainly should have produced the best effect if properly managed," had not a round of ammunition, and could not be fired.[2] The Forty-first regiment was almost mutinous, but had it been in the best condition it could not have held against serious attack. The whole strength of the Forty-first was only three hundred and fifty-six rank-and-file, or four hundred and eight men all told.[3] The numbers of the regiment actually in the field were reported as three hundred

[1] Richardson, pp. 122, 139.
[2] Richardson, p. 136.
[3] James, i. 278.

and fifteen rank-and-file, or three hundred and sixty-seven men all told.[1] The dragoons were supposed not to exceed twenty. This petty force was unable to see either the advancing enemy or its own members. The only efficient corps in the field was the Indians, who were estimated by the British sometimes at five hundred, at eight hundred, and twelve hundred in number, and who were in some degree covered by the swamp.

Harrison came upon the British line soon after two o'clock in the afternoon, and at once formed his army in regular order of battle. As the order was disregarded, and the battle was fought, as he reported, in a manner "not sanctioned by anything that I had seen or heard of,"[2] the intended arrangement mattered little. In truth, the battle was planned as well as fought by Richard M. Johnson, whose energy impressed on the army a new character from the moment he joined it. While Harrison drew up his infantry in order of battle, Johnson, whose mounted regiment was close to the British line, asked leave to charge,[3] and Harrison gave him the order, although he knew no rule of war that sanctioned it.

Johnson's tactics were hazardous, though effective. Giving to his brother, James Johnson, half the regiment to lead up the road against the six-pound gun and the British Forty-first regiment, R. M. Johnson with the other half of his regiment wheeled to the left, at an angle with the road, and crossed the swamp to attack twice his number of Indians posted in a thick wood.

James Johnson, with his five hundred men, galloped directly through the British first line,[4] receiving a confused fire, and passing immediately to the rear of the British second line, so rapidly as almost to capture Proctor himself, who fled at full speed.[5] As the British soldiers straggled in bands or singly toward the rear, they found themselves among the American mounted riflemen, and had no choice but to surrender. About fifty men, with a single lieutenant,

[1] Report of Lieutenant Bullock, Dec. 6, 1813; Richardson, p. 140.
[2] Harrison's Report of Oct. 9, 1813; Official Letters, p. 233.
[3] R. M. Johnson to Armstrong, Dec. 22, 1834; Armstrong's Notices, i. 232.
[4] Report of Lieutenant Bullock, Dec. 6, 1813; Richardson, p. 140.
[5] Richardson, p. 136.

A. B. Advance Guard on foot at head of 5 Collumns—the 1st Battalion of the mounted Regiments.

C D. Capt. Stocker's Comp. of 100 men on foot at head of 2 Collumns

NOTE: five Brigades & Reserved Corps, Governor Shelbys troops

G. D. E. represents the whole of the 2d Battalion after I was wounded & finding it impracticable on account of logs & the thickness of the woods to break through the Indian line & form in their rear, I ordered the men to dismount & fight the Indians in their own way; part of the time the Indians contended for the ground at the 2d Swamp.

Indian line

3d Swamp

2d Swamp

Brigade

Indian line

Bruk line

Reserve line

Brigade

Brigade

1st Swamp

Charging Collumns

Brigade

Brigade

3rd Brigade

River Thames

ACCOMPANYING COL. R. M. JOHNSON'S LETTER OF NOV. 21st 1813, DETAILING THE AFFAIR OF THE 5th AT THE RIVER THAMES, ETC.—WAR DEPARTMENT ARCHIVES, MSS.

contrived to escape through the woods; all the rest became prisoners.

R. M. Johnson was less fortunate. Crossing the swamp to his left, he was received by the Indians in underbrush which the horses could not penetrate. Under a sharp fire his men were obliged to dismount and fight at close quarters. At an early moment of the battle, Johnson was wounded by the rifle of an Indian warrior who sprang forward to despatch him, but was killed by a ball from Johnson's pistol. The fighting at that point was severe, but Johnson's men broke or turned the Indian line, which was uncovered after the British defeat, and driving the Indians toward the American left, brought them under fire of Shelby's infantry, when they fled.

In this contest Johnson maintained that his regiment was alone engaged. In a letter to Secretary Armstrong, dated six weeks after the battle, he said:[1] —

> "I send you an imperfect sketch of the late battle on the river Thames, fought solely by the mounted regiment; at least, so much so that not fifty men from any other corps assisted. . . . Fought the Indians, twelve hundred or fifteen hundred men, one hour and twenty minutes, driving them from the extreme right to the extreme left of my line, at which last point we came near Governor Shelby, who ordered Colonel Simrall to reinforce me; but the battle was over, and although the Indians were pursued half a mile, there was no fighting."

Harrison's official report gave another idea of the relative share taken by the Kentucky infantry in the action; but the difference in dispute was trifling. The entire American loss was supposed to be only about fifteen killed and thirty wounded. The battle lasted, with sharpness, not more than twenty minutes; and none but the men under Johnson's command enjoyed opportunity to share in the first and most perilous assault.

The British loss was only twelve men killed and thirty-six wounded. The total number of British prisoners taken on the field and in the Moravian town, or elsewhere on the day of

[1] R. M. Johnson to Armstrong, Nov. 21, 1813; MSS. War Department Archives.

battle, was four hundred and seventy-seven; in the whole campaign, six hundred. All Proctor's baggage, artillery, small arms, stores, and hospital were captured in the Moravian town. The Indians left thirty-three dead on the field, among them one reported to be Tecumthe. After the battle several officers of the British Forty-first, well acquainted with the Shawnee warrior, visited the spot, and identified his body. The Kentuckians had first recognized it, and had cut long strips of skin from the thighs, to keep, as was said, for razor-straps, in memory of the river Raisin.[1]

After Perry's victory on Lake Erie, Tecumthe's life was of no value to himself or his people, and his death was no subject for regret; but the manner chosen for producing this result was an expensive mode of acquiring territory for the United States. The Shawnee warrior compelled the government to pay for once something like the value of the lands it took. The precise cost of the Indian war could not be estimated, being combined in many ways with that of the war with England; but the British counted for little, within the northwestern territory, except so far as Tecumthe used them for his purposes. Not more than seven or eight hundred British soldiers ever crossed the Detroit River; but the United States raised fully twenty thousand men, and spent at least five million dollars and many lives in expelling them. The Indians alone made this outlay necessary. The campaign of Tippecanoe, the surrender of Detroit and Mackinaw, the massacres at Fort Dearborn, the river Raisin, and Fort Meigs, the murders along the frontier, and the campaign of 1813 were the price paid for the Indian lands in the Wabash Valley.

No part of the war more injured British credit on the American continent than the result of the Indian alliance. Except the capture of Detroit and Mackinaw at the outset, without fighting, and the qualified success at the river Raisin, the British suffered only mortifications, ending with the total loss of their fleet, the abandonment of their fortress, the flight of their army, and the shameful scene before the Moravian town, where four hundred British regulars allowed themselves to be ridden over and captured by five hundred Kentucky horsemen, with

[1] Richardson, p. 125. Lewis Cass to Armstrong, Oct. 28, 1813; MSS. War Department Archives.

hardly the loss of a man to the assailants. After such a disgrace the British ceased to be formidable in the northwest. The Indians recognized the hopelessness of their course, and from that moment abandoned their dependence on England.

The battle of the Thames annihilated the right division of the British army in Upper Canada. When the remnants of Proctor's force were mustered, October 17, at Ancaster, a hundred miles from the battlefield, about two hundred rank-and-file were assembled.[1] Proctor made a report of the battle blaming his troops, and Prevost issued a severe reprimand to the unfortunate Forty-first regiment on the strength of Proctor's representations. In the end the Prince Regent disgraced both officers, recognizing by these public acts the loss of credit the government had suffered; but its recovery was impossible.

So little anxiety did General Harrison thenceforward feel about the Eighth Military District which he commanded, that he returned to Detroit October 7; his army followed him, and arrived at Sandwich, October 10, without seeing an enemy. Promptly discharged, the Kentucky Volunteers marched homeward October 14; the mounted regiment and its wounded colonel followed a few days later, and within a fortnight only two brigades of the regular army remained north of the Maumee.

At Detroit the war was closed, and except for two or three distant expeditions was not again a subject of interest. The Indians were for the most part obliged to remain within the United States jurisdiction. The great number of Indian families that had been collected about Detroit and Malden were rather a cause for confidence than fear, since they were in effect hostages, and any violence committed by the warriors would have caused them, their women and children, to be deprived of food and to perish of starvation. Detroit was full of savages dependent on army supplies, and living on the refuse and offal of the slaughter-yard; but their military strength was gone. Some hundreds of the best warriors followed Proctor to Lake Ontario, but Tecumthe's northwestern confederacy was broken up, and most of the tribes made submission.

[1] Return of Right Division, Richardson, p. 129.

Chapter VII

THE NEW SECRETARIES of War and Navy who took office in January, 1813, were able in the following October to show Detroit recovered. Nine months solved the problem of Lake Erie. The problem of Lake Ontario remained insoluble.

In theory nothing was simpler than the conquest of Upper Canada. Six months before war was declared, Jan. 2, 1812, John Armstrong, then a private citizen, wrote to Secretary Eustis a letter containing the remark,—

"In invading a neighboring and independent territory like Canada, having a frontier of immense extent; destitute of means strictly its own for the purposes of defence; separated from the rest of the empire by an ocean, and having to this but one outlet,—this outlet forms your true object or point of attack."

The river St. Lawrence was the true object of attack, and the Canadians hardly dared hope to defend it.

"From St. Regis to opposite Kingston," said the Quebec "Gazette" in 1814, "the southern bank of the river belongs to the United States. It is well known that this river is the only communication between Upper and Lower Canada. It is rapid and narrow in many places. A few cannon judiciously posted, or even musketry, could render the communication impracticable without powerful escorts, wasting and parcelling the force applicable to the defence of the provinces. It is needless to say that no British force can remain in safety or maintain itself in Upper Canada without a ready communication with the lower province."

Closure of the river anywhere must compel the submission of the whole country above, which could not provide its supplies. The American, who saw his own difficulties of transport between New York and the Lakes, thought well of his energy in surmounting them; but as the war took larger proportions, and great fleets were built on Lake Ontario, the difficulties of Canadian transport became insuperable. Toward the close of the war, Sir George Prevost wrote to Lord Bathurst[1] that six thirty-two-pound guns for the fleet, hauled in winter four hundred miles from Quebec to Kingston, would cost at least £2000 for transport. Forty twenty-four-pounders hauled on the snow had cost £4,800; a cable of the largest size hauled from Sorel to Kingston, two hundred and fifty-five miles, cost £1000 for transport. In summer, when the river was open, the difficulties were hardly less. The commissary-general reported that the impediments of navigation were incalculable, and the scarcity of workmen, laborers, and voyageurs not to be described.[2]

If these reasons for attacking and closing the river St. Lawrence had not been decisive with the United States government, other reasons were sufficient. The political motive was as strong as the military. Americans, especially in New England, denied that treasonable intercourse existed with Canada; but intercourse needed not to be technically treasonable in order to have the effects of treason. Sir George Prevost wrote to Lord Bathurst, Aug. 27, 1814,[3] when the war had lasted two years,—

"Two thirds of the army in Canada are at this moment eating beef provided by American contractors, drawn principally from the States of Vermont and New York. This circumstance, as well as that of the introduction of large sums of specie into this province, being notorious in the United States, it is to be expected Congress will take steps to deprive us of those resources, and under that apprehension large droves are daily crossing the lines coming into Lower Canada."

This state of things had then lasted during three campaigns, from the beginning of the war. The Indians at Malden, the British army at Niagara, the naval station at Kingston were largely fed by the United States. If these supplies could be stopped, Upper Canada must probably fall; and they could be

---

[1] Prevost to Bathurst, Feb. 14, 1815; MSS. British Archives.

[2] W. H. Robinson to Prevost, Aug. 27, 1814; MSS. British Archives.

[3] Prevost to Bathurst, Aug. 27, 1814; MSS. British Archives, Lower Canada, vol. cxxviii. no. 190.

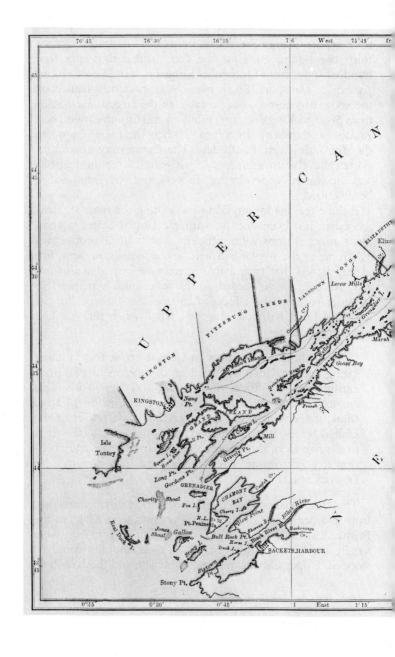

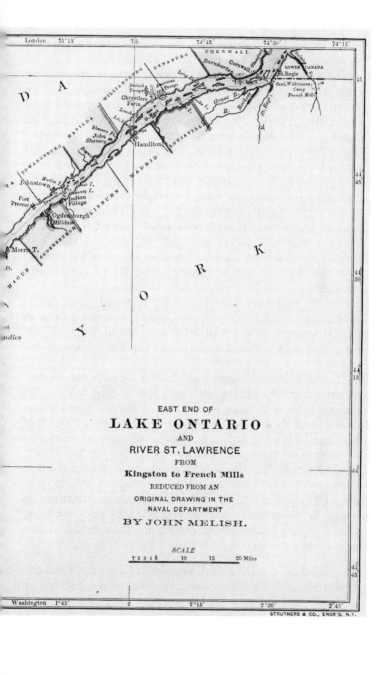

EAST END OF

LAKE ONTARIO

AND

RIVER ST. LAWRENCE

FROM

Kingston to French Mills

REDUCED FROM AN

ORIGINAL DRAWING IN THE
NAVAL DEPARTMENT

BY JOHN MELISH.

SCALE

1 2 3 4 5   10   15   20 Miles

easily stopped by interrupting the British line of transport anywhere on the St. Lawrence.

The task was not difficult. Indeed, early in the war an enterprising officer of irregulars, Major Benjamin Forsyth, carried on a troublesome system of annoyance from Ogdensburg, which Sir George Prevost treated with extreme timidity.[1] The British commandant at Prescott, Major Macdonnell, was not so cautious as the governor-general, but crossed the river on the ice with about five hundred men, drove Forsyth from the town, destroyed the public property, and retired in safety with a loss of eight killed and fifty-two wounded.[2] This affair, Feb. 23, 1813, closed hostilities in that region, and Major Forsyth was soon ordered to Sackett's Harbor. His experience, and that of Major Macdonnell, proved how easy the closure of such a river must be, exposed as it was for two hundred miles to the fire of cannon and musketry.

The St. Lawrence was therefore the proper point of approach and attack against Upper Canada. Armstrong came to the Department of War with that idea fixed in his mind. The next subject for his consideration was the means at his disposal.

During Monroe's control of the War Department for two months, between Dec. 3, 1812, and Feb. 5, 1813, much effort had been made to increase the army. Monroe wrote to the chairman of the Military Committee Dec. 22, 1812, a sketch of his ideas.[3] He proposed to provide for the general defence by dividing the United States into military districts, and apportioning ninety-three hundred and fifty men among them as garrisons. For offensive operations he required a force competent to overpower the British defence, and in estimating his wants, he assumed that Canada contained about twelve thousand British regulars, besides militia, and three thousand men at Halifax.

"To demolish the British force from Niagara to Quebec," said Monroe, " would require, to make the thing secure, an

[1] James, i. 140.
[2] Report of Major Macdonnell, Feb. 23, 1813; James, i. Appendix no. 16.
[3] State Papers, Military Affairs, i. 608.

efficient regular army of twenty thousand men, with an army of reserve of ten thousand. . . . If the government could raise and keep in the field thirty-five thousand regular troops, . . . the deficiency to be supplied even to authorize an expedition against Halifax would be inconsiderable. Ten thousand men would be amply sufficient; but there is danger of not being able to raise that force, and to keep it at that standard. . . . My idea is that provision ought to be made for raising twenty thousand men in addition to the present establishment."

Congress voted about fifty-eight thousand men, and after deducting ten thousand for garrisons, counted on forty-eight thousand for service in Canada. When Armstrong took control, Feb. 5, 1813, he began at once to devise a plan of operation for the army which by law numbered fifty-eight thousand men, and in fact numbered, including the staff and regimental officers, eighteen thousand nine hundred and forty-five men, according to the returns in the adjutant-general's office February 16, 1813. Before he had been a week in the War Department, he wrote, February 10, to Major-General Dearborn announcing that four thousand men were to be immediately collected at Sackett's Harbor, and three thousand at Buffalo. April 1, or as soon as navigation opened, the four thousand troops at Sackett's Harbor were to be embarked and transported in boats under convoy of the fleet across the Lake at the mouth of the St. Lawrence, thirty-five miles, to Kingston. After capturing Kingston, with its magazines, navy-yards, and ships, the expedition was to proceed up the Lake to York (Toronto) and capture two vessels building there. Thence it was to join the corps of three thousand men at Buffalo, and attack the British on the Niagara River.[1]

In explaining his plan to the Cabinet, Armstrong pointed out that the attack from Lake Champlain on Montreal could not begin before May 1; that Kingston, between April 1 and May 15, was shut from support by ice; that not more than two thousand men could be gathered to defend it; and that by beginning the campaign against Kingston rather than

[1] Armstrong to Dearborn, Feb. 10, 1813; Armstrong's Notices, i. 221.

against Montreal, six weeks' time would be gained before reinforcements could arrive from England.[1]

Whatever defects the plan might have, Kingston, and Kingston alone, possessed so much military importance as warranted the movement. Evidently Armstrong had in mind no result short of the capture of Kingston.

Dearborn received these instructions at Albany, and replied, February 18, that nothing should be omitted on his part in endeavoring to carry into effect the expedition proposed.[2] Orders were given for concentrating the intended force at Sackett's Harbor. During the month of March the preparations were stimulated by a panic due to the appearance of Sir George Prevost at Prescott and Kingston. Dearborn hurried to Sackett's Harbor in person, under the belief that the governor-general was about to attack it.

Armstrong estimated the British force at Kingston as nine hundred regulars, or two thousand men all told; and his estimate was probably correct. The usual garrison at Kingston and Prescott was about eight hundred rank-and-file. In both the British and American services, the returns of rank-and-file were the ordinary gauge of numerical force. Rank-and-file included corporals, but not sergeants or commissioned officers; and an allowance of at least ten sergeants and officers was always to be made for every hundred rank-and-file, in order to estimate the true numerical strength of an army or garrison. Unless otherwise mentioned, the return excluded also the sick and disabled. The relative force of every army was given in effectives, or rank-and-file actually present for duty.

In the distribution of British forces in Canada for 1812–1813, the garrison at Prescott was allowed three hundred and seventy-six rank-and-file, with fifty-two officers including sergeants. To Kingston three hundred and eighty-four rank-and-file were allotted, with sixty officers including sergeants. To Montreal and the positions between Prescott and the St. John's River about five thousand rank-and-file were allotted.[3]

---

[1] Note presented to Cabinet, Feb. 8, 1813; Wilkinson's Memoirs, iii. Appendix xxvi.; State Papers, Military Affairs, i. 439.

[2] State Papers; Military Affairs, i. 440.

[3] Distribution of Forces in Canada; Canadian Archives, Freer Papers, 1812–1813, p. 47.

At Prescott and Kingston, besides the regular troops, the men employed in ship-building or other labor, the sailors, and the local militia were to be reckoned as part of the garrison, and Armstrong included them all in his estimate of two thousand men.

The British force should have been known to Dearborn nearly as well as his own. No considerable movement of troops between Lower and Upper Canada could occur without his knowledge. Yet Dearborn wrote to Armstrong, March 9, 1813, from Sackett's Harbor,[1] —

> "I have not yet had the honor of a visit from Sir George Prevost. His whole force is concentrated at Kingston, probably amounting to six or seven thousand,—about three thousand of them regular troops. The ice is good, and we expect him every day. . . . As soon as the fall [fate?] of this place [Sackett's Harbor] shall be decided, we shall be able to determine on other measures. If we hold this place, we will command the Lake, and be able to act in concert with the troops at Niagara."

A few days later, March 14, Dearborn wrote again.[2]

> "Sir George," he said, had "concluded that it is too late to attack this place. . . . We are probably just strong enough on each side to defend, but not in sufficient force to hazard an offensive movement. The difference of attacking and being attacked, as it regards the contiguous posts of Kingston and Sackett's Harbor, cannot be estimated at less than three or four thousand men, arising from the circumstance of militia acting merely on the defensive."

Clearly Dearborn did not approve Armstrong's plan, and wished to change it. In this idea he was supported, or instigated, by the naval commander on the Lake, Isaac Chauncey, a native of Connecticut, forty years of age, who entered the service in 1798 and became captain in 1806. Chauncey and Dearborn consulted together, and devised a new scheme, which Dearborn explained to Armstrong about March 20:[3] —

[1] Dearborn to Armstrong, March 9, 1813; State Papers, Military Affairs, i. 441.
[2] Dearborn to Armstrong, March 9, 1813; State Papers, Military Affairs, i. 442.
[3] State Papers, Military Affairs, i. 442.

"To take or destroy the armed vessels at York will give us the complete command of the Lake. Commodore Chauncey can take with him ten or twelve hundred troops to be commanded by Pike; take York; from thence proceed to Niagara and attack Fort George by land and water, while the troops at Buffalo cross over and carry Forts Erie and Chippewa, and join those at Fort George; and then collect our whole force for an attack on Kingston. After the most mature deliberation the above was considered by Commodore Chauncey and myself as the most certain of ultimate success."

Thus Dearborn and Chauncey inverted Armstrong's plan. Instead of attacking on the St. Lawrence, they proposed to attack on the Niagara. Armstrong acquiesced. "Taking for granted," as he did[1] on Dearborn's assertion, "that General Prevost . . . has assembled at Kingston a force of six or eight thousand men, as stated by you," he could not require that his own plan should be pursued. "The alteration in the plan of campaign so as to make Kingston the last object instead of making it the first, would appear to be necessary, or at least proper," he wrote to Dearborn, March 29.[2]

The scheme proposed by Dearborn and Chauncey was carried into effect by them. The contractors furnished new vessels, which gave to Chauncey for a time the control of the Lake. April 22 the troops, numbering sixteen hundred men, embarked. Armstrong insisted on only one change in the expedition, which betrayed perhaps a shade of malice, for he required Dearborn himself to command it, and Dearborn was suspected of shunning service in the field.

From the moment Dearborn turned away from the St. Lawrence and carried the war westward, the naval and military movements on Lake Ontario became valuable chiefly as a record of failure. The fleet and army arrived at York early in the morning of April 27. York, a village numbering in 1806, according to British account, more than three thousand inhabitants, was the capital of Upper Canada, and contained

---

[1] Armstrong to Dearborn, April 19, 1813; State Papers, Military Affairs, i. 442.

[2] State Papers, Military Affairs, i. 442.

the residence of the lieutenant-governor and the two brick buildings where the Legislature met. For military purposes the place was valueless, but it had been used for the construction of a few war-vessels, and Chauncey represented, through Dearborn, that "to take or destroy the armed vessels at York will give us the complete command of the Lake." The military force at York, according to British account, did not exceed six hundred men, regulars and militia; and of these, one hundred and eighty men, or two companies of the Eighth or King's regiment, happened to be there only in passing.[1]

Under the fire of the fleet and riflemen, Pike's brigade was set ashore; the British garrison, after a sharp resistance, was driven away, and the town capitulated. The ship on the stocks was burned; the ten-gun brig "Gloucester" was made prize; the stores were destroyed or shipped; some three hundred prisoners were taken; and the public buildings, including the houses of Assembly, were burned. The destruction of the Assembly houses, afterward alleged as ground for retaliation against the capitol at Washington, was probably the unauthorized act of private soldiers. Dearborn protested that it was done without his knowledge and against his orders.[2]

The success cost far more than it was worth. The explosion of a powder magazine, near which the American advance halted, injured a large number of men on both sides. Not less than three hundred and twenty Americans were killed or wounded in the battle or explosion,[3] or about one fifth of the entire force. General Pike, the best brigadier then in the service, was killed. Only two or three battles in the entire war were equally bloody.[4] "Unfortunately the enemy's armed ship the 'Prince Regent,' " reported Dearborn,[5] "left this place for Kingston four days before we arrived."

Chauncey and Dearborn crossed to Niagara, while the troops remained some ten days at York, and were then disem-

[1] James, i. 143, 149.
[2] Letter of Dearborn, Oct. 17, 1814; Niles, viii. 36.
[3] Niles, iv. 238.
[4] Table of Land Battles; Niles, x. 154.
[5] Dearborn to Armstrong, April 28, 1813; State Papers, Military Affairs, i. 443.

barked at Niagara, May 8, according to Dearborn's report, "in a very sickly and depressed state; a large proportion of the officers and men were sickly and debilitated."[1] Nothing was ready for the movement which was to drive the British from Fort George, and before active operations could begin, Dearborn fell ill. The details of command fell to his chief-of-staff, Colonel Winfield Scott.

The military organization at Niagara was at best unfortunate. One of Secretary Armstrong's earliest measures was to issue the military order previously arranged by Monroe, dividing the Union into military districts. Vermont and the State of New York north of the highlands formed the Ninth Military District, under Major-General Dearborn. In the Ninth District were three points of activity,—Plattsburg on Lake Champlain, Sackett's Harbor on Lake Ontario, and the Niagara River. Each point required a large force and a commander of the highest ability; but in May, 1813, Plattsburg and Sackett's Harbor were denuded of troops and officers, who were all drawn to Niagara, where they formed three brigades, commanded by Brigadier-Generals John P. Boyd, who succeeded Pike, John Chandler, and W. H. Winder. Niagara and the troops in its neighborhood were under the command of Major-General Morgan Lewis, a man of ability, but possessing neither the youth nor the energy to lead an army in the field, while Boyd, Chandler, and Winder were competent only to command regiments.

Winfield Scott in effect assumed control of the army, and undertook to carry out Van Rensselaer's plan of the year before for attacking Fort George in the rear, from the Lake. The task was not very difficult. Chauncey controlled the Lake, and his fleet was at hand to transfer the troops. Dearborn's force numbered certainly not less than four thousand rank-and-file present for duty. The entire British regular force on the Niagara River did not exceed eighteen hundred rank-and-file, and about five hundred militia.[2] At Fort George about one thousand regulars and three hundred militia were stationed, and the military object to be gained by the Americans was

[1] Dearborn to Armstrong, May 13, 1813; State Papers, Military Affairs, i. 444.

[2] James, i. p. 151.

not so much the capture of Fort George, which was then not defensible, as that of its garrison.

Early on the morning of May 27, when the mist cleared away, the British General Vincent saw Chauncey's fleet, "in an extended line of more than two miles," standing toward the shore. When the ships took position, "the fire from the shipping so completely enfiladed and scoured the plains, that it became impossible to approach the beach," and Vincent could only concentrate his force between the Fort and the enemy, waiting attack. Winfield Scott at the head of an advance division first landed, followed by the brigades of Boyd, Winder, and Chandler, and after a sharp skirmish drove the British back along the Lake shore, advancing under cover of the fleet. Vincent's report continued:[1] —

"After awaiting the approach of the enemy for about half an hour I received authentic information that his force, consisting of from four to five thousand men, had reformed his columns and was making an effort to turn my right flank. Having given orders for the fort to be evacuated, the guns to be spiked, and the ammunition destroyed, the troops under my command were put in motion, and marched across the country in a line parallel to the Niagara River, toward the position near the Beaver Dam beyond Queenston mountain. . . . Having assembled my whole force the following morning, which did not exceed sixteen hundred men, I continued my march toward the head of the Lake."

Vincent lost severely in proportion to his numbers, for fifty-one men were killed, and three hundred and five were wounded or missing, chiefly in the Eighth or King's regiment.[2] Several hundred militia were captured in his retreat. The American loss was about forty killed and one hundred and twenty wounded. According to General Morgan Lewis, Col. Winfield Scott "fought nine-tenths of the battle."[3] Dearborn watched the movements from the fleet.

[1] Vincent to Sir George Prevost, May 28, 1813; James, i. 407; Appendix no. 21.

[2] Return of killed, etc.; James, i. 410.

[3] Morgan Lewis to Armstrong, July 5, 1813; MSS. War Department Archives.

For a time this success made a deep impression on the military administration of Canada, and the abandonment of the whole country west of Kingston was thought inevitable.[1] The opportunity for achieving a decided advantage was the best that occurred for the Americans during the entire war; but whatever might be said in public, the battle of Fort George was a disappointment to the War Department[2] as well as to the officers in command of the American army, who had hoped to destroy the British force. The chief advantage gained was the liberation of Perry's vessels at Black Rock above the Falls, which enabled Perry to complete his fleet on Lake Erie.

On Lake Ontario, May 31, Chauncey insisted, not without cause, on returning to Sackett's Harbor. Dearborn, instead of moving with his whole force, ordered Brigadier-General Winder, June 1, to pursue Vincent. Winder, with eight hundred or a thousand men marched twenty miles, and then sent for reinforcements. He was joined, June 5, by General Chandler with another brigade. Chandler then took command, and advanced with a force supposed to number in the aggregate two thousand men[3] to Stony Creek, within ten miles of Vincent's position at Hamilton, where sixteen hundred British regulars were encamped. There Chandler and Winder posted themselves for the night, much as Winchester and his Kentuckians had camped at the river Raisin four months earlier.[4]

Vincent was not to be treated with such freedom. Taking only seven hundred rank-and-file,[5] he led them himself against Chandler's camp. The attack began, in intense darkness, at two o'clock in the morning of June 6. The British quickly broke the American centre and carried the guns. The lines became mixed, and extreme confusion lasted till dawn. In the darkness both American generals, Chandler and Winder, walked into the British force in the centre, and were

[1] James, i. 203.

[2] Armstrong to Dearborn, June 19, 1813; State Papers, Military Affairs, i. 449.

[3] Table of land battles; Niles, x. 154.

[4] Morgan Lewis to Armstrong, June 14, 1813; Official Letters, p. 165. Chandler to Dearborn, June 18, 1813; Official Letters, p. 169.

[5] Vincent to Prevost, June 6, 1813; James, i. p. 431.

captured.[1] With difficulty the two armies succeeded in recovering their order, and then retired in opposite directions. The British suffered severely, reporting twenty-three killed, one hundred and thirty-four wounded, and fifty-five missing, or two hundred and twelve men in all; but they safely regained Burlington Heights at dawn.[2] The American loss was less in casualties, for it amounted only to fifty-five killed and wounded, and one hundred missing; but in results the battle at Stony Creek was equally disgraceful and decisive. The whole American force, leaving the dead unburied, fell back ten miles, where Major-General Lewis took command in the afternoon of June 7. An hour later the British fleet under Sir James Yeo made its appearance, threatening to cut off Lewis's retreat. Indians hovered about. Boats and baggage were lost. Dearborn sent pressing orders to Lewis directing him to return, and on the morning of June 8 the division reached Fort George.[3]

These mortifications prostrated Dearborn, whose strength had been steadily failing. June 8 he wrote to Armstrong: "My ill state of health renders it extremely painful to attend to the current duties; and unless my health improves soon, I fear I shall be compelled to retire to some place where my mind may be more at ease for a short time."[4] June 10, his adjutant-general, Winfield Scott, issued orders devolving on Major-General Morgan Lewis the temporary command not only of the Niagara army but also of the Ninth Military district.[5] "In addition to the debility and fever he has been afflicted with," wrote Dearborn's aid, S. S. Connor, to Secretary Armstrong, June 12,[6] "he has, within the last twenty-four hours, experienced a violent spasmodic attack on his breast, which has obliged him to relinquish business altogether." "I have doubts whether he will ever again be fit for service," wrote Morgan Lewis to Armstrong, June 14;[7] "he has been repeatedly in a

[1] Chandler's Report of June 18, 1813; State Papers, Military Affairs, i. p. 448.

[2] Report of Colonel Harvey, June 6, 1813; Canadiana, April, 1889. Report of General Vincent, June 6, 1813; James, i. p. 431.

[3] Morgan Lewis to Armstrong, June 14 (8?), 1813; Official Letters, p. 165.

[4] State Papers; Military Affairs, i. 445.

[5] State Papers; Military Affairs, i. 447.

[6] State Papers; Military Affairs, i. 448.

[7] State Papers; Military Affairs, i. 446.

state of convalescence, but relapses on the least agitation of mind." June 20 Dearborn himself wrote in a very despondent spirit both in regard to his health and to the military situation: "I have been so reduced in strength as to be incapable of any command. Brigadier-General Boyd is the only general officer present."[1]

The sudden departure of Morgan Lewis, ordered to Sackett's Harbor, left General Boyd for a few days to act as the general in command at Niagara. Boyd, though well known for his success at Tippecanoe, was not a favorite in the army. "A compound of ignorance, vanity, and petulance," wrote his late superior, Morgan Lewis,[2] "with nothing to recommend him but that species of bravery in the field which is vaporing, boisterous, stifling reflection, blinding observation, and better adapted to the bully than the soldier."

Galled by complaints of the imbecility of the army, Boyd, with Dearborn's approval,[3] June 23, detached Colonel Boerstler of the Fourteenth Infantry with some four hundred men and two field-pieces, to batter a stone house at Beaver Dam, some seventeen miles from Fort George.[4] Early in the morning of June 24 Boerstler marched to Beaver Dam. There he found himself surrounded in the woods by hostile Indians, numbering according to British authority about two hundred. The Indians, annoying both front and rear, caused Boerstler to attempt retreat, but his retreat was stopped by a few militia-men, said to number fifteen.[5] A small detachment of one hundred and fifty men came to reinforce Boerstler, and Lieutenant Fitzgibbon of the British Forty-ninth regiment, with forty-seven men, reinforced the Indians. Unable to extricate himself, and dreading dispersion and massacre, Boerstler decided to surrender; and his five hundred and forty men accordingly capitulated to a British lieutenant with two hundred and sixty Indians, militia, and regulars.

Dearborn reported the disaster as "an unfortunate and

[1] State Papers; Military Affairs, i. 449.
[2] Morgan Lewis to Armstrong, July 5, 1813; MSS. War Department Archives.
[3] Memoir of Dearborn, etc., compiled by Charles Coffin, p. 139.
[4] Court of Inquiry on Colonel Boerstler, Feb. 17, 1815; Niles x. 19.
[5] James, i. 216.

unaccountable event;"[1] but of such events the list seemed endless. A worse disaster, equally due to Dearborn and Chauncey, occurred at the other end of the Lake. Had they attacked Kingston, as Armstrong intended, their movement would have covered Sackett's Harbor; but when they placed themselves a hundred and fifty miles to the westward of Sackett's Harbor, they could do nothing to protect it. Sackett's Harbor was an easy morning's sail from Kingston, and the capture of the American naval station was an object of infinite desire on the part of Sir George Prevost, since it would probably decide the result of the war.

Prevost, though not remarkable for audacity, could not throw away such an opportunity without ruining his reputation. He came to Kingston, and while Dearborn was preparing to capture Fort George in the night of May 26–27, Prevost embarked his whole regular force, eight hundred men all told,[2] on Yeo's fleet at Kingston, set sail in the night, and at dawn of May 27 was in sight of Sackett's Harbor.[3]

Had Yeo and Prevost acted with energy, they must have captured the Harbor without serious resistance. According to Sir George's official report, "light and adverse winds" prevented the ships from nearing the Fort until evening.[4] Probably constitutional vacillation on the part of Sir James Yeo caused delay, for Prevost left the control wholly to him and Colonel Baynes.[5]

At Sackett's Harbor about four hundred men of different regular regiments, and about two hundred and fifty Albany volunteers were in garrison; and a general alarm, given on appearance of the British fleet in the distance, brought some hundreds of militia into the place; but the most important reinforcement was Jacob Brown, a brigadier-general of State militia who lived in the neighborhood, and had been requested by Dearborn to take command in case of an emer-

[1] Dearborn to Armstrong, June 25, 1813; State Papers, Military Affairs, i. 449.

[2] James, i. 165; Colonel Baynes to Prevost, May 30, 1813; James, i. 413.

[3] Report of Sir George Prevost, June 1, 1813; MSS. British Archives.

[4] Prevost to Bathurst, June 1, 1813; MSS. British Archives. Prevost's Life, p. 82, 83.

[5] James, i. 165, 166. Brenton to Freer, May 30, 1813; MSS. Canadian Archives, Freer Papers, 1812–1813, p. 183.

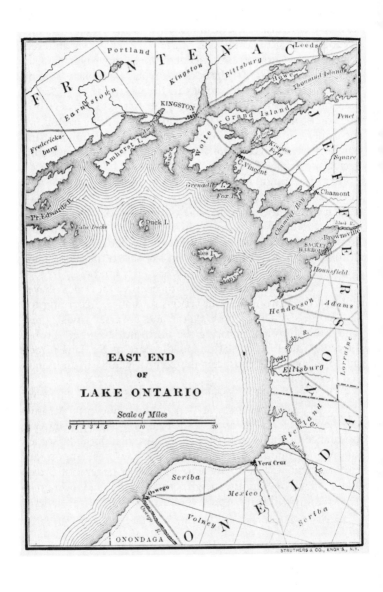

EAST END

OF

LAKE ONTARIO

Scale of Miles

0 1 2 3 4 5 10 20

gency. Brown arrived at the Harbor in time to post the men in order of battle. Five hundred militia were placed at the point where the British were expected to land; the regulars were arranged in a second line; the forts were in the rear.

At dawn of May 28, under command of Colonel Baynes, the British grenadiers of the One Hundredth regiment landed gallantly under "so heavy and galling a fire from a numerous but almost invisible foe, as to render it impossible to halt for the artillery to come up."[1] Pressing rapidly forward, without stopping to fire, the British regulars routed the militia and forced the second line back until they reached a block-house at the edge of the village, where a thirty-two pound gun was in position, flanked by log barracks and fallen timber. While Brown with difficulty held his own at the military barracks, the naval lieutenant in charge of the ship-yard, being told that the battle was lost, set fire to the naval barracks, shipping, and store-houses. Brown's indignation at this act was intense.

> "The burning of the marine barracks was as infamous a transaction as ever occurred among military men," he wrote to Dearborn.[2] "The fire was set as our regulars met the enemy upon the main line; and if anything could have appalled these gallant men it would have been the flames in their rear. We have all, I presume, suffered in the public estimation in consequence of this disgraceful burning. The fact is, however, that the army is entitled to much higher praise than though it had not occurred. The navy are alone responsible for what happened on Navy Point, and it is fortunate for them that they have reputations sufficient to sustain the shock."

Brown's second line stood firm at the barracks, and the British attack found advance impossible. Sir George Prevost's report admitted his inability to go farther:[3] —

> "A heavier fire than that of musketry having become necessary in order to force their last position, I had the mortification to learn that the continuation of light and adverse

---

[1] Report of Colonel Baynes, May 30, 1813; James, i. 413.
[2] Brown to Dearborn, July 25, 1813; Dearborn MSS.
[3] Prevost's Report of June 1, 1813; MSS. British Archives.

winds had prevented the co-operation of the ships, and that the gunboats were unequal to silence the enemy's elevated batteries, or to produce any effect on their block houses. Considering it therefore impracticable without such assistance to carry the strong works by which the post was defended, I reluctantly ordered the troops to leave a beaten enemy whom they had driven before them for upwards of three hours, and who did not venture to offer the slightest opposition to the re-embarkation, which was effected with proper deliberation and in perfect order."

If Sir George was correct in regarding the Americans as "a beaten enemy," his order of retreat to his own troops seemed improper; but his language showed that he used the words in a sense of his own, and Colonel Baynes's report gave no warrant for the British claim of a victory.[1]

"At this point," said Baynes,[2] "the further energies of the troops became unavailing. Their [American] block-houses and stockaded battery could not be carried by assault, nor reduced by field-pieces had we been provided with them. . . . Seeing no object within our reach to attain that could compensate for the loss we were momentarily sustaining from the heavy fire of the enemy's cannon, I directed the troops to take up the position we had charged from. From this position we were ordered to re-embark, which was performed at our leisure and in perfect order, the enemy not presuming to show a single soldier without the limits of his fortress."

Another and confidential report was written by E. B. Brenton of Prevost's staff to the governor's military secretary, Noah Freer.[3] After describing the progress of the battle until the British advance was stopped, Brenton said that Colonel Baynes came to Sir George to tell him that the men could not approach nearer the works with any prospect of success:—

"It was however determined to collect all the troops at a

[1] James, i. 175.
[2] Report of Colonel Baynes, May 30, 1813; James, i. 413.
[3] Brenton to Freer, May 30, 1813; MSS. Canadian Archives. Freer Papers, 1812–1813.

point, to form the line, and to make an attack immediately upon the battery and barracks in front. For this purpose the men in advance were called in, the line formed a little without the reach of the enemy's musketry, and though evidently much fagged, was, after being supplied with fresh ammunition, again led in line. At this time I do not think the whole force collected in the lines exceeded five hundred men."

The attack was made, and part of the Hundred-and-fourth regiment succeeded in getting shelter behind one of the American barracks, preparing for a farther advance. Sir George Prevost, under a fire which his aid described as tremendous,—"I do not exaggerate when I tell you that the shot, both of musketry and grape, was falling about us like hail,"—watched the American position through a glass, when, "at this time those who were left of the troops behind the barracks made a dash out to charge the enemy; but the fire was so destructive that they were instantly turned by it, and the retreat was sounded. Sir George, fearless of danger and disdaining to run or to suffer his men to run, repeatedly called out to them to retire in order; many however made off as fast as they could."

These reports agreed that the British attack was totally defeated, with severe loss, before the retreat was sounded. Such authorities should have silenced dispute; but Prevost had many enemies in Canada, and at that period of the war the British troops were unused to defeat. Both Canadians and English attacked the governor-general privately and publicly, freely charging him with having disgraced the service, and offering evidence of his want of courage in the action.[1] Americans, though not interested in the defence of Prevost, could not fail to remark that the British and Canadian authorities who condemned him, assumed a condition of affairs altogether different from that accepted by American authorities. The official American reports not only supported the views taken by Prevost and Baynes of the hopelessness of the British attack, but added particulars which made Prevost's retreat necessary. General Brown's opinion was emphatic: "Had not

[1] Quarterly Review, xxvii. 419; Christie, ii. 81; James, i. 177.

General Prevost retired *most rapidly* under the guns of his vessels, he would never have returned to Kingston."[1] These words were a part of Brown's official report. Writing to Dearborn he spoke with the same confidence:[2] —

"The militia were all rallied before the enemy gave way, and were marching perfectly in his view towards the rear of his right flank; and I am confident that even then, if Sir George had not retired with the utmost precipitation to his boats, he would have been cut off."

Unlike the Canadians, Brown thought Prevost's conduct correct and necessary, but was by no means equally complimentary to Sir James Yeo, whom he blamed greatly for failing to join in the battle. The want of wind which Yeo alleged in excuse, Brown flatly denied. From that time Brown entertained and freely expressed contempt for Yeo, as he seemed also to feel little respect for Chauncey. His experience with naval administration on both sides led him to expect nothing but inefficiency from either.

Whatever were the true causes of Prevost's failure, Americans could not admit that an expedition which cost the United States so much, and which so nearly succeeded, was discreditable to the British governor-general, or was abandoned without sufficient reason. The British return of killed and wounded proved the correctness of Prevost, Baynes, and Brown in their opinion of the necessity of retreat. According to the report of Prevost's severest critics, he carried less than seven hundred and fifty rank-and-file to Sackett's Harbor.[3] The returns showed forty-four rank-and-file killed; one hundred and seventy-two wounded, and thirteen missing,— in all, two hundred and twenty-nine men, or nearly one man in three. The loss in officers was relatively even more severe; and the total loss in an aggregate which could hardly have numbered much more than eight hundred and fifty men all told, amounted to two hundred and fifty-nine killed, wounded, and missing, leaving Prevost less than six hundred

[1] Brown's Report of June 1, 1813; Niles, iv. 260.
[2] Brown to Dearborn, July 25, 1813; Dearborn MSS.
[3] James, i. 165.

men to escape,[1] in the face of twice their numbers and under the fire of heavy guns.[2]

The British attack was repulsed, and Jacob Brown received much credit as well as a commission of brigadier-general in the United States army for his success; but the injury inflicted by the premature destruction at the navy-yard was very great, and was sensibly felt. Such a succession of ill news could not but affect the Government. The repeated failures to destroy the British force at Niagara; the disasters of Chandler, Winder, and Boerstler; the narrow and partial escape of Sackett's Harbor; the total incapacity of Dearborn caused by fever and mortification,—all these evils were not the only or the greatest subjects for complaint. The two commanders, Dearborn and Chauncey, had set aside the secretary's plan of campaign, and had substituted one of their own, on the express ground of their superior information. While affirming that the garrison at Kingston had been reinforced to a strength three or four times as great as was humanly possible, they had asserted that the capture of York would answer their purpose as well as the capture of Kingston, to "give us the complete command of the Lake." They captured York, April 27, but the British fleet appeared June 6, and took from them the command of the Lake. These miscalculations or misstatements, and the disasters resulting from them, warranted the removal of Chauncey as well as Dearborn from command; but the brunt of dissatisfaction fell on Dearborn alone. Both Cabinet and Congress agreed in insisting on Dearborn's retirement, and the President was obliged to consent. July 6, Secretary Armstrong wrote,—

"I have the President's orders to express to you the decision that you retire from the command of District No. 9, and of the troops within the same, until your health be reestablished and until further orders."

[1] Return, etc.; James, i. 417.
[2] Baynes's Report of May 30, 1813; James, i. 413.

Chapter VIII

ARMSTRONG'S EMBARRASSMENT was great in getting rid of the generals whom Madison and Eustis left on his hands. Dearborn was one example of what he was obliged to endure, but Wilkinson was a worse. According to Armstrong's account,[1] New Orleans was not believed to be safe in Wilkinson's keeping. The senators from Louisiana, Tennessee, and Kentucky remonstrated to the President, and the President ordered his removal. Armstrong and Wilkinson had been companions in arms, and had served with Gates at Saratoga. For many reasons Armstrong wished not unnecessarily to mortify Wilkinson, and in conveying to him, March 10, the abrupt order[2] to proceed with the least possible delay to the headquarters of Major-General Dearborn at Sackett's Harbor, the Secretary of War added, March 12, a friendly letter of advice:[3] —

"Why should you remain in your land of cypress when patriotism and ambition equally invite to one where grows the laurel? Again, the men of the North and East want you; those of the South and West are less sensible of your merits and less anxious to have you among them. I speak to you with a frankness due to you and to myself, and again advise, Come to the North, and come quickly! If our cards be well played, we may renew the scene of Saratoga."

The phrase was curious. Saratoga suggested defeated invasion rather than conquest; the surrender of a British army in the heart of New York rather than the capture of Montreal. The request for Wilkinson's aid was disheartening. No one knew better than Armstrong the feebleness of Wilkinson's true character. "The selection of this unprincipled imbecile was not the blunder of Secretary Armstrong," said Winfield

[1] Strictures on General Wilkinson's Defence; from the Albany "Argus." Niles, ix. 425.

[2] Armstrong to Wilkinson, March 10, 1813; Wilkinson's Memoirs, iii. 341.

[3] Armstrong to Wilkinson, March 12, 1813; Wilkinson's Memoirs, iii. 342.

Scott long afterward;[1] but the idea that Wilkinson could be chief-of-staff to Dearborn,—that one weak man could give strength to another,—was almost as surprising as the selection of Wilkinson to chief command would have been. Armstrong did not intend that Wilkinson should command more than a division under Dearborn;[2] but he must have foreseen that in the event of Dearborn's illness or incapacity, Wilkinson would become by seniority general-in-chief.

Wilkinson at New Orleans received Armstrong's letter of March 10 only May 19,[3] and started, June 10, for Washington, where he arrived July 31, having consumed the greater part of the summer in the journey. On arriving at Washington, he found that Dearborn had been removed, and that he was himself by seniority in command of the Ninth Military District.[4] This result of Dearborn's removal was incalculably mischievous, for if its effect on Wilkinson's vanity was unfortunate, its influence on the army was fatal. Almost every respectable officer of the old service regarded Wilkinson with antipathy or contempt.

Armstrong's ill-fortune obliged him also to place in the position of next importance Wilkinson's pronounced enemy, Wade Hampton. A major-general was required to take command on Lake Champlain, and but one officer of that rank claimed employment or could be employed; and Wade Hampton was accordingly ordered to Plattsburg.[5] Of all the major-generals Hampton was probably the best; but his faults were serious. Proud and sensitive even for a South Carolinian; irritable, often harsh, sometimes unjust, but the soul of honor,[6] Hampton was rendered wholly intractable wherever Wilkinson was concerned, by the long-standing feud which had made the two generals for years the heads of hostile sections in the army.[7] Hampton loathed Wilkinson. At the time of his appointment to command on Lake Champlain he had

[1] Autobiography, p. 94, *note*.
[2] Strictures; Niles, ix. 425.
[3] Wilkinson to Armstrong, May 23, 1813; Wilkinson's Memoirs, iii. 341.
[4] Armstrong's Notices, ii. 23.
[5] Armstrong's Notices, ii. 23.
[6] Scott's Autobiography, p. 50.
[7] Scott's Autobiography, p. 36.

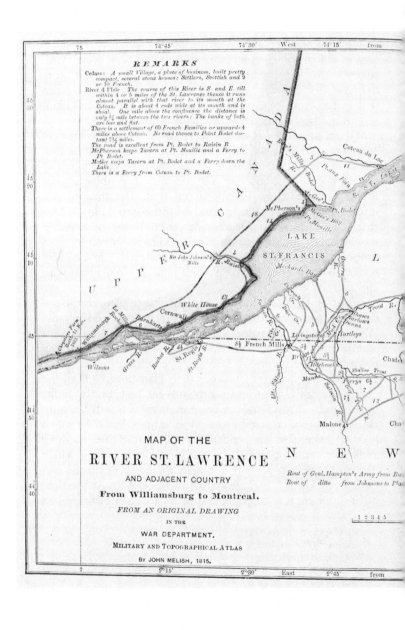

REMARKS

Cedars: A small Village, a place of business, built pretty compact, several stone houses: Settlers, Scottish and 9 or 10 French.

River d l'Isle The course of this River is S. and E. till within 4 or 5 miles of the St. Lawrence thence it runs almost parallel with that river to its mouth at the Coteau. It is about 4 rods wide at its mouth and is shoal. One mile above the confluence the distance is only ¾ mile between the two rivers: The banks of both are low and flat.

There is a settlement of 60 French Families or upwards 4 miles above Coteau. No road thence to Point Bodet distant 7½ miles.

The road is excellent from Pt. Bodet to Raisin R

McPherson keeps Tavern at Pt. Mouille and a Ferry to Pt. Bodet.

McGee keeps Tavern at Pt. Bodet and a Ferry down the Lake

There is a Ferry from Coteau to Pt. Bodet.

MAP OF THE

RIVER ST. LAWRENCE

AND ADJACENT COUNTRY

From Williamsburg to Montreal.

FROM AN ORIGINAL DRAWING

IN THE

WAR DEPARTMENT.

MILITARY AND TOPOGRAPHICAL ATLAS

BY JOHN MELISH, 1815.

Rout of Genl. Hampton's Army from Bur

Rout of   ditto   from Johnsons to Plat

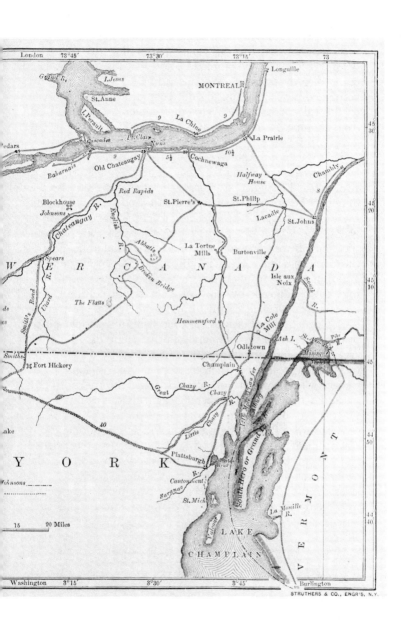

Longuille

MONTREAL

Grand R.
I.Jesus
St.Anne
I.Perault
Cascades

La Chine

La Prairie

Cedars
Baharnais
Old Chateaugay
Nuns
Pt.Clair
9
Cochnewaga
5½
10½

Halfway House

Chambly
8

Blockhouse
Johnsons
Red Rapids
St.Pierre's
St.Philip
Lacadie
St.Johns

Chateaugay R.
English R.

W
E
R
C
A
N
A
D
A

Spears
Abbatis
La Tortue Mills
Burtonville
Isle aux Noix

Smith's Road
Gisard R.
Broken Bridge
South R.

The Flatts

Hemmensford
La Cole Mill
Ash I.
St.Armand
Pike R.

Smiths
Odletown
Misisqui Bay

Fort Hickory
Champlain
45

Great Chazy R.
Chazy
Chazy R.

Lake
40
Little
Plattsburgh
Johnsons
Cantonment
Saranac
St.Michel
Y
O
R
K

South Hero or Grand I.

La Mouille R.

V
E
R
M
O
N
T

LAKE
CHAMPLAIN

15   20 Miles

Burlington

no reason to expect that Wilkinson would be his superior; but though willing and even wishing to serve under Dearborn, he accepted only on the express understanding that his was a distinct and separate command,[1] and that his orders were to come directly from the War Department. Only in case of a combined movement uniting different armies, was he to yield to the rule of seniority. With that agreement he left Washington, June 15, and assumed command, July 3, on Lake Champlain.

Nearly a month afterward Wilkinson arrived in Washington, and reported at the War Department. By that time Armstrong had lost whatever chance he previously possessed of drawing the army at Niagara back to a position on the enemy's line of supply. Three insuperable difficulties stood in his way,—the season was too late; the army was too weak; and the generals were incompetent. Armstrong found his generals the chief immediate obstacle, and struggled perseveringly and good-humoredly to overcome it. Wilkinson began, on arriving at Washington, by showing a fancy for continuing the campaign at Niagara.[2] Armstrong was obliged to give an emphatic order, dated August 8, that Kingston should be the primary object of the campaign, but he left Wilkinson at liberty to go there by almost any route, even by way of Montreal.[3] Disappointed at the outset by finding Wilkinson slow to accept responsibility or decided views,[4] he was not better pleased when the new general began his duties in Military District No. 9.

Wilkinson left Washington August 11, and no sooner did he reach Albany than he hastened to write, August 16, two letters to General Hampton, assuming that every movement of that general was directly dependent on Wilkinson's orders.[5] Considering the relations between the two men, these letters warranted the inference that Wilkinson intended to drive

[1] Hampton to Armstrong, Aug. 23, 1813; Wilkinson's Memoirs, iii. Appendix xxxvi.

[2] Memorandum by Armstrong, July 23, 1813; Wilkinson to Armstrong, Aug. 6, 1813; State Papers, Military Affairs, i. 463; Armstrong's Notices, ii. 31.

[3] Armstrong to Wilkinson, Aug. 8, 1813; State Papers, Military Affairs, i. 464.

[4] Armstrong's Notices, ii. 32.

[5] Wilkinson's Memoirs, iii. Appendix xxxv.

Hampton out of his Military District, and if possible from the service. Hampton instantly leaped to that conclusion, and wrote to Armstrong, August 23, offering his resignation in case Wilkinson's course was authorized by government.[1] Wilkinson also wrote to the secretary August 30, substantially avowing his object to be what Hampton supposed:[2] —

"You have copies of my letters to Major-General Hampton, which I know he has received, yet I have no answer. The reflection which naturally occurs is that if I am authorized to command he is bound to obey; and if he will not respect the obligation, he should be turned out of the service."

Armstrong pacified Hampton by promising once more that all his orders and reports should pass through the Department. Hampton promised to serve cordially and vigorously through the campaign, but he believed himself intended for a sacrifice, and declared his intention of resigning as soon as the campaign was ended.[3] Wilkinson, after having at Albany provoked this outburst, started for Sackett's Harbor, where he arrived August 20.

At Sackett's Harbor Wilkinson found several general officers. Morgan Lewis was there in command, Commodore Chauncey was there with his fleet. Jacob Brown was also present by virtue of his recent appointment as brigadier-general. The quartermaster-general, Robert Swartwout, a brother of Burr's friend who went to New Orleans, was posted there. Wilkinson summoned these officers to a council of war August 26, which deliberated on the different plans of campaign proposed to it, and unanimously decided in favor of one called by Armstrong "No. 3 of the plans proposed by the government."[4] As defined in Wilkinson's language[5] the scheme was—

[1] Hampton to Armstrong, Aug. 23, 1813; Memoirs, iii. Appendix xxxvi.

[2] Wilkinson's Memoirs, iii. 358.

[3] Hampton to Armstrong, Aug. 31, 1813; MSS. War Department Archives. Armstrong to Wilkinson, Sept. 6, 1813; Wilkinson's Memoirs, iii. Appendix xxxvii.

[4] Armstrong's Notices, ii. 33; Memorandum of July 23, 1813; State Papers, Military Affairs, i. 463.

[5] Minutes, etc.; Wilkinson's Memoirs, iii. Appendix no. 1.

"To rendezvous the whole of the troops on the Lake in this vicinity, and in co-operation with our squadron to make a bold feint upon Kingston, slip down the St. Lawrence, lock up the enemy in our rear to starve or surrender, or oblige him to follow us without artillery, baggage, or provisions, or eventually to lay down his arms; to sweep the St. Lawrence of armed craft, and in concert with the division under Major-General Hampton to take Montreal."

Orders were given, August 25, for providing river transport for seven thousand men, forty field-pieces, and twenty heavy guns, to be in readiness by September 15.[1]

The proposed expedition closely imitated General Amherst's expedition against Montreal in 1760, with serious differences of relative situation. After Wolfe had captured Quebec and hardly twenty-five hundred French troops remained to defend Montreal, in the month of July Amherst descended the river from Lake Ontario with more than ten thousand men, chiefly British veterans, capturing every fortified position as he went. Wilkinson's council of war proposed to descend the river in October or November with seven thousand men, leaving a hostile fleet and fortresses in their rear, and running past every fortified position to arrive in the heart of a comparatively well populated country, held by a force greater than their own, with Quebec to support it, while Wilkinson would have no certain base of supplies, reinforcements, or path of escape. Knowledge of Wilkinson's favorite Quintus Curtius or of Armstrong's familiar Jomini was not required to satisfy any intelligent private, however newly recruited, that under such circumstances the army would be fortunate to escape destruction.[2]

Wilkinson next went to Niagara, where he arrived September 4, and where he found the army in a bad condition, with Boyd still in command, but restrained by the President's orders within a strict defensive. Wilkinson remained nearly a month at Fort George making the necessary preparations for a movement. He fell ill of fever, but returned October 2 to

[1] Wilkinson to Swartwout, Aug. 25, 1813; Wilkinson's Memoirs, iii. 51.
[2] Cf. Wilkinson to Armstrong, Oct. 19, 1813; State Papers, Military Affairs, i. 472.

Sackett's Harbor, taking with him all the regular troops at Niagara. At that time Chauncey again controlled the Lake.

Secretary Armstrong also came to Sackett's Harbor, September 5, and established the War Department at that remote point for nearly two months.[1] When Wilkinson arrived, October 2, Armstrong's difficulties began. Wilkinson, then fifty-six years old, was broken by the Lake fever. "He was so much indisposed in mind and body," according to Brigadier-General Boyd,[2] "that in any other service he would have perhaps been superseded in his command." According to Wilkinson's story, he told Secretary Armstrong that he was incapable of commanding the army, and offered to retire from it; but the secretary said there was no one to take his place, and he could not be spared. In private Armstrong was believed to express himself more bluntly, and Wilkinson was told that the secretary said: "I would feed the old man with pap sooner than leave him behind."[3] Wilkinson's debility did not prevent him from giving orders, or from becoming jealous and suspicious of every one, but chiefly of Armstrong.[4] Whatever was suggested by Armstrong was opposed by Wilkinson. Before returning to Sackett's Harbor, October 4, Wilkinson favored an attack on Kingston.[5] On reaching Sackett's Harbor, finding that Armstrong also favored attacking Kingston, Wilkinson argued "against my own judgment" in favor of passing Kingston and descending upon Montreal.[6] Ten days afterward Armstrong changed his mind. Yeo had succeeded in returning to Kingston, bringing reinforcements.

"He will bring with him about fifteen hundred effectives," wrote Armstrong;[7] "and thanks to the storm and our snail-like movements down the Lake, they will be there before we can reach it. The manœuvre intended is lost, so

---

[1] Armstrong to Wilkinson, Sept. 6, 1813; Wilkinson's Memoirs, iii. Appendix xxxvii.

[2] Testimony of Brigadier-General Boyd; Wilkinson's Memoirs, iii. 80.

[3] Wilkinson's Memoirs, iii. 354.

[4] Wilkinson's Memoirs, iii. 357.

[5] Wilkinson's Memoirs, iii. 353.

[6] Wilkinson's Memoirs, iii. 190; Paper A, *note*.

[7] Armstrong to Hampton, Oct. 16, 1813; Wilkinson's Memoirs, iii. 361.

far as regards Kingston. What we now do against that place must be done by hard blows, at some risk."

Accordingly, October 19, Armstrong wrote to Wilkinson a letter advising abandonment of the attack on Kingston, and an effort at "grasping the safer and the greater object below."[1]

"I call it the safer and greater object, because at Montreal you find the weaker place and the smaller force to encounter; at Montreal you meet a fresh, unexhausted, efficient reinforcement of four thousand men; at Montreal you approach your own resources, and establish between you and them an easy and an expeditious intercourse; at Montreal you occupy a point which must be gained in carrying your attacks home to the purposes of the war, and which, if seized now, will save one campaign; at Montreal you hold a position which completely severs the enemy's line of operations, which shuts up the Ottawa as well as the St. Lawrence against him, and which while it restrains all below, withers and perishes all above itself."

As Armstrong veered toward Montreal Wilkinson turned decidedly toward Kingston, and wrote the same day to the secretary a letter[2] of remonstrance, closing by a significant remark:—

"Personal considerations would make me prefer a visit to Montreal to the attack of Kingston; but before I abandon this attack, which by my instructions I am ordered to make, it is necessary to my justification that you should by the authority of the President direct the operations of the army under my command particularly against Montreal."

The hint was strong that Wilkinson believed Armstrong to be trying to evade responsibility, as Armstrong believed Wilkinson to be trying to shirk it. Both insinuations were probably well-founded; neither Armstrong nor Wilkinson expected to capture Kingston, and still less Montreal. Wilkinson

[1] Armstrong to Wilkinson, Oct. 19, 1813; State Papers, Military Affairs, i. 472.
[2] Wilkinson to Armstrong, Oct. 19, 1813; State Papers, Military Affairs, i. 472.

plainly said as much at the time. "I speak conjecturally," he wrote; "but should we surmount every obstacle in descending the river we shall advance upon Montreal ignorant of the force arrayed against us, and in case of misfortune, having no retreat, the army must surrender at discretion." Armstrong's conduct was more extraordinary than Wilkinson's, and could not be believed except on his own evidence. He not only looked for no capture of Montreal, but before writing his letter of October 19 to Wilkinson, he had given orders for preparing winter quarters for the army sixty or eighty miles above Montreal, and did this without informing Wilkinson. In later years he wrote:[1] —

"Suspecting early in October, from the lateness of the season, the inclemency of the weather, and the continued indisposition of the commanding general, that the campaign then in progress would terminate as it did,—'with the disgrace of doing nothing, but without any material diminution of physical power,'—the Secretary of War, then at Sackett's Harbor, hastened to direct Major-General Hampton to employ a brigade of militia attached to his command, in constructing as many huts as would be sufficient to cover an army of ten thousand men during the winter."

The order dated October 16 and addressed to the quartermaster-general,[2] prescribed the cantonment of ten thousand men within the limits of Canada, and plainly indicated the secretary's expectation that the army could not reach Montreal. In other ways Armstrong showed the same belief more openly.

All the available troops on or near Lake Ontario were concentrated at Sackett's Harbor about the middle of October, and did not exceed seven thousand effectives, or eight thousand men.[3] "I calculate on six thousand combatants," wrote Wilkinson after starting,[4] "exclusive of Scott and Randolph,

[1] Armstrong's Notices, ii. 63.

[2] Armstrong to Swartwout, Oct. 16, 1813; Wilkinson's Memoirs, iii. 70.

[3] Council of War, Nov. 8, 1813; Wilkinson's Memoirs, iii. Appendix xxiv. Report of Adjutant-General, Dec. 1, 1813, Appendix vii.

[4] Wilkinson to Armstrong, Oct. 28, 1813; MSS. War Department Archives.

neither of whom will, I fear, be up in season." The army was divided into four brigades under Generals Boyd, Swartwout, Jacob Brown, and Covington,—the latter a Maryland man, forty-five years old, who entered the service in 1809 as lieutenant-colonel of dragoons. The brigades of Boyd and Covington formed a division commanded by Major-General Morgan Lewis. The second division was intended for Major-General Hampton; a reserve under Colonel Macomb, and a park of artillery under Brigadier-General Moses Porter, completed the organization.[1]

The men were embarked in bateaux, October 17, at Henderson's Bay, to the westward of Sackett's Harbor. The weather had been excessively stormy, and continued so. The first resting-point to be reached was Grenadier Island at the entrance of the St. Lawrence, only sixteen or eighteen miles from the starting-point; but the bateaux were dispersed by heavy gales of wind, October 18, 19, and 20, and the last detachments did not reach Grenadier Island until November 3. "All our hopes have been nearly blasted," wrote Wilkinson October 24; but at length, November 5, the expedition, numbering nearly three hundred boats, having safely entered the river, began the descent from French Creek. That day they moved forty miles, and halted about midnight six miles above Ogdensburg. The next day was consumed in running the flotilla past Ogdensburg under the fire of the British guns at Prescott. The boats floated down by night and the troops marched by land. November 7 the army halted at the White House, about twenty miles below Ogdensburg. There Wilkinson called a council of war, November 8, to consider whether the expedition should proceed. Lewis, Boyd, Brown, and Swartwout voted simply in favor of attacking Montreal. Covington and Porter were of the opinion "that we proceed from this place under great danger, . . . but . . . we know of no other alternative."[2]

More than any other cause, Armstrong's conduct warranted Wilkinson in considering the campaign at an end. If the attack on Montreal was seriously intended, every motive

---

[1] General Order of Encampment; Wilkinson's Memoirs, iii. 126; Order of October 9, Appendix iii.

[2] Minutes etc.; Wilkinson's Memoirs, iii. Appendix xxiv.

required Armstrong to join Hampton at once in advance of Wilkinson's expedition. No one knew so well as he the necessity of some authority to interpose between the tempers and pretensions of these two men in case a joint campaign were to be attempted, or to enforce co-operation on either side. Good faith toward Hampton, even more than toward Wilkinson, required that the secretary who had led them into such a situation should not desert them. Yet Armstrong, after waiting till Wilkinson was fairly at Grenadier Island, began to prepare for return to Washington. From the village of Antwerp, half way between Sackett's Harbor and Ogdensburg, the secretary wrote to Wilkinson, October 27, "Should my fever continue I shall not be able to approach you as I intended."[1] Three days later he wrote again from Denmark on the road to Albany, —

> "I rejoice that your difficulties are so far surmounted as to enable you to say with assurance when you will pass Prescott. I should have met you there; but bad roads, worse weather, and a considerable degree of illness admonished me against receding farther from a point where my engagements call me about the 1st proximo. The resolution of treading back my steps was taken at Antwerp."[2]

From Albany Armstrong wrote, November 12, for the last time, "in the fulness of my faith that you are in Montreal,"[3] that he had sent orders to Hampton to effect a junction with the river expedition. Such letters and orders, whatever Armstrong meant by them, were certain to impress both Wilkinson and Hampton with a conviction that the secretary intended to throw upon them the whole responsibility for the failure of an expedition which he as well as they knew to be hopeless.

Doubtless a vigorous general might still have found means if not to take Montreal, at least to compel the British to

[1] Armstrong to Wilkinson, Oct. 27, 1813; Wilkinson's Memoirs, iii. Appendix xli.

[2] Armstrong to Wilkinson, Oct. 30, 1813; State Papers, Military Affairs, i. 474.

[3] Armstrong to Wilkinson, Nov. 12, 1813; State Papers, Military Affairs, i. 474.

evacuate Upper Canada; but Wilkinson was naturally a weak man, and during the descent of the river he was excessively ill, never able to make a great exertion. Every day his difficulties increased. Hardly had his flotilla begun its descent, when a number of British gunboats commanded by Captain Mulcaster, the most energetic officer in the British naval service on the Lake, slipping through Chauncey's blockade, appeared in Wilkinson's rear, and caused him much annoyance. Eight hundred British rank-and-file from Kingston and Prescott were with Mulcaster, and at every narrow pass of the river, musketry and artillery began to open on Wilkinson from the British bank. Progress became slow. November 7, Macomb was landed on the north bank with twelve hundred men to clear away these obstructions.[1] The day and night of November 8 were consumed at the White House in passing troops across the river. Brown's brigade was landed on the north shore to reinforce Macomb. The boats were delayed to keep pace with Brown's march on shore, and made but eleven miles November 9, and the next day, November 10, fell down only to the Long Saut, a continuous rapid eight miles in length. The enemy pressed close, and while Brown marched in advance to clear the bank along the rapid, Boyd was ordered to take all the other troops and protect the rear.

The flotilla stopped on the night of November 10 near a farm called Chrystler's on the British bank; and the next morning, November 11, at half-past ten o'clock Brown having announced that all was clear below, Wilkinson was about to order the flotilla to run the rapids when General Boyd sent word that the enemy in the rear were advancing in column. Wilkinson was on his boat, unable to leave his bed;[2] Morgan Lewis was in no better condition; and Boyd was left to fight a battle as he best could. Boyd never had the confidence of the army; Brown was said to have threatened to resign rather than serve under him,[3] and Winfield Scott, who was that day with Macomb and Brown in the advance, described[4] Boyd as

---

[1] Journal etc.; State Papers, Military Affairs, i. 477.

[2] Evidence of General Boyd; Wilkinson's Memoirs, iii. 84; Evidence of Doctor Bull; Wilkinson's Memoirs, iii. 214.

[3] Wilkinson's Memoirs, iii. 364.

[4] Autobiography, pp. 93, 94.

amiable and respectable in a subordinate position, but "vacillating and imbecile beyond all endurance as a chief under high responsibilities."

The opportunity to capture or destroy Mulcaster and his eight hundred men was brilliant, and warranted Wilkinson in turning back his whole force to accomplish it. Boyd actually employed three brigades, and made an obstinate but not united or well-supported attempt to crush the enemy. Colonel Ripley with the Twenty-first regiment drove in the British skirmishers, and at half-past two o'clock the battle became general. At half-past four, after a stubborn engagement, General Covington was killed; his brigade gave way, and the whole American line fell back, beaten and almost routed.

This defeat was the least creditable of the disasters suffered by American arms during the war. No excuse or palliation was ever offered for it.[1] The American army consisted wholly of regulars, and all the generals belonged to the regular service. Wilkinson could hardly have had less than three thousand men with him, after allowing for his detachments, and was alone to blame if he had not more. Boyd, according to his own account, had more than twelve hundred men and two field-pieces under his immediate command on shore.[2] The reserve, under Colonel Upham of the Eleventh regiment, contained six hundred rank-and-file,[3] with four field-pieces. Wilkinson's official report admitted that eighteen hundred rank-and-file were engaged; Colonel Walbach, his adjutant-general, admitted two thousand,[4] while Swartwout thought that twenty-one hundred were in action. The American force was certainly not less than two thousand, with six field-pieces.

The British force officially reported by Lieutenant-Colonel Morrison of the Eighty-ninth regiment, who was in command, consisted of eight hundred rank-and-file, and thirty Indians. The rank-and-file consisted of three hundred and forty-two men of the Forty-ninth regiment, about as many more of the Eighty-ninth, and some Canadian troops. They had three

---

[1] Wilkinson's Defence, Memoirs, iii. 451; Ripley's Evidence, Wilkinson's Memoirs, iii. 139.

[2] Evidence of General Boyd; Wilkinson's Memoirs, iii. 85.

[3] Wilkinson to Armstrong, Nov. 18, 1813; Niles, v. 235.

[4] Evidence of Colonel Walbach; Wilkinson's Memoirs, iii. 151.

six-pound field-pieces, and were supported on their right flank by gunboats.[1]

On the American side the battle was ill fought both by the generals and by the men. Wilkinson and Morgan Lewis, the two major-generals, who were ill on their boats, never gave an order. Boyd, who commanded, brought his troops into action by detachments, and the men, on meeting unexpected resistance, broke and fled. The defeat was bloody as well as mortifying. Wilkinson reported one hundred and two killed, and two hundred and thirty-seven wounded, but strangely reported no missing,[2] although the British occupied the field of battle, and claimed upward of one hundred prisoners.[3] Morrison reported twenty-two killed, one hundred and forty-eight wounded, and twelve missing. The American loss was twice that of the British, and Wilkinson's reports were so little to be trusted that the loss might well have been greater than he represented it. The story had no redeeming incident.

If three brigades, numbering two thousand men, were beaten at Chrystler's farm by eight hundred British and Canadians, the chance that Wilkinson could capture Montreal, even with ten thousand men, was small. The conduct of the army showed its want of self-confidence. Late as it was, in the dusk of the evening Boyd hastened to escape across the river. "The troops being much exhausted," reported Wilkinson,[4] "it was considered most convenient that they should embark, and that the dragoons with the artillery should proceed by land. The embarkation took place without the smallest molestation from the enemy, and the flotilla made a harbor near the head of the Saut on the opposite shore." In truth, neither Wilkinson nor his adjutant gave the order of embarkation,[5] nor was Boyd willing to admit it as his.[6] Apparently the army by common consent embarked without orders.

Early the next morning, November 12, the flotilla ran the

---

[1] James, i. 323–325, 467.

[2] Return, etc., State Papers, Military Affairs, i. 476.

[3] Morrison's Report of Nov. 12, 1813; James, i. 451.

[4] Journal, Nov. 11, 1813; State Papers, Military Affairs, i. 478.

[5] Evidence of Colonel Walbach; Wilkinson's Memoirs, iii. 145; Evidence of Colonel Pinkney, iii. 311.

[6] Evidence of Brigadier-General Boyd; Wilkinson's Memoirs, iii. 91.

rapids and rejoined Brown and Macomb near Cornwall, where Wilkinson learned that General Hampton had taken the responsibility of putting an end to an undertaking which had not yet entered upon its serious difficulties.

Four months had passed since Hampton took command on Lake Champlain. When he first reached Burlington, July 3, neither men nor material were ready, nor was even a naval force present to cover his weakness. While he was camped at Burlington, a British fleet, with about a thousand regulars, entered the Lake from the Isle aux Noix and the Richelieu River, and plundered the American magazines at Plattsburg, July 31, sweeping the Lake clear of American shipping.[1] Neither Hampton's army nor McDonough's small fleet ventured to offer resistance. Six weeks afterward, in the middle of September, Hampton had but about four thousand men, in bad condition and poor discipline.

Wilkinson, though unable to begin his own movement, was earnest that Hampton should advance on Montreal.[2] Apparently in order to assist Wilkinson's plans, Hampton moved his force, September 19, to the Canada line. Finding that a drought had caused want of water on the direct road to Montreal, Hampton decided to march his army westward to the Chateaugay River, forty or fifty miles, and established himself there, September 26, in a position equally threatening to Montreal and to the British line of communication up the St. Lawrence. Armstrong approved the movement,[3] and Hampton remained three weeks at Chateaugay, building roads and opening lines of communication while waiting for Wilkinson to move.

October 16 Armstrong ordered Hampton, in view of Wilkinson's probable descent of the river, to "approach the mouth of the Chateaugay, or other point which shall better favor our junction, and hold the enemy in check."[4] Hampton

[1] James, i. 242; Christie, ii. 94.
[2] Wilkinson to Armstrong, Aug. 30, 1813; State Papers, Military Affairs, i. 466.
[3] Armstrong to Hampton, Sept. 28, 1813; State Papers, Military Affairs, i. 460. Cf. Armstrong's Notices, ii. 25.
[4] State Papers, Military Affairs, i. 461.

instantly obeyed, and moved down the Chateaugay to a point about fifteen miles from its mouth. There he established his army, October 22, and employed the next two days in completing his road, and getting up his artillery and stores.

Hampton's movements annoyed the British authorities at Montreal. Even while he was still within American territory, before he advanced from Chateaugay Four Corners, Sir George Prevost reported, October 8, to his government,[1] —

"The position of Major-General Hampton at the Four Corners on the Chateaugay River, and which he continued to occupy, either with the whole or a part of his force, from the latest information I have been able to obtain from thence, is highly judicious,—as at the same time that he threatens Montreal and obliges me to concentrate a considerable body of troops in this vicinity to protect it, he has it in his power to molest the communication with the Upper Province, and impede the progress of the supplies required there for the Navy and Army."

If this was the case, October 8, when Hampton was still at Chateaugay, fifty miles from its mouth, the annoyance must have been much greater when he advanced, October 21, to Spear's, within ten miles of the St. Lawrence on his left, and fifteen from the mouth of the Chateaugay. Hampton accomplished more than was expected. He held a position equally well adapted to threaten Montreal, to disturb British communication with Upper Canada, and to succor Wilkinson.

That Hampton, with only four thousand men, should do more than this, could not fairly be required. The defences of Montreal were such as required ten times his force to overcome. The regular troops defending Montreal were not stationed in the town itself, which was sufficiently protected by a broad river and rapids. They were chiefly at Chambly, St. John's, Isle aux Noix, or other points on the Richelieu River, guarding the most dangerous line of approach from Lake Champlain; or they were at Coteau du Lac on the St. Lawrence about twenty miles northwest of Hampton's position. According to the general weekly return of British forces

[1] Prevost to Bathurst, Oct. 8, 1813; MSS. British Archives.

serving in the Montreal District under command of Major-General Sir R. H. Sheaffe, Sept. 15, 1813, the aggregate rank-and-file present for duty was five thousand seven hundred and fifty-two. At Montreal were none but sick, with the general staff. At Chambly were nearly thirteen hundred effectives; at St. John's nearly eight hundred; at Isle aux Noix about nine hundred. Excluding the garrison at Prescott, and including the force at Coteau du Lac, Major-General Sheaffe commanded just five thousand effectives.[1]

Besides the enrolled troops, Prevost could muster a considerable number of sailors and marines for the defence of Montreal; and his resources in artillery, boats, fortifications, and supplies of all sorts were ample. In addition to the embodied troops, Prevost could count upon the militia, a force almost as good as regulars for the defence of a forest-clad country where axes were as effective as musketry in stopping an invading army. In Prevost's letter to Bathurst of October 8, announcing Hampton's invasion, the governor-general said: —

"Measures had been in the mean time taken by Major-General Sir Roger Sheaffe commanding in this district, to resist the advance of the enemy by moving the whole of the troops under his command nearer to the frontier line, and by calling out about three thousand of the sedentary militia. I thought it necessary to increase this latter force to nearly eight thousand by embodying the whole of the sedentary militia upon the frontier, this being in addition to the six battalions of incorporated militia amounting to five thousand men; and it is with peculiar satisfaction I have to report to your Lordship that his Majesty's Canadian subjects have a second time answered the call to arms in defence of their country with a zeal and alacrity beyond all praise."

Thus the most moderate estimate of the British force about Montreal gave at least fifteen thousand rank-and-file under arms.[2] Besides this large array of men, Prevost was amply

[1] Weekly General Return, Sept. 15, 1813; MSS. Canadian Archives, Freer Papers, 1813, p. 35.
[2] Cf. Wilkinson's Memoirs, iii. Appendix xxiv.; Council of War, Nov. 8, 1813; Wilkinson's Defence, Memoirs, iii. 449.

protected by natural defences. If Hampton had reached the St. Lawrence at Caughnawaga, he would still have been obliged to cross the St. Lawrence, more than two miles wide, under the fire of British batteries and gunboats. Hampton had no transports. Prevost had bateaux and vessels of every description, armed and unarmed, above and below the rapids, besides two river steamers constantly plying to Quebec.

Hampton's command consisted of four thousand infantry new to service, two hundred dragoons, and artillery.[1] With such a force, his chance of suffering a fatal reverse was much greater than that of his reaching the St. Lawrence. His position at the Chateaugay was not less perilous than that of Harrison on the Maumee, and far more so than that which cost Dearborn so many disasters at Niagara.

The British force in Hampton's immediate front consisted at first of only three hundred militia, who could make no resistance, and retired as Hampton advanced. When Hampton made his movement to Spear's, Lieutenant-Colonel de Salaberry in his front commanded about eight hundred men, and immediately entrenched himself and obstructed the road with abattis.[2] Hampton felt the necessity of dislodging Salaberry, who might at any moment be reinforced; and accordingly, in the night of October 25, sent a strong force to flank Salaberry's position, while he should himself attack it in front.

The flanking party failed to find its way, and the attack in front was not pressed.[3] The American loss did not exceed fifty men. The British loss was reported as twenty-five. Sir George Prevost and his officers were greatly pleased by their success;[4] but Prevost did not attempt to molest Hampton, who fell back by slow marches to Chateaugay, where he waited to hear from the Government. The British generals at Montreal showed little energy in thus allowing Hampton to escape; and the timidity of their attitude before Hampton's little army was the best proof of the incompetence alleged against Prevost by many of his contemporaries.

[1] Hampton to Armstrong, Oct. 12, 1813; State Papers, Military Affairs, i. 460.

[2] James, i. 307.

[3] Hampton to Armstrong, Nov. 1, 1813; State Papers, Military Affairs, i. 461.

[4] Prevost to Bathurst, Oct. 30, 1813; James, i. 462.

Hampton's retreat was due more to the conduct of Armstrong than to the check at Spear's or to the movements of Prevost. At the moment when he moved against Salaberry, October 25, a messenger arrived from Sackett's Harbor, bringing instructions from the quartermaster-general for building huts for ten thousand men for winter quarters. These orders naturally roused Hampton's suspicions that no serious movement against Montreal was intended.

"The papers sunk my hopes," he wrote to Armstrong, November 1,[1] "and raised serious doubts of receiving that efficacious support that had been anticipated. I would have recalled the column, but it was in motion, and the darkness of the night rendered it impracticable."

In a separate letter of the same date[2] which Hampton sent to Armstrong by Colonel King, assuming that the campaign was at an end, he carried out his declared purpose of resigning. "Events," he said, "have had no tendency to change my opinion of the destiny intended for me, nor my determination to retire from a service where I can neither feel security nor expect honor. The campaign I consider substantially at an end." The implication that Armstrong meant to sacrifice him was certainly disrespectful, and deserved punishment; but when Colonel King, bearing these letters, arrived in the neighborhood of Ogdensburg, he found that Armstrong had already done what Hampton reproached him for intending to do. He had retired to Albany, "suspecting . . . that the campaign . . . would terminate as it did."

A week afterward, November 8, Hampton received a letter from Wilkinson, written from Ogdensburg, asking him to forward supplies and march his troops to some point of junction on the river below St. Regis.[3] Hampton replied from Chateaugay that he had no supplies to forward; and as, under such circumstances, his army could not throw itself on Wilkinson's scanty means, he should fall back on Plattsburg, and

---

[1] Hampton to Armstrong, Nov. 1, 1813; State Papers, Military Affairs, i. 461.

[2] Hampton to Armstrong, Nov. 1, 1813; Wilkinson's Memoirs iii. Appendix lxix.

[3] Wilkinson to Hampton, Nov. 6, 1813; State Papers, Military Affairs, i. 462.

attempt to act against the enemy on some other road to be indicated.[1] Wilkinson received the letter on his arrival at Cornwall, November 12, the day after his defeat at Chrystler's farm; and with extraordinary energy moved the whole expedition the next day to French Mills, six or seven miles up the Salmon River, within the United States lines, where it went into winter quarters.

Armstrong and Wilkinson made common cause in throwing upon Hampton the blame of failure. Wilkinson at first ordered Hampton under arrest, but after reflection decided to throw the responsibility upon Armstrong.[2] The secretary declined to accept it, but consented after some delay to accept Hampton's resignation when renewed in March, 1814. Wilkinson declared that Hampton's conduct had blasted his dawning hopes and the honor of the army.[3] Armstrong sneered at Wilkinson for seizing the pretext for abandoning his campaign.[4] Both the generals believed that Armstrong had deliberately led them into an impossible undertaking, and deserted them, in order to shift the blame of failure from himself.[5] Hampton behaved with dignity, and allowed his opinion to be seen only in his contemptuous silence; nor did Armstrong publicly blame Hampton's conduct until Hampton was dead. The only happy result of the campaign was to remove all the older generals—Wilkinson, Hampton, and Morgan Lewis—from active service.

The bloodless failure of an enterprise which might have ended in extreme disaster was not the whole cost of Armstrong's and Wilkinson's friendship and quarrels. In November nearly all the regular forces, both British and American, had been drawn toward the St. Lawrence. Even Harrison and his troops, who reached Buffalo October 24, were sent to Sackett's Harbor, November 16, to protect the navy. Not a regiment of the United States army was to be seen between

---

[1] Hampton to Wilkinson, Nov. 8, 1813; State Papers, Military Affairs, 462.

[2] Wilkinson to Hampton; Wilkinson's Memoirs, iii. Appendix v. Wilkinson to Armstrong, Nov. 24, 1813; State Papers, Military Affairs, i. 480.

[3] Wilkinson to Armstrong, Nov. 17, 1813; State Papers, Military Affairs, i. 478.

[4] Armstrong's Notices, ii. 43.

[5] Wilkinson's Memoirs, iii. 362, *note*.

Sackett's Harbor and Detroit. The village of Niagara and Fort George on the British side were held by a few hundred volunteers commanded by Brigadier-General McClure of the New York militia. As long as Wilkinson and Hampton threatened Montreal, Niagara was safe, and needed no further attention.

After November 13, when Wilkinson and Hampton withdrew from Canada, while the American army forgot its enemy in the bitterness of its own personal feuds, the British generals naturally thought of recovering their lost posts on the Niagara River. McClure, who occupied Fort George and the small town of Newark under its guns, saw his garrison constantly diminishing. Volunteers refused to serve longer on any conditions.[1] The War Department ordered no reinforcements, although ten or twelve thousand soldiers were lying idle at French Mills and Plattsburg. December 10 McClure had about sixty men of the Twenty-fourth infantry, and some forty volunteers, at Fort George, while the number of United States troops present for duty at Fort George, Fort Niagara, Niagara village, Black Rock, and Buffalo, to protect the people and the magazines, amounted to four companies, or three hundred and twenty-four men.

As early as October 4, Armstrong authorized McClure to warn the inhabitants of Newark that their town might suffer destruction in case the defence of Fort George should render such a measure proper.[2] No other orders were given, but Wilkinson repeatedly advised that Fort George should be evacuated,[3] and Armstrong did nothing to protect it, further than to issue a requisition from Albany, November 25, upon the Governor of New York for one thousand militia.[4]

The British, though not rapid in their movements, were not so slow as the Americans. Early in December Lieutenant-General Gordon Drummond came from Kingston to York, and from York to the head of the Lake where the British had maintained themselves since losing the Niagara posts in May.

[1] McClure to Armstrong, Dec. 10, 1813; State Papers, Military Affairs, i. 486.

[2] Armstrong to McClure, Oct. 4, 1813; State Papers, Military Affairs, i. 484.

[3] Wilkinson to Armstrong, Sept. 16, 1813; Sept. 20, 1813; State Papers, Military Affairs, i. 467, 469.

[4] Armstrong to McClure, Nov. 25, 1813; State Papers, Military Affairs, i. 485.

Meanwhile General Vincent had sent Colonel Murray with five hundred men to retake Fort George. McClure at Fort George, December 10, hearing that Murray had approached within ten miles, evacuated the post and crossed the river to Fort Niagara; but before doing so he burned the town of Newark and as much as he could of Queenston, turning the inhabitants, in extreme cold, into the open air. He alleged as his motive the wish to deprive the enemy of winter quarters;[1] yet he did not destroy the tents or military barracks,[2] and he acted without authority, for Armstrong had authorized him to burn Newark only in case he meant to defend Fort George.

"The enemy is much exasperated, and will make a descent on this frontier if possible," wrote McClure from the village of Niagara, December 13; "but I shall watch them close with my handful of men until a reinforcement of militia and volunteers arrives. . . . I am not a little apprehensive that the enemy will take advantage of the exposed condition of Buffalo and our shipping there. My whole effective force on this extensive frontier does not exceed two hundred and fifty men."

Five days passed, and still no reinforcements arrived, and no regular troops were even ordered to start for Niagara. "I apprehended an attack," wrote McClure;[3] and he retired thirty miles to Buffalo, "with a view of providing for the defence." On the night of December 18 Colonel Murray, with five hundred and fifty regular rank-and-file, crossed the river from Fort George unperceived; surprised the sentinels on the glacis and at the gates of Fort Niagara; rushed through the main gate; and, with a loss of eight men killed and wounded, captured the fortress with some three hundred and fifty prisoners.

Nothing could be said on the American side in defence or excuse of this disgrace. From Armstrong at the War Department to Captain Leonard who commanded the fort, every one concerned in the transaction deserved whatever punish-

---

[1] McClure to Armstrong, Dec. 10 and 13, 1813; State Papers, Military Affairs, i. 486.

[2] James, ii. 77.

[3] McClure to Armstrong, Dec. 22, 1813; State Papers, Military Affairs, i. 487.

ment the law or army regulations could inflict. The unfortunate people of Niagara and Buffalo were victims to official
misconduct. The British, thinking themselves released from
ordinary rules of war by the burning of Newark and Queenston, showed unusual ferocity. In the assault on Fort Niagara
they killed sixty-seven Americans, all by the bayonet, while
they wounded only eleven. Immediately afterward they "let
loose"[1] their auxiliary Indians on Lewiston and the country
around. On the night of December 29, Lieutenant-General
Drummond sent a force of fifteen hundred men including
Indians[2] across the river above the falls, and driving away the
militia, burned Black Rock and Buffalo with all their public
stores and three small war-schooners.[3]

These acts of retaliation were justified by Sir George Prevost in a long proclamation[4] dated Jan. 12, 1814, which promised that he would not "pursue further a system of warfare so
revolting to his own feelings and so little congenial to the
British character unless the future measures of the enemy
should compel him again to resort to it." The Americans
themselves bore Drummond's excessive severity with less
complaint than usual. They partly suspected that the destruction effected on the Thames, at York and at Newark, by
American troops, though unauthorized by orders, had warranted some retaliation; but they felt more strongly that their
anger should properly be vented on their own government
and themselves, who had allowed a handful of British troops
to capture a strong fortress and to ravage thirty miles of frontier, after repeated warning, without losing two hundred men
on either side, while thousands of regular troops were idle
elsewhere, and the neighborhood ought without an effort to
have supplied five thousand militia.

Fort Niagara, which thus fell into British hands, remained,
like Mackinaw, in the enemy's possession until the peace.

[1] Christie, ii. 140.
[2] James, ii. 20, 21.
[3] James, ii. 23.
[4] Christie, ii. 143; Niles, v. 382.

Chapter IX

MILITARY MOVEMENTS in the Southern department attracted little notice, but were not the less important. The Southern people entered into the war in the hope of obtaining the Floridas. President Madison, like President Jefferson, gave all the support in his power to the scheme. Throughout the year 1812 United States troops still occupied Amelia Island and the St. Mary's River, notwithstanding the refusal of Congress to authorize the occupation. The President expected Congress at the session of 1812–1813 to approve the seizure of both Floridas, and took measures in advance for that purpose.

October 12, 1812, Secretary Eustis wrote to the Governor of Tennessee calling out fifteen hundred militia for the defence of the "lower country." The force was not intended for defence but for conquest; it was to support the seizure of Mobile, Pensacola, and St. Augustine by the regular troops. For that object every man in Tennessee was ready to serve; and of all Tennesseeans, Andrew Jackson was the most ardent. Governor Blount immediately authorized Jackson, as major-general of the State militia, to call out two thousand volunteers. The call was issued November 14; the volunteers collected at Nashville December 10; and Jan. 7, 1813, the infantry embarked in boats to descend the river, while the mounted men rode through the Indian country to Natchez.

> "I have the pleasure to inform you," wrote Jackson to Eustis in departing,[1] "that I am now at the head of two thousand and seventy volunteers, the choicest of our citizens, who go at the call of their country to execute the will of the Government; who have no Constitutional scruples, and if the Government orders, will rejoice at the opportunity of placing the American eagle on the ramparts of Mobile, Pensacola, and Fort St. Augustine."

The Tennessee army reached Natchez, February 15, and went into camp to wait orders from Washington, which were expected to direct an advance on Mobile and Pensacola.

[1] Parton's Jackson, i. 372.

While Jackson descended the Mississippi, Monroe, then acting Secretary of War, wrote, January 13, to Major-General Pinckney,[1] whose military department included Georgia: "It is intended to place under your command an adequate force for the reduction of St. Augustine should it be decided on by Congress, before whom the subject will be in a few days." A fortnight later, January 30, Monroe wrote also to Wilkinson,[2] then commanding at New Orleans: "The subject of taking possession of West Florida is now before Congress, and will probably pass. You will be prepared to carry into effect this measure should it be decided on."

Neither Madison nor Monroe raised objection to the seizure of territory belonging to a friendly power; but Congress showed no such readiness to act. Senator Anderson of Tennessee, as early as Dec. 10, 1812, moved,[3] in secret session of the Senate, that a committee be appointed to consider the expediency of authorizing the President "to occupy and hold the whole or any part of East Florida, including Amelia Island, and also those parts of West Florida which are not now in the possession and under the jurisdiction of the United States." After much debate the Senate, December 22, adopted the resolution by eighteen votes to twelve, and the committee, consisting of Anderson, Samuel Smith, Tait of Georgia, Varnum of Massachusetts, and Goodrich of Connecticut, reported a bill,[4] January 19, authorizing the President to occupy both Floridas, and to exercise government there, "provided . . . that the section of country herein designated that is situated to the eastward of the river Perdido may be the subject of future negotiation."

The bill met opposition from the President's personal enemies, Giles, Leib, and Samuel Smith, as well as from the Federalists and some of the Northern Democrats. January 26, Samuel Smith moved to strike out the second section, which authorized the seizure of Florida east of the Perdido; and the Senate, February 2, by a vote of nineteen to sixteen, adopted Smith's motion. The vote was sectional. North and South

[1] Monroe to Pinckney, Jan. 13, 1813; MSS. War Department Records.
[2] Monroe to Wilkinson, Jan. 30, 1813; MSS. War Department Records.
[3] Annals of Congress, 1812–1813, p. 124.
[4] Annals of Congress, 1812–1813, p. 127.

Carolina, Georgia, Tennessee, and Louisiana supported the bill; Maryland, Delaware, Pennsylvania, New York, Connecticut, and Rhode Island opposed it; Virginia, Kentucky, Ohio, Massachusetts, New Hampshire, and Vermont were divided; New Jersey threw one vote in its favor, the second senator being absent. Had Leib not changed sides the next day, the whole bill would have been indefinitely postponed; but the majority rallied, February 5, and by a vote of twenty-one to eleven authorized the President to seize Florida west of the Perdido, or, in other words, to occupy Mobile. The House passed the bill in secret session February 9, and the President signed it February 12.[1]

In refusing to seize East Florida, the Senate greatly disarranged Madison's plans. Three days afterward, February 5, Armstrong took charge of the War Department, and his first orders were sent to Andrew Jackson directing him to dismiss his force, "the causes of embodying and marching to New Orleans the corps under your command having ceased to exist."[2] Jackson, ignorant that the Administration was not to blame, and indignant at his curt dismissal, marched his men back to Tennessee, making himself responsible for their pay and rations. On learning these circumstances, Armstrong wrote, March 22, a friendly letter thanking him for the important services his corps would have rendered "had the Executive policy of occupying the two Floridas been adopted by the national legislature."[3]

After the Senate had so persistently refused to support Madison's occupation of East Florida, he could hardly maintain longer the illegal possession he had held during the past year of Amelia Island. February 15, Armstrong wrote to Major-General Pinckney,[4] "The late private proceedings of Congress have resulted in a decision not to invade East Florida at present;" but not until March 7, did the secretary order Pinckney to withdraw the troops from Amelia Island and Spanish territory.[5]

The troops were accordingly withdrawn from Amelia Island,

---

[1] Act of Feb. 12, 1813; Wilkinson's Memoirs, iii. 339.
[2] Parton's Jackson, i. 377.
[3] Armstrong to Jackson, March 22, 1813; MSS. War Department Records.
[4] Armstrong to Pinckney, Feb. 15, 1813; MSS. War Department Records.
[5] Armstrong to Pinckney, March 7, 1813; MSS. War Department Records.

May 16; but nothing could restore East Florida to its former repose, and the anarchy which had been introduced from the United States could never be mastered except by the power that created it. Perhaps Madison would have retained possession, as the least of evils, in spite of the Senate's vote of February 3, had not another cause, independent of legislative will, overcome his repugnance to the evacuation. The Russian offer of mediation arrived while the President was still in doubt. The occupation of Florida, being an act of war against Spain, could not fail to excite the anger of England, and in that feeling of displeasure the Czar must inevitably share. From the moment their cause against Napoleon was common, Russia, England, and Spain were more than likely to act together in resistance to any territorial aggression upon any member of their alliance. The evacuation of East Florida by the United States evaded a serious diplomatic difficulty; and probably not by mere coincidence, Armstrong's order to evacuate Amelia Island was dated March 7, while Daschkoff's letter offering the Czar's mediation was dated March 8.

The Cabinet was so little united in support of the Executive policy that Madison and Monroe ordered the seizure of Mobile without consulting Gallatin, whose persistent hostility to the Florida intrigues was notorious. When Monroe in April gave to Gallatin and Bayard the President's instructions[1] for the peace negotiations, among the rest he directed them to assert "a right to West Florida by cession from France, and a claim to East Florida as an indemnity for spoliations." On receiving these instructions, Gallatin wrote to Monroe, May 2, asking,[2] —

"Where is the importance of taking possession of Mobile this summer? We may do this whenever we please, and is it not better to delay every operation of minor importance which may have a tendency to impede our negotiations with Great Britain and Russia? You know that to take by force any place in possession of another nation, whatever our claim to that place may be, is war; and you must be aware that both Russia and Great Britain will feel disposed,

[1] Gallatin's Works, i. 539, *note*.
[2] Gallatin to Monroe, May 2, 1813; Gallatin's Writings, i. 539.

if not to support the pretensions of Spain against us, at least to take part against the aggressor."

Monroe quickly replied:[1] "With respect to West Florida, possession will be taken of it before you get far on your voyage. That is a question settled." In fact, possession had been taken of it three weeks before he wrote, in pursuance of orders sent in February, apparently without Gallatin's knowledge. Monroe added views of his own, singularly opposed to Gallatin's convictions.

"On the subject of East Florida," wrote Monroe to Gallatin, May 6,[2] "I think I intimated to you in my last that Colonel Lear was under the most perfect conviction, on the authority of information from respectable sources at Cadiz, that the Spanish regency had sold that and the other province to the British government, and that it had done so under a belief that we had, or should soon get, possession of it. My firm belief is that if we were possessed of both, it would facilitate your negotiations in favor of impressment and every other object, especially if it was distinctly seen by the British ministers or minister that, instead of yielding them or any part of either, we would push our fortunes in that direction, and in Canada, if they did not hasten to accommodate."

Gallatin, on the eve of sailing for Russia, replied with good temper, expressing opinions contrary to those of the President and Secretary of State.

"On the subject of Florida," Gallatin said,[3] "I have always differed in opinion with you, and am rejoiced to have it in our power to announce the evacuation of the province. Let it alone until you shall, by the introduction of British troops, have a proof of the supposed cession. In this I do not believe. It can be nothing more than a permission to occupy it in order to defend it for Spain. By withdrawing our troops, we withdraw the pretence; but the impolitic occupancy of Mobile will, I fear, renew our difficulties. The

[1] Monroe to Gallatin, May 5, 1813; Gallatin's Writings, i. 540.
[2] Monroe to Gallatin, May 6, 1813; Gallatin's Writings, i. 542.
[3] Gallatin to Monroe, May 8, 1813; Gallatin's Writings, i. 544.

object is at present of very minor importance, swelled into consequence by the representations from that quarter, and which I would not at this moment have attempted, among other reasons, because it was a Southern one, and will, should it involve us in a war with Spain, disgust every man north of Washington. You will pardon the freedom with which, on the eve of parting with you, I speak on this subject. It is intended as a general caution, which I think important, because I know and see every day the extent of geographical feeling, and the necessity of prudence if we mean to preserve and invigorate the Union."

No sooner did the Act of February 12 become law than Armstrong wrote, February 16, to Wilkinson at New Orleans, enclosing a copy of the Act, and ordering him immediately to take possession of Mobile and the country as far as the Perdido.[1] Wilkinson, who had for years looked forward to that step, hastened to obey the instruction. When Gallatin remonstrated, the measure had been already taken and could not be recalled.

Since July 9, 1812, Wilkinson had again commanded at New Orleans. No immediate attack was to be feared, nor could a competent British force be collected there without warning; but in case such an attack should be made, Wilkinson had reason to fear the result, for his regular force consisted of only sixteen hundred effectives, ill equipped and without defences.[2] The War Department ordered him to depend on movable ordnance and temporary works rather than on permanent fortifications;[3] but with his usual disregard of orders he began the construction or the completion of extensive works at various points on the river and coast, at a cost which the government could ill afford.

While engaged in this task Wilkinson received, March 14, Armstrong's order of February 16 for the invasion of West Florida. When the government's orders were agreeable to Wilkinson, they reached him promptly and were executed with rapidity. Within three weeks he collected at Pass

[1] Armstrong to Wilkinson, Feb. 16, 1813; Wilkinson's Memoirs, iii. 339.
[2] Minutes of a Council of War, Aug. 4, 1813; Wilkinson's Memoirs, i. 498–503.
[3] Eustis to Wilkinson, April 15, 1812; Wilkinson's Memoirs, i. 495.

Christian a force of about six hundred men, supported by gunboats, and entered the Bay of Mobile on the night of April 10, while at the same time the garrison at Fort Stoddert descended the Tensaw River, and cut the communication by land between Mobile and Pensacola. At that time Mobile Point was undefended. The only Spanish fortress was Fort Charlotte at Mobile, garrisoned by one hundred and fifty combatants. Wilkinson summoned the fort to surrender, and the commandant had no choice but to obey, for the place was untenable and without supplies. The surrender took place April 15. Wilkinson then took possession of the country as far as the Perdido, and began the construction of a fort, to be called Fort Bowyer, on Mobile Point at the entrance of the Bay, some sixty miles below the town.[1]

This conquest, the only permanent gain of territory made during the war, being effected without bloodshed, attracted less attention than it deserved. Wilkinson committed no errors, and won the President's warm approval.[2] Wilkinson was greatly pleased by his own success, and wished to remain at New Orleans to carry out his projected defences; but Armstrong had written as early as March 10, ordering him to the Lakes. As so often happened with orders that displeased the general, Armstrong's letter, though dated March 10, and doubtless arriving in New Orleans before April 10, was received by Wilkinson only on his return, May 19. After another delay of three weeks, he started northward, and travelled by way of Mobile through the Creek country to Washington.

Wilkinson's departure, June 10, and the evacuation of Amelia Island by General Pinckney May 16, closed the first chapter of the war in the South. Armstrong wrote to Wilkinson, May 27:[3] "The mission to Petersburg and the instructions to our envoys will put a barrier between you and Pensacola for some time to come at least, and permanently in case of peace." The sudden stop thus put by the Senate and the Russian mediation to the campaign against Pensacola and St. Augustine deranged the plans of Georgia and Tennessee, arrested the career of Andrew Jackson, and caused

[1] Wilkinson's Memoirs, i. 507–522.
[2] Armstrong to Wilkinson, May 22, 1813; Wilkinson's Memoirs, i. 521.
[3] Armstrong to Wilkinson, May 27, 1813; MSS. War Department Records.

the transfer of Wilkinson from New Orleans to the Lakes. The government expected no other difficulties in the Southern country, and had no reason to fear them. If new perils suddenly arose, they were due less to England, Spain, or the United States than to the chance that gave energy and influence to Tecumthe.

The Southern Indians were more docile and less warlike than the Indians of the Lakes. The Chickasaws and Choctaws, who occupied the whole extent of country on the east bank of the Mississippi River from the Ohio to the Gulf, gave little trouble or anxiety; and even the great confederacy of Muskogees, or Creeks, who occupied the territory afterward called the State of Alabama and part of Georgia, fell in some degree into a mode of life which seemed likely to make them tillers of the soil. In 1800 the Creeks held, or claimed, about three hundred miles square from the Tennessee River to the Gulf, and from the middle of Georgia nearly to the line which afterward marked the State of Mississippi. The Seminoles, or wild men, of Florida were a branch of the Muskogees, and the Creek warriors themselves were in the habit of visiting Pensacola and Mobile, where they expected to receive presents from the Spanish governor.

Two thirds of the Creek towns were on the Coosa and Tallapoosa rivers in the heart of Alabama. Their inhabitants were called Upper Creeks. The Lower Creeks lived in towns on the Chattahoochee River, the modern boundary between Alabama and Georgia. The United States government, following a different policy in 1799 from that of Jefferson toward the Northwestern Indians, induced the Creeks to adopt a national organization for police purposes; it also helped them to introduce ploughs, to learn cotton-spinning, and to raise crops. The success of these experiments was not at first great, for the larger number of Indians saw no advantage in becoming laborers, and preferred sitting in the squares of the towns, or hunting; but here and there chiefs or half-breeds had farms, slaves, stock, orchards, and spinning-wheels.

Large as the Creek country was, and wild as it had ever been, it did not abound in game. A good hunter, passing in any direction through the three hundred miles of Alabama and Georgia, found difficulty in obtaining game enough for

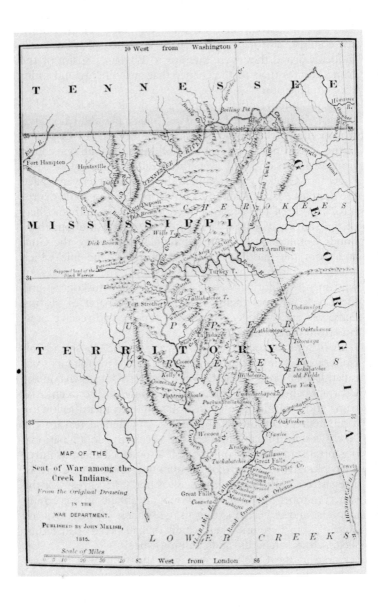

MAP OF THE
Seat of War among the
Creek Indians.
From the Original Drawing
IN THE
WAR DEPARTMENT.
PUBLISHED BY JOHN MELISH,
1815.
Scale of Miles

his support.[1] For that reason the Seminoles left their old towns and became wild people, as their name implied, making irregular settlements in Florida, where game and food were more plenty. The mass of the Creek nation, fixed in the villages in the interior, clung to their habits of hunting even when obliged to cultivate the soil, and their semi-civilization rendered them a more perplexing obstacle to the whites than though they had obstinately resisted white influence.

Had the Indian problem been left to the people of Georgia and Tennessee, the Indians would soon have disappeared; but the national government established under President Washington in 1789 put a sharp curb on Georgia, and interposed decisively between the Georgians and the Creeks.[2] President Washington in 1796 appointed Benjamin Hawkins of North Carolina as Indian agent among the Creeks, and Hawkins protected and governed them with devotion; but the result of his friendliness was the same as that of others' greed. The Indians slowly lost ground.

The Creeks complained of grievances similar to those of the Northwestern Indians, and their position was even more helpless. They had no other outlet than Pensacola and Mobile. Except from the Spaniards they could expect no aid in case of trouble, and the Spanish governors of Florida, after the abdication of Carlos IV. in 1807, could scarcely maintain their own position, much less supply the Creeks with arms or gunpowder. While the Northwestern Indians could buy at Malden all the weapons and ammunition they wanted, the Creeks possessed few firearms, and these in bad condition; nor were they skilful in using guns.

The United States government prevented the Georgians from compelling the Indians to sell their lands, but nothing could prevent them from trespass; and the Indian woods along the frontier were filled with cattle, horses, and hogs belonging to the whites, while white men destroyed the game, hunting the deer by firelight, and scaring the Indian hunters from their hunting-grounds. "Every cane-swamp where they go to look for a bear—which is part of their

[1] Hawkins's Sketch, p. 24.
[2] U. S. Commissioners to Governor Irwin, July 1, 1796; State Papers, Indian Affairs, i. 611.

support—is near eat out by the stocks put over by the citizens of Georgia."[1] This complaint was made in 1796, and as
time went on the Indian hunting-grounds were more rapidly
narrowed. Not only from Georgia but also from Fort Stoddert, along the course of the Tombigbee River, above Mobile,
intruders pressed into the Creek country. The Indians had no
choice but to sell their lands for annuities, and under this
pressure the Creeks, in 1802 and 1803, were induced to part
with the district between the Oconee and Ocmulgee in the
centre of Georgia. They retained their towns on the Chattahoochee, where Hawkins's agency was established in the
town of Coweta, on the edge of the Creek country.

Hawkins was satisfied with their behavior, and believed the
chiefs to be well disposed. They showed none of the restlessness which characterized the Northwestern Indians, until Tecumthe conceived the idea of bringing them into his general
league to check the encroachments of the whites. After Tecumthe's interview with Governor Harrison at Vincennes, in
July, 1811, he made a long journey through the Chickasaw and
Choctaw country, and arrived among the Creeks in October,
bringing with him a score of Indian warriors. The annual
council of the Creeks was held in that month at the village of
Tuckaubatchee,—an ancient town of the Upper Creeks on
the Tallapoosa. The rumor that Tecumthe would be present
brought great numbers of Indians, even Cherokees and Choctaws, to the place, while Hawkins attended the council in his
character as agent.

Tecumthe and his warriors marched into the centre of the
square and took their places in silence. That night "they
danced the dance of the Indians of the Lakes," which became
thenceforward a political symbol of their party among the
Creeks. Some nights afterward Tecumthe addressed the council. Versions more or less untrustworthy have been given of
the speech;[2] but the only official allusion to it by a person
entitled to credit seemed to show that it was in substance the
address made by Tecumthe at Vincennes. Hawkins, recalling
to the Creek chiefs in 1814 the course of events which had

[1] Talk of the Creek Indians, June 24, 1796; State Papers, Indian Affairs, i.
604.
[2] Life of Sam Dale, p. 59.

caused their troubles, reminded them how "Tecumseh, in the square of Tuckaubatchee, . . . told the Creeks not to do any injury to the Americans; to be in peace and friendship with them; not to steal even a bell from any one of any color. Let the white people on this continent manage their affairs their own way. Let the red people manage their affairs their own way."[1] Hawkins and the old chiefs would have certainly interfered had Tecumthe incited the Creeks to war or violence; but according to Hawkins the speech was a pacific "talk," delivered by Tecumthe in the name of the British. Indian tradition preserved another form of Tecumthe's rhetoric, which seemed to complete the identity with the Vincennes address. Unable to express himself in the Muskogee language, Tecumthe used pantomime familiar to Indians. Holding his war-club with outstretched arm, he opened first the little finger, then the next and the next, till the club fell from his hand.

Indian union was unquestionably the chief theme of all Tecumthe's public addresses. Whether in private he taught other doctrines must be matter of surmise; but he certainly brought into the Creek nation a religious fanaticism of a peculiar and dangerous kind. Prophets soon appeared, chiefly among the Alabamas, a remnant of an ancient race, not of Creek blood, but members of the Creek confederacy.[2] The prophets, with the usual phenomena of hysteria, claimed powers of magic, and promised to bring earthquakes to destroy an invading army. They preached the total destruction of everything, animate and inanimate, that pertained to civilization. As the nation generally was badly armed, and relied chiefly on their bows, arrows, and war-clubs for battle,[3] the moral support of magic was needed to give them confidence.

So secret was the influence of Tecumthe's friends that no suspicion of the excitement reached Hawkins even when the war with England began; and the old chiefs of the nation—

[1] Hawkins to the Creek Chiefs, June 16, 1814; State Papers, Indian Affairs, i. 845.

[2] Report of Alexander Cornells, June 22, 1813; State Papers, Indian Affairs, i. 845, 846.

[3] Hawkins to General Pinckney, July 9, 1813; State Papers, Indian Affairs, i. 848.

known to be devoted to peace and to the white alliance—
were kept in ignorance of all that was done among the young
warriors. The Alabamas, or Coosadas, lived below the junction of the Coosa and Tallapoosa, on the west bank of the
Alabama River, about eight miles above the modern town of
Montgomery; they were considered by Hawkins the most industrious and best behaved of all the Creeks, whose fields
were the granaries of the upper towns and furnished supplies
even to Mobile. Their town was the last place in which
Hawkins expected to see conspiracy, violence, or fanaticism.
The young men "sang the song of the Indians of the Lakes,
and danced the dance" in secret for eighteen months after
Tecumthe's visit, without public alarm, and probably would
have continued to do so except for an outbreak committed by
some of their nation three hundred miles away.

In 1812 a band of six Indians led by the Little Warrior of
Wewocau, a Creek town on the Coosa, was sent by the nation
on a public mission to the Chickasaws.[1] Instead of delivering
their "talks" and returning, they continued their journey to
the northern Lakes and joined Tecumthe at Malden. They
took part in the massacre at the river Raisin, Jan. 22, 1813, and
soon afterward began their return, bringing talks from the
Shawanese and British and also a letter from some British
officer at Malden to the Spanish officials at Pensacola, from
whom they hoped to obtain weapons and powder. According
to common report, Tecumthe told the Little Warrior that he
was about to aid the British in capturing Fort Meigs, and as
soon as the fort was taken he would come to join the Creeks.[2]
Until then his friends were to increase their party by the secret means and magic that had proved so successful, but were
not to begin open war.[3]

The Little Warrior and his party, including a warrior from
Tuskegee, a Creek town at the fork of the Coosa and Tallapoosa, after crossing Indiana in the month of February
reached the north bank of the Ohio River about seven miles

[1] Hawkins to the Creek Chiefs, March 29, 1813; State Papers, Indian Affairs,
i. 839.

[2] Hawkins to Armstrong, Aug. 23, 1813; State Papers, Indian Affairs, i. 851.

[3] Report of Alexander Cornells, June 23, 1813; State Papers, Indian Affairs,
i. 846.

above its mouth, where were two cabins occupied by white families.[1] Unable to resist the temptation to spill blood, the band murdered the two families with the usual Indian horrors. This outrage was committed February 9; and the band, crossing the Ohio, passed southward through the Chickasaw country, avowing the deed and its motive.[2]

The Little Warrior arrived at home about the middle of March, and reported that he brought talks from the Shawanese and British. The old chiefs of the Upper Creeks immediately held a council March 25, and after listening to the talks, reprimanded the Little Warrior and ordered him to leave the Council House.[3] On the same day Hawkins wrote to them from Coweta, demanding delivery of the Little Warrior and his six companions to answer for the murders they had committed. On hearing this demand, the old chiefs at Tuckaubatchee under the lead of the Big Warrior held another council, while the Little Warrior, the Tuskegee Warrior, and the murderers took to the woods. The old chiefs in council decided to execute the murderers, and sent out parties to do it. The Little Warrior was found in the swamp, well armed, but was decoyed out and killed by treachery; "the first and second man's gun snapped at him, but the third man's gun fired and killed; . . . four men that had on pouches kept them shaking following after him, so that he could not hear the gun snap; if he had found out that, he would have wounded a good many with his arrows."[4]

The Tuskegee Warrior and four others were found in a house on the Hickory Ground at the fork of the rivers. As long as they had ammunition, they held the attack at a distance, but at last the house was fired. The Tuskegee Warrior being wounded, was burned in the house, while his two young brothers were taken out and tomahawked. One warrior broke away, but was caught and killed; two more were

[1] Letter from Kaskaskias, Feb. 27, 1813; Niles, iv. 135.

[2] Hawkins to the Creek Chiefs, March 29, 1813; State Papers, Indian Affairs, i. 839.

[3] Hawkins to Armstrong, March 25, 1813; State Papers, Indian Affairs, i. 840.

[4] Report of the Big Warrior, April 26, 1813; State Papers, Indian Affairs, i. 843.

killed elsewhere. One escaped, and "set out the morning after to kill white people." Warriors were sent after him.

"He made battle, firing at the warriors, and was near killing one; the bullet passed near his ear. He then drew his knife and tomahawk, defended himself, and the warriors shot three balls through him. He fell, retained the power of speech till next day, and died. He said he had been to the Shawanese helping of them, and had got fat eating white people's flesh. Every one to the very last called on the Shawanese general, Tecumseh."[1]

Such political executions, in the stifled excitement of the moment, could not but rouse violent emotion throughout the Creek nation. The old chiefs, having given life for life, felt the stronger for their assertion of authority; but they knew nothing of the true situation. For several weeks no open outbreak occurred, but the prophets were more active than ever. About June 4 the old chiefs at Tuckaubatchee, hearing that the prophets "kept as usual their fooleries," sent a runner to the Alabamas with a message:[2] —

"You are but a few Alabama people. You say that the Great Spirit visits you frequently; that he comes in the sun and speaks to you; that the sun comes down just above your heads. Now we want to see and hear what you say you have seen and heard. Let us have the same proof you have had, and we will believe what we see and hear. You have nothing to fear; the people who committed murders have suffered for their crimes, and there is an end of it."

The runner who carried this message was one of the warriors who had aided in killing the seven murderers. The Alabamas instantly put him to death, and sent his scalp to their friends at the forks of the river. Then began a general uprising, and every warrior who had aided in killing the murderers was himself killed or hunted from the Upper Creek country. The chiefs of Tuckaubatchee with difficulty escaped to the

[1] Report of Nimrod Doyell, May 3, 1813; State Papers, Indian Affairs, i. 843.
[2] Report of Alexander Cornells, June 22, 1813; State Papers, Indian Affairs, i. 845.

agency at Coweta, where they were under the protection of Georgia.

The Lower Creek towns did not join the outbreak; but of the Upper Creek towns twenty-nine declared for war, and only five for peace. At least two thousand warriors were believed to have taken the war-club by August 1, and got the name of Red Clubs, or Red Sticks, for that reason. Everywhere they destroyed farms, stock, and all objects of white civilization, and killed or drove away their opponents.[1]

With all this the Spaniards had nothing to do. The outbreak was caused by the Indian War in the Northwest, and immediately by the incompetence of General Winchester and by the massacre at the river Raisin. The Creeks were totally unprepared for war, except so far as they trusted to magic; they had neither guns, powder, nor balls. For that reason they turned to the Spaniards, who could alone supply them. When the Little Warrior was put to death, the British letter which he carried from Malden for the Spanish officials at Pensacola came into the charge of another Creek warrior, Peter McQueen, a half-breed. In July, McQueen, with a large party of warriors started for Pensacola, with the letter and four hundred dollars, to get powder.[2] On arriving there they saw the Spanish governor, who treated them civilly, and in fear of violence gave them, according to McQueen's account,[3] "a small bag of powder each for ten towns, and five bullets to each man." With this supply, which the governor represented as a friendly present for hunting purposes, they were obliged to content themselves, and started on their return journey.

News that McQueen's party was at Pensacola instantly reached the American settlements above Mobile, where the inhabitants were already taking refuge in stockades.[4] A large number of Americans, without military organization, under several leaders, one of whom was a half-breed named Dixon Bailey, started July 26 to intercept McQueen, and succeeded in surprising the Indians July 27 at a place called Burnt Corn,

[1] Talosee Fixico to Hawkins, July 5, 1813; State Papers, Indian Affairs, i. 847.
[2] Hawkins to Armstrong, July 20, 1813; State Papers, Indian Affairs, i. 849.
[3] Hawkins to Armstrong, Aug. 23, 1813; State Papers, Indian Affairs, i. 851.
[4] Carson to Claiborne, July 29, 1813; Life of Dale, p. 78.

about eighty miles north of Pensacola. The whites at first routed the Indians, and captured the pack-mules with the ammunition; but the Indians quickly rallied, and in their turn routed the whites, with a loss of two killed and fifteen wounded,—although they failed to recover the greater part of the pack-animals. With the small amount of powder left to him, McQueen then returned to his people.

Angry at the attack and eager to revenge the death of his warriors, McQueen summoned the warriors of thirteen towns, some eight hundred in number, and about August 20 started in search of his enemies. The Creek war differed from that on the Lakes in being partly a war of half-breeds. McQueen's strongest ally was William Weatherford, a half-breed, well known throughout the country as a man of property and ability, as nearly civilized as Indian blood permitted, and equally at home among Indians and whites. McQueen and Weatherford were bitterly hostile to the half-breeds Bailey and Beasley, who were engaged in the affair of Burnt Corn.[1] Both Beasley and Bailey were at a stockade called Fort Mims, some thirty-five miles above Mobile, on the eastern side of the Alabama River, where about five hundred and fifty persons were collected,—a motley crowd of whites, half-breeds, Indians, and negroes, old and young, women and children, protected only by a picket wall, pierced by five hundred loopholes three and a half feet from the ground, and two rude gates.[2] Beasley commanded, and wrote, August 30, that he could "maintain the post against any number of Indians."[3] To Fort Mims the Creek warriors turned, for the reason that Beasley and Bailey were there, and they arrived in the neighborhood, August 29, without giving alarm. Twice, negroes tending cattle outside rushed back to the fort reporting that painted warriors were hovering about; but the horsemen when sent out discovered no sign of an enemy, and Beasley tied up and flogged the second negro for giving a false alarm.

At noon, August 30, when the drum beat for dinner no patrols were out, the gates were open, and sand had drifted against that on the eastern side so that it could not quickly be

[1] Hawkins to Floyd, Sept. 30, 1813; State Papers, Indian Affairs, i. 854.
[2] Pickett's Alabama, ii. 264.
[3] Life of Dale, 106.

closed. Suddenly a swarm of Indians raising the warwhoop rushed toward the fort. Beasley had time to reach the gate, but could not close it, and was tomahawked on the spot. The Indians got possession of the loop-holes outside, and of one inclosure. The whites, under Dixon Bailey, held the inner inclosure and fought with desperation; but at last the Indians succeeded in setting fire to the house in the centre, and the fire spread to the whole stockade. The Indians then effected an entrance, and massacred most of the inmates. Fifteen persons escaped, and among these was Dixon Bailey mortally wounded. Most of the negroes were spared to be slaves. Two hundred and fifty scalps became trophies of the Creek warriors,—a number such as had been seldom taken by Indians from the white people on a single day.

Chapter X

THE BATTLE AT Burnt Corn was regarded by the Indians as a declaration of war by the whites. Till then they seemed to consider themselves engaged in a domestic quarrel, or civil war;[1] but after the massacre at Fort Mims they could not retreat, and yet knew that they must perish except for supernatural aid. Their destiny was controlled by that of Tecumthe. Ten days after the massacre at Fort Mims, Perry won his victory on Lake Erie, which settled the result of the Indian wars both in the North and in the South. Tecumthe had expected to capture Fort Meigs, and with it Fort Wayne and the line of the Maumee and Wabash. On the impulse of this success he probably hoped to raise the war-spirit among the Chickasaws and Choctaws, and then in person to call the Creeks into the field. Proctor's successive defeats blasted Indian hopes, and the Creeks had hardly struck their first blow in his support when Tecumthe himself fell, and the Indians of the Lakes submitted or fled to Canada.

At best, the Creek outbreak would have been hopeless. Although the number of hostile Creek warriors was matter of conjecture, nothing showed that they could exceed four thousand. At Pensacola, Peter McQueen was said to have claimed forty-eight hundred "gun-men" on his side.[2] At such a moment he probably exaggerated his numbers. The Big Warrior, who led the peace party, estimated the hostile Creeks, early in August, as numbering at least twenty-five hundred warriors.[3] If the number of gun-men was four thousand, the number of guns in their possession could scarcely be more than one thousand. Not only had the Creeks few guns, and those in poor condition, but they had little powder or lead, and no means of repairing their weapons. Their guns commonly missed fire, and even after discharging them, the Creeks seldom reloaded, but resorted to the bow-and-arrows which they always carried. As warriors they felt their inferiority to the Shawanese and Indians of

[1] Hawkins to Armstrong, July 20, 1813; State Papers, Indian Affairs, i. 849.
[2] Hawkins to Floyd, Sept. 30, 1813; State Papers, Indian Affairs, i. 854.
[3] Big Warrior to Hawkins, Aug. 4, 1813; State Papers, Indian Affairs, i. 851.

the Lakes, while their position was more desperate, for the Choctaws and Cherokees behind them refused to join in their war.

Four thousand warriors who had never seen a serious war even with their Indian neighbors, and armed for the most part with clubs, or bows-and-arrows, were not able to resist long the impact of three or four armies, each nearly equal to their whole force, coming from every quarter of the compass. On the other hand, the military difficulties of conquering the Creeks were not trifling. The same obstacles that stopped Harrison in Ohio, stopped Pinckney in Georgia. Pinckney, like Harrison, could set in motion three columns of troops on three converging lines, but he could not feed them or make roads for them. The focus of Indian fanaticism was the Hickory Ground at the fork of the Coosa and Tallapoosa, about one hundred and fifty miles distant from the nearest point that would furnish supplies for an American army coming from Georgia, Tennessee, or Mobile. Pinckney's natural line of attack was through Georgia to the Lower Creek towns and the American forts on the Chattahoochee, whence he could move along a good road about eighty miles to the Upper Creek towns, near the Hickory Ground. The next convenient line was from Mobile up the Alabama River about one hundred and fifty miles to the same point. The least convenient was the pathless, mountainous, and barren region of Upper Alabama and Georgia, through which an army from Tennessee must toil for at least a hundred miles in order to reach an enemy.

The State of Georgia was most interested in the Creek war, and was chiefly to profit by it. Georgia in 1813 had a white population of about one hundred and twenty-five thousand, and a militia probably numbering thirty thousand. Military District No. 6, embracing the two Carolinas and Georgia, was supposed to contain two thousand regular troops, and was commanded by Major-General Pinckney. Under Pinckney's command, a thousand regulars and three thousand militia, advancing from Georgia by a good road eighty miles into the Indian country, should have been able to end the Creek war within six months from the massacre at Fort Mims; but for some reason the attempts on that side were not so successful as they should have been, and were neither rapid nor vigorous. Tennessee took the lead.

In respect of white population, the State of Tennessee was more than double the size of Georgia; but it possessed a greater advantage in Andrew Jackson, whose extreme energy was equivalent to the addition of an army. When news of the Mims massacre reached Nashville about the middle of September, Jackson was confined to his bed by a pistol-shot, which had broken his arm and nearly cost his life ten days before in a street brawl with Thomas H. Benton. From his bed he issued an order calling back into service his two thousand volunteers of 1812; and as early as October 12, little more than a month after the affair at Fort Mims, he and his army of twenty-five hundred men were already camped on the Tennessee River south of Huntsville in Alabama. There was his necessary base of operations, but one hundred and sixty miles of wilderness lay between him and the Hickory Ground.

On the Tennessee River Jackson's position bore some resemblance to that of Harrison on the Maumee a year before. Energy could not save him from failure. Indeed, the greater his energy the more serious were his difficulties. He depended on supplies from east Tennessee descending the river; but the river was low, and the supplies could not be moved. He had taken no measures to procure supplies from Nashville. Without food and forage he could not safely advance, or even remain where he was. Under such conditions, twenty-five hundred men with half as many horses could not be kept together. Harrison under the same difficulties held back his main force near its magazines till it disbanded, without approaching within a hundred miles of its object. Jackson suffered nearly the same fate. He sent away his mounted men under General Coffee to forage on the banks of the Black Warrior River, fifty miles to the southwest, where no Creeks were to be feared. He forced his infantry forward through rough country some twenty miles, to a point where the river made its most southern bend, and there, in the mountainous defile, he established, October 23, a camp which he called Deposit, where his supplies were to be brought when the river should permit.

Coffee's mounted men returned October 24. Then,

October 25, in the hope of finding food as he went, Jackson plunged into the mountains beyond the river, intending to make a raid, as far as he could, into the Creek country. Except fatigue and famine, he had nothing to fear. The larger Creek towns were a hundred miles to the southward, and were busy with threatened attacks nearer home. After a week's march Jackson reached the upper waters of the Coosa. Within a short distance were two or three small Creek villages. Against one of these Jackson sent his mounted force, numbering nine hundred men, under General Coffee. Early in the morning of November 3, Coffee surrounded and destroyed Talishatchee. His report represented that the Indians made an obstinate resistance.[1] "Not one of the warriors escaped to tell the news,—a circumstance unknown heretofore." According to Coffee's estimate, Talishatchee contained two hundred and eighty-four Indians of both sexes and all ages. If one in three could be reckoned as capable of bearing arms, the number of warriors was less than one hundred. Coffee's men after the battle counted one hundred and eighty-six dead Indians, and estimated the total loss at two hundred. In every attack on an Indian village a certain number of women and children were necessarily victims, but the proportion at Talishatchee seemed large.

"I lost five men killed, and forty-one wounded," reported Coffee,—"none mortally, the greater part slightly, a number with arrows. Two of the men killed was with arrows; this appears to form a very principal part of the enemy's arms for warfare, every man having a bow with a bundle of arrows, which is used after the first fire with the gun until a leisure time for loading offers."

Meanwhile Jackson fortified a point on the Coosa, about thirty-five miles from his base on the Tennessee, and named it Fort Strother. There he expected to be joined by a division of east Tennessee militia under General Cocke, approaching from Chattanooga, as he hoped, with supplies; but while waiting, he received, November 7, a message from Talladega, a Creek village thirty miles to the southward, reporting that

[1] Report of General Coffee, Nov. 4, 1813; Niles, v. 218.

the town, which had refused to join the war-party, was besieged and in danger of capture by a large body of hostile
warriors. Jackson instantly started to save Talladega, and
marched twenty-four miles November 8, surrounding and attacking the besieging Creeks the next morning.

"The victory was very decisive," reported Jackson to
Governor Blount,[1] November 11; "two hundred and ninety
of the enemy were left dead, and there can be no doubt
but many more were killed who were not found. . . . In
the engagement we lost fifteen killed, and eighty-five
wounded."

Coffee estimated the number of Indians, on their own
report,[2] at about one thousand. Jackson mentioned no
wounded Indians, nor the number of hostile Creeks engaged.
Male Indians, except infants, were invariably killed, and probably not more than five or six hundred were in the battle, for
Coffee thought very few escaped unhurt.

At Talladega Jackson was sixty miles from the Hickory
Ground, and still nearer to several large Indian towns, but he
had already passed the limit of his powers. News arrived that
the army of eastern Tennessee had turned eastward toward
the Tallapoosa, and that his expected supplies were as remote
as ever. Returning to Fort Strother November 10, Jackson
waited there in forced inactivity, as Harrison had waited at
Fort Meigs, anxious only to avoid the disgrace of retreat. For
two weeks the army had lived on the Indians. A month more
passed in idle starvation, until after great efforts a supply train
was organized, and difficulties on that account ceased; but at
the same moment the army claimed discharge.

The claim was reasonable. Enlisted Dec. 10, 1812, for one
year, the men were entitled to their discharge Dec. 10, 1813.
Had Jackson been provided with fresh levies he would doubtless have dismissed the old; but in his actual situation their
departure would have left him at Fort Strother to pass the
winter alone. To prevent this, he insisted that the men had no
right to count as service, within the twelve months for which

[1] Jackson to Blount, Nov. 11, 1813; Niles, v. 267.
[2] Parton's Jackson, i. 445.

they had enlisted, the months between May and October when they were dismissed to their homes. The men, unanimous in their own view of the contract, started to march home December 10; and Jackson, in a paroxysm of anger, planted two small pieces of artillery in their path and threatened to fire on them. The men, with good-temper, yielded for the moment; and Jackson, quickly recognizing his helplessness, gave way, and allowed them to depart December 12, with a vehement appeal for volunteers who made no response.

Fort Strother was then held for a short time by east Tennessee militia, about fourteen hundred in number, whose term of service was a few weeks longer than that of the west Tennesseeans. Jackson could do nothing with them, and remained idle. The Governor of Tennessee advised him to withdraw to the State frontier; but Jackson, while admitting that his campaign had failed, declared that he would perish before withdrawing from the ground he considered himself to have gained.[1] Fortunately he stood in no danger. The Creeks did not molest him, and he saw no enemy within fifty miles.

While Jackson was thus brought to a stand-still, Major-General Cocke of east Tennessee, under greater disadvantages, accomplished only results annoying to Jackson. Cocke with twenty-five hundred three-months militia took the field at Knoxville October 12, and moving by way of Chattanooga reached the Coosa sixty or seventy miles above Camp Strother. The nearest Creek Indians were the Hillabees, on a branch of the Tallapoosa about sixty miles from Cocke's position, and the same distance from Jackson. The Hillabees, a group of four small villages, numbered in 1800 one hundred and seventy warriors.[2] Unaware that the Hillabees were making their submission to Jackson, and were to receive his promise of protection, Cocke sent a large detachment, which started November 12 into the Indian country, and surprised one of the Hillabee villages November 18, massacring sixty-one warriors, and capturing the other inmates, two hundred

[1] Blount to Jackson, Dec. 22, 1813; Parton's Jackson, i. 479, 480–484.
[2] Hawkins's Sketch, pp. 43, 44.

and fifty in number, without losing a drop of blood or meeting any resistance.[1]

Jackson was already displeased with General Cocke's conduct, and the Hillabee massacre increased his anger. Cocke
had intentionally kept himself and his army at a distance in
order to maintain an independent command.[2] Not until Jackson's troops disbanded and marched home, December 12, did
Cocke come to Fort Strother. There his troops remained a
month, guarding Jackson's camp, until January 12, 1814, when
their three months' term expired.

While five thousand men under Jackson and Cocke wan-
dered about northern Alabama, able to reach only small and
remote villages, none of which were actively concerned in the
outbreak, the Georgians organized a force to enter the heart
of the Creek country. Brigadier-General John Floyd commanded the Georgia army, and neither Major-General Pinckney nor any United States troops belonged to it. Jackson's
battle of Talladega was fought November 9; Cocke's expedition against the Hillabees started November 12, and surprised
the Hillabee village November 18. Floyd entered the hostile
country November 24. The Georgians though nearest were
last to move, and moved with the weakest force. Floyd had
but nine hundred and forty militia, and three or four hundred
friendly warriors of the Lower Creek villages.

Floyd had heard that large numbers of hostile Indians were
assembled at Autossee,—a town on the Tallapoosa River near
Tuckaubatchee, in the centre of the Upper Creek country. He
crossed the Chattahoochee November 24 with five days rations, and marched directly against Autossee, arriving within
nine or ten miles without meeting resistance. At half-past six
on the morning of November 29 he formed his troops for
action in front of the town.[3]

The difference between the Northwestern Indians and the
Creeks was shown in the battle of Autossee compared with
Tippecanoe. Floyd was weaker than Harrison, having only
militia and Indians, while Harrison had a regular regiment
composing one third of his rank-and-file. The Creeks were

[1] Cocke to the Secretary of War, Nov. 28, 1813; Niles, v. 282, 283.
[2] Cocke to White; Parton's Jackson, i. 451.
[3] Floyd to Pinckney, Dec. 4, 1813; Niles, v. 283.

probably more numerous than the Tippecanoe Indians, although in both cases the numbers were quite unknown. Probably the Creeks were less well armed, but they occupied a strong position and stood on the defensive. Floyd reported that by nine o'clock he drove the Indians from their towns and burned their houses,—supposed to be four hundred in number. He estimated their loss at two hundred killed. His own loss was eleven killed and fifty-four wounded. That of Harrison at Tippecanoe was sixty-one killed or mortally wounded, and one hundred and twenty-seven not fatally injured. The Creeks hardly inflicted one fourth the loss caused by the followers of the Shawnee Prophet.

General Floyd,—himself among the severely wounded,—immediately after the battle ordered the troops to begin their return march to the Chattahoochee. The Georgia raid into the Indian country was bolder, less costly, and more effective than the Tennessee campaign; but at best it was only a raid, like the Indian assault on Fort Mims, and offered no immediate prospect of regular military occupation. Another attempt, from a third quarter, had the same unsatisfactory result.

The successor of General Wilkinson at New Orleans and Mobile, and in Military District No. 7, was Brigadier-General Thomas Flournoy. Under his direction an expedition was organized from Fort Stoddert, commanded by Brigadier-General Claiborne of the Mississippi volunteers. Claiborne was given the Third United States Infantry, with a number of militia, volunteers, and Choctaw Indians,—in all about a thousand men. He first marched to a point on the Alabama River, about eighty-five miles above Fort Stoddert, where he constructed a military post, called Fort Claiborne. Having established his base there, he marched, December 13, up the river till he reached, December 23, the Holy Ground, where the half-breed Weatherford lived. There Claiborne approached within about fifty miles of the point which Floyd reached a month before, but for want of co-operation he could not maintain his advantage. He attacked and captured Weatherford's town, killing thirty Indians, with a loss of one man; but after destroying the place he retreated, arriving unharmed at Fort Claiborne, on the last day of the year.

Thus the year 1813 ended without closing the Creek war. More than seven thousand men had entered the Indian country from four directions; and with a loss of thirty or forty lives had killed, according to their reports, about eight hundred Indians, or one fifth of the hostile Creek warriors; but this carnage had fallen chiefly on towns and villages not responsible for the revolt. The true fanatics were little harmed, and could offer nearly as much resistance as ever. The failure and excessive expense of the campaign were the more annoying, because they seemed beyond proportion to the military strength of the fanatics. Major-General Pinckney wrote to the War Department at the close of the year:[1] —

"The force of the hostile Creeks was estimated by the best judges to have consisted of three thousand five hundred warriors; of these it is apprehended that about one thousand have been put *hors de combat*."

To Andrew Jackson, Pinckney wrote, Jan. 19, 1814,[2]

"Your letter, dated December 26, did not reach me until the last evening. Your preceding dispatches of December 14 had led me to conclude what would probably soon be the diminished state of your force. I therefore immediately ordered to your support Colonel Williams's regiment of twelve-months men, and wrote to the Governor of Tennessee urging him to complete the requisition of fifteen hundred for the time authorized by law. I learn from the person who brought your letter that Colonel Williams's regiment is marching to join you; if the fifteen hundred of the quota should also be furnished by Governor Blount, you will in my opinion have force sufficient for the object to be attained. The largest computation that I have heard of the hostile Creek warriors, made by any competent judge, is four thousand. At least one thousand of them have been killed or disabled; they are badly armed and supplied with ammunition; little doubt can exist that two thousand of our men would be infinitely superior to any number they can collect."

[1] Pinckney to Armstrong, Dec. 28, 1813; MSS. War Department Archives.
[2] Pinckney to Jackson, Jan. 19, 1814; MSS. War Department Archives.

Jackson at Fort Strother on the departure of the east Tennesseeans, January 14, received a reinforcement of sixty-day militia, barely nine hundred in number.[1] Determined to use them to the utmost, Jackson started three days afterward to co-operate with General Floyd in an attack on the Tallapoosa villages, aiming at a town called Emuckfaw, some forty miles north of Tuckaubatchee. The movement was much more dangerous than any he had yet attempted. His own force was fresh, motley, and weak, numbering only nine hundred and thirty militia, including "a company of volunteer officers headed by General Coffee, who had been abandoned by his men," and assisted by two or three hundred friendly Creeks and Cherokees. The sixty-day militia were insubordinate and unsteady, the march was long, and the Creek towns at which he aimed were relatively large. Emuckfaw was one of seven villages belonging to Ocfuskee, the largest town in the Creek nation,—in 1800 supposed to contain four hundred and fifty warriors.[2]

As far as Enotachopco Creek, twelve miles from Emuckfaw, Jackson had no great danger to fear; but beyond that point he marched with caution. At daylight, January 22, the Indians, who were strongly encamped at about three miles distance, made an attack on Jackson's camp, which was repulsed after half an hour's fighting. Jackson then sent Coffee with four hundred men to burn the Indian camp, but Coffee returned without attempting it. "On viewing the encampment and its strength the General thought it most prudent to return to my encampment," reported Jackson.[3] Immediately after Coffee's return the Indians again attacked, and Coffee sallied out to turn their flank, followed by not more than fifty-four men. The Indians were again repulsed with a loss of forty-five killed, but Coffee was severely wounded, and Jackson "determined to commence a return march to Fort Strother the following day."

At that moment Jackson's situation was not unlike that of Harrison after the battle of Tippecanoe, and he escaped less happily. Fortifying his camp, he remained during the night of

[1] Parton, i. 864.

[2] Hawkins's Sketch, p. 45.

[3] Jackson to Pinckney, Jan. 29, 1814; Niles, v. 427.

January 22 undisturbed. At half-past ten, January 23, he began his return march, "and was fortunate enough to reach Eno-tachopco before night, having passed without interruption a dangerous defile occasioned by a hurricane."[1] Enotachopco Creek was twelve or fifteen miles from Emuckfaw Creek, and the Hillabee towns were about the same distance beyond.

At Enotachopco Jackson again fortified his camp. His position was such as required the utmost caution in remaining or moving. So hazardous was the passage of the deep creek and the defile beyond, through which the army had marched in its advance, that Jackson did not venture to return by the same path, but on the morning of January 24 began cautiously crossing the creek at a safer point:—

> "The front guard had crossed with part of the flank columns, the wounded were over, and the artillery in the act of entering the creek, when an alarm-gun was heard in the woods. . . . To my astonishment and mortification, when the word was given by Colonel Carrol to halt and form, and a few guns had been fired, I beheld the right and left columns of the rear guard precipitately give way. This shameful retreat was disastrous in the extreme; it drew along with it the greater part of the centre column, leaving not more than twenty-five men, who being formed by Colonel Carrol maintained their ground as long as it was possible to maintain it, and it brought consternation and confusion into the centre of the army,—a consternation which was not easily removed, and a confusion which could not soon be restored to order."[2]

The Indians were either weak or ignorant of warfare, for they failed to take advantage of the panic, and allowed themselves to be driven away by a handful of men. Jackson's troops escaped unharmed, or but little injured, their loss in the engagements of January 22 and 24 being twenty-four men killed and seventy-one wounded. Probably the Creek force consisted of the Ocfuskee warriors, and numbered about half that of Jackson.[3] Coffee supposed them to be eight hundred or a

[1] Jackson to Pinckney, Jan. 29, 1814; Niles, v. 427.
[2] Jackson to Pinckney, Jan. 29, 1814; Niles, v. 427.
[3] Pickett's Alabama, ii. 336.

thousand in number, but the exaggeration in estimating Indian forces was always greater than in estimating white enemies in battle. An allowance of one third was commonly needed for exaggeration in reported numbers of European combatants; an allowance of one half was not unreasonable in estimates of Indian forces.

In letting Jackson escape from Emuckfaw the Creeks lost their single opportunity. Jackson never repeated the experiment. He arrived at Fort Strother in safety January 29, and did not again leave his intrenchment until the middle of March, under much better conditions.

General Floyd was no more successful. Jackson started from Fort Strother for Emuckfaw January 17; Floyd left Fort Mitchell, on the Chattahoochee, January 18, for Tuckaubatchee, only forty miles south of Emuckfaw.[1] Floyd's army, like Jackson's, was partly composed of militia and partly of Lower Creek warriors, in all about seventeen hundred men, including four hundred friendly Creeks. From the best information to be obtained at the time, the effective strength of the hostile Indians did not then exceed two thousand warriors,[2] scattered along the Coosa and Tallapoosa rivers; while experience proved the difficulty of concentrating large bodies of Indians, even when supplies were furnished them. The British commissariat in Canada constantly issued from five to ten thousand rations for Indians and their families, but Proctor never brought more than fifteen hundred warriors into battle. The Creeks, as far as was known, never numbered a thousand warriors in any battle during the war. Floyd, with seventeen hundred men well armed, was able to face the whole Creek nation, and meant to move forward, fortifying military posts at each day's march, until he should establish himself on the Tallapoosa in the centre of the Creek towns, and wait for a junction with Jackson.

When Jackson was repulsed at Emuckfaw January 22, Floyd was about forty miles to the southward, expecting to draw the chief attack of the Indians. Having advanced forty-eight miles from the Chattahoochee he arrived at a point about seven or eight miles south of Tuckaubatchee, where he for-

---

[1] Jackson to Pinckney, Jan. 29, 1814; Niles v. 427.
[2] Letter from Milledgeville, March 16, 1814; "The War," April 5, 1814.

tified, on Calibee Creek, a camp called Defiance. There, before daybreak on the morning of January 27, he was sharply attacked, as Harrison was attacked at Tippecanoe, and with the same result. The attack was repulsed, but Floyd lost twenty-two killed and one hundred and forty-seven wounded,—the largest number of casualties that had yet occurred in the Indian war. The Indians "left thirty-seven dead on the field; from the effusion of blood and the number of head-dresses and war-clubs found in various directions, their loss must have been considerable independent of their wounded."[1]

The battle of Calibee Creek, January 27, was in substance a defeat to Floyd. So decided were his militia in their determination to go home, that he abandoned all his fortified posts and fell back to the Chattahoochee, where he arrived February 1, four days after the battle.[2]

Six months had then elapsed since the outbreak of hostilities at Burnt Corn; a year since the Little Warrior murders on the Ohio River, yet not a post had been permanently occupied within eighty miles of the fanatical centre at the fork of the Coosa and Tallapoosa.

Pinckney was obliged to apply to the governors of North and South Carolina to furnish him with men and equipments. The Governor of Georgia also exerted himself to supply the deficiencies of the national magazines.[3] By their aid Pinckney was able to collect an army with which to make another and a decisive movement into the Creek country; but before he could act, Jackson succeeded in striking a final blow.

Jackson's success in overcoming the obstacles in his path was due to his obstinacy in insisting on maintaining himself at Fort Strother, which obliged Governor Blount to order out four thousand more militia in January for six months. Perhaps this force alone would have been no more effectual in 1814 than in 1813, but another reinforcement was decisive. The Thirty-ninth regiment of the regular army, authorized by the Act of January 29, 1813, had been officered and recruited in Tennessee, and was still in the State. Major-General Pinckney

[1] Floyd to Pinckney, Jan. 27, 1814; Niles, v. 411.
[2] Floyd to Pinckney, Feb. 2, 1814; Military and Naval Letters, p. 306. Hawkins to Armstrong, June 7, 1814; State Papers, Indian Affairs, i. 858.
[3] Pinckney to the Governor of Georgia, Feb. 20, 1814; Niles, vi. 132.

sent orders, Dec. 23, 1813, to its colonel, John Williams, to join Jackson.[1] The arrival of the Thirty-ninth regiment February 6, 1814, gave Jackson the means of coping with his militia. February 21 he wrote to his quartermaster, Major Lewis, that he meant to use his regulars first to discipline his own army.[2] "I am truly happy in having the Colonel [Williams] with me. His regiment will give strength to my arm, and quell mutiny." His patience with militia-men had been long exhausted, and he meant to make a warning of the next mutineer.

The first victim was no less a person than Major-General Cocke of the east Tennessee militia. Cocke's division of two thousand men, mustered for six months, began January 17 its march from Knoxville to Fort Strother.[3] Learning on the march that the west Tennessee division, mustered at the same time for the same service, had been accepted to serve only three months, Cocke's men mutinied, and Cocke tried to pacify them by a friendly speech. Jackson, learning what had passed, despatched a sharp order to one of Cocke's brigadiers to arrest and send under guard to Fort Strother every officer of whatever rank who should be found exciting the men to mutiny. Cocke was put under arrest when almost in sight of the enemy's country; his sword was taken from him, and he was sent to Nashville for trial.[4] His division came to Fort Strother, and said no more about its term of service.

Having dealt thus with the officers, Jackson selected at leisure a test of strength with the men. The conduct of the Fayetteville company of the Twenty-eighth regiment of west Tennessee light infantry gave him ground for displeasure. Not only had they refused to obey the call for six months' service and insisted on serving for three months or not at all, but they had halted on their march, and had sent their commanding officer to bargain with Jackson for his express adhesion to their terms. Learning that Jackson made difficulties, they marched home without waiting for an official reply. Jackson

[1] Pinckney to Colonel Williams, Dec. 23, 1813; MSS. War Department Archives.

[2] Parton's Jackson, i. 503.

[3] Parton's Jackson, i. 454.

[4] Cocke's Defence; "National Intelligencer," October, 1852. Parton's Jackson, i. 455. Eaton's Jackson, p. 155.

ordered the whole body to be arrested as deserters, accompanying his order by an offer of pardon to such as returned to duty on their own understanding of the term of service. The company was again mustered, and arrived at Fort Strother not long after the arrival of the Thirty-ninth United States Infantry.

A few weeks later an unfortunate private of the same company, named Woods, refused to obey the officer of the day, and threatened to shoot any man who arrested him. Jackson instantly called a court-martial, tried and sentenced Woods, and March 14 caused him to be shot. The execution was a harsh measure; but Jackson gave to it a peculiar character by issuing a general order in which he misstated facts that made Wood's case exceptional,[1] in order to let the company understand that their comrade was suffering the penalty which they all deserved.

Without giving his army time to brood over this severity, Jackson ordered a general movement, and within forty-eight hours after Woods's execution, all were well on their way toward the enemy. Jackson had with him about five thousand men, four fifths of whom expected their discharge in a month. He left them not a day's repose.

Two lines of advance were open to him in approaching the fork of the Coosa and Tallapoosa, which was always the objective point. He might descend the Coosa, or cross to the Tallapoosa by the way he had taken in January. He descended the Coosa thirty miles, and then struck a sudden blow at the Tallapoosa towns.

The Ocfuskee Indians, elated by their success in January, collected their whole force, with that of some neighboring towns, in a bend of the Tallapoosa, where they built a sort of fortress by constructing across the neck of the Horse-shoe a breastwork composed of five large logs, one above the other, with two ranges of port-holes.[2] The interior was covered with trees and fallen timber along the river side, and caves were dug in the bank. Seven or eight hundred Indian warriors together with many women and children were within the enclosure of eighty or a hundred acres.

[1] Parton's Jackson, i. 511.
[2] Col. Gideon Morgan to Governor Blount, April 1, 1814; Niles, vi. 148.

Jackson, after leaving a garrison at a new fort which he constructed on the Coosa, about half way to the Horse-shoe, had somewhat less than three thousand effectives.[1] With these he camped, on the evening of March 28, about six miles northwest of the bend, and the next morning advanced to attack it. "Determined to exterminate them," he reported,[2] he detached Coffee with the mounted force of seven hundred men and six hundred friendly Indians[3] to surround the bend, along the river bank, while Jackson himself with all his infantry took position before the breastwork. At half-past ten o'clock he planted his cannon about two hundred yards[4] from the centre of the work, and began a rapid fire of artillery and musketry, which continued for two hours without producing apparent effect. Meanwhile the Cherokee allies swam the river in the rear of the Creek warriors, who were all at the breastwork, and seizing canoes, brought some two hundred Indians and whites into the Horse-shoe, where they climbed the high ground in the rear of the breastwork and fired on the Creeks, who were occupied in defending their front.

Jackson then ordered an assault on the breastwork, which was carried, with considerable loss, by the Thirty-ninth regiment, in the centre. The Creeks sought shelter in the thickets and under the bluffs, where they were hunted or burned out, and killed. "The slaughter was greater than all we had done before," wrote Coffee; it was continued all day and the next morning. When the Horse-shoe had been thoroughly cleared, five hundred and fifty-seven dead bodies were counted within the bend; many were killed in the river, and about twenty were supposed to have escaped. According to Coffee, " we killed not less than eight hundred and fifty or nine hundred of them, and took about five hundred squaws and children prisoners." The proportion of squaws and children to the whole number of Indians showed the probable proportion of warriors among the dead. "I lament that two or three women and children were killed by accident," reported Jackson.[5]

[1] Eaton's Jackson, p. 156.
[2] Jackson to Pinckney, March 28, 1814; Military and Naval Letters, p. 319.
[3] Coffee to Jackson, April 1, 1814; Niles, vi. 148.
[4] Colonel Morgan to Governor Blount, April 1, 1814; Niles, vi. 148.
[5] Jackson to Governor Blount, March 31, 1814; Niles, vi. 147.

Jackson's loss was chiefly confined to the Thirty-ninth regiment and the friendly Indians, who were most actively engaged in the storm. The Thirty-ninth lost twenty killed and fifty-two wounded. Among the severely wounded was Ensign Samuel Houston, struck by an arrow in the thigh. The major and two lieutenants were killed. The Cherokees lost eighteen killed and thirty-five wounded. The friendly Creeks lost five killed and eleven wounded. The Tennessee militia, comprising two thirds of the army, lost only eight killed and fifty-two wounded. The total loss was fifty-one killed and one hundred and forty-eight wounded.

Jackson's policy of extermination shocked many humane Americans, and would perhaps have seemed less repulsive had the Creeks shown more capacity for resistance. The proportion between two hundred casualties on one side and seven or eight hundred killed on the other would have been striking in any case, but was especially so where the advantages of position were on the side of the defence. A more serious criticism was that the towns thus exterminated were not the towns chiefly responsible for the outbreak. The Alabamas and the main body of fanatical Creeks escaped.

Jackson was obliged to return to his new fort on the Coosa, a march of five days; and was delayed five days more by preparations to descend the river. When at length he moved southward, scouring the country as he went, he could find no more enemies. He effected his junction with the Georgia troops April 15, and the united armies reached the fork of the Coosa and Tallapoosa April 18, where Major-General Pinckney joined them, April 20, and took command;[1] but the Red Sticks had then fled southward. A few of the hostile leaders, including Weatherford, made submission, but McQueen and the chief prophets escaped to continue the war from Florida. The friendly Creeks did not consider the war to be finished; they reported to Hawkins[2] —

"They did not believe the hostile Indians were ready for peace, although a part of them had suffered so severely in

[1] Jackson to Governor Blount, April 18, 1814; Niles, vi. 212. April 25, 1814; Niles, vi. 219.

[2] Hawkins to Pinckney, April 25, 1814; State Papers, Indian Affairs, i. 858.

battle against our armies. They were proud, haughty, brave, and mad by fanaticism: Those of the towns of Tallapoosa below Tuckaubatchee and Alabama had suffered the least, although they were the most culpable; and it was probable they would mistake our object in offering terms of peace to them."

The number of refugees was never precisely known, but Hawkins reported that eight of the Tallapoosa towns had migrated in a body to Spanish territory,[1] and probably a larger proportion of the Coosa and Alabama towns accompanied them. The Indians themselves gave out that a few more than a thousand Red Stick warriors survived, who meant to die fighting. In May the British admiral Cochrane sent Captain Pigot of the "Orpheus" to the Appalachicola to communicate with the refugee Creek Indians and supply them with arms. Pigot received ten of the principal chiefs on board his vessel May 20, and reported[2] on their authority that "the number of the warriors of the Creek Nation friendly to the English and ready to take up arms was about twenty-eight hundred, exclusive of one thousand unarmed warriors who had been driven by the Americans from their towns into the marshes near Pensacola, and who were expected to rejoin the main body." The Creek warriors friendly to the Americans were estimated at about twelve hundred, and the fugitive Red Sticks at one thousand. Whatever their number, they included the most fanatical followers of Tecumthe, and their obstinate outlawry caused long and costly difficulties to the United States government.

Meanwhile the whites were conquerors and could take as much of the Creek lands as suited them; but an irregularity of form could not be avoided. Secretary Armstrong first authorized General Pinckney to conclude a treaty of peace with the hostile Creeks, containing a cession of land and other provisions.[3] A few days later Armstrong saw reason to prefer that the proposed treaty with the Creeks should take a form

[1] Hawkins to Armstrong, July 19, 1814; State Papers, Indian Affairs, i. 860.

[2] Abstract of Correspondence, Expedition to New Orleans, 1814–1815; MSS. British Archives.

[3] Armstrong to Pinckney, March 17, 1814; State Papers, Indian Affairs, i. 836.

altogether military, and be in the nature of a capitulation.[1] His idea required a treaty with the hostile Creek chiefs;[2] but the hostile Creeks were not a separate organization capable of making a treaty or granting lands of the Creek nation; and besides that difficulty the hostile chiefs had fled, and refused either to submit or negotiate. The friendly chiefs could hardly capitulate in "a form altogether military," because they had never been at war. They had fought in the United States service and were entitled to reward as allies, not to punishment as enemies.

The solution of this legal problem was entrusted to Andrew Jackson, whose services in the war earned for him the appointment of major-general in the regular army, and the command of Military District No. 7, with headquarters at Mobile. Jackson met the Creek chiefs in July. The Indians, parties to the negotiation, were friendly chiefs, deputies, and warriors, representing perhaps one third of the entire Creek nation. To these allies and friends Jackson presented a paper, originally intended for the hostile Indians, entitled "Articles of Agreement and Capitulation," requiring as indemnity for war expenses a surrender of two thirds of their territory. They were required to withdraw from the southern and western half of Alabama, within the Chattahoochee on the east and the Coosa on the west. The military object of this policy was to isolate them from the Seminoles and Spaniards on one side, and from the Choctaws and Chickasaws on the other. The political object was to surround them with a white population.

Unanimously the Creeks refused to accept the sacrifice. Jackson told them in reply that their refusal would show them to be enemies of the United States; that they might retain their own part of the country, but that the part which belonged to the hostile Indians would be taken by the government; and that the chiefs who would not consent to sign the paper might join the Red Sticks at Pensacola,—although, added Jackson, he should probably overtake and destroy them

---

[1] Armstrong to Pinckney, March 20, 1814; State Papers, Indian Affairs, i. 837.

[2] Madison to Armstrong, May 20, 1814; Madison's Works, iii. 399. Madison's Works, iii. 400, 401.

before they could get there. Such arguments could not be answered. A number of the Creeks at last, after long resistance, signed the capitulation or agreement, although they continued to protest against it, and refused their aid to carry it out.

Jackson's capitulation of Aug. 9, 1814,[1] which, without closing the Creek war, appropriated to the government the larger part of the Creek lands, was nearly simultaneous with a treaty[2] signed July 22 by William Henry Harrison and Lewis Cass, at Greenville in Ohio, with chiefs of the Wyandots, Delawares, Shawanese, Senecas, and Miamis. This treaty contained no land-cession, but established peace between the parties, and obliged the Indian signers to declare war on the British. Neither Harrison's nor Jackson's treaty embraced the chief body of hostile Indians; but Harrison's treaty served another purpose of no small value in appearing to remove an obstacle to negotiation with England.

[1] State Papers, Indian Affairs, i. 826.
[2] State Papers, Indian Affairs, i. 826.

BADLY AS THE United States fared in the campaign of 1813, their situation would have been easy had they not suffered under the annoyances of a blockade continually becoming more stringent. The doctrine that coasts could be blockaded was enforced against America with an energy that fell little short of demonstration. The summer was well advanced before the whole naval force to be used for the purpose could be posted at the proper stations. Not until May 26 did Admiral Warren issue at Bermuda his proclamation of "a strict and rigorous blockade of the ports and harbors of New York, Charleston, Port Royal, Savannah, and of the river Mississippi," which completed the blockade of the coast, leaving only the ports of New England open to neutrals. From that time nothing entered or left the blockaded coast except swift privateers, or occasional fast-sailing vessels which risked capture in the attempt. Toward the close of the year Admiral Warren extended his blockade eastward. Notice of the extension was given at Halifax November 16, and by the blockading squadron off New London December 2, thus closing Long Island Sound to all vessels of every description.[1]

The pressure of the blockade was immediately felt. In August[2] superfine flour sold at Boston for $11.87 a barrel, at Baltimore for $6.00, and at Richmond for $4.50. Upland cotton sold at Boston for twenty cents a pound; at Charleston for nine cents. Rice sold at Philadelphia for $12.00 a hundred weight; in Charleston and Savannah for $3.00. Sugar sold in Boston for $18.75 a hundred weight; in Baltimore for $26.50. Already the American staples were unsalable at the places of their production. No rate of profit could cause cotton, rice, or wheat to be brought by sea from Charleston or Norfolk to Boston. Soon speculation began. The price of imported articles rose to extravagant points. At the end of the year coffee sold for thirty-eight cents a pound, after selling for twenty-one cents in August. Tea which could be bought for $1.70 per pound in August, sold for three and four dollars in

[1] Proclamation and Notice; Niles, v. 264.
[2] Prices Current; Niles, v. 41.

December. Sugar which was quoted at nine dollars a hundred weight in New Orleans, and in August sold for twenty-one or twenty-two dollars in New York and Philadelphia, stood at forty dollars in December.

More sweeping in its effects on exports than on imports, the blockade rapidly reduced the means of the people. After the summer of 1813, Georgia alone, owing to its contiguity with Florida, succeeded in continuing to send out cotton. The exports of New York, which exceeded $12,250,000 in 1811, fell to $209,000 for the year ending in 1814. The domestic exports of Virginia diminished in four years from $4,800,000 to $3,000,000 for 1812, $1,819,000 for 1813, and $17,581 for the year ending Sept. 30, 1814. At the close of 1813 exports, except from Georgia and New England, ceased.[1]

On the revenue the blockade acted with equal effect. Owing to the increase of duties and to open ports, the New England States rather increased than diminished their customs receipts. Until the summer of 1813, when the blockade began in earnest, New York showed the same result; but after that time the receipts fell, until they averaged less than $50,000 a month instead of $500,000, which would have been a normal average if peace had been preserved. Philadelphia suffered sooner. In 1810 the State of Pennsylvania contributed more than $200,000 a month to the Treasury; in 1813 it contributed about $25,000 a month. Maryland, where was collected in 1812 no less than $1,780,000 of net revenue, paid only $182,000 in 1813, and showed an actual excess of expenditures in 1814. After the summer, the total net revenue collected in every port of the United States outside of New England did not exceed $150,000 a month, or at the rate of $1,800,000 a year.[2]

No ordinary operations of war could affect the United States so severely as this inexorable blockade. Every citizen felt it in every action of his life. The farmer grew crops which he could not sell, while he paid tenfold prices for every necessity. While the country was bursting with wealth, it was ruined. The blockade was but a part of the evil. The whole coast was systematically swept of the means of industry. Especially the Virginians and Marylanders felt the heavy hand

[1] Table No. II.; Pitkin, p. 56.
[2] Table No. I.; Pitkin, p. 415.

of England as it was felt nowhere else except on the Niagara River. A large British squadron occupied Chesapeake Bay, and converted it into a British naval station. After the month of February, 1813, the coasts of Virginia and Maryland enjoyed not a moment's repose. Considering the immense naval power wielded by England, the Americans were fortunate that their chief losses were confined to the farm-yards and poultry of a few islands in Chesapeake Bay, but the constant annoyance and terror were not the less painful to the people who apprehended attack.

Fortunately the British naval officers showed little disposition to distinguish themselves, and their huge line-of-battle ships were not adapted to river service. The squadron under the general command of Admiral Sir John Borlase Warren seemed contented for the most part to close the bay to commerce. The only officer in the fleet who proved the energy and capacity to use a part of the great force lying idle at Lynnhaven Bay was Rear-Admiral Sir George Cockburn, whose efficiency was attested by the execration in which his name was held for fifty years in the United States. His duties were not of a nature to make him popular, and he was an admiral of the old school, whose boisterous energy seemed to take needless pleasure in the work.

Early in April, 1813, Admiral Warren sent Cockburn with a light flotilla to the head of Chesapeake Bay to destroy everything that could serve a warlike purpose, and to interrupt, as far as possible, communication along the shore.[1] The squadron consisted of only one light frigate, the "Maidstone," thirty-six guns; two brigs, the "Fantome" and "Mohawk;" and three or four prize schooners, with four or five hundred seamen, marines, and soldiers. With this petty force Cockburn stationed himself at the mouth of the Susquehanna River, and soon threw Maryland into paroxysms of alarm and anger. Taking possession of the islands in his neighborhood, he obtained supplies of fresh food for the whole British force in Chesapeake Bay. He then scoured every creek and inlet above his anchorage. He first moved into the Elk River, and sent his boats, April 28, with one hundred and fifty marines,

[1] Admiral Warren to J. W. Croker, May 28, 1813; London "Gazette," July 6, 1813.

to Frenchtown,—a village of a dozen buildings, which had acquired a certain importance for the traffic between Baltimore and Philadelphia since the stoppage of transit by sea. Without losing a man, the expedition drove away the few Americans who made a show of resistance, and burned whatever property was found, "consisting of much flour, a large quantity of army clothing, of saddles, bridles, and other equipments for cavalry, etc., together with various articles of merchandise," besides five vessels lying near the place.[1]

Cockburn next sent the same force to destroy a battery lately erected at Havre de Grace. The attack was made on the morning of May 3, and like the attack on Frenchtown, met with only resistance enough to offer an excuse for pillage. The militia took refuge in the woods; Cockburn's troops destroyed or carried away the arms and cannon, and set fire to the town of some sixty houses, "to cause the proprietors (who had deserted them and formed part of the militia who had fled to the woods) to understand and feel what they were liable to bring upon themselves by building batteries and acting toward us with so much useless rancor."[2] While engaged in this work Cockburn was told that an extensive cannon-foundry existed about four miles up the Susquehanna River; and he immediately started for it in his boats. He met no resistance, and destroyed the foundry with several small vessels. His handful of men passed the day undisturbed on the banks of the Susquehanna, capturing fifty-one cannon, mostly heavy pieces, with one hundred and thirty stand of small arms. The party then returned to their ships, " where we arrived at ten o'clock, after being twenty-two hours in constant exertion, without nourishment of any kind; and I have much pleasure in being able to add that, excepting Lieutenant Westphall's wound, we have not suffered any casualty whatever."

These expeditions cleared every inlet in the Upper Chesapeake except the Sassafras River on the eastern shore. During the night of May 5 Cockburn sent his boats into the Sassafras. Militia in considerable numbers assembled on both banks and opened a fire which Cockburn described as "most heavy," aided by one long gun. Cockburn landed, dispersed the

[1] Warren's Report of May 28, 1813; London "Gazette."
[2] Cockburn to Warren, May 3, 1813; London "Gazette," July 6, 1813.

militia, and destroyed Fredericktown and Georgetown, with the vessels and stores he found there. This expedition cost him five men wounded, one severely. The next day, May 6, he reported to Admiral Warren,—

"I had a deputation from Charleston in the Northeast River to assure me that that place is considered by them at your mercy, and that neither guns nor militia-men shall be suffered there; and as I am assured that all the places in the upper part of Chesapeake Bay have adopted similar resolutions, and as there is now neither public property, vessels, nor warlike stores remaining in this neighborhood, I propose returning to you with the light squadron to-morrow morning."

Thus in the course of a week, and without loss of life on either side, Cockburn with a few boats and one hundred and fifty men terrorized the shores of the Upper Chesapeake, and by his loud talk and random threats threw even Baltimore into a panic, causing every one to suspend other pursuits in order to garrison the city against an imaginary attack. The people, harassed by this warfare, remembered with extreme bitterness the marauding of Cockburn and his sailors; but where he met no resistance he paid in part for what private property he took, and as far as was recorded, his predatory excursions cost the Marylanders not a wound.

For six weeks after Cockburn's return to Warren's station at Lynnhaven Bay, the British fleet remained inactive. Apparently the British government aimed at no greater object than that of clearing from Chesapeake Bay every vessel not engaged in British interests under British protection. The small craft and privateers were quickly taken or destroyed; but the three chief depots of commerce and armaments—Norfolk, Baltimore, and Washington—required a greater effort. Of these three places Norfolk seemed most open to approach, and Admiral Warren determined to attack it.

The British navy wished nothing more ardently than to capture or destroy the American frigates. One of these, the "Constellation," lay at Norfolk, where it remained blockaded throughout the war. Admiral Warren could earn no distinction so great as the credit of capturing this frigate, which not only threatened to annoy British commerce should she escape to sea, but even when blockaded in port required a considerable squadron to watch her, and neutralized several times her force.

Another annoyance drew Warren's attention to Norfolk. June 20, fifteen gunboats issued from the harbor before daylight, and under cover of darkness approached within easy range of a becalmed British frigate, the "Junon" of forty-six guns. For half an hour, from four o'clock till half-past four, the gunboats maintained, according to the official report of Commodore Cassin who commanded them, "a heavy, galling fire at about three quarters of a mile distance."[1] Their armament was not mentioned, but probably they, like the gunboats on the Lakes, carried in part long thirty-two and twenty-four-pound guns. The attack was intended to test the offensive value of gunboats, and the result was not satisfactory. The fire of fifteen heavy guns for half an hour on a defenceless frigate within easy range should have caused great injury, but did not. When a breeze rose and enabled the "Junon" and a neighboring frigate, the "Barrosa," to get under weigh, the gunboats were obliged to retire with the loss of one man killed and two wounded. The "Junon" also had one man killed, but received only one or two shots in her hull.[2]

The "Constellation" lay, under the guns of two forts and with every possible precaution, five miles up the Elizabeth River, at the Portsmouth navy-yard. The utmost pains had been taken to provide against approach by water. Whatever incompetence or neglect was shown elsewhere, Norfolk was under the command of able officers in both services, who neglected no means of defence. General Wade Hampton had fortified the interior line immediately below the town, where two strong forts were constructed under the direction of Captain Walker Keith Armistead of the Engineers, the first graduate of the West Point Academy in 1803. Five miles below these forts, where the river widened into Hampton Roads, Brigadier-General Robert Taylor of the Virginia militia, and Captain John Cassin commanding at the navy-yard, established a second line of defence, resting on Craney

[1] Cassin to Secretary Jones, June 21, 1813; Niles, iv. 291.
[2] James, ii. 55.

Island on the left, supported by fifteen or twenty gunboats moored across the channel. A battery of seven guns was established on the island covering the approach to the gunboats, so that the capture of the island was necessary to the approach by water. The force on the island consisted of about seven hundred men, of whom less than a hundred were State troops. The rest were infantry of the line, riflemen, seamen, and marines.[1] The town and forts were strongly garrisoned, and a large body of State militia was constantly on service.

To deal with the defences of Norfolk, Admiral Warren brought from Bermuda, according to newspaper account, a detachment of battalion marines eighteen hundred strong; three hundred men of the One Hundred-and-second regiment of the line, commanded by Lieut.-Colonel Charles James Napier, afterward a very distinguished officer; two hundred and fifty chasseurs, or French prisoners of war who had entered the British service; and three hundred men of the royal marine artillery,[2] — in all, two thousand six hundred and fifty rank-and-file, or about three thousand men all told, besides the sailors of the fleet. At that time no less than thirteen sail of British ships, including three ships-of-the-line and five frigates, lay at anchor within thirteen miles of Craney Island.

The attack was planned for June 22. The land forces were commanded by Sir Sydney Beckwith, but the general movement was directed by Admiral Warren.[3] The main attack, led by Major-General Beckwith in person, was to land and approach Craney Island from the rear, or mainland; the second division, under command of Captain Pechell of the flagship "San Domingo," 74, was to approach the island in boats directly under fire of the American guns on the island, but not exposed to those in the gunboats.

The plan should have succeeded. The island was held by less than seven hundred men in an open earthwork easily assaulted from the rear. The water was so shallow as to offer little protection against energetic attack. The British force was

[1] Report of Robert Taylor, July 4, 1813; Niles, iv. 324.
[2] James, ii. 54.
[3] Warren's Report of June 24, 1813; James, ii. 414.

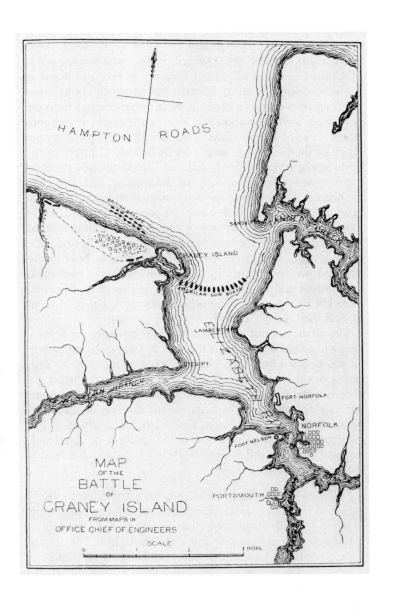

HAMPTON ROADS

BRITISH BARGES

CRANEY ISLAND

AMERICAN GUN BOATS

SANDY KNEK

LAMBERTS

TESIPT

AN BRANCH

FORT NORFOLK

NORFOLK

FORT NELSON

PORTSMOUTH

MAP
OF THE
BATTLE
OF
CRANEY ISLAND
FROM MAPS IN
OFFICE CHIEF OF ENGINEERS
SCALE
0   1   2   3 miles

more than twice the American, and the plan of attack took from the gunboats the chance of assisting the land-battery.

At daylight on the morning of June 22 Beckwith, with about eight hundred men, landed on the main shore outside of Craney Island, and pushed forward to take the island in the rear. Soon afterward Captain Pechell, with about seven hundred men in fifteen boats, approached the island from the northwest along the shore, far out of the reach of the gunboats. Toward eleven o'clock the British boats came within range of the American battery on the island. Contrary to the opinions of several officers, Captain Pechell insisted on making the attack independently of Beckwith's approach, and pushed on. Two or three hundred yards from land the leading boats grounded in shoal water. Apparently the men might have waded ashore; but "one of the seamen, having plunged his boat-hook over the side, found three or four feet of slimy mud at the bottom;"[1] the leading officer's boat being aground was soon struck by a six-pound shot, the boat sunk, and himself and his crew, with those of two other launches, were left in the water. The other boats took a part of them in, and then quickly retired.

The affair was not improved by the fortunes of Sir Sydney Beckwith, who advanced to the rear of Craney Island, where he was stopped by creeks which he reported too deep to ford, and accordingly re-embarked his troops without further effort; but the true causes of the failure seemed not to be understood. Napier thought it due to the division of command between three heads, Warren, Cockburn, and Beckwith;[2] but incompetence was as obvious as the division of command. Admiral Warren's official report seemed to admit that he was also overmatched:[3] —

"Upon approaching the island, from the extreme shoalness of the water on the seaside and the difficulty of getting across from the land, as well as the island itself being fortified with a number of guns and men from the frigate ['Constellation'] and the militia, and flanked by fifteen gun-

[1] James, ii. 59.
[2] Napier's Life, i. 221.
[3] Warren's Report of June 24, 1813; London "Gazette," Aug. 10, 1813.

boats, I considered, in consequence of the representation of the officer commanding the troops of the difficulty of their passing over from the land, that the persevering in the attempt would cost more men than the number with us would permit, as the other forts must have been stormed before the frigate and dockyard could be destroyed. I therefore directed the troops to be re-embarked."

On neither side were the losses serious. The American battery inflicted less injury than was to be expected. Fifteen British boats containing at least eight hundred men, all told, remained some two hours under the fire of two twenty-four-pound and four six-pound guns, at a range differently estimated from one hundred to three hundred yards, but certainly beyond musketry fire, for the American troops had to wade out before firing. Three boats were sunk; three men were killed, and sixteen were wounded.[1] Sixty-two men were reported missing, twenty-two of whom came ashore from the boats, while forty deserted from Beckwith's land force.[2] The Americans suffered no loss.

To compensate his men for their check at Craney Island, Admiral Warren immediately afterward devised another movement, which proved, what the Craney Island affair suggested, that the large British force in the Chesapeake was either ill constructed or ill led. Opposite Craney Island, ten miles away on the north shore of James River, stood the village of Hampton, a place of no importance either military or commercial. Four or five hundred Virginia militia were camped there, covering a heavy battery on the water's edge. The battery and its defenders invited attack, but Admiral Warren could have no military object to gain by attacking them. His official report[3] said "that the enemy having a post at Hampton defended by a considerable corps commanding the communication between the upper part of the country and Norfolk, I considered it advisable, and with a view to cut off their resources, to direct it to be attacked." Hampton could not fairly be said to "command" communication with

---

[1] Return, etc.; James, ii. 414, 415.
[2] Colonel Beatty's Report of June 25, 1813; Niles, iv. 324.
[3] Warren's Report of June 27, 1813; James, ii. 414.

Norfolk, a place which lay beyond ten miles of water wholly commanded by the British fleet; but Warren was not obliged to excuse himself for attacking wherever he pleased, and Hampton served his object best.

At dawn of June 25, Beckwith's troops were set ashore about two miles above the village, and moved forward to the road, taking Hampton in the rear, while Cockburn's launches made a feint from the front. The militia, after resistance costing Beckwith a total loss of nearly fifty men, escaped, and the British troops entered the town, where they were allowed to do what they pleased with property and persons. Lieutenant-Colonel Napier of the One Hundred-and-second regiment, who commanded Beckwith's advance, wrote in his diary that Sir Sydney Beckwith "ought to have hanged several villains at Little Hampton; had he so done, the Americans would not have complained; but every horror was perpetrated with impunity,—rape, murder, pillage,—and not a man was punished." The British officers in general shared Napier's disgust, but alleged that the English troops took no part in the outrages, which were wholly the work of the French chasseurs.

Warren made no attempt to hold the town; the troops returned two days afterward to their ships, and the Virginia militia resumed their station; but when the details of the Hampton affair became known, the story roused natural exasperation throughout the country, and gave in its turn incitement to more violence in Canada. Admiral Warren and Sir Sydney Beckwith did not deny the wrong; they dismissed their Frenchmen from the service, and the United States had no further reason to complain of that corps; but the double mortification seemed to lower the British officers even in their own eyes to the level of marauders.

After the failure to destroy the "Constellation," Admiral Warren could still indulge a hope of destroying the twenty-eight-gun frigate "Adams," and the navy-yard at Washington; for the defence of the Potomac had been totally neglected, and only one indifferent fort, about twelve miles below the Federal city, needed to be captured. July 1 the British squadron entered the Potomac; but beyond rousing a panic at Washington it accomplished nothing, except to gain some knowledge of the shoals and windings that impeded the ascent of the river. Leaving the Potomac, Warren turned up Chesapeake Bay toward Annapolis and Baltimore, but made no attempt on either place. During the rest of the year he cruised about the bay, meeting little resistance, and keeping the States of Virginia and Maryland in constant alarm.

Cockburn was more active. In the month of July he was detached with a squadron carrying Napier's One Hundred-and-second regiment, and arrived, July 12, off Ocracoke Inlet, where he captured two fine privateers,—the "Atlas" and "Anaconda." Thence he sailed southward, and established himself for the winter on Cumberland Island, near the Florida boundary, where he vexed the Georgians. Besides the property consumed or wasted, he gave refuge to many fugitive slaves, whom he assisted to the West Indies or Florida. "Strong is my dislike," wrote Napier, "to what is perhaps a necessary part of our job: namely, plundering and ruining the peasantry. We drive all their cattle, and of course ruin them. *My* hands are clean; but it is hateful to see the poor Yankees robbed, and to be the robber."

Compared with the widespread destruction which war brought on these regions half a century afterward, the injury inflicted by the British navy in 1813 was trifling, but it served to annoy the Southern people, who could offer no resistance, and were harassed by incessant militia-calls. To some extent the same system of vexation was pursued on the Northern coast. The Delaware River was blockaded and its shores much annoyed. New York was also blockaded, and Nantucket with the adjacent Sounds became a British naval station. There Sir Thomas Hardy, Nelson's favorite officer, commanded, in his flag-ship the "Ramillies." Hardy did not encourage marauding such as Cockburn practised, but his blockade was still stringent, and its efficiency was proved by the failure of Decatur's efforts to evade it.

Decatur commanded a squadron composed of the "United States," its prize frigate the "Macedonian," and the sloop-of-war "Hornet," which lay in the harbor of New York, waiting for a chance to slip out. Impatient at the steady watch kept by the British fleet off Sandy Hook, Decatur brought his three ships through the East River into Long Island Sound. He reached Montauk Point, May 29, only to find Hardy's squadron waiting for him. June 1 he made an attempt to run out, but was chased back, and took refuge in the harbor of New London. A large British squadron immediately closed upon the harbor, and Decatur not only lost hope of getting to sea but became anxious for the safety of his ships. He withdrew them as far as he could into the river, five miles above the town, and took every precaution to repel attack. The British officers were said to have declared that they would get the "Macedonian" back "even if they followed her into a cornfield." They did not make the attempt, but their vigilance never relaxed, and Decatur was obliged to remain all summer idle in port. He clung to the hope that when winter approached he might still escape; but in the month of December the country was scandalized by the publication of an official letter from Decatur to the Secretary of the Navy, charging the people of New London with the responsibility for his failure.

"Some few nights since," he wrote,[1] Dec. 20, 1813, "the weather promised an opportunity for this squadron to get to sea, and it was said on shore that we intended to make the attempt. In the course of the evening two blue lights were burned on both the points at the harbor's mouth as signals to the enemy; and there is not a doubt but that they have, by signals and otherwise, instantaneous information of our movements. Great but unsuccessful exertions have been made to detect those who communicated with the enemy by signal. . . . Notwithstanding these signals have been repeated, and have been seen by twenty persons at least in this squadron, there are men in New London who have the hardihood to affect to disbelieve it, and the effrontery to avow their disbelief."

Decatur's charge roused much ill feeling, and remained a subject of extreme delicacy with the people of New London. Perhaps Decatur would have done better not to make such an assertion until he could prove its truth. That blue lights, as well as other lights, were often seen, no one denied; but whether they came from British or from American hands, or

[1] Niles, v. 302.

were burned on sea or on shore, were points much disputed. The town of New London was three miles from the river's mouth, and Decatur's squadron then lay at the town. At that distance the precise position of a light in line with the British fleet might be mistaken. Decatur's report, if it proved anything, proved that the signals were concerted, and were burnt from "both the points at the river's mouth." If the British admiral wanted information, he could have found little difficulty in obtaining it; but he would hardly have arranged a system of signals as visible to Decatur as to himself. Even had he done so, he might have employed men in his own service as well as Americans for the purpose. Decatur's letter admitted that he had made great exertions to detect the culprits, but without success.

The rigor of the British blockade extended no farther north than the Vineyard and Nantucket. Captain Broke in the "Shannon," with a companion frigate, cruised off Boston harbor rather to watch for ships-of-war than to interfere with neutral commerce. Along the coast of Maine an illicit trade with the British provinces was so actively pursued that one of the few American sloops-of-war, the "Enterprise," cruised there, holding smugglers, privateers, and petty marauders in check. On no other portion of the coast would an armed national vessel have been allowed to show itself, but the "Enterprise," protected by the bays and inlets of Maine, and favored by the absence of a blockade, performed a useful service as a revenue cutter. She was not a first-rate vessel. Originally a schooner, carrying twelve guns and sixty men, she had taken part in the war with Tripoli. She was afterward altered into a brig, and crowded with sixteen guns and a hundred men. In 1813 she was commanded by Lieutenant William Burrows, a Pennsylvanian, who entered the navy in 1799, and, like all the naval heroes, was young,—not yet twenty-eight years old.

On the morning of September 5, as the "Enterprise" was cruising eastward, Burrows discovered in a bay near Portland a strange brig, and gave chase. The stranger hoisted three English ensigns, fired several guns, and stood for the "Enterprise." Perhaps escape would have been impossible; but the British captain might, without disgrace, have declined to fight, for he was no match for the American. The "Enterprise" measured about ninety-seven feet in length; the "Boxer," as the British brig was named, measured about eighty-four. The "Enterprise" was nearly twenty-four feet in extreme width; the "Boxer" slightly exceeded twenty-two feet. The "Enterprise" carried fourteen eighteen-pound carronades and two long-nines; the "Boxer" carried twelve eighteen-pound carronades and two long-sixes. The "Enterprise" had a crew of one hundred and two men; the "Boxer" had only sixty-six men on board. With such odds against him, the British captain might have entertained some desperate hope of success, but could not have expected it.

The behavior of Captain Blyth of the "Boxer" showed consciousness of his position, for he nailed his colors to the mast, and told his men that they were not to be struck while he lived. The day was calm, and the two brigs manœuvred for a time before coming together; but at quarter-past three in the afternoon they exchanged their first broadside within a stone's throw of one another. The effect on both vessels was destructive. Captain Blyth fell dead, struck full in the body by an eighteen-pound shot. Lieutenant Burrows fell, mortally wounded, struck by a canister shot. After another broadside, at half-past three the "Enterprise" ranged ahead, crossed the "Boxer's" bow, and fired one or two more broadsides, until the "Boxer" hailed and surrendered, her colors still nailed to the mast.

Considering the disparity of force, the two brigs suffered nearly in equal proportion. The "Boxer" lost seven men killed or mortally wounded; the "Enterprise" lost four. The "Boxer" had thirteen wounded, not fatally; the "Enterprise" had eight. The "Boxer's" injuries were not so severe as to prevent her captors from bringing her as a prize to Portland; and no incident in this quasi-civil war touched the sensibilities of the people more deeply than the common funeral of the two commanders,—both well known and favorites in the service, buried, with the same honors and mourners, in the graveyard at Portland overlooking the scene of their battle.

Neither the battle between the "Enterprise" and "Boxer," nor any measures that could be taken by sea or land, prevented a constant traffic between Halifax and the New-England ports not blockaded. The United States government seemed afraid to interfere with it. The newspapers asserted that hundreds of Americans were actually in Halifax carrying on a direct trade, and that thousands of barrels of flour were constantly arriving there from the United States in vessels carrying the Swedish or other neutral flag. In truth the government could do little to enforce its non-intercourse, and even that little might prove mischievous. Nothing could be worse than the spirit of the people on the frontier. Engaged in a profitable illicit commerce, they could only be controlled by force, and any force not overwhelming merely provoked violence or treason. The Navy Department had no vessels to send there, and could not have prevented their capture if vessels in any number had been sent. The Secretary of War had abandoned to the State governments the defence of the coast. When Armstrong allotted garrisons to the various military districts, he stationed one regiment, numbering three hundred and fifty-two effectives, besides two hundred and sixty-three artillerists, in Military District No. 1, which included the whole coast north of Cape Cod, with the towns of Boston, Marblehead, Salem, Gloucester, Portsmouth, Portland, and Eastport. Such a provision was hardly sufficient for garrisoning the fort at Boston. The government doubtless could spare no more of its small army, but for any military or revenue purpose might almost as well have maintained in New England no force whatever.

Chapter XII

DURING THE MONTH of April, 1813, four American frigates lay in Boston Harbor fitting for sea. The "President" and "Congress" returned to that port Dec. 31, 1812. The "Constitution," after her battle with the "Java," arrived at Boston February 27, 1813. The "Chesapeake" entered in safety April 9, after an unprofitable cruise of four months. The presence of these four frigates at Boston offered a chance for great distinction to the British officer stationed off the port, and one of the best captains in the service was there to seize it. In order to tempt the American frigates to come out boldly, only two British frigates, the "Shannon" and "Tenedos," remained off the harbor. They were commanded by Captain P. B. V. Broke of the "Shannon." Broke expected Rodgers with his ships, the "President" and "Congress," to seize the opportunity for a battle with two ships of no greater force than the "Shannon" and "Tenedos;" but either Rodgers did not understand the challenge or did not trust it, or took a different view of his duties, for he went to sea on the night of April 30, leaving Broke greatly chagrined and inclined to be somewhat indignant with him for escaping.[1]

After May 1, Broke on the watch outside, as he ran in toward Nahant, could see the masts of only the "Constitution" and "Chesapeake" at the Charlestown navy-yard, and his anxiety became the greater as he noticed that the "Chesapeake" was apparently ready for sea.[2] May 25 Broke sent away his consort, the "Tenedos," to cruise from Cape Sable southward, ostensibly because the two frigates cruising separately would have a better chance of intercepting the "Chesapeake" than if they kept together.[3] His stronger reason was to leave a fair field for the "Chesapeake" and "Shannon," as he had before kept all force at a distance except the "Shannon" and "Tenedos" in order to tempt Rodgers to fight.[4] That there might be no second misunderstanding, he sent several messages to

[1] Broke to Lawrence, June 1, 1813; Broke's Life, 159. Niles, v. 29.
[2] Broke's Life, pp. 150, 151.
[3] Broke's Life, p. 156.
[4] Broke's Life, pp. 160, 383.

Captain Lawrence commanding the "Chesapeake," inviting a combat.

Nothing showed so clearly that at least one object of the war had been gained by the Americans as the habit adopted by both navies in 1813 of challenging ship-duels. War took an unusual character when officers like Hardy and Broke countenanced such a practice, discussing and arranging duels between matched ships, on terms which implied that England admitted half-a-dozen American frigates to be equal in value to the whole British navy. The loss of a British frigate mattered little to a government which had more than a hundred such frigates actually at sea, not to speak of heavier ships; but the loss of the "Chesapeake" was equivalent to destroying nearly one fourth of the disposable American navy. Already the "Constellation" was imprisoned at Norfolk; the "United States" and "Macedonian" were blockaded for the war; the "Congress" though at sea was unseaworthy and never cruised again; the "Adams" was shut in the Potomac; the "Essex" was in the Pacific. The United States Navy consisted, for active service on the Atlantic, of only the "President," 44, at sea; the "Constitution," 44, replacing her masts at the Charlestown navy-yard; the "Chesapeake," 38, ready for sea; and a few sloops-of-war. Under such circumstances, British officers who like Broke considered every American frigate bound to offer them equal terms in a duel, seemed to admit that the American service had acquired the credit it claimed.

The first duty of a British officer was to take risks; the first duty of an American officer was to avoid them, and to fight only at his own time, on his own terms. Rodgers properly declined to seek a battle with Broke's ships. Captain James Lawrence of the "Chesapeake" was less cautious, for his experience in the war led him to think worse of the British navy than it deserved. Lawrence commanded the "Hornet" in Bainbridge's squadron at the time of the "Java's" capture. Bainbridge and Lawrence blockaded the "Bonne Citoyenne," a twenty-gun sloop-of-war at San Salvador in Brazil. Lawrence sent a message to the captain of the "Bonne Citoyenne" inviting him to come out and meet the "Hornet." The British captain declined, doubtless for proper reasons; but the reason he gave seemed to Lawrence insufficient, for it was merely that Commodore Bainbridge, in spite of his pledged word, might interfere.[1] Bainbridge sailed about Christmas, and was absent till January 3, capturing the "Java" in the interval. January 6 he sailed for Boston, leaving Lawrence in the "Hornet" still blockading the "Bonne Citoyenne," which showed no more disposition to fight the "Hornet" in Bainbridge's absence than before, although the British captain's letter had said that "nothing could give me greater satisfaction than complying with the wishes of Captain Lawrence" if the single alleged objection were removed.

The conduct of the "Bonne Citoyenne"—a vessel at least the equal of the "Hornet"[2]—gave Lawrence a low opinion of the British service, and his respect was not increased by his next experience. A British seventy-four arrived at San Salvador, January 24, and obliged the "Hornet" to abandon the "Bonne Citoyenne." During the next month the little vessel cruised northward along the Brazil coast, making a few prizes, until February 24 off the mouth of Demerara River, at half-past three o'clock in the afternoon, Captain Lawrence discovered a sail approaching him. Within the bar at the mouth of the river, seven or eight miles distant, he saw another vessel at anchor. Both were British sloops-of-war. The one at anchor was the "Espiègle," carrying eighteen thirty-two-pound carronades. The other, approaching on the "Hornet's" weather-quarter, was the "Peacock," carrying eighteen twenty-four-pound carronades, two long-sixes, and one or two lighter pieces.

The "Peacock," according to British report,[3] had long been "the admiration of her numerous visitors," and was remarkable for the elegance of her fittings; but in size she was inferior to the "Hornet." Lawrence reported his ship to be four feet the longer, but the British believed the "Hornet" to measure one hundred and twelve feet in length, while the "Peacock" measured one hundred.[4] Their breadth was the same. The "Hornet" carried eighteen thirty-two-pounders, while the British captain, thinking his sloop too light for thirty-

[1] Letter of Captain Greene; James, Appendix, no. 35.
[2] James, p. 209.
[3] James, p. 202.
[4] James, p. 206; Roosevelt's Naval War of 1812, p. 48.

twos, had exchanged them for twenty-fours, and carried only sixteen. The American crew numbered one hundred and thirty-five men fit for duty; the British numbered one hundred and twenty-two men and boys.

At ten minutes past five, Lawrence tacked and stood for the brig. Fifteen minutes afterward the two vessels, sailing in opposite directions, passed each other and exchanged broadsides within a stone's-throw. The British fire, even at point-blank range of forty or fifty feet, did no harm, while the "Hornet's" broadside must have decided the battle; for although both vessels instantly wore, and Lawrence at thirty-five minutes past five ran his enemy close aboard, the "Peacock" almost immediately struck at thirty-nine minutes past five in a sinking condition, and actually went down immediately afterward, carrying with her nine of the "Peacock's" wounded and three of the "Hornet's" crew.

The ease of this victory was beyond proportion to the odds. The British captain and four men were killed outright, thirty-three officers and men were wounded, and the brig was sunk in an action of less than fifteen minutes; while the "Hornet" lost one man killed and two wounded, all aloft, and not a shot penetrated her hull. If the facility of this triumph satisfied Lawrence of his easy superiority in battle, the conduct of the "Espiègle" convinced him that the British service was worse than incompetent. Lawrence, expecting every moment to see the "Espiègle" get under weigh, made great exertions to put his ship in readiness for a new battle, but to his astonishment the British brig took no notice of the action.[1] Subsequent investigation showed that the "Espiègle" knew nothing of the battle until the next day; but Lawrence, assuming that the British captain must have seen or heard, or at least ought to have suspected what was happening, conceived that cowardice was a trait of the British navy.

When Lawrence reached New York he became famous for his victory, and received at once promotion. The "Hornet," given to Captain Biddle, was attached to Decatur's squadron and blockaded at New London, while Lawrence received command of the "Chesapeake." Lawrence was then thirty-two

[1] Lawrence's Report of March 19, 1813; Niles, iv. 84.

years old; he was born in New Jersey in 1781, entered the navy in 1798, and served in the war with Tripoli. He was first lieutenant on the "Constitution," and passed to the grade of commander in 1810, commanding successively the "Vixen," the "Wasp," the "Argus," and the "Hornet." His appointment to the "Chesapeake" was an accident, owing to the ill health of Captain Evans, who commanded her on her recent cruise. The "Chesapeake's" reputation for ill luck clung to her so persistently that neither officers nor men cared greatly to sail in her, and Lawrence would have preferred to remain in the "Hornet;"[1] but his instructions were positive, and he took command of the "Chesapeake" about the middle of May. Most of the officers and crew were new. The old crew on reaching port, April 9, had been discharged, and left the ship, dissatisfied with their share of prize-money, and preferring to try the privateer service. The new crew was unequal in quality and required training; they neither knew their officers nor each other.

Lawrence's opponent, Captain Broke of the "Shannon," was an officer whose courage could as little be questioned as his energy or skill. Among all the commanders in the British service Broke had profited most by the lessons of the war. More than seven years' experience of his ship and crew gave him every advantage of discipline and system. Nearly every day the officers at the Charlestown navy-yard could see the "Shannon" outside, practising her guns at floating targets as she sailed about the bay. Broke's most anxious wish was to fight the "Chesapeake," which he considered to be of the same size with the "Shannon."[1] The two frigates were the same length within a few inches,—between one hundred and fifty, and one hundred and fifty-one feet. Their breadth was forty feet within a few inches. The "Chesapeake" carried eighteen thirty-two-pound carronades on the spar-deck; the "Shannon" carried sixteen. Each carried twenty-eight long eighteen-pounders on the gun-deck. The "Chesapeake" carried also two long twelve-pounders and a long eighteen-pounder, besides a twelve-pound carronade. The "Shannon"

---

[1] Biography; from "The Portfolio." Niles, Supplement to vol. v. p. 29. Cooper's Naval History, ii. 247.

[2] Broke's Life, p. 333.

carried four long nine-pounders, a long six-pounder, and three twelve-pound carronades. The "Chesapeake's" only decided advantage was in the number of her crew, which consisted of three hundred and seventy-nine men, while the "Shannon" carried three hundred and thirty all told.

Broke sent the "Tenedos" away May 25, but Lawrence was not aware of it, and wrote, May 27, to Captain Biddle of the "Hornet" a letter, showing that till the last moment he hoped not to sail in the "Chesapeake:"[1] —

> "In hopes of being relieved by Captain Stewart, I neglected writing to you according to promise; but as I have given over all hopes of seeing him, and the 'Chesapeake' is almost ready, I shall sail on Sunday, provided I have a chance of getting out clear of the 'Shannon' and 'Tenedos,' who are on the look-out."

Sunday, May 30, the ship was ready, though the crew was not as good or as well disciplined as it should have been, and showed some discontent owing to difficulties about prize-money. On the morning of June 1 the frigate was lying in President's Roads, when between eight and nine o'clock the second lieutenant, George Budd, reported a sail in sight. Captain Lawrence went up the main rigging, and having made out the sail to be a large frigate, ordered the crew to be mustered, and told them he meant to fight. At midday he stood down the harbor and out to sea. The "Shannon," outside, stood off under easy sail, and led the way until five o'clock, when she luffed and waited till the "Chesapeake" came up. As the wind was westerly, Lawrence had the choice of position, but he made no attempt to profit by his advantage, although it might have been decisive. Bringing the "Chesapeake" with a fresh breeze directly down on the "Shannon's" quarter, at half-past five he luffed, at about fifty yards distance, and ranged up abeam on the "Shannon's" starboard side.

The "Shannon" opened fire as her guns began to bear, but discharged only her two sternmost guns when the "Chesapeake" replied. The two ships ran on about seven minutes, or about the length of time necessary for two discharges of the

[1] Cooper's Naval History, ii. 247.

first guns fired, when, some of the "Shannon's" shot having cut away the "Chesapeake's" foretopsail tie and jib-sheet, the ship came up into the wind and was taken aback. Lying with her larboard quarter toward the "Shannon's" side, at some forty or fifty yards distance, she began to drift toward her enemy. None of the "Chesapeake's" guns then bore on the "Shannon," and the American frigate wholly ceased firing.

From the moment the "Chesapeake" was taken aback she was a beaten ship, and the crew felt it. She could be saved only by giving her headway, or by boarding the "Shannon;" but neither expedient was possible. The effort to make sail forward was tried, and proved futile. The idea of boarding was also in Lawrence's mind, but the situation made it impracticable. As the "Chesapeake" drifted stern-foremost toward the "Shannon," every gun in the British broadside swept the American deck diagonally from stern to stem, clearing the quarter-deck and beating in the stern-ports, while the musketry from the "Shannon's" tops killed the men at the "Chesapeake's" wheel, and picked off every officer, sailor, or marine in the after-part of the ship. Boarders could not be rallied under a fire which obliged them to seek cover. The men on the spar-deck left their stations, crowding forward or going below.

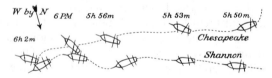

Nevertheless, Lawrence ordered up his boarders,—he could do nothing else; but the affair hurried with such rapidity to its close that almost at the same instant the "Chesapeake's" quarter touched the "Shannon" amidships. From the moment when the "Chesapeake" was taken aback until the moment when she fell foul, only four minutes were given for Lawrence to act. Before these four minutes were at an end, he was struck and mortally wounded by a musket-ball from the "Shannon." His first lieutenant, Ludlow, had already been carried below, wounded. His second lieutenant, Budd, was stationed below. His third lieutenant, Cox, improperly assisted Lawrence to reach the gun-deck. Not an officer remained on the spar-deck, and neither an officer nor a living man was on the quarter-deck when the "Chesapeake's" quarter came against the "Shannon's" gangway, as though inviting the British captain to take possession.

As the ships fouled, Broke ran forward and called for boarders. With about twenty men he stepped on the "Chesapeake's" quarter-deck, and was followed by thirty more before the ships parted. The error should have cost him his life and the lives of all who were with him, for the Americans might easily have killed every man of the boarding-party in spite of the fire from the "Shannon." For several moments Broke was in the utmost peril, not only from the American crew but from his own. His first lieutenant, Watt, hastening to haul down the American ensign, was killed by the discharge of a cannon from the "Shannon;" and when Broke, leaving the "Chesapeake's" quarter-deck, went forward to clear the forecastle, enough of the American crew were there to make a sharp resistance. Broke himself was obliged to take part in the scuffle. According to his report, he "received a severe sabre-wound at the first onset, whilst charging a part of the enemy who had rallied on their forecastle." According to another British account he was first knocked down with the butt-end of a musket, and then was cut by a broadsword. Of his fifty boarders, not less than thirty-seven were killed or wounded.[1]

Had the American crew been in a proper state of discipline, the struggle would have taken an extraordinary character, and the two ships might have renewed the combat, without officers, and in a more or less unmanageable condition. Fortunately for Broke, his fifty men outnumbered the Americans on the spar-deck, while the men below, for the most part, would not come up. About a score of sailors and marines were on the forecastle, and about a dozen more rushed up from below, led by the second lieutenant, George Budd, as soon as he, at his station on the main-deck, learned what was happening above; but so rapidly did the whole affair pass, that in two minutes the scuffle was over, the Americans were killed or thrown down the hatchway, and the ship was help-

[1] Life of Broke, p. 203.

less, with its spar-deck in the hands of Broke's boarders. The guns ceased firing, and the crew below surrendered after some musket-shots up and down the hatchways.

The disgrace to the Americans did not consist so much in the loss of a ship to one of equal force, as in the shame of suffering capture by a boarding-party of fifty men. As Lawrence lay wounded in the cock-pit, he saw the rush of his men from the spar-deck down the after-ladders, and cried out repeatedly and loudly, "Don't give up the ship! blow her up!" He was said to have added afterward: "I could have stood the wreck if it had not been for the boarding."

Doubtless the "Shannon" was the better ship, and deserved to win. Her crew could under no circumstances have behaved like the crew of the "Chesapeake." In discipline she was admittedly superior; but the question of superiority in other respects was not decided. The accident that cut the "Chesapeake's" jib-sheet and brought her into the wind was the only decisive part of the battle, and was mere ill luck, such as pursued the "Chesapeake" from the beginning. As far as could be seen, in the favorite American work of gunnery the "Shannon" showed no superiority.

On that point the reports agreed. The action began at half-past five o'clock in the afternoon at close range. In seven minutes the "Chesapeake" forged ahead, came into the wind and ceased firing, as none of her guns could be made to bear. Seven minutes allowed time at the utmost for two discharges of some of her guns. No more guns were fired from the "Chesapeake" till she drifted close to the "Shannon." Then her two sternmost guns, the thirteenth and fourteenth on the main deck, again bore on the enemy, and were depressed and fired by Lieutenant Cox while the boarders were fighting on the spar-deck.[1] Thus the number of discharges from the "Chesapeake's" guns could be known within reasonable certainty. She carried in her broadside nine thirty-two-pounders and fourteen or fifteen eighteen-pounders, besides one twelve-pounder,—twenty-five guns. Assuming them to have been all discharged twice, although the forward guns could scarcely have been discharged more than once, the "Chesa-

[1] Evidence of Midshipman Edmund Russell; Court-Martial of Lieutenant Cox. MSS. Navy Department Archives.

peake" could have fired only fifty-two shot, including the two eighteen-pounders fired by Lieutenant Cox at the close.

According to the official report nearly every shot must have taken effect. The "Shannon" was struck by thirteen thirty-two-pound shot; the "Chesapeake" fired only eighteen, if she discharged every gun twice. The "Shannon" was struck by twelve eighteen-pound shot, fourteen bar-shot, and one hundred and nineteen grape-shot; the "Chesapeake's" fifteen eighteen-pounders could hardly have done more in the space of seven minutes. In truth, every shot that was fired probably took effect.

The casualties showed equal efficiency of fire, and when compared with other battles were severe. When the "Guerriere" struck to the "Constitution" in the previous year, she had lost in half an hour of close action twenty-three killed or mortally wounded and fifty-six more or less injured. The "Shannon" seems to have lost in eleven minutes, before boarding, twenty-seven men killed or mortally wounded and nineteen more or less injured.[1]

The relative efficiency of the "Shannon's" gunnery was not so clear, because the "Shannon's" battery continued to fire after the "Chesapeake" ceased. As the "Chesapeake" drifted down on the "Shannon" she was exposed to the broadside of the British frigate, while herself unable to fire a gun.

> "The shot from the 'Shannon's' aftermost guns now had a fair range along the 'Chesapeake's' decks," said the British account,[2] "beating in the stern-ports and sweeping the men from their quarters. The shots from the foremost guns at the same time entering the ports from the mainmast aft did considerable execution."

Broke's biographer[3] said that the "Chesapeake" fired but one broadside, and then coming into the wind drifted down, "exposed while making this crippled and helpless movement to the 'Shannon's' second and most deliberate broadside." The "Chesapeake" was very near, almost touching the British frigate during the four or five minutes of this fire, and every

[1] List of killed and wounded; Life of Broke, p. 203.
[2] James, p. 216.
[3] Life of Broke, p. 170.

shot must have taken effect. Broke ordered the firing to cease when he boarded, but one gun was afterward discharged, and killed the British first lieutenant as he was lowering the American flag on the "Chesapeake's" quarter-deck.

The "Shannon's" fire lasted eleven or twelve minutes. She carried twenty-five guns in broadside.[1] Eight of these were thirty-two-pound carronades, and the official report showed that the "Chesapeake" was struck by twenty-five thirty-two-pound shot, showing that three full broadsides were fired from the "Shannon," and at least one gun was discharged four times. The "Shannon's" broadside also carried fourteen eighteen-pounders, which threw twenty-nine shot into the "Chesapeake," besides much canister and grape. Considering that at least half the "Shannon's" shot were fired at so close a range that they could not fail to take effect, nothing proved that her guns were better served than those of the "Chesapeake." The "Shannon," according to the British account, fired twice as many shot under twice as favorable conditions, but the injury she inflicted was not twice the injury inflicted in return. Setting aside the grape-shot, the "Chesapeake" struck the "Shannon" thirty-nine times; the "Shannon" struck the "Chesapeake" fifty-seven times. Including the grape-shot, which Broke used freely, the "Shannon" probably did better, but even with a liberal allowance for grape and canister, nothing proved her superiority at the guns.

The loss in men corresponded with the injury to the ships. The "Shannon" lost eighty-three killed and wounded; the "Chesapeake" lost one hundred and forty-six. Thirty-three of the "Shannon's" men were killed or died of their wounds; sixty-one of the "Chesapeake's" number were killed or mortally wounded.

The injuries suffered by the "Chesapeake" told the same story, for they were chiefly in the stern, and were inflicted by the "Shannon's" second and third broadsides, after the "Chesapeake" ceased firing. The "Chesapeake's" bowsprit received no injury, and not a spar of any kind was shot away. The "Shannon" carried her prize into Halifax with all its masts standing, and without anxiety for its safety.

[1] Broke's letter of challenge; James, Appendix, p. 36.

The news of Broke's victory was received in England and by the British navy with an outburst of pleasure that proved the smart of the wound inflicted by Hull, Decatur, and Bainbridge. The two official expressions of Broke's naval and civil superiors probably reflected the unexaggerated emotion of the service.

"At this critical moment," wrote Admiral Warren[1] by a curious coincidence the day before his own somewhat less creditable defeat at Craney Island, "you could not have restored to the British naval service the pre-eminence it has always preserved, or contradicted in a more forcible manner the foul aspersions and calumnies of a conceited, boasting enemy, than by the brilliant act you have performed."

A few days later he wrote again:[2] —

"The relation of such an event restores the history of ancient times, and will do more good to the service than it is possible to conceive."

In Parliament, July 8, John Wilson Croker said:[3]

"The action which he [Broke] fought with the 'Chesapeake' was in every respect unexampled. It was not—and he knew it was a bold assertion which he made—to be surpassed by any engagement which graced the naval annals of Great Britain."

The Government made Broke a baronet, but gave him few other rewards, and his wound was too serious to permit future hard service. Lawrence died June 5, before the ships reached Halifax. His first lieutenant, Ludlow, also died. Their bodies were brought to New York and buried September 16, with formal services at Trinity Church.

By the Americans the defeat was received at first with incredulity and boundless anxiety, followed by extreme discouragement. The news came at a dark moment, when every hope had been disappointed and the outlook was gloomy beyond all that had been thought possible.

[1] Broke's Life, p. 298.
[2] Broke's Life, p. 300.
[3] Cobbett's Debates, xxvi. 1160.

"I remember," wrote Richard Rush in later life,—"what American does not!—the first rumor of it. I remember the startling sensation. I remember at first the universal incredulity. I remember how the post-offices were thronged for successive days by anxious thousands; how collections of citizens rode out for miles on the highway, accosting the mail to catch something by anticipation. At last, when the certainty was known, I remember the public gloom; funeral orations and badges of mourning bespoke it. 'Don't give up the ship!'—the dying words of Lawrence—were on every tongue."

Six weeks afterward another American naval captain lost another American vessel-of-war by reason of the same over-confidence which caused Lawrence's mistakes, and in a manner equally discreditable to the crew. The "Argus" was a small brig, built in 1803, rating sixteen guns. In the summer of 1813 she was commanded by Captain W. H. Allen, of Rhode Island, who had been third officer to Barron when he was attacked in the "Chesapeake" by the "Leopard." Allen was the officer who snatched a coal from the galley and discharged the only gun that was fired that day. On leaving the "Chesapeake," Allen was promoted to be first officer in the "United States." To his exertions in training the men to the guns, Decatur attributed his superiority in gunnery over the "Macedonian." To him fell one of the most distinguished honors that ever came to the share of an American naval officer,— that of successfully bringing the "Macedonian" to port. Promoted to the rank of captain, he was put in command of the "Argus," and ordered to take William Henry Crawford to his post as Minister to France.

On that errand the "Argus" sailed, June 18, and after safely landing Crawford, July 11, at Lorient in Brittany, Captain Allen put to sea again, three days afterward, and in pursuance of his instructions cruised off the mouth of the British Channel. During an entire month he remained between the coast of Brittany and the coast of Ireland, destroying a score of vessels and creating a panic among the ship-owners and underwriters of London. Allen performed his task with as much forbearance as the duty permitted, making no attempt to save his prizes for the sake of prize-money, and permitting all passengers to take what they claimed as their own without inspection or restraint. The English whose property he destroyed spoke of him without personal ill-feeling.

The anxiety and labor of such a service falling on a brig of three hundred tons and a crew of a hundred men, and the impunity with which he defied danger, seemed to make Allen reckless. On the night of August 13 he captured a brig laden with wine from Oporto. Within sight of the Welsh coast and within easy reach of Milford Haven, he burned his prize, not before part of his crew got drunk on the wine. The British brig "Pelican," then cruising in search of the "Argus," guided by the light of the burning prize, at five o'clock on the morning of August 14 came down on the American brig; and Captain Allen, who had often declared that he would run from no two-masted vessel, waited for his enemy.

According to British measurements, the "Argus" was ninety-five and one-half feet long; the "Pelican," one hundred. The "Argus" was twenty-seven feet, seven and five-eighths inches in extreme breadth; the "Pelican" was thirty feet, nine inches. The "Argus" carried eighteen twenty-four-pound carronades, and two long twelve-pounders; the "Pelican" carried sixteen thirty-two-pound carronades, four long six-pounders, and a twelve-pound carronade. The number of the "Argus's" crew was disputed. According to British authority, it was one hundred and twenty-seven,[1] while the "Pelican" carried one hundred and sixteen men and boys.[2]

At six o'clock in the morning, according to American reckoning,[3] — at half-past five according to the British report, — the "Argus" wore, and fired a broadside within grape-distance, which was returned with cannon and musketry. Within five minutes Captain Allen was struck by a shot which carried away his left leg, mortally wounding him; and five minutes afterward the first lieutenant was wounded on the head by a grape-shot. Although the second lieutenant fought the brig well, the guns were surprisingly inefficient. During the first fifteen minutes the "Argus" had the advantage of position,

[1] Report of Captain Maples, Aug. 14, 1813; James, Appendix no. 42, p. lxv.
[2] James, pp. 275–282.
[3] Report of Lieutenant Watson, March 2, 1815; Niles, viii. 43.

and at eighteen minutes after six raked the "Pelican" at close range, but inflicted no great injury on the enemy's hull or rigging, and killed at the utmost but one man, wounding only five. According to an English account,[1] "the 'Argus' fought well while the cannonading continued, but her guns were not levelled with precision, and many shots passed through the 'Pelican's' royals." The "Pelican," at the end of twenty-five minutes, succeeded in cutting up her opponent's rigging so that the "Argus" lay helpless under her guns. The "Pelican" then took a position on her enemy's starboard quarter, and raked her with eight thirty-two-pound carron-ades for nearly twenty minutes at close range, without receiv-ing a shot in return except from musketry. According to the report of the British captain, the action "was kept up with great spirit on both sides forty-three minutes, when we lay her alongside, and were in the act of boarding when she struck her colors."[2]

The "Argus" repeated the story of the "Chesapeake," except that the action lasted three quarters of an hour instead of fif-teen minutes. During that time, the "Pelican" should have fired all her broadside eight or ten times into the "Argus" at a range so close that no shot should have missed. Sixty thirty-two-pound shot fired into a small brig less than one hundred feet long should have shivered it to atoms. Nine thirty-two-pound shot from the "Hornet" seemed to reduce the "Pea-cock" to a sinking condition in fifteen minutes; yet the "Argus" was neither sunk nor dismasted. The British account of her condition after the battle showed no more injury than was suffered by the "Peacock," even in killed and wounded, by one or at the utmost two broadsides of the "Hornet."

> "The 'Argus' was tolerably cut up in her hull. Both her lower masts were wounded, although not badly, and her fore-shrouds on one side nearly all destroyed; but like the 'Chesapeake,' the 'Argus' had no spar shot away. Of her carronades several were disabled. She lost in the action six seamen killed; her commander, two midshipmen, the car-

[1] Niles, v. 118.
[2] Report of Captain Maples, Aug. 14, 1813; Niles, v. 118. James, Appendix no. 42.

penter, and three seamen mortally, her first lieutenant and five seamen severely, and eight others slightly wounded,—total twenty-four; chiefly, if not wholly by the cannon-shot of the 'Pelican.' "[1]

"The "Pelican" lost seven men killed or wounded, chiefly by musketry. On both sides the battle showed little skill with the guns; but perhaps the "Pelican," considering her undisputed superiority during half the combat, showed even less than the "Argus." As in the "Chesapeake's" battle, the discredit of the defeated ship lay in surrender to boarders.

Two such defeats were calculated to shake confidence in the American navy. That Allen should have been beaten in gunnery was the more strange, because his training with the guns gave him his chief credit with Decatur. Watson, the second lieutenant of the "Argus," attributed the defeat to the fatigue of his crew. Whatever was the immediate cause, no one could doubt that both the "Chesapeake" and "Argus" were sacrificed to the over-confidence of their commanders.

[1] James, p. 273.

Chapter XIII

THE PEOPLE OF the Atlantic coast felt the loss of the "Chesapeake" none too keenly. Other nations had a history to support them in moments of mortification, or had learned by centuries of experience to accept turns of fortune as the fate of war. The American of the sea-coast was not only sensitive and anxious, but he also saw with singular clearness the bearing of every disaster, and did not see with equal distinctness the general drift of success. The loss of the "Chesapeake" was a terrible disaster, not merely because it announced the quick recovery of England's pride and power from a momentary shock, but also because it threatened to take away the single object of American enthusiasm which redeemed shortcomings elsewhere. After the loss of the "Chesapeake," no American frigate was allowed the opportunity to fight with an equal enemy. The British frigates, ordered to cruise in company, gave the Americans no chance to renew their triumphs of 1812.

Indeed, the experience of 1813 tended to show that the frigate was no longer the class of vessel best suited to American wants. Excessively expensive compared with their efficiency, the "Constitution," "President," and "United States" could only with difficulty obtain crews; and when after much delay they were ready for sea, they could not easily evade a blockading squadron. The original cost of a frigate varied from two hundred thousand dollars to three hundred thousand; that of a sloop-of-war, like the "Hornet," "Wasp," or "Argus," varied between forty and fifty thousand dollars. The frigate required a crew of about four hundred men; the sloop carried about one hundred and fifty. The annual expense of a frigate in active service was about one hundred and thirty-four thousand dollars; that of the brig was sixty thousand. The frigate required much time and heavy timber in her construction; the sloop could be built quickly and of ordinary material. The loss of a frigate was a severe national disaster; the loss of a sloop was not a serious event.

For defensive purposes neither the frigate nor the brig counted heavily against a nation which employed ships-of-the-line by dozens; but even for offensive objects the frigate was hardly so useful as the sloop-of-war. The record of the frigates for 1813 showed no results equivalent to their cost. Their cruises were soon told. The "President," leaving Boston April 30, ran across to the Azores, thence to the North Sea, and during June and July haunted the shores of Norway, Scotland, and Ireland, returning to Newport September 27, having taken thirteen prizes. The "Congress," which left Boston with the "President," cruised nearly eight months in the Atlantic, and returned to Boston December 14, having captured but four merchantmen. The "Chesapeake," which sailed from Boston Dec. 13, 1812, cruised four months in the track of British commerce, past Madeira and Cape de Verde, across the equator, and round through the West Indies, returning to Boston April 9, having taken six prizes; at the beginning of her next cruise, June 1, the "Chesapeake" was herself captured. The adventures of the "Essex" in the Pacific were such as might have been equally well performed by a sloop-of-war, and belonged rather to the comparative freedom with which the frigates moved in 1812 than to the difficult situation that followed. No other frigates succeeded in getting to sea till December 4, when the "President" sailed again. The injury inflicted by the frigates on the Atlantic was therefore the capture of twenty-three merchantmen in a year. At the close of 1813, the "President" and the "Essex" were the only frigates at sea; the "Constitution" sailed from Boston only Jan. 1, 1814; the "United States" and "Macedonian" were blockaded at New London; the "Constellation" was still at Norfolk; the "Adams" was at Washington, and the "Congress" at Boston.

When this record was compared with that of the sloops-of-war, the frigates were seen to be luxuries. The sloop-of-war was a single-decked vessel, rigged sometimes as a ship, sometimes as a brig, but never as a sloop, measuring about one hundred and ten feet in length by thirty in breadth, and carrying usually eighteen thirty-two-pound carronades and two long twelve-pounders. Of this class the American navy possessed in 1812 only four examples,—the "Hornet," the "Wasp," the "Argus," and the "Syren." The "Wasp" was lost Oct. 18, 1812, after capturing the "Frolic." The "Syren" remained at New Orleans during the first year of the war, and then came to Boston, but saw no ocean service of importance during 1813. The "Hornet" made three prizes, including the sloop-of-war "Peacock," and was then blockaded with the "United States" and "Macedonian;" but the smaller vessel could do what the frigates could not, and in November the "Hornet" slipped out of New London and made her way to New York, where she waited an opportunity to escape to sea. The story will show her success. Finally, the "Argus" cruised for a month in the British Channel, and made twenty-one prizes before she was captured by the "Pelican."

The three frigates, "President," "Congress," and "Chesapeake," captured twenty-three prizes in the course of the year, and lost the "Chesapeake." The two sloops, the "Hornet" and "Argus," captured twenty-four prizes, including the sloop-of-war "Peacock," and lost the "Argus."

The government at the beginning of the war owned four smaller vessels,—the "Nautilus" and "Vixen" of fourteen guns, and the "Enterprise" and "Viper" of twelve. Another brig, the "Rattlesnake," sixteen, was bought. Experience seemed to prove that these were of little use. The "Nautilus" fell into the hands of Broke's squadron July 16, 1812, within a month after the declaration of war. The "Vixen" was captured Nov. 22, 1812, by Sir James Yeo. The "Viper," Jan. 17, 1813, became prize to Captain Lumley in the British frigate "Narcissus." The "Enterprise" distinguished itself by capturing the "Boxer," and was regarded as a lucky vessel, but was never a good or fast one.[1] The "Rattlesnake," though fast, was at last caught on a lee shore by the frigate "Leander," July 11, 1814, and carried into Halifax.[2]

In the enthusiasm over the frigates in 1812, Congress voted that six forty-fours should be built, besides four ships-of-the-line. The Act was approved Jan. 2, 1813. Not until March 3 did Congress pass an Act for building six new sloops-of-war. The loss of two months was not the only misfortune in this legislation. Had the sloops been begun in January, they might have gone to sea by the close of the year. The six sloops were all launched within eleven months from the passage of the bill, and the first of them, the "Frolic," got to sea within that

[1] Lieutenant Creighton to Secretary Jones, March 9, 1814; Niles, vi. 69.
[2] Niles, vi. 391.

time, while none of the frigates or line-of-battle ships could get to sea within two years of the passage of the law. A more remarkable oversight was the building of only six sloops, when an equal number of forty-fours and four seventy-fours were ordered. Had Congress voted twenty-four sloops, the proportion would not have been improper; but perhaps the best policy would have been to build fifty such sloops, and to prohibit privateering. The reasons for such a course were best seen in the experiences of the privateers.

The history of the privateers was never satisfactorily written. Neither their number, their measurements, their force, their captures, nor their losses were accurately known. Little ground could be given for an opinion in regard to their economy. Only with grave doubt could any judgment be reached even in regard to their relative efficiency compared with government vessels of the same class. Yet their experience was valuable, and their services were very great.

In the summer of 1812 any craft that could keep the sea in fine weather set out as a privateer to intercept vessels approaching the coast. The typical privateer of the first few months was the pilot-boat, armed with one or two long-nine or twelve-pound guns. Of twenty-six privateers sent from New York in the first four months of war, fifteen carried crews of eighty men or less. These small vessels especially infested the West Indies, where fine weather and light breezes suited their qualities. After the seas had been cleared of such prey as these petty marauders could manage, they were found to be unprofitable,—too small to fight and too light to escape. The typical privateer of 1813 was a larger vessel,—a brig or schooner of two or three hundred tons, armed with one long pivot-gun, and six or eight lighter guns in broadside; carrying crews which varied in number from one hundred and twenty to one hundred and sixty men; swift enough to escape under most circumstances even a frigate, and strong enough to capture any armed merchantman.

After the war was fairly begun, the British mercantile shipping always sailed either under convoy or as armed "running ships" that did not wait for the slow and comparatively rare opportunities of convoy, but trusted to their guns for defence. The new American privateer was adapted to meet both chances. Two or three such craft hanging about a convoy could commonly cut off some merchantman, no matter how careful the convoying man-of-war might be. By night they could run directly into the fleet and cut out vessels without even giving an alarm, and by day they could pick up any craft that lagged behind or happened to stray too far away. Yet the "running ships" were the chief objects of their search, for these were the richest prizes; and the capture of a single such vessel, if it reached an American port in safety, insured success to the cruise. The loss of these vessels caused peculiar annoyance to the British, for they sometimes carried considerable amounts of specie, and usually were charged with a mail which was always sunk and lost in case of capture.

As the war continued, experience taught the owners of privateers the same lesson that was taught to the government. The most efficient vessel of war corresponded in size with the "Hornet" or the new sloops-of-war building in 1813. Tonnage was so arbitrary a mode of measurement that little could be learned from the dimensions of five hundred tons commonly given for these vessels; but in a general way they might be regarded as about one hundred and fifteen or one hundred and twenty feet long on the spar-deck and thirty-one feet in extreme breadth. Unless such vessels were swift sailers, particularly handy in working to windward, they were worse than useless; and for that reason the utmost effort was made both by the public and private constructors to obtain speed. At the close of the war the most efficient vessel afloat was probably the American sloop-of-war, or privateer, of four or five hundred tons, rigged as a ship or brig, and carrying one hundred and fifty or sixty men, with a battery varying according to the ideas of the captain and owners, but in the case of privateers almost invariably including one "long Tom," or pivot-gun.

Yet for privateering purposes the smaller craft competed closely with the larger. For ordinary service no vessel could do more effective work in a more economical way than was done by Joshua Barney's "Rossie" of Baltimore, or Boyle's "Comet" of the same port, or Champlin's "General Armstrong" of New York,—schooners or brigs of two or three hundred tons, uncomfortable to their officers and crews, but most dangerous enemies to merchantmen. Vessels of this class came into favor long before the war, because of their speed, quickness in handling, and economy during the experience of twenty years in blockade-running and evasion of cruisers. Such schooners could be built in any Northern sea-port in six weeks or two months at half the cost of a government cruiser.

The government sloop-of-war was not built for privateering purposes. Every government vessel was intended chiefly to fight, and required strength in every part and solidity throughout. The frame needed to be heavy to support the heavier structure; the quarters needed to be thick to protect the men at the guns from grape and musketry; the armament was as weighty as the frame would bear. So strong were the sides of American frigates that even thirty-two-pound shot fired at forty or fifty feet distance sometimes failed to penetrate, and the British complained as a grievance that the sides of an American forty-four were thicker than those of a British seventy-four.[1] The American ship-builders spared no pains to make all their vessels in every respect—in size, strength, and speed—superior to the vessels with which they were to compete; but the government ship-carpenter had a harder task than the private ship-builder, for he was obliged to obtain greater speed at the same time that he used heavier material than the British constructors. As far as the navy carpenters succeeded in their double object, they did so by improving the model and increasing the proportions of the spars.

The privateer was built for no such object. The last purpose of a privateer was to fight at close range, and owners much preferred that their vessels, being built to make money, should not fight at all unless much money could be made. The private armed vessel was built rather to fly than to fight, and its value depended far more on its ability to escape than on its capacity to attack. If the privateer could sail close to the wind, and wear or tack in the twinkling of an eye; if she could spread an immense amount of canvas and run off as fast as a frigate before the wind; if she had sweeps to use in a calm, and one long-range gun pivoted amidships, with plenty of men in case boarding became necessary,—she was perfect.

[1] James, p. 18.

To obtain these results the builders and sailors ran excessive risks. Too lightly built and too heavily sparred, the privateer was never a comfortable or a safe vessel. Beautiful beyond anything then known in naval construction, such vessels roused boundless admiration, but defied imitators. British constructors could not build them, even when they had the models; British captains could not sail them; and when British admirals, fascinated by their beauty and tempted by the marvellous qualities of their model, ordered such a prize to be taken into the service, the first act of the carpenters in the British navy-yards was to reduce to their own standard the long masts, and to strengthen the hull and sides till the vessel should be safe in a battle or a gale. Perhaps an American navy-carpenter must have done the same; but though not a line in the model might be altered, she never sailed again as she sailed before. She could not bear conventional restraints.

Americans were proud of their privateers, as they well might be; for this was the first time when in competition with the world, on an element open to all, they proved their capacity to excel, and produced a creation as beautiful as it was practical. The British navy took a new tone in regard to these vessels. Deeply as the American frigates and sloops-of-war had wounded the pride of the British navy, they never had reduced that fine service to admitted inferiority. Under one pretext or another, every defeat was excused. Even the superiority of American gunnery was met by the proud explanation that the British navy, since Trafalgar, had enjoyed no opportunity to use their guns. Nothing could convince a British admiral that Americans were better fighters than Englishmen; but when he looked at the American schooner he frankly said that England could show no such models, and could not sail them if she had them. In truth, the schooner was a wonderful invention. Not her battles, but her escapes won for her the open-mouthed admiration of the British captains, who saw their prize double like a hare and slip through their fingers at the moment when capture was sure. Under any ordinary condition of wind and weather, with an open sea, the schooner, if only she could get to windward, laughed at a frigate.

As the sailing rather than the fighting qualities of the

privateer were the chief object of her construction, those were the points best worth recording; but the newspapers of the time were so much absorbed in proving that Americans could fight, as to cause almost total neglect of the more important question whether Americans could sail better than their rivals. All great nations had fought, and at one time or another every great nation in Europe had been victorious over every other; but no people, in the course of a thousand years of rivalry on the ocean, had invented or had known how to sail a Yankee schooner. Whether ship, brig, schooner, or sloop, the American vessel was believed to outsail any other craft on the ocean, and the proof of this superiority was incumbent on the Americans to furnish. They neglected to do so. No clear evidence was ever recorded of the precise capacities of their favorite vessels. Neither the lines of the hull, the dimensions of the spars, the rates of sailing by the log in different weather, the points of sailing,—nothing precise was ever set down.

Of the superiority no doubts could be entertained. The best proof of the American claim was the British admission. Hardly an English writer on marine affairs—whether in newspapers, histories, or novels—failed to make some allusion to the beauty and speed of American vessels. The naval literature of Great Britain from 1812 to 1860 was full of such material. The praise of the invention was still commonly accompanied by some expression of dislike for the inventor, but even in that respect a marked change followed the experiences of 1812–1814. Among the Englishmen living on the island of Jamaica, and familiar with the course of events in the West Indies from 1806 to 1817, was one Michael Scott, born in Glasgow in 1789, and in the prime of his youth at the time of the American war. In the year 1829, at the age of forty, he began the publication in "Blackwood's Magazine" of a series of sketches which rapidly became popular as "Tom Cringle's Log." Scott was the best narrator and probably the best informed man who wrote on the West Indies at that period; and his frequent allusions to the United States and the war threw more light on the social side of history than could be obtained from all official sources ever printed.

"I don't like Americans," Scott said; "I never did and

never shall like them. I have seldom met an American gentleman in the large and complete sense of the term. I have no wish to eat with them, drink with them, deal with or consort with them in any way; but let me tell the whole truth, — *nor fight* with them, were it not for the laurels to be acquired by overcoming an enemy so brave, determined, and alert, and every way so worthy of one's steel as they have always proved."

The Americans did not fight the War of 1812 in order to make themselves loved. According to Scott's testimony they gained the object for which they did fight. "In gunnery and small-arm practice we were as thoroughly weathered on by the Americans during the war as we overtopped them in the bull-dog courage with which our boarders handled those genuine English weapons, — the cutlass and the pike." Superiority in the intellectual branches of warfare was conceded to the Americans; but even in regard to physical qualities, the British were not inclined to boast.

"In the field," said Scott, "or grappling in mortal combat on the blood-slippery quarter-deck of an enemy's vessel, a British soldier or sailor is the bravest of the brave. No soldier or sailor of any other country, saving and excepting those damned Yankees, can stand against them."

Had English society known so much of Americans in 1807, war would have been unnecessary.

Yet neither equality in physical courage nor superiority in the higher branches of gunnery and small-arms was the chief success of Americans in the war. Beyond question the schooner was the most conclusive triumph. Readers of Michael Scott could not forget the best of his sketches, — the escape of the little American schooner "Wave" from two British cruisers, by running to windward under the broadside of a man-of-war. With keen appreciation Scott detailed every motion of the vessels, and dwelt with peculiar emphasis on the apparent desperation of the attempt. Again and again the thirty-two-pound shot, as he described the scene, tore through the slight vessel as the two crafts raced through the heavy seas within musket-shot of one another, until at last the firing from the corvette ceased. "The breeze had taken off, and the 'Wave,' resuming her superiority in light winds, had escaped." Yet this was not the most significant part of "Tom Cringle's" experience. The "Wave," being afterward captured at anchor, was taken into the royal service and fitted as a ship-of-war. Cringle was ordered by the vice-admiral to command her, and as she came to report he took a look at her:—

"When I had last seen her she was a most beautiful little craft, both in hull and rigging, as ever delighted the eye of a sailor; but the dock-yard riggers and carpenters had fairly bedevilled her, at least so far as appearances went. First they had replaced the light rail on her gunwale by heavy solid bulwarks four feet high, surmounted by hammock nettings at least another foot; so that the symmetrical little vessel that formerly floated on the foam light as a sea-gull now looked like a clumsy, dish-shaped Dutch dogger. Her long, slender wands of masts which used to swing about as if there were neither shrouds nor stays to support them were now as taut and stiff as church-steeples, with four heavy shrouds of a side, and stays and back-stays, and the Devil knows what all."

"If them heave-'emtaughts at the yard have not taken the speed out of the little beauty I am a Dutchman" was the natural comment,—as obvious as it was sound.

The reports of privateer captains to their owners were rarely published, and the logs were never printed or deposited in any public office. Occasionally, in the case of a battle or the loss of guns or spars or cargo in a close pursuit, the privateer captain described the causes of his loss in a letter which found its way into print; and from such letters some idea could be drawn of the qualities held in highest regard, both in their vessels and in themselves. The first and commonest remark was that privateers of any merit never seemed to feel anxious for their own safety so long as they could get to windward a couple of gunshots from their enemy. They would risk a broadside in the process without very great anxiety. They chiefly feared lest they might be obliged to run before the wind in heavy weather. The little craft which could turn on itself like a flash and dart away under a frigate's guns into the wind's eye long before the heavy ship could come about, had little to fear on that point of sailing; but when she was obliged to run to leeward, the chances were more nearly equal. Sometimes, especially in light breezes or in a stronger wind, by throwing guns and weighty articles overboard privateers could escape; but in heavy weather the ship-of-war could commonly outcarry them, and more often could drive them on a coast or into the clutches of some other man-of-war.

Of being forced to fly to leeward almost every privateer could tell interesting stories. A fair example of such tales was an adventure of Captain George Coggeshall, who afterward compiled, chiefly from newspapers, an account of the privateers, among which he preserved a few stories that would otherwise have been lost.[1] Coggeshall commanded a two-hundred-ton schooner, the "David Porter," in which he made the run to France with a cargo and a letter-of-marque. The schooner was at Bordeaux in March, 1814, when Wellington's army approached. Afraid of seizure by the British if he remained at Bordeaux, Coggeshall sailed from Bordeaux for La Rochelle with a light wind from the eastward, when at daylight March 15, 1814, he found a large ship about two miles to windward. Coggeshall tried to draw his enemy down to leeward, but only lost ground until the ship was not more than two gunshots away. The schooner could then not run to windward without taking the enemy's fire within pistol-shot, and dared not return to Bordeaux. Nothing remained but to run before the wind. Coggeshall got out his square-sail and studding-sails ready to set, and when everything was prepared he changed his course and bore off suddenly, gaining a mile in the six or eight minutes lost by the ship in spreading her studding-sails. He then started his water-casks, threw out ballast, and drew away from his pursuer, till in a few hours the ship became a speck on the horizon.

Apparently a similar but narrower escape was made by Captain Champlin of the "Warrior," a famous privateer-brig of four hundred and thirty tons, mounting twenty-one guns and carrying one hundred and fifty men.[2] Standing for the

[1] Coggeshall's History of American Privateers, p. 188.
[2] Extract of letter from Captain Champlin; Niles, viii. 110.

harbor of Fayal, Dec. 15, 1814, he was seen by a British man-of-war lying there at anchor. The enemy slipped her cables and made sail in chase. The weather was very fresh and squally, and at eight o'clock in the evening the ship was only three miles distant. After a run of about sixty miles, the man-of-war came within grape-shot distance and opened fire from her two bow-guns. Champlin luffed a little, got his long pivot-gun to bear, and ran out his starboard guns as though to fight, which caused the ship to shorten sail for battle. Then Champlin at two o'clock in the morning threw overboard eleven guns, and escaped. The British ship was in sight the next morning, but did not pursue farther.

Often the privateers were obliged to throw everything overboard at the risk of capsizing, or escaped capture only by means of their sweeps. In 1813 Champlin commanded the "General Armstrong," a brig of two hundred and forty-six tons and one hundred and forty men. Off Surinam, March 11, 1813, he fell in with the British sloop-of-war "Coquette," which he mistook for a letter-of-marque, and approached with the intention of boarding. Having come within pistol-shot and fired his broadsides, he discovered his error. The wind was light, the two vessels had no headway, and for three quarters of an hour, if Champlin's account could be believed, he lay within pistol-shot of the man-of-war. He was struck by a musket-ball in the left shoulder; six of his crew were killed and fourteen wounded; his rigging was cut to pieces; his fore-mast and bowsprit injured, and several shots entered the brig between wind and water, causing her to leak; but at last he succeeded in making sail forward, and with the aid of his sweeps crept out of range. The sloop-of-war was unable to cripple or follow him.[1]

Sometimes the very perfection of the privateer led to dangers as great as though perfection were a fault. Captain Shaler of the "Governor Tompkins," a schooner, companion to the "General Armstrong," chased three sail Dec. 25, 1812, and on near approach found them to be two ships and a brig. The larger ship had the appearance of a government transport; she had boarding-nettings almost up to her tops,

---

[1] Extract from log, March 11, 1813; Niles, iv. 133.

but her ports appeared to be painted, and she seemed prepared for running away as she fought. Shaler drew nearer, and came to the conclusion that the ship was too heavy for him; but while his first officer went forward with the glass to take another look, a sudden squall struck the schooner without reaching the ship, and in a moment, before the light sails could be taken in, "and almost before I could turn round, I was under the guns, not of a transport, but of a large frigate, and not more than a quarter of a mile from her." With impudence that warranted punishment, Shaler fired his little broadside of nine or twelve pounders into the enemy, who replied with a broadside of twenty-four-pounders, killing three men, wounding five, and causing an explosion on deck that threw confusion into the crew; but the broadside did no serious injury to the rigging. The schooner was then just abaft the ship's beam, a quarter of a mile away, holding the same course and to windward. She could not tack without exposing her stern to a raking fire, and any failure to come about would have been certain destruction. Shaler stood on, taking the ship's fire, on the chance of outsailing his enemy before a shot could disable the schooner. Side by side the two vessels raced for half an hour, while twenty-four-pound shot fell in foam about the schooner, but never struck her, and at last she drew ahead beyond range. Even then her dangers were not at an end. A calm followed; the ship put out boats; and only by throwing deck-lumber and shot overboard, and putting all hands at the sweeps, did Shaler "get clear of one of the most quarrelsome companions that I ever met with."[1]

The capacities of the American privateer could to some extent be inferred from its mishaps. Notwithstanding speed, skill, and caution, the privateer was frequently and perhaps usually captured in the end. The modes of capture were numerous. April 3, 1813, Admiral Warren's squadron in the Chesapeake captured by boats, after a sharp action, the privateer "Dolphin" of Baltimore, which had taken refuge in the Rappahannock River. April 27 the "Tom" of Baltimore, a schooner of nearly three hundred tons, carrying fourteen

---

[1] Shaler's Report of Jan. 1, 1813; Niles, v. 429.

guns, was captured by his Majesty's ships "Surveillante" and "Lyra" after a smart chase. Captain Collier of the "Surveillante" reported: "She is a remarkably fine vessel of her class, and from her superior sailing has already escaped from eighteen of his Majesty's cruisers." May 11, the "Holkar" of New York was driven ashore off Rhode Island and destroyed by the "Orpheus" frigate. May 19, Captain Gordon of the British man-of-war "Ratler," in company with the schooner "Bream," drove ashore and captured the "Alexander" of Salem, off Kennebunk, "considered the fastest sailing privateer out of the United States," according to Captain Gordon's report.[1] May 21, Captain Hyde Parker of the frigate "Tenedos," in company with the brig "Curlew," captured the "Enterprise" of Salem, pierced for eighteen guns. May 23, the "Paul Jones," of sixteen guns and one hundred and twenty men, fell in with a frigate in a thick fog off the coast of Ireland, and being crippled by her fire surrendered. July 13, Admiral Cockburn captured by boats at Ocracoke Inlet the fine privateer-brig "Anaconda" of New York, with a smaller letter-of-marque. July 17, at sea, three British men-of-war, after a chase of four hours, captured the "Yorktown" of twenty guns and one hundred and forty men. The schooner "Orders in Council" of New York, carrying sixteen guns and one hundred and twenty men, was captured during the summer, after a long chase of five days, by three British cutters that drove her under the guns of a frigate. The "Matilda," privateer of eleven guns and one hundred and four men, was captured off San Salvador by attempting to board the British letter-of-marque "Lyon" under the impression that she was the weaker ship.

In these ten instances of large privateers captured or destroyed in 1813, the mode of capture happened to be recorded; and in none of them was the privateer declared to have been outsailed and caught by any single British vessel on the open seas. Modes of disaster were many, and doubtless among the rest a privateer might occasionally be fairly beaten in speed, but few such cases were recorded, although British naval officers were quick to mention these unusual victories. Unless

[1] London Gazette for 1813, p. 1574.

the weather gave to the heavier British vessel-of-war the advantage of carrying more sail in a rough sea, the privateer was rarely outsailed.

The number of privateers at sea in 1813 was not recorded. The list of all private armed vessels during the entire war included somewhat more than five hundred names.[1] Most of these were small craft, withdrawn after a single cruise. Not two hundred were so large as to carry crews of fifty men. Nearly two hundred and fifty, or nearly half the whole number of privateers, fell into British hands. Probably at no single moment were more than fifty sea-going vessels on the ocean as privateers, and the number was usually very much less; while the large privateer-brigs or ships that rivalled sloops-of-war in size were hardly more numerous than the sloops themselves.

The total number of prizes captured from the British in 1813 exceeded four hundred, four fifths of which were probably captured by privateers, national cruisers taking only seventy-nine. If the privateers succeeded in taking three hundred and fifty prizes, the whole number of privateers could scarcely have exceeded one hundred. The government cruisers "President," "Congress," "Chesapeake," "Hornet," and "Argus" averaged nearly ten prizes apiece. Privateers averaged much less; but they were ten times as numerous as the government cruisers, and inflicted four times as much injury.

Such an addition to the naval force of the United States was very important. Doubtless the privateers contributed more than the regular navy to bring about a disposition for peace in the British classes most responsible for the war. The colonial and shipping interests, whose influence produced the Orders in Council, suffered the chief penalty. The West India colonies were kept in constant discomfort and starvation by swarms of semi-piratical craft darting in and out of every channel among their islands; but the people of England could have borne with patience the punishment of the West Indies had not the American cruisers inflicted equally severe retribution nearer home.

Great Britain was blockaded. No one could deny that man-

[1] Emmons's Navy of the United States, pp. 170–197.

ifest danger existed to any merchant-vessel that entered or left British waters. During the summer the blockade was continuous. Toward the close of 1812 an American named Preble, living in Paris, bought a small vessel, said to have belonged in turn to the British and French navy, which he fitted as a privateer-brig, carrying sixteen guns and one hundred and sixty men. The "True-Blooded Yankee," commanded by Captain Hailey, sailed from Brest March 1, 1813, and cruised thirty-seven days on the coasts of Ireland and Scotland, capturing twenty-seven valuable vessels; sinking coasters in the very bay of Dublin; landing and taking possession of an island off the coast of Ireland, and of a town in Scotland, where she burned seven vessels in the harbor. She returned safely to Brest, and soon made another cruise. At the same time the schooner "Fox" of Portsmouth burned or sunk vessel after vessel in the Irish Sea, as they plied between Liverpool and Cork. In May, the schooner "Paul Jones" of New York, carrying sixteen guns and one hundred and twenty men, took or destroyed a dozen vessels off the Irish coast, until she was herself caught in a fog by the frigate "Leonidas," and captured May 23 after a chase in which five of her crew were wounded.

While these vessels were thus engaged, the brig "Rattlesnake" of Philadelphia, carrying sixteen guns and one hundred and twenty men, and the brig "Scourge" of New York, carrying nine guns and one hundred and ten men, crossed the ocean and cruised all the year in the northern seas off the coasts of Scotland and Norway, capturing some forty British vessels, and costing the British merchants and ship-owners losses to the amount of at least two million dollars. In July the "Scourge" fell in with Commodore Rodgers in the "President," and the two vessels remained several days in company off the North Cape, while the British admiralty sent three or four squadrons in search of them without success. July 19, after Rodgers had been nearly a month in British waters, one of these squadrons drove him away, and he then made a circuit round Ireland before he turned homeward. At the same time, from July 14 to August 14, the "Argus" was destroying vessels in the British Channel at the rate of nearly one a day. After the capture of the "Argus," August 14, the

"Grand Turk" of Salem, a brig carrying sixteen guns and one hundred and five men, cruised for twenty days in the mouth of the British Channel without being disturbed. Besides these vessels, others dashed into British waters from time to time as they sailed forward and back across the ocean in the track of British commerce.

No one disputed that the privateers were a very important branch of the American navy; but they suffered under serious drawbacks, which left doubtful the balance of merits and defects. Perhaps their chief advantage compared with government vessels was their lightness,—a quality which no government would have carried to the same extent. The long-range pivot-gun was another invention of the privateer, peculiarly successful and easily adapted for government vessels. In other respects, the same number or even half the number of sloops-of-war would have probably inflicted greater injury at less cost. The "Argus" showed how this result could have been attained. The privateer's first object was to save prizes; and in the effort to send captured vessels into port the privateer lost a large proportion by recapture. Down to the moment when Admiral Warren established his blockade of the American coast from New York southward, most of the prizes got to port. After that time the New England ports alone offered reasonable chance of safety, and privateering received a check.[1] During the war about twenty-five hundred vessels all told were captured from the British. Many were destroyed; many released as cartels; and of the remainder not less than seven hundred and fifty, probably one half the number sent to port, were recaptured by the British navy. Most of these were the prizes of privateers, and would have been destroyed had they been taken by government vessels. They were usually the most valuable prizes, so that the injury that might have been inflicted on British commerce was diminished nearly one half by the system which encouraged private war as a money-making speculation.

Another objection was equally serious. Like all gambling ventures, privateering was not profitable. In the list of five

[1] Memorial of Baltimore merchants, Feb. 19, 1814; State Papers, Naval Affairs, p. 300.

hundred privateers furnished by the Navy Department,[1] three hundred were recorded as having never made a prize. Of the remainder, few made their expenses. One of the most successful cruises of the war was that of Joshua Barney on the Baltimore schooner "Rossie" at the outbreak of hostilities, when every prize reached port. Barney sent in prizes supposed to be worth fifteen hundred thousand dollars; but after paying charges and duties and selling the goods, he found that the profits were not sufficient to counterbalance the discomforts, and he refused to repeat the experiment. His experience was common. As early as November, 1812, the owners of twenty-four New York privateers sent to Congress a memorial declaring that the profits of private naval war were by no means equal to the hazards, and that the spirit of privateering stood in danger of extinction unless the government would consent in some manner to grant a bounty for the capture or destruction of the enemy's property.

If private enterprise was to fail at the critical moment, and if the government must supply the deficiency, the government would have done better to undertake the whole task. In effect, the government in the end did so. The merchants asked chiefly for a reduction of duties on prize-goods. Gallatin pointed out the serious objections to such legislation, and the little probability that the measure would increase the profits of privateering or the number of privateers. The actual privateers, he said, were more than enough for the food offered by the enemy's trade, and privateering, like every other form of gambling, would always continue to attract more adventurers than it could support.[2]

Congress for the time followed Gallatin's advice, and did nothing; but in the summer session of 1813, after Gallatin's departure for Europe, the privateer owners renewed their appeal, and the acting Secretary of the Treasury, Jones, wrote to the chairman of the Naval Committee July 21, 1813,[3] —

"The fact is that . . . privateering is nearly at an end; and from the best observation I have been enabled to make,

[1] Emmons's Navy of the United States.
[2] Gallatin to Langdon Cheves, Dec. 8, 1812; Annals, 1812–1813, p. 434.
[3] Annals, 1813–1814, i. 473.

it is more from the deficiency of remuneration in the net proceeds of their prizes than from the vigilance and success of the enemy in recapturing."

In deference to Jones's opinion, Congress passed an Act, approved Aug. 2, 1813, reducing one third the duties on prize-goods. Another Act, approved August 3, granted a bounty of twenty-five dollars for every prisoner captured and delivered to a United States agent by a private armed vessel. A third Act, approved August 2, authorized the Secretary of the Navy to place on the pension list any privateersman who should be wounded or disabled in the line of his duty.

These complaints and palliations tended to show that the privateer cost the public more than the equivalent government vessel would have cost. If instead of five hundred privateers of all sizes and efficiency, the government had kept twenty sloops-of-war constantly at sea destroying the enemy's commerce, the result would have been about the same as far as concerned injury to the enemy, while in another respect the government would have escaped one of its chief difficulties. Nothing injured the navy so much as privateering. Seamen commonly preferred the harder but more profitable and shorter cruise in a privateer, where fighting was not expected or wished, to the strict discipline and murderous battles of government ships, where wages were low and prize-money scarce. Of all towns in the United States, Marblehead was probably the most devoted to the sea; but of nine hundred men from Marblehead who took part in the war, fifty-seven served as soldiers, one hundred and twenty entered the navy, while seven hundred and twenty-six went as privateersmen.[1] Only after much delay and difficulty could the frigates obtain crews. The "Constitution" was nearly lost by this cause at the beginning of the war; and the loss of the "Chesapeake" was supposed to be chiefly due to the determination of the old crew to quit the government service for that of the privateers.

Such drawbacks raised reasonable doubts as to the balance of advantages and disadvantages offered by the privateer system. Perhaps more careful inquiry might show that, valuable as the privateers were, the government would have done

[1] Roads's Marblehead, p. 255.

better to retain all military and naval functions in its own hands, and to cover the seas with small cruisers capable of pursuing a system of thorough destruction against the shipping and colonial interests of England.

Chapter XIV

GALLATIN AND BAYARD, having sailed from the Delaware May 9, arrived at St. Petersburg July 21, only to find that during the six months since the Czar offered to mediate, Russia had advanced rapidly in every direction except that of the proposed mediation. Napoleon after being driven from Russia in December, 1812, passed the winter in Paris organizing a new army of three hundred thousand men on the Elbe, between Dresden and Magdeburg, while a second army of more than one hundred thousand was to hold Hamburg and Bremen. Russia could not prevent Napoleon from reconstructing a force almost as powerful as that with which he had marched to Moscow, for the Russian army had suffered very severely and was unfit for active service; but the Czar succeeded in revolutionizing Prussia, and in forcing the French to retire from the Vistula to the Elbe, while he gained a reinforcement of more than one hundred thousand men from the fresh and vigorous Prussian army. Even with that assistance the Czar could not cope with Napoleon, who, leaving Paris April 17, during the month of May fought furious battles at Lützen and Bautzen, which forced the allied Russian and Prussian armies back from the Elbe to the Oder.

At that point Austria interfered so energetically as to oblige Napoleon to accept an armistice for the purpose of collecting new forces. During the armistice the Czar stationed himself at Gitschin in Bohemia, nine hundred miles from St. Petersburg, and about the same distance from London by the path that couriers were obliged to take. When Gallatin and Bayard reached St. Petersburg, July 21, the armistice, which had been prolonged until August 10, was about to expire, and the Czar could not be anxious to decide subordinate questions until the issue of the coming campaign should be known.

Meanwhile the government of England had in May, with many friendly expressions, declined the Russian mediation.[1] Castlereagh probably hoped that this quiet notification to Lieven, the Russian envoy in London, would end the matter; but toward the month of July news reached London that the

[1] Diary of J. Q. Adams, June 22, 1813, ii. 479.

American commissioners, Gallatin and Bayard, had arrived at Gothenburg on their way to Russia, and Castlereagh then saw that he must be more explicit in his refusal. Accordingly he took measures for making the matter clear not only to the Russian government but also to the American commissioners.

With the Russian government he was obliged by the nature of their common relations to communicate officially, and he wrote instructions to Lord Cathcart, dated July 5, directing communication to be made.

"I am afraid," said Castlereagh's letter,[1] "this tender of mediation which on a question of maritime right cannot be listened to by Great Britain, however kindly and liberally intended, will have had the unfortunate effect of protracting the war with the United States. It is to be lamented that the formal offer was made to America before the disposition of the British government was previously sounded as to its acceptance of a mediation. It has enabled the President to hold out to the people of America a vague expectation of peace, under which he may reconcile them with less repugnance to submit to the measures of the Government. This evil, however, cannot now be avoided, and it only remains to prevent this question from producing any embarrassment between Great Britain and Russia."

Embarrassment between Great Britain and Russia was no new thing in European politics, and commonly involved maritime objects for which the United States were then fighting. Castlereagh had much reason for wishing to avoid the danger. The most fortunate result he could reasonably expect from the coming campaign was a defeat of Bonaparte that should drive him back to the Rhine. Then Russia and Austria would probably offer terms to Napoleon; England would be obliged to join in a European Congress; Napoleon would raise the question of maritime rights, and on that point he would be supported by Russian sympathies. Napoleon and Russia might insist that the United States should take part in the Congress, and in that case England might be obliged to retire from it. Castlereagh felt uneasy at the prospect, and ordered

[1] Castlereagh to Cathcart, July 5, 1813; MSS. British Archives.

Cathcart to "press the Emperor of Russia in the strongest manner not to push his personal interference on this point further." Cathcart was to use his utmost endeavors to persuade the Czar "pointedly to discountenance a design so mischievously calculated to promote the views of France."

Another week of reflection only increased Castlereagh's anxieties, and caused the British government to take a step intended to leave the Czar no opening for interference. July 13 Castlereagh wrote Cathcart new instructions,[1] directing him to present a formal note acquainting the Czar that the Prince Regent was "ready immediately to name plenipotentiaries to meet and treat with the American plenipotentiaries in the earnest desire" of peace, either in London or at Gothenburg; although he could "not consent that these discussions should be carried on in any place which might be supposed to imply that they were in any way connected with any other negotiations." He wrote privately to Cathcart that the mere knowledge of the intervention of a third power in any arrangement with the United States would probably decide the British people against it.[2]

Thus in July, 1813, when the war was barely a year old, Castlereagh reached the point of offering to negotiate directly with the United States. This advantage was gained by the Russian offer of mediation, and was intended not to pacify America but to silence Alexander and Roumanzoff. Castlereagh was frank and prompt in his declarations. His offer of direct negotiation was dated July 13, at a time when Alexander Baring received a letter from Gallatin announcing his arrival at Gothenburg and inviting assistance for the proposed mediation. Baring consulted Castlereagh, and wrote, July 22, a long letter to Gallatin, to inform the American commissioners what the British government had done and was willing to do. "Before this reaches you," said Baring,[3] "you will have been informed that this mediation has been refused, with expressions of our desire to treat separately and directly here; or, if more agreeable to you, at Gothenburg." To leave no room for

[1] Castlereagh to Cathcart, July 13, 1813; MSS. British Archives.
[2] Castlereagh to Cathcart, July 14, 1813; Castlereagh Papers, Third Series, i. 35.
[3] Baring to Gallatin, July 22, 1813; Gallatin's Writings, i. 546.

misunderstanding, Baring added that if the American commissioners were obliged by their instructions to adhere pertinaciously to the American demands in respect to impressments, he should think negotiation useless.

In regular succession all these expressions of British policy were received at St. Petersburg in the Czar's absence, and in the doubtful state of mind which followed the battles of Lützen and Bautzen. Alexander had left Count Roumanzoff at St. Petersburg, continuing to act as Chancellor of the Empire and Foreign Secretary; but in truth the Minister of Foreign Affairs, as far as the Czar then required such an officer, was Count Nesselrode, who attended Alexander in person and received his orders orally. Nesselrode at that time was rather an agent than an adviser; but in general he represented the English alliance and hostility to Napoleon, while Roumanzoff represented the French alliance and hostility to England.

Of English diplomacy Americans knew something, and could by similarity of mind divine what was not avowed. Of French diplomacy they had long experience, and their study was rendered from time to time more easy by Napoleon's abrupt methods. Of Russian diplomacy they knew little or nothing. Thus far Minister Adams had been given his own way. He had been allowed to seem to kindle the greatest war of modern times, and had been invited to make use of Russia against England; but the Czar's reasons for granting such favor were mysterious even to Adams, for while Napoleon occasionally avowed motives, Alexander never did. Russian diplomacy moved wholly in the dark.

Only one point was certain. For reasons of his own, the Czar chose to leave Roumanzoff nominally in office until the result of the war should be decided, although Roumanzoff was opposed to the Czar's policy. The chancellor did not stand alone in his hostility to the war; probably a majority of the Russian people shared the feeling. Even the army and its old General Koutousoff, though elated with an immense triumph, grumbled at being obliged to fight the battles of Germany, and would gladly have returned to their own soil. The Czar himself could not afford to break his last tie with the French interest, but was wise to leave a path open by which he could still retreat in case his war in Germany failed. If Napoleon should succeed once more in throwing the Russian army back upon Russian soil, Alexander might still be obliged to use Roumanzoff's services if not to resume his policy. Such a suspicion might not wholly explain Alexander's course toward Roumanzoff and Koutousoff, but no one could doubt that it explained the chancellor's course toward the Czar. Indeed, Roumanzoff made little concealment of his situation or his hopes. Adams could without much difficulty divine that the failure of the Czar in Germany would alone save Roumanzoff in St. Petersburg, and that the restoration of Roumanzoff to power was necessary to reinvigorate the mediation.

Castlereagh's first positive refusal to accept the mediation was notified to Count Lieven in May, and was known to Roumanzoff in St. Petersburg about the middle of June. Early in July the Czar received it, and by his order Nesselrode, in a despatch to Lieven dated July 9, expressed "the perfect satisfaction which his Imperial Majesty felt in the reasons which actuated the conduct of this [British] government on a point of so much delicacy and importance."[1] The Czar was then in the midst of difficulties. The result of the war was doubtful, and depended on Austria.

Just as news of the armistice arrived in St. Petersburg, Minister Adams went to Roumanzoff, June 22, to inform him of Gallatin's and Bayard's appointment. Roumanzoff in return gave Adams explicit information of England's refusal to accept the Czar's offer. Adams immediately recorded it in his Diary:[2] —

"He [Roumanzoff] said that he was very sorry to say he had received since he had seen me [June 15] further despatches from Count Lieven, stating that the British government, with many very friendly and polite assurances that there was no mediation which they should so readily and cheerfully accept as that of the Emperor of Russia, had however stated that their differences with the United States of America involving certain principles of the internal gov-

[1] Castlereagh to Cathcart, Sept. 1, 1813; MSS. British Archives.
[2] Diary of J. Q. Adams, June 22, 1813, ii. 479.

ernment of England were of a nature which they did not think suitable to be settled by a mediation."

Adams expected this answer, and at once assumed it to be final; but Roumanzoff checked him. "It would now be for consideration," he continued, "whether, after the step thus taken by the American government [in sending commissioners to St. Petersburg], it would not be advisable to renew the proposition to Great Britain; upon which he should write to the Emperor." Not because of any American request, but wholly of his own motion, Roumanzoff proposed to keep the mediation alive. His motives were for Adams to fathom. The chancellor did not avow them, but he hinted to Adams that the chances of war were many. "Perhaps it might be proper not to be discouraged by the ill success of his first advances. After considerations might produce more pacific dispositions in the British government. Unexpected things were happening every day; 'and in our own affairs,' said the count, 'a very general report prevails that an armistice has taken place.'" A Congress had been proposed, and the United States were expressly named among the Powers to be invited to it.

Adams reported this conversation to his Government in a despatch dated June 26,[1] and waited for his two new colleagues, who arrived July 21. Personally the colleagues were agreeable to Adams, and the proposed negotiation was still more so, for the President sent him official notice that in case the negotiations were successful, Adams's services would be required as minister in London; but with the strongest inducements to press the mediation, Adams could not but see that he and his colleagues depended on Roumanzoff, and that Roumanzoff depended not on Alexander, but on Napoleon. Roumanzoff's only chance of aiding them was by clinging to office until the Czar should be weary of war.

Unwilling as Gallatin was to be thus made the sport of imperial policy, he was obliged, like his colleagues, to submit. Two days after their arrival, Roumanzoff told them that he meant, if possible, to begin the whole transaction anew.

"The count said he regretted much that there was such

reason to believe the British would decline the mediation; but on transmitting the copy of the credential letter to the Emperor, he would determine whether to renew the proposal, as the opposition in England might make it an embarrassing charge against the Ministry if they should under such circumstances reject it."[1]

Roumanzoff had written soon after June 22 to ask the Czar whether, on the arrival of the American commissioners, the offer of mediation should be renewed. The Czar, overwhelmed with business, wrote back, about July 20, approving Roumanzoff's suggestion, and authorizing him to send a despatch directly to Count Lieven in London renewing the offer. The Czar's letter was communicated to Adams August 10[2] by Roumanzoff, who was evidently much pleased and perhaps somewhat excited by it.

Such a letter warranted some excitement, for Roumanzoff could regard it only as a sign of hesitation and anxiety. Alexander was in a degree pledged to England to press the mediation no further. While he assured England through Nesselrode, July 9, that he was perfectly satisfied with the British reasons for refusing his offer of mediation "on a point of so much delicacy and importance," he authorized Roumanzoff only ten days afterward to annoy England a second time with an offer which he had every reason to know must be rejected; and he did this without informing Nesselrode.

Gallatin and Bayard found themselves, August 10, condemned to wait two or three months for the British answer, which they knew must be unfavorable, because Gallatin received August 17 Baring's letter announcing the determination of Castlereagh to negotiate separately. Roumanzoff's conduct became more and more mysterious to the commissioners. He did not notify them of Castlereagh's official offer to negotiate directly. He confounded Adams, August 19, by flatly denying his own information, given two months before, that England rejected mediation in principle because it involved doctrines of her internal government. Roumanzoff insisted that England had never refused to accept the

[1] Diary of J. Q. Adams, July 23, 1813, ii. 489.
[2] Diary of J. Q. Adams, July 23, 1813, ii. 501.

mediation, although he held in his hands at least two despatches from Lieven, written as late as July 13, officially communicating England's determination to negotiate directly or
not at all. Castlereagh, foreseeing the possibility of misunderstanding, had read to Lieven the instructions of July 13 for
communication to Roumanzoff, besides authorizing Cathcart
to show them *in extenso* to the Czar.[1] In denying that such
instructions had been given, Roumanzoff could not have expected the American commissioners to believe him.

The motive of Roumanzoff's persistence might be open to
the simple explanation that the chancellor hoped to recover
power, and within a few months to re-establish his policy of
antagonism to England. Alexander's conduct could be explained by no such obvious interest. When Castlereagh's
letters of July 13 and 14 reached Cathcart at the Czar's
headquarters in Bohemia about August 10, they arrived at the
most critical moment of the war. On that day the armistice
expired. The next day Austria declared war on Napoleon. The
combined armies of Russia, Prussia, and Austria concentrated
behind the mountains, and then marched into Saxony. While
starting on that campaign, August 20, the Czar was told by
Lord Cathcart the reasons why his offer of mediation was
rejected, and answered at once that in this case he could do
nothing more.[2] Cathcart wrote to Nesselrode a formal note
on the subject August 23 or 24, but did not at once communicate it,[3] because the campaign had then begun; the great
battle of Dresden was fought August 26 and 27, and the allies,
again beaten, retired into Bohemia August 28. The Czar saw
his best military adviser Moreau killed by his side at Dresden,
and he returned to Töplitz in no happy frame of mind.

At Töplitz, September 1, Cathcart delivered to Nesselrode
his formal note,[4] refusing Russian mediation and communicating the offer of England to negotiate directly. In an ordinary condition of government Nesselrode should have taken
care that the British note should be made known without

[1] Castlereagh to Cathcart, July 14, 1813; Castlereagh's Papers, Third Series,
i. 35.
[2] Diary of J. Q. Adams, Nov. 23, 1813, ii. 539, 542.
[3] Diary of J. Q. Adams, April 2, 1814, ii. 593.
[4] Cathcart to Nesselrode, Sept. 1, 1813; State Papers, iii. 622.

delay to the American commissioners at St. Petersburg, but the Czar kept in his own hands the correspondence with Roumanzoff and the Americans, and neither he nor Nesselrode communicated Cathcart's act to Roumanzoff.[1] Possibly their silence was due to the new military movements. August 29 the French marshal Vandamme with forty thousand men, pursuing the allies into Bohemia, was caught between the Prussians and Austrians August 30 and crushed. During the month of September severe fighting, favorable to the allies, occurred, but no general advance was made by the allied sovereigns.

Alexander next received at Töplitz toward September 20 a letter from Roumanzoff enclosing a renewal of the offer of mediation, to be proposed in a despatch to Lieven, read by Roumanzoff to the American commissioners August 24, and sent to London August 28. The Czar must have known the futility of this new step, as well as the mistake into which Roumanzoff had been led, and the awkward attitude of the American commissioners. Only a fortnight before, he had received Cathcart's official note, and a few days earlier he had assured Cathcart that he should do no more in the matter. Yet, September 20, Alexander wrote with his own hand a note of four lines to Roumanzoff, approving his despatch to Lieven, and begging him to follow up the affair as he had begun it.[2]

The Czar's letter of September 20 completed the embroglio, which remained unintelligible to every one except himself. Cathcart was the most mystified of all the victims to the Czar's double attitude. At the time when Alexander thus for the second time authorized Roumanzoff to disregard the express entreaties of the British government, Cathcart was making an effort to explain to Castlereagh the Czar's first interference. If Castlereagh understood his minister's ideas, he was gifted with more than common penetration.

"I believe the not communicating the rescript of the Emperor concerning the American plenipotentiaries to have been the effect of accident," wrote Cathcart[3] from Töplitz

[1] Diary of J. Q. Adams, April 23, 1814, ii. 599.
[2] Diary of J. Q. Adams, Sept. 10, 1813, ii. 531.
[3] Cathcart to Castlereagh, Sept. 25, 1813; MSS. British Archives.

September 25; "but what is singular is that notwithstanding his [Nesselrode's] letter of the ninth [July], by the Emperor's command, to Count Lieven, this communication from and instruction to Roumanzoff was not known to Count Nesselrode till this day, when I mentioned it to him, having received no caution to do otherwise, and he was not at all pleased with it. It was during the advance to Dresden. But I cannot help thinking that there must have been some policy of Roumanzoff's stated in regard to keeping hold of the mediation, which, whether it was detailed or not, would not escape the Emperor's penetration, and upon which he may have been induced to act as far as sanctioning the proposal of treating at *London* under Russia's mediation, which the Prince Regent's government might accept or reject as they pleased; and that not wishing to go at that time into a discussion of maritime rights with either Nesselrode or me, he afterward forgot it."

Cathcart's style was involved, but his perplexity was evident. His remarks related only to the Czar's first letter to Roumanzoff, written about July 20, not "during the advance to Dresden." He knew nothing of the Czar's second letter to Roumanzoff, dated September 20, renewing the same authority, only five days before Cathcart's labored attempt to explain the first. Of the second letter, as of the first, neither Nesselrode nor Cathcart was informed.

The Czar's motive in thus ordering each of his two ministers to act in ignorance and contradiction of the other's instructions perplexed Roumanzoff as it did Cathcart. Lieven first revealed to Roumanzoff the strange misunderstanding by positively refusing to present to Castlereagh the chancellor's note of August 28 renewing the offer of mediation. Roumanzoff was greatly mortified. He told Gallatin that the mediation had been originally the Czar's own idea; that it had been the subject of repeated discussions at his own motion, and had been adopted notwithstanding Roumanzoff's hints at the possibility of English reluctance.[1] The chancellor sent Lieven's despatch immediately to the Czar without comment, requesting the Czar to read it and give his orders. The British

[1] Diary of J. Q. Adams, Nov. 3, 1813, ii. 541.

officials, unwilling to blame Alexander, attacked Roumanzoff. Lord Walpole, who came directly from Bohemia to St. Petersburg to act as British ambassador, said "he was as sure as he was of his own existence, and he believed he could prove it, that Roumanzoff had been cheating us all."[1] Cathcart wrote, December 12, to Castlereagh,—

"I think Nesselrode knows nothing of the delay of communicating with the American mission; that it was an intrigue of the chancellor's, if it is one; and that during the operations of war the Emperor lost the clew to it, so that something has been unanswered."[2]

Perhaps the Czar's conduct admitted of several interpretations. He might wish to keep the mediation alive in order to occupy Roumanzoff until the campaign should be decided; or he might in his good nature prefer to gratify his old favorite by allowing him to do what he wished; or he took this method of signifying to Roumanzoff his disgrace and the propriety of immediate retirement. Apparently Roumanzoff took the last view, for he sent his resignation to the Czar, and at the close of the year quitted his official residence at the Department of Foreign Affairs, telling Gallatin that he remained in office only till he should receive authority to close the American mission.

The American commissioners in private resented Alexander's treatment, but were unable to leave Russia without authority. Gallatin learned, October 19, that the Senate had refused to confirm his appointment, but he remained at St. Petersburg, chiefly in deference to Roumanzoff's opinion, and probably with ideas of assisting the direct negotiation at London or elsewhere. Meanwhile the campaign was decided, October 18, by Napoleon's decisive overthrow at Leipzig, which forced him to retreat behind the Rhine. Still the Czar wrote nothing to Roumanzoff, and the American commissioners remained month after month at St. Petersburg. Not until Jan. 25, 1814, did Gallatin and Bayard begin their winter journey to Amsterdam, where they arrived March 4 and remained a month. Then Gallatin received, through Baring,

[1] Diary of J. Q. Adams, April 2, 1814, ii. 591.
[2] Cathcart to Castlereagh, Dec. 12, 1813; Castlereagh Papers.

permission to enter England, and crossed the Channel to hasten if he could the direct negotiation which Castlereagh had
offered and Madison accepted.

The diplomatic outlook had changed since March, 1813,
when the President accepted the offer of Russian mediation;
but the change was wholly for the worse. England's triumphs
girdled the world, and found no check except where Perry's
squadron blocked the way to Detroit. The allied armies
crossed the Rhine in December and entered France on the
east. At the same time Wellington after a long campaign
drove Joseph from Spain, and entering France from the south
pressed against Bordeaux. The government and people of England, in their excitement and exultation at daily conquests,
thought as little as they could of the American war. Society
rarely mentioned it. Newspapers alone preserved a record of
British feelings toward the United States during the year 1813.
The expressions of newspapers, like those of orators, could
not be accepted without allowance, for they aimed at producing some desired effect, and said either more or less than the
truth; as a rule, they represented the cool opinion neither of
the person who uttered nor of the audience who heard them;
but in the absence of other records, public opinion was given
only in the press, and the London newspapers alone furnished
evidence of its character.

The "Morning Chronicle"—the only friend of the United
States in the daily press of England—showed its friendship
by silence. Whatever the liberal opposition thought in private,
no one but Cobbett ventured in public to oppose the war.
Cobbett having become a radical at the time of life when
most men become conservative, published in his "Weekly
Register" many columns of vigorous criticism on the American war without apparent effect, although in truth he expressed opinions commonly held by intelligent people. Even
Lord Castlereagh, Cobbett's antipathy, shared some of Cobbett's least popular opinions in the matter of the American
war.

English society, whatever shades of diversity might exist,
was frank and free in expressing indifference or contempt. Of
the newspapers which made a duty of reflecting what was
believed to be the prevailing public opinion, the "Times,"

supposed to favor the interests of Wellesley and Canning, was probably the ablest. During the early part of the war, the "Times" showed a disposition to criticise the Ministry rather than the Americans. From the "Times" came most of the bitter complaints, widely copied by the American press, of the naval defeats suffered by the "Guerriere," the "Java," and the "Macedonian." British successes were belittled, and abuse of Americans was exaggerated, in order to deprive ministers of credit. "The world has seen President Madison plunge into a war from the basest motives, and conduct it with the most entire want of ability," said the "Times" of February 9, 1813. "The American government has sounded the lowest depth of military disgrace, insomuch that the official records of the campaign take from us all possibility of exulting in our victories over such an enemy." The "Times" found in such reflections a reason for not exulting in ministerial victories, but it bewailed defeats the more loudly, and annoyed the Ministry by the violence of its attacks on naval administration.

As the year passed, and England's triumph in Europe seemed to overshadow the world, the "Times," probably recognizing the uselessness of attacking the Ministry, showed worse temper toward the United States. The Americans were rarely mentioned, and always with language of increasing ill humor. "Despicable in the cabinet, ridiculous in the field,"[1] the Americans disappeared from sight in the splendor of victory at Vittoria and Leipzig. No wish for peace was suggested, and if the "Times" expressed the true feelings of the respectable middle class, as it was supposed to aim at doing, no wish for peace could be supposed to exist.

Of the ministerial papers the "Courier" was the best, and of course was emphatic in support of the American war. The Ministry were known to be lukewarm about the United States, and for that reason they thought themselves obliged to talk in public as strongly as the strongest against a peace. When the Russian mediation called for notice, May 13, the "Courier" at once declared against it:—

"Before the war commenced, concession might have been proper; we always thought it unwise. But the hour of

[1] The Times, Oct. 17, 1813.

concession and compromise is passed. America has rushed unnecessarily and unnaturally into war, and she must be made to feel the effects of her folly and injustice; peace must be the consequence of punishment, and retraction of her insolent demands must precede negotiation. The thunders of our cannon must first strike terror into the American shores."

The "Courier" felt that Americans were not Englishmen, and could not forgive it, but was unable to admit that they might still exercise a considerable influence on human affairs:—

"They have added nothing to literature, nothing to any of the sciences; they have not produced one good poet, not one celebrated historian! Their statesmen are of a mixed breed,—half metaphysicians, half politicians; all the coldness of the one with all the cunning of the other. Hence we never see anything enlarged in their conceptions or grand in their measures."[1]

These reasons were hardly sufficient to prove the right of impressing American seamen. The literary, metaphysical, or social qualities of Americans, their "enlarged conceptions," and the grandeur or littleness of their measures, had by common consent ceased to enter into discussion, pending a settlement of the simpler issue, whether Americans could fight. For a long time the English press encouraged the belief that Americans were as incapable of fighting as of producing poets and historians. Their naval victories were attributed to British seamen. Perhaps the first turn of the tide was in November, 1813, when news of Perry's victory on Lake Erie crossed in London the news of Napoleon's defeat at Leipzig. Perry's victory, like those of Hull, Decatur, and Bainbridge, was too complete for dispute: "It may, however, serve to diminish our vexation at this occurrence to learn that the flotilla in question was not any branch of the British navy, . . . but a local force, a kind of mercantile military."[2]

By a curious coincidence, Castlereagh's official letter to

[1] The Courier, July 27, 1813.
[2] The Courier, Nov. 4, 1813.

Monroe, offering direct negotiation, was dated the same day, November 4, when news of the victory at Leipzig met in London news of the defeat on Lake Erie, and Castlereagh probably meant to allow no newspaper prejudices to obstruct a peace; but public opinion was slow to recover its balance. When news arrived that the Americans had captured Malden, recovered Detroit, and destroyed Proctor's army on the Thames, the "Courier" showed the first symptom of change in opinion by expressing a somewhat simple-minded wish to hear no more about the Americans:—

"The intelligence is unpleasant, but we confess that we do not view, and have never from the beginning of the war viewed, the events in America with any very powerful interest. The occurrences in Europe will no doubt produce a very decisive effect upon the American government; and unless it is more obstinate and stupid in its hostility than even *we* think it, it will do as the other allies of Bonaparte have done,—abandon him."

If the national extravagance could be expected to show its full force in one direction rather than in another, naturalized Americans taken in arms were certain to produce it. The issue was regularly raised after Van Rensselaer's defeat at Queenston in 1812. When the American prisoners arrived at Quebec, they were mustered, and twenty-three native-born subjects of Great Britain, belonging to the First, Sixth, and Thirteenth U. S. Infantry, were taken from the ranks and shipped to England to be put on trial as British subjects for bearing arms against their king. The American agent in London reported to the President that the men had arrived there for the reason given. Secretary Armstrong, May 15, 1813, then ordered twenty-three British soldiers into close confinement as hostages. The British government directed Sir George Prevost to put double the number of Americans in close confinement, and Sir George, in giving notice of this measure to General Wilkinson, October 17, 1813,[1] added:—

"I have been further instructed by his Majesty's govern-

[1] Prevost to Wilkinson, Oct. 17, 1813; State Papers, Foreign Relations, iii. 635. Bathurst to Prevost, Aug. 12, 1813; State Papers, Foreign Relations, iii. 641.

ment to notify to you for the information of the government of the United States that the commanders of his Majesty's armies and fleets on the coasts of America have received instructions to prosecute the war with unmitigated severity against all cities, towns, and villages belonging to the United States, and against the inhabitants thereof, if, after this communication shall have been made to you, and a reasonable time given for its being transmitted to the American government, that government shall unhappily not be deterred from putting to death any of the soldiers who now are or who may hereafter be kept as hostages for the purposes stated in the letter from Major-General Dearborn."

The limit of retaliation was soon reached, for the number of prisoners was small on both sides. The British government somewhat carefully refrained from committing itself too far; but the press treated the matter as though it were vital.

"If Mr. Madison," said the "Courier" of July 24, "dare to retaliate by taking away the life of one English prisoner in revenge for a British subject fully proved to be such being taken in the act of voluntarily bearing arms against his country, America puts herself out of the protection of the law of nations, and must be treated as an outlaw. An army and navy acting against her will then be absolved from all obligation to respect the usages and laws of war. Hostilities may be carried on against her in any mode until she is brought to a proper sense of her conduct."

The "Morning Post" of December 28 called for the execution of British subjects taken in arms, and for retaliation on retaliation in defiance of "the brutal wretches who, after betraying, are still suffered to govern America." The "Times" of May 24 spoke with hardly less vehemence. Probably such talk was not shared by the government, for the government never tested its sincerity by bringing the men to trial; but at the close of 1813 public opinion in England was supposed to be tending toward extreme measures against the United States. The approaching fall of Napoleon threatened to throw America outside the pale of civilization. Englishmen seemed ready to accept the idea that Madison and Napoleon should be coupled together, and that no peace should be made which did not include the removal of both from office and power. Of all periods in American history this was probably the least adapted to negotiation, but while England was at the moment of her most extravagant sense of power, President Madison received and accepted Castlereagh's offer to negotiate, and Gallatin went with Bayard to London to hasten the approach of peace.

Chapter XV

CONGRESS ASSEMBLED Dec. 6, 1813, at a time of general perplexity. The victories of Perry and Harrison, September 10 and October 5, had recovered Detroit and even conquered a part of West Canada, but their successes were already dimmed by the failures of Wilkinson and Hampton before Montreal, and the retreat of both generals November 13 within United States territory. In the Creek country the Georgians had failed to advance from the east, and Jackson was stopped at Fort Strother by want of supplies and men. At sea the navy was doing little, while the British blockade from New London southward was becoming more and more ruinous to the Southern and Middle States, and through them to the government. Abroad the situation was not yet desperate. The latest news from Europe left Napoleon at Dresden, victorious for the moment, before the great battles of October. From the American commissioners at St. Petersburg no news had arrived, but England's refusal to accept mediation was unofficially known. With this material the President was obliged to content himself in framing his Annual Message.

The Message sent to Congress December 7 began by expressing regret that the British government had disappointed the reasonable anticipation of discussing and, if possible, adjusting the rights and pretensions in dispute. From France nothing had been received on the subjects of negotiation. Madison congratulated Congress on the success of the navy upon the ocean and the Lakes, and the victory won by Harrison and R. M. Johnson in Canada. He mentioned briefly the failure of the armies on the St. Lawrence, and at greater length the success of Jackson on the Coosa; and he entered in detail into the retaliatory measures taken on either side in regard to naturalized soldiers. The finances were treated with more show of confidence than was warranted by the prospects of the Treasury; and the Message closed by a succession of paragraphs which seemed written in a spirit of panegyric upon war:—

"The war has proved moreover that our free government

871

like other free governments, though slow in its early movements, acquires in its progress a force proportioned to its
freedom; and that the Union of these States, the guardian
of the freedom and safety of all and of each, is strengthened
by every occasion that puts it to the test. In fine, the war
with its vicissitudes is illustrating the capacity and the destiny of the United States to be a great, a flourishing, and a
powerful nation."

The rule that feeble and incompetent governments acquire
strength by exercise, and especially in war, had been as well
understood in 1798 as it was in 1813, and had been the chief
cause of Republican antipathy to war; but had Madison publicly expressed the same sentiment in 1798 as in 1813, he would
have found himself in a better position to enforce the rights
for which he was struggling when the extreme discontent of
nearly one third of the States contradicted his congratulations
on "the daily testimony of increasing harmony throughout
the Union." Whatever the ultimate result of the war might
be, it had certainly not thus far strengthened the Union. On
the contrary, public opinion seemed to be rapidly taking the
shape that usually preceded a rupture of friendly relations between political societies. Elections in the Middle States
showed that the war, if not actually popular, had obliged the
people there to support the government for fear of worse
evils. New Jersey by a small majority returned to its allegiance, and the city of New York elected a Republican to represent it in Congress; but the steady drift of opinion in the
Middle States toward the war was simultaneous with an
equally steady drift in the Eastern States against it.

The evidences of chronic discontent in the Eastern States
were notorious. Less than a month before Madison wrote his
Annual Message, Governor Chittenden of Vermont, by proclamation November 10, recalled the State militia from national service:[1]

"He cannot conscientiously discharge the trust reposed
in him by the voice of his fellow-citizens, and by the
Constitution of this and the United States, without an

[1] Proclamation of Nov. 10, 1813; Niles, v. 212.

unequivocal declaration that in his opinion the military strength and resources of this State must be reserved for its own defence and protection exclusively, excepting in cases provided for by the Constitution of the United States, and then under orders derived only from the commander-in-chief."

The intercourse between the Eastern States and the enemy was notorious. The Federalist press of Massachusetts, encouraged by Russian and English success in Europe, discussed the idea of withdrawing the State from all share in the war, and making a separate arrangement with England. The President's first act, after sending to Congress his Annual Message, was to send a special Message incidentally calling attention to the want of harmony that paralyzed the energy of the government.

The special and secret Message of December 9 asked Congress once more to impose an embargo. Considering the notorious antipathy of the Eastern States to the system of embargo, the new experiment was so hazardous as to require proof of its necessity. That it was directed against the commerce of the New England States was evident, for the blockade answered the purposes of embargo elsewhere. The Message seemed to propose that all commerce should cease because any commerce must favor the enemy; in effect, it urged that New England should be forbidden to sell or buy so long as the rest of the country was prevented from doing so.

"The tendency of our commercial and navigation laws in their present state to favor the enemy," said Madison,[1] "and thereby prolong the war, is more and more developed by experience. Supplies of the most essential kinds find their way not only to British ports and British armies at a distance, but the armies in our neighborhood with which our own are contending derive from our ports and outlets a subsistence attainable with difficulty if at all from other sources. Even the fleets and troops infesting our coasts and waters are by like supplies accommodated and encouraged in their predatory and incursive warfare. Abuses having a like tendency take place in our import trade. British fabrics

---

[1] Message of Dec. 9, 1813; Annals, 1813–1814, p. 2031.

and products find their way into our ports under the name and from the ports of other countries, and often in British vessels disguised as neutrals by false colors and papers. . . . To shorten as much as possible the duration of the war, it is indispensable that the enemy should feel all the pressure that can be given to it."

Although Madison pointed to the notorious supply of food for the British forces in Canada as one of the motives for imposing an embargo, no one supposed that motive to be decisive. Other laws already forbade and punished such communication with the enemy; and experience proved that a general embargo would be no more effective than any special prohibition. The idea that England could be distressed by an embargo seemed still less likely to influence Government. Congress knew that Russia, Prussia, Denmark, Sweden and Norway, Spain, and South America were already open to English commerce, and that a few days must decide whether Napoleon could much longer prevent Great Britain from trading with France. The possibility of distressing England by closing Boston and Salem, New Bedford and Newport to neutral ships was not to be seriously treated.

Whatever was the true motive of the President's recommendation, Congress instantly approved it. The next day, December 10, the House went into secret session, and after two days of debate passed an Embargo Act by a vote of eighty-five to fifty-seven, which quickly passed the Senate by a vote of twenty to fourteen, and received the President's approval December 17, being the first legislation adopted at the second session of the Thirteenth Congress.[1] The Act was at once enforced with so much severity that within a month Congress was obliged to consider and quickly adopted another Act[2] relieving from its operation the people of Nantucket, who were in a state of starvation, all communication with the main land having been forbidden by the law; but nothing proved that the illicit communication with Canada ceased.

This beginning of legislation at a time when the crisis of the war could be plainly seen approaching suggested much

[1] Act laying an Embargo, Dec. 17, 1813; Annals, 1813–1814, p. 2781.
[2] Act of Jan. 25, 1814; Annals, 1813–1814, p. 2788.

besides want of harmony. The embargo strengthened the antipathy of New England to the war,—a result sufficiently unfortunate; but it also led to a number of other consequences that were doubtless foreseen by the Administration, since they were prophesied by the Federalists. The Act was approved December 17. Hardly had it gone into operation when the British schooner "Bramble" arrived at Annapolis, December 30, bringing a letter from Castlereagh to Monroe offering to negotiate directly, though declining mediation. Important as this news was, it did not compare with that in the newspapers brought by the "Bramble." These contained official reports from Germany of great battles fought at Leipzig October 16, 18, and 19, in which the allies had overwhelmed Napoleon in defeat so disastrous that any hope of his continuing to make head against them in Germany was at an end. Except France, the whole continent of Europe already was open to British commerce, or soon must admit it. From that moment the New England Federalists no longer doubted their own power. Their tone rose; their opposition to the war became more threatening; their schemes ceased to be negative, and began to include plans for positive interference; and the embargo added strength to their hatred of Madison and the Union.

Madison was seldom quick in changing his views, but the battle of Leipzig was an event so portentous that optimism could not face it. Other depressing news poured in. Fort George was evacuated; Fort Niagara was disgracefully lost; Lewiston, Black Rock, and Buffalo were burned, and the region about Niagara was laid waste; blue lights were seen at New London. Every prospect was dark, but the battle of Leipzig was fatal to the last glimmer of hope that England could be brought to reason, or that New England could be kept quiet. A change of policy could not safely be delayed.

Castlereagh's offer was instantly accepted. January 5 Monroe replied, with some complaint at the refusal of mediation, that the President acceded to the offer of negotiating at Gothenburg. The next day Madison sent the correspondence to Congress, with a warning not to relax "vigorous preparations for carrying on the war." A week afterward, January 14, he nominated J. Q. Adams, J. A. Bayard, Henry Clay, and

Jonathan Russell as commissioners to negotiate directly with Great Britain, and the Senate confirmed the nominations, January 18, with little opposition except to Jonathan Russell's further nomination as Minister to Sweden, which was confirmed by the narrow vote of sixteen to fourteen. Three weeks later, February 8, Albert Gallatin was added to the commission, George W. Campbell being nominated to the Treasury.

The prompt acceptance of Castlereagh's offer, the addition of Henry Clay to the negotiators, and the removal of Gallatin from the Treasury showed that diplomacy had resumed more than its old importance. The hope of peace might serve to quiet New England for a time, but mere hope with so little to nourish it could not long pacify any one, if the embargo was to remain in force. Several signs indicated there also a change of policy. Besides the embargo, and in support of its restrictions, Madison had recommended the passage of bills prohibiting collusive captures, ransoming vessels captured by the enemy, and interference by the courts, as well as the introduction of British woollens, cottons, and spirits. The bill prohibiting woollens and other articles was reported to the Senate December 30, the day when the "Bramble" reached Annapolis. The Senate waited nearly a month, till January 27, and then passed the bill, January 31, by a vote of sixteen to twelve. The House referred it to the Committee on Foreign Relations February 3, where it remained. On the other hand, the bill prohibiting ransoms was introduced in the House December 30, and passed January 26 by a vote of eighty to fifty-seven. The Senate referred it January 28 to the Committee on Foreign Relations, which never reported it. The fate of these measures foreshadowed the destiny of the embargo.

Yet the President clung to his favorite measure with a degree of obstinacy that resembled desperation. Congress showed by its indifference to the two supplementary bills that it had abandoned the President's system as early as January, but the embargo continued throughout the winter, and the month of March passed without its removal. The news from Europe at the close of that month left no doubt that Napoleon could offer little effectual resistance even in France to the allies, whose armies were known to have crossed the Rhine, while Wellington advanced on Bordeaux. Holland was restored to her ancient independence, and Napoleon was understood to have accepted in principle, for a proposed Congress at Mannheim, the old boundaries of France as a basis of negotiation. In theory, the overthrow of Napoleon should have not essentially affected the embargo or the Non-importation Acts, which were expected to press upon England independently of Napoleon's Continental system; but in practice the embargo having produced no apparent effect on Europe during the war, could not be expected to produce an effect after England had succeeded in conquering France, and had abandoned her blockades as France had abandoned her decrees. For that reason avowedly Madison at last yielded, and sent a Message to Congress March 31, recommending that the system of commercial restriction should cease:—

"Taking into view the mutual interests which the United States and the foreign nations in amity with her have in a liberal commercial intercourse, and the extensive changes favorable thereto which have recently taken place; taking into view also the important advantages which may otherwise result from adapting the state of our commercial laws to the circumstances now existing,"—

Taking into view only these influences, Madison seemed to ignore the supposed chief motive of the embargo in stopping supplies for Canada, and to admit that embargo was an adjunct of Napoleon's Continental system; but in truth Madison's motives, both political and financial, were deeper and more decisive than any he alleged. His retreat was absolute. He recommended that Congress should throw open the ports, and should abandon all restriction on commerce beyond a guaranty of war duties for two years after peace as a measure of protection to American manufactures. The failure of the restrictive system was not disguised.

The House received the Message with a mixed sense of relief and consternation, and referred it to Calhoun's committee, which reported April 4 a bill for repealing the Embargo and Non-importation Acts, together with the reasons which led the committee to unite with the Executive in abandoning the restrictive system.

Calhoun had always opposed the commercial policy of

Jefferson and Madison. For him the sudden Executive change was a conspicuous triumph; but he showed remarkable caution in dealing with the House. Instead of attempting to coerce the majority, according to his habit, by the force of abstract principles, he adopted Madison's reasoning and softened his own tone, seeming disposed to coax his Southern and Western friends from making a display of useless ill-temper. "Men cannot go straight forward," he said, "but must regard the obstacles which impede their course. Inconsistency consists in a change of conduct when there is no change of circumstances which justify it." The changes in the world's circumstances required a return to free trade; but the manufactures would not be left unprotected,—on the contrary, "he hoped at all times and under every policy they would be protected with due care."[1]

As an example of political inconsistency, as Calhoun defined it, his pledge to protect American manufactures deserved to be remembered; but hardly had Calhoun's words died on the echoes of the House when another distinguished statesman offered a prospective example even more striking of what Calhoun excused. Daniel Webster rose, and in the measured and sonorous tones which impressed above all the idea of steadfastness in character, he pronounced a funeral oration over the restrictive system:—

"It was originally offered to the people of this country as a kind of political faith; it was to be believed, not examined; . . . it was to be our political salvation, nobody knew exactly how; and any departure from it would lead to political ruin, nobody could tell exactly why."

Its opponents had uniformly contended that it was auxiliary to Napoleon's Continental system, in co-operation with Napoleon's government; and its abandonment with the fall of Napoleon showed the truth. While thus exulting in the overthrow of the first "American system," Webster qualified his triumph by adding that he was, "generally speaking," not the enemy of manufactures; he disliked only the rearing them in hot-beds:—

[1] Annals, 1813–1814, p. 1965.

"I am not in haste to see Sheffields and Birminghams in America. . . . I am not anxious to accelerate the approach of the period when the great mass of American labor shall not find its employment in the field; when the young men of the country shall be obliged to shut their eyes upon external Nature,—upon the heavens and the earth,—and immerse themselves in close and unwholesome workshops; when they shall be obliged to shut their ears to the bleatings of their own flocks upon their own hills, and to the voice of the lark that cheers them at the plough, that they may open them in dust and smoke and steam, to the perpetual whirl of spools and spindles and the grating of rasps and saws."

Potter of Rhode Island, where the new manufactures centred, spoke hotly against the change. Much Federalist capital had been drawn into the manufacturing business as well as into speculation in all articles of necessity which the blockade and the embargo made scarce. At heart the Federalists were not unanimous in wishing for a repeal of the restrictive system, and Potter represented a considerable class whose interests were involved in maintaining high prices. He admitted that the average duties would still give American manufactures an advantage of thirty-six per cent, without including freight and marine risks, but he insisted that the bill was intended to encourage importations of British goods "that we do not want and can do very well without, in order to raise a revenue from the people in an indirect way."

Probably Potter's explanation of the change in system was correct. The necessities of the Treasury were doubtless a decisive cause of Madison's step; but these necessities were foreseen by the Federalists when Madison recommended the embargo, and the neglect to give them due weight exposed the Administration to grave reproach. "A government which cannot administer the affairs of a nation," said Webster, "without producing so frequent and such violent alterations in the ordinary occupations and pursuits of private life, has in my opinion little claim to the regard of the community."

The Republicans made no attempt to defend themselves from such criticisms. Among the small number who refused to follow Calhoun was Macon, who sat in his seat during the debate writing to his friend Judge Nicholson.

> "Those who voted the embargo so very lately," he said,[1] "and those or him who recommended it must, I think, feel a little sore under Webster's rubs. . . . I have not for a long time seen the Feds look in so good humor. They have all a smile on their countenances, and look at each other as if they were the men which had brought this great and good work about. . . . The Republicans have not the most pleasing countenances. Those who support the bill do not look gay or very much delighted with their majority, and those who expect to be in the minority have a melancholy gloom over their faces."

That the system of commercial restrictions had failed was admitted, but the failure carried no conviction of error to its friends. Physical force had also apparently failed. The Southern Republicans had no choice but to adopt strong measures, giving to the government powers which in their opinion they had no constitutional right to confer; but they remained unshaken in their opinions.

> "I confess to you," wrote Macon, "that the parties seem by their acts to be approaching each other, and I fear that tough times is a strong argument with many of us to stretch the Constitution; and the difference between expediency and constitutionality becomes every day less. Notwithstanding this, I do not despair of the republic, because my dependence has always been on the people; and their influence was felt in laying the embargo, and probably that of the Executive in repealing it."

No one understood or represented so well as Macon the instincts and ideas of the Southern people at that time, and he never represented them more truly than in the matter of the embargo. Virginia and the Carolinas were with him at heart. Macon's hopes for the republic depended on his confidence in the people; and that confidence in its turn depended on his belief that the people were still true to a dogma which

[1] Macon to Nicholson, April 6, 1814; Nicholson MSS.

the Government had abandoned as impracticable. The belief was well founded, as the course of events proved. The House, April 7, by a vote of one hundred and fifteen to thirty-seven, passed the bill repealing the Embargo and Non-importation Acts; the Senate also passed it, April 12, by a vote of twenty-six to four; the President, April 14, approved it; and from that day the restrictive system, which had been the cardinal point of Jefferson's and Madison's statesmanship, seemed to vanish from the public mind and the party politics of the country. Yet so deeply riveted was the idea of its efficacy among the Southern people, that at the next great crisis of their history they staked their lives and fortunes on the same belief of their necessity to Europe which had led them into the experiment of coercing Napoleon and Canning by commercial deprivations; and their second experiment had results still more striking than those which attended their first.

The explanation of this curious popular trait certainly lay in the nature of Southern society; but the experience was common to the whole Union. When the restrictive system was abandoned of necessity in April, 1814, it had brought the country to the verge of dissolution. The Government could neither make war nor peace; the public seemed indifferent or hostile; and the same traits which characterized the restrictive system continued to paralyze the efforts of Congress to adopt more energetic methods.

"I will yet hope we may have no more war," wrote Mrs. Madison to Mrs. Gallatin Jan. 7, 1814.[1] "If we do, alas! alas! we are not making ready as we ought to do. Congress trifle away the most precious of their days,—days that ought to be devoted to the defence of their divided country."

Mrs. Madison doubtless echoed the language she heard used at the White House; yet the leaders of Congress were neither triflers nor idlers, and they did all that public opinion permitted. Within a week after Mrs. Madison's complaint, the military committee of the House reported a bill for encouraging enlistments. Viewed as a means of embodying the whole military strength of the republic to resist the whole

[1] Gallatin MSS.

military strength of Great Britain, about to be released from service in Europe, Troup's bill[1] was not an efficient measure; but it terrified Congress.

During the campaign of 1813, as the story has shown, the Government never succeeded in placing more than ten or eleven thousand effective rank-and-file in the field in a single body. About as many more were in garrison, and the sick-list was always large. Armstrong reported to the Ways and Means Committee that the aggregate strength of the army in February, 1813, was 18,945; in June, 27,609; in December, 34,325; and Jan. 17, 1814, it was 33,822.[2] Discouraging as this report was, it concealed the worst part of the situation. In truth, the abstract furnished by the adjutant-general's office gave the number of regular troops in service for January, 1814, not as 33,822, but as 23,614; and to the return a note was appended, explaining that "although the numerical force in January, 1814, was 23,614, the actual strength of the army at that time was less than half that number, arising from the expiration of the term of service of the troops raised in 1809 and enlisted for five years, and of the twelve and eighteen-months men enlisted in 1812–1813."[3] The establishment consisted of 58,254 men authorized by law; but the legal establishment was not half filled. The European news showed that England would soon be able to reinforce her army in Canada and take the offensive. Instead of sixty thousand men, Armstrong needed twice that number for a moderately safe defence, since every part of the sea-coast stood at the enemy's mercy, and no adequate defence was possible which did not include an offensive return somewhere on the Canadian frontier. Needing more than one hundred thousand,—authorized by law to enlist sixty thousand,—he could depend on less than thirty thousand men. Yet so far from attempting to increase the establishment, Armstrong hoped only to fill the ranks.

Troup's bill aimed at that object, purporting to be "A Bill making further provision for filling of the ranks of the regular army." No system of draft was suggested. Troup's committee

[1] Annals, 1813–1814, p. 928.
[2] Armstrong to Eppes, Feb. 10, 1814; Niles, vi. 94.
[3] Note to abstract of regular troops in service, January, 1814; adjutant-general's office. MSS. War Department Archives.

proposed to treble the bounty rather than raise the pay,—a system which might be economical in a long war; but if the war should last only one year, the soldier must gain four fifths of his bounty without return. Troup first suggested one hundred dollars as bounty, which Congress raised to one hundred and twenty-four dollars, together with three hundred and twenty acres of land as already fixed. The pay of privates remained at ten dollars. Twenty-four dollars of the bounty was to be paid only on the soldier's discharge. Recruiting-agents were to receive eight dollars for each recruit.

Such a provision for filling the ranks could not be called excessive. Even if the whole bounty were added to the pay, and the soldier were to serve but twelve months, he would receive only twenty dollars a month and his land-certificate. If he served his whole term of five years, he received little more than twelve dollars a month. The inducement was not great in such a community as the United States. The chance that such a measure would fill the ranks was small; yet the measure seemed extravagant to a party that had formerly pledged itself against mercenary armies.

If the bill showed the timidity of the Republicans, it called out worse qualities in the Federalists. The speeches of the opposition were for the most part general in their criticisms and denunciations, and deserved little attention; but that of Daniel Webster was doubly interesting, because Webster was not only the ablest but among the most cautious of his party. His speech[1] suggested much of the famous eloquence of his later oratory, but dwelt on ideas to which his later life was opposed, and followed lines of argument surprising in a statesman of his great intellectual powers. His chief theme was the duty of government to wage only a defensive war, except on the ocean. "Give up your futile projects of invasion. Extinguish the fires that blaze on your inland frontiers." He wished the government to use its forces only to repel invasion.

"The enemy, as we have seen, can make no permanent stand in any populous part of the country. Its citizens will drive back his forces to the line; but at that line where defence ceases and invasion begins, they stop. They do not

[1] Annals, 1813–1814, p. 940.

pass it because they do not choose to pass it. Offering no serious obstacle to their actual power, it rises like a Chinese wall against their sentiments and their feelings."

This advice, which echoed a Federalist idea reasonable or excusable in 1812, was out of place in January, 1814. The battles of Leipzig and Vittoria had settled the question of offensive and defensive in Canada. The offensive had passed into British hands, and a successful defence was all that the United States could hope. The interests of New England as well as of New York and of the whole Union required that the defensive campaign should, if possible, be fought on Canadian soil rather than at Plattsburg, Washington, or New Orleans; and even the most extreme Federalist could scarcely be believed blind to an idea so obvious.

Moderate as the bill was, fifty-eight members voted against it, while ninety-seven voted in its favor. In the Senate the bill passed without a division, and received, January 27, the President's approval. Meanwhile the Senate passed bills for converting the twelve-months regiments into regiments enlisted for the war, as well as for raising three rifle regiments for the same term, and any number of volunteers that in the President's opinion the public service required, offering to all recruits for these corps the same inducements as to the regular regiments. These bills produced another and a longer debate, but were passed without serious opposition. No further addition was made to the regular army, and no other effort to obtain recruits.

Thus organized, the army consisted of forty-six regiments of infantry enlisted for five years,—four rifle regiments; an artillery corps and a regiment of light artillery; a regiment of dragoons; the engineer corps, the rangers, and sea-fencibles,—an aggregate of 62,773 men authorized by law, an increase of only five thousand men over that of the previous year.

The appropriations for the military establishment amounted to nearly twenty-five million dollars, the Federalists alone voting against them. The naval appropriations amounted to seven millions, and were voted without opposition. The Secretary of the Navy discouraged the building of more cruisers, owing to want of timber and seamen; but Congress showed more than ordinary sagacity by appropriating half a million dollars for the construction of floating batteries with steam-power.

Such provision for the coming campaign offered little evidence of increasing energy to make head against the vastly increased military and naval power of England; but the financial outlook was much worse than the military, and Congress dared not face it. The acting Secretary of the Treasury, William Jones, sent his annual report to the House January 8, and so far as his balance-sheet went, no difficulties were apparent. He had disbursed thirty million dollars during the past fiscal year, and needed nearly forty millions for the current year. These sums were not excessive when compared with the wealth of the country or its exertions at other periods of national danger. Half a century afterward the people of the Southern States, not much more numerous than the people of the Union in 1812, and with a far larger proportion of slaves, supported during four years the burden of an army numbering nearly five hundred thousand men. For the same period the Northern people, not much exceeding twenty millions in number, lent their government more than five hundred million dollars a year. The efforts of 1864, proportioned to the population, were nearly ten times as great as those of 1814, when Secretary Jones looked with well-founded alarm at the prospect of borrowing thirty millions for the year, and of maintaining an army which could scarcely be expected to number forty thousand rank-and-file.

The United States, with a proper currency and untouched resources, should have found no serious difficulty in borrowing thirty or even fifty millions a year in 1814; but they were in reality on the verge of bankruptcy, although the national resources were probably ample. The amount of private capital available for loans was uncertain, and the amount of circulating medium was equally doubtful. Timothy Pitkin of Connecticut, perhaps the best authority in Congress, thought that the paid bank capital of the United States did not much exceed sixty millions,[1] and that the notes of these banks in

---

[1] Speech of Timothy Pitkin, Feb. 10, 1814; Annals, 1813–1814, p. 1297.

circulation did not reach thirty millions. His estimate of paid bank capital was probably liberal, but his estimate of the circulation was eight or ten millions too small. Had the Treasury been able to count on the use of these resources, they might have answered all necessary purposes; but between the mistakes of the government and the divisions of the people, the Treasury was left with no sound resources whatever.

The first and fatal blow to the Treasury was the loss of the Bank of the United States, which left the government without financial machinery or a sound bank-note circulation. The next blow, almost equally severe, was the loss of the Massachusetts and Connecticut banks, which were the strongest in the Union. Whether the responsibility for the loss rested on the Executive, Congress, or the two States might be a subject for dispute; but whoever was responsible, the effect was ruinous. The New England banks were financial agents of the enemy. The bank capital of Massachusetts including Maine was about twelve and a quarter million dollars; that of Connecticut exceeded three millions. The whole bank capital of New England reached eighteen millions,[1] or nearly one third of the paid bank capital of the whole country, if Pitkin's estimate was correct. That nearly one third of the national resources should be withdrawn from the aid of government was serious enough; but in reality the loss was much greater, for New England held a still larger proportion of the specie on which the bank circulation of other States depended.

The system of commercial restrictions was responsible for thus, at the most critical moment of the war, throwing the control of the national finances into the hands of the Boston Federalists. Against the protests of the Federalists, manufactures had been forced upon them by national legislation until New England supplied the Union with articles of necessary use at prices practically fixed by her own manufacturers. From the whole country specie began to flow toward Boston as early as the year 1810, and with astonishing rapidity after the war was declared. The British blockade stimulated the movement, and the embargo of December, 1813, which lasted till April, 1814, cut off every other resource from the Southern

[1] Considerations on Currency, etc. By Albert Gallatin, 1831. Statements II. and III., pp. 101, 103.

and Western States. Unable longer to send their crops even to New England for a market, they were obliged to send specie, and they soon came to the end of their supply. The Massachusetts banks, which reported about $820,000 in specie in 1809, returned more than $3,680,000 in June, 1812; which rose to $5,780,000 in June, 1813, and reached nearly $7,000,000 in June, 1814. In five years the Massachusetts banks alone drew more than six million dollars in specie from the Southern and Middle States,[1] besides what they sent to Canada in payment for British bills.

No one knew how much specie the country contained. Gallatin afterward estimated it at seventeen million dollars,[2] and of that amount the banks of New England in 1814 probably held nearly ten millions. The Massachusetts banks, with seven millions in specie, had a bank-note circulation of less than three millions. The Middle, Southern, and Western States must have had a bank-note circulation approaching forty millions in paper, with seven or eight millions in specie to support it,[3] while the paper was constantly increasing in quantity and the specie constantly diminishing. Bank paper, as was believed, could not with safety exceed the proportion of three paper dollars to every specie dollar in the bank vaults; but the banks in 1814 beyond New England were circulating at least four paper dollars to every silver or gold dollar, and in many cases were issuing paper without specie in their possession.

Already the banks of New England were pressing their demands on those of New York, which in their turn called on Philadelphia and Baltimore. The specie drained to New England could find its way back only by means of government loans, which New England refused to make in any large amount. On the other hand, Boston bought freely British Treasury notes at liberal discount, and sent coin to Canada in payment of them.[4] Probably New England lent to the British government during the war more money than she lent to her

---

[1] Schedule, 1803–1837; Senate Document No. 38. Massachusetts Legislature, 1838.

[2] Gallatin's Considerations, p. 45.

[3] Gallatin's Considerations, p. 45. Schedules II. and III., pp. 101, 103. Gallatin's Writings, iii. 286, 357, 359.

[4] Gallatin's Writings, iii. 284.

own. The total amount subscribed in New England to the United States loans was less than three millions.

This situation was well understood by Congress. In the debate of February, 1814, the approaching dangers were repeatedly pointed out. The alarm was then so great that the Committee of Ways and Means reported a bill to incorporate a new national bank with a capital of thirty million dollars, while Macon openly advocated the issue of government paper,[1] declaring that "paper money never was beat." Congress after a diffuse debate passed only a loan bill for twenty-five millions, and an Act for the issue of five million interest-bearing Treasury notes, leaving with the President the option to issue five millions more in case he could not borrow it. The legislation was evidently insufficient, and satisfied no one. "You have authorized a loan for twenty-five millions," said Grundy in the debate of April 2, "and have provided for the expenditure of so much money. Where is the money?"

Without attempting to answer this question, April 18 Congress adjourned.

[1] Annals, 1813–1814, p. 1787.

Chapter XVI

WHILE CONGRESS was thus employed, much occurred behind the scenes that bore directly on the movements of war. The French minister, Serurier, alone made official reports, and his letters became less interesting as his importance diminished; but occasionally he still threw a ray of light on Madison's troubles. At midsummer in 1813 he was in high spirits.

"Within the past week," Serurier wrote, July 21, 1813,[1] "we have received, one after another, news of the fresh successes at the beginning of the campaign,—the battle of Lützen, the offer of armistice, and the battle of Bautzen. These events, so glorious for France, have been so many thunder-strokes for the enemy in America. Their consternation is equal to their previous confidence, which had no bounds. The Republicans of Congress, on the other hand, have received these news in triumph. All have come to congratulate me, and have told me that they, not less than we, had been victorious at Lützen. The ascendency, henceforward irresistible, which his Majesty is acquiring over his enemies, will, I hope, supply a little tone and vigor to this Government, which had need of them."

When the President returned to Washington, Oct. 25, 1813, Serurier reported with less enthusiasm, but still with confidence, that Madison remained firm:

"He expressed himself in very proper, though very measured, terms on the monstrous coalition that has been renewed against his Majesty. I remarked to him that among our advantages we must doubtless count the fact that the coalition had ten heads, while France had but one. 'And what a powerful head!' replied the President, instantly, with less grace than conviction in his whole countenance."

The vigor of Napoleon postponed for a few months the total downfall of Serurier's influence, but it slowly waned,

[1] Serurier to Bassano, July 21, 1813; Archives des Aff. Étr. MSS.

and he became more and more grateful for consideration shown him. The President's Annual Message, December 7, met his approval. "All agree that nothing more energetic or more warlike has yet come from Mr. Madison's Cabinet."[1] The secret Message of December 9 and the embargo pleased him more.

> "Mr. Monroe assured me three days ago," continued Serurier, writing December 10, "that the Government had been informed of supplies to the extent of nearly thirty thousand barrels of flour furnished to Canada from ports of the United States. A rigorous embargo can alone prevent such criminal speculations, and give the war a decisive character which will shorten its duration and assure its success. . . . In this affair is seen a new proof of Mr. Madison's obstinacy (*roideur*) which prevents him from abandoning a measure he has once put forward, and judges to be for the public interest."

The arrival of the "Bramble" with news of the battle of Leipzig, and with Castlereagh's offer to negotiate, left Serurier helpless. "In this state of things," he wrote,[2] January 14, "it would have been difficult for the Executive to refuse to negotiate; and I cannot but think that he accedes to it only with regret and without illusions." In deference to Serurier's opinion, the President appointed Henry Clay as commissioner to treat for peace rather than Crawford, then American envoy to Napoleon; but in the last week of March news arrived from Bordeaux to February 10, announcing that the allies had reached Troyes and were advancing on Paris, while Napoleon had accepted their conditions of negotiation.

> "For the moment the public believed everything to be lost," reported Serurier, April 15.[3] "I ought in justice to say that the President and his Cabinet showed more coolness and did not share the universal alarm, and that they continued to show me great confidence in the Emperor's genius. I did not find them excessively disturbed by the march of

[1] Serurier to Bassano, Dec. 10, 1813; Archives des Aff. Étr. MSS.
[2] Serurier to Bassano, Jan. 14, 1814; Archives des Aff. Étr. MSS.
[3] Serurier to Bassano, April 15, 1814; Archives des Aff. Étr. MSS.

the allies, or doubtful of our power to repulse them; but I know that his Majesty's adhesion to the preliminary conditions of the allies, and yet more the Congress of Chatillon, and the irresistible influence necessarily acquired for the British minister, greatly (*vivement*) alarmed Mr. Madison. He thought he saw, in the announcement of our adoption of those conditions, our renunciation of every kind of power and control over Spain and Germany, where England was to rule. He believed that a peace, dictated by Lord Castlereagh, must already have been signed, and that the United States were to remain alone on the field of battle. It was then that Mr. Madison, abruptly and without having in any way prepared the public for it, addressed to Congress the Message recommending an immediate repeal of the embargo and a partial repeal of the non-importation."

While Serurier explained the suddenness of Madison's action by the need of conciliating the Continental powers and the manufacturing cities of England, he added that domestic difficulties had a large share in the decision. Contraband trade had become general in the Eastern States. A sort of civil war, he said, was beginning between the officers of customs and the smugglers; the Government also felt serious anxiety for the success of its loan, and began to doubt its ability to maintain payments for the army and navy. Revenue had become necessary. Such was the terror caused by the French news that the capitalists who had offered to contract for the loan began to withdraw their offers and to say that it was no longer practicable. "Analyze it as you please," said Serurier, "you will still find that it was the passage of the Rhine and the progress of the allies in France which, in spite of all I could say, decided this retrograde movement of a Government which I have hitherto always found firm, wise, and consequent. But fear does not reason."

Serurier failed even to obtain permission for French letters-of-marque to be received with their prizes in American ports. The President recommended it to Congress, but Monroe told Serurier that the committee of Congress had not dared to make a report, being persuaded that it would be rejected.[1]

[1] Serurier to Bassano, April 25, 1814; Archives des Aff. Étr. MSS.

"Mr. Monroe agreed to all I said; granted that Congress was in the wrong, and I entirely in the right; but nevertheless Congress has adjourned without considering the question." Serurier was disposed to advise the withdrawal by France of the liberties granted to American privateers,—a measure which, he might almost have foreseen, was likely in any case soon to be taken.

With the repeal of the embargo ended the early period of United States history, when diplomatists played a part at Washington equal in importance to that of the Legislature or the Executive. The statecraft of Jefferson and Madison was never renewed. Thenceforward the government ceased to balance between great foreign Powers, and depended on its own resources. As far as diplomacy had still a part to play in the year 1814, its field of action was in Europe; and there the ablest men in civil life were sent. Gallatin, Bayard, J. Q. Adams, and Crawford were already on the spot; and Henry Clay, after resigning the Speaker's chair, Jan. 19, 1814, sailed for Gothenburg to take part in the negotiation.

President Madison sought in vain for men of equal ability to supply the gaps made by transferring so many of his strongest supporters to Europe. The House of Representatives, January 19, elected Langdon Cheves Speaker; but the choice was a defeat for Madison, whose friends supported Felix Grundy. The Federalists, joining those Republicans who were hostile to commercial restrictions, numbered ninety-four against fifty-nine votes for Grundy,—and the success of Cheves foreshadowed the overthrow of the embargo. In providing for other vacancies the President fared worse. Cheves was a man of ability, and in general policy was a friend of the Administration; but most of the other material upon which the President must depend was greatly inferior to Cheves. The Cabinet needed partial reconstruction, and Madison was at a loss for choice.

The President's favorite candidate for the Treasury, after Gallatin showed his determination to remain abroad, was Alexander James Dallas of Pennsylvania. Dallas was one of Gallatin's strongest personal friends, an old Republican, and a lawyer of undoubted ability. Born in Jamaica in 1759, like Gallatin and Hamilton he had become a citizen of the United

States before the Constitution or the confederation was adopted. He had been a leader of the Republican party in Federalist times, and was made district-attorney of Pennsylvania by Jefferson; but Duane and the "Aurora" destroyed his influence and left him isolated. In Pennsylvania Dallas commanded no support. Both the senators, Leib and Lacock, opposed his appointment to the Treasury, and were able to procure his rejection had Madison ventured to make it.[1]

Obliged to abandon Dallas, the President offered the appointment to Richard Rush, the comptroller, who declined it. At last Madison pitched upon G. W. Campbell, of Tennessee. Since Crawford's departure Campbell had represented the Administration in the Senate, but neither as senator nor as representative had he won great distinction. Best known for his duel with Barent Gardenier, his physical courage was more apparent than his financial fitness. Campbell brought no strength to the Administration, and rather weakened its character among capitalists; but Madison could think of no one better qualified for the place. The Republicans were at a loss for leaders. "I do not complain that Campbell is unfit," wrote Macon to Nicholson;[2] "indeed, if the choice of secretary must be made out of Congress, I do not know that a better could be made." Yet the selection was unfortunate.

Madison was also obliged to select a new attorney-general in place of William Pinkney. Till then the attorney-general had not been regarded as standing on the same footing with other members of the Cabinet. The Secretaries of State and Treasury were paid five thousand dollars a year; those of the War and Navy were paid forty-five hundred; but the attorney-general was paid only three thousand. He had neither office-room nor clerks, and was not required to reside permanently at Washington, but pursued the private business of his profession where he liked, attending to the business of government rather as a counsel under general retainer than as a head of Department. Pinkney lived in Baltimore, and his abilities were so valuable that the President was glad to employ them on any terms, and was not inclined to impose conditions of residence which Pinkney could not accept without a greater

[1] Ingersoll's History, ii. 253.
[2] Macon to Nicholson, Feb. 8, 1814; Nicholson MSS.

sacrifice than he was ready to make.[1] Congress was not so forbearing as the President. John W. Taylor, a member from New York, moved a resolution January 5, directing the Judiciary Committee to inquire into the expediency of requiring the attorney-general to reside in Washington during the session of Congress. The committee reported a bill, January 22, requiring permanent residence from the attorney-general, with an increase of salary. The bill failed to become law, but Pinkney at once resigned.

Madison offered the post to Richard Rush, who accepted it. Rush's abilities were more than respectable, and caused regret that he had not accepted the Treasury, for which he was better fitted than Campbell; but these changes did not improve the Cabinet. "His predecessor, Pinkney, I believe considered him the best lawyer in the nation," wrote Macon;[2] "but that Campbell and Rush are equal to Gallatin and Pinkney is not, I imagine, believed by any one who knows them." In the case of Pinkney and Rush, the advantages of permanent residence balanced in part the loss of ability; but no such consideration affected the change of Campbell for Gallatin.

Fortunately Madison lost enemies as well as friends. Time worked steadily in his favor. The old Smith faction, the Clinton party, and the "Aurora" were already broken. Senators who claimed too much independence of action found public opinion setting strongly against them. Samuel Smith and Giles were near the end of their terms, and had no chance of re-election. The legislature of North Carolina, in December, 1813, censured so severely the conduct of Senator Stone that the senator resigned his seat.[3] At the same time, Pennsylvania succeeded in ridding herself of Senator Leib, and Madison was able to punish the postmaster-general, Gideon Granger, whose friendship for Leib made him obnoxious to his party.

Granger was not a member of the Cabinet, but his patronage was the more important because at that time, by some anomaly in the law, it was not subject to approval by the Senate. Early in January one of his best post-offices, that of Philadelphia, became vacant. One senator of the United States

[1] Madison to Pinkney, Jan. 29, 1814; Works, ii. 581.
[2] Macon to Nicholson, Feb. 17, 1814; Nicholson MSS.
[3] Report and Resolution of Dec. 16, 1814; Niles, v. 356.

had already resigned his seat to become postmaster of New York; and the Pennsylvanians had reason to fear that Leib, whose term was about to expire, would resign to become postmaster of Philadelphia, and that Granger wished to gratify him. Immediately all the Administration Republicans, including members of Congress and of the State legislature, joined in recommending another man, and warned Granger in private that his own removal from office would follow the appointment of Leib.[1] C. J. Ingersoll—a young member from Pennsylvania, among the warmest supporters of Madison and the war—reinforced the threat by moving the House, January 7, for a committee to amend the laws with a view to making postmasters subject to the usual rule of confirmation. The committee was appointed.

Irritated by this treatment, Granger in defiance of President and party appointed Michael Leib to the office, and Leib instantly resigned his seat and hastened to assume the duties of his new post. In this transaction Madison was the chief gainer. Not only did he rid himself of Leib, but he gained a warm ally in the person of Leib's successor; for the Pennsylvania legislature, February 28, transferred Jonathan Roberts from the House to take Leib's place in the Senate. Madison's advantage was not limited by Leib's departure or Roberts's accession. He was able also to punish Granger in a manner at that time almost or quite without parallel. Executive offices ran, as a rule, during good behavior; and although Jefferson made removals of party enemies, neither he nor Madison had ventured to remove party friends, except in cases of misbehavior. Granger's conduct exasperated the Pennsylvanians to a point where no rules were regarded. Eighty-six members of the Pennsylvania legislature joined in addressing a memorial to the President demanding the removal of Granger as the only means of getting rid of Leib, who had not only opposed Madison's election, but who, " when entrusted with one of the highest offices in the gift of the State, . . . acted in direct hostility to her wishes and interests, and aided as far as possible her political enemies." Madison needed little urging. February 25 he nominated to the Senate as postmaster-general

[1] Granger to John Todd, February, 1814; New England "Palladium," March 4, 1814.

the governor of Ohio, Return Jonathan Meigs. After some little delay, the Senate confirmed the appointment, March 17, without a division.

Scarcely was this matter settled, when Congress yielded to Madison's opinion in another instance where for ten years the House had obstinately resisted his wishes. The Yazoo bill became law. For this concession several reasons combined. The Supreme Court, through Chief-Justice Marshall, by an elaborate decision in February, 1810, settled the law in favor of the claimants. John Randolph's defeat removed from Congress the chief obstacle to the proposed agreement. The threatening attitude of New England made every palliative necessary. Under these inducements, the Senate passed the bill, February 28, by a vote of twenty-four to eight, and the House passed it, March 26, by a vote of eighty-four to seventy-six.

Little by little the pressure of necessity compelled Congress and the country to follow Madison's lead. Whether for good or for evil, he had his way. His enemies were overcome and driven from the field; his friends were rewarded, and his advice followed. Of revolt within the party he stood no longer in fear. Already political intrigue and factiousness began to take a direction which concerned him only so far as he felt an interest in the choice of his successor. Three years more would complete Madison's public career, and in all probability if another President of the United States were ever elected, he would be one of Madison's friends; but many persons doubted whether the country would reach another Presidential election, and the jealousy which actuated New England against the South was not the only ground for that opinion. In Madison's immediate circle of friends, the jealousy between Virginia and New York threatened to tear the government in pieces. These States did not, like Massachusetts, threaten to leave the Union, but their struggles for power promised to bring government to a standstill.

The antipathy of New York for Virginia was not lessened by the success of Virginia in overthrowing Aaron Burr and DeWitt Clinton. The Republican party in New York quickly produced two new aspirants to the Presidency, whose hopes were founded on public weariness of Virginian supremacy. One of the two candidates was Governor Daniel D. Tompkins, whose services as war-governor of New York were great, and were rewarded by great popularity. Governor Tompkins was too remote from the capital to annoy Madison by direct contact with factions or activity in intrigue; but the other rival stood at the centre of Executive patronage. John Armstrong was a man capable of using power for personal objects, and not easily to be prevented from using it as he pleased.

Armstrong was an unusual character. The local influences which shaped Americans were illustrated by the leaders whom New York produced, and by none better than by Armstrong. Virginians could not understand, and could still less trust, such a combination of keenness and will, with absence of conventional morals as the Secretary of War displayed. The Virginians were simple in everything; even their casuistry was old-fashioned. Armstrong's mind belonged to modern New York. The Virginians were a knot of country gentlemen, inspired by faith in rural virtues, and sustained by dislike for the city tendencies of Northern society. Among themselves they were genial, reluctant to offend, and eager to remove causes of offence. The domestic history of the government at Washington repeated the Virginian traits. Jefferson and his friends passed much time in making quarrels, and more in making peace. Unlike Pennsylvania, New York, and New England, Virginia stood stoutly by her own leaders; and however harsh Virginians might be in their judgment of others, they carried delicacy to an extreme in their treatment of each other. Even John Randolph and W. B. Giles, who seemed to put themselves beyond the social pale, were treated with tenderness and regarded with admiration.

The appearance of a rough and harshly speaking friend in such a society was no slight shock, and for that reason William Henry Crawford was regarded with some alarm; but Crawford was socially one of themselves, while Armstrong belonged to a different type and class. The faculty of doing a harsh act in a harsh way, and of expressing rough opinions in a caustic tone, was not what the Virginians most disliked in Armstrong. His chief fault in their eyes, and one which they could not be blamed for resenting, was his avowed want of admiration for the Virginians themselves. Armstrong's opinion on that subject, which was but the universal opinion of

New York politicians, became notorious long before he entered the Cabinet, and even then annoyed Madison.[1] The newspapers gossiped about the mean estimate which Armstrong expressed for the capacities of the Virginia statesmen. So old and fixed was the feud, that from the first the Virginians lost no opportunity to express their opinion of Armstrong, especially in the Senate, whenever he was nominated for office. Madison unwillingly selected him for the post of secretary after Crawford refused it, but neither of the Virginia senators voted on the question of confirmation. In appointing Armstrong, Madison bestowed on him neither respect nor confidence. He afterward declared the reasons that caused him to invite a person whom he distrusted into a position of the highest importance.

"Should it be asked," wrote Madison ten years after the war,[2] " why the individual in question was placed, and after such developments of his career continued, at the head of the War Department, the answer will readily occur to those best acquainted with the circumstances of the period. Others may be referred for an explanation to the difficulty, which had been felt in its fullest pressure, of obtaining services which would have been preferred, several eminent citizens to whom the station had been offered having successively declined it. It was not unknown at the time that objections existed to the person finally appointed, as appeared when his nomination went to the Senate, where it received the reluctant sanction of a scanty majority [eighteen to fifteen]. Nor was the President unaware or unwarned of the temper and turn of mind ascribed to him, which might be uncongenial with the official relations in which he was to stand. But these considerations were sacrificed to recommendations from esteemed friends; a belief that he possessed, with known talents, a degree of military information which might be useful; and a hope that a proper mixture of conciliating confidence and interposing control would render objectionable peculiarities less in practice than in prospect."

[1] Madison to Jefferson, April 19, 1811; Works, ii. 493.
[2] Works, iii. 384.

Possibly Armstrong took a different view of Madison's conduct, and regarded his own acceptance of the War Department in January, 1813, as proof both of courage and disinterestedness. He knew that he could expect no confidence from Virginians; but apparently he cared little for Virginian enmity, and was chiefly fretted by what he thought Virginian incompetence. No one could fail to see that he came into the Government rather as a master than a servant. According to General Wilkinson, he was quite as much feared as hated. "I am indeed shocked," wrote Wilkinson in his Memoirs,[1] "when I take a retrospect of the evidence of the terror in which that minister kept more than one great man at Washington." Wilkinson, who hated Madison even more than he hated Armstrong, evidently believed that the President was afraid of his secretary. Madison himself explained that he thought it better to bear with Armstrong's faults than to risk another change in the Department of War.

In that decision Madison was doubtless right. Whatever were Armstrong's faults, he was the strongest Secretary of War the government had yet seen. Hampered by an inheritance of mistakes not easily corrected, and by a chief whose methods were unmilitary in the extreme, Armstrong still introduced into the army an energy wholly new. Before he had been a year in office he swept away the old generals with whom Madison and Eustis had encumbered the service, and in their place substituted new men. While Major-Generals Dearborn, Pinckney, and Morgan Lewis were set over military districts where active service was unnecessary, and while Major-General Wilkinson was summoned to the last of his many courts of inquiry, the President sent to the Senate, January 21 and February 21, the names of two new major-generals and six brigadiers of a totally different character from the earlier appointments.

The first major-general was George Izard of South Carolina, born at Paris in 1777, his father Ralph Izard being then American commissioner with Franklin and Deane. Returning to America only for a few years after the peace, George Izard at the age of fifteen was sent abroad to receive a military

[1] Wilkinson's Memoirs, i. 762.

education in England, Germany, and France in the great school of the French Revolution. As far as education could make generals, Izard was the most promising officer in the United States service. Appointed in March, 1812, colonel of the Second Artillery, promoted to brigadier in March, 1813, he served with credit under Hampton at Chateaugay, and received his promotion over the heads of Chandler, Boyd, and one or two other brigadiers his seniors. He was intended to succeed Hampton on Lake Champlain.

The second new major-general was Jacob Brown, who after receiving the appointment of brigadier, July 19, 1813, was suddenly promoted to major-general at the same time with Izard. The selection was the more remarkable because Brown had no military education, and was taken directly from the militia. Born in Pennsylvania in 1775 of Quaker parentage, Brown began life as a schoolmaster. At the instance of the Society of Friends, he taught their public school in New York city for several years with credit.[1] He then bought a large tract of land near Sackett's Harbor, and in 1799 undertook to found a town of Brownville. He soon became a leading citizen in that part of New York, and in 1809 was appointed to the command of a militia regiment. In 1811 he was made a brigadier of militia, and at the beginning of the war distinguished himself by activity and success at Ogdensburg. His defence of Sackett's Harbor in 1813 won him a brigade in the regular service, and his share in Wilkinson's descent of the St. Lawrence led to his further promotion.

Wilkinson, who regarded Brown as one of his enemies, declared that he knew not enough of military duty to post the guards of his camp,[2] and that he compelled his battery to form in a hollow for the advantage of elevating the pieces to fire at the opposite heights.[3] Winfield Scott, who was one of Brown's warmest friends, described him as full of zeal and vigor, but not a technical soldier, and but little acquainted with organization, tactics, police, and camp-duties in general.[4] The promotion of an officer so inexperienced to the most

---

[1] Memoir of Brown from the "Port Folio;" Niles, vii. 32.

[2] Wilkinson's Memoirs, iii. 402.

[3] Wilkinson's Memoirs, iii. 65.

[4] Autobiography, p. 118.

important command on the frontier, gave a measure of Armstrong's boldness and judgment.

The six new brigadiers were also well chosen. They were Alexander Macomb, T. A. Smith, Daniel Bissell, Edmund P. Gaines, Winfield Scott, and Eleazer W. Ripley, all colonels of the regular army, selected for their merits. Armstrong supplied Brown's defects of education by giving him the aid of Winfield Scott and Ripley, who were sent to organize brigades at Niagara.

The energy thus infused by Armstrong into the regular army lasted for half a century; but perhaps his abrupt methods were better shown in another instance, which brought upon him the displeasure of the President. Against Harrison, Armstrong from the first entertained a prejudice. Believing him to be weak and pretentious, the Secretary of War showed the opinion by leaving him in nominal command in the northwest, but sending all his troops in different directions, without consulting him even in regard to movements within his own military department. Harrison, taking just offence, sent his resignation as major-general, May 11, 1814, but at the same time wrote to Governor Shelby of Kentucky a letter which caused the governor to address to the President a remonstrance against accepting the resignation.[1]

At that moment Armstrong and Madison were discussing the means of promoting Andrew Jackson in the regular service for his success in the Creek campaigns. No commission higher than that of brigadier was then at their disposal, and a commission as brigadier was accordingly prepared for Jackson May 22, with a brevet of major-general.[2] Harrison's resignation had been received by Armstrong two days before issuing Jackson's brevet, and had been notified to the President, who was then at Montpelier.[3] The President replied May 25, suggesting that in view of Harrison's resignation, the better way would be to send a commission as major-general directly to Jackson: "I suspend a final decision, however, till I see you, which will be in two or three days after the arrival of this."[4]

---

[1] Dawson, p. 436; Lossing, p. 563.
[2] Armstrong to Jackson, May 23, 1814; Madison's Works, iii. 376.
[3] Armstrong to Madison, May 20, 1814; Madison's Works, iii. 375.
[4] Madison's Works, iii. 375.

No sooner did Armstrong receive the letter, than without waiting for the President's return he wrote to Jackson, May 28: "Since the date of my letter of the 24th Major-General Harrison has resigned his commission in the army, and thus is created a vacancy in that grade, which I hasten to fill with your name."[1]

Armstrong's course was irregular, and his account to Jackson of the circumstances was incorrect; for Harrison's resignation had been received before, not after, Armstrong's letter of the 24th. Madison believed that Armstrong wished to appear as the source of favor to the army. Armstrong attributed Madison's hesitation to the wish of Madison and Monroe that Harrison, rather than Jackson, should take command of Mobile and New Orleans.[2] Both suspicions might be wrong or right; but Armstrong's conduct, while betraying the first motive, suggested the fear that the President might change his mind; and Harrison believed that the President would have done so, had not Armstrong's abrupt action made it impossible. "The President expressed his great regret," said Harrison's biographer,[3] "that the letter of Governor Shelby had not been received earlier, as in that case the valuable services of General Harrison would have been preserved to the nation in the ensuing campaign."

Little as the President liked his Secretary of War, his antipathy was mild when compared with that of Monroe. The failure of the Canada campaign gave a serious blow to Armstrong; but he had still recovered Detroit, and was about to finish the Creek war. His hold upon the army was becoming strong. His enemies charged him with ambition; they said he was systematically engaged in strengthening his influence by seducing the young officers of talents into his personal support, teaching them to look for appreciation not to the President but to himself, and appointing to office only his own tools, or the sons of influential men. He was believed to favor a conscription, and to aim at the position of lieutenant-general. These stories were constantly brought to Monroe,

[1] Madison's Works, iii. 377.
[2] Kosciusko Armstrong's Notice of J. Q. Adams's Eulogy on James Monroe, p. 32, *note*.
[3] Dawson, p. 436.

and drove him to a condition of mind only to be described as rabid. He took the unusual step of communicating them to the President,[1] with confidential comments that, if known to Armstrong, could hardly have failed to break up the Cabinet.

"It is painful to me to make this communication to you," wrote the Secretary of State Dec. 27, 1813;[2] "nor should I do it if I did not most conscientiously believe that this man, if continued in office, will ruin not you and the Administration only, but the whole Republican party and cause. He has already gone far to do it, and it is my opinion, if he is not promptly removed, he will soon accomplish it. Without repeating other objections to him, if the above facts are true, . . . he wants a head fit for his station. Indolent except to improper purposes, he is incapable of that combination and activity which the times require. My advice to you, therefore, is to remove him at once. The near prospect of a conscription, adopted and acted on without your approbation or knowledge, is a sufficient reason. The burning of Newark, if done by his orders, is another. The failure to place troops at Fort George is another. In short there are abundant reasons for it. His removal for either of the three would revive the hopes of our party now desponding, and give a stimulus to measures. I do not however wish you to act on my advice,—consult any in whom you have confidence. Mr. A. has, as you may see, few friends, and some of them cling to him rather as I suspect from improper motives, or on a presumption that you support him."

Armstrong's faults were beyond dispute, but his abilities were very considerable; and the President justly thought that nothing would be gained by dismissing him, even to restore Monroe to the War Department. Armstrong, struggling with the load of incapable officers and insufficient means, for which Madison and Congress were responsible, required the firm support of his chief and his colleagues, as well as of the army and of Congress, to carry the burden of the war; but he had not a friend to depend upon. Secretary Jones was as

[1] Gilman's Monroe, p. 114.
[2] Monroe to Madison, Dec. 27, 1813; Monroe MSS. State Department Archives.

hostile as Monroe. Pennsylvania and Virginia equally distrusted him, and the fate of any public man distrusted by
Pennsylvania and Virginia was commonly fixed in advance.
Armstrong was allowed to continue his preparations for the
next campaign, but Monroe remained actively hostile. In a
private letter to Crawford, written probably about the month
of May, 1814, and preserved with a memorandum that it was
not sent, Monroe said:[1] —

> "There is now no officer free to command to whom the
> public looks with any sort of confidence or even hope. Iz-
> ard stands next, but he is as you see otherwise engaged [on
> a court of inquiry on Wilkinson]. Thus the door is left
> open for some new pretender, and Mr. Armstrong is that
> pretender. This has been his object from the beginning.
> . . . The whole affair is beyond my control."

Thus the elements of confusion surrounding Armstrong
were many. A suspicious and hesitating President; a powerful
and jealous Secretary of State; a South Carolinian major-general, educated in the French engineers, commanding on Lake
Champlain; a Pennsylvania schoolmaster, of Quaker parentage, without military knowledge, commanding at Sackett's
Harbor and Niagara; a few young brigadiers eager to distinguish themselves, and an army of some thirty thousand
men,—these were the elements with which Armstrong was
to face the whole military power of England; for Paris capitulated March 31, and the war in Europe was ended.

In one respect, Armstrong's conduct seemed inconsistent
with the idea of selfishness or intrigue. The duty of organizing a court martial for the trial of William Hull fell necessarily
upon him. Hull's defence must inevitably impeach Hull's superiors; his acquittal was possible only on the ground that the
Government had been criminally negligent in supporting
him. As far as Armstrong was interested in the result, he was
concerned in proving the incapacity of his predecessor Eustis,
and of the President, in their management of the war. He
could have had no personal object to gain in procuring the
conviction of Hull, but he might defend his own course by
proving the imbecility of Dearborn.

[1] Monroe MSS. State Department Archives.

The President ordered a court martial on Hull before Armstrong entered the War Department. A. J. Dallas drew up the specifications, and inserted, contrary to his own judgment, a charge of treason made by the Department. The other charges were cowardice, neglect of duty, and unofficer-like conduct. Monroe, while temporarily at the head of the Department, organized the first court to meet at Philadelphia Feb. 25, 1813. Major-General Wade Hampton was to preside.

Before the trial could be held, Armstrong came into office, and was obliged to order the members of the court to active service. Hampton was sent to Lake Champlain, and when his campaign ended in November, 1813, he returned under charges resembling those against Hull.[1] Finding that neither Wilkinson nor Armstrong cared to press them, and satisfied that no inquiry could be impartial, Hampton determined to settle the question by once more sending in his resignation,[2] which he did in March, 1814, when it was accepted. Armstrong in effect acquitted Hampton by accepting his resignation, and never publicly affirmed any charge against him until after Hampton's death, when he attributed to the major-general "much professional error and great moral depravity."[3] Hampton's opinion of Armstrong could be gathered only from his conduct and his letters to the Secretary of War, but was not materially different from Armstrong's opinion of Hampton.

Meanwhile Hull waited for trial. During the summer of 1813 he saw nearly all his possible judges disgraced and demanding courts martial like himself. Hampton was one; Wilkinson another; Dearborn a third. Dearborn had been removed from command of his army in face of the enemy, and loudly called for a court of inquiry. Instead of granting the request, the President again assigned him to duty in command of Military District No. 3, comprising the city of New York, and also made him President of the court martial upon General Hull.

The impropriety of such a selection could not be denied.

---

[1] Wilkinson to Armstrong, Nov. 24, and Dec. 8, 1813. State Papers, Military Affairs, p. 480. Order of Arrest. Wilkinson's Memoirs, iii. Appendix v.

[2] Defence of General Hampton; "National Intelligencer," June 7, 1814.

[3] Notices, etc., ii. 26.

Of all men in the United States, Dearborn was most deeply interested in the result of Hull's trial, and the President, next to Dearborn, would be most deeply injured by Hull's acquittal. The judgment of Dearborn, or of any court over which Dearborn presided, in a matter which affected both court and government so closely could not command respect. That Armstrong lent himself to such a measure was a new trait of character never explained; but that Madison either ordered or permitted it showed that he must have been unconscious either of Dearborn's responsibility for Hull's disaster, or of his own.

Hull offered no objection to his court, and the trial began at Albany, Jan. 3, 1814, Dearborn presiding, and Martin Van Buren acting as special judge-advocate. March 26 the court sentenced Hull to be shot to death for cowardice, neglect of duty, and unofficer-like conduct. April 25 President Madison approved the sentence, but remitted the execution, and Hull's name was ordered to be struck from the army roll.

That some one should be punished for the loss of Detroit was evident, and few persons were likely to complain because Hull was a selected victim; but many thought that if Hull deserved to be shot, other men, much higher than he in office and responsibility, merited punishment; and the character of the court-martial added no credit to the Government, which in effect it acquitted of blame.

Chapter I

AT THE BEGINNING of the year 1814, the attitude of New England pleased no one, and perhaps annoyed most the New England people themselves, who were conscious of showing neither dignity, power, courage, nor intelligence. Nearly one half the people of the five New England States supported the war, but were paralyzed by the other half, which opposed it. Of the peace party, one half wished to stop the war, but was paralyzed by the other half, which threatened to desert their leaders at the first overt act of treason. In this dead-lock every one was dissatisfied, but no one seemed disposed to yield.

Such a situation could not last. In times of revolution treason might be necessary, but inert perversity could at no time serve a useful purpose. Yet the Massachusetts Federalists professed only a wish to remain inert. Josiah Quincy, who fretted at restraints, and whose instincts obliged him to act as energetically as he talked, committed his party to the broad assertion that "a moral and religious people" could not express admiration for heroism displayed in a cause they disapproved. They would defend Massachusetts only by waiting to be invaded; and if their safety depended on their possessing the outlet of Lake Champlain, they would refuse to seize it if in doing so they should be obliged to cross the Canadian line. With one accord Massachusetts Federalists reiterated that until their territory should be actually invaded, they would not take arms. After January 1, 1814, when news of the battle of Leipzig arrived, the dreaded invasion of New England became imminent; but the Federalists, officially and privately, insisted on their doctrine of self-defence.

"In the tumult of arms," said Governor Strong in his speech to the legislature, January 12, 1814, "the passions of men are easily inflamed by artful misrepresentations; they are apt to lose sight of the origin of a contest, and to forget, either in the triumph of victory or the mortification of defeat, that the whole weight of guilt and wretchedness occasioned by war is chargeable upon that government which unreasonably begins the conflict, and upon those of its subjects who, voluntarily and without legal obligation, encourage and support it."

The Massachusetts Senate echoed the sentiment in language more emphatic: —

"Beyond that submission which laws enacted agreeably to the Constitution make necessary, and that self-defence which the obligation to repel hostile invasions justifies, a people can give no encouragement to a war of such a character without becoming partakers in its guilt, and rendering themselves obnoxious to those just retributions of Divine vengeance by which, sooner or later, the authors and abettors of such a war will be assuredly overtaken."

The House of Representatives could see but one contingency that warranted Massachusetts in making voluntary exertion: —

"It is only after the failure of an attempt to negotiate, prosecuted with evidence of these dispositions on the part of our Administration, that any voluntary support of this unhappy war can be expected from our constituents."

In thus tempting blows from both sides, Massachusetts could hardly fail to suffer more than by choosing either alternative. Had she declared independence, England might have protected and rewarded her. Had she imitated New York in declaring for the Union, probably the Union would not have allowed her to suffer in the end. The attempt to resist both belligerents forfeited the forbearance of both. The displeasure of Great Britain was shown by a new proclamation, dated April 25, 1814, including the ports of New England in the blockade; so that the whole coast of the Union, from New Brunswick to Texas, was declared to be closed to commerce by "a naval force adequate to maintain the said blockade in the most rigorous and effective manner."[1]

However annoying the blockade might be, it was a trifling evil compared with other impending dangers from Great

[1] Proclamation of Admiral Cochrane, April 25, 1814; Niles, vi. 182.

Britain. Invasion might be expected, and its object was notorious. England was known to regret the great concessions she
had made in the definitive treaty of 1783. She wished especially
to exclude the Americans from the fisheries, and to rectify the
Canadian boundary by recovering a portion of Maine, then a
part of Massachusetts. If Massachusetts by her neutral attitude
should compel President Madison to make peace on British
terms, Massachusetts must lose the fisheries and part of the
District of Maine; nor was it likely that any American outside
of New England would greatly regret her punishment.

The extreme Federalists felt that their position could not be
maintained, and they made little concealment of their wish to
commit the State in open resistance to the Union. They represented as yet only a minority of their party; but in conspiracies, men who knew what they wanted commonly ended by
controlling the men who did not. Pickering was not popular;
but he had the advantage of following a definite plan, familiar
for ten years to the party leaders, and founded on the historical idea of a New England Confederation.[1] For Pickering,
disunion offered no terrors. "On the contrary," he wrote, July
4, 1813, "I believe an immediate separation would be a real
blessing to the 'good old thirteen States,' as John Randolph
once called them."[2] His views on this subject were expressed
with more or less fidelity and with much elaboration in a
pamphlet published in 1813 by his literary representative, John
Lowell.[3] His policy was as little disguised as his theoretical
opinions; and in the early part of the year 1814, under the
pressure of the embargo, he thought that the time had come
for pressing his plan for a fourth time on the consideration of
his party. Without consulting his old associates of the Essex
Junto, he stimulated action among the people and in the State
legislature.

The first step was, as usual, to hold town-meetings and
adopt addresses to the General Court. Some forty towns followed this course, and voted addresses against the embargo
and the war. Their spirit was fairly represented by one of the

[1] Pickering to John Lowell, Nov. 7, 1814; New England Federalism, p. 404.

[2] Pickering to George Logan, July 4, 1813; New England Federalism, p. 391.

[3] Thoughts in Answer to a Question respecting the Division of the States;
by a Massachusetts Farmer.

most outspoken, adopted by a town-meeting at Amherst, over which Noah Webster presided Jan. 3, 1814.[1] The people voted—

"That the representatives of this town in the General Court are desired to use their influence to induce that honorable body to take the most vigorous and decisive measures compatible with the Constitution to put an end to this hopeless war, and to restore to us the blessings of peace. What measures it will be proper to take, we pretend not to prescribe; but whatever measures they shall think it expedient to adopt, either separately or in conjunction with the neighboring States, they may rely upon our faithful support."

The town of Newbury in Essex County made itself conspicuous by adopting, January 31, a memorial inviting bloodshed:—

"We remember the resistance of our fathers to oppressions which dwindle into insignificance when compared with those which we are called on to endure. The rights 'which we have received from God we will never yield to man.' We call on our State legislature to protect us in the enjoyment of those privileges to assert which our fathers died, and to defend which we profess ourselves ready to resist unto blood. We pray your honorable body to adopt measures immediately to secure to us especially our undoubted right of trade within our State. We are ourselves ready to aid you in securing it to us to the utmost of our power, 'peaceably if we can, forcibly if we must;' and we pledge to you the sacrifice of our lives and property in support of whatever measures the dignity and liberties of this free, sovereign, and independent State may seem to your wisdom to demand."

The voters of Newbury were constituents of Pickering. Their address could not have reached him at Washington when a few days afterward he wrote to Samuel Putnam, an active member of the General Court, then in session, urging

[1] The Palladium, Feb. 1, 1814.

that the time for remonstrances had passed, and the time for action had come:[1] —

> "Declarations of this sort by Massachusetts, especially if concurred in by the other New England States, would settle the business at once. But though made now by Massachusetts alone, you surely may rely on the co-operation of New Hampshire, Rhode Island, and Connecticut, and I doubt not of Vermont and New York. With the executives and legislatures of most, and the representatives of all of them, you can freely communicate. Ought there not to be a proposal of a convention of delegates from those six States?"

The project of a New England convention was well understood to violate the Constitution, and for that reason alone the cautious Federalists disliked and opposed it. Doubtless a mere violence done to the law did not necessarily imply a wish for disunion. The Constitution was violated more frequently by its friends than by its enemies, and often the extent of such violations measured the increasing strength of the Union. In such matters intent was everything; and the intent of the proposed New England convention was made evident by the reluctance with which the leaders slowly yielded to the popular demand.

The addresses of the towns to the General Court were regularly referred to a committee, which reported February 18,[2] in a spirit not altogether satisfactory to the advocates of action: —

> "Whenever the national compact is violated and the citizens of this State are oppressed by cruel and unauthorized laws, the legislature is bound to interpose its power and wrest from the oppressor his victim. This is the spirit of our Union, and thus it has been explained by the very man who now sets at defiance all the principles of his early political life. . . . On the subject of a convention, the committee observe that they entertain no doubt of the right of the legislature to invite other States to a convention and to

[1] Pickering to Putnam, Feb. 4, 1814; New England Federalism, p. 391.
[2] Report of Committee; Niles, vi. 4–8.

join it themselves for the great purposes of consulting for
the general good, and of procuring Amendments to the
Constitution whenever they find that the practical construction given to it by the rulers for the time being is contrary
to its true spirit and injurious to their immediate constituents. . . . This was the mode proposed by Mr. Madison[1]
in answer to objections made as to the tendency of the general government to usurp upon that of the States."

The *argumentum ad personam* commonly proved only
weakness. Madison's authority on these points had always
been rejected by the Federalists when in power; and even he
had never asserted the right of States to combine in convention for resistance to measures of the national government, as
the General Court was asked to do. So revolutionary was the
step that the committee of both Houses shrank from it:
"They have considered that there are reasons which render it
inexpedient at the present moment to exercise this power."
They advised that the subject should not be immediately decided, but should be referred to the representatives soon to
be returned for the next General Court, who would "come
from the people still more fully possessed of their views and
wishes as to the all-important subject of obtaining by future
compact, engrafted into the present Constitution, a permanent security against future abuses of power, and of seeking
effectual redress for the grievances and oppressions now
endured."

To the people, therefore, the subject of a New England
convention was expressly referred. The issue was well understood, and excluded all others in the coming April election.
So serious was the emergency, and so vital to the Administration and the war was the defeat of a New England convention, that the Republicans put forward no party candidate,
but declared their intention to vote for Samuel Dexter, a Federalist,—although Dexter, in a letter dated February 14, reiterated his old opinions hostile to the embargo, and professed
to be no further a Republican than that he offered no indis-
criminate opposition to the war. His Federalism was that of
Rufus King and Bayard.

[1] Federalist, no. 46.

"What good is to be expected," he asked,[1] "from creating division when engaged in war with a powerful nation that has not yet explicitly shown that she is willing to agree to reasonable terms of peace? Why make publications and speeches to prove that we are absolved from allegiance to the national government, and hint that an attempt to divide the empire might be justified? . . . The ferocious contest that would be the effect of attempting to skulk from a participation of the burdens of war would not be the greatest calamity."

Under such circumstances the load of the embargo became too heavy for the Massachusetts Republicans to carry. They tried in every manner to throw it off, as persistently as President Madison tried to hold it on. Their candidate, Dexter, argued strongly against the restrictive system in his letter consenting to stand. They drew a distinction between the restrictive system and the war; but even in regard to the war they required not active support, but only abstinence from active resistance. The Federalists used the embargo to stimulate resistance to the war, and advocated a New England convention under cover of the unpopularity of commercial restrictions.

With the pertinacity which was his most remarkable trait, Madison clung to the embargo all winter in face of overwhelming motives to withdraw it. A large majority in Congress disliked it. England having recovered her other markets could afford to conquer the American as she had conquered the European, and to wait a few months for her opportunity. The embargo bankrupted the Treasury, threatened to stop the operations of war, and was as certain as any ordinary antecedent of a consequent result to produce a New England convention. Yet the President maintained it until the news from Europe caused a panic in Congress.

The Massachusetts election took place in the first days of April, while Congress was engaged in repealing the embargo and the system of commercial restrictions. The result showed that Dexter might have carried the State and defeated the project of a New England convention, had the embargo been repealed a few weeks earlier. A very large vote, about one

[1] Dexter to the Electors of Massachusetts, Feb. 14, 1814; Niles, vi. 9.

hundred and two thousand in aggregate, was cast. The Federalists, whose official vote in 1813 was 56,754, threw 56,374 votes; while the Republicans, who cast 42,789 votes in 1813, numbered 45,359 in 1814.

The reduction of the Federalist majority from fourteen thousand to eleven thousand was not the only reason for believing that Dexter might have carried Massachusetts but for the embargo. At the same time William Plumer, supported like Dexter by the Republicans, very nearly carried New Hampshire, and by gaining a majority of the executive council, precluded the possibility that New Hampshire as a State could take part in a New England convention. The President's Message recommending a repeal of the embargo was sent to Congress March 31, and the Act of Repeal was signed April 14. Two weeks later, April 28, the New York election took place. To this election both parties anxiously looked. The Administration press admitted that all was lost if New York joined Massachusetts,[1] and the New England Federalists knew that a decisive defeat in New York would leave them to act alone. The returns were watched with such anxiety as had seldom attended a New York election, although no general State officer was to be chosen.

In May, 1813, Governor Tompkins carried the State by a majority of only 3,506, and the Federalists in the House of Assembly numbered sixty, while the Republicans numbered fifty-two. The city of New York and the counties of Queens, Westchester, Dutchess, Columbia, Rensselaer, and Washington—the entire range of counties on the east shore of the Hudson—were then Federalist. The counties of Albany, Montgomery, Oneida, Otsego, Madison, and Ontario in the centre of the State were also Federalist. At the congressional election of 1812, twenty Federalists and six Republicans had been chosen. The May election of 1814 was for the State Assembly and for Congress. No opportunity was given for testing the general opinion of the State on a single issue, but no one could mistake what the general opinion was. City and State reversed their political character. The Republicans recovered possession of the Assembly with a large majority of

[1] National Intelligencer, May 5, 1814.

seventy-four to thirty-eight, and the Congressional delegation numbered twenty-one Republicans and only six Federalists.

The result was supposed to be largely due to a dislike of the New England scheme and to a wish among New York Federalists that it should be stopped. The energy of the demonstration in New York marked the beginning of an epoch in national character; yet the change came too late to save Massachusetts from falling for the first time into the hands of the extreme Federalists. The towns of Massachusetts chose as their representatives to the General Court a majority bent on taking decisive action against the war. Connecticut and Rhode Island were controlled by the same impulse, and the discouraged Republicans could interpose no further resistance. A New England convention could be prevented only by a treaty of peace.

The effect of the attitude of New England was felt throughout the Union, and, combined with the news from Europe, brought a general conviction that peace must be made. No man in the Union was more loyal to the war than Governor Shelby of Kentucky, but Shelby already admitted that peace had become necessary.

"I may in confidence confess to you," wrote Shelby, April 8,[1] "that I lament over my country that she has in her very bosom a faction as relentless as the fire that is unquenchable, capable of thwarting her best interests, and whose poisonous breath is extending to every corner of the Union. There is but one way to cure the evil, and that is an awful and desperate one; and in the choice of evils we had better take the least. Were we unanimous I should feel it less humiliating to be conquered, as I verily believe that the Administration will be driven to peace *on any terms* by the opposition to the war."

If Governor Shelby had reached this conclusion before he knew the result of the Massachusetts election, the great mass of citizens who had been from the first indifferent to the war felt that peace on any terms could no longer be postponed. Mere disunion was not the result chiefly to be feared. That

[1] Shelby to J. J. Crittenden, April 8, 1814; Life of Crittenden, p. 31.

disunion might follow a collapse of the national government was possible; but for the time, Massachusetts seemed rather disposed to sacrifice the rest of the Union for her own power than to insist on a separation. Had the Eastern States suffered from the hardships of war they might have demanded disunion in despair; but in truth New England was pleased at the contrast between her own prosperity and the sufferings of her neighbors. The blockade and the embargo brought wealth to her alone. The farming and manufacturing industries of New England never grew more rapidly than in the midst of war and commercial restrictions.[1] "Machinery for manufactures, etc., and the fruits of household industry increase beyond calculation," said a writer in the "Connecticut Herald" in July, 1813. "Wheels roll, spindles whirl, shuttles fly. We shall export to other States many more productions of industry than ever were exported in any one former season." Manufactures were supposed to amount in value to fifteen or twenty million dollars a year. The Federalists estimated the balance due by the Southern States to New England at six million dollars a year.[2] The New England banks were believed to draw not less than half a million dollars every month from the South.

> "We are far from rejoicing at this state of things," wrote a Connecticut Federalist;[3] "and yet we cannot but acknowledge the hand of retributive justice in inflicting the calamities of war with so much more severity on that section of the Union which has so rashly and so unmercifully persisted in their determination to commence hostilities. The pressure of this balance is sensibly felt, and will continue to increase as long as the war continues."

John Lowell declared[4] that "the banks are at their wits' end to lend their capital, and money is such a drug . . . that men against their consciences, their honor, their duty, their professions and promises, are willing to lend it secretly to support the very measures which are intended and calculated for their ruin." To avoid the temptation of lending money to support

[1] Letter of Jan. 15, 1814; "National Intelligencer," Jan. 27, 1814.
[2] The Palladium, July 15, 1814.
[3] The Palladium, July 15, 1814.
[4] Road to Ruin, No. 5; The Examiner, Jan. 8, 1814.

Madison's measures, many investors bought British government bills of exchange at twenty to twenty-two per cent discount. These bills were offered for sale in quantities at Boston; and perhaps the most legitimate reason for their presence there was that they were taken by New England contractors in payment for beef and flour furnished to the British commissariat in Canada.

While New England thus made profits from both sides, and knew not what to do with the specie that flowed into her banks, the rest of the country was already insolvent, and seemed bent on bankruptcy. In March, 1814, the legislature of Pennsylvania passed a bill for the creation of forty-one new banks. March 19 Governor Snyder vetoed it.[1]

> "It is a fact well ascertained," said Governor Snyder, "that immense sums of specie have been withdrawn from the banks in Pennsylvania and certain other States to pay balances for British goods which Eastern mercantile cupidity has smuggled into the United States. The demand for specie has in consequence been and is still so great that the banks in Philadelphia and in some other parts have stopped discounting any new paper. I ask a patriotic legislature, Is this an auspicious era to try so vast an experiment? Shall we indirectly aid our internal and external enemies to destroy our funds and embarrass the government by the creating of forty-one new banks which must have recourse for specie to that already much exhausted source? Is there at this time an intelligent man in Pennsylvania who believes that a bank-note of any description is the representative of specie?"

The Pennsylvania legislature instantly overrode Governor Snyder's veto and chartered the new banks, which were, according to the governor, insolvent before they had legal existence. In ordinary times such follies punished and corrected themselves in regular course; but in 1814 the follies and illusions of many years concentrated their mischiefs on the national government, which was already unequal to the burden of its own. The war was practically at an end as far as the

[1] Niles, vi. 94.

government conducted it. The army could not show a regiment with ranks more than half full.[1] The first three months of the year produced less than six thousand recruits.[2] The government could defend the frontier only at three or four fortified points. On the ocean, government vessels were scarcely to be seen. The Treasury was as insolvent as the banks, and must soon cease even the pretence of meeting its obligations.

The Secretary of the Treasury, authorized by law to borrow twenty-five millions and needing forty, offered a loan for only ten millions shortly before Congress adjourned. In Boston the government brokers advertised that the names of subscribers should be kept secret,[3] while the Boston "Gazette" of April 14 declared that "any man who lends his money to the government at the present time will forfeit all claim to common honesty and common courtesy among all true friends to the country." The offers, received May 2, amounted to thirteen millions, at rates varying from seventy-five to eighty-eight. Jacob Barker, a private banker of New York, offered five million dollars on his single account. The secretary knew that Barker's bid was not substantial, but he told the President that if it had been refused "we could not have obtained the ten millions without allowing terms much less favorable to the government."[4] The terms were bad at best. The secretary obtained bids more or less substantial for about nine millions at eighty-eight, with the condition that if he should accept lower terms for any part of the sixteen millions still to be offered, the same terms should be conceded to Barker and his associates. The operation was equivalent to borrowing nine millions on an understanding that the terms should be fixed at the close of the campaign. Of this loan Boston offered two millions, and was allotted about one million dollars.

The event proved that Campbell would have done better to accept all solid bids without regard to rate, for the government could have afforded to pay two dollars for one within a

[1] Scott's Autobiography, pp. 114, 118, 121.
[2] Return, etc.; State Papers, Military Affairs, i. 521.
[3] Advertisement of Gilbert & Deane, Boston "Chronicle," April 14, 1814.
[4] Secretary Campbell to Madison, May 4, 1814; Madison MSS., State Department Archives.

twelve-month, rather than stop payments; but Campbell was earnest to effect his loan at eighty-eight, and accordingly accepted only four million dollars besides Barker's offer. With these four millions, with whatever part of five millions could be obtained from Barker, with interest-bearing Treasury notes limited to ten million dollars,[1] and with the receipts from taxes, the Treasury was to meet demands aggregating about forty millions for the year; for the chance was small that another loan could succeed, no matter what rate should be offered.

For this desperate situation of the government New England was chiefly responsible. In pursuing their avowed object of putting an end to the war the Federalists obtained a degree of success surprising even to themselves, and explained only by general indifference toward the war and the government. No one could suppose that the New England Federalists, after seeing their object within their grasp, would desist from effecting it. They had good reason to think that between Madison's obstinacy and their own, the national government must cease its functions,—that the States must resume their sovereign powers, provide for their own welfare, and enter into some other political compact; but they could not suppose that England would forego her advantages, or consent to any peace which should not involve the overthrow of Madison and his party.

In such conditions of society morbid excitement was natural. Many examples in all periods of history could be found to illustrate every stage of a mania so common. The excitement of the time was not confined to New England. A typical American man-of-the-world was Gouverneur Morris. Cool, easy-tempered, incredulous, with convictions chiefly practical, and illusions largely rhetorical, Morris delivered an oration on the overthrow of Napoleon to a New York audience, June 29, 1814.

"And thou too, Democracy! savage and wild!" began Morris's peroration,—"thou who wouldst bring down the virtuous and wise to the level of folly and guilt! thou child of squinting envy and self-tormenting spleen! thou per-

[1] Act of March 4, 1814; Annals, 1813–1814, p. 2795.

secutor of the great and good!—see! though it blast thine eyeballs,—see the objects of thy deadly hate! See lawful princes surrounded by loyal subjects! . . . Let those who would know the idol of thy devotion seek him in the island of Elba!"

The idea that American democracy was savage and wild stood in flagrant contrast to the tameness of its behavior; but the belief was a part of conservative faith, and Gouverneur Morris was not ridiculed, even for bad taste, by the society to which he belonged, because he called by inappropriate epithets the form of society which most of his fellow-citizens preferred. In New England, where democracy was equally reviled, kings and emperors were not equally admired. The austere virtue of the Congregational Church viewed the subject in a severer light, and however extreme might be the difference of conviction between clergymen and democrats, it was not a subject for ridicule.

To men who believed that every calamity was a Divine judgment, politics and religion could not be made to accord. Practical politics, being commonly an affair of compromise and relative truth,—a human attempt to modify the severity of Nature's processes,—could not expect sympathy from the absolute and abstract behests of religion. Least of all could war, even in its most necessary form, be applauded or encouraged by any clergyman who followed the precepts of Christ. The War of 1812 was not even a necessary war. Only in a metaphysical or dishonest sense could any clergyman affirm that war was more necessary in 1812 than in any former year since the peace of 1783. Diplomacy had so confused its causes that no one could say for what object Americans had intended to fight,—still less, after the peace in Europe, for what object they continued their war. Assuming the conquest of Canada and of Indian Territory to be the motive most natural to the depraved instincts of human nature, the clergy saw every reason for expecting a judgment.

In general, the New England clergy did not publicly or violently press these ideas. The spirit of their class was grave and restrained rather than noisy. Yet a few eccentric or exceptional clergymen preached and published Fast-day sermons that threw discredit upon the whole Congregational Church. The chief offenders were two,—David Osgood, of the church at Medford, and Elijah Parish, a graduate of Dartmouth College, settled over the parish of Byfield in the town of Newbury, where political feeling was strong. Parish's Fast-day sermon of April 7, 1814, immediately after the election which decided a New England convention, was probably the most extreme made from the pulpit:—

"Israel's woes in Egypt terminated in giving them the fruits of their own labors. This was a powerful motive for them to dissolve their connection with the Ancient Dominion. Though their fathers had found their union with Egypt pleasant and profitable, though they had been the most opulent section in Egypt, yet since the change of the administration their schemes had been reversed, their employments changed, their prosperity destroyed, their vexations increased beyond all sufferance. They were tortured to madness at seeing the fruit of their labors torn from them to support a profligate administration. . . . They became discouraged; they were perplexed. Moses and others exhorted them not to despair, and assured them that *one* mode of relief would prove effectual. Timid, trembling, alarmed, they hardly dared to make the experiment. Finally they dissolved the Union: they marched; the sea opened; Jordan stopped his current; Canaan received their triumphant banners; the trees of the field clapped their hands; the hills broke forth into songs of joy; they feasted on the fruits of their own labors. Such success awaits a resolute and pious people."

Although Parish's rhetoric was hardly in worse taste than that of Gouverneur Morris, such exhortations were not held in high esteem by the great body of the Congregational clergy, whose teachings were studiously free from irreverence or extravagance in the treatment of political subjects.[1] A poor and straitened but educated class, of whom not one in four obtained his living wholly from his salary, the New England ministers had long ceased to speak with the authority of their

[1] Defence of the Clergy; Concord, July, 1814.

predecessors, and were sustained even in their moderate protest against moral wrong rather by pride of class and sincerity of conviction than by sense of power. Some supported the war; many deprecated disunion; nearly all confined their opposition within the limits of non-resistance. They held that as the war was unnecessary and unjust, no one could give it voluntary aid without incurring the guilt of blood.

The attitude was clerical, and from that point of view commanded a degree of respect such as was yielded to the similar conscientiousness of the Friends; but it was fatal to government and ruinous to New England. Nothing but confusion could result from it if the war should continue, while the New England church was certain to be the first victim if peace should invigorate the Union.

Chapter II

AFTER THE CLOSE of the campaign on the St. Lawrence, in November, 1813, General Wilkinson's army, numbering about eight thousand men, sick and well, went into winter-quarters at French Mills, on the Canada line, about eight miles south of the St. Lawrence. Wilkinson was unfit for service, and asked leave to remove to Albany, leaving Izard in command; but Armstrong was not yet ready to make the new arrangements, and Wilkinson remained with the army during the winter. His force seemed to stand in a good position for annoying the enemy and interrupting communications between Upper and Lower Canada; but it lay idle between November 13 and February 1, when, under orders from Armstrong, it was broken up.[1] Brigadier-General Brown, with two thousand men, was sent to Sackett's Harbor. The rest of the army was ordered to fall back to Plattsburg,—a point believed most likely to attract the enemy's notice in the spring.[2]

Wilkinson obeyed, and found himself, in March, at Plattsburg with about four thousand effectives. He was at enmity with superiors and subordinates alike; but the chief object of his antipathy was the Secretary of War. From Plattsburg, March 27, he wrote a private letter to Major-General Dearborn,[3] whose hostility to the secretary was also pronounced: "I know of his [Armstrong's] secret underworkings, and have therefore, to take the bull by the horns, demanded an arrest and a court-martial. . . . Good God! I am astonished at the man's audacity, when he must be sensible of the power I have over him." Pending the reply to his request for a court-martial, Wilkinson determined to make a military effort. "My advanced post is at Champlain on this side. I move to-day; and the day after to-morrow, if the ice, snow, and frost should not disappear, we shall visit the Lacolle, and take possession of that place. This is imperiously enjoined to check

[1] Armstrong to Wilkinson, Jan. 20, 1814; Wilkinson's Memoirs, i. 625.
[2] Armstrong's Notices, ii. 64.
[3] Wilkinson to Dearborn, March 27, 1814; Dearborn MSS.

the reinforcements he [Prevost] continues to send to the Upper Province."[1]

The Lacolle was a small river, or creek, emptying into the Sorel four or five miles beyond the boundary. According to the monthly return of the troops commanded by Major-General de Rottenburg, the British forces stationed about Montreal numbered, Jan. 22, 1814, eight thousand rank-and-file present for duty. Of these, eight hundred and eighty-five were at St. John's; six hundred and ninety were at Isle aux Noix, with outposts at Lacadie and Lacolle of three hundred and thirty-two men.[2]

Wilkinson knew that the British outpost at the crossing of Lacolle Creek, numbering two hundred men all told,[3] was without support nearer than Isle aux Noix ten miles away; but it was stationed in a stone mill, with thick walls and a solid front. He took two twelve-pound field-guns to batter the mill, and crossing the boundary, March 30, with his four thousand men, advanced four or five miles to Lacolle Creek. The roads were obstructed and impassable, but his troops made their way in deep snow through the woods until they came within sight of the mill. The guns were then placed in position and opened fire; but Wilkinson was disconcerted to find that after two hours the mill was unharmed. He ventured neither to storm it nor flank it; and after losing more than two hundred men by the fire of the garrison, he ordered a retreat, and marched his army back to Champlain.

With this last example of his military capacity Wilkinson disappeared from the scene of active life, where he had performed so long and extraordinary a part. Orders arrived, dated March 24, relieving him from duty under the form of granting his request for a court of inquiry. Once more he passed the ordeal of a severe investigation, and received the verdict of acquittal; but he never was again permitted to resume his command in the army.

The force Wilkinson had brought from Lake Ontario, though united with that which Wade Hampton had orga-

[1] Wilkinson to Dearborn, March 27, 1814; Dearborn MSS.

[2] State of the Left Division, Jan. 22, 1814; MSS. Canadian Archives. Freer Papers, 1814, p. 17.

[3] James, ii. 82, 83.

nized, was reduced by sickness, expiration of enlistments, and other modes of depletion to a mere handful when Major-General Izard arrived at Plattsburg on the first day of May. Izard's experience formed a separate narrative, and made a part of the autumn campaign. During the early summer the war took a different and unexpected direction, following the steps of the new Major-General Brown; for wherever Brown went, fighting followed.

General Brown marched from French Mills, February 13, with two thousand men. February 28, Secretary Armstrong wrote him a letter suggesting an attack on Kingston, to be covered by a feint on Niagara.[1] Brown, on arriving at Sackett's Harbor, consulted Chauncey, and allowed himself to be dissuaded from attacking Kingston. "By some extraordinary mental process," Armstrong thought,[2] Brown and Chauncey "arrived at the same conclusion,—that the main action, an attack on Kingston, being impracticable, the *ruse*, intended merely to mask it, might do as well." Brown immediately marched with two thousand men for Niagara.

When the secretary learned of this movement, although it was contrary to his ideas of strategy, he wrote an encouraging letter to Brown, March 20:[3]

"You have mistaken my meaning. . . . If you hazard anything by this mistake, correct it promptly by returning to your post. If on the other hand you left the Harbor with a competent force for its defence, go on and prosper. Good consequences are sometimes the result of mistakes."

The correspondence showed chiefly that neither the secretary nor the general had a distinct idea, and that Brown's campaign, like Dearborn's the year before, received its direction from Chauncey, whose repugnance to attacking Kingston was invincible.

Brown was shown his mistake by Gaines, before reaching Buffalo March 24, and leaving his troops, he hurried back to Sackett's Harbor, "the most unhappy man alive."[4] He

---

[1] Armstrong to Brown, Feb. 28, 1814; Notices, ii. 213.
[2] Armstrong's Notices, ii. 66.
[3] Lossing, p. 793.
[4] Brown to Armstrong, March 24, 1814; Lossing, p. 793.

resumed charge of such troops as remained at the Harbor, while Winfield Scott formed a camp of instruction at Buffalo, and, waiting for recruits who never came, personally drilled the officers of all grades. Scott's energy threw into the little army a spirit and an organization strange to the service. Three months of instruction converted the raw troops into soldiers.

Meanwhile Brown could do nothing at Sackett's Harbor. The British held control of the Lake, while Commodore Chauncey and the contractor Eckford were engaged in building a new ship which was to be ready in July. The British nearly succeeded in preventing Chauncey from appearing on the Lake during the entire season, for no sooner did Sir James Yeo sail from Kingston in the spring than he attempted to destroy the American magazines. Owing to the remote situation of Sackett's Harbor in the extreme northern corner of the State, all supplies and war material were brought first from the Hudson River to Oswego by way of the Mohawk River and Oneida Lake. About twelve miles above Oswego the American magazines were established, and there the stores were kept until they could be shipped on schooners, and forwarded fifty miles along the Lake-shore to Sackett's Harbor,—always a hazardous operation in the face of an enemy's fleet. The destruction of the magazines would have been fatal to Chauncey, and even the capture or destruction of the schooners with stores was no trifling addition to his difficulties.

Sir James Yeo left Kingston May 4, and appeared off Oswego the next day, bringing a large body of troops, numbering more than a thousand rank-and-file.[1] They found only about three hundred men to oppose them, and having landed May 6, they gained possession of the fort which protected the harbor of Oswego. The Americans made a resistance which caused a loss of seventy-two men killed and wounded to the British, among the rest Captain Mulcaster of the Royal Navy, an active officer, who was dangerously wounded. The result was hardly worth the loss. Four schooners were captured or destroyed, and some twenty-four hundred barrels of flour,

[1] James, ii. 100.

pork, and salt, but nothing of serious importance.[1] Yeo made no attempt to ascend the river, and retired to Kingston after destroying whatever property he could not take away.

Although the chief American depot escaped destruction, the disgrace and discouragement remained, that after two years of war the Americans, though enjoying every advantage, were weaker than ever on Lake Ontario, and could not defend even so important a point as Oswego from the attack of barely a thousand men. Their coastwise supply of stores to Sackett's Harbor became a difficult and dangerous undertaking, to be performed mostly by night.[2] Chauncey remained practically blockaded in Sackett's Harbor; and without his fleet in control of the Lake the army could do nothing effectual against Kingston.

In this helplessness, Armstrong was obliged to seek some other line on which the army could be employed against Upper Canada; and the idea occurred to him that although he had no fleet on Lake Ontario he had one on Lake Erie, which by a little ingenuity might enable the army to approach the heart of Upper Canada at the extreme western end of Lake Ontario. "Eight or even six thousand men," Armstrong wrote[3] to the President, April 30, "landed in the bay between Point Abino and Fort Erie, and operating either on the line of the Niagara, or more directly if a more direct route is found, against the British post at the head of Burlington Bay, cannot be resisted with effect without compelling the enemy so to weaken his more eastern posts as to bring them within reach of our means at Sackett's Harbor and Plattsburg."

Armstrong's suggestion was made to the President April 30. Already time was short. The allies had entered Paris March 31; the citadel of Bayonne capitulated to Wellington April 28. In a confidential despatch dated June 3, Lord Bathurst notified the governor-general of Canada that ten thousand men had been ordered to be shipped immediately for Quebec.[4] July 5, Major-General Torrens at the Horse-guards informed Prevost that four brigades,—Brisbane's, Kempt's,

---

[1] Report of Sir James Yeo; James, ii. 428–430.
[2] M. T. Woolsey to Chauncey, June 1, 1814; Niles, vi. 266.
[3] Armstrong's Notices, ii. 216.
[4] Prevost to Bathurst, Aug. 27, 1814; MSS. British Archives.

Power's, and Robinson's; fourteen regiments of Wellington's best troops,—had sailed from Bordeaux for Canada.[1] Prevost could afford in July to send westward every regular soldier in Lower Canada, sure of replacing them at Montreal by the month of August.

"A discrepancy in the opinions of the Cabinet," according to Armstrong,[2] delayed adoption of a plan till June, when a compromise scheme was accepted,[3] but not carried out.

"Two causes prevented its being acted upon *in extenso*," Armstrong afterward explained,[4]—"the one, a total failure in getting together by militia calls and volunteer overtures a force deemed competent to a campaign of demonstration and manœuvre on the peninsula; the other, an apprehension that the fleet, which had been long inactive, would not yet be found in condition to sustain projects requiring from it a vigorous co-operation with the army."

Brown might have been greatly strengthened at Niagara by drawing from Detroit the men that could be spared there; but the Cabinet obliged Armstrong to send the Detroit force—about nine hundred in number—against Mackinaw. Early in July the Mackinaw expedition, commanded by Lieutenant-Colonel Croghan, started from Detroit, and August 4 it was defeated and returned. Croghan's expedition did not even arrive in time to prevent a British expedition from Mackinaw crossing Wisconsin and capturing, July 19, the distant American post at Prairie du Chien.[5]

Armstrong did not favor Croghan's expedition, wishing to bring him and his two batteries to reinforce Brown, but yielded to the Secretary of the Navy, who wished to capture Mackinaw,[6] and to the promises of Commodore Chauncey that on or before July 1 he would sail from Sackett's Harbor, and command the Lake. In reliance on Chauncey, the

[1] Torrens to Prevost, July 5, 1805; MSS. Canadian Archives.
[2] Armstrong's Notices, ii. 74, 82.
[3] Armstrong to Izard, June 11, 1814; Izard's Correspondence, p. 33.
[4] Armstrong's Notices, ii. 82.
[5] Colonel McKay to Colonel McDouall, July 27, 1814; Report on Canadian Archives by Douglas Brymner, 1887, p. cv.
[6] Madison to the Secretary of Navy, May 4, 1814; Madison's Works, iii. 396.

Cabinet, except Monroe, decided that Major-General Brown should cross to the Canadian side, above the Falls of Niagara, and march, with Chauncey's support, to Burlington Heights and to York.[1]

This decision was made June 7, and Armstrong wrote to Brown, June 10, describing the movement intended.[2] The Secretary of the Navy, he said, thought Chauncey could not be ready before July 15:

> "To give, however, immediate occupation to your troops, and to prevent their blood from stagnating, why not take Fort Erie and its garrison, stated at three or four hundred men? Land between Point Abino and Erie in the night; assail the Fort by land and water; push forward a corps to seize the bridge at Chippawa; and be governed by circumstances in either stopping there or going farther. Boats may follow and feed you. If the enemy concentrates his whole force on this line, as I think he will, it will not exceed two thousand men."

Brown had left Sackett's Harbor, and was at Buffalo when these orders reached him. He took immediate measures to carry them out. Besides his regular force, he called for volunteers to be commanded by Peter B. Porter; and he wrote to Chauncey, June 21,[3] an irritating letter, complaining of having received not a line from him, and giving a sort of challenge to the navy to meet the army before Fort George, by July 10. The letter showed that opinion in the army ran against the navy, and particularly against Chauncey, whom Brown evidently regarded as a sort of naval Wilkinson. In truth, Brown could depend neither upon Chauncey nor upon volunteers. The whole force he could collect was hardly enough to cross the river, and little exceeded the three thousand men on whose presence at once in the boats Alexander Smyth had insisted eighteen months before, in order to capture Fort Erie.

So famous did Brown's little army become, that the details

---

[1] Madison's Cabinet Memorandum, June 7, 1814; Madison's Works, iii. 403.

[2] Armstrong to Brown, June 10, 1814; MSS. War Department Records.

[3] Brown to Chauncey, June 21, 1814; enclosed in Brown to Armstrong, June 22, 1814; MSS. War Department Archives.

of its force and organization retained an interest equalled only by that which attached to the frigates and sloops-of-war. Although the existence of the regiments ceased with the peace, and their achievements were limited to a single campaign of three or four months, their fame would have insured them in any other service extraordinary honors and sedulous preservation of their identity. Two small brigades of regular troops, and one still smaller brigade of Pennsylvania volunteers, with a corps of artillery, composed the entire force. The first brigade was commanded by Brigadier-General Winfield Scott, and its monthly return of June 30, 1814, reported its organization and force as follows:[1] —

Strength of the First, or Scott's, Brigade.

	PRESENT FOR DUTY.		AGGREGATE.
	Non-com. Officers, rank-and-file.	Officers.	Present and absent.
Ninth Regiment	332	16	642
Eleventh Regiment	416	17	577
Twenty-second Regiment. . . .	217	12	287
Twenty-fifth Regiment	354	16	619
General Staff		4	4
Total	1319	65	2129

The Ninth regiment came from Massachusetts, and in this campaign was usually commanded by its lieutenant-colonel, Thomas Aspinwall, or by Major Henry Leavenworth. The Eleventh was raised in Vermont, and was led by Major John McNeil. The Twenty-second was a Pennsylvania regiment, commanded by its colonel, Hugh Brady. The Twenty-fifth was enlisted in Connecticut, and identified by the name of T. S. Jesup, one of its majors. The whole brigade, officers and privates, numbered thirteen hundred and eighty-four men present for duty on the first day of July, 1814.

The Second, or Ripley's, brigade was still smaller, and became even more famous. Eleazar Wheelock Ripley was born in New Hampshire, in the year 1782. He became a resident of Portland in Maine, and was sent as a representative to the State legislature at Boston, where he was chosen speaker of the Massachusetts House of Representatives, Jan. 17, 1812, on the retirement of Joseph Story to become a Justice of the

[1] Monthly Returns, etc., MSS. War Department Archives.

Supreme Court of the United States. A few weeks afterward, March 12, 1812, Ripley took the commission of lieutenant-colonel of the Twenty-first regiment, to be enlisted in Massachusetts. A year afterward he became colonel of the same regiment, and took part in the battle of Chrystler's Field. Secretary Armstrong made him a brigadier-general April 15, 1814, his commission bearing date about a month after that of Winfield Scott. Both the new brigadiers were sent to Niagara, where Scott formed a brigade from regiments trained by himself; and Ripley was given a brigade composed of his old regiment, the Twenty-first, with detachments from the Seventeenth and Nineteenth and Twenty-third. The strength of the brigade, July 1, 1814, was reported in the monthly return as follows:—

Strength of the Second, or Ripley's, Brigade.

	PRESENT FOR DUTY.		AGGREGATE.
	Non-com. Officers, rank-and-file.	Officers.	Present and absent.
Twenty-first Regiment	651	25	917
Twenty-third Regiment	341	8	496
General staff		2	2
Total	992	35	1415

Ripley's old regiment, the Twenty-first, was given to Colonel James Miller, who had served in the Tippecanoe campaign as major in the Fourth Infantry, and had shared the misfortune of that regiment at Detroit. The other regiment composing the brigade—the Twenty-third—was raised in New York, and was usually commanded by one or another of its majors, McFarland or Brooke. Ripley's brigade numbered one thousand and twenty-seven men present for duty, on the first day of July.

The artillery, under the command of Major Hindman, was composed of four companies.

Strength of Hindman's Battalion of Artillery.

	PRESENT FOR DUTY.	AGGREGATE.
Towson's Company	89	101
Biddle's Company	80	104
Ritchie's Company	96	133
Williams's Company	62	73
Total	327	413

The militia brigade was commanded by Peter B. Porter, and consisted of six hundred Pennsylvania volunteer militia, with about the same number of Indians, comprising nearly the whole military strength of the Six Nations.[1]

Strength of Major-General Brown's Army, Buffalo, July 1, 1814.

	PRESENT FOR DUTY.		AGGREGATE.
	Non-com. Officers, rank-and-file.	Officers.	Present and absent.
Artillery	330	15	413
Scott's Brigade	1312	65	2122
Ripley's Brigade	992	36	1415
Porter's Brigade	710	43	830
Total	3344	159	4780

Thus the whole of Brown's army consisted of half-a-dozen skeleton regiments, and including every officer, as well as all Porter's volunteers, numbered barely thirty-five hundred men present for duty. The aggregate, including sick and absent, did not reach five thousand.

The number of effectives varied slightly from week to week, as men joined or left their regiments; but the entire force never exceeded thirty-five hundred men, exclusive of Indians.

According to the weekly return of June 22, 1814, Major-General Riall, who commanded the right division of the British army, had a force of four thousand rank-and-file present for duty; but of this number the larger part were in garrison at York, Burlington Heights, and Fort Niagara. His headquarters were at Fort George, where he had nine hundred and twenty-seven rank-and-file present for duty. Opposite Fort George, in Fort Niagara on the American side, five hundred and seventy-eight rank-and-file were present for duty. At Queenston were two hundred and fifty-eight; at Chippawa, four hundred and twenty-eight; at Fort Erie, one hundred and forty-six. In all, on the Niagara River Riall commanded two thousand three hundred and thirty-seven rank-and-file present for duty. The officers, musicians, etc., numbered three hundred and thirty-two. At that time only about one hundred and seventy men were on the sick list. All told, sick and well, the regular force numbered two thousand eight

[1] Stone's Life of Red Jacket, p. 328.

hundred and forty men.[1] They belonged chiefly to the First, or Royal Scots; the Eighth, or King's; the Hundredth, the Hundred-and-third regiments, and the Artillery, with a few dragoons.

As soon as Porter's volunteers were ready, the whole American army was thrown across the river. The operation was effected early in the morning of July 3; and although the transport was altogether insufficient, the movement was accomplished without accident or delay. Scott's brigade with the artillery landed below Fort Erie; Ripley landed above; the Indians gained the rear; and the Fort, which was an open work, capitulated at five o'clock in the afternoon. One hundred and seventy prisoners, including officers of all ranks,[2] being two companies of the Eighth and Hundredth British regiments were surrendered by the major in command.

The next British position was at Chippawa, about sixteen miles below. To Chippawa Major-General Riall hastened from Fort George, on hearing that the American army had crossed the river above; and there, within a few hours, he collected about fifteen hundred regulars and six hundred militia and Indians, behind the Chippawa River, in a position not to be assailed in front. The American army also hastened toward Chippawa. On the morning of July 4 Scott's brigade led the way, and after an exhausting march of twelve hours, the enemy tearing up the bridges in retiring, Scott reached Chippawa plain toward sunset, and found Riall's force in position beyond the Chippawa River. Scott could only retire a mile or two, behind the nearest water, —a creek, or broad ditch, called Street's Creek,—where he went into camp. Brown and Ripley, with the second brigade and artillery, came up two or three hours later, at eleven o'clock in the night.[3] Porter followed the next morning.

Brown, knowing his numbers to be about twice those of Riall, was anxious to attack before Riall could be reinforced; and on the morning of July 5, leaving Ripley and Porter's

---

[1] Weekly Distribution Return, June 22, 1814; MSS. Canadian Archives, Freer Papers, 1814, p. 53.

[2] James, ii. 117.

[3] Brown's Report of July 7, 1814; Official Letters, p. 368.

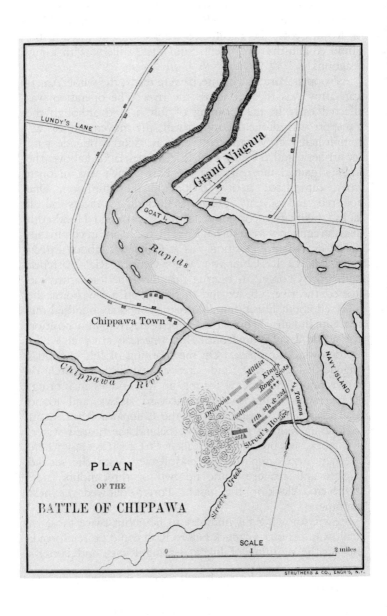

LUNDY'S LANE

Grand Niagara

GOAT I.

Rapids

Chippawa Town

Chippawa River

Militia

King's

Royal Scots

Dragoons

100th

11th 9th & 22d

25th

Street's Ho.

NAVY ISLAND

Towson

PLAN

OF THE

BATTLE OF CHIPPAWA

Street's Creek

SCALE

0   1   2 miles

brigades encamped in the rear, he reconnoitred the line of the Chippawa River, and gave orders for constructing a bridge above Riall's position. The bridge was likely to be an affair of several days, and Riall showed a disposition to interfere with it. His scouts and Indians crossed and occupied the woods on the American left, driving in the pickets and annoying the reconnoitring party, and even the camp. To dislodge them, Porter's volunteers and Indians were ordered forward to clear the woods; and at about half-past four o'clock in the afternoon, Porter's advance began to drive the enemy's Indians back, pressing forward nearly to the Chippawa River. There the advancing volunteers and Indians suddenly became aware that the whole British army was in the act of crossing the Chippawa Bridge on their flank. The surprise was complete, and Porter's brigade naturally broke and fell back in confusion.[1]

No one could have been more surprised than Brown, or more incredulous than Scott, at Riall's extraordinary movement. The idea that a British force of two thousand men at most should venture to attack more than three thousand, with artillery, covered by a deep, miry creek, had not entered their minds. Riall drew up his little army in three columns on the Chippawa plain,—the King's regiment four hundred and eighty strong in advance, supported by the Royal Scots five hundred strong, and the Hundredth four hundred and fifty strong, with a troop of dragoons and artillerists; in all about fifteen hundred regular troops, with two twenty-four-pound field-pieces and a five-and-a-half inch howitzer. Six hundred militia and Indians occupied the woods.[2] The whole force advanced in order of battle toward Street's Creek.

Brown was at the front when this movement was made. Porter was routed. Ripley with the second brigade was in the rear. Scott, having rested his brigade in the morning and given them a dinner to celebrate the Fourth of July, had ordered a grand parade "to keep his men in breath," as he said; and while Riall's regular force, fifteen hundred strong, formed on the Chippawa plain a mile away, Scott's brigade—which a week before had been reported as containing thirteen

[1] Stone's Life of Red Jacket, p. 352.
[2] Riall's Report of July 6, 1814; James, ii. 431.

hundred men present for duty, and if all its details had been called in could hardly have exceeded thirteen hundred men in the ranks on the afternoon of July 5—was forming, before crossing the little bridge over Street's Creek to parade on the plain already occupied by the British. Owing to the brushwood that lined the creek Scott could not see the plain, and received no notice of danger until he approached the bridge at the head of his brigade. At that moment General Brown in full gallop from the front rode by, calling out in passing, "You will have a battle!"[1] Scott remarked that he did not believe he should find three hundred British to fight, and crossed the bridge.

If Riall was unwise to attack, Scott tempted destruction by leaving his secure position behind the creek; but at that moment he was in his happiest temper. He meant to show what he and his brigade could do. As his thin column crossed the bridge, the British twenty-four-pound guns opened upon it; but the American line moved on, steady as veterans, and formed in order of battle beyond. Towson's three twelve-pounders were placed in position near the river on the extreme right, and opened fire on the heavier British battery opposite. The infantry deployed in three battalions,—the right, under Major Leavenworth of the Ninth; the centre, under Major McNeil of the Eleventh; the left, under Major Jesup of the Twenty-fifth. Throwing the flanks obliquely forward, and extending Jesup's battalion into the woods on the left to prevent outflanking, Scott ordered an advance; and at the same time Riall directed the Royal Scots and the Hundredth to charge.[2] The two lines advanced, stopping alternately to fire and move forward, while Towson's guns, having blown up a British caisson, were turned on the British column. The converging American fire made havoc in the British ranks, and when the two lines came within some sixty or seventy paces of each other in the centre, the flanks were actually in contact. Then the whole British line broke and crumbled away.[3] Ripley's brigade, arriving soon afterward, found

[1] Scott's Autobiography, p. 128.
[2] Riall's Report, July 6, 1814; James, ii. 432.
[3] Scott's Autobiography, p. 130. Jesup's Narrative; Ingersoll, ii. 90, 91. Mansfield's Scott, pp. 105–110.

no enemy on the plain. The battle had lasted less than an hour.

Riall's report made no concealment of his defeat.[1]

"I placed two light twenty-four-pounders and a five-and-a-half inch howitzer," he said, "against the right of the enemy's position, and formed the Royal Scots and Hundredth regiment with the intention of making a movement upon his left, which deployed with the greatest regularity and opened a very heavy fire. I immediately moved up the King's regiment to the right, while the Royal Scots and Hundredth regiments were directed to charge the enemy in front, for which they advanced with the greatest gallantry under a most destructive fire. I am sorry to say, however, in this attempt they suffered so severely that I was obliged to withdraw them, finding their further efforts against the superior numbers of the enemy would be unavailing."

For completeness, Scott's victory at Chippawa could be compared with that of Isaac Hull over the "Guerriere;" but in one respect Scott surpassed Hull. The "Constitution" was a much heavier ship than its enemy; but Scott's brigade was weaker, both in men and guns, than Riall's force. Even in regulars, man against man, Scott was certainly outnumbered. His brigade could not have contained, with artillerists, more than thirteen hundred men present on the field,[2] while Riall officially reported his regulars at fifteen hundred, and his irregular corps at six hundred. Scott's flank was exposed and turned by the rout of Porter. He fought with a creek in his rear, where retreat was destruction. He had three twelve-pound field-pieces, one of which was soon dismounted, against two twenty-four-pounders and a five-and-a-half inch howitzer. He crossed the bridge and deployed under the enemy's fire. Yet the relative losses showed that he was the superior of his enemy in every respect, and in none more than in the efficiency of his guns.

Riall reported a total loss in killed, wounded, and missing of five hundred and fifteen men,[3] not including Indians. Scott

[1] James, ii. 432.
[2] Mansfield's Scott, p. 112.
[3] James, ii. 434.

and Porter reported a total loss of two hundred and ninety-seven, not including Indians. Riall's regular regiments and artillery lost one hundred and thirty-seven killed, and three hundred and five wounded. Scott's brigade reported forty-eight killed and two hundred and twenty-seven wounded. The number of Riall's killed was nearly three times the number of Scott's killed, and proved that the battle was decided by the superior accuracy or rapidity of the musketry and artillery fire, other military qualities being assumed to be equal.

The battle of Chippawa was the only occasion during the war when equal bodies of regular troops met face to face, in extended lines on an open plain in broad daylight, without advantage of position; and never again after that combat was an army of American regulars beaten by British troops. Small as the affair was, and unimportant in military results, it gave to the United States army a character and pride it had never before possessed.

Riall regained the protection of his lines without further loss; but two days afterward Brown turned his position, and Riall abandoned it with the whole peninsula except Fort George.[1] Leaving garrisons in Fort George and Fort Niagara, he fell back toward Burlington Bay to await reinforcements. Brown followed as far as Queenston, where he camped July 10, doubtful what next to do. Fretting under the enforced delay, he wrote to Commodore Chauncey, July 13, a letter that led to much comment:[2] —

"I have looked for your fleet with the greatest anxiety since the 10th. I do not doubt my ability to meet the enemy in the field, and to march in any direction over his country, your fleet carrying for me the necessary supplies. . . . There is not a doubt resting in my mind but that we have between us the command of sufficient means to conquer Upper Canada within two months, if there is a prompt and zealous co-operation and a vigorous application of these means."

Brown, like Andrew Jackson, with the virtues of a militia

[1] Riall to Drummond, July 8, 1814; MSS. Canadian Archives.
[2] Brown to Chauncey, July 13, 1814; Niles, vii. 38.

general, possessed some of the faults. His letter to Chauncey expressed his honest belief; but he was mistaken, and the letter tended to create a popular impression that Chauncey was wholly to blame. Brown could not, even with Chauncey's help, conquer Upper Canada. He was in danger of being himself destroyed; and even at Queenston he was not safe. Riall had already received, July 9, a reinforcement of seven hundred regulars;[1] at his camp, only thirteen miles from Brown, he had twenty-two hundred men; in garrison at Fort George and Niagara he left more than a thousand men; Lieutenant-General Drummond was on his way from Kingston with the Eighty-ninth regiment four hundred strong, under Colonel Morrison, who had won the battle of Chrystler's Field, while still another regiment, DeWatteville's, was on the march. Four thousand men were concentrating on Fort George, and Chauncey, although he might have delayed, could not have prevented their attacking Brown, or stopping his advance.

Brown was so well aware of his own weakness that he neither tried to assault Fort George nor to drive Riall farther away, although Ripley and the two engineer officers McRee and Wood advised the attempt.[2] After a fortnight passed below Queenston, he suddenly withdrew to Chippawa July 24, and camped on the battle-field. Riall instantly left his camp at eleven o'clock in the night of July 24, and followed Brown's retreat with about a thousand men, as far as Lundy's Lane, only a mile below the Falls of Niagara. There he camped at seven o'clock on the morning of July 25, waiting for the remainder of his force, about thirteen hundred men, who marched at noon, and were to arrive at sunset.

The battle of Chippawa and three weeks of active campaigning had told on the Americans. According to the army returns of the last week in July, Brown's army at Chippawa, July 25, numbered twenty-six hundred effectives.[3]

[1] James, ii. 132.
[2] Ripley's "Facts relative to the Campaign on the Niagara," p. 8. Jesup's Narrative; Ingersoll, ii. 106.
[3] Ripley's "Facts," 1815.

Strength of Major-General Brown's Army,
Chippawa, July 25, 1814.

	PRESENT FOR DUTY. Non-com. Officers and Privates.	AGGREGATE. Present and absent.
Scott's Brigade.	1072	1422
Ripley's Brigade	895	1198
Porter's Brigade	441	538
Artillery	236	260
Total	2644	3418

Thus Brown at Chippawa bridge, on the morning of July 25, with twenty-six hundred men present for duty, had Riall within easy reach three miles away at Lundy's Lane, with only a thousand men; but Brown expected no such sudden movement from the enemy, and took no measures to obtain certain information. He was with reason anxious for his rear. His position was insecure and unsatisfactory except for attack. From the moment it became defensive, it was unsafe and needed to be abandoned.

The British generals were able to move on either bank of the river. While Riall at seven o'clock in the morning went into camp within a mile of Niagara Falls, Lieutenant-General Gordon Drummond with the Eighty-ninth regiment disembarked at Fort George, intending to carry out a long-prepared movement on the American side.[1]

Gordon Drummond, who succeeded Major-General de Rottenburg in the command of Upper Canada in December, 1813, and immediately distinguished himself by the brilliant capture of Fort Niagara and the destruction of Buffalo, was regarded as the ablest military officer in Canada. Isaac Brock's immediate successors in the civil and military government of Upper Canada were Major-Generals Sheaffe and De Rottenburg. Neither had won distinction; but Gordon Drummond was an officer of a different character. Born in 1772, he entered the army in 1789 as an ensign in the First regiment, or Royal Scots, and rose in 1794 to be lieutenant-colonel of the Eighth, or King's regiment. He served in the Netherlands, the West Indies, and in Egypt, before being ordered to Canada in 1808. In 1811 he became lieutenant-general. He was at Kingston when his subordinate officer, Major-

[1] Harvey to Lieut.-Colonel Tucker, July 23, 1814; MSS. Canadian Archives.

General Riall, lost the battle of Chippawa and retired toward Burlington Heights. Having sent forward all the reinforcements he could spare, Drummond followed as rapidly as possible to take command in person.

No sooner did Drummond reach Fort George than, in pursuance of orders previously given, he sent a detachment of about six hundred men across the river to Lewiston. Its appearance there was at once made known to Brown at Chippawa, only six or seven miles above, and greatly alarmed him for the safety of his base at Fort Schlosser, Black Rock, and Buffalo. Had Drummond advanced up the American side with fifteen hundred men, as he might have done, he would have obliged Brown to recross the river, and might perhaps have destroyed or paralyzed him; but Drummond decided to join Riall, and accordingly, recalling the detachment from Lewiston at four o'clock in the afternoon, he began his march up the Canadian side with eight hundred and fifteen rank-and-file to Lundy's Lane.[1]

At five o'clock, July 25, the British army was nearly concentrated. The advance under Riall at Lundy's Lane numbered nine hundred and fifty rank-and-file, with the three field-pieces which had been in the battle of Chippawa, and either two or three six-pounders.[2] Drummond was three miles below with eight hundred and fifteen rank-and-file, marching up the river; and Colonel Scott of the One Hundred-and-third regiment, with twelve hundred and thirty rank-and-file and two more six-pound field-pieces, was a few miles behind Drummond.[3] By nine o'clock in the evening the three corps, numbering three thousand rank-and-file, with eight field-pieces, were to unite at Lundy's Lane.

At a loss to decide on which bank the British generals meant to move, Brown waited until afternoon, and then, in great anxiety for the American side of the river, ordered Winfield Scott to march his brigade down the road toward Queenston on the Canadian side, in the hope of recalling the enemy from the American side by alarming him for the safety of his rear. Scott, always glad to be in motion, crossed

[1] James, ii. 142.
[2] James, ii. 139.
[3] James, ii. 144.

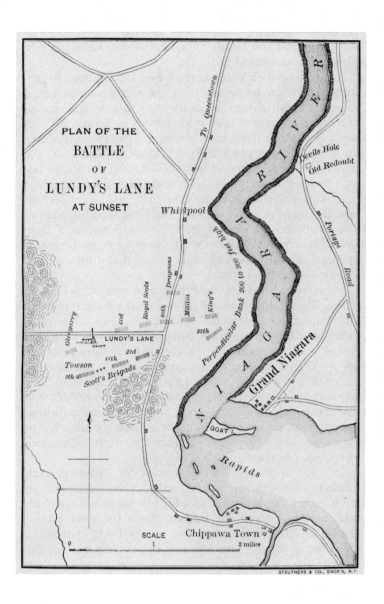

PLAN OF THE
BATTLE
OF
LUNDY'S LANE
AT SUNSET

To Queenstown

Whirlpool

Devils Hole
Old Redoubt

Portage Road

Perpendicular Bank 200 to 300 feet high

Glengarry
41st
Royal Scots
89th
Dragoons
Militia
King's
25th

LUNDY'S LANE

Towson
11th
22d
9th
Scott's Brigade

N I A G A R A   R I V E R

Grand Niagara

GOAT I.

Rapids

SCALE
0
1
2 miles

Chippawa Town

STRUTHERS & CO., ENGR'S, N.Y.

Chippawa bridge, with his brigade and Towson's battery, soon after five o'clock, and to his great surprise, in passing a house near the Falls, learned that a large body of British troops was in sight below. With his usual audacity he marched directly upon them, and reaching Lundy's Lane, deployed to the left in line of battle. Jesup, Brady, Leavenworth, and McNeil placed their little battalions, numbering at the utmost a thousand rank-and-file, in position, and Towson opened with his three guns. The field suited their ambition. The sun was setting at the end of a long, hot, midsummer day. About a mile to their right the Niagara River flowed through its chasm, and the spray of the cataract rose in the distance behind them.

At the first report that the American army was approaching, Riall ordered a retreat, and his advance was already in march from the field when Drummond arrived with the Eighty-ninth regiment, and countermanded the order.[1] Drummond then formed his line, numbering according to his report sixteen hundred men, but in reality seventeen hundred and seventy rank-and-file,[2] — the left resting on the high road, his two twenty-four-pound brass field-pieces, two six-pounders, and a five-and-a-half-inch howitzer a little advanced in front of his centre on the summit of the low hill, and his right stretching forward so as to overlap Scott's position in attacking. Lundy's Lane, at right angles with the river, ran close behind the British position. Hardly had he completed his formation, when, in his own words, "the whole front was warmly and closely engaged."

With all the energy Scott could throw into his blow, he attacked the British left and centre. Drummond's left stopped slightly beyond the road, and was assailed by Jesup's battalion, the Twenty-fifth regiment, while Scott's other battalions attacked in front. So vigorous was Jesup's assault that he forced back the Royal Scots and Eighty-ninth, and got into the British rear, where he captured Major-General Riall himself, as he left the field seriously wounded. "After repeated attacks," said Drummond's report, "the troops on the left were partially forced back, and the enemy gained a mo-

[1] Drummond's Report of July 27, 1814; James, ii. 436.
[2] James, ii. 143.

mentary possession of the road." In the centre also Scott attacked with obstinacy; but the British artillery was altogether
too strong and posted too high for Towson's three guns,
which at last ceased firing.[1] There the Americans made no
impression, while they were overlapped and outnumbered by
the British right.

From seven till nine o'clock Scott's brigade hung on the
British left and centre, charging repeatedly close on the enemy's guns; and when at last with the darkness their firing
ceased from sheer exhaustion, they were not yet beaten. Brady's battalion, the Ninth and Twenty-second, and McNeil's,
the Eleventh, were broken up; their ammunition was exhausted, and most of their officers were killed or wounded.
The Eleventh and Twenty-second regiments lost two hundred
and thirty men killed, wounded, and missing, or more than
half their number; many of the men left the field, and only
with difficulty could a battalion be organized from the de-
bris.[2] McNeil and Brady were wounded, and Major Leavenworth took command of the remnant. With a small and
exhausted force which could not have numbered more than
six hundred men, and which Drummond by a vigorous movement might have wholly destroyed, Scott clung to the enemy's flank until in the darkness Ripley's brigade came down
on the run. The American line was also reinforced by Porter's
brigade; by the First regiment, one hundred and fifty strong,
which crossed from the American side of the river; and by
Ritchie's and Biddle's batteries.

At about the same time the rest of Riall's force, twelve
hundred and thirty rank-and-file, with two more six-pound
guns, appeared on the field, and were placed in a second line
or used to prolong the British right. If Scott had lost four
hundred men from the ranks Drummond had certainly lost
no more, for his men were less exposed. Brown was obliged
to leave details of men for camp duty; Drummond brought
three thousand rank-and-file on the field. At nine o'clock
Drummond could scarcely have had fewer than twenty-six
hundred men in Lundy's Lane, with seven field-pieces, two
of which were twenty-four-pounders. Brown could scarcely

[1] Letter of Major Leavenworth, Jan. 15, 1815; Ripley's "Facts," p. 21.
[2] Letter of Major Leavenworth, Jan. 15, 1815; Ripley's "Facts," pp. 18–27.

have had nineteen hundred, even allowing Porter to have brought five hundred of his volunteers into battle.[1] He had also Towson's, Ritchie's, and Biddle's batteries,—seven twelve-pound field-pieces in all.

As long as the British battery maintained its fire in the centre, victory was impossible and escape difficult.[2] Ripley's brigade alone could undertake the task of capturing the British guns, and to it the order was given. Colonel Miller was to advance with the Twenty-first regiment against the British battery in front.[3] Ripley himself took command of the Twenty-third regiment on the right, to lead it by the road to attack the enemy's left flank in Lundy's Lane. According to the story that for the next fifty years was told to every American school-boy as a model of modest courage, General Brown gave to Miller the order to carry the enemy's artillery, and Miller answered, "I'll try!"[4]

The two regiments thus thrown on the enemy's centre and left numbered probably about seven hundred men in the ranks, according to Ripley's belief. The Twenty-first regiment was the stronger, and may have contained four hundred and fifty men, including officers; the Twenty-third could scarcely have brought three hundred into the field. In a few minutes both battalions were in motion. The Twenty-third, advancing along the road on the right, instantly attracted the enemy's fire at about one hundred and fifty yards from the hill, and was thrown back. Ripley reformed the column, and in five minutes it advanced again.[5] While the Twenty-third was thus engaged on the right, the Twenty-first silently advanced in front, covered by shrubbery and the darkness, within a few rods of the British battery undiscovered, and with a sudden rush carried the guns, bayoneting the artillery-men where they stood.

So superb a feat of arms might well startle the British general, who could not see that less than five hundred men were

---

[1] Strength of the Army, July 25, 1814; Ripley's "Facts," Appendix.

[2] Mansfield's Scott, p. 129; *note* 2.

[3] Miller's Letter in the Boston "Patriot," Sept. 4, 1814; Ripley's "Facts," p. 27.

[4] Lossing, p. 820, *note*.

[5] Evidence of Captain McDonald; Ripley's "Facts," p. 12.

engaged in it; but according to the British account[1] the guns stood immediately in front of a British line numbering at least twenty-six hundred men in ranks along Lundy's Lane. Drummond himself must have been near the spot, for the whole line of battle was but five minutes' walk; apparently he had but to order an advance, to drive Miller's regiment back without trouble. Yet Miller maintained his ground until Ripley came up on his right. According to the evidence of Captain McDonald of Ripley's staff, the battle was violent during fifteen or twenty minutes:—

"Having passed the position where the artillery had been planted, Colonel Miller again formed his line facing the enemy, and engaged them within twenty paces distance. There appeared a perfect sheet of fire between the two lines. While the Twenty-first was in this situation, the Twenty-third attacked the enemy's flank, and advanced within twenty paces of it before the first volley was discharged,—a measure adopted by command of General Ripley, that the fire might be effectual and more completely destructive. The movement compelled the enemy's flank to fall back immediately by descending the hill out of sight, upon which the firing ceased."[2]

Perhaps this feat was more remarkable than the surprise of the battery. Ripley's Twenty-third regiment, about three hundred men, broke the British line, not in the centre but on its left, where the Eighty-ninth, the Royal Scots, King's, and the Forty-first were stationed,[3] and caused them to retire half a mile from the battle-field before they halted to reform.

When the firing ceased, Ripley's brigade held the hill-top, with the British guns, and the whole length of Lundy's Lane to the high-road. Porter then brought up his brigade on the left; Hindman brought up his guns, and placed Towson's battery on Ripley's right, Ritchie's on his left, while Biddle's two guns were put in position on the road near the corner of Lundy's Lane. Jesup with the Twenty-fifth regiment was put

---

[1] Drummond's Report, July 27, 1814; James, ii. 437.
[2] Evidence of Captain McDonald; Ripley's "Facts," p. 13.
[3] Drummond's Report; James, ii. 143.

in line on the right of Towson's battery; Leavenworth with the remnants of the Ninth, Eleventh, and Twenty-second formed a second line in the rear of the captured artillery; and thus reversing the former British order of battle, the little army stood ranked along the edge of Lundy's Lane, with the British guns in their rear.

The British force was then in much confusion, a part of it marching into the American line by mistake, and suffering a destructive fire; a part of it firing into the regiment on its own right, and keeping up the fire persistently.[1] In order to re-cover their artillery they must assault, without guns, a steep hill held by an enemy with several field-pieces. Had Brown been able to put a reserve of only a few hundred men into the field, his victory was assured; but the battle and exhaus-tion were rapidly reducing his force. He had at ten o'clock not more than fifteen hundred men in the ranks, and almost every officer was wounded.

After a long interval the British line was reformed, and brought to the attack. General Drummond's report said noth-ing of this movement, but according to the American account the two lines were closely engaged their whole length at a distance of ten or twelve yards. In the darkness the troops could aim only at the flash of the muskets. "We having much the advantage of the ground, the enemy generally fired over our heads," said Captain McDonald of Ripley's staff; "but the continual blaze of light was such as to enable us distinctly to see their buttons." After a sharp combat of some twenty min-utes the enemy retreated. Three times, at intervals of half an hour or more, the British line moved up the hill, and after the exchange of a hot fire retired; between the attacks, for half an hour at a time, all was darkness and silence, hardly inter-rupted by a breath of air. Brown and Scott were with Porter on the extreme left. In the centre, by the captured cannon, Ripley sat on his horse, ten or twelve paces in rear of his line. Two bullets passed through his hat, but he was unhurt. Captain Ritchie was killed at his battery on the left; Jesup was wounded on the right. Each attack sorely diminished the number of men in the ranks, until at the close of the third

[1] James, ii. 145.

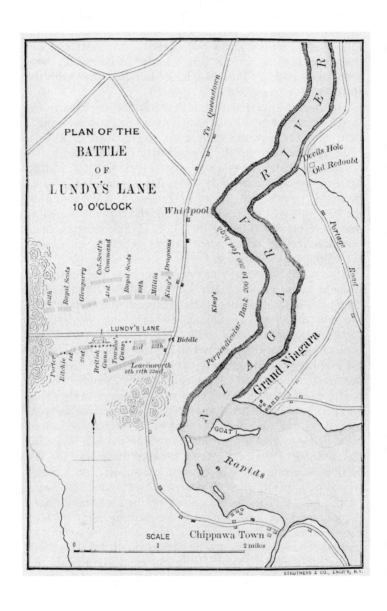

PLAN OF THE
BATTLE
OF
LUNDY'S LANE
10 O'CLOCK

To Queenstown

Whirlpool

Devils Hole

Old Redoubt

Portage Road

N I A G A R A   R I V E R

King's

Perpendicular Bank 200 to 300 feet high

Grand Niagara

104th

Royal Scots

Glengarry

Col. Scott's Command

41st

Royal Scots

89th

Militia

King's Dragoons

LUNDY'S LANE

Porter

Ritchie

1st

21st

British Guns

Towson's Guns

23d

25th

Biddle

Leavenworth
9th 11th 22nd

GOAT I.

Rapids

SCALE
0   1   2 miles

Chippawa Town

STRUTHERS & CO., ENGR'S, N.Y.

about seven hundred rank-and-file, with few officers, were believed to remain in position.[1]

Scott, with Leavenworth's consolidated battalion, after
ranging somewhat wildly the entire length of the line in the
attempt to turn the enemy's flank, and receiving the fire of
both armies, joined Jesup's Twenty-fifth regiment on the
right, and was at last severely wounded.[2] At about the same
time Brown was wounded on the extreme left,[3] where Porter's volunteers held the line. Major Leavenworth, with the
remnants of the first brigade, moving from the left to reinforce Jesup on the right after the third repulse of the enemy,
met Scott retiring from the field, and soon afterward was
hailed by General Brown, who was also returning to camp
severely wounded. The time was then about eleven o'clock,
and every one felt that the army must soon retreat.[4] Farther
in the rear General Brown met Major Hindman of the artillery, who was bringing up his spare ammunition wagons.
Brown ordered Hindman to collect his artillery as well as he
could, and retire immediately; " we shall all march to camp."
He said that they had done as much as they could do; that
nearly all their officers were killed or wounded; that he was
himself wounded, and he thought it best to retire to camp.
Hindman on arriving at the hill, firing having wholly ceased,
immediately began to withdraw the guns. Ripley first learned
the order to withdraw by discovering the artillery to be
already gone.[5] Next came a peremptory order to collect the
wounded and retire.[6] The order was literally obeyed. The enemy in no way molested the movement; and at about midnight the wearied troops marched for camp, in as good order
and with as much regularity as they had marched to the
battle-field.[7]

[1] Evidence of Captain McDonald; Ripley's "Facts," p. 16.

[2] Cf. Wilkinson's Memoirs, i. 712.

[3] Letter of Major Leavenworth, Jan. 15, 1815; Ripley's "Facts," p. 23. Jesup's
Narrative; Ingersoll, ii. 107.

[4] Letter of Major Leavenworth, Jan. 15, 1815; Ripley's "Facts," p. 23. Jesup's
Narrative; Ingersoll, ii. 107.

[5] Ripley's "Facts," Appendix.

[6] Letter of Captain Clarke, March 15, 1815; Ripley's "Facts," p. 30. Letter of
Adjutant Livingston, March 6, 1815; Ripley's "Facts," p. 31.

[7] Letter of Major Leavenworth, Jan. 15, 1815; Ripley's "Facts," p. 25.

Hindman withdrew his own guns, and having with some difficulty procured horses to haul off the British pieces, on returning to the hill after Ripley's withdrawal found the enemy again in possession, and some men and wagons captured.[1] He left the field at once, with the British in possession of their guns, and followed the retreating column.

Lieutenant-General Drummond's report of the battle, though silent as to the repeated British repulses, declared that the Americans fought with uncommon gallantry: —

> "In so determined a manner were the attacks directed against our guns that our artillery-men were bayoneted by the enemy in the act of loading, and the muzzles of the enemy's guns were advanced within a few yards of ours. The darkness of the night during this extraordinary conflict occasioned several uncommon incidents; our troops having for a moment been pushed back, some of our guns remained for a few minutes in the enemy's hands."

Drummond's "few minutes" were three hours. According to the British account, the One-Hundred-and-third regiment, with its two field-pieces, arrived on the field just at nine, and "passed by mistake into the centre of the American army now posted upon the hill."[2] The regiment "fell back in confusion" and lost its two field-pieces, which were captured by Miller, with Riall's five pieces. By British report, Miller was at nine o'clock "in possession of the crest of the hill and of seven pieces of captured artillery."[3] Drummond admitted that in retiring "about midnight" the Americans carried away one of his light pieces, having limbered it up by mistake and leaving one of their own. During the entire action after nine o'clock Drummond did not fire a cannon, although, according to Canadian authority, the fighting was desperate: —

> "The officers of the army from Spain who have been engaged in Upper Canada have acknowledged that they never saw such determined charges as were made by the Americans in the late actions. . . . In the action on the

---

[1] Colonel Hindman's statement; Ripley's "Facts," p. 43.
[2] James, ii. 144–145.
[3] James, ii. 146.

25th July the Americans charged to the very muzzles of our cannon, and actually bayoneted the artillery-men who were at their guns. Their charges were not once or twice only, but repeated and long, and the steadiness of British soldiers alone could have withstood them."[1]

[1] Letter in Halifax newspaper; Niles, vii. 410.

Chapter III

THE BATTLE of Lundy's Lane lasted five hours, and Drummond believed the American force to be five thousand men. In truth, at no moment were two thousand American rank-and-file on the field.[1] "The loss sustained by the enemy in this severe action," reported Drummond,[2] "cannot be estimated at less than fifteen hundred men, including several hundred prisoners left in our hands." Drummond's estimate of American losses, as of American numbers, was double the reality. Brown reported a total loss, certainly severe enough, of eight hundred and fifty-three men,—one hundred and seventy-one killed, five hundred and seventy-two wounded, one hundred and ten missing. Drummond reported a total loss of eight hundred and seventy-eight men,—eighty-four killed, five hundred and fifty-nine wounded, one hundred and ninety-three missing, and forty-two prisoners. On both sides the battle was murderous. Brown and Scott were both badly wounded, the latter so severely that he could not resume his command during the war. Drummond and Riall were also wounded. On both sides, but especially on the American, the loss in officers was very great.

The effect of the British artillery on Scott's brigade, while daylight lasted, had been excessive, while at that period of the battle the British could have suffered comparatively little. Among Scott's battalions the severest loss was that of Brady's Twenty-second regiment, from Pennsylvania,—at the opening of the campaign two hundred and twenty-eight strong, officers and men. After Lundy's Lane the Twenty-second reported thirty-six killed, ninety wounded, and seventeen missing. The Ninth, Leavenworth's Massachusetts regiment, which was returned as numbering three hundred and forty-eight officers and men June 31, reported sixteen killed, ninety wounded, and fifteen missing at Lundy's Lane. The Eleventh, McNeil's Vermont battalion, which numbered three hundred

[1] Strength of the American army; Ripley's "Facts," Appendix.
[2] Drummond's Report of July 27, 1814; James, ii. 438.

and four officers and men June 31, returned twenty-eight killed, one hundred and two wounded, and three missing. The Twenty-fifth, Jesup's Connecticut corps, numbering three hundred and seventy officers and men at the outset, reported twenty-eight killed, sixty-six wounded, and fifteen missing. These four regiments, composing Scott's brigade, numbered thirteen hundred and eighty-eight officers and men June 31, and lost in killed, wounded, and missing at Lundy's Lane five hundred and six men, after losing two hundred and fifty-seven at Chippawa.

Ripley's brigade suffered less; but although, after the British guns were captured, the Americans were exposed only to musketry fire, the brigades of Ripley and Porter reported a loss of two hundred and fifty-eight men, killed, wounded, and missing. The three artillery companies suffered a loss of forty-five men, including Captain Ritchie. The total loss of eight hundred and fifty-three men was as nearly as possible one third of the entire army, including the unengaged pickets and other details.

When Ripley, following the artillery, arrived in camp toward one o'clock in the morning,[1] Brown sent for him, and gave him an order to return at day-break to the battle-field with all the force he could collect, "and there to meet and beat the enemy if he again appeared."[2] The order was impossible to execute. The whole force capable of fighting another battle did not exceed fifteen or sixteen hundred effectives, almost without officers, and exhausted by the night battle.[3] The order was given at one o'clock in the morning; the army must employ the remainder of the night to reorganize its battalions and replace its officers, and was expected to march at four o'clock to regain a battle-field which Brown had felt himself unable to maintain at midnight, although he then occupied it, and held all the enemy's artillery. The order was futile. Major Leavenworth of the Ninth regiment, who though wounded commanded the first brigade after the disability of Scott, Brady, Jesup, and McNeil, thought it "the most con-

[1] Letter of Capt. McDonald, March 20, 1815; Ripley's "Facts," p. 29.
[2] Brown's Report of the battle of July 25; Niles, vi. 433.
[3] Letter of Major Leavenworth, Jan. 15, 1815; Ripley's "Facts," p. 27.

summate folly to attempt to regain possession of the field of battle," and declared that every officer he met thought like himself.[1]

Yet Ripley at dawn began to collect the troops, and after the inevitable delay caused by the disorganization, marched at nine o'clock, with about fifteen hundred men, to reconnoitre the enemy. At about the same time Drummond advanced a mile, and took position in order of battle near the Falls, his artillery in the road, supported by a column of infantry. A month earlier Drummond, like Riall, would have attacked, and with a force greater by one half could hardly have failed to destroy Ripley's shattered regiments; but Chippawa and Lundy's Lane had already produced an effect on the British army. Drummond believed that the Americans numbered five thousand, and his own force in the ranks was about twenty-two hundred men. He allowed Ripley to retire unmolested, and remained at the Falls the whole day.

Ripley returned to camp at noon and made his report to Brown. The question requiring immediate decision was whether to maintain or abandon the line of the Chippawa River. Much could be said on both sides, and only officers on the spot could decide with certainty how the enemy could be placed under most disadvantage, and how the army could be saved from needless dangers. Ripley, cautious by nature, recommended a retreat to Fort Erie. With the assent, as he supposed, of Brown and Porter,[2] Ripley immediately broke up the camp at Chippawa, and began the march to Fort Erie, sixteen miles in the rear. Although complaint was made of the retreat as confused, hasty, and unnecessary, it was conducted with no more loss or confusion than usual in such movements,[3] and its military propriety was to be judged by its effects on the campaign.

The same evening, July 26, the army arrived at Fort Erie and camped. Brown was taken from Chippawa across the river to recover from his wound. Scott was also removed to safe quarters. Ripley was left with the remains of the army camped on a plain, outside the unfinished bastions of Fort

[1] Letter of Major Leavenworth, Jan. 15, 1815; Ripley's "Facts," p. 27.
[2] Ripley's "Facts." Cf. Brown's Narrative; Ingersoll, ii. 105.
[3] Letter of Major Leavenworth, Jan. 15, 1815; Ripley's "Facts," p. 383.

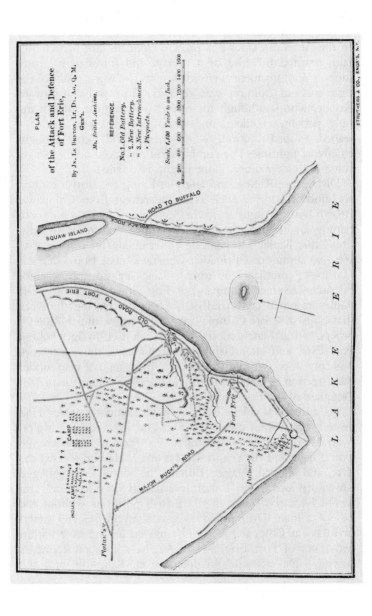

PLAN

of the Attack and Defence
of Fort Erie,

By Js. Le Breton, Lt. Dy. As. Q. M.
Genl.

Ms. British Archives.

REFERENCE

No 1. Old Battery.
" 2. New Battery.
" 3. New Intrenchment.
x Picquets.

Scale, 1,750 Yards to an Inch,

0   200   400   600   800   1000 1200 1400 1600

ROAD TO BUFFALO

SQUAW ISLAND

BLACK ROCK

OLD ROAD TO FORT ERIE

CAMP

INDIAN CAMP

MAJOR BUCK'S ROAD

Pletne's W.

Fort Erie

Petiner's

L   A   K   E   E   R   I   E

STRUTHERS & CO., ENGR'S, N.Y.

Erie, where the destruction of his entire force was inevitable in case of a reverse. Ripley favored a withdrawal of the army to the American side; but Brown, from his sick bed at Buffalo, rejected the idea of a retreat, and fortunately Drummond's reinforcements arrived slowly. The worst result of the difference in opinion was to make Brown harsh toward Ripley, who—although his record was singular in showing only patient, excellent, and uniformly successful service—leaned toward caution, while Brown and Scott thought chiefly of fighting. The combination produced admirable results; but either officer alone might have failed.

Distrusting Ripley, and angry at losing the British cannon at Lundy's Lane as well as at the retreat from Chippawa, Brown wrote, August 7, to the Secretary of War a report containing an improper implication, which he afterward withdrew, that Ripley was wanting either in courage or capacity.[1] He also summoned Brigadier-General Gaines from Sackett's Harbor to command the army.[2] Gaines arrived, and as senior brigadier assumed command at Fort Erie, August 4, while Ripley resumed command of his brigade. During the week that elapsed before Gaines's arrival, the army, under Ripley's orders, worked energetically to intrench itself in lines behind Fort Erie; and after Gaines took command the same work was continued without interruption or change of plan, under the direction of Major McRee, Major Wood, and Lieutenant Douglass of the Engineers.

The result was chiefly decided by Drummond's errors. Had he followed Ripley closely, and had he attacked instantly on overtaking the retreating army at Fort Erie or elsewhere, he would have had the chances in his favor. Had he crossed the river and moved against Buffalo, he would have obliged Brown to order the instant evacuation of Fort Erie, and would have recovered all the British positions without the loss of a man. Drummond took neither course. He waited two days at Chippawa before he moved up the river within two miles of Fort Erie. About August 1 his reinforcements arrived,—DeWatteville's regiment from Kingston, and the

[1] Report of Aug. 7, 1814; Niles, vi. 434. Brown to Dallas, May, 1815; Ripley's "Facts," p. 46.
[2] Brown's Diary; Ingersoll's History, ii. 105.

Forty-first from Fort George,—replacing his losses, and giving him three thousand one hundred and fifty rank-and-file;[1] but he seemed still undecided what course to adopt. The battles of Chippawa and Lundy's Lane had given the British army respect for American troops, and Drummond hesitated to assault the unfinished works at Fort Erie, although he was fully one half stronger in men than Gaines and Ripley, who had barely two thousand rank-and-file after obtaining such reinforcements as were at hand.

Strength of Scott's Brigade, Fort Erie, July 31, 1814.

	PRESENT FOR DUTY.		AGGREGATE.
	Non-com. Officers, rank-and-file.	Officers.	Present and absent.
Ninth Regiment	139	8	569
Eleventh Regiment	293	11	624
Twenty-second Regiment. . . .	218	10	408
Twenty-fifth Regiment	255	7	676
General Staff	___	4	4
Total	905	40	2281

Strength of Ripley's Brigade.

First Regiment	141	6	220
Twenty-first Regiment	441	20	849
Twenty-third Regiment	292	12	713
General Staff	___	4	4
Total	874	42	1786

Monthly return of troops under Major-General Brown,
Fort Erie, July 31, 1814.

Bombardiers, etc.	58	2	69
Light Dragoons	47	1	64
Artillery Corps	241	12	364
First Brigade	905	40	2281
Second Brigade	874	42	1786
Total of Brown's army . . .	2125	97	4564

Drummond began operations by ordering a detachment of six hundred men to cross the river and destroy the magazines at Black Rock and Buffalo.[2] During the night of August 3 Colonel Tucker of the Forty-first, with four hundred and sixty rank-and-file of his own and other regiments,[3] landed two or three miles below Black Rock, and advanced against it. They

[1] James, ii. 161, 162.
[2] Drummond to Prevost, Aug. 4, 1814; MSS. Canadian Archives.
[3] James, ii. 162, 163.

were met at the crossing of a creek by two hundred and forty men of Morgan's Rifles, then garrisoning Black Rock, with some volunteers. The effect of the rifles was so deadly that the British troops refused to face them, and Tucker returned after losing twenty-five men. This repulse, as creditable in its way to the American army as the battles at Chippawa and Lundy's Lane, caused much annoyance to Drummond, who issued an order, August 5, expressing "the indignation excited by discovering that the failure of an expedition, the success of which . . . would have compelled the enemy's forces to surrender or . . . encounter certain defeat, was attributable to the misbehavior of the troops employed."[1] The only success achieved by British detachments was the cutting out of two American schooners which covered the approach to Fort Erie, near the shore.

Drummond having decided not to assault the lines of Fort Erie until he had made an impression on the works, next sent for guns of heavy calibre.[2] Ten days were passed in opening trenches and constructing batteries. Gaines and Ripley employed the time in completing their defences. Of these, the so-called Fort Erie was the smallest part, and made only the salient angle toward Drummond's approaches. As the British had constructed the fort, it was a small, unfinished work, about one hundred and fifty yards from the Lake-shore, open in the rear, and mounting three guns. The American engineers completed its rear bastions, and constructed an earthwork seven feet high, with a ditch, to the shore, where a small stone-work completed the defence on that side, and brought the lines to the water's edge. The stone-work was called the Douglass battery, after the lieutenant of engineers who built it. Fort Erie, Battery Douglass, and their connecting breastwork secured the camp on the right. A similar breastwork, nearly at right angles with the first, was extended three hundred and fifty yards westward parallel with the Lake-shore, then turning slightly ran three hundred and fifty yards farther till it neared the Lake-shore, where it was finished on Snake Hill by a projecting battery called Towson's. Traverses

---

[1] Ingersoll's History, ii. 145. Cf. Report of Major Morgan, Aug. 5, 1814; Niles, vi. 437.

[2] Drummond to Prevost, Aug. 4, 1814; MSS. Canadian Archives.

were constructed, and a strongly intrenched camp, about seven hundred yards by two hundred and fifty, was thus formed, open on its rear to the Lake.

Hindman had general charge of the artillery. Battery Douglass mounted one gun; another was mounted on the neighboring line; Fort Erie contained six,[1] under Captain Williams; Biddle's and Fanning's (Ritchie's) four guns were placed on the long line in the front; and Towson had six field-pieces at the extreme left.[2] Scott's brigade, commanded by Lieutenant-Colonel Aspinwall, was posted on the right; Porter's volunteers and the First Rifles occupied the centre; and Ripley with the Twenty-first and Twenty-third regiments defended the left.

Drummond opened with six guns, August 13, and prepared for assault the following day. His arrangements were somewhat complicated. He divided the attacking force into three columns, retaining another division in reserve. The strongest column, commanded by Lieutenant-Colonel Fischer of DeWatteville's regiment, was composed of portions of four regular regiments, and numbered about thirteen hundred men; these were to assault Towson and Ripley on Snake Hill. The centre column, commanded by Lieutenant-Colonel Drummond of the One-Hundred-and-fourth, numbered only one hundred and ninety rank-and-file, including a party of seamen and marines;[3] these were to attack Fort Erie. The third column, under Colonel Scott of the One-Hundred-and-third regiment, numbered six hundred and fifty rank-and-file; these were to assault the breastworks between Fort Erie and Battery Douglass.[4] According to these numbers, Drummond meant to assault with twenty-one hundred and forty rank-and-file, or about twenty-four hundred men all told. His reserve numbered one thousand men.[5] Some further number must have been detailed in camp duty.

Drummond's instructions, dated August 14, to Colonel

---

[1] Charges of Lieutenant-Colonel Trimble against General Gaines; Niles, xi. 219.

[2] Report of General Gaines, August, 1814; Niles, vii. 19.

[3] James, ii. 170, 171.

[4] Drummond's orders of Aug. 14, 1814; Niles, vii. 21. James, ii. 169–171.

[5] James, ii. 178.

Fischer were minute.[1] Fischer's column was to march immediately, in order to pass through the woods before dark, and
halt for the night opposite the point of attack, with every
precaution against discovery: —

"You are to advance to the attack precisely at two
o'clock. You are to enter the enemy's position betwixt
Snake Hill and the Lake, which is represented to be sufficiently open; but this is not to prevent your making your
arrangements for assaulting any other part of the position
by means of the short ladders and hay-bags with which you
will be furnished. In order to *insure success*, the Lieutenant-
General most strongly recommends that the flints be taken
out of the firelocks, with the exception of a reserve of select
and steady men who may be permitted to retain their flints,
if you think it necessary or advisable, not exceeding one
third of your force. This reserve, with the detachment of
artillery, should take post on Snake Hill."

A demonstration was to be made a few minutes before two
o'clock against the American pickets opposite the centre of
the line.

Drummond's general orders concluded by encouraging his
men to consider their task easy:[2] —

"The Lieutenant-General most strongly recommends a
free use of the bayonet. The enemy's force does not exceed
fifteen hundred fit for duty, and those are represented as
much dispirited."

The British general underestimated Gaines's force, which
probably contained at least two thousand rank-and-file fit for
duty August 14, who though possibly overworked and inclined to grumble, were ready to fight. Neither Gaines nor
Ripley, nor any of the excellent officers of engineers and
artillery who defended the lines of Fort Erie, were likely to
allow themselves to be surprised or even approached by a
force no greater than their own without ample resistance.
They kept strong pickets far in advance of their lines, and

[1] Instructions to Lieutenant-Colonel Fischer, Aug. 14, 1814; MSS. Canadian
Archives.
[2] Lieutenant-General Drummond's Order for attack [Secret]; Niles, vii. 21.

were alive to every sign of attack. Soon after midnight of August 14 the fire of the British siege-guns slackened and ceased. At the same moment Gaines left his quarters and Ripley ordered his brigade to turn out. Both officers looked for an assault, and were not mistaken. At two o'clock the pickets fired and fell back, and at half-past two o'clock Colonel Fischer's advancing column moved against Snake Hill.

There at the breastworks were Towson's guns and the Twenty-first regiment commanded by Major Wood of the Engineers, only two hundred and fifty strong, but as steady as at Lundy's Lane.[1] A part of Fischer's brigade marched gallantly up to the abattis, bayonets charged and guns without flints, and approached within ten feet of the breastwork, but failed to reach it. The other column, DeWatteville's regiment at its head, "marching too near the Lake," according to Colonel Fischer's report,[2] "found themselves entangled between the rocks and the water, and by the retreat of the flank companies were thrown in such confusion as to render it impossible to give them any kind of formation during the darkness of the night, at which time they were exposed to a most galling fire of the enemy's battery." A part of DeWatteville's regiment waded through the water round the American line, and came into the camp on the flank, but found there two companies posted to meet such an attempt, and were all captured, so that Colonel Fischer, writing his report the next day, seemed ignorant what had become of them.

The attack and repulse of Colonel Fischer on the extreme American left were soon over, and the story was easy to understand; but the attack on Fort Erie and the extreme right was neither quickly ended nor easily understood. There a column of more than seven hundred men, all told, under Colonel Scott of the One-Hundred-and-third, was to attack the Douglass battery. Another column, numbering somewhat more than two hundred men, all told, under Lieutenant-Colonel Drummond of the One-Hundred-and-fourth, was to assault Fort Erie. The American line between Battery Douglass and Fort Erie was held by the Ninth regiment and the

[1] Gaines's Report of Aug. 23, 1814; Niles, vii. 19. Ripley's Report of Aug. 17, 1814; Niles, vii. Supplement, p. 139.

[2] Report of Lieutenant-Colonel Fischer, Aug. 15, 1814; James, ii. 453.

volunteers, and was covered by the battery. Fort Erie was defended by about one hundred and eighteen men of the Nineteenth regiment under Major Trimble, and about sixty artillerists[1] under Captain Williams.

The most intelligible account of the battle at the eastern end of the lines was given neither in Gaines's nor Drummond's reports, but in some charges afterward brought against Gaines by Major Trimble, who was angry at the language of Gaines's report. Trimble's charges were judged to be frivolous, but his story of the battle was more precise than any other.

According to Major Trimble, Lieutenant-Colonel Drummond's column was directed against the north curtain of the fort, and was repulsed, but continued the assault. Colonel Scott's column at the same time advanced within about sixty yards of the Douglass battery, but deterred by the fire of the guns served under the direction of Major McRee and Lieutenant Douglass of the Engineers, and by the loss of its commanding officer Colonel Scott, who fell before the American line, the column moved quickly to the right, gained the ditch of the northeast bastion of Fort Erie, and under cover of the smoke and darkness entered the bastion. There they were joined by Drummond's men. They surprised the artillerists, and in the scuffle Captain Williams and his lieutenants— McDonough, Fontaine, and Watmough—were killed or disabled.

Without support the British columns could do no more, and Lieutenant-General Drummond did not come to their support. None of the reports mentioned the time at which the bastion was captured; but the small British force, which could not have exceeded six or seven hundred men, remained for more than two hours in or about the bastion, exposed to the American fire, to which they could not reply with effect, and waiting for Drummond and the reserve, which the Americans also expected and trained their guns to enfilade. The British in the bastion repeatedly attempted to advance from the bastion to gain possession of the Fort, and twice tried to force the door of the stone mess-house from which the men of the Nineteenth regiment kept up a destructive fire. They

[1] Charges of Major Trimble; Niles, xi. 219.

repulsed the attacks made by reinforcements ordered by Gaines into the Fort to recover the bastion; yet their destruction was inevitable as soon as the dawn should arrive, for they could neither advance nor escape, nor remain where they were, under the guns of the garrison.

After maintaining themselves till five o'clock in this difficult position, the British soldiers and sailors in the bastion were panic-struck by the explosion of an ammunition-chest under the platform. According to General Drummond's official report, "Some ammunition, which had been placed under the platform, caught fire from the firing of guns in the rear, and a most tremendous explosion followed, by which almost all the troops which had entered the place were dreadfully mangled. Panic was instantly communicated to the troops, who could not be persuaded that the explosion was accidental; and the enemy at the same time pressing forward and commencing a heavy fire of musketry, the Fort was abandoned, and our troops retreated toward the battery."

The explosion merely hastened the rout. Probably the attacking columns would have fared still worse, had they remained. Even their panic-stricken flight saved only a remnant. Of Drummond's column, said to number one hundred and ninety rank-and-file, one hundred and eighty-eight officers and men were reported as missing, wounded, or killed. Of Scott's column, said to number six hundred and fifty rank-and-file,—the Royal Scots and the One-Hundred-and-third regiments,—four hundred and ninety-six officers and men were returned as killed, wounded, or missing. Of the whole rank-and-file engaged under Fischer, Scott, and Drummond, numbering two thousand one hundred and fifty men, if the British report was correct, seven hundred and eighty were officially reported among the casualties. The loss in officers was equally severe. Colonel Scott was killed before the lines. Lieutenant-Colonel Drummond was killed in the bastion. One major, ten captains, and fifteen lieutenants were killed, wounded, or missing. The total British loss was nine hundred and five among some twenty-four hundred engaged. The total American loss was eighty-four men.[1]

---

[1] British Return; James, ii. 454. American Return; Niles, vii. 21.

General Drummond was excessively mortified by his failure, in truth the severest blow that British arms could suffer at that moment. For the fourth time in six weeks a large body of British troops met a bloody and unparalleled check, if not rout, from an inferior force. In a private letter to Prevost, dated August 16, Drummond attributed the disaster to the misconduct of DeWatteville's regiment, a foreign corps, which was struck by panic:[1] —

"It appears that part of the forlorn hope and about half of Watteville's Light Company, by wading through the water, though the footing was excessively rough and rocky along the Lake-shore, turned the left flank of an abattis which extended from the enemy's battery on Snake Hill, the left of their position, to the Lake, and part penetrated through the abattis itself, and thereby gained the rear of the enemy's works. The fire of the enemy at this time being extremely heavy both from artillery and musketry, it would seem as if a simultaneous shock of panic pervaded the greater part of those not in immediate advance; and the forlorn hope, not finding itself sufficiently supported, was reluctantly under the necessity of relinquishing the advantages they had gained, and of retiring again through the water under a most galling fire. They lost many men, and DeWatteville's Light Company nearly half their number. The Light Company of the Eighty-ninth, notwithstanding they were almost overwhelmed by the grenadiers of DeWatteville in the precipitancy of their retreat, was the only body that preserved its order and remained firm upon its ground. By this act of steadiness they fortunately lost scarcely a man. The main body of DeWatteville's regiment retreated in such confusion that they carried the King's regiment before them like a torrent. Thus by the misconduct of this foreign corps has the opportunity been totally lost."

The mortification of Drummond was acute in having to charge both his attacking columns with being panic-stricken: "The agony of mind I suffer from the present disgraceful and unfortunate conduct of the troops committed to my superin-

[1] Drummond to Prevost, Aug. 16, 1814; MSS. Canadian Archives.

tendence, wounds me to the soul!" Yet he offered no evidence to show that his troops fled before they were beaten, nor did he explain why he had thought it useless to order the reserve to their support after they had captured the bastion. In reality the battle of Fort Erie was more creditable to the British than the battles of Chippawa or Lundy's Lane, and the Americans could not admit that in either of the three the conduct of Drummond's troops was "disgraceful."

The defeat so much weakened Drummond that he could no longer keep the field without support, and immediately sent for two more regiments,—the Sixth and the Eighty-second from Burlington and York,—numbering about one thousand and forty rank-and-file, and making good his losses.[1]

At that time Chauncey was in control of Lake Ontario. The anxieties and delays in fitting out his new ship had ended in a fever, under which he was still suffering when he received General Brown's challenge of July 13 to meet him opposite Fort George. Chauncey did not immediately reply except by message through General Gaines. July 31, everything being at last ready, he was carried on board his ship, and the next day he sailed, arriving August 5 off Fort George. Brown's army was then besieged in Fort Erie, and could not approach the fleet. This situation gave to Chauncey the opportunity of writing a letter to Brown, repaying the harshness that Brown had shown to him.

"Was it friendly or just or honorable," asked Chauncey,[2] "not only to furnish an opening for the public, but thus to assist them to infer that I had pledged myself to meet you on a particular day at the head of the Lake, for the purpose of co-operation, and in case of disaster to your army, thus to turn their resentment from you, who are alone responsible, upon me, who could not by any possibility have prevented, or retarded even, your discomfiture? You well know, sir, that the fleet could not have rendered you the least service during your late incursion upon Upper

[1] James, ii. 814. Drummond to Prevost, Aug. 16, 1814; MSS. Canadian Archives.

[2] Chauncey to Brown, Aug. 10, 1814; Niles, vii. 38.

Canada. You have not been able to approach Lake Ontario on any point nearer than Queenston."

Brown's quarrel with Chauncey made much noise in its day, and, like the less defensible quarrel with Ripley, proved that Brown was unnecessarily aggressive; but in the situation of the United States, aggressiveness was the most valuable quality in the service. That Brown might have become a great general was possible, had his experience been larger; but whatever was his merit as a general, his qualities as a fighter were more remarkable than those of any other general officer in the war. Except immediately after receiving his wound at Lundy's Lane, when his army was exhausted by four hours of extreme effort, he never seemed satiated with fighting. Among all the American major-generals, he alone made raw troops as steady as grenadiers, and caused militia to storm entrenched lines held by British regulars.

Brown might have been well satisfied to let Drummond exhaust his strength in attacking Fort Erie. From a military point of view, Fort Erie was worthless for any other purpose than to draw the enemy to the extreme end of their line, where they could with difficulty obtain supplies, and could take no part in the serious campaigning intended on Lake Champlain. For that object, no more pitched battles were needed. Drummond's force was wasting away by sickness and exposure.[1]

After the battle of August 15, the British continued to bombard Fort Erie. No great damage was done; but a shell exploded in Gaines's quarters August 29, injuring him severely and obliging him to relinquish command. Brown was still unfit for service, but was bent upon more fighting, and knew that Ripley preferred to abandon Fort Erie altogether. Accordingly he resumed command at Buffalo, September 2, and set himself to study the situation.

The situation was uncomfortable, but in no way perilous. The lines of Fort Erie were stronger than ever, and beyond danger of capture from any British force that could be brought to assault them, until Drummond should discover some new means of supplying troops with subsistence. The

[1] James, ii. 230.

army return of August 31 gave the precise strength of the garrison.

Strength of the Army at Fort Erie, Aug. 31, 1814.

| | PRESENT FOR DUTY. | | AGGREGATE. |
	Non-com. Officers, rank-and-file.	Officers.	Present and absent.
Dragoons	27	1	48
Bombardiers, etc..	34		51
Artillery Corps	206	10	369
First Brigade	725	39	2311
Second Brigade	698	42	1646
Porter's Brigade	220	16	599
First and Fourth Rifles	217	11	504
Total	2127	119	5528

The regular force in Fort Erie numbered two thousand and thirty-three effectives[1] September 4, and though annoyed by the enemy's fire and worn by hard work, they were in both these respects better situated than the besiegers. Sooner or later the British would be obliged to retreat; and Brown was informed by deserters that Drummond was then contemplating withdrawal.[2] Brown estimated the British force very loosely at three or four thousand;[3] and it was in fact about the smaller number.

Drummond's situation was told in his reports to Sir George Prevost. September 8 he wrote[4] that he should not fail to seize any favorable opportunity to attack; "but should no such opportunity present itself, I feel it incumbent on me to prepare your Excellency for the possibility of my being compelled by sickness or suffering of the troops, exposed as they will be to the effects of the wet and unhealthy season which is fast approaching, to withdraw them from their present position to one which may afford them the means of cover. Sickness has, I am sorry to say, already made its appearance in several of the corps." Three days afterward, September 11,[5] Drummond was warned by several signs that his

[1] Ripley to Armstrong, Sept. 4, 1814; MSS. War Department.
[2] Lossing, p. 837.
[3] Brown to Izard, Sept. 10, 1814; Izard's Correspondence, p. 86.
[4] Drummond to Prevost, Sept. 8, 1814; MSS. Canadian Archives.
[5] Drummond to Prevost, Sept. 11, 1814; MSS. Canadian Archives.

lines were to be attacked by Brown, although "whether the account which is *invariably* given by deserters of his intention to act offensively . . . be correct, I have not yet been able accurately to ascertain." Drummond's batteries had been almost silent for several days for want of ammunition, and he could do nothing till the arrival of reinforcements,—the Ninety-seventh regiment,—unaccountably delayed. Rain had begun, and he dreaded its effect on the troops. In his next despatch, dated September 14,[1] he said that the rain had been incessant, and "as the whole of the troops are without tents, and the huts in which they are placed are wholly incapable of affording shelter against such severe weather, their situation is most distressing." The roads were impassable; the nearest depot of supplies was Fort George, and Drummond had not cattle enough to move a third of his heavy ordnance if a sudden movement should be necessary. The enemy seemed about to cross the river in his rear, and the Ninety-seventh regiment had not yet arrived:—

"In the mean time I have strong grounds for thinking that the enemy will risk an attack,—an event which though from the necessity of defending my batteries in the first instance with the pickets alone I shall have to meet under every possible disadvantage, yet I am very much disposed to hope may be the most fortunate circumstance which can happen, as it will bring us in contact with the enemy at a far cheaper rate than if we were to be the assailants."

While Drummond struggled between the necessity of retreat and the difficulty of retreating, Brown was bent on attacking his lines. The plan was open to grave objections, and a council of war, September 9, discouraged the idea. Brown was much disappointed and irritated at the result of the council, especially with Ripley; but while giving the impression that he acquiesced, he brought over all the volunteers he could obtain.[2] The number was never precisely given, but according to the official reports of General Peter B. Porter who commanded them, and of General Brown himself, they did

[1] Drummond to Prevost, Sept. 14, 1814; MSS. Canadian Archives.
[2] Jesup's Narrative; Lossing, p. 837, *note*; Ingersoll, ii. 151.

not exceed one thousand.[1] With these, and an equal number of regular troops, Brown undertook to assault Drummond's entrenchments.

The nearest British line was about six hundred yards from old Fort Erie. From the first British battery on the Lakeshore, to Battery No. 3 in the woods, the line extended nearly half a mile, covered by abattis, but defended only by the brigade of troops on actual duty. If carried, the first line could not be held without capturing the second line, about fifty yards distant, and a third line, farther in the rear; while the main British force was encamped, for reasons of health and comfort, a mile behind, and was supposed to number at least three thousand six hundred men, or quite sufficient to recover their works. Brown professed no intention of fighting the British army. He proposed only "to storm the batteries, destroy the cannon, and roughly handle the brigade upon duty, before those in reserve could be brought into action."[2]

Although Drummond expected and wished to be attacked, he kept no proper pickets or scouts in the woods, and all day of September 16 American fatigue parties were at work opening a path through the forest the distance of a mile, from Snake Hill on the extreme left to the extremity of the British line in the woods. So little precaution had Drummond's engineers taken that they left the dense forest standing within pistol-shot of the flank and rear of their Battery No. 3 on their extreme right, and the American parties opened a path within one hundred and fifty yards of the flank of the British line without being discovered.

At noon, September 17, General Porter led a column of sixteen hundred men—of whom one thousand were militia volunteers, and a part were the Twenty-third regiment—along the path through the woods, in three divisions, commanded by Colonel Gibson of the Fourth Rifles, Colonel E. D. Wood of the Engineers, and Brigadier-General Davis of the New York militia. At three o'clock, under cover of heavy rain, the whole force fell suddenly on the blockhouse which covered the flank and rear of the British battery No. 3, and succeeded

[1] Porter's Report of Sept. 22, 1814, and Brown's Report of Sept. 29, 1814; Niles, vii. 100, 101.

[2] Brown's Report of Sept. 29, 1814; Niles, vii. 100.

in capturing the blockhouse and mastering the battery held by DeWatteville's regiment. While detachments spiked the guns and blew up the magazine, the main column advanced on Battery No. 2, while at the same time General Miller, promoted to the command of Scott's old brigade, moved with "the remains of the Ninth and Eleventh Infantry and a detachment of the Nineteenth" from a ravine in front of Battery No. 3 to pierce the centre of the British line between Battery No. 3 and Battery No. 2.[1]

Within half an hour after the first gun was fired, Porter and Miller had effected their junction within the British lines, had captured Battery No. 2, and moved on Battery No. 1, by the Lake-shore. There the success ended. Battery No. 1 could not be carried. By that time the Royal Scots, the Eighty-ninth, the Sixth, and the Eighty-second British regiments had arrived,—probably about one thousand men.[2] A sharp engagement followed before Brown, after ordering his reserve under Ripley to the assistance of Porter and Miller, could disengage his troops. The three commanders of Porter's divisions —Gibson, Wood, and Davis—were killed or mortally wounded,—Gibson at the second battery, Davis and Wood in assaulting the shore battery. Ripley was desperately wounded at the same time. General Porter, Lieutenant-Colonel Aspinwall of the Ninth, and Major Trimble of the Nineteenth, as well as a number of other officers, were severely wounded. That the last action was sharp was proved by the losses suffered by the British reinforcements. According to the British official return, the four regiments which came last into the field—the Royal Scots, Sixth, Eighty-second, and Eighty-ninth—lost thirty-six killed, one hundred and nine wounded, and fifty-four missing,—a total of two hundred men, in a short action of half an hour at the utmost, without artillery.

The American forces were recalled by Brown and Miller as soon as their progress was stopped, and they retired without serious pursuit beyond the British lines. Their losses were very severe, numbering five hundred and eleven killed,

[1] Brown's Report of Oct. 1, 1814; Official Letters, p. 445.
[2] James, ii. 232, 233. Report of Major-General DeWatteville, Sept. 19, 1814; James, ii. 469.

wounded, and missing, or about one fourth of their number. Among them were several of the best officers in the United States service, including Ripley, Wood, and Gibson. Drummond's loss was still more severe, numbering six hundred and nine,[1] probably almost one man in three of the number engaged. The British killed numbered one hundred and fifteen. The Americans reported seventy-nine killed,—sixty regulars, and nineteen militia.

The next day Drummond issued a general order claiming a victory over an American force of "not less than five thousand men, including militia;" but his situation, untenable before the sortie, became impossible after it. Three out of six battering cannon were disabled;[2] he had lost six hundred men in battle, and his losses by sickness were becoming enormous. "My effective numbers are reduced to considerably less than two thousand firelocks," he reported, September 21. Immediately after the sortie, although reinforced by the Ninety-seventh regiment, he made his arrangements to retreat.

"Within the last few days," he wrote to Prevost, September 21,[3] "the sickness of the troops has increased to such an alarming degree, and their situation has really become one of such extreme wretchedness from the torrents of rain which have continued to fall for the last thirteen days, and from the circumstance of the Division being entirely destitute of camp-equipage, that I feel it my duty no longer to persevere in a vain attempt to maintain the blockade of so vastly superior and increasing a force of the enemy under such circumstances. I have therefore given orders for the troops to fall back toward the Chippawa, and shall commence my movement at eight o'clock this evening."

[1] James, ii. 234.
[2] James, ii. 236.
[3] Drummond to Prevost, Sept. 21, 1814; MSS. Canadian Archives.

Chapter IV

WEAK AS WAS the army at Niagara, it was relatively
stronger than the defence at any other threatened
point. Sackett's Harbor contained only seven hundred effectives.[1] On Lake Champlain, Major-General Izard tried to
cover Plattsburg and Burlington with about five thousand
regular troops.[2] Already Armstrong knew that large British
reinforcements from Wellington's army were on their way to
Canada;[3] and within a few weeks after the battle of Lundy's
Lane eleven thousand of the best troops England ever put in
the field were camped on or near the Sorel River, about to
march against Izard's five thousand raw recruits.

They could march nowhere else. Not only was the line of
Lake Champlain the natural and necessary path of an invading army, but the impossibility of supplying any large number
of troops in Upper Canada made Lake Champlain the only
region in which a large British force could exist. Sir George
Prevost had reached the limit of his powers in defending Upper Canada. His commissary-general, W. H. Robinson, wrote
to him, August 27, expressing "the greatest alarm" on account
of deficient supplies at Burlington Heights and Niagara,
where instead of nine thousand rations daily as he expected,
he was required to furnish fourteen thousand, half of them to
Indians.[4] Much as Prevost wanted to attack Sackett's Harbor,
and weak as he knew that post to be, he could not attempt it,
although he had thirteen or fourteen thousand rank-and-file
idle at Montreal. In October he went to Kingston expressly
to arrange such an attack, and found it impossible.

"An investigation of the state of the stores at this post,"
he wrote to Lord Bathurst October 18,[5] "proved that the
articles for the armament and equipment for a ship of the
class of the 'St. Lawrence,' carrying upward of one hundred
guns, had absorbed almost the whole of the summer trans-

[1] Chauncey to Jones, Aug. 10, 1814; Niles, vii. 37.
[2] Izard to Armstrong, July 19, 1814; Izard's Correspondence, p. 54.
[3] Armstrong to Izard, July 2, 1814; Izard's Correspondence, p. 51.
[4] W. H. Robinson to Sir G. Prevost, Aug. 27, 1814; MSS. British Archives.
[5] Prevost to Bathurst, Oct. 18, 1814; MSS. British Archives.

port-service from Montreal, leaving the materials for an undertaking of the magnitude of the destruction of Sackett's Harbor still at the extremity of the line of communication; and now, by giving precedence to that supply of provisions and stores without which an army is no longer to be maintained in Upper Canada, its removal is inevitably postponed until the winter roads are established."

Not only were military operations on a large scale impossible in Upper Canada, but for the opposite reason occupation of Lake Champlain by a British force was necessary. Northern New York and Vermont furnished two thirds of the fresh beef consumed by the British armies. General Izard reported to Armstrong, July 31,[1] —

"From the St. Lawrence to the ocean, an open disregard prevails for the laws prohibiting intercourse with the enemy. The road to St. Regis is covered with droves of cattle, and the river with rafts, destined for the enemy. The revenue officers see these things, but acknowledge their inability to put a stop to such outrageous proceedings. On the eastern side of Lake Champlain the high roads are found insufficient for the supplies of cattle which are pouring into Canada. Like herds of buffaloes they press through the forest, making paths for themselves. . . . Nothing but a cordon of troops from the French Mills to Lake Memphramagog could effectually check the evil. Were it not for these supplies, the British forces in Canada would soon be suffering from famine, or their government be subjected to enormous expense for their maintenance."

After Chauncey, August 1, regained possession of Lake Ontario, any British campaign against Sackett's Harbor or Detroit became doubly impossible, and the occupation of Lake Champlain became doubly necessary. Prevost wrote to Bathurst, August 27,[2] —

"In fact, my Lord, two thirds of the army in Canada are at this moment eating beef provided by American contractors, drawn principally from the States of Vermont and

[1] Izard's Correspondence, p. 57.
[2] Prevost to Bathurst, Aug. 27, 1814; MSS. British Archives.

New York. This circumstance, as well as that of the introduction of large sums in specie into this province, being notorious in the United States, it is to be expected that Congress will take steps to deprive us of those resources; and under that apprehension large droves are daily crossing the lines coming into Lower Canada."

The fear that Izard might at any moment take efficient measures to cut off the British supplies gave double force to the reasons for occupying Lake Champlain, and forcing the military frontier back beyond Plattsburg and Burlington.

The political reasons were not less strong or less notorious than the military. England made no secret of her intention to rectify the Canadian frontier by lopping away such territory as she could conquer. July 5, the day of the battle of Chippawa, Lieutenant-Colonel Pilkington sailed from Halifax, and under the naval protection of Sir Thomas Hardy in the "Ramillies," landed at Eastport, July 11, with the One-Hundred-and-second regiment, some engineers and artillery,—a detachment of six hundred men,—and took possession of Moose Island.[1] Fort Sullivan, with six officers and eighty men, capitulated, and Great Britain took permanent possession of the place.

Moose Island was disputed territory, and its occupation was not necessarily conquest; but the next step showed wider views. August 26, Lieutenant-General Sir J. C. Sherbrooke, the British governor of Nova Scotia, set sail from Halifax with a powerful fleet, carrying near two thousand troops, and arrived September 1 at the Penobscot.[2] At his approach, the American garrison of the small battery at Castine blew up their fort and dispersed. In all Massachusetts, only about six hundred regular troops were to be found, and beyond the Penobscot, in September, 1814, hardly a full company could have been collected. The able-bodied, voting, male population of the counties of Kennebeck and Hancock, on either side of the Penobscot River, capable of bearing arms, was at that time about twelve thousand, on an estimate of one in

---

[1] Lieut.-Colonel Pilkington to Lieut.-General Sherbrooke, July 12, 1814; James, ii. 472.

[2] Sherbrooke to Bathurst, Sept. 18, 1814; James, ii. 475.

five of the total population; but they offered no resistance to the British troops.

One misfortune led to another. A few days before Sherbrooke's arrival at Castine the United States ship "Adams," a heavy corvette carrying twenty-eight guns, having escaped from Chesapeake Bay and cruised some months at sea struck on a reef on the Isle of Haut, and was brought into the Penobscot in a sinking condition. Captain Morris, who commanded her, took the ship up the river about twenty-five miles, as far as Hampden near Bangor, and removed her guns in order to repair her. Sherbrooke, on occupying Castine, sent a detachment of some six hundred men in boats up the river to destroy the ship, while he occupied Belfast with another regiment.[1] Captain Morris hastily put his guns in battery, and prepared to defend the ship with his crew, numbering probably more than two hundred men, relying on the militia to cover his flanks. On the morning of September 3, in a thick fog, the enemy's boats approached and landed their infantry, which attacked and routed the militia, and obliged Captain Morris to set fire to the "Adams," abandon his guns, and disperse his men.[2] The British force then marched to Bangor, which they occupied without opposition. Their entire loss was one man killed and eight wounded.[3] At Bangor they remained nearly a week, destroying vessels and cargoes; but Sir John Sherbrooke had no orders to occupy the country west of the Penobscot, and his troops returned September 9 to Castine.

At Castine the British remained, while another detachment occupied Machias. All the province of Maine east of the Penobscot was then in Sherbrooke's hands. The people formally submitted. One hundred miles of Massachusetts sea-coast passed quietly under the dominion of the King of England. The male citizens were required to take, and took, the oath of allegiance to King George,[4] and showed no unwillingness to remain permanently British subjects. After September 1 the United States government had every reason to expect that

---

[1] Sherbrooke to Bathurst, Sept. 18, 1814; James, ii. 475.
[2] Morris to Jones, Sept. 20, 1814; Niles, vii. 63.
[3] James, ii. 482.
[4] Lossing, p. 903, *note*.

Great Britain would require, as one condition of peace, a cession of the eastern and northern portions of Maine.

For this purpose the British needed also to occupy Lake Champlain, in order to make their conquests respectable. The British general might move on Plattsburg or on Burlington; but in order to maintain his position he must gain naval possession of the Lake. In such a case the difficulties of the American government would be vastly increased, and the British position would be impregnable. Armstrong knew these circumstances almost as well as they were known to Sir George Prevost.

In May the British flotilla entered Lake Champlain from the Sorel River, and cruised, May 9, as far southward as Otter Creek, terrifying Vermont for the safety of the American flotilla under Lieutenant Thomas Macdonough at Vergennes. Irritated and alarmed by this demonstration, Armstrong ordered Izard to seize and fortify Rouse's Point, or the mouth of Lacolle River, or Ash Island, and so close the entrance to the Lake.[1] Apparently Armstrong gave the order in ignorance that Lacolle River and Ash Island were strongly fortified British positions,[2] and that a battery established at Rouse's Point, in the relative situation of forces, must have fallen into British hands. On this point the opinion of Izard was more valuable than that of Armstrong; and Izard, after much study and inquiry, decided to erect his fortifications at Plattsburg. He preferred the task of taking a position which he could certainly hold, although it would not prevent the enemy from passing if they chose to leave it behind them. At Plattsburg, therefore, he collected his troops, amounting to five or six thousand men, and constructed strong forts, while Macdonough's fleet took position in the bay.

While thus occupied, Izard cast anxious glances westward, doubting whether, in case of a reverse at Niagara or Sackett's Harbor, he ought not to move on the St. Lawrence and threaten the British communications between Montreal and Kingston.[3] The same idea occurred to Armstrong, who in a

---

[1] Armstrong to Izard, May 25 and June 30, 1814; Izard's Correspondence, pp. 23, 48.

[2] Izard to Armstrong, July 12, 1814; Izard's Correspondence, p. 52.

[3] Izard to Armstrong, July 19, 1814; Izard's Correspondence, p. 54.

letter dated July 27 recommended Izard to carry it out.[1] The letter reached Izard August 10, when he had advanced with his army to Chazy, and had learned enough of the concentration of British troops in his front to be assured that they meant to direct their serious attack against Lake Champlain. He wrote Armstrong a letter, August 11, which failed only in saying too little, rather than too much, of the dangers risked in obeying Armstrong's order:[2] —

"I will make the movement you direct, if possible; but I shall do it with the apprehension of risking the force under my command, and with the certainty that everything in this vicinity but the lately erected works at Plattsburg and Cumberland Head will in less than three days after my departure be in the possession of the enemy. He is in force superior to mine in my front; he daily threatens an attack on my position at Champlain; we are in hourly expectation of a serious conflict. That he has not attacked us before this time is attributable to caution on his part, from exaggerated reports of our numbers, and from his expectation of reinforcements. . . . It has always been my conviction that the numerical force of the enemy has been under-rated. I believe this to be the strong point of our frontier for either attack or defence, and I know that a British force has been kept in check in Lower Canada for many weeks past, greatly superior to that which I could oppose to it."

Izard was right. Every week new British forces poured into Quebec and were forwarded to Montreal. The arrival of the first division at Quebec was announced in the American newspapers early in August. Within a few weeks three brigades arrived and were sent to the front. When Izard wrote, he was probably faced by ten thousand veteran British troops within twenty or thirty miles of his position, and more were known to be on their way. At such a moment the danger of attempting a diversion was great; but Armstrong refused to believe it. Irritated by Izard's remonstrance, the secretary not only persisted in his own opinion, but, abandoning the idea of a movement against the British communications along the St. Law-

[1] Armstrong to Izard, July 27, 1814; Izard's Correspondence, p. 64.
[2] Izard to Armstrong, Aug. 11, 1814; Izard's Correspondence.

rence, ordered Izard to march his army to Sackett's Harbor, and from there to operate either directly in force against Kingston,[1] or to go on to Niagara and assist Brown, then hard pressed at Fort Erie. "It is very distinctly my opinion," wrote the secretary August 12,[2] "that it has become good policy on our part to carry the war as far to the westward as possible, particularly while we have an ascendency on the Lakes."

Izard obeyed. His troops, numbering four thousand men, began their march August 29 for Sackett's Harbor, and for several weeks at the crisis of the campaign ceased to exist for military purposes. Within the fortifications at Plattsburg Izard left a miscellaneous body of three thousand, three hundred men,[3] without an organized battalion except four companies of the Sixth regiment. Brigadier-General Alexander Macomb, who as senior officer was left in command, reported his force as not exceeding fifteen hundred effectives.[4]

Armstrong's policy of meeting the enemy's main attack by annihilating the main defence never received explanation or excuse. At times Armstrong seemed to suggest that he meant to rely on the navy,[5]—and indeed nothing else, except Izard's forts, was left to rely upon; but in truth he rather invited the invasion of a British army into New York to "renew the scene of Saratoga."[6] As Izard predicted, the enemy crossed the frontier at once after his departure, occupying Chazy September 3, and approaching, September 5, within eight miles of Plattsburg.

Great Britain had never sent to America so formidable an armament. Neither Wolfe nor Amherst, neither Burgoyne nor Cornwallis, had led so large or so fine an army as was under the command of Sir George Prevost. According to his proposed arrangement, the light brigade, under Major-General Robinson, contained four battalions of the Twenty-seventh, Thirty-ninth, Seventy-sixth, and Eighty-eighth foot, with artillery, and numbered two thousand eight hundred and

[1] Armstrong to Izard, July 27, 1814; Izard's Correspondence, p. 64.
[2] Armstrong to Izard, Aug. 12, 1814; Izard's Correspondence, p. 69.
[3] Izard's Correspondence, p. 144.
[4] Macomb to Armstrong, Sept. 15, 1814; Niles, vii. 60.
[5] Armstrong to Izard, Aug. 2, 1814; Izard's Correspondence, p. 61.
[6] See ante, p. 740.

eighty-four rank-and-file. The second brigade, under Major-General Brisbane, contained battalions of the Eighth, Thirteenth, and Forty-ninth, De Meuron's regiment and Canadian voltigeurs and chasseurs, numbering four thousand and forty-eight rank-and-file. The third brigade, under Major-General Power, contained battalions of the Third, Fifth, Twenty-seventh, and Fifty-eighth, and numbered three thousand eight hundred and one rank-and-file. The reserve, under Major-General Kempt, contained battalions of the Ninth, Thirty-seventh, Fifty-seventh, and Eighty-first, numbering three thousand five hundred and forty-nine rank-and-file. Finally, fourteen hundred and eighty-eight men of the Sixteenth and Seventieth regiments, under the command of Major-General DeWatteville, were stationed between Coteau du Lac and Gananoque on the St. Lawrence.[1]

Thus the left division of the British army in Canada numbered fifteen thousand seven hundred and seventy effectives, or, including officers, probably eighteen thousand men, without reckoning the Canadian militia, either incorporated or sedentary. Two lieutenant-generals and five major-generals were in command. Amply provided with artillery and horses, every brigade well equipped, they came fresh from a long service in which the troops had learned to regard themselves as invincible. As they were at last organized, four brigades crossed the border, numbering not less than "eleven thousand men with a proportionate and most excellent train of artillery, commanded in chief by Sir George Prevost, and under him by officers of the first distinction in the service."[2] A reserve of about five thousand men remained behind.

The fleet was almost as formidable as the army. As the force of the flotilla was reported to Prevost, it consisted of a thirty-six-gun ship, the "Confiance;" an eighteen-gun brig, the "Linnet;" two ten-gun sloops and twelve gunboats, carrying sixteen guns,[3]—all commanded by Captain Downie, of the Royal Navy, detached by Sir James Yeo for the purpose.

[1] Proposed Distribution of the Forces in the Left Division; MSS. Canadian Archives, Freer Papers, 1812–1813, p. 107.

[2] James, ii. 206.

[3] Comparative Force of the Flotillas; MSS. Canadian Archives. Prevost's Report; James, ii. 462; Christie, ii. 211, *note*.

Such an expedition was regarded with unhesitating confidence, as able to go where it pleased within the region of Lake Champlain. About every other undertaking in America the British entertained doubts, but in regard to this affair they entertained none.[1] Every movement of the British generals showed conviction of their irresistible strength. Had Prevost doubted the result of attacking Plattsburg, he could have advanced by St. Albans on Burlington,[2] which would have obliged Macomb and Macdonough to leave their positions. So little did his army apprehend difficulty, that in advancing to Plattsburg in face of Macomb's skirmishers they did not once form in line, or pay attention to the troops and militia who obstructed the road. "The British troops did not deign to fire on them except by their flankers and advanced patrols," reported Macomb.[3] "So undaunted was the enemy that he never deployed in his whole march, always pressing on in column."

The fleet felt the same certainty. According to the best Canadian authority,[4] "the strongest confidence prevailed in the superiority of the British vessels, their weight of metal, and in the capacity and experience of their officers and crews." Captain Downie informed Sir George Prevost's staff-officer that he considered himself with the "Confiance" alone a match for the whole American squadron.[5] Taking the British account of the "Confiance" as correct, she was one hundred and forty-six feet long on the gun-deck, and thirty-six feet broad; she carried a crew of three hundred officers and men;[6] her armament was thirty-seven guns,—twenty-seven long twenty-four-pounders, six thirty-two-pound carronades, and four twenty-four-pound carronades,—throwing in all nine hundred and thirty-six pounds.[7] The American account, which was more trustworthy because the "Confiance" became better known in the American than in the British service,

[1] Christie, ii. 221, 222.
[2] Montreal Herald, Sept. 24, 1814.
[3] Report of Sept. 15, 1814; Niles, vii. 50.
[4] Christie, ii. 212.
[5] Christie, ii. 212.
[6] London Naval Chronicle, xxxii. 292. Niles, viii.; Supplement, p. 173.
[7] James, p. 413.

gave her thirty-one long twenty-four-pounders and six carronades.[1]

Macdonough's best ship was the "Saratoga." Her dimensions were not recorded. Her regular complement of men was two hundred and ten, but she fought with two hundred and forty; she carried eight twenty-four-pounders, twelve thirty-two and six forty-two-pound carronades,—or twenty-six guns, throwing eight hundred and twenty-eight pounds. Her inferiority to the "Confiance" at long range was immense, and within carronade range it was at least sufficient to satisfy Captain Downie. He believed that a few broadsides would dispose of the "Saratoga," and that the other American vessels must then surrender.

Assuming Sir George Prevost's report to have been correct, the two fleets compared as follows:[2]—

Force of British Fleet.

Vessels.	Guns.	Long.	Short.	Long metal.	Short metal.	Weight of metal.
Confiance	37	31	6	744	192	936
Linnet	16	16		192		192
Chubb	11	1	10	6	180	186
Finch	10	4	6	24	108	132
Twelve Gunboats	16	8	8	162	256	418
Total	90	60	30	1128	736	1864

Force of American Fleet.

Vessels.	Guns.	Long.	Short.	Long metal.	Short metal.	Weight of metal.
Saratoga	26	8	18	192	636	828
Eagle	20	8	12	144	384	528
Ticonderoga	17	12	5	168	146	314
Preble	7	7		63		63
Ten Gunboats	16	10	6	192	108	300
Total	86	45	41	759	1274	2033

In this calculation the possible error consists only in one disputed eighteen-pound columbiad on the "Finch," and

[1] Cooper's Naval History, ii. 429.

[2] Macdonough's Report of Sept. 12, 1814; Niles, vii. 42. Cooper's Naval History, chap. xxviii. James's Naval Occurrences, pp. 414, 415. Roosevelt's Naval War of 1812, pp. 378–384.

three disputed guns—one long and two short—on the British gunboats. In one case the British would have thrown about nineteen hundred pounds of metal,—in the other, about eighteen hundred. A glance at the two tables shows that in one respect Downie held a decisive superiority in his guns. He had no less than sixty long-range pieces, while Macdonough had but forty-five. Downie's long-range guns threw at least eleven hundred pounds of metal; Macdonough's threw but seven hundred and sixty. If Downie chose his own distance beyond range of the thirty-two-pound carronades, and fought only his long guns, nothing could save Macdonough except extreme good fortune, for he had but fourteen twenty-four-pound guns against Downie's thirty-four. Firing by broadsides, Downie could throw from his single ship, the "Confiance," sixteen twenty-four-pound shot, to which Macdonough could reply only with eight, even if he used all his long guns on the same side.

The Americans had a decided advantage only in their commander. Thomas Macdonough, born in Delaware in 1783, was thirty years old when this responsibility fell upon him. He had been educated, like most of the naval heroes, in the hard service of the Tripolitan war, and had been sent to construct and command the naval force on Lake Champlain in the spring of 1813. Macdonough's superiority over ordinary commanders consisted in the intelligent forethought with which he provided for the chances of battle. His arrangement showed that he foresaw, and as far as possible overcame in advance, every conceivable attack. He compelled the enemy to fight only as pleased himself.

Macdonough anchored his four large vessels across Plattsburg Bay, where it was a mile and a half wide, and placed his gunboats in their rear to fill the gaps. Cumberland Head on his left and front, and Crab Island on his right obliged the enemy to enter in a line so narrow that Downie would find no room to anchor on his broadside out of carronade range, but must sail into the harbor under the raking fire of the American long guns, and take a position within range of the American carronades.[1] As the battle was to be fought at

[1] Cooper's Naval History, ii. 427, 431.

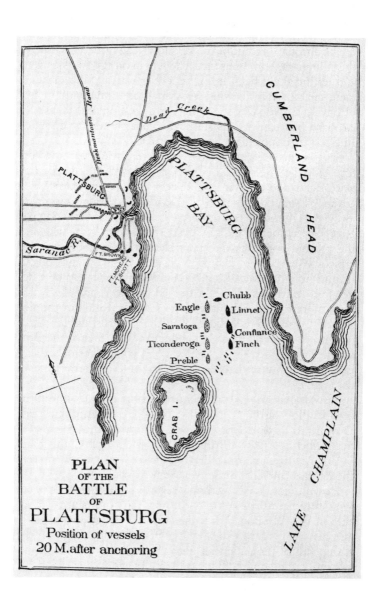

PLAN
OF THE
BATTLE
OF
PLATTSBURG
Position of vessels
20 M. after anchoring

anchor, both squadrons would as a matter of course be anchored with springs on their cables; but Macdonough took the additional precaution of laying a kedge off each bow of the "Saratoga," bringing their hawsers in on the two quarters, and letting them hang in bights under water.[1] This arrangement enabled him to wind his ship at any time without fear of having his cables cut by the enemy's shot, and to use his larboard broadside if his starboard guns should be disabled. In effect, it doubled his fighting capacity.

Sir George Prevost and the army were ready to move before Downie's fleet could be prepared. Marching directly forward with the utmost confidence, Sir George turned the advanced American position at Dead Creek Bridge and drove away the gunboats that covered it. He reached the Saranac River September 6, and saw beyond it a ridge "crowned with three strong redoubts and other field-works, and blockhouses armed with heavy ordnance, with their flotilla at anchor out of gunshot from the shore."[2] The description was not exaggerated. Izard was himself a trained engineer, and the works built by him, under the direction of Major Totten of the Engineer Corps, were believed capable of resisting for three weeks a combined attack by land and water, even if the British fleet were victorious.[3] Three good companies of artillery manned the guns. Excellent officers of every arm were in command.

Prevost properly halted, and declined to assault without the co-operation of the fleet. He waited five days impatiently for Downie to appear. Not till seven o'clock on the morning of September 11 did the British flotilla sail round Cumberland Head. At the same time Prevost ordered his troops to cross the Saranac and storm the American works.

Downie intended, without regarding his superiority in long-range guns, to sail in and to lay the "Confiance" alongside of the "Saratoga;" but the wind was light and baffling, and his approach was so slow that he could not long bear the raking fire of the American guns. As he came within carronade range the wind baffling, he was obliged to anchor at two

[1] Cooper's Naval History, ii. 432.
[2] Prevost's Report of Sept. 11, 1814; James, ii. 461.
[3] Izard to Monroe, Oct. 7, 1814; Izard's Correspondence, p. 97.

cables' lengths,[1] or three hundred yards,[2] and begin action. With the same discipline that marked the movements of the troops on shore, Downie came to, anchored, made everything secure, and then poured a full broadside into Macdonough's ship. The "Saratoga" shivered under the shock of sixteen twenty-four-pound shot and canister charges striking her hull; almost one-fifth of her crew were disabled; but she stood stoutly to her work, and the whole line was soon hotly engaged.

Americans usually had a decided advantage in their better gunnery, but three hundred yards was a long range for thirty-two-pound carronades, which at point-blank carried less than two hundred and fifty yards, and lost accuracy in proportion to elevation.[3] Macdonough was slow to prove superiority. Early in the battle the British suffered a severe, and perhaps in the experience of this war a decisive, loss in their commander, Captain Downie, instantly killed by one of his own guns thrown off its carriage against him by a solid shot. Yet at the end of two hours' combat the British squadron was on the whole victorious, and the American on the point of capture. Of the three smaller American vessels, the "Preble" on the extreme right was driven out of the engagement, and the British gunboats, turning the American flank, attacked the "Ticonderoga," which maintained a doubtful battle. The American left was also turned, the "Eagle" having been driven to take refuge between the "Saratoga" and "Ticonderoga," in the centre. Macdonough's ship was then exposed to the concentrated fire of the "Confiance" and "Linnet," and his battery was soon silenced. The "Saratoga" could no longer use a gun on the engaged side, and the battle was nearly lost.

Then Macdonough's forethought changed the impending defeat into victory. His fire had nearly silenced the "Confiance," and disregarding the "Linnet," he ceased attention to the battle in order to direct the operation of winding ship. Little by little hauling the ship about, he opened on the "Confiance" with one gun after another of the fresh broadside, as they bore; and the "Confiance," after trying in vain to

[1] Report of Captain Pring, Sept. 12, 1814; James, Appendix no. 90.
[2] Report of Commodore Macdonough, Sept. 13, 1814; Niles, vii. 41.
[3] Howard Douglas's Naval Gunnery, p. 115. (Fourth edition).

effect the same operation, struck her colors. Then the British fleet was in the situation which Downie had anticipated for the Americans in the event of silencing the "Saratoga." The three smaller vessels were obliged to surrender, and the gunboats alone escaped. The battle had lasted from quarter past eight till quarter before eleven.

By land, the British attack was much less effective than by water. The troops were slow in reaching their positions, and had time to make no decisive movement. A column under Major-General Robinson was ordered to move round by the right flank to a ford previously reconnoitred, some distance up the Saranac, in order to gain a position whence they could reverse the American works and carry them by assault; but Robinson's column missed its way, and before reaching the ford heard the cheers of the American troops, and halted to ascertain its cause.[1] The remainder of the army waited for Robinson's column to assault. The casualties showed that nothing like a serious engagement took place. The entire loss of the British army from September 6 to September 14 was officially reported as only thirty-seven killed and one hundred and fifty wounded, and of this loss a large part occurred previous to the battle of September 11. The entire American loss was thirty-seven killed and sixty-two wounded.

In the naval battle, Macdonough reported fifty-two killed and fifty-eight wounded, among about eight hundred and eighty men. The British reported fifty-seven killed and seventy-two wounded, in crews whose number was never precisely known, but was probably fully eight hundred. In neither case was the loss, though severe, as great relatively to the numbers as the severity of the action seemed to imply. The "Saratoga" lost twenty-eight killed in a crew of two hundred and forty. In Perry's battle on Lake Erie, the "Lawrence" lost twenty-two men killed in a crew of one hundred and thirty-one. About one man in eight was killed on Macdonough's ship; about one man in six on Perry's.

With needless precipitation, Prevost instantly retreated the next day to Champlain, sacrificing stores to a very great amount, and losing many men by desertion. The army was

[1] Christie, ii. 215, 216.

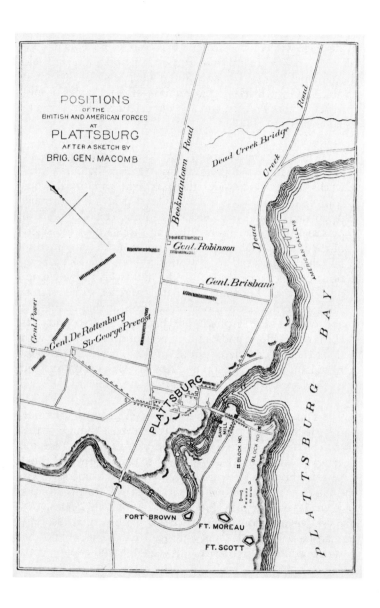

POSITIONS
OF THE
BRITISH AND AMERICAN FORCES
AT
PLATTSBURG
AFTER A SKETCH BY
BRIG. GEN. MACOMB

Beekmantown Road

Dead Creek Bridge

Dead Creek

AMERICAN GALLEYS

Genl. Robinson

Genl. Brisbane

Genl. Power

Genl. De Rottenburg

Sir George Prevost

PLATTSBURG

PLATTSBURG BAY

SAW MILL

BLOCK HO.

BLOCK HO.

FORT BROWN

FT. MOREAU

FT. SCOTT

cruelly mortified, and Prevost lost whatever military reputation he still preserved in Canada. In England the impression of disgrace was equally strong. "It is scarcely possible to conceive the degree of mortification and disappointment," said the "Annual Register,"[1] " which the intelligence of this defeat created in Great Britain." Yeo brought official charges of misconduct against Prevost, and Prevost defended himself by unusual arguments.

"With whatever sorrow I may think of the unfortunate occurrences to which I allude," he wrote to Bathurst, three weeks later,[2] "I consider them as light and trivial when compared to the disastrous results which, I am solemnly persuaded, would have ensued had any considerations of personal glory, or any unreflecting disregard of the safety of the province, or of the honor of the army committed to my charge, induced me to pursue those offensive operations by land, independent of the fleet, which it would appear by your Lordship's despatch were expected of me. Such operations, my Lord, have been attempted before, and on the same ground. The history of our country records their failure; and had they been undertaken again with double the force placed under my command, they would have issued in the discomfiture of his Majesty's arms, and in a defeat not more disastrous than inevitable."

The Duke of Wellington was not so severe as other critics, and hesitated to say that Prevost was wrong; "though of this I am certain, he must equally have returned . . . after the fleet was beaten; and I am inclined to think he was right. I have told the ministers repeatedly that a naval superiority on the Lakes is a *sine qua non* of success in war on the frontier of Canada, even if our object should be wholly defensive."[3] Yet the Duke in conversation seemed to think that his army in Canada was also at fault. "He had sent them some of his best troops from Bordeaux," he said five-and-twenty years

---

[1] Annual Register for 1814, p. 332.
[2] Prevost to Bathurst, Oct. 6, 1814; Christie, ii. 395.
[3] Wellington to Sir George Murray, Dec. 22, 1814; Despatches, xii. 224.

afterward,[1] "but they did not turn out quite right; they wanted this iron fist to command them."

Meanwhile Major-General Izard, by Armstrong's order, marched his four thousand men as far as possible from the points of attack. Starting from Champlain, August 29, the army reached Sackett's Harbor September 17, having marched about two hundred and eighty miles in twenty days. At Sackett's Harbor Izard found no orders from the government, for the government at that time had ceased to perform its functions; but he received an earnest appeal from General Brown to succor Fort Erie. "I will not conceal from you," wrote Brown, September 10,[2] "that I consider the fate of this army very doubtful unless speedy relief is afforded." Izard, who had no means of testing the correctness of this opinion, decided to follow Brown's wishes, and made, September 17, the necessary preparations. Violent storms prevented Chauncey from embarking the troops until September 21; but September 27 the troops reached Batavia, and Izard met Brown by appointment. The army had then been a month in movement. The distance was more than four hundred miles, and no energy could have shortened the time so much as to have affected the result of the campaign. At one end of the line Sir George Prevost retreated from Plattsburg September 12; at the other end, Lieutenant-General Drummond retreated from Fort Erie September 21; and Izard's force, constituting the largest body of regular troops in the field, had been placed where it could possibly affect neither result.

Izard was a friend of Monroe, and was therefore an object of Armstrong's merciless criticism.[3] Brown was a favorite of Armstrong, and shared his prejudices. The position of Izard at Buffalo was calculated to excite jealousy. He had implicitly obeyed the wishes of Armstrong and Brown; in doing so, he had sacrificed himself,—yielding to Macomb the credit of repulsing Prevost, and to Brown, who did not wait for his arrival, the credit of repulsing Drummond. As far as could be seen, Izard had acted with loyalty toward both Armstrong and Brown; yet both distrusted him. Brown commonly

[1] Stanhope's Conversations, p. 252.
[2] Brown to Izard, Sept. 10, 1814; Izard's Correspondence, p. 86.
[3] Notices, ii. 102–107.

inclined toward severity, and was the more sensitive because Izard, as the senior officer, necessarily took command.

Until that moment Izard had enjoyed no chance of showing his abilities in the field, but at Niagara he saw before him a great opportunity. Drummond lay at Chippawa, with an army reduced by battle and sickness to about twenty-five hundred men. Izard commanded fifty-five hundred regular troops and eight hundred militia.[1] He had time to capture or destroy Drummond's entire force before the winter should set in, and to gather the results of Brown's desperate fighting. Brown was eager for the attack, and Izard assented. October 13 the army moved on Chippawa, and stopped. October 16, Izard wrote to the War Department,[2] —

"I have just learned by express from Sackett's Harbor that Commodore Chauncey with the whole of his fleet has retired into port, and is throwing up batteries for its protection. This defeats all the objects of the operations by land in this quarter. I may turn Chippawa, and should General Drummond not retire, may succeed in giving him a good deal of trouble; but if he falls back on Fort George or Burlington Heights, every step I take in pursuit exposes me to be cut off by the large reinforcements it is in the power of the enemy to throw in twenty-four hours upon my flank or rear."

In this state of mind, notwithstanding a successful skirmish, October 19, between Bissell's brigade and a strong detachment of the enemy, Izard made a decision which ruined his military reputation and destroyed his usefulness to the service. He reported to the Department, October 23,[3] —

"On the 21st, finding that he [Drummond] still continued within his works, which he had been assiduously engaged in strengthening from the moment of our first appearance, the weather beginning to be severe, and a great quantity of our officers and men suffering from their con-

[1] Izard to Monroe, Oct. 16, 1814; Izard's Correspondence, p. 100.

[2] Izard to Monroe, Oct. 16, 1814; Izard's Correspondence, p. 103.

[3] Izard to Monroe, Oct. 23, 1814; Izard's Correspondence, p. 105. Cf. Brown to Armstrong, Nov. 28, 1814; Kosciusko Armstrong's "Notice of J. Q. Adams's Eulogy on James Monroe," p. 29.

tinued fatigues and exposure, at twelve at noon I broke up my encampment, and marched to this ground [opposite Black Rock] in order to prepare winter quarters for the troops."

Nothing remained but to break up the army. Brown was sent at his own request to Sackett's Harbor, where the next fighting was expected. A division of the army went with him. The remainder were placed in winter quarters near Buffalo. Fort Erie was abandoned and blown up, November 5, and the frontier at Niagara relapsed into repose.

Izard felt the mortification of his failure. His feelings were those of a generous character, and his tone toward Brown contrasted to his advantage both in candor and in temper with Brown's language toward him; but great energy generally implied great faults, and Brown's faults were better suited than Izard's virtues for the work of an American general at Niagara. Greatly to Izard's credit, he not only saw his own inferiority, but advised the government of it. He wrote to the Secretary of War, November 20,[1] —

"The success of the next campaign on this frontier will in a great measure depend on concert and good understanding among the superior officers. . . . General Brown is certainly a brave, intelligent, and active officer. Where a portion of the forces is composed of irregular troops, I have no hesitation in acknowledging my conviction of his being better qualified than I to make them useful in the public service."

So sensitive was Izard to the public feeling and his loss of standing that he sent his resignation to the secretary, December 18,[2] in terms which betrayed and even asserted his consciousness of shrinking under the weight of responsibility: —

"I am fully aware that attempts have been made to lessen the confidence of government as well as of the public in my ability to execute the important duties intrusted to me,— duties which were imposed unexpectedly and much against my inclination. It is therefore not improbable that my vol-

[1] Izard to Monroe, Nov. 20, 1814; Izard's Correspondence, p. 119.
[2] Izard to Monroe, Dec. 18, 1814; Izard's Correspondence, p. 130.

untary retirement will relieve the Department of War from some embarrassment, and that my individual satisfaction will accord with the public advantage,—especially as my view of the connection between military command and responsibility differs materially from that entertained by persons in high authority."

A man who showed so little confidence in himself could not claim the confidence of others, and in contact with stronger characters like Armstrong, Brown, Scott, or Andrew Jackson could play no part but that of a victim. His resignation was not accepted, but his career was at an end. When he relieved the pressure kept by Brown constantly applied to the extremity of the British line, the movement of war necessarily turned back to its true object, which was Sackett's Harbor. Drummond no sooner saw Fort Erie evacuated and his lines re-established, November 5, than he hurried on board ship with a part of his troops, and reached Kingston, November 10,[1] where Sir George Prevost had already prepared for an attack on Sackett's Harbor as soon as supplies could be brought from Quebec to Kingston over the winter roads. Soon afterward Sir George Prevost was recalled to England, and a new commander-in-chief, Sir George Murray, supposed to be a man of higher capacity, was sent to take direction of the next campaign. Reinforcements continued to arrive.[2] About twenty-seven thousand regular troops, including officers, were in Canada;[3] a seventy-four-gun ship and a new frigate were launched at Kingston; and no one doubted that, with the spring, Sackett's Harbor would be formally besieged. Izard remained at Buffalo, doing nothing, and his only influence on the coming as on the past campaign was to leave the initiative to the enemy.

[1] James, ii. 241.
[2] James, ii. 393.
[3] MSS. Canadian Archives. Freer Papers, 1814, p. 31.

Chapter V

ARMSTRONG'S management of the Northern campaign caused severe criticism; but his neglect of the city of Washington exhausted the public patience. For two years Washington stood unprotected; not a battery or a breastwork was to be found on the river bank except the old and untenable Fort Washington, or Warburton.[1] A thousand determined men might reach the town in thirty-six hours, and destroy it before any general alarm could be given.[2] Yet no city was more easily protected than Washington, at that day, from attack on its eastern side; any good engineer could have thrown up works in a week that would have made approach by a small force impossible. Armstrong neglected to fortify. After experience had proved his error, he still argued in writing to a committee of Congress[3] that fortifications would have exhausted the Treasury; "that bayonets are known to form the most efficient barriers; and that there was no reason in this case to doubt beforehand the willingness of the country to defend itself,"—as though he believed that militia were most efficient when most exposed! He did not even provide the bayonets.

In truth, Armstrong looking at the matter as a military critic decided that the British having no strategic object in capturing Washington, would not make the attempt. Being an indolent man, negligent of detail, he never took unnecessary trouble; and having no proper staff at Washington, he was without military advisers whose opinion he respected. The President and Monroe fretted at his indifference, the people of the District were impatient under it, and every one except Armstrong was in constant terror of attack; but according to their account the secretary only replied: "No, no! Baltimore is the place, sir; that is of so much more consequence."[4]

[1] Lieutenant Edwards's Report of July 25, 1814; State Papers, Military Affairs, i. 545.

[2] Winder to Armstrong, July 9, 1814; State Papers, Military Affairs, i. 543.

[3] Letter of Secretary Armstrong, Oct. 17, 1814; State Papers, Military Affairs, i. 538.

[4] Letter of J. P. Van Ness, Nov. 23, 1814; State Papers, Military Affairs, i. 581.

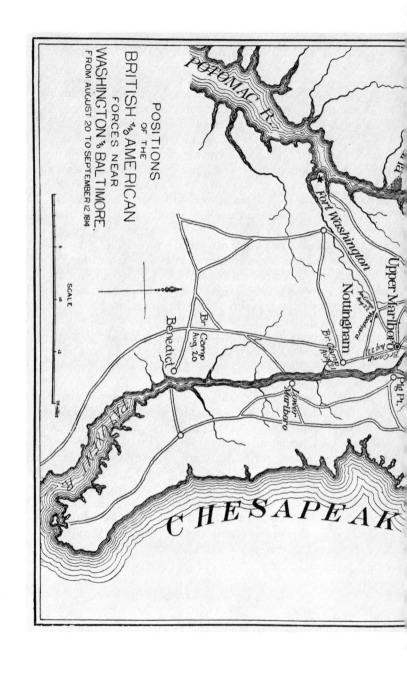

POSITIONS
OF THE
BRITISH AND AMERICAN
FORCES NEAR
WASHINGTON AND BALTIMORE.
FROM AUGUST 20 TO SEPTEMBER 12 1814.

SCALE
5   10   5   20 Miles

POTOMAC R.

Fort Washington

Upper Marlboro

Nottingham

Br. Camp
Aug. 20

Benedict

Br. Camp
Aug. 21

Pig Pt.

Lower
Marlboro

CHESAPEAK

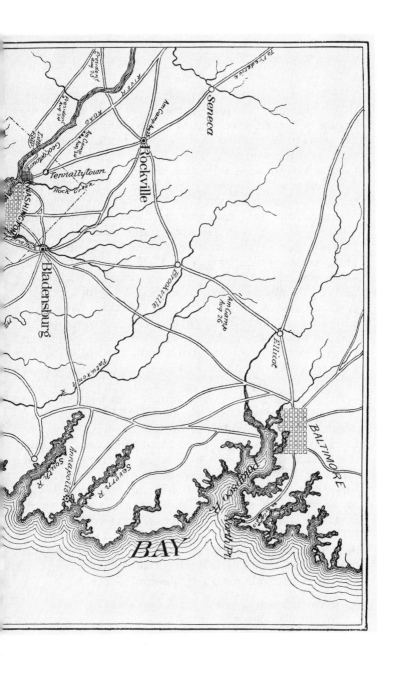

Probably he was right, and the British would have gone first to Baltimore had his negligence not invited them to Washington.

In May the President began to press Armstrong for precautionary measures.[1] In June letters arrived from Gallatin and Bayard in London which caused the President to call a Cabinet meeting. June 23 and 24 the Cabinet met and considered the diplomatic situation.[2] The President proposed then for the first time to abandon impressment as a *sine qua non* of negotiation, and to approve a treaty that should be silent on the subject. Armstrong and Jones alone supported the idea at that time, but three days afterward, June 27, Monroe and Campbell acceded to it. The Cabinet then took the defences of Washington in hand, and July 1 decided to organize a corps of defence from the militia of the District and the neighboring States. July 2, the first step toward efficient defence was taken by creating a new military district on the Potomac, with a military head of its own. Armstrong wished to transfer Brigadier-General Moses Porter from Norfolk, to command the new Potomac District;[3] but the President selected Brigadier-General Winder, because his relationship to the Federalist governor of Maryland was likely to make co-operation more effective.

Political appointments were not necessarily bad; but in appointing Winder to please the governor of Maryland Madison assumed the responsibility, in Armstrong's eyes, for the defence of Washington. The Secretary of War seemed to think that Madison and Monroe were acting together to take the defence of Washington out of his hands, and to put it in hands in which they felt confidence. Armstrong placed Winder instantly in command, and promptly issued the orders arranged in Cabinet; but he left further measures to Winder, Monroe, and Madison. His conduct irritated the President; but no one charged that the secretary refused to carry out the orders, or to satisfy the requisitions of the President or of General Winder. He was merely passive.[4]

[1] Madison to Armstrong, May 20, 1814; Madison's Works, iii. 399.
[2] Madison's Works, iii. 408, 409.
[3] Notices, ii. 140.
[4] Madison's Works, iii. 422, 426.

Winder received his appointment July 5, and went to Washington for instructions. He passed the next month riding between Washington, Baltimore, and points on the lower Potomac and Patuxent,[1] obtaining with great fatigue a personal knowledge of the country. August 1 he established his permanent headquarters at Washington, and the entire result of his labors till that time was the presence of one company of Maryland militia at Bladensburg. No line of defence was selected, no obstructions to the roads were prepared, and not so much as a ditch or a breastwork was marked out or suggested between Annapolis and Washington. Another fortnight passed, and still Winder was not further advanced. He had no more men, arms, fortifications, and no more ideas, on the 18th of August than on the 5th of July. "The call for three thousand militia under the requisition of July 4 had produced only two hundred and fifty men at the moment the enemy landed at Benedict."[2] Winder had then been six weeks in command of the Washington defences.

Meanwhile a British expedition under command of Major-General Robert Ross, a distinguished officer of the Peninsula army, sailed from the Gironde, June 27, to Bermuda. Ross was instructed "to effect a diversion on the coasts of the United States of America in favor of the army employed in the defence of Upper and Lower Canada." The point of attack was to be decided by Vice-Admiral Cochrane, subject to the general's approval; but the force was not intended for "any extended operation at a distance from the coast," nor was Ross to hold permanent possession of any captured district.[3]

"When the object of the descent which you may make on the coast is to take possession of any naval or military stores, you will not delay the destruction of them in preference to the taking them away, if there is reasonable ground of apprehension that the enemy is advancing with superior force to effect their recovery. If in any descent you shall be enabled to take such a position as to threaten the

[1] Winder to Armstrong, July 27, 1814; State Papers, Military Affairs, i. 546.
[2] Winder's letter of Sept. 26, 1814; State Papers, Military Affairs, i. 552.
[3] Bathurst to Ross, 1814; War Office Despatches, MSS. British Archives.

inhabitants with the destruction of their property, you are hereby authorized to levy upon them contributions in return for your forbearance; but you will not by this understand that the magazines belonging to the government, or their harbors, or their shipping, are to be included in such an arrangement. These, together with their contents, are in all cases to be taken away or destroyed."

Negroes were not to be encouraged to rise upon their masters, and no slaves were to be taken away as slaves; but any negro who should expose himself to vengeance by joining the expedition or lending it assistance, might be enlisted in the black corps, or carried away by the fleet.

Nothing in these orders warranted the destruction of private or public property, except such as might be capable of military uses. Ross was not authorized, and did not intend, to enter on a mere marauding expedition; but Cochrane was independent of Ross, and at about the time when Ross reached Bermuda Cochrane received a letter from Sir George Prevost which gave an unexpected character to the Chesapeake expedition. A small body of American troops had crossed Lake Erie to Long Point, May 15, and destroyed the flour-mills, distilleries, and some private houses there. The raid was not authorized by the United States government, and the officer commanding it was afterward court-martialed and censured; but Sir George Prevost, without waiting for explanations, wrote to Vice-Admiral Cochrane, June 2, suggesting that he should "assist in inflicting that measure of retaliation which shall deter the enemy from a repetition of similar outrages."[1]

When Cochrane received this letter, he issued at Bermuda, July 18, orders to the ships under his command, from the St. Croix River to the St. Mary's, directing general retaliation.[2] The orders were interesting as an illustration of the temper the war had taken.

"You are hereby required and directed," wrote the Vice-

[1] Cochrane to Prevost, July 22, 1814; MSS. Canadian Archives. C. 684, p. 221.

[2] Orders of Vice-Admiral Cochrane, July 18, 1814; MSS. Canadian Archives, C. 684, p. 204.

Admiral to the British blockading squadrons, "to destroy and lay waste such towns and districts upon the coast as you may find assailable. You will hold strictly in view the conduct of the American army toward his Majesty's unoffending Canadian subjects, and you will spare merely the lives of the unarmed inhabitants of the United States. For only by carrying this retributory justice into the country of our enemy can we hope to make him sensible of the impropriety as well as of the inhumanity of the system he has adopted. You will take every opportunity of explaining to the people how much I lament the necessity of following the rigorous example of the commander of the American forces. And as these commanders must obviously have acted under instructions from the Executive government of the United States, whose intimate and unnatural connection with the late government of France has led them to adopt the same system of plunder and devastation, it is therefore to their own government the unfortunate sufferers must look for indemnification for their loss of property."

This ill-advised order was to remain in force until Sir George Prevost should send information "that the United States government have come under an obligation to make full remuneration to the injured and unoffending inhabitants of the Canadas for all the outrages their troops have committed." Cochrane further wrote to Prevost that "as soon as these orders have been acted upon," a copy would be sent to Washington for the information of the Executive government.

Cochrane's retaliatory order was dated July 18, and Ross's transports arrived at Bermuda July 24. As soon as the troops were collected and stores put on board, Cochrane and Ross sailed, August 3, for Chesapeake Bay. They arrived a few days in advance of the transports, and passing up the bay to the mouth of the Potomac, landed, August 15, with Rear Admiral Cockburn, to decide on a plan for using to best effect the forces under their command.

Three objects were within reach. The first and immediate aim was a flotilla of gunboats, commanded by Captain Joshua Barney, which had taken refuge in the Patuxent River, and was there blockaded. The next natural object of desire was Baltimore, on account of its shipping and prize-money. The third was Washington and Alexandria, on account of the navy-yard and the vessels in the Potomac. Baltimore was the natural point of attack after destroying Barney's flotilla; but Cockburn, with a sailor's recklessness, urged a dash at Washington.[1] Ross hesitated, and postponed a decision till Barney's flotilla should be disposed of.

Two days afterward, August 17, the troops arrived, and the squadron, commanded by Vice-Admiral Cochrane, moved twenty miles up the bay to the mouth of the Patuxent,—a point about fifty miles distant from Annapolis on the north, and from Washington on the northwest. Having arrived there August 18, Cochrane wrote, or afterward ante-dated, an official letter to Secretary Monroe:[2]—

"Having been called on by the Governor-General of the Canadas to aid him in carrying into effect measures of retaliation against the inhabitants of the United States for the wanton destruction committed by their army in Upper Canada, it has become imperiously my duty, conformably with the nature of the Governor-General's application, to issue to the naval force under my command an order to destroy and lay waste such towns and districts upon the coast as may be found assailable."

The notice was the more remarkable because Cochrane's order was issued only to the naval force. The army paid no attention to it. Ross's troops were landed at Benedict the next day, August 19; but neither there nor elsewhere did they destroy or lay waste towns or districts. They rather showed unusual respect for private property.

At Benedict, August 19, the British forces were organized in three brigades, numbering, according to different British accounts, four thousand five hundred, or four thousand rank-and-file.[3] Cockburn with the boats of the fleet the next day, August 20, started up the river in search of Barney's flotilla;

[1] James, ii. 275, 276; Cockburn to Cochrane, Aug. 27, 1814; Ross to Bathurst, Aug. 30, 1814; James, ii. 492–499.

[2] Cochrane to Monroe, Aug. 18, 1814; State Papers, Foreign Affairs, iii. 693.

[3] Gleig's Washington and New Orleans, p. 51. James, ii. 283.

while the land force began its march at four o'clock in the afternoon abreast of the boats, and camped four miles above Benedict without seeing an enemy, or suffering from a worse annoyance than one of the evening thunder-storms common in hot weather.

The next day at dawn the British army started again, and marched that day, Sunday, August 21, twelve miles to the village of Nottingham, where it camped.[1] The weather was hot, and the march resembled a midsummer picnic. Through a thickly wooded region, where a hundred militia-men with axes and spades could have delayed their progress for days, the British army moved in a solitude apparently untenanted by human beings, till they reached Nottingham on the Patuxent,—a deserted town, rich in growing crops and full barns.

At Nottingham the army passed a quiet night, and the next morning, Monday, August 22, lingered till eight o'clock, when it again advanced. Among the officers in the Eighty-fifth regiment was a lieutenant named Gleig, who wrote afterward a charming narrative of the campaign under the title, "A Subaltern in America." He described the road as remarkably good, running for the most part through the heart of thick forests, which sheltered it from the rays of the sun. During the march the army was startled by the distant sound of several heavy explosions. Barney had blown up his gunboats to prevent their capture. The British naval force had thus performed its part in the enterprise, and the army was next to take the lead. Ross halted at Marlboro after a march of only seven miles, and there too he camped, undisturbed by sight or sound of an armed enemy, although the city of Washington was but sixteen miles on his left, and Baltimore thirty miles in his front. Ross had then marched twenty or twenty-one miles into Maryland without seeing an enemy, although an American army had been close on his left flank, watching him all day.

At Marlboro Ross was obliged to decide what he should next do. He was slow in forming a conclusion. Instead of marching at daybreak of August 23, and moving rapidly on Baltimore or Washington, the army passed nearly the whole

[1] Map of General Ross's Route; Wilkinson's Memoirs.

day at Marlboro in idleness, as though it were willing to let the Americans do their utmost for defence. "Having advanced within sixteen miles of Washington," Ross officially reported,[1] "and ascertained the force of the enemy to be such as might authorize an attempt to carry his capital, I determined to make it, and accordingly put the troops in movement on the evening of the 23d." More exactly, the troops moved at two o'clock in the afternoon, and marched about six miles on the road to Washington, when they struck American outposts at about five o'clock, and saw a force posted on high ground about a mile in their front. As the British formed to attack, the American force disappeared, and the British army camped about nine miles from Washington by way of the navy-yard bridge over the Eastern Branch.

Thus for five days, from August 18 to August 23, a British army, which though small was larger than any single body of American regulars then in the field, marched in a leisurely manner through a long-settled country, and met no show of resistance before coming within sight of the Capitol. Such an adventure resembled the stories of Cortez and De Soto; and the conduct of the United States government offered no contradiction to the resemblance.

News of the great fleet that appeared in the Patuxent August 17 reached Washington on the morning of Thursday, August 18, and set the town in commotion. In haste the President sent fresh militia requisitions to the neighboring States, and ordered out the militia and all the regular troops in Washington and its neighborhood. Monroe started again as a scout, arriving in the neighborhood of Benedict at ten o'clock on the morning of August 20, and remaining there all day and night without learning more than he knew before starting.[2] Winder was excessively busy, but did, according to his own account, nothing. "The innumerably multiplied orders, letters, consultations, and demands which crowded upon me at the moment of such an alarm can more easily be conceived than described, and occupied me nearly day and night, from Thursday the 18th of August till Sunday the 21st,

---

[1] Ross's Report of Aug. 30, 1814; Niles, vii. 277.

[2] Monroe to Madison, Aug. 20 and 21, 1814; State Papers, Military Affairs, i. 537. Winder's Narrative, Ibid. 554.

and had nearly broken down myself and assistants in preparing, dispensing, and attending to them." Armstrong, at last alive to the situation, made excellent suggestions,[1] but could furnish neither troops, means, nor military intelligence to carry them out; and the President could only call for help. The single step taken for defence was taken by the citizens, who held a meeting Saturday evening, and offered at their own expense to erect works at Bladensburg. Winder accepted their offer. Armstrong detailed Colonel Wadsworth, the only engineer officer near the Department, to lay out the lines, and the citizens did such work as was possible in the time that remained.

After three days of confusion, a force was at last evolved. Probably by Winder's order, although no such order was preserved, a corps of observation was marched across the navy-yard bridge toward the Patuxent, or drawn from Bladensburg, to a place called the Woodyard, twelve miles beyond the Eastern Branch. The force was not to be despised. Three hundred infantry regulars of different regiments, with one hundred and twenty light dragoons, formed the nucleus; two hundred and fifty Maryland militia, and about twelve hundred District volunteers or militia, with twelve six-pound field-pieces, composed a body of near two thousand men,[2] from whom General Brown or Andrew Jackson would have got good service. Winder came out and took command Sunday evening, and Monroe, much exhausted, joined them that night.

There the men stood Monday, August 22, while the British army marched by them, within sight of their outposts, from Nottingham to Marlboro. Winder rode forward with his cavalry and watched all day the enemy's leisurely movements close in his front,[3] but the idea of attack did not appear to enter his mind. "A doubt at that time," he said,[4] "was not entertained by anybody of the intention of the enemy to

[1] State Papers, Military Affairs, i. 547, 549.

[2] Winder's Narrative; State Papers, Military Affairs, i. 554. General W. Smith's Statement; State Papers, Military Affairs, i. 563.

[3] Winder's Narrative; State Papers, Military Affairs, i. 554. General W. Smith's Statement, i. 563.

[4] Winder's Narrative; State Papers, Military Affairs, i. 555.

proceed direct to Washington." At nine o'clock that evening Monroe sent a note to the President, saying that the enemy was in full march for Washington; that Winder proposed to retire till he could collect his troops; that preparations should be made to destroy the bridges, and that the papers in the government offices should be removed.[1] At the same time Monroe notified Serurier, the only foreign minister then in Washington, that the single hope of saving the capital depended on the very doubtful result of an engagement, which would probably take place the next day or the day after, at Bladensburg.[2]

At Bladensburg, of necessity, the engagement must take place, unless Winder made an attack or waited for attack on the road. One of two courses was to be taken,—Washington must be either defended or evacuated. Perhaps Winder would have done better to evacuate it, and let the British take the undefended village; but no suggestion of the sort was made, nor did Winder retreat to Bladensburg as was necessary if he meant to unite his troops and make preparations for a battle. Instead of retreating to Bladensburg as soon as he was satisfied—at noon of Monday, August 22—that the British were going there, he ordered his troops to fall back, and took position at the Old Fields, about five miles in the rear of the Woodyard, and about seven miles by road from the navy-yard. Another road led from the Old Fields to Bladensburg about eight miles away. The American force might have been united at Bladensburg Monday evening, but Winder camped at the Old Fields and passed the night.

That evening the President and the members of the Cabinet rode out to the camp, and the next morning the President reviewed the army, which had been reinforced by Commodore Barney with four hundred sailors, the crews of the burned gunboats. Winder then had twenty-five hundred men, of whom near a thousand were regulars, or sailors even better fighting troops than ordinary regulars. Such a force vigorously led was sufficient to give Ross's army a sharp check, and at that moment Ross was still hesitating whether to attack Washington. The loss of a few hundred men might have

[1] State Papers, Military Affairs, i. 538.
[2] Serurier to Talleyrand, Aug. 22, 1814; Archives des Aff. Étr. MSS.

turned the scale at any moment during Tuesday, August 23;
but Winder neither fought nor retreated, but once more
passed the day on scout. At noon he rode with a troop of
cavalry toward Marlboro. Satisfied that the enemy was not in
motion and would not move that day, he started at one
o'clock for Bladensburg, leaving his army to itself. He wished
to bring up a brigade of militia from Bladensburg.[1]

Winder had ridden about five miles, when the British at
two o'clock suddenly broke up their camp and marched directly on the Old Fields. The American army hastily formed
in line, and sent off its baggage to Washington. Winder was
summoned back in haste, and arrived on the field at five
o'clock as the British appeared. He ordered a retreat. Every
military reason required a retreat to Bladensburg. Winder
directed a retreat on Washington by the navy-yard bridge.

The reasons which actuated him to prefer the navy-yard to
Bladensburg, as explained by him, consisted in anxiety for the
safety of that "direct and important pass," which could not
without hazard be left unguarded.[2] In order to guard a bridge
a quarter of a mile long over an impassable river covered by
the guns of war-vessels and the navy-yard, he left unguarded
the open high-road which led through Bladensburg directly
to the Capitol and the White House. After a very rapid retreat
that "literally became a run of eight miles,"[3] Winder encamped in Washington near the bridge-head at the navy-yard
at eight o'clock that night, and then rode three miles to the
White House to report to the President. On returning to
camp, he passed the night until three or four o'clock in the
morning making in person arrangements to destroy the
bridge " when necessary," assuring his officers that he expected the enemy to attempt a passage there that night.[4]
Toward dawn he lay down, exhausted by performing a
subaltern's duty all day, and snatched an hour or two of sleep.

The British in their camp that evening were about eight
miles from Bladensburg battle-field. Winder was about five
miles distant from the same point. By a quick march at dawn

[1] Winder's Narrative; State Papers, Military Affairs, pp. 555, 556.
[2] Winder's Narrative; State Papers, Military Affairs, pp. 556, 557.
[3] Statement of John Law; State Papers, Military Affairs, i. 585.
[4] Winder's Narrative; State Papers, Military Affairs, i. 557.

he might still have arrived there, with six hours to spare for arranging his defence. He preferred to wait till he should know with certainty that the British were on their way there. On the morning of Wednesday, August 24, he wrote to Armstrong:[1] —

> "I have found it necessary to establish my headquarters here, the most advanced position convenient to the troops, and nearest information. I shall remain stationary as much as possible, that I may be the more readily found, to issue orders, and collect together the various detachments of militia, and give them as rapid a consolidation and organization as possible. . . . The news up the river is very threatening. Barney's or some other force should occupy the batteries at Greenleaf's Point and the navy-yard. I should be glad of the assistance of counsel from yourself and the Government. If more convenient, I should make an exertion to go to you the first opportunity."

This singular note was carried first to the President, who, having opened and read it, immediately rode to headquarters. Monroe, Jones, and Rush followed. Armstrong and Campbell arrived last. Before Armstrong appeared, a scout arrived at ten o'clock with information that the British army had broken up its camp at daylight, and was probably more than half way to Bladensburg.[2]

Winder's persistence in remaining at the navy-yard was explained as due to the idea that the enemy might move toward the Potomac, seize Fort Washington or Warburton, secure the passage of his ships, and approach the city by the river.[3] The general never explained how his presence at the navy-yard was to prevent such a movement if it was made.

The whole eastern side of Washington was covered by a broad estuary called the Eastern Branch of the Potomac, bridged only at two points, and impassable, even by pontoons, without ample warning. From the Potomac River to

[1] State Papers, Military Affairs, i. 548.
[2] Captain Burch's Statement, Oct. 12, 1814; State Papers, Military Affairs, i. 574.
[3] Rush's Narrative; State Papers, Military Affairs, i. 542. Winder's Narrative; State Papers, Military Affairs, i. 557.

Bladensburg, a distance of about seven miles, the city was effectually protected. Bladensburg made the point of a right angle. There the Baltimore road entered the city as by a pass; for beyond, to the west, no general would venture to enter, leaving an enemy at Bladensburg in his rear. Roads were wanting, and the country was difficult. Through Bladensburg the attacking army must come; to Bladensburg Winder must go, unless he meant to retreat to Georgetown, or to re-cross the Eastern Branch in the enemy's rear. Monroe notified Serurier Monday evening that the battle would be fought at Bladensburg. Secretary Jones wrote to Commodore Rodgers, Tuesday morning, that the British would probably "advance to-day toward Bladensburg."[1] Every one looked instinctively to that spot,[2] yet Winder to the last instant persisted in watching the navy-yard bridge, using the hours of Wednesday morning to post Barney's sailors with twenty-four-pound guns to cover an approach[3] where no enemy could cross.

No sooner did Winder receive intelligence at ten o'clock Wednesday morning that the British were in march to Bladensburg, than in the utmost haste he started for the same point, preceded by Monroe and followed by the President and the rest of the Cabinet and the troops. Barney's sailors and their guns would have been left behind to guard the navy-yard bridge had Secretary Jones not yielded to Barney's vigorous though disrespectful remonstrances, and allowed him to follow.[4]

In a long line the various corps, with their military and civil commanders, streamed toward Bladensburg, racing with the British, ten miles away, to arrive first on the field of battle. Monroe was earliest on the ground. Between eleven and twelve o'clock he reached the spot where hills slope gently toward the Eastern Branch a mile or more in broad incline, the little straggling town of Bladensburg opposite, beyond a shallow stream, and hills and woods in the distance. Several militia corps were already camped on the ground, which had

[1] Review of J. Q. Adams by Kosciusko Armstrong, p. 7.
[2] William Pinkney's Statement; State Papers, Military Affairs, i. 572.
[3] Secretary Jones's Report, Oct. 3, 1814; State Papers, Military Affairs, i. 576.
[4] Armstrong's Letter; State Papers, Military Affairs, i. 540. Ingersoll's History, ii. 173.

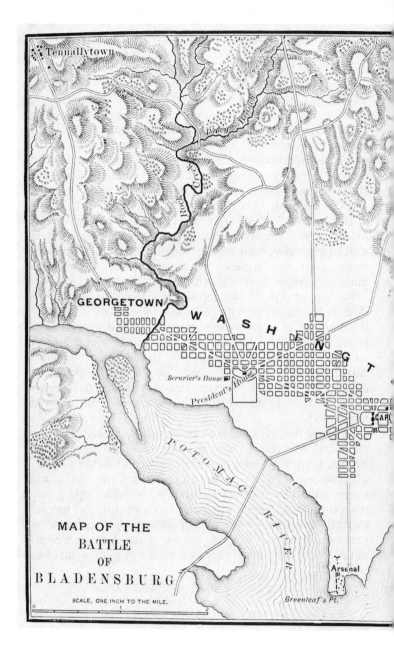

MAP OF THE
BATTLE
OF
BLADENSBURG

SCALE, ONE INCH TO THE MILE.

0   1   2

Tennallytown

Rock Creek

GEORGETOWN

WASHINGTON

Serurier's House

President's House

CAPI

Arsenal

Greenleaf's Pt.

POTOMAC RIVER

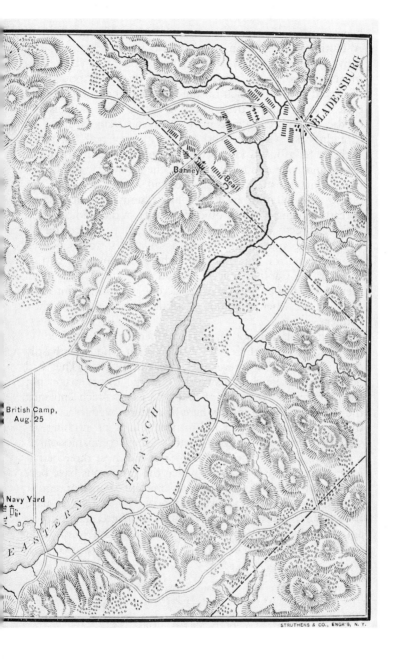

BLADENSBURG

Barne Beall

British Camp,
Aug. 25

Navy Yard

EASTERN BRANCH

been from the first designated as the point of concentration. A Baltimore brigade, more than two thousand strong, had arrived there thirty-six hours before. Some Maryland regiments arrived at the same time with Monroe. About three thousand men were then on the field, and their officers were endeavoring to form them in line of battle. General Stansbury of the Baltimore brigade made such an arrangement as he thought best. Monroe, who had no military rank, altered it without Stansbury's knowledge.[1] General Winder arrived at noon, and rode about the field. At the same time the British light brigade made its appearance, and wound down the opposite road, a mile away, a long column of redcoats, six abreast, moving with the quick regularity of old soldiers,[2] and striking directly at the American centre. They reached the village on one side of the stream as Winder's troops poured down the hill on the other; and the President with two or three of his Cabinet officers, considerably in advance of all their own troops, nearly rode across the bridge into the British line, when a volunteer scout warned them of their danger.[3]

Much the larger portion of the American force arrived on the ground when the enemy was in sight, and were hastily drawn up in line wherever they could be placed.[4] They had no cover. Colonel Wadsworth's intrenchments were not used,[5] except in the case of one field-work which enfiladed the bridge at close range, where field-pieces were placed. Although some seven thousand men were present, nothing deserving the name of an army existed. "A few companies only," said the Subaltern, "perhaps two or at the most three battalions, wearing the blue jacket which the Americans have borrowed from the French, presented some appearance of regular troops. The rest seemed country-people, who would have been much more appropriately employed in attending to their agricultural occupations than in standing with muskets in

[1] Stansbury's Report; Monroe's Letter; State Papers, Military Affairs, i. 561, 536.

[2] Gleig's Subaltern, p. 68.

[3] Letter of William Simmons; State Papers, Military Affairs, i. 596.

[4] Winder's Narrative; State Papers, Military Affairs, i. 557. Stansbury's Report; State Papers, Military Affairs, i. 562.

[5] Van Ness's Letter; State Papers, Military Affairs, i. 580.

their hands on the brow of a bare, green hill." Heterogeneous as the force was, it would have been sufficient had it enjoyed the advantage of a commander.

The British light brigade, some twelve or fifteen hundred men, under Colonel Thornton of the Eighty-fifth regiment, without waiting for the rear division, dashed across the bridge, and were met by a discharge of artillery and musketry directly in their face. Checked for an instant, they pressed on, crossed the bridge or waded the stream, and spread to the right and left, while their rockets flew into the American lines. Almost instantly a portion of the American line gave way; but the rest stood firm, and drove the British skirmishers back under a heavy fire to the cover of the bank with its trees and shrubs. Not until a fresh British regiment, moving well to the right, forded the stream and threatened to turn the American left, did the rout begin. Even then several strong corps stood steady, and in good order retired by the road that led to the Capitol; but the mass, struck by panic, streamed westward toward Georgetown and Rockville.

Meanwhile Barney's sailors, though on the run, could not reach the field in time for the attack, and halted on the hillside, about a mile from Bladensburg, at a spot just outside the District line. The rout had then begun, but Barney put his five pieces in position and waited for the enemy. The American infantry and cavalry that had not fled westward moved confusedly past the field where the sailors stood at their guns. Winder sent Barney no orders, and Barney, who was not acting under Winder, but was commander-in-chief of his own forces under authority of the Navy Department, had no idea of running away. Four hundred men against four thousand were odds too great even for sailors, but a battle was not wholly disgraceful that produced such a commander and such men. Barney's account of the combat was as excellent as his courage:[1] —

"At length the enemy made his appearance on the main road in force and in front of my battery, and on seeing us made a halt. I reserved our fire. In a few minutes the enemy again advanced, when I ordered an eighteen-pounder to be

[1] Barney's Report of Aug. 29, 1814; State Papers, Military Affairs, i. 579.

fired, which completely cleared the road; shortly after, a second and a third attempt was made by the enemy to come forward, but all were destroyed. They then crossed over into an open field, and attempted to flank our right. He was met there by three twelve-pounders, the marines under Captain Miller, and my men acting as infantry, and again was totally cut up. By this time not a vestige of the American army remained, except a body of five or six hundred posted on a height on my right, from which I expected much support from their fine situation."

Such a battle could not long continue. The British turned Barney's right; the corps on the height broke and fled,[1] and the British, getting into the rear, fired down upon the sailors. The British themselves were most outspoken in praise of Barney's men. "Not only did they serve their guns with a quickness and precision that astonished their assailants," said the Subaltern, "but they stood till some of them were actually bayoneted with fuses in their hands; nor was it till their leader was wounded and taken, and they saw themselves deserted on all sides by the soldiers, that they left the field." Barney held his position nearly half an hour, and then, being severely wounded, ordered his officers to leave him where he lay. There he was taken by the British advance, and carried to their hospital at Bladensburg. The British officers, admiring his gallantry, treated him, he said, " with the most marked attention, respect, and politeness as if I was a brother,"—as though to show their opinion that Barney instead of Winder should have led the American army.

After the sailors retired, at about four o'clock, the British stopped two hours to rest. Their victory, easy as it seemed, was not cheaply bought. General Ross officially reported sixty-four killed and one hundred and eighty-five wounded.[2] A loss of two hundred and fifty men among fifteen hundred said to be engaged[3] was not small; but Gleig, an officer of the light brigade, himself wounded, made twice, at long intervals, an assertion which he must have intended as a contra-

[1] Colonel Beall's Statement; State Papers, Military Affairs, i. 571.
[2] James, ii. 499.
[3] Cockburn to Cochrane, Aug. 27, 1814; James, ii. 493.

diction of the official report. "The loss on the part of the English was severe," he said,[1] "since out of two thirds of the army which were engaged upward of five hundred men were killed and wounded." According to this assertion, Ross lost five hundred men among three thousand engaged, or one in six. Had Winder inflicted that loss while the British were still on the Patuxent, Ross would have thought long before risking more, especially as Colonel Thornton was among the severely injured. The Americans reported only twenty-six killed and fifty-one wounded.

At six o'clock, after a rest of two hours, the British troops resumed their march; but night fell before they reached the first houses of the town. As Ross and Cockburn, with a few officers, advanced before the troops, some men, supposed to have been Barney's sailors, fired on the party from the house formerly occupied by Gallatin, at the northeast corner of Capitol Square. Ross's horse was killed, and the general ordered the house to be burned, which was done. The army did not enter the town, but camped at eight o'clock a quarter of a mile east of the Capitol. Troops were then detailed to burn the Capitol, and as the great building burst into flames, Ross and Cockburn, with about two hundred men, marched silently in the darkness to the White House, and set fire to it. At the same time Commodore Tingey, by order of Secretary Jones, set fire to the navy-yard and the vessels in the Eastern Branch. Before midnight the flames of three great conflagrations made the whole country light, and from the distant hills of Maryland and Virginia the flying President and Cabinet caught glimpses of the ruin their incompetence had caused.

Serurier lived then in the house built by John Tayloe in 1800, called the Octagon, a few hundred yards from the War and Navy Departments and the White House.[2] He was almost the only civil official left in Washington, and hastened to report the event to Talleyrand:[3] —

"I never saw a scene at once more terrible and more magnificent. Your Highness, knowing the picturesque nature

[1] Campaigns, p. 67; Cf. Barney to the National Intelligencer. Niles, vii. Supplement, p. 159.
[2] Benjamin Ogle Tayloe. In Memoriam, p. 154.
[3] Serurier to Talleyrand, Aug. 22 and 27, 1814. Archives des Aff. Étr. MSS.

and the grandeur of the surroundings, can form an idea of it. A profound darkness reigned in the part of the city that I occupy, and we were left to conjectures and to the lying reports of negroes as to what was passing in the quarter illuminated by these frightful flames. At eleven o'clock a colonel, preceded by torches, was seen to take the direction of the White House, which is situated quite near mine; the negroes reported that it was to be burned, as well as all those pertaining to government offices. I thought best, on the moment, to send one of my people to the general with a letter, in which I begged him to send a guard to the house of the Ambassador of France to protect it. . . . My messenger found General Ross in the White House, where he was collecting in the drawing-room all the furniture to be found, and was preparing to set fire to it. The general made answer that the King's Hotel should be respected as much as though his Majesty were there in person; that he would give orders to that effect; and that if he was still in Washington the next day, he would have the pleasure to call on me."

Ross and Cockburn alone among military officers, during more than twenty years of war, considered their duty to involve personal incendiarism. At the time and subsequently various motives were attributed to them,—such as the duty of retaliation,—none of which was alleged by either of them as their warranty.[1] They burned the Capitol, the White House, and the Department buildings because they thought it proper, as they would have burned a negro kraal or a den of pirates. Apparently they assumed as a matter of course that the American government stood beyond the pale of civilization; and in truth a government which showed so little capacity to defend its capital, could hardly wonder at whatever treatment it received.

A violent thunder-storm checked the flames; but the next morning, Thursday, August 25, fresh detachments of troops were sent to complete the destruction of public property. Without orders from his Government, Ross converted his campaign, which till then had been creditable to himself and

[1] Reports of Ross and Cockburn; James, ii. 499.

flattering to British pride, into a marauding raid of which no sensible Englishman spoke without mortification. Cockburn amused himself by revenging his personal grievances on the press which had abused him. Mounted on a brood mare, white, uncurried, with a black foal trotting by her side, the Admiral attacked the office of the "National Intelligencer," and superintended the destruction of the types. "Be sure that all the C's are destroyed," he ordered, "so that the rascals cannot any longer abuse my name."[1] Ross was anxious to complete the destruction of the public buildings with the least possible delay, that the army might retire without loss of time;[2] and the work was pressed with extreme haste. A few private buildings were burned, but as a rule private property was respected, and no troops except small detachments were allowed to leave the camp.

Soon after noon, while the work was still incomplete, a tornado burst on the city and put an end to the effort. An accidental explosion at the navy-yard helped to check destruction. Ross could do no more, and was in haste to get away. No sooner had the hurricane, which lasted nearly two hours and seemed especially violent at the camp, passed over, than Ross began preparations to retire. With precautions wholly unnecessary, leaving its camp-fires burning, the British column in extreme silence, after nine o'clock at night, began its march. Passing Bladensburg, where the dead were still unburied, Ross left his wounded in the hospital to American care, and marched all night till seven o'clock Friday morning, when the troops, exhausted with fatigue, were allowed a rest. At noon they were again in motion, and at night-fall, after marching twenty-five miles within twenty-four hours, they arrived at Marlboro. Had the advance from Benedict been equally rapid, Ross would have entered Washington without a skirmish.

[1] Ingersoll's History, ii. 189.
[2] Ross's Report of Aug. 30, 1814; James, ii. 496.

Chapter VI

WHILE ROSS and Cockburn were hastily burning the White House and the Department buildings, anxious only to escape, and never sending more than two hundred soldiers beyond Capitol Square, the President, his Cabinet, his generals, and his army were performing movements at which even the American people, though outraged and exasperated beyond endurance, could not but laugh.

The President, after riding over the battle-field until the action began, remarked to Monroe and Armstrong that "it would be now proper for us to retire in the rear, leaving the military movement to military men," which they did.[1] A moment afterward the left of the line gave way, and the panic-stricken militia poured along the road leading westward toward the point which in later times became known as the Soldier's Home. The President retired with them, "continuing to move slowly toward the city," according to Monroe, in company with Attorney-General Rush. The slowness of movement, on which Monroe seemed to lay stress, was compensated by steadiness. The President left Bladensburg battle-field toward two o'clock. He had already ridden in the early morning from the White House to the navy-yard, and thence to Bladensburg,—a distance of eight miles at the least. He had six miles to ride, on a very hot August day, over a road encumbered by fugitives. He was sixty-three years old, and had that day already been in the saddle since eight o'clock in the morning, probably without food. Soon after three o'clock he reached the White House, where all was confusion and flight.[2] He had agreed with his Cabinet, in case of disaster, to meet them at Frederick in Maryland, fifty miles away, but he did not go toward Frederick. Before six o'clock he crossed the Potomac in a boat from the White House grounds, and started by carriage westward, apparently intending to join his wife and accompany her to his residence at Montpelier in

[1] Monroe's Letter, Nov. 13, 1814; State Papers, Military Affairs, i. 537.
[2] Mrs. Madison to her sister, Aug. 24, 1814; Memoirs and Letters of Dolly Madison, p. 108.

Loudoun County, adjoining Frederick County, on the south side of the Potomac. Secretary Jones, Attorney-General Rush, and one or two other gentlemen accompanied him. In the midst of a troop of fugitives they travelled till dark, and went about ten miles, passing the night at a house "a few miles above the lower falls."[1]

The next morning, August 25, the President travelled about six miles and joined his wife at an inn on the same road, where he remained during the tornado, subjected to no little discomfort and some insult from fugitives who thought themselves betrayed. Although far beyond reach of the British troops and some twenty miles from their camp, the panic was still so great as to cause an alarm on the following night, which drove Madison from his bed for refuge in the Virginia woods,[2] at the time when Ross's army, more than twenty miles distant, was marching at the utmost speed in the opposite direction.

Of all the rulers, monarchical or republican, whose capitals were occupied by hostile armies in the Napoleonic wars, Madison was personally the most roughly treated. Monroe's adventures were not less mortifying. As a scout the Secretary of State's services were hardly so valuable as those of a common trooper, for he was obliged to be more cautious; as a general, his interference with the order of battle at Bladensburg led to sharp criticisms from General Stansbury, whose arrangements he altered,[3] and to the epithet of "busy and blundering tactician" from Armstrong.[4] After the battle he was not less busy, and opinions greatly differed whether he was less blundering. He did not return to the White House with Madison, but joined Winder and rode with him to the Capitol, where he assented to an evacuation, and retired after the flying troops through Georgetown, passing the night on the Maryland side of the Potomac. The next morning, August 25, he crossed the river and overtook the President. After an

[1] Memorandum of Colonel Monroe; MSS. State Department Archives.
[2] Ingersoll's History, ii. 208; Memoirs and Letters of Dolly Madison, p. 116.
[3] Report of General Stansbury, Nov. 15, 1814; State Papers, Military Affairs, i. 560.
[4] Notices, ii. 148.

interview with him, Monroe recrossed the river to Winder's headquarters at Montgomery Court House, where he resumed military functions.

The Secretary of the Treasury, G. W. Campbell, on the morning of the battle went to the Cabinet meeting at the navy-yard, but his health, which had become much affected, obliged him to return to his lodgings instead of riding to Bladensburg. In parting from Madison, Campbell lent him a pair of pistols, which the President put in his holsters. Federalists were curious to know whether the pistols were the same with which he shot Barent Gardenier, but learned only that they were fine duelling pistols, and that they were stolen from the President's holsters during his short stay at the White House after the battle. The secretary's duelling pistols became the best known of all the weapons unused that day; but the secretary himself made no further appearance on the scene. He went to Frederick. The Secretary of the Navy and the Attorney-General accompanied the President, and shared his fortunes.

Although ridicule without end was showered on the President and the other civilians, their conduct was on the whole creditable to their courage and character; but of the commanding general no kind word could be said. Neither William Hull, Alexander Smyth, Dearborn, Wilkinson, nor Winchester showed such incapacity as Winder either to organize, fortify, fight, or escape. When he might have prepared defences, he acted as scout; when he might have fought, he still scouted; when he retreated, he retreated in the wrong direction; when he fought, he thought only of retreat; and whether scouting, retreating, or fighting, he never betrayed an idea. In the brief moment of his preparations on the field at Bladensburg he found time to give the characteristic order to his artillery: "When you retreat, take notice that you must retreat by the Georgetown road."[1] When he left the field of Bladensburg he rode past Barney's sailors, at their guns, and sent his aid to Colonel Beall, on the hill covering Barney's right, with an order to retreat.[2] "After accompanying the

[1] Statement of John Law, Nov. 10, 1814; State Papers, Military Affairs, p. 585.

[2] Wilkinson's Memoirs, i. 786.

retreating army within two miles of the Capitol, I rode forward for the purpose of selecting a position."[1] He reached the Capitol first, and was presently joined there by Monroe and Armstrong. Having decided not to fight at the Capitol, or at any point between the Capitol and Georgetown, he rode to Georgetown.[2] Behind Rock Creek his army would have been safe, and he could certainly have rallied more than a thousand men to stop the panic; but he thought a farther retreat necessary, and went on to the heights. On the heights nothing could reach him without hours of warning, but he rode three miles farther to Tenallytown. At Tenallytown his exhausted men stopped a moment from inability to run farther, yet he seemed angry at their fatigue. Struck by a fresh panic at the glare of the burning city, he pressed his men on at midnight. "After waiting in this position [Tenallytown] until I supposed I collected all the force that could be gathered, I proceeded about five miles farther on the river road, which leads a little wide to the left of Montgomery Court House, and in the morning gave orders for the whole to assemble at Montgomery Court House." The river road was the road that led farthest from the enemy westward, when every motive required retreat toward Baltimore if anywhere. The next morning Winder returned to the Rockville road, till he reached Rockville, or Montgomery Court House, sixteen miles from Washington, where at last he paused.

From the beginning to the end of the campaign Winder showed no military quality. In other respects his conduct tallied with his behavior in the field. He lost no opportunity of throwing responsibility on the President and on his troops, and he so far succeeded as to save himself from public anger by encouraging the idea that the President and the Cabinet had directed the campaign. Universal as that belief was, and continued to be, it was without foundation. While Winder courted advice from every quarter, and threw on the President at every instant the responsibility for every movement, neither the President nor the Cabinet showed a disposition to interfere with his authority in any way except to give the

[1] Winder's Narrative; State Papers, Military Affairs, p. 558.

[2] Armstrong's Notices, ii. 231; Appendix no. 28. Winder's Narrative; State Papers, Military Affairs, p. 559.

support he asked. Under the strongest temptation they abstained even from criticism.

More than all the rest, Armstrong refrained from interference with the movements of Winder. Of all the unfortunate or incapable generals of the war, Winder was the one whom Armstrong treated with least bitterness,[1] although he was not Armstrong's choice, and was the direct cause of the secretary's ruin. So careful was Armstrong not to interfere, that his non-interference became the chief charge against him. At one moment the President told the secretary that he interfered too much, at another moment that he should interfere more; but in truth Armstrong was the only man connected with the defence of Washington whom no one charged with being ridiculous. After August 20 his conduct was not open to reproach. He was cool when others were excited; he tried to check the panic; his suggestions were sensible; he gave all possible aid both to Winder and to the citizens; he attended the President in his expeditions, used wisely such power as he had, and indulged in few words.[2] At the President's request he went to Bladensburg to support and assist Winder; at the President's order he retired after the battle began. He returned, after Winder, to the Capitol, hoping to convert that strong building into a fortress,—a measure not unreasonable, if the regulars and sailors were rallied to make a stand there. When Winder decided to retire to Georgetown, the secretary acquiesced without a word. Then, in pursuance of a Cabinet decision made a few hours before, he set out in company with Secretary Campbell for Frederick, and arrived there in the course of the next day.

Armstrong and Campbell were at Frederick when the British army began its retreat Thursday night; the President was in Virginia, sixteen miles up the river; Winder and Monroe, with the remaining troops, were at Montgomery Court House sixteen miles from Washington. There they learned, Friday morning, that the British had marched toward Bladensburg, probably going to Baltimore; and at about ten o'clock in the morning Winder marched from Montgomery Court House toward Brookville and Baltimore with all his

[1] Notices, vol. ii. chap. v.
[2] Madison's Memorandum, Aug. 24, 1814; Works, iii.. 422.

force. Passing through Brookville, they camped, Friday night, "about half way between Montgomery Court House and Ellicott's upper mills,"[1] and Winder there left them, starting late that evening alone for Baltimore, and leaving Monroe and Stansbury in command, with directions to follow.

Meanwhile the President had crossed the Potomac that morning, expecting to find Winder and Monroe at Montgomery Court House; but on arriving there at six o'clock in the evening, and learning that the army had marched toward Baltimore, he followed as far as Brookville, about ten miles, where he passed the night.[2] Attorney-General Rush was with him. Saturday morning, August 27, the President sent notes to all his Cabinet requesting them to unite in Washington.[3] The same afternoon he returned with Monroe and Rush to the city, which they reached at about six o'clock, after three days' absence.

Armstrong and Campbell, ignorant of the change in plan, waited at Frederick for the President's arrival, while the President and Monroe, Sunday, August 28, began the task of restoring the functions of government. The task was difficult, not so much on account of the British ravages, which had been confined to public property, as on account of the general irritation and the continued panic. Hardly had Ross's army disappeared when a squadron of British war-vessels, under Captain Gordon of the frigate "Seahorse," worked its way up the river, approaching Fort Washington or Warburton August 27. The commander of that post, misunderstanding his orders, abandoned it and crossed the river with his men. Gordon's squadron reached Alexandria the next day, and the town capitulated, since it could not resist. Until August 31 the frigates remained at Alexandria, loading such vessels as were there with the tobacco and other produce which the warehouses contained.[4]

The citizens of Washington and Georgetown, expecting to be visited in their turn, and conscious of their inability to

[1] Stansbury's Report; State Papers, Military Affairs, i. 562.
[2] Madison to Monroe, Aug. 26, ten o'clock P.M.; Ingraham's "Sketch of the Events," p. 61.
[3] Note of Aug. 27, 1814; MSS. War Department Archives.
[4] Report of Captain Gordon, Sept. 9, 1814; James, Appendix no. 84.

resist, talked of a capitulation. Public feeling ran strong against the President. Armstrong was absent. Winder was at Baltimore. Monroe alone was in a position to act, and upon Monroe the President was obliged to depend.

"Under these circumstances," said Monroe in the only authentic account of the event which remains,[1] "the President requested Mr. Monroe to take charge of the Department of War and command of the District *ad interim*, with which he immediately complied. On the 28th, in the morning, the President with Mr. Monroe and the Attorney-General visited the navy-yard, the arsenal at Greenleaf's Point, and passing along the shore of the Potomac up toward Georgetown. Mr. Monroe, as Secretary of War and military commander, adopted measures under sanction of the President for the defence of the city and of Georgetown."

Colonel W[adsworth?] who was placing some guns on the opposite shore refused to obey an order of Monroe to change their position. Monroe rode across the bridge and gave the order in person. The colonel replied that he did not know Mr. Monroe as Secretary of War or commanding general. Monroe ordered him to obey or leave the field, and the colonel left the field.

Monroe's act, whether such was his intention or not, was a *coup d'état*. The citizens, unable to punish the President, were rabid against Armstrong. No one could deny that they had reason for their anger, although the blame for their misfortunes was so evenly distributed between every officer and every branch of government that a single victim could not justly be selected for punishment. Monroe, instead of giving to Armstrong in his absence such support as might have sustained him, took a position and exercised an authority that led necessarily to his overthrow. The influence of such acts on the citizens was obvious. That evening the first brigade of militia held a meeting, and passed a formal and unanimous resolution that they would no longer serve under the orders or military administration of General Armstrong, whom they

---

[1] Monroe's Memorandum; Gilman's Monroe, p. 119.

denounced as the willing cause of the fate of Washington.[1] This mutinous resolution, adopted in the immediate presence of the enemy, was taken to the President by two officers of the brigade, one of whom at least was a strong friend of Monroe.[2]

The resolution of the first brigade was communicated to the President the next morning, Monday, August 29. All the President's recorded acts and conversation for months after the capture of Washington implied that he was greatly shaken by that disaster. He showed his prostration by helplessness. He allowed Monroe for the first time to control him; but he did not dismiss Armstrong. At one o'clock on the afternoon of the same day the Secretary of War arrived in Washington.[3] The President that evening rode to his lodgings. Madison preserved a memorandum of their conversation, and Armstrong also immediately afterward recorded what passed.[4] The President described to the secretary the violent prejudices which existed in the city against the Administration, and especially against himself and the Secretary of War. "Before his arrival there was less difficulty, as Mr. Monroe, who was very acceptable to them, had, as on preceding occasions of his absence, though very reluctantly on this, been the medium for the functions of Secretary of War;" but since Armstrong had returned, something must be done.

Armstrong replied that he was aware of the excitement, and knew its sources; that evidently he could not remain if his functions were exercised by any one else; that he would resign, or retire from Washington at once, as the President preferred.

Madison deprecated resignation, and recommended "a temporary retirement, as he suggested;" and after some further conversation, in which the President complained of the secretary's mistakes, they parted with the understanding that Armstrong should leave Washington the next morning. Armstrong behaved with dignity and with his usual pride; but he

[1] Williams; Capture of Washington, p. 105.

[2] McKenney's Memoirs, p. 47.

[3] Madison's Memorandum; Works, iii. 424. Letter of Jacob Barker, Feb. 8, 1843; Life of Barker, pp. 114, 115.

[4] Armstrong's Letter of Sept. 13, 1814; Niles, vii. 6.

understood, if Madison did not, the necessary consequences of his retirement, and on reaching Baltimore sent his resignation to the President. At the same time he announced it to the public in a letter, dated September 3, containing comments on the weakness of Madison's conduct calculated to close their relations.

Between conscious intrigue and unconscious instinct no clear line of division was ever drawn. Monroe, by the one method or the other, gained his point and drove Armstrong from the Cabinet; but the suspicion that he had intrigued for that object troubled his mind to the day of his death.[1] Even after Armstrong's departure, the dangers and disadvantages of appointing Monroe his successor were so great that for three weeks the post remained unfilled, until, after many doubts and hesitations, Monroe wrote to Madison a letter claiming the appointment of Secretary of War.

"I have thought much of the state of the Departments at this time," he informed the President, September 25,[2] "and of the persons whom it may be proper to place in them, and have concluded that whatever may be the arrangement with respect to other Departments, the Department of War ought to be immediately filled. I think also that I ought to take charge of it. . . . By taking charge of the Department twice, and withdrawing from it a second time, it may be inferred that I shrink from the responsibility from a fear of injuring my reputation; and this may countenance the idea that the removal of the others was an affair of intrigue in which I partook, especially in the latter instance, from selfish and improper motives, and did not proceed from his incompetency or misconduct. It seems due, therefore, to my own reputation to go through with the undertaking by accepting permanently a trust which I have not sought, never wished, and is attended with great responsibility and hazard. By taking the place, all clamor will be silenced. It is known, here at least, that I was put into it when the other could no longer hold it.

[1] McKenney's Memoirs, p. 44.
[2] Monroe to Madison, Sept. 25, 1814; Madison MSS. State Department Archives.

Those who wished it in the first instance will be satisfied, and I shall go on with your support and a favorable expectation of the public that I shall discharge to advantage its duties."

While Monroe in private communications with Madison thus treated Armstrong's retirement as a "removal," due to his "incompetency or misconduct," and Madison apparently acquiesced in that view, in public Madison seemed inclined to convey the idea that Armstrong was not removed or meant to be removed from office, but rather deserted it. Whichever view was correct, Madison certainly dreaded the political effect of appearing to remove Armstrong; and while he gave to Monroe the appointment of Secretary of War, he wrote, September 29, to Governor Tompkins of New York, offering him the State Department.

Governor Tompkins declined the offer. Apart from the great need of his services as governor, the experience of Northern men in Virginia Cabinets was not calculated to encourage any aspirant to the Presidency in seeking the position. Monroe remained Secretary of State as well as Secretary of War. As Secretary of State he had little or nothing to do, which was partly the cause of his activity in military matters; but as Secretary of War he was obliged to undertake a task beyond the powers of any man.

During an entire month after the appearance of the British in the Patuxent, the United States government performed few or none of its functions. The war on the frontiers was conducted without orders from Washington. Every energy of the government was concentrated on its own immediate dangers, as though Washington were a beleaguered fortress. Slowly the tide of war ebbed from the Potomac and Chesapeake, and not until it had wholly subsided could men cease to dread its possible return.

Captain Gordon's squadron began its descent of the river September 1, greatly annoyed[1] by batteries erected on the banks by Commodore Rodgers, Perry, and Porter, who were sent from Baltimore, by order of Secretary Jones, for the purpose. Not until September 6 did Captain Gordon escape from

[1] Report of Captain Gordon, Sept. 9, 1814; James, ii. Appendix no. 84.

his perilous position and rejoin the fleet. Meanwhile the shores of Chesapeake Bay continued to be ravaged with all the severity threatened by Cochrane. Frederick Chamier, afterward the author of several popular sea-stories, was then a lieutenant on the "Menelaus" in Cochrane's squadron, and his recollections in "The Life of a Sailor" gave a lively picture of the marauding in which he took part.[1] Like Napier, Chamier was too tender-hearted for his work. "I am willing to make oath," he wrote, in reply to Captain Scott's contradictions, "that on the day that the 'Menelaus' entered the Potomac, three houses were burning at the same time on the left-hand bank of the river. We burnt more than five ourselves." War was commonly accompanied by destruction, but the war in the Chesapeake was remarkable for the personal share taken by the highest officers, especially by Cockburn and Ross, in directing the actual operation of setting fire to private and public property.[2]

At last the practice caused a disaster that cost the British navy a life more valuable than all the property it could destroy or carry away. The "Menelaus," commanded by Sir Peter Parker, was sent up Chesapeake Bay to divert attention from the general movement of troops and ships on the Potomac.[3] The "Menelaus" took position off the Sassafras River, which Cockburn had cleared of vessels the year before. Nothing in the river could injure the navy, but the "Menelaus" was ordered to make a diversion; and Sir Peter Parker learned from negroes that two hundred militia, encamped behind a wood half a mile from the beach, intended to cross the bay for the protection of Baltimore.[4] One hundred and twenty-four men were landed at eleven o'clock on the night of August 30, and went in search of the militia. Instead of half a mile, they were led by their guides three or four miles, and at last found the militia drawn up, ready to receive them. Sir Peter Parker ordered an attack, and while cheering it on in the moonlight was struck by a buckshot,

---

[1] Chamier's "Life of a Sailor." Preface to Second Edition, chap. xviii.
[2] Life of a Sailor, Bentley, 1850, p. 180.
[3] James, ii. 276.
[4] Report of Acting-Commodore Crease, Sept. 1, 1814; Niles, vii., Supplement, p. 150.

which severed the femoral artery. The sailors carried him back to the ship, but he died long before reaching it.[1] His party escaped with a loss of thirteen killed and twenty-seven wounded besides their captain.

The Americans regretted only that the punishment had fallen on the wrong person, for Cochrane and Cockburn rather than Parker were the true marauders; but the lesson was effectual, and the British became more cautious after Parker's death. Indeed, their activity in the Chesapeake centred thenceforward in an effort to capture Baltimore, which required all their strength.

Baltimore should have been first attacked, but Cockburn's influence by diverting Ross to Washington gave the larger city time to prepare its defence. The citizens themselves, headed by the mayor, took charge of the preparations; and their first act, contrary to the course pursued by Armstrong and Winder at Washington, was to construct intrenchments round the city, and to erect semi-circular batteries at a number of points, mounted with cannon and connected by a line of works. After the capture of Washington the citizens toiled still more earnestly at their task, until a formidable line of redoubts protected the town, and, though not wholly finished, gave cover to the militia. The batteries were manned by sailors, commanded by officers of the navy. The harbor was protected by Fort McHenry, small but capable of defence, and occupied by a strong force of regular troops, sailors, and volunteer artillerists numbering about one thousand, under the command of Lieutenant-Colonel Armistead of the Artillery.[2]

These precautions made the capture of Baltimore impossible by such a force as had taken Washington, even though aided by the fleet. The precise number of troops present in the city, according to the official return for September 10, was twelve thousand nine hundred and ninety-one men present for duty, with eight hundred and ninety-seven officers. The aggregate of present and absent was sixteen thousand eight hundred and five men.[3] The force was ample to man the

[1] Chamier's "Life of a Sailor," pp. 183–191.
[2] Report of Lieutenant-Colonel Armistead, Sept. 24, 1814; Niles, vii. 40.
[3] Army Returns; MSS. Adjutant-General's office, War Department.

works, but the fortifications chiefly decided the result. No army on either side during the war succeeded in storming works in face, except by surprise; and to turn the works of Baltimore a larger army was required than Ross had at his command.

The militia major-general commanding at Baltimore was no other than Samuel Smith, senator of the United States. He had lately passed his sixty-second year. The brigadier-general in the United States service who commanded the military district was W. H. Winder, whose defence of Washington ended abruptly August 24, and who left that neighborhood on the evening of August 26 to take command of the defences of Baltimore. Winder was a Baltimore lawyer, only three years Smith's junior, when Eustis and Madison gave him a regiment in March, 1812. Smith was not disposed to accept the idea of subordination to a man of inferior rank, military and civil, who knew no more of war than Smith knew, and whose career had been twice marked by unusual ridicule. Winder on arriving in Baltimore notified Smith that he should take command, and was astonished when the senator declined to surrender his authority. Winder appealed to the President and to the governor of Maryland, his cousin Levin Winder; but nothing could be done to assist him, and in the end he submitted. Samuel Smith remained in command.

The British leaders having succeeded in turning their demonstration up the Patuxent into an attack on Washington, next decided to make "a demonstration upon the city of Baltimore, which might be converted into a real attack should circumstances appear to justify it,"[1] and sailed from the Potomac September 6 for the Patapsco River. They anchored September 11 off its mouth. From that point Ross's army when landed had only fourteen miles to march, and no water in their way, while Cochrane's fleet had but twelve miles to sail. Compared with the approaches to Washington, the approach to Baltimore was easy.

Ross's troops were all landed at daylight on the northern point, and were in motion by eight o'clock September 12, without firing a shot. Their numbers were differently given

[1] Cochrane's Report of Sept. 17, 1814; James, ii. Appendix no. 73.

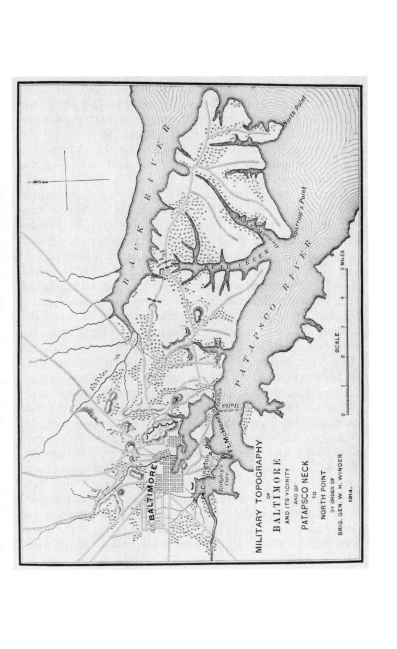

MILITARY TOPOGRAPHY
OF
BALTIMORE
AND ITS VICINITY
AND OF
PATAPSCO NECK
TO
NORTH POINT
BY ORDER OF
BRIG. GEN. W. H. WINDER
1814.

by British authorities,—one reporting them at three thousand two hundred and seventy rank-and-file;[1] the other reckoning them at upward of five thousand.[2] Ross made on the
Patapsco no such leisurely movements as on the Patuxent, but
began his march at once, and proceeded about five miles
without meeting resistance. The light brigade with the
Eighty-fifth regiment was in advance; the second brigade, under Colonel Brooke of the Forty-fourth, followed; and the
third brigade, under Colonel Patterson of the Twenty-first,
formed the rear. At the same time the fleet moved up the
channel toward Fort Henry.

The city was naturally excited at the news that the British
had arrived. General Smith, on receiving the intelligence September 11, detached a brigade of Baltimore militia, under
General Stricker, to check the enemy if possible, and Stricker
advanced that evening about seven miles toward North Point.
His force numbered about three thousand two hundred
men;[3] and with that body of raw militia, a part of whom had
been routed at Bladensburg only a fortnight before, General
Stricker attempted to fight a battle with five thousand old
soldiers. On the morning of September 12 he formed his
troops in three lines three hundred yards apart, apparently in
close order, without cover or protection of any kind, standing
in fields more or less open, and with an exposed flank.[4] Of all
his arrangements, the only one which showed ordinary caution was to send a detachment of cavalry and riflemen a mile
or two in his front. As the British advance approached, the
American outposts fell back, and General Stricker sent forward some four hundred men, partly rifles, as skirmishers.
The British advanced guard coming up, the skirmishing party
fired, but was soon driven back. Ross and Cockburn were
walking together with the advance, and after the firing ceased,
Ross turned back alone to order up the light companies in
anticipation of more serious resistance. On his way he was
shot through the breast from the wood, and fell in the road,

[1] James, ii. 313, 314.
[2] Gleig's Campaigns, p. 116.
[3] Report of General Stricker, Sept. 15, 1814; Niles, vii. 26.
[4] Drawing of line of battle; Lossing, p. 953. Report of Colonel Brooke,
Sept. 17, 1814; James, ii. Appendix no. 71.

where he lay till he was found by the light companies hurrying forward to the scene of the firing. He barely spoke afterward.[1]

The loss of their commanding general was the second heavy penalty paid by the British for their contempt of militia. Colonel Brooke immediately took command, and the advance was not checked; but the loss was not the less serious. When Brooke saw Stricker's line stretching across the field, he did not dash at them at once with the light brigade as Thornton had attacked the larger force and stronger position at Bladensburg, but deployed the whole army and formed a regular order of battle. Although his force easily overlapped and outflanked the American, the engagement that followed was sharp, and the Americans were not routed without considerable loss to the British, who reported forty-six killed and two hundred and seventy-three wounded,—or more than they reported at Bladensburg. The Americans, though routed, suffered less, losing only twenty-four killed, one hundred and thirty-nine wounded, and fifty prisoners, with two fieldpieces.

This spirited little battle detained the British so long that they bivouacked on the field, and passed the night in a drenching rain, resuming their march the next morning, September 13, when they found the roads obstructed, and were obliged to move so slowly that evening arrived before they came in sight of Baltimore.[2] When at last they saw on the distant heights the long line of intrenchments that surrounded Baltimore on the side of their approach, they stopped short. Colonel Brooke had gone forward with the advance, and was engaged all day, at about a mile and a half distance, in studying the American lines. He made arrangements for a night attack, hoping to avoid the effects of the American artillery,[3] and then waited for the fleet to support him.

The fleet all day bombarded the forts and batteries that covered the entrance to the harbor, and continued the bombardment till past midnight. Unlike most naval engagements

[1] James, ii. 315.
[2] Gleig's Campaigns, p. 102.
[3] Brooke's Report of Sept. 17, 1814; James, ii. Appendix no. 71, p. 508.

during the war, this battle was harmless to either party. The heavier British ships feared to approach within range, owing to a barrier of sunken vessels, covered by the guns on shore and by gunboats. Without the heavy ships, the lighter vessels could not maintain a position. The fort sustained no great injury, and only four men were killed and twenty-four wounded.[1] The fleet as far as was reported sustained no injury whatever. The firing ceased toward midnight, and Admiral Cochrane sent word to Colonel Brooke that he could do no more.[2]

"Under these circumstances," reported Colonel Brooke, "and keeping in view your Lordship's instructions, it was agreed between the Vice-admiral and myself that the capture of the town would not have been a sufficient equivalent to the loss which might probably be sustained in storming the heights."

Sir George Prevost at Plattsburg only two days before, with three times the number of troops and a much smaller number of opponents, came to the same conclusion. That both officers were probably wise was shown by the experience of Lieutenant-General Drummond, a month earlier, in attempting to storm the lines of Fort Erie. Brooke and Prevost followed the same course in another respect, for Brooke withdrew his army so rapidly that at noon of September 14 it had already passed the battle-field of two days before, and in another day the whole force was re-embarked.[3]

As soon as the wind allowed, the fleet returned to the lower Chesapeake; and September 19 Admiral Cochrane sailed for Halifax to prepare for a new expedition. The troops remained till October 14 in their transports in the bay, and then set sail for Jamaica, leaving Virginia and Maryland to a long repose, which the vexed shores sorely needed.

[1] Armistead's Report, Sept. 24, 1814; Niles, vii. 40.
[2] Cochrane's Report of Sept. 17, 1814; James, ii. 514.
[3] Subaltern, chap. xiii.

Chapter VII

AFTER BALANCING gains and losses, the result of the campaign favored Great Britain by the amount of plunder which the navy obtained in Alexandria, and by the posts which Governor Sherbrooke occupied between the Penobscot and the Passamaquoddy in Maine. Considering the effort made and the waste of money, the result was a total disappointment to the British people; but even these advantages on land could not be regarded as secure until the British navy and mercantile marine had summed up their profits and losses on the ocean.

At the beginning of the year 1814 the American navy had almost disappeared. Porter in the "Essex" still annoyed British interests in the Pacific; but of the five large frigates only the "President" was at sea. January 1 the "Constitution," Captain Charles Stewart, left Boston and cruised southward, making a few prizes and destroying a British fourteen-gun schooner, but fighting no battle and effecting no object equivalent to her cost. In returning to Boston, April 3, she narrowly escaped capture by the two British frigates blockading the port, and with difficulty got into Marblehead harbor. The "Constitution" did not again go to sea until December 17. During her cruise of three months, from January 1 to April 3, she made four prizes.

The "President" regained New York February 18, and was blockaded during the rest of the year. The "United States" and "Macedonian" remained blockaded at New London. The "Constellation" remained blockaded at Norfolk. The corvette "Adams," twenty-eight guns, ran the blockade of Chesapeake Bay January 18, and cruised until August 17, making nine prizes and several narrow escapes before striking on the Isle of Haut and taking refuge in the Penobscot as the British forces occupied Castine. The story of her destruction has been told. Her fate was the same she would have met had she remained in Washington, where a week earlier the new forty-four-gun frigate "Columbia" and the new twenty-two-gun sloop-of-war "Argus" were burned to prevent them from falling prize to the British army.

This short abstract accounted for all the frigates except the "Essex," whose fortune was no happier than that of the larger ships. October 27, 1812, the "Essex," Captain David Porter, left the Delaware, intending to meet Bainbridge and form part of a squadron under his command. Failing to meet Bainbridge, though constantly near him, Porter at last decided to sail southward; and when Bainbridge in the "Constitution" reached Boston February 27, 1813, the "Essex" had already passed Cape Horn, and was running up the western coast of South America to Valparaiso.

At Valparaiso Porter arrived March 14, 1813, to the consternation of commerce. Chili had recently asserted independence of Spain, and as yet no English war-vessels were stationed in the Pacific. The chief British interest was the whale fishery which centred in the Galapagos Islands,—a group lying under the equator, about a thousand miles from Panama. Although the influence of England was supreme, on account of her naval power, her commerce, and her political alliance with the Spanish people, and although Porter had neither a harbor of his own, nor the support of a diplomatic officer on the Pacific, he had nothing to fear. He was well received at Valparaiso, where since 1811 J. R. Poinsett had held the post of United States Consul-General for Buenos Ayres, Chili, and Peru; but the "Essex" tarried only for supplies, and soon sailed for the Galapagos Islands. There she arrived in April, 1813, and in the course of the summer captured all the British whalers known to be in those seas. These were twelve in number, and after sending some of them away, Porter still had a fleet of five armed ships besides his own, and nothing more to do.

The "Essex" had then been a year at sea, and needed repairs. Porter determined to take his entire fleet of six vessels about three thousand miles to the Marquesas Islands,—as though to make a voyage of discovery, or to emulate the mutineers of the "Bounty." The squadron sailed three weeks over the southern seas, until, October 23, the Marquesas Islands were sighted. There Porter remained seven weeks, amusing himself and his crew by intervention in native Marquesan politics, ending in his conquest of the principal tribes, and taking possession of the chief island in the name of his Government.

That he should have brought away his whole crew after such relaxation, without desertion, was surprising. The men were for a time in a state of mutiny on being ordered to sea; but they did not desert, and the squadron sailed, Dec. 12, 1813, for Valparaiso.

Porter would have done better to sail for the China seas or the Indian Ocean. He knew that British war-vessels were searching for him, and that Valparaiso was the spot where he would be directly in their way. He arrived February 3, and five days afterward two British vessels of war sailed into the harbor, making directly for the "Essex" with the appearance of intending to attack and board her. The crew of the "Essex" stood at quarters ready to fire as the larger ship ran close alongside, until her yards crossed those of the "Essex," and Porter probably regretted to the end of his life that he did not seize the opportunity his enemy gave him; but the British captain, from his quarter-deck only a few feet away, protested that the closeness of his approach was an accident, and that he intended no attack. The moment quickly passed, and then Porter found himself overmatched.

The British frigate "Phœbe," thirty-six guns, had sailed from England in March, 1813, under secret orders to break up the United States fur-establishment on the Columbia River.[1] At Rio Janeiro the "Phœbe" was joined by the "Cherub," a sloop-of-war rated at eighteen guns, and both sailed in search of the "Essex." The "Phœbe" was one hundred and forty-three and three quarters feet in length, by thirty-eight and a quarter in breadth; the "Essex" was one hundred and thirty-eight and a half feet in length, and thirty-seven and a quarter in breadth. The "Phœbe" carried a crew of three hundred men and boys; the "Essex" carried two hundred and fifty-five. The "Essex" was the better sailer, and the result of an action depended on her ability to use this advantage. The broadside of the "Essex" consisted of seventeen thirty-two-pound carronades and six long twelve-pounders; the "Phœbe" showed only eight carronades, but had thirteen long eighteen-pounders, one long twelve-pounder, and one long nine-pounder. At close range, Porter's battery would overpower

[1] James, p. 305.

the "Phœbe's" long guns, but the "Phœbe's" thirteen long-range eighteen-pounders could destroy her enemy without receiving a shot in return. Porter knew all this, and knew also that he could not depend on Chilian protection. No British captain in such a situation could afford to be delicate in regard to the neutrality of Chili, which was not even a recognized nation. At most Porter could hope for immunity only in the port of Valparaiso.

Captain Hillyar of the "Phœbe" made no mistakes. During an entire month he blockaded the "Essex" with his two vessels, acting with extreme caution. At last Porter determined to run out, trusting to a chase to separate the blockading cruisers; and March 28, 1814, with a strong southerly wind, he got under way. As he rounded the outermost point a violent squall carried away his maintopmast. The loss threw on Porter a sudden emergency and a difficult, instantaneous decision. He decided to return to harbor. A young midshipman, David Farragut, who made his first cruise in the "Essex," gave his high authority in after years to the opinion that Porter's decision was wrong. "Being greatly superior in sailing powers," said Farragut, "we should have borne up, and run before the wind." The chance of outsailing the "Phœbe," or separating her from her consort, was better than that of regaining the anchorage.

The wind did not allow of a return to port, and the "Essex" was run into a small bay three miles from Valparaiso, and anchored within pistol-shot of the shore. There Hillyar had her wholly at his mercy. At first he attacked somewhat timidly. Although Porter could bring only three long twelve-pounders to bear, he damaged the "Phœbe's" rigging until Hillyar, in half an hour, hauled off to repair the injury,—or, according to Hillyar's account, the "Phœbe" was prevented by the freshness of the wind from holding a position.[1] Finally the "Phœbe" anchored, and began firing her broadsides of long eighteen-pounders into the "Essex's" quarter. The "Cherub" kept under way, using only her bow guns. Reply was impossible. The crew of the "Essex" fired what guns would bear, and got the ship under way; but the "Phœbe"

[1] Report of Captain Hillyar; James, ii. Appendix no. 71. Naval History, vi. 153.

kept her distance, throwing thirteen eighteen-pound shot into the "Essex" every five or ten minutes, until the "Essex" was cut to pieces and her decks were shambles.

The last attack continued, according to Captain Hillyar, from 5.35 till 6.20 P. M., when the "Essex" struck. The entire battle lasted from four o'clock until the surrender. The carnage was frightful and useless. Porter declared that fifty-eight of his crew were killed. Hillyar claimed one hundred and nineteen unwounded prisoners, while Porter declared the number of unwounded prisoners to be seventy-five. The British ships, with five hundred men, lost only fifteen killed and wounded.

The loss of the "Essex," like the loss of the "Chesapeake" and "Argus," was unnecessary. Porter need not have gone to Valparaiso, or might have tried to run out at night, or might have fought, even after the loss of his maintopmast, under less disadvantage. The disaster completed the unfortunate record of the frigates for the year. They made some sixteen prizes and busied many British cruisers, but won no victories and suffered one bloody defeat.

The sloops told a different story. Early in 1814 three of the new sloops-of-war were ready for sea,—the "Frolic," the "Peacock," and the "Wasp." They were heavy vessels of their class, about one hundred and twenty feet long on the maindeck, and thirty-two feet in extreme breadth; carrying crews of about one hundred and sixty men, with an armament of twenty thirty-two-pound carronades and two long eighteen-pounders. Although only one third the tonnage of the forty-four-gun frigates, and carrying only one third the crew, the new sloops-of-war threw nearly half the weight of metal,— for the broadside of the "Constitution" commonly exceeded but little the weight of seven hundred pounds, while the sloops threw three hundred and thirty-eight. The difference was due not to the weight, but to the range. The frigates carried thirty long twenty-four-pounders; the sloops carried only two long eighteen-pounders. The sloops were rigged as ships, and built with the usual solidity of war-vessels, costing about seventy-five thousand dollars each.

The first to sail was the "Frolic," from Boston, in February. She captured only two prizes before she was herself taken,

April 20, off Matanzas, after a chase by the thirty-six-gun British frigate "Orpheus," assisted by a twelve-gun schooner.

The second sloop-of-war, the "Peacock," commanded by Lewis Warrington, sailed from New York in March. Warrington was a Virginian, thirty-two years old and fourteen years in the service, with the rank of master-commandant in 1813. Cruising down the coast, the "Peacock" first ran in to St. Mary's on the Florida frontier; and then continuing southward, on the morning of April 29, off the Indian River Inlet, she discovered a small convoy on its way from Havana to Bermuda, under charge of the British eighteen-gun brig "Epervier." The British brig was no match for the American ship. She was smaller, and carried only sixteen thirty-two and two eighteen-pound carronades, with a crew of one hundred and three men and fifteen boys.[1] The inferiority was something like four to three; but Captain Wales of the "Epervier" gallantly brought his vessel into action at the usual close-range of these murderous combats.

Captain Wales told the result in an official report, dated May 8, to Vice-Admiral Cochrane.[2] The report was not published, the British Admiralty having become sensitive to the popular outcry against their naval management.

"At eight A. M.," reported Captain Wales, "the wind being about east-south-east, I saw a strange sail in the southwest apparently in chase of us; at nine, perceiving her to near very fast and to be a square-rigged vessel-of-war, I shortened sail and hauled to the wind on the larboard tack to be between her and the convoy, being rather ahead of them. The wind at this time veering round to the southward enabled the stranger to lay up for us. . . . At 9.50 A. M. we weathered her and exchanged broadsides; having passed her beam, we tacked, shortened sail, and continued in close action until eleven A. M., when—five of our larboard guns being disabled by the breeching-bolts giving way, and three others by shot, and unable to manœuvre so as to get the

[1] Commander R. W. Wales to Sir Alexander Cochrane, May 8, 1814; MSS. British Archives.

[2] Commander R. W. Wales to Sir Alexander Cochrane, May 8, 1814; MSS. British Archives.

starboard guns to bear in consequence of the rigging and sails being cut to pieces in the early part of the action by star-shot, the main boom shot away, the foremast wounded in several places, and several shot between wind and water, with four-and-a-half feet of water in the hold, and the enemy seemingly in a state to continue the action—I deemed it prudent to surrender."

The giving way of the breeching-bolts did not wholly disable the guns, for Captain Wales specially commended "Mr. Lawrence Kennedy the Purser, who rendered much service in his exertions at the after-guns by getting them in a fighting state again when unshipped by the fighting-bolts coming out of their places."

At the close of the battle the "Peacock's" hull had not been touched; aloft, her foreyard was disabled and a few upper stays were cut away; of her crew, two men were slightly wounded,—but this was all the injury sustained in running for three quarters of an hour under the close fire of nine heavy guns.[1] The "Epervier" was reported by Captain Warrington as showing forty-five shot-holes in her hull; masts and rigging much cut up, and twenty-three men killed or wounded in a crew of one hundred and twenty-eight. The difference between the force of the two vessels amply accounted for the capture; but the Admiralty might well show unwillingness to admit the bad condition of the vessels-of-war to which it intrusted the duty of convoying British mercantile shipping.[2] So complete was the "Epervier's" disaster that no excuse was offered for it, except the plea that she was in almost every respect inferior to the standard that British vessels of her class were supposed to maintain.

Captain Warrington saved the "Epervier" and brought her into Savannah in spite of two British frigates encountered on the way. He sailed again early in June, and passed the months of July and August in British waters or in the track of British commerce from the Faroe Islands to the Canaries. He burned or sunk twelve prizes, besides making cartels of two more, and brought his ship through the blockade into New York

[1] James's Naval History, vi. 160.
[2] James, pp. 342–347.

harbor, October 30, without injury, with only one man lost and the crew in fine health.[1]

The third new sloop was named the "Wasp" after the famous victor over the "Hornet." The new "Wasp" sailed from Portsmouth, New Hampshire, May 1, under command of Johnston Blakeley. Born in Ireland in 1781, Blakeley was from infancy a North Carolinian. He became in 1800 an officer in the navy. Blakeley and the "Wasp" of 1814, like Jones and the "Wasp" of 1813, ran a career in which tragedy gave a deeper tinge than usual to the bloody colors they won; but their success was on the whole greater than that of any other national cruiser from the beginning to the end of the war. Merely as a story of adventure Blakeley's career was exciting, but romance was its smallest interest. For several reasons the sloop battles and cruises afforded one of the best relative tests of American character and skill among all that were furnished in the early period of the national history; and among the sloops, Blakeley's "Wasp" was the most distinguished.

Blakeley ran directly across the ocean into soundings at the mouth of the British Channel. There he remained during the month of June, searching every vessel that passed. The number of neutrals constantly diverting his attention kept him actively employed, and led him farther into the Channel than was intended; but although three British frigates and fourteen sloops were at sea for the protection of British waters, the "Wasp" continued to burn and sink such British merchantmen as she met,—the first, June 2, and subsequently June 13, 18, 23, and 26,—until on the morning of June 28 a man-of-war brig appeared to windward, and bore down on the American ship.

The day was warm and overcast. During the whole morning the two vessels approached each other so slowly that each had more than time to study his opponent. Once more the foresight of the American ship-builders secured a decisive advantage. The British brig, the "Reindeer," was altogether unequal to the contest. In tonnage she resembled the "Epervier," and her armament was even lighter. Captain Manners, her commander, had substituted twenty-four-pound carronades for the usual thirty-two-pounders, and his broad-side of ten guns threw only two hundred and ten pounds of metal,[1] while the "Wasp's" eleven guns threw three hundred and thirty-eight pounds. The American crew numbered one hundred and seventy-three men; the British numbered one hundred and eighteen. Contest under such conditions was a forlorn hope, but the "Reindeer's" crew were the pride of Portsmouth, and Manners was the idol of his men. They might cripple the "Wasp" if they could not capture her; and probably the fate of the "Argus," a year before, encouraged the hope that the "Reindeer" could do at least as well as the "Pelican."

Each captain manœuvred for the weather-gauge, but the Englishman gained it, and coming up on the "Wasp's" weather-quarter, repeatedly fired his light twelve-pound bow-carronade, filled with round and grape shot, into the American ship. Blakeley, "finding the enemy did not get sufficiently on the beam to enable us to bring our guns to bear, put the helm a-lee," and fired as his guns bore. The firing began at 3.26 P. M. and lasted until 3.40, fourteen minutes, at close range. In that space of time each gun in the broadside could be fired at the utmost three times. Apparently Manners felt that he had no chance with his guns, for he brought his vessel's bow against the "Wasp's" quarter and repeatedly attempted boarding. Early in the action the calves of his legs were shot away; then a shot passed through both his thighs; yet he still climbed into the rigging to lead his boarders, when two balls at the same moment struck him in the head. His fall ended the battle; and such had been the losses of his company that the highest officer remaining unhurt on the British brig to surrender the vessel was said to be the captain's clerk. At 3.45 the "Reindeer's" flag was struck,—the whole action, from the "Wasp's" first gun, having lasted nineteen minutes.

Had every British vessel fought like the "Reindeer," Englishmen would have been less sensitive to defeat. In this desperate action the "Wasp" suffered severely. Her foremast was shot through; her rigging and spars were much injured; her hull was struck by six round shot and much grape; eleven

---

[1] Blakeley's Report of July 8, 1814; Niles, vii. 114.

men were killed and fifteen wounded, or nearly one man in six, "chiefly in repelling boarders," reported Blakeley. The "Reindeer" was a wreck, and was blown up as soon as the wounded could be removed. Of her crew, numbering one hundred and eighteen, thirty-three lost their lives; thirty-four were wounded,—in all, sixty-seven, or more than half the brig's complement.

Ten days afterward Blakeley ran into Lorient, where his ship was well received by the French, whose British antipathies were increased rather than lessened by their enforced submission. After refitting, the "Wasp" sailed again August 27, and four days later cut out a valuable ship from a convoy under the eyes of a seventy-four. The same evening, September 1, at half-past six, Blakeley sighted four vessels, two on either bow, and hauled up for the one most to windward. At 9.26 at night the chase, a brig, was directly under the "Wasp's" lee-bow, and Blakeley began firing a twelve-pound bow-carronade, which he must have taken from the "Reindeer," for no such gun made part of his regular armament.

The battle in the dark which followed has been always deeply interesting to students of naval history, the more because the British Admiralty suppressed the official reports, and left an air of mystery over the defeat which rather magnified than diminished its proportions. The British brig was the sloop-of-war "Avon," commanded by Captain James Arbuthnot, and carrying the usual armament of sixteen thirty-two-pound carronades with two long six-pounders. Her crew was reported as numbering one hundred and four men and thirteen boys. Captain Arbuthnot's official report[1] said that the "Avon" had been cruising in company with the sloop-of-war "Castilian," when at daylight, September 1, he "discovered an enemy's schooner in the rear of the Kangaroo convoy," and gave chase. The "Castilian" also gave chase, and at seven o'clock the twenty-gun ship "Tartarus" was signalled, also in chase.[2] All day the three British sloops-of-war chased the privateer schooner, until at half-past six o'clock in the evening the "Castilian's" superiority in sailing free left the

[1] Report of Captain James Arbuthnot, Sept. 1, 1814; MSS. British Archives.
[2] Report of Lieutenant George Lloyd of the "Castilian," Sept. 2, 1814; MSS. British Archives.

"Avon" out of sight, nine miles astern. The position of the
"Tartarus" was not mentioned in the reports, but she could
hardly have been ahead of the "Castilian." The three British
sloops were then within ten miles of each other, under full
sail, with a ten-knot wind. The weather was hazy, and neither
the "Castilian" nor the "Tartarus" could see that the "Avon"
was signalling the "Castilian" a recall. The "Avon" saw at four
o'clock a large sail on her weather-beam standing directly for
her, and knowing that the "Wasp" was cruising in these waters, Captain Arbuthnot felt natural anxiety to rejoin his
consort.

Captain Arbuthnot's report continued: —

"The stranger closing with us fast, I kept away and set
the weather studding-sails in hopes of nearing the 'Castilian' or 'Tartarus,' the latter of which I had only lost sight
of at 3 P. M. At 7.30 P. M. the stranger had approached
within hail, and being unable to get a satisfactory answer I
had not a doubt of her being an enemy's corvette. At 8.30
he fired a shot over us which was instantly returned with a
broadside. He then bore up and endeavored to rake us, but
was prevented. The action then became general within half
pistol-shot, and continued without intermission until 10.30
P. M., when—having seven feet of water in the hold, the
magazine drowned; tiller, foreyard, main-boom, and every
shroud shot away, and the other standing and the running
rigging cut to pieces; the brig quite unmanageable, and the
leak gaining fast on the pumps; with forty killed and
wounded, and five of the starboard guns dismounted; and
conceiving further resistance only would cause a useless sacrifice of lives—I was under the painful necessity of ordering the colors to be struck to the American corvette 'Wasp,'
the mainmast, almost immediately after, going over the
side."

Lieutenant George Lloyd, commanding the "Castilian," reported September 2 the circumstances attending the loss of
the "Avon," as far as they concerned his share in the matter.[1]
At nine o'clock the "Castilian" heard a very heavy firing in the

[1] Lieutenant Lloyd to Vice-Admiral Sawyer, Sept. 2, 1814; MSS. British
Archives.

north-northeast, and immediately wore and made all possible sail in that direction, burning blue lights. At quarter past ten the firing ceased, "and on coming up I had the mortification to observe the 'Avon' a totally dismantled and ungovernable wreck, with her mainmast gone,—the enemy, apparently a large ship corvette, lying to, to leeward of her, who on my closing made all sail, and evinced every wish to avoid a contest with us."

"I immediately used means to enable me to bring her to close action; and from our superior sailing I had in a few minutes the gratification to be within half a cable's length on her weather quarter. But I lament to state at this anxious crisis the 'Avon's' situation became most alarming; she had commenced firing minute guns, and making every other signal of distress and of being in want of immediate assistance. I must here (as my pen can but inadequately describe) leave you, sir, to judge the feelings of myself, officers, and crew, as, from the confusion which evidently prevailed on board the enemy, the damage she had sustained, and her bad steerage, together with the cool and steady conduct of the officers and men I have the honor to command, I had no doubt of her falling an easy prey could we have persisted in attacking her, but which was not to be done without sacrificing the lives of the surviving gallant crew of our consort. Thus situated . . . I was obliged . . . to leave the flying enemy to escape; but I feel somewhat gratified the situation of the 'Castilian' enabled me to give him a raking, and I doubt not from the closeness of the vessels a most destructive broadside, which he did not return even with a single gun,—a circumstance that, I trust, cannot fail to prove how destructive the 'Avon's' fire must have been."

Lieutenant Lloyd did not explain how his enemy was to bring guns to bear under the circumstances, the "Castilian" tacking under the "Wasp's" stern at half a cable's length distance, and immediately standing in the opposite direction, nor did he say what had become of the "Tartarus." Doubtless the "Wasp" steered badly, her rigging being much damaged; and Blakeley was chiefly intent on keeping off till he could reeve new braces. The "Castilian's" broadside cut the "Wasp's" rigging and sails, and shot away a lower main cross-tree, but did no other serious damage.

The "Avon" lost ten men killed and thirty-two wounded, besides being reduced to a sinking condition in an hour of night action in a ten-knot wind, with two more ships-of-war in sight and hearing. The "Wasp" lost two men killed and one wounded, four round shot in the hull, and the "rigging and sails suffered a great deal."[1]

Blakeley had done enough, and could hardly do more. Besides two eighteen-gun brigs, he made in his cruise fourteen prizes, which he destroyed, several of great value. In that year all the frigates in the United States service had not done as much. With a single-decked ship of five hundred tons, armed with carronades, Blakeley blockaded the British Channel for two months, capturing vessels in sight of ships-of-the-line, and destroying two sloops-of-war in rapid succession, without serious injury to himself, and to the consternation of the British marine.

After sinking the "Avon," September 1, Blakeley held on his course toward Madeira, and there, September 21, captured the brig "Atlanta," which he sent to Savannah. Still later, October 9, near the Cape de Verde Islands, he spoke a Swedish brig, which reported him. After that day no word of tidings was ever received from the "Wasp." Somewhere under the waters of the Atlantic, ship and crew found an unknown grave.

Besides the large sloops-of-war, three smaller vessels — the "Syren," "Enterprise," and "Rattlesnake" — went to sea in 1814. The "Syren" was captured after a chase of eleven hours, nearly on a wind, by the "Medway," seventy-four; her sixteen guns, and everything else that could be spared, were thrown overboard during the chase. The "Rattlesnake" and "Enterprise" cruised in company toward the West Indies, and made some prizes. The "Rattlesnake" was fast, the "Enterprise" a very dull sailer; but after repeated hairbreadth escapes, the "Rattlesnake" was caught, July 11, by the frigate "Leander," with Cape Sable to windward, and was obliged to surrender.[2]

[1] Blakeley's Report, Sept. 11, 1814; Niles, vii. 191.
[2] Letter from the Purser, July 29, 1814; Niles, vi. 391.

The "Enterprise," with her usual good fortune, was never taken, but became a guardship.

After November 1 the United States government had not a ship at sea. In port, three seventy-fours were building, and five forty-fours were building or blockaded. Three thirty-six-gun frigates were laid up or blockaded. Four sloops-of-war were also in port, the "Peacock" having just returned from her long cruise. Such a result could not be called satisfactory. The few war-vessels that existed proved rather what the government might have done than what the British had to fear from any actual or probable American navy. The result of private enterprise showed also how much more might easily have been done by government.

The year 1814 was marked by only one great and perhaps decisive success on either side, except Macdonough's victory. This single success was privateering. Owners, captains, and crews had then learned to build and sail their vessels, and to hunt their prey with extraordinary skill. A few rich prizes stimulated the building of new vessels as the old were captured, and the ship-yards turned them out as rapidly as they were wanted. In the neighborhood of Boston, in the summer of 1814, three companion ships were built,—the "Reindeer," "Avon," and "Blakeley;" and of these the "Reindeer" was said to have been finished in thirty-five working days, and all three vessels were at sea in the following winter. No blockade short of actual siege could prevent such craft from running out and in. Scores of them were constantly on the ocean.

On the Atlantic privateers swarmed. British merchantmen were captured, recaptured, and captured again, until they despaired of ever reaching port. One British master who was three times taken and as often retaken, reported that he had seen ten American privateers crossing his course. A letter from Halifax printed in the London "Times" of December 19 said: "There are privateers off this harbor which plunder every vessel coming in or going out, notwithstanding we have three line-of-battle ships, six frigates, and four sloops here." The West Indies and the Canaries were haunted by privateers. The "Rambler," "Hyder Ali," and "Jacob Jones" of Boston penetrated even the Chinese seas, and carried prize-goods into Macao and Canton. Had these pests confined their ravages to the colonies or the ocean, the London clubs and the lobbies of Parliament would have thought little about them; but the privateer had discovered the weakness of Great Britain, and frequented by preference the narrow seas which England regarded as her own. The quasi-blockade of the British coasts which American cruisers maintained in 1813 became a real and serious blockade in 1814. Few days passed without bringing news of some inroad into British waters, until the Thames itself seemed hardly safe.

The list of privateers that hung about Great Britain and Ireland might be made long if the number were necessary to the story, but the character of the blockade was proved by other evidence than that of numbers. A few details were enough to satisfy even the English. The "Siren," a schooner of less than two hundred tons, with seven guns and seventy-five men,[1] had an engagement with her Majesty's cutter "Landrail" of four guns, as the cutter was crossing the British Channel with despatches. The "Landrail" was captured after a somewhat sharp action, and sent to America, but was recaptured on the way. The victory was not remarkable, but the place of capture was very significant; and it happened July 12, only a fortnight after Blakeley captured the "Reindeer" farther westward. The "Siren" was but one of many privateers in those waters. The "Governor Tompkins" burned fourteen vessels successively in the British Channel. The "Young Wasp" of Philadelphia cruised nearly six months about the coasts of England and Spain and in the course of West India commerce. The "Harpy" of Baltimore, another large vessel of some three hundred and fifty tons and fourteen guns, cruised nearly three months off the coast of Ireland, in the British Channel and in the Bay of Biscay, and returned safely to Boston filled with plunder, including, as was said, upward of £100,000 in British Treasury notes and bills of exchange. The "Leo," a Boston schooner of about two hundred tons, was famous for its exploits in these waters, but was captured at last by the frigate "Tiber" after a chase of eleven hours. The "Mammoth," a Baltimore schooner of nearly four hundred tons, was seventeen days off Cape Clear, the southernmost

[1] James, p. 361.

point of Ireland. The most mischievous of all was the "Prince of Neufchatel" of New York, which chose the Irish Channel as its favorite haunt, where during the summer it made ordinary coasting traffic impossible. The most impudent was probably the "Chasseur," commanded by Captain Boyle, who cruised three months, and amused himself, when off the British coast, by sending to be posted at Lloyd's a "Proclamation of Blockade" of "all the ports, harbors, bays, creeks, rivers, inlets, outlets, islands, and sea-coast of the United Kingdom." The jest at that moment was too sardonic to amuse the British public.

As the announcement of these annoyances, recurring day after day, became a practice of the press, the public began to grumble in louder and louder tones. "That the whole coast of Ireland, from Wexford round by Cape Clear to Carrickfergus," said the "Morning Chronicle" of August 31, "should have been for above a month under the unresisted dominion of a few petty 'fly-by-nights' from the blockaded ports of the United States, is a grievance equally intolerable and disgraceful." The Administration mouthpiece, the "Courier," admitted, August 22, that five brigs had been taken in two days between the Smalls and the Tuskar, and that insurance on vessels trading between Ireland and England had practically ceased. The "Annual Register" for 1814 recorded as "a most mortifying reflection," that with a navy of nearly a thousand ships of various sizes, and while at peace with all Europe, "it was not safe for a vessel to sail without convoy from one part of the English or Irish Channel to another." Such insecurity had not been known in the recent wars.

As early as August 12, the London Assurance Corporations urged the government to provide a naval force competent to cope with the privateers. In September the merchants of Glasgow, Liverpool, and Bristol held meetings, and addressed warm remonstrances to government on the want of protection given to British commerce. The situation was serious, and the British merchants did not yet know all. Till that time the East India and China trade had suffered little, but at last the American privateers had penetrated even the Chinese seas; and while they were driving the British flag into port there, they attacked the East India Company's ships, which were really men-of-war, on their regular voyages. In August the "Countess of Harcourt" of more than five hundred tons, carrying six heavy guns and ninety men, was captured in the British Channel by the privateer "Sabine" of Baltimore, and sent safely to America. The number and value of the prizes stimulated new energy in seeking them, and British commerce must soon yield to that of neutral nations if the war continued.

The merchants showed that a great change had come over their minds since they incited or permitted the Tories to issue the Impressment Proclamation and the Orders in Council seven years before. More than any other class of persons, the ship-owners and West India merchants were responsible for the temper which caused the war, and they were first to admit their punishment. At the Liverpool meeting, where Mr. Gladstone, who took the chair, began by declaring that some ports, particularly Milford, were under actual blockade,[1] a strong address was voted; and at a very numerous meeting of merchants, manufacturers, ship-owners, and underwriters at Glasgow, September 7, the Lord Provost presiding, resolutions were unanimously passed—

"That the number of American privateers with which our channels have been infested, the audacity with which they have approached our coasts, and the success with which their enterprise has been attended, have proved injurious to our commerce, humbling to our pride, and discreditable to the directors of the naval power of the British nation, whose flag till of late waved over every sea and triumphed over every rival.

"That there is reason to believe, in the short space of twenty-four months, above eight hundred vessels have been captured by the Power whose maritime strength we have hitherto impolitically held in contempt."

The war was nearly at an end, and had effected every possible purpose for the United States, when such language was adopted by the chief commercial interests of Great Britain. Yet the Glasgow meeting expressed only a part of the com-

[1] Morning Chronicle, Sept. 6, 1814.

mon feeling. The rates of insurance told the whole story. The press averred that in August and September underwriters at Lloyd's could scarcely be induced to insure at any rate of premium, and that for the first time in history a rate of thirteen per cent had been paid on risks to cross the Irish Channel. Lloyd's list then showed eight hundred and twenty-five prizes lost to the Americans, and their value seemed to increase rather than diminish.

Weary as the merchants and ship-owners were of the war, their disgust was not so intense as that of the navy. John Wilson Croker, Secretary of the Admiralty Board, whose feelings toward America were at best unkind, showed a temper that passed the limits of his duties. When the London underwriters made their remonstrance of August 12, Croker assured them, in a letter dated August 19,[1] that at the time referred to "there was a force adequate to the purpose of protecting the trade both in St. George's Channel and the Northern Sea." The news that arrived during the next two weeks threw ridicule on this assertion; and Croker was obliged to reply to a memorial from Bristol, September 16, in a different tone.[2] He admitted that the navy had not protected trade, and could not protect it; but he charged that the merchants were to blame for losing their own ships. His letter was a valuable evidence of the change in British sentiment:—

"Their Lordships take this opportunity of stating to you, for the information of the memorialists, that from the accounts which their Lordships have received of the description of vessels which had formed the largest proportion of the captures in the Irish and Bristol channels, it appears that if their masters had availed themselves of the convoys appointed for their protection from foreign ports, or had not in other instances deserted from the convoys under whose protection they had sailed, before the final conclusion of the voyage, many of the captures would not have been made. It is their Lordships' determination, as far as they may be enabled, to bring the parties to punishment

[1] Niles, vii. 174.
[2] Croker to the Mayor of Bristol, Sept. 16, 1814; Niles, viii. Supplement, p. 186.

who may have been guilty of such illegal acts, and which are attended with such injurious consequences to the trade of the country."

Little by little the Americans had repaid every item of the debt of insult they owed, and after Croker's letter the account could be considered settled. Even the "Times" was not likely to repeat its sneer of 1807, that the Americans could hardly cross to Staten Island without British permission. Croker's official avowal that no vessel could safely enter or leave one port in the British Islands for another except under guard of a man-of-war, was published on the same page with the memorialists' assertion that the rate of insurance had gradually risen till it exceeded twofold the usual rates prevailing during the wars on the Continent.

The spirit of exasperation shown by Croker extended through the navy. The conduct of Cochrane and Cockburn has been already told. That of Captain Hillyar at Valparaiso was equally significant. Under the annoyance of their mortifications the British commanders broke through ordinary rules. Captain Lloyd of the "Plantagenet," seventy-four, on arriving in the harbor of Fayal, September 26, saw a large brig in the roads, which he must have known to be an American privateer. He was so informed by his pilot. It was the "General Armstrong," Captain Samuel C. Reid, a brig which for two years had fretted and escaped the British navy. The "Plantagenet," with two other ships-of-war, appeared at sunset. Reid dared not run out to sea, and the want of wind would in any case have prevented success. A little after dusk, Reid, seeing the suspicious movements of the enemy, began to warp his vessel close under the guns of the castle. While doing so, at about eight o'clock four boats filled with men left the ships and approached him. As they came near he repeatedly hailed and warned them off, and at last fired. His fire was returned, but the boats withdrew with the loss of a number of men.[1]

Captain Lloyd, in a somewhat elaborate report to explain the propriety of his conduct, enclosed affidavits to prove that the Americans had violated the neutrality of the port. The

---

[1] Letter of Consul Dabney, Oct. 5, 1814; Niles, vii. 253.

affidavits proved that, knowing the character of the vessel, he sent two boats from his own ship to assist the boats of the "Carnation" to "watch" the privateer. His report told the story as he wished it to be understood:[1]

"On the evening of the 26th instant I put into this port for refreshments, previous to my return to Jamaica. In shore was discovered a suspicious vessel at anchor. I ordered Captain Bentham of the 'Carnation' to watch her movements, and sent the pinnace and cutter of this ship to assist him on that service; but on his perceiving her under way, he sent Lieut. Robert Faussett in the pinnace, about eight o'clock, to observe her proceedings. On his approaching the schooner, he was ordered to keep off or they would fire into him, upon which the boat was immediately backed off; but to his astonishment he received a broadside of round, grape, and musketry, which did considerable damage. He then repeatedly requested them to leave off firing, as he was not come to molest them; but the enemy still continued his destructive fire until they had killed two men and wounded seven, without a musket being returned by the boat."

Lieutenant Faussett's affidavit threw more light on this curious story of British naval management. He deposed —

"That on Monday, the 26th instant, about eight o'clock in the evening, he was ordered to go in the pinnace as guard-boat unarmed on board her Majesty's brig 'Carnation,' to know what armed vessel was at anchor in the bay, when Captain Bentham of said brig ordered him to go and inquire of said vessel (which by information was said to be a privateer). When said boat came near the privateer, they hailed (to say, the Americans), and desired the English boat to keep off or they would fire into her; upon which said Mr. Faussett ordered his men to back astern, and with a boat-hook was in the act of so doing, when the Americans in the most wanton manner fired into said English boat, killed two men and wounded seven, some of them mor-

[1] Robert Lloyd to Rear-Admiral Brown, Sept. 28, 1814; MSS. British Archives.

tally,—and this notwithstanding said Faussett frequently called out not to murder them, that they struck and called for quarter. Said Faussett solemnly declares that no resistance of any kind was made, nor could they do it, not having any arms, nor of course sent to attack said vessel."

Lieutenant Faussett's affidavit proved that the "General Armstrong" had good reason for firing into the British boats. The "Carnation" had anchored within pistol-shot of the privateer; four boats of the "Plantagenet" and "Carnation," filled with men, were on the water watching her in the moonlight; every act of the British squadron pointed to an attack, when Captain Bentham ordered the pinnace "to go and inquire" of the vessel, known to be an American privateer, what armed vessel it was. If Captain Bentham did not intend to provoke a shot from the privateer, his order was wanting in intelligence. Lieutenant Faussett accordingly approached in the pinnace, the other boats being not far behind. That his men were unarmed was highly improbable to the privateer, which affirmed that their fire killed one of the American crew and wounded the first lieutenant;[1] but their armament had little to do with the matter. They approached as enemies, in the night, with a large armed force immediately behind them. The privateer repeatedly warned them off. Instead of obeying the order, Lieutenant Faussett came alongside. When he was fired on, he was so near that by his own account he shoved off with the boat-hook. Considering who and where he was, he had reason to be thankful that any of his boat's-crew escaped.

Captain Lloyd's report continued:—

"This conduct, in violating the neutrality of this port, I conceive left me no alternative but that of destroying her. I therefore repeatedly ordered Captain Bentham to tow in the brig and take that step immediately. All the boats of this ship and the 'Rota' were sent under his orders to tow him alongside or assist him in the attack, as circumstances might require; but from continued light baffling winds and a lee tide he was not able, as he informed me, with his utmost exertions to put my orders in execution."

[1] Letter of Captain Reid, Oct. 4, 1814; Niles, vii. Supplement, p. 167.

Meanwhile Captain Reid of the "General Armstrong" warped his vessel close to the beach, under the fort, and made all his preparations for the attack which he knew must come. The people of the town, with the governor among them, lined the shore, and witnessed the affair. Captain Lloyd's report told the result: —

"Finding the privateer was warping under the fort very fast, Captain Bentham judged it prudent to lose no time, and about twelve o'clock ordered the boats to make the attack. A more gallant, determined one never was made, led on by Lieutenants Matterface of the 'Rota' and Bowerbank of this ship; and every officer and man displayed the greatest courage in the face of a heavy discharge of great guns and musketry. But from her side being on the rocks (which was not known at the time), and every American in Fayal, exclusive of part of the crew, being armed and concealed in these rocks, which were immediately over the privateer, it unfortunately happened when these brave men gained the deck they were under the painful necessity of returning to their boats, from the very destructive fire kept up by those above them from the shore, who were in complete security, — and I am grieved to add, not before many lives were lost exclusive of the wounded."

As far as the accounts[1] agree, the boats were twelve in number, with about two hundred men. The privateersmen numbered ninety. As the boats approached, the guns opened on them; and when they came alongside the privateer they found the boarding-nettings up, with a desperate crew behind. So vigorously did the British seamen attack, that they gained the forecastle for a time. All three American lieutenants were killed or disabled, and Captain Reid fought his brig alone; but the deck was at last cleared, and the surviving assailants dropped into their boats or into the water.

Proverbially, an unsuccessful boat-attack was the most fatal of all services. The British loss was excessive. According to their report at the time, "Lieutenants Bowerbank, Coswell,

[1] Niles, vii. 255. James's Naval History, vi. 509. Cf. Letter from Fayal, Oct. 15, 1814. Cobbett's "Weekly Register," reprinted in Niles, vii. Supplement, p. 171.

and Rogers of the 'Rota' were killed, as well as thirty-eight
seamen, and eighty-three wounded; the first, fourth, and fifth
lieutenants of the 'Plantagenet' were wounded, and twenty-
two seamen killed, and twenty-four wounded."[1] According to
the official report, thirty-four were killed and eighty-six were
wounded. The "Guerriere" in her battle with the "Constitution" lost only seventy-eight men altogether. The "Macedonian" lost only one hundred and four. The attack on the
"General Armstrong" was one of the bloodiest defeats suffered by the British navy in the war. Not only was the privateer untaken, but she lost few of her crew,—nine in all, killed
and wounded.

Captain Lloyd then declared that he would destroy the privateer if he had to destroy Fayal in doing it, and ordered
Captain Bentham of the "Carnation" to attack her with his
guns. Reid abandoned and scuttled the "General Armstrong,"
taking his men on shore. The "Carnation's" shot inflicted
some injury on the town, before the privateer was set on fire
by the "Carnation's" boats.[2]

If the British navy cared to pay such a price for the shell of
an old privateer brig, which had already cost British commerce, as Captain Lloyd believed, a million dollars,[3] the privateers were willing to gratify the wish, as was shown a few
days afterward when the "Endymion" tried to carry the
"Prince of Neufchatel" by boarding. This privateer had made
itself peculiarly obnoxious to the British navy by the boldness
of its ravages in British waters. It was coming to America
filled with plunder, and with a prize in company, when off
Gay Head the "Endymion" was sighted, October 11, and gave
chase.

Captain Hope of the "Endymion" made an official report,
explaining with much detail that he chased the privateer till
evening, when the wind failed, and he then sent out his
boats:[4] —

[1] Niles, vii. 255.
[2] Dabney's Letter; Niles, vii. 254. Reid's Letter of Oct. 4, 1814; State
Papers, Naval Affairs, p. 495.
[3] Report of Captain Lloyd, Oct. 4, 1814; MSS. British Archives.
[4] Captain Hope to Rear Admiral Hotham, Oct. 11, 1814; MSS. British
Archives.

"I sent all the boats under command of Lieutenants Hawkins, Ormond, and Fanshaw. In approaching the ship an alarm was fired. The boats had been previously rowing up under a shoal, and had not felt the effects of a rapid tide which they almost instantaneously became exposed to. The second barge in taking the station assigned by Lieutenant Hawkins on the schooner's starboard bow, having her larboard oars shot away, unfortunately was swept by the stream athwart the first barge; thereby all the boats became entangled; and it is with extreme concern I acquaint you that the attack was in consequence at this moment only partially made. Notwithstanding this disadvantage at the first onset, every exertion that human skill could devise was resorted to to renew the contest; and they succeeded in again getting alongside, but not in the position intended. Their failure, therefore, is to be ascribed in the first instance to the velocity of the tide, the height of the vessel's side, not having channel plates to assist the men in getting on her deck, and her very superior force (a schooner of the largest dimensions, the 'Prince of Neufchatel,' three hundred and twenty tons, eighteen guns, long-nine and twelve-pounders, with a complement of one hundred and forty men of all nations, commanded by Mons. Jean Ordronaux). The boats' painters being now shot away, they again fell astern without ever being able to repeat the attack, and with great difficulty regained the ship, with the exception of the second barge."

Captain Ordronaux of the privateer had a crew of less than forty men then at quarters, and they suffered severely, only nine men escaping injury. The boarders gained the deck, but were killed as fast as they mounted; and at last more than half the British party were killed or captured. According to the British account, twenty-eight men, including the first lieutenant of the "Endymion," were killed; and thirty-seven men, including the second lieutenant, were wounded.[1] This report did not quite agree with that of the privateer, which claimed also twenty-eight prisoners, including the second lieutenant, who was unhurt. In any case, more than seventy men of the

[1] James's Naval History, vi. 527.

"Endymion's" crew, besides her first and second lieutenant, were killed, wounded, or captured; and the "Prince of Neufchatel" arrived in safety in Boston.

In the want of adjacent rocks lined with armed Americans, such as Captain Lloyd alleged at Fayal, Captain Hope was reduced to plead the tides as the cause of his defeat. These reports, better than any other evidence, showed the feelings of the British naval service in admitting discomfiture in the last resort of its pride. Successively obliged to plead inferiority at the guns, inferiority in sailing qualities, inferiority in equipment, the British service saw itself compelled by these repeated and bloody repulses to admit that its supposed preeminence in hand-to-hand fighting was a delusion. Within a single fortnight two petty privateers, with crews whose united force did not amount to one hundred and fifty men, succeeded in repulsing attacks made by twice their number of the best British seamen, inflicting a loss, in killed and wounded, officially reported at one hundred and eighty-five.

Such mortifying and bloody experiences made even the British navy weary of the war. Valuable prizes were few, and the service, especially in winter, was severe. Undoubtedly the British cruisers caught privateers by dozens, and were as successful in the performance of their duties as ever they had been in any war in Europe. Their blockade of American ports was real and ruinous, and nothing pretended to resist them. Yet after catching scores of swift cruisers, they saw scores of faster and better vessels issue from the blockaded ports and harry British commerce in every sea. Scolded by the press, worried by the Admiralty, and mortified by their own want of success, the British navy was obliged to hear language altogether strange to its experience.

"The American cruisers daily enter in among our convoys," said the "Times" of February 11, 1815, "seize prizes in sight of those that should afford protection, and if pursued 'put on their sea-wings' and laugh at the clumsy English pursuers. To what is this owing? Cannot we build ships? . . . It must indeed be encouraging to Mr. Madison to read the logs of his cruisers. If they fight, they are sure to conquer; if they fly, they are sure to escape."

Chapter VIII

IN THE TEMPEST of war that raged over land and ocean during the months of August and September, 1814, bystanders could not trust their own judgment of the future; yet shrewd observers, little affected either by emotion or by interest, inclined to the belief that the United States government was near exhaustion. The immediate military danger on Lake Champlain was escaped, and Baltimore was saved; but the symptoms of approaching failure in government were not to be mistaken, and the capture of Washington, which was intended to hurry the collapse, produced its intended effect.

From the first day of the war the two instruments necessary for military success were wanting to Madison,—money and men. After three campaigns, the time came when both these wants must be supplied, or the national government must devolve its duties on the States. When the President, preparing his Annual Message, asked his Cabinet officers what were the prospects of supplying money and men for another campaign, he received answers discouraging in the extreme.

First, in regard to money. In July, Secretary Campbell advertised a second loan, of only six million dollars. He obtained but two and a half millions at eighty. His acceptance of this trifling sum obliged him to give the same terms to the contractors who had taken the nine millions subscribed in the spring at eighty-eight. Barker found difficulty in making his payments, and from both loans the Treasury could expect to obtain only $10,400,000, owing to the contractors' failures.[1] The authorized loan was twenty-five millions. The secretary could suggest no expedient, except Treasury notes, for filling the deficit.

Bad as this failure was,—though it showed Secretary Campbell's incapacity so clearly as to compel his retirement, and obliged the President to call a special session of Congress,—the Treasury might regard it as the least of its embarrassments. Commonly governments had begun their

[1] Report of Secretary Campbell, Sept. 26, 1814; State Papers, Finance, ii. 840.

most desperate efforts only after ordinary resources failed; but the United States government in 1814 had so inextricably involved its finances that without dictatorial powers of seizing property its functions could not much longer be continued. The general bankruptcy, long foreseen, at length occurred.

The panic caused by the capture of Washington, August 24, obliged the tottering banks of Philadelphia and Baltimore to suspend specie payments. The banks of Philadelphia formally announced their suspension, August 31, by a circular explaining the causes and necessity of their decision.[1] The banks of New York immediately followed, September 1; and thenceforward no bank between New Orleans and Albany paid its obligations except in notes. Only the banks of New England maintained specie payments, with the exception of those in least credit, which took the opportunity to pay or not pay as they pleased. The suspension was admitted to be permanent. Until the blockade should be raised and domestic produce could find a foreign market, the course of exchange was fixed, and specie payments could not be resumed. The British navy and the Boston Federalists held the country firmly bound, and peace alone could bring relief.

Suspension mattered little, and had the National Bank been in existence the failure might have been an advantage to the government; but without a central authority the currency instantly fell into confusion. No medium of exchange existed outside of New England. Boston gave the specie standard, and soon the exchanges showed wide differences. New York money stood at twenty per cent discount, Philadelphia at twenty-four per cent, Baltimore at thirty per cent. Treasury notes were sold in Boston at twenty-five per cent discount, and United States six-per-cents stood at sixty in coin.[2] The Treasury had no means of transferring its bank deposits from one part of the country to another. Unless it paid its debts in Treasury notes, it was unable to pay them at all. No other money than the notes of suspended banks came into the Treasury. Even in New England, taxes, customs-duties, and loans were paid in Treasury notes, and rarely in local currency.

[1] Niles, vii.; Supplement, p. 176.
[2] Niles, vii.; Supplement, p. 176.

Thus, while the government collected in the Middle and Southern States millions in bank-notes, it was obliged to leave them in deposit at the local banks where the collection was made, while its debts in Boston and New York remained unpaid. The source of revenue was destroyed. The whole South and West, and the Middle States as far north as New York, could contribute in no considerable degree to the support of government.

The situation was unusual. The government might possess immense resources in one State and be totally bankrupt in another; it might levy taxes to the amount of the whole circulating medium, and yet have only its own notes available for payment of debt; it might borrow hundreds of millions and be none the better for the loan. All the private bank-notes of Pennsylvania and the Southern country were useless in New York and New England where they must chiefly be used. An attempt to transfer such deposits in any quantity would have made them quite worthless. The Treasury already admitted bankruptcy. The interest on the national obligations could not be paid.

The President's second inquiry regarded men. The new Secretary of War, Monroe, gave him such information as the Department possessed on the numbers of the army. A comparative account showed that in June, 1813, the regular troops numbered 27,609; in December, 34,325. In January, 1814, the number was nominally 33,822;[1] in July the aggregate was 31,503, the effectives being 27,010.[2] Since July the recruits had declined in numbers. The three months of March, April, and May produced 6,996 recruits; the three months of July, August, and September were reported as furnishing 4,477.[3] The general return of September 30 reported the strength of the army at 34,029 men.[4] The government was not able to provide the money necessary to pay bounties due for the last

---

[1] Armstrong to Eppes, Feb. 10, 1814; Niles, vi. 94. See *ante*, p. 882.

[2] Report; State Papers, Military Affairs, i. 535.

[3] Return of Enlistments, Nov. 2, 1814; State Papers, Military Affairs, i. 521. Letter of Assistant Inspector-General, Oct. 22, 1814; State Papers, Military Affairs, p. 518.

[4] The Inspector-General's Letter of Nov. 2, 1814; State Papers, Military Affairs, p. 520.

three months' recruiting.[1] The Secretary of War admitted the failure of the recruiting service, and attributed it to the high bounties given for substitutes in the militia detached for United States service.[2]

The smallness of the armies in the field showed worse results than were indicated by the returns. Macomb at Plattsburg claimed to have only fifteen hundred effectives. Izard carried with him to Buffalo only four thousand men. Brown's effectives at Fort Erie numbered two thousand. Apparently these three corps included the entire force in the field on the Canada frontier, and their combined effective strength did not exceed eight thousand men. The year before, Wilkinson and Hampton commanded fully eleven thousand effectives in their movements against Montreal. Nothing showed that the victories at Niagara and Plattsburg had stimulated enlistments, or that the army could be raised above thirty thousand effectives even if the finances were in a condition to meet the expense.

Much was said of the zeal shown by the State militia in hastening to the defence of their soil, and the New England Federalists were as loud as the Kentucky and Tennessee Democrats in praise of the energy with which the militia rose to resist invasion; but in reality this symptom was the most alarming of the time. Both in the military and in the political point of view, the persistence in depending on militia threatened to ruin the national government.

The military experience of 1814 satisfied the stanchest war Democrats that the militia must not be their dependence. In Maine the militia allowed themselves with hardly a show of resistance to be made subjects of Great Britain. At Plattsburg volunteers collected in considerable numbers, but the victory was won by the sailors and the engineers. At Niagara, Brown never could induce more than a thousand volunteers to support him in his utmost straits. Porter's efforts failed to create a brigade respectable in numbers, and at Chippawa his Indians outnumbered his whites. Four days after the repulse of Drummond's assault on Fort Erie, at the most anxious

[1] Report of the Paymaster, Oct. 26, 1814; State Papers, Military Affairs, p. 519.
[2] Monroe to Giles, Oct. 26, 1814; State Papers, Military Affairs, p. 518.

moment of the Niagara campaign, Major-General Brown wrote to Secretary Armstrong,[1]—

"I very much doubt if a parallel can be found for the state of things existing on this frontier. A gallant little army struggling with the enemies of their country, and devoting their lives for its honor and its safety, left by that country to struggle alone, and that within sight and within hearing."

A month afterward Brown succeeded in obtaining a thousand volunteers, and by some quality of his own made them assault and carry works that old soldiers feared to touch. The feat was the most extraordinary that was performed on either side in the remarkably varied experience of the war; but it proved Brown's personal energy rather than the merits of a militia system. At Washington the militia were thoroughly tested; their rout proved chiefly the incompetence of their general, but the system was shown, before the battle, to be more defective than the army it produced. At Baltimore the militia were again routed, and the town was saved chiefly by the engineers and sailors. In Virginia, where more than forty thousand militia were in the field, they protected nothing, and their service was more fatal to themselves than though they had fought severe battles. Nearly all the Virginia militia summoned for the defence of Norfolk suffered from sickness, and the mortality when compared with that of the regular service was enormous; five militia-men sickened and died where one regular soldier suffered.[2] In Tennessee and Georgia the experience was equally unfortunate; the Georgia militia could do nothing with the Creeks, and Andrew Jackson himself was helpless until he obtained one small regiment of regulars.

Besides its military disadvantages the militia service was tainted with fraud. Habitually and notoriously in New England and New York, the militia-men when called out attended muster, served a few days in order to get their names on the pay-roll, and then went home. The United States government wasted millions of dollars in pay and pensions for

[1] Brown to Armstrong, July [August] 19, 1814; MSS. War Department Archives.
[2] Niles, vii.; Supplement, p. 188.

such men. Another source of waste was in the time required
to place them in the field. The government struggled to avoid
a call of militia, even though risking great disasters by the
neglect.

The worst of all evils lay still further in the background.
The militia began by rendering a proper army impossible, and
ended by making government a form. The object of Massachusetts in praising the conduct of militia, and in maintaining
its own at a high state of efficiency, was notorious. The Federalists knew that the national government must sooner or
later abandon the attempt to support an army. When that
time should come, the only resource of the government
would lie in State armies, and Massachusetts was the best
equipped State for that object. Her militia, seventy thousand
strong, well-armed, well-drilled, and as yet untouched by war,
could dictate to the Union. Whenever Massachusetts should
say the word, the war must stop; and Massachusetts meant to
say the word when the government fairly ceased to possess
either money or arms.

That moment, in the belief of the Massachusetts Federalists, had come. Their course in the summer and autumn of
1814 left no doubt of their intentions. No act of open rebellion could be more significant than their conduct when Sherbrooke's expedition occupied Castine. Then at last Governor
Strong consented to call out the militia, which he refused to
do two years before, because, he asserted, Castine and the
other coast towns were sufficiently defended;[1] but the governor was careful to avoid the suspicion that these troops were
in the national service. He acted independently of the national
government in the terms of his general order of September,
1814,[2] placing his militia under the command of a major-
general of their own, and making only a bare inquiry of the
Secretary of War whether their expenses would be re-
imbursed,[3] — an inquiry which Monroe at once answered in
the negative.[4] The force was a State army, and could not fail

[1] Strong to Eustis, Aug. 5, 1812; State Papers, Military Affairs, i. 610.
[2] General Orders, Sept. 6, 1814; State Papers, Military Affairs, p. 613.
[3] Strong to the Secretary of War, Sept. 7, 1814; State Papers, Military
Affairs, p. 613.
[4] Monroe to Strong, Sept. 17, 1814; State Papers, Military Affairs, p. 614.

to cause the President more anxiety than it was likely ever to cause the Prince Regent.

At the same time the governor of Connecticut withdrew from the command of Brigadier-General Cushing the brigade of State militia then in the national service, and placed it under a major-general of State militia, with injunctions to obey no orders except such as were issued by State authority.[1] The evil of these measures was greatly aggravated by coinciding with the crisis which stopped the course of national government. Connecticut withdrew her militia, August 24; Washington was captured the same day; the Philadelphia banks suspended payment August 29; Castine was taken August 31; and Governor Strong called out the Massachusetts militia September 6. The government was prostrate, and New England was practically independent when Sir George Prevost crossed the frontier, September 3. So complete was the paralysis that Governor Chittenden of Vermont, on receiving official notice[2] that the British army and navy were advancing on Lake Champlain, refused to call out the militia, because neither the Constitution nor the laws gave him authority to order the militia out of the State.[3] He could only recommend that individuals should volunteer to assist in the defence of Plattsburg. Chittenden's conduct was the more suggestive because of his undoubted honesty and the absence of factious motive for his refusal.

The full meaning of Governor Strong's course was avowed a few days afterward. Having called a special meeting of the State legislature for October 5, he addressed to it a message narrating the steps he had taken, and the refusal of the President to assume the expenses of the militia called into service for the defence of the State.

"The situation of this State is peculiarly dangerous and perplexing," said Governor Strong;[4] " we have been led by the terms of the Constitution to rely on the government of the Union to provide for our defence. We have resigned to

[1] Cushing to the Secretary of War, Sept. 12, 1814; State Papers, Military Affairs, p. 620.
[2] Macomb to Chittenden, Sept. 4, 1814; Niles, vii. 102.
[3] Chittenden to General Newell, Sept. 5, 1814; Niles, vii. 103.
[4] Message of Oct. 5, 1814; Niles, vii. 113.

that government the revenues of the State with the expectation that this object would not be neglected. . . . Let us then, relying on the support and direction of Providence, unite in such measures for our safety as the times demand and the principles of justice and the law of self-preservation will justify."

The sense which this invitation was intended to bear could be best understood by appreciating the temper of the body thus addressed and the time when the appeal was made. The national government had for practical purposes ceased. The Boston "Centinel," a newspaper of large circulation, said to reach six thousand copies, announced September 10, 1814, that the Union was already practically dissolved, and that the people must rise in their majesty, protect themselves, and compel their unworthy servants to obey their will. Governor Strong knew that the legislature was controlled by extreme partisans of the Pickering type, who wished, to use his phrase, to "let the ship run aground." Even Josiah Quincy, one of the most vehement Federalists, was aware that the members of the General Court stood in danger of doing too much rather than too little.[1]

Strong's message of October 5 was echoed by Pickering from Washington, October 12, in a letter which closed with the exhortation to seize the national revenues:—

"As, abandoned by the general government except for taxing us, we must defend ourselves, so we ought to secure and hold fast the revenues indispensable to maintain the force necessary for our protection against the foreign enemy and the still greater evil in prospect,—domestic tyranny."[2]

The Massachusetts legislature could not fail to understand Governor Strong's message as an invitation to resume the powers with which the State had parted in adopting the Constitution.

The legislature referred the message to a committee, which

[1] Quincy's Life of Quincy, p. 357.
[2] Pickering to Strong, Oct. 12, 1814; New England Federalism, p. 394.

reported only three days afterward through its chairman, Harrison Gray Otis:[1] —

> "The state of the national Treasury as exhibited by the proper officer requires an augmentation of existing taxes; and if in addition to these the people of Massachusetts, deprived of their commerce and harassed by a formidable enemy, are compelled to provide for the indispensable duty of self-defence, it must soon become impossible for them to sustain this burden. There remains to them therefore no alternative but submission to the enemy, or the control of their own resources to repel his aggressions. It is impossible to hesitate in making the election. This people are not ready for conquest or submission; but being ready and determined to defend themselves, they have the greatest need of those resources derivable from themselves which the national government has hitherto thought proper to employ elsewhere."

The report further showed that the United States Constitution had failed to secure to New England the rights and benefits expected from it, and required immediate change. The prescribed mode of amendment was insufficient: —

> "When this deficiency becomes apparent, no reason can preclude the right of the whole people who were parties to it to adopt another. . . . But as a proposition for such a convention from a single State would probably be unsuccessful, and our danger admits not of delay, it is recommended by the committee that in the first instance a conference should be invited between those States the affinity of whose interests is closest."

Thus, after ten years' delay, the project of a New England Convention was brought forward by State authority, through the process of war with England, which George Cabot from the first declared to be the only means of producing it.[2] As Otis's committee presented the subject, the conference was in the first place to devise some mode of common defence; and,

---

[1] Report of Oct. 8, 1814; Niles, vii. 149.
[2] Cabot to Pickering, Feb. 14, 1804; Lodge's Cabot, p. 341. See *ante*, p. 413.

in the second, "to lay the foundation for a radical reform in the national compact by inviting to a future convention a deputation from all the States in the Union." The report closed by offering seven Resolutions, recommending the enlistment of a State army of ten thousand men, a loan of a million dollars at six per cent, and the appointment of delegates "to meet and confer with delegates from the States of New England or any of them" on the defence of those States and the redress of their grievances.

The Senate committee also made a strenuous argument against the President's decision that State militia were in State service unless called for by a United States officer and placed under his direction,[1] and recommended that the subject should be referred to the next session. To the proposition for a conference of the New England States, and to Otis's other Resolutions, the Senate and House assented, October 13, by large majorities, varying in numbers, but amounting to two hundred and sixty against ninety in the case of the proposed convention. The minority in both Houses presented protests, charging the majority with intending more than was avowed. "The reasoning of the report," said the Protest signed by seventy-six members of the House,[2] "is supported by the alarming assumption that the Constitution has failed in its objects, and the people of Massachusetts are absolved from their allegiance, and at liberty to adopt another. In debate it has been reiterated that the Constitution is no longer to be respected, and that revolution is not to be deprecated." The House refused to receive the Protest, as disrespectful. The minority withdrew from further share in these proceedings; and the majority then, October 19, chose twelve delegates "to meet and confer on the 15th December next with such as may be chosen by any or all of the other New England States upon our public grievances and concerns." The choice was marked by a conservative spirit not altogether pleasing to Timothy Pickering. George Cabot and Harrison Gray Otis stood at the head of the delegation.

The remonstrances and threats of the minority made the majority cautious, but did not check them. The legislature of

[1] Senate Report of Oct. 18, 1814; Niles, vii. 151.
[2] Niles, vii. 154.

Connecticut immediately appointed seven delegates to meet those of Massachusetts at Hartford, December 15, for the purpose of recommending "such measures for the safety and welfare of these States as may consist with our obligations as members of the national Union."[1] In this clause the legislature intended to draw a distinction between obligations to the Union and obligations to the Constitution. To the former the people avowed no hostility; to the latter they thought the war had put an end. On that point the committee's report was clear.[2]

Besides Massachusetts and Connecticut the legislature of Rhode Island, by a vote of thirty-nine to twenty-three, appointed, November 5, four delegates to confer at Hartford upon the measures which might be in their power to adopt to restore their rights under the Constitution, "consistently with their obligations."[3] These three States alone chose delegates. The governor and legislature of New Hampshire would probably have joined them had not the Republican council stood in the way. The legislature of Vermont, including its Federalist minority, unanimously declined the invitation.

Immediately after these steps were taken, the autumn elections occurred. Members of Congress were to be chosen, and the people were obliged to vote for or against the Hartford Convention as the issue expressly avowed. President Madison might safely assume that no man voted for Federalist Congressmen in November, 1814, unless he favored the project of a New England Convention. The result was emphatic. Massachusetts chose eighteen Federalists and two Republicans; Vermont, New Hampshire, Rhode Island, and Connecticut chose only Federalists. In all, New England chose thirty-nine Federalist Congressmen and two Republicans[4] for the Fourteenth Congress. In the Thirteenth Congress, chosen in 1812, when the feeling against the war was supposed to be strongest, the Federalist members from New England numbered thirty, the Republicans eleven.[5]

[1] Niles, vii. 165.
[2] Report; Niles, vii. 164.
[3] Niles, vii. 181.
[4] Niles, ix. 281.
[5] Niles, iv. 268.

Beyond New England the autumn elections were less significant, but were still unsatisfactory to the Administration. New Jersey returned to her true sympathies, and as far as her Congressmen expressed her opinions gave unanimous support to the war; but Pennsylvania, owing to local quarrels, elected five Federalist members; and Maryland elected five Federalists and four Republicans. In spite of the great loss in Federalist members which had occurred in the spring elections in New York, the Federalists numbered sixty-five in the Fourteenth Congress; in the Thirteenth they numbered sixty-eight. The Administration had hoped, and freely asserted, that a strong reaction in favor of the war had followed the burning of Washington and the avowal of England's designs against Maine and the Northwestern Territory. The elections showed no such reaction. The war was no more popular than before.

The public apathy was the more alarming because, whatever was the true object of the Hartford Convention, all Republicans believed it to be intended as a step to dissolve the Union, and they supported the Administration chiefly because Madison represented the Union. Federalists might deceive themselves. Probably the men who voted for the Hartford Convention saw its necessary consequences less clearly than they were seen by the men who voted against it. The Republican vote represented the strength of Union sentiment more closely than the disunion sentiment was represented by the Federalist vote. Yet the States from Maryland to Maine chose a majority of Congressmen who were not Republicans. The New England States, New York, New Jersey, Pennsylvania, Delaware, and Maryland returned much more than half the members of Congress,—one hundred and eight in one hundred and eighty-two; and of these fifty-seven were Federalists, while only fifty-one were Republicans. The unpopularity of the Administration was not easily overestimated when Madison could win no more support than this, at a time when the public believed a vote for Federalism to be a vote for disunion.

"I give you the most serious assurance," wrote Randolph in an open letter to James Lloyd, of Massachusetts,[1]

[1] Randolph's Letter to Lloyd, Dec. 15, 1814; Niles, vii. 258.

remonstrating against the Convention, "that nothing less than the shameful conduct of the enemy and the complection of certain occurrences to the eastward could have sustained Mr. Madison after the disgraceful affair at Washington. The public indignation would have overwhelmed in one common ruin himself and his hireling newspapers."

Randolph's political judgments were commonly mistaken, but in this instance he proved himself to be at least partially right; for at the next election, six months later, when the current had turned decidedly in Madison's favor, Randolph after a sharp contest defeated Eppes and recovered control of his district. Virginia could hardly have chosen a representative less calculated to please Madison.

The President himself betrayed unusual signs of distress. Nothing in Madison's character was more remarkable than the placidity with which he commonly met anxieties that would have crushed a sensitive man; but the shock of defeat at Bladensburg, the flight from Washington, and the anxieties that followed broke him down. William Wirt visited Washington October 14, before the action of the Massachusetts legislature was yet completed. After viewing the ruins of the White House, a "mournful monument of American imbecility and improvidence," he called upon the President at Colonel Tayloe's Octagon House, which Serurier had occupied, but which Madison took for his residence after his return.

"P—— and I called on the President," wrote Wirt in a private letter.[1] "He looks miserably shattered and woe-begone. In short, he looked heart-broken. His mind is full of the New England sedition. He introduced the subject and continued to press it, painful as it obviously was to him. I denied the probability, even the possibility, that the yeomanry of the North could be induced to place themselves under the power and protection of England, and diverted the conversation to another topic; but he took the first opportunity to return to it, and convinced me that his heart and mind were painfully full of the subject."

[1] Kennedy's Life of Wirt, i. 339.

No misconduct of New England alone would have so un-manned a Virginia President. Madison's worst troubles lay nearer home; Massachusetts made only the last straw in his burden. Jefferson, with his usual kindliness, tried to console and encourage him; but Jefferson's consolations proved only the difficulty of finding words or arguments to warrant satisfaction with the past or hope for the future.

"In the late events at Washington," wrote Jefferson, September 24,[1] "I have felt so much for you that I cannot withhold the expression of my sympathies. For although every reasonable man must be sensible that all you can do is to order,—that execution must depend on others, and failures be imputed to them alone,—yet I know that when such failures happen they affect even those who have done everything they could to prevent them. Had General Washington himself been now at the head of our affairs, the same event would probably have happened."

Jefferson's estimate of Washington's abilities was lower than that commonly accepted; and his rule that a President's responsibility ceased after giving an order, besides ignoring the President's responsibility for the selection of agents, seemed to destroy the foundation of the public service. "I never doubted that the plans of the President were wise and sufficient," wrote Jefferson to Monroe.[2] "Their failure we all impute, (1) to the insubordinate temper of Armstrong, and (2) to the indecision of Winder." The rule that an administrator might select any agent, however incompetent, without incurring responsibility for the agent's acts, was one which in private affairs Jefferson would hardly have accepted.

Yet Jefferson's opinions probably expressed Republican sentiment in Virginia, and showed better than any other evidence the course of thought among Madison's friends. In that respect his expressions retained permanent value. The Virginians were willing to throw off responsibility for public disaster; and they naturally threw it on New England, since New England challenged it. Writing to his friend William

[1] Jefferson to Madison, Sept. 24, 1814; Works, vi. 385.
[2] Jefferson to Monroe, Jan. 1, 1815; Works, vi. 407.

Short, Jefferson spoke of the threatening attitude of Massachusetts:[1] —

"Some apprehend danger from the defection of Massachusetts. It is a disagreeable circumstance, but not a dangerous one. If they become neutral, we are sufficient for one enemy without them, and in fact we get no aid from them now."

Probably most Virginians shared this belief, at least so far as concerned the aid rendered by Massachusetts to the war. In truth, Massachusetts gave little aid, and made a profession of her wish to give none at all; but the difficulty did not end there. Massachusetts and Virginia were States of the first class. The census of 1810 allotted to Massachusetts, including Maine, a population of about seven hundred thousand; to Virginia, a white population of five hundred and fifty-one thousand, and a colored population of four hundred and twenty-three thousand,—nine hundred and seventy-four thousand in all. In the ratio of representation Massachusetts counted for twenty, Virginia for twenty-three. The quota of Massachusetts in the direct tax was $316,000; that of Virginia was $369,000. On the scale furnished by these data, Virginia should have contributed in support of the war about one eighth or one seventh more men and money than were required from Massachusetts. The actual result was different.

The amount of money contributed by Massachusetts could not be compared with that contributed by Virginia, partly because of the severe blockade which closed the Virginian ports. The net revenue from customs derived from Virginia in 1814 was $4,000; that from Massachusetts was $1,600,000.[2] Unlike the customs revenue, the receipts from internal revenue were supposed to be reasonably equalized, so that each State should contribute in due proportion. According to the official return, dated Nov. 24, 1815, the total internal duties which had then been paid to the collectors for the year 1814 in Massachusetts was $198,400; in Virginia it was $193,500. The total amount then paid to the Treasury was

[1] Jefferson to Short, Nov. 28, 1814; Works, vi. 398.
[2] Seybert, p. 436; Pitkin, p. 415.

$178,400 in Massachusetts, and $157,300 in Virginia.[1] The direct tax was fixed by Congress and was assumed by the State in Virginia, but regularly assessed in Massachusetts. One paid $316,000; the other, $369,000. The total revenue derived from Massachusetts was therefore $2,114,400 in the year 1814; that from Virginia, $566,500. Of the loans effected in the same year, Massachusetts took a small part considering her means,—hardly a million dollars. Virginia took still less,—only two hundred thousand.[2]

In money, Massachusetts contributed four times as much as Virginia to support the war, and her contributions were paid in Treasury notes or paper equivalent to coin,—not in the notes of banks worthless beyond the State. In men, the estimate was affected by the inquiry whether the militia were to be considered as protecting the national government or the State. Owing to the presence of the British in the Chesapeake, Virginia kept a large force of militia on foot, some of which were in garrison at Norfolk, and a few were on the field of Bladensburg. Massachusetts also was obliged to call out a considerable force of militia to protect or garrison national posts.

The relative numbers of regular troops were also somewhat doubtful; but the paymaster of the army reported Oct. 26, 1814, that he had distributed in bounties during the year $237,400 for Massachusetts, and $160,962 for Virginia.[3] During the year, six regular regiments—the Ninth, Twenty-first, Thirty-third, Thirty-fourth, Fortieth, and Forty-fifth—recruited in Massachusetts. Three—the Twelfth, Twentieth, and Thirty-fifth—recruited in Virginia. Perhaps the military aid furnished by the different sections of the seaboard could be better understood by following the familiar divisions. New England furnished thirteen regiments. New York, New Jersey, and Pennsylvania furnished fifteen. The Southern States, from Delaware to South Carolina inclusive, furnished ten. Of all the States in the Union New York alone supplied more regular soldiers than Massachusetts, and Massachusetts supplied as

---

[1] Statement, etc.; State Papers, Finance, iii. 44–48.
[2] State Papers, Finance, ii. 846, 847.
[3] Letter of Paymaster Brent, Oct. 26, 1814; State Papers, Military Affairs, i. 519.

many as were furnished by Virginia and the two Carolinas together.

Judged by these standards, either Massachusetts had done more than her share, or Virginia had done less than hers. The tests were material, and took no moral element in account; but in moral support the relative failure of Massachusetts was not beyond dispute. Public opinion in New England was almost equally divided, and the pronounced opposition to the war was much greater in the Eastern States than in the Southern; but in the serious work of fighting, New England claimed a share of credit. In the little army at Niagara New York supplied the Major-General, Virginia and Massachusetts the two brigadiers; but Winfield Scott's brigade was chiefly composed of New England men; and when, nearly half a century afterward, Scott in his old age was obliged to choose between his allegiance to his State and allegiance to the Union, the memory of the New England troops who had won for him his first renown had its influence in raising his mind above the local sympathies which controlled other Virginia officers. Without reflecting on Virginia courage or patriotism, the New England Republicans were warranted in claiming that not the Virginia regiments, but the Massachusetts Ninth, the Vermont Eleventh, the Massachusetts Twenty-first, and the Connecticut Twenty-fifth routed the Royal Scots at Chippawa, and bayoneted the British artillerymen at Lundy's Lane, and stormed Drummond's intrenchments at Fort Erie. They could add that without their sailors the war might have been less successful than it was; and they would have been justified had they asked Jefferson to glance at his latest newspaper as he wrote that Massachusetts gave no aid to the war, and read the despatch of Johnston Blakeley reporting that the New England crew of the "Wasp" had sunk the "Avon" in the middle of a British fleet.[1] Virginians did not take kindly to the ocean; and on land, owing to the accidents of war, no Virginia regiment was offered a chance to win distinction.

These comparisons were of little weight to prove that New England was either better or worse than other parts of the

[1] Niles's Register, Nov. 26, 1814.

Union, but they showed that the difficulties that depressed Madison's mind were not merely local. He might have disregarded the conduct of the State governments of Massachusetts and Connecticut had he enjoyed the full support of his own great Republican States, Pennsylvania, Virginia, and North Carolina. Except New York, Kentucky, Tennessee, and perhaps Ohio, no State gave to the war the full and earnest co-operation it needed. Again and again, from the beginning of the troubles with England, Madison had acted on the conviction that at last the people were aroused; but in every instance he had been disappointed. After the burning of Washington, he was more than ever convinced that the moment had come when the entire people would rally in their self-respect; but he was met by the Hartford Convention and the November elections. If the people would not come to the aid of their government at such a moment, Madison felt that nothing could move them. Peace was his last hope.

Chapter IX

ONGRESS WAS summoned to meet in extra session September 19, by a proclamation issued August 8, before the capture of Washington. On the appointed day the members appeared, but found their building in ashes, and met like vagrants, without a shelter they could call their own. The President caused the only public office that had been spared, to be fitted for their use. Partly owing to the exertions of Dr. Thornton, the head of the Bureau of Patents, partly owing to the tornado of August 25, the building used as Post and Patent Office was not burned. There Congress was obliged to hold its sessions, in such discomfort as it had never before known.

The President sent his Annual Message September 20, which informed Congress that it had been specially summoned to supply "any inadequacy in the existing provision for the wants of the Treasury," as well as to be ready for whatever result might be reached by the negotiation at Ghent. Two thirds of the Message related to the operations of war, and the President seemed rather disposed to suppress than to avow his difficulties, but the little he said of them was heavy with anxiety. He announced that July 1 five million dollars remained in the Treasury, and that "large sums" must be provided; but he did not add that the loan had failed, or that the banks and Treasury had suspended specie payments. He did not say that the regular army and the militia system were inadequate to national defence; but he declared "the necessity of immediate measures for filling the ranks of the regular army," and of giving "the requisite energy and efficiency" to the militia:—

"From this view of the national affairs Congress will be urged to take up, without delay, as well the subject of pecuniary supplies as that of military force, and on a scale commensurate with the extent and the character which the war has assumed. It is not to be disguised that the situation of our country calls for its greatest efforts. . . . From such an adversary, hostility in its greatest force and in its worst forms may be looked for."

The President threw on the Secretaries of the Treasury and of War the ungrateful task of announcing the details of their need. Secretary Campbell was first to address Congress, and the tone of his report on the state of the finances received emphasis from the resignation which he sent at the same time to the President. Campbell's annual report of September 23 was an admission of incompetence. He had paid, he said, nearly twenty millions from the Treasury between January and July; twenty-seven millions more were payable between July and the following January. For the year 1815 the Treasury would require at least as much as for 1814. Congress must therefore speedily provide at least seventy-four millions for the service between July 1, 1814, and Dec. 31, 1815. He ventured to suggest no means of obtaining this sum, or any amount approaching it.

July 1 the Treasury contained $4,722,000. From its various sources of revenue it could expect $4,840,000 during the remainder of the year; from loans already contracted, $4,320,000. In all, $13,822,000 might be considered as in hand, which was one half the sum immediately required. For the year 1815 the revenue in all its branches might produce $8,200,000, leaving $39,000,000 to be provided. Twenty-two millions were the extent of Campbell's resources, but fifty-two million dollars more must be raised merely to carry on the government as it had been administered in the past year.

The plan of finance adopted by Gallatin at the outset of the war assumed that all deficits could be covered by loans.

"The experience of the present year," said Campbell, "furnishes ground to doubt whether this be practicable, at least in the shape in which loans have hitherto been attempted. Nor is it even certain that the establishing and pledging of revenues adequate to the punctual payment of the interest and eventual reimbursement of the principal of the sums which will be required for the year 1815, would enable the Treasury to obtain them through the medium of loans effected in the ordinary way."

Loans being impracticable, Campbell discussed the possibility of using Treasury notes. Eight millions were already in issue, and of these more than four millions would fall due before December 31. Campbell considered that six millions in Treasury notes was about as large a sum as could easily be circulated, but by issuing notes of small denominations he hoped to raise the amount to ten millions.

From all sources Campbell hoped to obtain about twenty-four million dollars of the seventy-four millions required. For the remaining fifty millions he had no suggestion to offer. The means for new and extraordinary exertions, he said, "ought to be provided." He declared that the resources of the nation were ample,—which was true, but was also the most discouraging symptom of the time; for if the people, with ample resources, as he asserted, refused to come to the support of their own government on any terms, their decision must be accepted as final. Besides throwing upon Congress all these difficulties, without a suggestion of his own, Campbell added that Congress would be required to exert its powers to remedy the evils of the currency and the suspension of specie payments.

Congress on hearing this financial statement regarded the situation as desperate. "Tell Dr. Madison," Senator Lacock was reported[1] to have said to the President's private secretary, "that we are now willing to submit to his Philadelphia lawyer for head of the Treasury. The public patient is so very sick that we must swallow anything, however nauseous." Dallas was nominated October 5, and confirmed the next day without opposition, as Secretary of the Treasury. No stronger proof could have been given of the helplessness of Congress, for Dallas was a man who under no other circumstances could have obtained a ray of popular favor.

Dallas's character was high, his abilities undoubted, his experience large; but for ten years he had been one of the least popular men in Pennsylvania, the target of newspaper abuse and the champion of political independence. The people reasonably required that their leaders should more or less resemble some popular type, and if the result was monotonous the fault was in the society, not in its politics or its politicians; but Dallas was like no ordinary type in any people. His tone of intellectual and social superiority, his powdered hair, old-

---

[1] Ingersoll's History, ii. 253.

fashioned dress and refined manners, his free habits of expense, and the insubordination even more than the vivacity of his temper irritated the prejudices of his party.[1] He had little respect for Presidents, and none for Congress. For Jefferson and Virginia doctrines he felt distrust, which was returned. Earnest in temper and emphatic in tone, even to the point of tears and tropical excitability, Dallas came to Washington as though to lead a forlorn hope,—caring little for parties and less for ambition, but bent upon restoring to the government the powers that his friend Gallatin, too easily as he thought, had allowed to slip from its grasp.

The difficulties of the Treasury when Dallas took charge of it were not easily exaggerated. His own description,[2] given some six weeks afterward, made no disguise of them. "The Treasury," he said, "was suffering under every kind of embarrassment. The demands upon it were great in amount, while the means to satisfy them were comparatively small, precarious in collection, and difficult in their application. . . . The means consisted, first, of the fragment of an authority to borrow money when nobody was disposed to lend, and to issue Treasury notes which none but necessitous creditors or contractors in distress . . . seemed willing to accept;" second, of bank-credits, chiefly in the South and West, rendered largely useless by the suspension of specie payments; third, of the current receipts of taxes, also useless because paid chiefly in Treasury notes. The Treasury was bankrupt. The formal stoppage of payments in interst on the debt was announced, November 9, by an official letter from the secretary, notifying holders of government securities in Boston that the Treasury could not meet its obligations, and that "the government was unable to avert or to control this course of events."[3] After that date the Treasury made no further pretence of solvency.

From this situation the government could be rescued only by a great effort; and obviously the currency must be first restored, for until some system of exchange could be established, every increase of taxation would merely increase

<hr/>

[1] Ingersoll's History, ii. 254, 257.

[2] Dallas to William Lowndes, Nov. 27, 1814; State Papers, Finance, ii. 872.

[3] Dallas to the Commissioner of Loans at Boston, Nov. 9, 1814; Niles, vii. 270.

unavailable bank deposits. Fifty millions of Southern bank-notes, locked in the vaults of Southern banks, would not pay the over-due interest on government bonds at Boston.

To this subject every one turned, but the schemes that seemed to have a chance of adoption were only two. The first came from President Jefferson, and was strongly pressed by the South. As Jefferson explained it, the plan seemed as simple as his plans were apt to be; he proposed to issue twenty millions in promissory notes every year as long as might be necessary. "Our experience," he told the President,[1] "has proved it [a paper currency] may be run up to two or three hundred millions without more than doubling what would be the prices of things under a sufficient medium, or say a metallic one." His plan included an increase of taxation by two million dollars every year to redeem the same amount of Treasury issues.

Obviously the insuperable obstacle to this plan was the paper money of the State banks, which already stood at discounts varying from ten to fifty per cent in specie, and in any large quantity could not be discounted at all. Until private paper should be abolished, public or government paper could not be brought into common use. Jefferson's views on this, as on the whole subject, were interesting.

"The banks have discontinued themselves," he explained.[2] "We are now without any medium; and necessity, as well as patriotism and confidence, will make us all eager to receive Treasury notes if founded on specific taxes. Congress may now borrow of the public, and without interest, all the money they may want, to the amount of a competent circulation, by merely issuing their own promissory notes of proper denominations for the larger purposes of circulation, but not for the small. Leave that door open for the entrance of metallic money. . . . The State legislatures should be immediately urged to relinquish the right of establishing banks of discount. Most of them will comply on patriotic principles, under the convictions of the moment;

[1] Jefferson to Madison, Oct. 15, 1814; Works, vi. 391.
[2] Jefferson to Thomas Cooper, Sept. 10, 1814; Works, vi. 375.

and the non-complying may be crowded into concurrence by legitimate devices."

Instead of "banks of discount," Jefferson probably meant to say banks of issue, although the Virginia school was hostile to all banks, and possibly he wished to destroy the whole system. If the scheme were adopted, twenty million dollars in paper money would not supply the wants of the Treasury, which required at least fifty millions within a year. The resource was limited, even if the States could be compelled to stop the issue of private notes, — which was extremely doubtful in the temper of Massachusetts and with the leanings of Chief-Justice Marshall. Jefferson did not touch upon legal tender; but the assumption of power implied in the issue of paper money seemed to require that the government should exercise the right of obliging its creditors to accept it. The actual interest-bearing Treasury notes stood then at a discount of about twenty per cent. The proposed paper money could hardly circulate at a better rate, and coin was not to be obtained. Under such conditions the notes must be a forced currency if they were to circulate at all.

The scheme was reported to the House by the Committee of Ways and Means through its chairman, John W. Eppes, Jefferson's son-in-law.[1] For the report Eppes was alone responsible, and the plan in his hands varied in some points from that of Jefferson. Starting from the admitted premise that loans were not to be obtained, and that money could not be transferred from one point to another in any existing medium at the disposition of government, Eppes proposed to issue Treasury notes "in sums sufficiently small for the ordinary purposes of society," which were not to be made payable on demand in coin, but might at any time be exchanged for eight per cent bonds, and were to be received "in all payments for public lands and taxes." Nothing was said of legal tender, or of driving bank-notes from circulation; but Eppes proposed to double the taxes at one stroke.

Eppes's scheme lost the advantages of Jefferson's without gaining any of its own. It abandoned the hope of abolishing bank paper; and in want of such a restraint on private issues,

[1] Report of Oct. 10, 1814; State Papers, Finance, ii. 854.

the proposed government paper would merely add one more element of confusion to the chaos already existing. Eppes further altered Jefferson's plan by adding some ten millions instead of two millions to the burden of taxation; but even Jefferson protested that this part of the scheme was impracticable.

"This is a dashing proposition," he wrote to Monroe;[1] "but if Congress pass it, I shall consider it sufficient evidence that their constituents generally can pay the tax. No man has greater confidence than I have in the spirit of the people to a rational extent. Whatever they can, they will. But without either market or medium, I know not how it is to be done. All markets abroad and all at home are shut to us, so that we have been feeding our horses on wheat. Before the day of collection, bank-notes will be but as oak-leaves; and of specie there is not within all the United States one half of the proposed amount of the taxes."

This was the situation of the Virginia scheme when Dallas took the matter in hand. Immediately after entering into office, Dallas wrote to Eppes an official letter, dated October 17, expressing views wholly at variance with the Virginia plan.

"Under favorable circumstances and to a limited extent," he said,[2] "an emission of Treasury notes would probably afford relief; but Treasury notes are an expensive and precarious substitute either for coin or for bank-notes, charged as they are with a growing interest, productive of no countervailing profit or emolument, and exposed to every breath of popular prejudice or alarm. The establishment of a national institution operating upon credit combined with capital, and regulated by prudence and good faith, is after all the only efficient remedy for the disordered condition of our circulating medium. While accomplishing that object, too, there will be found under the auspices of such an institution a safe depository for the public treasure and a constant auxiliary to the public credit. But whether the issues of a paper currency proceed from the national Treasury or

[1] Jefferson to Monroe, Oct. 16, 1814; Works, vi. 394.
[2] Dallas to Eppes, Oct. 17, 1814; State Papers, Finance, ii. 866.

from a national Bank, the acceptance of the paper in a course of payments and receipts must be forever optional with the citizens. The extremity of that day cannot be anticipated when any honest and enlightened statesman will again venture upon the desperate expedient of a tender-law."

Without a tender-law the Virginia scheme would hardly answer the purposes required, since the government must restrain the issue of paper within a limit too narrow for usefulness. Dallas did not press this point, but developed his own scheme, which required, like that of Eppes, a duplication of taxes to produce twenty-one million dollars, and the creation of a national Bank with a capital of fifty million dollars.

Either Eppes's or Dallas's plan might answer the immediate object of providing a currency, and both required the exercise of implied powers by Congress. Apparently Congress had only to choose, but in truth choice was most difficult. The House readily adopted Dallas's recommendation in principle, and voted, October 24, by sixty-six to forty, that it was expedient to establish a national Bank; but the problem of establishing a specie-paying bank without specie passed its powers. Dallas abandoned the attempt at the outset. He proposed a bank of fifty millions capital, of which forty-four millions might be subscribed in government bonds and Treasury notes, and six millions in coin. The bank was at once to lend to government thirty millions,—of course in bank-notes,—and no one denied that an immediate suspension of specie payments must follow such an issue. To any bank, strong or weak, the old Virginia influence represented by Eppes was hostile; and to a bank insolvent from the start the Federalists also were opposed.

When the bill, reported November 7, was printed, it was found to contain a provision authorizing the suspension of specie payments at the President's discretion. The discussion began November 14, and every successive day revealed objections and increased the opposition. Calhoun complicated the subject still further by bringing forward, November 16, a plan of his own, requiring the capital to consist "one tenth in specie, and the remainder in specie or in Treasury notes to be hereafter issued," and taking away all government control. Ingham of Pennsylvania, representing Dallas, combated Calhoun with force, but could not make his own measure agreeable to the House. His phrase in regard to the suspension of specie payments was significant. Congress, he said, would be to blame for "frantic enthusiasm" if it did not provide for the case. "It may happen, and probably will happen, that their specie payments cannot be continued, and what will then be the situation of the bank? Failing to fulfil the purposes designed, its credit is blighted, its operations are stopped, and its charter violated; and if this should take place before your Treasury notes are sold, the government will scarce obtain a moment's relief." That the new bank could not pay specie was obvious. The Bank of England itself could not pay specie, and had not attempted to do so for nearly twenty years.

The House in committee adopted Calhoun's amendment by a majority of about sixty, in spite of Ingham's opposition; and thus substituted for Dallas's scheme a large private bank, over which the government was to exercise no control, with a capital of fifty millions, nine tenths of which were to be Treasury notes. The House then discovered so many unforeseen difficulties, that November 25 it recommitted the bill to a select committee, of which Lowndes, Calhoun, Ingham, Forsyth, and two Federalists were members.

Dallas was obliged openly to enter the lists against Calhoun, and wrote to the committee a letter, dated November 27,[1] sounding like a defiance: "The dividend on the funded debt has not been punctually paid; a large amount of Treasury notes has already been dishonored; and the hope of preventing further injury and reproach in transacting business with the Treasury is too visionary to afford a moment's consolation." Calhoun's scheme, he plainly intimated, was impracticable and mischievous.

The next day, November 28, Lowndes brought back Calhoun's bill to the House, together with Dallas's letter, and told the House that the committee could come to no agreement. Upon this admission of helplessness, Hanson addressed

[1] Dallas to Lowndes, Nov. 27, 1814; State Papers, ii. 872.

the House in a speech which seemed to carry Federalist exultation to the extremest point. Protesting his anxiety to defend the country, Hanson uttered a cry of triumph over the destruction of the government: —

"Not only had government bills been dishonored and the interest of the public debt remained unpaid, but . . . so completely empty was the Treasury and destitute of credit, that funds could not be obtained to defray the current ordinary expenses of the different Departments. Disgraceful, humiliating as the fact was, it ought not to be concealed from the nation, and he felt it his duty to state to the House that the Department of State was so bare of money as to be unable to pay even its stationery bill. The government was subsisting upon the drainings of unchartered banks in the District, which felt themselves compelled to contribute their means lest the rod *in terrorem* which was held over them should be applied, and an Act of incorporation refused."

No one contradicted or answered Hanson. The House wavered in incapacity that suggested dissolution. At last Richard M. Johnson, in order to force a decision right or wrong, moved the previous question and brought the House to a vote. Then the majority turned against Calhoun, as they had before turned against Dallas, and rejected the bill by a vote of one hundred and four to forty-nine.

The Southern preference for government paper currency lay at the bottom of Calhoun's scheme as of Jefferson's, and seemed to Dallas to combine ignorance with dishonesty. Treasury notes bearing interest could not be made to serve as a currency, and were useless as a foundation for government paper. "What use is there," asked Ingersoll,[1] "in such a mass of banking machinery to give circulation to some millions of Treasury notes? Why not issue them at once without this unwieldy, this unnecessary medium?" Yet when Bolling Hall of Georgia, in pursuance of Macon's aphorism that "paper money never was beat," moved, November 12, Resolutions authorizing the issue of Treasury notes as legal tender, the

[1] Annals of Congress, 1814–1815, p. 606.

House refused to consider it by a vote of ninety-five to forty-two. Eppes did not vote; Calhoun voted against it, and of the twenty-five Southern members who supported it Macon and Stanford were the most prominent.

Nothing could be plainer than that the House must ultimately come to inconvertible government paper, whether issued by the Treasury or by a Bank. Dallas, Eppes, and Calhoun were all agreed on that point, if on no other; but after Congress had sat two months and a half, the House was no nearer a decision than when it met. The Federalists, voting at one time with Calhoun, at another with Dallas, were able to paralyze action. Eppes wrote to Dallas, December 2, inviting further information; and Dallas wrote back the same day, recounting the needs of the Treasury for the current month, merely on account of the national debt. Dallas reported that $5,726,000 in Treasury notes and dividends were due, or would fall due by January 1; and that including unavailable bank-credits, and subject to possible contingencies, the Treasury might contain resources to meet these demands to the amount of $3,972,000.[1] Eppes could do no more for immediate relief than report a bill for the issue of some ten millions more of interest-bearing Treasury notes, which was passed without debate and became law, December 26, without improving the situation.

The House also passed the heavy tax-bills without much opposition except from Federalists who wished to stop military operations on the part of the government. Between thirty and forty members, or about one half of the Federalists, carried their opposition to that point. The bill raising the direct tax to six million dollars passed the House, December 22, by a vote of one hundred and six to fifty-three, and passed the Senate, January 5, 1815, by twenty-three to seven. Dallas and Eppes hoped to raise about twenty million dollars through the new taxation, or twice what had been previously attempted. Jefferson held that these taxes could not be paid, and expressed his opinion without reserve.

"If anything could revolt our citizens against the war,"

[1] Dallas to Eppes, Dec. 2, 1814; State Papers, Finance, ii. 877.

wrote Jefferson, November 28,[1] "it would be the extravagance with which they are about to be taxed. . . . The taxes proposed cannot be paid. How can a people who cannot get fifty cents a bushel for their wheat, while they pay twelve dollars a bushel for their salt, pay five times the amount of taxes they ever paid before? Yet this will be the case in all the States south of the Potomac."

If any conclusion was intended to be drawn from the official return[2] sent to Congress, October 13, of internal taxes received to that date in each State, the evil predicted by Jefferson seemed already to exist. In Massachusetts, of taxes to the amount of $200,000, accrued for the first two quarters of the year, $170,000 had been received before October 10. In New York $393,000 had accrued, and $303,000 had been received; thus New York was nearly one fourth in arrears. Pennsylvania was worse; of $470,000 accrued the government had received $280,000,—leaving two fifths in arrears. Virginia was in somewhat worse condition than Pennsylvania; of $247,000 accrued $136,000 had been paid,—leaving four ninths in arrears.

Yet Pennsylvania and Virginia paid taxes in their own depreciated bank paper, while New York and New England paid chiefly in Treasury notes. The new taxes were still to be paid in the same medium, although the laws gave no express authority for it. In the next Congress, when the subject was discussed, Wright of Maryland said:[3] "When Congress passed the revenue laws and imposed the six million and three million land tax, did they contemplate the payment of specie? No! they knew the people had it not, and of course could not pay it. . . . Does any man doubt that Congress intended these taxes being paid in bank paper? Nay, has not the Secretary of the Treasury . . . sealed this construction of the law by taking the bank paper in discharge for these taxes?" That the bank paper was worth less than Treasury notes was shown by the Southern States paying their taxes in such paper, when they might equally well have paid them in Treasury notes except for the difference in value.

[1] Jefferson to Short, Nov. 28, 1814; Works, vi. 398.
[2] Statement, etc.; State Papers, Finance, ii. 861.
[3] Annals of Congress, 1815–1816, p. 1435.

The medium of depreciated and depreciating bank paper in which the taxes were to be paid, secured the States outside of New England from intolerable pressure by giving the means of indefinite depreciation; but to the government such a resource meant merely a larger variety of bank-credits, which were of no certain value even in the towns where the banks existed, and were of no value at all elsewhere. The burden of taxation would be thrown chiefly on New England; and if the Hartford Convention did nothing else, it was sure to take measures for sequestering the proceeds of taxation in New England for military purposes. The hope of restoring the finances by taxation was faint. Until the currency could be established and exchanges made secure, the government was helpless.

The House having broken down November 28, the Senate next took the matter in hand. Rufus King reported, December 2, a bill to incorporate a bank, which was in effect the bill recommended by Dallas. After a week's consideration the Senate passed the bill, December 9, by the vote of seventeen to fourteen, — King and the Federalists, with four Republican senators, voting against it. The House referred it to the Committee of Ways and Means, which reported it, December 14, with amendments. The debate began December 23, and was cut short December 27 by C. J. Ingersoll, who by the close vote of seventy-two to seventy obliged the House to call for the previous question, and order the bill to its third reading. This energy was followed by a reaction; the bill was recommitted for amendment, again reported, and vehemently attacked.

Never had the House shown itself more feeble. The Federalists took the lead in debate; and January 2 Daniel Webster, in a speech that placed him at the head of the orators of the time, dictated the action of Congress: —

"What sort of an institution, sir, is this? It looks less like a bank than like a department of government. It will be properly the paper-money department. Its capital is government debts; the amount of issues will depend on government necessities; government in effect absolves itself from its own debts to the bank, and by way of compensation absolves the bank from its own contracts with others. This is indeed a wonderful scheme of finance. The government is to grow rich because it is to borrow without the obligation of repaying, and is to borrow of a bank which issues paper without the liability to redeem it. . . . They provide for an unlimited issue of paper in an entire exemption from payment. They found their bank in the first place on the discredit of government, and then hope to enrich government out of the insolvency of the bank."

Webster was a master of antithesis, and the proposed bank was in effect what he described; but had he been a member of the British Parliament he might have made the same objections, with little alteration, to the Bank of England. The Hartford Convention was in session while he spoke. Every word of his speech was a shock to the government and the Union, for his only suggestion was equivalent to doing nothing. He moved to instruct the committee to report a bill creating a bank with thirty millions of capital, composed one fourth of specie and three fourths of government securities; without power to suspend specie payments, and without obligation to lend three fifths of its capital to the government. To such a bank he would give his support, "not as a measure of temporary policy, or an expedient to find means of relief from the present poverty of the Treasury," but as an institution most useful in times of peace.

The House came to a vote the same day, and divided eighty-one to eighty. Then the Speaker, Langdon Cheves, rose, and after denouncing the proposed bank as "a dangerous, unexampled, and he might almost say a desperate resort," gave his casting vote against the bill.

No sooner had the House struck this blow at Dallas than it shrank back. The next day, amid complaints and objections, it reconsidered its matured decision by the sudden majority of one hundred and seven to fifty-four. Once more the bill was recommitted, and once more reported, January 6, in the form that Webster proposed. Weary of their own instability, the majority hastened to vote. Most of the Federalists supported the bill; but Grosvenor of New York, one of the ablest, frankly said what every one felt, that the proposed institution could not be a specie bank, or get a million of its notes into circulation. "The government relying on it would be disappointed, and ruin soon stare them in the face." With this understanding the House passed the bill, January 7, by a vote of one hundred and twenty to thirty-eight; and the Senate, after a struggle with the House, accepted it, January 20, by a vote of twenty to fourteen.

Dallas was not a man to be easily daunted even in so desperate a situation. After ten days deliberation, the President sent to Congress a veto message.

"The most the bank could effect," said Madison, "and the most it could be expected to aim at, would be to keep the institution alive by limited and local transactions . . . until a change from war to peace should enable it, by a flow of specie into its vaults and a removal of the external demand for it, to derive its contemplated emoluments from a safe and full extension of its operations."

"I hope this will satisfy our friends," wrote Webster to his brother,[1] "that it was not a bank likely to favor the Administration." Either with or without such a bank, the Administration was equally helpless. The veto left the Treasury, February 1, without a resource in prospect. The unsatisfied demands reached nearly twenty millions. The cash balance, chiefly in bank-credits, was little more than six millions. A further deficit of forty millions remained to be provided above the estimated revenue of 1815. United States six-per-cents commanded only a nominal price, between fifty and sixty cents on the dollar,[2] and were quoted in Boston at a discount of forty cents.[3] Treasury notes being in demand for taxes, were worth about seventy-five cents in the dollar. Dallas had no serious hope of carrying on the government. In a letter to the Committee of Ways and Means, dated January 17, he could only propose to add six millions more to the taxes, issue fifteen millions in Treasury notes, and borrow twenty-five millions on any terms that could be obtained. In making these recom-

[1] Letter to E. Webster, Jan. 30, 1814; Webster's Correspondence, i. 250, 251.
[2] Review of Dallas's Report; Boston "Advertiser," Dec. 1815.
[3] Niles, vii.; Supplement, p. 176.

mendations he avowed in grave words his want of confidence in their result:[1] —

> "In making the present communication I feel, sir, that I have performed my duty to the Legislature and to the country; but when I perceive that more than forty millions of dollars must be raised for the service of the year 1815, by an appeal to public credit through the medium of the Treasury notes and loans, I am not without sensations of extreme solicitude."

Young George Ticknor of Boston happened to be in the gallery of the House of Representatives when Eppes read this letter, January 21, and the next day he wrote,[2] —

> "The last remarkable event in the history of this remarkable Congress is Dallas's report. You can imagine nothing like the dismay with which it has filled the Democratic party. All his former communications were but emollients and palliations compared with this final disclosure of the bankruptcy of the nation. Mr. Eppes as Chancellor of the Exchequer, or Chairman of the Committee of Ways and Means, read it in his place yesterday, and when he had finished, threw it upon the table with expressive violence, and turning around to Mr. Gaston, asked him with a bitter levity between jest and earnest,—
> " 'Well, sir! will your party take the government if we will give it up to them?'
> " 'No, sir!' said Gaston; . . . 'No, sir! Not unless you will give it to us as we gave it to you!' "

[1] Dallas to Eppes, Jan. 17, 1817; State Papers, Finance, ii. 885.
[2] Life of George Ticknor, i. 31.

Chapter X

WHILE DALLAS struggled with Congress to obtain the means of establishing a currency in order to pay the army, Monroe carried on a similar struggle in order to obtain an army to pay. On this point, as on the financial issue, Virginian ideas did not accord with the wishes of Government. The prejudice against a regular army was stimulated by the evident impossibility of raising or supporting it. Once more Jefferson expressed the common feeling of his Virginia neighbors.[1]

> "We must prepare for interminable war," he wrote to Monroe, October 16. "To this end we should put our house in order by providing men and money to an indefinite extent. The former may be done by classing our militia, and assigning each class to the description of duties for which it is fit. It is nonsense to talk of regulars. They are not to be had among a people so easy and happy at home as ours. We might as well rely on calling down an army of angels from heaven."

As Jefferson lost the habits of power and became once more a Virginia planter, he reverted to the opinions and prejudices of his earlier life and of the society in which he lived. As Monroe grew accustomed to the exercise and the necessities of power, he threw aside Virginian ideas and accepted the responsibilities of government. On the same day when Jefferson wrote to Monroe that it was nonsense to talk of regulars, Monroe wrote to Congress that it was nonsense to talk of militia. The divergence between Monroe and Jefferson was even greater than between Dallas and Eppes.

> "It may be stated with confidence," wrote Monroe to Congress,[2] "that at least three times the force in militia has been employed at our principal cities, along the coast and on the frontier, in marching to and returning thence, that would have been necessary in regular troops; and that the

[1] Jefferson to Monroe, Oct. 16, 1814; Works, vi. 394.
[2] Monroe to Giles, Oct. 17, 1814; State Papers, Military Affairs, i. 514.

expense attending it has been more than proportionately augmented from the difficulty if not the impossibility of preserving the same degree of system in the militia as in the regular service."

In Monroe's opinion a regular force was an object "of the highest importance." He told the Senate committee that the army, which was only thirty-four thousand strong on the first of October, should be raised to its legal limit of sixty-two thousand, and that another permanent army of forty thousand men should be raised for strictly defensive service. In the face of Jefferson's warning that he might as well call down an army of angels from heaven, Monroe called for one hundred thousand regular troops, when no exertions had hitherto availed to keep thirty thousand effectives on the rolls.

The mere expression of such a demand carried with it the train of consequences which the people chiefly dreaded. One hundred thousand troops could be raised only by draft. Monroe affirmed the power as well as the need of drafting. "Congress have a right by the Constitution," he said, "To raise regular armies, and no restraint is imposed on the exercise of it. . . . It would be absurd to suppose that Congress could not carry this power into effect otherwise than by accepting the voluntary service of individuals." Absurd as it was, such had been the general impression, and Monroe was believed to have been one of the most emphatic in maintaining it. "Ask him," suggested Randolph, "what he would have done, while governor of Virginia and preparing to resist Federal usurpation, had such an attempt been made by Mr. Adams and his ministers, especially in 1800. He *can* give the answer." Doubtless the silence of the Constitution in respect to conscription was conclusive to some minds in favor of the power; but the people preferred the contrary view, the more because militia service seemed to give more pay for less risk.

The chance of carrying such a measure through Congress was not great, yet Monroe recommended it as his first plan for raising men. He proposed to enroll the free male population between eighteen and forty-five years of age into classes of one hundred, each to furnish four men and to keep their places supplied.[1] The second plan varied from the first only in the classification, not in the absence of compulsion. The militia were to be divided into three sections according to age, with the obligation to serve, when required, for a term of two years. A third plan suggested the exemption from militia service of every five militia-men who could provide one man for the war. If none of these schemes should be approved by Congress, additional bounties must be given under the actual system. Of the four plans, the secretary preferred the first.

The Senate committee immediately summoned Monroe to an interview. They wished an explanation of the failure in the recruiting service, and were told by Monroe that the failure was chiefly due to the competition of the detached militia for substitutes.[2] The military committee of the House then joined with the military committee of the Senate in sounding the members of both bodies in order to ascertain the most rigorous measure that could be passed. According to the report of Troup of Georgia, chairman of the House committee,[3] they "found that no efficacious measure, calculated certainly and promptly to fill the regular army, could be effectually resorted to. Measures were matured and proposed by the [House] committee, but were not pressed on the House, from the solemn conviction that there was no disposition in the Legislature to act finally on the subject."

Yet the issue was made at a moment of extreme anxiety and almost despair. In October, 1814, the result of the war was believed to depend on the establishment of an efficient draft. The price of United States six-per-cents showed better than any other evidence the opinion of the public; but the military situation, known to all the world, warranted deep depression. Sir George Prevost, about to be succeeded by an efficient commander,—Sir George Murray,—was then at Kingston organizing a campaign against Sackett's Harbor, with an army of twenty thousand regular troops and a fleet that con-

[1] Explanatory Observations, State Papers, Military Affairs, i. 515.

[2] Monroe to Giles, Oct. 26, 1814; State Papers, Military Affairs, i. 518.

[3] Annals of Congress, Feb. 6, 1815, p. 1130.

trolled the Lake. Another great force, military and naval, was known to be on its way to New Orleans; and the defences of New Orleans were no stronger than those of Washington. One half the province of Maine, from Eastport to Castine, was already in British possession.

To leave no doubt of England's intentions, despatches from Ghent, communicating the conditions on which the British government offered peace, arrived from the American commissioners and were sent, October 10, to Congress. These conditions assumed rights of conquest. The British negotiators demanded four territorial or proprietary concessions, and all were vital to the integrity of the Union. First, the whole Indian Territory of the Northwest, including about one third of the State of Ohio, two thirds of Indiana, and nearly the entire region from which the States of Illinois, Wisconsin, and Michigan were afterward created, was to be set aside forever as Indian country under British guaranty. Second, the United States were to be excluded from military or naval contact with the Lakes. Third, they had forfeited their rights in the fisheries. Fourth, they were to cede a portion of Maine to strengthen Canada.

These demands, following the unparalleled insult of burning Washington, foreshadowed a war carried to extremities, and military preparations such as the Union had no means ready to repel. Monroe's recommendations rested on the conviction that the nation must resort to extreme measures. Dallas's financial plan could not have been suggested except as a desperate resource. Congress understood as well as the Executive the impending peril, and stood in even more fear of it.

Under these circumstances, when Troup's committee refused to act, Giles reported, on behalf of the Senate committee, two military measures. The first, for filling the regular army, proposed to extend the age of enlistment from twenty-one to eighteen years; to double the land-bounty; and to exempt from militia duty every militia-man who should furnish a recruit for the regular service.

The second measure, reported the same day, November 5, purported to authorize the raising an army of eighty thousand militia-men by draft, to serve for two years within the limits of their own or an adjoining State.[1] The provisions of this measure were ill-conceived, ill-digested, and unlikely to answer their purpose. The moment the debate began, the bill was attacked so vigorously as to destroy whatever credit it might have otherwise possessed.

Of all the supporters of the war, Senator Varnum of Massachusetts was one of the steadiest. He was also the highest authority in the Senate on matters pertaining to the militia. When Giles's bill came under discussion November 16, Varnum began the debate by a speech vehemently hostile to the proposed legislation. He first objected that although the bill purported to call for an army of eighty thousand men, "yet in some of the subsequent sections of it we find that instead of realizing the pleasing prospect of seeing an ample force in the field, the force is to be reduced to an indefinite amount,—which contradiction in terms, inconsistency in principle, and uncertainty in effect, cannot fail to produce mortification and chagrin in every breast." Varnum objected to drafting men from the militia for two years' service because the principle of nine months' service was already established by the common law. If the nation wanted a regular force, why not make it a part of the regular army without a system of drafting militia "unnecessary, unequal, and unjust?" The machinery of classification and draft was " wholly impracticable." The limit of service to adjoining States abandoned the objects for which the Union existed. The proffered bounties would ruin the recruiting service for the regular army; the proffered exemptions and reductions in term of duty left no permanency to the service. The bill inflicted no penalties and charged no officers with the duty of making the draft. "I consider the whole system as resolving into a recommendation upon the patriotism of the States and Territories and upon the patriotism of the classes."

The justice of Varnum's criticism could not fairly be questioned. The bill authorized the President "to issue his orders to such officers of the militia as he may think proper," and left the classification and draft in the hands of these militia officers. Every drafted man who had performed any tour of

[1] A Bill, etc.; Niles, vii. 181.

duty in the militia since the beginning of the war was entitled to deduct a corresponding term from his two years of service; and obviously the demand created for substitutes would stop recruiting for the regular army.

Hardly had Varnum sat down when Senator Daggett of Connecticut spoke.

"The bill," said the Connecticut senator, "is incapable of being executed, as well as unconstitutional and unjust. It proceeds entirely upon the idea that the State governments will lend their aid to carry it into effect. If they refuse, it becomes inoperative. Now, sir, will the Executives, who believe it a violation of the Constitution, assist in its execution? I tell you they will not."

Every member of the Senate who heard these words knew that they were meant to express the will of the convention which was to meet at Hartford within a month. The sentiment thus avowed was supported by another New England senator, whose State was not a party to the Convention. Jeremiah Mason of New Hampshire was second to no one in legal ability or in personal authority, and when he followed Daggett in the debate, he spoke with full knowledge of the effect his words would have on the action of the Hartford Convention and of the State executives.

"In my opinion," he said, "this system of military conscription thus recommended by the Secretary of War is not only inconsistent with the provisions and spirit of the Constitution, but also with all the principles of civil liberty. In atrocity it exceeds that adopted by the late Emperor of France for the subjugation of Europe. . . . Such a measure cannot, it ought not to be submitted to. If it could in no other way be averted, I not only believe, but I hope, it would be resisted."

Mason pointed to the alternative,—which Massachusetts was then adopting, as the necessary consequence of refusing power to the government,—that the States must resume the powers of sovereignty:

"Should the national defence be abandoned by the

general government, I trust the people, if still retaining a good portion of their resources, may rally under their State governments against foreign invasion, and rely with confidence on their own courage and virtue."

At that time the State of Massachusetts was occupied for one hundred miles of its sea-coast by a British force, avowedly for purposes of permanent conquest; and the State legislature, October 18, refused to make an inquiry, or to consider any measure for regaining possession of its territory, or to cooperate with the national government for the purpose,[1] but voted to raise an army of ten thousand men. The object of this State army was suggested by Christopher Gore, the Federalist senator from Massachusetts who followed Mason in the debate. In personal and political influence Gore stood hardly second to Mason, and his opinions were likely to carry the utmost weight with the convention at Hartford. With this idea necessarily in his mind, Gore told the Senate,—

"This [bill] is the first step on the odious ground of conscription,—a plan, sir, which never will and never ought to be submitted to by this country while it retains one idea of civil freedom; a plan, sir, which if attempted will be resisted by many States, and at every hazard. In my judgment, sir, it should be resisted by all who have any regard to public liberty or the rights of the several States."

These denunciations were not confined to New England. Senator Goldsborough of Maryland, also a Federalist, affirmed that the sentiment of abhorrence for military duty was almost universal:—

"Sir, you dare not—at least I hope you dare not—attempt a conscription to fill the ranks of your regular army. When the plan of the Secretary of War made its appearance, it was gratifying to find that it met with the abhorrence of almost every man in the nation; and the merit of the bill before you, if such a measure can be supposed to have merit at all, is that it is little else, as regards the militia, than a servile imitation of the secretary's plan."

[1] Message of Governor Strong, with documents, Jan. 18, 1815.

Nevertheless, when Goldsborough took his seat the Senate passed the Militia Bill by a vote of nineteen to twelve,—Anderson of Tennessee and Varnum of Massachusetts joining the Federalists in opposition. The Regular Army Bill, which was in effect a bill to sacrifice the regular army, passed November 11, without a division. Both measures then went to the House and were committed, November 12, to the Committee of the Whole.

Ordinarily such a measure would have been referred to the Military Committee, but in this instance the Military Committee would have nothing to do with the Senate bill. Troup, the chairman, began the debate by denouncing it.[1] The measure, he said, was inadequate to its object. "It proposed to give you a militia force when you wanted, not a militia, but a regular force . . . You have a deficiency of twenty-odd thousand to supply. How will you supply it? Assuredly the [Regular Army] bill from the Senate will not supply it. No, sir, the recruiting system has failed." On the nature of the force necessary for the next campaign Troup expressed his own opinion and that of his committee, as well as that of the Executive, in language as strong as he could use at such a time and place. "If, after what has happened, I could for a moment believe there could be any doubt or hesitation on this point, I would consider everything as lost; then indeed there would be an end of hope and of confidence." Yet on precisely this point Congress showed most doubt. Nothing could induce it to accept Troup's view of the necessity for providing a regular army. "The bill from the Senate," remonstrated Troup, "instead of proposing this, proposes to authorize the President to call upon the States for eighty thousand raw militia; and this is to be our reliance for the successful prosecution of the war! Take my word for it, sir, that if you do rely upon it (the military power of the enemy remaining undivided) defeat, disaster, and disgrace, must follow."

The House refused to support Troup or the President. Calhoun was first to yield to the general unwillingness, and declared himself disposed to accept the Senate bill as a matter

[1] Debate of Dec. 2, 1814; Annals of Congress, 1814–1815, iii. 705.

of policy. Richard M. Johnson, though sympathizing with Troup, still preferred to accept the bill as the only alternative to nothing: "If it was rejected, they would have no dependence for defence but on six months' militia."[1] On the other hand, Thomas K. Harris of Tennessee protested that if the British government had it in their power to control the deliberations of Congress, they could not devise the adoption of a measure of a military character better calculated to serve their purposes. The people, he said, were in his part of the country prepared to make every sacrifice, and expected Congress, after the news from Ghent, to do its share; but Congress was about to adopt a measure of all others the best calculated to prolong the war.[2]

While the friends of the government spoke in terms of open discouragement and almost despair of the strongest military measure which Congress would consent to consider, the Federalists made no concealment of their wishes and intentions. Daniel Webster used similar arguments to those of his friend Jeremiah Mason in the Senate, affirming that the same principle which authorized the enlistment of apprentices would equally authorize the freeing of slaves,[3] and echoing pathetic threats of disunion.[4] Other Federalists made no professions of sadness over the approaching dissolution of government. Artemas Ward of Massachusetts spoke December 14, the day before the Hartford Convention was to meet, and announced the course which events were to take:[5] —

"That the Treasury is empty I admit; that the ranks of the regular army are thin I believe to be true; and that our country must be defended in all events, I not only admit but affirm. But, sir, if all the parts of the United States are defended, of course the whole will be defended. If every State in the Union, with such aid as she can obtain from her neighbors, defends herself, our whole country will be defended. In my mind the resources of the States will be

[1] Annals of Congress, 1814–1815, iii. 974.
[2] Annals of Congress, 1814–1815, iii. 891, 895.
[3] Annals of Congress, 1814–1815, iii. 734.
[4] Speech of C. J. Ingersoll, Dec. 9, 1814; Annals, 1814–1815, iii. 809.
[5] Annals of Congress, 1814–1815, iii. 907.

applied with more economy and with greater effect in defence of the country under the State governments than under the government of the United States."

Such avowals of the intent to throw aside Constitutional duties were not limited to members from New England. Morris S. Miller of New York made a vehement speech on the failure of national defence, and declared the inevitable result to be "that the States must and will take care of themselves; and they will preserve the resources of the States for the defence of the States."[1] He also declared that conscription would be resisted, and echoed the well-remembered declamation of Edward Livingston against the Alien Bill in 1798, when the Republican orator prayed to God that the States would never acquiesce in obedience to the law.

"This House," replied Duvall of Kentucky, "has heard discord and rebellion encouraged and avowed from more than one quarter." Indeed, from fully one fourth of its members the House heard little else. Under the shadow of the Hartford Convention the Federalist members talked with entire frankness. "This great fabric seems nodding and tottering to its fall," said Z. R. Shipherd of New York, December 9;[2] "and Heaven only knows how long before the mighty ruin will take place." J. O. Moseley of Connecticut "meant no improper menace" by predicting to the House, "if they were determined to prosecute the war by a recourse to such measures as are provided in the present bill, that they would have no occasion for future committees of investigation into the causes of the failure of their arms."[3] The latest committee of investigation had recently made a long report on the capture of Washington, carefully abstaining from expressing opinions of its own, or imputing blame to any one, and Moseley's remark involved a double sneer. None of these utterances were resented. Richard Stockton of New Jersey was allowed unanswered to denounce in measured terms the mild Militia Bill then under debate, from which the committee had already struck the term of two years' service by substituting one year;

[1] Annals of Congress, 1814–1815, iii. 790, 791.
[2] Annals of Congress, 1814–1815, iii. 829.
[3] Annals of Congress, 1814–1815, iii. 833.

and Stockton concluded his fine-drawn arguments by equally studied menace:[1] —

> "This bill also attacks the right and sovereignty of the State governments. Congress is about to usurp their undoubted rights,—to take from them their militia. By this bill we proclaim that we will have their men, as many as we please, when and where and for as long a time as we see fit, and for any service we see proper. Do gentlemen of the majority seriously believe that the people and the State governments will submit to this claim? Do they believe that all the States of this Union will submit to this usurpation? Have you attended to the solemn and almost unanimous declaration of the legislature of Connecticut? Have you examined the cloud arising in the East? Do you perceive that it is black, alarming, portentous?"

The Resolution of the Connecticut legislature to which Stockton referred was adopted in October, and authorized the governor in case of the passage of the Militia Bill to convoke the General Assembly forthwith, to consider measures "to secure and preserve the rights and liberties of the people of this State, and the freedom, sovereignty, and independence of the same."[2] Stockton's speech was made December 10, and "the cloud arising in the East," as he figured the Hartford Convention, was to take form December 15. The Republican speakers almost as earnestly used the full influence of these national fears to rouse the energies of the House. They neither denied nor disguised the helplessness of government. All admitted dread of approaching disaster. Perhaps C. J. Ingersoll was the only member who declared that the war had been successful, and that Americans need no longer blush to be Americans; but Ingersoll disliked the Militia Bill as cordially as it was disliked by Troup or Varnum, and voted for it only because "something must be done."[3]

> "When our army," said Samuel Hopkins of Kentucky, in closing the debate, "is composed of a mere handful of men,

[1] Annals of Congress, 1814–1815, iii. 848.
[2] Resolution; Niles, vii.; Supplement, p. 107.
[3] Annals of Congress, 1814–1815, iii. 808.

and our treasury empty so that it cannot provide for this gallant handful; when an enemy, powerful and active, is beating against our shores like the strong wave of the ocean; when everything is at stake,— . . . surely such is not the moment for parsimonious feelings in raising taxes, or for forced constructions to defeat the means for raising men."

Notwithstanding every effort of the war-leaders, the opposition steadily won control over the House. Daniel Webster during his entire lifetime remembered with satisfaction that he shared with Eppes the credit of overthrowing what he called Monroe's conscription.[1] December 10, at Eppes's motion, the House voted by a majority of sixty-two to fifty-seven to reduce the term of service from two years to one.[2] A motion made by Daniel Webster to reduce the term to six months was lost by only one voice, the vote standing seventy-eight to seventy-nine.[3] The bill passed at last, December 14, by a vote of eighty-four to seventy-two, in a House where the true war majority was forty-six. When the Senate insisted on its provision of two years' service, Troup, in conference committee, compromised on eighteen months. Then the House, December 27, by a vote of seventy-three to sixty-four, rejected the report of its conference committee. The next day, December 28, in the Senate, Rufus King made an unpremeditated motion for indefinite postponement. Some members were absent; no debate occurred. The question was immediately put, and carried by a vote of fourteen to thirteen.[4] The effect of this action was to destroy the bill.

With this failure the attempt to supply an army was abandoned, and Congress left the government to conduct the war in 1815, as in 1814, with thirty thousand regular troops and six months' militia. Monroe's effort to fill the ranks of the army ended in doubling the land-bounty; in authorizing the enlistment of minors, who had till then been enlisted without authorization; and in exempting from militia duty such persons

[1] Curtis's Life of Webster, i. 139.
[2] Annals of Congress, 1814–1815, iii. 869.
[3] Annals of Congress, 1814–1815, iii. 882.
[4] Curtis's Life of Webster, i. 139 *note*.

as should furnish a recruit for the regular army.[1] The prospect
was remote that such inducements could do more than repair
the waste of the actual force; but the government was unable
to pay a larger number even if the force could be raised, and
Monroe was obliged to prepare for the next campaign with
such slight means of defence as remained to him. The last
effort to induce the House to consider a serious method of
raising troops was made February 6, and was referred to the
Committee of the Whole, with a tacit understanding that the
ordinary process of recruiting was not to be disturbed.[2] According to the returns in the adjutant-general's office, the
whole number of men—non-commissioned officers, privates,
musicians, and artificers, present or absent, sick or well—in
the regular army Feb. 16, 1815, was thirty-two thousand one
hundred and sixty. During the previous two months it had
remained stationary, the returns of December, 1814, reporting
thirty-two thousand three hundred and sixty men. Nothing
showed a possibility of greatly increasing the force by the
means prescribed by Congress.

The navy requiring little new legislation, readily obtained
the little it asked. Almost the first Act of the session, approved
Nov. 15, 1814, authorized the purchasing or building of twenty
sixteen-gun sloops-of-war. Another Act of Feb. 7, 1815, created
a Board of Commissioners for the navy to discharge all the
ministerial duties of the secretary, under his superintendence.

This legislation, with the various tax-bills, comprised all
that was accomplished by Congress between the months of
September and February toward a vigorous prosecution of
the war. For the navy the prospect of success in the coming
year was sufficiently fair, and privateering promised to be
more active than ever; but the army was threatened with
many perils. The most serious of all dangers to the military
service of the Union was supposed by Federalists to be the
establishment of armies by the separate States. The attempt
to establish such an army by Massachusetts in time of peace
had been one of the causes which led to the Constitution of
1789;[3] and at the close of 1814, when Massachusetts voted to

[1] Act of Dec. 10, 1814; Annals of Congress, 1814–1815, p. 1837.
[2] Annals of Congress, 1814–1815, pp. 1125–1130.
[3] Madison's Debates, ii. 712.

raise an army of ten thousand men, the significance of the step was more clearly evident than in the time of the Confederation.

The State of Massachusetts might be supposed to act in a spirit of hostility to the Constitution; but no such motive actuated States outside of New England. If they followed the same course, they did so because the national government was believed to be incompetent to the general defence. Of all the States Massachusetts alone possessed considerable resources, and could command both credit and specie; yet the creation of a State army of ten thousand men overburdened her finances, and obliged her to claim her share of the national revenues. No other State could expect to support an army without immediate financial trouble. Yet Governor Tompkins of New York recommended to the legislature in September the establishment of a State army of twenty thousand men,[1] and the legislature passed Acts for the purpose. The legislature of Pennsylvania took a similar measure into consideration. The legislature of Maryland passed an Act for raising five thousand State troops. Virginia decided also to create a State army, with two major-generals. South Carolina passed a law for raising a brigade of State troops, and appointed the officers. Kentucky took measures for raising a State army of ten thousand men.

The national government, unable to create an efficient army of its own, yielded to necessity, and looked already to the State armies as levies to be taken into the national service in case of need. The States, on their side, unable to bear the expense of separate armies, expected to be relieved of the burden by the national government. Yet for the moment the States, however deficient their means might be, seemed better able than the general government not only to raise men but to support them. In January, 1815, the financial resources of the government were exhausted, so that the Treasury could not meet the drafts drawn by Major-General Jackson and the pressing demands of the paymaster at New Orleans. The Secretary of War was obliged to go from bank to bank of Washington and Georgetown asking, as a personal favor, loans of

[1] Message of Sept. 30, 1814; Niles, vii. 97.

their bank-notes already depreciated about fifty per cent. So desperate, according to Monroe's account, was the situation that his success depended on adding his own guaranty to that of the government.[1] At no time of his life were Monroe's means sufficient to supply his private needs, and nothing could express so strongly his sense of national bankruptcy as the assertion that his credit was required to support that of the United States.[2]

The State armies were the natural result of such a situation. Congress could not resist the movement, and passed an Act, approved Jan. 27, 1815, authorizing the President to receive into the national service a certain proportion of the State troops, not exceeding forty thousand men in the aggregate. Little was said in debate on the bearings of the Act, which seemed to concede the demand of Massachusetts that the States should be allowed to raise troops at the expense of the United States. The Hartford Convention had then met, deliberated, and adjourned. Its report had been published, and among its demands was one that "these States might be allowed to assume their own defence." The Federalists considered the Act of Jan. 27, 1815, as a "full and ample" concession of the demand.[3] Senator Gore wrote to Governor Strong, January 22, while the measure was before the President, commenting on the financial and military expedients of Dallas and Monroe:[4]

"These appear to me the spasms of a dying government. . . . The bill authorizing the raising of State troops by the States, and at the expense of the United States, according to the plan sent you some time since, has passed both Houses. Thus one part of the recommendation of the Hartford Convention seems to be adopted. The other,— that to authorize the States to receive the taxes,—will probably be more difficult to be attained. The accession to this seems not to accord with Mr. Monroe's intimation in

[1] Monroe's Memoir; Deposition of Tench Ringgold, Feb. 14, 1826, pp. 13, 58.
[2] Eulogy of James Monroe by J. Q. Adams, p. 75.
[3] H. G. Otis's Letters in Defence of the Hartford Convention, 1824, pp. 38, 39.
[4] Lodge's Cabot, p. 561.

your letter, or rather in his letter to you. Indeed, if they have fears of the State governments, one can hardly account for this government's authorizing the States to raise and keep in pay, at the expense of the United States, troops which may be used for purposes hostile to, or not conformable with, the views of the paymaster."

The accession to the principle of State armies which surprised Gore could be explained only by the government's consciousness of helplessness. Gore was somewhat careful to express no opinion of the probable consequences, but other Federalists spoke with entire candor. Timothy Pickering expected a division of the Union.[1] Less extreme partisans looked only to a dissolution of government. A year afterward, in the calmer light of peace and union, Joseph Hopkinson, a very distinguished Federalist of Philadelphia, not deluded like the New Englanders by local pride or prejudice, declared publicly in Congress the common conviction of his party on the probable consequences of another year of war:[2]

"The federal government was at the last gasp of existence. But six months longer and it was no more. . . . The general government would have dissolved into its original elements; its powers would have returned to the States from which they were derived; and they doubtless would have been fully competent to their defence against any enemy. Does not everybody remember that all the great States, and I believe the small ones too, were preparing for this state of things, and organizing their own means for their own defence?"

Calhoun contradicted Hopkinson and denied his assertions; but on that subject Hopkinson was at least an equal authority. Calhoun knew well his own State, but he knew little of New England; and he had yet to learn, perhaps to his own surprise, how easily a section of the Union could be wrought to treason.

[1] Pickering to John Lowell, Jan. 24, 1815; New England Federalism, p. 425.
[2] Debate of Jan. 29, 1816; Annals of Congress, 1815–1816, p. 795.

Chapter XI

THE MASSACHUSETTS legislature issued, October 17, its invitation to the New England States for a conference,[1] and on the same day the newspapers published the despatches from Ghent, to August 20, containing British conditions of peace,—which required, among greater sacrifices, a cession of Massachusetts territory, and an abandonment of fisheries and fishing rights conceded with American independence. Two counties of the State beyond the Penobscot were then in British military possession, and a third, Nantucket, was a British naval station. Yet even under these circumstances the British demands did not shock the Federalist leaders. Governor Strong, after reading the Ghent documents October 17, wrote to Pickering at Washington,[2]—

> "If Great Britain had discovered a haughty or grasping spirit, it might naturally have excited irritation; but I am persuaded that in the present case there is not a member of Congress who, if he was a member of Parliament, would have thought that more moderate terms ought in the first instance to have been offered."

The argument seemed to prove only that members of Congress could also be haughty and grasping; but Governor Strong thought the British demands reasonable, and began at once to sound his friends in regard to the proposed concessions. The following day he wrote[3] that the Essex people expected to lose the fisheries, but were ready to give up a portion of Maine to retain them.

Pickering wrote in reply, acquiescing in the proposed barter of territory for fisheries, and also in the more extravagant British demands for the Indians and the Lakes. "I was gratified," said Pickering,[4] "to find my own sentiments cor-

---

[1] Letter of Invitation, Oct. 17, 1814; Niles, vii. 179.
[2] Lodge's Memoir of Strong; Proceedings of Massachusetts Historical Society, 1879.
[3] Lodge's Memoir of Strong; Proceedings of Massachusetts Historical Society, 1879.
[4] Pickering to Strong, Oct. 29, 1814; Lodge's Cabot, p. 535.

responding with yours." The leading Federalists united with Pickering and Strong in blaming the American negotiators and the government for rejecting the British offers. The same view was taken by the chief Federalist newspaper of the State, the Boston "Centinel."[1]

Thus in the November election, a few weeks later, two issues were impressed on the people of New England. In regard to neither issue did the Federalist leaders attempt concealment. The people were invited, as far as the press of both parties could decide the points of dispute, to express their opinion,—first, whether the British conditions of peace should have been taken into consideration; second, whether the States should be represented at the Hartford Convention. The popular response was emphatic. Everywhere in New England the Republican candidates were defeated; and the Federalists, encouraged by the result,—believing the Hartford Convention to be the most popular action taken by Massachusetts since the State adopted the Federal Constitution,[2]—prepared to support measures, looking to the restoration of peace and to the establishment of a new Federal compact comprising either the whole or a portion of the actual Union.

However varied the wishes of the majority might be, they agreed in requiring a radical change in the organic law. This intention was their chief claim to popularity. The Boston "Centinel," announcing November 9 the adhesion of Connecticut and Rhode Island to the Hartford Convention, placed over the announcement the head-line, "Second and third Pillars of a new Federal Edifice reared." During November and December, almost every day, the newspapers discussed the question what the convention should do; and the chief divergence of opinion seemed to regard rather the immediate than the ultimate resort to forcible means of stopping the war. The extremists, represented in the press by John Lowell, asked for immediate action.

"Throwing off all connection with this wasteful war,"—wrote "A New England Man" in the "Centinel" of December 17,—"making peace with our enemy and opening once

[1] Boston Centinel, Oct. 19, 1814.
[2] Otis's Letters in Defence of the Hartford Convention, p. 10.

more our commerce with the world, would be a wise and manly course. The occasion demands it of us, and the people at large are ready to meet it."

Apparently Lowell was right. The people showed no sign of unwillingness to meet any decision that might be recommended by the convention. As the moment approached, the country waited with increasing anxiety for the result. The Republican press—the "National Intelligencer" as well as the Boston "Patriot"—at first ridiculed the convention, then grew irritable, and at last betrayed signs of despair. On both sides threats were openly made and openly defied; but in Massachusetts the United States government had not five hundred effective troops, and if the convention chose to recommend that the State should declare itself neutral and open its ports, no one pretended that any national power existed in Massachusetts capable of preventing the legislature from carrying the recommendation into effect if it pleased.

From immediate extravagance Massachusetts was saved by the leaders who, knowing the popular excitement, feared lest the convention should be carried too fast into disorder, and for that reason selected representatives who could be trusted to resist emotion. When George Cabot was chosen as the head of the State delegation, the character of the body was fixed. The selection of Cabot did not please the advocates of action. Pickering wrote to Lowell suggesting doubts whether Cabot was the fittest choice.[1] Lowell replied that he shared these doubts, and that in consequence he had been led to oppose the convention altogether, because it would not withdraw the State resources from the general government.[2] Cabot, he said, was "most reluctantly dragged in like a conscript to the duty of a delegate;" he had always been despondent as to the course of public affairs, and felt no confidence in the possibility of awakening the people to their true disease,—which was not the war or the Union, but democracy. Lowell did not know "a single bold and ardent man" among the Massachusetts or Connecticut delegates. In the "Centinel"

[1] Pickering to Lowell, Nov. 7, 1814; Lodge's Cabot, p. 541.
[2] Lowell to Pickering, Dec. 3, 1814; Lodge's Cabot, p. 545.

of December 7 he described Cabot's tendencies in language evidently intended as a warning to Cabot himself:—

"There are men who know that our troubles are not the offspring of this war alone, and will not die with it. But they despair of relief, and think resistance unavailing. They consider the people in their very nature democratic, and that nothing but the severity of their sufferings has driven them from those men and that system out of which have grown all our evils; that should they be restored to that state of prosperity which they once enjoyed, the same passions and opinions would diffuse themselves through the country, and the same course of conduct be again followed out."

Cabot shocked Pickering by expressing all his favorite political views in one brief question: "Why can't you and I let the world ruin itself its own way?"[1] Such a turn of mind was commonly the mark of a sceptical spirit, which doubted whether the world at best was worth the trouble of saving; and against this inert and indifferent view of human affairs New England offered a constant protest. Yet the Massachusetts delegation to Hartford was in sympathy with Cabot, while the Massachusetts legislature seemed to sympathize with Pickering. William Prescott, another member of the delegation, was chiefly remarkable for prudence and caution; Nathan Dane bore the same stamp; Harrison Gray Otis took character and color from his surroundings. The Connecticut delegation—James Hillhouse, Chauncey Goodrich, Roger M. Sherman, and others—were little likely to recommend "effectual measures." The convention consisted of men supposed to be inclined to resist popular pressure, and Cabot was probably serious in replying to a young friend who asked him what he was to do at Hartford: "We are going to keep you young hot-heads from getting into mischief."[2]

In the Council Chamber of the State House at Hartford the delegates assembled, December 15, and gave instant evidence of their intention to discourage appeals to popular emotion. Their earliest steps decided their whole course. They chose

[1] Lodge's Cabot, p. 541.
[2] Lodge's Cabot, p. 519.

George Cabot as their President, and they made their sessions secret. Under no circumstances could the convention have regarded itself as a popular body, for the delegates numbered only twenty-three persons, mostly cautious and elderly men, who detested democracy, but disliked enthusiasm almost as much. Two new members, appointed by popular meetings in New Hampshire, were next admitted; and toward the close of the sessions another member, representing the county of Windham in Vermont, was given a seat. Thus enlarged, the convention over which George Cabot presided numbered twenty-six members besides the secretary, Theodore Dwight.

Excess of caution helped to give the convention an air of conspiracy, which warned future conspirators to prefer acting, or appearing to act, in public. The secrecy of the Hartford conference was chiefly intended to secure freedom for the exchange of opinion, and also in some degree to prevent premature excitement and intrusion of popular feeling; but the secrecy created a belief that the debates would not bear publicity. Possibly much was said which verged on treasonable conspiracy; but the members were not men of a class likely to act beyond their instructions, and they adhered strictly to the practical task imposed on them. Some years afterward, Harrison Gray Otis, laboring to clear his political reputation from the stigma of membership, caused the official journal of the convention to be published; and the record, though revealing nothing of what was said, proved that nothing was formally done or proposed which contradicted the grave and restrained attitude maintained in its public expressions.

On the first day of its meeting the convention appointed a committee to consider and report upon the business to be done. Chauncey Goodrich, Otis, and three other members formed this committee, which reported the next day the points in dispute between the States and the national government,—the militia power, conscription power, duty and means of defence, and matters of a like nature. After two days of discussion, the convention appointed another committee to frame a general project of measures, and again placed a Connecticut man—Nathaniel Smith—at its head, with Otis second. Still another committee was appointed, December 21, to prepare a report showing the reasons which guided the convention to its results; and of that committee Otis was chairman.

Clearly, Otis took the chief burden of business; and the result could scarcely fail to reflect in some degree the character of the man as well as of the body for which he was acting. Though ambitious of leading, Otis never led. John Lowell described his character, as it was understood in Boston, perhaps somewhat harshly, for Otis was no favorite with any class of men who held fixed opinions:[1] —

"Mr. Otis is naturally timid and frequently wavering, — to-day bold, and to-morrow like a hare trembling at every breeze. It would seem by his language that he is prepared for the very boldest measures, but he receives anonymous letters every day or two threatening him with bodily harm. It seems the other party suspect his firmness. He is sincere in wishing thorough measures, but a thousand fears restrain him."

Otis was the probable author of the report, adopted December 24, recommending a course to the convention; and he was chairman of the larger committee to which that report was referred, and within which the final report—after a discussion lasting from December 24 to December 30—was framed. The discussions, both in committee and in convention, took much time and caused some difficulties; but nothing was ever known of the speeches made, or of the motions proposed, or of the amendments offered. All the reports were finally adopted by the convention; and all proposed business then having been finished, January 5 the convention adjourned without delay, authorizing Cabot to call another meeting at Boston if he should at any time see occasion for it.

The report, therefore, contained all the information which the convention intended to make public, and only from that document could the ultimate object of the members be inferred. It was immediately published in Connecticut, and at the meeting of the legislatures of Massachusetts and Connecticut in January it was laid before them for approval.

Considering the conservative temper of the delegates and

[1] Lodge's Cabot, p. 548.

their dislike for extreme measures, the report bore striking evidence of the popular passion which urged them forward. A few paragraphs in its first pages showed the spirit of its recommendations, and a few more showed the effect expected from them: —

> "It is a truth not to be concealed that a sentiment prevails to no inconsiderable extent . . . that the time for a change is at hand. . . . This opinion may ultimately prove to be correct; but as the evidence on which it rests is not yet conclusive, . . . some general considerations are submitted in the hope of reconciling all to a course of moderation and firmness which may . . . probably avert the evil, or at least insure consolation and success in the last resort. . . . A severance of the Union by one or more States against the will of the rest, and especially in time of war, can be justified only by absolute necessity."

Having thus discouraged precipitation, and argued in favor of firm and moderate measures as a probable means of preserving the Union, the report sketched the limits of the Union that was to be preserved. In a paragraph closely following the precedent of the Virginia Resolutions of 1798, the report asserted the right and duty of a State to "interpose its authority" for the protection of its citizens from infractions of the Constitution by the general government. In the immediate crisis, this interposition should take the form of State laws to protect the militia or citizens from conscriptions and drafts; of an arrangement with the general government authorizing the States to assume their own defence, and to retain "a reasonable portion of the taxes collected within the said States" for the purpose; and of State armies to be held in readiness to serve for the defence of the New England States upon the request of the governor of the State invaded.

Such measures involved the establishment of a New England Confederation. The proposed union of the New England States for their own defence ignored any share to be taken by the general government in the defence of the national territory, and reduced that government to helplessness. What could be done by New England might be done by all; and the Federalists assumed that all would be obliged to do it.

If the general government should reject the request for the proposed arrangement, the ultimate emergency must arise; but with the measures to be then taken the convention would not interfere.

"It would be inexpedient for this convention to diminish the hope of a successful issue to such an application by recommending, upon supposition of a contrary event, ulterior proceedings. Nor is it indeed within their province. In a state of things so solemn and trying as may then arise, the legislatures of the States, or conventions of the whole people, or delegates appointed by them for the express purpose in another convention, must act as such urgent circumstances may then require."

Besides the measures of urgency which must be immediately accepted by the national government, the convention recommended seven amendments to the Constitution; but on these no immediate action was required. The single issue forced on the government by the convention was that of surrendering to Massachusetts, Connecticut, and Rhode Island "a reasonable portion of the taxes collected within said States," and consenting to some arrangement " whereby the said States may, separately or in concert, be empowered to assume upon themselves the defence of their territory against the enemy." If the United States government should decline such an arrangement, the State legislatures were to send delegates to another convention to meet at Boston, June 15, " with such powers and instructions as the exigency of a crisis so momentous may require."

While the convention was preparing its report, from December 15 to January 5, the public waited with the utmost curiosity for the result. Major Jesup, famous at Chippawa and Lundy's Lane, was then recruiting for the Twenty-fifth United States Infantry at Hartford, and reported constantly to the President and War Department; but he could tell nothing of the convention that was not notorious. His letters were mere surmises or unmilitary comments on the treasonable intentions of the meeting.[1] The Federalists knew no more

---

[1] Ingersoll's History, ii. 232–238; MSS. War Department Archives.

than was known to the Republicans; but while they waited, they expressed fear only lest the convention should fall short of their wishes.

"I care nothing more for your actings and doings," wrote Gouverneur Morris to Pickering in Congress.[1] "Your decree of conscriptions and your levy of contributions are alike indifferent to one whose eyes are fixed on a star in the East, which he believes to be the day-spring of freedom and glory. The traitors and madmen assembled at Hartford will, I believe, if not too tame and timid, be hailed hereafter as the patriots and sages of their day and generation."

As far as newspapers reflected public opinion, the people of New England held the same views as those expressed by Gouverneur Morris. The Boston "Centinel" contained, December 28, an address to the Hartford Convention announcing that the once venerable Constitution had expired: "At your hands, therefore, we demand deliverance. New England is unanimous. And we announce our irrevocable decree that the tyrannical oppression of those who at present usurp the powers of the Constitution is beyond endurance. And we will resist it." A meeting at Reading in Massachusetts, January 5, pledged itself to make no more returns for taxation and to pay no more national taxes until the State should have made its decision known.

A newspaper paragraph copied by the Federalist press[2] advised the President to provide himself with a swifter horse than he had at Bladensburg if he meant to attempt to subjugate the Eastern States. "He must be able to escape at a greater rate than forty miles a day, or the swift vengeance of New England will overtake the wretched miscreant in his flight." Such expressions of the press on either side were of little authority, and deserved no great attention; but the language of responsible and representative bodies could not be denied weight. Opposition to the convention seemed cowed. Apparently the State was ready for immediate action; and the convention, in recommending a delay of six months, risked general disapproval.

[1] Morris to Pickering, Dec. 22, 1814; Morris's Works, iii. 324.
[2] Boston Gazette, Jan. 5, 1815.

While the public was in this temper, the convention adjourned, and its report was given to the press. No one doubted that moderate men would approve it. The only persons whose approval was in question were "bold and ardent" partisans, like Gouverneur Morris, Pickering, and John Lowell, who wanted instant action. Chiefly for the sake of unanimity, these men gave in their adhesion. John Lowell hastened to publish his acquiescence in the convention's report.[1] Pickering also approved it, although Pickering's approval was partly founded on the belief that the Union was already dissolved, and no further effort in that direction need be made.

"If the British succeed in their expedition against New Orleans," Pickering wrote to Lowell,[2] — "and if they have tolerable leaders I see no reason to doubt of their success, — I shall consider the Union as severed. This consequence I deem inevitable. I do not expect to see a single representative in the next Congress from the Western States."

Governor Strong and Senator Gore also approved the convention's report. On receiving it at Washington, January 14, Gore wrote to Strong: "The result of the Hartford Convention is here, and affords satisfaction to most if not to all, — to some because they see not the point nor consequence of the recommendation as relates to taxes." The point and consequence of that recommendation were clear to Gore, and he approved of both.

If any leading Federalist disapproved the convention's report, he left no record of the disapproval. In such a case, at such a moment, silence was acquiescence. As far as could be inferred from any speeches made or letters written at the time, the Federalist party was unanimous in acquiescing in the recommendations of the Hartford Convention.

In Massachusetts and Connecticut the acquiescence was express. The legislature, convened at Boston, January 18, hastened to refer the convention's report to a joint committee, which reported, January 24, Resolutions that the legislature "do highly approve" the proceedings of the convention, and that State commissioners should immediately proceed to

[1] Boston Centinel, Jan. 14, 1815.
[2] Pickering to Lowell, Jan. 23, 1815; Lodge's Cabot, p. 561.

Washington to effect the arrangement proposed.[1] By a very large majority of three to one, the legislature adopted the Resolutions, making the acts of the convention their own. Three commissioners were quickly appointed,—Harrison Gray Otis at their head,—and in the early days of February started for Washington.

Massachusetts was then more than ever convinced that it must peremptorily insist on taking its share of the national revenue into its own hands. Already the first step toward providing a State army had plunged the State treasury into financial difficulties, and measures for defence were stopped until new resources could be obtained. To the surprise of Governor Strong, the Massachusetts banks, restrained by their charters, applied to the State government the same rigorous refusal of credit which they had applied to the national government, and Strong found himself unable to obtain even the loan of one million dollars authorized by the legislature at its autumn session. The miscarriage cast a shade of ridicule on the character of the State which criticised so severely the failure of the national government to defend it, and found itself unable to take the first step toward defence without the aid of the national government, bankrupt and impotent though it was. Governor Strong sent to the legislature on the first day of its winter session a message[2] that might have been sent by Madison to Congress. He reminded the legislature that it had, by a Resolution of Oct. 11, 1814, authorized a loan of a million dollars from the banks.

> "At that time," continued Strong's message, "it was supposed that there would be no difficulty in procuring the requisite sums from that source, and the treasurer soon obtained loans to a considerable amount; but the directors of some of the banks declared themselves unable to lend, and others have expressed such reluctance as forbids an expectation that the whole amount can be obtained in that way during the continuance of the present cautious operations of the banks."

The treasurer had obtained $631,000, and with the expen-

[1] Report of Committee, Jan. 24, 1815; Niles, vii. 372.
[2] Niles, vii.; Supplement, p. 97.

diture of that sum the work of defence and the organization of the State army ceased. "The efforts of defensive preparation which were made in this State the last year," Governor Strong declared, "will, if continued at the expense of the Commonwealth, be fatal to our finances." The necessary consequence followed, that the State must take the national revenues. Accordingly the committee of both Houses, to which the subject was referred, reported[1] an approval of suspending the organization of State troops "until in virtue of some arrangement to be made with the national government sufficient funds can be provided for their pay and support, without recourse to additional taxes." Under such circumstances the national government was little likely to surrender its resources, and every symptom showed that the State then meant to seize them.

The same committee formally approved the governor's course in declining to co-operate with the national government in expelling the enemy from Maine. The public excuse for the refusal was founded on the condition of the Treasury. In Federalist society the weightier motive was supposed to be the wish to leave on the national government the odium of failure to defend the State.[2]

While Massachusetts sustained the Hartford Convention, and pressed to an issue the quarrel with the national government, Connecticut acted with equal zeal in the same sense. The governor, John Cotton Smith, was an old man, and neither his opinions nor his passions were extreme; but as far as concerned the Hartford Convention, his views differed little from those of Pickering and Lowell. He called a special session of the legislature for January 25, to act on the delegates' report; and his speech at the opening of the session would have been taken for irony, had his moderation of character not been known.[3] "The temperate and magnanimous course proposed for our adoption cannot fail to allay the apprehensions which many have professed to entertain, and to enliven the hopes of all who cherish our national Union, and are disposed to place it on a solid and durable basis." The legislature

---

[1] Boston Centinel, Feb. 4, 1815.
[2] Sumner's East Boston, p. 739.
[3] Speech to the Connecticut Legislature; Niles, vii.; Supplement, p. 95.

without delay approved the measures recommended by the convention, and appointed delegates to accompany those sent from Massachusetts to effect the proposed arrangement with the government at Washington.

In later times the Hartford Convention was often and vigorously defended by writers whose works were friendly to the national government, and whose influence was popular.[1] The wisdom, loyalty, and patriotism of George Cabot and his associates became the theme of authors whose authority was above dispute. Nearly always the defence rested on the argument that popular opinion went beyond the convention's report, and that the convention risked its credit by refusing to advise instant withdrawal from the Union.[2] This view was apparently correct. The efforts of the moderate Federalists to praise the moderation of the report, and the labored protests of the extremists against the possible suspicion that they objected to its moderation,[3] showed that the convention was then believed to have offered resistance to what Governor Smith stigmatized as "rash councils or precipitate measures." The tone of the press and the elections bore out the belief that a popular majority would have supported an abrupt and violent course.

The tone of the minority at the time showed a similar belief that Massachusetts favored disunion. During all the proceedings of the State legislatures and the convention, the loyal press and citizens never ceased to point out the dangerous, treasonable, and absurd results to be expected from the course pursued. In the Massachusetts Senate John Holmes of Maine attacked the convention and its doings in a speech that gave him wide reputation.[4] Threats of civil war were freely uttered and defied. Among the least violent of Federalists was James Lloyd, recently United States senator from Massachusetts; and to him as a man of known patriotism John Randolph addressed a letter, Dec. 15, 1814, remonstrating against the Hartford Convention that day to meet. Lloyd replied in a

---

[1] Lodge's Cabot, pp. 504–526; Lossing, p. 1015; Goodrich's Recollections, ii. pp. 9–61.

[2] Lodge's Cabot, p. 518.

[3] Pickering to Lowell, Jan. 23, 1815; Lodge's Cabot, p. 561.

[4] Niles, vii.; Supplement, pp. 49–53.

letter also published, advising Randolph and the Virginians to coerce Madison into retirement, and to place Rufus King in the Presidency as the alternative to a fatal issue.[1] The assertion of such an alternative showed how desperate the situation was believed by the moderate Federalists to be.

A long letter of a similar kind was written, Nov. 26, 1814, by Jonathan Mason to Wilson Cary Nicholas.[2] The opinion of the men among whom Mason lived was expressly declared by Mason to the effect that "Great Britain will not treat with Mr. Madison. He must retire, or the country and the Union are at an end. . . . This is plain language, but in my soul I believe it true. We shall not be destroyed to-day or to-morrow, but it will come; and the end of these measures [of the Administration] will be disunion and disgrace."

In the Republican party the belief was universal that the Hartford Convention could lead only to a New England Confederation; and the belief was not confined to partisans. An anecdote that George Ticknor delighted in telling, illustrated the emotion that then agitated men far beyond the passing and fitful excitements of party politics. Ticknor, a young Federalist twenty-three years old, wished for letters of introduction to Virginia, and asked them from John Adams, then a man of eighty, whose support of the war made him an object of antipathy to the party he had led.

"When I visited him in Quincy to receive these letters," related Ticknor,[3] "I had a remarkable interview with him, which at the time disturbed me not a little. . . . Soon after I was seated in Mr. Adams's parlor,—where was no one but himself and Mrs. Adams, who was knitting,—he began to talk of the condition of the country with great earnestness. I said not a word; Mrs. Adams was equally silent; but Mr. Adams, who was a man of strong and prompt passions, went on more and more vehemently. He was dressed in a single-breasted dark-green coat, buttoned tightly by very large white metal buttons over his somewhat rotund

[1] Palladium, Jan. 24, 1815. Cf. Pickering to Lowell, Jan. 24, 1815; New England Federalism, p. 426.
[2] Mason to Nicholas, Nov. 26, 1814; Nicholas MSS.
[3] Life of Ticknor, i. 12.

person. As he grew more and more excited in his discourse, he impatiently endeavored to thrust his hand into the breast of his coat. The buttons did not yield readily; at last he *forced* his hand in, saying, as he did so, in a very loud voice and most excited manner: 'Thank God! thank God! George Cabot's close-buttoned ambition has broke out at last: he wants to be President of New England, sir!' "

Whether George Cabot wanted it or not, he was in danger of becoming what John Adams predicted. He was far from being the first man who had unwillingly allowed himself to be drawn into a position from which escape was impossible. After going so far, neither leaders nor people could retreat. The next and easy step of sequestrating the direct and indirect taxes was one to which the State stood pledged in the event of a refusal by President Madison and Congress to surrender them. After such an act, the establishment of a New England Confederation could hardly be matter of choice.

If so considerable a mass of concurrent testimony did not prove the gravity of the occasion, as it was understood by the most intelligent and best-informed men of the time, ample evidence could be drawn from other sources. William Wirt described the painful anxiety of Madison as early as the month of October. Throughout Virginia the depression was akin to despair. John Randolph and Wilson Cary Nicholas gave expression to it in letters to prominent New Englanders; but Jefferson in private was still more pronounced in his fears. "The war, had it proceeded, would have upset our government," he wrote to Gallatin a year later,[1] "and a new one, whenever tried, will do it." George Ticknor, after obtaining at Quincy his letter of introduction from John Adams to Jefferson, delivered it at Monticello at a time when the anxiety for the safety of New Orleans was acute. He found Jefferson convinced that the city must fall, and Jefferson expressed the expectation that the British would hold it indefinitely.[2] Pickering felt the same conviction, and regarded the event as a dissolution of the Union.

The "Federal Republican" of Baltimore published, January 5,

[1] Jefferson to Gallatin; Works, vi. 498.
[2] Life of Ticknor, i. 37.

the day when the Hartford Convention adjourned, a letter from Washington announcing "an explosion at hand; that the President would be called on to resign; and there must be peace by that or a future Administration." The fall of New Orleans was to be the signal for a general demand that Madison should resign, and the Federalist press already prepared the ground by insisting that "Mr. Madison has scarcely raised his little finger to preserve New Orleans," and would finally determine to abandon the State of Louisiana.[1] That Madison's authority could survive two such blows as the capture of Washington and the loss of Louisiana seemed improbable; but that he should resign was impossible, though the alternative was a collapse of government.

When the month of February arrived, government and people were waiting with keen apprehension for some new disaster, and the least probable solution was that England knowing the situation would consent to any tolerable peace. The "Federal Republican" of January 28, commenting on the expected bank veto, summed up the consequences, not unfairly from its point of view, in few words:—

"It is impossible, as Mr. Giles said in his luminous and eloquent argument upon the measure [of a national bank], that the government can stand these reiterated shocks. . . . The interest upon the public debt remains unpaid, and there exists not the means, without making the most ruinous sacrifices, to pay it. The government is in arrears to the army upward of nine million dollars; to the navy, about four millions. . . . The condition of our finances is known to the enemy; and is it possible he will be such a fool as to give us peace, after the mortal blow we aimed at him, when he knows we cannot pay the interest on the public debt, that we cannot pay our army or our navy, and when he finds us unable to defend any part of the country at which he strikes?"

[1] The Federal Republican, Jan. 14 and 16, 1815.

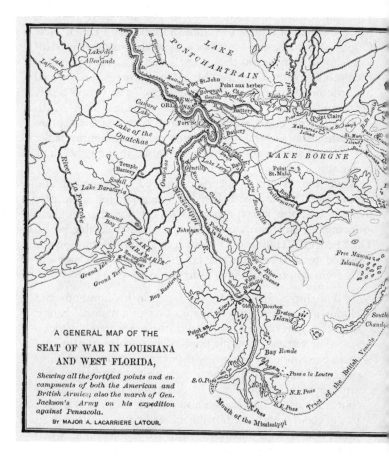

A GENERAL MAP OF THE

SEAT OF WAR IN LOUISIANA
AND WEST FLORIDA,

Shewing all the fortified points and en-
campments of both the American and
British Armies; also the march of Gen.
Jackson's Army on his expedition
against Pensacola.

BY MAJOR A. LACARRIERE LATOUR.

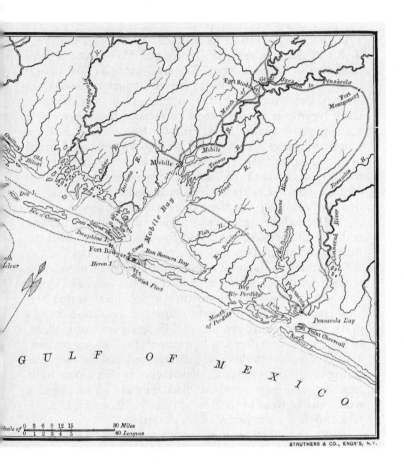

Pascagoula R.

Fort Stoddart

Gen'l Jackson to Pensacola

Marsh of

Fort Montgomery

Old Biloxi

Ceriton

Cedar R.

Mobile

Mobile

Dos Fume R.

Tensaw R.

Minet

Minet R.

Stone River

Escambia R.

Conecuh River

Dog I.

Isle d'Orne

Merchant

Dauphine I.

Fort Bowyer

R. Camy

Mobile Bay

Fish R.

R. Sebastian

Bon Secours Bay

Rio Bodiny

Pensacola

Heron I.

British Fleet

Bay
Rio Perdido

Fort

Mouth
of Perdido

Pensacola Bay

Point Chevreull

Sea Kant I.

G   U   L   F   O   F   M   E   X   I   C   O

Scale of   0 3 6 9 12 15   30 Miles
           0 1 2 3 4 5   40 Leagues

STRUTHERS & CO., ENGR'S, N.Y.

Chapter XII

A DESPATCH from Lord Bathurst, marked "most secret," and dated July 30, 1814, informed Major-General Ross that, after finishing his operations in Chesapeake Bay, he was to sail with his whole force to Jamaica, where he would join an expedition then preparing in England to rendezvous at Cape Negril on the west coast of Jamaica about November 20. Lieutenant-General Lord Hill was to command the combined land-forces.[1] These orders were given before the arrival of a long report from Vice-Admiral Cochrane concerning the military condition of the American territories on the Gulf of Mexico, which Cochrane considered such "that he had no doubt in his mind that three thousand British troops landed at Mobile, where they would be joined by all the Indians, with the disaffected French and Spaniards, would drive the Americans entirely out of Louisiana and the Floridas."[2]

Circumstances induced the British government to defer sending Lord Hill, with a large force, to the Gulf; and Cochrane was informed by a despatch, dated August 10, that Major-General Ross was directed to carry out the Vice-Admiral's plans, which required fewer men.[3] Orders were sent to Ross, of the same date, informing him that reinforcements amounting to more than twenty-one hundred rank-and-file were preparing to sail from England, which with the Fifth West India regiment and two hundred black pioneers from Jamaica would enable Ross to carry more than five thousand effective rank-and-file to the theatre of his operations.[4]

Ross's detailed instructions were dated September 6.[5] They began by recounting the force which was intended to act against New Orleans. The brigade from the Gironde which Ross took to the Chesapeake was estimated at about twenty-three hundred effectives, and a battalion which he had taken from Bermuda was supposed to have raised his rank-and-

[1] Bathurst to Ross, July 30, 1814; MSS. British Archives.
[2] Cochrane to Croker, June 20, 1814; MSS. British Archives.
[3] Croker to Cochrane, Aug. 10, 1814; MSS. British Archives.
[4] Bathurst to Ross, Aug. 10, 1814; MSS. British Archives.
[5] Bathurst to Ross, Sept. 6, 1814; MSS. British Archives.

file to thirty-four hundred men. In addition to this force, a brigade under Major-General Keane, numbering twenty-one hundred and fifty men, was under orders for Jamaica, which with the black troops would enable Ross to proceed to his destination " with near six thousand men, exclusive of the marines and seamen. . . . About the same time you will be joined by the First West India regiment from Guadeloupe."

The objects which rendered the success of the expedition "extremely important" were two: first, the command of the mouth of the Mississippi, so as to deprive the back settlements of America of their communication with the sea; second, "to occupy some important and valuable possession by the restoration of which we may improve the conditions of peace, or which may entitle us to exact its cession as the price of peace."

The point of attack was left to the discretion of Cochrane and Ross. They might proceed directly against New Orleans, or move in the first instance into the back parts of Georgia and the country of the friendly Indians. In either case, the second object in view could not be attained against the will of the inhabitants. "With their favor and co-operation, on the other hand, we may expect to rescue the whole province of Louisiana from the United States."

"If therefore you shall find in the inhabitants a general and decided disposition to withdraw from their recent connection with the United States, either with the view of establishing themselves as an independent people or of returning under the dominion of the Spanish Crown, you will give them every support in your power; you will furnish them with arms and clothing, and assist in forming and disciplining the several levies, provided you are fully satisfied of the loyalty of their intentions, which will be best evinced by their committing themselves in some act of decided hostility against the United States. . . . You will discountenance any proposition of the inhabitants to place themselves under the dominion of Great Britain; and you will direct their disposition toward returning under the protection of the Spanish Crown rather than to the attempting to maintain what it will be much more difficult to secure substantially,—their independence as a separate State; and you must give them clearly to understand that Great Britain cannot pledge herself to make the independence of Louisiana, or its restoration to the Spanish Crown, a *sine qua non* of peace with the United States."

After occupying New Orleans, Ross and Cochrane were to decide whether any further military operations could be carried on; and if nothing of material importance could be attempted, they were to send the disposable part of their force to Bermuda.

Ross's report of the capture of Washington reached Lord Bathurst September 27, and caused so much satisfaction that the British government decided to show its approval by placing another major-general, Lambert, with a brigade numbering twenty-two hundred rank-and-file, under Ross's command, to be used without restriction, either in the Middle or the Southern States.[1] The Prince Regent highly applauded the ability with which Ross had conducted the capture of Washington, "an enterprise so creditable to his Majesty's arms, and so well calculated to humble the presumption of the American government, which contrary to the real interests, and as it is believed contrary to the prevailing wish, of the nation has involved that country in an unnecessary and unjust war against his Majesty."[2] Only in one respect did Bathurst hint a criticism on the course pursued by Ross. While informing him, September 29, that reinforcements were on their way which would place upward of ten thousand men under his command, to be used very much at his discretion, Bathurst added,[3] —

"You and your troops have gained great credit in the discipline you observed at Washington. It is no disparagement of your merit to say that it was prudent as well as merciful to show such forbearance. If, however, you should attack Baltimore, and could, consistent with that discipline *which it is essential for you not to relax*, make its inhabitants *feel* a little more the effects of your visit than what has been

[1] Bathurst to Ross, Sept. 28, 1814; MSS. British Archives.
[2] Bathurst to Ross, Sept. 29, 1814; MSS. British Archives.
[3] Bathurst to Ross, Sept. 29, 1814; MSS. British Archives.

experienced at Washington, you would make that portion of the American people experience the consequences of the war who have most contributed to its existence."

When this despatch was written, Ross had made his attack on Baltimore, and had failed. The report of his failure and death was received by the War Department in London October 17, and Bathurst as soon as possible selected a new commander for the expedition to New Orleans. Orders, dated October 24, were sent to Major-Generals Sir Edward Pakenham and Gibbs to join Vice-Admiral Cochrane forthwith, detailing the force at their command. Pakenham was to follow the instructions already given to Ross, and was especially enjoined to conciliate the people of Louisiana:—

"You will for that purpose cause the force under your command to observe the strictest discipline; to respect the lives and the property of all those who are inclined to a peaceable deportment, and by no means to excite the black population to rise against their masters."

The "Statira" received orders, October 28, to convey Major-Generals Pakenham and Gibbs to the rendezvous at Negril Bay in Jamaica, whither the large force intended for New Orleans was already moving from several distant quarters. The day for beginning the movement on New Orleans was already fixed for November 20, and Pakenham could at that season hardly expect to reach Jamaica in time to sail with his troops. Meanwhile the English press talked openly of the expedition and its object.

Military District No. 7, in which New Orleans and Mobile were situated, had not been neglected by the United States government. The regular force assigned by Secretary Armstrong for its defence consisted of five regiments of United States Infantry,—the Second, Third, Seventh, Thirty-ninth, and Forty-fourth, with three hundred and fifty artillerists,—an aggregate of two thousand three hundred and seventy-eight men. The provision was relatively liberal. District No. 5, on Chesapeake Bay, contained an aggregate of two thousand two hundred and eight regular troops; District No. 6, including North and South Carolina and Georgia, was allotted two thousand two hundred and forty-four men. One half the regular army was employed in such garrison duty, and a greater number could not have been allotted consistently with retaining an army in the field. Indeed, the only means by which Armstrong could provide so strong a defence, aggregating nearly eight thousand men, for the Southern States was by stripping Massachusetts. District No. 1, including Massachusetts and Maine, contained only six hundred and fifty-five regular troops; and District No. 2, including Rhode Island and Connecticut, contained only seven hundred and fourteen. Besides the regular troops, New Orleans enjoyed the protection of gunboats and one or two larger armed vessels. The city needed only an efficient commander to defy any ordinary attack.

Armstrong supplied a commander who might, as he believed, be safely considered efficient. In the month of May Andrew Jackson was appointed to the command of Military District No. 7, with headquarters at Mobile. At that moment Jackson, having finished the Creek war, was about to make the necessary arrangements for the future control of the Creek nation, and he did not take immediate command of his district. No occasion for haste existed. During the summer of 1814 no British force of consequence approached the Gulf of Mexico, or was likely to approach it until the frosts began. Jackson was detained in the centre of Alabama, undisturbed by fears for New Orleans, until the so-called Treaty or Capitulation of August 9 with the Creeks released him from further duties in that region. He left the Creek country August 11, with his regular troops, going by water down the Alabama River, and arriving at Mobile about August 15.

At the same moment government was brought to a standstill at Washington by the appearance of General Ross's army in the Patuxent, and the raids on Washington and Baltimore. Between August 20 and September 25 the War Department could do little more than attend to its own pressing dangers. Jackson was left independent, substantially dictator over the Southwest. If New England carried out its intentions, and the government sank, as seemed probable, into helplessness, his dictatorship was likely to be permanent.

When Jackson arrived at Mobile, August 15, the defence of New Orleans was not in his mind. The people of Tennessee and Georgia had long been bent on the seizure of the Floridas, and Jackson had been one of the most ardent in favoring the step. The Creek war and the escape of the hostile Creeks to East Florida strengthened his conviction that the Spaniards must be expelled. He had begun the war with the idea of pushing his army directly through the Creek country to Pensacola, which he meant to hold.[1] The instant he succeeded in destroying the military power of the Creeks, he began preparations for invading Florida. As early as July he wrote to the War Department suggesting an attack on Pensacola:—

"Will you only say to me, Raise a few hundred militia (which can be quickly done), and with such a regular force as can be conveniently collected, make a descent upon Pensacola and reduce it?"[2]

At the same time Jackson entered, July 12, into an angry correspondence with the Spanish governor of Pensacola, and requested him to deliver up the Creek warriors who had taken refuge in East Florida,—a demand with which he knew that the Spaniard had no means of complying. August 10 he wrote to Armstrong announcing that he had given orders for the reoccupation of Mobile Point. "The United States in possession of Pensacola and Mobile, well defended, our whole coast and country in this quarter would be secure."[3] A direct attack by the British on New Orleans had not occurred to his mind.

Although Jackson received no answer from Washington to his suggestion, he came to Mobile, August 15, determined to pursue his object; and his decision was confirmed by the eccentric conduct of Major Nicholls, an Irish officer, who was sent to Pensacola, July 23, with the sloops-of-war "Hermes" and "Carron," with four officers, eleven non-commissioned officers, and ninety-seven privates of the Royal Marines, taking two howitzers, a field-piece, a thousand stand of arms, and three hundred suits of clothing for the Creek warriors.[4]

[1] Eaton's Jackson, p. 210.
[2] Eaton's Jackson, p. 212.
[3] Jackson to Armstrong, Aug. 10, 1814; MSS. War Department Archives.
[4] Sir Alexander Cochrane to Croker, July 23, 1814; MSS. British Archives.

Nicholls landed his marines, seized Fort Barrancas, disembarked arms, and began to collect the fugitive Creeks, commonly known as Red Sticks, with a view to invading Louisiana, while he spread extravagant stories of his plans.

Had the British government sent Nicholls to Pensacola expressly to divert Jackson's attention from New Orleans, he could not have used his means more successfully for his purpose. Jackson at Mobile, some sixty miles away, learned within forty-eight hours what Nicholls was doing at Pensacola, and wrote instantly, August 27, to Governor Blount of Tennessee,[1] calling out the whole quota of Tennessee militia, twenty-five hundred men, who were to march instantly to Mobile. "It is currently reported in Pensacola," he added, "that the Emperor of Russia has offered his Britannic Majesty fifty thousand of his best troops for the conquest of Louisiana, and that this territory will fall a prey to the enemy before the expiration of one month."

During the next three months Nicholls with a mere handful of men distracted Jackson's whole attention. From Pensacola, August 29, Nicholls issued a proclamation calling on the natives of Louisiana to assist him "in liberating from a faithless, imbecile government" their paternal soil.[2] A few days afterward, September 3, a British sloop-of-war, the "Sophie," appeared at Barataria, forty miles south of New Orleans. There for several years smugglers and pirates had established a station, to the scandal of society and with its connivance.[3] Three Frenchmen, the brothers Laffite,—Jean, Pierre, and Dominique,—ruled over this community, and plundered impartially the commerce of England and Spain, while defying the laws of the United States and the power of the national government.[4] The British sloop-of-war brought to Jean Laffite a letter from Major Nicholls asking him and his men, with their vessels, to enter into British service, under penalty of destruction to their establishment.[5] Laffite, preferring to make terms with the United States, and knowing that the authorities at

[1] Jackson to Governor Blount, Aug. 27, 1814; Niles, vii. 47.
[2] Military and Naval Letters, p. 407.
[3] Latour, p. 14.
[4] National Intelligencer, Oct. 22, 1814.
[5] Latour, Appendix, p. ix.

New Orleans were about to break up his establishment in any case, sent to Governor Claiborne the letters he received from Captain Lockyer of the "Sophie," and offered his services to defend Barataria.

Nothing in these demonstrations suggested a direct attack on New Orleans. Nicholls constantly gave out that he meant to attack Mobile, and from there "push for New Orleans;"[1] but his force was wholly inadequate, and his rank was much too low, to warrant the belief that he intended a serious campaign. Yet such noisy and insulting conduct was adapted to irritate a man of Jackson's temper, and to keep his attention fixed on Mobile and Pensacola. Nicholls even undertook to annoy Jackson in his headquarters.

On a bare sand-point at the entrance of Mobile Bay, General Wilkinson, on taking possession of Mobile in April, 1813, established a battery which he armed with Spanish cannon. The redoubt, which was called Fort Bowyer, could not hold against a land attack properly supported, and offered a temptation to the enemy; but in the absence of a land force competent to besiege it, the fortification was useful to close the entrance of Mobile Bay against marauders. In Fort Bowyer Jackson placed one hundred and sixty men of the Second United States Infantry, commanded by Major William Lawrence. Twenty guns were mounted on the platforms, but according to the American account only two twenty-four pounders and six twelve-pounders were likely to prove serviceable.[2]

The British force at Pensacola consisted chiefly of four sloops, commanded by Captain W. H. Percy,—the "Hermes," twenty-two guns, the "Carron," twenty, and the "Sophie" and "Childers" of eighteen guns each. The usual armament of such vessels consisted of thirty-two-pound carronades, with two long-nines or sixes. Apparently the British squadron threw thirty-four thirty-two-pound shot, and four nine or six pound balls at a broadside. Whether the armament was greater or smaller mattered little, for Captain Percy was unable to use with effect the batteries of either the "Carron" or the "Childers." With much difficulty, owing to the shoals,

[1] Anonymous Letter of Aug. 8, 1814; Latour, Appendix, p. v.
[2] Latour, p. 34.

he brought his squadron within range of Fort Bowyer, and with more gallantry than discretion prepared for the attack.

According to the British account, the land force at Percy's command consisted of sixty marines and one hundred and twenty Indians, with one five-and-a-half-inch howitzer. According to the American account, a twelve-pound field-piece was placed ashore in battery with the howitzer. Such a force was insufficient to do more than intercept the garrison if it should be driven out of the fort. The brunt of the action fell on the ships, and experience did not warrant Percy in believing that his sloops, with their carronades, could silence a work like Fort Bowyer.

Nevertheless Percy gallantly made the attempt. At half-past four of the afternoon of September 15, he brought the "Hermes" close in, and opened fire within musket-shot of the fort. The "Sophie" came to anchor some distance astern, but within range. The "Carron" and the "Childers" anchored so far out that their carronades were useless, and apparently even the American twenty-four-pounders did not touch them. The "Hermes" and the "Sophie" alone sustained injury,[1] but their experience was decisive. After an hour's action, the cable of the "Hermes" being cut, she became unmanageable, and at last grounded and was abandoned. Captain Percy set her on fire, and carried his crew, including the wounded, with much difficulty to his other vessels. The "Sophie" withdrew from fire, and the squadron returned at once to Pensacola.

Assuming that Captain Percy could use with effect only the twenty guns of the broadsides of the "Hermes" and "Sophie" against the twenty guns of the fort, the American gunnery was evidently superior to the British. The "Hermes" lost twenty-five men killed and twenty-four wounded,—a very severe loss in a crew which could not much have exceeded one hundred and fifty men. A better test of marksmanship was offered by the "Sophie," which received comparatively little attention from the fort, but lost six killed and sixteen wounded. The whole American loss was reported as four killed and five wounded,[2] under the combined fire of both ships at close range, the fort having no casemates, and

[1] James, ii. 344.
[2] General Orders of Sept. 17, 1814; Niles, vii. 95.

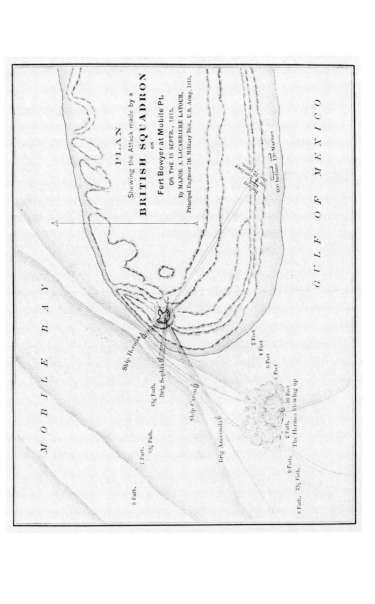

PLAN

Shewing the Attack made by a

BRITISH SQUADRON

ON

Fort Bowyer at Mobile Pt.

ON THE 15 SEPTR., 1815.

By MAJOR A. LACARRIERE LATOUR,

Principal Engineer 7th Military Dist., U.S. Army, 1815.

MOBILE BAY

GULF OF MEXICO

Ship Hermes 4

Brig Sophia 2

Ship Caron 8

Brig Anaconda 6

Battery

the Fort

600 Indians 130 Marines

8 Fath.

7 Fath.   6½ Fath.

6½ Fath.

2 Feet

4 Feet

6 Feet

8 Feet

10 Feet

8 Fath. 2½ Fath.   2 Fath.   The Hermes blowing up

parapets only on the front and flanks.[1] Three guns were dismounted.

Greatly pleased by this success, Jackson issued a counter-
proclamation[2] to the people of Louisiana, somewhat in the
style of that which Nicholls had issued three weeks before.

"The base, the perfidious Britons," it began, "have attempted to invade your country. They had the temerity to
attack Fort Bowyer with their incongruous horde of Indians and negro assassins. . . . The proud, vain-glorious
boaster Colonel Nicholls, when he addressed you, Louisianians and Kentuckians, had forgotten that you were the
votaries of freedom. . . . I ask you, Louisianians, can we
place any confidence in the honor of men who have courted
an alliance with pirates and robbers? Have not these noble
Britons, these honorable men, Colonel Nicholls and the
honorable Captain W. H. Percy, the true representatives of
their royal master, done this? Have they not made offers to
the pirates of Barataria to join them and their holy cause?
And have they not dared to insult you by calling on you to
associate as brethren with them and this hellish banditti?"

With the exception of this proclamation and another[3] of
the same date to the free negroes of Louisiana, Jackson paid
no attention to the defence of New Orleans, but left it entirely to Governor Claiborne. He disregarded a memorial
from the citizens, dated September 18, urging his personal attention and presence. "My whole force would not satisfy the
demands they make," he wrote to the War Department, October 10.[4] "As soon as security is given to this section of my
district, which is first indispensably necessary, I shall hasten
to New Orleans," he wrote from Mobile, October 14.[5] He
entertained no doubt that at Mobile he stood between the
British and their object. "Unless Pensacola were reduced,"
said his confidential biographer[6] ten years afterward, "it was

[1] Latour, p. 33.
[2] Latour, Appendix, p. xxix.
[3] Latour, Appendix, p. xxxi.
[4] Jackson to Monroe, Oct. 10, 1814; MSS. War Department Archives.
[5] Jackson to Monroe, Oct. 14, 1814; MSS. War Department Archives.
[6] Eaton, pp. 239, 240.

vain to think of defending the country. . . . The attack on Mobile Point was a confirmation of his previous conjectures as to the views of the enemy."

The Government at Washington became alarmed. While Jackson waited at Mobile for the arrival of General Coffee with his Tennesseeans to attack Pensacola, Monroe at Washington received warnings from Europe, Halifax, and Bermuda that the British force which had just laid Washington in ashes was but a division of a larger army on its way to attack New Orleans. He wrote to Jackson, September 25,[1] —

> "There is great cause to believe that the enemy have set on foot an expedition against Louisiana, through the Mobile, in the expectation that while so strong a pressure was made from Canada and in this quarter, whereby the force of the country and attention of the government would be much engaged, a favorable opportunity would be afforded them to take possession of the lower part of that State, and of all the country along the Mobile."

The President, he continued, had ordered five thousand additional troops from Tennessee to march to Jackson's aid, and had directed the governor of Georgia to hold twenty-five hundred more subject to Jackson's orders. He had also sent one hundred thousand dollars in Treasury notes to Governor Blount of Tennessee, to be applied to the necessary expenses of the campaign, and Jackson could draw on him for the necessary funds. The orders to the governor of Tennessee were sent the same day, September 25. A week later, October 3, Monroe wrote to Governor Shelby of Kentucky, requesting him to send twenty-five hundred men to Jackson. Again, October 10, Monroe wrote to Jackson, informing him that not less than twelve thousand five hundred men were already subject to his orders, from Kentucky, Tennessee, and Georgia:

> "There is strong reason to presume, from intelligence just received from our ministers at Ghent, that a British force consisting of twelve or fifteen thousand men sailed from Ireland early in September for New Orleans and the

[1] Monroe to Jackson, Sept. 25, 1814; MSS. War Department Records. Monroe MSS.

Mobile, with intention to take possession of that city and of the country through which the great rivers on which the whole of the United States westward of the Alleghany Mountains so essentially depends."

When Monroe received a letter from Jackson, dated September 9, indicating his intention of attacking Pensacola, the secretary replied October 21,[1] forbidding the step. "I hasten to communicate to you the directions of the President that you should at present take no measures which would involve this government in a contest with Spain." He reiterated the warning that British forces would probably be directed against Louisiana; but he did not order Jackson to New Orleans, nor did he notify him that arms would be sent there. Not until November 2 were orders given that four thousand stand of arms should be sent from Pittsburg, and only November 11 and 15 were the arms shipped, not by steamer but by the ordinary flatboat.[2] Even then the arms were in advance of the men. The governor of Tennessee could not appoint an earlier day than November 13 for mustering the new levies, and on that day three thousand men assembled at Nashville, while two thousand collected at Knoxville. Not till November 20 did the Nashville division start down the river, to arrive a month later at New Orleans.

Jackson quietly waited at Mobile for the twenty-five hundred men he had summoned from Tennessee by his letter of August 27. Two months were consumed in this manner. The Tennessee brigade, under command of General Coffee, marched promptly, and passing through the Indian country arrived October 25 at Mobile. Coffee brought with him somewhat more than the number of men required by the call. His force was about twenty-eight hundred.[3] Jackson held at Mobile the Second, Third, Thirty-ninth, and Forty-fourth United States Infantry, besides some Mississippi troops and Choctaw Indians.[4] With the Tennesseeans he could dispose of more than four thousand troops.

[1] Monroe to Jackson, Oct. 21, 1814; MSS. War Department Records.

[2] Monroe to Hugh L. White, Feb. 9, 1827; Monroe MSS., State Department Archives.

[3] Eaton, p. 243.

[4] Jackson to Governor Blount, Nov. 14, 1814; Official Letters, p. 451.

Notwithstanding Monroe's warning letter of September 25, Jackson still paid no immediate attention to New Orleans. October 28 he wrote to Monroe, acknowledging a letter from him of September 27, and announcing that he was then organizing an attack on Pensacola. Having no authority for the act, and aware that the Government was anxious about New Orleans, he added: "I hope in a few weeks to place this quarter in perfect security, and to be able to move to New Orleans with General Coffee's mounted men."[1] October 31 Jackson wrote, apparently for the first time, that he needed arms, and that half the arms of the militia were not fit for use.[2]

Taking four thousand one hundred men,[3] without trains, Jackson marched November 3 against Pensacola, which he occupied, November 7, with little resistance, although "Spanish treachery," he said,[4] "kept us out of possession of the fort until nearly twelve o'clock at night." The next morning the British blew up Fort Barrancas, six miles below, where they had established themselves, and Colonel Nicholls sailed away no farther than the Appalachicola River, leaving Jackson to do what he pleased with Pensacola, a position of no value to either party.

Even Armstrong, who favored Jackson against what he thought the ill-will of Madison and Monroe, afterward condemned the movement against Pensacola. "The general's attack and capture of the town on the 7th of November, 1814, was to say the least of it decidedly ill-judged, involving at once an offence to a neutral power, and a probable misapplication of both time and force as regarded the defence of New Orleans."[5] Jackson remained only two days at the place, and then returned to Mobile, where he arrived November 11 and remained until November 22, as though still in doubt. He detached Major Blue of the Thirty-ninth United States Infantry, with a thousand mounted men, to the Appalachicola to break up the depot established there for supplying assistance

[1] Jackson to Monroe, Oct. 28, 1814; MSS. War Department Archives.
[2] Jackson to Monroe, Oct. 31, 1814; MSS. War Department Archives.
[3] Jackson to Monroe, Nov. 14, 1814; MSS. War Department Archives.
[4] Jackson to Monroe, Nov. 14, 1814; MSS. War Department Archives.
[5] Armstrong's Notices, ii. 176.

to the Red Stick Indians.[1] Nothing indicated that he felt anxiety for the safety of New Orleans, although the British expedition, comprising some fifty vessels, was then at Jamaica, and November 26 actually sailed for the Mississippi.[2]

Jackson's conduct greatly alarmed the President and the Secretary of War. When the despatches arrived at Washington announcing what was taking place at Mobile and Pensacola, Monroe hastened to order General Gaines to Mobile. He wrote to Jackson, December 7,[3] —

> "General Gaines is ordered to join you and act under you in the defence of New Orleans and of the district under your command. Full confidence is entertained that this appointment of an officer of his merit will afford to you a very acceptable aid in the discharge of your highly important duties. . . . Much anxiety is felt lest you should remain too long on the Mobile. The city [New Orleans], it is presumed, is the principal object of the enemy, and it cannot be defended on either of the passes by which it may be approached,—one by the river Mississippi itself, another by the Fourche, the third by Lake Pontchartrain,— without occupying the ground bearing on these passes."

Three days afterward, December 10, Monroe wrote again in stronger terms:[4] —

> "It is hoped that you will have long since taken a suitable position on the river to afford complete protection to that city. Mobile is a comparatively trifling object with the British government. Your presence at such a point on the river with the main body of your troops will be of vital importance."

Jackson left Mobile November 22, four days before the British expedition under Sir Edward Pakenham sailed from Jamaica. Both Jackson and Pakenham were moving to New Orleans at the same time. Pakenham brought with him an immense fleet and a large army. Jackson, instead of taking, as

[1] Eaton, p. 257.
[2] Subaltern, p. 101.
[3] Monroe to Jackson, Dec. 7, 1814; MSS. War Department Records.
[4] Monroe to Jackson, Dec. 10, 1814; MSS. War Department Records.

Monroe hoped, "the main body" of his troops, left at Mobile the main body, consisting of the Second, Third, and Thirty-ninth regiments, about a thousand or twelve hundred men.

According to his friend's biography, probably founded on his own information, Jackson's "principal fears at present were that Mobile might fall, the left bank of the Mississippi be gained, all communication with the Western States cut off, and New Orleans be thus unavoidably reduced."[1] That the British should advance against the Mississippi by way of Mobile was improbable, as Monroe pointed out; but they could have taken no course which better suited the resources of Jackson. A march of near two hundred miles, through a barren and wooded country, with Jackson's whole force concentrated in their front, was an undertaking that promised little success.

Leaving at Mobile three regular regiments, Jackson ordered the Forty-fourth regiment to New Orleans, and directed Coffee with two thousand of his mounted brigade to march to Baton Rouge. He was himself ill and suffering, and made no excessive haste. "I leave this for New Orleans on the 22d instant," he wrote to Monroe, November 20,[2] "and if my health permits, shall reach there in twelve days. I travel by land, to have a view of the points at which the enemy might effect a landing." Starting from Mobile November 22, he arrived at New Orleans, about one hundred and twenty-five miles, only December 2.[3] His troops were then much scattered. The main body was at Mobile. The Forty-fourth regiment was in march from Mobile to New Orleans, where the Seventh regiment was already stationed. A thousand volunteer horsemen, part of Coffee's brigade, under Major Blue of the Thirty-ninth Infantry, were scouring the Escambia, Yellow Water, and other remote Florida recesses. The remainder of Coffee's brigade was at Baton Rouge December 4, greatly reduced by various causes, and numbering only twelve hundred men.[4] A few Mississippi dragoons were near them. A division of Tennessee militia, twenty-five hundred strong, under General Carroll,

[1] Eaton, pp. 261, 282.
[2] Jackson to Monroe, Nov. 20, 1814; MSS. War Department Archives.
[3] Jackson to Monroe, Dec. 2, 1814; MSS. War Department Archives.
[4] Eaton, p. 290.

had started from Nashville November 20, and might be expected at New Orleans about December 20. A division of Kentucky militia, also twenty-five hundred strong, was on its way, and might arrive about the new year. Meanwhile the British expedition was sailing, with much deliberation, past the shores of Cuba, toward Florida.[1]

At New Orleans nothing had yet been done for defence; but inaction was not the worst. Jackson found the people despondent and distrustful.[2] The legislature showed incompetence and, as Jackson believed, indifference. The whole population of Louisiana was but small, containing certainly not more than fifty thousand white inhabitants; while the city of New Orleans probably numbered hardly more than twenty thousand persons including slaves. The State government supplied one thousand militia under the general requisition of the President.[3] The city raised a battalion of volunteers nearly three hundred strong, a rifle company numbering sixty-two men when in the field, and a battalion of free mulattoes, chiefly refugees from St. Domingo, which produced two hundred and ten men,—in all, between five and six hundred troops. Jackson immediately reviewed the companies, December 2, and could expect no further aid from these sources. No arms were in store, even if men could be found, and none of the necessary supplies of an army had been provided.

Jackson's first act after arriving at New Orleans showed no consciousness of danger. Armstrong, criticising his measures, afterward said:[4] "Had the general been better acquainted with military history, he would not have suffered a single day of the twenty he had for preparation to have passed without forming one or more intrenched camps for the protection of the city." Instead of doing this, Jackson did what had been done by Armstrong and Winder at Washington in August. Having arrived in the city December 2, he started two days afterward to inspect Fort St. Philip on the river sixty miles below. He returned to New Orleans December 11,[5] believing

---

[1] Subaltern, p. 193.
[2] Eaton, p. 286; Latour, p. 53.
[3] General Orders of Aug. 6, 1814; Latour, Appendix, p. xvii.
[4] Notices, ii. 177.
[5] Jackson to Monroe, Dec. 12, 1814; MSS. War Department Archives.

that the British would approach by the river, and prepared works to arrest their advance.[1] He then rode out to Chef Menteur and Lake Pontchartrain on the north, which he thought the next probable point of attack. He was still absent, December 15, examining the situation of different works northward of the city, when the British expedition struck its first blow.[2]

Six American gunboats, the whole force on the lakes, watched the entrance of Lake Borgne through which the British must pass if they attacked New Orleans by way of the lakes. They were stationed for observation rather than for resistance,—although for observation a few fishermen's boats would have been more useful. The British expedition, upward of fifty sail, made land December 10,[3] and was seen by the gunboats, which retired within the lake. The British land-forces were transferred from the heavy ships into the lighter vessels, and under convoy of sloops-of-war entered Lake Borgne December 13. The boats of the squadron, carrying about a thousand seamen and marines,[4] left the ships during the night of December 12 in search of the American gunboats, which tried to escape, but were becalmed and obliged by the tide to anchor. After a tedious row of thirty-six hours the British boats overtook the gunboat flotilla December 14, and after a sharp struggle succeeded in capturing the whole, with a loss of seventeen men killed and seventy-seven wounded.[5] The American crews numbered one hundred and eighty-two men, and lost six killed and thirty-five wounded.

News of the capture of the gunboats, which occurred at noon December 14 about forty miles to the eastward of New Orleans, arrived on the evening of December 15, and produced the utmost consternation.[6] Jackson hurried back to the city, where his presence was no longer a matter of choice but necessity. Instantly on hearing the news he sent expresses to

[1] Eaton, p. 272.
[2] Eaton, p. 282.
[3] Sir Alexander Cochrane to J. W. Croker, Dec. 16, 1814; Latour, Appendix, p. cxxxviii.
[4] James, ii. 349.
[5] Report of Captain Lockyer, Dec. 18, 1814; James, ii. 523.
[6] Letter of Dec. 16, 1814; Niles, vii. 316.

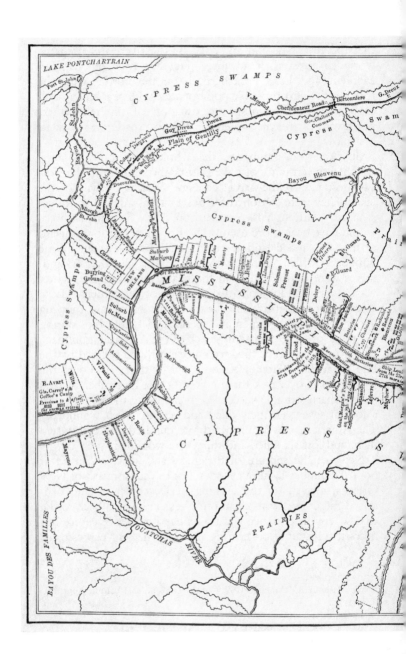

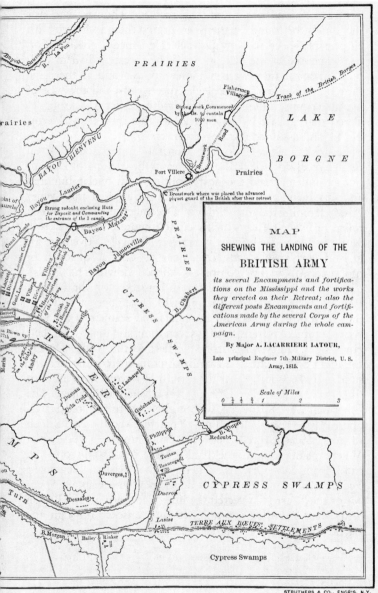

MAP

SHEWING THE LANDING OF THE

BRITISH ARMY

its several Encampments and fortifications on the Mississippi and the works they erected on their Retreat; also the different posts Encampments and fortifications made by the several Corps of the American Army during the whole campaign.

By Major A. LACARRIERE LATOUR,

Late principal Engineer 7th Military District, U. S. Army, 1815.

Scale of Miles

0 ¼ ½ ¾ 1   2   3

STRUTHERS & CO., ENGR'S, N.Y.

Coffee at Baton Rouge, and to Carroll and Thomas, wherever they might be found on the river, urging them to hasten with all possible speed to New Orleans. He issued a proclamation to the people of the city, in which he threatened them with punishment if they were not unanimous,[1] and at the same time he recommended the legislature to suspend the writ of habeas corpus. Finding the legislature hesitate, Jackson declared martial law by proclamation[2] the same day, December 16, and assumed dictatorial powers.

Feverish activity followed. General Coffee above Baton Rouge received Jackson's summons on the evening of December 17, and marched the next morning with twelve hundred and fifty men. In two days he made one hundred and twenty miles, camping on the night of December 19 within fifteen miles of New Orleans, with eight hundred men.[3] Carroll, with the Tennessee brigade which left Nashville November 27, arrived at New Orleans December 21, and a squadron of mounted Mississippi volunteers hurried down. The British also lost no time. Their advance disembarked on the Isle aux Poix in Lake Borgne on the night of December 14, and during the following week all the boats and seamen of the fleet were occupied in transporting seven thousand men, with their equipment, thirty miles from the fleet to the island. During the night of December 18 two British officers reconnoitred the head of Lake Borgne.[4] At the mouth of Bayou Bienvenu, not fifteen miles from New Orleans, was a fishermen's village. The fishermen were Spaniards, with no love for the United States, and ready to accept British pay. They received the two British officers, and conveyed them in a canoe up the bayou to the Villeré plantation on the bank of the Mississippi only six miles from New Orleans.[5] There, at their leisure, Lieutenant Peddie of the quartermaster's department and Captain Spencer of the "Carron" selected the line of advance for the British army, and returned, unmolested and unseen, through the bayou to the lake and the Isle aux Poix.

---

[1] General Orders, Dec. 16, 1814; Niles, vii. 316.
[2] General Orders, Dec. 16, 1814; Niles, vii. 317.
[3] Eaton, p. 290.
[4] Report of Major-General Keane, Dec. 26, 1814; James, ii. 529.
[5] Admiral Cochrane to Mr. Croker, Jan. 18, 1815; James, ii. 550.

Only December 21, two days after the British reconnaissance, was an American picket of eight men and a sergeant
placed at the fishermen's village,[1] where they remained thirty-
six hours without learning that British officers had been on
the spot, or that the fishermen were all away, acting as pilots
for the approaching British boats. Meanwhile the troops at
Isle aux Poix were ready to move almost as soon as Lieutenant Peddie could return to show them the way. At ten o'clock
on the morning of December 22 the light brigade—sixteen
hundred and eighty-eight rank-and-file,[2] under Colonel
Thornton, who had led the advance at Bladensburg—embarked in boats, and after a day on the lake arrived the next
morning, December 23, at daylight, without giving alarm, at
the fishermen's village, where they surprised and captured the
picket, and then passing up the bayou five miles, landed at a
point about three miles from the Mississippi River. No attempt at concealment was made.[3] The troops were formed in
column, and found no obstacles to their march except the soft
ground and the ditches. Through reeds and cypress swamp
they made their way about three miles, when their advance
suddenly entered open fields skirted by an orange-grove, with
the broad Mississippi beyond. They were on the Villeré plantation; and they surprised and captured Major Villeré and his
militia company, in his own house at noon-day, after a march
of three miles with sixteen hundred men, from a point which
had been recognized by Jackson as one of two or three necessary avenues of approach.

The record of American generalship offered many examples
of misfortune, but none so complete as this. Neither Hull nor
Harrison, neither Winder nor Samuel Smith, had allowed a
large British army, heralded long in advance, to arrive within
seven miles unseen and unsuspected, and without so much as
an earth-work, a man, or a gun between them and their object. The disaster was unprecedented, and could be repaired
only by desperate measures.

[1] Latour, p. 77; Jackson's Report of Dec. 27, 1814; Latour, Appendix, p. xlv.
[2] James, ii. 355.
[3] Subaltern, p. 212.

Chapter XIII

THE DEFENCE of New Orleans resembled the defence of Washington until the moment when in each case the British expedition came within sight. Jackson was even slower than Winder to see the point of danger or to concentrate his forces. At Washington, Winder took command July 1, and the British expedition arrived August 16; at Mobile, Jackson took command August 16, and the British expedition arrived December 14. In neither case was the interval seriously employed for defence. So much was Jackson misled that he collected no troops, and made no inquiry as to the military means at his disposal at New Orleans. Had he gone there September 1, he would have felt the want of arms and equipment, and would have been able to supply them. During the summer, while yet among the Creeks, he was said to have made requisition for a quantity of war material to be sent to New Orleans;[1] but he certainly showed no interest in its shipment or the causes for its delay in arrival. The arms should have reached New Orleans in October, when he would have had ample time to correct any failure or want of supply. He could have used, in case of necessity, the steamboat "Enterprise," which was then regularly plying on the Mississippi, and was not the only steamboat on those waters.[2] If New Orleans was deficient in many articles of military necessity, the fault was not wholly in the War Department.

A similar criticism applied to the political situation at New Orleans. Governor Claiborne wanted authority to control the factions in his legislature, and the legislature wanted an impulse sufficiently energetic to overcome its inertia. Probably Jackson's presence would at any time have given authority to Claiborne and energy to the entire State government. From the moment of his actual arrival, difficulties of this kind seemed to cease. "It is hardly possible," said the military historian of the campaign,[3] "to form an idea of the change which his arrival produced on the minds of the people."

[1] Latour, p. 66.
[2] Eaton, p. 293, *note*.
[3] Latour, p. 53.

When the British expedition was once known to have appeared at the entrance of Lake Borgne, Jackson's task was perhaps simpler than Winder's, for Winder might doubt whether the British meant to attack Washington, and in fact General Ross took the decision only at the last moment; but no one could doubt that New Orleans was the object of Pakenham's expedition. Jackson had only to choose his positions and collect his resources. These were small; but on the other hand the British were opposed by natural difficulties much greater at New Orleans than at Washington. Even their greater numbers were a disadvantage when they were obliged to move in widely separated detachments, in open boats, from a point far distant from their column's head, and toward a point easily fortified.

If until the moment of the enemy's appearance Jackson showed no more military capacity than was shown by Winder, his conduct thenceforward offered a contrast the more striking because it proved how Washington might have been saved. Winder lost his head when he saw an enemy. Jackson needed to see his enemy in order to act; he thought rightly only at the moment when he struck. At noon, December 23, New Orleans was in greater danger than Washington on the afternoon of August 23, when the British advanced from the Patuxent. Had Colonel Thornton followed his impulses and marched directly on the city, he must have reached it before a gun could have been fired by the Americans; his own muskets would have given the first news of his arrival. Major-General Keane, his commanding officer, preferred caution,[1] and his delay gave a few hours time for Jackson to show his qualities.

News that a British column had reached the Villeré plantation was brought to Jackson at headquarters in New Orleans, at about half-past one o'clock, much as the news was brought to Winder, August 24, that the British were marching on Bladensburg. The distances were about the same. Winder and Jackson both allowed the enemy to approach within seven miles before anything had been done for defence. In one respect Jackson was more unfortunate than Winder, for

[1] Subaltern, p. 215 (American edition, 1833).

his troops were not ready to march; they were not even collected. Jackson sent orders to the different corps, but several hours passed before the men could be brought down and posted between the city and the British.

Fortunately Major Latour, chief-engineer in Military District No. 7, had been sent that morning to examine the approaches from Lake Borgne, and as he rode down the road at noon he met persons flying toward town with news that the British had penetrated through the canal to Villeré's house. Latour was a trained French engineer, whose services were extremely valuable, not only during the campaign but afterward; for he subsequently wrote a "History of the War in West Florida and Louisiana," which was far the best military work published in the United States till long after that time, and furnished the only accurate maps and documents of the campaign at New Orleans.[1] On the morning of December 23 Latour approached within rifle-shot of the British force, and judged their number accurately as sixteen or eighteen hundred men.[2] Such exact information, which could not have been gained from any ordinary scout, was invaluable. Latour hastened to headquarters, and reported at two o'clock to Jackson the position and numbers of the enemy. The general, on that information, decided to attack.

For such a purpose Jackson's resources were ample. Four miles above the city his Tennessee militia were camped,—Carroll's brigade numbering probably about two thousand effectives, and the remnants of Coffee's mounted brigade numbering some seven hundred men in the field. The Mississippi and New Orleans volunteers could be reckoned at about seven hundred men,[3] besides three regiments of city militia. The Seventh United States Infantry produced four hundred and sixty-five men in the ranks; the Forty-fourth counted three hundred and thirty-one; while a detachment of artillerists, twenty-two in number, with two six-pound field-pieces, added greatly to the numerical strength of the Infantry.[4]

[1] See Memoir of Latour in Cullum's Campaigns of the War of 1812–1815, p. 309.
[2] Latour, p. 88.
[3] Latour, p. 105.
[4] Latour, p. 105.

Against Thornton's force, numbering one thousand six hundred and eighty-eight rank-and-file, or about nineteen hundred men all told, Jackson could oppose about five thousand Infantry with two field-pieces.

Besides these land forces Jackson was provided with another resource. In the river at New Orleans lay a war-schooner, the "Carolina," rated at fourteen guns, armed with one long twelve-pounder and six twelve-pound carronades on a broadside.[1] A sixteen-gun sloop-of-war, the "Louisiana," was also at New Orleans, but not ready for immediate use. The "Carolina" could be brought instantly into action, and her broadside of seven twelve-pounders, added to the field-battery of two six-pounders, gave Jackson immense advantage over the British, who had no artillery except two three-pounders and rockets, and whose lines must be enfiladed by the "Carolina's" fire.

Jackson, aware of his superiority, expected with reason to destroy the British detachment. He did not even think more than half his force necessary for the purpose, but detached the whole of Carroll's brigade and the three regiments of city militia,—fully twenty-five hundred men,—to guard the town against an apprehended attack from the north. Without giving the reasons which led him to believe that the British could approach on that side without ample warning, his report said,—

> "Apprehending a double attack by the way of Chef Menteur, I left General Carroll's force and the militia of the city posted on the Gentilly road, and at five o'clock P. M. marched to meet the enemy, whom I was resolved to attack in his first position, with Major Hind's dragoons, General Coffee's brigade, parts of the Seventh and Forty-fourth regiments, the uniformed companies of militia under the command of Major Plauché, two hundred men of color chiefly from St. Domingo, raised by Colonel Savary and acting under the command of Major Daquin, and a detachment of artillery under the direction of Colonel McRea, with two six-pounders under the command of Lieutenant Spots,— not exceeding in all fifteen hundred."

[1] Captain Henley's Letter of Dec. 28, 1814; Niles, vii. 387.

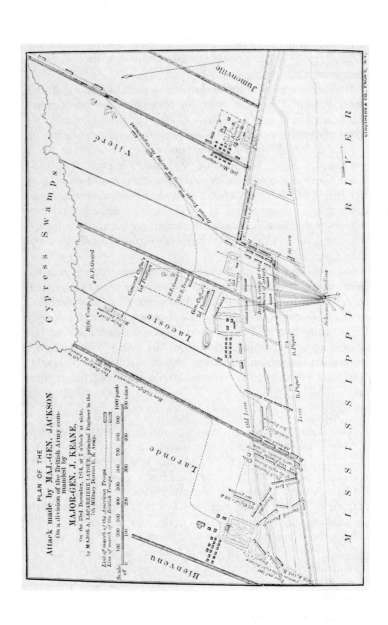

PLAN OF THE
Attack made by MAJ.-GEN. JACKSON
On a division of the British Army commanded by
MAJOR-GEN. J. KEANE,
On the 23rd December, 1814, at 7 o'clock at night,
by MAJOR A. LACARRIERE LATOUR, principal Engineer in the
7th Military District U. S. Army.

Line of march of the American Troops
Line of march of the British Troops

Scale of 0 100 200 300 400 500 600 700 800 900 1000 yards
500 toises

STRUTHERS & CO., ENGRS., N. Y.

More exact returns showed that Jackson carried with him eight hundred and eighty-four regular troops and two field-pieces, five hundred and sixty-three mounted riflemen of Coffee's brigade, five hundred and fifty-nine Louisiana militia, one hundred and seven Mississippians, and eighteen Choctaw Indians, — in all, twenty-one hundred and thirty-one men and two guns, besides the "Carolina," which dropped down the river at four o'clock.[1]

Jackson did not, like Winder, pass the hours in looking at his enemy, nor did he, like General Smith at Baltimore, send out militia under militia officers, to stand in close order on an open field and wait attack. His chief difficulty was due to the ground, which obliged him to make his main assault in a narrow column along the road. To gain the advantage of his numbers, he detached Coffee with seven hundred and thirty-two men, mostly armed with rifles, to make a detour toward the left and fall on the British flank and rear, while Jackson himself, with fourteen hundred men and two guns, should strike the British advance where it was posted on the levee.

The signal for battle was to be given by the "Carolina's" guns. Commodore Patterson in the "Carolina" received his orders at half-past six, and getting out sweeps, brought his vessel in a few minutes abreast of the British camp, where he anchored close in shore and began a heavy fire,[2] soon after seven o'clock. Ten minutes later, Jackson, waiting about two miles above, ordered his men to advance, and moving down the road with his regulars and New Orleans companies struck the British outposts about a mile below his point of departure, at a few minutes before eight o'clock. At the same time Coffee, as he marched along the edge of the swamp, hearing the signal, wheeled to the right, and moved toward the British flank.

Night had then fallen. The weary British troops had lain down, when their sentries on the levee gave the alarm, and immediately afterward the roar of seven cannon close beside them threw their camp into confusion. About half an hour afterward, while the "Carolina" still swept the camp with its

[1] Latour, p. 104. Parton, i. 617. Commodore Patterson's Report of Dec. 28, 1814; Latour, Appendix, p. xliii.

[2] Patterson's Report of Dec. 28, 1814; Latour, Appendix, p. xliii.

shot, the British sentries on the levee a mile above gave another alarm, and in a few moments the outposts were sharply attacked.

The accounts of the battle fought along the levee, under the command of Jackson in person, were both confused and contradictory. Thornton's brigade was composed of the Eighty-fifth and Ninety-fifth regiments, a company of rocketeers, one hundred sappers and miners, and the Fourth regiment as a support,—in all, sixteen hundred and eighty-eight rank-and-file.[1] At the point where the fighting began the British had merely an outpost, which was forced back by Jackson's attack, with some difficulty, about one hundred and fifty yards.[2] Colonel Thornton ordered two of his regiments—the Eighty-fifth and Ninety-fifth, eight hundred rank-and-file[3]— to support the outpost, and their arrival checked Jackson's advance. Indeed, the American line was driven back and lost ground, until the two field-pieces were in danger, and were hastily withdrawn.[4] Each party claimed that the other first withdrew from fire; but the American report admitted that the battle which began on the levee at eight ceased before nine, while Jackson seemed not to regard his attack as successful. His first brief report, written December 26,[5] said,—

"The heavy smoke occasioned by an excessive fire rendered it necessary that I should draw off my troops, after a severe conflict of upward of an hour."

Jackson's official report of December 27 said,[6]—

"There can be but little doubt that we should have succeeded on that occasion with our inferior force in destroying or capturing the enemy, had not a thick fog which arose about eight o'clock occasioned some confusion among the different corps. Fearing the consequences, under this circumstance, of the further prosecution of a night

[1] James, ii. 355.
[2] Latour's Plan.
[3] James, ii. 355. Keane's Report of Dec, 26, 1814; James, ii. 529.
[4] Latour, pp. 96, 97. Parton, ii. 90.
[5] Report of Dec. 26, 1815; Latour, Appendix, p. xliv.
[6] Report of Dec. 27, 1814; Niles, vii. 357.

attack with troops then acting together for the first time, I contented myself with lying on the field that night."

Although the battle was severest where Jackson commanded, it was most successful where Coffee attacked. On hearing the "Carolina" open fire, Coffee turning to the right advanced on the British flank, striking it nearly opposite to the "Carolina's" position. The British, thus surrounded, were placed in a situation which none but the steadiest troops could have maintained. So great was the confusion that no organized corps opposed Coffee's men. Squads of twenty or thirty soldiers, collecting about any officer in their neighborhood, made head as they best could against Coffee's riflemen, and the whole British position seemed encircled by the American fire. Forced back toward the river, the British rallied behind an old levee which happened at that point to run parallel with the new levee, at a distance of about three hundred yards.[1] Knots of men, mixed in great disorder, here advancing, there retreating, carried on a desultory battle over the field, often fighting with clubbed weapons, knives, and fists. At last the British centre, finding a strong protection in the old levee which answered for an earthwork, held firm against Coffee's further advance, and were also sheltered by the new levee in their rear from the fire of the "Carolina's" guns. At about the same time several companies of the Twenty-first and Ninety-third regiments arrived from Lake Borgne, and raised the British force to two thousand and fifty rank-and-file.[2] Coffee then despaired of further success, and withdrew his men from the field.

"My brigade," wrote Coffee immediately afterward,[3] "met the enemy's line near four hundred yards from the river. The fire on both sides was kept up remarkably brisk until we drove them to the river-bank, where they gave a long, heavy fire, and finally the enemy fell behind the levee or river-bank that is thrown up. The battle had now lasted near two and a half hours. The regulars had ceased firing near one hour before I drew my men back."

[1] Latour's Plan of the Battle of December 23; Peddie's Sketch.
[2] James, ii. 362. Keane's Report; James, ii. 530.
[3] Parton, ii. 100.

The "Carolina" began firing soon after seven o'clock, and ceased at nine.[1] Jackson's attack with the regulars began at eight o'clock, and his force ceased firing before nine. Coffee withdrew his men at about half-past nine. The hope of destroying the British force was disappointed; and brilliant as the affair was, its moral effect was greater than the material injury it inflicted. Major-General Keane officially reported his loss as forty-six killed, one hundred and sixty-seven wounded, and sixty-four missing,—two hundred and sixty-seven in all.[2] Jackson reported twenty-four killed, one hundred and fifteen wounded, and seventy-four missing,—two hundred and thirteen in all. The two regular regiments suffered most, losing fifteen killed and fifty-four wounded. Coffee's Tennesseeans lost nine killed and forty-three wounded. The New Orleans volunteer corps and the colored volunteers lost seventeen wounded.

Compared with the night battle at Lundy's Lane, the night battle of December 23 was not severe. Brown's army, probably not more numerous than Jackson's, lost one hundred and seventy-one men killed, while Jackson lost twenty-four. Brown lost five hundred and seventy-one wounded, while Jackson lost one hundred and fifteen. Drummond at Lundy's Lane reported a British loss of eighty-four killed, while Keane reported forty-six. Drummond reported five hundred and fifty-nine wounded, while Keane reported one hundred and sixty-seven. The total British loss at Lundy's Lane was eight hundred and seventy-eight men; that of December 23 was two hundred and sixty-seven. Jackson's battle was comparatively short, lasting an hour and a half, while the fighting at Lundy's Lane continued some five hours. Lundy's Lane checked the enemy only for a day or two, and the battle of December 23 could hardly be expected to do more.

Conscious that the British army would advance as soon as its main body arrived, Jackson, like Brown, hastened to place his men under cover of works. Falling back the next morning about two miles, he took position behind an old canal or ditch which crossed the strip of cultivated ground where it was narrowest. The canal offered no serious obstacle to an

[1] Patterson to Secretary of Navy, Dec. 28, 1814; Latour, Appendix, p. xliii.
[2] Report of Major-General Keane, Dec. 26, 1814; James, ii. 529.

enemy, for although ten feet wide it was shallow and dry, and fully three quarters of a mile long. Had the British been able to advance in force at any time the next day, December 24, directing their attack toward the skirts of the swamp to avoid the "Carolina's" fire, they might have forced Jackson back upon New Orleans; but they were in no disposition to do on the 24th what they had not ventured to do on the 23d, when they possessed every advantage. Keane believed that Jackson's force in the night battle amounted to five thousand men.[1] Keane's troops, weary, cold, without food, and exposed to the "Carolina's" fire, which imprisoned them all day between the two levees,[2] were glad to escape further attack, and entertained no idea of advance. The day and night of December 24 were occupied by the British in hurrying the main body of their troops from the Isle aux Poix across Lake Borgne to the Bayou Bienvenu.

By very great efforts the boats of the fleet transported the whole remaining force across the lake, until, on the morning of December 25, all were concentrated at the Villeré plantation. With them arrived Major-General Sir Edward Pakenham, and took command. Hitherto the frequent British disasters at Plattsburg, Sackett's Harbor, Fort Erie, and the Moravian towns had been attributed to their generals. Sir George Prevost, Major-Generals Drummond and Riall, and Major-General Proctor were not officers of Wellington's army. The British government, in appointing Sir Edward Pakenham to command at New Orleans, meant to send the ablest officer at their disposal. Pakenham was not only one of Wellington's best generals, but stood in the close relation of his brother-in-law, Pakenham's sister being Wellington's wife. In every military respect Sir Edward Pakenham might consider himself the superior of Andrew Jackson. He was in the prime of life and strength, thirty-eight years of age, while Jackson, nearly ten years older, was broken in health and weak in strength. Pakenham had learned the art of war from Wellington, in the best school in Europe. He was supported by an efficient staff and a military system as perfect as experience and expenditure could make it, and he commanded as fine an

[1] Keane's Report of December 26, 1814; James, ii. 531.
[2] Subaltern, pp. 228, 229.

army as England could produce, consisting largely of Peninsula veterans.

Their precise number, according to British authority, was five thousand and forty rank-and-file, on Christmas Day, when Pakenham took command.[1] Afterward many more arrived, until January 6, when ten regiments were in camp at Villeré's plantation,—Royal Artillery; Fourteenth Light Dragoons; Fourth, Seventh, Twenty-first, Forty-third, Forty-fourth, Eighty-fifth, Ninety-third, and Ninety-fifth Infantry, —numbering, with sappers and miners and staff-corps, five thousand nine hundred and thirteen rank-and-file; or with a moderate allowance of officers, an aggregate of at least sixty-five hundred Europeans. Two West India regiments of black troops accompanied the expedition, numbering ten hundred and forty-three rank-and-file. The navy provided about twelve hundred marines and seamen, perhaps the most efficient corps in the whole body. Deducting eight hundred men for camp-duty, Pakenham, according to British official reports, could put in the field a force of eight thousand disciplined troops, well-officered, well-equipped, and confident both in themselves and in their commander. More were on their way.

The Duke of Wellington believed such a force fully competent to capture New Orleans, or to rout any American army he ever heard of; and his confidence would have been, if possible, still stronger, had he known his opponent's resources, which were no greater and not very much better than those so easily overcome by Ross at Bladensburg. The principal difference was that Jackson commanded.

Jackson's difficulties were very great, and were overcome only by the desperate energy which he infused even into the volatile creoles and sluggish negroes. When he retired from the field of the night battle, he withdrew, as has been told, only two miles. About five miles below New Orleans he halted his troops. Between the river and the swamp, the strip of open and cultivated land was there somewhat narrower than elsewhere. A space of a thousand yards, or about three fifths of a mile, alone required strong defence. A shallow, dry

[1] James, ii. 363.

canal, or ditch, ten feet wide, crossed the plain and opened into the river on one side and the swamp on the other. All day the troops, with the negroes of the neighborhood, worked, deepening the canal, and throwing up a parapet behind it. The two six-pound field-pieces commanded the road on the river-bank, and the "Louisiana" descended the river to a point about two miles below Jackson's line. A mile below the "Louisiana" the "Carolina" remained in her old position, opposite the British camp. By nightfall the new lines were already formidable, and afforded complete protection from musketry. For further security the parapet was continued five hundred yards, and turned well on the flank in the swamp; but this task was not undertaken until December 28.[1]

The first act of Sir Edward Pakenham gave the Americans at least three days for preparation. Even veteran soldiers, who were accustomed to storming mountain fortresses held by French armies, were annoyed at exposing their flank to the fire of fifteen or twenty heavy guns, which hampered not only every military movement but also every motion beyond cover of the bank. Pakenham sent instantly to the fleet for cannon to drive the ships away. In reality he could not so relieve himself, for the American commodore soon placed one twenty-four-pound gun and two twelve-pounders in battery on the opposite bank of the river, where they answered every purpose of annoyance, while the ships after December 28 took little part in action.[2] Pakenham gained nothing by waiting; but he would not advance without artillery, and the sailors, with much labor, brought up a number of light guns,—nine field-pieces, it was said,[3] two howitzers, and a mortar. Pakenham passed two days, December 25 and 26, organizing his force and preparing the battery. At daylight, December 27, the guns were ready. Five pieces suddenly opened with hot shot and shell on the "Carolina," and in half an hour obliged the crew to abandon her.[4] The "Louisiana," by extreme exertion, was hauled beyond range while the British battery was occupied in destroying the "Carolina."

[1] Latour, p. 121.
[2] Patterson's Report of Jan. 2, 1815; Latour, Appendix, p. 1, no. xxviii.
[3] Gleig's Campaigns, p. 165.
[4] Report of J. D. Henley, Dec. 28, 1814; Niles, vii. 387.

Nothing then prevented Pakenham's advance, and the next morning, December 28, the whole army moved forward.

"On we went," said the Subaltern, "for about three miles, without any halt or hindrance, either from man or inanimate nature coming in our way. But all at once a spectacle was presented to us, such indeed as we ought to have looked for, but such as manifestly took our leaders by surprise. The enemy's army became visible. It was posted about forty yards in rear of a canal, and covered, though most imperfectly, by an unfinished breastwork."

The British left, coming under the fire of the "Louisiana," was immediately halted and placed as far as possible under cover. The skirmishers in the swamp were recalled. In the evening the whole army was ordered to retire beyond cannon-shot and hut themselves.[1] They obeyed; but "there was not a man among us who failed to experience both shame and indignation."[2]

Beyond doubt, such caution was not expected from Sir Edward Pakenham. Sir George Prevost at Sackett's Harbor and Plattsburg, and Colonel Brooke at Baltimore had retired before American works; but those works had been finished forts, strongly held and situated on elevated points. Even with such excuses, and after suffering severe losses, Prevost was discredited for his retreats. Pakenham did not live to make a report, and his reasons remained unavowed; but Admiral Cochrane reported that it was "thought necessary to bring heavy artillery against this work, and also against the ship which had cannonaded the army when advancing."[3] The decision implied that Pakenham considered the chances unfavorable for storming the American line.

In effect, Pakenham's withdrawal December 28 was equivalent to admitting weakness in his infantry, and to calling on the artillery as his strongest arm. The experiment showed little self-confidence. Not only must he sacrifice two or three days in establishing batteries, but he must challenge a contest

[1] Journal of Major Forrest; Latour, Appendix, p. cxlvii.
[2] Subaltern, p. 235.
[3] Cochrane's Report of Jan. 18, 1815; James, ii. 552.

with cannon,—weapons which the Americans were famous for using, both afloat and ashore, with especial skill. Jackson could also mount heavy guns and allow Pakenham to batter indefinite lines. Sooner or later Pakenham must storm, unless he could turn the American position.

The seamen were once more set to work, and " with incredible labor" rowed their boats, laden with heavy guns, from the fleet to the bayou, and dragged the guns through three miles of bog to the British headquarters. The Americans also prepared batteries. From the lines one thirty-two-pounder, three twenty-four-pounders, and one eighteen-pounder commanded the plain in their front. Besides these heavy guns, three twelve-pounders, three six-pounders, a six-inch howitzer or mortar, and a brass carronade, useless from its bad condition,[1]—in all, twelve or thirteen guns, capable of replying to the British batteries, were mounted along the American lines. On the west bank of the river, three quarters of a mile away, Commodore Patterson established, December 30 and 31, a battery of one twenty-four-pounder and two long twelve-pounders, which took the British batteries in flank.[2] Thus the Americans possessed fifteen effective guns, six of which were heavy pieces of long range. They were worked partly by regular artillerists, partly by sailors, partly by New Orleans militia, and partly by the "hellish banditti" of Barataria, who to the number of twenty or thirty were received by General Jackson into the service and given the care of two twenty-four-pounders.

The number and position of the British guns were given in Lieutenant Peddie's sketch of the field. Before the reconnaissance of December 28, field-pieces had been placed in battery on the river-side to destroy the "Carolina" and "Louisiana." Canon Gleig said that "nine field-pieces, two howitzers, and one mortar" were placed in battery on the river-side during the night of December 25.[3] Captain Henley of the "Carolina" reported that five guns opened upon him on the morning of December 26.[4] Captain Peddie's sketch marked seven pieces

[1] Latour, pp. 147, 148.
[2] Patterson's Report of Jan. 2, 1815; Latour, Appendix, p. i, no. xxviii.
[3] Campaigns, p. 166.
[4] Henley's Report of December 28; Niles, vii. 387.

Sketch of the Position of the British and American Forces

NEAR NEW ORLEANS, FROM THE 23rd OF DECEMBER TO THE 8th OF JANUARY, 1815.

From original by John Peddie, D. A. Q. M. Genl., endorsed "Enclosure in M. Genl. Lambert's of 29 Jany., 1815."—British Archives.

REFERENCES.

A. Enemy's position on the night of the 23rd of December when he attacked.
B. Bivouac of the troops for the 23rd of December.
C. Position on the night of the 23rd of December.
D. Position on the night of the 24th of December.
E. Position after the advance on the 28th of December.
F. Col. Thornton's attack on the morning of the 8th of January.
G. Col. Thornton's furthest advance.
1, 2, 3, 4, 5, 6, 7, 8. Redoubt and batteries constructed after the advance of the 28th.
H. The enemy retiring.

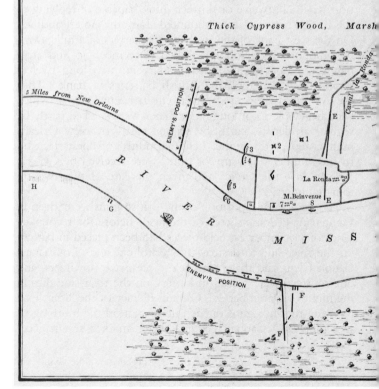

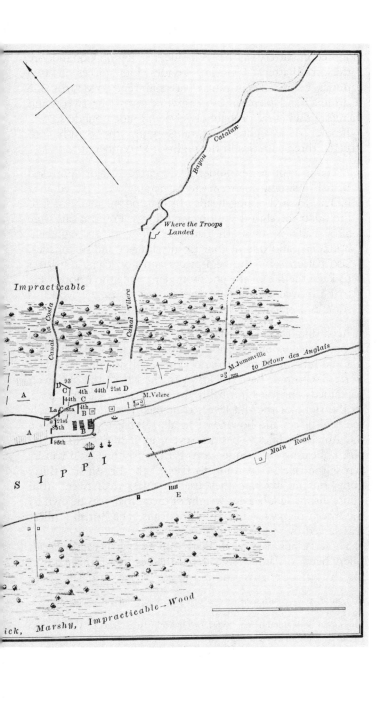

Bayou Catalan

Where the Troops
Landed

Impracticable

Canal Costa

Canal Vilere

to Detour des Anglais

M.Jumonville

D | 93
C | 4th | 44th | 21st D
44th | C
La Costa | 4th
B
A | 121st
95th
A
95th

M.Velere

Main Road

S I P P I

E

ick, Marshy, Impracticable—Wood

mounted in battery on the river-side, bearing on Commodore Patterson's battery opposite, besides four pieces in two batteries below. Their range was sufficient to destroy the "Carolina" and pierce the breastwork across the river,[1] and therefore they were probably twelve and nine pounders.

Besides these lighter long-range guns, the British constructed three batteries in the night of December 31.

"Four eighteen-pounders," reported Major Forrest,[2] British assistant-quartermaster-general, "were placed in a battery formed of hogsheads of sugar, on the main road, to fire upon the ship if she dropped down. Preparations were also made to establish batteries,—one of six eighteen-pounders, and one of four twenty-four-pound carronades; also batteries for the field-pieces and howitzers, the latter to keep the fire of the enemy under, while the troops were to be moved forward in readiness to storm the works as soon as a practicable breach was effected."

According to Peddie's sketch the Battery No. 6, on the road or new levee, contained not four but two guns. Battery No. 5, some fifty yards from No. 6, contained six guns, as Major Forrest reported. Battery No. 4, to the left of the old levee, contained four guns, probably the carronades. Battery No. 3, to the right of the old levee, contained five guns, probably the field-pieces and howitzers. In all, seventeen guns bore on the American lines,—besides seven, in Batteries No. 7 and No. 8, bearing on Commodore Patterson's three-gun battery across the river. According to Gleig,[3] the British had thirty guns; but in any case they used not less than twenty-four guns, throwing a heavier weight of metal than was thrown by the fifteen pieces used by the Americans. The British artillery was served by regular artillerists.

These details were particularly interesting, because the artillery battle of Jan. 1, 1815, offered the best test furnished during the war of relative skill in the use of that arm. The attack

[1] Latour, p. 136. Patterson's Report of Jan. 2, 1815; Latour, Appendix, p. 1, no. xxviii.

[2] Journal of Major Forrest, Assistant-Quartermaster-General; MSS. British Archives. Latour, Appendix, p. cxlvii.

[3] Subaltern, p. 249. Gleig's Campaigns, p. 173.

had every advantage over the defence. The British could concentrate their fire to effect a breach for their troops to enter; the Americans were obliged to disperse their fire on eight points. The American platforms being elevated, offered a better target than was afforded by the low British batteries, and certainly were no better protected. Three of the American guns were in battery across the river, three quarters of a mile from the main British battery of six eighteen-pounders, while the "Louisiana's" carronades were beyond range, and the "Louisiana" herself was not brought into action.[1] On the American side the battle was fought entirely by the guns in Jackson's lines and in Patterson's battery across the river,— one thirty-two-pounder, four twenty-four-pounders, one eighteen-pounder, five twelve-pounders, three six-pounders, and a howitzer,—fifteen American guns in all, matched against ten British eighteen-pounders, four twenty-four-pound carronades, and ten field-pieces and howitzers,— twenty-four guns in all. If the British field-pieces were twelves and nines, the weight of metal was at least three hundred and fifty pounds on the British side against two hundred and twenty-four pounds on the American side, besides two howitzers against one.

The main British batteries were about seven hundred yards distant from Jackson's line. Opposite to the battery of six eighteen-pounders were the American thirty-two and three twenty-four-pounders. Behind the British batteries the British army waited for the order to assault. Toward eight o'clock on the morning of Jan. 1, 1815, the British opened a hot fire accompanied by a shower of rockets. The American guns answered, and the firing continued without intermission until toward noon, when the British fire slackened, and at one o'clock the British artillerists abandoned their batteries, leaving the guns deserted.

No other battle of the war, except that at Chrystler's Farm, left the defeated party with so little excuse for its inferiority. Commonly apologists ascribed greater force to the victor than to the vanquished, or dwelt upon some accident or oversight which affected the result. For the defeat of the British

[1] Patterson's Report of Jan. 2, 1815; Latour, Appendix, p. 1, no. xxviii.

artillery, Jan. 1, 1815, no excuse was ever suggested.[1] The British army and navy frankly admitted that the misfortune was due to American superiority in the use of artillery. British evidence on that point was ample, for their surprise and mortification were extreme; while the Americans seemed never fully to appreciate the extraordinary character of the feat they performed. The most detailed British account was also the most outspoken.

"Never was any failure more remarkable or unlooked-for than this," said Gleig.[2] . . . "The sun, as if ashamed to shine upon our disgrace, was slow of making its appearance; a heavy mist obscured him, and the morning was far advanced before it cleared away. At last, however, the American lines were visible, and then began a fire from our batteries, so brisk and so steadily kept up that we who were behind made not the smallest doubt of its effect. It was answered for a while faintly, and with seeming difficulty. By and by, however, the enemy's salutation became more spirited, till it gradually surpassed our own, both in rapidity and precision. We were a good deal alarmed at this, and the more that a rumor got abroad that our batteries were not proof against the amazing force of the American shot. We had, it may be stated, imprudently rolled into the parapets barrels filled with sugar, under the impression that sugar would prove as effectual as sand in checking the progress of cannon-balls. But the event showed that we had been completely mistaken. The enemy's shot penetrated these sugar-hogsheads as if they had been so many empty casks, dismounting our guns and killing our artillery-men in the very centre of their works. There could be small doubt, as soon as these facts were established, how the cannonading would end. Our fire slackened every moment; that of the Americans became every moment more terrible, till at length, after not more than two hours and a half of firing, our batteries were all silenced. The American works, on the other hand, remained as little injured as ever, and we were completely foiled."

[1] James, ii. 369.
[2] Subaltern, p. 249 (American edition, 1833).

Admiral Codrington, writing from the British headquarters three days after the battle, expressed equal astonishment and annoyance:[1] —

"On the 1st we had our batteries, by severe labor, ready in situations from which the artillery people were, as a matter of course, to destroy and silence the opposing batteries, and give opportunity for a well-arranged storm. But instead of so doing, not a gun of the enemy appeared to suffer, and our firing too high was not made out until we had expended too much of our hardly-collected ammunition to push the matter further. Such a failure in this boasted arm was not to be expected, and I think it a blot in the artillery escutcheon."

Codrington somewhat under-estimated the effect of the British fire. Three of the American guns, including the thirty-two-pounder, were more or less damaged, and the cotton-bales which formed the cheeks of the embrasures proved to be as little serviceable as the hogsheads of sugar in the British river battery.[2] Two artillery caissons were exploded by the British rockets. Thirty-four men were killed or wounded; while the British reported a loss of seventy-six killed and wounded between Jan. 1 and 5, 1815, most of whom fell in the artillery battle.[3]

The British official reports said less, but their silence was equally significant.

"Our batteries made little impression upon the enemy's parapet," wrote Major Forrest.[4] "The order for the assault was therefore not carried into effect. The troops remained in this advanced position, and orders were given to retire the guns in the night. The evening changed to wet, and the ground became in consequence so deep that it required the exertions of the whole army as a working-party, aided by the seamen, to retire the guns a short distance before daylight. The army then fell back to the position it occupied on the 31st."

[1] Life of Codrington, i. 334.
[2] Latour, pp. 133, 134.
[3] Return of Casualties; James, ii. 543.
[4] Journal; Latour, Appendix, p. cxlvii.

Admiral Cochrane's official report was still more brief, and best understood by the comments already quoted from his friend Admiral Codrington:—

> "On the 1st instant batteries were opened; but our fire not having the desired effect, the attack was deferred until the arrival of the troops under Major-General Lambert, which was daily expected."

If the Subaltern was right, the British defeat resulted in the loss of several guns.

> "The enemy having made no attempt to carry off our heavy guns, which we abandoned to their fate," continued Gleig, "it was judged advisable to bring them into the camp as soon as circumstances would allow; and for this purpose working parties were again sent out as soon as the darkness screened them. It was my fortune to accompany them. The labor of dragging a number of huge ship's guns out of the soft soil into which they had sunk, crippled too as most of them were in their carriages, was more extreme by far than any one expected to find it. Indeed, it was not till four o'clock in the morning that our task came to a conclusion, and even then it had been very imperfectly performed. Five guns were eventually left behind. These were rendered useless, it is true, by breaking their trunnions; but it cannot be said that in the course of the late operations the British army came off without the loss of some of its artillery."

Chapter XIV

EFFECTUALLY STOPPED by these repeated miscarriages, General Pakenham, with fully five thousand good soldiers at his command, decided to wait an entire week for Major-General Lambert, who was then on his way with two fresh regiments. In the meanwhile Pakenham adopted a suggestion made first by Vice-Admiral Cochrane,[1] to prepare for throwing a force across the river to turn Jackson's line from the opposite bank. The plan required that the Villeré canal should be extended through the levee to the river without the knowledge of the Americans. Perhaps Pakenham would have done better by dragging his boats across the intervening space; but he preferred to dig a canal, and the work, begun January 4, was done so successfully that until January 6, when it was completed, Jackson did not suspect the movement. On the same day Lambert's division arrived.

From this week of inaction the Americans gained little advantage. The lines were strengthened; but although the Kentucky reinforcements, more than two thousand in number, under General Thomas and John Adair, arrived January 4, they were ill provided with arms, and Jackson could furnish them neither with arms, clothing, nor equipment. The Louisiana militia were in the same condition. Jackson did his utmost to supply these wants; the people of New Orleans did more, and lent at last the few hundred muskets reserved against the danger of a slave insurrection,[2] until in the end, if Adair was correct, a thousand of the Kentuckians were placed in the line of battle. Yet after all the reinforcements had been mustered, Jackson's main dependence was still on his artillery and his intrenchments. In the open field he could not meet the British force.

In his immediate front, Jackson had little to fear. Three thousand marksmen, behind intrenchments everywhere at least five feet high, defended by heavy guns and supported

[1] Life of Codrington, i. 336. Lambert's Report of Jan. 28, 1815; Latour, Appendix, p. clxvi.

[2] Adair's letters of Oct. 21, 1817; Letters of Adair and Jackson, Lexington, 1817.

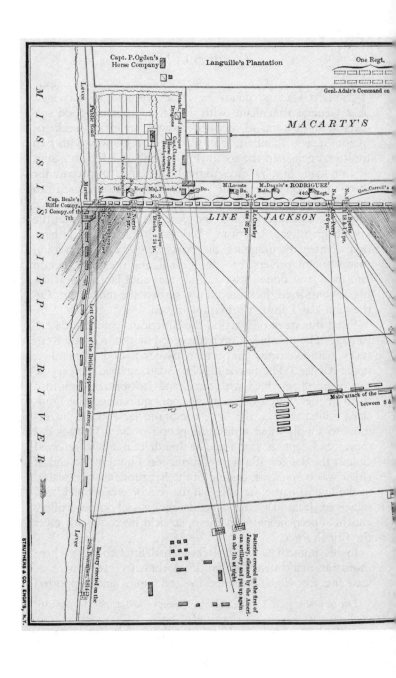

MISSISSIPPI RIVER

Levee

Public Road

Capt. P. Ogden's Horse Company

Languille's Plantation

One Regt.

Genl. Adair's Command on

MACARTY'S

Detachmt. of Attacapas Dragoons

Capt. Chauveau's Horse Company Headquarters

Powder Magazine

Cap. Beale's Rifle Compy.
1 Compy. of the 7th

Mortar

No. 1

7th Regt. Maj. Plauché's No. 3

Bn. M. Lacoste Bn.

M. Daquin's Batn. No. 4

RODRIGUEZ 44th Regt.

Gen. Carroll's

No. 5 Col. Perry. 26 pr.

Lt. Spotts 18 & 14 pr.

LINE JACKSON

Capt. Dominingue Blache. 9 24 pr.

No. 2 Mr. Norris 24 pr.

Lt. Crawley one 32 pr.

Left Column of the British supposed 1300 strong

Main attack of the

between 8 &

Levee

Battery erected on the 28th December, 1814.

Batteries erected on the first of January, silenced by the American artillery and put up again on the 7th at night.

STRUTHERS & CO., ENGR'S, N. Y.

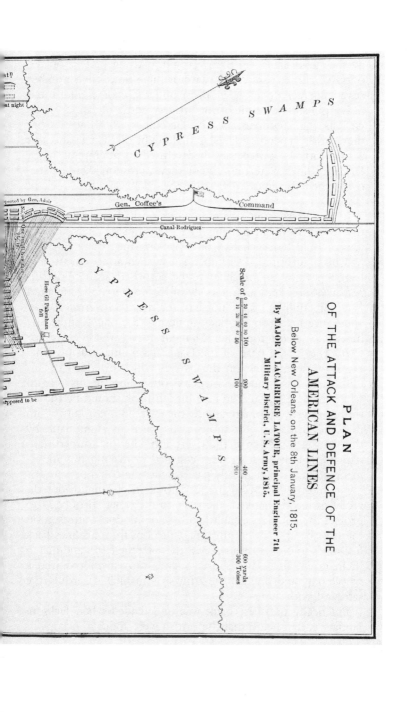

CYPRESS SWAMPS

at night

Gen. Coffee's Command

Canal Rodriguez

ported by Gen. Adair

One small quarter D. E. m.

Here Gl Pakenham fell

CYPRESS SWAMPS

upposed to be

PLAN

OF THE ATTACK AND DEFENCE OF THE

AMERICAN LINES

Below New Orleans, on the 8th January, 1815.

By MAJOR A. LACARRIÈRE LATOUR, principal Engineer 7th

Military District, U. S. Army, 1815.

Scale of 0 20 40 60 80 100   200   400   600 yards
          0 10 20 30 40 60   100   200   300 Toises

by the "Louisiana" on the river and a strong battery on the opposite shore, could defy twice or three times their number advancing across an open plain under fire of eight or ten heavy guns. The result of the artillery battle of January 1, as well as the reconnaissance of December 28, showed what the British general and his staff thought of their chances in a front attack. Twice they had refused to attempt it when Jackson's lines were unfinished; they were not likely to succeed when the lines were strengthened by another week of labor.

In his direct front, therefore, Jackson had reason to think that the British did not intend serious attack. Their next attempt could hardly fail to be a flanking movement. Jackson had been surprised, December 23, by such a movement, and feared nothing so much as to be surprised again. For this reason he still kept a large body of troops, three regiments of Louisiana militia, on the north of the city.[1] "His greatest fear, and hence his strongest defence next to the one occupied by himself, was on the Chef Menteur road, where Governor Claiborne, at the head of the Louisiana militia, was posted." He kept close watch on the bayous which extended on his immediate flank, and constructed other lines in his rear to which he could retreat in case his left flank should be turned through the swamp. Apparently the idea did not occur to him that the British might more easily turn his right flank by throwing a force across the river; and when he learned, January 7, that the British were engaged in making this movement, the time had already passed when he could prevent it.

No means had been provided for transporting troops directly from one bank of the river to the other. If obliged to protect the batteries established by Commodore Patterson on the west bank, Jackson must march troops from his lines back five miles to New Orleans, cross them by the ferry, and march them down the other shore. Such a movement required a whole day, and divided the army in a manner hazarding the safety of both wings.

Practically the west bank was undefended when Jackson, January 7, first heard that the British were about to occupy it.

[1] Eaton, p. 359.

Commodore Patterson had mounted there, as has been told, a number of heavy guns in battery, but these guns were not in position to cover their own bank against attack from below. Major Latour was engaged with negroes in laying out lines of defence, but nothing was completed. In an advanced position, about a mile below the line of Jackson's works, a bastion had been raised close to the river, and near it a small redan, or salient, had been constructed. This work, which was untenable in case of attack in flank or rear, was occupied by four hundred and fifty Louisiana militia, commanded by General David Morgan. During the afternoon of January 7, after the British plan of attack was suspected, General Morgan caused three guns—one twelve-pounder and two six-pounders—to be mounted on his line. Late the same evening General Jackson ordered four hundred men of the Kentucky division to New Orleans, where they were to obtain muskets, then to cross the river, and march down the opposite shore to reinforce Morgan. The Kentuckians obeyed their orders, but they found only about seventy muskets at New Orleans; and not more than two hundred and fifty armed men, weary with marching and faint from want of food, reached Morgan's quarters at four o'clock on the morning of January 8.[1] Adair, who should have known the number best, declared that only one hundred and seventy men were then in the ranks.[2] They were sent a mile farther and stationed as an advanced line, with one hundred Louisiana militia.

Thus seven or eight hundred tired, ill-armed, and unprotected militia, divided in two bodies a mile apart, waited on the west bank to be attacked by a British column which was then in the act of crossing the river. Their defeat was almost certain. A thousand British troops could easily drive them away, capture all the batteries on the west bank, destroy the "Louisiana" as they had destroyed the "Carolina," thus turning all Jackson's lines, and probably rendering necessary the evacuation of New Orleans. For this work Pakenham detached the Eighty-fifth regiment, about three hundred strong, the Fifth West India, two hundred seamen and two hundred

[1] Latour, p. 170.
[2] Adair to Jackson, March 20, 1815; Letters of Adair and Jackson, 1817; Latour, Appendix, p. cxxxii.

marines,—about twelve hundred men in all,[1]—under command of Colonel Thornton, who had led the light brigade at
Bladensburg and across Lake Borgne to the Mississippi. The
movement was ordered for the night of January 7, and was to
be made in boats already collected in the Villeré canal.

With some hesitation[2] Pakenham decided to make a simultaneous attack on Jackson. The arrangements for this assault
were simple. The usual store of fascines and ladders was provided. Six of the eighteen-pound guns were once more
mounted in battery about eight hundred yards from the
American line, to cover the attack. The army, after detaching
Thornton's corps, was organized in three divisions,—one,
under Major-General Gibbs, to attack Jackson's left; another,
under Major-General Keane, to attack along the river-side; a
third, the reserve, to be commanded by Major-General
Lambert.

"The principal attack was to be made by Major-General
Gibbs," said the British official report.[3] The force assigned to
Gibbs consisted of the Fourth, Twenty-first, and Forty-fourth
regiments, with three companies of the Ninety-fifth,—about
two thousand two hundred rank-and-file.[4] The force assigned
to Keane consisted of "the Ninety-third, two companies of
the Ninety-fifth, and two companies of the Fusileers and
Forty-third,"[5]—apparently about twelve hundred rank-and-
file. "The first brigade, consisting of the Fusileers and Forty-
third, formed the reserve" under Major-General Keane,
apparently also twelve hundred strong. Adding two hundred
artillerists and five hundred black troops of the First West India regiment, employed as skirmishers along the edge of the
swamp, the whole body of troops engaged on the east bank
in the assault, according to the official report and returns of
wounded,[6] numbered about five thousand three hundred
rank-and-file, consisting of the Fourth, Seventh (Fusileers),

---

[1] Journal of Major Forrest, Assistant-Quartermaster-General; MSS. British
Archives. Lambert's Report, Jan. 10, 1815; James, ii. 543.

[2] Life of Codrington, i. 336.

[3] Lambert's Report of Jan. 10, 1815; Niles, viii. 177.

[4] James, ii. 373.

[5] Lambert's Report; Niles, viii. 177.

[6] Niles, viii. 180.

Twenty-first, Forty-third, Forty-fourth, Ninety-third, and Ninety-fifth regiments, of whom twenty-two hundred were to attack on the right, twelve hundred on the left, and twelve hundred were to remain in reserve.

Thus of the whole British force, some eight thousand rank-and-file, fifty-three hundred were to assault Jackson's line; twelve hundred were to cross the river and assault Morgan; eight hundred and fifty men were detailed for various duties; and the seamen, except two hundred with Colonel Thornton, must have been in the boats.

To meet this assault, Jackson held an overwhelming force, in which his mere numbers were the smallest element. According to a detailed account given by Jackson two years afterward, his left wing, near the swamp, was held by Coffee's brigade of eight hundred and four men; his centre, by Carroll's brigade of fourteen hundred and fourteen men; his right, near the river, by thirteen hundred and twenty-seven men, including all the regulars; while Adair's Kentucky brigade, numbering five hundred and twenty-five men, were in reserve.[1] Adair claimed that the Kentuckians numbered fully one thousand. The dispute mattered little, for barely one third of the entire force, whatever it was, discharged a gun.

Besides three thousand or thirty-five hundred men on the parapets and a thousand in reserve, Jackson had twelve pieces of artillery distributed along the line, covering every portion of the plain. The earth-wall behind which his men rested was in every part sufficiently high to require scaling, and the mud was so slippery as to afford little footing.[2] Patterson's battery on the opposite shore increased in force till it contained three twenty-four-pounders and six twelve-pounders,[3] covered the levee by which the British left must advance. The "Louisiana" took no part in the action, her men being engaged in working the guns on shore; but without the "Louisiana's" broadside, Jackson had more than twenty cannon in position. Such a force was sufficient to repel ten thousand men if the attack were made in open day.

---

[1] Jackson to Adair, July 23, 1817.
[2] Latour, pp. 147–152.
[3] Patterson's Report of Jan. 13, 1815; Latour, Appendix, p. ix.

Pakenham, aware of the probable consequences of attacking by daylight, arranged for moving before dawn; but his plan required a simultaneous advance on both banks of the river, and such a combination was liable to many accidents. According to the journal of Major Forrest, the British Assistant-Quartermaster-General,[1] forty-seven boats were brought up the bayou on the evening of January 7:

> "As soon as it was dark, the boats commenced to be crossed over into the river. A dam erected below the stern-most boat had raised the water about two feet. Still there was a very considerable fall from the river; and through which, for an extent of two hundred and fifty yards, the boats were dragged with incredible labor by the seamen. It required the whole night to effect this, and the day had dawned before the first detachment of Colonel Thornton's corps (about six hundred men) had embarked; and they just reached the opposite bank when the main attack commenced on the enemy's line."

At six o'clock in broad dawn the columns of Gibbs and Keane moved forward toward Jackson's works, which were lined with American troops waiting for the expected attack. Gibbs's column came first under fire, advancing near the swamp in close ranks of about sixty men in front.[2] Three of the American batteries opened upon them. Coming within one hundred and fifty yards of the American line, the British column obliqued to the left to avoid the fire of the battery directly in face. As they came within musketry range the men faltered and halted, beginning a confused musketry fire. A few platoons advanced to the edge of the ditch, and then broke. Their officers tried in vain to rally them for another advance. Major-General Gibbs was mortally wounded, according to the official report, "within twenty yards of the glacis."[3] Pakenham himself rode forward to rally Gibbs's column, and was instantly struck by a grape-shot and killed, nearly three

---

[1] Journal of Major Forrest, Assistant-Quartermaster-General; MSS. British Archives.

[2] Latour, p. 154.

[3] Lambert's Report of Jan. 10, 1815; Latour, Appendix, p. cxlix.

hundred yards from the American line.[1] "As I advanced with the reserve," said Lambert's report, "at about two hundred and fifty yards from the line, I had the mortification to observe the whole falling back upon me in the greatest confusion."

Keane's column on the left moved along the road and between the river and the levee. Pressing rapidly forward, greatly annoyed by Patterson's battery on the west bank, the head of this column reached the American line, and stormed an unfinished redoubt outside the main work at the edge of the river. The concentrated fire of the whole American right almost immediately drove the column back in disorder; the men who reached the redoubt were killed; Major-General Keane was severely wounded and carried off the field, while the casualties among officers of a lower grade were excessive. The Ninety-third regiment in Keane's brigade lost its lieutenant-colonel and two captains killed, and four more captains severely wounded; three hundred and forty-eight rank-and-file were wounded, ninety-nine were reported missing, and fifty-eight killed. These losses amounted to five hundred and five in seven hundred and seventy-five rank-and-file.[2]

Lambert's report continued:[3] —

"In this situation, finding that no impression had been made; that though many men had reached the ditch, they were either drowned or obliged to surrender, and that it was impossible to restore order in the regiments where they were,—I placed the reserve in position until I could obtain such information as to determine me how to act to the best of my judgment, and whether or not I should resume the attack; and if so, I felt it could be done only by the reserve."

Just as the main attack ended, Colonel Thornton with his six hundred rank-and-file, having landed on the west bank, advanced against Morgan's line, routed it, turned the redoubt, and advanced on Patterson's heavy battery beyond. Patterson unable to use his guns had no choice but to spike

[1] Latour's Plan.
[2] Return of Casualties; James, ii. 554.
[3] James, ii. 373.

his pieces and retreat. Thornton passed up the river a mile beyond Jackson's line,[1] and needed only a field-piece and some hot shot to burn the "Louisiana" and march opposite New Orleans.

From the eastern shore Jackson watched the progress of Thornton with alarm. His official report of January 9 gave an idea of his emotions.

"Simultaneously with his advance on my lines," Jackson said, "the enemy had thrown over in his boats a consider-able force to the other side of the river. These having landed were hardy enough to advance against the works of General Morgan; and what is strange and difficult to ac-count for, at the very moment when their entire discom-fiture was looked for with a confidence approaching to certainty, the Kentucky reinforcements ingloriously fled, drawing after them by their example the remainder of the forces, and thus yielding to the enemy that most formidable position. The batteries which had rendered me for many days the most important service, though bravely defended, were of course now abandoned, not however until the guns had been spiked. This unfortunate rout had totally changed the aspect of affairs. The enemy now occupied a position from which they might annoy us without hazard, and by means of which they might have been enabled to defeat in a great measure the effect of our success on this side the river."

John Adair, who was then in command of the Kentucky brigade, General Thomas being unwell, took great offence at Jackson's account of the battle on the west bank. "The detach-ment on the other side of the river," he reported to Governor Shelby,[2] " were obliged to retire before a superior force. They have been calumniated by those who ought to have fought with them, but did not." The tone of Jackson's report, and his language afterward, showed a willingness to load the Ken-tucky troops on the west bank with the responsibility for a military oversight with which they had nothing to do; but the oversight was not the less serious, whoever was respon-

[1] Latour's Plan.
[2] Letter of Jan. 13, 1815; Niles, vii. 389.

sible for it. The Kentucky and Louisiana troops did not easily yield. The British returns of killed and wounded showed that Thornton's column suffered a considerable loss. Thornton himself was wounded; his regiment, the Eighty-fifth, numbering two hundred and ninety-eight rank-and-file, reported a loss of forty-three men killed, wounded, and missing, besides their colonel. Of one hundred sailors employed in the attack[1] twenty were killed or wounded, besides Captain Money of the royal navy, "who, I am sorry to say, was severely wounded," said Thornton. The Americans made as good a resistance as could have been expected, and had they resisted longer they would merely have been captured when the next detachment of Thornton's column came up. The chief blame for the disaster did not rest on them.

Jackson was helpless to interpose. As he and his men, lining the river bank, watched the progress of Thornton's column on the opposite shore, Jackson could do nothing; but he ordered his men "that they should take off their hats, and give our troops on the right bank three cheers." Adair, who inclined to a severe judgment of Jackson's generalship, told the story more picturesquely:[2] —

"I was standing by him when he gave his order, and with a smile, not of approbation, observed I was afraid they could not hear us. The distance from us to them, on a straight line, was upward of one mile and a half; there was a thick fog, and I confess I could not see the troops of either army. All I could discover was the blaze from the guns; and seeing that continue to progress up the river was the only knowledge we had that our men were retreating."

Jackson then ordered General Humbert, a French officer acting as a volunteer, to take four hundred men and cross the river at New Orleans to repulse the enemy, cost what it might;[3] but had the enemy pressed his advantage, no force at Jackson's command could have stopped their advance, without causing the sacrifice of Jackson's lines. Fortunately the

[1] Thornton's Report of Jan. 8, 1815; James, ii. 547.
[2] Letters of General Adair and General Jackson, 1817.
[3] Latour, p. 175.

only remaining British general, Lambert, was not disposed to make another effort. The eight regiments of regular troops which made the bulk of Pakenham's army had suffered severely in the assault. One of these regiments, the Eighty-fifth, was with Thornton on the west shore. Two, the Seventh and Forty-third, had been in the reserve, and except two companies had never approached the works within musket-shot, yet had lost fifty-two killed, and about one hundred wounded and missing, in an aggregate of less than eighteen hundred. The five remaining regiments—the Fourth, Twenty-first, Forty-fourth, Ninety-third, and Ninety-fifth—were nearly destroyed. They went into battle probably about three thousand strong;[1] they lost seventeen hundred and fifty men killed, wounded, and missing. The total British loss was two thousand and thirty-six.[2] The American loss was seventy-one. Even on the west bank the American loss was much less than that of the British.

The loss of three major-generals was almost as serious as the loss of one third of the regular Infantry. Lambert, the fourth major-general, weighed down by responsibility and defeat, had no wish but to escape. He recalled Thornton's corps the same evening from its position on the opposite bank, and the next day, January 9, began preparations for his difficult and hazardous retreat.[3]

Pakenham's assault on Jackson's lines at New Orleans, January 8, repeated the assault made by Drummond, August 15, at Fort Erie. According to the British account of that battle, Drummond's engaged force numbered twenty-one hundred and forty men; the reserve, about one thousand.[4] Drummond's direct attack, being made by night, was more successful than Pakenham's; his troops approached nearer and penetrated farther than those of Gibbs and Keane; but the consequences were the same. Of three thousand men, Drummond lost nine hundred and five. Of six thousand, engaged in the double action of Jan. 8, 1815, Pakenham lost two thousand and thirty-six. In each case the officers commanding the

[1] James, ii. 373.
[2] James, ii. 382.
[3] Report of General Lambert, Jan. 28, 1815; James, ii. 565.
[4] James, ii. 179.

assaulting columns were killed or wounded, and the repulse was complete.

After the battle General Lambert's position was critical. His withdrawal of Thornton's corps from the west bank betrayed his intention of retiring, and his line of retreat was exposed to attack from the bayou which headed near Jackson's camp. Fortunately for him, Jackson was contented with checking his advance.

> "Whether, after the severe loss he has sustained," wrote Jackson, five days after the battle,[1] "he is preparing to return to his shipping, or to make still mightier efforts to attain his first object, I do not pretend to determine. It becomes me to act as though the latter were his intention."

If Jackson's inaction allowed Lambert to escape, it was likely to hazard a renewal of the attack from some other quarter; but the armies remained for ten days in their old positions without further hostilities, except from artillery fire, until on the night of January 18, after making careful preparations, the whole British force silently withdrew to fortified positions at the mouth of the bayou, disappearing as suddenly and mysteriously as it came, and leaving behind it only eight or, according to the American report, fourteen[2] of the guns which had covered the river and held the "Louisiana" at a distance.[3] At the mouth of the bayou the army remained until January 27, when it was re-embarked in the ships off Chandeleur's Island.

On the day of the battle of January 8, a British squadron appeared in the river below Fort St. Philip. Two bomb-vessels, under the protection of a sloop, a brig, and a schooner, bombarded the fort without effect until January 18, when they withdrew at the same time with the army above.

Notwithstanding the disastrous failure of the campaign before New Orleans, the British expedition, as it lay off Chandeleur Island February 1, still possessed nearly as much strength as when it appeared there December 11. Reinforced by a thousand fresh soldiers, Lambert determined to attack

---

[1] Jackson to the Secretary of War, Jan. 13, 1815; Niles, vii. 374.
[2] Latour, p. 185.
[3] Lambert's Report of Jan. 28, 1815; Latour, Appendix, p. clxvi.

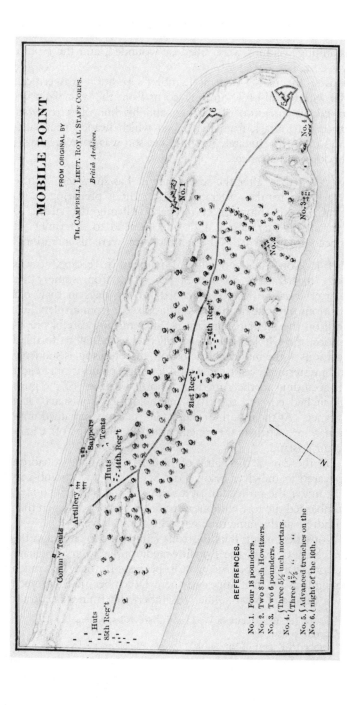

MOBILE POINT

FROM ORIGINAL BY

Th. Campbell, Lieut. Royal Staff Corps.

British Archives.

REFERENCES.

No. 1. Four 18 pounders.
No. 2. Two 8 inch Howitzers.
No. 3. Two 6 pounders.
No. 4. {Three 5½ inch mortars.
       {Three 4¾   "   "
No. 5. {Advanced trenches on the
No. 6. {night of the 10th.

Comm'y Tents

Artillery
Sappers
Tents
Huts
44th Reg't

21st Reg't

4th Reg't

Huts
55th Reg't

Mobile. "It was decided," reported Lambert,[1] "that a force should be sent against Fort Bowyer, situated on the eastern point of the entrance of the bay, and from every information that could be obtained it was considered that a brigade would be sufficient for this object, with a respectable force of artillery." At daylight on the morning of February 8 a whole brigade and a heavy battering-train were disembarked in the rear of Fort Bowyer.

Jackson's determination to defend Mobile had already deprived him of the use of more than half the regular troops assigned to his military district, who remained inactive at Mobile during the months of December and January. They were commanded by General Winchester, whose record as a military officer was not reassuring. Although Fort Bowyer was known to be untenable against attack by land, Jackson not only retained Lieutenant-Colonel Lawrence there, but increased his force until he had three hundred and sixty men in his command,—equal to the average strength of an entire regiment, or half the force of regulars which Jackson commanded at New Orleans. This garrison was only large enough to attract, not to repel, an enemy. The obvious criticism on such a course was afterward made by Armstrong:[2] —

> "After the arrival of the British armament the garrison of Fort Bowyer was not only continued but increased, though from its locality wholly unable to aid in any important purpose of the campaign. Nor was this the whole extent of the evil, for by the disposition made of this gallant corps it was not only subjected to present inaction, but ultimately . . . to the perils of a siege and the humiliation of a surrender."

Colonel Lawrence had no choice but to capitulate, which he did February 11. He had not even the opportunity to resist, for the British made regular approaches, and could not be prevented from capturing the place without the necessity of assault. Jackson reported to the Secretary of War[3] that this event was one which he "little expected to happen but after the most gallant resistance; that it should have taken place

---

[1] Report of Feb. 14, 1815; Latour, Appendix, p. clxxii.
[2] Notices, ii. 176.
[3] Jackson's Report of Feb. 24, 1815; Latour, Appendix, p. xcvii.

without even a fire from the enemy's batteries is as astonishing as it is mortifying." In truth, the military arrangements, not Lawrence's defence, were responsible for the result; and Jackson had reason to fear that a greater disaster was at hand, for unless General Winchester should promptly evacuate Mobile, the disaster of the River Raisin was likely to be repeated on a larger scale.

Chapter I

DURING THE SPRING and summer of 1814 the task of diplomacy was less hopeful than that of arms. Brown and Izard with extreme difficulty defended the frontier; but Gallatin and Bayard could find no starting-point for negotiation. Allowed by Castlereagh's courtesy to visit England, they crossed the Channel in April, and established themselves in London. There Gallatin remained until June 21, waiting for the British government to act, and striving with tact, caution, and persistency to bring both governments on common ground; but the attempt was hopeless. England was beside herself with the intoxication of European success.

Although the English newspapers expressed a false idea of the general will, and were even at cross purposes with the Ministry in American matters, their tone was in some respects an indifferent barometer for measuring the elation or depression of the public temper, and exercised some influence, rather apparent than real, on the momentary attitudes of government. Had Castlereagh and his colleagues been really controlled by the press, no American peace could have been made. Whatever spirit of friendship for America might exist was necessarily silent, and only extravagant enmity found expression either in the press or in society.

Perhaps because ministers were believed to wish for peace with the United States, the London "Times," which was not a ministerial journal, made itself conspicuous in demanding war. The "Times" had not previously shown a vindictive spirit, but it represented the Wellesley and Canning interest, which could discover no better course than that of being more English than England, and more patriotic than the Government. The "Times" was always ably written and well edited, but its language toward the United States showed too strong a connection with that of the Federalists, from whose public and private expressions the press of England formed its estimate of American character.

The "Times" indulged to excess in the pleasure of its antipathy. Next to Napoleon, the chief victim of English hatred was Madison. For so mild a man Madison possessed a remarkable faculty of exciting invective. The English press surpassed the American Federalists in their allusions to him, and the "Times" was second to no English newspaper in the energy of its vituperation. "The lunatic ravings of the philosophic statesman of Washington" were in its political category of a piece with "his spaniel-like fawning on the Emperor of Russia.[1] . . . The most abject of the tools of the deposed tyrant; . . . doubtless he expected to be named Prince of the Potomack or Grand Duke of Virginia."[2] The "Sun" somewhat less abusively spoke of "that contemptible wretch Madison, and his gang;"[3] but the "Times" habitually called him liar and impostor.

"Having disposed of all our enemies in Europe," the "Times" in the middle of April turned its attention to the United States. "Let us have no cant of moderation," was its starting-point. "There is no public feeling in the country stronger than that of indignation against the Americans; . . . conduct so base, so loathsome, so hateful. . . . As we urged the principle, No peace with Bonaparte! so we must maintain the doctrine of, No peace with James Madison!"[4] To this rule the "Times" steadily adhered with a degree of ill-temper not easily to be described, and with practical objects freely expressed. "Mr. Madison's dirty, swindling manœuvres in respect to Louisiana and the Floridas remain to be punished," it declared April 27; and May 17 it pursued the idea: "He must fall a victim to the just vengeance of the Federalists. Let us persevere. Let us unmask the impostor. . . . Who cares about the impudence which they call a doctrine? . . . We shall demand indemnity. . . . We shall insist on security for Canada. . . . We shall inquire a little into the American title to Louisiana; and we shall not permit the base attack on Florida to go unpunished." May 18 it declared that Madison had put himself on record as a liar in the cause of his Corsican master. "He has lived an impostor, and he deserves to meet

[1] The Times, Feb. 4 and 10, 1814.
[2] The Times, April 23, 1814.
[3] The Sun, Aug. 4, 1814.
[4] The Times, April 15, 1814.

the fate of a traitor. That fate now stares him in the face."
May 24 the "Times" resumed the topic: "They are struck to
the heart with terror for their impending punishment; and oh
may no false liberality, no mistaken lenity, no weak and cow-
ardly policy, interpose to save them from the blow! Strike!
chastise the savages, for such they are! . . . With Madison
and his perjured set no treaty can be made, for no oath can
bind them." When British commissioners were at last announced as ready to depart for Ghent to negotiate for peace
with the United States, June 2, the "Times" gave them
instructions: "Our demands may be couched in a single
word, — Submission!"

The "Morning Post," a newspaper then carrying higher authority than the "Times," used language if possible more abusive, and even discovered, Jan. 18, 1814, "a new trait in the
character of the American government. Enjoying the reputation of being the most unprincipled and the most contemptible on the face of the earth, they were already known to be
impervious to any noble sentiment; but it is only of late that
we find them insensible of the shame of defeat, destitute even
of the brutish quality of being beaten into a sense of their
unworthiness and their incapacity." Of Madison the "Morning Post" held the lowest opinion. He was "a despot in disguise; a miniature imitation" and miserable tool of Bonaparte,
who wrote his Annual Message; a senseless betrayer of his
country.[1]

The "Times" and "Morning Post" were independent newspapers, and spoke only for themselves; but the "Courier" was
supposed to draw inspiration from the Government, and
commonly received the first knowledge of ministers' intentions. In temper the "Courier" seemed obliged to vie with its
less favored rivals. The President's Annual Message of 1813
resembled in its opinion "all the productions of that vain and
vulgar Cabinet;" it was "a compound of canting and hypocrisy, of exaggeration and falsehood, of coarseness without
strength, of assertions without proof, of the meanest prejudices, and of the most malignant passions; of undisguised
hatred of Great Britain, and of ill-concealed partiality and

---

[1] The Morning Post, Jan. 27 and Feb. 1, 1814.

servility toward France."[1] "We know of no man for whom we feel greater contempt than for Mr. Madison," said the "Courier" of May 24. These illustrations of what the "Courier" called "exaggeration and falsehood, of coarseness without strength, of assertions without proof, of the meanest prejudices, and of the most malignant passions" were probably in some degree a form as used by the "Courier," which would at a hint from the Ministry adopt a different tone; but announcements of official acts and intentions were more serious, and claimed more careful attention.

Immediately after the capitulation of Paris, March 31, the Ministry turned its attention to the United States, and the "Courier" announced, April 15, that twenty thousand men were to go from the Garonne to America. Mr. Madison, the "Courier" added, had "made a pretty kettle of fish of it." Twenty thousand men were about two thirds of Wellington's English force, and their arrival in America would, as every Englishman believed, insure the success of the campaign. Not until these troops were embarked would the Ministry begin to negotiate; but in the middle of May the military measures were complete, and then the "Courier" began to prepare the public mind for terms of peace.

These terms were the same as those announced by the "Times," except that the "Courier" did not object to treating with Madison. The United States were to be interdicted the fisheries; Spain was to be supported in recovering Louisiana; the right of impressment must be expressly conceded,—anything short of this would be unwise and a disappointment. "There are points which must be conceded by America before we can put an end to the contest."[2] Such language offered no apparent hope of peace; yet whatever hope existed lay in Castlereagh, who inspired it. Extravagant as the demands were, they fell short of the common expectation. The "Courier" admitted the propriety of negotiation; it insisted neither on Madison's retirement nor on a division of the Union, and it refrained from asserting the whole British demand, or making it an ultimatum.

The chief pressure on the Ministry came from Canada, and

[1] The Courier, Jan. 27, 1814.
[2] The Courier, May 19 and 24, 1814.

could not be ignored. The Canadian government returned to its old complaint that Canadian interests had been ignorantly and wantonly sacrificed by the treaty of 1783, and that the opportunity to correct the wrong should not be lost. The Canadian official "Gazette" insisted that the United States should be required to surrender the northern part of the State of New York, and that both banks of the St. Lawrence should be Canadian property.[1] A line from Plattsburg to Sackett's Harbor would satisfy this necessity; but to secure Canadian interests, the British government should further insist on acquiring the east bank of the Niagara River, and on a guaranty of the Indian Territory from Sandusky to Kaskaskias, with the withdrawal of American military posts in the Northwest. A pamphlet was published in May to explain the subject for the use of the British negotiators, and the required territorial cessions were marked on a map.[2] The control of the Lakes, the Ohio River as the Indian boundary, and the restitution of Louisiana were the chief sacrifices wished from the United States. The cession of a part of Maine was rather assumed than claimed, and the fisheries were to be treated as wholly English. A memorial from Newfoundland, dated Nov. 8, 1813,[3] pointed out the advantages which the war had already brought to British trade and fisheries by the exclusion of American competition, to the result of doubling the number of men employed on the Labrador shores; and the memorialists added,—

"They cannot too often urge the important policy . . . of wholly excluding foreigners from sharing again in the advantages of a fishery from which a large proportion of our best national defence will be derived."

British confidence was at its highest point when the Emperor of Russia and the King of Prussia visited London, June 7, and received an enthusiastic welcome. Gallatin obtained an interview with the Czar, June 17, and hoped that Russian influence might moderate British demands; but the Czar could

[1] Niles, vi. 322.
[2] Compressed view of the Points to be discussed in treating with America. London, 1814.
[3] Niles, vi. 238.

give him no encouragement.[1] Gallatin wrote home an often-quoted despatch, dated June 13, warning the President that fifteen or twenty thousand men were on their way to America, and that the United States could expect no assistance from Europe.

"I have also the most perfect conviction," Gallatin continued, "that under the existing unpropitious circumstances of the world, America cannot by a continuance of the war compel Great Britain to yield any of the maritime points in dispute, and particularly to agree to any satisfactory arrangement on the subject of impressment; and that the most favorable terms of peace that can be expected are the *status ante bellum.*"

Even these terms, Gallatin added, depended on American success in withstanding the shock of the campaign. He did not say that at the time he wrote, the *status ante bellum* would be scouted by public opinion in England as favorable to the United States; but his estimate of the situation was more nearly exact than though he had consulted only the apparent passions of the British press.

"Lord Castlereagh," wrote Gallatin to Clay,[2] "is, according to the best information I can collect, the best disposed man in the Cabinet." Yet Castlereagh did not venture at that stage to show a disposition for peace. He delayed the negotiation, perhaps wisely, six weeks after the American negotiators had assembled at Ghent; and his instructions[3] to the British commissioners, dated July 28, reflected the demands of the press. They offered, not the *status ante bellum*, but the *uti possidetis*, as the starting-point of negotiation. "The state of possession must be considered as the territorial arrangement which would revive upon a peace, except so far as the same may be modified by any new treaty." The state of possession, in view of the orders that had then been given, or were to be given, for the invasion of the United States, was likely to cost the Americans half of Maine, between the Penobscot and the Passamaquoddy; Plattsburg, and the northern part of New York,

[1] Adams's Gallatin, p. 514.
[2] Gallatin to Clay, April 22, 1814; Adams's Gallatin, p. 506.
[3] Castlereagh Correspondence, x. 67.

Vermont, and New Hampshire; Fort Niagara, Mackinaw, and possibly New Orleans and Mobile. Besides this concession of the *uti possidetis*, or military occupation at the date of peace, the Americans were required at the outset to admit as a *sine qua non*, or condition precedent to any negotiation, that England's Indian allies, the tribes of the Northwestern Territory, should be included in the pacification, and that a definite boundary should be assigned to them under a mutual guaranty of both Powers. Eastport, or Moose Island, and the fishing privileges were to be regarded as British. With these instructions of July 28, the British commissioners, early in August, started for Ghent.

Between Castlereagh's ideas and those of Madison no relation existed. Gallatin and his colleagues at Ghent were provided with two sets of instructions. The first set had been written in 1813, for the expected negotiation at Petersburg. The second set was written in January, 1814, and was brought to Europe by Clay. Neither authorized the American commissioners to discuss such conditions as Castlereagh proposed. The President gave his negotiators authority to deal with questions of maritime law; but even there they were allowed to exercise no discretion on the chief issue in dispute. Monroe's latest letter, dated January 28, was emphatic. "On impressment, as to the right of the United States to be exempted from it, I have nothing to add," said the secretary;[1] "the sentiments of the President have undergone no change on that important subject. This degrading practice must cease; our flag must protect the crew, or the United States cannot consider themselves an independent nation." The President would consent to exclude all British seamen, except those already naturalized, from American vessels, and to stipulate the surrender of British deserters; but the express abandonment of impressment was a *sine qua non* of treaty. "If this encroachment of Great Britain is not provided against," said Monroe, "the United States have appealed to arms in vain. If your efforts to accomplish it should fail, all further negotiations will cease, and you will return home without delay."

On territorial questions the two governments were equally

[1] Instructions of Jan. 28, 1814; State Papers, Foreign Affairs, iii. 701.

wide apart. So far from authorizing a cession of territorial rights, Monroe instructed the American commissioners, both at St. Petersburg and at Ghent, "to bring to view the advantage to both countries which is promised by a transfer of the upper parts and even the whole of Canada to the United States."[1] The instructions of January 1 and January 28, 1814, reiterated the reasoning which should decide England voluntarily to cede Canada. "Experience has shown that Great Britain cannot participate in the dominion and navigation of the Lakes without incurring the danger of an early renewal of the war."[2]

These instructions were subsequently omitted from the published documents, probably because the Ghent commissioners decided not to act upon them;[3] but when the American negotiators met their British antagonists at Ghent, each party was under orders to exclude the other, if possible, from the Lakes, and the same divergence of opinion in regard to the results of two years' war extended over the whole field of negotiation. The British were ordered to begin by a *sine qua non* in regard to the Indians, which the Americans had no authority to consider. The Americans were ordered to impose a *sine qua non* in regard to impressments, which the British were forbidden to concede. The British were obliged to claim the basis of possession; the Americans were not even authorized to admit the status existing before the war. The Americans were required to negotiate about blockades, contraband and maritime rights of neutrals; the British could not admit such subjects into dispute. The British regarded their concessions of fishing-rights as terminated by the war; the Americans could not entertain the idea.

The diplomacy that should produce a treaty from such discordant material must show no ordinary excellence; yet even from that point of view the prospect was not encouraging. The British government made a peculiar choice of negotiators. The chief British commissioner, Lord Gambier, was unknown in diplomacy, or indeed in foreign affairs. A writer in the London "Morning Chronicle" of August 9 expressed the

---

[1] Monroe's Instructions of June 23, 1813; MSS. State Department Records.
[2] Instructions of Jan. 1 and Jan. 28, 1814; MSS. State Department Records.
[3] Diary of J. Q. Adams, iii. 51.

general surprise that Government could make no better selection for the chief of its commission than Lord Gambier, " who was a post-captain in 1794, and happened to fight the 'Defence' decently in Lord Howe's action; who slumbered for some time as a Junior Lord of the Admiralty; who sung psalms, said prayers, and assisted in the burning of Copenhagen, for which he was made a lord."

Gambier showed no greater fitness for his difficult task than was to be expected from his training; and the second member of the commission, Henry Goulburn, could not supply Gambier's deficiencies. Goulburn was Under-Secretary of State to Lord Bathurst; he was a very young man, but a typical under-secretary, combining some of Francis James Jackson's temper with the fixed opinions of the elder Rose, and he had as little idea of diplomacy as was to be expected from an Under-Secretary of State for the colonies. The third and last member was William Adams, Doctor of Civil Law, whose professional knowledge was doubtless supposed to be valuable to the commission, but who was an unknown man, and remained one.

Experience had not convinced the British government that in dealing with the United States it required the best ability it could command. The mistake made by Lord Shelburne in 1783 was repeated by Lord Castlereagh in 1814. The miscalculation of relative ability which led the Foreign Office to assume that Gambier, Goulburn, and William Adams were competent to deal with Gallatin, J. Q. Adams, J. A. Bayard, Clay, and Russell was not reasonable. Probably the whole British public service, including Lords and Commons, could not at that day have produced four men competent to meet Gallatin, J. Q. Adams, Bayard, and Clay on the ground of American interests; and when Castlereagh opposed to them Gambier, Goulburn, and Dr. Adams, he sacrificed whatever advantage diplomacy offered; for in diplomacy as in generalship, the individual commanded success.

The only serious difficulty in the American commission was its excess of strength. By a natural reaction against the attempt to abolish diplomatic offices, the United States government sent into diplomacy its most vigorous men. Under favorable conditions, four minds and wills of so decided a character could not easily work together; but in the Ghent commission an additional difficulty was created by the unfortunate interference of the Senate. Originally Gallatin, as was due to his age, services, and ability, had been the head of the St. Petersburg commission; but the Senate refused to confirm the appointment. The President at last removed Gallatin from the Treasury, and renominated him as a member of the Ghent commission after the other members had been nominated and confirmed. The Senate then gave its approval,—thus making Gallatin the last member of the commission instead of the first, and placing J. Q. Adams above them all.

Gallatin was peculiarly fitted to moderate a discordant body like the negotiators, while Adams was by temperament little suited to the post of moderator, and by circumstances ill-qualified to appear as a proper representative of the commission in the eyes of its other members. Unless Gallatin were one of the loftiest characters and most loyal natures ever seen in American politics, Adams's chance of success in controlling the board was not within reasonable hope. Gallatin was six years the senior, and represented the President, with the authority of close and continuous personal friendship. The board, including Adams himself, instinctively bowed to Gallatin's authority; but they were deferential to no one else, least of all to their nominal head. Bayard, whose age was the same as that of Adams, was still in name a Federalist; and although his party trusted him little more than it trusted Adams or William Pinkney, who had avowedly become Republicans, he was not the more disposed to follow Adams's leadership. Clay, though ten years their junior, was the most difficult of all to control; and Jonathan Russell, though a New Englander, preferred Clay's social charm, and perhaps also his political prospects, to the somewhat repellent temper and more than doubtful popularity of Adams.

Personal rivalry and jealousies counted for much in such a group; but these were not the only obstacles to Adams's influence. By a misfortune commonly reserved for men of the strongest wills, he represented no one but himself and a powerless minority. His State repudiated and, in a manner, ostracized him. Massachusetts gave him no support, even in defending her own rights; by every means in her power she deprived him of influence, and loaded him with the burden of her own unpopularity. Adams represented a community not only hostile to the war, but avowedly laboring to produce peace by means opposed to those employed at Ghent. If the Ghent commission should succeed in making a treaty, it could do so only by some sacrifice of Massachusetts which would ruin Adams at home. If the Ghent commission should fail, Adams must be equally ruined by any peace produced through the treasonable intrigues or overt rebellion of his State.

Such a head to a commission so constituted needed all the force of character which Adams had, and some qualities he did not possess, in order to retain enough influence to shape any project into a treaty that he could consent to sign; while Gallatin's singular tact and nobility of character were never more likely to fail than in the effort to make allowance for the difficulties of his chief's position. Had Castlereagh improved the opportunity by sending to Ghent one competent diplomatist, or even a well-informed and intelligent man of business, like Alexander Baring, he might probably have succeeded in isolating Adams, and in negotiating with the other four commissioners a treaty sacrificing Massachusetts.

The five American commissioners were ready to negotiate in June; but Castlereagh, for obvious reasons, wished delay, and deferred action until August, doubtless intending to prevent the signature of a treaty on the basis of *uti possidetis* until after September, when Sherbrooke and Prevost should have occupied the territory intended to be held. In May and June no one in England, unless it were Cobbett, entertained more than a passing doubt of British success on land and water; least of all did the three British commissioners expect to yield British demands. They came to impose terms, or to break negotiation. They were not sent to yield any point in dispute, or to seek a cessation of arms.

At one o'clock on the afternoon of August 8, the first conference took place in the Hotel des Pays Bas at Ghent. After the usual civilities and forms had passed, Goulburn took the lead, and presented the points which he and his colleagues were authorized to discuss,—(1) Impressment and allegiance; (2) the Indians and their boundary, a *sine qua non*; (3) the Canadian boundary; (4) the privilege of landing and drying fish within British jurisdiction. Goulburn declared that it was not intended to contest the right of the United States to the fisheries, by which he probably meant the deep-sea fisheries; and he was understood to disavow the intention of acquiring territory by the revision of the Canada boundary; but he urged an immediate answer upon the question whether the Americans were instructed on the point made a *sine qua non* by the British government.

The Americans, seeing as yet only a small part of the British demands, were not so much surprised at Goulburn's points as unable to answer them. The next day they replied in conference that they had no authority to admit either Indian boundary or fisheries into question, being without instructions on these points; and in their turn presented subjects of discussion,—Blockades and Indemnities; but professed themselves willing to discuss everything.

In the conversation following this reply, the British commissioners, with some apparent unwillingness, avowed the intention of erecting the Indian Territory into a barrier between the British possessions and the United States; and the American commissioners declined even to retire for consultation on the possibility of agreeing to such an article. The British commissioners then proposed to suspend conferences until they could receive further instructions, and their wish was followed. Both parties sent despatches to their Governments.

Lord Castlereagh was prompt. As soon as was reasonably possible he sent more precise instructions. Dated August 14,[1] these supplementary instructions gave to those of July 28 a distinct outline. They proposed the Indian boundary fixed by the Treaty of Greenville for the permanent barrier between British and American dominion, beyond which neither government should acquire land. They claimed also a "rectification" of the Canadian frontier, and the cession of Fort Niagara and Sackett's Harbor, besides a permanent prohibition on the United States from keeping either naval forces or land fortifications on the Lakes. Beyond these demands the British commissioners were not for the present to go, nor were they to ask for a direct cession of territory for Canada

[1] Castlereagh Correspondence, x. 86.

" with any view to an acquisition of territory as such, but for the purpose of securing her possessions and preventing future disputes;"[1] yet a small cession of land in Maine was necessary for a road from Halifax to Quebec, and an arrangement of the Northwestern boundary was required to coincide with the free navigation of the Mississippi.

As soon as the new instructions reached Ghent the British commissioners summoned the Americans to another conference, August 19; and Goulburn, reading from Castlereagh's despatch, gave to the Americans a clear version of its contents.[2] When he had finished, Gallatin asked what was to be done with the American citizens—perhaps one hundred thousand in number—already settled beyond the Greenville line, in Ohio, Indiana, Illinois, and Michigan? Goulburn and Dr. Adams replied that these people must shift for themselves. They added also that Moose Island and Eastport belonged to Great Britain as indisputably as the county of Northamptonshire, and were not a subject for discussion; but they would not then make a *sine qua non* of the proposition regarding the Lakes. The conference ended, leaving the Americans convinced that their answer to these demands would close the negotiation. Clay alone, whose knowledge of the Western game of brag stood him in good stead, insisted that the British would recede.[3]

The British commissioners the next day, August 20, sent an official note containing their demands, and the Americans before sending their reply forwarded the note to America, with despatches dated August 19 and 20, announcing that they intended to return "a unanimous and decided negative."[4] They then undertook the task of drawing up their reply. Upon Adams as head of the commission fell the duty of drafting formal papers,—a duty which, without common consent, no other member could assume. His draft met with little mercy, and the five gentlemen sat until eleven o'clock of August 24, "sifting, erasing, patching, and amending until we were all

[1] Note of British Commissioners, Aug. 19, 1814; State Papers, Foreign Affairs, iii. 710.
[2] Diary of J. Q. Adams, iii. 17, 18.
[3] Diary of J. Q. Adams, iii. 20, 101.
[4] Despatch of Aug. 19, 1814; State Papers, Foreign Affairs, iii. 708.

wearied, though none of us was yet satiated with amendment." At the moment when they gave final shape to the note
which they believed would render peace impossible, the army
of General Ross was setting fire to the Capitol at Washington,
and President Madison was seeking safety in the Virginia
woods.

Only to persons acquainted with the difficulties of its composition did the American note of August 24 show signs of
its diverse origin.[1] In dignified temper, with reasoning creditable to its authors and decisive on its issues, it assured the
British negotiators that any such arrangement as they required for the Indians was contrary to precedent in public
law, was not founded on reciprocity, and was unnecessary for
its professed object in regard to the Indians. The other demands were equally inadmissible:—

"They are founded neither on reciprocity, nor on any of
the usual bases of negotiation, neither on that of *uti possidetis* nor of *status ante bellum*. They are above all dishonorable to the United States in demanding from them to
abandon territory and a portion of their citizens; to admit
a foreign interference in their domestic concerns, and to
cease to exercise their natural rights on their own shores
and in their own waters. A treaty concluded on such terms
would be but an armistice."

The negotiators were ready to terminate the war, both parties restoring whatever territory might have been taken, and
reserving their rights over their respective seamen; but such
demands as were made by the British government could not
be admitted even for reference.

The American reply was sent to the British commissioners
August 25, "and will bring the negotiation," remarked J. Q.
Adams, "very shortly to a close."[2] The American commissioners prepared to quit Ghent and return to their several posts,
while the British commissioners waited for instructions from
London. Even Gallatin, who had clung to the hope that he
could effect an arrangement, abandoned the idea, and believing that the British government had adopted a system of

[1] Note of Aug. 24, 1814; State Papers, Foreign Affairs, iii. 711.
[2] Diary of J. Q. Adams, Aug. 25, 1814, iii. 23.

conquest, prepared for an immediate return to America.[1] Goulburn also notified his Government that the negotiation was not likely to continue, and reported some confidential warnings from Bayard that such conditions of peace would not only insure war, but would sacrifice the Federalist party. "It has not made the least impression upon me or upon my colleagues," reported Goulburn to Bathurst.[2]

At that point the negotiation remained stationary for two months, kept alive by Liverpool, Castlereagh, and Bathurst, while they waited for the result of their American campaign. The despatch of August 20 crossed the Atlantic, and was communicated to Congress October 10, together with all other papers connected with the negotiation; but not until October 25 did the American commissioners write again to their Government.

[1] Adams's Gallatin, p. 524.
[2] Goulburn to Bathurst, Aug. 23, 1814; Wellington, Supplementary Despatches, ix. 189.

Chapter II

THE BRITISH NOTE of August 19 and the American rejoinder of August 24, brought about a situation where Lord
Castlereagh's influence could make itself felt. Castlereagh had
signed the British instructions of July 28 and August 14,[1] and
himself brought the latter to Ghent, where he passed August
19, before going to Paris on his way to the Congress at
Vienna. He was at Ghent when Goulburn and his colleagues
held their conference and wrote their note of August 19;[2] and
he could not be supposed ignorant of their language or acts.
Yet when he received at Paris letters from Goulburn, dated
August 24 and 26,[3] he expressed annoyance that the American
commissioners should have been allowed to place England in
the attitude of continuing the war for purposes of conquest,
and still more that the British commissioners should be willing to accept that issue and break off negotiation upon it. In
a letter to Lord Bathurst, who took charge of the negotiation
in his absence, Castlereagh suggested ideas altogether different from those till then advanced in England.[4]

"The substance of the question is," said Castlereagh,
"Are we prepared to continue the war for territorial arrangements? And if not, is this the best time to make our
peace, saving all our rights, and claiming the fisheries,
which they do not appear to question? In which case the
territorial questions might be reserved for ulterior discussion. Or is it desirable to take the chance of the campaign,
and then to be governed by circumstances? . . . If we
thought an immediate peace desirable, as they are ready to
waive all the abstract questions, perhaps they might be prepared to sign a provisional article of Indian peace as distinct
from limits, and relinquish their pretensions to the islands

[1] Castlereagh Correspondence, x. 67, 86.
[2] Diary of J. Q. Adams, Aug. 19 and 20, 1814, iii. 19, 21.
[3] Goulburn to Bathurst, Aug. 24, 1814; Wellington Supplementary Despatches, ix. 190. Goulburn to Castlereagh, Aug. 26, 1814; Wellington Supplementary Despatches, ix. 193.

[4] Castlereagh to Bathurst, Aug. 28, 1814; Castlereagh Correspondence,
x. 100.

in Passamaquoddy Bay, and possibly to admit minor adjustments of frontier, including a right of communication from Quebec to Halifax across their territory. But while I state this, I feel the difficulty of so much letting down the question under present circumstances."

At the same time Castlereagh wrote to Goulburn, directing him to wait at Ghent for new instructions from London.[1] Lord Liverpool shared his disapproval of the manner in which the British commissioners had managed the case, and replied to Castlereagh, September 2, that the Cabinet had already acted in the sense he wished:[2] —

"Our commissioners had certainly taken a very erroneous view of our policy. If the negotiation had been allowed to break off upon the two notes already presented, or upon such an answer as they were disposed to return, I am satisfied that the war would have become quite popular in America."

The idea that the war might become popular in America was founded chiefly on the impossibility of an Englishman's conceiving the contrary; but in truth the Ministry most feared that the war might become unpopular in England.

"It is very material to throw the rupture of the negotiation, if it is to take place, upon the Americans," wrote Liverpool, the same day, to the Duke of Wellington;[3] "and not to allow them to say that we have brought forward points as ultimata which were only brought forward for discussion, and at the desire of the American commissioners themselves. The American note is a most impudent one, and, as to all its reasoning, capable of an irresistible answer."

New instructions were accordingly approved in Cabinet.[4]

[1] Castlereagh to Goulburn, Aug. 28, 1814; Castlereagh Correspondence, x. 102.
[2] Liverpool to Castlereagh, Sept. 2, 1814; Wellington Supplementary Despatches, ix. 214.
[3] Liverpool to Wellington, Sept. 2, 1814; Wellington Supplementary Despatches, ix. 212.
[4] Draft of note, etc., Sept. 1, 1814; Wellington Supplementary Despatches, ix. 245.

Drawn by Bathurst, and dated September 1, they contained what Liverpool considered an "irresistible answer" to the American note of August 24; but their force of logic was weakened by the admission that the previous British demands, though certainly stated as a *sine qua non*, were in reality not to be regarded as such. In private this retreat was covered by the pretext that it was intended only to keep the negotiation alive until better terms could be exacted.

"We cannot expect that the negotiation will proceed at present," continued Liverpool's letter to Castlereagh; "but I think it not unlikely, after our note has been delivered in, that the American commissioners will propose to refer the subject to their Government. In that case the negotiation may be adjourned till the answer is received, and we shall know the result of the campaign before it can be resumed. If our commander does his duty, I am persuaded we shall have acquired by our arms every point on the Canadian frontier which we ought to insist on keeping."

Lord Gambier and his colleagues communicated their new instructions to the American negotiators in a long note dated September 4, and were answered by a still longer note dated September 9, which was also sent to London, and considered in Cabinet. Bathurst felt no anxiety about the negotiation in its actual stage. Goulburn wrote to him that "as long as we answer their notes, I believe that they will be ready to give us replies," and urged only that Sir George Prevost should hasten his reluctant movements in Canada.[1] Bathurst wrote more instructions, dated September 16, directing his commissioners to abandon the demands for Indian territory and exclusive control of the Lakes, and to ask only that the Indians should be included in the peace.[2] The British commissioners sent their note with these concessions to the Americans September 19; and then for the first time the Americans began to suspect the possibility of serious negotiation. For six weeks they had

[1] Goulburn to Bathurst, Sept. 5 and 16, 1814; Wellington Supplementary Despatches, ix. 221, 265.

[2] Draft of note, etc., Sept. 16, 1814; Wellington Supplementary Despatches, ix. 263.

dealt only with the question whether they should negotiate at all.

The demand that the Indians should be included in the treaty was one that under favorable circumstances the Americans would have rejected; but none of them seriously thought of rejecting it as their affairs then stood. When the American commissioners discussed the subject among themselves, September 20, Adams proposed to break off the negotiation on that issue; but Gallatin good-naturedly overruled him, and Adams would not himself, on cool reflection, have ventured to take such responsibility. Indeed, he suggested an article for an Indian amnesty, practically accepting the British demand.[1] He also yielded to Gallatin the ungrateful task of drafting the answers to the British notes; and thus Gallatin became in effect the head of the commission.

All Gallatin's abilities were needed to fill the place. In his entire public life he had never been required to manage so unruly a set of men. The British commissioners were trying, and especially Goulburn was aggressive in temper and domineering in tone; but with them Gallatin had little trouble. Adams and Clay were persons of a different type, as far removed from British heaviness as they were from the Virginian ease of temper which marked the Cabinet of Jefferson, or the incompetence which characterized that of Madison. Gallatin was obliged to exert all his faculties to control his colleagues; but whenever he succeeded, he enjoyed the satisfaction of feeling that he had colleagues worth controlling. They were bent on combat, if not with the British, at all events with each other; and Gallatin was partly amused and partly annoyed by the unnecessary energy of their attitude.

The first divergence occurred in framing the reply to the British note of September 19, which while yielding essentials made a series of complaints against the United States,—and among the rest reproached them for their attempt to conquer Canada, and their actual seizure of Florida. Adams, who knew little about the secrets of Jefferson's and Madison's Administrations, insisted on resenting the British charges, and especially on justifying the United States government in its

[1] Diary of J. Q. Adams, Sept. 20, 1814, iii. 38.

attacks upon Florida. Bayard protested that he could not support such a view, because he had himself publicly in Congress denounced the Government on the subject of Florida; and Gallatin was almost equally committed, for, as he frankly said, he had opposed in Cabinet for a whole year what had been done in Florida before he could succeed in stopping it.[1] Clay said nothing, but he had strong reasons for wishing that the British negotiators should not be challenged to quote his notorious speeches on the conquest of Canada. Adams produced Monroe's instructions, and in the end compelled his colleagues to yield. His mistake in pressing such an issue was obvious to every one but himself, and would have been evident to him had he not been blinded by irritation at the British note. His colleagues retaliated by summarily rejecting as cant his argument that moral and religious duty required the Americans to take and settle the land of the Indians.[2]

After much discussion their note was completed and sent, September 26, to the British commissioners,[3] who forwarded it as usual to London, with a letter from Goulburn of the same date, written in the worst possible temper, and charging the American commissioners with making a variety of false and fraudulent statements.[4] While the British Cabinet detained it longer than usual for consideration, the Americans at Ghent felt their position grow weaker day by day.

Nothing warranted a serious hope of peace. Goulburn and his colleagues showed no thought of yielding acceptable conditions. The London "Courier" of September 29 announced what might be taken for a semi-official expression of the Ministry:—

"Peace they [the Americans] may make, but it must be on condition that America has not a foot of land on the waters of the St. Lawrence, . . . no settlement on the Lakes, . . . no renewal of the treaties of 1783 and 1794; . . . and they must explicitly abandon their new-fangled principles of the law of nations."

[1] Diary of J. Q. Adams, Sept. 25, 1814, iii. 41.
[2] Diary of J. Q. Adams, Sept. 25, 1814, iii. 42.
[3] American note of Sept. 26, 1814; State Papers, Foreign Affairs, iii. 719.
[4] Goulburn to Bathurst, Sept. 26, 1814; Wellington Supplementary Despatches, ix. 287.

Liverpool, writing to Castlereagh September 23,[1] said that in his opinion the Cabinet had "now gone to the utmost justifiable point in concession, and if they [the Americans] are so unreasonable as to reject our proposals, we have nothing to do but to fight it out. The military accounts from America are on the whole satisfactory." The news of the cruel humiliation at Bladensburg and the burning of Washington arrived at Ghent October 1, and caused British and Americans alike to expect a long series of British triumphs, especially on Lake Champlain, where they knew the British force to be overwhelming.

Goulburn exerted himself to produce a rupture. His letter of September 26 to Bathurst treated the American offer of an Indian amnesty as a rejection of the British ultimatum. Again Lord Bathurst set him right by sending him, October 5, the draft of a reciprocal article replacing the Indians in their situation before the war; and the British commissioners in a note dated October 8, 1814, communicated this article once more as an ultimatum.[2] Harrison's treaty of July 22 with the Wyandots, Delawares, Shawanees, and other tribes, binding them to take up arms against the British, had then arrived, and this news lessened the interest of both parties in the Indian question. None of the American negotiators were prepared to break off negotiations on that point at such a time, and Clay was so earnest to settle the matter that he took from Gallatin and Adams the task of writing the necessary acceptance of the British ultimatum. Gallatin and Clay decided to receive the British article as according entirely with the American offer of amnesty, and the note was so written.[3]

With this cordial admission of the British ultimatum the Americans coupled an intimation that the time had come when an exchange of general projects for the proposed treaty should be made. More than two months of discussion had then resulted only in eliminating the Indians from the dispute, and in agreeing to maintain silence in regard to the Lakes. Another great difficulty which had been insuperable

[1] Liverpool to Castlereagh, Sept. 23, 1814; Wellington Supplementary Despatches, ix. 278.

[2] British note of Oct. 8, 1814; State Papers, Foreign Affairs, iii. 721.

[3] American note of Oct. 13, 1814; State Papers, Foreign Affairs, iii. 723.

was voluntarily removed by President Madison and his Cabinet, who after long and obstinate resistance at last authorized the commissioners, by instructions dated June 27, to omit impressment from the treaty. Considering the frequent positive declarations of the United States government, besides the rejection of Monroe's treaty in 1807 and of Admiral Warren's and Sir George Prevost's armistice of 1812 for want of an explicit concession on that point, Monroe's letter of June 27 was only to be excused as an act of common-sense or of necessity. The President preferred to represent it as an act of common-sense, warranted by the peace in Europe, which promised to offer no further occasion for the claim or the denial of the British right. On the same principle the subject of blockades was withdrawn from discussion; and these concessions, balanced by the British withdrawal from the Indian ultimatum and the Lake armaments, relieved the American commissioners of all their insuperable difficulties.

The British commissioners were not so easily rescued from their untenable positions. The American note of October 13, sent as usual to London, was answered by Bathurst October 18 and 20,[1] in instructions revealing the true British terms more completely than had yet been ventured. Bathurst at length came to the cardinal point of the negotiation. As the American commissioners had said in their note of August 24, the British government must choose between the two ordinary bases of treaties of peace,—the state before the war, or *status ante bellum*; and the state of possession, or *uti possidetis*. Until the middle of October, 1814, the *uti possidetis*, as a basis of negotiation, included whatever country might have been occupied by Sir George Prevost in his September campaign. Bathurst from the first intended to insist on the state of possession, but had not thought proper to avow it. His instructions of October 18 and 20 directed the British commissioners to come to the point, and to claim the basis of *uti possidetis* from the American negotiators:—

"On their admitting this to be the basis on which they are ready to negotiate, but not before they have admitted it, you will proceed to state the mutual accommodations

[1] Castlereagh Correspondence, x. 168–173.

which may be entered into in conformity with this basis. The British occupy Fort Michillimackinaw, Fort Niagara, and all the country east of the Penobscot. On the other hand the forces of the United States occupy Fort Erie and Fort Amherstburg [Malden]. On the government of the United States consenting to restore these two forts, Great Britain is ready to restore the forts of Castine and Machias, retaining Fort Niagara and Fort Michillimackinaw."

Thus the British demand, which had till then been intended to include half of Maine and the whole south bank of the St. Lawrence River from Plattsburg to Sackett's Harbor, suddenly fell to a demand for Moose Island, a right of way across the northern angle of Maine, Fort Niagara with five miles circuit, and the Island of Mackinaw. The reason for the new spirit of moderation was not far to seek. On the afternoon of October 17, while the British Cabinet was still deliberating on the basis of *uti possidetis*, news reached London that the British invasion of northern New York, from which so much had been expected, had totally failed, and that Prevost's large army had precipitately retreated into Canada. The London "Times" of October 19 was frank in its expressions of disappointment: —

"This is a lamentable event to the civilized world. . . . The subversion of that system of fraud and malignity which constitutes the whole policy of the Jeffersonian school . . . was an event to which we should have bent and yet must bend all our energies. The present American government must be displaced, or it will sooner or later plant its poisoned dagger in the heart of the parent State."

The failure of the attempt on Baltimore and Drummond's bloody repulse at Fort Erie became known at the same time, and coming together at a critical moment threw confusion into the Ministry and their agents in the press and the diplomatic service throughout Europe. The "Courier" of October 25 declared that "peace with America is neither practicable nor desirable till we have wiped away this late disaster;" but the "Morning Chronicle" of October 21–24 openly intimated that the game of war was at an end. October 31, the Paris correspondent of the London "Times" told of the cheers that rose from the crowds in the Palais Royal gardens at each recital of the Plattsburg defeat; and October 21 Goulburn wrote from Ghent to Bathurst,[1] —

"The news from America is very far from satisfactory. Even our brilliant success at Baltimore, as it did not terminate in the capture of the town, will be considered by the Americans as a victory and not as an escape. . . . If it were not for the want of fuel in Boston, I should be quite in despair."

In truth the blockade was the single advantage held by England; and even in that advantage the Americans had a share as long as their cruisers surrounded the British Islands.

Liverpool wrote to Castlereagh, October 21,[2] commenting severely on Prevost's failure, and finding consolation only in the thought that the Americans showed themselves even less patriotic than he had supposed them to be: —

"The capture and destruction of Washington has not united the Americans: quite the contrary. We have gained more credit with them by saving private property than we have lost by the destruction of their public works and buildings. Madison clings to office, and I am strongly inclined to think that the best thing for us is that he should remain there."

Castlereagh at Vienna found himself unable to make the full influence of England felt, so long as such mortifying disasters by land and sea proved her inability to deal with an enemy she persisted in calling contemptible.

On the American commissioners the news came, October 21, with the effect of a reprieve from execution. Gallatin was deeply moved; Adams could not believe the magnitude of the success; but as far as regarded their joint action, the overthrow of England's scheme produced no change. Their tone had always been high, and they saw no advantage to be gained by altering it. The British commissioners sent to them,

[1] Goulburn to Bathurst; Wellington Supplementary Despatches, ix. 366.

[2] Liverpool to Castlereagh, Oct. 21, 1814; Wellington Supplementary Despatches, ix. 367.

October 21, the substance of the new instructions, offering the basis of *uti possidetis*, subject to modifications for mutual convenience.[1] The Americans by common consent, October 23, declined to treat on that basis, or on any other than the mutual restoration of territory.[2] They thought that the British government was still playing with them, when in truth Lord Bathurst had yielded the chief part of the original British demand, and had come to what the whole British empire regarded as essentials,—the right of way to Quebec, and the exclusion of American fishermen from British shores and waters.

The American note of October 24, bluntly rejecting the basis of *uti possidetis*, created a feeling akin to consternation in the British Cabinet. At first, ministers assumed that the war must go on, and deliberated only on the point to be preferred for a rupture. "We still think it desirable to gain a little more time before the negotiation is brought to a close," wrote Liverpool to the Duke of Wellington,[3] October 28; and on the same day he wrote to Castlereagh at Vienna to warn him that the American war " will probably now be of some duration," and treating of its embarrassments without disguise.[4] The Czar's conduct at Vienna had annoyed and alarmed all the great Powers, and the American war gave him a decisive advantage over England; but even without the Russian complication, the prospect for ministers was not cheering.

"Looking to a continuance of the American war, our financial state is far from satisfactory," wrote Lord Liverpool; ". . . the American war will not cost us less than £10,000,000, in addition to our peace establishment and other expenses. We must expect, therefore, to hear it said that the property tax is continued for the purpose of securing a better frontier for Canada."

A week passed without bringing encouragement to the

---

[1] British note of Oct. 21, 1814; State Papers, Foreign Affairs, iii. 724.

[2] American note of Oct. 24, 1814; State Papers, Foreign Affairs, iii. 725.

[3] Liverpool to Wellington, Oct. 28, 1814; Wellington Supplementary Despatches, ix. 384.

[4] Liverpool to Castlereagh, Oct. 28, 1814; Wellington Supplementary Despatches, ix. 382.

British Cabinet. On the contrary the Ministry learned that a vigorous prosecution of hostilities would cost much more than ten million pounds, and when Liverpool next wrote to Castlereagh, November 2,[1] although he could still see "little prospect for our negotiations at Ghent ending in peace," he added that "the continuance of the American war will entail upon us a prodigious expense, much more than we had any idea of." A Cabinet meeting was to be held the next day, November 3, to review the whole course of policy as to America.

Throughout the American difficulties, from first to last, the most striking quality shown by the British government was the want of intelligence which caused the war, and marked the conduct of both the war and the negotiations. If the foreign relations of every government were marked by the same character, politics could be no more than rivalry in the race to blunder; but in October, 1814, another quality almost equally striking became evident. The weakness of British councils was as remarkable as their want of intelligence. The government of England had exasperated the Americans to an animosity that could not forget or forgive, and every dictate of self-interest required that it should carry out its policy to the end. Even domestic politics in Parliament might have been more easily managed by drawing public criticism to America, while in no event could taxes be reduced to satisfy the public demand.[2] Another year of war was the consistent and natural course for ministers to prefer.

So the Cabinet evidently thought; but instead of making a decision, the Cabinet council of November 3 resorted to the expedient of shifting responsibility upon the Duke of Wellington. The Duke was then Ambassador at Paris. His life had been threatened by angry officers of Napoleon, who could not forgive his victories at Vittoria and Toulouse. For his own security he might be sent to Canada, and if he went, he should go with full powers to close the war as he pleased.

The next day, November 4, Liverpool wrote to Wellington,

---

[1] Liverpool to Castlereagh, Nov. 2, 1814; Wellington Supplementary Despatches, ix. 382.

[2] Liverpool to Castlereagh, Jan. 16, 1815; Castlereagh Correspondence, x. 240.

explaining the wishes of the Cabinet, and inviting him to take the entire command in Canada, in order to bring the war to an honorable conclusion.[1] Wellington replied November 9,— and his words were the more interesting because, after inviting and receiving so decided an opinion from so high an authority, the Government could not easily reject it. Wellington began by reviewing the military situation, and closed by expressing his opinion on the diplomatic contest:[2] —

"I have already told you and Lord Bathurst that I feel no objection to going to America, though I don't promise to myself much success there. I believe there are troops enough there for the defence of Canada forever, and even for the accomplishment of any reasonable offensive plan that could be formed from the Canadian frontier. I am quite sure that all the American armies of which I have ever read would not beat out of a field of battle the troops that went from Bordeaux last summer, if common precautions and care were taken of them. That which appears to me to be wanting in America is not a general, or a general officer and troops, but a naval superiority on the Lakes."

These views did not altogether accord with those of Americans, who could not see that the British generals made use of the Lakes even when controlling them, but who saw the troops of Wellington retire from one field of battle after another,—at Plattsburg, Baltimore, and New Orleans,—while taking more than common precautions. Wellington's military comments showed little interest in American affairs, and evidently he saw nothing to be gained by going to Canada. His diplomatic ideas betrayed the same bias:—

"In regard to your present negotiations, I confess that I think you have no right, from the state of the war, to demand any concession of territory from America. . . . You have not been able to carry it into the enemy's territory, notwithstanding your military success and now undoubted

[1] Liverpool to Wellington, Nov. 4, 1814; Liverpool to Castlereagh, Nov. 4, 1814; Wellington Supplementary Despatches, ix. 404, 405.
[2] Wellington to Castlereagh, Nov. 9, 1814; Wellington Supplementary Despatches, i. 426.

military superiority, and have not even cleared your own territory on the point of attack. You cannot on any principle of equality in negotiation claim a cession of territory excepting in exchange for other advantages which you have in your power. . . . Then if this reasoning be true, why stipulate for the *uti possidetis*? You can get no territory; indeed, the state of your military operations, however creditable, does not entitle you to demand any."

After such an opinion from the first military authority of England, the British Ministry had no choice but to abandon its claim for territory. Wellington's letter reached London about November 13, and was duly considered in the Cabinet. Liverpool wrote to Castlereagh, November 18, that the Ministry had made its decision; the claim for territory was to be abandoned. For this retreat he alleged various excuses,—such as the unsatisfactory state of the negotiations at Vienna, and the alarming condition of France; the finances, the depression of rents, and the temper of Parliament.[1] Such reasoning would have counted for nothing in the previous month of May, but six months wrought a change in public feeling. The war had lost public favor. Even the colonial and shipping interests and the navy were weary of it, while the army had little to expect from it but hard service and no increase of credit. Every Englishman who came in contact with Americans seemed to suffer. Broke, the only victor by sea, was a life-long invalid; and Brock and Ross, the only victors on land, had paid for their success with their lives. Incessant disappointment made the war an unpleasant thought with Englishmen. The burning of Washington was an exploit of which they could not boast. The rate of marine insurance was a daily and intolerable annoyance. So rapidly did the war decline in favor, that in the first half of December it was declared to be decidedly unpopular by one of the most judicious English liberals, Francis Horner; although Horner held that the Americans, as the dispute then stood, were the aggressors.[2] The tone of the press showed the same popular tendency, for while the

---

[1] Liverpool to Castlereagh, Nov. 18, 1814; Wellington Supplementary Despatches, ix. 438.

[2] Horner to J. A. Murray, Dec. 10, 1814; Horner's Memoirs, ii. 213.

"Times" grumbled loudly over the Canada campaign, the "Morning Chronicle" no longer concealed its hostility to the war, and ventured to sneer at it, talking of "the entire defeat and destruction of the last British fleet but one; for it has become necessary to particularize them now."[1]

While the Cabinet still waited, the first instalment of Ghent correspondence to August 20, published in America October 10, returned to England November 18, and received no flattering attention. "We cannot compliment our negotiators," remarked the "Morning Chronicle;" and the "Times" was still less pleased. "The British government has been tricked into bringing forward demands which it had not the power to enforce. . . . Why treat at all with Mr. Madison?" In Parliament, November 19, the liberal opposition attacked the Government for setting up novel pretensions. Ministers needed no more urging, and Bathurst thenceforward could not be charged with waste of time.

During this interval of more than three weeks the negotiators at Ghent were left to follow their own devices. In order to provide the Americans with occupation, the British commissioners sent them a note dated October 31 calling for a counter-project, since the basis of *uti possidetis* was refused.[2] This note, with all the others since August 20, was sent by the Americans to Washington on the same day, October 31; and then Gallatin and Adams began the task of drafting the formal project of a treaty. Immediately the internal discords of the commission broke into earnest dispute. A struggle began between the East and the West over the fisheries and the Mississippi.

The treaty of 1783 coupled the American right of fishing in British waters and curing fish on British shores with the British right of navigating the Mississippi River. For that arrangement the elder Adams was responsible. The fisheries were a Massachusetts interest. At Paris in 1783 John Adams, in season and out of season, with his colleagues and with the British negotiators, insisted, with the intensity of conviction, that the fishing rights which the New England people held while subjects of the British crown were theirs by no grant or

[1] The Morning Chronicle, Nov. 19, 1814.
[2] British note of Oct. 31, 1814; State Papers, Foreign Relations, iii. 726.

treaty, but as a natural right, which could not be extinguished by war; and that where British subjects had a right to fish, whether on coasts or shores, in bays, inlets, creeks, or harbors, Americans had the same right, to be exercised wherever and whenever they pleased. John Adams's persistence secured the article of the definitive treaty, which, without expressly admitting a natural right, coupled the in-shore fisheries and the navigation of the Mississippi with the recognition of independence. In 1814 as in 1783 John Adams clung to his trophies, and his son would have waged indefinite war rather than break his father's heart by sacrificing what he had won; but at Ghent the son stood in isolation which the father in the worst times had never known. Massachusetts left him to struggle alone for a principle that needed not only argument but force to make it victorious. Governor Strong did not even write to him as he did to Pickering, that Massachusetts would give an equivalent in territory for the fisheries. As far as the State could influence the result, the fisheries were to be lost by default.

Had Adams encountered only British opposition he might have overborne it as his father had done; but since 1783 the West had become a political power, and Louisiana had been brought into the Union. If the fisheries were recognized as an indefeasible right by the treaty of 1783, the British liberty of navigating the Mississippi was another indefeasible right, which must revive with peace. The Western people naturally objected to such a proposition. Neither they nor the Canadians could be blamed for unwillingness to impose a mischievous servitude forever upon their shores, and Clay believed his popularity to depend on preventing an express recognition of the British right to navigate the Mississippi. Either Clay or Adams was sure to refuse signing any treaty which expressly sacrificed the local interests of either.

In this delicate situation only the authority and skill of Gallatin saved the treaty. At the outset of the discussion, October 30, Gallatin quietly took the lead from Adams's hands, and assumed the championship of the fisheries by proposing to renew both privileges, making the one an equivalent for the other. Clay resisted obstinately, while Gallatin gently and patiently overbore him. When Gallatin's proposal was put to the vote November 5, Clay and Russell alone opposed it,—and the support then given by Russell to Clay was never forgotten by Adams. Clay still refusing to sign the offer, Gallatin continued his pressure, until at last, November 10, Clay consented to insert, not in the project of treaty, but in the note which accompanied it, a paragraph declaring that the commissioners were not authorized to bring into discussion any of the rights hitherto enjoyed in the fisheries: "From their nature, and from the peculiar character of the treaty of 1783 by which they were recognized, no further stipulation has been deemed necessary by the Government of the United States to entitle them to the full enjoyment of all of them."

Clay signed the note,[1] though unwillingly; and it was sent, November 10, with the treaty project, to the British commissioners, who forwarded it to London, where it arrived at the time when the British Cabinet had at last decided on peace. Bathurst sent his reply in due course; and Goulburn's disgust was great to find that instead of breaking negotiation on the point of the fisheries as he wished,[2] he was required once more to give way. "You know that I was never much inclined to give way to the Americans," he wrote, November 25.[3] "I am still less inclined to do so after the statement of our demands with which the negotiation opened, and which has in every point of view proved most unfortunate."

The British reply, dated November 26,[4] took no notice of the American reservation as to the fisheries, but inserted in the project the old right of navigating the Mississippi. Both Bathurst and Goulburn thought that their silence, after the American declaration, practically conceded the American right to the fisheries, though Gambier and Dr. Adams thought differently.[5] In either case the British note of November 26, though satisfactory to Adams, was far from agreeable to Clay, who was obliged to endanger the peace in order

[1] American note of Nov. 10, 1814; State Papers, Foreign Relations, iii. 733.

[2] Goulburn to Bathurst, Nov. 10, 1814; Wellington Supplementary Despatches, ix. 427.

[3] Goulburn to Bathurst, Nov. 10, 1814; Wellington Supplementary Despatches, ix. 452.

[4] British note of Nov. 26, 1814; State Papers, Foreign Relations, iii. 740.

[5] Goulburn to Bathurst, Nov. 25, 1814; Wellington Supplementary Despatches, ix. 452.

to save the Mississippi. Adams strongly inclined to take the British project precisely as it was offered,[1] but Gallatin overruled him, and Clay would certainly have refused to sign. In discussing the subject, November 28, Gallatin proposed to accept the article on the navigation of the Mississippi if the British would add a provision recognizing the fishing rights. Clay lost his temper, and intimated something more than willingness to let Massachusetts pay for the pleasure of peace;[2] but during the whole day of November 28, and with the same patience November 29, Gallatin continued urging Clay and restraining Adams, until at last on the third day he brought the matter to the point he wished.

The result of this long struggle saved not indeed the fisheries, but the peace. Clay made no further protest when, in conference with the British commissioners December 1, the Americans offered to renew both the disputed rights.[3] Their proposal was sent to London, and was answered by Bathurst December 6, in a letter offering to set aside for future negotiation the terms under which the old fishing liberty and the navigation of the Mississippi should be continued for fair equivalents.[4] The British commissioners communicated this suggestion in conference December 10, and threw new dissension among the Americans.

The British offer to reserve both disputed rights for future negotiation implied that both rights were forfeited, or subject to forfeit, by war,—an admission which Adams could not make, but which the other commissioners could not reject. At that point Adams found himself alone. Even Gallatin admitted that the claim to the natural right of catching and curing fish on British shores was untenable, and could never be supported. Adams's difficulties were the greater because the question of peace and war was reduced to two points,—the fisheries and Moose Island,—both interesting to Massachusetts alone. Yet the Americans were unwilling to yield without another struggle, and decided still to resist the British claim

[1] Diary of J. Q. Adams, Nov. 27, 1814, iii. 70.
[2] Diary of J. Q. Adams, iii. 72.
[3] Protocol of Dec. 1, 1814; State Papers, Foreign Relations, iii. 742.
[4] Bathurst to the Commissioners, Dec. 6, 1814; Castlereagh Correspondence, x. 214.

as inconsistent with the admitted basis of the *status ante bellum*.

The struggle with the British commissioners then became warm. A long conference, December 12, brought no conclusion. The treaty of 1783 could neither be followed nor ignored, and perplexed the Englishmen as much as the Americans. During December 13 and December 14, Adams continued to press his colleagues to assert the natural right to the fisheries, and to insist on the permanent character of the treaty of 1783; but Gallatin would not consent to make that point an ultimatum. All the commissioners except Adams resigned themselves to the sacrifice of the fisheries; but Gallatin decided to make one more effort before abandoning the struggle, and with that object drew up a note rejecting the British stipulation because it implied the abandonment of a right, but offering either to be silent as to both the fisheries and the Mississippi, or to admit a general reference to further negotiation of all subjects in dispute, so expressed as to imply no abandonment of right.

The note was signed and sent December 14,[1] and the Americans waited another week for the answer. Successful as they had been in driving their British antagonists from one position after another, they were not satisfied. Adams still feared that he might not be able to sign, and Clay was little better pleased. "He said we should make a damned bad treaty, and he did not know whether he would sign it or not."[2] Whatever Adams thought of the treaty, his respect for at least two of his colleagues was expressed in terms of praise rarely used by him. Writing to his wife, September 27,[3] Adams said: "Mr. Gallatin keeps and increases his influence over us all. It would have been an irreparable loss if our country had been deprived of the benefit of his talents in this negotiation." At the moment of final suspense he wrote again, December 16:—

"Of the five members of the American mission, the Chevalier [Bayard] has the most perfect control of his temper, the most deliberate coolness; and it is the more meri-

[1] American note of Dec. 14, 1814; State Papers, Foreign Relations, iii. 743.
[2] Diary of J. Q. Adams, Dec. 14, 1814, iii. 118.
[3] J. Q. Adams to his wife, Sept. 27, 1814; Adams MSS.

torious because it is real self-command. His feelings are as quick and his spirits as high as those of any one among us, but he certainly has them more under government. I can scarcely express to you how much both he and Mr. Gallatin have risen in my esteem since we have been here living together. Gallatin has not quite so constant a supremacy over his own emotions; yet he seldom yields to an ebullition of temper, and recovers from it immediately. He has a faculty, when discussion grows too warm, of turning off its edge by a joke, which I envy him more than all his other talents; and he has in his character one of the most extraordinary combinations of stubbornness and of flexibility that I ever met with in man. His greatest fault I think to be an ingenuity sometimes trenching upon ingenuousness."

Gallatin's opinion of Adams was not so enthusiastic as Adams's admiration for him. He thought Adams's chief fault to be that he lacked judgment "to a deplorable degree."[1] Of Clay, whether in his merits or his faults, only one opinion was possible. Clay's character belonged to the simple Southern or Virginia type, somewhat affected, but not rendered more complex, by Western influence,—and transparent beyond need of description or criticism.

The extraordinary patience and judgment of Gallatin, aided by the steady support of Bayard, carried all the American points without sacrificing either Adams or Clay, and with no quarrel of serious importance on any side. When Lord Bathurst received the American note of December 14, he replied December 19, yielding the last advantage he possessed:[2] "The Prince Regent regrets to find that there does not appear any prospect of being able to arrive at such an arrangement with regard to the fisheries as would have the effect of coming to a full and satisfactory explanation on that subject;" but since this was the case, the disputed article might be altogether omitted.

Thus the treaty became simply a cessation of hostilities, leaving every claim on either side open for future settlement. The formality of signature was completed December 24, and

[1] Adams's Gallatin, p. 599.
[2] Castlereagh Correspondence, x. 221.

closed an era of American history. In substance, the treaty sacrificed much on both sides for peace. The Americans lost their claims for British spoliations, and were obliged to admit question of their right to Eastport and their fisheries in British waters; the British failed to establish their principles of impressment and blockade, and admitted question of their right to navigate the Mississippi and trade with the Indians. Perhaps at the moment the Americans were the chief losers; but they gained their greatest triumph in referring all their disputes to be settled by time, the final negotiator, whose decision they could safely trust.

Chapter III

ENGLAND RECEIVED the Treaty of Ghent with feelings of mixed anger and satisfaction. The "Morning Chronicle" seemed surprised at the extreme interest which the news excited. As early as November 24, when ministers made their decision to concede the American terms, the "Morning Chronicle" announced that "a most extraordinary sensation was produced yesterday" by news from Ghent, and by reports that ministers had abandoned their ground. When the treaty arrived, December 26, the same Whig newspaper, the next morning, while asserting that ministers had "humbled themselves in the dust and thereby brought discredit on the country," heartily approved what they had done; and added that "the city was in a complete state of hurricane during the whole of yesterday, but the storm did not attain its utmost height until toward the evening. . . . Purchases were made to the extent of many hundred thousand pounds." The importance of the United States to England was made more apparent by the act of peace than by the pressure of war. "At Birmingham," said the "Courier," "an immense assemblage witnessed the arrival of the mail, and immediately took the horses out, and drew the mail to the post-office with the loudest acclamations,"—acclamations over a treaty universally regarded as discreditable.

The "Times" admitted the general joy, and denied only that it was universal. If the "Times" in any degree represented public opinion, the popular satisfaction at the peace was an extraordinary political symptom, for in its opinion the Government had accepted terms such as "might have been expected from an indulgent and liberal conqueror. . . . We have retired from the combat," it said, December 30, "with the stripes yet bleeding on our back,—with the recent defeats at Plattsburg and on Lake Champlain unavenged." During several succeeding weeks the "Times" continued its extravagant complaints, which served only to give the Americans a new idea of the triumph they had won.

In truth, no one familiar with English opinion during the past ten years attempted to deny that the government of

England must admit one or the other of two conclusions,—either it had ruinously mismanaged its American policy before the war, or it had disgraced itself by the peace. The "Morning Chronicle," while approving the treaty, declared that the Tories were on this point at odds with their own leaders:[1] "Their attachment to the ministers, though strong, cannot reconcile them to this one step, though surely if they would look back with an impartial eye on the imbecility and error with which their idols conducted the war, they must acknowledge their prudence in putting an end to it. One of them very honestly said, two days ago, that if they had not put an end to the war, the war would have put an end to their Ministry." Whatever doubts existed about the temper of England before that time, no one doubted after the peace of Ghent that war with the United States was an unpopular measure with the British people.

Nevertheless the "Times" and the Tories continued their complaints until March 9, when two simultaneous pieces of news silenced criticism of the American treaty. The severe defeat at New Orleans became known at the moment when Napoleon, having quitted Elba, began his triumphal return to Paris. These news, coming in the midst of Corn Riots, silenced further discussion of American relations, and left ministers free to redeem at Waterloo the failures they had experienced in America.

In the United States news of peace was slow to arrive. The British sloop-of-war "Favorite" bore the despatches, and was still at sea when the month of February began. The commissioners from Massachusetts and Connecticut, bearing the demands of the Hartford Convention, started for Washington. Every one was intent on the situation of New Orleans, where a disaster was feared. Congress seemed to have abandoned the attempt to provide means of defence, although it began another effort to create a bank on Dallas's plan. A large number of the most intelligent citizens believed that two announcements would soon be made,—one, that New Orleans was lost; the other, that the negotiation at Ghent had ended in rupture. Under this double shock, the

[1] The Morning Chronicle, Dec. 30, 1814.

collapse of the national government seemed to its enemies inevitable.

In this moment of suspense, the first news arrived from New Orleans. To the extreme relief of the Government and the Republican majority in Congress, they learned, February 4, that the British invasion was defeated and New Orleans saved. The victory was welcomed by illuminations, votes of thanks, and rejoicings greater than had followed the more important success at Plattsburg, or the more brilliant battles at Niagara; for the success won at New Orleans relieved the Government from a load of anxiety, and postponed a crisis supposed to be immediately at hand. Half the influence of the Hartford Convention was destroyed by it; and the commissioners, who were starting for the capital, had reason to expect a reception less favorable by far than they would have met had the British been announced as masters of Louisiana. Yet the immediate effect of the news was not to lend new vigor to Congress, but rather to increase its inertness, and to encourage its dependence on militia, Treasury notes, and good fortune.

A week afterward, on the afternoon of Saturday, February 11, the British sloop-of-war "Favorite" sailed up New York harbor, and the city quickly heard rumors of peace. At eight o'clock that evening the American special messenger landed, bringing the official documents intrusted to his care; and when the news could no longer be doubted, the city burst into an uproar of joy. The messenger was slow in reaching Washington, where he arrived only on the evening of Tuesday, February 13, and delivered his despatches to the Secretary of State.

Had the treaty been less satisfactory than it was, the President would have hesitated long before advising its rejection, and the Senate could hardly have gained courage to reject it. In spite of rumors from London and significant speculations on the London Exchange, known in America in the middle of January, no one had seriously counted on a satisfactory peace, as was proved by the steady depression of government credit and of the prices of American staples. The reaction after the arrival of the news was natural, and so violent that few persons stopped to scrutinize the terms. Contrary to Clay's forebodings, the treaty, mere armistice though it seemed to be, was probably the most popular treaty ever negotiated by the United States. The President sent it to the Senate February 15; and the next day, without suggestion of amendment, and apparently without a criticism, unless from Federalists, the Senate unanimously confirmed it, thirty-five senators uniting in approval.

Yet the treaty was not what the Government had expected in declaring the war, or such as it had a right to demand. The Republicans admitted it in private, and the Federalists proclaimed it in the press. Senator Gore wrote to Governor Strong:[1] "The treaty must be deemed disgraceful to the Government who made the war and the peace, and will be so adjudged by all, after the first effusions of joy at relief have subsided." Opinions differed widely on the question where the disgrace belonged,—whether to the Government who made the war, or to the people who refused to support it; but no one pretended that the terms of peace, as far as they were expressed in the treaty, were so good as those repeatedly offered by England more than two years before. Yet the treaty was universally welcomed, and not a thought of continued war found expression.

In New England the peace was received with extravagant delight. While the government messenger who carried the official news to Washington made no haste, a special messenger started from New York at ten o'clock Saturday night, immediately on the landing of the government messenger, and in thirty-two hours arrived in Boston. Probably the distance had rarely been travelled in less time, for the Boston "Centinel" announced the expense to be two hundred and twenty-five dollars; and such an outlay was seldom made for rapidity of travel or news. As the messenger passed from town to town he announced the tidings to the delighted people.[2] Reaching the "Centinel" office, at Boston, early Monday morning, he delivered his bulletin, and a few minutes after it was published all the bells were set ringing; schools and shops were closed, and a general holiday taken; flags were hoisted, the British with the American; the militia paraded, and in the

[1] Gore to Strong, Feb. 18, 1815; Lodge's Cabot, p. 563.
[2] Goodrich's Recollections, i. 503—505.

evening the city was illuminated. Yet the terms of peace were wholly unknown, and the people of Massachusetts had every reason to fear that their interests were sacrificed for the safety of the Union. Their rejoicing over the peace was as unreasoning as their hatred of the war.

Only along the Canadian frontier where the farmers had for three years made large profits by supplying both armies, the peace was received without rejoicing.[1] South of New York, although less public delight was expressed, the relief was probably greater than in New England. Virginia had suffered most, and had felt the blockade with peculiar severity. A few weeks before the treaty was signed, Jefferson wrote:[2]—

"By the total annihilation in value of the produce which was to give me sustenance and independence, I shall be like Tantalus,—up to the shoulders in water, yet dying with thirst. We can make indeed enough to eat, drink, and clothe ourselves, but nothing for our salt, iron, groceries, and taxes which must be paid in money. For what can we raise for the market? Wheat?—we only give it to our horses, as we have been doing ever since harvest. Tobacco?—it is not worth the pipe it is smoked in."

While all Virginia planters were in this situation February 13, they awoke February 14 to find flour worth ten dollars a barrel, and groceries fallen fifty per cent. They were once more rich beyond their wants.

So violent and sudden a change in values had never been known in the United States. The New York market saw fortunes disappear and other fortunes created in the utterance of a single word. All imported articles dropped to low prices. Sugar which sold Saturday at twenty-six dollars a hundred-weight, sold Monday at twelve dollars and a half. Tea sank from two dollars and a quarter to one dollar a pound; tin fell from eighty to twenty-five dollars a box; cotton fabrics declined about fifty per cent. On the other hand flour, cotton, and the other chief staples of American produce rose in the same proportion. Nominally flour was worth seven and a half dollars on Saturday, though no large amounts could have

[1] Montreal Herald, March 18, 1815; Niles, viii. 132.
[2] Jefferson to W. Short, Nov. 28, 1814; Works, vi. 398.

been sold; on Monday the price was ten dollars, and all the wheat in the country was soon sold at that rate.

Owing to the derangement of currency, these prices expressed no precise specie value. The effect of the peace on the currency was for a moment to restore an apparent equilibrium. In New York the specie premium of twenty-two per cent was imagined for a time to have vanished. In truth, United States six-per-cents rose in New York from seventy-six to eighty-eight in paper; Treasury-notes from ninety-two to ninety-eight. In Philadelphia, on Saturday, six-per-cents sold at seventy-five; on Monday, at ninety-three. The paper depreciation remained about twenty per cent in New York, about twenty-four per cent in Philadelphia, and about thirty per cent in Baltimore. The true value of six-per-cents was about sixty-eight; of Treasury notes about seventy-eight, after the announcement of peace.

As rapidly as possible the blockade was raised, and ships were hurried to sea with the harvests of three seasons for cargo; but some weeks still passed before all the operations of war were closed. The news of peace reached the British squadron below Mobile in time to prevent further advance on that place; but on the ocean a long time elapsed before fighting wholly ceased.

Some of the worst disasters as well as the greatest triumphs of the war occurred after the treaty of peace had been signed. The battle of New Orleans was followed by the loss of Fort Bowyer. At about the same time a British force occupied Cumberland Island on the southern edge of the Georgia coast, and January 13 attacked the fort at the entrance of the St. Mary's, and having captured it without loss, ascended the river the next day to the town of St. Mary's, which they seized, together with its merchandise and valuable ships in the river. Cockburn established his headquarters on Cumberland Island January 22, and threw the whole State of Georgia into agitation, while he waited the arrival of a brigade with which an attack was to be made on Savannah.

The worst disaster of the naval war occurred January 15, when the frigate "President"—one of the three American forty-fours, under Stephen Decatur, the favorite ocean hero of the American service—suffered defeat and capture within fifty miles of Sandy Hook. No naval battle of the war was more disputed in its merits, although its occurrence in the darkest moments of national depression was almost immediately forgotten in the elation of the peace a few days later.

Secretary Jones retired from the Navy Department Dec. 19, 1814, yielding the direction to B. W. Crowninshield of Massachusetts, but leaving a squadron ready for sea at New York under orders for distant service. The "Peacock" and "Hornet," commanded by Warrington and Biddle, were to sail with a store-ship on a long cruise in Indian waters, where they were expected to ravage British shipping from the Cape of Good Hope to the China seas. With them Decatur was to go in the "President," and at the beginning of the new year he waited only an opportunity to slip to sea past the blockading squadron. January 14 a strong westerly wind drove the British fleet out of sight. The "President" set sail, but in crossing the bar at night grounded, and continued for an hour or more to strike heavily, until the tide and strong wind forced her across. Decatur then ran along the Long Island coast some fifty miles, when he changed his course to the southeast, hoping that he had evaded the blockading squadron. This course was precisely that which Captain Hayes, commanding the squadron, expected;[1] and an hour before daylight the four British ships, standing to the northward and eastward, sighted the "President," standing to the southward and eastward, not more than two miles on the weather-bow of the "Majestic,"—the fifty-six-gun razee commanded by Captain Hayes.

The British ships promptly made chase. Captain Hayes's squadron, besides the "Majestic," consisted of the "Endymion," a fifty-gun frigate, with the "Pomone" and "Tenedos," frigates like the "Guerriere," "Macedonian," and "Java," armed with eighteen-pound guns. Only from the "Endymion" had Decatur much to fear, for the "Majestic" was slow and the other ships were weak; but the "Endymion" was a fast sailer, and especially adapted to meet the American frigates. The "Endymion," according to British authority, was about one hundred and fifty-nine feet in length on the lower

[1] Report of Captain Hayes, Jan. 17, 1815; James, Appendix, p. clxxx; Niles, viii. 175.

deck, and nearly forty-three feet in extreme breadth; the "President," on the same authority, was about one hundred and seventy-three feet in length, and forty-four feet in breadth. The "Endymion" carried twenty-six long twenty-four-pounders on the main deck; the "President" carried thirty. The "Endymion" mounted twenty-two thirty-two pound carronades on the spar deck; the "President" mounted twenty. The "Endymion" had also a long brass eighteen-pounder as a bow-chaser; the "President" a long twenty-four-pounder as a bow-chaser, and another as a stern-chaser. The "Endymion" was short-handed after her losses in action with the "Prince de Neufchatel," and carried only three hundred and forty-six men; the "President" carried four hundred and fifty. The "Endymion" was the weaker ship, probably in the proportion of four to five; but for her immediate purpose she possessed a decisive advantage in superior speed, especially in light winds.

At two o'clock in the afternoon, the "Endymion" had gained so much on the "President" as to begin exchanging shots between the stern and bow-chasers.[1] Soon after five o'clock, as the wind fell, the "Endymion" crept up on the "President's" starboard quarter, and "commenced close action."[2] After bearing the enemy's fire for half an hour without reply, Decatur was obliged to alter his course and accept battle, or suffer himself to be crippled.[3] The battle lasted two hours and a half, until eight o'clock, when firing ceased; but at half-past nine, according to the "Pomone's" log, the "Endymion" fired two guns, which the "President" returned with one.[4] According to Decatur's account the "Endymion" lay for half an hour under his stern, without firing, while the "President" was trying to escape. In truth the "Endymion" had no need to fire; she was busy bending new sails, while Decatur's ship, according to his official report, was crippled, and in the want of wind could not escape.

In a letter written by Decatur to his wife immediately after

[1] Log of the "Pomone;" Niles, viii. 133. Log of the "Endymion;" James, p. 427.
[2] Report of Captain Hayes; Niles, viii. 175.
[3] Decatur's Report of Jan. 18, 1815; Niles, viii. 8.
[4] Log of the "Pomone;" Niles, viii. 133.

the battle, he gave an account of what followed, as he understood it.[1]

"The 'Endymion,' " he began, . . . "was the leading ship of the enemy. She got close under my quarters and was cutting my rigging without my being able to bring a gun to bear upon her. To suffer this was making my capture certain, and that too without injury to the enemy. I therefore bore up for the 'Endymion' and engaged her for two hours, when we silenced and beat her off. At this time the rest of the ships had got within two miles of us. We made all the sail we could from them, but it was in vain. In three hours the 'Pomone' and 'Tenedos' were alongside, and the 'Majestic' and 'Endymion' close to us. All that was now left for me to do was to receive the fire of the nearest ship and surrender."

The "Pomone's" account of the surrender completed the story:[2] —

"At eleven, being within gunshot of the 'President' who was still steering to the eastward under a press of sail, with royal, top-gallant, topmast, and lower studding-sails set, finding how much we outsailed her our studding-sails were taken in, and immediately afterward we luffed to port and fired our starboard broadside. The enemy then also luffed to port, bringing his larboard broadside to bear, which was momentarily expected, as a few minutes previous to our closing her she hoisted a light abaft, which in night actions constitutes the ensign. Our second broadside was fired, and the 'President' still luffing up as if intent to lay us on board, we hauled close to port, bracing the yards up, and setting the mainsail; the broadside was again to be fired into his bows, raking, when she hauled down the light, and we hailed demanding if she had surrendered. The reply was in the affirmative, and the firing immediately ceased. The 'Tenedos,' who was not more than three miles off, soon afterward came up, and assisted the 'Pomone' in securing the prize and removing the prisoners. At three quarters past

[1] Niles, vii. 364.
[2] Niles, viii. 133.

twelve the 'Endymion' came up, and the 'Majestic' at three in the morning."

Between the account given by Decatur and that of the "Pomone's" log were some discrepancies. In the darkness many mistakes were inevitable; but if each party were taken as the best authority on its own side, the connected story seemed to show that Decatur, after beating off the "Endymion," made every effort to escape, but was impressed by the conviction that if overtaken by the squadron, nothing was left but to receive the fire of the nearest ship, and surrender. The night was calm, and the "President" made little headway. At eleven o'clock one of the pursuing squadron came up, and fired two broadsides. "Thus situated," reported Decatur, "with about one fifth of my crew killed and wounded, my ship crippled, and a more than fourfold force opposed to me, without a chance of escape left, I deemed it my duty to surrender."

The official Court of Inquiry on the loss of the "President" reported, a few months afterward, a warm approval of Decatur's conduct:[1] —

> "We fear that we cannot express in a manner that will do justice to our feelings our admiration of the conduct of Commodore Decatur and his officers and crew. . . . As well during the chase as through his contest with the enemy [he] evinced great judgment and skill, perfect coolness, the most determined resolution, and heroic courage."

The high praise thus bestowed was doubtless deserved, since the Court of Inquiry was composed of persons well qualified to judge; but Decatur's battle with the "Endymion" was far from repeating the success of his triumph over the "Macedonian." Anxious to escape rather than to fight, Decatur in consequence failed either to escape or resist with effect. The action with the "Endymion" lasted three hours from the time when the British frigate gained the "President's" quarter. For the first half hour the "President" received the "Endymion's" broadsides without reply. During the last half hour the firing slackened and became intermittent. Yet for two hours the ships were engaged at close range, a part of the

[1] Niles, viii. 147.

time within half musket-shot, in a calm sea, and in a parallel
line of sailing.[1] At all times of the battle, the ships were well
within point-blank range,[2] which for long twenty-four-
pounders and thirty-two-pound carronades was about two
hundred and fifty yards.[3] Decatur had needed but an hour
and a half to disable and capture the "Macedonian," although
a heavy swell disturbed his fire, and at no time were the ships
within easy range for grape, which was about one hundred
and fifty yards. The "Endymion" was a larger and better ship
than the "Macedonian," but the "President" was decidedly
less efficient than the "United States."

According to Captain Hope's report, the "Endymion" lost
eleven men killed and fourteen wounded. The "President" reported twenty-five killed and sixty wounded. Of the two ships
the "President" was probably the most severely injured.[4] The
masts of both were damaged, and two days afterward both
were dismasted in a gale; but while the "President" lost all
her masts by the board, the "Endymion" lost only her fore
and main masts considerably above deck. On the whole, the
injury inflicted by the "President" on the "Endymion" was
less than in proportion to her relative strength, or to the
length of time occupied in the action. Even on the supposition that the "President's" fire was directed chiefly against the
"Endymion's" rigging, the injury done was not proportional to
the time occupied in doing it. According to the "Pomone's"
log, the "Endymion" was able to rejoin the squadron at
quarter before one o'clock in the night. According to the "Endymion's" log, she repaired damages in an hour, and resumed
the chase at nine o'clock.[5]

The British ships were surprised that Decatur should have
surrendered to the "Pomone" without firing a shot. Apparently the "Pomone's" broadside did little injury, and the
"Tenedos" was not yet in range when the "Pomone" opened

[1] Log of the "Endymion;" James, p. 428.

[2] Cooper's Naval History, ii. 466.

[3] Adye's Bombardier, p. 197. Douglas's Naval Gunnery (Fourth edition),
p. 103.

[4] Report of Injuries received by the "President;" James, Appendix, p. cxciv,
no. 107.

[5] James's Naval Occurrences, p. 429.

fire. The question of the proper time to surrender was to be judged by professional rules; and if resistance was hopeless, Decatur was doubtless justified in striking when he did; but his apparent readiness to do so hardly accorded with the popular conception of his character.

As usual the sloops were more fortunate than the frigate, and got to sea successfully, January 22, in a gale of wind which enabled them to run the blockade. Their appointed rendezvous was Tristan d'Acunha. There the "Hornet" arrived on the morning of March 23, and before she had time to anchor sighted the British sloop-of-war "Penguin,"—a new brig then cruising in search of the American privateer "Young Wasp."

Captain Biddle of the "Hornet" instantly made chase, and Captain Dickinson of the "Penguin" bore up and stood for the enemy. According to British authority the vessels differed only by a "trifling disparity of force."[1] In truth the American was somewhat superior in size, metal, and crew, although not so decisively as in most of the sloop battles. The "Hornet" carried eighteen thirty-two-pound carronades and two long twelve-pounders; the "Penguin" carried sixteen thirty-two-pound carronades, two long guns differently reported as twelve-pounders and six-pounders, and a twelve-pound carronade. The crews were apparently the same in number,— about one hundred and thirty-two men. Captain Dickinson had equipped his vessel especially for the purpose of capturing heavy privateers, and was then looking for the "Young Wasp,"—a vessel decidedly superior to the "Hornet."[2] Although he had reason to doubt his ability to capture the "Young Wasp," he did not fear a combat with the "Hornet," and showed his confidence by brushing up close alongside and firing a gun, while the "Hornet," all aback, waited for him.

The result was very different from that of Decatur's two-hour battle with the "Endymion." In little more than twenty minutes of close action the "Penguin's" foremast and bowsprit were gone, her captain killed, and thirty-eight men killed or wounded, or more than one fourth the crew. The brig was

[1] James, p. 498.
[2] Admiral Tyler to Captain Dickinson, Jan. 31, 1815; Niles, viii. 345.

"a perfect wreck," according to the British official report, when the senior surviving officer hailed and surrendered.[1] The "Hornet" was not struck in the hull, but was very much cut up in rigging and spars. She had two killed, and nine wounded. "It was evident," said Captain Biddle's report, "that our fire was greatly superior both in quickness and effect."

The "Penguin" was destroyed, and the "Hornet" and "Peacock" continued their cruise until April 27, when they chased for twenty-four hours a strange sail, which proved to be the British seventy-four "Cornwallis." On discovering the character of the chase Biddle made off to windward, but found that the enemy "sailed remarkably fast and was very weatherly." At daylight of the 29th, the "Cornwallis" was within gunshot on the "Hornet's" lee-quarter. Her shot did not take effect, and Biddle, by lightening his ship, drew out of fire; but a few hours later the enemy again came up within three quarters of a mile, in a calm sea, and opened once more. Three shot struck the "Hornet," but without crippling her. Biddle threw over everything that could be spared, except one long gun; and a fortunate change of wind enabled him a second time to creep out of fire. He escaped; but the loss of his guns, anchors, cables, and boats obliged him to make for San Salvador, where he heard the news of peace.[2]

Captain Warrington in the "Peacock" continued his cruise to the Indian Ocean, and captured four Indiamen. In the Straits of Sunda, June 30, he encountered a small East India Company's cruiser, whose commander hailed and announced peace. Warrington replied, "directing him at the same time to haul his colors down if it were the case, in token of it,— adding that if he did not, I should fire into him." The brig refused to strike its colors, and Warrington nearly destroyed her by a broadside.[3] For this violence little excuse could be offered, for the "Nautilus" was not half the "Peacock's" strength, and could not have escaped. Warrington, like most officers of the American navy, remembered the "Chesapeake" too well.

[1] Report of Lieutenant McDonald, April 6, 1815; James, Appendix, p. cc, no. iii.

[2] Biddle's Report of June 10, 1815; Niles, viii. 438.

[3] Warrington's Letter of Nov. 11, 1815; Niles, x. 58.

The cruise of the "President," "Peacock," and "Hornet" ended in the loss of the "President," the disabling of the "Hornet," and the arrival of the "Peacock" alone at the point intended for their common cruising-ground. No other national vessels were at sea after peace was signed, except the "Constitution," which late in December sailed from Boston under the command of Captain Charles Stewart,—a Philadelphian of Irish descent, not thirty-nine years old, but since 1806 a captain in the United States service.

Cruising between Gibraltar and Madeira, at about one o'clock on the afternoon of February 20 Captain Stewart discovered two sail ahead, which he chased and overtook at six o'clock. Both were ship-rigged sloops-of-war. The larger of the two was the "Cyane." Americans preferred to call her a frigate, but that designation, though vague at best, could hardly be applied to such a vessel. The "Cyane" was a frigate-built sloop-of-war, or corvette, like the "Little Belt," carrying a regular complement of one hundred and eighty-five men. Her length on the lower deck was one hundred and eighteen feet; her breadth was thirty-two feet. She carried thirty-three guns, all carronades except two long-nines or twelves. Her companion, the "Levant," was also a sloop-of-war of the larger sort, though smaller than the "Cyane." She mounted twenty-one guns, all carronades except two long nine-pounders. Her regular crew was one hundred and thirty-five men and boys.

Either separately or together the British ships were decidedly unequal to the "Constitution," which could, by remaining at long range, sink them both without receiving a shot in return. The "Constitution" carried thirty-two long twenty-four-pounders; while the two sloops could reply to these guns only by four long nine-pounders. The "Constitution" carried four hundred and fifty men; the two sloops at the time of the encounter carried three hundred and thirty-six seamen, marines, and officers.[1] The "Constitution" was built of great strength; the two sloops had only the frames of their class. The utmost that the British captains could hope was that one of the two vessels might escape by the sacrifice of the other.

---

[1] Statement of the actual force, etc., Stewart's Report; Niles, viii. 219.

Instead of escaping, the senior officer, Captain George Douglass of the "Levant," resolved to engage the frigate, "in the hopes, by disabling her, to prevent her intercepting two valuable convoys that sailed from Gibraltar about the same time as the 'Levant' and 'Cyane.' "[1] Captain Douglass knew his relative strength, for he had heard that the American frigate was on his course.[2] Yet he seriously expected to disable her, and made a courageous attempt to do so.

The two ships, close together, tried first for the weather-gauge, but the "Constitution" outsailed them also on that point. They then bore up in hope of delaying the engagement till night, but the "Constitution" overhauled them too rapidly for the success of that plan. They then stood on the starboard tack, the "Cyane" astern, the "Levant" a half-cable length ahead, while the "Constitution" came up to windward and opened fire. Commodore Stewart's report described the result:[3] —

"At five minutes past six ranged up on the starboard side of the sternmost ship [the 'Cyane'], about three hundred yards distant, and commenced the action by broadsides, — both ships returning our fire with great spirit for about fifteen minutes. Then the fire of the enemy beginning to slacken, and the great column of smoke collected under our lee, induced us to cease our fire to ascertain their positions and conditions. In about three minutes the smoke clearing away, we found ourselves abreast of the headmost ship [the 'Levant'], the sternmost ship luffing up for our larboard quarter."

Three hundred yards was a long range for carronades, especially in British sloops whose marksmanship was indifferent at best. According to the British court-martial on the officers of the "Cyane" and "Levant," their carronades had little effect.[4] If Stewart managed his ship as his duty required, the two sloops until that moment should have been allowed to make little effective return of the "Constitution's" broadside of

[1] James, Naval Occurrences, p. 458.
[2] James, Naval Occurrences, p. 458.
[3] Minutes of the Action; Niles, viii. 219.
[4] Niles, viii. 363. Cf. Letter of Lieutenant Shubrick; Niles, viii. 383.

sixteen twenty-four-pounders except by two nine-pounders. They were in the position of the "Essex" at Valparaiso. The "Cyane" naturally luffed up, in order to bring her carronades to bear, but she was already cut to pieces, and made the matter worse by closing.

"We poured a broadside into the headmost ship," continued the American account, "and then braced aback our main and mizzen topsails and backed astern under cover of the smoke abreast the sternmost ship, when the action was continued with spirit and considerable effect until thirty-five minutes past six, when the enemy's fire again slackened."

The "Levant," after receiving two stern-raking fires, bore up at forty minutes past six and began to repair damages two miles to leeward. The "Cyane," having become unmanageable, struck at ten minutes before seven. The most remarkable incident of the battle occurred after the "Cyane" struck, when the "Constitution" went after the "Levant" which was in sight to leeward. The little "Levant," instead of running away, stood directly for the huge American frigate, more than three times her size, and ranging close alongside fired a broadside into her as the two ships passed on opposite tacks. Although the sloop received the "Constitution's" broadside in return, she was only captured at last after an hour's chase, at ten o'clock, much cut up in spars and rigging, but still seaworthy, and with seven men killed and sixteen wounded, or only one casualty to six of her crew.

In truth, the injury inflicted by the "Constitution's" fire was not so great as might have been expected. The "Cyane" lost twelve killed and twenty-six wounded, if the American report was correct. Neither ship was dismasted or in a sinking condition. Both arrived safely, March 10, at Porto Praya. On the other hand, the "Constitution" was struck eleven times in the hull, and lost three men killed and twelve wounded, three of the latter mortally. She suffered more than in her battle with the "Guerriere,"—a result creditable to the British ships, considering that in each case the "Constitution" could choose her own range.

Stewart took his prizes to the Cape de Verde Islands. At noon, March 11, while lying in port at Porto Praya, three

British frigates appeared off the harbor, and Stewart instantly stood to sea, passing the enemy's squadron to windward within gunshot. The three frigates made chase, and at one o'clock, as the "Cyane" was dropping astern, Stewart signalled to her to tack ship, and either escape, if not pursued, or return to Porto Praya. The squadron paid no attention to the "Cyane," but followed the "Constitution" and "Levant." At three o'clock, the "Levant" falling behind, Stewart signalled her also to tack. Immediately the whole British squadron abandoned pursuit of the "Constitution" and followed the "Levant" to Porto Praya, where they seized her under the guns of the Portuguese batteries. Meanwhile the "Constitution" and "Cyane" escaped, and reached the United States without further accident. The extraordinary blunders of the British squadron were never satisfactorily explained.

These combats and cruises, with the last ravages of the privateers, closed the war on the ocean as it had long ceased on land; and meanwhile the people of the United States had turned their energies to undertakings of a wholly different character.

Chapter IV

THE LONG, EXCITING, and splendid panorama of revolution and war, which for twenty-five years absorbed the world's attention and dwarfed all other interests, vanished more quickly in America than in Europe, and left fewer elements of disturbance. The transformation scene of a pantomime was hardly more sudden or complete than the change that came over the United States at the announcement of peace. In a single day, almost in a single instant, the public turned from interests and passions that had supplied its thought for a generation, and took up a class of ideas that had been unknown or but vaguely defined before.

At Washington the effect of the news was so extraordinary as to shake faith in the seriousness of party politics. Although the peace affected in no way party doctrine or social distinctions, a new epoch for the Union began from the evening of February 13, when the messenger from Ghent arrived with the treaty. No one stopped to ask why a government, which was discredited and falling to pieces at one moment, should appear as a successful and even a glorious national representative a moment afterward. Politicians dismissed the war from their thoughts, as they dismissed the treaty, with the single phrase: "Not an inch ceded or lost!"[1] The commissioners from Massachusetts and Connecticut who appeared at Washington with the recommendations of the Hartford Convention, returned home as quietly as possible, pursued by the gibes of the press. The war was no more popular then than it had been before, as the subsequent elections proved; but the danger was passed, and passion instantly subsided.

Only by slow degrees the country learned to appreciate the extraordinary feat which had been performed, not so much by the people as by a relatively small number of individuals. Had a village rustic, with one hand tied behind his back, challenged the champion of the prize-ring, and in three or four rounds obliged him to draw the stakes, the result would have been little more surprising than the result of the American campaign of 1814. The most intelligent and best educated part

[1] Ingersoll, ii. 311.

of society both in the United States and in Great Britain could not believe it, and the true causes of British defeat remained a subject of conjecture and angry dispute. The enemies of the war admitted only that peace had saved Madison; but this single concession, which included many far-reaching consequences, was granted instantly, and from that moment the national government triumphed over all its immediate dangers.

While the Senate unanimously ratified the treaty February 16, the House set to work with much more alacrity than was its habit to dispose of the business before it. Haste was necessary. Barely fourteen days remained before the Thirteenth Congress should expire, and in that interval some system of peace legislation must be adopted. The struggle over the proposed Bank charter was still raging, for the Senate had passed another bill of incorporation February 11, over which the House was occupied the whole day of February 13 in a sharp and close contest. The first effect of the peace was to stop this struggle. By a majority of one vote, seventy-four to seventy-three, February 17, the House laid the subject aside.

Three days afterward, February 20, the President sent to Congress a Message transmitting the treaty with its ratifications, and congratulating the country on the close of a war " waged with the success which is the natural result of the wisdom of the legislative councils, of the patriotism of the people, of the public spirit of the militia, and of the valor of the military and naval forces of the country." After recommending to Congress the interests of the soldiers and sailors, the Message passed to the reduction of expenditures, which required immediate attention:

> "There are, however," continued Madison, "important considerations which forbid a sudden and general revocation of the measures that have been produced by the war. Experience has taught us that neither the pacific dispositions of the American people, nor the pacific character of their political institutions, can altogether exempt them from that strife which appears, beyond the ordinary lot of nations, to be incident to the actual period of the world;

and the same faithful monitor demonstrates that a certain degree of preparation for war is not only indispensable to avert disasters in the onset, but affords also the best security for the continuance of peace."

The avowal that experience had shown the error of the principle adopted by the nation in 1801 was not confined to President Madison. Monroe spoke even more plainly. In a letter to the military committee, February 24, Monroe urged that an army of twenty thousand men should be retained on the peace establishment. Each soldier of the rank-and-file was supposed to cost in peace about two hundred dollars a year, and Monroe's proposal involved an annual expense of more than five million dollars.

As far as concerned Madison and Monroe the repudiation of old Republican principles seemed complete; but the people had moved less rapidly than their leaders. Had Congress, while debating the subject February 25, known that Napoleon was then quitting Elba to seize once more the control of France, and to rouse another European convulsion with all its possible perils to neutrals, the President's views might have been adopted without serious dispute; but in the absence of evident danger, an army of twenty thousand men seemed unnecessary. The finances warranted no such extravagance. Dallas wrote to Eppes, the chairman of the Ways and Means Committee, a letter[1] dated February 20, sketching a temporary financial scheme for the coming year. He proposed to fund at seven per cent the outstanding Treasury notes, amounting to $18,637,000; and even after thus sweeping the field clear of pressing claims, he still required the extravagant war-taxes in order to meet expenses, and depended on a further issue of Treasury notes, or a loan, to support the peace establishments of the army and navy. The state of the currency was desperate, and the revenue for the year 1815 was estimated at $18,200,000 in the notes of State banks,—a sum little in excess of the estimated civil necessities.

The military committee of the House showed no sympathy with the new principles urged upon Congress by the Executive. Troup of Georgia reported a bill, February 22, fixing the

[1] Annals of Congress, 1814–1815; iii. 1178.

peace establishment at ten thousand men, with two major-generals and four brigadiers. In submitting this proposal, Troup urged the House, February 25, to accept the reduction to ten thousand as the lowest possible standard, requiring only the expense of two and a half millions; but no sooner did he take his seat than Desha of Kentucky moved to substitute "six" for "ten," and a vigorous debate followed, ending in the adoption of Desha's amendment in committee by a majority of nineteen votes. The war leaders were greatly annoyed by this new triumph of the peace party. As a matter of principle, the vote on Desha's amendment affirmed Jefferson's pacific system and condemned the Federalist heresies of Madison and Monroe. The war leaders could not acquiesce in such a decision, and rallying for another effort, February 27, they remonstrated hotly. Forsyth of Georgia was particularly emphatic in defining the issue:[1] —

"He had hoped that the spirit of calculation falsely styled economy, whose contracted view was fixed upon present expense, and was incapable of enlarging it to permanent and eventual advantage, had been laid forever by the powerful exorcisms of reason and experience. It would seem however that it had been only lulled by the presence of a more powerful demon. Since the potent spell of necessity had been broken, the troubled spirit of petty calculation was again awakened to vex the counsels and destroy the best hopes of the country."

For three years the friends of strong government, under the pressure of war, had been able to drive Congress more or less in their own direction; but at the announcement of peace their power was greatly lessened, and their unwilling associates were no longer disposed to follow their lead or to tolerate their assumptions of superiority. Desha retaliated in the tone of 1798: —

"Do they suppose that the House do not understand the subject; or do they suppose that by this great flow of eloquence they can make the substantial part of the House change their opinions in so short a time? When I speak of

[1] Annals of Congress, 1814–1815, pp. 1213, 1250.

the substantial part of the House, I mean those who think much and speak but little; who make common-sense their guide, and not theoretical or visionary projects. . . . Some gentlemen advocate ten thousand and others twenty thousand of a standing army. The policy is easy to be seen through. The advocates of a perpetual system of taxation discover that if they cannot retain a considerable standing army, they will have no good plea of riveting the present taxes on the people."

In the process of national growth, public opinion had advanced since 1801 several stages in its development; but the speeches of Forsyth, Calhoun, and Lowndes on one side, like that of Desha on the other, left still in doubt the amount of change. While Forsyth admitted that he had under-estimated the strength of the economical spirit, Desha certainly over-estimated the force of the men "who think much and speak but little." With Federalist assistance, Desha's friends passed the bill for an army of six thousand men by a vote of seventy-five to sixty-five; but the Senate, by a more decided vote of eighteen to ten, substituted "fifteen" for "six." With this amendment the bill was returned to the House March 2, which by an almost unanimous vote refused to concur. The bill was sent to a conference committee, which reported the original plan of ten thousand men; and in the last hours of the session, March 3, the House yielded. By a vote of seventy to thirty-eight the peace establishment was fixed at ten thousand men.

The movement of public opinion was more evident in regard to the navy. Instead of repeating the experiments of 1801, Congress maintained the whole war establishment, and appropriated four million dollars chiefly for the support of frigates and ships-of-the-line. The vessels on the Lakes were dismantled and laid up; the gunboats, by an Act approved February 27, were ordered to be sold; but the sum of two hundred thousand dollars was appropriated for the annual purchase of ship-timber during the next three years, and the whole navy thenceforward consisted of cruisers, which were to be kept as far as possible in active service. As the first task of the new ships, an Act, approved March 3, authorized hostilities against the Dey of Algiers, who had indulged in the plunder of American commerce.

These hasty arrangements for the two services, coupled with an equally hasty financial makeshift, completed the career of the Thirteenth Congress, which expired March 4, as little admired or regretted as the least popular of its predecessors. Not upon Congress but upon the Executive Departments fell the burden of peace as of war, and on the Executive the new situation brought many embarrassments.

The first and most delicate task of the Government was the reduction of the army. No one could greatly blame Monroe for shrinking from the invidious duty of dismissing two thirds of the small force which had sustained so well and with so little support the character of the country; but the haste which he showed in leaving the War Department suggested also how keenly he must have suffered under its burdens. His name was sent to the Senate, February 27, as Secretary of State; no Secretary of War was nominated, but Dallas, with the courage that marked his character, undertook to manage the War Department as well as the Treasury until the necessary arrangements for the new army should be made.

April 8 Dallas wrote to six generals,—Brown, Jackson, Scott, Gaines, Macomb, and Ripley,—requesting their attendance at Washington to report a plan for the new army. Jackson and Gaines were unable to attend. The rest of the board reported a scheme dividing the country into two military districts, north and south; and into nine departments, five in the northern, four in the southern division,—allotting to each the troops needed for its service. May 17 the new arrangements were announced. Brown was ordered to command the northern district, with Ripley and Macomb as brigadiers. Jackson took the southern district, with Scott and Gaines as brigadiers. Eight regiments of infantry, one of riflemen, and one of light artillery were retained, together with the corps of artillery and engineers. As far as possible, all the officers whose names became famous for a generation received rank and reward.

No such operation was necessary for the navy, where no reduction was required. In the civil service, Madison enjoyed the satisfaction of rewarding the friends who had stood by him in his trials. February 27 he sent to the Senate, with the nomination of Monroe as Secretary of State, the name of J. Q. Adams as Minister to England. At the same time Bayard was appointed to St. Petersburg, and Gallatin to Paris. The nomination of Bayard proved to be an empty compliment, for he arrived, August 1, in the Delaware River, in the last stages of illness, and was carried ashore the next day only to die.

These appointments were well received and readily confirmed by the Senate; but Madison carried favoritism too far for the Senate's approval when, March 1, he nominated Major-General Dearborn to be Secretary of War. Dearborn had few or no enemies, but the distinction thus shown him roused such strong remonstrance that Madison hastened to recall the nomination, and substituted Crawford in Dearborn's place. The Senate had already rejected Dearborn, but consented to erase the record from their journal,[1] and Crawford became Secretary of War.

Thus the government in all its branches glided into the new conditions, hampered only by the confusion of the currency, which could not be overcome. The people were even more quick than the government to adapt themselves to peace. In New Orleans alone a few weeks of alarm were caused by extraordinary acts of arbitrary power on the part of General Jackson during the interval before the peace became officially known; but public order was not seriously disturbed, and the civil authority was restored March 13. Elsewhere the country scarcely stopped to notice the cost or the consequences of the war.

In truth the cost was moderate. Measured by loss of life in battle, it was less than that reported in many single battles fought by Napoleon. An army which never exceeded thirty thousand effectives, or placed more than four thousand regular rank-and-file in a single action, could not sacrifice many lives. According to the received estimates the number of men killed in battle on land did not much exceed fifteen hundred, including militia, while the total of killed and wounded little

[1] Madison to Dearborn, March 4, 1815; Madison's Works, ii. 598.

exceeded five thousand.[1] Sickness was more fatal than wounds, but a population of eight millions felt camp-diseases hardly more than its periodical malarial fevers.

The precise financial cost of the war, measured only by increase of debt, was equally moderate. During three years,—from February, 1812, until February, 1815,—the government sold six per cent bonds at various rates of discount, to the amount of fifty million dollars, and this sum was the limit of its loans, except for a few bank discounts of Treasury notes not exceeding a million in all. By forcing Treasury notes on its creditors the Treasury obtained the use of twenty millions more. After the peace it issued bonds and new Treasury notes, which raised the aggregate amount of war debt, as far as could be ascertained, to about eighty million five hundred thousand dollars, which was the war-addition to the old nominal capital of debt, and increased the total indebtedness to one hundred and twenty-seven millions at the close of the year 1815.[2]

The debt had exceeded eighty millions twenty years before, and in the interval the country had greatly increased its resources. The war debt was a trifling load, and would not have been felt except for the confusion of the currency and the unnecessary taxation imposed at the last moments of the war. That the currency and the war taxes were severe trials was not to be denied, but of other trials the people had little to complain.

Considering the dangers to which the United States were exposed, they escaped with surprising impunity. The shores of Chesapeake Bay and of Georgia were plundered; but the British government paid for the slaves carried away, and no town of importance except Washington was occupied by an enemy. Contrary to the usual experience of war, the richest parts of the country suffered least. Only the Niagara frontier was systematically ravaged. When the blockade of the coast was raised, every seaboard city was able instantly to resume its commercial habits without having greatly suffered from the interruption. The harvests of two seasons were ready for immediate export, and the markets of Europe were waiting

[1] Niles, x. 154.
[2] Dallas's Report of Dec. 6, 1815; State Papers, Finance, iii. 8.

to receive them. Every man found occupation, and capital instantly returned to its old channels. From the moment of peace the exports of domestic produce began to exceed five million dollars a month, while four millions was the highest average for any previous twelvemonth, and the average for the seven years of embargo and blockade since 1807 fell much short of two and a half millions. The returns of commerce and navigation showed that during the seven months from March 1 to October 1, 1815, domestic produce valued at forty-six million dollars was exported, and American shipping to the amount of eight hundred and fifty-four thousand tons was employed in the business of export.[1]

The ease and rapidity of this revolution not only caused the war to be quickly forgotten, but also silenced political passions. For the first time in their history as a nation, the people of the United States ceased to disturb themselves about politics or patronage. Every political principle was still open to dispute, and was disputed; but prosperity put an end to faction. No evidence could be given to prove that the number or weight of persons who held the opinions commonly known as Federalist, diminished either then or afterward. Massachusetts showed no regret for the attitude she had taken. At the April election, six weeks after the proclamation of peace, although Samuel Dexter was the Republican candidate, the State still gave to Governor Strong a majority of about seven thousand in a total vote of ninety-five thousand. The Federalists reasonably regarded this vote as an express approval of the Hartford Convention and its proposed measures, and asked what would have been their majority had peace not intervened to save the Government from odium. They believed not only that their popular support would have been greater, but that it would also have shown a temper beyond control; yet the Federalist majority in April was no longer hostile to the Government.

The other elections bore the same general character. Even in New York the popular reaction seemed rather against the war than in its favor. New York city in April returned Federalist members to the State legislature, causing a tie in the

[1] State Papers, Commerce and Navigation, ii. 647.

Assembly, each party controlling sixty-three votes.[1] In Virginia the peace produced no change so decided as to warrant a belief that the war had become popular. In April John Randolph defeated Eppes and recovered control of his district. The State which had chosen sixteen Republicans and seven opposition congressmen in 1813, elected in 1815 seventeen Republicans and six opposition members. The stability of parties was the more remarkable in New York and Virginia, because those States were first to feel the effects of renewed prosperity.

After the excitement of peace was past, as the summer drew toward a close, economical interests dwarfed the old political distinctions and gave a new character to parties. A flood of wealth poured into the Union at a steady rate of six or seven million dollars a month, and the distribution of so large a sum could not fail to show interesting results. The returns soon proved that the larger portion belonged to the Southern States. Cotton, at a valuation of twenty cents a pound, brought seventeen and a half millions to the planters; tobacco brought eight and a quarter millions; rice produced nearly two million eight hundred thousand dollars. Of fifty millions received from abroad in payment for domestic produce within seven or eight months after the peace, the slave States probably took nearly two thirds, though the white population of the States south of the Potomac was less than half the white population of the Union. The stimulus thus given to the slave system was violent, and was most plainly shown in the cotton States, where at least twenty million dollars were distributed in the year 1815 among a white population hardly exceeding half a million in all, while the larger portion fell to the share of a few slave-owners.[2]

Had the Northern States shared equally in the effects of this stimulus, the situation would have remained relatively as before; but the prosperity of the North was only moderate. The chief export of the Northern States was wheat and Indian corn. Even of these staples, Maryland and Virginia furnished a share; yet the total value of the wheat and corn exported from the Union was but eight million three hundred and fifty

[1] Hammond, i. 401.
[2] State Papers, Commerce and Navigation, ii. 23.

thousand dollars, while that of tobacco alone was eight and a quarter millions. While flour sold at nine or ten dollars a barrel, and Napoleon's armies were vying with the Russians and Austrians in creating an artificial demand, the Middle States made a fair profit from their crops, although much less than was made by the tobacco and cotton planters; but New England produced little for export, and there the peace brought only ruin.

Ordinarily shipping was the source of New England's profits. For twenty-five years the wars in Europe had given to New England shipping advantages which ceased with the return of peace. At first the change of condition was not felt, for every ship was promptly employed; but the reappearance of foreign vessels in American harbors showed that competition must soon begin, and that the old rates of profit were at an end.

Had this been all, Massachusetts could have borne it; but the shipping on the whole suffered least among New England interests. The new manufactures, in which large amounts of capital had been invested, were ruined by the peace. If the United States poured domestic produce valued at fifty million dollars into the markets of Great Britain, Great Britain and her dependencies poured in return not less than forty million dollars' worth of imports into the United States, and inundated the Union with manufactured goods which were sold at any sacrifice to relieve the British markets. Although the imported manufactures paid duties of twenty-five per cent or more, they were sold at rates that made American competition impossible.

The cotton manufacturers of Rhode Island, in a memorial to Congress, dated October 20, 1815, declared that their one hundred and forty manufactories, operating one hundred and thirty thousand spindles, could no longer be worked with profit, and were threatened with speedy destruction.[1] New England could foresee with some degree of certainty the ultimate loss of the great amount of capital invested in these undertakings; but whether such fears for the future were just or not, the loss of present profits was not a matter of specu-

---

[1] Annals of Congress, 1815–1816, p. 1651.

lation, but of instant and evident notoriety. Before the close of the year 1815 little profit was left to the new industries. The cotton manufacture, chiefly a New England interest, was supposed to employ a capital of forty million dollars, and to expend about fifteen millions a year in wages.[1] The woollen manufacture, largely in Connecticut, was believed to employ a capital of twelve million dollars.[2] Most of the large factories for these staples were altogether stopped.

From every quarter the peace brought distress upon New England. During the war most of the richer prizes had been sent to New England ports, and the sale of their cargoes brought money and buyers into the country; but this monopoly ceased at the same moment with the monopoly of manufactures. The lumber trade was almost the last surviving interest of considerable value, but in November Parliament imposed duties on American lumber which nearly destroyed the New England trade. The fisheries alone seemed to remain as a permanent resource.

The effect of these changes from prosperity to adversity was shown in the usual forms. Emigration became active. Thousands of native New Englanders transferred themselves to the valley of the Mohawk and Western New York. All the cities of the coast had suffered a check from the war; but while New York and Philadelphia began to recover their lost ground, Boston was slow to feel the impulse. The financial reason could be partly seen in the bank returns of Massachusetts. In January, 1814, the Massachusetts banks held about $7,300,000 in specie.[3] In January and February, 1815, when peace was declared, the same banks probably held still more specie, as the causes which led to the influx were not removed. In June, about three months later, they held only $3,464,000 in specie, and the drain steadily continued, until in June, 1816, the specie in their vaults was reduced to $1,260,000, while their discounts were not increased and their circulation was diminished.[4]

[1] Report on Manufactures, Feb. 13, 1816; Niles, ix. 447.
[2] Report on Woollen Manufactures, March 6, 1816; Niles, x. 82.
[3] Niles's Articles on the New England Convention, Dec. 8, 1814; Niles, vii. 196.
[4] Schedule etc.; Massachusetts Senate Document, No. 38, Jan. 17, 1838.

The state of the currency and the policy pursued by the Treasury added to the burden carried by New England. There alone the banks maintained specie payments. In the autumn of 1815, while the notes of the Boston banks were equivalent to gold, Treasury notes were at eleven per cent discount in Boston; New York bank-notes were at eleven and a half per cent discount; Philadelphia at sixteen; Baltimore at seventeen and eighteen; and United States six-per-cent bonds sold at eighty-six. In New England the Government exacted payments either in Treasury notes or in the notes of local banks equivalent to specie. Elsewhere it accepted the notes of local banks at a rate of depreciation much greater than that of Treasury notes. This injustice in exacting taxes was doubled by an equivalent injustice in paying debts. In New England the Treasury compelled creditors to take payment in whatever medium it had at hand, or to go unpaid. Elsewhere the Treasury paid its debts in the currency it received for its taxes.

Dallas admitted the wrong, but made no serious attempt to correct it. So complicated was the currency that the Treasury was obliged to keep four accounts with each of its ninety-four banks of deposit,—(1) in the currency of the bank itself; (2) in special deposits of other bank currency; (3) in special deposits of Treasury notes bearing interest; (4) in small Treasury notes not bearing interest. In New England, and also in the cities of New York and Philadelphia, for some months after the peace the taxes were paid in Treasury notes. So little local currency was collected at these chief centres of business that the Treasury did not attempt to discharge its warrants there in currency. As the Treasury notes gradually appreciated in value above the local bank-notes of the Middle States, tax-payers ceased to make payments in them, and paid in their local bank-notes. Little by little the accumulation of local currency in the Treasury deposits at Philadelphia and New York increased, until the Treasury was able to draw on them in payment of its warrants; but even at those points this degree of credit was not attained in 1815, and in New England the Treasury still made no payments except in Treasury notes, or the notes of distant banks at a discount still greater than that of Treasury notes. This exceptional severity toward New

England was admitted by Dallas, and excused only for the reason that if he were just to New England he must be severe to the rest of the country. Every holder of a Treasury warrant would have demanded payment at the place where the local medium was of the highest value, which was Boston; and as the Treasury could not pay specie at Boston without exacting specie elsewhere, Dallas paid no attention to Constitutional scruples or legal objections, but arbitrarily excluded Boston from the number of points where warrants were paid in local currency.[1]

The people of Boston criticised, with much severity and with apparent justice, Dallas's management of the finances, which seemed to require some explanation not furnished in his reports. By an Act approved March 3, Congress authorized a loan of $18,452,800 to absorb the outstanding Treasury notes. At that time, under the momentary reaction of peace excitement, Treasury notes were supposed to be worth about ninety-four cents in the dollar, and Dallas expected to convert them nearly dollar for dollar into six-per-cent bonds. His proposals were issued March 10, inviting bids for twelve millions, and requiring only "that the terms of the proposals should bear some relation to the actual fair price of stock in the market of Philadelphia or New York." When the bids were received, Dallas rejected them all, because in his opinion they were below the market rates. "In point of fact," he afterward said, "no direct offer was made to subscribe at a higher rate than eighty-nine per cent, while some of the offers were made at a rate even lower than seventy-five per cent." Although the old six-per-cents were then selling at eighty-nine, eighty-eight, and eighty-seven in Boston and New York, Dallas held that "the real condition of the public credit" required him to insist upon ninety-five as the value of the new stock.

After failing to obtain ninety-five or even ninety as the price of his bonds, Dallas resorted to expedients best described in his own words. As he could not fund the Treasury notes at the rate he wished, he abandoned the attempt, and used the loan only to supply the local wants of the Treasury: —

[1] Dallas's Report of Dec. 3, 1816; State Papers, Finance, iii. 130.

"The objects of the loan being to absorb a portion of the Treasury-note debt, and to acquire a sufficiency of local currency for local purposes, the price of the stock at the Treasury was of course independent of the daily up-and-down prices of the various stock markets in the Union, and could only be affected by the progress toward the attainment of those objects. Thus while the wants of the Treasury were insufficiently supplied, offers to subscribe were freely accepted, and the parties were sometimes authorized and invited to increase the amount of their offers; but where the local funds had so accumulated as to approach the probable amount of the local demands, the price of the stock was raised at the Treasury, and when the accumulation was deemed adequate to the whole amount of the local demands the loan was closed."[1]

Governments which insisted upon borrowing at rates higher than the money market allowed, could do so only by helping to debase the currency. Dallas's course offered encouragement to the suspended banks alone. The schedule of his loans proved that he paid a premium to insolvency. Of all places where he most needed "a sufficiency of local currency for local purposes," Boston stood first; but he borrowed in Boston less than one hundred thousand dollars, and this only in Treasury notes. Next to Boston stood New York; but in New York Dallas borrowed only $658,000, also in Treasury notes. In Philadelphia he obtained more than three millions, and took $1,845,000 in the depreciated local currency. In Baltimore he took nearly two millions in local currency; and in the bank paper of the District of Columbia, which was the most depreciated of all, he accepted $2,282,000 in local currency.[2] Thus the loan which he had asked Congress to authorize for the purpose of absorbing the excess of Treasury notes, brought into the Treasury only about three millions in these securities, while it relieved the banks of Philadelphia, Baltimore, and Washington of six millions of their depreciated paper, worth about eighty cents in the dollar, and provided

[1] Report of the Secretary of the Treasury, Dec. 6, 1815; State Papers, Finance, iii. 11.

[2] Report of Dec. 6, 1815; State Papers, Finance, iii. 11.

nothing to redeem the government's overdue bills at Boston and New York.

Had Dallas pursued a different course and funded all the overdue Treasury notes at the market rate, he might not have relieved New England, but he would have placed the government in a position to deal effectually with the suspended banks elsewhere. The immediate result of his refusal to redeem the dishonored Treasury notes was to depress their market value, and to discredit the government. Treasury notes fell to eighty-eight and eighty-seven, while the six-per-cents fell as low as eighty-one. In Washington, Baltimore, and Philadelphia Dallas obtained enough local currency to meet local obligations, and doubtless saved to the government a small percentage by thus trafficking in its own discredit; but in gaining this advantage he offered encouragement to the overissues of the suspended banks, and he helped to embarrass the solvent banks in the chief commercial centres as well as those in New England.[1]

At the close of the year 1815 the general effect of the peace was already well defined. The Southern States were in the full enjoyment of extraordinary prosperity. The Middle States were also prosperous and actively engaged in opening new sources of wealth. Only the Eastern States suffered under depression; but there it was so severe as to warrant a doubt whether New England could recover from the shock. The new epoch of American history began by the sudden decline of Massachusetts to the lowest point of relative prosperity and influence she had ever known, and by an equally sudden stimulus to the South and West. So discredited was Massachusetts that she scarcely ventured to complain, for every complaint uttered by her press was answered by the ironical advice that she should call another Hartford Convention.

---

[1] Gallatin to Jefferson, Nov. 27, 1815; Gallatin's writings, i. 666. Gallatin to Macon, April 23, 1816; Gallatin's writings, i. 697.

Chapter V

BETWEEN 1801 and 1815, great changes in the American people struck the most superficial observer. The Rights of Man occupied public thoughts less, and the price of cotton more, in the later than in the earlier time. Although in 1815 Europe was suffering under a violent reaction against free government, Americans showed little interest and no alarm, compared with their emotions of twenty years before. Napoleon resumed his empire, and was overthrown at Waterloo, without causing the people of the United States to express a sign of concern in his fate; and France was occupied by foreign armies without rousing among Americans a fear of England. Foreign affairs seemed reduced to the question whether England would consent to negotiate a treaty of commerce.

After excluding most of the American demands, Lord Castlereagh consented to a commercial convention abolishing discriminating duties, and admitting American commerce with the East Indies. This treaty, signed July 3, seemed to satisfy American demands, and the British Ministry showed no wish to challenge new disputes. With France, the disturbed condition of government permitted no diplomatic arrangement. The only foreign country that required serious attention was Algiers; and Decatur, with a strong squadron of the new American cruisers, speedily compelled the Dey to sign a treaty more favorable to the United States than he had yet signed with any other nation. Tunis and Tripoli showed a similar disposition, and Decatur returned home in the autumn, having settled to his satisfaction all the matters intrusted to his care.

Under such circumstances, without an anxiety in regard to foreign or domestic affairs, President Madison sent his Annual Message to Congress December 5, 1815. It told a pleasant story of successful administration and of rapidly growing income; but its chief historical interest lay in the lines of future party politics that Madison more or less unconsciously sketched. The Message proved, or seemed to prove, that Madison's views and wishes lay in the direction of strong government. He advised "liberal provision" for defence; more military academies; an improved and enlarged navy; effectual protection to manufactures; new national roads and canals; a national university; and such an organization of the militia as would place it promptly and effectually under control of the national government. Madison seemed to take his stand, beyond further possibility of change, on the system of President Washington.

Dallas's report echoed the tone of Alexander Hamilton. Very long, chiefly historical, and interesting beyond the common, this Treasury Report of 1815 recommended a scale of annual expenditure exceeding twenty-seven millions, in place of the old scale of ten millions. The expenditure was to be but a part of the system. A protective tariff of customs duties was assumed to be intended by Congress, and a national bank was urged as the only efficient means by which the government could recover control over the currency.

Although the President was less emphatic than the secretary in holding a national bank to be the only cure for the disorders of the currency, he was prepared to go a step further by issuing government paper as a national currency, and suggested that alternative in his Message. A national bank or a national currency was an equally energetic exercise of supreme central powers not expressly granted by the Constitution and much disputed by theorists. Dallas's objection to the national currency did not relate to its inefficiency, but to the practical difficulty of issuing paper and keeping it in issue. Either course of action implied a recurrence to the principles of President Washington. The Executive proposed to start afresh in 1816 from its point of departure in 1790.

The Fourteenth Congress was well disposed to support the attempt. Under the stress of war the people had selected as their representatives the ablest and most vigorous men of their generation. The war leaders were mostly returned,— Calhoun, Clay, Lowndes, Richard M. Johnson, Peter B. Porter, and John Forsyth,—while the old peace party was strongly represented by Timothy Pickering, Daniel Webster, John Randolph, Grosvenor of New York, and Stanford of North Carolina; but perhaps the most distinguished member of all was William Pinkney of Maryland. A swarm of younger men, far above the average, reinforced both sides of the House. Philip P. Barbour sat again for Virginia. John McLean sat again for Ohio. Henry St. George Tucker came for the first time into the House. Joseph Hopkinson, Samuel D. Ingham, and John Sergeant raised the character of the Pennsylvania delegation; and Samuel Smith, at last ejected from the Senate by a Federalist legislature in Maryland, reappeared in the House for the first time since 1803.

The Senate was also improved. The disappearance of Leib and Samuel Smith was made more suggestive by the resignation of Giles. David Stone of North Carolina, another independent much given to opposition at critical moments, also resigned; and another of the same class, Joseph Anderson of Tennessee, who had been a member of the Senate since 1797, retired to become First Comptroller of the Treasury. These retirements removed the chief abettors of faction, and changed the character of the Senate until it seemed to belong to a different epoch. Jonathan Roberts still sat in the place of Leib. Armistead Mason took the seat of Giles, and with James Barbour gave Madison for the first time the full support of Virginia. Macon took the place of David Stone. George W. Campbell took the place of Joseph Anderson. Robert G. Harper, the old champion of Federalism, succeeded Samuel Smith from Maryland. The Senate scarcely recognized itself as the same body that since 1808 had so persistently thwarted and fretted the President.

In the arrangement of new party divisions the Fourteenth Congress, unlike its recent predecessors, consciously aimed to take a decided share. The House seemed for the first time in many years to pride itself on intellectual superiority. William Pinkney, Calhoun, Lowndes, Clay, Daniel Webster, John Randolph, and their associates were not men who bowed to authority, even of the people, but rather looked on the task of government as a function of superior intellect. They proposed to correct what they considered mistaken popular tendencies. Each expressed his ideas with sufficient clearness in the form natural to him. Calhoun generalized before descending to particulars.[1]

---

[1] Speech of Jan. 31, 1816; Annals of Congress, 1815–1816, p. 830.

"In the policy of nations," reasoned Calhoun, "there are two extremes: one extreme, in which justice and moderation may sink in feebleness; another, in which that lofty spirit which ought to animate all nations, particularly free ones, may mount up to military violence. These extremes ought to be equally avoided; but of the two, I consider the first far the most dangerous. . . . I consider the extreme of weakness not only the most dangerous of itself, but as that extreme to which the people of this country are peculiarly liable."

Clay, aiming at the same objects, dwelt chiefly on foreign dangers as the motive of the strong government he wished to establish. "That man must be blind to the indications of the future," he declared,[1] " who cannot see that we are destined to have war after war with Great Britain, until, if one of the two nations be not crushed, all grounds of collision shall have ceased between us." He wished to create a government that should control the destinies of both American continents by a display of armed force. "He confessed with infinite regret that he saw a supineness throughout the country which left him almost without hope that what he believed the correct policy would be pursued," toward aiding the Spanish colonies against their mother country. Both Calhoun and Clay admitted that they wished to govern in a sense not approved by an apparent majority of the nation; and the sympathies of the House were openly or secretly with them.

Of the contrary sentiment, John Randolph was the champion. Although his early career had ended in the most conspicuous failure yet known in American politics, he returned to the House, with intelligence morbidly sharpened, to begin a second epoch of his life with powers and materials that gave him the position of equal among men like Calhoun, Pinkney, and Webster. Randolph held a decisive advantage in wishing only to obstruct. He had no legislation to propose, and his political philosophy suited that extreme "to which," according to Calhoun, "the people of this country are peculiarly liable." Early in the session Randolph showed that he understood even better than Calhoun and Clay the division between him-

[1] Speech of Jan. 29, 1816; Annals of Congress, 1815–1816, p. 787.

self and them. "If the warning voice of Patrick Henry," he said in the debate of January 31, 1816,[1] "had not apprised me long ago, the events of this day would have taught me that this Constitution does not comprise one people, but that there are two distinct characters in the people of this nation." In every growing people two or more distinct characters were likely to rise, else the people would not grow; but the primal character, which Randolph meant to represent, enjoyed the political advantage of passive resistance to impulse from every direction.

In reply to Calhoun, Randolph defined the issue with his usual skill of words:[2] —

"As the gentleman from South Carolina has presented the question to the House, they and the nation cannot have the slightest difficulty in deciding whether they will give up the States or not; whether they will, in fact, make this an elective monarchy. The question is whether or not we are willing to become one great consolidated nation; or whether we have still respect enough for those old, respectable institutions to regard their integrity and preservation as a part of our policy."

Randolph's eccentricities, which amounted to insanity, prevented him from exercising in the House the influence to which his experience and abilities entitled him, but did not prevent him from reflecting the opinions of a large part of the nation, particularly in the South. Between these two impulses the Fourteenth Congress was to choose a path, subject to the future judgment of their constituents.

The Executive urged them on. Dallas began by sending to Calhoun, the chairman of the Committee on Currency, a plan for a national bank with a capital of thirty-five millions and power to increase it to fifty millions; with twenty-five directors, five of whom were to be appointed by the government to represent its share in the bank stock, of which the government was to subscribe one fifth.[3]

In another report, dated Feb. 12, 1816, Dallas recommended

[1] Annals of Congress, 1815–1816, p. 841.
[2] Annals of Congress, 1815–1816, p. 844.
[3] Dallas to Calhoun, Dec. 24, 1815; Annals of Congress, 1815–1816, p. 505.

a protective tariff and sketched its details. Upon cotton fabrics he proposed a duty of thirty-three and one half per cent on their value; on woollens, twenty-eight per cent; on linen, hemp, and silk, twenty per cent; on paper, leather, etc., thirty-five per cent; on earthenware, glassware, etc., thirty per cent; on bar-iron, seventy-five cents per hundred weight; on rolled iron, a dollar and a half; and on unenumerated articles, fifteen per cent. These duties were avowedly protective, intended to serve as the foundation of a system, and to perpetuate the policy to which the Government stood pledged by its legislation for the last six years. In connection with a proposed reduction of internal taxes, the Bank and the Tariff covered the financial field.

The House first grappled with the subject of revenue. The Committee of Ways and Means, through William Lowndes, reported, Jan. 9, 1816, a scheme embodied in twelve Resolutions intended to serve as the guide to definite legislation. Lowndes assumed a net annual revenue of $25,369,000; and to obtain this sum he proposed to shift the burden of about seven million dollars from internal taxation to the customs, by an addition of forty-two per cent to the rates of permanent duty.[1] The direct tax was to be retained to the amount of three million dollars, and an annual fund of $13,500,000 was to be set aside for the interest and principal of the national debt.

Hardly had the debate begun when Randolph, January 16, dragged the question of a protective system into the prominence it was thenceforward to maintain. Two years of repose had singularly improved his skill in the choice of language and in the instigation of class against class.

"The manufacturer," said he,[2] "is the citizen of no place or any place; the agriculturist has his property, his lands, his all, his household Gods to defend,—and like that meek drudge the ox, who does the labor and ploughs the ground, then for his reward takes the refuse of the farm-yard, the blighted blades and the mouldy straw, and the mildewed shocks of corn for his support. . . . Alert, vigi-

---

[1] Report of Committee; Annals of Congress, 1815–1816, p. 516.
[2] Annals of Congress, 1815–1816, p. 687.

lant, enterprising, and active, the manufacturing interest are collected in masses, and ready to associate at a moment's warning for any purpose of general interest to their body. Do but ring the fire-bell, and you can assemble all the manufacturing interest of Philadelphia in fifteen minutes. Nay, for the matter of that they are always assembled; they are always on the Rialto, and Shylock and Antonio meet there every day as friends, and compare notes, and possess in trick and intelligence what, in the goodness of God to them, the others can never possess."

Randolph's political sagacity was nowhere better shown than in replying, Jan. 31, 1816, to a speech of Calhoun: "On whom do your impost duties bear?" he asked.[1] "Upon whom bears the duty on coarse woollens and linens and blankets, upon salt, and all the necessaries of life? On poor men, and on slaveholders." With a perception abnormally keen, Randolph fixed on the tariff and the slaveholders as the necessary combination to oppose the nationalizing efforts of Calhoun and Clay.

No leader of note supported Randolph. He stood alone, or with only the support of Stanford, as far as concerned debate; but he led nearly half the House. Upon Benjamin Hardin's motion, February 3, to repeal the direct tax immediately and altogether, a motion which struck at the root of Dallas's scheme, the House decided by eighty-one votes against seventy-three to sustain the secretary. On the passage of the bill to continue the direct tax of three million dollars for one year, the minority lacked but a change of three votes to defeat it. The bill passed, March 4, by a vote of sixty-seven to sixty-three.

On the tariff the House was more closely divided. The Committee of Ways and Means consisted of seven members. Lowndes was chairman. Three other members were from the South, one of whom, Robertson of Louisiana, wished protection for sugar. Three members were from the North, one of whom, Ingham of Pennsylvania, represented Dallas's views. The chief question concerned the duty on cottons and woollens. So close was the division that Ingham, to use his own

[1] Annals of Congress, 1815–1816, p. 842.

words, was struck dumb with astonishment when the committee, after adopting a duty of fifty-six per cent for the protection of sugar, voted to impose a duty of only twenty per cent on cottons and woollens. "It was, however, too glaringly inconsistent and palpably wrong to be persisted in, and therefore it was that the Committee of Ways and Means, upon reconsideration, substituted the twenty-five per cent which was reported in the bill."[1]

When the bill came before the House, Clay moved, March 21, to substitute the rate of thirty-three and one third per cent for that of twenty-five per cent on cottons, for the express purpose of testing the sense of the House. Clay and the Northern protectionists held that the committee's bill did not afford protection enough. The committee, also admitting the propriety of protection, maintained that twenty-five per cent was sufficient. On both sides some temper was shown, and charges of sectionalism were made. By a vote of sixty-eight to sixty-one, the House in committee voted, March 22, to impose a duty of thirty per cent. Daniel Webster then moved to limit this rate to two years, after which the duty should be twenty-five per cent for two years more, when it should be reduced to twenty per cent. Finally the House adopted a duty of twenty-five per cent for three years. Webster also carried, March 27, a motion to reduce the proposed duty on bar-iron from seventy-five to forty-five cents a hundred weight.

All the members of note, except Randolph, professed to favor protection. Calhoun was as decided as Ingham. "He believed the policy of the country required protection to our manufacturing establishments."[2] The bill was assumed to offer protection enough, and the House disputed only whether the adopted duties were or were not sufficient. The actual free-trade sentiment was shown, April 8, when Randolph made a final motion to postpone, and was beaten by a vote of ninety-five to forty-seven.

The bill promptly passed the Senate, and was approved by the President April 27; but the true issue was undecided. No one could deny that if the duty of twenty-five per cent on

[1] Annals of Congress, 1815–1816, p. 1245.
[2] Annals of Congress, 1815–1816, p. 1272.

cottons and woollens should prove to be insufficient, the House was pledged to increase it. The bill was avowedly protective. In regard to the coarser Indian cottons, it was practically prohibitive, since it valued them all, for tariff purposes, at twenty-five cents a yard,—a rate which on the cheaper fabrics raised the duty above one hundred per cent. Yet when the tariff of 1816 proved to be little protective, in after years it was commonly represented as a revenue and not a protective tariff. In substance, Randolph's opinions controlled the House.

Dallas was more fortunate in regard to the Bank. Randolph's hostility to State banks was greater than to the Bank of the United States. Calhoun reported, January 8, the bill to incorporate for twenty years a new National Bank with a capital of thirty-five million dollars, and supported it, February 26, by a speech showing that the Bank was a proper means for attaining the Constitutional object of restoring the money of the country to its true medium. Active opposition came chiefly from the Federalists. Even Samuel Smith seemed to plead rather that the State banks should be gently treated than that the National Bank should be opposed. Randolph, while professing hostility to the new Bank on any and every ground suggested by others, concluded by pledging himself to support any adequate means for reducing the overpowering influence of the State banks. Clay thought himself obliged to leave the Speaker's chair in order to recant in the most public manner his errors of 1811. Forsyth, one of Calhoun's ablest allies, went so far in his support of the measure as to assert without reserve that the power to suspend specie payments— a power expressly reserved to the government by Calhoun's bill—belonged undoubtedly to Congress, an opinion which the House did not share. In the Republican ranks open opposition to the Bank seemed almost silenced; and the member who made himself most conspicuous in hostility to the bill was Daniel Webster,—the last of all in whom such a course was natural.

Webster's criticism on Calhoun's Constitutional argument was made in his loftiest manner. The currency, he said, needed no reform, for it was, by the Constitution and the law, gold and silver; nor had Congress the right to make any other medium current. The true remedy was for Congress to interdict the bills of the suspended banks.[1] Had he been content to rest his opposition on that ground alone, Webster could not have been answered, although he might have been regarded as an impracticable politician; but as the bill came toward its passage, and as several Federalists declared in its favor, he pressed his hostility so far, and with so much dogmatism, that several of his own party revolted, and Grosvenor of New York replied sharply that he did not propose to be drilled to vote on whatever any one might choose to call a principle.

In spite of determined opposition from Webster, Pitkin, John Sergeant, and other Federalists, the House passed the bill, March 14, by a vote of eighty to seventy-one. The majority was small, but of the minority not less than thirty-eight were Federalists; and, omitting Randolph and Stanford, only thirty-one Republicans voted against the bill. The House contained one hundred and seventeen Republicans. In the Senate the opposition was almost wholly confined to Federalists, and the bill passed by a majority much larger than that in the House. Twenty-two senators voted in its favor; only twelve voted against it, and of the twelve only four were Republicans. The President approved it April 10; and thus, after five years of financial disorder, the Republican party reverted to the system of Washington, and resumed powers it had found indispensable to government.

The Federalists of New England were in a situation too alarming to bear even the little delay required to organize the Bank. For them a general return to specie payments was the only escape from imminent ruin; and acting on this conviction, Webster moved, April 26, a joint Resolution ordering that all taxes should be collected after Feb. 1, 1817, in some medium equivalent to specie, thus allowing but nine months for the work of resumption. The same day the House passed the Resolution by the decisive majority of seventy-one to thirty-four. The Senate substituted February 20 as the day of resumption, and passed the Resolution April 29, which was approved by the President the next day.

In contrast with the imbecility of many previous Con-

[1] Annals of Congress, 1815–1816, p. 1091.

gresses, the vigor of the Fourteenth Congress in thus settling the new scale of government was remarkable; but other measures of importance were not wanting. An Act approved April 29 appropriated one million dollars annually for three years to build ships of war; an Act approved April 19 authorized the people of Indiana to form a State government. A bill, which passed the House but was postponed by the Senate and became law at the next session, provided for the admission of Mississippi. In still another direction the House showed its self-confidence in a manner that caused unusual popular excitement. It undertook to increase the pay of its own members and of senators.

The scale of salary for public officials was low. The President, relatively highly paid, received twenty-five thousand dollars. The Secretaries of State and Treasury received five thousand; those of War and Navy, four thousand; the Attorney-General, three thousand; Chief-Justice Marshall was paid four thousand, and the six associate justices received thirty-five hundred dollars each.

While the Executive and Judiciary were paid regular salaries, Congress stood on a different footing. Legislators had never been paid what was considered an equivalent for their time and services. They were supposed to be unpaid; but such a rule excluded poor men from the public service, and therefore the colonial legislatures adopted a practice, which Congress continued, of allowing what were supposed to be the reasonable expenses of members. The First Congress fixed upon six dollars a day, and six dollars for every twenty miles of estimated journey, as a suitable scale of expense both for senators and representatives;[1] and the same rate had been continued for twenty-five years. No one supposed it sufficient to support a household, but poor men could live upon it. Desha of Kentucky averred that it was a fair allowance for the average representative. According to him, board was twelve or thirteen dollars a week, and the total cost of a session of one hundred and fifty days amounted to five hundred and seventy or eighty dollars; so that the western and southwestern members, with whose habits he was familiar, carried

[1] Act of Sept. 22, 1789. Act of March 10, 1796.

home, with their mileage, about four hundred and fifty dollars in savings.[1]

In the pride of conscious superiority the Fourteenth Congress undertook to change the system; and Richard M. Johnson, probably the most popular member of the House, assumed the risk of popular displeasure. In moving for a committee, March 4, Johnson repudiated the idea of increasing the pay; and his committee, including Webster, Pitkin, Jackson, the President's brother-in-law, Grosvenor, and McLean of Ohio, reported through him that fifteen hundred dollars a year was the correct equivalent of six dollars a day.

The bill known as the Compensation Bill was reported March 6, and was debated for two days with some animation. Among its supporters John Randolph was prominent, and gave offence to the opponents of the measure by his usual tactics. Most of the friends of the bill stoutly insisted that it did not increase the pay; most of its opponents averred that it more than doubled the amount. Calhoun admitted the increase of pay, and favored it, in order to retain "young men of genius without property" in the public service. The bill was hurried through the House.

"The Compensation Bill," said Forsyth at the next session,[2] " was the only one of any interest pushed through the Committee of the whole House and ordered to a third reading in a single day. All motions to amend were rejected; for the committee to rise and report progress and ask leave to sit again, met with a similar fate. . . . The House refused repeated propositions to adjourn, and continued its sittings until the bill was ordered to be engrossed."

No time was lost. Johnson moved for a committee March 4; the committee reported the bill March 6; the House in committee took it up March 7, and reported it the same day. The House passed it March 8, by a vote of eighty-one to sixty-seven. In the Senate the bill was read for a second time March 12. In the course of the debate one of the New Jersey

[1] Annals of Congress; 1816–1817, p. 492.
[2] Annals of Congress; 1816–1817, p. 559.

senators, commenting on the haste shown by the House to pass the bill, added that also "in the Senate postponement, commitment, and amendment are all refused, and it is to be pushed through by main strength with a haste altogether unusual." The Senate passed it March 14, by a vote of twenty-one to eleven; and it received the President's signature March 19, barely a fortnight after Johnson's request for a committee.

At the time when the bill was still under consideration by the President, and the House had just passed the Bank Act, the Republican members of both Houses met to nominate a candidate to succeed Madison as President. Three candidates were in the field,—Daniel D. Tompkins, William H. Crawford, and James Monroe.

The choice was a matter of small consequence, for any candidate of the Republican party was sure of almost unanimous election, and all were respectable men; but Tompkins could expect little support at a time when Congress selected the candidate, for only men well known in the national service were likely to satisfy the standard of Congressmen. The true contest lay between Crawford and Monroe, and was complicated, as far as the candidates themselves understood it, by personal intrigues on both sides. Perhaps Crawford's strength was the greater, for four fifths of the New York members favored him rather than the Virginian.[1] In cases where no strong feeling fixed results, dexterity in management might overcome a preference between persons; and by some means never explained, the preference of the New York members for Crawford was overcome. One of these members—a competent observer— believed that Martin Van Buren and Peter B. Porter, for reasons of their own, prevented New York from declaring for Crawford when such a declaration would have decided the result.[2] Crawford himself at the last professed to withdraw from the contest,[3] and several of his warm friends did not attend the caucus. On the evening of March 15, one hundred and nineteen senators and representatives appeared in the hall

[1] Hammond's New York, i. 409.
[2] Hammond's New York, i. 409.
[3] Crawford to Gallatin, May 10, 1816; Gallatin's Writings, i. 702.

of the House of Representatives in obedience to an anonymous notice addressed to one hundred and forty-three Republican members. Sixty-five, or less than half the Republican representation, voted for Monroe; fifty-four voted for Crawford; and eighty-five then united in nominating Governor Tompkins as Vice-President.

Monroe's character was well known, and his elevation to the Presidency was a result neither of great popularity nor of exceptional force, but was rather due to the sudden peace which left him the residuum of Madison's many Cabinets. A long list of resignations alone remained to recall the memory of his associates. Robert Smith, Cæsar Rodney, William Eustis, Paul Hamilton, Gallatin, G. W. Campbell, William Jones, William Pinkney, and John Armstrong had all resigned in succession, leaving Monroe and Dallas in possession of the government when peace was declared. Dallas was not a popular character, whatever were his abilities or services; and no other man occupied high ground. Under such circumstances the strength shown by Crawford was surprising, and proved that Monroe, notwithstanding his advantages, was regarded with no exclusive favor.

In truth Monroe had no party. His original friends were the old Republicans,—John Taylor of Caroline, Littleton Tazewell, John Randolph, and their associates, from whom he had drawn apart. His new friends were chiefly northern Democrats, whose motives for preferring him to Crawford were selfish. In any case an epoch of personal politics could be foreseen, for men like Crawford, Calhoun, and Clay never submitted long to a superior; and for such an epoch Monroe was probably the best choice.

Shortly after the nomination Dallas gave notice to the President that he meant to retire from the Treasury in order to resume his practice at the bar.[1] Madison immediately wrote to Gallatin, April 12, inviting him to resume charge of the Treasury; but Gallatin was weary of domestic politics, and preferred diplomacy. He went as minister to France, while Dallas remained at the Treasury until October, to set the new Bank in motion.

[1] Life and Writings of A. J. Dallas, p. 139.

These arrangements closed the first session of the Fourteenth Congress, which adjourned April 30, leaving Madison in unaccustomed peace, harassed by no more enemies or dissensions, to wait the close of his public life.

Chapter VI

THE PROSPERITY that followed the Peace of Ghent suffered no check during the year 1816, or during the remainder of Madison's term. The exports of domestic produce, officially valued at $45,000,000 for the year ending Sept. 30, 1815, were valued at nearly $65,000,000 for the following year, and exceeded $68,000,000 for 1817. The Southern States still supplied two thirds of the exported produce. Cotton to the amount of $24,000,000, tobacco valued at nearly $13,000,000, and rice at $3,500,000, contributed more than forty of the sixty-five millions of domestic exports in 1816. The tables[1] showed that while South Carolina, Georgia, and Louisiana gained with unparalleled rapidity, New England lost ground, and New York only maintained its uniform movement. While the domestic exports of Georgia and Louisiana trebled in value, those of New York increased from eight to fourteen millions.

Notwithstanding the great importations from Europe which under ordinary conditions would have counterbalanced the exports, the exchanges soon turned in favor of the United States. Before the close of 1816 specie in considerable quantities began to flow into the country. Canada, being nearest, felt the drain first, and suffered much inconvenience from it; but during the summer of 1816 and 1817 Europe also shipped much specie to America. Every ship brought some amount, until the export began to affect the Bank of England, which at last found its bullion diminishing with alarming rapidity. The returns showed a drain beginning in July or August, 1817, when the Bank of England held £11,668,000, until August, 1819, when the supply was reduced to £3,595,000; and in the interval a commercial crisis, with a general destruction of credit, occurred. The reaction could not fail in the end to affect America as it affected England, but the first result was stimulating beyond all previous experience. In England the drain of specie embarrassed government in returning to specie payments. In the United States the influx of specie made the return easy, if not necessary.

[1] State Papers; Commerce and Navigation, i. 929.

The recovery of internal exchanges kept pace with the influx of specie. At Boston, July 27, 1816, United States six-per-cent bonds were quoted at eighty-five, and Treasury notes at ninety-four to ninety-four and one-half; at New York six-per-cents stood at ninety, and Treasury notes at par; in Philadelphia six-per-cents were worth ninety-eight, and Treasury notes one hundred and seven; in Baltimore six-per-cents were selling at one hundred and two, and Treasury notes at one hundred and twelve. During the next five months the recovery was steady and rapid. The banks of New York, September 26, began to cash their one-dollar notes, thus relieving the community from the annoyance of fractional currency. October 26 the six-per-cents stood at ninety-two in Boston, at ninety-three and one-half in New York, at ninety-eight in Philadelphia, and at one hundred and one and one-half in Baltimore. November 28 they sold at ninety-six in Boston; November 30 they sold at ninety-six and one-quarter in New York, at one hundred and one and one-half in Philadelphia, and at one hundred and five in Baltimore. January 1, 1817, the Treasury resumed payments at Boston in Boston money, and no further discredit attached to government securities.

The banks of the Middle States were less disposed than the government to hasten the return of specie payments. In order to do so, they were obliged to contract their circulation and discounts to an extent that would have been unendurable in any time but one of great prosperity; and only the threats of Dallas overcame their reluctance, even under most favorable conditions. Both Dallas and the President were irritated by their slowness.[1] July 22, 1816, the Secretary of the Treasury issued a circular warning them that, at whatever cost, the Treasury must carry into effect the order of Congress to collect the revenue, after Feb. 20, 1817, only in specie or its equivalent. "The banks in the States to the South," he said,[2] "and to the west of Maryland, are ready and willing, it is believed, to co-operate in the same measure. The objection, or the obstacle to the measure, principally rests with the banks of the Middle States." Dallas invited them to assist the Treasury in resuming specie payments with the least possible delay; and

[1] Madison to Dallas, July 16, 1816; Life of A. J. Dallas, p. 453.
[2] Niles, x. 376.

accordingly the banks of the Middle States held a convention at Philadelphia, August 6, to consider their course.

This convention, on discussing the possibility of resumption, agreed that the banks needed more time than the government was disposed to allow. Credit had been necessarily expanded by the unusual scale of commerce and enterprise. So sudden and violent a contraction as was required for specie payments could not fail to distress the public, and might cause great suffering. Yet in some degree the new United States Bank could relieve this pressure; and therefore the resumption should not be attempted by the State banks until the National Bank should be fairly opened and ready to begin its discounts. The State banks in convention foresaw, or imagined, that the United States Bank could not begin operations so early as Feb. 20, 1817, and they declined to risk resumption without its aid. Acting on this impression, they met Dallas's urgency by a formal recommendation that their banks should begin to pay specie, not on the 20th of February, but on the first Monday of July, 1817.

This decision, though unsatisfactory to Dallas and the President, could not be considered unreasonable. Credit was expanded beyond the limit of safety, and the government was largely responsible for the expansion. Many of the State banks were probably unsound from the first, and needed careful management. Between 1810 and 1830, on a total capital of one hundred and forty millions, the bank failures amounted to thirty millions, or more than one fifth of the whole.[1] In Pennsylvania the country banks reduced their issues from $4,756,000 in November, 1816, to $1,318,000 in November, 1819. The latter moment was one of extreme depression, but the former was probably not that of the greatest expansion. When the banks of the Middle States held their convention, Aug. 6, 1816, contraction had already begun, and steadily continued, while specie flowed into the country to supply a foundation for bank paper. Under such circumstances the banks asked no extravagant favor in recommending that eleven months, instead of seven, should be allowed for resumption.

Dallas was not disposed to concede this favor. Having at

[1] Gallatin, Banks and Currency; Works, iii. 293.

last the necessary machinery for controlling the State banks, he used it with the same vigor that marked all his acts. No sooner had the convention announced its unwillingness to co-operate with the Treasury in executing the order of Congress, than Dallas issued instructions, August 16,[1] hastening the preparations for opening the National Bank as early as Jan. 1, 1817. Soon afterward, September 12, he renewed his notice that the notes of suspended banks would be rejected by the Treasury after Feb. 20, 1817.

The Bank subscription was filled in August, a deficit of three million dollars being taken by Stephen Girard in a sin-gle mass.[2] In October the board of directors was chosen by the shareholders, and in November the directors met and elected as President the former Secretary of the Navy, William Jones. One of their first acts was much debated, and was strongly opposed in the board of directors by J. J. Astor. They sent John Sergeant, of Philadelphia, abroad with au-thority to purchase some millions of bullion; and his mission was calculated to impress on the public the conviction that specie payments were to be resumed as soon as the Bank could open its doors.

Hurried by Dallas, the Bank actually began its operations in January, 1817, and under the double pressure from the Trea-sury the State banks had no choice but to yield. Another meeting was held at Philadelphia, February 1, consisting of delegates from the banks of New York, Philadelphia, Balti-more, and Richmond. The convention entered into a compact with the Secretary of the Treasury to resume payments, on certain conditions, at the day fixed by Congress. The compact was carried into effect February 20, a few days before the close of Madison's Presidency. Its success was magical. In New York, at ten o'clock on the morning of February 20, specie was at two and one half per cent premium. The banks opened their doors, and in half an hour all was once more regular and normal.

Thus the worst financial evil of the war was removed within two years after the proclamation of peace. A debt of about one hundred and thirty millions remained; but the

[1] Niles, x. 423.
[2] Dallas to Madison, Aug. 27, 1816; Life of Dallas, p. 471.

people which only twenty years before had shrunk with fear and disgust from a debt of eighty millions, gave scarcely a thought in 1816 to their funded obligations. The difference between the two periods was not so much economical as political. Population and wealth had increased, but the experience of the people had advanced more rapidly than their numbers or capital. In measuring the political movement shrewd judges might easily err, for the elections of 1816 showed little apparent change in parties; but in truth parties had outgrown their principles, and in politics, as in finance, the close of Madison's Administration obliterated old distinctions.

Neither party admitted the abandonment of its dogmas. The New York election in the spring of 1816 showed no considerable change in votes. In 1810 Governor Tompkins was elected by ten thousand majority; even in the dark days of 1813 he had a majority of thirty-six hundred; in 1816, notwithstanding his popularity and the success of his war administration, his majority was less than seven thousand. In Massachusetts John Brooks, who succeeded Governor Strong as candidate of the Federalist party, received forty-nine thousand five hundred votes, while Samuel Dexter received forty-seven thousand four hundred. Six years before, in 1810, the Republican candidate, Elbridge Gerry, had received more than forty-six thousand five hundred, and Governor Strong had polled only forty-four thousand. Apparently the Republicans had lost ground in Massachusetts since 1810. In Connecticut, where the election turned on church issues, the result was somewhat different. The Anglican church, a small body but rich and influential, strongly Federalist in politics and conservative in character, joined the Democrats to overthrow the reign of the Congregational clergy. Oliver Wolcott, a Federalist who supported the war, was their candidate; and the combination nearly carried the State. Wolcott received about ten thousand two hundred votes; his Federalist opponent was elected by eleven thousand three hundred and seventy votes. The Federalists also carried Rhode Island, once a strongly Democratic State, and seemed socially as well as politically to be little affected by their many mistakes and misfortunes.

Yet every one felt that real distinctions of party no longer existed. The Anglicans of Connecticut, the Unitarians of Boston, the Universalists and Baptists, looked chiefly to the overthrow of the established New England church; and the Democrats of New York, like the Republicans of Virginia and North Carolina, labored for a system of internal improvements and for increased energy in national government. Parties, no longer held together by discipline, were liable at any moment to fall into confusion; and, as frequently happened in such stages of public opinion, they were extraordinarily affected by influences seemingly trivial. In 1816 the relaxation of party spirit resulted in a phenomenon never before witnessed. The whole community rose against its own representatives, and showed evident pleasure in condemning them. The occasion for this outbreak of popular temper was the Compensation Bill; but the instinct that could alone account for the public pleasure in punishing public men, could not be explained by a cause so trifling as that Act.

At the next session of Congress, Calhoun, lapsing in the middle of a speech into his usual meditative speculation, remarked, as though he were perplexed to account for his own theory, that in his belief the House of Representatives was not a favorite with the American people.[1] Had he expressed the opinion that freedom of thought or speech was not a favorite with the American people, he would have said nothing more surprising. If the House was not a favorite, what part of the government was popular, and what could be hoped for representative government itself? Of all the machinery created by the Constitution, the House alone directly reflected and represented the people; and if the people disliked it, they disliked themselves.

The people best knew whether Calhoun was right. Certainly the House, owing in part to its size, its frequent elections and changes, its lack of responsibility and of social unity, was the least steady and least efficient branch of government. Readers who have followed the history here closed, have been surprised at the frequency with which the word *imbecility* has risen in their minds in reading the proceedings of the House. So strong was the same impression at the time,

---

[1] Annals of Congress, 1816–1817, pp. 392, 505, 604.

that in the year 1814, at the close of the war, every earnest patriot in the Union, and many men who were neither earnest nor patriotic, were actively reproaching the House for its final failure, at an apparent crisis of the national existence, to call out or organize any considerable part of the national energies. The people in truth, however jealous of power, would have liked in imagination, though they would not bear in practice, to be represented by something nobler, wiser, and purer than their own average honor, wisdom, and purity. They could not make an ideal of weakness, ignorance, or vice, even their own; and as they required in their religion the idea of an infinitely wise and powerful deity, they revolted in their politics from whatever struck them as sordid or selfish. The House reflected their own weaknesses; and the Compensation Act seemed to them an expression of their own least agreeable traits. They rebelled against a petty appropriation of money, after enduring for years a constant succession of worse offences.

"Who would have believed," asked John Randolph,[1] six months afterward,—"who would have believed," he repeated, "that the people of the United States would have borne all the privations and losses of the late war, and of the measures that led to it; that they would have quietly regarded a national debt, swelled to an amount unknown,—to an amount greater than the whole expense of our seven years' war; that they would have seen the election of President taken out of their hands [by the caucus]; that they would have borne with abuse and peculation through every department of the government,—and that the great Leviathan, which slept under all these grievances, should be roused into action by the Fifteen-Hundred-Dollar Law?"

Only with difficulty could members persuade themselves that the public anger was real. They could not at first conceive that the people should be seriously angry because Congress had thought proper to pay its members a sum not in itself extravagant or adequate to their services. Not until the members returned to their homes did they appreciate the force of

[1] Annals of Congress, 1816–1817, p. 501.

public feeling; but they soon felt themselves helpless to resist it. Richard M. Johnson and Henry Clay, the two most popular men in Kentucky, found their entire constituency attacking them. "When I went home," said Clay,[1] "I do not recollect to have met with one solitary individual of any description of party who was not opposed to the Act,—who did not, on some ground or other, think it an improper and unjust law." Benjamin Hardin,[2] another of the Kentucky victims, said: "If a man came into the county court to be appointed a constable or surveyor of the road, he entered his solemn protest against the Compensation Law. If a petty demagogue wanted to get into the legislature, he must post up, or put in the newspapers, his protest against it."

"There was at first a violent excitement," said Philip P. Barbour of Virginia;[3] "gentlemen might call it, if they pleased, a storm. But that storm, even when its fury abated, subsided into a fixed and settled discontent at the measure; it met the disapprobation and excited the discontent of the grave, the reflecting, and the deliberate; and such he believed to be the case with an immense majority of the American people."

Grand juries denounced it in Vermont and Georgia; the State legislature denounced it in Massachusetts; town-meetings protested against it; county conventions sat upon it; all classes and parties united in condemning it, and the brunt of this sweeping popular reproval fell upon the House of Representatives. Close as the House stood to the people, its want of popularity was evident,—as Calhoun, with his usual insight, bore witness. The House had as a body few friends and no protection against popular tempests. The first to suffer, it was always the last to escape. One after another the weaker members gave way, and either declined re-election or were not re-elected. The chiefs succeeded for the most part by personal popularity in maintaining their hold on their districts, although several leading members lost their seats.

Even against so feeble and factious a body as the Thirteenth

[1] Annals of Congress, 1816–1817, p. 497.
[2] Annals of Congress, 1816–1817, p. 535.
[3] Annals of Congress, 1816–1817, p. 517.

Congress, such condemnation would have seemed exceptional; but the peculiarity that made this popular reproof singular and suggestive was the popular admission that the Fourteenth Congress, for ability, energy, and usefulness, never had a superior, and perhaps, since the First Congress, never an equal. Such abilities were uncommon in any legislative body, American or European. Since Federalist times no Congress had felt such a sense of its own strength, and such pride in its own superiority; none had filled so fully the popular ideal of what the people's representatives should be. That this remarkable body of men should have incurred almost instantly the severest popular rebuke ever visited on a House of Representatives, could not have been mere accident.

The politics of 1816 seemed absorbed in the Compensation Act, and in the union of parties to condemn their representatives. The Senate escaped serious censure; and President Madison, so far from being called to account for errors real or imaginary, seemed to enjoy popularity never before granted to any President at the expiration of his term. The apparent contentment was certainly not due to want of grievances. The internal taxes pressed hard on the people, especially in New England, where the suffering was general and in some places severe; but no popular cry for reduction of taxes disturbed the elections. No portion of the country seemed displeased that a fourth Virginian should be made President by the intrigues of a Congressional caucus. The State legislatures for the most part chose as usual the Presidential electors; and in December the public learned, almost without interest, that James Monroe had received one hundred and eighty-three electoral votes, representing sixteen States, while Rufus King had received thirty-four electoral votes, representing Massachusetts, Connecticut, and Delaware. Daniel D. Tompkins of New York was made Vice-President by the same process. Nothing in the elections, either for President or for Congress, showed that the people were disposed to scrutinize sharply the workings of any part of their government except the House of Representatives.

As the winter approached when Madison was to meet Congress for the last time, the sixteen years of his official service, which had been filled with excitement and violence, were ending in political stagnation. Party divisions had so nearly disappeared that nothing prevented the President elect from selecting as the head of his Cabinet the son of the last Federalist President, who had been the object of more violent attack from the Republican party than had been directed against any other Federalist. Old Republicans, like Macon and John Randolph, were at loss to know whether James Monroe or J. Q. Adams had departed farthest from their original starting-points. At times they charged one, at times the other, with desertion of principle; but on the whole their acts tended to betray a conviction that J. Q. Adams was still a Federalist in essentials, while Monroe had ceased to be an old Republican. In the political situation of 1817, if Jefferson and his contemporaries were right in their estimates, Federalist views of government were tending to prevail over the views of the Jeffersonian party.

With this tendency, the national prosperity and the state of the Treasury had much to do. Dallas carried out his purpose, and in October quitted the Treasury. In retiring, he left with the President a sketch of the condition of the finances such as no previous secretary had been so fortunate as to present. For the year ending Sept. 30, 1816, the receipts amounted to $47,670,000.[1] From the customs, which Dallas had estimated at $21,000,000, duties to the amount of $36,000,000 were received. A surplus of more than $20,000,000 was likely to accumulate in the Treasury before the close of the year.

Old ideas of economy and strict restraints on expenditure could not long maintain themselves in the presence of such an income; but besides the temptation to expand the sphere of government in expenditures, other influences were at work to establish Federalist principles in the system itself. Dallas remained in office chiefly in order to organize the Bank, and to render certain the resumption of specie payments. When he retired, in October, 1816, both objects were practically attained. His administration of the Treasury had then lasted two years. He found the government bankrupt; he left it with a surplus of twenty millions for the year. His measures not only relieved the country from financial disorders equalled

[1] Statement, etc.; State Papers, Finances, iii. 487.

only by those of the Revolutionary War, but also fixed the financial system in a firm groove for twenty years. He failed only in his attempt to obtain from Congress a larger degree of protection for domestic industries. Had his scheme of protection been adopted, possibly the violence of subsequent changes in revenue and legislation might have been moderated, and certainly the result could have been no more mischievous than it was.

Dallas retired to private life by his own wish, and the public three months afterward heard with surprise and regret the news of his sudden death. Like most of the men who rendered decisive services during the war, he received no public reward commensurate with his deserts. He fared better than Armstrong, who created the army; but even Gallatin, who shaped the diplomatic result, was content to retire into the comparative obscurity of the mission to Paris; while Perry and Macdonough, whose personal qualities had decided the fortunes of two campaigns and won the military basis on which peace could be negotiated, received no more reward than fell to the lot of third-rate men. In the case of Dallas and Gallatin, the apparent neglect was their own choice. Gallatin might have returned to the Treasury, but declined it; and the President transferred W. H. Crawford from the War Department to the charge of the finances, while Clay was offered the War Department in succession to Crawford.

These arrangements affected Madison but little. He had no longer an object to gain from the disposal of patronage, and he sought to smooth the path of his successor rather than to benefit himself. Few Presidents ever quitted office under circumstances so agreeable as those which surrounded Madison. During the last two years of his Administration almost every month brought some difficulty to an end, or accomplished some long-desired result. The restoration of the finances was perhaps his greatest source of satisfaction; but the steadiness with which the whole country, except New England, recovered prosperity and contentment afforded him a wider and more constant pleasure. The ravages of war left few traces. Even at Washington the new public buildings were pressed forward so rapidly that the effects of fire were no longer seen. The Capitol began to rise from its ruins. The new halls of

Congress promised to do honor to Madison's judgment. Benjamin Latrobe was the architect in charge; and his Representative Chamber, without reproducing that which Jefferson had helped to design, was dignified and worthy of its object. The old sandstone columns were replaced by another material. On the shore of the Potomac, near Leesburg, Latrobe noticed a conglomerate rock, containing rounded pebbles of various sizes and colors, and capable of being worked in large masses. His love of novelty led him to employ this conglomerate as an ornamental stone for the columns of the Hall of Representatives; and the effect was not without elegance.

Several years were still to pass before Congress occupied its permanent quarters, and Madison did not return to the White House; but the traces of national disaster disappeared in the process of reconstruction before he quitted the Presidency.

Surrounded by these pleasant conditions, Madison saw Congress assemble for the last time to listen to his requests. The Message which he sent to the legislature December 3 showed the extinction of party issues, and suggested no action that seemed likely to revive party disputes in any new form. The President expressed regret at the depression in shipping and manufactures, the branches of industry unfavorably affected by the peace. He suggested that Congress should consider especially the need of laws counteracting the exclusive navigation system of Great Britain. He recommended once more the time-worn subjects of the Militia and a National University. He asked for legislation against the Slave Trade, and urged a re-modification of the Judiciary. He requested Congress to create a new Executive department for Home or Interior Affairs, and to place the Attorney-General's office on the footing of a department. He gave a flattering account of the finances; and his Message closed with a panegyric on the people and their government, for seeking "by appeals to reason, and by its liberal examples, to infuse into the law which governs the civilized world a spirit which may diminish the frequency or circumscribe the calamities of war, and meliorate the social and beneficent relations of peace: a government, in a word, whose conduct, within and without, may bespeak the most noble of all ambitions,—that of promoting peace on earth and good-will to man."

For the moment, Congressmen were too much interested in their own quarrel to sympathize strongly with panegyrics on the people or their government. The members of the House returned to Washington mortified, angry, and defiant, disgusted alike with the public and with the public service. No sooner were the standing committees announced, December 4, than Richard M. Johnson moved for a special committee on the repeal of the Compensation Law, and supported his motion in an unusually elaborate speech, filled with argument, complaint, and irritation. The committee was appointed, — Johnson at its head; William Findley of Pennsylvania, second; Daniel Webster, third, with four other members. After twelve days' consideration, December 18, the committee presented a report, written by Webster, defending the Act, but recommending a return to the *per diem* system, in deference to the popular wish. The scale of the new allowance was left for Congress to determine.

Until this personal quarrel was discussed, no other business received attention. The debate — postponed till Jan. 14, 1817, to save the dignity of the House — lasted, to the exclusion of other business, until January 23. As an exhibition of personal and corporate character, it was entertaining; but it contained little of permanent interest or value. Calhoun, always above his subject, spoke with much force against yielding to popular outcry. "This House," he said, "is the foundation of the fabric of our liberty. So happy is its constitution, that in all instances of a general nature its duty and its interests are inseparable. If he understood correctly the structure of our government, the prevailing principle is not so much a balance of power, as a well-connected chain of responsibility. That responsibility commenced here, and this House is the centre of its operation." The idea that the people had "resolved the government into its original elements, and resumed to themselves their primitive power of legislation," was inconsistent with the idea that responsibility commenced and centred in the House. "Are we bound in all cases to do what is popular?" asked Calhoun. Could the House shift responsibility from itself to the people without destroying the foundation of the entire fabric?

Like most of Calhoun's speculations, this question could

receive its answer only in some distant future. The Compensation Law lowered permanently the self-respect of the House, which had already declined from the formation of the government. "Of that House," said Richard Henry Wilde of Georgia,[1] "he feared it might be said in the words of Claudian: 'A fronte recedant imperii.' Yes, sir, they were receding,—they had receded from the front of empire. That House, formerly the favorite of the American nation, the first and most important branch of the government, the immediate image of the people, had been losing, and continued to lose,—certainly by no fault of theirs, but by the working of causes not for him to develop,—that rank and power in the government originally belonging to them, and which others at their expense had been secretly acquiring." Yet the House, while repealing the law, refused to admit itself in the wrong. The law was repealed only so far as it applied to subsequent Congresses. Leaving its successors to fix whatever compensation they thought proper for their services, the Fourteenth Congress adhered to its own scale, and took the money it was expected to refund.

Having disposed of this personal affair, the House turned to serious business, and completed its remarkable career by enacting several measures of far-reaching importance.

The first of these measures was a Navigation Act, approved March 1, 1817, imposing on foreign vessels the same restrictions and prohibitions which were imposed by foreign nations on Americans. The second resembled the first in its object, but related only to the importation of plaster of Paris from Nova Scotia and New Brunswick. These two Acts began a struggle against the foreign navigation systems, which ended in their overthrow.

For the present the House postponed the establishment of an Interior Department, and allowed the Attorney-General to remain without an office or a clerk; but it passed an Act, approved March 3, 1817, concentrating in the Treasury the accounting business of government, and appointing four more auditors and one more comptroller for the purpose.

The fourth and most important measure that became law

[1] Annals of Congress, 1816–1817, p. 604.

was a Neutrality Act, approved March 3, 1817, which authorized collectors of customs to seize and detain "any vessel manifestly built for warlike purposes, . . . when the number of men shipped on board, or other circumstances, shall render it probable that such vessel is intended by the owner" to cruise against the commerce of a friendly State. Nearly fifty years were to pass before the people of the United States learned to realize the full importance of this Act, which laid the foundation for all the subsequent measures taken by the United States and Great Britain for preserving neutrality in their relations with warring countries.[1] The Neutrality Act of 1817 furnished the measure of neutral obligations.

Besides these important laws, the Fourteenth Congress passed another bill, which closed its own activity and that of President Madison. None of the previous measures bore any direct relation to party politics, either past or future; but the bill for internal improvements, which Congress passed and the President vetoed, was an event of no small meaning in party history.

Calhoun moved, December 16, "that a committee be appointed to inquire into the expediency of setting apart . . . a permanent fund for internal improvement." The committee was appointed the same day,—Calhoun, Sheffey of Virginia, Creighton of Ohio, Grosvenor of New York, and Ingham of Pennsylvania. December 23 Calhoun reported a bill[2] setting aside the bonus paid by the Bank, $1,500,000, and the future dividends from Bank stock, "as a fund for constructing roads and canals." February 4 he introduced his bill by a speech, showing that a system of internal improvements was necessary, and could, in certain instances, be created by the national government alone.

"Let it not be forgotten," said Calhoun,[3] with the air of sombre forecast which marked his mind and features, "let it be forever kept in mind, that the extent of our republic exposes us to the greatest of all calamities, next to the loss of liberty, and even to that in its consequence,— *disunion*.

[1] Dana's Wheaton, pp. 541–542, *note*.
[2] Annals of Congress, 1816–1817, p. 361.
[3] Annals of Congress, 1816–1817, pp. 853, 854.

We are great, and rapidly—I was about to say fearfully—growing. This is our pride and danger, our weakness and our strength. Little does he deserve to be intrusted with the liberties of this people, who does not raise his mind to these truths. We are under the most imperious obligation to counteract every tendency to disunion. . . . If . . . we permit a low, sordid, selfish, and sectional spirit to take possession of this House, this happy scene will vanish. We will divide, and in its consequences will follow misery and despotism."

The Constitutional question Calhoun reserved for the future; he thought it scarcely worth discussion, since the good sense of the States might be relied on to prevent practical evils. Nevertheless he discussed it, and drew sufficient authority from the "general welfare" clause, and from the power to "establish" post-roads. Granting that the Constitution was silent, he saw no restraint on Congress:—

"If we are restricted in the use of our money to the enumerated powers, on what principle can the purchase of Louisiana be justified? . . . If it cannot, then are we compelled either to deny that we had the power to purchase, or to strain some of the enumerated powers to prove our right."

The debate was interesting. Timothy Pickering, with the accumulated experience of seventy years, suggested that the right to regulate commerce among the several States, as in the case of light-houses and beacons, covered the proposed appropriation. Clay supported the bill with his usual energy, avowing that among his strongest motives was the wish to add this new distinction to the Fourteenth Congress, so harshly judged by the people. The chief Constitutional argument against the measure was made by Philip P. Barbour of Virginia; but other members opposed it on different grounds, and chiefly because as long as the internal taxes were still exacted, internal improvements should not be undertaken.

If the final vote was a correct test, Constitutional objections had but little weight with Congress. The bill passed the House, February 8, by the small majority of eighty-six to eighty-four. Of the minority no less than thirty-three were New England Federalists, whose opposition was founded on local and sectional reasons. From the slave States about forty-two votes were given against the bill; but a number of these were Federalist, and others were influenced by peculiar reasons. Two thirds of the Virginians voted against the bill; two thirds of the South Carolinians voted in its favor. Probably not more than twenty-five or thirty members, in the total number of one hundred and seventy, regarded the Constitutional difficulty as fatal to the bill.

In the Senate the bill passed by a vote of twenty to fifteen. Of the minority nine represented New England, and six represented Southern States. Every senator from the Middle States, as well as both senators from Virginia, supported the bill. Both senators from Massachusetts, the Republican Varnum and the Federalist Ashmun, opposed it; while Jeremiah Mason of New Hampshire and Rufus King of New York voted in its favor. The confusion of parties was extreme; but the States-rights school of old Republicans seemed to command not more than five or six votes in thirty-five.

The divisions on this bill seemed to leave no question that Congress by an overwhelming majority regarded the Constitutional point as settled. No one doubted that the Judiciary held the same opinion. The friends of the bill had reason to feel secure in regard to the Constitutional issue if on nothing else, and were the more disappointed when, March 3, President Madison exercised for the last time his official authority by returning the bill with a veto founded on Constitutional objections.

"The power to regulate commerce among the several States," he said, "cannot include a power to construct roads and canals, and to improve the navigation of water-courses in order to facilitate, improve, and secure such a commerce, without a latitude of construction departing from the ordinary import of the terms, strengthened by the known inconveniences which doubtless led to the grant of this remedial power to Congress. To refer the power in question to the clause 'to provide for the common defence and general welfare' would be contrary to the established and consistent rules of interpretation, as rendering the special and careful enumeration of powers which follow the clause nugatory and improper. Such a view of the Constitution would have the effect of giving to Congress a general power of legislation."

Every one who looked at the Constitution as an instrument or machine to be employed for the first time, must have admitted that Madison was right. Interpreted by no other aid than its own terms and the probable intent of a majority of the Convention which framed and the States which adopted it, the Constitution contained, and perhaps had been intended to contain, no power over internal improvements. The wide difference of opinion which so suddenly appeared between the President and Congress could not have been the result so much of different views of the Constitution, as of conclusions reached since the Constitution was framed. Congress held the bill to be Constitutional, not because it agreed with the strict interpretation of the text, but because it agreed with the interpretation which for sixteen years the Republican party, through Congress and Executive, had imposed upon the text.

On that point Calhoun's argument left no doubt; and his question—the last of his speculations pregnant with future history—echoed unanswered: "On what principle can the purchase of Louisiana be justified?" Dismissing all other violations or violence offered to the Constitution by President Madison or his predecessors,—such as the Bank, the Embargo, the Enforcement laws, the laws for the government of Orleans Territory, the seizure of West Florida,—Calhoun's question went to the heart of the issue between President and Congress.

From the Virginia side only one answer was possible. In returning to their early views of resistance to centralization, Madison and Jefferson must have maintained the invalidity of precedents to affect the Constitution. The veto seemed to create a new classification of public acts into such as were Constitutional; such as were unconstitutional, but still valid; and such as were both unconstitutional and invalid. The admitted validity of an act, like the purchase of Louisiana, even though it were acknowledged to be unconstitutional, did not create a precedent which authorized a repetition of a similar act.

Viewed only from a political standpoint, the veto marked the first decided reaction against the centralizing effect of the war. Unfortunately for the old Republican party, whose principles were thus for a second time to be adopted in appearance by a majority of the people, sixteen years had affected national character; and although precedents might not bind Congress or Executive, they marked the movement of society.

The Veto Message of March 3, 1817, was Madison's Farewell Address. The next day he surrendered to Monroe the powers of government, and soon afterward retired to Virginia, to pass, with his friend Jefferson, the remaining years of a long life, watching the results of his labors.

Chapter VII

THE UNION, which contained 5,300,000 inhabitants in 1800, numbered 7,240,000 in 1810, and 9,634,000 in 1820. At the close of Madison's Administration, in 1817, the population probably numbered not less than 8,750,000 persons. The average rate of annual increase was about three and five-tenths per cent, causing the population to double within twenty-three years.

The rate of increase was not uniform throughout the country, but the drift of population was well defined. In 1800 the five New England States contained about 1,240,000 persons. Virginia and North Carolina, united, then contained nearly 1,360,000, or ten per cent more than New England. In 1820 the two groups were still nearer equality. New England numbered about 1,665,000; the two Southern States numbered 1,700,000, or about two per cent more than New England. While these two groups, containing nearly half the population of the Union, increased only as one hundred to one hundred and twenty-nine, the middle group, comprising New York, New Jersey, and Pennsylvania, increased in the relation of one hundred to one hundred and ninety-two,—from 1,402,000 in 1800, to 2,696,000 in 1820. Their rate was about the average ratio for the Union; and the three Western States,—Ohio, Kentucky, and Tennessee,—grew proportionally faster. Their population of 370,000 in 1800 became 1,567,000 in 1820, in the ratio of one hundred to four hundred and twenty-three.

Careful study revealed a situation alarming to New England and Virginia. If only Connecticut, Rhode Island, and Massachusetts, without its district of Maine, were considered, a total population numbering 742,000 in 1800 increased only to 881,000 in 1820, or in the ratio of one hundred to one hundred and eighteen in twenty years. If only the white population of Virginia and North Carolina were taken into the estimate, omitting the negroes, 852,000 persons in 1800 increased to 1,022,000 in 1820, or in the ratio of one hundred to one hundred and twenty. Maryland showed much the same result, while Delaware, which rose from 64,270 in 1800 to

72,674 in 1810, remained stationary, numbering only 72,749 in 1820,—a gain of seventy-five persons in ten years. The white population showed a positive decrease, from 55,361 in 1810 to 55,282 in 1820.

Probably a census taken in 1817 would have given results still less favorable to the sea-coast. The war affected population more seriously than could have been reasonably expected, and stopped the growth of the large cities. New York in 1800 contained 60,000 persons; in 1810 it contained 96,400, but a corporation census of 1816 reported a population of only one hundred thousand, although two of the six years were years of peace and prosperity. From that time New York grew rapidly, numbering 124,000 in 1820,—a gain of about twenty-five per cent in four years. Even the interior town of Albany, which should have been stimulated by the war, and which increased four thousand in population between 1800 and 1810, increased only three thousand between 1810 and 1820. Philadelphia fared worse, for its population of 96,000 in 1810 grew only to 108,000 in 1820, and fell rapidly behind New York. Baltimore grew from 26,000 in 1800 to 46,000 in 1810, and numbered less than 63,000 in 1820. Boston suffered more than Baltimore; for its population, which numbered 24,000 in 1800, grew only to 32,000 in 1810, and numbered but 43,000 in 1820. Charleston was still more unfortunate. In 1800 its population numbered about eighteen thousand; in 1810, 24,700; in 1817 a local census reported a decrease to 23,950 inhabitants, and the national census of 1820 reported 24,780, or eighty persons more than in 1810. The town of Charleston and the State of Delaware increased together by the same numbers.

Although the war lasted less than three years, its effect was so great in checking the growth of the cities that during the period from 1810 to 1820 the urban population made no relative increase. During every other decennial period in the national history the city population grew more rapidly than that of the rural districts; but between 1810 and 1820 it remained stationary, at four and nine-tenths per cent of the entire population. While Boston, Philadelphia, and Charleston advanced slowly, and New York only doubled its population in twenty years, Western towns like Pittsburg, Cincinnati, and

Louisville grew rapidly and steadily, and even New Orleans, though exposed to capture, more than trebled in size; but the Western towns were still too small to rank as important. Even in 1820 the only cities which contained a white population of more than twenty thousand were New York, Philadelphia, Baltimore, and Boston.

The severest sufferers from this situation were the three southern States of New England,—Connecticut, Rhode Island, and Massachusetts, excluding the district of Maine, which was about to become a separate State. Fortunately the northern part of New England, notwithstanding the war, increased much more rapidly than the southern portion; but this increase was chiefly at the cost of Massachusetts, and returned little in comparison with the loss. The situation of Massachusetts and Connecticut was dark. Had not wealth increased more rapidly than population, Massachusetts would have stood on the verge of ruin; yet even from the economical point of view, the outlook was not wholly cheerful.

Judged by the reports of Massachusetts banks, the increase of wealth was surprising. The official returns of 1803, the first year when such returns were made, reported seven banks in the State, with a capital of $2,225,000 and deposits of $1,500,000. In June, 1816, twenty-five banks returned capital stock amounting nearly to $11,500,000 and deposits of $2,133,000. The deposits were then small, owing to the decline of industry and drain of specie that followed the peace, but the capital invested in banks had more than quintupled in thirteen years.

This multiplication was not a correct measure of the general increase in wealth. Indeed, the banks were in excess of the public wants after the peace, and their capital quickly shrunk from $11,500,000 in June, 1816, to $9,300,000 in June, 1817, a decline of nearly twenty per cent in a year. From that time it began to increase again, and held its improvement even in the disastrous year 1819. Assuming 1803 and 1817 as the true terms of the equation, the banking capital of Massachusetts increased in fourteen years from $2,225,000 to $9,300,000, or more than quadrupled.

Gauged by bank discounts the increase of wealth was not so great. In 1803 the debts due to the banks were returned at

$3,850,000; in June, 1817, they were $12,650,000. If the discounts showed the true growth of industry, the business of the State somewhat more than trebled in fourteen years. Probably the chief industries that used the increased banking capital were the new manufactures, for the older sources of Massachusetts wealth showed no equivalent gain. Tested by the imports, the improvement was moderate. In 1800 the gross amount of duties collected in Massachusetts was less than $3,200,000; in 1816 it somewhat exceeded $6,100,000, but had not permanently doubled in sixteen years. Tested by exports of domestic produce, Massachusetts showed no gain. In 1803 the value of such produce amounted to $5,400,000; in 1816, to $5,008,000.[1]

Other methods of calculating the increase of wealth gave equally contradictory results. The registered tonnage of Massachusetts engaged in foreign trade exceeded two hundred and ten thousand tons in 1800; in 1816 it was two hundred and seventy-four thousand tons. In the coasting-trade Massachusetts employed seventy-five thousand tons in 1800, and one hundred and twenty-nine thousand in 1816. The tonnage employed in the fisheries showed no growth. The shipping of Massachusetts seemed to indicate an increase of about forty per cent in sixteen years.

The system of direct taxation furnished another standard of comparison. In 1798 a valuation was made in certain States of houses and lands for direct taxes; another was made in 1813; a third in 1815. That of 1798 amounted to eighty-four million dollars for Massachusetts; that of 1813, to one hundred and forty-nine millions; that of 1815, to one hundred and forty-three millions,—a gain of seventy per cent in sixteen years; but such a valuation in 1817 would probably have shown a considerable loss on that of 1815.

Evidently the chief increase in wealth consisted in the growth of manufactures, but after the prostration of the manufacturing interest in 1816 no plausible estimate of their true value could be made, unless the bank discounts measured their progress. The result of the whole inquiry, though vague, suggested that wealth had increased in Massachusetts more

[1] Pitkin, pp. 55–56.

rapidly than population, and had possibly gained seventy or eighty per cent in sixteen years;[1] but in spite of this increase the State was in a pitiable situation. Neither steamboats, canals, nor roads could help it. Thousands of its citizens migrated to New York and Ohio, beyond the possibility of future advantage to the land they left. Manufactures were prostrate. Shipping was driven from the carrying trade. Taxation weighed far more heavily than ever before. A load of obloquy rested on the State on account of its war policy and the Hartford Convention. The national government treated it with severity, and refused to pay for the Massachusetts militia called into service by the President during the war, because the governor had refused to place them under national officers.

The condition of Massachusetts and Maine was a picture of New England. Democratic Rhode Island suffered equally with Federalist Connecticut. Maine, New Hampshire, and Vermont showed growth, but the chief possibility of replacing lost strength lay in immigration. During the European wars, no considerable number of immigrants were able to reach the United States; but immediately after the return of peace, emigration from Europe to America began on a scale as alarming to European governments as the movement to western New York and Ohio was alarming to the seaboard States of the Union. During the year 1817 twenty-two thousand immigrants were reported as entering the United States.[2] Twelve or fourteen thousand were probably Irish; four thousand were German. More than two thousand arrived in Boston, while about seven thousand landed in New York and the same number in Philadelphia. The greater part probably remained near where they landed, and in some degree supplied the loss of natives who went west. The rapid growth of the northern cities of the sea-coast began again only with the flood of immigration.

Although the three southern States of New England were the severest sufferers, the Virginia group—comprising Delaware, Maryland, Virginia, and North Carolina—escaped little better. In twenty years their white population increased nine-

[1] Pitkin, p. 373.
[2] Niles, 1817.

teen and five tenths per cent, while that of Massachusetts, Connecticut, and Rhode Island increased eighteen per cent. The wealth of Southern States consisted largely in slaves; and the negro population of the Virginia group increased about twenty-five per cent in numbers during the sixteen years from 1800 to 1816. The exports of domestic produce increased about forty per cent in value, comparing the average of 1801–1805 with that of 1815–1816. The net revenue collected in Virginia increased nearly seventy per cent, comparing the year 1815 with the average of the five years 1800–1804; while that collected in North Carolina more than doubled.

Measured by these standards, the growth of wealth in the Virginia group of States was not less rapid than in Massachusetts, and the same conclusion was established by other methods. In 1816 Virginia contained two State banks, with branches, which returned for January 1 a capital stock of $4,590,000, with a note circulation of $6,000,000, and deposits approaching $2,500,000. Their discounts amounted to $7,768,000 in January, 1816, and were contracted to $6,128,000 in the following month of November.[1] Although Virginia used only half the banking capital and credits required by Massachusetts, the rate of increase was equally rapid, and the tendency toward banking was decided. In 1817 the legislature created two new banks, one for the valley of Virginia, the other for western Virginia, with a capital stock of $600,000, and branches with capital stock of $100,000 for each. Between 1800 and 1817, banking capital exceeding five million dollars was created in Virginia, where none had existed before.

If the estimates made by Timothy Pitkin, the best statistician of the time, were correct, the returns for direct taxes showed a greater increase of wealth in Virginia than in Massachusetts.[2] The valuation of Virginia for 1799 was $71,000,000; that of 1815 was $165,000,000. The valuation of North Carolina in 1799 was $30,000,000; that of 1815 was $51,000,000. Maryland was estimated at $32,000,000 in 1799, at $106,000,000 in 1815. The average increase for the three States was in the ratio of one hundred to two hundred and

[1] Niles, ix. 427; xi. 196.
[2] Pitkin, p. 372.

forty, while that for Massachusetts, Rhode Island, and Connecticut was nearer one hundred to one hundred and seventy-five. The normal increase for the Union was in the ratio of one hundred to two hundred and sixty-three.

The result obtained from the estimates for direct taxes was affected by a doubt in regard to the correctness of the valuation of 1799, which was believed to have been too low in the Southern States; but the general conclusion could not be doubted that the Virginia group of States increased steadily in wealth. The rapidity of increase was concealed by an equally rapid impoverishment of the old tobacco-planting aristocracy, whose complaints drowned argument. As the lands of the ancient families became exhausted, the families themselves fell into poverty, or emigrated to the richer Ohio valley. Their decline or departure gave rise to many regrets and alarms. With the impressions thus created, the people associated the want of economical machinery as a cause of their backwardness, and became clamorous for roads, canals, and banks. The revolution in their ideas between 1800 and 1816 was complete.

The North Carolinians were first to denounce their old habits of indifference, and to declare their State in danger of ruin on that account. A committee of the State legislature reported Nov. 30, 1815, that vigorous measures for self-protection could no longer be postponed:[1] —

"With an extent of territory sufficient to maintain more than ten millions of inhabitants, . . . we can only boast of a population something less than six hundred thousand, and it is but too obvious that this population under the present state of things already approaches its maximum. Within twenty-five years past more than two hundred thousand of our inhabitants have removed to the waters of the Ohio, Tennessee, and Mobile; and it is mortifying to witness the fact that thousands of our wealthy and respectable citizens are annually moving to the West, . . . and that thousands of our poorer citizens follow them, being literally driven away by the prospect of poverty. In this state of things our agriculture is at a stand."

[1] Niles, ix., Supplement, p. 165.

The Virginians showed an equally strong sense of their perils. Twelve months after the North Carolina legislature took the matter in hand, a committee of the Virginia legislature in December, 1816, discussed the same topic and reached the same conclusion.[1] Although something had been done by corporations to open canals on the Potomac, the James River, and to the Dismal Swamp, the State of Virginia had in sixteen years made little advance in material welfare. While New England had built turnpikes wherever a profit could be expected, in Virginia, said the committee, "the turnpike-roads of the Commonwealth, except a few short passes of particular mountains and a road recently begun from Fredericksburg to the Blue Ridge, are confined principally to the county of Loudon, the adjacent counties of Fairfax, Fauquier, and Frederick, and to the vicinity of the seat of government." In other respects the situation was worse.

"While many other States," said the committee,[2] "have been advancing in wealth and numbers with a rapidity which has astonished themselves, the ancient Dominion and elder sister of the Union has remained stationary. A very large proportion of her western territory is yet unimproved, while a considerable part of her eastern has receded from its former opulence. How many sad spectacles do her low-lands present of wasted and deserted fields, of dwellings abandoned by their proprietors, of churches in ruins! The genius of her ancient hospitality, benumbed by the cold touch of penury, spreads his scanty hoard in naked halls, or seeks a coarser but more plenteous repast in the lonely cabins of the West. The fathers of the land are gone where another outlet to the ocean turns their thoughts from the place of their nativity, and their affections from the haunts of their youth."

Another committee reported to the House of Delegates Jan. 5, 1816, in favor of extending the banking system of the State.[3] The report used language new as an expression of Virginian opinions.

[1] Niles, ix., Supplement, p. 149.
[2] Niles, ix., Supplement, p. 150.
[3] Niles, ix., Supplement, p. 155.

"Your committee believe that a prejudice has gone abroad, which they confidently trust experience will prove to be unfounded even to the satisfaction of those by whom it is entertained, that the policy of Virginia is essentially hostile to commerce and to the rights of commercial men. Upon the removal of this prejudice must depend the future contributions of this Commonwealth toward the prosperity and glory if not the happiness and safety of the United States. Without the confidence of foreigners there can exist no foreign commerce. Without foreign commerce there can exist neither ships, seamen, nor a navy; and a tremendous lesson has taught Virginia that without a navy she can have no security for her repose."

Notwithstanding the gloom of these recitals, the evidence tended to show that while the white population of Virginia increased only about nineteen per cent in sixteen years, its wealth nearly doubled. Comparison with the quicker growth of the Middle States—New York, New Jersey, and Pennsylvania—caused much of the uneasiness felt by New England and Virginia. The banking capital of New York, which probably did not much exceed three million dollars in 1800, amounted in 1816 to nearly $19,000,000; that of Pennsylvania exceeded $16,000,000. The valuation of houses and lands for the direct tax rose in New York from $100,000,000 in 1799 to nearly $270,000,000 in 1815; and in Pennsylvania, from $102,000,000 in 1799 to $346,000,000 in 1815.[1] The net revenue collected in New York was $2,700,000 in 1800, and $14,500,000 in 1815; that collected in Pennsylvania was $1,350,000 in 1800, and $7,140,000 in 1815. This rate of increase did not extend to exports. The value of the domestic exports from New York in 1803 was about $7,500,000; in 1816 it exceeded $14,000,000; while the value of Pennsylvanian exports increased little,—being $4,021,000 in 1803 and $4,486,000 in 1816. The population of New York doubled while that of Massachusetts and Virginia hardly increased one third. Pennsylvania grew less rapidly in numbers, but still about twice as fast as New England.

Although this rate of progress seemed to leave New

[1] Pitkin, p. 372.

England and Virginia far behind the Middle States, it was less striking than the other economical changes already accomplished or foreseen. The movement of population or of wealth was not so important as the methods by which the movement was effected. The invention of the steamboat gave a decisive advantage to New York over every rival. Already in 1816 the system had united New York city so closely with distant places that a traveller could go from New York to Philadelphia by steamboat and stage in thirteen hours; or to Albany in twenty-four hours; and taking stage to Whitehall in twelve hours could reach Montreal in thirty hours, and go on to Quebec in twenty-four hours,—thus consuming about five and a half successive days in the long journey from Philadelphia to Quebec, sleeping comfortably on his way, and all at an expense of fifty dollars. This economy of time and money was a miracle; but New York could already foresee that it led to other advantages of immeasurable value. The steamboat gave impetus to travel, and was a blessing to travellers; but its solid gain for the prosperity of the United States lay not in passenger traffic so much as in freight, and New York was the natural centre of both.

While Pennsylvania, Virginia, and the Carolinas were building roads and canals across a hundred miles of mountains, only to reach at last an interior region which enjoyed an easier outlet for freight, New York had but to people a level and fertile district, nowhere fifty miles from navigable water, in order to reach the great Lake system, which had no natural outlet within the Union except through the city of New York. So obvious was the idea of a canal from the Lakes to the Hudson that it was never out of men's minds, even before the war; and no sooner did peace return than the scheme took large proportions. Active leaders of both political parties pressed the plan,—De Witt Clinton, Gouverneur Morris, and Peter B. Porter were all concerned in it; but the legislature and people then supposed that so vast an undertaking as a canal to connect Lake Erie with the ocean, national in character and military in its probable utility, required national aid. Supposing the Administration to be pledged to the policy outlined by Gallatin and approved by Jefferson in the Annual Message of 1806, the New York commissioners applied to Congress for assistance, and uniting with other local interests procured the passage of Calhoun's bill for internal improvements.

They were met by Madison's veto. This act, although at first it seemed to affect most the interests of New York, was in reality injurious only to the Southern States. Had the government lent its aid to the Erie Canal, it must have assisted similar schemes elsewhere, and in the end could hardly have refused to carry out Gallatin's plan of constructing canals from the Chesapeake to the Ohio, and from the Santee to the Tennessee River. The veto disappointed New York only for the moment, but was fatal to Southern hopes. After the first shock of discouragement, the New York legislature determined to persevere, and began the work without assistance. The legislature of Pennsylvania at the same time appropriated half a million dollars for roads and canals, and for improvements of river navigation, devoting nearly one hundred and fifty thousand dollars to aid the turnpike-road to Pittsburg. The fund established by the State of Ohio, as a condition of its admission to the Union, had in 1816 produced means to construct the National or Cumberland Road to the hundred and thirteenth mile. The indifference to internal improvements which had been so marked a popular trait in 1800, gave place to universal interest and activity in 1816; but the Middle States were far in advance of the Eastern and Southern in opening communications with the West; and New York, owing in no small degree to the veto, could already foresee the time when it would wrest from Pennsylvania the supply of the valley of the Ohio, while expanding new tributary territory to an indefinite extent along the Lakes.

When Madison retired from the Presidency, the limits of civilization, though rapidly advancing, were still marked by the Indian boundary, which extended from the western end of Lake Erie across Indiana, Kentucky, Tennessee, and the Southwestern territory. Only weak and helpless tribes remained east of the Mississippi, waiting until the whites should require the surrender of their lands; but the whites, already occupying land far in advance of their needs, could not yet take the whole. Not until 1826 were the Indian titles generally extinguished throughout Indiana. The military work was done, and the short space of sixteen years had practically accomplished the settlement of the whole country as far as the Mississippi; but another generation was needed in order to take what these sixteen years had won.

As population spread, the postal service struggled after it. Except on the Hudson River, steamboats were still irregular in their trips; and for this reason the mails continued to be carried on horseback through the interior. In 1801 the number of post-offices was 957; in 1817 it was 3,459. In 1801 the length of post-roads was less than 25,000 miles; in 1817 it was 52,689. In 1800 the gross receipts from postage were $280,000; in 1817 they slightly exceeded $1,000,000. In each case the increase much surpassed the ratio for population, and offered another means for forming some estimate of the increase of wealth. The Fourteenth Congress pressed the extension of post-routes in western New York, Ohio, and Indiana; they were already established beyond the Mississippi. Rapidity of motion was also increased on the main routes. From New York to Buffalo, four hundred and seventy-five miles, the traveller went at an average rate of five miles an hour, and, sleeping every night, he arrived in about four days. Between Philadelphia and Pittsburg, where no watercourse shortened the distance, the stage-coach consumed five and a half days, allowing for stoppage at night. These rates of travel were equal to those common on routes of similar length in Europe; but long after 1817 the mail from Washington to New Orleans, by a route 1,380 miles in length, required twenty-four days of travel.

Had the steamboat system been at once perfected, the mail could have been carried with much more rapidity; but the progress of the new invention was slow. After the trial trip of the "Clermont," Aug. 17, 1807, five years elapsed before the declaration of war; yet in 1812 New York possessed no other steam-line than the Albany packets. Steam-ferries plied to Hoboken, Amboy, and other places in the immediate neighborhood; but neither Newport, New London, nor New Haven enjoyed steam communication with New York until after the war. In the spring of 1813 eight or nine steamboats belonged to the city of New York, but only three, which ran to Albany, were more than ferries. At the same time Philadelphia possessed six such ferry-boats. From Baltimore a steamer ran to the head of Chesapeake Bay; but the southern coast and the town of Charleston saw no steamboat until a year after the war was ended.

The West was more favored. In 1811 a boat of four hundred tons was built at Pittsburg and sent down the river to New Orleans, where it plied between New Orleans and Natchez. Two more were built at the same place in 1813–1814; and one of them, the "Vesuvius," went down the river in the spring of 1814, rousing general interest in the midst of war by making the trip in nine days and a half, or two hundred and twenty-seven hours. The "Vesuvius" remained on the Mississippi for the next two years, but was burned with her cargo in the summer of 1816. By that time the world was thinking much of steamboats, and their use was rapidly extending, though regular trips were still uncommon except in the east.

The result of the sixteen years, considered only in the economical development of the Union, was decisive. Although population increased more rapidly than was usual in human experience, wealth accumulated still faster. From such statistics as the times afforded, a strong probability has been shown that while population doubled within twenty-three years, wealth doubled within twenty. Statistics covering the later period of national growth, warrant the belief that a valuation of $1,742,000,000 in 1800 corresponded to a valuation of $3,734,000,000 in 1820; and that if a valuation of $328 per capita is assumed for 1800, a valuation of $386 per capita may be estimated for 1820.[1]

These sixteen years set at rest the natural doubts that had attended the nation's birth. The rate of increase both in population and wealth was established and permanent, unless indeed it should become even more rapid. Every serious difficulty which seemed alarming to the people of the Union in 1800 had been removed or had sunk from notice in 1816. With the disappearance of every immediate peril, foreign or domestic, society could devote all its energies, intellectual and physical, to its favorite objects. This result was not the only or even the chief proof that economical progress was to be at least as rapid in the future as at the time when the nation had

[1] The Wealth of the United States and the Rate of its Increase. By Henry Gannett, International Review, May, 1882.

to struggle with political difficulties. Not only had the people during these sixteen years escaped from dangers, they had also found the means of supplying their chief needs. Besides clearing away every obstacle to the occupation and development of their continent as far as the Mississippi River, they created the steamboat, the most efficient instrument yet conceived for developing such a country. The continent lay before them, like an uncovered ore-bed. They could see, and they could even calculate with reasonable accuracy, the wealth it could be made to yield. With almost the certainty of a mathematical formula, knowing the rate of increase of population and of wealth, they could read in advance their economical history for at least a hundred years.

Chapter VIII

THE MOVEMENT of thought, more interesting than the movement of population or of wealth, was equally well defined. In the midst of political dissension and economical struggles, religion still took precedence; and the religious movement claimed notice not merely for its depth or for its universality, but also and especially for its direction. Religious interest and even excitement were seen almost everywhere, both in the older and in the newer parts of the country; and every such movement offered some means of studying or illustrating the development of national character. For the most part the tendency seemed emotional rather than intellectual; but in New England the old intellectual pre-eminence, which once marked the Congregational clergy, developed a quality both new and distinctive.

The Congregational clergy, battling with the innate vices of human nature, thought themselves obliged to press on their hearers the consequences of God's infinite wrath rather than those of his infinite love. They admitted that in a worldly sense they erred, and they did not deny that their preaching sometimes leaned to severity; but they would have been false to their charge and undeserving of their high character had they lost sight of their radical doctrine that every man was by nature personally depraved, and unless born again could not hope to see the kingdom of God. Many intellectual efforts had been made by many ages of men to escape the logic of this doctrine, but without success. The dogma and its consequences could not be abandoned without abandoning the Church.

From this painful dilemma a group of young Boston clergymen made a new attempt to find a path of escape. Their movement drew its inspiration from Harvard College, and was simultaneous with the sway of Jefferson's political ideas; but the relationship which existed between religious and political innovation was remote and wholly intellectual. Harvard College seemed to entertain no feeling toward Jefferson but antipathy, when in 1805 the corporation appointed Henry Ware, whose Unitarian tendencies were well known, to be

Hollis Professor of Theology. The Unitarianism of Henry Ware and his supporters implied at that time no well-defined idea beyond a qualified rejection of the Trinity, and a suggestion of what they thought a more comprehensible view of Christ's divine character; but it still subverted an essential dogma of the Church, and opened the way to heresy. The Calvinists could no longer regard Harvard College as a school proper for the training of clergy; and they were obliged to establish a new theological seminary, which they attached to a previously existing Academy at Andover, in Essex County, Massachusetts. The two branches of the New England Calvinists—known then as old Calvinism and Hopkinsianism—united in framing for the instructors of the Andover school a creed on the general foundation of the Westminster Assembly's Shorter Catechism, and thus provided for the future education of their clergy in express opposition to Unitarians and Universalists.

Thenceforward the theological school of Harvard College became more and more Unitarian. The Massachusetts parishes, divided between the two schools of theology, selected, as pleased a majority of their church-members, either Orthodox or Unitarian pastors; and while the larger number remained Calvinistic, though commonly preferring ministers who avoided controversy, the Boston parishes followed the Unitarian movement, and gradually filled their pulpits with young men. The Unitarian clergy soon won for themselves and for their city a name beyond proportion with their numbers.

Joseph Stevens Buckminster, the first, and while he lived the most influential, of these preachers, began his career in 1805 by accepting a call from one of the old Boston churches. He died in 1812 at the close of his twenty-eighth year. His influence was rather social and literary than theological or controversial. During his lifetime the Unitarian movement took no definite shape, except as a centre of revived interest in all that was then supposed to be best and purest in religious, literary, and artistic feeling. After his death, Unitarians learned to regard William Ellery Channing as their most promising leader. Channing had accepted the charge of a Boston church as early as 1803, and was about four years older than Buckminster. A third active member of the Boston clergy was Samuel Cooper Thacher, who took charge of a Boston parish in 1811, and was five years younger than Channing. In all, some seven or eight churches were then called Unitarian; but they professed no uniform creed, and probably no two clergymen or parishes agreed in their understanding of the precise difference between them and the Orthodox church. Shades of difference distinguished each Unitarian parish from every other, and the degree of their divergence from the old creed was a subject of constant interest and private discussion, although the whole body of churches, Congregational as well as Unitarian, remained in external repose.

The calm was not broken until the close of the war relieved New England from a political anxiety which for fifteen years had restrained internal dissensions. No sooner did peace restore to New England the natural course of its intellectual movement than the inevitable schism broke out. In June, 1815, the "Panoplist," the mouthpiece of the Congregational clergy, published an article charging the Unitarians with pursuing an unavowed propaganda, and calling upon the Church to refuse them communion. Channing and his friends thought the attack to require reply, and, after consultation, Channing published a "Letter to the Rev. Samuel C. Thacher," which began a discussion and a theological movement of no slight interest to American history.

Channing's theology at that time claimed no merit for originality. His letter to Thacher betrayed more temper than he would afterward have shown; but in no particular was he more earnest than in repelling the idea that he or his brethren were innovators. In whatever points they disagreed, they were most nearly unanimous in repudiating connection with the English Unitarians who denied the divinity of Christ. Channing declared "that a majority of our brethren believe that Jesus Christ is more than man; that he existed before the world; that he literally came from heaven to save our race; that he sustains other offices than those of a teacher and witness to the truth; and that he still acts for our benefit, and is our intercessor with the Father." So far was Channing from wishing to preach a new theology that he would gladly have accepted the old had he thought it intelligible:

"It is from deep conviction that I have stated once and again that the differences between Unitarians and Trinitarians lie more in sounds than in ideas; that a barbarous phraseology is the chief wall of partition between these classes of Christians; and that could Trinitarians tell us what they mean, their system would generally be found little else than a mystical form of the Unitarian doctrine."

Calvinists could not be blamed for thinking that their venerable creed, the painful outcome of the closest and most strenuous reasoning known in the Christian world, was entitled to more respect than to be called "little else than a mystical form of the Unitarian doctrine." The Unitarians themselves scarcely attempted to make the infinite more intelligible to the finite by any new phraseology. They avowed a dislike for dogma as their merit. During these early years they systematically avoided controversy; in the pulpit they never assailed and seldom mentioned other forms of Christian faith, or even the scheme of Trinity which caused their schism.

"So deeply are we convinced," said Channing's letter, "that the great end of preaching is to promote a spirit of love, a sober, righteous, and godly life, and that every doctrine is to be urged simply and exclusively for this end, that we have sacrificed our ease, and have chosen to be less striking preachers rather than to enter the lists of controversy."

Yet the popular dislike of Calvinistic severity could not wholly make good the want of doctrinal theology. The Unitarian clergy, however unwilling to widen the breach between themselves and the old Church, were ill at ease under the challenges of Orthodox critics, and could not escape the necessity of defining their belief.

"According to your own concession," rejoined Dr. Samuel Worcester to Channing's letter, "the party in whose behalf you plead generally deny the essential divinity of the Saviour, and hold him to be a being entirely 'distinct from God,' entirely 'dependent,'—in other words, a mere creature. . . . You doubtless do not suppose that by any mere creature atonement could be made for the sins of an apostate world of sufficient merit for the pardon, sanctification, and eternal salvation of all who should trust in him; therefore if you hold to atonement in any sense, yet unquestionably not in the sense of a proper propitiatory sacrifice. Upon this denial of atonement must follow of course the denial of pardon procured by the blood of Christ, of justification through faith in him, of redemption from eternal death unto everlasting life by him. Connected, and generally if not invariably concomitant, with the denial of these doctrines is a denial of the Holy Spirit in his personal character and offices, and of the renewal of mankind unto holiness by his sovereign agency, as held by Orthodox Christians. Now, sir, are these small and trivial points of difference between you and us?"

Channing protested against these inferences; but he did not deny—indeed, he affirmed—that Unitarians regarded dogma as unnecessary to salvation. "In our judgment of professed Christians," he replied, " we are guided more by their temper and lives than by any peculiarities of opinion. We lay it down as a great and indisputable opinion, clear as the sun at noonday, that the great end for which Christian truth is revealed is the sanctification of the soul, the formation of the Christian character; and wherever we see the marks of this character displayed in a professed disciple of Jesus, we hope, and rejoice to hope, that he has received all the truth which is necessary to his salvation." The hope might help to soothe anxiety and distress, but it defied conclusions reached by the most anxious and often renewed labors of churchmen for eighteen hundred years. Something more than a hope was necessary as the foundation of a faith.

Not until the year 1819, did Channing quit the cautious attitude he at first assumed. Then, in his "Sermon on the Ordination of Jared Sparks" at Baltimore, he accepted the obligation to define his relation to Christian doctrine, and with the support of Andrews Norton, Henry Ware, and other Unitarian clergymen gave a doctrinal character to the movement. With this phase of his influence the present story has nothing to do. In the intellectual development of the country, the earlier stage of Unitarianism was more interesting than the later, for it marked a general tendency of national thought. At a time when Boston grew little in population and but moderately in wealth, and when it was regarded with antipathy, both political and religious, by a vast majority of the American people, its society had never been so agreeable or so fecund. No such display of fresh and winning genius had yet been seen in America as was offered by the genial outburst of intellectual activity in the early days of the Unitarian schism. No more was heard of the Westminster doctrine that man had lost all ability of will to any spiritual good accompanying salvation, but was dead in sin. So strong was the reaction against old dogmas that for thirty years society seemed less likely to resume the ancient faith in the Christian Trinity than to establish a new Trinity, in which a deified humanity should have place. Under the influence of Channing and his friends, human nature was adorned with virtues hardly suspected before, and with hopes of perfection on earth altogether strange to theology. The Church then charmed. The worth of man became under Channing's teachings a source of pride and joy, with such insistence as to cause his hearers at last to recall, almost with a sense of relief, that the Saviour himself had been content to regard them only as of more value than many sparrows.

The most remarkable quality of Unitarianism was its high social and intellectual character. The other more popular religious movements followed for the most part a less ambitious path, but were marked by the same humanitarian tendency. In contrast with old stringency of thought, the religious activity of the epoch showed warmth of emotion. The elder Buckminster, a consistent Calvinist clergyman, settled at Portsmouth in New Hampshire, while greatly distressed by his son's leanings toward loose theology, was at the same time obliged to witness the success of other opinions, which he thought monstrous, preached by Hosea Ballou, an active minister in the same town. This new doctrine, which took the name of Universalism, held as an article of faith "that there is one God, whose nature is love, revealed in one Lord Jesus Christ, by one Holy Spirit of grace, who will finally restore the whole family of mankind to holiness and happiness." In former times any one who had publicly professed belief in universal salvation would not have been regarded as a Christian. With equal propriety he might have preached the divinity of Ammon or Diana. To the old theology one god was as strange as the other; and so deeply impressed was Dr. Buckminster with this conviction, that he felt himself constrained in the year 1809 to warn Hosea Ballou of his error, in a letter pathetic for its conscientious self-restraint. Yet the Universalists steadily grew in numbers and respectability, spreading from State to State under Ballou's guidance, until they became as well-established and as respectable a church as that to which Buckminster belonged.

A phenomenon still more curious was seen in the same year, 1809, in western Pennsylvania. Near the banks of the Monongahela, in Washington County, a divergent branch of Scotch Presbyterianism established a small church, and under the guidance of Thomas Campbell, a recent emigrant from Scotland, issued, Sept. 7, 1809, a Declaration:

> "Being well aware from sad experience of the heinous nature and pernicious tendency of religious controversy among Christians, tired and sick of the bitter jarrings and janglings of a party spirit, we would desire to be at rest; and were it possible, would also desire to adopt and recommend such measures as would give rest to our brethren throughout all the churches, as would restore unity, peace, and purity to the whole Church of God. This desirable rest, however, we utterly despair either to find for ourselves, or to be able to recommend to our brethren, by continuing amid the diversity and rancor of party contentions the varying uncertainty and clashings of human opinions; nor indeed can we reasonably expect to find it anywhere but in Christ and his simple word, which is the same yesterday, to-day, and forever. Our desire, therefore, for ourselves and our brethren would be that rejecting human opinions and the inventions of men as of any authority, or as having any place in the Church of God, we might forever cease from further contentions about such things, returning to and holding fast by the original standard."

Campbell's Declaration expressed so wide a popular want that his church, in a few years, became one of the largest branches of the great Baptist persuasion. Perhaps in these instances of rapid popular grouping, love of peace was to some extent supplemented by jealousy of learning, and showed as much spirit of social independence as of religious instinct. The growth of vast popular sects in a democratic community might testify to intellectual stagnation as well as to religious or social earnestness; but whatever was the amount of thought involved in such movements, one character was common to them all, as well as to the Unitarians,—they agreed in relaxing the strictness of theological reasoning. Channing united with Campbell in suggesting that the Church should ignore what it could not comprehend. In a popular and voluntary form they proposed self-restraints which should have the same effect as the formal restraints of the hierarchies. "Rejecting," like Campbell, "human opinions and the inventions of men,"—preaching, like Channing and Ballou, "that there is one God, whose nature is love," and that doctrine was useless except to promote a spirit of love,—they founded new churches on what seemed to resemble an argument that the intellectual difficulties in their path must be unessential because they were insuperable.

Wide as the impulse was to escape the rigor of bonds and relax the severity of thought, organizations so deeply founded as the old churches were not capable of destruction. They had seen many similar human efforts, and felt certain that sooner or later such experiments must end in a return to the old standards. Even the Congregational Church of New England, though reduced in Boston to a shadow of its old authority, maintained itself at large against its swarm of enemies,— Unitarian, Universalist, Baptist, Methodist,—resisting, with force of character and reasoning, the looseness of doctrine and vagueness of thought which marked the time. Yale College remained true to it. Most of the parishes maintained their old relations. If the congregations in some instances crumbled away or failed to increase, the Church could still stand erect, and might reflect with astonishment on its own strength, which survived so long a series of shocks apparently fatal. For half a century the Congregational clergy had struggled to prevent innovation, while the people emigrated by hundreds of thousands in order to innovate. Obliged to insist on the infinite justice rather than on the infinite mercy of God, they shocked the instincts of the new generation, which wanted to enjoy worldly blessings without fear of future reckoning. Driven to bay by the deistic and utilitarian principles of Jefferson's democracy, they fell into the worldly error of defying the national instinct, pressing their resistance to the war until it amounted to treasonable conspiracy. The sudden peace swept away much that was respectable in the old society of America, but perhaps its noblest victim was the unity of the New England Church.

The Church, whether Catholic or Protestant, Lutheran or Calvinistic, always rested in the conviction that every divergence from the great highways of religious thought must be temporary, and that no permanent church was possible except on foundations already established; but the State stood in a position less self-confident. The old principles of government were less carefully developed, and Democrats in politics were more certain than Unitarians or Universalists in theology that their intellectual conclusions made a stride in the progress of thought. Yet the sixteen years with which the century opened were singularly barren of new political ideas. Apparently the extreme activity which marked the political speculations of the period between 1775 and 1800, both in America and in Europe, had exhausted the energy of society, for Americans showed interest only in the practical working of their experiments, and added nothing to the ideas that underlay them. With such political thought as society produced, these pages have been chiefly filled; the result has been told. The same tendency which in religion led to reaction against dogma, was shown in politics by general acquiescence in practices which left unsettled the disputed principles of government. No one could say with confidence what theory of the Constitution had prevailed. Neither party was satisfied, although both acquiesced. While the Legislative and Executive branches of the government acted on no fixed principle, but established precedents at variance with any consistent theory, the Judiciary rendered so few decisions that Constitutional law stood nearly still. Only at a later time did Chief-Justice Marshall begin his great series of judicial opinions,—McCulloch against the State of Maryland in 1819; Dartmouth College in the same year; Cohens against the State of Virginia in 1821. No sooner were these decisive rulings announced, than they roused the last combative energies of Jefferson against his old enemy the Judiciary: "That body, like gravity, ever acting, with noiseless foot and unalarming advance, gaining ground step by step, and holding what it gains, is engulfing insidiously the special governments."

Marshall had few occasions to decide Constitutional points during the Administrations of Jefferson and Madison, but the opinions he gave were emphatic. When Pennsylvania in 1809 resisted, in the case of Gideon Olmstead, a process of the Supreme Court, the chief-justice, without unnecessary words, declared that "if the legislatures of the several States may at will annul the judgments of the courts of the United States, and destroy the rights acquired under those judgments, the Constitution itself becomes a solemn mockery, and the nation is deprived of the means of enforcing its laws by the instrumentality of its own tribunals." Pennsylvania yielded; and Marshall, in the following year, carried a step further the authority of his court. He overthrew the favorite dogma of John Randolph and the party of States rights, so long and vehemently maintained in the Yazoo dispute.

The Yazoo claims came before the court in the case of Fletcher against Peck, argued first in 1809 by Luther Martin, J. Q. Adams, and Robert G. Harper; and again in 1810 by Martin, Harper, and Joseph Story. March 16, 1810, the chief-justice delivered the opinion. Declining, as "indecent in the extreme," to enter into an inquiry as to the corruption of "the sovereign power of a State," he dealt with the issue whether a legislature could annul rights vested in an individual by a law in its nature a contract.

> "It may well be doubted," he argued, " whether the nature of society and government does not prescribe some limits to the legislative power; and if any are to be prescribed, where are they to be found if the property of an individual, fairly and honestly acquired, may be seized without compensation? To the legislature all legislative power is granted; but the question whether the act of transferring the property of an individual to the public be in the

nature of the legislative power, is well worthy of serious reflection. It is the peculiar province of the legislature to prescribe general rules for the government of society: the application of those rules to individuals in society would seem to be the duty of other departments. How far the power of giving the law may involve every other power, in cases where the Constitution is silent, never has been and perhaps never can be definitely stated."

In the case under consideration, Marshall held that the Constitution was not silent. The provision that no State could pass any law impairing the obligation of contracts, as well as "the general principles which are common to our free institutions," restrained the State of Georgia from passing a law whereby the previous contract could be rendered void. His decision settled, as far as concerned the Judiciary, a point regarded as vital by the States-rights school. Four years afterward Congress gave the required compensation for the contract broken by Georgia.

The chief-justice rendered no more leading Constitutional decisions during Madison's term of office; but his influence was seen in a celebrated opinion delivered by Justice Story in 1816, in the case of Martin against Hunter's Lessee. There the court came in conflict with the State of Virginia. The Court of Appeals of that State refused to obey a mandate of the Supreme Court, alleging that the proceedings of the Supreme Court were *coram non judice*, or beyond its jurisdiction, being founded on section 25 of the Judiciary Act of 1789, which was unconstitutional in extending the appellate jurisdiction of the Supreme Court over the State courts.

The Court of Appeals was unfortunate in the moment of its resistance to the authority of the national courts. While the case was passing through its last stage peace was declared, and the national authority sprang into vigor unknown before. The chief-justice would not with his own hand humiliate the pride of the Court of Appeals, for which as a Virginian and a lawyer he could feel only deep respect. He devolved the unpleasant duty on young Justice Story, whose own State of Massachusetts was then far from being an object of jealousy to Virginia, and who, a Republican in politics, could not be prejudiced by party feeling against the Virginia doctrine. Much of the opinion bore the stamp of Marshall's mind; much showed the turn of Story's intelligence; yet the same principle lay beneath the whole, and no one could detect a divergence between the Federalism of the Virginia chief-justice and the Democracy of the Massachusetts lawyer.

"It has been argued," said the court, "that such an appellate jurisdiction over State courts is inconsistent with the genius of our governments and the spirit of the Constitution; that the latter was never designed to act upon State sovereignties, but only upon the people; and that if the power exists, it will materially impair the sovereignty of the States and the independence of their courts. We cannot yield to the force of this reasoning; it assumes principles which we cannot admit, and draws conclusions to which we do not yield our assent. It is a mistake that the Constitution was not designed to operate upon States in their corporate capacity. It is crowded with provisions which restrain or annul the sovereignty of the States in some of the highest branches of their prerogatives. . . . When, therefore, the States are stripped of some of the highest attributes of sovereignty, and the same are given to the United States; when the legislatures of the States are in some respects under the control of Congress, and in every case are, under the Constitution, bound by the paramount authority of the United States,—it is certainly difficult to support the argument that the appellate power over the decisions of State courts is contrary to the genius of our institutions."

So far were the political principles of the people from having united in a common understanding, that while the Supreme Court of the United States thus differed from the Virginia Court of Appeals in regard to the genius of the government and the spirit of the Constitution, Jefferson still publicly maintained that the national and state governments were "as independent, in fact, as different nations," and that the function of one was foreign, while that of the other was domestic. Madison still declared that Congress could not build a road or clear a watercourse; while Congress believed itself authorized to do both, and in that belief passed a law which Madison vetoed. In politics as in theology, the practical system which resulted from sixteen years of experience seemed to rest on the agreement not to press principles to a conclusion.

No new idea was brought forward, and the old ideas, though apparently incapable of existing together, continued to exist in rivalry like that of the dogmas which perplexed the theological world; but between the political and religious movement a distinct difference could be seen. The Church showed no tendency to unite in any creed or dogma,—indeed, religious society rather tended to more divisions; but in politics public opinion slowly moved in a fixed direction. The movement could not easily be measured, and was subject to reaction; but its reality was shown by the protests of Jefferson, the veto of Madison, and the decisions of the Supreme Court. No one doubted that a change had occurred since 1798. The favorite States-rights dogma of that time had suffered irreparable injury. For sixteen years the national government in all its branches had acted, without listening to remonstrance, on the rule that it was the rightful interpreter of its own powers. In this assumption the Executive, the Legislature, and the Judiciary had agreed. Massachusetts and Pennsylvania, as well as Virginia and Georgia, yielded. Louisiana had been bought and admitted into the Union; the Embargo had been enforced; one National Bank had been destroyed and another established; every essential function of a sovereignty had been performed, without an instance of failure, though not without question. However unwilling the minority might be to admit in theory the overthrow of their principles, every citizen assented in daily practice to the rule that the national government alone interpreted its own powers in the last resort. From the moment the whole people learned to accept the practice, the dispute over theory lost importance, and the Virginia Resolutions of 1798 marked only a stage in the development of a sovereignty.

The nature of the sovereignty that was to be the result of American political experiment, the amount of originality which could be infused into an idea so old, was a matter for future history to settle. Many years were likely to elapse before the admitted practice of the government and people could be fully adopted into the substance of their law, but the process thus far had been rapid. In the brief space of thirty years, between 1787 and 1817,—a short generation,—the Union had passed through astonishing stages. Probably no great people ever grew more rapidly and became more mature in so short a time. The ideas of 1787 were antiquated in 1815, and lingered only in districts remote from active movement. The subsidence of interest in political theories was a measure of the change, marking the general drift of society toward practical devices for popular use, within popular intelligence. The only work that could be said to represent a school of thought in politics was written by John Taylor of Caroline, and was probably never read,—or if read, certainly never understood,—north of Baltimore by any but curious and somewhat deep students, although to them it had value.

John Taylor of Caroline might without irreverence be described as a *vox clamantis*,—the voice of one crying in the wilderness. Regarded as a political thinker of the first rank by Jefferson, Monroe, John Randolph, and the Virginia school, he admitted, with the geniality of the class to which he belonged, that his disciples invariably deserted in practice the rules they praised in his teaching; but he continued to teach, and the further his scholars drifted from him the more publicly and profusely he wrote. His first large volume, "An Inquiry into the Principles and Policy of the Government of the United States," published in 1814, during the war, was in form an answer to John Adams's "Defence of the Constitutions" published in London twenty-five years before. In 1787 John Adams, like Jefferson, Hamilton, Madison, Jay, and other constitution-makers, might, without losing the interest of readers, indulge in speculations more or less visionary in regard to the future character of a nation yet in its cradle; but in 1814 the character of people and government was formed; the lines of their activity were fixed. A people which had in 1787 been indifferent or hostile to roads, banks, funded debt, and nationality, had become in 1815 habituated to ideas and machinery of the sort on a great scale. Monarchy or aristocracy no longer entered into the public mind as factors in future development. Yet Taylor resumed the discussions of 1787 as though the interval were a blank; and his only conclusion from the experience of thirty years was that both political parties were equally moving in a wrong direction.

"The two parties, called Republican and Federal," he concluded, "have hitherto undergone but one revolution. Yet each when in power preached Filmer's old doctrine of passive obedience in a new form, with considerable success; and each, out of power, strenuously controverted it. The party in power asserted that however absurd or slavish this doctrine was under other forms of the numerical analysis, the people under ours were *identified* (the new term to cog this old doctrine upon the United States) with the government; and that therefore an opposition to the government was an opposition to the nation itself. . . . This identifying doctrine . . . puts an end to the idea of a responsibility of the government to the nation; . . . it renders useless the freedom of speech and of the press; it converts the representative into the principal; it destroys the division of power between the people and the government, as being themselves indivisible; and in short it is inconsistent with every principle by which politicians and philosophers have hitherto defined a free government."

The principle to which Taylor so strenuously objected was nevertheless the chief political result of national experience. Somewhere or another a point was always reached where opposition became treasonable,—as Virginia, like Massachusetts, had learned both when in power and when out. Taylor's speculations ended only in an admission of their own practical sterility, and his suggestions for restraining the growth of authority assumed the possibility of returning to the conditions of 1787. Banks were his horror. Stocks and bonds, or paper evidences of indebtedness in any form, he thought destructive to sound principles of government. The Virginia and Kentucky Resolutions of 1798 were his best resource for the preservation of civil liberty. However well-founded his fears might be, his correctives could no longer be applied. Political philosophers of all ages were fond of devising systems for imaginary Republics, Utopias, and Oceanas, where practical difficulties could not stand in their way. Taylor was a political philosopher of the same school, and his Oceana on the banks of the Rappahannock was a reflection of his own virtues.

Chapter IX

SOCIETY SHOWED great interest in the statesmen or preachers who won its favor, and earnestly discussed the value of political or religious dogmas, without betraying a wish to subject itself ever again to the rigor of a strict creed in politics or religion. In a similar spirit it touched here and there, with a light hand, the wide circuit of what was called *belles lettres*, without showing severity either in taste or temper.

For the first four or five years of the century, Dennie's "Portfolio" contained almost everything that was produced in the United States under the form of light literature. The volumes of the "Portfolio" for that period had the merit of representing the literary efforts of the time, for Philadelphia insisted on no standard of taste so exacting as to exclude merit, or even dulness, in any literary form. Jacobins, as Dennie called Democrats, were not admitted into the circle of the "Portfolio;" but Jacobins rarely troubled themselves with *belles lettres*.

The "Portfolio" reflected a small literary class scattered throughout the country, remarkable chiefly for close adhesion to established English ideas. The English standard was then extravagantly Tory, and the American standard was the same. At first sight the impression was strange. A few years later, no ordinary reader could remember that ideas so illiberal had seriously prevailed among educated Americans. By an effort, elderly men could, in the next generation, recall a time when they had been taught that Oliver Cromwell was a monster of wickedness and hypocrisy; but they could hardly believe that at any period an American critic coldly qualified "Paradise Lost," and "Avenge, O Lord, thy slaughtered saints," as good poetry, though written by a Republican and an enemy of established order. This was the tone of Dennie's criticism, and so little was it confined to him that even young Buckminster, in his Phi Beta Kappa Oration of 1809, which was regarded as making almost an epoch in American literature, spoke of Milton's eyes as "quenched in the service of a vulgar and usurping faction," and of Milton's life as "a memorable instance of the temporary degradation of learning." Buckminster was then remonstrating against the influence of politics upon letters rather than expressing a political sentiment, but his illustration was colored by the general prejudices of British Toryism. Half a century before, Dr. Johnson had taken the tone of Tory patronage toward Milton's genius, and Johnson and Burke were still received in America as final authorities for correct opinion in morals, literature, and politics. The "Portfolio" regarded Johnson not only as a "superlative" moralist and politician, but also as a "sublime" critic and a "transcendent" poet. Burke and Cicero stood on the same level, as masters before whose authority criticism must silently bow.

Yet side by side with these conventional standards, the "Portfolio" showed tendencies which seemed inconsistent with conservatism,—a readiness to welcome literary innovations contradicting every established canon. No one would have supposed that the critic who accepted Johnson and Pope as transcendent poets, should also delight in Burns and Wordsworth; yet Dennie was unstinted in praise of poetry which, as literature, was hardly less revolutionary than the writings of Godwin in politics. Dennie lost no opportunity of praising Coleridge, and reprinted with enthusiasm the simplest ballads of Wordsworth. Moore was his personal friend, and Moore's verses his models. Wherever his political prejudices were untouched, he loved novelty. He seemed to respect classical authority only because it was established, but his literary instincts were broader than those of Jefferson.

The original matter of the "Portfolio" was naturally unequal, and for the most part hardly better than that of a college magazine. Dennie was apt to be commonplace, trivial, and dull. His humor was heavy and commonly coarse; he allowed himself entire freedom, and no little grossness of taste. Of scholarship, or scholarly criticism, his paper showed great want. He tried to instruct as well as to amuse, but society soon passed the stage to which his writing belonged. The circulation of the "Portfolio" probably never exceeded fifteen hundred copies, and Dennie constantly complained that the paper barely supported itself. When the Bostonians, in the year 1805, began to feel the spirit of literary ambition, they took at once a stride beyond Dennie's power, and established a monthly magazine called the "Anthology and Boston Review," which in 1806 numbered four hundred and forty subscribers. The undertaking was doubly remarkable; for the Anthology Society which supported the Review combined with it the collection of a library, limited at first to periodical publications, which expanded slowly into the large and useful library known as the Boston Athenæum. The Review and Library quickly became the centre of literary taste in Boston, and, in the words of Josiah Quincy many years afterward, might be considered as a revival of polite learning in America. The claim was not unreasonable, for the Review far surpassed any literary standards then existing in the United States, and was not much inferior to any in England; for the Edinburgh was established only in 1802, and the Quarterly not till 1809.

The Anthology Society, which accomplished the feat of giving to Boston for the first time the lead of American literary effort, consisted largely of clergymen, and represented, perhaps unintentionally, the coming Unitarian movement. Its president and controlling spirit had no sympathy with either division of the Congregational Church, but was a clergyman of the Church of England. John Sylvester John Gardiner, the rector of Trinity, occupied a peculiar position in Boston. Of American descent, but English birth and education, he was not prevented by the isolation of his clerical character from taking an active part in affairs, and his activity was sometimes greater than his discretion. His political sermons rivalled those of the Congregational ministers Osgood and Parish, in their violence against Jefferson and the national government; his Federalism was that of the Essex Junto, with a more decided leaning to disunion; but he was also an active and useful citizen, ready to take his share in every good work. When he became president of the Anthology Society, he was associated with a clergyman of Unitarian opinions as vice-president,—the Rev. William Emerson, a man of high reputation in his day, but better known in after years as the father of Ralph Waldo Emerson. The first editor was Samuel Cooper Thacher, to whom, ten years afterward, Channing addressed his earliest controversial letter. Young Buckminster and William Tudor, a Boston man, who for the next twenty years was active in the literary life of Massachusetts, were also original members. The staff of the "Anthology" was greatly superior to ordinary editorial resources; and in a short time the Review acquired a reputation for ability and sharpness of temper never wholly forgiven. Its unpopularity was the greater because its aggressiveness took the form of assaults on Calvinism, which earned the ill-will of the Congregational clergy.

Buckminster and Channing were the editor's closest friends, and their liberality of thought was remarkable for the time and place; yet the point from which the liberality of Boston started would have been regarded in most parts of the Union as conservative. Channing's fear of France and attachment to England were superstitious.

> "I will not say," began his Fast Day Sermon in 1810, "that the present age is as strongly marked or distinguished from all other ages as that in which Jesus Christ appeared; but with that single exception, perhaps the present age is the most eventful the world has ever known. We live in times which have no parallel in past ages; in times when the human character has almost assumed a new form; in times of peculiar calamity, of thick darkness, and almost of despair. . . . The danger is so vast, so awful, and so obvious, that the blindness, the indifference, which prevail argue infatuation, and give room for apprehension that nothing can rouse us to those efforts by which alone the danger can be averted. Am I asked what there is so peculiar and so tremendous in the times in which we live? . . . I answer: In the very heart of Europe, in the centre of the civilized world, a new power has suddenly arisen on the ruins of old institutions, peculiar in its character, and most ruinous in its influence."

While Channing felt for France the full horror of his Federalist principles, he regarded England with equivalent affection.

> "I feel a peculiar interest in England," he explained in a note appended to the Fast Day Sermon; "for I believe that there Christianity is exerting its best influences on the human character; that there the perfections of human nature,

wisdom, virtue, and piety are fostered by excellent institutions, and are producing the delightful fruits of domestic happiness, social order, and general prosperity."

The majority of Americans took a different view of the subject; but even those who most strongly agreed with Channing would have been first to avow that their prejudice was inveterate, and its consequences sweeping. Such a conviction admitted little room for liberalism where politics were, directly or remotely, involved. Literature bordered closely on politics, and the liberalism of Unitarian Boston was bounded even in literature by the limits of British sympathies. Buckminster's Phi Beta Kappa Oration of 1809 was as emphatic on this point as Channing's Fast Day Sermon of 1810 was outspoken in its political antipathies.

"It is our lot," said Buckminster, "to have been born in an age of tremendous revolution, and the world is yet covered with the wrecks of its ancient glory, especially of its literary renown. The fury of that storm which rose in France is passed and spent, but its effects have been felt through the whole system of liberal education. The foul spirit of innovation and sophistry has been seen wandering in the very groves of the Lyceum, and is not yet completely exorcised, though the spell is broken."

The liberalism of Boston began in a protest against "the foul spirit of innovation," and could hardly begin at any point more advanced. "Infidelity has had one triumph in our days, and we have seen learning as well as virtue trampled under the hoofs of its infuriated steeds, let loose by the hand of impiety." From this attitude of antipathy to innovation, the Unitarian movement began its attempts to innovate, and with astonishing rapidity passed through phases which might well have required ages of growth. In five years Channing began open attack upon the foundation, or what had hitherto been believed the foundation, of the Church; and from that moment innovation could no longer be regarded as foul.

Of the intellectual movement in all its new directions, Harvard College was the centre. Between 1805 and 1817 the college inspired the worn-out Federalism of Boston with life till then unimagined. Not only did it fill the pulpits with Buck-minsters, Channings, and Thachers, whose sermons were an unfailing interest, and whose society was a constant stimulus, but it also maintained a rivalry between the pulpit and the lecture-room. The choice of a new professor was as important and as much discussed as the choice of a new minister. No ordinary political event caused more social interest than the appointment of Henry Ware as Professor of Theology in 1805. In the following year J. Q. Adams was made Professor of Rhetoric, and delivered a course of lectures, which created the school of oratory to which Edward Everett's generation ad-hered. Four younger men, whose influence was greatly felt in their branches of instruction, received professorships in the next few years,—Jacob Bigelow, who was appointed Profes-sor of Medicine in 1813; Edward Everett, Greek Professor in 1815; John Collins Warren, Professor of Anatomy in the same year; and George Ticknor, Professor of *Belles Lettres* in 1816. In the small society of Boston, a city numbering hardly forty thousand persons, this activity of college and church pro-duced a new era. Where thirty-nine students a year had en-tered the college before 1800, an average number of sixty-six entered it during the war, and took degrees during the four or five subsequent years. Among them were names familiar to the literature and politics of the next half century. Besides Ticknor and Everett, in 1807 and 1811, Henry Ware graduated in 1812, and his brother William, the author of "Zenobia," in 1816; William Hickling Prescott, in 1814; J. G. Palfrey, in 1815; in 1817, George Bancroft and Caleb Cushing graduated, and Ralph Waldo Emerson entered the college. Boston also drew resources from other quarters, and perhaps showed no stronger proof of its vigor than when, in 1816, it attracted Daniel Webster from New Hampshire to identify himself with the intellect and interests of Massachusetts. Even by re-action the Unitarians stimulated Boston,—as when, a few years afterward, Lyman Beecher accepted the charge of a Bos-ton church in order to resist their encroachments.

The "Anthology," which marked the birth of the new lit-erary school, came in a few years to a natural end, but was revived in 1815 under the name of the "North American Re-view," by the exertions of William Tudor. The life of the new

Review belonged to a later period, and was shaped by other influences than those that surrounded the "Anthology." With the beginning of the next epoch, the provincial stage of the Boston school was closed. More and more its influence tended to become national, and even to affect other countries. Perhaps by a natural consequence rather than by coincidence, the close of the old period was marked by the appearance of a short original poem in the "North American Review" for September, 1817: —

> ". . . The hills,
> Rock-ribbed and ancient as the sun; the vales
> Stretching in pensive quietness between;
> The venerable woods; the floods that move
> In majesty, and the complaining brooks
> That wind among the meads and make them green, —
> Are but the solemn declarations all,
> Of the great tomb of man. The golden sun,
> The planets, all the infinite host of heaven
> Are glowing on the sad abodes of death
> Through the still lapse of ages. All that tread
> The globe are but a handful to the tribes
> That slumber in its bosom. Take the wings
> Of morning, and the Borean desert pierce;
> Or lose thyself in the continuous woods
> That veil Oregan, where he hears no sound
> Save his own dashings, — yet the dead are there;
> And millions in these solitudes, since first
> The flight of years began, have laid them down
> In their last sleep: the dead reign there alone.
> So shalt thou rest: and what if thou shalt fall
> Unnoticed by the living, and no friend
> Take note of thy departure? Thousands more
> Will share thy destiny. The tittering world
> Dance to the grave. The busy brood of care
> Plod on, and each one chases as before
> His favorite phantom. Yet all these shall leave
> Their mirth and their employments, and shall come
> And make their bed with thee."

The appearance of "Thanatopsis" and "Lines to a Water-fowl" in the early numbers of the "North American Review," while leaving no doubt that a new national literature was close at hand, proved also that it was not to be the product of a single source; for Bryant, though greatly tempted to join the Emersons, Channing, Dana, Allston, and Tudor in Boston, turned finally to New York, where influences of a different kind surrounded him. The Unitarian school could not but take a sober cast, and even its humor was sure to be tinged with sadness, sarcasm, or irony, or some serious purpose or passion; but New York contained no atmosphere in which such a society could thrive. Busy with the charge of practical work, — the development of industries continually exceeding their power of control, — the people of New York wanted amusement, and shunned what in Boston was considered as intellectual. Their tastes were gratified by the appearance of a writer whose first book created a school of literature as distinctly marked as the Unitarian school of Boston, and more decidedly original. "The History of New York, by Diedrich Knickerbocker," appeared in 1809, and stood alone. Other books of the time seemed to recognize some literary parentage. Channing and Buckminster were links in a chain of theologians and preachers. "Thanatopsis" evidently drew inspiration from Wordsworth. Diedrich Knickerbocker owed nothing to any living original.

The "History of New York" was worth more than passing notice. In the development of a national character, as well as of the literature that reflected it, humor was a trait of the utmost interest; and Washington Irving was immediately recognized as a humorist whose name, if he fulfilled the promise of his first attempt, would have a chance of passing into the society of Rabelais, Cervantes, Butler, and Sterne. Few literary tasks were more difficult than to burlesque without vulgarizing, and to satirize without malignity; yet Irving in his first effort succeeded in doing both. The old families, and serious students of colonial history, never quite forgave Irving for throwing an atmosphere of ridicule over the subject of their interest; but Diedrich Knickerbocker's History was so much more entertaining than ordinary histories, that even historians could be excused for regretting that it should not be true.

Yet the book reflected the political passions which marked the period of the Embargo. Besides the burlesque, the "History" contained satire; and perhaps its most marked trait was the good-nature which, at a time when bitterness was universal in politics, saved Irving's political satire from malignity. Irving meant that no one should mistake the character of the universal genius, Governor Wilhelmus Kieft, surnamed the Testy, who as a youth had made many curious investigations into the nature and operations of windmills, and who came well-nigh being smothered in a slough of unintelligible learning,—"a fearful peril, from the effects of which he never perfectly recovered."

> "No sooner had this bustling little man been blown by a whiff of fortune into the seat of government, than he called together his council and delivered a very animated speech on the affairs of the government; . . . and here he soon worked himself into a fearful rage against the Yankees, whom he compared to the Gauls who desolated Rome, and to the Goths and Vandals who overran the fairest plains of Europe. . . . Having thus artfully wrought up his tale of terror to a climax, he assumed a self-satisfied look, and declared with a nod of knowing import that he had taken measures to put a final stop to these encroachments,—that he had been obliged to have recourse to a dreadful engine of warfare, lately invented, awful in its effects but authorized by direful necessity; in a word, he was resolved to conquer the Yankees—by Proclamation."

Washington Irving's political relations were those commonly known as Burrite, through his brother Peter, who edited in Burr's interest the "Morning Chronicle." Antipathy to Jefferson was a natural result, and Irving's satire on the President was the more interesting because the subject offered temptations for ill-tempered sarcasm such as spoiled Federalist humor. The Knickerbocker sketch of Jefferson was worth comparing with Federalist modes of expressing the same ideas:—

> "The great defect of Wilhelmus Kieft's policy was that though no man could be more ready to stand forth in an

hour of emergency, yet he was so intent upon guarding the national pocket that he suffered the enemy to break its head. . . . All this was a remote consequence of his education at the Hague; where, having acquired a smattering of knowledge, he was ever a great conner of indexes, continually dipping into books without ever studying to the bottom of any subject, so that he had the scum of all kinds of authors fermenting in his pericranium. In some of these titlepage researches he unluckily stumbled over a grand political *cabalistic word*, which with his customary facility he immediately incorporated into his great scheme of government, to the irretrievable injury and delusion of the honest province of Nieuw Nederlands, and the eternal misleading of all experimental rulers."

Little was wanting to make such a sketch bitter; but Irving seemed to have the power of deadening venom by a mere trick of hand. Readers of the "History," after a few years had passed, rarely remembered the satire, or supposed that the story contained it. The humor and the style remained to characterize a school.

The originality of the Knickerbocker humor was the more remarkable because it was allowed to stand alone. Irving published nothing else of consequence until 1819, and then, abandoning his early style, inclined to imitate Addison and Steele, although his work was hardly the less original. Irving preceded Walter Scott, whose "Waverley" appeared in 1814, and "Guy Mannering" in 1815; and if either author could be said to influence the other, the influence of Diedrich Knickerbocker on Scott was more evident than that of "Waverley" on Irving.

In the face of the spontaneous burst of genius which at that moment gave to English literature and art a character distinct even in its own experience, Americans might have been excused for making no figure at all. Other periods produced one poet at a time, and measured originality by single poems; or satisfied their ambition by prose or painting of occasional merit. The nineteenth century began in England with genius as plenty as it was usually rare. To Beattie, Cowper, and Burns, succeeded Wordsworth, Coleridge, Scott, Byron,

Crabbe, Campbell, Charles Lamb, Moore, Shelley, and Keats. The splendor of this combination threw American and even French talent into the shade, and defied hope of rivalry; but the American mind, as far as it went, showed both freshness and originality. The divergence of American from English standards seemed insignificant to critics who required, as they commonly did, a national literature founded on some new conception, — such as the Shawanee or Aztecs could be supposed to suggest; but to those who expected only a slow variation from European types, the difference was well marked. Channing and Irving were American in literature, as Calhoun and Webster were American in politics. They were the product of influences as peculiar to the country as those which produced Fulton and his steamboat.

While Bryant published "Thanatopsis" and Irving made his studies for the "Sketch-Book," another American of genius perhaps superior to theirs—Washington Allston—was painting in London, before returning to pass the remainder of his life in the neighborhood of Boston and Harvard College. Between thirty and forty years of age, Allston was then in the prime of his powers; and even in a circle of artists which included Turner, Wilkie, Mulready, Constable, Callcott, Crome, Cotman, and a swarm of others equally famous, Allston was distinguished. Other Americans took rank in the same society. Leslie and Stuart Newton were adopted into it, and Copley died only in 1815, while Trumbull painted in London till 1816; but remarkable though they were for the quality of their art, they belonged to a British school, and could be claimed as American only by blood. Allston stood in a relation somewhat different. In part, his apparent Americanism was due to his later return, and to his identification with American society; but the return itself was probably caused by a peculiar bent of character. His mind was not wholly English.

Allston's art and his originality were not such as might have been expected from an American, or such as Americans were likely to admire; and the same might be said of Leslie and Stuart Newton. Perhaps the strongest instance of all was Edward Malbone, whose grace of execution was not more remarkable than his talent for elevating the subject of his exquisite work. So far from sharing the imagination of

Shawanee Indians or even of Democrats, these men instinctively reverted to the most refined and elevated schools of art. Not only did Allston show from the beginning of his career a passion for the nobler standards of his profession, but also for technical quality,—a taste less usual. Washington Irving met him in Rome in 1805, when both were unknown; and they became warm friends.

> "I do not think I have ever been more captivated on a first acquaintance," wrote Irving long afterward. "He was of a light and graceful form, with large blue eyes and black silken hair. Everything about him bespoke the man of intellect and refinement. . . . He was exquisitely sensitive to the graceful and the beautiful, and took great delight in paintings which excelled in color; yet he was strongly moved and aroused by objects of grandeur. I well recollect the admiration with which he contemplated the sublime statue of Moses, by Michael Angelo."

The same tastes characterized his life, and gave to his work a distinction that might be Italian, but was certainly not English or usual.

"It was Allston," said Leslie, " who first awakened what little sensibility I may possess to the beauties of color. For a long time I took the merit of the Venetians on trust, and if left to myself should have preferred works which I now feel to be comparatively worthless. I remember when the picture of 'The Ages' by Titian was first pointed out to me by Allston as an exquisite work, I thought he was laughing at me." Leslie, if not a great colorist, was seldom incorrect; Stuart Newton had a fine eye for color, and Malbone was emphatically a colorist; but Allston's sensibility to color was rare among artists, and the refinement of his mind was as unusual as the delicacy of his eye.

Allston was also singular in the liberality of his sympathies. "I am by nature, as it respects the arts, a wide liker," he said. In Rome he became acquainted with Coleridge; and the remark of Coleridge which seemed to make most impression on him in their walks "under the pines of the Villa Borghese" was evidently agreeable because it expressed his own feelings. "It was there he taught me this golden rule: never to judge of any work of art by its defects." His admiration for the classics did not prevent him from admiring his contemporaries; his journey through Switzerland not only showed him a new world of Nature, but also "the truth of Turner's Swiss scenes,—the poetic truth,—which none before or since have given." For a young American art-student in 1804, such sympathies were remarkable; not so much because they were correct, as because they were neither American nor English. Neither in America nor in Europe at that day could art-schools give to every young man, at the age of twenty-five, eyes to see the color of Titian, or imagination to feel the "poetic truth" of Turner.

Other painters, besides those whose names have been mentioned, were American or worked in America, as other writers besides Bryant and Irving, and other preachers besides Buckminster and Channing, were active in their professions; but for national comparisons, types alone serve. In the course of sixteen years certain Americans became distinguished. Among these, suitable for types, were Calhoun and Clay in Congress, Pinkney and Webster at the bar, Buckminster and Channing in the pulpit, Bryant and Irving in literature, Allston and Malbone in painting. These men varied greatly in character and qualities. Some possessed strength, and some showed more delicacy than vigor; some were humorists, and some were incapable of a thought that was not serious; but all were marked by a keen sense of form and style. So little was this quality expected, that the world inclined to regard them as un-American because of their refinement. Frenchmen and Italians, and even Englishmen who knew nothing of America but its wildness, were disappointed that American oratory should be only a variation from Fox and Burke; that American literature should reproduce Steele and Wordsworth; and that American art should, at its first bound, go back to the ideals of Raphael and Titian. The incongruity was evident. The Americans themselves called persistently for a statesmanship, religion, literature, and art which should be American; and they made a number of experiments to produce what they thought their ideals. In substance they continued to approve nothing which was not marked by style as its chief merit. The oratory of Webster and Calhoun, and even of John

Randolph bore the same general and common character of style. The poetry of Bryant, the humor of Irving, the sermons of Channing, and the painting of Allston were the objects of permanent approval to the national mind. Style remained its admiration, even when every newspaper protested against the imitation of outworn forms. Dennie and Jefferson, agreeing in nothing else, agreed in this; the South Carolinian Allston saw color as naturally as the New Englander Bryant heard rhythm; and a people which seemed devoid of sense or standards of beauty, showed more ambition than older societies to acquire both.

Nothing seemed more certain than that the Americans were not artistic, that they had as a people little instinct of beauty; but their intelligence in its higher as in its lower forms was both quick and refined. Such literature and art as they produced, showed qualities akin to those which produced the swift-sailing schooner, the triumph of naval architecture. If the artistic instinct weakened, the quickness of intelligence increased.

Chapter X

UNTIL 1815 nothing in the future of the American Union was regarded as settled. As late as January, 1815, division into several nationalities was still thought to be possible. Such a destiny, repeating the usual experience of history, was not necessarily more unfortunate than the career of a single nationality wholly American; for if the effects of divided nationality were certain to be unhappy, those of a single society with equal certainty defied experience or sound speculation. One uniform and harmonious system appealed to the imagination as a triumph of human progress, offering prospects of peace and ease, contentment and philanthropy, such as the world had not seen; but it invited dangers, formidable because unusual or altogether unknown. The corruption of such a system might prove to be proportionate with its dimensions, and uniformity might lead to evils as serious as were commonly ascribed to diversity.

The laws of human progress were matter not for dogmatic faith, but for study; and although society instinctively regarded small States, with their clashing interests and incessant wars, as the chief obstacle to improvement, such progress as the world knew had been coupled with those drawbacks. The few examples offered by history of great political societies, relieved from external competition or rivalry, were not commonly thought encouraging. War had been the severest test of political and social character, laying bare whatever was feeble, and calling out whatever was strong; and the effect of removing such a test was an untried problem.

In 1815 for the first time Americans ceased to doubt the path they were to follow. Not only was the unity of their nation established, but its probable divergence from older societies was also well defined. Already in 1817 the difference between Europe and America was decided. In politics the distinction was more evident than in social, religious, literary, or scientific directions; and the result was singular. For a time the aggressions of England and France forced the United States into a path that seemed to lead toward European methods of government; but the popular resistance, or inertia, was so great that the most popular party leaders failed to overcome it, and no sooner did foreign dangers disappear than the system began to revert to American practices; the national government tried to lay aside its assumed powers. When Madison vetoed the bill for internal improvements he could have had no other motive than that of restoring to the government, as far as possible, its original American character.

The result was not easy to understand in theory or to make efficient in practice; but while the drift of public opinion, and still more of practical necessity, drew the government slowly toward the European standard of true political sovereignty, nothing showed that the compromise, which must probably serve the public purpose, was to be European in form or feeling. As far as politics supplied a test, the national character had already diverged from any foreign type. Opinions might differ whether the political movement was progressive or retrograde, but in any case the American, in his political character, was a new variety of man.

The social movement was also decided. The war gave a severe shock to the Anglican sympathies of society, and peace seemed to widen the breach between European and American tastes. Interest in Europe languished after Napoleon's overthrow. France ceased to affect American opinion. England became an object of less alarm. Peace produced in the United States a social and economical revolution which greatly curtailed the influence of New England, and with it the social authority of Great Britain. The invention of the steamboat counterbalanced ocean commerce. The South and West gave to society a character more aggressively American than had been known before. That Europe, within certain limits, might tend toward American ideas was possible, but that America should under any circumstances follow the experiences of European development might thenceforward be reckoned as improbable. American character was formed, if not fixed.

The scientific interest of American history centred in national character, and in the workings of a society destined to become vast, in which individuals were important chiefly as types. Although this kind of interest was different from that of European history, it was at least as important to the world. Should history ever become a true science, it must expect to establish its laws, not from the complicated story of rival European nationalities, but from the economical evolution of a great democracy. North America was the most favorable field on the globe for the spread of a society so large, uniform, and isolated as to answer the purposes of science. There a single homogeneous society could easily attain proportions of three or four hundred million persons, under conditions of undisturbed growth.

In Europe or Asia, except perhaps in China, undisturbed social evolution had been unknown. Without disturbance, evolution seemed to cease. Wherever disturbance occurred, permanence was impossible. Every people in turn adapted itself to the law of necessity. Such a system as that of the United States could hardly have existed for half a century in Europe except under the protection of another power. In the fierce struggle characteristic of European society, systems were permanent in nothing except in the general law, that, whatever other character they might possess they must always be chiefly military.

The want of permanence was not the only or the most confusing obstacle to the treatment of European history as a science. The intensity of the struggle gave prominence to the individual, until the hero seemed all, society nothing; and what was worse for science, the men were far more interesting than the societies. In the dramatic view of history, the hero deserved more to be studied than the community to' which he belonged; in turth, he was the society, which existed only to produce him and to perish with him. Against such a view historians were among the last to protest, and protested but faintly when they did so at all. They felt as strongly as their audiences that the highest achievements were alone worth remembering either in history or in art, and that a reiteration of commonplaces was commonplace. With all the advantages of European movement and color, few historians succeeded in enlivening or dignifying the lack of motive, intelligence, and morality, the helplessness characteristic of many long periods in the face of crushing problems, and the futility of human efforts to escape from difficulties religious, political, and social. In a period extending over four or five thousand years, more or less capable of historical treatment, historians were content to illustrate here and there the most dramatic moments of the most striking communities. The hero was their favorite. War was the chief field of heroic action, and even the history of England was chiefly the story of war.

The history of the United States promised to be free from such disturbances. War counted for little, the hero for less; on the people alone the eye could permanently rest. The steady growth of a vast population without the social distinctions that confused other histories,—without kings, nobles, or armies; without church, traditions, and prejudices,—seemed a subject for the man of science rather than for dramatists or poets. To scientific treatment only one great obstacle existed. Americans, like Europeans, were not disposed to make of their history a mechanical evolution. They felt that they even more than other nations needed the heroic element, because they breathed an atmosphere of peace and industry where heroism could seldom be displayed; and in unconscious protest against their own social conditions they adorned with imaginary qualities scores of supposed leaders, whose only merit was their faculty of reflecting a popular trait. Instinctively they clung to ancient history as though conscious that of all misfortunes that could befall the national character, the greatest would be the loss of the established ideals which alone ennobled human weakness. Without heroes, the national character of the United States had few charms of imagination even to Americans.

Historians and readers maintained Old-World standards. No historian cared to hasten the coming of an epoch when man should study his own history in the same spirit and by the same methods with which he studied the formation of a crystal. Yet history had its scientific as well as its human side, and in American history the scientific interest was greater than the human. Elsewhere the student could study under better conditions the evolution of the individual, but nowhere could he study so well the evolution of a race. The interest of such a subject exceeded that of any other branch of science, for it brought mankind within sight of its own end.

Travellers in Switzerland who stepped across the Rhine where it flowed from its glacier could follow its course among

mediæval towns and feudal ruins, until it became a highway
for modern industry, and at last arrived at a permanent equilibrium in the ocean. American history followed the same
course. With prehistoric glaciers and mediæval feudalism the
story had little to do; but from the moment it came within
sight of the ocean it acquired interest almost painful. A child
could find his way in a river-valley, and a hoy could float on
the waters of Holland; but science alone could sound the
depths of the ocean, measure its currents, foretell its storms,
or fix its relations to the system of Nature. In a democratic
ocean science could see something ultimate. Man could go no
further. The atom might move, but the general equilibrium
could not change.

Whether the scientific or the heroic view were taken, in
either case the starting-point was the same, and the chief object of interest was to define national character. Whether the
figures of history were treated as heroes or as types, they must
be taken to represent the people. American types were especially worth study if they were to represent the greatest democratic evolution the world could know. Readers might judge
for themselves what share the individual possessed in creating
or shaping the nation; but whether it was small or great, the
nation could be understood only by studying the individual.
For that reason, in the story of Jefferson and Madison individuals retained their old interest as types of character, if not
as sources of power.

In the American character antipathy to war ranked first
among political traits. The majority of Americans regarded
war in a peculiar light, the consequence of comparative security. No European nation could have conducted a war, as the
people of America conducted the War of 1812. The possibility
of doing so without destruction explained the existence of the
national trait, and assured its continuance. In politics, the divergence of America from Europe perpetuated itself in the
popular instinct for peaceable methods. The Union took
shape originally on the general lines that divided the civil
from the military elements of the British constitution. The
party of Jefferson and Gallatin was founded on dislike of
every function of government necessary in a military system.
Although Jefferson carried his pacific theories to an extreme,

and brought about a military reaction, the reactionary movement was neither universal, violent, nor lasting; and society showed no sign of changing its convictions. With greater strength the country might acquire greater familiarity with warlike methods, but in the same degree was less likely to suffer any general change of habits. Nothing but prolonged intestine contests could convert the population of an entire continent into a race of warriors.

A people whose chief trait was antipathy to war, and to any system organized with military energy, could scarcely develop great results in national administration; yet the Americans prided themselves chiefly on their political capacity. Even the war did not undeceive them, although the incapacity brought into evidence by the war was undisputed, and was most remarkable among the communities which believed themselves to be most gifted with political sagacity. Virginia and Massachusetts by turns admitted failure in dealing with issues so simple that the newest societies, like Tennessee and Ohio, understood them by instinct. That incapacity in national politics should appear as a leading trait in American character was unexpected by Americans, but might naturally result from their conditions. The better test of American character was not political but social, and was to be found not in the government but in the people.

The sixteen years of Jefferson's and Madison's rule furnished international tests of popular intelligence upon which Americans could depend. The ocean was the only open field for competition among nations. Americans enjoyed there no natural or artificial advantages over Englishmen, Frenchmen, or Spaniards; indeed, all these countries possessed navies, resources, and experience greater than were to be found in the United States. Yet the Americans developed, in the course of twenty years, a surprising degree of skill in naval affairs. The evidence of their success was to be found nowhere so complete as in the avowals of Englishmen who knew best the history of naval progress. The American invention of the fast-sailing schooner or clipper was the more remarkable because, of all American inventions, this alone sprang from direct competition with Europe. During ten centuries of struggle the nations of Europe had labored to obtain superiority over each other in ship-construction, yet Americans instantly made improvements which gave them superiority, and which Europeans were unable immediately to imitate even after seeing them. Not only were American vessels better in model, faster in sailing, easier and quicker in handling, and more economical in working than the European, but they were also better equipped. The English complained as a grievance that the Americans adopted new and unwarranted devices in naval warfare; that their vessels were heavier and better constructed, and their missiles of unusual shape and improper use. The Americans resorted to expedients that had not been tried before, and excited a mixture of irritation and respect in the English service, until Yankee smartness became a national misdemeanor.

The English admitted themselves to be slow to change their habits, but the French were both quick and scientific; yet Americans did on the ocean what the French, under stronger inducements, failed to do. The French privateer preyed upon British commerce for twenty years without seriously injuring it; but no sooner did the American privateer sail from French ports, than the rates of insurance doubled in London, and an outcry for protection arose among English shippers which the Admiralty could not calm. The British newspapers were filled with assertions that the American cruiser was the superior of any vessel of its class, and threatened to overthrow England's supremacy on the ocean.

Another test of relative intelligence was furnished by the battles at sea. Instantly after the loss of the "Guerriere" the English discovered and complained that American gunnery was superior to their own. They explained their inferiority by the length of time that had elapsed since their navy had found on the ocean an enemy to fight. Every vestige of hostile fleets had been swept away, until, after the battle of Trafalgar, British frigates ceased practice with their guns. Doubtless the British navy had become somewhat careless in the absence of a dangerous enemy, but Englishmen were themselves aware that some other cause must have affected their losses. Nothing showed that Nelson's line-of-battle ships, frigates, or sloops were as a rule better fought than the "Macedonian" and "Java," the "Avon" and "Reindeer." Sir Howard Douglas, the chief authority on the subject, attempted in vain to explain British reverses by the deterioration of British gunnery. His analysis showed only that American gunnery was extraordinarily good. Of all vessels, the sloop-of-war,—on account of its smallness, its quick motion, and its more accurate armament of thirty-two-pound carronades,—offered the best test of relative gunnery, and Sir Howard Douglas in commenting upon the destruction of the "Peacock" and "Avon" could only say,—

> "In these two actions it is clear that the fire of the British vessels was thrown too high, and that the ordnance of their opponents were expressly and carefully aimed at and took effect chiefly in the hull."

The battle of the "Hornet" and "Penguin" as well as those of the "Reindeer" and "Avon," showed that the excellence of American gunnery continued till the close of the war. Whether at point-blank range or at long-distance practice, the Americans used guns as they had never been used at sea before.

None of the reports of former British victories showed that the British fire had been more destructive at any previous time than in 1812, and no report of any commander since the British navy existed showed so much damage inflicted on an opponent in so short a time as was proved to have been inflicted on themselves by the reports of British commanders in the American war. The strongest proof of American superiority was given by the best British officers, like Broke, who strained every nerve to maintain an equality with American gunnery. So instantaneous and energetic was the effort that, according to the British historian of the war, "a British forty-six-gun frigate of 1813 was half as effective again as a British forty-six-gun frigate of 1812;" and, as he justly said, "the slaughtered crews and the shattered hulks" of the captured British ships proved that no want of their old fighting qualities accounted for their repeated and almost habitual mortifications.[1]

Unwilling as the English were to admit the superior skill of

[1] James, pp. 525, 528.

Americans on the ocean, they did not hesitate to admit it, in certain respects, on land. The American rifle in American hands was affirmed to have no equal in the world. This admission could scarcely be withheld after the lists of killed and wounded which followed almost every battle; but the admission served to check a wider inquiry. In truth, the rifle played but a small part in the war. Winchester's men at the river Raisin may have owed their over-confidence, as the British Forty-first owed its losses, to that weapon, and at New Orleans five or six hundred of Coffee's men, who were out of range, were armed with the rifle; but the surprising losses of the British were commonly due to artillery and musketry fire. At New Orleans the artillery was chiefly engaged. The artillery battle of January 1, according to British accounts, amply proved the superiority of American gunnery on that occasion, which was probably the fairest test during the war. The battle of January 8 was also chiefly an artillery battle; the main British column never arrived within fair musket range; Pakenham was killed by a grape-shot, and the main column of his troops halted more than one hundred yards from the parapet.

The best test of British and American military qualities, both for men and weapons, was Scott's battle of Chippawa. Nothing intervened to throw a doubt over the fairness of the trial. Two parallel lines of regular soldiers, practically equal in numbers, armed with similar weapons, moved in close order toward each other, across a wide open plain, without cover or advantage of position, stopping at intervals to load and fire, until one line broke and retired. At the same time two three-gun batteries, the British being the heavier, maintained a steady fire from positions opposite each other. According to the reports, the two infantry lines in the centre never came nearer than eighty yards. Major-General Riall reported that then, owing to severe losses, his troops broke and could not be rallied. Comparison of the official reports showed that the British lost in killed and wounded four hundred and sixty-nine men; the Americans, two hundred and ninety-six. Some doubts always affect the returns of wounded, because the severity of the wound cannot be known; but dead men tell their own tale. Riall reported one hundred and forty-eight killed; Scott reported sixty-one. The severity of the losses showed that the battle was sharply contested, and proved the personal bravery of both armies. Marksmanship decided the result, and the returns proved that the American fire was superior to that of the British in the proportion of more than fifty per cent if estimated by the entire loss, and of two hundred and forty-two to one hundred if estimated by the deaths alone.

The conclusion seemed incredible, but it was supported by the results of the naval battles. The Americans showed superiority amounting in some cases to twice the efficiency of their enemies in the use of weapons. The best French critic of the naval war, Jurien de la Gravière said: "An enormous superiority in the rapidity and precision of their fire can alone explain the difference in the losses sustained by the combatants."[1] So far from denying this conclusion the British press constantly alleged it, and the British officers complained of it. The discovery caused great surprise, and in both British services much attention was at once directed to improvement in artillery and musketry. Nothing could exceed the frankness with which Englishmen avowed their inferiority. According to Sir Francis Head, "gunnery was in naval warfare in the extraordinary state of ignorance we have just described, when our lean children, the American people, taught us, rod in hand, our first lesson in the art." The English text-book on Naval Gunnery, written by Major-General Sir Howard Douglas immediately after the peace, devoted more attention to the short American war than to all the battles of Napoleon, and began by admitting that Great Britain had "entered with too great confidence on war with a marine much more expert than that of any of our European enemies." The admission appeared "objectionable" even to the author;[2] but he did not add, what was equally true, that it applied as well to the land as to the sea service.

No one questioned the bravery of the British forces, or the ease with which they often routed larger bodies of militia; but the losses they inflicted were rarely as great as those they suffered. Even at Bladensburg, where they met little resistance, their loss was several times greater than that of the Americans. At Plattsburg, where the intelligence and quickness of Mac-

[1] Guerres Maritimes, ii. 286, 287.
[2] Naval Gunnery (Second edition), p. 3.

donough and his men alone won the victory, his ships were in effect stationary batteries, and enjoyed the same superiority in gunnery. "The 'Saratoga,'" said his official report, "had fifty-five round-shot in her hull; the 'Confiance,' one hundred and five. The enemy's shot passed principally just over our heads, as there were not twenty whole hammocks in the nettings at the close of the action."

The greater skill of the Americans was not due to special training, for the British service was better trained in gunnery, as in everything else, than the motley armies and fleets that fought at New Orleans and on the Lakes. Critics constantly said that every American had learned from his childhood the use of the rifle, but he certainly had not learned to use cannon in shooting birds or hunting deer, and he knew less than the Englishman about the handling of artillery and muskets. As if to add unnecessary evidence, the battle of Chrystler's Farm proved only too well that this American efficiency was not confined to citizens of the United States.

Another significant result of the war was the sudden development of scientific engineering in the United States. This branch of the military service owed its efficiency and almost its existence to the military school at West Point, established in 1802. The school was at first much neglected by government. The number of graduates before the year 1812 was very small; but at the outbreak of the war the corps of engineers was already efficient. Its chief was Colonel Joseph Gardner Swift, of Massachusetts, the first graduate of the academy: Colonel Swift planned the defences of New York harbor. The lieutenant-colonel in 1812 was Walker Keith Armistead, of Virginia,—the third graduate, who planned the defences of Norfolk. Major William McRee, of North Carolina, became chief engineer to General Brown, and constructed the fortifications at Fort Erie, which cost the British General Gordon Drummond the loss of half his army, besides the mortification of defeat. Captain Eleazer Derby Wood, of New York, constructed Fort Meigs, which enabled Harrison to defeat the attack of Proctor in May, 1813. Captain Joseph Gilbert Totten, of New York, was chief engineer to General Izard at Plattsburg, where he directed the fortifications that stopped the advance of Prevost's great army. None of the works constructed by a graduate of West Point was captured by the enemy; and had an engineer been employed at Washington by Armstrong and Winder, the city would have been easily saved.

Perhaps without exaggeration the West Point Academy might be said to have decided, next to the navy, the result of the war. The works at New Orleans were simple in character, and as far as they were due to engineering skill were directed by Major Latour, a Frenchman; but the war was already ended when the battle of New Orleans was fought. During the critical campaign of 1814, the West Point engineers doubled the capacity of the little American army for resistance, and introduced a new and scientific character into American life.

In the application of science the steamboat was the most striking success; but Fulton's invention, however useful, was neither the most original nor the most ingenious of American efforts, nor did it offer the best example of popular characteristics. Perhaps Fulton's torpedo and Stevens's screw-propeller showed more originality than was proved by the "Clermont." The fast-sailing schooner with its pivot-gun—an invention that grew out of the common stock of nautical intelligence—best illustrated the character of the people.

That the individual should rise to a higher order either of intelligence or morality than had existed in former ages was not to be expected, for the United States offered less field for the development of individuality than had been offered by older and smaller societies. The chief function of the American Union was to raise the average standard of popular intelligence and well-being, and at the close of the War of 1812 the superior average intelligence of Americans was so far admitted that Yankee acuteness, or smartness, became a national reproach; but much doubt remained whether the intelligence belonged to a high order, or proved a high morality. From the earliest ages, shrewdness was associated with unscrupulousness; and Americans were freely charged with wanting honesty. The charge could neither be proved nor disproved. American morality was such as suited a people so endowed, and was high when compared with the morality of many older societies; but, like American intelligence, it discouraged excess. Probably the political morality shown by the government and by public men during the first sixteen years of the century offered a fair gauge of social morality. Like the character of the popular inventions, the character of the morals corresponded to the wants of a growing democratic society; but time alone could decide whether it would result in a high or a low national ideal.

Finer analysis showed other signs of divergence from ordinary standards. If Englishmen took pride in one trait more than in another, it was in the steady uniformity of their progress. The innovating and revolutionary quality of the French mind irritated them. America showed an un-English rapidity in movement. In politics, the American people between 1787 and 1817 accepted greater changes than had been known in England since 1688. In religion, the Unitarian movement of Boston and Harvard College would never have been possible in England, where the defection of Oxford or Cambridge, and the best educated society in the United Kingdom, would have shaken Church and State to their foundations. In literature the American school was chiefly remarkable for the rapidity with which it matured. The first book of Irving was a successful burlesque of his own ancestral history; the first poem of Bryant sang of the earth only as a universal tomb; the first preaching of Channing assumed to overthrow the Trinity; and the first paintings of Allston aspired to recover the ideal perfection of Raphael and Titian. In all these directions the American mind showed tendencies that surprised Englishmen more than they struck Americans. Allston defended himself from the criticism of friends who made complaint of his return to America. He found there, as he maintained, not only a growing taste for art, but "a quicker appreciation" of artistic effort than in any European land. If the highest intelligence of American society were to move with such rapidity, the time could not be far distant when it would pass into regions which England never liked to contemplate.

Another intellectual trait, as has been already noticed, was the disposition to relax severity. Between the theology of Jonathan Edwards and that of William Ellery Channing was an enormous gap, not only in doctrines but also in methods. Whatever might be thought of the conclusions reached by

Edwards and Hopkins, the force of their reasoning commanded respect. Not often had a more strenuous effort than theirs been made to ascertain God's will, and to follow it without regard to weaknesses of the flesh. The idea that the nature of God's attributes was to be preached only as subordinate to the improvement of man, agreed little with the spirit of their religion. The Unitarian and Universalist movements marked the beginning of an epoch when ethical and humanitarian ideas took the place of metaphysics, and even New England turned from contemplating the omnipotence of the Deity in order to praise the perfections of his creatures.

The spread of great popular sects like the Universalists and Campbellites, founded on assumptions such as no Orthodox theology could tolerate, showed a growing tendency to relaxation of thought in that direction. The struggle for existence was already mitigated, and the first effect of the change was seen in the increasing cheerfulness of religion. Only when men found their actual world almost a heaven, could they lose overpowering anxiety about the world to come. Life had taken a softer aspect, and as a consequence God was no longer terrible. Even the wicked became less mischievous in an atmosphere where virtue was easier than vice. Punishments seemed mild in a society where every offender could cast off his past, and create a new career. For the first time in history, great bodies of men turned away from their old religion, giving no better reason than that it required them to believe in a cruel Deity, and rejected necessary conclusions of theology because they were inconsistent with human self-esteem.

The same optimism marked the political movement. Society was weary of strife, and settled gladly into a political system which left every disputed point undetermined. The public seemed obstinate only in believing that all was for the best, as far as the United States were concerned, in the affairs of mankind. The contrast was great between this temper of mind and that in which the Constitution had been framed; but it was no greater than the contrast in the religious opinions of the two periods, while the same reaction against severity marked the new literature. The rapid accumulation of wealth and increase in physical comfort told the same story from the standpoint of economy. On every side society showed that ease was for a time to take the place of severity, and enjoyment was to have its full share in the future national existence.

The traits of intelligence, rapidity, and mildness seemed fixed in the national character as early as 1817, and were likely to become more marked as time should pass. A vast amount of conservatism still lingered among the people; but the future spirit of society could hardly fail to be intelligent, rapid in movement, and mild in method. Only in the distant future could serious change occur, and even then no return to European characteristics seemed likely. The American continent was happier in its conditions and easier in its resources than the regions of Europe and Asia, where Nature revelled in diversity and conflict. If at any time American character should change, it might as probably become sluggish as revert to the violence and extravagances of Old-World development. The inertia of several hundred million people, all formed in a similar social mould, was as likely to stifle energy as to stimulate evolution.

With the establishment of these conclusions, a new episode in American history began in 1815. New subjects demanded new treatment, no longer dramatic but steadily tending to become scientific. The traits of American character were fixed; the rate of physical and economical growth was established; and history, certain that at a given distance of time the Union would contain so many millions of people, with wealth valued at so many millions of dollars, became thenceforward chiefly concerned to know what kind of people these millions were to be. They were intelligent, but what paths would their intelligence select? They were quick, but what solution of insoluble problems would quickness hurry? They were scientific, and what control would their science exercise over their destiny? They were mild, but what corruptions would their relaxations bring? They were peaceful, but by what machinery were their corruptions to be purged? What interests were to vivify a society so vast and uniform? What ideals were to ennoble it? What object, besides physical content, must a democratic continent aspire to attain? For the treatment of such questions, history required another century of experience.

Index

ACTS OF CONGRESS, of July 14, 1798, concerning sedition, 395; of June 28, 1809, restoring intercourse with Great Britain, 58; of June 28, 1809, suspending the recruiting service, 62; of June 28, 1809, reducing the naval establishment, 62; of March 1, 1810, concerning the commercial intercourse between the United States and Great Britain and France, 137–40 (see Non-intercourse); of Feb. 14, 1810, appropriating sixty thousand dollars for the Cumberland Road, 148; of March 26, 1810, providing for the Third Census, 148; of March 30, 1810, appropriating five thousand dollars for experiments on the submarine torpedo, 148; of Feb. 20, 1811, admitting the State of Louisiana into the Union, 227; of Jan. 15, 1811, authorizing the occupation of East Florida, 228; of March 2, 1811, reviving non-intercourse against Great Britain, 235–46 (see Non-intercourse); of Jan. 11, 1812, to raise an additional military force of twenty-five thousand men, 396–97, 400; of Feb. 6, 1812, to accept volunteers, 404–06; of March 14, 1812, authorizing a loan for eleven million dollars, 411; of April 4, 1812, laying an embargo for ninety days, 433–34; of April 8, 1812, admitting the State of Louisiana into the Union, 456; of April 10, 1812, authorizing a call for one hundred thousand militia, 435; of April 14, 1812, to enlarge the limits of the State of Louisiana, 456; of May 14, 1812, to enlarge the boundaries of the Mississippi Territory, 456–57; of June 18, 1812, declaring war against Great Britain, 451–52; of July 1, 1812, doubling the duties on imports, 456; of Dec. 12, 1812, increasing the pay of the army, 598; of Jan. 20, 1813, increasing the bounty for recruits, 598; of Jan. 2, 1813, for building four seventy-fours and six frigates, 598; of Jan. 5, 1813, remitting fines, forfeitures, etc., 603; of Jan. 29, 1813, for raising twenty regiments for one year, 607; of Feb. 8, 1813, authorizing loan of sixteen millions, 606; of Feb. 24, 1813, for appointing six major-generals and six brigadiers, 607; of Feb. 25, 1813, authorizing the issue of Treasury notes for five millions, 606–07; of March 3, 1813, to provide for the supplies of the army, 607; of March 3, 1813, for the better organization of the general staff, 607; of March 3, 1813, for building six sloops-of-war, 607; of March 3, 1813, for the regulation of seamen on board the public and private vessels of the United States, 610–13; of Feb. 24, 1813, for appointing six major-generals and six brigadiers, 645–46; of March 3, 1813, for the regulation of seamen, etc., 652; of July 22, 1813, for the assessment and collection of direct taxes and internal revenue, 657, 668; of July 24, 1813, laying duties on carriages, 657, 668; of July 24, 1813, laying duties on licenses to distillers, 657, 668; of July 24, 1813, laying duties on sales at auction, 668; of July 29, 1813, laying a duty on imported salt, 668; of Aug. 2, 1813, to lay and collect a direct tax, 668; of Aug. 2, 1813, laying duties on licenses to retailers, 668; of Aug. 2, 1813, authorizing a loan for seven million, five hundred thousand dollars, 668; of Aug. 2, 1813, laying stamp duties, 668; of Aug. 2, 1813, to prohibit British licenses of trade, 668; secret, of Feb. 12, 1813, authorizing the President to seize West Florida, 765–66; of Aug. 2, 1813, reducing duties on prize goods, 852; of Aug. 3, 1813, allowing a bounty for prisoners taken by privateers, 852; of Aug. 2, 1813, extending the pension law to privateers, 852; of Dec. 17, 1813, laying an embargo, 874; of Jan. 25, 1814, relieving Nantucket from the Embargo Act, 874; of Jan. 27, 1814, for filling the ranks of the regular army, 882–84; of March 9, 1814, for building steam-batteries, 885; of March 24, 1814, authorizing a loan for twenty-five millions, 888; of March 4, 1814, authorizing the issue of ten million treasury notes, 888; of March 31, 1814, for the indemnification of Mississippi land claimants (Yazoo Act), 896; of Nov. 15, 1814, for building twenty 16-gun sloops-of-war, 1104; of Dec. 10, 1814, making further provision for filling the ranks of the army, 1095, 1099; of Dec. 21, 1814, laying additional duties on stills, 1081–82, 1086; of Dec. 23, 1814, doubling the internal revenue taxes, 1081–82, 1086; of Dec. 26, 1814, authorizing the issue of treasury notes to the amount of ten million five hundred thousand dollars, 1086; of Jan. 9, 1815, raising the direct tax to six million dollars, 1081–82, 1086; of Jan. 18, 1815, increasing the customs duties, 1082, 1086–87; of January 18, 1815, increasing the duties on household furniture, etc., 1082, 1086–87; of Jan. 27, 1815, authorizing the President to accept the services of State troops, 1105–06; of Feb. 7, 1815, creating a board of navy commissioners, 1104; of March 2, 1815, fixing the military peace establishment, 1238–39; of Feb. 27, 1815, concerning the flotilla service and gunboats, 1241; of March 3, 1815, for the support of the navy, 1241–42; of March 3, 1815, for protecting commerce against Algerine cruisers, 1241–42; of March 3, 1815, authorizing a loan for eighteen millions, 1250–51; of March 5, 1816, to reduce the amount of direct tax, 1258, 1259; of April 10, 1816, to incorporate the subscribers to the Bank of the United States, 1261–62; of April 27,

1816, to regulate the duties on imports, 1259–61; of April 29, 1816, for the gradual increase of the navy, 1263; of March 19, 1816, to change the mode of Compensation to the members of the Senate and House of Representatives, 1264–65; of April 19, 1816, to admit Indiana into the Union, 1263; of Feb. 6, 1817, to repeal the Compensation Act, 1280–81; of March 1, 1817, concerning the navigation of the United States, 1281; of March 3, 1817, to regulate the trade in plaster of Paris, 1281; of March 3, 1817, to provide for the prompt settlement of public accounts, 1281; of March 3, 1817, more effectually to preserve the neutral relations of the United States, 1282.

Act of the territorial legislature of Indiana, permitting the introduction of slaves, 350.

Acts of Parliament, of 6th Anne, naturalizing foreign seamen, 634–35; of 13th George II, naturalizing foreign seamen, 634–35.

Adair, John, senator from Kentucky, commands Kentucky militia at New Orleans, 1169; his dispute with Jackson, 1173, 1175, 1178; his account of the battle on the west bank, 1178.

Adams, John, expenditures of his administration, 141, 145, 146; Randolph's allusion to, in 1814, 1093; George Ticknor's account of his remarks on the Hartford Convention, 1121–22; his struggle for the fisheries in 1783, 1213–14; his "Defence of the Constitutions," 1314.

Adams, John Quincy, nominated as minister to Russia, 13; renominated and confirmed, 62; nominated and confirmed Justice of the Supreme Court, 249; sails for Russia, 283; arrives, 283; his negotiations in 1809, 283, 284–85; his negotiations in 1810, 285–89; his success, 290, 292; receives and forwards the Czar's offer of mediation, 639–40; nominated as joint envoy to treat of peace at St. Petersburg, 660; his appointment confirmed, 661; ignorant of the Czar's motives, 857; informed by Roumanzoff that England refused mediation, 858; designated as minister to London, 859; informed that the Czar would renew offer, 860; surprised by Roumanzoff's contradictions, 860; nominated and confirmed as joint envoy to treat of peace at Ghent, 875–76; chief of the commission, 1200; his difficulties, 1194–95; his account of the American note of August 24, 1198; despairs of peace, 1199; insists on defending the Florida policy, 1203–04; struggles to preserve the fisheries, 1213–17; his opinion of Gallatin and Bayard, 1218; appointed minister to England, 1243; appointed Secretary of State by Monroe, 1277; Professor of Rhetoric at Harvard College, 1322.

Adams, William, LL.D., British commissioner at Ghent, 1193; states British demands, 1197; on the fisheries, 1215.

"Adams," brig, launched at Detroit, 504; captured and recaptured, 539; destroyed, 539.

"Adams," 28-gun corvette, 551; at Washington, 658, 813, 819, 835; her cruise in 1814, 975; her destruction in the Penobscot, 975.

"Aeolus," case of, 482.

"Aeolus," British frigate, 554.

"Africa," British frigate, 554.

Alabama Indians, members of the Creek nation, 775; the centre of Creek fanaticism, 775–76; outbreak among, 778; escape of, 798.

Albany, headquarters of Dearborn, 504, 506–08; increase in population of, 1288.

"Alert," British sloop-of-war, her action with the "Essex," 319, 560.

"Alexander," Salem privateer captured, 847.

Alexander, Czar of Russia, with Napoleon at Erfurt, 20–21; his alliance with Napoleon, 96, 182; his approaching rupture with Napoleon, 267, 282–92; interferes for American commerce in Denmark, 284–85; his reply to Napoleon's demands, 286; gives special orders to release American ships, 287; his attachment to the United States, 287; his ukase on foreign trade, 289; offers mediation, 638–40, 648, 863; continues war in Germany, 854, 857–58; forced back to Silesia, 854; at Gitschin during armistice, 854; his difficulties and hesitations, 857–58; orders Nesselrode, July 9, 1813, to acquiesce in British refusal of mediation, 858, 860; orders Roumanzoff, July 20, to renew offer of mediation, 860, 863; acquiesces, August 20, in British refusal of mediation, 861; orders Roumanzoff, September 20, to renew offer of mediation, 862–63; his motives, 863–64; takes no notice of American commissioners, 862, 863–64; Andrew Jackson's report of, 1132; visits London, 1189; his conduct at Vienna, 1209.

Alexandria, town of, capitulates to British fleet, 1021.

Algiers, hostilities against, in 1815, 1241–42, 1253.

Alien and sedition laws. (See Acts of Congress.)

Allen, John, colonel of Kentucky Rifles, 679–80; killed at the River Raisin, 685.

Allen, W. H., commander in U. S. navy, 829; commands "Argus," 830; his action with the "Pelican," 831; killed, 831.

Allston, Washington, 1324; his art, 1327–29.

Amelia Island, 117, 764, 765, 766.

Amendments of the Constitution, proposed by the Hartford Convention, 1113–15.

Amherst, town-meeting address voted, January, 1814, 910.

Amherst, Jeffery, British major-general, his expedition against Montreal in 1760, 746.

"Anaconda," privateer, captured, 812, 847.

Anderson, Joseph, senator from Tennessee, defeats mission to Russia, 14; criticises Giles, 398; chairman of committee on declaration of war, 451; chairman of committee on Gallatin's mission, 660–61; member of committee on Swedish mission, 662; reports bill for seizing Florida, 765; votes against Giles's militia bill, 1098–99; appointed first comptroller, 1255.

Andover, foundation of theological school at, 1302.

"Annual Register," on the battle of Plattsburg, 988; on privateers in 1814, 1048.

"Anthology and Boston Review," 1319–20, 1322–23.

Arbuthnot, James, captain of British sloop-of-war "Avon," 1042; his report of action with the "Wasp," 1042–43.

"Argus," sloop-of-war, 550–51, 560, 562; carries W. H. Crawford to France, 830; captured by the "Pelican," 831–33; number of her prizes, 836, 849–50.

Armistead, George, major of Artillery Corps, commands Fort McHenry at Baltimore, 1027.

Armistead, Walker Keith, captain of U. S. engineers, fortifies Norfolk, 807, 1341.

Armistice, between Dearborn and Prevost, 519–20, 577; known to Brock, 524; disavowed by Madison, 534–35, 577, 1206; an advantage to Dearborn, 537; proposed by Monroe, 576–77; proposed by Admiral Warren, 585.

Armstrong, John, minister at Paris, his discontent, 23; his relations with Roumanzoff, 24; his complaints in 1809, 25–26; communicates Non-intercourse Act of March 1, 1809, 97, 166; his comments on the right of search, 104; his interview with King Louis of Holland, 105; his despatch on Fouché and Montalivet, 158–59; on Napoleon's motives, 159; his minute for a treaty, 161; his recall asked by Napoleon, 161, 162, 178; his remonstrance against the doctrine of

retaliation, 165; his report of Jan. 10, 1810, 168; inquires condition of revoking decrees, 178; communicates Non-intercourse Act of May 1, 1810, 178; his reception of Cadore's letter of Aug. 5, 1810, 183–84; returns to America, 184, 264; declares Napoleon's conditions to be not precedent, 184; silent about indemnity, 183–84, 207; Virginian jealousy of, 256; on Napoleon's designs on the Baltic, 289; becomes brigadier-general, 592; his attitude toward Monroe and Madison, 592; nominated Secretary of War, 593; his character, 593; a source of discord, 643; Dallas's opinion of, 643; nominates Monroe as major-general, 645; intends to command in chief, 645–46; alienates Gallatin, 647–48; comments on military diplomacy, 689; changes the plan of campaign in the northwest, 690–91, 698; comments on Harrison and Proctor, 690; comments on strategy, 718; his plan for attacking Kingston, in April, 1813, 723–24; his plan changed by Dearborn and Chauncey, 726; issues order dividing the Union into military districts, 728; removes Dearborn from command, 739; orders Wilkinson to Sackett's Harbor, 740, 770; orders Hampton to Plattsburg, 741; orders Wilkinson to attack Kingston, 744; goes to Sackett's Harbor, 747; his difficulties with Wilkinson, 747–49; orders Hampton to prepare winter quarters, 749; returns to Washington, 751, 759; his treatment of Hampton, 760; his orders for the defence of Fort George, 761; his responsibility for the loss of Fort Niagara, 762; dismisses Andrew Jackson's corps, 766; orders withdrawal from Amelia Island, 766; orders Wilkinson to seize Mobile, 769; his instructions on capitulation of the Creeks, 799–800; orders the confinement of hostages for naturalized soldiers, 868; disliked by Virginians, 897; disliked by Madison, 898; feared, 899; introduces new energy into the army, 899–901; his irregular conduct in the appointment of Andrew Jackson, 902; his removal urged by Monroe, 902–04; his share in the court-martial of William Hull, 904; his treatment of Hampton, 905; Wilkinson's remarks on, 921; orders Brown to attack Kingston, 925; his letter to Brown on mistakes, 925; his plan of a campaign at Niagara, 927–29; orders Brown to cross the Niagara River, 929; orders Izard to fortify Rouse's Point, 976; orders Izard to move his army to Sackett's Harbor, 976–78; his severity toward Izard, 989; his neglect of the defences of Washington, 996; his excuses, 996; his attitude toward the defence of Washington, 996; after August 20 alive to the situation, 1003; joins Winder on the morning of August 24, 1006; on Bladensburg battle-field, 1016; his conduct during the British advance, 1020; retires to Frederick, 1020–21; militia refuse to serve under, 1022; returns to Washington, 1023; goes to Baltimore and resigns, 1024; cause of his retirement, 1025; his provision for the defence of New Orleans, 1129–30; his criticism on Jackson's Pensacola campaign, 1139; his criticism on Jackson's first measures at New Orleans, 1142; his criticism on Jackson's loss of Fort Bowyer, 1183.

Army, enlistments stopped in June, 1809, 62; its condition in 1809, 116, 120–21; encampment of, at Terre aux Bœufs, 121–24; debate on reduction of, in 1810, 141–46; raised to thirty-five thousand men by Act of Jan. 11, 1812, 396–97, 399, 400; useless, 408; condition of, 492, 494; recruiting for, in May, 1812, 495; war establishment in 1812, corps of engineers, two regiments of light dragoons, one regiment of light artillery, three regiments of artillerists, one regiment of riflemen, and twenty-five regiments of infantry,—by law thirty-five thousand men, 496; enlistments in, 529,

567, 575; difficulty of filling ranks of, 570; acts of Congress for filling ranks of, 598, 599; war establishment of 1813, corps of engineers, two regiments of light dragoons, one regiment of light artillery, three regiments of artillery, one regiment of riflemen, and forty-four regiments of infantry, rangers, and sea-fencibles,—by law, fifty-eight thousand men, 607, 722–23, 882; Monroe's estimate of number of troops required in 1813, 722–23; actual force, in February, 1813, nineteen thousand men, 723, 882; mode of stating force of, in rank-and-file, 724; aggregate strength of, in February, June, and December, 1813, and January, 1814, 882; Troup's bill for filling ranks of, 882–83; bounty and pay of, 882–83; appropriations for, in 1814, 884; organization of, in 1814, 884; condition of, in 1814, 918; aggregate strength of, June and December, 1813, January, July, and September, 1814, 1060–61; weakness of, in the field, 1061; bounties for, paid in Massachusetts and Virginia, 1073; Monroe recommends raising to one hundred thousand men by draft, 1093; failure in recruiting service for, 1094; Congress unwilling to adopt efficacious measures for, 1094; Giles's bill for filling, 1095, 1099, 1103; "a mere handful of men," 1102; aggregate strength of, December, 1814, and Feb. 16, 1815, 1104; allotment of, to military districts, 1129–30; peace establishment discussed, 1239–41; peace establishment fixed at ten thousand men, 1241; reduction of, 1242. (See Artillery, Infantry, Engineers.)

Artillery, two regiments of, added in 1812, 496, 538, 539; corps of, 884; Hindman's battalion of, 931; Towson's company at Chippawa, 937; Hindman's battalion at Lundy's Lane, 941–44, 946–49; and at Fort Erie, 959, 961–62, 967; in military district No. 7, 1129; in the night battle at New Orleans, 1149–50, 1154; in

Jackson's lines, 1158–59, 1161, 1164, 1165; in the battle of Jan. 1, 1815, 1164–68; in the battle of Jan. 8, 1176. (See Gunnery.)

Ash Island in the Richelieu River, a fortified British post, 976.

Ashmun, Eli Porter, senator from Massachusetts, votes against internal improvements, 1284.

"Asia," American ship, burned by French squadron, 428, 431.

Aspinwall, Thomas, lieutenant-colonel of the Ninth Infantry, 930; commands Scott's brigade, 959; wounded in the sortie from Fort Erie, 970.

Astor, John Jacob, 502; shares loan of 1813, 650–51; director of United States Bank, 1271.

"Atlas," privateer, captured, 813.

Attorney General. (See Cæsar A. Rodney, William Pinkney, Richard Rush.)

Austria, 23, 96; fights battles of Essling and Wagram, 77; interferes in Russian war, 854; declares war on Napoleon, 861.

"Avon," British 18-gun sloop-of-war, sunk by the "Wasp," 1042–45.

"Avon," privateer, 1046.

BACON, EZEKIEL, member of Congress from Massachusetts, chairman of ways and means committee, 402; votes against frigates, 408; moves war taxes, 408–09.

Baen, William C., captain of Fourth U. S. Infantry, killed at Tippecanoe, 368.

Bailey, Dixon, Creek half-breed, attacks Peter McQueen at Burnt Corn, 779; surprised and killed at Fort Mims, 780–81.

Bainbridge, William, captain in U. S. navy, 564; takes command of the "Constitution," 564; captures "Java," 564–65; blockades the "Bonne Cito-yenne," 819.

Ball, James V., lieutenant-colonel of Second U. S. Light Dragoons, 707.

Ballou, Hosea, his Universalism, 1306–07.

Baltimore, population in 1810, 203; threatened by Cockburn, 806; chief object of British attack, 993, 1000; defences of, 1027–28; British attack on, 1028–32; banks suspend payment, 1059; saved by engineers and sailors, 1062; inhabitants to feel Ross's visit, 1128–29; effect of repulse at Ghent, 1208–09; depreciation of currency, 1225; shares loan of 1815, 1251; growth of, 1288; steamboat at, 1298–99.

Baltimore riot, July 27, 1812, 578–80.

Bancroft, George, 1322.

Bangor, in Maine, plundered by British expedition, 975.

Bank of England, drain of specie from, 1817–1819, 1268.

Bank of the United States, Gallatin's dependence on, 118–19; bill introduced for rechartering, 146–47; hostile influence of State Banks, 228, 230, 231, 233–34; pretexts for opposition to charter of, 228–29; necessity for, 229; Crawford's bill for rechartering, 231; debate on, 231–34; defeat of, 234; a fatal loss to the Treasury, 886, 1059; plan for, with fifty millions' capital, recommended by Dallas in October, 1814, 1083; Dallas's plan of, approved by House, October 24, 1083; Calhoun's plan of, approved by House, 1084; Senate bill, 1088; defeated in the House, 1088–89; Webster's plan adopted by Congress, 1089–90; vetoed, 1090; new bill introduced, passes the Senate Feb. 11, 1815, 1221, 1238; postponed by the House, 1238; recommended by Dallas in his annual report of 1815, 1254; Dallas's scheme of 1816, 1257; bill for incorporating, 1261; bill passes and becomes law, 1262; capital subscribed, 1271; begins operations, January, 1817, 1271.

Banks, State, popularity of, in 1812, 438; their capital in 1813, 885–86; their circulation, 885–86, 887; of New England financial agents of the enemy, 886; capital of New England, 886; specie in New England, 886–87;

pressure of New England on other, 887; suspend specie payments in September, 1814, except in New England, 1059; worthlessness of the suspended notes of, 1059–60, 1079–81; suspended notes taken in payment of taxes, 1087–88; of Massachusetts refuse loans to State government, 1118–19; currency of, affected by the peace, 1225, 1249–52; of Massachusetts drained of specie after the peace, 1248; discount on notes of, in the autumn of 1815, 1249; special treasury accounts in notes of, 1249; resist return to specie payments, 1269–70; resume specie payments, Feb. 20, 1817, 1271; increase of, in Massachusetts, 1289; increase of, in Virginia,, 1292; in New York and Pennsylvania, 1295.

Bankhead, Dr., 583.

Bankruptcy, of the national government, in 1814, 1058–60; formally announced, Nov. 9, 1814, 1079, 1085, 1086, 1090–91.

Baptists, 1273.

Barataria, smuggling station at, 1132; "hellish banditti" of, 1136; work guns at New Orleans, 1161.

Barbour, James, senator from Virginia, 1255.

Barbour, Philip P., member of the Fourteenth Congress, from Virginia, 1255; on the effect of the Compensation Act, 1275; opposes internal improvements, 1283.

Barclay, Captain Robert Heriot, of the Royal Navy, sent to command the British squadron on Lake Erie, 701; his fleet, 701; his report of the battle, 704; his losses, 706.

Baring, Alexander, on British policy, 484; on impressment, 636; correspondence with Gallatin in July, 1813, 856, 860; assists Gallatin to negotiate, 864–65.

Barker, Jacob, takes five millions of the loan in 1814, 918; fails to make his payments, 1058, 1077.

Barlow, Joel, on Robert Smith's appointment, 13; on Smith's opposition

to Macon's bill, 132; his defence of the President, 209, 211, 262; appointed minister to France, 249; his instructions on revocation of French Decrees, 295; his departure delayed by Monroe, 330; ready to start, 333; order for his departure countermanded, 334; order finally given, 337; his instructions, 341; his want of success, 444; arrives in Paris, Sept. 19, 1811, 463; his negotiation with Bassano, 465–75; his journey to Wilna, 475; his death, 476.

Barney, Joshua, commands privateer "Rossie," 838; his cruise, 851; commands gunboats in Chesapeake Bay, 999; burns his gunboats, 1001; joins Winder's army, 1004; ordered to defend the navy-yard bridge, 1006; remonstrates and marches to Bladensburg, 1007; his battle and capture, 1011–12.

"Barrosa," 42-gun British frigate, 807.

Bassano, Duc de. (See Maret.)

Bassett, Burwell, member of Congress from Virginia, 146.

Bathurst, Lord, on the Orders in Council, 483; on the right of impressment, 631; sends ten thousand men to Canada, 927; his instructions to Cochrane and Ross regarding an expedition to the Chesapeake, 997–98; his instructions to Ross regarding an expedition to the Gulf of Mexico, 1126–28; approves Ross's Washington campaign, 1128; advises severity to Baltimore, 1128–29; sends Pakenham to succeed Ross, 1129; his under-secretary commissioner at Ghent, 1193; keeps the Ghent negotiation alive, 1199; takes charge of the negotiation, 1194; his instructions of Sept. 1, 1814, 1201–02; yields the Indian *sine qua non*, 1205; claims the basis of *uti possidetis*, 1206–07, 1208–09; hastens the peace, 1213; concedes the fisheries, 1215, 1218–19.

Baton Rouge, seizure of, 213–15; Jackson orders troops to, 1141, 1146.

Bayard, James A., senator from Delaware, 451; appointed peace commissioner to Russia, 649; sails for St. Petersburg, 651; nominated and confirmed, 660, 661; arrives at St. Petersburg, 854; obliged to wait at St. Petersburg, 860; goes to London with Gallatin, 864–65, 870, 1185; nominated and confirmed as joint commissioner to Ghent, 875–76; at Ghent, 1193–94; his remarks to Goulburn, 1198; on the Florida policy, 1203–04; Adams's opinion of, 1218; secures the success of the negotiation, 1218; appointed minister to Russia, 1243; his death, 1243.

Baynes, Edward, colonel of Glengarry Light Infantry, British adjutant-general, negotiates armistice with Dearborn, 519; commands expedition against Sackett's Harbor, 733–35; his report, 736.

Bayou Bienvenu, selected as line of British advance to New Orleans, 1146–47.

Beall, William D., colonel of Maryland militia at Bladensburg, 1012, 1018.

Beasley, Daniel, commands at Fort Mims, 780; surprised and killed, 781.

Beckwith, Sir Sydney, British major-general, repulsed at Craney Island, 808, 810; captures Hampton, 812.

Beecher, Lyman, 1322.

"Belvidera," British frigate, blockading New York, 551–52; escapes from Rodgers' squadron, 553; chases "Constitution," 554, 555.

Benedict on the Patuxent, Ross's army lands at, 997, 1000; Monroe scouts to, 1002.

Bentham, George, commander of British sloop-of-war "Carnation," his part in destroying the "General Armstrong," 1051–55.

Benton, Thomas Hart, his brawl with Andrew Jackson, 784.

Bermuda, governor of, licenses importation from eastern States, 641.

Bernadotte, Jean Baptiste. (See Sweden.)

Bibb, William A., member of Congress from Georgia, on the annexation of West Florida to Louisiana, 226.

Biddle, James, commander in U. S. navy, commands the "Hornet," 823, 1226; captures "Penguin," 1231–32; escapes "Cornwallis," 1232.

Biddle, Thomas, captain of artillery in Hindman's battalion, 931; at Lundy's Lane, 944, 946; at Fort Erie, 959.

Bidwell, Barnabas, member of Congress from Massachusetts, a defaulter, 249.

Bigelow, Jacob, professor of medicine at Harvard College, 1322.

Bingham, A. B., captain of the British corvette "Little Belt," his account of his action with the "President," 316–17, 318–19.

Birmingham, remonstrates against Orders in Council, 480; treaty of Ghent received at, 1220.

Bissell, Daniel, colonel of Fifth U. S. Infantry, promoted to brigadier, 901; his skirmish with Drummond's forces in October, 1814, 990.

Bladensburg, designated as the point of concentration for the defence of Washington, 997, 1005, 1007–10; citizens erect works at, 1003; the necessary point of British attack, 1004, 1005, 1007; battle-field of, 1007–10; battle of, 1011–12; Ross retreats through, 1015; relative losses at, 1340.

Blakeley, Johnston, commander in U. S. navy, commands the "Wasp" in 1814, 1040, 1074; cruises in the British Channel, 1040; captures British sloop-of-war "Reindeer," 1041, 1047; sinks the "Avon," 1042–45; lost at sea, 1045.

"Blakeley," privateer, 1046.

Bleecker, Harmanus, member of Congress from New York, 440.

Blockade, Napoleon's definition of, 106, 161, 177; Pinkney's definition of, 201, 303; Napoleon abandons for municipal regulations, 278–79; alleged by Madison as the third *casus belli*, 447; offered by American Ghent commissioners for discussion, 1192, 1196; omitted from treaty, 1206, 1219.

Blockades, British, (Fox's) of the French and German coasts, May 16, 1806, Pinkney inquires whether still in force, 194–96; Wellesley's conduct regarding, 196; express withdrawal of, required by Madison, 222, 266; withdrawal of, demanded by Pinkney, 298–99, 308; British reply to demand of withdrawal of, 300, 302, 306, 311; becomes the only apparent *casus belli*, 446–47.

———of Venice, July 27, 1806, 196.

———of all ports and places under the government of France, April 26, 1809, 47–48, 75, 194; repeal of, demanded by Pinkney, 298, 301–02; offered by Wellesley on condition that the French decrees should be effectually withdrawn, 302; repeal refused by Wellesley, 308; repeal again asked by Pinkney and refused by Wellesley, 308. (See Order in Council of April 26, 1809.)

———of the ports and harbors of Chesapeake Bay and Delaware River, Dec. 26, 1812, 640, 642; raised, 1225.

———of New York, Charleston, Port Royal, Savannah, and the River Mississippi, May 26, 1813, 802; effects of, 802–04, 850, 1059; raised, 1225.

———of New London and Long Island Sound, 802, 813; raised, 1225.

———of the coast of New England, April 25, 1814, 908, 1208; raised, 1225.

Blockades, French, of Great Britain, Nov. 21, 1806. (See Decree of Berlin.)

Blockades, *quasi*, of New York, in 1811, 313, 377, 447.

Blockades of Great Britain by American cruisers in 1813–1814, 848–49; in 1814, 1047–51.

Bloomfield, Joseph, brigadier-general, 493; at Plattsburg, 548.

Blount, Willie, governor of Tennessee, orders out two thousand militia for service in Florida, 764; advises Jackson to withdraw from the Creek country, 787; orders out four thousand militia, 794; required to provide for defence of New Orleans, 1132, 1137.

Blue, Uriah, major of Thirty-ninth U. S. Infantry, commands expedition to the Appalachicola, 1139–40, 1141.

Blyth, Samuel, commander of British sloop-of-war "Boxer," his death and burial, 816.

Boerstler, C. G., colonel of Fourteenth U. S. Infantry, 732; his surrender at Beaver Dam, 732.

Bonaparte, Joseph, deserted by Napoleon, 23; driven from Spain, 865.

Bonaparte. (See Napoleon.)

Bonds, U. S., six per cent., their market value, Feb. 1, 1815, 1059, 1090, 1094; on Feb. 13, 1815, 1225; in March, 1815, 1290; in 1816, 1269.

"Bonne Citoyenne," British sloop-of-war, 564; blockaded at San Salvador, 819.

Bordeaux, Wellington advances on, 876.

Borodino, battle of, 638.

Boston, reception of F. J. Jackson in, 151–52, 153; population in 1810, 203; takes one million of loan of 1814, 918; blockaded, 1208; welcomes peace, 1223; harshly treated by Dallas, 1249–50; treasury payments resumed at, 1269; growth of, 1288; immigrants to, 1291; its society in 1817, 1306; takes the lead of American literature, 1318–19, 1321–23.

Boston town-meeting on Baltimore riot, 580.

Bowyer, Fort. (See Fort Bowyer.)

"Boxer," British sloop-of-war, captured by "Enterprise," 815–17.

Boyd, Adam, member of Congress from New Jersey, 146.

Boyd, John Parke, colonel of Fourth U. S. Infantry, 360–61; arrives at Vincennes, 362; brigadier-general, 728; Morgan Lewis's opinion of, 730; ordered to cease offensive operations, 746; commands brigade in Wilkinson's expedition, 750; favors moving on Montreal, 750; covers the rear, 752; Brown's and Scott's opinion of,

752; his defeat at Chrystler's Field, 754.

Boyle, Thomas, commands Baltimore privateer "Comet," 838; commands "Chasseur," and notifies a blockade of the British coast, 1048.

Bradley, Stephen R., senator from Vermont, votes against occupying East Florida, 461.

Brady, Hugh, colonel of Twenty-second Infantry, 930; at Lundy's Lane, 942; wounded, 944.

Brazil, glutted with British goods in 1808, 36.

Brenton, E. B., staff officer of Sir George Prevost, his account of the attack on Sackett's Harbor, 736–37.

Brisbane, major-general in British army, commanding a brigade at Plattsburg, 978.

Bristol, memorial of merchants in September, 1814, 1048, 1050.

Brock, Isaac, governor of Upper Canada, his career, 514; his military precautions, 515; his military force, 515; his civil difficulties, 515–17; orders expedition to Mackinaw, 517; his proclamation, 517; dismisses his legislature, 517; passes Long Point, 518; arrives at Malden, 523; decides to cross the Detroit River, 524; his march on Detroit, 525; returns to Niagara, 536; his military wishes, 536; distressed by loss of vessels, 539; his force at Niagara, 540; surprised at Queenston Heights, 541; his death, 541, 1212.

Broke, P. B. V., captain of British frigate "Shannon," commands squadron, 554; chases "Constitution," 555; invites battle with Rodgers, 818; challenges "Chesapeake," 819; his qualities, 822; his battle with the "Chesapeake," 823–29; captures "Nautilus," 836; a life-long invalid, 1212; his gunnery, 1338.

Brooke, Arthur, colonel of the British Forty-fourth Infantry, at the advance on Baltimore, 1030; succeeds Ross in command, 1031; studies the lines of

Baltimore, 1031; decides to retreat, 1032.

Brooke, G. M., major in Twenty-third Infantry, 931.

Brooks, John, elected governor of Massachussetts, in 1816, 1272.

Brookville, in Maryland, 1020–21.

Brougham, Henry, organizes agitation against Orders in Council, 480, 486, 488; his speech of March 3, 1812, 483; obliges ministers to grant a committee of inquiry, 488–89; moves repeal, 490.

Brown, Jacob, brigadier-general of N. Y. militia, 733, 900; takes command at Sackett's Harbor, 735; his remarks on the battle at Sackett's Harbor, 735, 738; appointed brigadier-general in the U. S. army, 739; commands a brigade in Wilkinson's expedition, 745, 750; favors moving on Montreal, 750; landed on north bank of the St. Lawrence, 752; clears the bank, 752, 755; his opinion of Boyd, 752; appointed major-general, 900; his fitness described by Wilkinson and Scott, 900; ordered to Sackett's Harbor in February, 1814, 923; carries his army to Niagara, 925; returns to Sackett's Harbor, 925; at Buffalo in June, ordered to capture Fort Erie, 929; his forces, 930–32; crosses the Niagara River, 933; fights the battle of Chippawa, 935–37; his letter to Commodore Chauncey, 938; falls back from Queenston to Chippawa, 939–40; orders Scott to march toward Queenston, 941; his order to Miller at Lundy's Lane, 945; his position at Lundy's Lane, 947; wounded, 949; orders the army to retire, 949; orders Ripley to return to Lundy's Lane, 953; taken to Buffalo, 954; summons Gaines to Fort Erie, 956; his quarrels with Chauncey and Ripley, 965; his qualities, 966, 1062; resumes command, 966–67; his sortie from Fort Erie, 968–71; asks Izard's aid, 989; meets Izard at Batavia, 989; distrusts Izard, 989; favors attack on Chippawa in October,

1814, 990; sent to Sackett's Harbor, 991; Izard's opinion of, 991; his letter of August 19, 1814, complaining of being left to struggle alone, 1062; head of army board for reducing the army, 1242; commands northern military district, 1242.

Bryant, William Cullen, his poem "Thanatopsis," 1323–24, 1327, 1329–30, 1343.

Buckminster, Joseph, remonstrates with Hosea Ballou, 1306–07.

Buckminster, Joseph Stevens, 1302; his Phi Beta Kappa oration, 1317, 1321; one of the Anthology Club, 1319–20.

Budd, George, second lieutenant of the "Chesapeake," 823; stationed below, 824; leads boarders, 825.

Buffalo, burned by British, 763.

Burnt Corn Creek, Indians attacked at, 779, 782.

Burr, Aaron, Vice-President, his memoir to Napoleon, 169.

Burrows, William, lieutenant in U. S. Navy, captures the "Boxer," 815–16; his death and burial, 816–17.

Burwell, William A., member of Congress from Virginia, on reducing the army and navy in 1810, 142–43.

CABINET. (See Robert Smith, James Monroe, William Jones, Secretaries of State; Albert Gallatin, G. W. Campbell, A. J. Dallas, W. H. Crawford, Secretaries of the Treasury; Henry Dearborn, William Eustis, James Monroe, John Armstrong, A. J. Dallas, Secretaries of War; William Jones, B. W. Crowninshield, Secretaries of the Navy; Cæsar A. Rodney, William Pinkney, Richard Rush, Attorneys General.)

Cabot, George, at the head of the Massachusetts delegation to the Hartford Convention, 1066, 1067, 1109; his conservative character, 1110–11; chosen president of the Hartford Convention, 1111–12; authorized to call another meeting, 1113; defence of,

1120; John Adams's remark about, 1122.

Cadore, Duc de (see Champagny).

"Caledonia," 2-gun British brig, captured by Lieutenant Elliott, 539; in Perry's squadron, 699, 702, 703; in Perry's action, 704, 705.

Calhoun, John C., member of Congress from South Carolina, 380; on Committee of Foreign Relations, 381, 384; his war-speech of Dec. 12, 1811, 393–94; votes for frigates, 408; warns Quincy of the embargo, 433; on the conquest of Canada, 440; his war-report, 450; his bill declaring war, 451; his speech of June 24, 1812, against the restrictive system, 454; favors war-taxation, 456; opposes compromise of forfeitures under Nonimportation Act, 602–03; favors high import duties, 603; his remark on inconsistency, 877–78; his plan for a national bank, 1083–85; votes against legal tender, 1086; accepts Giles's militia bill, 1099; not a good judge of treason, 1107; in the Fourteenth Congress, 1254; his view of extremes in government, 1256; chairman of committee on currency, 1257; favors protection, 1260; reports bill for a national bank, 1261; supports compensation bill, 1264; his remark that the House of Representatives was not a favorite with the American people, 1273, 1275; his defence of the House, 1280; his bill for internal improvements, 1282–83, 1285, 1297.

Calvinism, rupture of church in 1815, 1301–09.

Campbell, George W., member of Congress from Tennessee, his report reaches Canning, 38; not a member of the Eleventh Congress, 55; senator from Tennessee, his criticism of Giles, 398; appointed Secretary of the Treasury, 874, 893; negotiates loan in May, 1814, 918, 918; accedes to abandoning impressment as a *sine qua non*, 996; at Winder's headquarters, August 24, 1006; goes to Frederick,

1018; fails to negotiate loan of six millions in July, 1814, 1058–59; his annual report of Sept. 23, 1814, 1077; announces the impracticability of raising loans, 1077; makes no suggestion for supplying deficit, 1078; resigns, 1077; returns to the Senate, 1255.

Campbell, Thomas, his Declaration of Sept. 9, 1809, 1307–08, 1344.

Canada, intended conquest of, 389, 392, 395, 398, 440; invasion planned at Washington, 497; ordered by Eustis, 502; conquest attempted by Hull, 497; invaded by Hull, 502–03; evacuated, 513–14; difficulties of defending, 514–17; extent of Upper, 514; military force in 1812, 515, 529; Jefferson and Madison on campaign in, 528–29; invasion of, at Niagara, 537–38; Van Rensselaer's attack on, 539–43; Smyth's attempts against, 544–47; Dearborn's march to, 548; British garrisons in, 724–25, 756–58; reinforcements for, in 1814, 972, 977–79; proper method of attacking, 718–22; difficulties of defence, 718, 972, 973; frontier to be rectified, 974–76; regular troops in, December, 1814, 992; demands of, at Ghent, 1188–89; cession of, asked by Monroe, 1192; British reproach about, 1203–04.

Canals. (See Erie Canal.)

Canning, George, his character, 42; his reply to Napoleon and Alexander, 21; his notice to Pinkney of possible change in the Orders, 33; his note of Dec. 24, 1808, announcing a change, 33; his anger at Pinkney's reply, 34–35; his willingness for further relaxations, 35; his discontent with Castlereagh and Perceval, 37, 76–77; his reception of Erskine's despatches and Campbell's Report, 38–39; his assertion as to the cause of the embargo, 38–39; his instructions to Erskine of Jan. 23, 1809, 40–43, 49, 51–54, 66; his influence declining, 43–44; his speech of March 6, 1809, on the Orders, 45; his remark to Pinkney on the Order of April 26, 46; his dis-

avowal of Erskine's arrangement, 64–69; his statement to the House of Commons, 71; his instructions to F. J. Jackson, July 1, 1809, 71–76; his charge of duplicity against Madison, 72–73, 82, 90; his resignation, 77; his duel with Castlereagh, 77–78; his relations with Wellesley, 187–88; his speech on the renewal of intercourse between the United States and Great Britain, 193–94; his speech of March 3, 1812, on the Orders in Council and licenses, 484; on the loss of the "Guerriere" and "Macedonian," 624; on the conduct of the war, 627, 636; his failure as a minister, 634–36; his view of British naturalization acts, 634–36.

Capitol at Washington, burned, 1013; rebuilt, 1278–79.

Carden, J. S., captain of the British frigate "Macedonian," 562–63.

"Carnation," British sloop-of-war, attacks and destroys the "General Armstrong," 1051–55.

"Carolina," American 14-gun sloop-of-war, at New Orleans, 1151; her share in the night battle, 1153–54, 1155, 1156; her fire imprisons the British troops, 1157, 1159; destroyed, Dec. 27, 1814, 1159, 1161–62.

Carroll, William, major-general of Tennessee militia, arrives at New Orleans, 1146; his brigade, 1150; posted on the Gentilly road, 1151.

"Carron," 20-gun British sloop-of-war, sent to Pensacola, 1131, 1133; attacks Fort Bowyer, 1133–34.

Carronades, their range, 985.

Cass, Lewis, colonel of Ohio militia, 500; refuses to abandon Detroit, 514; his discontent with Hull, 521; detached to open an interior road to the river Raisin, 522; ordered to return, 523; included in Hull's capitulation, 526; brigadier-general U. S. army, 707; treats with Indians, 801.

Cassin, John, captain in U. S. navy, 807.

"Castilian," British sloop-of-war, cruises in company with the "Avon,"

1042; her commander's report on the loss of the "Avon," 1043–45.

Castine, occupied by British expedition, 975; offered to be restored at Ghent, 1207.

Castlereagh, Lord, his supposed failures as Secretary of War, 37, 76–77; his quarrel with Canning, 42–43; his duel with Canning, 77–78; retires from the cabinet, 77; becomes Foreign Secretary, 443; his instructions to Foster of April 10, 1812, 443, 446; announces suspension of Orders in Council, 490; his statement of number of American seamen in British service, 612; his remarks to Jonathan Russell, Aug. 24, 1812, 584, 622; defends course of ministry, 627; his remarks on impressment, 633; his remarks on the Czar's offer of mediation, 640; declines Russian mediation in May, 1813, 854–55, 858; his letter of July 5, declining mediation, 855; his letter to Cathcart, July 13, offering direct negotiation with United States, 856, 860–61, 864–65; lukewarm about the American war, 865, 866, 868; his letter to Monroe, November 4, offering to negotiate directly, 867–68, 875; his offer accepted by Madison, 870, 875; his irresistible influence, 891; his disposition toward America, 1185, 1188, 1190; his instructions of July 28, 1190, 1200; his choice of negotiators, 1193; delays negotiation until August, 1195; his instructions of August 14, 1196; keeps the negotation alive until October, 1199; at Ghent, August 19, 1200; his letter to Bathurst suggesting immediate peace, 1200–01; at Vienna, embarrassed by the American war, 1208; negotiates commercial convention with the United States, 1253.

Cathcart, Lord, British ambassador at St. Petersburg, 639; his instructions of July 5, 1813, 855–56; his comments on the Czar's conduct, 861–64.

Caulaincourt, Duc de Vicence, French ambassador in Russia, 285; recalled, 289; congratulates Adams, 200.

Census, of 1810, Act for, 148.

"Centinel," Boston newspaper, of Sept. 10, 1814, quoted, 1065, 1109, 1110–11, 1116, 1117; publishes peace, 1223.

Chamier, Frederick, lieutenant on the British frigate "Menelaus," his account of house-burning on the Potomac, 1026.

Champagny, Jean Baptiste de, his instructions to Turreau in defence of the Decrees, Dec. 10, 1808, 26; in defence of the Spanish colonies, 27; his remonstrances to Napoleon against severity to the United States, 99–100; complains of the Non-intercourse Act, 100; his instructions to Hauterive, June 13, 1809, on concessions to the United States, 100; his note on the right of search and blockade, 106–07, 176–77; his efforts on behalf of neutral commerce, 157; his interview with Armstrong, Jan. 25, 1810, 162; his note of Feb. 14, 1810, announcing reprisals for the Non-intercourse Act, 164; his letter of August 5, 1810, announcing that the decrees are revoked, 179–81, 200–01, 207–11, 266, 286–87, 301; creates a contract by letter of August 5, 237; his report on the decrees, 242, 265, 269, 301; his phrase *bien entendu*, 269; declares the decrees revoked on Feb. 2, 1811, 267–68, 270; removed from office, 278.

Champlain, Lake. (See Plattsburg.)

Champlin, Guy R., captain of the privateer "General Armstrong," 838; his escapes, 844–45.

Chandler, John, brigadier-general in U. S. army, 728; engaged in capturing Fort George, 729; advances to Stony Creek, 730; captured, 730.

Channing, William Ellery, takes charge of church at Boston, 1302; his letter to Thacher, 1303; his Unitarianism, 1303–06; his Fast-Day Sermon in 1810, 1320–21.

Charleston, in Maryland, 806.

Charleston, S. C., in 1816, 1288.

"Chasseur," privateer, her blockade, 1048.

Chateaugay, Hampton's campaign at, 756–59.

Chatillon, Congress of, 891.

Chauncey, Isaac, captain in U. S. navy, takes command on Lake Ontario, 538; arranges plan of campaign with Dearborn, 725–27; controls the lake, 726; crosses to Niagara, 727; aids capture of Fort George, 729; returns to Sackett's Harbor, 730; loses control of the lake, 739; recovers control of the lake, 747; dissuades Brown from attacking Kingston, 925; shut up in Sackett's Harbor in the spring of 1814, 926–27, 929; Brown's irritating letters to, 929, 938, 939; sails from Sackett's Harbor, 965; his reply to Brown's letters, 965; carries Izard's army to the Genesee River, 989; loses control of the lake in October, 1814, 990.

Cherokee Indians, with Jackson in the Creek war, 791.

"Cherub," British 18-gun sloop-of-war, 1035; assists the "Phoebe" to blockade and capture the "Essex," 1036–37.

"Chesapeake," 38-gun frigate, 315, 320, 657, 835; arrives at Boston, April 9, 1813, 818, 819; her force, 822; her action with the "Shannon," 823–30; effect of capture, 830, 834; cause of capture, 852.

"Chesapeake Affair," Canning's instructions of Jan. 23, 1809, for settling, 40–41; Erskine's settlement of the, 50; settlement disavowed, 65–66; Canning's instructions of July 1, 1809, for settling, 73; Jackson's offer to settle, 90–91, 93; untouched by Wellesley, 200; Foster's instructions to settle, 311; American indifference to settlement, 321; its effect on the Indians, 352; settled by Foster, 379, 480; remembered too well, 1232.

Chesapeake Bay, British naval force in, 630, 636; blockade of, announced Dec. 26, 1812, 640–41, 642; severity of blockade in, 803, 804; Admiral Cockburn's operations in, 804–06; Admiral Warren's operations in, 812–

13; Cochrane's marauding in, 1026; in October, 1814, left to repose, 1032; steamboat on, 1298–99.

Cheves, Langdon, member of Congress from South Carolina, asserts contract with Napoleon, 238; in the Twelfth Congress, 380; chairman of naval committee, 381; on Committee on Ways and Means, 381; his opinion on the war-power, 405; his motion to build a navy, 406; his argument in favor of seventy-fours, 406–07; his hostility to non-importation, 435, 453, 454, 605–06; favors war-taxation, 456; opposes forfeitures under Non-importation Act, 602; on war-taxes, 603–04; elected speaker, Jan. 19, 1814, 892; defeats Dallas's scheme for a national bank, 1089.

Chew, Captain Samuel, deposition of, 427, 429.

Chicago. (See Fort Dearborn.)

Chickasaw Indians, 771.

"Childers," 18-gun British sloop-of-war sent to Pensacola, 1133; in the attack on Fort Bowyer, 1133–34.

Chippawa, British force at, 932; Riall takes position at, 933; battle at, 935–38; Brown withdraws to, 939–41; Ripley retreats from, 954–56; Drummond's delay at, 956; Drummond retires to, 971; Izard's failure at, 991.

"Chippeway," 1-gun British schooner on Lake Erie, 701.

Chittenden, Martin, governor of Vermont, his proclamation recalling the State militia, Nov. 10, 1813, 872; refuses to call out the State militia to defend Plattsburg, 1064.

Choctaw Indians, 771; with Jackson at Mobile, 1138; at New Orleans, 1153.

Christie, John, lieutenant-colonel of Thirteenth Infantry, 541–42.

Chrystler's Farm, battle at, 752–54.

Cintra, convention of, 37.

Claiborne, Ferdinand Leigh, brigadier-general of Mississippi militia, 789; penetrates Creek country, 789.

Claiborne, William Charles Cole, takes possession of West Florida, 217–19;

left by Jackson in charge of military defence of New Orleans, 1136; his want of authority, 1148; commands on the Chef Menteur Road, 1172.

Claims, American, on France (see French spoliations).

Clay, Green, brigadier-general of Kentucky militia, surprises Proctor, 692, 693; commands Fort Meigs, 694, 698.

Clay, Henry, senator from Kentucky, his war-speech of Feb. 22, 1810, 134; his speech on the occupation of West Florida, 223–24; his speech on the Bank Charter, 232–33; elected speaker, 380, 381; favors army of thirty-five thousand men, 399; favors war-power, 405; favors navy, 407; supposed to have coerced Madison to war, 430; urges embargo, 433; suppresses discussion in the House, 450; his vote defeats repeal of non-importation, 455; his account of the military efforts of Kentucky, 567–70; his comments on Hull's surrender, 569–70; opposes compromise of forfeitures under Non-importation Act, 602; elected speaker of Thirteenth Congress, 656; assists Harrison, 670; nominated and confirmed as joint envoy to negotiate peace at Ghent, 875–76, 890; resigns speakership and sails for Europe, 892, 1191; at Ghent, 1193, 1194; insists that the British will recede, 1197; combative, 1203; his speeches, 1204; drafts Indian article, 1205; opposed to recognizing the British right of navigating the Mississippi, 1214–16; his opinion of the treaty, 1217, 1222–23; his character, 1218; Speaker in the Fourteenth Congress, 1254–55; favors strong foreign policy, 1256; favors protection, 1259–60; recants his errors in regard to the national bank, 1261; attacked on account of the Compensation Act, 1275; offered the War Department, 1278; supports internal improvements, 1283.

Clergy, of New England, their attitude toward the war, 920–22; their divi-

sion into Orthodox, Unitarian, and Universalist, 1301–09.

Clinton, De Witt, nominated for the Presidency by New York, 442; his canvass, 580–81; his electoral vote, 582, 653; favors Erie Canal, 1296.

Clinton, George, Vice-President, presides in the Senate, 55, 134; his vote against the Bank Charter, 234; his political capacity, 252; his death, 442.

Coasting trade under the embargo, tonnage employed in 1807–1810, 16.

Cobbett, William, his "Weekly Register" on the American war, 865.

Cochrane, Sir Alexander, British vice-admiral succeeding Sir John Borlase Warren, communicates with refugee Creeks, 799; joint commander with Ross of expedition in the Chesapeake, 997; his instructions, 998; his orders for general retaliation, 998–99; his letter to Monroe, 1000; fails to capture Fort McHenry, 1031–32; sails for Halifax, 1032; recommends expedition to Mobile, 1126; at New Orleans, 1168; suggests canal, 1169.

Cockburn, Sir George, British rear-admiral, his operations in Chesapeake Bay, 804–06, 810, 812; at Ocracoke, 813, 847; at Cumberland Island, 813; lands with Ross, and urges attack on Washington, 999; pursues and destroys Barney's flotilla, 1000–01; enters Washington and burns the White House, 1013–14; destroys the type of the "National Intelligencer," 1015; an incendiary, 1026; at the attack on Baltimore, 1030.

Cocke, John, major-general of Tennessee militia, 787; surprises Hillabee village, 788; put under arrest, 795.

Codrington, Sir Edward, British admiral, his account of the artillery battle at New Orleans, 1167.

Coffee, John, colonel of Tennessee militia, commands mounted force in Jackson's Creek campaign, 784; destroys Talishatchee, 785; at Talladega, 785; abandoned by his men, 791; wounded at Emuckfaw, 791; engaged at the Horseshoe, 795; his account of the slaughter, 797; marches with Tennessee militia to Mobile, 1137, 1138; ordered to Baton Rouge, 1141; hurries to New Orleans, 1146; his brigade, 1150; his share in the night battle, 1151–53, 1155–56; stationed on the left of Jackson's line, 1175.

Coggeshall, George, author of "History of American Privateers," 844; his escape in privateer "David Porter," 844.

Coleridge, Samuel Taylor, 1328.

"Comet," Baltimore privateer, 838.

Commerce, foreign and domestic, nature and value of American, 203–04.

Commercial Intercourse, Act of May 1, 1810, regarding (see Non-intercourse).

Commercial restrictions, list of measures of, 109, 137; Madison's devotion to, 205, 206–07; Madison's return to, 212.

Compensation Act, 1263–65; popular protest against, 1273–76; repeal of, 1280–81.

"Confiance," British 36-gun ship, on Lake Champlain, 979; her armament and crew, 980–82; fights the battle of Plattsburg, 984–86, 1341.

Congress, first session of Eleventh, meets, May 22, 1809, 55; proceedings of, 56–63; adjourns June 28, 63; second session meets, Nov. 27, 1809, 125; proceedings of, 126–48; adjourns, May 2, 1810, 148; character of, 221; election of Twelfth, 221; third session of Eleventh, 223–48; close of Eleventh, 248; first session of Twelfth, meets Nov. 4, 1811, 377; its composition, 380; chooses Henry Clay speaker, 381; war-debate in, 387–400; proceedings of, 387–415, 433–34, 435; declares war against England, 451–52; adjourns, July 6, 1812, 456; decline of influence, 599; second session of Twelfth, 598–613; meeting of Thirteenth, May 24, 1813, 656; proceedings of first session, 657–63, 665, 667–68; meeting of second session, Dec. 6, 1813, 871; proceedings of, 874, 876–81, 882–88; Federalist strength

in, 1068; meeting of third session, Sept. 19, 1814, 1058–59; proceedings of, 1081–91, 1094–1103; peace legislation of, 1238–42; close of, 1242; meeting of Fourteenth, 1254–55; superiority of Fourteenth, 1255–57, 1276; proceedings of first session of, 1258–65; close of first session, 1267; popular rebuke of, 1276; second session of, 1279; proceedings of second session, 1280–86. (See Acts of.)

"Congress," 38-gun frigate, 550; at Boston, 560; her cruise in 1812, 562; returns to Boston, Dec. 31, 1812, 818; goes to sea, April 30, 1813, 818; unseaworthy, 819; returns to Boston, Dec. 14, 1813, 835.

Connecticut, disaffection of, 642–43, 915; prosperity of, during the war, 916; withdraws militia, Aug. 24, 1814, from national service, 1064; appoints delegates to the Hartford Convention, 1068; resolutions of legislature against the militia bill, in October, 1814, 1102; approves report of the Hartford Convention, 1119–20; regular troops stationed in, 1130; elections of 1816, 1272, 1276; growth of population, 1287; increase of wealth in, 1289.

"Constellation," 38-gun frigate, at Washington, 551, 556, 560; at Norfolk, 806, 807, 810, 819.

"Constitution," 44-gun frigate, chased by British squadron, 551, 554–56; captures "Guerriere," 557–58; captures "Java," 564–65; arrives at Boston, Feb. 27, 1813, 818; replaces her masts, 819; goes to sea, Jan. 1, 1814, 835; imperilled by privateering, 852; sails from Boston in December, 1814, 1233; her action with the "Cyane" and "Levant," 1234–36; escapes British squadron, 1236.

Constitution, the (see War Power, Militia, Internal Improvement, Amendment, Bank of the United States, Embargo, New England Convention, Marshall, and Story).

Coosa River, home of the Upper Creeks, 771, 776, 783; Jackson's march to the, 785; Cocke's march to the, 787.

Coosadas (see Alabamas).

Copley, John Singleton, 1327.

"Cornwallis," British seventy-four, chases "Hornet," 1232.

Cotton, manufacturers of, 16; American, prohibited in France, 108; price of, affected by blockade, 802; value of export in 1815, 1246; manufactures depressed by the peace, 1247; fabrics, in the tariff of 1816, 1258, 1259, 1260–61; export in 1816, 1268.

"Courier," the, London newspaper, on the American war, 866; on the Americans, 867; on Perry's victory, 867; on Proctor's defeat, 868; on the necessity of retaliation, 869; on privateers, 1048; on Madison, 1188; on terms of peace, 1188, 1204, 1207; on the news of peace, 1220.

Covington, Leonard, brigadier-general in the U. S. army, commands brigade in Wilkinson's expedition, 750; his opinion in council of war, 750; killed at Chrystler's Farm, 753.

Coxe, William S., third lieutenant on the "Chesapeake," 824; fires the last guns, 826.

Craig, Sir James, governor-general of Canada, recalls John Henry, 62.

Craney Island, fortified, 807–08; attacked, 808–11.

Crawford, William H., senator from Georgia, opposes mission to Russia, 14; on the message of Jan. 3, 1810, 127; represents the Treasury, 128; votes with Samuel Smith, 135; his character, 230–31; introduces Bank Charter, 231; his speech on Bank Charter, 231–32; reports bill for fifty thousand volunteers, 248; party to revolutionizing East Florida, 459; his comments on the conduct of the war, 570–71; sent as minister to Paris, 653; sails in the "Argus," 830; reason of not being a peace commissioner, 890; appointed Secretary of War, 1243; candidate for the Presidency in 1816, 1265–66; appointed Secretary of the Treasury, 1278.

Creek Indians, Tecumthe visits, 360, 371; their confederacy and grievances, 771–74; Tecumthe's visit to, 774–76; secret excitement among, 775–76; murders on the Ohio by warriors of, 776; execution of murderers, 777–78; outbreak of fanaticism among, 779; attacked at Burnt Corn, 779; capture Fort Mims, 780–81; number of hostile warriors among, 782, 790, 793; Andrew Jackson's campaign of 1813 among, 784–87; Cocke's campaign against, 787–88; Floyd's campaign against, 788–89; Claiborne's campaign against, 789; Jackson's second campaign against, 790–92; Floyd's second campaign against, 793–94; Jackson's last campaign against, 796–98; number of Red Stick refugees among, 799; Andrew Jackson's capitulation with, 799–801, 1130; effect of their war on the Florida difficulties, 1131.

Crillon, Count Edward de, his family, 416; acts as John Henry's agent, 417–18; his social success, 417, 418; his evidence, 421; sails for France, 421; an impostor, 422; an agent of French police, 422–23.

Croghan, George, major of the Seventeenth U. S. Infantry, his defence of Fort Stephenson, 695–98; his expedition against Mackinaw, 928.

Croker, John Wilson, Secretary to the Admiralty, 44; on British naturalization laws, 634, 635; on the "Chesapeake" and "Shannon," 829; on the captures in British waters, 1050–51.

Crowninshield, Benjamin Williams, appointed Secretary of the Navy, 1226.

Cuba, Jefferson's policy toward, 30.

Cumberland Island in Georgia, occupied by Admiral Cockburn, 813; again occupied in 1815, 1225.

Cumberland Road, 148; in 1816, 1297.

Currency (see Banks, national and State).

Cushing, Caleb, 1322.

Cushing, T. H., brigadier-general, 1064.

Cutts, Charles, senator from New Hampshire, 653.

"Cyane," British corvette, captured by "Constitution," 1233–36.

DACRES, J. R., captain of the "Guerriere," 314, 320, 557; his action with the "Constitution," 557–58; censured by the "Times," 623, 629; on the cause of his defeat, 624, 629.

Daggett, David, senator from Connecticut, his speech against Giles's bill for drafting militia, 1097.

Dalberg, Duc, negotiates with Joel Barlow, 472; his remonstrances to Bassano against Napoleon's treatment of the United States, 474.

Dallas, Alexander James, his opinion of Armstrong, 643–44; Madison's favorite candidate for the treasury, 892; defeated by senators, 893; author of specifications against William Hull, 905; appointed Secretary of the Treasury, Oct. 5, 1814, 1078; his character and temper, 1078–79; his account of the condition of the Treasury in October, 1814, 1079; opposes treasury-note issues and recommends a bank, 1082, 1083–90, 1221; describes the condition of the Treasury in November, 1814, 1084; describes the condition of the Treasury in December, 1814, 1086; describes the condition of the Treasury in January, 1815, 1090–91; sketches financial scheme for first year of peace, 1239; acts as Secretary of War to reduce the army, 1242; his severity to New England, 1249–50; fails to fund treasury-notes, 1250–52; his report of 1815, 1254; recommends a national bank and a protective tariff, 1257–58, 1259; announces his retirement from the Treasury, 1266; restores specie payments, 1269–71; his success as Secretary of the Treasury, 1277–78; his death, 1278.

Dallas, Alexander James, third lieutenant of the frigate "President," 315, 318.

Dana, Samuel Whittlesey, senator from Connecticut, 663.

Dane, Nathan, delegate to the Hartford Convention, 1111.

Daquin, ———, major commanding battalion of men of color at New Orleans, 1151.

Daschkoff, André, Russian chargé at Washington, 648, 767.

Daveiss, Joseph H., offers to serve as a volunteer in Harrison's campaign, 361; urges an attack on Tippecanoe, 365; his death, 368, 370.

"David Porter," privateer schooner, escape of, 844.

Davis, Daniel, 969–70.

Davout, Marshal, 283, 294, 467.

Davy, William R., appointed Major-General, 645.

Dearborn, Henry, appointed collector at Boston, 12; his orders, as Secretary of War, to Wilkinson, Dec. 2, 1808, 120; appointed senior major-general, 492; his plan of campaign, 497, 505, 534–35; reaches Albany, 504; goes to Boston, 504; his difficulties at Boston, 506, 507–08; returns to Albany, 508; ignorant that he commands operations at Niagara, 508, 518, 534; sends militia to Niagara, 518; negotiates armistice, 519, 534; effect of armistice, 520, 536–37; armistice rejected by the President, 534–35; his opinion of Van Rensselaer, 543; his campaign against Montreal, 548; his reflections on the campaign of 1812, 548–49; Monroe's criticisms of, 571–72; George Hay's remark on, 588; continued in command, 645–47; releases Perry's vessels, 700, 730; ordered to attack Kingston, 723; his estimate of British force at Kingston, 725; decides not to attack Kingston, 725–26, 739; captures York, 726–27; arrives at Niagara, 727; captures Fort George, 729; devolves command on Morgan Lewis, 731; reports Boerstler's disaster, 732; removed from command, 739, 905; put in command of New York, 899, 905; president of court-martial on William Hull, 905;

nominated Secretary of War in 1815, 1243.

Dearborn, Fort, at Chicago, murders at, 372; garrison at, 495; evacuated, 527.

Debt, Public (see Finances).

Decatur, Stephen, commands squadron, 550; his orders, 550–51, 554; his advice, 551; his first cruise in 1812, 552, 554, 558; his second cruise, 562; captures the "Macedonian," 562–63; returns to port with prize, 563; takes refuge with squadron in New London, 813–14; reports on blue lights, 814–15; commands "President," 1225; runs blockade, 1226; his battle with the "Endymion," 1226–27, 1229–30; his surrender, 1230–31.

Decrees, French, of 1798, 391.

Decree of Berlin, Nov. 21, 1806, declaring Great Britain in a state of blockade, and excluding from French ports all vessels coming from British ports, Napoleon's varying objects in using, 20–21.

Decrees of Berlin, Milan, and Bayonne, 21, 109, 208; their rigid enforcement, 25; Champagny's argument in defence of, 26; their effect on England, 35–36; their effect on France, 99; Napoleon drafts, June 10, 1809, decree repealing that of Milan, 100–01; lays aside draft of repealing decree, 101; drafts Vienna decree of August, 1809, retaliating the Non-intercourse Act, 102–03, 107, 162; Louis's resistance to, 106, 169–71; Napoleon's condition of repeal, 162, 173–74, 177; null and void for licensed vessels, 175; declared by Champagny revoked on Nov. 1, 1810, 180; declared revoked by Madison, 212, 222, 241; Russell's reports on the revocation, 264–75; declared revoked by Champagny for Feb. 2, 1811, 268, 270–71; not revoked, 273–74; declared fundamental laws by Napoleon, 275, 282; declared successful by Napoleon, 276; considered suspended by Madison, 278; recognized by United States, 278–79; their revocation doubted by Russell,

274, 277, 281; their revocation affirmed by Russell, 280; enforced on the Baltic, 294–95; Barlow instructed that they are considered revoked, 295; revocation asserted by Pinkney, 298, 299, 300, 304; evidence of revocation asked by Wellesley, 299; argued by Pinkney, 300, 301; revocation denied by Wellesley, 311–12; affirmed to be still in force by Foster, 323; affirmed by Monroe to be revoked as far as America has a right to expect, 324; their international and municipal characters, 325; argued by Monroe, 325–26; their revocation unknown to the President, 334; argued by Serurier, 337; disputed by Madison, 339; their revocation a personal affair with Madison, 340; their effect on the northwestern Indians, 354–55; declared not repealed by British courts, 377; their repeal doubted by Madison and Monroe, 378, 423–25; repeal asserted in annual message, 382; repeal assumed by House committee, 387–88; repeal denied by Monroe, 428–29, 433; repeal assumed by Monroe, 430–31; Bassano's report on validity of, 443, 468; repeal assumed by Madison, 444, 448; repeal maintained by Monroe till June, 1812, 453; Bassano's instructions on repeal of, 465; repeal asserted by Barlow, 467; evidence of repeal required by Barlow, 468–69; repealing decree produced by Bassano, 469–71; still enforced, 473; revocation unknown to the French authorities, 474–75; Webster's resolutions on repeal of, 657, 659.

Decree of Rambouillet, March 23, 1810, sequestering American property in retaliation for the Non-importation Act, 167, 171, 192.

—— of July 25, 1810, regarding licenses, 175; of July 22, 1810, confiscating American property in Dutch and Spanish ports, 182; of Aug. 5, 1810, confiscating American property in France, 182.

———— of St. Cloud, dated April 28, 1811, repealing the Decrees of Berlin and Milan from Nov.1, 1810, 469–71, 472.

Decrès, Denis, Duc, Napoleon's Minister of Marine, asks instructions in the case of American schooner at San Sebastian, 102; Marmont's story of, 157.

Defiance, old Fort, 671–74, 677, 678.

Delaware, growth of population of, 1287–88.

Delaware Indians, murders of, 347.

Denmark, spoliations of American commerce in, 283, 284.

Dennie, Joseph, character and influence of his "Portfolio," 1317–19.

De Rottenburg, Baron, forces under his command in Montreal district, 924; one of Brock's successors, 940.

De Salaberry, A., lieutenant-colonel of Canadian voltigeurs, defeats Hampton, 756.

Desha, Joseph, member of Congress from Kentucky, insists on reducing the army in 1815, 1239–41; on expenses of western members, 1263.

Detroit, military situation of, 495, 496, 502; measures for protection of, 496; Hull's difficulties in defending, 511–12, 519, 520; Hull besieged in, 520–25; Brock's attack on, 525–27; Hull's surrender of, 527, 569; reinforcements for, 568; expedition to recover, to be commanded by Harrison, 569; Harrison receives *carte blanche* to recover, 670–71; Harrison's views on military value of, 670, 672, 675–76; failure of Harrison's campaign against, 688–89; evacuated by Proctor, 708; occupied by Harrison, 709.

"Detroit," 19-gun British ship on Lake Erie, 701; her armament, 702; captured, 706.

De Watteville, major-general in British army, 979. (See Infantry, British regiments of.)

Dexter, Samuel, defeats project of State convention in Massachusetts, 576; republican candidate for governor of Massachusetts in April, 1814, 912–14; again in 1815, 1245; again in 1816, 1272.

Dickinson, James, captain of the British sloop-of-war "Penguin," 1231; killed in action with "Hornet," 1231–32.

"Dolphin," Baltimore privateer, captured, 846.

Douglas, Sir Howard, on American gunnery, 1336–37, 1340, 1341.

Douglass, David B., lieutenant of engineers, at Fort Erie, 958, 962.

Douglass, George, captain of British sloop-of-war "Levant," his action with the "Constitution," 1234–36.

Downie, George, captain in the British navy, commanding flotilla on Lake Champlain, 979; his confidence in the superiority of his fleet, 980, 982; brings his fleet into action, 984; killed, 985.

Dresden, battle of, 861.

Drummond, Gordon, lieutenant-general in British army, and governor of Upper Canada, 761; burns Black Rock and Buffalo, 763; his military career, 940–41; arrives at Fort George, July 25, 1814, 940–41; reaches Lundy's Lane, 943; his battle at Lundy's Lane, 943–50; his losses, 952; his delays after Lundy's Lane, 956; moves on Fort Erie, 957; censures his troops at Black Rock, 958; assaults Fort Erie, 959–63; censures De Watteville's regiment, 964; his agony of mind, 964–65; expects a sortie, 967–69; claims victory, 971; retires to Chippawa, 971; his force, 990–91; returns to Kingston, 992; compared with Pakenham, 1180–81.

Drummond, ————, lieutenant-colonel of the Hundred-and-Fourth British Infantry, leads assault on Fort Erie, 959, 961; killed in the bastion, 963.

Duane, William, editor of the "Aurora," his attacks on Gallatin, 250, 252; appointed adjutant-general, 648.

Dudley, William, colonel of Kentucky militia, killed at the Maumee Rapids, 692.

Duval, Gabriel, appointed Justice of the Supreme Court, 593.

Duvall, William P., member of Congress from Kentucky, 1101.

Dwight, Theodore, secretary of the Hartford Convention, 1112.

"EAGLE," 20-gun brig, in Macdonough's squadron on Lake Champlain, 981; in the battle of Plattsburg, 985.

Eastern Branch of the Potomac, navy-yard bridge over, 1002; Winder's position beyond, 1003, 1004; Winder retreats across, 1005; protects Washington on the eastern side, 1006–07; extends to Bladensburg, 1007; ships burned in, 1013.

Eastport in Maine, claimed and occupied by Great Britain, 974.

Eckford, Henry, naval contractor at Sackett's Harbor, 926.

Eel River Miami Indians, 346, 349.

Effectives, rank-and-file present for duty, 724.

Eldon, Lord, on the differences with America, 632.

Election, State, in 1809, 14, 113; in 1810, 152, 221; in Massachusetts in April, 1811, 375; in April, 1812, 435; in May, 1812, 439; in New York, May, 1812, 439; presidential, of 1812, 580–81, 582–83; in the spring of 1813, 653–54; in the autumn of 1813, 872; in the spring of 1814, 912–15; congressional in November, 1814, 1068–69, 1075, 1109; of April, 1815, 1245–46; of April, 1816, 1272; presidential of 1816, 1276.

Electoral College in 1808 and 1812, 582.

Elk River, Cockburn's operations in, 804–05.

Elliott, Jesse D., lieutenant U. S. navy, 538; cuts out British vessels at Fort Erie, 539; commander in U. S. Navy, commands "Niagara," in Perry's squadron, 702; fails to close with the enemy, 703; Perry's, Barclay's, and Yarnall's remarks on, 704–06; dispute about, 705.

Ellsworth, Oliver, chief-justice, sent to France as envoy extraordinary, 649.

Embargo of Dec. 22, 1807, repeal of, 27; Turreau's complaints of repeal, 28, 29–30; Canning's note on, 33; revocation of orders attributed to, 55, 56; John Taylor's explanation of repeal, 138–39; approved by Napoleon, 179; causes France to lose her colonies, 180; its effect on the northwestern Indians, 354–55.

Embargo for sixty days, recommended by the President, March 31, 1812, 427–29, 430–31; Foster's report on, 432; act passed by Congress, April 4, 1812, 433–34.

Embargo, of Dec. 17, 1813, rejected by the Senate, 667–68; recommended by the President, December 9, 873, 874; adopted by Congress, 874; repeal recommended by Madison, March 31, 1814, 877; debate on, 876–80; repealed, 880–81, 914; effect of, on the currency, 886–87; effect of, on the elections, 913–14; on Massachusetts, 916.

Emerson, Ralph Waldo, 1319, 1322.

Emerson, Rev. William, 1319.

Emuckfaw, Andrew Jackson's campaign against, 791, 793.

"Endymion," 50-gun British frigate, boats beaten off by the "Prince of Neufchatel," 1055–57; her action with the "President," 1226–30.

Enforcement Act (see Embargo and Acts of Congress).

Engineers, Corps of, services of, in the war, 1341–42. (See Walker Keith Armistead, David Bates Douglass, William McRee, Joseph Gilbert Totten, Eleazar Derby Wood.)

England, financial dangers of, in 1809, 36; political decline of, 43–44; distress of, in 1811, 297–98; apathy of, upon American questions, 312; change of tone between 1807 and 1812, 449, 479–80, 490; war declared against, 451–52; distress of, in 1812, 478–79; attitude toward the war, 578; slow to accept war with United States, 621; sensitive on right of impressment, 622; in consternation at the loss of the "Guerriere," 622–23, 636; angry with United States, 625, 627, 630; her naturalization acts, 634–36; *quasi* blockade of, in 1813, 848–50; her exultation at Napoleon's overthrow, 865; her indifference in 1813 to the American war, 865–67; her demands at Ghent, 1095; her intentions at New Orleans 1127; intoxication of, in the spring of 1814, 1185–87, 1190; conditions of peace required by, 1188–91, 1195–97; her reception of the Treaty of Ghent, 1220–21.

Enotachopco Creek, Jackson's rout at, 791–92.

"Enterprise," Mississippi steamboat, 1148.

"Enterprise," Salem privateer, captured, 847.

"Enterprise," sloop-of-war, captures the "Boxer," 815–16, 836; escapes capture, 1046.

"Epervier," British 18-gun sloop-of-war, 1038; captured by "Peacock," 1038, 1039; brought into Savannah, 1039.

Eppes, John W., member of Congress from Virginia, chairman of Committee of Ways and Means in Eleventh Congress, 55; his appropriation bills for 1810, 142; his bill for reviving non-intercourse against Great Britain, 235; maintains doctrine of contract with France, 236–37; waits arrival of Serurier, 240; amends his non-intercourse bill, 244; quarrels with John Randolph, 244; defeats John Randolph for Congress, 654; chairman of Ways and Means committee, 656; defeated for the Fourteenth Congress by Randolph, 1070; his treasury-note scheme, 1081–83; silent about legal tender, 1081, 1086; reports treasury-note bill, 1086; favors doubling taxes, 1086; Ticknor's report of his remark to Gaston, 1091; moves to reduce term of military service, 1103; defeated for the Fourteenth Congress, 1246.

Erie Canal, 1296–97.

Erie, Fort (see Fort Erie).

Erie, Lake, armaments on, 496, 504, 515, 538; Perry's victory on, 698–707.

Erskine, Lord Chancellor, on the American war, 632.

Erskine, David Montague, his report, March 17, 1809, of Turreau's anger at the repeal of embargo, 28; his threatening despatches of November and December, 1808, 37–38; his instructions of Jan. 23, 1809, 40–43, 49, 52–53, 66, 68, 80; his reasons for exceeding instructions, 49, 51, 68–69; his settlement of the "Chesapeake affair," 50; his "Chesapeake" settlement disavowed by Canning, 65; his settlement of commercial disputes, 52–53; his commercial arrangement received in England, 64; disavowed, 65–66, 69; his explanation of the Order of April 26, 1809, 60; his reply to Canning's criticisms, 68–69; his recall, 69; effect of his disavowal in the United States, 79; Jackson's opinion of, 86; his farewell audience, 86; effect of his arrangement on Napoleon, 100; comparison between his pledges and those of Champagny, 210.

"Espiègle," British sloop-of-war, 820–21.

Essex county in Massachusetts, declaration of meeting, July 21, 1812, 575.

"Essex," 32-gun frigate, her action with the "Alert," 319, 560; arrives with despatches, 331, 334; sails in July, 1812, 559; returns to port, 560; in the Pacific, 819, 835, 1034–35; her force, 1035; blockaded at Valparaiso, 1036; tries to run the blockade, 1036; driven back and captured, 1036–37.

Eustis, Dr. William, appointed Secretary of War, 12; orders Wilkinson not to camp at Terre aux Bœufs, 122, 123; authorizes Harrison to buy Indian land in the Wabash valley, 354; approves Harrison's purchase, 355; orders Harrison to preserve peace with Indians, 358, 361; orders the Fourth

Regiment to Indiana, 360; his lost letter of Sept. 18, 1811, to Harrison, 362; appears before the Committee of Foreign Relations, 384–85; his supposed incompetence, 410, 436, 568–69, 570–73; his duties in 1812, 410; on recruiting, 495; his letters to William Hull, announcing war, 500–01; and ordering conquests in Canada, 502; his orders to Dearborn to repair to Albany, 505, 506–07; and to take direction of militia at Niagara, 508, 518, 534–35; resigns, 589, 674; orders out fifteen hundred Tennessee militia for service in Florida, 764.

Evans, Samuel, captain in U. S. navy, commands "Chesapeake," 822.

"Evening Star," London newspaper, on American frigates, 621.

Everett, Edward, 1322.

Exchange, turn of, against England, in 1808, 36; rates of internal in the United States, 1814–1815, 1059, 1269; favorable turn of foreign, in 1816, 1268.

Exports and Imports in 1815, 1245, 1246–48; in 1816, 1268; in Massachusetts, 1290; in Virginia, 1291–92; in New York and Pennsylvania, 1295.

FAGAN, ———, agent of Fouché, 168.

Fanning, Alexander C. W., captain of artillery at Fort Erie, 959.

"Fantome," British sloop-of-war, 804.

Farragut, David Glasgow, midshipman in U. S. navy, his criticism on Captain Porter, 1036.

Faussett, Robert, lieutenant of the British seventy-four "Plantagenet," his affidavit about the "General Armstrong," 1052–53.

"Favorite," British sloop-of-war, arrives at New York with treaty from Ghent, 1221–22.

Fayal, destruction of the "General Armstrong" at, 1051–55.

"Federal Republican," Baltimore newspaper, mobbed, 578–79; of Jan. 28,

1815, on the impossibility that government should stand, 1123.

Federalists (see Party).

Fenwick, John R., lieutenant-colonel of Light Artillery, 543.

Ferdinand, Prince of the Austrias (Ferdinand VII.), proposed kingdom for, in America, 169; cedes Florida by treaty of 1819, 457.

Fernandina in East Florida, seized by United States, 459; occupation disavowed and maintained, 460–61, 764; evacuated, 766–67.

Finances, national, in 1809, 116, 126; customs-revenue in 1807, 1808, 1809, 1810, 203–04, 223; military and naval appropriations of the Eleventh Congress, 247; in 1811, 383; Gallatin's estimates for war, 402–04; war-taxes proposed by Gallatin, 408; approved by the House, 409; laid aside, 409–10; in 1812, 596; in 1813, 599–607; in 1813, mentioned in annual message, 871; condition of, 885–88, 891; in 1814, 918–19, 1059–60; mentioned in annual message, 1076; Campbell's annual report on, 1077–78; Dallas's account of, in November, 1814, 1079, 1084; Dallas's account of, in December, 1814, 1086; Dallas's account of, in January, 1815, 1090–91; Monroe's account of, in January, 1815, 1106; the "Federal Republican's" account of, Jan. 28, 1815, 1123; Dallas's sketch of, for the first year of peace, 1239; condition of, after the peace, 1244, 1249–52; Lowndes's report on, January, 1816, 1258; Dallas's sketch of, in October, 1816, 1277; (See Gallatin, Jones, Campbell, Dallas, Taxes, Loans, Treasury Notes.)

Findlay, James, colonel of Ohio volunteers, 500, 514, 521.

Findley, William, member of Congress from Pennsylvania, favors war, 395; in the Fourteenth Congress, 1280.

Finnis, Captain R., of the Royal Navy, commands British squadron on Lake Erie, 699, 700; commands the "Queen Charlotte" in action, 701.

Fischer, British lieutenant-colonel in

De Watteville's regiment, leads assault on Snake Hill at Fort Erie, 959–62.

Fisheries, England's wish to exclude the United States from, 909, 1095, 1108; Governor Strong's views on, 1108; to be interdicted to the United States, 1188; Newfoundland memorial on, 1189; Castlereagh's instructions of July 28 on, 1190–91, 1192, 1209; discussed by the British commissioners, at Ghent, 1196; question of, under the treaty of 1783, 1213–17; Adams's struggle for, 1214–17; Gallatin's championship of, 1214–17; Clay's indifference to, 1214–17; British silence regarding, 1215; British offer to reserve right, 1216; Gallatin's offer regarding, 1217; omission of, in the Treaty of Ghent, 1218.

Fletcher against Peck, Marshall's decision in case of, 1310–11.

Florida, Napoleon's retention of, 26–27; Napoleon insinuates an idea regarding, 282; Foster instructed to protest against the seizure of, 311; his protest, 321; Monroe's reception of the protest, 321–22; Madison's designs on, 642, 764–66; Russian influence on, 767; supposed sale to England, 767–68; a southern object, 768–69, 1131; in the negotiation at Ghent, 1202–04.

Florida, East, Madison asks authority to occupy, 227; Congress authorizes occupation of, 228; commissioners sent to take possession of, 228; revolutionized, 457–61; bill for occupation of, 461; occupation continued, 764; bill for the seizure of, 765; bill amended, 765; troops withdrawn from, 766–67.

Florida, West, revolution in, 214–20; Madison orders occupation of, 217–18, 222; Claiborne takes possession of, 219; organized as part of Orleans Territory, 219; protest of British *chargé*, 220; Giles's bill for annexing to Orleans Territory, 223; debate on annexation, 223–25; Macon's bill, admitting, as a part of Lousiana, 225–

26; remains a separate territory, 227; divided by act of Congress, 456; ceded by Spain in 1819, 457. (See Mobile.)

Flour, price of, its effect in repealing the embargo, 139; affected by the blockade, 802; affected by peace, 1224.

Flournoy, Thomas, brigadier-general, in U. S. army, succeeds Wilkinson at New Orleans, 789.

Floyd, John, brigadier-general of Georgia militia, his campaign to Autossee, 788–89; his battle at Calibee Creek, 793–94.

Fontaine, John, lieutenant of artillery in Fort Erie, 962.

Forfeitures under the Non-importation Act, 598–603.

Forrest, C. R., major of the British Thirty-fourth Infantry, Assistant Quarter-Master General before New Orleans, his account of the British batteries, 1164, 1167; his account of the canal, 1176.

Forsyth, Benjamin, major in U. S. Rifle Regiment, 722.

Forsyth, John, member of Congress from Georgia, 656; on bank committee, 1084; objects to economy, 1240; in the Fourteenth Congress, 1254; supports the bank, 1261; his remarks on the Compensation Bill, 1264.

Fort Barrancas at Pensacola, occupied by British expedition, 1132; evacuated and blown up, 1139.

Fort Bowyer, on Mobile Point, constructed by Wilkinson, 770; occupied by Jackson, 1131, 1133; attacked by British sloops-of-war, 1133–36; captured, 1181–84.

Fort Dearborn, Chicago, 372, 495; garrison massacred, 527.

Fort Erie, 536, 540, 547; evacuated by British, 700, 730; re-occupied by Drummond, 761; Brown ordered to attack, 929; British garrison at, 932; captured by Brown, 933; Ripley's retreat to, 954; entrenched American camp at, 956, 958–59, 1341; Drummond's repulse at, 959–65; strength of army at, 957, 967; Brown's sortie from, 967–71; Drummond retires from, 971; abandoned and blown up by Izard, 990–91, 992; in the negotiation at Ghent, 1207.

Fort George, 501, 536, 540, 726; Brock's headquarters, 536, 540–41, 542; captured by Dearborn, 729; held by McClure, 761; evacuated, 762; Riall's headquarters, 932; Brown unable to attack, 938–39.

Fort Harrison, 362, 369, 495; attacked by Indians, 669.

Fort McHenry, at Baltimore, strength of, 1027; bombardment of, 1027–28.

Fort Meigs, constructed in February, 1813, 683, 688, 689; besieged by Proctor, 691–93; siege abandoned, 693–94; threatened by Proctor, 694.

Fort Mims, surprise and massacre of, 780–81.

Fort Niagara, bombarded, 545; captured by Drummond, 762, 763; British garrison at, 932; cession required, 1190–91, 1207.

Fort St. Philip, below New Orleans, 1142; bombarded, 1181.

Fort Schlosser, on the Niagara River, Brown's base of supplies, 941.

Fort Stephenson, Croghan's defence of, 695–96.

Fort Stoddert, 789.

Fort Strother, on the Coosa, Jackson's base, 786–87, 791.

Fort Sullivan, at Eastport, Maine, capitulates, 974.

Fort Washington (or Warburton), on the Potomac, 658, 993, 1006; abandoned, 1021.

Fort Wayne, 669.

Fortifications, appropriation for, in 1809, 62; appropriation asked in 1810, 223.

Foster, Augustus John, appointed British minister to the United States, 307, 310; F. J. Jackson's opinion of, 311; his instructions, 311–12; arrives at Washington, 321, 331; protests against the seizure of Florida, 321; reports Monroe's language about Spanish America, 321–22; protests against the

non-importation, 322; narrows the issue to Fox's blockade and the Orders in Council, 322–23; reports Monroe's language on the revocation of the French decrees, 324; threatens retaliation for the non-importation, 325; reports that the Orders in Council are the single object of irritation, 326; settles the "Chesapeake affair," 379–80; his report of executive temper in November, 1811, 386; his report of Gallatin's language about taxes, 402; his report of the conduct of Federalists in Congress, 413–15; receives instructions, March 21, 1812, 426; communicates them, 427; his report of Monroe's remarks on recent French spoliations, 429, 430–31; his report of Madison's and Monroe's remarks on the embargo of April, 1812, 432; suggests Madison's re-election, 441; on the American people, 630; his Florida protest, 642.

Fouché, Joseph, Duc d'Otrante, Napoleon's minister of police, 157; opposes Napoleon's commercial system, 159; sends an agent to the British government, 168; disgraced and exiled, 171.

"Fox," privateer, in British waters, 849.

France, alienation between United States and, 23–32, 101–08; difficulties of commerce with, 109, 173–74; value of spoliations in 1809, 1810, 172; contract with, 236; unfriendly language of the annual message toward, 382; Madison's language regarding, 423, 444, 448; theory of contract with, apparently abandoned, 448; Monroe's language regarding, 453; Napoleon driven back into, 875; invaded, 876, 890, 891. (See Armstrong, Barlow, Madison, Monroe, Talleyrand, Champagny, Maret.)

Franklin, Jesse, senator from North Carolina, 653.

Fremantle, Colonel, letter on the situation of Parliament, 44.

French Mills, Wilkinson's winter quarters, 760, 923.

French spoliations (see Spoliations, French).

Frenchtown, in Maryland, Cockburn's attack on, 804–05.

Frenchtown, on the river Raisin, 679. (See Raisin.)

Frigates, American, effect of their captures on England, 622–23, 626, 628–31, 636; cost of, 834; efficiency of, compared with sloops-of-war, 834–36; six new, ordered to be built, 836; their record in 1814, 1033–37. (See Navy, "President," "Constitution," "United States," "Chesapeake," "Congress," "Constellation," "Essex," and "Adams.")

"Frolic," American sloop-of-war, built in 1813, 836; sails in February, 1814, and is captured April 20, 1037.

"Frolic," British sloop-of-war, 561; her action with the "Wasp," 561–62.

Fulton, Robert, his torpedo, 148; his inventions, 1342. (See Steamboat.)

GAINES, EDMUND PENDLETON, promoted to brigadier, 901; corrects Brown, 925; takes command at Fort Erie, 956; his force, 960; repulses Drummond's assault, 960–65; wounded, relinquishes command, 966; ordered to Mobile, 1140; remains brigadier on peace establishment, 1242.

Gallatin, Albert, his appointment as Secretary of State defeated, 9–12; his quarrel with Samuel Smith, 13; his conversation with Turreau about the Floridas, 30–31; his remarks to Turreau on renewing intercourse with Great Britain, 54; his letters on Erskine's disavowal, 79–80; his expectations from Jackson's mission, 79–80, 83–84; his feud with Giles, Smith, and Leib, 113; his letter of remonstrance to Jefferson, 114, 116–17; his enemies, 118; his annual report of 1809, 126; his bill for excluding British and French ships, 130 (see Macon); his remarks on Napoleon's secret confiscations, 183; his remarks

to Turreau on revival of non-intercourse against England, 212; gives notice of revival of non-intercourse against England, 212; his annual report of 1810, 223; his dependence on the bank, 229, 233; asks an increase of duties, 247; his letter of resignation, 250–53; Serurier's estimate of, 327; his annual report of November, 1811, 382; attacked by Giles, 397–98; delays his estimates, 402; his war-taxes, 402–04, 408–09, 435; his war-taxes reported June 26, 456; his loan of 1812, 437; believed to think war unnecessary, 449; complains of Congress, 455–56; reports tax-bills to Congress, 456; his instructions at the outbreak of war, 501–02; his opinion of Eustis, 572–73; claims department of State, 590; his annual report of Dec. 5, 1812, 596, 600; his views on the forfeiture of merchandise imported in 1812, 600–01; his attitude toward war-taxation, 605; offended by Duane's appointment, 648; asks to go as peace commissioner to Russia, 649; regards his separation from the Treasury as final, 649; negotiates loan of 1813, 650; settles financial arrangements for the year, 651; sails for Russia, 651; on the incapacity of government, 655; his name sent to the Senate as envoy, 660; his nomination rejected, 660, 864; remonstrates against the seizure of Mobile, 767–68; objects to special legislation for privateers, 851; arrives at St. Petersburg, 854, 859; writes to Baring, 856; obliged to remain idle at St. Petersburg, 859–60; leaves St. Petersburg and arrives in London, 864–65, 870; nominated and confirmed as joint envoy to Ghent, 876; his estimate of bank capital, currency, and specie in 1814, 886–88; effect of his letters on the President, 996; Dallas's opinion of, 1079; remains in London until June 21, 1814, 1185; has interview with the Czar June 17, 1189; writes despatch of June 13, 1190; his position and authority among the negotiators, 1193–94; abandons hope of peace, 1198; takes control of the commission, 1203; on the Florida policy, 1204; accepts the Indian article, 1205; learns Prevost's defeat, 1208; becomes champion of the fisheries, 1214, 1216, 1217; Adams's opinion of, 1218; his opinion of Adams, 1218; appointed minister to France, 1243; declines the Treasury, 1266, 1278.

Gambier, Lord, appointed chief British commissioner at Ghent, 1193.

Gardenier, Barent, member of Congress from New York, his remarks on Jefferson and Madison, 57–58; supports Macon's bill, 131; cause of changing rule of previous question, 245.

Gardiner, John Sylvester John, president of the Anthology Club, 1319.

Gaston, William, member of Congress from North Carolina, his reply to Eppes, 1091.

Gaudin, Duc de Gaete, orders of, 241.

"General Armstrong," New York privateer brig, 838; escapes the "Coquette," 845; destroyed at Fayal, 1051–55.

George III., King of England, becomes insane, 202, 298.

George, Prince of Wales, his Whig associations, 298–99; becomes Prince Regent, Feb. 6, 1811, 306; retains Spencer Perceval's ministry, 306; his audience of leave for William Pinkney, 307, 308–10; his conditional declaration of April 21, 1812, that the Orders in Council should be withdrawn, 469, 488; his opinion of Major-General Proctor, 683–84; approves conduct of Major-General Ross, 1128.

Georgia, State of, relations with Creek Indians, 771–73; share in the Creek war, 783; militia campaigns of Floyd, 788–89, 793–94; militia fail to deal with the Creeks, 1062; regular troops in, 1129–30; agitated by British invasion, 1225.

German, Obadiah, senator from New York, 653.

Gerry, Elbridge, elected governor of Massachusetts in 1810 and 1811, 152, 375; defeated in 1812, 435; nominated for the Vice-Presidency, 442; elected, 582.

"Gershom," American brig, burned by French squadron, 428, 431.

Ghent, despatches dated Aug. 20, 1814, arrive at Washington from, 1095, 1199; American commissioners arrive at, 1190, 1195; first conference at, August 8, 1195; second conference at, August 19, 1197; despatches of August 20 from, 1199; Castlereagh visits, 1200; Treaty of, signed December 24, 1218; Treaty of, received in England, 1220–21; Treaty of, received in America, 1222–24; treaty confirmed and ratified, 1222–23, 1238; character of treaty, 1223; effect of treaty on party politics, 1237.

Gholson, Thomas, member of Congress from Virginia, moves new rule of previous question, 245.

Gibbs, Sir Samuel, British major-general, appointed second in command of British expedition to New Orleans, 1129; commands British right column at the battle of Jan. 8, 1815, 1174; attacks and is killed 1176, 1180–81.

Gibson, James, colonel of Fourth Rifles, leads sortie from Fort Erie, 969; killed, 970–71.

Giles, William Branch, senator from Virginia, defeats Gallatin's appointment as Secretary of State, 9–11; votes for mission to Russia, 14; his report on F. J. Jackson, 126–27, 129; wishes energy of government, 127–28, 134; his bill for the annexation of West Florida, 223; his speech on the Bank Charter, 232; his political capacity, 252; reports bill for raising twenty-five thousand troops, 396; his speech attacking Gallatin, 397–98; his factiousness, 398; his admission of errors, 401; his speech on the volunteer bill, 405; votes for war, 451; votes against occupying East Florida, 461; on seamen's bill, 610–11; in opposition, 653; votes against Gallatin's appointment to Russia, 660; charged by Monroe with schemes of usurpation, 662; votes against mission to Sweden, 663; no chance of re-election, 894; his bill for drafting eighty thousand militia, 1095–1103; thinks government cannot stand, 1123; resigns seat in Senate, 1255.

Girard, Stephen, shares loan of 1813, 650–51; subscribes for bank-stock, 1271.

Gitschin in Bohemia, the Czar's headquarters, 854.

Glasgow, meeting of merchants at, in September, 1814, 1049.

Gleig, George R., lieutenant in the British Eighty-fifth Regiment, his account of the capture of Washington, 1001, 1012–13; his account of the artillery at New Orleans, 1161–64, 1166–68.

Gold, premium in England in 1812, 623. (See Specie.)

Goldsborough, Robert Henry, senator from Maryland, 662–63; denounces conscription, 1098.

Goodrich, Chauncey, delegate to the Hartford Convention, 1111, 1112.

Gordon, James A., captain of British frigate "Seahorse," captures Alexandria, 1021; rejoins fleet, 1025–26.

Gore, Christopher, elected governor of Massachusetts in 1809, 14; invites F. J. Jackson to Boston, 151; defeated in the election of 1810, 152; and in 1811, 375; senator from Massachusetts, his speech on conscription, 1098; his letter on State armies, 1106–07; approves report of Hartford Convention, 1117; his opinion of the Treaty of Ghent, 1223.

Goulburn, Henry, under secretary of state for the colonies, appointed British commissioner at Ghent, 1193; presents subjects of discussion, 1195; states British demands, 1197; reports Bayard's remarks, 1199; checked by Castlereagh, 1200–01; anxious for Prevost to move, 1202; out of temper, 1204–05; again checked, 1205; quite in despair, 1208; thinks the fisheries conceded, 1215.

"Governor Tompkins," New York privateer schooner, her escape from man-of-war, 845–46; in the British Channel, 1047.

"Grace Ann Greene," American vessel released by Napoleon, 271.

Graham, John, his account of public opinion in Kentucky, 570.

"Grand Turk," privateer, in British waters, 849–50.

Grandpré, Louis, 214.

Granger, Gideon, removed from office by Madison, 894–96.

Great Britain (see England).

Greenleaf's Point (Arsenal), at Washington, 1006.

Grenville, Lord, on Canning, 38; on the American government, 627.

Grétry, 166.

Grosvenor, Thomas P., member of Congress from New York, on Webster's bank-bill, 1089–90; in the Fourteenth Congress, 1254; criticises Webster, 1262; on committee for internal improvements, 1282.

Grundy, Felix, member of Congress from Tennessee, 380, 390, 430; on Committtee of Foreign Relations, 381, 384; his speech in favor of war, 390–92; favors large army, 399; opposes war-power, 405; against frigates, 408; on embargo, 433; on the political effects of war, 441; on forfeitures, 603; reports bill for regulation of seamen, 609; on the state of the finances in April, 1813, 888; defeated as Speaker, 892.

"Guerriere," British frigate, 313; "Little Belt" mistaken for, 314–16; Captain Dacres, commander of, 320; joins Broke's squadron, 554; chases "Constitution," 555; captured by "Constitution," 556–58; consternation produced throughout Great Britain by capture of, 622, 636; Captain Dacres on capture of, 624; the "Times" on conduct of, 629; relative loss compared with "Shannon," 827; loss inflicted by, compared with that inflicted by "Cyane" and "Levant," 1235; effect of battle of, 1337.

Gunboats, Secretary Hamilton's remarks on, 119; attack British frigate "Junon," 807; captured on Lake Borgne, 1143; ordered to be sold, 1241.

Gunnery, naval, of American gunboats in the affair with the British frigate "Junon," 807; of the battery on Craney Island, 810–11; of the "Hornet" and "Peacock," 820–21; of the "Shannon" and "Chesapeake," 822, 826–28; of the "Argus" and "Pelican," 831–33; superiority of American, 840, 1057; Michael Scott on, 842; relative superiority at Plattsburg, 982, 985, 1340–41; of the "Peacock" and "Epervier," 1039–40; of the "Wasp" and "Reindeer," 1041–42; of the "Wasp" and "Avon," 1043–45; of the "President" and "Endymion," 1230; of the "Hornet" and "Penguin," 1231–32; of the "Constitution," "Cyane," and "Levant," 1234–36; relative superiority of American, 1337–41. (See Artillery.)

HALIFAX, blockaded by privateers in 1814, 1046–47.

Hall, Bolling, member of Congress from Georgia, moves resolutions authorizing issue of legal-tender treasury-notes, 1085–86.

Hamilton, Paul, appointed Secretary of the Navy, 12, 146; his orders to Commodore Rodgers of June 9, 1810, 313–14; of May 6, 1811, 313; his supposed incompetence, 411, 493, 570, 573; his orders to Rodgers, Decatur, and Hull, in June, 1812, 550–52, 554; his orders of September, 1812, 560; resigns, 593.

Hammond, George, Under Secretary for Foreign Affairs, 35.

Hampton, village of, captured and plundered, 811–12.

Hampton, Wade, brigadier-general in U. S. army, hostile to Wilkinson, 120; takes command at New Orleans,

124, 493; appointed Major-General, 645; sent to Lake Champlain, 741; his hostility to Wilkinson, 741; not under Wilkinson's orders, 741–44; ordered to prepare winter quarters, 749, 759; his force on Lake Champlain, 755; advances to Chateaugay, 755; reaches Spear's, 756; his force, 758; his check and retreat, 758–59; offers resignation, 759; falls back to Plattsburg, 759–60; blamed by Wilkinson and Armstrong, 760; his resignation accepted, 760, 905; fortifies Norfolk, 807; on Hull's court-martial, 905; Armstrong's treatment of, 905.

Hanson, A. C., a victim of the Baltimore riot, 579; on the popularity of the war, 666–67; his speech, Nov. 28, 1814, on the destitution of government, 1084–85.

Hardin, Benjamin, member of the Fourteenth Congress from Kentucky, moves to repeal the direct tax, 1259; on the effect of the Compensation Act, 1275.

Hardy, Sir Thomas M., captain in British navy, blockades New York, 813; countenances ship-duels, 819; escorts British expedition to Moose Island, 974.

Harper, Robert Goodloe, federalist leader in 1799, 394; senator from Maryland, 1255.

"Harpy," privateer, 1047.

Harris, Thomas K., member of Congress from Tennessee, on Giles's militia bill, 1100.

Harrison, Fort (see Fort Harrison).

Harrison, William Henry, governor of Indiana Territory, appointed governor, in 1800, 342; his account of Indian affairs, 343–48; his treaties of 1804 and 1805, 349, 351; his influence in the dispute about slavery in Indiana, 349–50; his interview with the Prophet in August, 1808, 352; his treaty of Sept. 30, 1809, 354–55; his interview with Tecumthe of Aug. 12, 1810, 356–58; his letter to Tecumthe, June 24, 1811, 359; his talk with

Tecumthe July 27, 1811, 359–60; instructed to avoid hostilities, 360–61; raises military forces, 361; sends army up the Wabash valley, 362; constructs Fort Harrison, 362; marches on Tippecanoe, 363; his arrival, 364–65; his camp, 366–67; attacked, 367; his return to Vincennes, 369; Humphrey Marshall's opinion of, 370; his estimate of the effect of his campaign, 370–71; appointed by Kentucky to command expedition to recover Detroit, 569, 587; unable to advance, 582; appointed major-general, 645; placed in command by Kentucky, 670; commissioned by the President as brigadier-general, 671; receives *carte blanche*, with no orders but to recover Detroit, 671, 674, 690; his autumn campaign, 671–77; his winter campaign, 677–78, 688–89; ordered to remain on the defensive, 690; besieged in Fort Meigs, 691–94; attacked at Sandusky, 694–98; his army of invasion, 707; embarks, 708; occupies Malden, 708–09; occupies Sandwich and Detroit, 709–10; defeats Proctor on the Thames, 713–16; returns to Detroit, 717; sent to Sackett's Harbor, 760; his treaty of peace with Indian tribes, 801, 1205; Armstrong's prejudice against, 901; resigns from the army, 901.

Hartford Convention (see New England Convention).

Harvard College, the source of Boston Unitarianism, 1301; its influence on Boston, 1321–22.

Hauterive, Alexandre Maurice, Comte d', charged with negotiations with Armstrong, 100.

Havre de Grace, in Maryland, Cockburn's attack on, 805.

Hawkesbury, Lord (see Liverpool).

Hawkins, Benjamin, Indian agent among the Creeks, 773; satisfied with behavior of Creeks, 774; his report of Tecumthe's addresss to the Creeks, 774–75; demands the delivery of Creek murderers, 777; his re-

port on the flight of the Red Sticks, 798–99.

Hay, George, District Attorney, his advice to Monroe, 588.

Hayes, John, captain of British 56-gun frigate "Majestic," commanding blockading squadron off New York, intercepts Decatur in the "President," 1226.

Head, Sir Francis, 1340.

Henley, John D., commander in the U. S. navy, his report on the destruction of the "Carolina" at New Orleans, 1161.

Henry, John, his report on disunion, 15; recalled, 62; demands money, 416; comes to Boston, 417; employs Crillon to negotiate with Monroe, 417; obtains fifty thousand dollars, 418; sails for Europe, 419; papers of, 420; supposed effect of, in Florida affairs, 459–60.

Henry, Patrick, quoted by Randolph, 1256–57.

"Hermes," 22-gun British sloop-of-war, sent to Pensacola, 1131, 1133; attacks Fort Bowyer, 1134; disabled and burned, 1134.

Hickory Ground, the focus of Creek fanaticism, 783.

Hill, Lord, intended to command British expedition to New Orleans, 1126.

Hillabee villages, 787, 792.

Hillhouse, James, delegate to the Hartford Convention, 1111.

Hillyar, James, captain of the British 36-gun frigate "Phoebe," blockades and captures the "Essex" at Valparaiso, 1036–37, 1051.

Hindman, Jacob, major of artillery corps, commands battalion in Brown's army, 931; at Lundy's Lane, 946; ordered to withdraw his guns, 949; commands artillery at Fort Erie, 959.

Hinds, Thomas, lieutenant-colonel of Mississippi volunteers, at New Orleans, 1151.

"Holkar," New York privateer, captured, 847.

Holland, exempted from the non-intercourse, 53, 66, 81; restored to independence, 876–77. (See Louis Bonaparte.)

Holland, Lord, on repeal of the orders, 483.

Holmes, John, of Maine, attacks report of Hartford Convention in the Massachusetts legislature, 1120.

Holstein, Duchy of, 286.

Hope, Henry, captain of the British frigate "Endymion," his report of attack on the "Prince of Neufchatel," 1055–56; his action with the "President," 1230.

Hopkins, Samuel, major-general of Kentucky militia, 670, 671, 673; member of the Thirteenth Congress, 1102.

Hopkinson, Joseph, member of the Fourteenth Congress, declares the federal government at its last gasp in January, 1815, 1107; represents Pennsylvania, 1255.

Horner, Francis, declares the American war unpopular, 1212.

"Hornet," sloop-of-war, brings despatches, 443; cruises with Rodgers' squadron, 552; at Boston, 560, 562; her second cruise, 564; blockades the "Bonne Citoyenne," 564, 819; Josiah Quincy's Resolution on victory of, 664; attached to Decatur's squadron, 813; sinks the "Peacock," 820–21; commanded by Biddle, 821, 823; blockaded at New London, 836; sails from New York, 1226, 1231; captures "Penguin," 1231–32; escapes "Cornwallis," 1232; gunnery of, 1338.

Horse-shoe, of the Tallapoosa River, battle at, 796–97.

Houston, Samuel, wounded at the Horse-shoe, 798.

Howell, Jeremiah B., senator from Rhode Island, votes against occupying West Florida, 461.

Hull, Isaac, captain in U. S. navy, commands "Constitution," 551; his orders, 551; chased by a British squadron, 554–55; captures "Guerriere," 556–58; takes command at New York, 563–64.

Hull, William, governor of Michigan Territory, 494; appointed brigadier-general, 493, 497; his advice regarding the defence of Detroit, 497; his march to Detroit, 500; his loss of papers, 501; arrives at Detroit, 502; invades Canada, 502–03, 515; his proclamation, 503; his required campaign, 509; decides to besiege Malden, 510–11; sudden discovery of his danger, 511–14; evacuates Canada, 514; his situation at Detroit, 519–23; his capitulation, 525–26, 527; Jefferson's opinion of, 528, 573; his proclamation, 642; criticised by Harrison, 676; his court-martial, 904, 905; sentenced to death, 906.

Humbert, Jean Joseph Amable, French general, a volunteer at the battle of New Orleans, 1179.

"Hunter," 10-gun British brig on Lake Erie, 701.

"Hyder Ali," privateer 1046.

ILLINOIS TERRITORY, population in 1810, 203.

Immigration in 1816, 1291.

Imports (see Exports).

Impressment of seamen, not a voice raised in 1809 against, 54; little complaint in 1810, 205; the House refuses to insist upon in February, 1811, 244; not expressly mentioned by Pinkney, 308; or in the annual message, 382; first made a *casus belli* in the autumn of 1811, 376–77; treated by House Committee of Foreign Relations, 387–88; mentioned by Grundy, 391; by Madison's war message, 447; only obstacle to peace, 594–96, 608–09; extent of, 609; cost and value of, 633; right of, partially conceded by Monroe's instructions, 652; abandonment of, a *sine qua non*, 652; Alexander Baring's remark on, 856–57; abandoned by the Cabinet June 27, 1814, as a *sine qua non*, 996, 1206; insisted upon by Monroe's instructions of Jan. 28, 1814, 1191.

Inaugural Address, first, of President

Madison, 7–9; second, of President Madison, 643.

India, career of Marquess Wellesley in, 187.

Indiana Territory, population in 1810, 203; created in 1800, 342; its dispute about the introduction of slavery, 349–50; adopts second grade of territorial government, 350; admitted into the Union, 1263; extinction of Indian titles in, 1297. (See Harrison.)

Indians, in 1810, 222; in the Northwest, 343; their condition described by Governor Harrison, 343; trespasses on their territory, 343; effects of intoxication upon, 346–47; murders committed upon, 347; Jefferson's policy toward, 348–49; Harrison's treaties with, in 1804 and 1805, 349; Tecumthe and the Prophet, 351; Jefferson's refusal to recognize them as a confederated body, 352; establishment at Tippecanoe Creek, 352–53; their hostility to cessions of land, 354, 356–57; their land-cession of Sept. 30, 1809, 354–55; their outbreak imminent in 1810, 356; outbreak delayed by British influence, 356; their interview with Harrison, Aug. 12, 1810, 356–58; government wishes peace with, 358; of the Six Nations in Upper Canada, wish to remain neutral, 516–17; their employment in war by the British, 517; murders by, 569–70; number of, at Frenchtown, 680; at the River Raisin, 684–85; at the siege of Fort Meigs, 691, 692–94; at the attack on Fort Stephenson, 694–98; at Amherstburg, 708; at the battle of the Thames, 713–15; in the Creek war, 782–83, 790, 797; at Talishatchee, 785; at Talladega, 785–86; at the Hillabee towns, 787–88; of the Six Nations in Porter's brigade at Niagara, 932, 933; in Riall's army, 935, 937; British rations furnished to, in Upper Canada, 972; to be guaranteed in the northwestern territory by treaty, 1095, 1189, 1191, 1192; boundary according to the Treaty of Greenville advanced as a *sine qua non* at Ghent, 1196–97; boundary abandoned as a *sine qua non*, 1200, 1202–03; amnesty accepted as a basis of peace, 1205; condition of, in 1816, 1297–98. (See Treaties.)

Infantry, American, First Regiment of, in 1813 (New Jersey), 669; prisoners from, sent to England for trial, 868; at Lundy's Lane, 944; at Fort Erie, 957.

——Second, at Fort Bowyer, 1129, 1133; capitulates, 1183.

——Third (Mississippi and Missouri Territories), at Mobile, penetrates Creek country, 789; remains at Mobile, 1129, 1138, 1141.

——Fourth, ordered to Indiana July, 1811, 360; arrives, 362; part of the expedition to Tippecanoe, 363; losses in the battle, 368; its share in the battle, 370; ordered to Detroit, 372; marches to Detroit, 500; at the battle of Maguaga, 521–22; at the surrender of Detroit, 931.

——Sixth (New York), prisoners from, sent to England for trial, 868; at Plattsburg, 978.

——Seventh (Kentucky), 669; at New Orleans, 1129, 1141; in the night battle, 1150–53, 1156.

——Ninth (Massachusetts), part of Scott's brigade, 930; at Chippawa, 936–37; at Lundy's Lane, 941, 947; its losses, 952; its strength at Fort Erie, 957; in the assault on Fort Erie, 961–62; in the sortie from Fort Erie, 970; recruited in Massachusetts, 1073.

——Eleventh (Vermont), part of Scott's brigade, 930, 1074; at Chippawa, 936; at Lundy's Lane, 941–43, 944, 947; its losses, 952–53; its strength at Fort Erie, 957; in the sortie from Fort Erie, 970.

——Twelfth, recruited in Virginia, 1073.

——Thirteenth (New York), at Queenston, 538, 541; prisoners from, sent to England for trial, 868.

——Fourteenth (Maryland), Winder's, 547; at Beaver Dam, 732.

——Seventeenth (Kentucky), 671,

679; at the River Raisin, 680–81, 684; at Fort Stephenson, 695; consolidated with the Nineteenth, 931.

——Nineteenth (Ohio), at Fort Meigs, 693; a part of Ripley's brigade, 931; defend Fort Erie, 962; in the sortie, 970.

——Twentieth, recruited in Virginia, 1073.

——Twenty-first (Massachusetts), Ripley's, at Chrystler's Field, 753; part of Ripley's brigade, 931; carries the British guns at Lundy's Lane, 945, 1074; its strength at Fort Erie, 957; holds Snake Hill, 958–59, 961; recruited in Massachusetts, 1073.

——Twenty-second (Pennsylvania), part of Scott's brigade, 930; at Lundy's Lane, 944, 947; its losses, 952; its strength at Fort Erie, 957.

——Twenty-third (New York), part of Ripley's brigade, 931; breaks the British left at Lundy's Lane, 945–46; its strength at Fort Erie, 957; holds Snake Hill, 959.

——Twenty-fifth (Connecticut), part of Scott's brigade, 930, 1074; at Chippawa, 936; at Lundy's Lane, 943, 946, 949; its losses, 953; at Fort Erie, 957.

——Thirty-third, recruited in Massachusetts, 1073.

——Thirty-fourth, recruited in Massachusetts, 1073.

——Thirty-fifth, recruited in Virginia, 1073.

——Thirty-ninth (Tennessee), ordered to join Jackson, 791, 794; arrives at Fort Strother, 795; storms Indian breastwork at the Horseshoe, 797; its losses, 798; at Mobile, 1129, 1138; sent to the Appalachicola, 1139, 1141; left by Jackson at Mobile, 1141.

——Fortieth, recruited in Massachusetts, 1073.

——Forty-fourth (Louisiana), at Mobile, 1129, 1138; ordered to New Orleans, 1141; in the night battle, 1150–53, 1156.

——Forty-fifth, recruited in Massachusetts, 1073.

Infantry, British, First Regiment of (Royal Scots), 933; in the battle of Chippawa, 935, 937; at Lundy's Lane, 944, 946–47; in the assault on Fort Erie, 963; at the sortie from Fort Erie, 970.

——Third, at Plattsburg, 979.

——Fourth, at New Orleans, 1154, 1158; in Gibbs's column, 1174, 1180.

——Fifth, at Plattsburg, 979.

——Sixth, reinforces Drummond at Fort Erie, 965; at the sortie from Fort Erie, 970.

——Seventh (Fusileers), at New Orleans, 1158; at the battle of Jan. 8, 1815, 1174–75, 1180.

——Eighth (King's), at York, 727; at the capture of Fort George, 729; part of Riall's army on the Niagara, 933; in the battle of Chippawa, 935, 937; at Lundy's Lane, 946; in the assault on Fort Erie, 964; at Plattsburg, 979.

——Ninth, at Plattsburg, 979.

——Thirteenth, at Plattsburg, 979.

——Sixteenth, on the St. Lawrence, 979.

——Twenty-first, at Baltimore, 1030; in the night battle at New Orleans, 1155; at Villeré's plantation, 1158; in the battle of Jan. 8, 1815, 1174–75, 1180.

——Twenty-seventh, at Plattsburg, 979.

——Thirty-seventh, at Plattsburg, 979.

——Thirty-ninth, at Plattsburg, 978.

——Forty-first, at Malden, 510, 511; with Brock in the attack on Detroit, 525; with Brock at Queenston, 540–41, 542; with Proctor at the River Raisin, 684; at the siege of Fort Meigs, 692; at the assault on Fort Stephenson, 696; on Barclay's fleet on Lake Erie, 701; defeated and captured at the battle of the Thames, 712–14, 716; at Lundy's Lane, 946; at

Fort Erie, 957; repulsed before Black Rock, 957–58.

——Forty-third, at New Orleans, 1158; in the battle of Jan. 8, 1815, 1174–75, 1180.

——Forty-fourth, at the attack on Baltimore, 1030; at New Orleans, 1158; in the battle of Jan. 8, 1815, 1174–75, 1180.

——Forty-ninth, Brock's regiment, 514; at Montreal, 515, 529; at Niagara, 540; at Queenston, 541; captures Boerstler, 732; at Chrystler's Farm, 753; at Plattsburg, 979.

——Fifty-seventh, at Plattsburg, 979.

——Fifty-eighth, at Plattsburg, 979.

——Seventieth, on the St. Lawrence, 979.

——Seventy-sixth, at Plattsburg, 978.

——Eighty-first, at Plattsburg, 979.

——Eighty-second, reinforces Drummond at Fort Erie, 965; at the sortie from Fort Erie, 970.

——Eighty-fifth, in Ross's army, 1001; leads the attack at Bladensburg, 1011; its losses, 1012–13; leads the advance to Baltimore, 1030; leads the advance across Lake Borgne to the Mississippi, 1147; in the night battle of Dec. 23, 1814, 1154; ordered to the west bank, 1173; captures Patterson's battery, 1177–78; losses of, 1179.

——Eighty-eighth, at Plattsburg, 978.

——Eighty-ninth, at Chrystler's Farm, 753; with Drummond at Niagara, 939; at Lundy's Lane, 943, 946; in the assault on Fort Erie, 964; at the sortie from Fort Erie, 970.

——Ninety-third, in the night battle at New Orleans, 1155; at Villeré's plantation, 1158; in the battle of Jan. 8, 1815, 1174–75; its losses, 1176, 1180.

——Ninety-fifth, in the night battle at New Orleans, 1154; at Villeré's plantation, 1158; in the battle of Jan. 8, 1815, 1174–75, 1180.

——Ninety-seventh, reinforces

Drummond at Fort Erie, 968, 971.

——One Hundredth, at the attack on Sackett's Harbor, 735; with Riall, 933; at Chippawa, 935, 936.

——One Hundred and Second, occupies Eastport, 974.

——One Hundred and Third, with Riall, 933; at Lundy's Lane, 941, 950; in the assault on Fort Erie, 959, 961–62, 963.

——One Hundred and Fourth, at the attack on Sackett's Harbor, 737; in the assault on Fort Erie, 959, 961–63.

——De Meuron's regiment, at Plattsburg, 979.

——De Watteville's regiment (German), reinforces Drummond, 956–57; in the assault on Fort Erie, 959, 961; Drummond's report on their disaster, 964; surprised in the sortie from Fort Erie, 969–70.

——Royal Newfoundland, at Malden, 510.

——First West India (colored), at New Orleans, 1158; employed as skirmishers, 1174–75.

——Fifth West India (colored), at New Orleans, 1158; in the action on the west bank, 1173.

Ingersoll, Charles Jared, member of Congress from Pennsylvania, attacks Granger, 895; criticises Calhoun's plan for a bank, 1085; calls for previous question on the bank bill, 1088; declares the war successful, 1102.

Ingham, Samuel Delucenna, member of Congress from Pennsylvania, opposes Calhoun's plan of a national bank, 1084; in the Fourteenth Congress, 1255; supports protective tariff, 1259; on committee of internal improvement, 1282.

Insurance, rates of British marine, in 1814, 1048–50, 1212.

Interior Department, recommended by Madison, 1279.

Internal improvements, bill for, 1283–85; vetoed, 1284, 1297.

Invisibles, the, 252.

Ireland, coast of, under the dominion of American privateers, 1048.

Irving, Washington, his "History of New York," 1324–26, 1343; his account of Allston, 1328.

Isle aux Noix, British force at, 924.

Isle aux Poix, British base in Lake Borgne, 1146.

Izard, George, major-general in U. S. army, his history, 899–900; takes command at Plattsburg in May, 1814, 925; his report on intercourse with the enemy, 973; fortifies Plattsburg, 976, 984; suggests moving toward the St. Lawrence, 976; ordered to move, 976–77; his remonstrance, 977; ordered to Sackett's Harbor, marches Aug. 29, 1814, 978, 989; arrives at Batavia, September 27, 989; his apparent loyalty, 989; moves on Chippawa, October 13, 990; his reports of October 16 and 23, 990–91; goes into winter quarters, 991; his mortification, 991; recommends Brown to command at Niagara, 991; offers to resign, 991–92; his career at an end, 992; his effectives, 1061.

JACKSON, ANDREW, ordered with two thousand men to support the seizure of Florida, 764; ordered to dismiss his force, 766; returns to Tennessee, 766, 770; recalls his force into service, 784; penetrates northern Alabama, 784; attacks Talishatchee, 785; relieves Talladega, 785–86; abandoned by his men, 786–87; his campaign to Emuckfaw, 791–93; his treatment of Cocke and Woods, 795–96; captures the Horse-shoe, 796–97; his treaty with the Creeks, 800–01; appointed major-general in the U. S. army, 901–02; helpless with militia, 1062; his drafts on the Treasury, 1105; appointed to command military district No. 7, 1130; arrives at Mobile Aug. 15, 1814, 1130; attacks Pensacola, 1130–39; occupies Mobile Point, 1131, 1133; his proclamations to the people of Louisiana, 1136; his ne-

glect of New Orleans, 1136–42; leaves Mobile November 22, 1140; arrives at New Orleans December 2, 1141; his military resources, 1142; goes down the river December 4, 1142; hurries back to the city December 15, 1143; surprised December 23, 1147; his measures of defence compared with Winder's, 1148–50; his military resources at New Orleans, 1150–53; his night attack of December 23, 1153–56; his entrenchments, 1156–57, 1158–59; his artillery, 1161, 1165; contrasted with Pakenham, 1157; his lines at New Orleans, 1169–73; his force, 1175–76; his account of the rout on the west bank, 1178; Adair's comments on, 1179; contented to let the British escape, 1181; his remarks on the surrender of Fort Bowyer, 1183–84; retained on peace establishment, 1242; his arbitrary conduct at New Orleans, 1243.

Jackson, Mrs. F. J., 83, 111–12.

Jackson, Francis James, his reputation, 70; appointed British minister to the United States, 70; his instructions, 72–76; sails for America, 76; Gallatin's expectations from, 80, 84; arrives at Washington, 84; his impressions, 84–88; his negotiation, 88–95; rupture with, 95; his anger, 110; his complaints, 111; his reception in Baltimore and New York, 112; discussed before Congress, 125, 126–27, 129; his letters from New York and Boston, 150–55; returns to England, 155; his treatment by Wellesley, 154–55, 189, 190–91; his influence with the British government, 305; his account of Pinkney's "inamicable leave," 309–10; his opinion of Augustus J. Foster, 311; his death, 311.

"Jacob Jones," privateer, 1046.

Jamaica, blockaded by American privateers, 628; rendezvous for British expedition against New Orleans Nov. 20, 1814, 1126, 1129, 1140.

"Java," British frigate, her action with the "Constitution," 564–65; effect of capture in England, 630.

Jay, Chief-Justice, sent to England by Washington, 649.

Jefferson, Thomas, Turreau's anger with, 28; Gallatin's remarks on, 30–31; the "National Intelligencer" on, 55; Randolph's remarks on, 57; Robert Smith's remarks on, 61; intermediates with Monroe, 115; expenditures of his administration, 141, 145; considered too timid by Robert Smith, 328; his Indian policy, 343, 348–49, 351–52, 353; his opinion of William Hull, 528, 573; his expectation of the conquest of Canada, 528; his opinion of Van Rensselaer, 573; his letter of sympathy with Madison, Sept. 24, 1814, 1071; his letter to Monroe on the capture of Washington, 1071; his letter to Short on the defection of Massachusetts, 1071–72; his plan for providing a paper currency, 1080–81; declares that more taxes cannot be paid, 1082, 1087; thinks it nonsense to talk of regulars, 1092; thinks that the war would have upset the government, 1122; expects the British to hold New Orleans indefinitely, 1122; describes the want of money in Virginia, 1224; denounces the Judiciary, 1310; reverts to his earlier theories, 1312; satirized by Washington Irving, 1325–26; results of his theories, 1335–36.

Jesup, Thomas Sidney, acting adjutant-general at Detroit, 523; major of the Twenty-fifth Infantry, 930; at Chippawa, 936; at Lundy's Lane, 943, 946; wounded, 947, 953; at Hartford, reports on the Convention, 1115.

Johnson, James, leads attack at the battle of the Thames, 713.

Johnson, Richard Mentor, member of Congress from Kentucky, favors manufactures, 139; denounces the timidity of Congress, 144; in the Twelfth Congress, 380; his war speech, 393; on the dangers of a navy, 407; on the treason of opposition, 440; colonel of Kentucky rangers, 707; crosses into Canada, 709–10; his energy, 713; wins the battle of the Thames, 715; returns home, 717; moves previous question on bank bill, 1085; accepts Giles's militia bill, 1100; in the Fourteenth Congress, 1254; author of the compensation bill, 1264, 1275; moves for committee on the Compensation Act, 1280.

Jones, Jacob, captain U. S. navy, commands the "Wasp," 561; his action with the "Frolic," 561; captured, 562; takes command of the "Macedonian," 563.

Jones, John Paul, 624.

Jones, Walter, his letter to Jefferson on dissensions in Madison's Cabinet, 133.

Jones, William, appointed Secretary of the Navy, 593; acting Secretary of the Treasury, 649–50; recommends legislation to encourage privateering, 851–52; his treasury report for 1813, 885; hostile to Armstrong, 903–04; sends Croghan's expedition to Mackinaw, 928–29; favors abandoning impressments as a *sine qua non*, 996; goes to navy-yard on the morning of Aug. 24, 1814, 1006; expects British advance through Bladensburg, 1007; permits Barney to go to Bladensburg, 1007; orders the vessels at the navy-yard to be burned, 1013; accompanies the President into Virginia, 1016–17; causes batteries to be erected on the Potomac, 1025; retires from the Navy Department, 1226; becomes president of the United States Bank, 1271.

"Junon," 46-gun British frigate, attacked by gunboats, 807.

KEANE, JOHN, British major-general, ordered on the New Orleans expedition, 1127; his caution in leading the advance, Dec. 23, 1814, 1149; after the night battle, 1157; commands assaulting column, Jan. 8, 1815, 1174; attacks and is severely wounded, 1177.

Kempt, ———, major-general in British army, commanding brigade at Plattsburg, 979.

Kennedy, Laurence, purser of the "Epervier," 1039.

Kentucky, enthusiasm for the war, 567; number of men in the field, 567, 569; distaste for the regular army, 567–68, 570; militia placed under Harrison's command, 670; three regiments at Fort Defiance, 673, 674, 678; march to the Maumee Rapids, 678; advance to the River Raisin, 680–81; massacred or captured, 684–87; appearance of, 685–86; failures of, 689; brigade of, sent to Fort Meigs, 692; massacred or captured, 692; two divisions, under Governor Shelby, invade Canada, 707; at the battle of the Thames, 715; State army raised by, 1105; twenty-five hundred militia ordered to New Orleans, 1137, 1142; arrive at New Orleans, 1169; ordered to cross the river, 1173; in reserve, 1175; routed, 1177–78, 1179; growth in population, 1287.

Key, Phillip Barton, member of Congress from Maryland, favors navigation bill, 131.

King, Rufus, his supposed opposition to Clinton, 581; elected senator from New York, 653; moves inquiry in regard to Gallatin's mission to Russia, 660; declares a minister in Sweden to be inexpedient, 662–63; reports bill to incorporate a national bank, 1088; defeats Monroe's conscription, 1103; to be placed in the Presidency, 1121; candidate for the Presidency in 1816, 1276; votes for internal improvements, 1284.

Kingston, on Lake Ontario, 721; Armstrong's plan of attacking, 723; British garrison at, 724–25; Dearborn decides not to attack, 725–26; Prevost embarks at, 733; Wilkinson ordered to attack, 744; Wilkinson decides to pass, 745–46; Armstrong and Wilkinson change opinions regarding, 747–49; Brown ordered to attack, in February, 1814, 925; Prevost visits, in October, 1814, 972, 992; preparations at, for the siege of Sackett's Harbor, 992.

"Knickerbocker" school of literature, 1324–26.

LABOUCHÈRE, 168–69.

Lacock, Abner, senator from Pennsylvania, opposes the appointment of Dallas to the Treasury, 893; consents to Dallas's appointment, 1078.

Lacolle River, Wilkinson's defeat at, 924; British force at, 924.

Lady "Prevost," 13-gun British schooner on Lake Erie, 701; in action, 704; crippled and captured, 706.

Laffite, Jean, Pierre, and Dominique, of Barataria, 1132–33.

Lambert, Henry, captain of the British frigate "Java," 565.

Lambert, John, British major-general, ordered on the expedition to New Orleans, 1128; arrives at New Orleans, 1169; commands reserve, 1174; his report of the assault, 1177; recalls Thornton, 1180; escapes, 1181; captures Fort Bowyer, 1181–84.

"Landrail," British cutter captured in the channel, 1047.

Langdon, John, of New Hampshire, nominated for the Vice-Presidency, 442.

Lansdowne, Marquess of, moves for a committee on the Orders in Council, 483; on British naval success, 631–32.

Latour, A. Lacarriere, chief engineer to Jackson at New Orleans, reports to Jackson the numbers of the British advance, 1150; lays out lines on the west bank, 1173; his services, 1342.

Latrobe, Benjamin H., rebuilds the capitol, 1278–79.

Lauriston, Marquis de, French ambassador to Russia, 289.

"Lawrence," Perry's flagship, 701, 706, 986.

Lawrence, James, captain in U. S. navy, commands "Hornet," 819; blockades "Bonne Citoyenne," 819–20; sinks "Peacock," 821; his previous career, 821–22; commands "Chesapeake," 821; his defeat and death, 823–29.

Lawrence, William, major of Second U. S. Infantry, commands Fort Bowyer, 1133; capitulates, 1183–84.

"Leander," British 50-gun frigate, captures "Rattlesnake," 836.

Lear, Tobias, quoted as authority on the ownership of Florida, 768.

Leavenworth, Henry, major of the Ninth Infantry, 930; commands right battalion at Chippawa, 936; at Lundy's Lane, 943, 944, 947, 949; wounded, commands brigade, 952, 953; his opinion of Brown's order, 953–54.

Lee, Henry, crippled by Baltimore rioters, 579.

Legal tender, Jefferson's silence about, in 1814, 1081; not a part of Eppes's scheme, 1081–82; denounced by Dallas, 1082–83; rejected by House of Representatives, 1085–86.

Leib, Michael, senator from Pennsylvania, 128, 134, 135, 451, 461; votes against Bank Charter, 234; his political capacity, 252; in opposition, 653, 660; his vote on seizing West Florida, 765; resigns to become postmaster of Philadelphia, 894–95, 1255.

Leipzig, battle of, 864; news reaches America, 875, 890.

"Leo," privateer, 1047.

Leonard, Nathaniel, captain in First Artillery, surprised and captured in Fort Niagara, 762.

Leslie, Charles Robert, 1327; his account of Allston, 1328.

"Levant," 20-gun British sloop-of-war, 1233; captured by the "Constitution," 1234–35; seized by British squadron in Portuguese waters, 1236.

Lewis, Captain, of the "Leander," 265.

Lewis, Morgan, appointed major-general, 645, 728; on the capture of Fort George, 729; withdraws from Stony Creek, 730; on Dearborn's health, 731–32; ordered to Sackett's Harbor, 732, 745; commands division under Wilkinson, 750; ill at Chrystler's Farm, 752, 754; commands district, 899.

Lewis, William, colonel of Fifth Kentucky militia, 679–80, 681; captured, 685.

Licenses of trade, British, prescribed by Orders in Council, 44, 48; scandal of, 482; debate on, 482–83; Canning's remarks on, 485, 486; Sidmouth's conditions on, 487; Castlereagh proposes to abandon, 446–47, 487; to be restricted in the war to New England vessels, 641.

Licenses, Napoleon's system of, 174–76; promised abandonment of, 272; continued issue of, 277; repudiated by Napoleon, 287, 288–89, 292; municipal character of, 325; their continued issue, 332–33; extension of, 466.

Lieven, Prince de, Russian ambassador in London, 854; informs Roumanzoff of Castlereagh's refusal of mediation, 858, 861; ordered to renew the offer, 860, 862; refuses to renew the offer, 863.

Lincoln, Levi, declines appointment as justice, 249.

Lingan, James Maccubin, killed by Baltimore rioters, 579.

"Linnet," British 18-gun brig, on Lake Champlain, 979; her armament, 981; in the battle of Plattsburg, 985.

Literature, American, in 1817, 1301–30, 1343.

"Little Belt," British sloop-of-war, affair of, 313–21, 326, 479.

"Little Belt," 3-gun British sloop, on Lake Erie, 701.

Little Warrior of Wewocau, joins Tecumthe, 776; murders white families on the Ohio, 776–77; is put to death, 777.

Livermore, Edward St. Loe, member of Congress from Massachusetts, 130.

Liverpool, meeting of merchants at, in September, 1814, 1049.

Liverpool, Earl of (Baron Hawkesbury), on American partiality to France, 38; succeeds Castlereagh at the War Department, 186; his view of American duty, 632; on the opening negotiations at Ghent, 1201–02; on the utmost point of concession, 1205; on the capture of Washington, 1208;

writes to Wellington, 1210–11; abandons claim to territory, 1212.

Livingston, Edward, his speech of 1798, 1101.

Lloyd, George, lieutenant in the British navy, commanding sloop-of-war "Castilian," his report on the loss of the "Avon," 1043–45.

Lloyd, James, senator from Massachusetts, 421; Randolph's letter to, on the Hartford Convention, 1069–70; his reply to Randolph, 1120–21.

Lloyd, Robert, captain of the British seventy-four "Plantagenet," finds the "General Armstrong" at Fayal, 1051; his report of the destruction of the "General Armstrong," 1051–55, 1057.

Loan of 1810, 126; of 1812, for eleven millions, 411; partial failure of, 437; of 1813, for twenty millions, 596, 606; for 1813, of sixteen millions, 650; for 1814, authorized for twenty-five millions, 888; threatened failure of, 891; nine millions obtained in May, 918; failure of, in July, 1814, 1058, 1077; amounts taken in Virginia and Massachusetts, 1072–73; of eighteen millions, in 1815, for funding treasury notes, 1239, 1250; failure of, in 1815, 1250–52.

Lockyer, Nicholas, captain of the British sloop-of-war "Sophie," negotiates with Jean Laffite, 1132–33.

Long, Charles, joint paymaster-general of the forces, 43.

Louis Bonaparte, king of Holland, resists Napoleon's decrees, 105; his interview with Armstrong, 106; threatened by Napoleon, 167, 169; stipulates seizure of American ships, 169, 192; abdicates, 171.

Louisiana, government offered to Monroe, 115; proposed as a kingdom for the French Bourbons, 169; admitted into the Union, 225–27, 456; objects of British expedition to, 1127–28; Nicholl's proclamation to natives of, 1132; Jackson's proclamation to people of, 1136; Jackson's proclamation to free negroes of, 1136; Monroe warns Jackson of expedition

to, 1137; population of, 1142; militia in the night battle at New Orleans, 1151–53; militia in want of arms, 1169; militia placed on the Chef Menteur road, 1172; militia on the west bank, 1173; militia routed, 1178; to be restored to Spain, 1186, 1188, 1189; Calhoun's question regarding purchase of, 1283, 1285. (See New Orleans.)

"Louisiana," American 16-gun sloop-of-war at New Orleans, 1151; descends the river, 1159; hauled beyond range of British guns, 1159, 1161; not brought into action, Jan. 1, 1815, 1165; supports Jackson's line, 1169–72; not in action of Jan. 8, 1175.

Lowell, John, his pamphlet on disunion, 909; on the condition of Massachusetts banks, 916; favors a separate peace, 1109–10; on the delegates to Hartford, 1110–11; on H. G. Otis, 1113; approves report of Convention, 1117.

Lowndes, William, member of the Twelfth Congress from South Carolina, 380, 407; his hostility to nonimportation, 435, 455, 604, 606; opposes compromise of forfeitures, 603; reports inability to decide between Dallas and Calhoun on a national bank, 1084; in the Fourteenth Congress, 1254–55; his report on the revenue, 1258; chairman of tariff committee, 1259.

Ludlow, Augustus C., first lieutenant on the "Chesapeake," mortally wounded, 824.

Lumber trade of New England, depressed in 1815, 1248.

Lumley, captain of British 32-gun frigate "Narcissus," 836.

Lundy's Lane, Riall advances to, 939; concentration of forces at, 941; battle of, 943–53.

Lyon, Matthew, favors defence, 248.

MacDONNELL, G., major in Glengarry Light Infantry, 722.

Macdonough, Thomas, commander in U. S. Navy, commands flotilla on Lake Champlain, 755, 976; takes position in Plattsburg Bay, 976; his force, 981; his previous career, 982; his forethought in preparing for action, 984; his victory, 985–86, 1340–41; his losses, 986; his reward, 1278.

"Macedonian," British frigate, capture of, 562–63; effect of capture in England, 624–25, 626, 628, 631; blockaded at New London, 813–14, 819, 835; action with, compared with that of "Endymion," 1229–30.

Mackinaw (see Michillimackinaw).

MacNeil, John, major of Eleventh U. S. Infantry, 930; at Chippawa, 936; at Lundy's Lane, 943; wounded, 944, 952.

Macomb, Alexander, colonel of Third Artillery, commands reserve in Wilkinson's expedition, 750; lands on north shore of St. Lawrence, 752; in the advance, 752, 755; promoted to brigadier, 901; takes command at Plattsburg, 978; his account of the British advance, 980; his effectives, 1061; retained on peace establishment, 1242.

Macon, Nathaniel, of North Carolina, votes with Federalists, 129; his bill for excluding British and French shipping, 130; bill defeated by Senate, 131, 135, 136; Samuel Smith's motives for defeating, 131–32, 136; his bill No. 2, 137; adopted by Congress, 139–40; his remark on manufacturing influence, 139; his speech on reducing the army and navy in 1810, 142; his bill admitting the State of Louisiana, with West Florida, into the Union, 225–27; not candidate for Speaker, 381; his account of the opinions prevailing at Washington, 384; supports war, 395; his remark on France and England, 429; his remarks on the repeal of the restrictive system, 880; favors legal-tender paper, 888, 1085–86; senator from North Carolina, 1255.

MacRee, William, lieutenant-colonel of artillery, at New Orleans, 1151.

Madison, Mrs., her remarks on Congress, 881.

Madison, James, inaugurated, 7; his Inaugural Address, 7–9; offers the Treasury to Robert Smith, 11, 263; appoints Robert Smith Secretary of State, 11; his Cabinet, 12–13; nominates J. Q. Adams to Russia, 13; his letter to Erskine accepting settlement of the "Chesapeake" affair, 50–52, 64–65; issues proclamation renewing intercourse with England, 53–54; his views of the change in British policy, 55, 59, 60; his message of May 23, 1809, 56; his popularity, 58, 62; on the disavowal of Erskine's arrangement, 80–81; revives non-intercourse against England, 82; his negotiation with F. J. Jackson, 84, 88–95; described by Jackson, 87; his ·message of Nov. 29, 1809, 125–26; special message of Jan. 3, 1810, asking for volunteers, 127; his opinions of Samuel and Robert Smith, 131–32; dissensions in his cabinet, 133; remarks on the experiment of unrestricted commerce, 148–49; his reply to Napoleon's note on the right of search and blockade, 176–77; his anger at Napoleon's confiscations, 205; his instructions of June 5, 1810, to Armstrong on Champagny's reprisals, 205–06; his devotion to commercial restrictions, 205, 206; his instructions of July 5, 1810, to Armstrong requiring indemnity, 207, 209; his decision to accept the conditions of Champagny's letter of August 5, 207–11; revives non-intercourse against Great Britain, 212; takes military possession of West Florida, 215–18, 222; his supposed character, 216; his annual message of Dec. 5, 1810, 219, 222–23; asks authority to take possession of East Florida, 228; appoints commissioners for East Florida, 228; decides to enforce the non-intercourse against Great Britain, 241; his doubts regarding Napoleon's folly, 243; his irritation at Smith's proposed inquiry from Serurier, 243–44; offers the State Department to Monroe, 254, 258, 259; his parting interview with

Robert Smith, 260–61; his anger with Smith, 262; his translation of *bien entendu*, 269; his success in maintaining his own system in the Cabinet, 337–38; his discontent with Napoleon's conduct, 339–40, 382, 423, 444, 448; his orders to maintain peace with the northwestern Indians, 358, 361; his attitude toward war with England, 377, 382, 385, 386, 415, 429–30, 441; his annual message of Nov. 5, 1811, 381; entertains Crillon, 417, 422; his message communicating Henry's papers, 419; his embargo message, 427, 431–32; his comments on the conduct of the Senate, 434; sustains non-importation, 436; re-nominated for the Presidency, 442; perplexed by the French decrees, 444; his letter to Barlow threatening war on France, 444, 472; his view of the "immediate impulse" to war with England, 446, 449; his war message, 447–50; signs declaration of war, and visits departments, 452; his measures regarding East Florida, 457, 459, 460, 461; his remarks on Napoleon's Russian campaign, 476; his remarks in August, 1812, on the Canadian campaign, 528–29; re-elected President, 582; wishes Monroe to command western army, 586–87, 591; his annual message of 1812, 594–96; his "fair calculation" on Napoleon's success, 621; his message on British "demoralizing and disorganizing contrivances," 641–42; his second Inaugural Address, 643; his relations toward Gallatin and Monroe, 647; consents to Gallatin's departure, 649–50; his annual message, May 25, 1813, 656–57; dangerous illness of, 657, 659; his reply to the Senate in regard to Gallatin's absence, 660–61; his skill in overthrowing an enemy, 663; goes to Montpelier, 667; his annual message of Dec. 7, 1813, 871–72; his embargo message of Dec. 9, 1813, 873–74, 876, 890; accepts Castlereagh's offer of direct negotiation, 875; nominates commissioners and a

Secretary of the Treasury, 875–76; his obstinacy, 876, 890; abandons system of commercial restrictions, 877–78, 881; causes of his abandonment of commercial restrictions, 877–78, 879, 891; his language about Napoleon, 889; appoints G. W. Campbell Secretary of the Treasury, 892–93; appoints Richard Rush attorney-general, 893–94; appoints R. J. Meigs postmaster-general, 896; overcomes his party enemies, 896; his dislike of Armstrong, 898, 904; offended by Armstrong's letter appointing Andrew Jackson a major-general, 901–02; his court-martial on William Hull, 905–06; his mode of resisting usurpations on States rights, 912; irritated by Armstrong's neglect to defend Washington, 993; calls a cabinet meeting, June 23, 1814, 996; selects General Winder to command at Washington, 996; calls for militia, 1002–03; reviews the army at the Old Fields, 1004; goes to Winder's headquarters at eight o'clock on the morning of August 24, 1006; arrives on the battle-field at Bladensburg, 1010; his movements, August 24–27, 1016–17, 1020–21, 1116, 1198; charges Monroe with the war department in Armstrong's absence, 1022; his interview with Armstrong, August 29, 1023–24; greatly shaken by the capture of Washington, 1023, 1070–71; appoints Monroe Secretary of War, 1025; his unpopularity, 1069–70; his disappointments, 1075; his annual message of Sept. 20, 1814, 1076; vetoes bill for incorporating a national bank, 1090; to be coerced into retiring, 1121, 1123, 1186–87; characterized by the London press, 1185–88; decides to omit impressment from treaty, 1206; Lord Liverpool's remark on, 1208; sends treaty of peace to the Senate, 1222; recommends preparation for war, 1238–39; his annual message of 1815, 1253–54; his annual message of 1816, 1279; his veto of internal improvements,

1284, 1297, 1313, 1332; his retirement, 1286.

Maguaga, battle of, 521.

"Maidstone," 36-gun British frigate, 804.

Mail routes, in 1816, 1298.

Maine, District of, 909, 974; two counties of, occupied by British expedition in 1814, 974–75, 1095, 1098, 1195; portion of, demanded by Great Britain, 1095, 1108; concessions proposed by Governor Strong, 1108; territory of, required by England, 1189; cession assumed by the *uti possidetis*, 1190–91; claimed at Ghent, 1197, 1200; claim partially abandoned, 1207; claim rejected, 1209; claim wholly abandoned, 1211, 1218; relative prosperity of, 1288–89, 1291.

"Majestic," 56-gun British frigate, intercepts the "President," 1226, 1228–29.

Malbone, Edward G., his painting, 1327–28.

Malden, British trading post on the Detroit River, 348, 352, 356, 501; to be besieged by Hull, 503, 511; British force at, 510; evacuated by Proctor, 708–09; occupied by Harrison, 709; in the negotiation at Ghent, 1207.

"Mammoth," privateer, in British waters, 1047.

Manners, William, captain of the British sloop-of-war "Reindeer," his action with the "Wasp," 1040–42.

Mannheim, proposed Congress at, 877.

Manufactures in New England, growth of, in 1809–1810, 16–19; political influence of, 139; protection of, 222; stimulated by the war, 916; depressed by the peace, 1247–48; protection of, recommended by Madison, 1253–54; protective tariff recommended by Dallas, 1254; Dallas's scheme for protecting, 1257–58; protection opposed by Randolph, 1258–59; protective tariff of 1816, 1259–61; value of, 1291.

Marblehead, privateersmen from, 852.

Maret, Hugues Bernard, Duc de Bassano, Napoleon's secretary, 102; succeeds Champagny as Minister of Foreign Affairs, 278; his report to

Napoleon of March 10, 1812, 443, 468; his negotiation with Joel Barlow, 465–75; his instructions to Serurier of October, 1811, on the revocation of the decrees, 465; communicates Decree of St. Cloud to Barlow and Serurier, 469–71; his instructions to Dalberg, 473; invites Barlow to Wilna, 475; dismisses his guests, 476.

Marlboro, in Maryland, Ross camps at, Aug. 22, 1814, 1001; returns to, Aug. 26, 1015.

Marmont, Marshal, his story of Decrès, 157.

Marshall, Humphrey, of Kentucky, on W. H. Harrison, 370.

Marshall, John, Chief-Justice, his judicial opinions, 1309–12.

Martin against Hunter's Lessee, Story's opinion in case of, 1311.

Maryland, her electoral vote, 578, 582; affected by the blockade, 803; Admiral Cockburn's operations against the shores of, 803–06; election of 1814, 1069; creates a State army, 1105; growth of population, 1287–88, 1291–92; increase of wealth in, 1293.

Mason, Armistead, succeeds Giles as senator from Virginia, 1255.

Mason, Jeremiah, elected senator from New Hampshire, 653; votes against a mission to Sweden, 663; his speech against Giles's bill for drafting militia, 1097; votes for internal improvements, 1284.

Mason, Jonathan, his letter to Nicholas on the alternative to disunion, 1121.

Massa, Duc de, letter from, 241.

Massac (see Fort Massac).

Massachusetts, tonnage of, 17; manufactures of, 17–19; resolutions of legislature regarding F. J. Jackson, 151–52; election of 1810, 152; republican control of, in 1810 and 1811, 375; Federalists recover control in 1812, 435; gives trouble to Dearborn, 504–05; refuses obedience to call for militia, 508; temper of, in 1812, 574–75; federalist majority in the elections of 1812, 582; disaffection of, 642; election in April, 1813, 653–54; delays action, 654; reports and resolutions of legislature in 1813, 661–62; banks of, their condition and influence, 886–87; expression of legislature in January, 1814, 907–08; blockaded April 25, 1814, 908; in danger from both sides, 909; town meetings in January, 1814, 909–11; report of legislature on a New England Convention, Feb. 18, 1814, 911–12; election in April, 1814, 912–14, 915; prosperity in 1814, 916; expressions of clergy, 920–22; regular troops in, 817, 974, 1130; territory of, occupied, 974–75; object of, in dependence on militia, 1063; places militia under State major-general, 1064, 1291; "dangerous and perplexing" situation of, 1064–66; calls a New England Convention at Hartford, 1066–68, 1108; election of November, 1814, a federalist triumph, 1068, 1109; Jefferson's remark that Virginia got no aid from, 1072; money furnished by, 1072–73; men furnished by, 1073–74; moral support furnished by, 1074; arrears of internal taxes in, 1087; legislature of, refuses to co-operate in expelling enemy from Maine, 1098, 1119; creates a State army of ten thousand men, 1098, 1104–05; her delegation to the Hartford Convention, 1110–11; accepts the report of the Hartford Convention, 1113, 1117; banks refuse to lend money to the State, 1118; suspends organization of State army, 1119; disunion sentiment of, 1120–22; her indifference to the negotiation at Ghent, 1194, 1214; alone interested in the obstacles to a treaty, 1216; election of April, 1815, 1245; interests affected by peace, 1247, 1248; suffers from Dallas's arrangements, 1249–52; election of April, 1816, 1272; legislature denounces Compensation Act, 1275; in Presidential election of 1816, 1276.

Massassinway, council at, 372.

"Matilda," privateer, captured, 847.

Matthews, George, appointed commissioner to take possession of East Florida, 457; his proceedings, 458–60; disavowed, 459–61.

McArthur, Duncan, colonel of Ohio militia, 500, 521, 522, 525, 526; brigadier-general, 707.

McClure, George, brigadier-general of New York militia, commands at Niagara, 760; evacuates Fort George and burns Newark, 762.

McDonald, William, captain in Nineteenth U. S. Infantry, on Ripley's staff, his account of the battle of Lundy's Lane, 946, 947.

McDonogh, P., lieutenant of artillery in Fort Erie, 962.

McFarland, D., major of Twenty-third U. S. Infantry, 931.

McKee, John, 457.

McLean, John, member of Congress from Ohio, 1255.

McQueen, Peter, half-breed Creek Indian, visits Pensacola, 779; attacked at Burnt Corn, 779; captures Fort Mims, 780–81; claims forty-eight hundred gun-men, 782; escapes to Florida, 798.

McRee, William, major of engineers, advises Brown to move against Riall, 939; directs entrenchments at Fort Erie, 956, 962, 1341.

Mecklenburg, Grand Duchy of, closes its ports to American commerce, 286.

Meigs, Return Jonathan, appointed postmaster-general, 896.

"Melampus," British frigate, 313.

"Menelaus," British frigate, engaged in house-burning on the Potomac, 1026; off Sassafras River, 1026.

Merry, Anthony, Jackson's allusions to, 85–87.

Message, first annual, of President Madison, May 23, 1809, 56; annual, of Nov. 29, 1809, 125–26; special, of Jan. 3, 1810, asking for volunteers, 127; annual, of Dec. 5, 1810, 222–23; special, of Feb. 19, 1811, on the revocation of the French decrees, 241; annual, of Nov. 5, 1811, 381–82; special, of March 9, 1812, communicating

John Henry's papers, 419; special, of April 1, 1812, recommending an embargo for sixty days, 431; of April 24, 1812, asking for two assistant Secretaries of War, 436; of June 1, 1812, recommending a declaration of war with England, 447–50; annual, of Nov. 4, 1812, 594–96; special, of Feb. 24, 1813, on British licenses of trade with New England, 641–42; annual, of May 25, 1813, 656–57; annual, of Dec. 7, 1813, 871, 1187; special, of Dec. 9, 1813, asking for an embargo, 873–74, 876; special, of March 31, 1814, recommending abandonment of commercial restrictions, 877–78; annual, of Sept. 20, 1814, 1076; veto, of Jan. 30, 1815, on the bill to incorporate the United States Bank, 1090; special, of Feb. 20, 1815, transmitting treaty of peace, 1238; annual, of Dec. 5, 1815, 1253–54; annual, of Dec. 3, 1816, 1279; special, of March 3, 1817, vetoing bill for internal improvements, 1284.

Michigan Territory, population in 1810, 203. (See Detroit.)

Michillimackinaw, Island of, 495; captured by British expedition, 511, 517; Croghan's expedition against, 928; demanded by British at Ghent, 1207.

Milan Decree (see Decrees).

Militia, constitutional power of Congress over, 404, 574; Cheves's opinion on the war power, 405; act authorizing call for one hundred thousand, 435, 567; refuses to cross the frontier, 542–43, 548; of Kentucky, 568, 569 (see Kentucky, Tennessee, Georgia, Washington City); praised by political parties, 1061; system a failure in 1814, 1061–62; tainted with fraud, 1062; intended for overthrowing the national government, 1063; of Massachusetts and Connecticut withdrawn from national service in September, 1814, 1063, 1064; of Vermont refused for defence of Plattsburg, 1064; views of the Massachusetts Senate regarding, 1067; Monroe's complaints of, 1092–93;

Monroe's scheme for drafting from, 1093–94; Giles's bill for raising eighty thousand by draft, 1095–1103; Troup's opinion of, 1099; Madison's recommendation for, 1253–54.

Miller, James, lieutenant-colonel of Fourth U. S. Infantry, at Detroit, 521, 522; appointed colonel of the Twenty-first Infantry, 931; at Lundy's Lane, captures the British guns, 945–46, 950; promoted to brigadier, takes command of Scott's brigade, 970; carries British battery in sortie from Fort Erie, 969–70.

Miller, John, colonel of Nineteenth U. S. Infantry, leads sortie at Fort Meigs, 693.

Miller, Morris S., member of Congress from New York, on the States taking care of themselves in 1814, 1101.

Miller, Samuel, captain of marines, at Bladensburg, 1012.

Mississippi militia, with Jackson at Mobile, 1138; at New Orleans, 1141, 1146, 1150–53.

Mississippi River, British right of navigating, under the treaty of 1783, 1213–14, 1219.

Mississippi Territory, admitted into the Union, 1263.

Mitchell, D. B., Governor of Georgia, 461.

Mobile, intended to be seized at the outbreak of the war, 764–65; Congress authorizes seizure of, 765–66; Gallatin's remonstrance against seizure of, 767–69; Armstrong orders seizure of, 769; Wilkinson takes possession of, 770; Vice-Admiral Cochrane recommends expedition to, 1126; Andrew Jackson arrives at, Aug. 15, 1814, 1131–32; Jackson waits at, 1132–33; Jackson leaves for New Orleans, Nov. 22, 1814, 1140–42.

Mobile Act, annexing Mobile to the Union, 457.

"Mohawk," British sloop-of-war, 804.

Money, Captain, of the British ship "Trave," commands sailors at the battle of Jan. 8, 1815, wounded, 1179.

Monroe, James, Madison's advances to,

113, 115; his state of mind, 115; offered the State Department, 254; his acceptance and policy, 255–59; takes charge, 264; Secretary of State, April 1, 1811, 330; his sensitiveness about the title to West Florida, 321; his reply to Foster's protest against the seizure of Florida, 321–22; blames Jonathan Russell for questioning the revocation of the French decrees, 324; asserts the revocation of the French decrees, 324–25; abandons task of reconciliation with England, 326; requires revocation of the Orders in Council, 326; delays Barlow's departure, 330; his remonstrances to Serurier about Napoleon's conduct, 330, 332, 424–25, 428, 432–33, 444; his remarks on protection accorded to commerce, 335; his acceptance of Madison's policy, 336–37; affirms to Foster the repeal of Napoleon's decrees, 340; his letter of June 13, 1812, to John Taylor of Caroline, 341; his language to Serurier, in October, 1811, 378; informs Serurier in November of executive plan, 385; agrees to assist the independence of Spanish America, 385; negotiates purchase of Henry's papers, 417–19; his remarks to Foster on Wellesley's instructions, 427; his conference with House Committee of Foreign Relations, March 31, 1812, 430; his remarks on the embargo, 432–33, 434; his relations toward Matthews and the occupation of East Florida, 458, 459–61; his criticisms on the conduct of the war, 571–72; assures Serurier he will not negotiate for peace, 583–84; proposes to negotiate, 584–85; proposes to take a military commission, 586–87; hesitates between civil or military control of the war, 588–89; becomes acting Secretary of War, 590; excites jealousy, 590–91; abandons military career, 591–92; offers to prohibit the employment of foreign seamen, 609; expected to command the army, 644, 645; declines commission as major-general, 645;

his protest against Armstrong's military control, 645–46; his reply to the Czar's offer of mediation, 648; acquiesces in Gallatin's departure, 649; his instructions to the peace commissioners in April, 1813, 652, 767; goes as scout to the lower Potomac, 658; acting Secretary of War, 675; his views on the force required for conquering Canada, 722–23; instructs commissioners to assert right to Florida, 767; his views on the seizure of Florida, 768–69; his remarks to Serurier on intercourse with Canada, 890; his antipathy to Armstrong, 902; advises the President to remove Armstrong, 902–03; charges Armstrong with improper ambition, 904; friendly to Izard, 989; irritated by Armstrong's indifference to the defence of Washington, 993; accedes to the abandonment of impressment as a *sine qua non*, 996; acts as a scout, August 19 and 20, 1002; joins Winder, August 21, 1003; notifies Madison and Serurier of expected battle at Bladensburg, 1004, 1007; goes to Winder's headquarters on the morning of August 24, 1006; arrives first on the battle-field at Bladensburg, 1007; changes the order of troops, 1010; returns to Washington, 1117; at Rockville, 1020; returns with the President to Washington, 1021; takes charge of the War Department, 1022, 1023; effect of his course on Armstrong, 1022; claims the War Department, 1024–25; appointed Secretary of War in September, 1814, 1025; admits failure of recruiting service, 1061, 1094; declines to receive Massachusetts militia into national service under a State major-general, 1063; asks Congress for one hundred thousand regular troops in October, 1814, 1092; recommends a draft, 1093; borrows national loans on his private credit, 1105–06; warns Jackson Sept. 25, 1814, of British expedition against Louisiana, 1137, 1139; his measures for the defence of Louisiana, 1137–38;

forbids attack on Pensacola, 1138; orders Gaines to Mobile, and Jackson to New Orleans, 1140; his instructions to the Ghent commissioners, 1191–92; his instructions of June 27, to omit impressment, 1206; recommends a peace establishment of twenty thousand men, 1239; returns to State department, 1242; nominated for the Presidency, 1265–66; elected President, 1276.

Montalivet, Comte de, Napoleon's Minister of the Interior, 157; his efforts for American commerce, 158.

Montgomery Court House (see Rockville).

Montreal, Wilkinson decides to attack, 746; Amherst's expedition against, in 1760, 746; Armstrong and Wilkinson change opinions about, 747–49; Hampton's advance toward, 755–56; British forces in district of, 756–58; British forces about, in January, 1814, 924.

Moore, Sir John, his Spanish campaign, 22, 36–37.

Moose Island, occupied by British troops in July, 1814, 974; disputed territory, 974; claimed at Ghent by England, 1191, 1197, 1200, 1207, 1216, 1219.

Moravian town, Proctor's defeat at, 709–17.

Moreau, Jean Victor, death of, 861.

Morgan, David, brigadier-general of Louisiana militia, commands on right bank at New Orleans, 1173; driven back, 1177.

Morgan, L., major of First Rifles, repulses British attack on Black Rock, 958.

Morier, J. P., British chargé at Washington, 155; his protest against the seizure of West Florida, 220.

"Morning Chronicle," the, silent toward the American war in 1813, 865; on American privateers, 1048; on the failure of the war, 1207, 1213; on the Ghent correspondence, 1213; on the

news from Ghent, 1220; on the treaty, 1220.

"Morning Post," the, on the American frigates, 628; calls for execution of British subjects taken in arms, 869; on the American government, 1187.

Morris, Charles, captain in U. S. navy, commands corvette "Adams," 975; destroys his ship in the Penobscot, 975.

Morris, Gouverneur, his oration on the overthrow of Napoleon, 919–20; his letter on the Hartford Convention, 1116; assists Erie Canal, 1296.

Morrison, J. W., lieutenant-colonel of British Eighty-ninth Regiment, commanding at Chrystler's Farm, 753–54; reinforces Drummond, 939.

Moscow, occupied by Napoleon, 623, 639; abandoned, 626, 640.

Moseley, Jonathan Ogden, member of Congress from Connecticut, 1101.

Mountmorris, Lord, 186.

Mulcaster, W. H., captain in British navy, commands flotilla in Wilkinson's rear, 752; wounded in attacking Oswego, 926.

Murray, Sir George, British major-general, succeeds Prevost as governor-general of Canada, 992, 1094.

Murray, J., colonel in British service, retakes Fort George, 762; captures Fort Niagara, 762.

Muscogee Indians (see Creeks).

NANTUCKET, British naval station, 813; relieved from operation of the embargo in 1814, 874.

Napier, Charles James, lieutenant-colonel of British infantry, 808; his remark on the Craney Island affair, 810; on the affair at Hampton, 812; on plundering the Yankees, 813.

Napoleon, his Spanish campaign, 20–23; his severity toward American commerce, 25–27; withholds Florida, 27; his causes for rupture with the United States, 31–32; his war with Austria in 1809, 76, 96; learns the repeal of the embargo and of the British Orders, 98; his first reply to Armstrong's communication, 98; drafts decree withdrawing the Milan Decree, 100; cause of his hesitation, 100–01; lays aside his repealing decree, 101; his view of the right of search, 98, 104, 106–07; his draft of Vienna Decree of Aug. 4, 1809, 103, 162, 164, 167; quarrels with his brother Louis, 105; his increased severity toward the United States, 107–09, 156; calls a Cabinet council on commerce, Dec. 19, 1809, 156; discussions with Montalivet, 157, 158; his note to Gaudin on American ships, 158; his want of money, 159–60, 167; calls for a report from Champagny, Jan. 10, 1810, 160; his dislike for Armstrong, 161–62; his condition for the revocation of his decrees, 162; his draft of note asserting retaliation on the Non-intercourse Act, 163; his reply to Armstrong's remonstrances, 165–66; his memory, 166; his Decree of Rambouillet, 167; his threats of annexing Holland, 168, 174; his annexation of Holland, 171; his reflections on Macon's act, 173–74; his license system, 174; his instructions to Champagny ordering announcement that the decrees will be withdrawn, 179; dictates letter of Aug. 5, 1810, 179; his idea of a trap, 182, 266; his instructions of Dec. 13, 1810, on the non-intercourse and the Floridas, 266; on commercial liberties, 267–68; his address of March 17, 1811, to the deputies of the Hanse Towns, 275; his address of March 24, 1811, to the Paris merchants, 276, 291; appoints Maret in place of Champagny, 278; orders a report on American commerce, 278–79; admits American cargoes, May 4, 1811, 280; his instruction of Aug. 28, 1811, about Spanish America and Florida, 282; his rupture with Russia and Sweden, 282–95; his order of May 4, 1811, opening his ports to American commerce, 325, 336; probable amount of his spoliations, 464; his restrictions on Amer-

ican commerce, 464; goes to Holland, Sept. 19, 1811, 465; his interview with Joel Barlow, 465; his extension of the license system in January, 1812, 466; his seizure of Swedish Pomerania, 467; his Decree of St. Cloud, April 28, 1811, 469–70; his departure for Poland, May 9, 1812, 471; enters Russia, 472, 491; his battle at Borodino, Sept. 7, 1812, 475; enters Moscow, Sept. 15, 1812, 475; begins his retreat, 476; his passage of the Beresina, 476; his return to Paris, December, 1812, 476; enters Moscow, 623, 638–39; begins retreat, 626; leaves his army, 627; returns to Paris, 640; organizes a new army, 854; wins battles of Lützen and Bautzen, 854, 857, 889; makes armistice, 854; wins battle at Dresden, 861; overthrown at Leipzig, 864, 868, 875, 890; approaching fall of, 869, 890; effects of overthrow on Congress and the President, 890–91; his return from Elba, 1221, 1239; overthrown at Waterloo, 1253.

"Narcissus," British 32-gun frigate, captures "Viper," 836.

"National Intelligencer," on renewal of intercourse with Great Britain, 55; on Erskine's disavowal, 79; Joel Barlow's letter in, 209; office destroyed by Cockburn, 1015.

Naturalization, British laws of, 634–36; issue raised, 868.

"Nautilus," East India Company's cruiser, 1232.

"Nautilus," sloop-of-war, captured, 554, 565, 836.

Navigation Act, moved by Macon, 130.

Navigation Act of 1816, 1281.

Navy, British, cost and pay-roll of, 633.

Navy Department (see Paul Hamilton, William Jones, B. W. Crowninshield).

Navy of the United States, in 1809, 119; reductions in 1810, 142–46; opposed by Republican party, 406; increase refused by Congress in January, 1812, 407; condition of, in June, 1812, 550–51; distribution of, in September,

1812, 559–60; movements and battles of, in 1812, 550–65; increase of, 598, 607; condition of, in 1813, 819; appropriations for, in 1814, 884–85; legislation for, in November, 1814, and February, 1815, 1104; war establishment retained in peace, 1241, 1263. (See Gunnery, "Constitution," "President," "United States," "Constellation," "Chesapeake," "Congress," "Essex," "Adams," "Wasp," "Hornet," "Argus," "Peacock," "Syren," "Nautilus," "Louisiana," "Carolina.")

Negril Bay (see Jamaica).

Nelson, Roger, on reduction of armaments in 1810, 143.

Nesselrode, Count, accompanies Czar Alexander as foreign secretary, 857; his despatch of July 9 to Lieven, 858, 860; ignorant of the Czar's orders to Roumanzoff, 860, 863, 864.

Neutrals, Napoleon's idea of, as exempt from interference, 98–99, 106–07; list of restrictions on commerce of, 109; of 1809, 117; Napoleon's declaration that, after the Milan Decree, there were no more, 160 (see Napoleon); defence of, by Russia and Sweden, 283–95 (see Impressment, Licenses, Spoliations); Madison's indifference to duties of, in West Florida, 216–17 (see Florida, East and West); Act of 1816, to preserve relations of, 1282.

Newark, on the Niagara River, burned by McClure, 762.

Newbury, memorial of town-meeting in January, 1814, 910.

New England, prosperity of shipping in, 1807–1810, 16; prosperity of manufactures in, 16–19; encouragement of manufactures in, 139; F. J. Jackson's reception in, 151–54; refuses to take the war loan of 1812, 437; favored by British government in the war, 641–42; furnishes money and supplies to Canada, 719, 873–74; benefited by the British blockade, 803, 816–17, 873; military force assigned to, 817; banks, their condition

and influence, 886, 887–88, 916; blockaded, April 25, 1814, 908; attitude toward the war in January, 1814, 915; prosperity in 1814, 916; attitude of clergy, 921–22; banks maintain specie payments, 1059; frauds in militia system of, 1062; practically independent in September, 1814, 1064; (see New England Convention); congressional elections of November, 1814, in, 1068; effect of sedition on Madison, 1071; furnishes thirteen regiments, 1073; supplies Scott's brigade, 1074; supplies Blakeley's crew, 1074; burden of taxation thrown on, 1088; probable consequence of her proposed action, 1130; delighted by news of peace, 1223–24; disastrous effects of peace on, 1247–52, 1268; church of, in 1816, 1272; representatives of, oppose internal improvements, 1284; increase of population in 1817, 1287; increase of wealth in, 1289–90; division of church in, 1301–09. (See Massachusetts, Connecticut, etc.)

New England Convention, in 1812, 576; in 1814, 909–15; project realized in October, 1814, 1066, 1108; Massachusetts delegates to, 1067, 1110–11; Rhode Island and Connecticut send delegates to, 1068; Vermont declines invitation to, 1068; project approved by the people in the November election, 1068–70; its intention to sequester the government taxes, 1088; its demand for State armies conceded by the national government, 1106; assembles at Hartford, Dec. 15, 1815, 1111; character of members of, 1111–12; proceedings of, 1112–15; report of, approved by Massachusetts and Connecticut, 1117–18, 1119–20; commissioners appointed to effect the arrangement proposed by, 1117–18; commissioners start for Washington, 1221; met by news of the battle of New Orleans, 1222; return home, 1237; sarcasms about, 1237, 1252, 1291.

New Hampshire, becomes Federalist in 1809, 14; sends no delegates to the

Hartford Convention, 1068; prosperous, 1291.

New Jersey, election in 1814, 1069; increase of population in, 1287.

New London, blue lights seen from, 814.

New Orleans, concentration of troops at, in 1809, 120–21; to be occupied by British expedition in 1814, 1126–28; military defences of, 1129–30; Jackson's delay in going to, 1130–32; Nicholl's talk of attacking, 1133; Jackson's neglect of, 1136–40; Monroe's anxiety for, 1140; Jackson arrives at, Dec. 2, 1814, 1141; population of, 1142; Jackson's measures at, 1143; news of British capture of gunboats reaches, 1143; martial law proclaimed at, 1146; in danger, 1149; its defences, 1150–51; volunteer companies of, 1150–51; volunteers of, in the night battle of Dec. 23, 1814, 1153, 1156; night battle of Dec. 23, 1814, 1153–56; artillery battle of Jan. 1, 1815, 1160–68; supplies militia, 1169; in danger from the west bank, 1173; battle of Jan. 8, 1815, 1176–81; news of battle reaches the government, 1222; civil authority restored at, 1243; growth of, 1289; fortifications at, 1342.

"New Orleans packet," seized under the Berlin and Milan Decrees, 301; by a "municipal operation," 324–25.

Newton, Gilbert Stuart, 1327–28.

New York city, described by F. J. Jackson, 151; population in 1810, 203; affected by the blockade, 803; depreciation of currency, 1225; increase of exports, 1268; increase of population, 1288; immigrants to, 1291; exports and imports of, 1295; steamboats in 1816, 1298, 1300.

New York State, election of 1809, 14; position of, in census of 1810, 203; banking mania in, 438; election in May, 1812, 439; nominates De Witt Clinton to the Presidency, 442; recruiting in, 504; politics of, in 1813, 653; suffrage in, 654; jealousy of Virginia, 896; elections in April, 1813

and 1814, 914–15; banks suspend payment, 1059; soldiers furnished by, 1073; arrears of internal taxes in, 1087; creates a State army, 1105; elections in April, 1815, 1245; election in April, 1816, 1272; growth of population, 1800–1816, 1287, 1296; growth of wealth in, 1295; begins the Erie Canal, 1296–97.

"Niagara," 20-gun brig on Lake Erie, commanded by Jesse D. Elliott, 702; her armament, 702; taken command of by Perry, 703–04; ill-fought by Elliott, 705.

Niagara, Fort (see Fort Niagara).

Niagara frontier, military importance of, 504, 508; force at, 509, 517–18, 535–36, 537–38; force raised to six thousand men, 538; Van Rensselaer's campaign at, 539–43; Alexander Smyth's campaign at, 543–47; sickness of troops at, 547; Brown's campaign at the, 923–71; British force at the, in June, 1814, 932–33; victories fail to stimulate enlistments, 1061–62; cession required as a condition of peace, 1189.

Nicholas, Wilson Cary, on the appointment of Gallatin as Secretary of State, 9–10; resigns from Congress, 55; his letter to Jonathan Mason in 1814, 1121, 1122.

Nicholls, Edward, major of the British marines, occupies Pensacola, 1131–32; issues proclamation to the natives of Louisiana, 1132, 1136; distracts Jackson's attention, 1133; evacuates Pensacola and goes to the Appalachicola, 1139.

Non-importation (see Non-intercourse).

Non-intercourse, lists of acts, 137. (See Embargo.)

Non-intercourse Act of March 1, 1809, its effect on commerce, 29; English view of, 46; affected by Erskine's arrangement, 58, 64, 66; revived by Erskine's disavowal, 80, 82–83; communicated to Napoleon, 97; communication denied by Napoleon, 164, 165–66, 174; Champagny's com-

1396

plaints of, 100; Napoleon's retaliation on, 103, 107–08, 162–63, 164, 180; its mischievous effects in America, 117–18, 126, 130; about to expire, 130; suspended, 137–40, 148; revived by proclamation of Nov. 2, 1810, 211–13.

—— of May 1, 1810, its passage, 137–40, 192; its effect on Napoleon, 173, 180; its effect in England, 192–94; its condition precedent to reviving non-intercourse, 208; creates a contract, 237, 274.

—— of March 2, 1811, reviving Act of March 1, 1809, moved by Eppes, Jan. 15, 1811, 235; decided upon, 241; amended, 244; reported, 244; passed, 245, 271; its effect on Napoleon, 272–73, 278, 280; Foster's instructions on the, 312; his protest against, 322; his threat of retaliation, 325, 381; not noticed by Napoleon, 334; an intolerable burden to the United States, 391; efforts to suspend, 437, 452–55, 606; not retaliated by England, 480; forfeitures under, 599–603; Calhoun on, 604; bill for stricter enforcement of, 606.

Norfolk, exposed to attack, 806; fortifications of, 807–08; attacked by British expedition, 808–12; sickness among militia at, 1062.

"North American Review," 1322.

North Carolina, in 1816, growth of population, 1287, 1291–92; growth of wealth, 1293; legislative report on internal improvements, 1293.

Norton, Rev. Andrews, 1305.

Nottingham, in Maryland, Ross's camp, Aug. 21, 1814, 1001.

Ocaña, battle at, 189.

Ocracoke Inlet, captured by Admiral Cockburn, 813.

Ogden, Aaron, appointed major-general, 645.

Ogdensburg, captured in 1813, 722; passed by Wilkinson, 750.

Ohio, population in 1810, 203; militia, 689; growth of, 1287.

Old Fields, Winder's army camps at, 1004; retreat from, 1005.

Olmstead, Gideon, case of, 15; Marshall's opinion in case of, 1310.

Ontario, Lake, armaments on, 536, 537. (See Sackett's Harbor.)

Order in Council, of Nov. 11, 1807, called Spencer Perceval's Order, asserted by Canning not to have caused the embargo, 39; Canning's conditions of repealing, 40–41, 42, 66, 68–69, 73–74; Grenville and Sidmouth's language regarding, 44–45; debate on, March 6, 1809, 45–46; Erskine's arrangement withdrawing, 52–54; disavowal of Erskine's arrangement, 64–69, 79–81.

—— of Dec. 21, 1808, suspending export duties on foreign produce, 33–34; further relaxations proposed, 35; their effect on English trade, 35–36.

—— of April 26, 1809, establishing a general blockade in place of the Orders of November, 1807, 47–48, 59, 75, 81, 91, 109; issue chosen by Madison and Monroe, 322–23, 326, 379, 433; conditions of repeal, 381, 446; enforced by British prize-courts, 377, 381, 478; alleged as Madison's fourth complaint, 447; revocation promised by Prince Regent on formal revocation of French decrees, 469, 488; popular agitation against, 480–81, 487, 488–89; debate of Feb. 28, 1811, in House of Lords, 483; debate of March 3 in House of Commons, 483–84; Rose's definition of, 483–84, 488; Canning's remarks on, 484–85; Perceval's account of, 486; ministers grant a committee on, 488–89; suspension of, June 16, 1812, 490–91, 576; suspension not satisfactory to the President, 577; repeal susceptible of satisfactory explanations, 595.

—— of May 24, 1809, repudiating Erskine's arrangement, and protecting vessels sailing under it, 64, 69; Canning's instructions of July 1, 1809, to F. J. Jackson, on, 73–76.

—— of Oct. 13, 1812, directing general reprisals against the United States, 622.

"Orders in Council," privateer, captured, 847.

Ordronnaux, John, captain of the privateer "Prince of Neufchatel," 1056.

Orleans, Territory of (see Louisiana).

"Orpheus," British 36-gun frigate, sent to communicate with Creek refugees, 799; captures "Frolic," 1038.

Osgood, David, minister of Medford, 921, 1319.

Oswego attacked in May, 1814, 926–27.

Otis, Harrison Gray, president of Massachusetts Senate, supports State convention in 1812, 576; supports Clinton for President, 581; his report of Oct. 8, 1814, on controlling their own resources, 1066; reports in favor of a New England Convention, 1066; chosen a delegate, 1067, 1111; publishes journal of, 1112; his activity in, 1112–13; Lowell's opinion of, 1113; appointed commissioner for, 1118.

Otter Creek in Vermont, station of Macdonough's flotilla in May, 1814, 976.

Ouvrard, Gabriel Julien, agent of the French Treasury, 169.

PAKENHAM, SIR EDWARD, British major-general, ordered to command the expedition to New Orleans, 1129; his instructions, 1129; his armament leaves Jamaica, 1140; on the way to Louisiana, 1142; makes land, Dec. 10, 1814, 1143; takes command Dec. 25, 1814, before New Orleans, 1157; contrasted with Jackson, 1157; sends for field-pieces, 1159; halts before Jackson's breastworks, Dec. 28, 1814, 1160; sends for heavy guns, 1160; digs canal, 1169; his plan of attack, 1173–76; killed in the assault, 1176–77; his assault compared with Drummond's, 1180.

Palfrey, John Gorham, 1322.

"Panoplist," the, 1303.

Papenberg, 117.

Paris, capitulates, March 31, 1814, 1188; pleased with the victory at Plattsburg, 1207–08; Napoleon's return to, 1221.

Parish, David, shares loan of 1813, 650.

Parish, Elijah, his Fast-Day sermon of April 7, 1814, 921, 1319.

Parker, Sir Peter, captain of British frigate "Menelaus," his death, 1026–27.

Parliament (see Acts of), meets Jan. 19, 1809, 38; debates the Orders in Council, 38–40, 44–46; on the Duke of York, 43–44; prorogued June 21, 1809, 71; prorogued June 15, 1810, 193; passes the Regency bill, January, 1811, 305–06; meets Jan. 7, 1812, 480; debates in, 480–86; orders a committee of inquiry into the Orders in Council, 488, 489; meets Nov. 24, 1812, 626; debates on the speech from the throne, 626–27; debates the American war, Feb. 18, 1813, 631–36; debate of Nov. 19, 1814, on the Ghent correspondence, 1213.

Parsons, Theophilus, chief-justice of Massachusetts, his opinion on the power of a State over its militia, 574; his assurance to Pickering, 655.

Party, the Federalist, deprived of grievances, 56; praise Madison, 56, 112; make common cause with Jackson, 112; described by Giles, 127–28; in Congress, Foster's reports of their conduct and advice, 420–21; their reception of Henry's documents, 424; cease attempts to discuss war, 451; their attitude toward the war, 573; support Clinton for the Presidency, 581; strength of, in 1813, 654–55; encouraged by overthrow of Napoleon, 875; divided on protection to manufactures, 879; their inert perversity, 907–08; divided on the question of a New England Convention, 912–15; praise militia, 1061; of New England believe the crisis arrived in September, 1814, 1063; call New England Convention at Hartford, 1066; victorious in the congressional elections of November, 1814, 1068; a majority of the members of Congress north of the Potomac, 1069; oppose tax-bills, 1086; approve report of Hartford Convention, 1117; influence British press, 1185; affected by peace, 1245.

Party, the Republican, its attitude toward the manufacturing interest in 1809, 139; attempt to restore its purity in 1810, 141–46; its attitude toward the Bank, 146–48, 228–34, 247; its attitude toward the Constitution in Florida, 223–27; its attitude on the previous question in Congress, 244–47; its attitude toward war in 1811, 389–403, 412–15; its attitude toward the militia, 404–06; its attitude toward a navy, 406–08; its attitude toward taxation, 411–12; its attitude toward war in 1812, 435, 450–52; its caucus of 1812, 442; De Witt Clinton's schism, 442, 581; its success in the election of 1812, 582–83; its change of attitude toward a navy, 598; its treatment of war-taxation, 605–06.

Passamaquoddy Bay (see Moose Island).

Patapsco River, at Baltimore, 1028.

Patterson, Daniel T., commander in U. S. Navy, brings the "Carolina" into action at New Orleans, 1153; establishes battery on west bank, 1161, 1164–65, 1172–73, 1175; abandons battery and spikes guns, 1177–78.

"Paul Jones," privateer, captured, 847, 849.

"Peacock," American 22-gun sloop-of-war built in 1813, 1037; goes to sea in March, 1814, 1038–39; captures "Epervier," 1038–39; returns to port October 30, 1040, 1046; sails from New York, 1226, 1230; fires into "Nautilus," 1232.

"Peacock," British sloop-of-war, 820; sunk by "Hornet," 821.

Pechell, S. G., captain of the British 74-gun ship "San Domingo," repulsed at Craney Island, 808–09.

Peddie, John, British lieutenant in Twenty-Seventh Infantry, deputy-as-

sistant-quartermaster-general, reconnoitres Bayou Bienvenu, 1147; his sketch of battle-fields at New Orleans, 1161–64.

"Pelican," British sloop-of-war, her force, 831; captures "Argus," 831–33.

"Penguin," British sloop-of-war, her action with the "Hornet," 1231–32, 1338.

Pennsylvania, resists mandate of Supreme Court, 14; decides Presidential election of 1812, 582; affected by blockade, 803; creates forty-one banks in 1814, 917; election of 1814, 1069; arrears of internal taxes in October, 1814, 1087; creates a State army, 1105; bank circulation in 1816–1817, 1270; growth of population, 1800–1816, 1287; increase of wealth in, 1295; internal improvements in, 1297, 1298.

Pensacola, visited by Creek Indians, 779; object of Jackson's Creek campaigns, 1130–31; occupied by Nicholls, 1131–32, 1133; seized by Jackson, 1136, 1139–40.

Perceval, Spencer, his relaxations of the Orders in Council, 33, 35, 47; decline of his authority in 1809, 43–44, 46–47; his difficulties with Canning and Castlereagh, 77; becomes First Lord of the Treasury, 186; invites Wellesley into the Cabinet, 188; Wellesley's opinion of, 197–98; prime minister of England, becomes ruler after the insanity of George III., 298; retained as prime minister by the Prince Regent, 306; his indifference to Wellesley's advice, 478; his remarks on an American war, 480; his persistence in the system of commercial restriction, 481; his remarks on licenses, 482; his silence toward Canning, 486; his bargain for Sidmouth's support, 487; concedes a committee on the Orders in Council, 488; his assassination, 489.

Percy, W. H., captain of British 22-gun sloop-of-war "Hermes," 1133, 1136; attacks Fort Bowyer, 1134; abandons his ship, 1134.

Perry, Oliver Hazard, commander in U. S. Navy, ordered to Lake Erie, 698; creates squadron, 699–700; destroys British fleet, 702–06; his despatch of Sept. 10, 1813, 707; effect of his victory on the Creek war, 782; its effect in England, 865, 867–68; erects batteries on the Potomac, 1025; his rewards, 1278.

Petry, M., 161–62.

Philadelphia, population of, in 1810, 203; banks suspend payment, Aug. 31, 1814, 1059; depreciation of currency, 1225, 1249; allotted share in loan of 1815, 1251; growth of population of, 1288; immigrants to, 1291; steamboats in 1816, 1298.

Phillimore, Dr. Joseph, his pamphlets on the license system, 482.

Piankeshaw Indians, 346, 349.

Pickering, Timothy, senator from Massachusetts, his toast at Jackson's dinner, 153; his speech on the occupation of West Florida, 224; loses his seat in the Senate, 375; his attempt to call a State convention in 1812, 575; favors disunion, 909–10; urges a New England Convention in January, 1814, 909–11; exhorts Governor Strong to seize the national revenues, 1065; acquiesces in British demands, 1108; suggests doubts of George Cabot's earnestness, 1110; approves the report of the Hartford Convention, 1117; considers the Union dissolved, 1117, 1122; member of the Fourteenth Congress, 1254; on the power of internal improvement, 1283.

Pigot, H., captain of British frigate "Orpheus," reports number of Creek warriors, 799.

Pike, Zebulon Montgomery, brigadier-general, 726; captures York, 726–27; killed, 727.

Pilkington, A., lieutenant-colonel commanding British expedition to Moose Island, 974.

"Pilot," British newspaper, on the American frigates, 630–31.

Pinckney, Thomas, appointed major-general, 492; ordered to prepare for seizing St. Augustine, 765; ordered to withdraw troops from Amelia Island, 766; his difficulties in the Creek war, 783; his estimate of the hostile Indians, 790; orders the Thirty-ninth Regiment to join Jackson, 790; prepares army against Creeks, 794; joins Jackson, 798.

Pinkney, William, minister in London, his reply, Dec. 28, 1808, to Canning's first advance, 34–35; his reception of Canning's further advances, 38, 39; opinion attributed to, by Canning, 40; his pleasure at the Order of April 26, 1809, 47; his opinion of Francis James Jackson, 70; his intimacy with Wellesley, 190, 193; his reports of Wellesley's intentions, 190; inquires whether Fox's blockade is in force, 194–97; notifies Wellesley of Champagny's letter of Aug. 5, 1810, 200–01; his "republican insolence," 202; demands repeal of the Orders, Nov. 3, 1811, 298; his argument that the French decrees were revoked and that Fox's blockade was illegal, 299–301, 302–04; his definition of blockade, 303; his demand for an audience of leave, 304, 306; his hesitation, 307; his note of Feb. 17, 1811, to Wellesley, 308; insists on "an inamicable leave," 308, 309; his final audience, 309–10; his character as minister, 310; sails for America, 310; appointed attorney-general, 594; resigns attorney-generalship, 893; member of the Fourteenth Congress, 1254.

Pitkin, Timothy, member of Congress from Connecticut, votes for war measures, 396; on the bank capital of the Union, 885; opposes national bank, 1262.

Pitt, William, his patronage of young men, 186–87.

Pittsburg, growth of, in 1816, 1288–89; steamboats built at, 1299.

"Plantagenet," British seventy-four, at Fayal, 1051–55.

Plattsburg, on Lake Champlain, military force at, in October, 1812, 537;

Dearborn's campaign from, 548; plundered by British expedition in July, 1813, 755; Wilkinson's headquarters in March, 1814, 923; fortified by Izard, 976–77; garrison at, 978; British armament against, 978–81; battle of, 982–88; effect of battle in England, 988; saved by engineers and sailors, 1061, 1341; effect of battle at London, Paris, and Ghent, 1207–09, 1220; at Washington, 1222.

Plauché, ——, major of New Orleans militia, 1151.

Plumer, William, Republican candidate for governor of New Hampshire, 914.

Poland, 182.

"Pomone," British 38-gun frigate, 1226; extracts from her log, 1227–28; Decatur's surrender to, 1229–30.

Population of the United States, in 1810, 203; of the Union in 1817, 1287; movements of, 1800–1817, 1287–89, 1291–92, 1293.

Porter, David, captain in U. S. navy, commands "Essex," 559; captures "Alert," 559; returns to port, 560; sails again, 564; erects batteries on the Potomac in August, 1814, 1025; his cruise in the Pacific with the "Essex," 1034–35; blockaded at Valparaiso, 1036; attacked and obliged to surrender, 1036–37.

Porter, Moses, colonel of Light Artillery, brevet brigadier-general, commands artillery in Wilkinson's expedition on the St. Lawrence, 750; his opinion on moving against Montreal, 750; intended by Armstrong to command at Washington, 996.

Porter, Peter Buell, member of Congress from New York, 380; on Committee of Foreign Relations, 381, 384; his report favoring war, 387–89; his war speech, 389; favors small army, 399; asks for provisional army, 408–10; introduces embargo bill, 433–41; calls for volunteers, 545; charges General Smyth with cowardice, 547; his duel with Smyth, 547; raises volunteer brigade under Brown, 929;

strength of his brigade, 932; at Chippawa, 935, 937; at Lundy's Lane, 944, 946, 949, 953; at Fort Erie, 961, 967; brings volunteers to Brown, 968; leads sortie from Fort Erie, 969–70; wounded, 970; fails to create a brigade respectable in numbers, 1061; in the Fourteenth Congress, 1254; helps to defeat Crawford, 1265; assists Erie canal, 1296.

"Portfolio," the, its character and influence, 1317–19.

Portland, Duke of, his death, 77.

Postal System of the United States, in 1816, 1298.

Postmaster-General (see Gideon Granger, R. J. Meigs).

Potomac (see Eastern Branch).

Pottawatomies, charged by Tecumthe with bad conduct, 373.

Potter, Elisha, member of Congress from Rhode Island, 118; opposes the repeal of the restrictive system, 879.

Power, ——, major-general in British army, commanding brigade at Plattsburg, 979.

Prairie du Chien, captured by British expedition, 928.

"Preble," 7-gun sloop, in Macdonough's fleet on Lake Champlain, 981; in the battle of Plattsburg, 985.

Prescott, opposite Ogdensburg, 722; British garrison at, 724; passed by Wilkinson, 750.

Prescott, William, delegate to the Hartford Convention, 1111.

Prescott, William Hickling, 1322.

"President," American 44-gun frigate, ordered to sea, May 6, 1811, 313; chases a British war-vessel, 314; fires into the "Little Belt," 316; at New York, 550, 552; goes to sea, 552; cruise of, 552, 554; returns to Boston, 558, 560; sails again, 562; returns to Boston, Dec. 31, 1812, 562, 818; goes to sea, April 30, 1813, 818; returns to Newport, Sept. 27, 1813, 834; goes to sea, Dec. 4, 1813, 835; in British waters, 849; captured by British squadron, Jan. 15, 1815, 1225–30.

Previous question, the rule of, adopted, 245–46; denounced by Stanford, 395.

Prevost, Sir George, governor general of Canada, 515; his report on the lukewarm and temporizing spirit in Upper Canada, 515–16; negotiates armistice with Dearborn, 519, 1206; his military superiority in August, 1812, 529–34; unable to assist Proctor, 694; on Proctor's defeat at Fort Stephenson, 697; unable to man the British fleet on Lake Erie, 700–01; his difficulties of transport, 718–19; his remarks on supplies from Vermont, 719, 973; charged with timidity, 722; visits Kingston in March, 1813, 724; his supposed force at Kingston, 724, 726; comes to Kingston in May, 1813, 733; embarks for Sackett's Harbor, 733; attacks Sackett's Harbor, 735; repulsed, 735–37; charged with want of courage, 737–38; his remarks on Hampton's movement, 756; his force for the defence of Montreal, 756–58; shows timidity toward Hampton, 758; his proclamation on the burning of Black Rock and Buffalo, 763; his letter to Wilkinson on the execution of hostages, 868; reinforced by ten thousand troops in July, 1814, 927, 972; his letter of Oct. 18, 1814, on the impossibility of supplying an army in Upper Canada, 972–73; his expedition against Plattsburg, 978–81, 984–88, 1032; recalled to England, 992; asks Cochrane to retaliate for American outrages in Canada, 998; at Kingston, 1094; effect of his campaign on the negotiation at Ghent, 1202, 1206–08.

Prices of American produce, affected by blockade, 802–03; speculative, in imported articles, 802–03.

"Prince of Neufchatel," in the Irish Channel, 1048; beats off the "Endymion's" boats, 1055–57.

Prince Regent (see George, Prince of Wales).

Privateers, American, their depredations in the West Indies in 1812, 628;

types of, 837; qualities of, 839–40, 840–41, 843–44; modes of capturing, 846–47; number of, 848; in British waters, 849–50; disadvantages of, 850–53; in 1814, 1046–57; their value as a test of national character, 1336–37.

Privateers, French, not received in American ports, 891.

Prizes, number captured in 1813, 848; American success in taking, in 1814, 1049–50.

Proclamation by President Jefferson, of July 2, 1807, on the "Chesapeake" affair, 39; by President Madison of April 19, 1809, renewing intercourse with Great Britain, 53, 83; of Aug. 9, 1809, reviving the Non-intercourse Act against Great Britain, 82–83; of Nov. 2, 1810, reviving the non-intercourse against Great Britain, 211–13, 235, 278; of Oct. 27, 1810, ordering the military occupation of West Florida, 217; of Nov. 2, 1810, announcing the repeal of the French decrees, 299, 334; by William Hull, of July 12, 1812, on invading Canada, 503, 517; by Isaac Brock in reply to Hull, 517; of Aug. 8, 1814, summoning Congress to meet Sept. 19, 1814, 1076; of Aug. 29, 1814, by Major Nicholls, of the Royal Marines, to the natives of Louisiana, 1132; of Sept. 21, 1814, by Andrew Jackson, to the people of Louisiana, 1136.

Proctor, Henry, colonel of the Forty-first British Infantry, arrives at Malden, 511; disapproves Brock's measures, 524; major-general, his incapacity officially censured by the Prince Regent, 683–84, 717; his victory over Winchester at the River Raisin, 685–87; returns to Malden, 688; besieges Fort Meigs, 691–93; repulsed at Fort Stephenson, 694–97; evacuates Malden and Detroit, 708–09; his retreat, 710–11; his defeat on the River Thames, 712–16; his report, 717.

Prophet, the Shawnee, begins Indian movement at Greenville, 351; removes to Tippecanoe Creek, 352; his talk with Gov. Harrison in August, 1808, 352–53; charged with beginning hostilities, 362; sends Indians to Harrison, 363, 365; blamed for the affair at Tippecanoe, 371.

Protection to American manufactures, measure of, recommended by Madison for two years, 877; promised by Calhoun, 878; opposed by Webster, 878–79; urged by Potter, 879; recommended by Madison and Dallas in 1815, 1254, 1257–58; opposed by Randolph, 1258–59; debated in Congress, 1259–60; avowed in tariff of 1816, 1260–61.

Prussia, spoliations by, 160; closes ports to American vessels, 286, 288; king of, visits London, 1189.

Putnam, Samuel, correspondent of Pickering, 910.

"QUEEN CHARLOTTE," 17-gun British ship, on Lake Erie, 701; in action, 704; captured, 706.

Queenston, battle at, 541–43.

Quincy, Josiah, declares the admission of Louisana a virtual dissolution of the Union, 226–27; votes for war-measures, 396, 399; gives warning of embargo, 433; moves that the war-debate be public, 450; opposes enlistment of minors, 598; opposes forfeitures, 603; his Resolution on the "Hornet's" victory, 664, 907; his opinion on the temper of Massachusetts, 1065; on the Boston "Anthology," 1319.

RAISIN, RIVER, defeat and massacre at the, 679, 688.

Rambouillet, Decree of (see Decrees).

"Ramilies," Sir Thomas Hardy's flagship, 974.

Randolph, John, his remarks on Jefferson, 57; on Erskine's arrangement, 57; on Madison's message, 125–26; his attempt to reduce expenditures in 1810, 141–47; on the incapacity of government, 148; on the contract with Napoleon, 239; his quarrel with Eppes, 244; denounces the previous question, 245; his remarks on President and Cabinet, February, 1811, 249–50; supports the Bank Charter, 251; his opinion of "the cabal," 251–52; his quarrel with Monroe, 254; his report on slavery in Indiana, 350; replies to Grundy on war, 393, 395; ridicules army bill, 400; declares war impossible, 433; his comments on Eustis and Hamilton, 436; his remarks on war, 440; criticises Gallatin, 605; defeated for Congress, in 1813, 654; quoted by Pickering, 909; his letter to Lloyd on the Hartford Convention, 1069, 1120; elected to the Fourteenth Congress, 1070, 1246; suggest inquiry of Monroe's opinions in 1800, 1093; in the Fourteenth Congress, 1254; leads minority, 1256–57; opposes manufacturers, 1258–59, 1260; hostile to State banks, 1261; supports Compensation Bill, 1264; not a friend of Monroe, 1266; on the popular action against the Compensation Act, 1274; his oratory, 1329–30.

Rank-and-file, mode of stating strength of armies, 724.

"Rattlesnake," American 16-gun sloop-of-war, 836; captured, 836, 1045.

"Rattlesnake," privateer, in British waters, 849.

Reading in Massachusetts, town of, votes to pay no more taxes, 1116.

Red Clubs, hostile Creeks, 779; their flight to Florida, 798; their number, 799; assisted by British, 1126, 1131–32; pursued by Jackson, 1131, 1139–40.

Regiments (see Infantry).

Reid, Samuel C., captain of privateer "General Armstrong," his battle at Fayal, 1051–55.

"Reindeer," British 18-gun sloop-of-war, captured by the "Wasp," 1040–42, 1338.

"Reindeer," privateer, built in thirty-five days, 1046.

Remusat, Mme. de, 166.

Republicans (see Party).

Revenue (see Finances).

Rhea, James, captain in the First United States Infantry, 669.

Rhea, John, member of Congress from Tennessee, on the annexation of West Florida to Louisiana, 226; asserts contract with Napoleon, 238.

Rhine, passed by the allied armies, 876.

Rhode Island, appoints delegates to the Hartford Convention, 1068; elects federalist congressmen in November, 1814, 1068; cotton manufactures of, depressed by the peace, 1247; federalist in 1816, 1272.

Riall, P., British major-general, his force, 932; takes position behind the Chippawa River, 933; advances in order of battle, 933–37; his report of his defeat, 937; his loss, 937–38; retires toward Burlington, 938; advances to Lundy's Lane, 940; orders retreat, 943; wounded and captured, 943.

Rice, value of export of, in 1815, 1246; in 1816, 1268.

Richardson, ———, lieutenant of Canadian militia, his account of the capture of Detroit, 526; his description of Kentucky militia, 685–86.

Rifles, efficiency of, 684, 1339; First Regiment of, 958; at Fort Erie, 967; Fourth Regiment of, at Fort Erie, 967; in the sortie, 969–71.

Ripley, Eleazer Wheelock, colonel of Twenty-first U. S. Infantry, at the battle of Chrystler's Farm, 753; promoted to brigadier and sent to Niagara, 901; his previous history, 930; his brigade, 931; crosses the Niagara, 933; arrives at Chippawa, 933; not in battle of Chippawa, 936; advises advance on Burlington Heights, 939; strength of his brigade, 940; arrives on the battle-field at Lundy's Lane, 944; captures the British position, 945–46; holds the hill-top, 947; ordered to retreat, 949; his losses, 953; ordered to regain the field of battle, 953–54; marches out and returns, 954; retreats to Fort Erie, 954, 958; his quarrel with Brown, 954–56, 966, 968; fortifies Fort Erie, 956; strength of his brigade, 957; repulses assault, 958–59, 960; discourages sortie, 968; desperately wounded in sortie, 970–71; retained on peace establishment, 1242.

Ritchie, John, captain of artillery in Hindman's battalion, 931; at Lundy's Lane, 945; killed, 947.

Roads and canals, national, recommended by Madison, 1254; encouraged by Virginia in 1816, 1293–94; popular demand for, 1296–97.

Roberts, Jonathan, elected senator, 895.

Robertson, Thomas Bolling, member of Congress from Louisiana, favors protection to sugar, 1259.

Robinson, W. H., British commissary-general, his report on the failure of supplies for Upper Canada, 972.

Robinson, ———, major-general in British army, commands light brigade at Plattsburg, 978; moves on the works, 986.

Rockingham, in New Hampshire, county meeting of, 576, 580.

Rockville, or Montgomery Court House, sixteen miles from Washington, 1011; Winder arrives at, 1019, 1020.

Rodgers, John, captain in the United States navy, ordered to sea in the "President," May 6, 1811, 313; chases the "Little Belt," 314; mistakes the "Little Belt" for the "Guerriere," 315–16; his action with the "Little Belt," 315–20; his orders in June, 1812, 550, 552, 553–54; chases the "Belvidera," 552; arrives with his squadron at Boston, 558; sails again with squadron, 560, 562; returns, Dec. 31, 1812, 562; goes to sea April 30, 1813, 818, 819; erects batteries on the Potomac, 1025.

Rodney, Cæsar A., attorney-general, his report on slavery in Indiana, 350; resigns attorney-generalship, 593.

Rose, George, on the Orders in Council, 483–84, 487, 488; yields to an inquiry, 488.

Rose, George Henry, sent as envoy for

the adjustment of the "Chesapeake" affair, 81; intended as minister to the United States to succeed Erskine, 69.

Ross, Robert, major-general of the British army, commands expedition to America, 997; arrives in the Potomac, 999; lands in the Patuxent, August 19, 1814, 1000; camps at Nottingham, August 21, 1001; camps at Marlboro, August 22, 1001; camps at Old Fields, August 23, 1002; his report of losses at Bladensburg, 1012; enters Washington, 1013, 1198; reported by Serurier as setting fire to furniture in the White House, 1014; retires from Washington, 1014–15; takes part in incendiarism, 1026; lands his army before Baltimore, 1028; killed, 1030, 1212; intended for command of New Orleans expedition, 1126–27; his capture of Washington highly approved by the Prince Regent, 1128–29; his movements synchronous with Jackson's, 1130.

"Rossie," Baltimore privateer, 838, 851.

"Rota," British 38-gun frigate, 1053–54.

Rottenburg (see De Rottenburg).

Roumanzoff, Count Nicholas, chancellor of the Russian empire, his language about Austria, 96; declines to interfere in Danish spoliations, 283–84; declines to release vessels at Archangel, 287; protests against ukase, 289; offers the Czar's mediation, 639, 640; left at St. Petersburg, 857; receives Castlereagh's refusal of mediation in May, 858; favors renewing offer, June 20, 859; authorized by the Czar, July 20, to renew offer, 860; his conduct perplexes the American commissioners, 860; his motives, 860; renews offer of mediation in note of August 28, 861, 863; mortified by the Czar's treatment, 863; assures Gallatin that mediation was the Czar's idea, 863; resigns and retires, 864.

Round Head, Indian chief, at the River Raisin, 684; captures Winchester, 685.

Rouse's Point, difficulty in fortifying, 976.

Rovigo, Duc de (see Savary).

Rule of the war of 1756, that trade illegal in peace should not be permitted in times of war, Canning's demand for express recognition of, 40, 41–42, 53, 75.

"Running ships," 837.

Rush, Richard, comptroller of the Treasury, 452; on the loss of the "Chesapeake," 803; offered the Treasury, 893; appointed attorney-general, 894; attends the President to Bladensburg, 1006, 1010; and in the subsequent flight, 1016–17; returns to Washington, 1021.

Russell, Jonathan, charged with legation at Paris, 184, 264; his reports on the revocation of the decrees, 264–74; blamed by Monroe for questioning the revocation of the French decrees, 324; blamed by Serurier for his tone, 332; sent as chargé to the legation at London, 467, 488; asks proofs that the French decrees are repealed, 467; his reports from London, 488; his interview with Castlereagh, Aug. 24, 1812, 622; nominated minister to Sweden, 660; nomination not confirmed by the Senate, 662–63, 668; confirmed, 663, 875–76; at Ghent, 1193, 1194, 1215.

Russia, mission to, declared inexpedient, 13–14; minister to, appointed, 62; her rupture with France in 1811, 267, 276, 285–93; annoyed by American war, 621, 638; loses and recovers Moscow, 626, 638–39, 640; drives Napoleon from Poland and Prussia, 627, 640; offers mediation to the United States, 639–40, 648. (See Alexander, Roumanzoff, Nesselrode.)

Ryland, Herman W., secretary to Sir James Craig, 62.

SACKETT'S HARBOR, military importance of, 536–37; force concentrated at, in March, 1813, 723–24; denuded of troops, 728, 733; attacked, 733; attack repulsed, 735–39; garrison at, in 1814, 972; to be besieged in the spring of 1815, 972, 992.

Sailors (see Seamen).

St. Augustine (see Florida, East).

"St. Lawrence," British line-of-battle ship, on Lake Ontario, 972.

St. Lawrence River, strategic importance of, 718–22; Wilkinson's expedition down, 746–54; difficulties of transport on, 973; both banks to be Canadian, 1189, 1190–91, 1204.

St. Mary's, seized by British, 1225.

St. Mary's River, 117.

Salaberry (see De Salaberry).

Salaries of cabinet officers, 893; of public officials, 1263–65.

Salt, repeal of duty on, 397–98; tax to be re-enacted, 402, 408–09.

"San Domingo," British ship-of-the-line, 808.

Sandusky River, base of Harrison's campaigns, 671, 673, 677, 694. (See Fort Stephenson.)

Sandwich, opposite Detroit, 503; occupied by Harrison, 709.

Saratoga, Armstrong's idea of renewing the scene of, 740, 978.

"Saratoga," Macdonough's flag-ship on Lake Champlain, 981; her armament, 981; in the battle of Plattsburg, 982–86; her losses, 986, 1340–41.

Sassafras River, in Maryland, Cockburn's expedition to, 805; Sir Peter Parker stationed off, 1026.

Savannah, threatened by British, 1225.

Savary, Duc de Rovigo, 171.

Sawyer, British vice-admiral, 554.

Sawyer, Lemuel, member of Congress from North Carolina, 130.

Scheldt, British expedition to, 77.

Schooner, the swiftest sailer in the world, 328; privateer, 837; a wonderful invention, 840–41, 1336, 1342; the triumph of the war, 842–43.

Scott, ———, British colonel of the Hundred-and-third Regiment, at Lundy's Lane, 941; leads assault on Fort Erie, 959, 961; killed, 962, 963.

Scott, Charles, governor of Kentucky, 670.

Scott, Michael, author of "Tom Cringle's Log," 841; his remarks on Yankee sailors and schooners, 841–42.

Scott, Walter, 1326.

Scott, Sir William, decides the French decrees to be still in force, 478.

Scott, Winfield, captain of artillery in 1808, 494; his description of the army, 494; lieutenant-colonel at Queenston Heights, 542; surrenders, 543; colonel of Second U. S. artillery, chief-of-staff to Dearborn, 728, 731; captures Fort George, 728–29; his opinion of Wilkinson, 740–41; his opinion of Hampton, 741; his opinion of Brown, 900; promoted to brigadier, 901; drills his brigade at Buffalo, 926, 931; organization and strength of his brigade, 930; lands below Fort Erie, 933; marches on Chippawa, 933; fights the battle of Chippawa, 935–38; ordered to march toward Queenston, 941; attacks British army at Lundy's Lane, 943–45; wounded, 948, 954; his brigade, 1074; retained on peace establishment, 1242.

"Scourge," privateer, in British waters, 849.

Seamen, foreign, in the American service, 611–13; to be excluded from American vessels, 652.

Search, right of, as understood by Napoleon, 98–99, 104.

Seaver, Ebenezer, member of Congress from Massachusetts, 574.

Sedition Law (see Acts of Congress).

Seminole Indians, 771–72.

Semonville, Comte de, his official address, 265, 269, 301.

Senate (see Congress).

"Serapis," British 44-gun frigate, 624.

Sergeant, John, member of Congress from Pennsylvania, 1255; opposes bank, 1262; sent to Europe, 1271.

Serurier, Jean Matthieu Philibert, succeeds Turreau as French minister at Washington, 240; his first interview with Robert Smith, 240; reports the government decided to enforce non-intercourse against Great Britain,

241; his estimates of Gallatin and Robert Smith, 327–30; the crisis of his fortune, 331; reports Monroe's anger at Napoleon's conduct, 330–31, 332–33, 334–35; remonstrates at Barlow's delay, 333; his letter of July 19, 1811, on the repeal of Napoleon's decrees, 337; his report of Monroe's and Madison's remarks on Napoleon's arrangements, July, 1811, 339; his report of Madison's warlike plans in November, 1811, 385; his reports on Crillon and John Henry's papers, 417–19; his report of Madison's language on the French spoliations, 423; his report of Monroe's language regarding the repeal of the French decrees, 424, 428–29; his report of Monroe's remarks on the embargo and war, 432–35; remonstrates against suspension of the Non-importation Act, 436; his remarks on the failure of the loan, 438; his report of angry feeling against France, 443–44; his report of Monroe's complaints in June, 1812, 453; his report of Monroe's language about the occupation of East Florida, 460; his report of Monroe's language about negotiation for peace, 584–85; his report of Monroe's military prospects, 644; his report of fears for the safety of Washington, in July, 1813, 658; his reports in 1813–1814, 889–92; his explanation of the abandonment of the restrictive system by Madison, 890–92; his report of the burning of Washington, 1013–14.

Shaler, Nathaniel, captain of privateer "Governor Tompkins," 845; his escape from a man-of-war, 846.

"Shannon," British frigate, 554; chases "Constitution," 555; stationed off Boston, 815; captures the "Chesapeake," 818–30.

Sheaffe, Sir R. H., major-general of the British army in Canada, 541, 542; his force in the district of Montreal, 757; Brock's successor in Upper Canada, 940.

Shelburne, Lord, his negotiation of 1783, 1193.

Shelby, Isaac, governor of Kentucky, 670; commands the Kentucky volunteers in Canada, 707, 715; remonstrates against Harrison's resignation, 901; his letter of April 8, 1814, on the necessity of peace, 915; sends Kentucky militia to New Orleans, 1137.

Sherbrooke, Sir J. C., British governor of Nova Scotia, occupies Castine and Machias, 974–75, 1033.

Sheridan, Richard Brinsley, 187.

Sherman, Roger Minot, delegate to the Hartford Convention, 1111.

Shipherd, Zebulon R., member of Congress from New York, on the approaching fall of the national government in 1814, 1101.

Shipping, its prosperity in 1809–1810, 15–16, 203; protection of, 223; growth of, in Massachusetts, 1800–1816, 1290.

Short, William, appointment negatived, 13.

Sidmouth, Lord, speech on the Orders in Council, 44; his weariness of the orders, 198; enters Cabinet, 487.

"Siren," privateer, captures "Landrail," 1047.

Slavery, in Indiana, 349–50; stimulus to, in 1815, 1246.

Sloops-of-war, in the U.S. navy (see "Wasp," "Hornet," "Argus," "Syren," "Nautilus"); act of Congress for building six, 607; their cost, 834; their size and force, 835; their efficiency compared with frigates, 836; six new, ordered to be built, 836; twenty authorized by Act of November 15, 1814, 1104; their record in 1814, 1037–45.

Smilie, John, member of Congress from Pennsylvania, 144.

Smith, John Cotton, governor of Connecticut, on the report of the Hartford Convention, 1119–20.

Smith, John Spear, chargé in London, 310, 478.

Smith, Nathaniel, delegate to the Hartford Convention, 1112.

Smith, Robert, offered the Treasury Department, 11, 263; becomes Secretary of State, 11, 12–13; his language about war with France, 28; his letter to Erskine accepting settlement of the "Chesapeake" affair, 50–51; his replies to Canning's three conditions, 52–53; his remarks to Turreau on Jefferson's weakness and indiscretions, 61; introduces F. J. Jackson to the President, 86; his interviews with Jackson, 88–89, 91; his incompetence, 113; Madison's resentment of his conduct on Macon's bill, 132; his supposed quarrels in the Cabinet, 133; opposed to Madison's course toward France, 208, 253, 259–60, 262; notifies Turreau of the President's intention to revive the non-intercourse against England, 211–12; explains to Turreau the occupation of West Florida, 218–19; his first interviews with Serurier, 240; irritates Madison by questioning Serurier, 243; his abilities, 252, 261; his removal from the State Department, 260–61; his Address to the People, 262; his retort against Madison, 263; Serurier's estimate of, 327–30; his remark about American schooners, 328; his comments on Jefferson, Madison, and Clinton, 328; his pamphlet reveals secrets annoying to Madison, 332.

Smith, Samuel, member of Congress from Maryland, defeats Gallatin's appointment as Secretary of State, 9–10; his quarrel with Gallatin, 13; votes for mission to Russia, 13–14; re-elected to the Senate, 113; his support of Giles, 128; defeats Macon's bill, 131, 136–37; his motives, 131–32, 135–36; reports bill of his own, 139–40; moves censure of Pickering, 225; his speech on the Bank Charter, 233–34; his abilities, 252; opposes every financial proposal, 455; votes against occupying East Florida, 461; in opposition, 653; votes against Gallatin's

Russian mission, 660; opposes seizure of East Florida, 765; no chance of re-election, 894; major-general of Maryland militia, refuses to yield command of Baltimore to Winder, 1028; sends Stricker's brigade to meet the enemy, 1030; member of the House in 1815–1817, 1255; supports Bank, 1261.

Smith, Thomas A., colonel of Rifles, promoted to brigadier-general, 901.

Smyth, Alexander, inspector-general of United States army, with rank of brigadier, 544; arrives at Buffalo with brigade, 539; his disagreement with Van Rensselaer, 539, 540; ordered to take command, 543; his Niagara campaign, 544–47; dropped from the army-roll, 547.

Snake Hill, western end of the American lines at Fort Erie, 958, 969; assaulted, 959–62, 964.

Snyder, Simon, chosen governor of Pennsylvania, 14; vetoes bill creating forty-one banks, 917.

"Sophie," 18-gun British sloop-of-war, appears off Barataria, 1132; attacks Fort Bowyer, 1133–34.

South Carolina, creates a State army, 1105.

Spain, Napoleon and Moore's campaigns in, 20–23; Wellesley's campaigns in, 189.

Spanish America, Napoleon's policy toward, 26–27, 266–67, 282; Jefferson's wishes regarding, 30–31; Madison's policy toward, 30–31, 213–20; Spencer Perceval's policy toward, 190, 199–200; movements for independence in, 213; Henry Clay's policy toward, 1256.

Specie, in the United States in 1810, 230; large sums of, sent to Canada, 721, 887, 974; drain of, to New England, 1810–1814, 886–87, 916–17; premium on, in New York, Philadelphia, and Baltimore, Feb. 1, 1815, 1059; premium on, in the autumn of 1815, 1249; influx of, in 1816, 1268.

Specie payments, suspended in August and September, 1814, by State banks, except in New England, 1059; suspended by Treasury of the United States, 1060; power to suspend, in Dallas's scheme for a national bank, 1094, 1261–62; ordered to be resumed by the Treasury, on Feb. 20, 1817, 1262, 1269; resisted by State banks, 1270; resumed Feb. 20, 1817, 1271.

Spencer, P., captain of the British sloop-of-war "Carron," reconnoitres Bayou Bienvenu, 1146.

Spoliations, British, indemnities asked for, at Ghent, 1196; abandoned, 1218–19.

—— French, in 1807–1808, 25; in 1809, 108, 156, 180; value of, 172; Madison's anger at, 205; Madison's demand for indemnity, 207; their municipal character, 209; their justification as reprisals, 162, 164, 165–66, 167, 178–80, 182–83, 269, 271, 274–75; in Denmark, 283, 285; not matter of discussion, 332, 382; Madison's language regarding, 423; Monroe's language regarding, 424–25; new, reported in March, 1812, 427, 448, 467; in June, 453; probable value of, 464.

Spotts, Samuel, first lieutenant of artillery, in the night battle at New Orleans, 1151.

Stanford, Richard, member of Congress from North Carolina, votes against Giles's resolution, 129; his retort on Calhoun, 397; his speech on war, 395; votes for legal tender paper, 1086; in the Fourteenth Congress, 1254, 1262.

Stanley, Lord, 488.

Stansbury, Tobias E., brigadier-general of Maryland militia commanding brigade at Bladensburg, 1010, 1021; criticises Monroe, 1017.

State armies, created by Massachusetts, 1063, 1067, 1098, 1104; one of the causes that led to the Constitution of 1789, 1104; created by New York, 1105; by Pennsylvania and Maryland, 1105; by Virginia, South Carolina, and Kentucky, 1105; demanded by

Hartford Convention, 1106, 1114; Joseph Hopkinson's remarks on, 1107; of Massachusetts, suspended for want of money, 1119.

State Department (see Robert Smith, James Monroe).

States rights, mentioned in Madison's Inaugural Address, 9; affected by the use of militia in war, 404–05; affected by the war, 665; asserted in Massachusetts in February, 1814, 909–12; asserted by New England in September, 1814, 1063–68; championed by Randolph in the Fourteenth Congress, 1257; affected by decisions of Supreme Court, 1310–13; affected by consistent action of government, 1313.

"Statira," British frigate, 1129.

Status ante bellum, the best terms of peace obtainable, 1190; not offered by Madison, 1192; not offered by England at Ghent, in August, 1814, 1197–98; opposed to *uti possidetis*, 1206; offered by American commissioners, 1208–09, 1216–17.

Steam-battery, appropriation for, 885.

Steamboat, use of, in 1816, 1296, 1297–99; relative character of invention, 1342.

Stephen, James, his speech of March 6, 1809, 45, 48; his remarks on Erskine's arrangement, 71; on the orders, 484; yields to a parliamentary inquiry, 489.

Stevens, John, relative merit of his invention, 1342.

Stewart, Charles, captain in U. S. navy, 823; commands "Constitution," 1233; his action with the "Cyane" and "Levant," 1233–34, 1235; escapes British squadron, 1235–36.

Stockton, Richard, member of Congress from New Jersey, threatens rebellion, 1101–02.

Stone, Senator David, re-elected senator from North Carolina, 653; censured and resigns, 894, 1255.

Stony Creek, battle of, 730–31.

Story, Joseph, retires from Congress, 55; obnoxious to Jefferson, 249;

Speaker of Massachusetts legislature, resigns to become Justice of Supreme Court, 930; his opinion in the case of Martin against Hunter's lessee, 1311–12.

Stowell, Lord (see Sir William Scott).

Street's Creek (see Chippawa).

Stricker, John, brigadier-general of Maryland militia, sent to meet Ross's army, 1030; his battle, 1030–31.

Strong, Caleb, re-elected governor of Massachusetts in April, 1812, 435; his Fast Proclamation, 574; declines to obey call for militia, 574; calls out three companies, 574; re-elected in 1813, 654; his speech to the legislature Jan. 12, 1814, 907; places militia under a State major-general, 1064; his address to the State legislature Oct. 5, 1814, 1064–65; his letter to Pickering on the British demands, 1108, 1214; approves report of Hartford Convention, 1117; his message of Jan. 18, 1815, announcing failure of loan, 1118; succeeded by Governor Brooks, 1272.

Strother (see Fort Strother).

"Subaltern in America" (see Gleig), quoted, 1001, 1010–11, 1012–13.

Suffrage in Massachusetts and New York, 654.

Sugar, price of, in February, 1815, 1224.

Sumter, Thomas, appointed minister to Brazil, 13.

"Sun," London newspaper, on Madison, 1186.

Supreme Court (see Marshall).

Swartwout, Robert, quartermaster-general under Wilkinson, 745; commands brigade, 750, 753.

Sweden, Bernadotte, Prince of, 293; his rupture with Napoleon, 294–95; Napoleon declares war on, 467; mission to, declared inexpedient by the Senate, 662–63.

Swedish Pomerania, 294.

Swift, Joseph Gardner, colonel of engineers, 1341.

"Syren," American 16-gun sloop-of-war, 560; captured July 12, 1814, 1045; at New Orleans, 835.

TALISHATCHEE, Creek village, destroyed by Jackson, 783.

Talladega, Creek village, relieved by Jackson, 784.

Tallapoosa River, home of the Upper Creeks, 769, 772, 785, 786; Jackson's first campaign to, 789–91; Jackson's second campaign to, 794–96.

Talleyrand, his letter of Dec. 21, 1804, on the boundaries of Louisiana, 224–25.

Tariff of 1816, 1258–61.

"Tartarus," British 20-gun sloop-of-war, with the "Avon" and "Castilian," 1042–43, 1044.

Taxes, war, 403, 408–09; postponed, 410, 435; reported June 26, 1812, 456; postponed by Congress, 456, 603–04; bill for, 606; bills passed in July and August, 1813, 656–57, 665; receipts of, paid in Treasury notes or the notes of suspended banks, 1079, 1087; doubled in 1814, 1083, 1086, 1090; arrears of, in October, 1814, 1087; internal, shifted to customs in 1816, 1258.

Taylor, James, 583.

Taylor, John, member of Congress from South Carolina, author of Macon's bill No. 2, 137; his speech, 137–38; introduces Bank Charter, 147.

Taylor, John, of Caroline, his advice to Monroe, 256; Monroe's letter to, June 13, 1812, 341; his remarks on the presidential election of 1812, 583, 585; his "Inquiry," 1314–16.

Taylor, John W., member of Congress from New York, 892.

Taylor, Robert, brigadier-general of Virginia militia at Norfolk, 805.

Taylor, Zachary, captain in the Seventh U. S. Infantry, 669.

Tazewell, Littleton Waller, 115, 1266.

Tea, price of, in February, 1815, 1224.

Tecumthe, his origin, 351; his plan of Indian confederation, 352; establishes himself at Tippecanoe, 352; character of his village, 352; joined by the Wyandots, 355; his conference with Harrison, Aug. 12, 1810, 356; seizes salt in June, 1811, 359; his talk at Vincennes, July 27, 1811, 360; starts for the Creek country, 360; his account of the affair at Tippecanoe, 369, 371; returns from the Creek country, 371; his reply to British complaints, 371; his speech of May 16, 1812, 372–73; joins the British at Malden, 523–24; routs Ohio militia, 511–14; at the battle of Maguaga, 520; at the capture of Detroit, 525; absent at the River Raisin, 684; at the siege of Fort Meigs, 691, 692; stops massacre, 693; reported to be moving against Harrison, 695–96; protests against evacuation of Malden, 708; killed at the battle of the Thames, 716–17; his visit to the Creeks in October, 1811, 772; his speech to the Creeks, 772–73; effect of his visit to the Creeks, 773–74; his intentions regarding the southern Indians, 780.

Tenallytown, near Washington, Winder's halt at, 1019.

"Tenedos," 46-gun British frigate, 816, 821; captures privateer "Enterprise," 845; chases "President," 1226, 1228.

Tennessee, militia, ordered into service, Dec. 10, 1812, 762; dismissed, 764; recalled into service, 782; claim discharge, 784; return home, 785; sixty-day, join Jackson, 789; routed at Enotachopco Creek, 789–90; disciplined by Jackson, 793–94; losses of, at the Horse-shoe, 795; the whole quota called out by Jackson, Aug. 27, 1814, 1132; march for Mobile, 1138; ordered to New Orleans, 1141–42; reach New Orleans, 1146; growth of population, 1287.

Terre aux Bœufs, encampment at, 121–24.

Thacher, Rev. Samuel Cooper, Unitarian clergyman, 1303; editor of the "Anthology," 1319.

Thames, Harrison's victory on the, 707–17.

"Thanatopsis," 1323–24.

Thiers, Louis Adolphe, on Napoleon, 159, 160, 167.

Thomas, John, major-general of Kentucky militia, ordered to New Or-

leans, 1146; arrives at New Orleans, 1169; unwell, 1178.

Thornton, Dr. William, 1076.

Thornton, William, colonel of British Eighty-fifth Light Infantry, leads attack at Bladensburg, 1011; severely wounded, 1013; leads the advance to New Orleans, 1147, 1149; his brigade, 1151, 1154; in the night battle of December 23, 1814, 1154; ordered to cross the river, 1174–75; crosses, 1176; captures Patterson's battery, 1178; wounded, 1179; recalled, 1181.

"Tiber," British frigate, captures privateer "Leo," 1047.

Ticknor, George, reports Eppes's remark to Gaston, 1091; reports John Adams's remark on George Cabot, 1121–22; reports Jefferson's remark on the British at New Orleans, 1122; professor of Belles Lettres in Harvard College, 1322.

"Ticonderoga," 17-gun schooner, in Macdonough's fleet on Lake Champlain, 981; in the battle of Plattsburg, 985.

"Times," the London, on the "Chesapeake" affair, 1051; on the Orders in Council, 46; on English apathy toward the United States, 312; on an American war, 491; on the "Guerriere," 623, 629; on the conduct of the war in 1812, 626, 863–64; on American privateers in the West Indies, 628; on the "Macedonian," 629; on the "Java," 630; on the Foreign Seamen Bill, 636; on President Madison, 864; on the execution of British subjects taken in arms, 867; on the American cruisers, 1057; on Madison, 1185–86; on terms of peace, 1187; on the defeat at Plattsburg, 1207; on the Ghent correspondence, 1213; on the Treaty, 1220–21.

Tin, price of, in February, 1815, 1224.

Tingey, Thomas, captain in U. S. navy, commandant of Washington navy-yard, sets fire to vessels in the Eastern Branch, 1013.

Tippecanoe Creek, 342, 352; Indian settlement at, 352; character of, 353; to be a large Indian resort, 360; to be broken up, 360, 361; Harrison's march on, 363; arrival at, 364; camp at, 366; battle of, 367–68; characterized by Tecumthe, 369, 371, 372–73; retreat from, 369; Harrison's estimate of effect of battle, 370; charged upon England, 391, 393.

Tobacco, value of exported, in 1815, 1246; in 1816, 1268.

Todd, Thomas, associate justice, 670.

"Tom," Baltimore privateer captured, 844.

"Tom Cringle's Log," 839–40.

Tompkins, Daniel D., his prevention of the Bank Charter, 438; re-elected governor of New York, in May, 1813, 654, 914; candidate for the Presidency, 894; offered the State Department, 1025; recommends a State army, 1105; nominated as Vice-President, 1265–66; elected Vice-President, 1276.

Töplitz in Bohemia, the Czar's headquarters, 859.

Toronto (see York).

Torpedo, Fulton's, 148.

Totten, Joseph G., captain of engineers, 542, 543; major of engineers, constructs the fortifications of Plattsburg, 984, 1341.

Town-meetings held in Massachusetts, in January, 1814, 909–11.

Towson, Nathan, captain of artillery, 539; captain of artillery company in Hindman's battalion, 931; attached to Scott's brigade at Chippawa, 936–37; at Lundy's Lane, 941–44, 945, 946; commands artillery on Snake Hill, 958–59, 961.

Treasury (see Gallatin, Jones, Campbell, Dallas).

Treasury Notes, five millions authorized in January, 1813, 607; ten millions authorized in March, 1814, 886, 919; Campbell's only resource, 1058, 1077–78; discount on, Feb. 1, 1815, 1059, 1090; six millions as much as could easily be circulated, 1078; no one willing to accept, 1079; fifteen millions to be issued, 1090; value of,

affected by the peace, 1225; issues of, 1244; Dallas's failure to fund, in 1815, 1239, 1249–52.

Treaties, with European powers, definitive, between the United States and Great Britain, Sept. 3, 1783, 1204, 1213–17; with England, of Dec. 1, 1806 (Monroe's), 1206; of Dec. 24, 1814, with Great Britain at Ghent, 1185–1219; of Feb. 22, 1819, between the United States and Spain, ceding Florida, 457.

——— Indian, of Greenville, Aug. 3, 1795, for the establishment of peace and boundaries with Wyandots, Delawares, Shawanese, Ottawas, Chippewas, Pottawatamies, Miamies, Eel Rivers, Weas, Kickapoos, Piankeshaws, and Kaskaskias, 352, 1196–97; of June 16, 1802, with the Creek nation, ceding land between the forks of the Oconee and Ocmulgee rivers in Georgia, 772; of Aug. 18, 1804, with the Delaware Indians ceding land, 349; of Aug. 27, 1804, with the Piankeshaw Indians, ceding land, 349, 351; of Nov. 3, 1804, with the Creek nation, ceding all the land between Oconee and Ocmulgee, 772; of Aug. 21, 1805, with the Delawares, Pottawatamies, Miamies, Eel River, and Weas, at Grouseland near Vincennes, ceding land, 349; of Nov. 7, 1807, with the Ottawas, Chippewas, Wyandots, and Pottawatamies, at Detroit, ceding lands, 354; of Sept. 30, 1809, with the Delawares, Pottawatamies, Miamies, and Eel River Miamies, at Fort Wayne, ceding lands, 354, 355, 357; or capitulation of Aug. 9, 1814, with Creek chiefs, ceding lands, 797–99; of peace, July 22, 1814, with Wyandots, Delawares, Shawanese, Senecas, and Miamies, 799, 1205.

Treaty of June 30, 1815, between the United States and Algiers, of peace and amity, 1253.

——— of July 3, 1815, between the United States and Great Britain, to regulate commerce, 1253.

Trimble, W. H., major of Nineteenth U. S. Infantry, in Fort Erie, 962; his account of the British assault, 962–63; wounded in sortie, 970.

Tripoli, visited by Decatur in 1815, 1253.

Tristan d'Acunha, scene of "Hornet's" battle with "Penguin," 1231.

Troup, George McIntosh, member of Congress from Georgia, opposes Macon's bill, 131; on maintaining the army, 143; on admission of West Florida, 226; his war-speech, 394–95; votes for frigates, 408; his report on the defences of Washington, 658; his bill for filling the ranks of the regular army, 880, 881–82; declares that no efficacious military measure could pass the House, 1094–95; denounces Giles's bill, 1099; his conference report rejected, 1103; his bill for a peace establishment, 1239.

"True-Blooded Yankee," privateer, in British waters, 847.

Trumbull, John, 1327.

Tuckaubatchee, Creek town on the Tallapoosa, council at, 772; Tecumthe's speech at, 773; councils at, 775; chiefs escape from, 776.

Tucker, ———, British colonel of Forty-First Regiment, repulsed at Black Rock, 958.

Tucker, Henry St. George, member of Congress from Virginia, 1255.

Tudor, William, 1319, 1322–24.

Tupper, Edward W., brigadier-general of Ohio militia, 672.

Turner, Charles, member of Congress from Massachusetts, assaulted in Plymouth, 574, 580.

Turner, J. M. W., 1327, 1329.

Turreau, Louis Marie, his anger with the American government in the spring of 1809, 27–32; his report on the repeal of the embargo, 28; on the Non-importation Act, 29; on disunion, 29; on the Spanish colonies, 30; his advice on rupture with the United States, in June, 1809, 31–32; his report of Gallatin's remarks on renewal of intercourse with Great Britain, 54; his report of Robert

Smith's remarks on Jefferson's weakness and indiscretions, 61; his note of June 14, 1809, remonstrating at the unfriendly conduct of the United States, 61; his recall ordered by Napoleon, 160; his successor arrives, 240.

Tuskegee Warrior, murders white families on the Ohio, 775; is put to death, 775, 777.

UKASE, Imperial, of Dec. 19, 1810, 289–90.

Union, dissolution of, a delicate topic, 15; a cause of repealing the embargo, 28; discussed by Turreau, 29; discussed in New England, 576, 580; affected by the seizure of Florida, 766–67; "increasing harmony throughout the," 870; jealousies in the, 894; Massachusetts federalists wish to resist the, 909, 912–13, 915, 921; southern section of, suffers most by the war, 916; its duty of defence neglected, 1064–65; practically dissolved, 1065; amount of sentiment for and against, in 1814, 1069; dissolution of, deprecated by Webster, 1100; dissolution of, encouraged and avowed in Congress, 1101; severance of, deprecated by Hartford Convention, 1114; already dissolved, 1117; alternative to dissolution of, 1121; political effect of peace on, 1237, 1245; difficulties of, overcome in 1816, 1299, 1313–14, 1331–32; its distinctive character, 1335.

Unitarians in New England, 1273; in Harvard College, 1301–02; churches in Boston, 1303; opinions of, in Boston churches, 1303–04; literary influence of, 1321–22, 1322–23; optimism of, 1343–44.

United States, population in 1810, 203; population of, in 1817, 1287; growth of population and wealth in, 1299–1300; character of people, 1331–45.

"United States," 44-gun frigate, 550; first cruise of, in 1812, 552; at Boston, 560; second cruise of, 562; captures the "Macedonian," 563; blockaded at New London, 811–12, 817, 833.

Universalists, 1273; growth of church, 1306–07; significance of movement, 1344.

University, national, Madison's recommendation of, 223; recommended by Madison in 1815, 1254; again in 1816, 1279.

Upham, Timothy, lieutenant-colonel commanding the Eleventh U. S. Infantry at Chrystler's Farm, 751.

Uti possidetis, claimed by England at Ghent, 1190, 1195, 1206; exceeded by British demands, 1198; opposed to *status ante bellum*, 1206–07; rejected, 1209; abandoned, 1211–12.

VAN BUREN, MARTIN, his support of De Witt Clinton, 580, 582; special judge advocate in Hull's trial, 904; prevents Crawford's nomination to the Presidency, 1265.

Van Rensselaer, Solomon, colonel of New York militia, commands attack on Queenston, 540.

Van Rensselaer, Stephen, major-general of New York militia, ordered to take command at Niagara, 518; forwards letter to Hull, 520; his force, Aug. 19, 1812, 535; his alarming position, 536–37; his force, Sept. 15, 537; expected to invade Canada with six thousand men, 538; his attack on Queenston, 539–40; retires from command, 543; Monroe's opinion of, 572; Jefferson's comment on, 573.

Varnum, Joseph B., member of Congress from Massachusetts, re-elected Speaker in the Eleventh Congress, 55; his rulings on the previous question, 245; elected senator, 375; defeated candidate for governor, 654; his speech on Giles's bill for drafting eighty thousand militia, 1096; votes against Giles's bill, 1099; votes against internal improvements, 1284.

Vermilion River, Indian boundary, 364.

Vermont, militia recalled from national service, 870; furnishes supplies to British army, 721, 973; militia not called out to defend Plattsburg, 1064; refuses to attend the Hartford Convention, 1068; chooses federalist Congressmen, 1068; prosperous, 1291.

"Vesuvius," steamboat on the Mississippi, 1299.

Vienna, Napoleon's draft for a decree of, 102–03, 107, 109; Congress of, 1200, 1208.

Villeré plantation, at New Orleans, seized by British advance, 1146, 1147.

Vincennes, territorial capital of Indiana, 342, 346, 352; the Shawnee prophet's talk at, 352; Tecumthe's talks at, 356, 359; citizens' meeting at, 360; Indian deputation at, 371; panic at, 372.

Vincent, John, British brigadier-general, evacuates Fort George, 727; attacks at Stony Creek, 728–29; recaptures Fort George, 760.

Virginia, creates manufactures in New England, 18–19; apathy of, toward the war, 582–83; exports of, affected by the blockade, 801–02; operations of war on the shores of, 802–11; militia, mortality of, 1062; her relative rank and obligations, 1072; money furnished by, 1072; men furnished by, 1073; soldiers and sailors of, 1074; arrears of internal taxes in, 1087; creates a State army, 1105; effect of peace on, 1224; congressional election in 1815, 1246; increase of population, 1800–1816, 1287; increase of wealth, 1291–96; legislative reports on roads and banks, 1294–95; judicial decision of, in case of Martin against Hunter's lessee, 1311–12; resolutions of 1798 obsolete in 1817, 1313.

"Vixen," sloop-of-war, captured, 565, 834.

WABASH, valley of, 342, 349, 351; Harrison's land purchase in, 354; war imminent in, 356.

Wadsworth, Decius, colonel commissary general of ordnance, detailed to erect fortifications at Bladensburg, 1003, 1010; refuses to obey Monroe's orders, 1022.

Wadsworth, William, brigadier-general of New York militia, 542; surrenders at Queenston, 543.

Wagner, Jacob, editor of the "Federal Republican," 578–79.

Walbach, John B., adjutant-general to Wilkinson at Chrystler's Farm, 751.

Wales, Prince of (see George, Prince of Wales).

Wales, R. W., captain of British sloop-of-war "Epervier," his report of action with the "Peacock," 1038–39.

Walpole, Lord, British ambassador at St. Petersburg, his remarks on Roumanzoff, 862.

War, cost of, 1812–1815, 1243–44.

War with England, declared by Monroe to be nearly decided in November, 1811, 385; recommended by House Committee of Foreign Relations, Nov. 29, 1811, 387–89; its objects explained by Peter B. Porter, 389; its probable effects discussed by Felix Grundy, 390–91, 392; Grundy's account of its causes, 391–92; Macon's view of its object, 395; Monroe's remarks on, 425; Madison's message recommending, 447–50; expediency of, 447–48; Calhoun's report on causes, 451; Calhoun's bill for, adopted by the House, 451; by the Senate, 451–52; and signed by the President, 452; criticisms on the conduct of, 568–74; opposition to, 573–77; apathy toward, 583; only attainable object of, 586; reasons of continuance, 594–96.

War Department (see Dearborn, Eustis, Armstrong, Monroe, Dallas).

War Power, over the militia, 404–05.

Ward, Artemas, member of Congress from (Boston) Massachusetts, on defence of the Union, 1100–01.

Ward, Robert Plumer, 485–86.

Ware, Henry, his Unitarianism, 1301, 1305, 1321.

Ware, Henry, the younger, 1322.

Ware, William, 1322.

Warren, Admiral Sir John Borlase, his authority to suspend hostilities, 623, 1206; his blockade of May 26, 1813, 800; his operations in Chesapeake Bay, 802–11; his remarks on Broke's victory, 827.

Warren, Dr. J. C., professor of anatomy at Harvard College, 1322.

Warrington, Lewis, commander in U. S. Navy, commands "Peacock," 1038; captures "Epervier," 1038, 1039; sails from New York, 1226; fires into "Nautilus," 1232.

"Warrior," privateer brig, her escape, 843.

Washington city, F. J. Jackson's impressions of, 84–86; threatened by British fleet in July, 1813, 658, 810; fears for safety of, 658; declared to be adequately defended, 659; neglect of its defences, 993; military district created to protect, 996; result of measures of defence, 997; British reasons for attacking, 993, 1000, 1002; measures of defence taken after August 18, 1002–03; Winder retreats to, 1005; natural defences of, 1006–07; capture and burning of, 1013–15, 1198; conduct of citizens of, 1021–23; militia system tested at, 1062; report of investigating committee on capture of, 1101; Ross's treatment of, approved by his government, 1128; defence of, compared with that of New Orleans, 1148–49; news of capture received at Ghent, 1205, 1212; Lord Liverpool on capture of, 1209; news from New Orleans and Ghent received at, 1222–23; banks share in loan of 1815, 1251; public buildings rebuilt, 1278–79.

Washington (or Warburton) Fort (see Fort Washington).

Washington, President, expenditures of his administration, 141; Jefferson's estimate of, 1071.

"Wasp," sloop-of-war, 551, 560; her action with the "Frolic," 561–62, 832, 833.

"Wasp," new American 22-gun sloop-of-war built in 1813, 1040, 1074; in the British Channel in June, 1814, 1040; captures the "Reindeer," 1040–41; sinks the "Avon," 1042–45; lost, 1045; gunnery of, 1338.

Waterloo, 1221.

Watmough, John G., lieutenant of artillery, in Fort Erie, 962.

Watson, W.H., first lieutenant of the "Argus," 829, 831.

Watt, first lieutenant of the "Shannon," killed, 823.

Wayne, Fort, 495.

Wea Indians, 346, 349, 357–58.

Weatherford, William, Creek half-breed, 778, 787, 796.

Webster, Daniel, his Rockingham Resolutions, 576; member of Congress from New Hampshire, 656; his resolutions on the repeal of French decrees, 657, 659; his speech on repealing the restrictive system, 876–77; his speech on a defensive war, 881–82; his speech on Dallas's bank scheme, 1088–89; his bank scheme adopted by Congress, 1089–90; deprecates disunion, 1100; defeats conscription, 1103; in the Fourteenth Congress, 1254–55, 1256; opposes protective duties, 1260; opposes bank, 1261–62; favors Compensation Act, 1264; his report on repeal of the Compensation Act, 1280; becomes resident of Boston, 1322; a type, 1329.

Webster, Noah, presides at Amherst town-meeting, 910.

Wellesley, Marquess, his character, 186–87, 189–90; appointed ambassador to the Supreme Junta, 188; becomes Foreign Secretary, 188–89; his friendship with Pinkney, 190, 194; his promises, 190; his note on Jackson, 191; his remark on American hatred, 191–92; his procrastination, 194–97, 200; his contempt for his colleagues, 198; resolves to retire, 200; his reply to Champagny's letter of August 5, 200–01; hopes for a Whig ministry in November, 1811, 298; his controversy with Pinkney over the French decrees and the law of blockade, 300, 302; abandons hope of a Whig ministry, 306; rejects Pinkney's demands, 306, 308; appoints a minister to Washington, 307; his instructions of April 10, 1811, to the new minister (see Foster), 311; criticises his colleagues for apathy toward America, 312; his instructions to Foster of Jan. 28, 1812, 426–27; settles the "Chesapeake" affair, 379, 480; urges his colleagues to choose a course, 478; resigns from the Cabinet, Jan. 16, 1812, 481; on the American government, 626.

Wellesley, Sir Arthur, Duke of Wellington, in India, 187; fights the battle of Talavera, 77; made a viscount, 186; general-in-chief, 188; retreats into Portugal, 189; fails in siege of Burgos, 623, 626; invades France, 863; his remarks on Prevost's retreat from Plattsburg, 988; his remarks on his troops sent to America, 988, 1158, 1211; brother-in-law of Pakenham, 1157; on the negotiations at Ghent, 1210–12.

Wellesley, Henry, 186; envoy in Spain, 189; on Perceval's commercial policy, 199–200.

Wells, Samuel, colonel of Seventeenth U. S. Infantry, 680–82, 684, 695.

West Point Military Academy, school at, 223; value of, in the war, 1341–42.

Wewocau, Little Warrior of (see Little Warrior).

Wheat, value of export of, in 1815, 1246–47.

Whitbread, Samuel, on the American war, 627, 634, 636.

White House, at Washington, burned by Ross, 1013–14, 1070; rebuilt, 1279.

Widgery, William, member of Congress from Massachusetts, 574.

Wilberforce, William, member of Parliament, 481, 486.

Wilde, Richard Henry, member of Congress from Georgia, on the decline of the House of Representatives, 1281.

Wilkinson, James, brigadier-general

and governor of the Louisiana Territory, his movements, 30; Gallatin's remarks on his character, 30–31; military court of inquiry on, 120; his influence on the army, 120; ordered to New Orleans, 120; his encampment at Terre aux Bœufs, 121–24; summoned to Washington for investigation, 124; senior brigadier, 493; appointed major-general, Feb. 27, 1813, 645; ordered from New Orleans to Sackett's Harbor, March 10, 1813, 738, 768; causes of his transfer, 738, 768–69; arrives at Washington, July 31, 739; takes command of military district No. 9, 742; his plan of campaign, 743–44; goes to Niagara, 744; returns to Sackett's Harbor, October 2, 744; his relations with Armstrong, 745–47; his expedition down the St. Lawrence, 748–53; goes into winter quarters at French Mills, 758; throws blame on Armstrong and Hampton, 758; advises evacuation of Fort George, 759; his administration at New Orleans, 767; seizes Mobile, 768, 1133; on Armstrong, 899; court-martialed, 899; on Jacob Brown, 900; at French Mills, 923; demands a court martial, 923; attacks Lacolle Mill, 924; relieved and court-martialed, 924.

Williams, A. J., captain of artillery in Hindman's battalion, 931; in Fort Erie, 959; killed, 962.

Williams, David R., not a member of the Eleventh Congress, 55; in the Twelfth Congress, 380; chairman of military committee, 381, 598.

Williams, John, colonel of Thirty-Ninth U. S. Infantry, ordered to join Jackson, 788, 793; arrives at Fort Strother, 793.

Wilna, in Poland, Barlow's journey to, 475.

Winchester, James, brigadier-general, 493; yields command to Harrison, 671; commands left division at Fort Defiance, 672–73; hardships of his men, 674; by Harrison's orders moves to the Maumee Rapids, 675,

678; his force, 679; sends detachment to Frenchtown, 679; follows to Frenchtown, 681; his account of the position, 681–82; defeated and captured, 685; effect of his defeat on the Creek Indians, 774, 776; commands at Mobile, 1183, 1184.

Winder, Levin, governor of Maryland in 1814, 996, 1028.

Winder, William H., colonel of Fourteenth Infantry, 546–47; brigadier-general, 726; takes part in capture of Fort George, 727; advances to Stony Creek, 728; captured, 728; appointed to command new military district at Washington, 996; his physical activity, 997, 1002–03; takes command of forces at the Woodyard, 1003; retreats to the Old Fields, 1004; retreats to the navy-yard, 1005; his letter to the Secretary of War, August 24, 1006; his supposed motives for occupying the navy-yard, 1005–06; starts for Bladensburg, 1007; rides about the field, 1010; retreats to the capitol, 1011; retreats to Georgetown, 1019, 1020; retreats to Rockville, 1019; his fear of responsibility, 1019; goes to Baltimore, 1020; yields command to Samuel Smith, 1028; his measures compared with Jackson's, 1148–50.

Windham, County of, in Vermont, sends delegate to the Hartford Convention, 1112.

Wirt, William, his description of Madison in October, 1814, 1070.

Wolcott, Alexander, 249.

Wolcott, Oliver, republican candidate for governor of Connecticut, 1272.

Wood, Eleazar Derby, major of engineers, constructs Fort Meigs, 682–83, 688, 691, 1341; his comments on the affair at the River Raisin, 683; with Brown on the Niagara, 939; directs entrenchments at Fort Erie, 956; takes command of Twenty-first Infantry, 961; leads sortie from Fort Erie, 969; killed, 970–71.

Woodyard, the, Winder's army camps at, 1004.

Wool, John E., captain of Thirteenth Infantry, gains Queenston Heights, 541.

Woollen manufacturers, 17; depressed by the peace, 1248; fabrics in the tariff of 1816, 1258, 1259–60.

Worcester, Dr. Samuel, his reply to Channing, 1304–05.

Wright, Robert, member of Congress from Maryland, his motion on impressments, 244; opposes Gallatin's taxes, 409; his threats against opposition, 441; on the payment of taxes in suspended bank paper, 1087.

YALE COLLEGE, remains orthodox, 1308.

Yarnall, John J., lieutenant in U. S. navy, Perry's first officer on the "Lawrence," 703; his comment on Elliott, 705.

Yazoo bill, passage of, 894; Marshall's decision on claims, 1310–11.

Yeo, Sir James Lucas, British commodore on Lake Ontario, 729; his attack on Sackett's Harbor, 732, 736; reinforces Kingston, 745; captures "Vixen," 834; attacks Oswego, 926–27; brings charges against Prevost, 988.

York, or Toronto, capital of Upper Canada, 514; captured by Dearborn, 724–25; public buildings burned, 725.

York, Duke of, 43, 76.

"Yorktown," privateer, captured, 845.

"Young Wasp," privateer, 1047.

Chronology

1838   Born in Boston, Massachusetts, on February 16, third son of Charles Francis Adams and Abigail Brooks Adams, great-grandson of President John Adams, and grandson of President John Quincy Adams, at whose home in Quincy he is a frequent summer visitor as a boy.

1854–58   Enters Harvard College. Contributes to the *Harvard Magazine* and is active in theatricals. Graduates as Class Orator.

1858   Sails, September 29, with several fellow graduates, for the traditional Grand Tour of Europe. Arrives at Liverpool on October 9. Attends the university as a student of civil law in Berlin after his arrival on October 22. Transfers to a German secondary school and writes an article on his winter's experience there (published in *American Historical Review*, Oct. 1947).

1859   In April resumes study of civil law in Dresden, where he lives until April 1, 1860. During intervals tours Austria and Germany and travels in northern Italy with his sister Louisa Kuhn before going on to Rome.

1860–61   Travels in Italy and Sicily until June. Interviews the Italian patriot Garibaldi just after the surrender of the Bourbon troops. Publishes his Italian travel letters in the *Boston Daily Courier*. Returns to Quincy, Massachusetts, in October. In December accompanies his father, who had been reelected to Congress, to Washington as his private secretary. December to mid-March 1861, serves as Washington correspondent of the Boston *Daily Advertiser*. Prepares "The Great Secession Winter, 1860–1861" (published in *Proceedings*, Massachusetts Historical Society, 1909–10).

1861–63   Sails for England, May 1. Serves as private secretary to his father, whom Lincoln has appointed as minister to Great Britain, until his father's resignation in May 1868. As London correspondent of *The New York Times* from June 1861 to January 1862, Adams reports British reaction to the American Civil War. His father sends Adams as a special messenger to the King of Denmark, December 1862. Tours Scotland and the Isle of Skye in August 1863 with his fifteen-year-old brother, Brooks.

1864–66   Grows restless with London society. Travels with mother,
           sister, and younger brother on the Continent. Returns to
           London; publishes unsigned scholarly articles.

1867   Publishes "Captaine John Smith" in the *North American
           Review*, demonstrating that that idol of Virginians had in-
           vented the tale of his rescue by Pocahontas. Also publishes
           "British Finance in 1816" and "The Bank of England Re-
           striction," the latter illustrating the futility of issuing in-
           convertible paper money.

1868   Publishes a long review article on Sir Charles Lyell's tenth
           edition of his *Principles of Geology* in the *North American
           Review*, challenging current theories of glaciation and Dar-
           win's theory of evolution as "in its nature incapable of
           proof." Returns to America in July with his parents and
           begins work in Washington as a free-lance political jour-
           nalist and lobbyist in favor of currency reform, free trade,
           and the establishment of civil service, contributing occa-
           sional pieces to the New York *Nation* toward the end of
           the year.

1869   Attacks the subservience of Congress to special interests
           and its reliance on the spoils system in "The Session" and
           "Civil Service Reform," articles published in the *North
           American Review*. Publishes "American Finance, 1865–
           1869," an article critical of the financial expedients of the
           period, in the *Edinburgh Review*. Continues brief contri-
           butions to the *Nation* into 1870.

1870   Publishes "The Legal-Tender Act" (with the assistance of
           Francis A. Walker), vigorously attacking that legislation
           and its sponsor, Elbridge G. Spaulding, and a second
           "Session" critical of Congress in the *North American Re-
           view*. Adams makes a holiday visit to England, but he is
           shortly summoned to his sister Louisa's bedside at Bagni
           di Lucca, where on July 13 she dies of tetanus, leaving
           Adams with a lasting impression of Nature's indifference
           to human suffering. Is appointed assistant professor of
           history by Charles W. Eliot, the new president of Harvard
           College. Begins teaching courses in medieval English and
           European history; later adds courses in American history.
           Assumes editorship of the *North American Review*, to

which he contributes two articles and over twenty reviews over the next seven years. Finally places his sensational exposé, "The New York Gold Conspiracy," in the *Westminster Review*. Drops the use of his middle name, Brooks.

1871 Publishes with his brother Charles Francis Adams, Jr., *Chapters of Erie*, a collection of some of their previously published articles. Travels to the Far West where he meets Clarence King of the United States Geological Survey. King soon afterward brings him into the circle of scientists connected with the Survey and the Smithsonian Institution.

1872–73 On June 27, Adams marries Marian (Clover) Hooper, daughter of the retired physician Dr. Robert William Hooper, a prominent Bostonian and a long-time widower. They sail July 9 on a wedding journey to England, the Continent, and Egypt. Adams renews friendships with Sir Robert Cunliffe, Charles Milnes Gaskell, Francis Palgrave, and Thomas Woolner, and consults European and English scholars such as Heinrich von Sybel, Ernst Curtius, Heinrich von Gneist, Georg H. Pertz, Theodor Mommsen, William Stubbs, John Richard Green, Sir Henry Maine, Robert Laing, and Benjamin Jowett. Returns to Boston August 1873.

1876 Publishes *Essays in Anglo-Saxon Law*, which includes his own essay "Anglo-Saxon Courts of Law" and three essays written by his doctoral candidates—Henry Cabot Lodge, Ernest Young, and James Lawrence Laughlin. Publishes "The Independents in the Canvass" in the *North American Review*, urging Republicans to break away from the conservative regular party. The article offends the publisher and leads to Adams' ending his connection with the *Review*. In December, Adams delivers his Lowell Institute lecture, "Primitive Rights of Women."

1877 Resigns from Harvard after accepting an invitation to work on the papers of Albert Gallatin, Thomas Jefferson's Secretary of the Treasury. As a friend of Secretary of State Evarts, Adams is given full access to the State Department archives. Publishes *Documents Relating to New England Federalism* in defense of the anti-Federalist policy of John Quincy Adams.

1879   Publishes *The Life of Albert Gallatin* and *The Writings of Albert Gallatin*. Forms friendships with Senator James D. Cameron and his wife, Elizabeth, and with John Hay, former private secretary of Abraham Lincoln. An inner circle of intimate friends is established of "The Five of Hearts"—the Adamses, John and Clara Hay, and Clarence King. Adams' wife presides over exclusive salon, which attracts friends such as Secretary of the Interior Carl Schurz, Attorney General Charles Devens, Senator Lucius Lamar of Mississippi, Congressman Abram Hewitt, Turkish minister Aristarchi Bey, and a procession of diplomats and foreign visitors. Adams begins acquaintance with a long succession of American presidents.

1879–80   Travels in Europe researching archives of London, Paris, and Madrid for his projected history of the administrations of Jefferson and Madison.

1880   Anonymously publishes *Democracy: An American Novel*, widely read in the United States and England for its depiction of political corruption in Washington.

1882   Publishes *John Randolph* in the American Statesmen Series.

1884   Under the pseudonym Frances Snow Compton, publishes *Esther: A Novel*. Adams and Hay begin construction of their residences on H Street facing Lafayette Square in Washington. The houses were designed by Adams' college mate, Henry Hobson Richardson. Circulates six copies, privately printed, of the first section of his *History of the United States during the Administrations of Thomas Jefferson and James Madison* to a few intimates for criticism.

1885   Circulates six copies of the second section of the *History*. Dr. Hooper, Adams' father-in-law, dies in April. On December 6, Adams' wife, Marian, commits suicide. Shortly afterward moves into the just-completed house at 1603 H Street.

1886   Commissions bronze figure to be executed by American sculptor Augustus Saint-Gaudens for the gravesite of Marian Adams in Rock Creek Cemetery. June to October, Adams tours Japan with artist John La Farge. November 21, Adams' father dies at Quincy at age seventy-nine.

1888   Circulates six copies of the third section of the *History*. (The fourth section was set directly from manuscript.) Adams makes his first visit to Cuba. Makes a circle tour of the Far West with his English friend Robert Cunliffe.

1889   Charles Scribner's Sons publishes the first two volumes of the trade edition of the *History* (four more volumes are published in 1890; the final three volumes and the volume of *Historical Essays* are published in 1891). June 6, Adams' mother dies at Quincy at age eighty-one. Adams becomes increasingly dependent on his friendship with Elizabeth Cameron.

1890–92 Adams travels with John La Farge to Hawaii, Samoa, Tahiti, Fiji, Australia, and Ceylon from August 1890 to September 1891. Writes poem "Buddha and Brahma" aboard ship en route from Ceylon (published in *The Yale Review*, Oct. 1915). Has a reunion with Elizabeth Cameron in France. Leaves England for America February 3, 1892.

1893   Commences intellectual collaboration with his brother Brooks, whose radical *Law of Civilization and Decay* will appear in 1895. Privately prints *Memoirs of Marau Taaroa, Last Queen of Tahiti*. Twice visits the World Columbian Exposition in Chicago, whose buildings seem to him to promise a renaissance in art and architecture.

1894   In December, sends his presidential address predicting the development of scientific history to the annual meeting of the American Historical Association to be delivered in absentia ("The Tendency of History," published in *Annual Report of the American Historical Association for the Year 1894*). Tours Cuba with Clarence King, February to March; travels to the Yellowstone and the Tetons with John Hay, July to September; tours Mexico and the Caribbean Islands with Chandler Hale, December 1894 to April 1895.

1895   Adams makes his first systematic study of the Gothic architecture of Normandy cathedrals and Mont-Saint-Michel in the company of Henry and Anna Cabot Lodge.

1896   Prepares "Recognition of Cuban Independence" for Senator Cameron, printed in the Senate Report. In April, travels to Mexico with the Camerons. Tours Europe with the Hays, May to October.

1897–98   Prolonged stay abroad is spent in London, Paris, Egypt (with the Hays), Turkey, Greece, the Balkans, Vienna, and Paris. Is in England, June to November. While visiting with Adams at Surrenden Dering in England, Hay is appointed U.S. Secretary of State, having served as ambassador to England since March 1897.

1899   Tours Italy and Sicily with the Lodges. Resides in Paris, June to January 1900. (Until 1911, in Paris for part of each year; from 1908 as member of Edith Wharton's circle.)

1900   Visits the Paris Exposition and is especially impressed by the Hall of Dynamos. Composes the poem "Prayer to the Virgin of Chartres," which includes a "Prayer to the Dynamo" (published 1920, in Mabel La Farge, *Letters to a Niece*).

1901   Revises and enlarges the Tahiti memoir as *Memoirs of Arii Taimai* for private distribution. Travels with the Lodges during July and August to Bayreuth, Vienna, Warsaw, Moscow, and St. Petersburg, then alone during September to Sweden and Norway.

1904   Privately prints *Mont Saint Michel and Chartres*. Contributes chapter on Clarence King in *Clarence King Memoirs*. In the spring, accompanies Secretary of State John Hay to the opening of the St. Louis Exposition.

1907   In February, issues the private edition of *The Education of Henry Adams*, containing the first formulation of his Dynamic Theory of History and his Law of Acceleration. Circulates the volume for correction to persons it comments on, including his brothers, Henry Cabot Lodge, Charles Gaskell, Theodore Roosevelt, Charles William Eliot, and Speck von Sternburg.

1908   Edits the *Letters of John Hay and Extracts from Diary*, but Adams surrenders completion to Hay's widow, who reduces the names to initials.

1909   Writes "The Rule of Phase Applied to History," in which he reformulates his theory of scientific history, now basing it on an analogy to Josiah Willard Gibbs's "Rule of Phase" contained in Gibbs's "On the Equilibrium of Heterogeneous Substances."

1910   Prints and distributes to university libraries and history
        professors the small volume *A Letter to American Teachers
        of History* proposing a theory of history based on the Sec-
        ond Law of Thermodynamics and the principle of en-
        tropy.

1911   Publishes *The Life of George Cabot Lodge*, prepared at the
        instance of the Lodges.

1912   Issues a second private edition, slightly revised, of *Mont
        Saint Michel and Chartres*. Is partially paralyzed by a cere-
        bral thrombosis, April to late July.

1913   Authorizes the American Institute of Architects to publish
        a trade edition of the *Chartres*, edited by Ralph Adams
        Cram and issued through Houghton Mifflin Company.
        The advance sale breaks the publisher's records.

1913–14 Spends summers again in France, first at the Chateau
        Marivault in the countryside north of Paris and sub-
        sequently at the Chateau Coubertin. Engages Aileen
        Tone, a musician, as secretary-companion and becomes
        engrossed in the study and performance of medieval
        chansons.

1914–18 Presides at his noontime breakfast table at 1603 H Street
        during the war years, entertaining nieces and "nieces in
        wish" and visiting dignitaries such as Arthur Balfour,
        Henri Bergson, and French Ambassador Jusserand.

1918   Dies in Washington March 27 at the age of eighty. Buried
        beside his wife in Rock Creek Cemetery. First trade pub-
        lication of *The Education of Henry Adams*. "Tendency of
        History," "Rule of Phase Applied to History," and "A
        Letter to American Teachers" are included by Brooks
        Adams in *The Degradation of the Democratic Dogma* (1919).
        The Pulitzer Prize is awarded posthumously in 1919 for
        The Education.

Note on the Texts

In the fall of 1879, with *The Life of Albert Gallatin* recently published, Henry Adams left America for London, Paris, Madrid, and Seville to do research in government archives. Adams wrote that he was in "pursuit of the larger subject, for which the Gallatin is only a preliminary study." This larger subject, a "History of the United States from 1801 to 1815," as he then called it, "will be an affair of at least ten years work, and will exhaust all that I have to say in this world, I hope. To compress this into three volumes and to expunge every unnecessary syllable, will be my great labor for several years. To make it readable is the great hope of my life."

As he continued to examine hitherto secret documents, his collection of relevant materials grew. In 1880, after taking stock of his European documents and beginning to write, Adams expressed a hope to publish in 1886; he gradually realized, however, that he would need more time—and more space—than he had planned. The history of Jefferson's two presidential administrations took shape during the early 1880s, and by the end of 1884 these first two parts of the *History* were written—and indeed were in print in private editions of six copies each for circulation among friends. Adams' progress in these years was rapid; in addition to the work on the *History*, he published the biography *John Randolph* and the novels *Democracy* and *Esther*. That progress was slowed, however, first by fatigue, and then by the suicide of his wife, Marian, in December 1885.

Adams returned from a restorative trip to Japan in the summer of 1886 with a new resolve to finish his history. Working sometimes ten hours a day, he moved ahead on the history of Madison's administrations while continuing to fill gaps in the first two parts. By 1888, after Adams had spent nearly a decade researching, writing, and expanding, the *History* had grown to a size that he thought would require eight published volumes—two for each of the four presidential administrations that his work considered. (Madison's second administration, combined with a long and detailed general index, eventually filled three volumes instead of two, bringing the trade edition to nine volumes.)

In June 1888 Adams' assistant, Theodore Dwight, a former State Department librarian, wrote to arrange for publication with Charles Scribner's Sons. Adams requested as printer the Cambridge, Massachusetts, firm of John Wilson & Son, which set type and prepared the stereotype plates that would be used for all subsequent printings during Adams' lifetime. Through the rest of 1888 and 1889, Adams supplied copy to Wilson, worked on proofs, and rewrote the later portions of the *History*. He also negotiated with Charles Scribner on nearly every aspect of production and design—binding, thickness of paper, page design, typography, reproduction of maps and plans, and indexing—and on subjects such as whether or not to have chapter titles and what system to use in running heads. The nine volumes of *History of the United States* (New York: Charles Scribner's Sons, 1889–91) were issued as a set of ten with Adams' *Historical Essays*. He himself was not at home to receive copies of his final volumes; after sending the last revised proofs to Wilson, he set off for Polynesia in August 1890, leaving Dwight in charge of final details.

Adams believed he was writing the *History* for "a continent of a hundred million people fifty years hence," as he told an English friend, and he strove to improve the work by constant revision and incorporation of new information. As late as September 1889, he was in Ottawa gathering material about the War of 1812, and in early 1890 he was still working in new documents arriving from England.

Revision did not end with publication. Adams knew, as he complained in one letter, "how impossible it is to make a first edition accurate in its statements and reasoning, to say nothing of its style." He returned to the French archives after his Polynesian trip, and he revised parts of the *History* at various times throughout the 1890s.

In January 1899, Adams requested Scribner's to "be so kind as to send me a set of my History for revision and correction, so that in future my absence may not interfere with your requests." In February he told his friend Elizabeth Cameron that he was enjoying reading his own work, " which I am correcting in case of further editions"; and by March he returned the set to Scribner's " with a list of the pages on which corrections are to be made." These final revisions were cut into the plates and appeared in new printings of parts of the *History* as Scribner's required more copies.

This Library of America volume contains the last two parts of Adams' work, *History of the United States of America during the First Administration of James Madison* and *History of the United States of America during the Second Administration of James Madison*. The companion volume contains the first two parts covering Thomas Jefferson's two administrations. In each case, the text is that of the last printing containing new revisions by Adams.

Adams began *History of the United States of America during the First Administration of James Madison* late in 1884, drawing on his extensive collection of manuscripts from foreign and State Department archives. Events of the following two years—Marian Adams' decline and death in 1885, the Japanese trip with John La Farge in 1886—slowed progress on the book. Work nevertheless went on, and a draft of this third part of the *History* was finished by summer 1887. Adams spent the summer at his ancestral home in Quincy, Massachusetts, where he hoped to begin the long process of revision. He soon found he was making such rapid progress, however— working six to ten hours a day and "making it just dance"— that he could finish before returning to Washington in the fall. To speed the work, Adams employed "a female called a caligraphess . . . meaning a type-writer," to whom he dictated portions of this second draft. "With this vile modern innovation I shall spoil my work," he wrote, "but I shall either be in my pleasant grave on this day two years, or my history will be done and out."

In the fall Adams arranged to have the manuscript printed by John Wilson & Son of Cambridge in a small private edition for his own use, as the first two parts of the *History* had been in 1883 and 1884. These "draft" volumes, with wide margins and interleaved blank pages, were intended to provide a clean text to revise for publication, safeguard the work, establish the priority of Adams' scholarship, and elicit comments and criticism from colleagues—including his brother Charles Francis Adams and the historian George Bancroft. The texts of each were divided into five "books"—an organization dropped in the trade edition. By the time the private edition of *First Administration of James Madison* was ready in late 1888, Dwight had already arranged for trade publication of the *History* with Charles Scribner's Sons.

Setting copy for the trade edition was a revised copy of the privately printed draft volume. As with the earlier parts of the *History*, Adams used the comments of the readers of his draft volumes in preparing printer's copy for Scribner's. Some further changes were made just before the work appeared in response to a protest on behalf of General William Hull's descendants, who sought to protect his reputation from any imputation of cowardice. The trade edition was issued in two volumes—fifth and sixth in the series—on September 26, 1890, in a printing of 2000. Subsequent impressions may have corrected the "small errata" that Dwight mentioned in an 1891 letter to Scribner's.

On October 7, 1896, Adams wrote to William Brownell of Scribner's: "A dozen changes, or thereabouts, ought to be made in my volumes V and VI. Most of these are trifling, but the last chapter of volume VI is considerably affected by Russian publications since I wrote. . . . If possible I will not overrun paging, but just now I am not quite sure of the subject." A revised printing of *First Administration of James Madison* was published later that year. New information about diplomatic relations between Czar Alexander I and Napoleon prompted some of the changes. "Roumanzoff answered his appeal" became "Alexander answered his appeal" (288.27); more precise information led Adams to change the sentence "Before many months had passed, he found himself winning successes that could be explained only by the direct interposition of the Czar against the resistance of Roumanzoff and the ambassador of France" to "By a good fortune almost equal to that which brought Monroe to Paris on April 12, 1803, Adams was officially received at St. Petersburg on October 25, 1809, only two days before the Czar first revolted against Napoleon's authority" (284.14–18). Documents Adams discovered in French archives after his Polynesian trip threw new light on the character of the Count de Crillon. Adams rewrote a passage at 422.36–423.2, citing an article on the subject that he had written to help launch the first volume of the *American Historical Review* in 1895. Other changes involved qualifications of assertions of fact. "Louis Grandpré alone defending his flag" was qualified to "almost alone" (214.25), for example, and the statement that "none" of the American brigadier-generals in 1812 had ever "commanded a regiment in face of an enemy" was altered to "Excepting Hull, none seems ever before" to have done so (494.5–7).

Adams made his final set of revisions in the entire four-part work in January 1899. They were cut into the plates and appeared in new printings of each volume as Scribner's required more copies. The only change in *First Administration of James Madison* was a new citation to Paul Leicester Ford's edition of *The Writings of Thomas Jefferson* (10 volumes, 1892–99) where a manuscript had been cited in the earlier printings. The change first appeared in the revised printing issued in 1901, which is the text presented here.

History of the United States of America during the Second Administration of James Madison was the only one of the four parts that did not have a private "draft" printing before trade publication. Adams worked on his manuscript during late 1887 and 1888, interrupting the writing to do research in the War Department, correct proofs for the private printing of the third part of the *History*, and to take short trips with friends. Back at the family library in Quincy during summer 1888, he wrote six to ten hours a day, confessing that "the frenzy of finishing the big book has seized me." The narrative portion was finished in September: "In imitation of Gibbon," Adams noted in his diary, "I walked in the garden among the yellow and red autumn flowers, blazing in sunshine, and meditated."

Adams began rewriting *Second Administration of James Madison* in 1889, while preparing printer's copy and correcting proofs of the earlier volumes. He set a typist to work at the beginning of the manuscript, and he rewrote—starting from the last chapter. Throughout the year, new documents were woven into the text: Adams' British friend Sir Robert Cunliffe helped secure naval reports in the London Foreign

Office, and Adams went to Ottawa in August to search out additional material in the Canadian War Office. As late as November, with *First Administration of Thomas Jefferson* already published, Adams told Cunliffe, "I shall still have time to use new material. . . . The more the better" as long as *Second Administration of James Madison* "is not in print." This new material, along with the engraved maps and plans Adams was supervising and the growing general index he was assembling, swelled the work until in January 1890 Adams wrote to Scribner that *Second Administration of James Madison* would "have to take three volumes or make uncomfortably thick ones." In August 1890, the final proofs of the index were left with Dwight, and Adams departed with John La Farge for Tahiti.

The trade edition, set from Adams' manuscript, was published in three volumes on January 10, 1891. By the end of the year, 2300 copies were in print, some of these perhaps incorporating the "one or two corrections" Dwight mentioned in an October 1891 letter to Scribner's. Adams' last changes in *Second Administration of James Madison*, made during the final revision of the *History* in 1899, first appeared in a 1904 printing. Of the changes, most of which were in the four concluding chapters, one was stylistic: "the men interested more than the societies" was revised to "the men were far more interesting than the societies" (1333.24–25). Two involved the change of "State-rights" to "States-rights" that Adams marked throughout the *History*. Most changes qualified or altered assertions of fact. In a discussion of the artillery battle at New Orleans, the first printing stated that "During the entire war, no other battle was fought in which the defeated party had not some excuse to offer for inferiority." This was qualified to "No other battle of the war, except that at Chrystler's Farm, left the defeated party with so little excuse for its inferiority" (1165.34–35). The claim about post-routes in 1817 that "none was yet established beyond the Mississippi" was altered to "they were already beyond the Mississippi" (1298.16–17); and the statement that American periodicals in 1817 were not much inferior to British "for neither the Edinburgh nor the Quarterly Review was established until several years later" was revised to read "for the Edinburgh was established only in 1802, and the Quarterly not till 1809" (1319.14–15). The text of the 1904 printing, where the changes first appeared, is the one printed here.

This Library of America volume presents the texts of the 1901 printing of *History of the United States of America during the First Administration of James Madison* and the 1904 printing of *History of the United States of America during the Second Administration of James Madison*, which incorporate Adams' final revisions in those works. Adams' large general index (which he himself assembled by reworking and expanding the indexes to the first three parts and adding entries for the fourth) has been separated into two indexes corresponding to this edition's two-volume format, and entries have been corrected where necessary. Maps and plans are reproduced from the *History* by courtesy of The Massachusetts Historical Society.

Adams treated the four administrations as distinct units, and insisted on four different title pages with four sets of volume numbers—"I" and "II" for each of the first three units and "I," "II," and "III" for the fourth. He compromised with Charles Scribner's desire for a series format, however, by allowing the spines of the volumes to bear the series title "History of the United States," inclusive dates, and consecutive volume numbers 1 through 9. The Library of America has followed an analogous practice in the present edition: different title pages for the two volumes with the series title and dates stamped on the binding.

This volume is concerned with presenting the texts of the 1901 and 1904 printings; it does not attempt to reproduce features of the typographic design, such as the display capitalization of chapter openings. The texts are reproduced without change, except for the correction of typographical errors. Spelling, punctuation, and capitalization often are expressive features, and they are not altered, even when inconsistent or irregular. The following is a list of the typographical errors, cited by page and line number: 110.19, Intelligencer; 160.22, *trouvons*)."; 266.39, Correspondance; 278.40, Correspondance; 317.38, iii,; 321.39, Papers; 418.39, Etr; 460.37, des.; 558.16, "Constitutution,"; 565.39, Brainbridge's; 662.39, p; 680.38, 185:; 757.32, praise"; 771.26, Chattahooche; 777.27, warrior; 796.40, Niles.; 797.36, Jackson.; 937.39, James; 945.11, Twenty third; 1045.38, Sept; 1073.38, Papers;; 1073.39, papers,; 1113.29, day,; 1151.30, dragoons; 1161.29−30, reconnaisance; 1248.36, Niles; 1284.19, State-rights; 1328.22−23, For long.

Notes

For more detailed notes, references to other studies, and further biographical background, see Ernest Samuels' *The Young Henry Adams*, *Henry Adams: The Middle Years*, and *Henry Adams: The Major Phase* (Cambridge, Mass.: The Belknap Press of Harvard University Press, 1967, 1958, 1964); Earl N. Harbert's "Henry Adams" in *Fifteen American Authors Before 1900: Bibliographical Essays on Research and Criticism* (Madison, Wis.: University of Wisconsin Press, 1984), edited by Harbert and Robert A. Rees; and *The Letters of Henry Adams*, 3 vols. (Cambridge, Mass.: The Belknap Press of Harvard University Press, 1982; volumes 4–6 forthcoming), edited by J. C. Levenson, Ernest Samuels, Charles Vandersee, and Viola Hopkins Winner. In the notes below, the numbers refer to the page and line of the present volume (the line count includes chapter titles). No note is made for material included in a standard desk-reference book. Notes printed at the foot of pages within the text are Adams' own.

7.25   voluntary]   The text of the Inaugural Address in the Madison Papers at the University of Virginia has "involuntary" here.

214.25   almost]   This qualification, marked by Adams in his copy of the first printing, first appeared in 1896.

218.14–19   By . . . nothing.]   In 1896 this passage replaced the following: "Before many months had passed, he found himself winning successes that could be explained only by the direct interposition of the Czar against the resistance of Roumanzoff and the ambassador of France. In the mysterious atmosphere of the Russian court, the effect of wielding this astounding power might well have turned his head; but Adams hardly realized his position." Adams had written Scribner's in October 1896 that this chapter of the *History* was "considerably affected by Russian publications since I wrote." The revisions he made in this chapter for the 1896 printing, all marked in his own copy of the first printing, were based on the new sources cited in an added footnote here: Sergei Spiridonovich Tatishchev's *Alexandre I*er *et Napoléon, d'après leur correspondance inédite, 1801–1812* (Librairie académique Didier: Paris, 1891) and Albert Vandal's *Napoléon et Alexandre I*er*: L'alliance russe sous le premier empire*, 3 vols. (E. Plon, Nourrit et cie: Paris, 1891–96).

288.27   Alexander]   "Roumanzoff " in the first printing.

288.31   rejoined:]   In the first printing: "dictated his reply to Roumanzoff 's argument."

293.28−29   had . . . Swedes,]   In the first printing: "happened to command the French army corps at Hamburg," etc.

294.31   commerce.]   In the first printing, "commerce by Bernadotte."

422.35−423.2   Although . . . accomplice.[1]]   In 1896 this replaced the following passage: "Although the truth was revealed only at a much later time that Crillon was an agent of Napoleon's secret police, no Frenchman, who had enjoyed the advantages of a diplomatic education, could have been wholly deceived in regard to the character of a person so evidently suspicious." Adams' research in French archives after the first printing of the *History* showed that "Crillon," whose real name was Soubiran, was not an agent of Napoleon's secret police (as Adams had claimed on Serurier's authority) but a fugitive from the French Imperial Police. In his article "Count Edward de Crillon," cited in the footnote, Adams drew upon diplomatic archives in Britain, France, and the United States to correct the historical record. The article also notes: "According to mathematicians, every man carries with him a personal error in his observation of facts, for which a certain allowance must be made before attaining perfect accuracy."

494.5−6   Excepting Hull,]   The qualification was added in 1896 to the text of the first printing, which claimed that "none belonged to the regular service, or had ever commanded a regiment in face of an enemy." In the spring of 1890, when *First Administration of James Madison* was ready to be printed, Adams exchanged letters with retired Confederate general Joseph Wheeler, who wrote on behalf of General Hull's grandchildren. Wheeler sought to learn if Adams' *History* would repeat the court-martial verdict of cowardice. Adams had proofs of the volume to use in preparing the index and agreed to "send you herewith all the sheets I can recall to mind, which contain allusions to William Hull." When Wheeler wrote with new wording, Adams promised to "give most careful consideration to your suggestions. As yet I cannot be certain of adopting them literally, but I will in any case make such changes as will tend to soften, if not to remove, the objectionable language." Adams changed "His army became mutinous from disgust at his vacillation and at their own idleness" to "His army lost respect for him in consequence of his failure to attack Malden" (511.21−23), and added that the court-martial "could not command respect" considering the bias of those constituting it (906.6).

800.6−8   The friendly . . . war.]   In 1904 this sentence replaced the following one: "No chiefs remained except among the friendly Creeks, who could not capitulate because they had never been at war."

1165.34−36   No . . . apologists]   In 1904 this passage replaced the following: "During the entire war, no other battle was fought in which the defeated party had not some excuse to offer for inferiority. Usually the excuse", etc.

1298.16   they . . . already]   In the first printing, "but none was yet" established there.

1319.14—15   for . . . 1809.]   In the first printing: "for neither the Edinburgh nor the Quarterly Review was established until seven years later."

1333.2   economical]   In the first printing, "methodical". In works such as "The Rule of Phase Applied to History" (1909) and *A Letter to American Teachers of History* (1910), Adams explored further the possibility of making history "a true science."

1333.24—25   science . . . societies]   The first printing reads, "what was worse for scientific purposes, the men interested more than the societies." Adams, in his copy of the first printing, first revised this to "the men attracted more interest than the societies" before adopting the wording of the 1904 printing.

1341.15—18   As . . . States.]   In 1904 this replaced the following sentence from the first printing: "The same intelligence that selected the rifle and the long pivot-gun for favorite weapons was shown in handling the carronade, and every other instrument however clumsy."

CATALOGING INFORMATION

Adams, Henry, 1838–1918.
    History of the United States of America during the admin-
    istrations of Thomas Jefferson and James Madison. 2 vols.
        Vol. 1 History of the United States of America during the
            administrations of Thomas Jefferson
        Vol. 2 History of the United States of America during the
            administrations of James Madison
    Edited by Earl N. Harbert.

    (The Library of America ; 31, 32)
    Includes indexes.
1. United States—Politics and government—1801–1809.
2. United States—Politics and government—1809–1817.
I. Title.   II. Series
E331.A192   1986   973.4′6′0924
ISBN 0–940450–34–8 (V. 1)
ISBN 0–940450–35–6 (V. 2)

This book is set in 10 point Linotron Galliard,
a face designed for photocomposition by Matthew Carter
and based on the sixteenth-century face Granjon. The paper
is acid-free Ecusta Nyalite and meets the requirements for perma-
nence of the American National Standards Institute. The binding
material is Brillianta, a 100% woven rayon cloth made by
Van Heek-Scholco Textielfabrieken, Holland. The com-
position is by Haddon Craftsmen, Inc., and The
Clarinda Company. Printing and binding
by R. R. Donnelley & Sons Company.
Designed by Bruce Campbell.